Twentieth-Century Literary Criticism

Guide to Gale Literary Criticism Series

For criticism on	Consult these Gale series
Authors now living or who died after December 31, 1999	***CONTEMPORARY LITERARY CRITICISM (CLC)***
Authors who died between 1900 and 1999	***TWENTIETH-CENTURY LITERARY CRITICISM (TCLC)***
Authors who died between 1800 and 1899	***NINETEENTH-CENTURY LITERATURE CRITICISM (NCLC)***
Authors who died between 1400 and 1799	***LITERATURE CRITICISM FROM 1400 TO 1800 (LC)*** ***SHAKESPEAREAN CRITICISM (SC)***
Authors who died before 1400	***CLASSICAL AND MEDIEVAL LITERATURE CRITICISM (CMLC)***
Authors of books for children and young adults	***CHILDREN'S LITERATURE REVIEW (CLR)***
Dramatists	***DRAMA CRITICISM (DC)***
Poets	***POETRY CRITICISM (PC)***
Short story writers	***SHORT STORY CRITICISM (SSC)***
Literary topics and movements	***HARLEM RENAISSANCE: A GALE CRITICAL COMPANION (HR)*** ***THE BEAT GENERATION: A GALE CRITICAL COMPANION (BG)***
Asian American writers of the last two hundred years	***ASIAN AMERICAN LITERATURE (AAL)***
Black writers of the past two hundred years	***BLACK LITERATURE CRITICISM (BLC)*** ***BLACK LITERATURE CRITICISM SUPPLEMENT (BLCS)***
Hispanic writers of the late nineteenth and twentieth centuries	***HISPANIC LITERATURE CRITICISM (HLC)*** ***HISPANIC LITERATURE CRITICISM SUPPLEMENT (HLCS)***
Native North American writers and orators of the eighteenth, nineteenth, and twentieth centuries	***NATIVE NORTH AMERICAN LITERATURE (NNAL)***
Major authors from the Renaissance to the present	***WORLD LITERATURE CRITICISM, 1500 TO THE PRESENT (WLC)*** ***WORLD LITERATURE CRITICISM SUPPLEMENT (WLCS)***

ISSN 0276-8178

PIERCE COLLEGE LIBRARY
PUYALLUP WA 98374
LAKEWOOD WA 98498
Volume 142

Twentieth-Century Literary Criticism

Criticism of the
Works of Novelists, Poets, Playwrights,
Short Story Writers, and Other Creative Writers
Who Lived between 1900 and 1999,
from the First Published Critical
Appraisals to Current Evaluations

Janet Witalec
Project Editor

Detroit • New York • San Diego • San Francisco • Cleveland • New Haven, Conn. • Waterville, Maine • London • Munich

THOMSON
GALE

Twentieth-Century Literary Criticism, Vol. 142

Project Editor
Janet Witalec

Editorial
Jenny Cromie, Scott Darga, Kathy D. Darrow, Julie Keppen, Allison Marion, Linda Pavlovski

Research
Michelle Campbell, Tracie A. Richardson

Rights & Acquisition Management
Edna Hedblad, Ann Taylor

Imaging and Multimedia
Lezlie Light, Luke Rademacher, Denay Wilding

Composition and Electronic Capture
Kathy Sauer

Manufacturing
Stacy L. Melson

© 2004 by Gale. Gale is an imprint of The Gale Group, Inc., a division of Thomson Learning, Inc.

Gale and Design® and Thomson Learning™ are trademarks used herein under license.

For more information, contact
The Gale Group, Inc.
27500 Drake Rd.
Farmington Hills, MI 48331-3535
Or you can visit our internet site at
http://www.gale.com

ALL RIGHTS RESERVED
No part of this work covered by the copyright herein may be reproduced or used in any form or by any means—graphic, electronic, or mechanical, including photocopying, recording, taping, Web distribution, or information storage retrieval systems—without the written permission of the publisher.

This publication is a creative work fully protected by all applicable copyright laws, as well as by misappropriation, trade secret, unfair competition, and other applicable laws. The authors and editors of this work have added value to the underlying factual material herein through one or more of the following: unique and original selection, coordination, expression, arrangement, and classification of the information.

For permission to use material from the product, submit your request via the Web at http://www.gale-edit.com/permissions, or you may download our Permissions Request form and submit your request by fax or mail to:

Permisssions Department
The Gale Group, Inc.
27500 Drake Rd.
Farmington Hills, MI 48331-3535
Permissions Hotline:
248-699-8006 or 800-877-4253, ext. 8006
Fax 248-699-8074 or 800-762-4058

Since this page cannot legibly accommodate all copyright notices, the acknowledgments constitute an extension of the copyright notice.

While every effort has been made to secure permission to reprint material and to ensure the reliability of the information presented in this publication, the Gale Group neither guarantees the accuracy of the data contained herein nor assumes any responsibility for errors, omissions or discrepancies. Gale accepts no payment for listing; and inclusion in the publication of any organization, agency, institution, publication, service, or individual does not imply endorsement of the editors or publisher. Errors brought to the attention of the publisher and verified to the satisfaction of the publisher will be corrected in future editions.

LIBRARY OF CONGRESS CATALOG CARD NUMBER 76-46132

ISBN 0-7876-7041-3
ISSN 0276-8178

Printed in the United States of America
10 9 8 7 6 5 4 3 2 1

Contents

Preface vii

Acknowledgments xi

Literary Criticism Series Advisory Board xiii

The Grail Theme in Twentieth-Century Literature
Introduction 1
Representative Works 1
Overviews and General Studies 2
Major Works 20
Further Reading 89

Literary Expressionism
Introduction 90
Representative Works 90
Overviews and General Studies 91
Themes in Literary Expressionism 138
Expressionism in Germany 161
Further Reading 184

Southern Gothic Literature
Introduction 186
Representative Works 186
Overviews and General Studies 187
Major Authors in Southern Gothic Literature 197
Structure and Technique in Southern Gothic Literature 230
Themes in Southern Gothic Literature 250
Further Reading 270

Twentieth-Century Danish Literature
Introduction 271
Representative Works 271
Major Works 272
Major Authors 284
Further Reading 343

Literary Criticism Series Cumulative Author Index 347

Literary Criticism Series Cumulative Topic Index 443

TCLC Cumulative Nationality Index 453

Preface

Since its inception more than fifteen years ago, *Twentieth-Century Literary Criticism* (*TCLC*) has been purchased and used by nearly 10,000 school, public, and college or university libraries. *TCLC* has covered more than 500 authors, representing 58 nationalities and over 25,000 titles. No other reference source has surveyed the critical response to twentieth-century authors and literature as thoroughly as *TCLC*. In the words of one reviewer, "there is nothing comparable available." *TCLC* "is a gold mine of information—dates, pseudonyms, biographical information, and criticism from books and periodicals—which many librarians would have difficulty assembling on their own."

Scope of the Series

TCLC is designed to serve as an introduction to authors who died between 1900 and 1999 and to the most significant interpretations of these author's works. Volumes published from 1978 through 1999 included authors who died between 1900 and 1960. The great poets, novelists, short story writers, playwrights, and philosophers of the period are frequently studied in high school and college literature courses. In organizing and reprinting the vast amount of critical material written on these authors, *TCLC* helps students develop valuable insight into literary history, promotes a better understanding of the texts, and sparks ideas for papers and assignments. Each entry in *TCLC* presents a comprehensive survey on an author's career or an individual work of literature and provides the user with a multiplicity of interpretations and assessments. Such variety allows students to pursue their own interests; furthermore, it fosters an awareness that literature is dynamic and responsive to many different opinions.

Every fourth volume of *TCLC* is devoted to literary topics. These topics widen the focus of the series from the individual authors to such broader subjects as literary movements, prominent themes in twentieth-century literature, literary reaction to political and historical events, significant eras in literary history, prominent literary anniversaries, and the literatures of cultures that are often overlooked by English-speaking readers.

TCLC is designed as a companion series to Gale's *Contemporary Literary Criticism,* (*CLC*) which reprints commentary on authors who died after 1999. Because of the different time periods under consideration, there is no duplication of material between *CLC* and *TCLC*.

Organization of the Book

A *TCLC* entry consists of the following elements:

- The **Author Heading** cites the name under which the author most commonly wrote, followed by birth and death dates. Also located here are any name variations under which an author wrote, including transliterated forms for authors whose native languages use nonroman alphabets. If the author wrote consistently under a pseudonym, the pseudonym will be listed in the author heading and the author's actual name given in parenthesis on the first line of the biographical and critical information. Uncertain birth or death dates are indicated by question marks. Single-work entries are preceded by a heading that consists of the most common form of the title in English translation (if applicable) and the original date of composition.

- A **Portrait of the Author** is included when available.

- The **Introduction** contains background information that introduces the reader to the author, work, or topic that is the subject of the entry.

- The list of **Principal Works** is ordered chronologically by date of first publication and lists the most important works by the author. The genre and publication date of each work is given. In the case of foreign authors whose works have been translated into English, the English-language version of the title follows in brackets. Unless otherwise indicated, dramas are dated by first performance, not first publication.

- Reprinted **Criticism** is arranged chronologically in each entry to provide a useful perspective on changes in critical evaluation over time. The critic's name and the date of composition or publication of the critical work are given at the beginning of each piece of criticism. Unsigned criticism is preceded by the title of the source in which it appeared. All titles by the author featured in the text are printed in boldface type. Footnotes are reprinted at the end of each essay or excerpt. In the case of excerpted criticism, only those footnotes that pertain to the excerpted texts are included.

- A complete **Bibliographical Citation** of the original essay or book precedes each piece of criticism. Source citations in the Literary Criticism Series follow University of Chicago Press style, as outlined in *The Chicago Manual of Style*, 14th ed. (Chicago: The University of Chicago Press, 1993).

- Critical essays are prefaced by brief **Annotations** explicating each piece.

- An annotated bibliography of **Further Reading** appears at the end of each entry and suggests resources for additional study. In some cases, significant essays for which the editors could not obtain reprint rights are included here. Boxed material following the further reading list provides references to other biographical and critical sources on the author in series published by Gale.

Indexes

A **Cumulative Author Index** lists all of the authors that appear in a wide variety of reference sources published by the Gale Group, including *TCLC*. A complete list of these sources is found facing the first page of the Author Index. The index also includes birth and death dates and cross references between pseudonyms and actual names.

A **Cumulative Nationality Index** lists all authors featured in *TCLC* by nationality, followed by the number of the *TCLC* volume in which their entry appears.

A **Cumulative Topic Index** lists the literary themes and topics treated in the series as well as in *Classical and Medieval Literature Criticism, Literature Criticism from 1400 to 1800, Nineteenth-Century Literature Criticism,* and the *Contemporary Literary Criticism* Yearbook, which was discontinued in 1998.

An alphabetical **Title Index** accompanies each volume of *TCLC*. Listings of titles by authors covered in the given volume are followed by the author's name and the corresponding page numbers where the titles are discussed. English translations of foreign titles and variations of titles are cross-referenced to the title under which a work was originally published. Titles of novels, dramas, nonfiction books, and poetry, short story, or essay collections are printed in italics, while individual poems, short stories, and essays are printed in roman type within quotation marks.

In response to numerous suggestions from librarians, Gale also produces an annual paperbound edition of the *TCLC* cumulative title index. This annual cumulation, which alphabetically lists all titles reviewed in the series, is available to all customers. Additional copies of this index are available upon request. Librarians and patrons will welcome this separate index; it saves shelf space, is easy to use, and is recyclable upon receipt of the next edition.

Citing *Twentieth-Century Literary Criticism*

When citing criticism reprinted in the Literary Criticism Series, students should provide complete bibliographic information so that the cited essay can be located in the original print or electronic source. Students who quote directly from reprinted criticism may use any accepted bibliographic format, such as University of Chicago Press style or Modern Language Association (MLA) style. Both the MLA and the University of Chicago formats are acceptable and recognized as being the current standards for citations. It is important, however, to choose one format for all citations; do not mix the two formats within a list of citations.

The examples below follow recommendations for preparing a bibliography set forth in *The Chicago Manual of Style,* 14th ed. (Chicago: The University of Chicago Press, 1993); the first example pertains to material drawn from periodicals, the second to material reprinted from books:

Morrison, Jago. "Narration and Unease in Ian McEwan's Later Fiction." *Critique* 42, no. 3 (spring 2001): 253-68. Reprinted in *Twentieth-Century Literary Criticism.* Vol. 127, edited by Janet Witalec, 212-20. Detroit: Gale, 2003.

Brossard, Nicole. "Poetic Politics." In *The Politics of Poetic Form: Poetry and Public Policy,* edited by Charles Bernstein, 73-82. New York: Roof Books, 1990. Reprinted in *Twentieth-Century Literary Criticism.* Vol. 127, edited by Janet Witalec, 3-8. Detroit: Gale, 2003.

The examples below follow recommendations for preparing a works cited list set forth in the *MLA Handbook for Writers of Research Papers,* 5th ed. (New York: The Modern Language Association of America, 1999); the first example pertains to material drawn from periodicals, the second to material reprinted from books:

Morrison, Jago. "Narration and Unease in Ian McEwan's Later Fiction." *Critique* 42.3 (spring 2001): 253-68. Reprinted in *Twentieth-Century Literary Criticism.* Ed. Janet Witalec. Vol. 127. Detroit: Gale, 2003. 212-20.

Brossard, Nicole. "Poetic Politics." *The Politics of Poetic Form: Poetry and Public Policy.* Ed. Charles Bernstein. New York: Roof Books, 1990. 73-82. Reprinted in *Twentieth-Century Literary Criticism.* Ed. Janet Witalec. Vol. 127. Detroit: Gale, 2003. 3-8.

Suggestions are Welcome

Readers who wish to suggest new features, topics, or authors to appear in future volumes, or who have other suggestions or comments are cordially invited to call, write, or fax the Project Editor:

Project Editor, Literary Criticism Series
The Gale Group
27500 Drake Road
Farmington Hills, MI 48331-3535
1-800-347-4253 (GALE)
Fax: 248-699-8054

Acknowledgments

The editors wish to thank the copyright holders of the criticism included in this volume and the permissions managers of many book and magazine publishing companies for assisting us in securing reproduction rights. We are also grateful to the staffs of the Detroit Public Library, the Library of Congress, the University of Detroit Mercy Library, Wayne State University Purdy/Kresge Library Complex, and the University of Michigan Libraries for making their resources available to us. Following is a list of the copyright holders who have granted us permission to reproduce material in this volume of *TCLC*. Every effort has been made to trace copyright, but if omissions have been made, please let us know.

COPYRIGHTED MATERIAL IN *TCLC*, VOLUME 142, WAS REPRODUCED FROM THE FOLLOWING PERIODICALS:

African American Review, v. 29, spring, 1995 for "Should Their Eyes Have Been Watching God?: Hurston's Use of Religious Experience and Gothic Horror" by Erik Curren. Copyright © 1995 by Erik Curren. All rights reserved. Reproduced by permission of the author.—*Arthuriana,* v. 4, winter, 1994. Copyright © 1994, by *Arthuriana.* All rights reserved. Reproduced by permission.—*Conradiana,* v. 13, 1981. Copyright © 1981, by *Conradiana.* All rights reserved. Reproduced by permission.—*Contemporary Literature,* v. 10, winter, 1969. Copyright © 1969 The Board of Regents of the University of Wisconsin System. All rights reserved. Reproduced by permission.—*Criticism: A Quarterly for Literature and the Arts,* v. 9, winter, 1967. Copyright, 1967, Wayne State University Press. Reproduced by permission of the publisher.—*Folklore,* v. 111, October, 2000 for "The Holy Grail: From Romance Motif to Modern Genre" by Juliette Wood. Copyright © 2000, by *Folklore.* All rights reserved. Reproduced by permission of the publisher and the author.—*The German Quarterly,* v. 54, May, 1981. Copyright © 1981 by the American Association of Teachers of German. Reproduced by permission.—*Mississippi Quarterly,* v. 50, fall, 1997. Copyright © 1997, *Mississippi Quarterly.* All rights reserved. Reproduced by permission.—*Rocky Mountain Review of Language and Literature,* v. 47, 1993. Copyright © 1993, by *Rocky Mountain Review of Language and Literature.* All rights reserved. Reproduced by permission.—*Scandinavian Studies,* v. 48, 1976 for "Documentarism and the Modern Scandinavian Novel" by George Bisztray; v. 71, spring, 1999 for "H. C. Branner and the Colors of Consciousness" by Mark Mussari. Copyright © 1976, 1999 by *Scandinavian Studies.* Both reproduced by permission of the publisher and the respective authors.—*South Dakota Review,* v. 20, summer, 1982. © 1982, University of South Dakota. All rights reserved. Reproduced by permission.—*Southern Literary Journal,* v. 4, fall, 1971. Copyright © 1971, by *Southern Literary Journal.* All rights reserved. Reproduced by permission.—*Southwest Review,* v. 50, summer, 1965. Copyright © 1965, *Southwest Review.* All rights reserved. Reproduced by permission.—*Victorian Poetry,* v. 11, winter, 1973 for "The Holy Grail: Subversion and Revival of a Tradition in Tennyson and T. S. Eliot" by Linda Ray Pratt. Copyright © 1973, *West Virginia University,* 1973. Reproduced by permission of the author.—*World Literature Today,* v. 57, winter, 1983. Copyright © 1983, *by World Literature Today.* Reproduced by permission.—*Wisconsin Studies in Contemporary Literature,* v. 4, autumn, 1963. Copyright © 1963, renewed 1991 The Board of Regents of the University of Wisconsin System. All rights reserved. Reproduced by permission.

COPYRIGHTED MATERIAL IN *TCLC*, VOLUME 142, WAS REPRODUCED FROM THE FOLLOWING BOOKS:

Andersen, Frank Egholm, and John Weinstock. From "Danish Literary Criticism since 1960," in *The Nordic Mind: Current Trends in Scandinavian Literary Criticism.* Edited by Frank Egholm Andersen and John Weinstock. Copyright © by University Press of America, Inc., 1986. All rights reserved. Reproduced by permission.—Appel, Alfred, Jr. From *A Season of Dreams: The Fiction of Eudora Welty.* Louisiana State University Press, 1965. Copyright © 1965, by Louisiana State University Press. All rights reserved. Reproduced by permission.—Barr, Marleen. From "Food for Postmodern Thought: Isak Dinesen's Female Artists as Precursors to Contemporary Feminist Fabulators," in *Feminism, Utopia, and Narrative.* Edited by Libby Falk Jones and Sarah Webster Goodwin. University of Tennessee Press, 1990. Copyright ©1990, by University of Tennessee. All rights reserved. Reproduced by permission.—Brostrøm, Torben. From *Contemporary Danish Poetry: An Anthology.* Twayne's, 1977. Copyright © by Gyldenalske Boghandel, Nordisk Forlag A/S, Copenhagen 1977. All rights reserved. Reproduced by permission.—Burns, Margie. From "A Good Rose Is Hard to Find: Southern Gothic as Signs of Social Dislocation in Faulkner and O'Connor," in *Image and Ideology in Modern/Postmodern Discourse.* Edited by David B. Browning and Susan Bazargan. State University of New York Press, 1991. Copyright © 1991, by State University of New York. All rights reserved. Reproduced by permission of the State University of New York Press.—Crowley,

J. Donald, and Sue Mitchell Crowley. From *King Arthur Through the Ages.* Garland Publishing Inc., 1990. Copyright © 1990, by Valerie M. Lagorio and Mildred Leake Day. All rights reserved. Reproduced by permission.—Furness, Raymond. From *Expressionism Reassessed.* University of Manchester, 1993. Copyright © Raymond Furness. Reproduced by permission of the author.—Gray, Charlotte Schiander. From *Klaus Rifbjerg.* Copyright © 1986 by Charlotte Schiander Gray. Reproduced by permission of Greenwood Publishing Group, Inc., Westport, CT.—Henriksen, Aage. From *Isak Dinesan/Karen Blixen: The Work and the Life.* Translated by William Mishler. St. Martin's Press, NY, 1988. Reproduced by permission.—Ingwersen, Faith, and Niels Ingwersen. From *Quests for a Promised Land: The Works of Martin Andersen Nexø.* Greenwood Press, 1984. Copyright © 1984 by Faith Ingwersen and Niels Ingwersen. Reproduced by permission of Greenwood Publishing Group, Inc., Westport, CT.—Kahane, Claire. From *The Female Gothic.* Eden Press, 1983. Copyright © 1983, Eden Press, Inc. Reproduced by permission of the author.—Krispyn, Egbert. From *Style and Society in German Literary Expressionism.* University of Florida Press, 1964. Copyright © by the Board of Commissioners of the State Institutions of Florida. Reproduced with the permission of the University Press of Florida.—Martin, Robert K. From "Haunted by Jim Crow: Gothic Fictions by Hawthorne and Faulkner," in *American Gothic: New Inventions in a National Narrative.* Edited by Robert K. Martin and Eric Savoy. University of Iowa Press, 1998. Copyright © 1998, by University of Iowa Press. All rights reserved. Reproduced by permission.—Moorman, Charles. From *The Grail: A Casebook.* Garland Publishing Inc., 2000. Copyright © 2000, by Dhira B. Mahoney. All rights reserved. Reproduced by permission.—Murphy, Richard. From *Theorizing the Avant-Garde: Modernism, Expressionism, and the Problem of Postmodernity.* Cambridge University Press, 1998. Copyright © 1998 Richard Murphy. Reproduced by permission.—Nicholls, Peter. From *Modernisms: A Literary Guide.* Macmillan, 1995. © Peter Nicholls 1995. All rights reserved. Reproduced by permission.—O'Connor, Theresa. From "Demythologizing Nationalism: Joyce's Dialogized Grail Myth," in *Joyce in Context.* Edited by Vince J. Cheng and Timothy Martin. Cambridge University Press, 1992. Copyright © 1992, by Cambridge University Press. All rights reserved. Reproduced by permission.—Olderman, Raymond M. From *Beyond the Waste Land: The American Novel in the Nineteen Sixties.* Yale University Press, 1972. Copyright, 1972, Yale University Press. Reproduced by permission.—Perry, J. Douglas. From *The Critical Response to Truman Capote.* Greenwood Press, 1999. Copyright © 1999. Reproduced by permission of Greenwood Publishing Group, Inc., Westport, CT. All rights reserved.—Schleifer, Ronald. From "Rural Gothic: The Sublime Rhetoric of Flannery O'Connor," in *Frontier Gothic: Terror and Wonder at the Frontier in American Literature.* David Mogen, Scott P. Sanders, Joanne B. Karpinski, eds. Associated University Presses, 1993. Copyright © 1993, by Associated University Presses, Inc. All rights reserved. Reproduced by permission.—Thompson, Raymond H. From *The Grail: A Casebook.* Garland Publishing Inc., 2000. Copyright © 2000, by Dhira B. Mahoney. All rights reserved. Reproduced by permission.—Vergo, Peter. From "The Origins of Expressionism and the Notion of Gesamtkunstwerk," in *Expressionism Reassessed.* Shulamith Behr, David Fanning, and Douglas Jarman, eds. University of Manchester, 1993. Copyright © Peter Vergo. Reproduced by permission of the author.—Waller, Christopher. From *Expressionist Poetry and Its Critics.* Institute of Germanic Studies, University of London, 1986. Copyright © 1986 by The Institute of Germanic Studies. All rights reserved. Reproduced by permission.

PHOTOGRAPHS AND ILLUSTRATIONS APPEARING IN *TCLC*, VOLUME 142, WERE RECEIVED FROM THE FOLLOWING SOURCES:

Dinesen, Isak, 1957, photograph. Corbis-Bettmann. Reproduced by permission.—Eliot, T. S., photograph. International Portrait Gallery. Reproduced by permission.—Jensen, Johannes V., 1945, photograph. Corbis-Bettmann. Reproduced by permission.—Kokoschka, Oscar, 1949, photograph. Hulton-Deutsch Collection/Corbis-Bettmann. © 2000 Artist Rights Society (ARS), New York/ ProLitteris, Zurich. Reproduced by permission.—Sir Percival and the Holy Grail, photograph. Corbis-Bettmann. Reproduced by permission.—Plantation house in Convent, Louisiana, photograph by Russell Lee. Getty Images. Reproduced by permission.

Gale Literature Product Advisory Board

The members of the Gale Group Literature Product Advisory Board—reference librarians from public and academic library systems—represent a cross-section of our customer base and offer a variety of informed perspectives on both the presentation and content of our literature products. Advisory board members assess and define such quality issues as the relevance, currency, and usefulness of the author coverage, critical content, and literary topics included in our series; evaluate the layout, presentation, and general quality of our printed volumes; provide feedback on the criteria used for selecting authors and topics covered in our series; provide suggestions for potential enhancements to our series; identify any gaps in our coverage of authors or literary topics, recommending authors or topics for inclusion; analyze the appropriateness of our content and presentation for various user audiences, such as high school students, undergraduates, graduate students, librarians, and educators; and offer feedback on any proposed changes/enhancements to our series. We wish to thank the following advisors for their advice throughout the year.

Barbara M. Bibel
Librarian
Oakland Public Library
Oakland, California

Dr. Toby Burrows
Principal Librarian
The Scholars' Centre
University of Western Australia Library
Nedlands, Western Australia

Celia C. Daniel
Associate Librarian, Reference
Howard University
Washington, D.C.

David M. Durant
Reference Librarian
Joyner Library
East Carolina University
Greenville, North Carolina

Nancy Guidry
Librarian
Bakersfield Community College
Bakersfield, California

Steven R. Harris
English Literature Librarian
University of Tennessee
Knoxville, Tennessee

Mary Jane Marden
Collection Development Librarian
St. Petersburg College
Pinellas Park, Florida

Heather Martin
Arts & Humanities Librarian
University of Alabama at Birmingham, Sterne Library
Birmingham, Alabama

Susan Mikula
Director
Indiana Free Library
Indiana, Pennsylvania

Thomas Nixon
Humanities Reference Librarian
University of North Carolina, Davis Library
Chapel Hill, North Carolina

Mark Schumacher
Jackson Library
University of North Carolina
Greensboro, North Carolina

Gwen Scott-Miller
Assistant Director
Sno-Isle Regional Library System
Marysville, Washington

Donald Welsh
Head, Reference Services
College of William and Mary, Swem Library
Williamsburg, Virginia

The Grail Theme in Twentieth-Century Literature

The following entry presents criticism on the Grail theme in twentieth-century literature.

INTRODUCTION

The legend of the Grail and the quest to locate it has been one of the most consistent motifs throughout Western literature. One of the earliest recorded instances of the legend itself was in Chrétien de Troyes's *Perceval ou Le conte du Graal* (c. 1190), which depicted the Grail as a chalice or vessel that was present during the Last Supper and later used to collect Jesus Christ's blood after his crucifixion. Though there are numerous interpretations and theories regarding the origin of the myth and the vessel, in its most basic form, the story of the Grail revolves around a quest for an object that sustains life. In most versions of the legend, the Grail is extremely difficult to find—hidden in a desolate castle, surrounded by barren land, and guarded by an ailing owner. The myth holds that the power of the Grail can only be restored if the questing knight is able to find the castle and ask the right question of its owner. Failure at any time during this journey implies a failure of the quest, which must then begin anew. The knight who succeeds in his quest becomes the new guardian of the castle and the Grail, replacing the previous caretaker, often referred to as the Fisher King. Although the legend is fundamentally connected to Christian beliefs and mythology, literary interpretations of the story have treated the Grail as both a secular and religious symbol. The most common association of the Grail quest in literature is with Arthurian legends, but scholars acknowledge that the concept of the Grail existed in Western mythology long before the tales of King Arthur and his Round Table were created.

Twentieth-century authors, in particular, have utilized the Grail legend in both realistic and fantasy fiction, notably in stories that revolve around time travel or the struggle between good and evil. One variation on the Grail myth—largely introduced by twentieth-century authors—has been the focus on characters that attempt to steal the Grail for their own purposes. Such selfish motivations are held in stark contrast to the traditional role of the Grail in literature, where the vessel is a holy talisman, representative of an individual's journey towards spiritual growth and enlightenment. In other works, the Grail appears as a representation of the disparity between the material and spiritual worlds. For example, in Arthur Machen's *The Great Return* (1915), the Grail serves as an inspiration to better oneself, while in T. S. Eliot's *The Waste Land* (1922), the legend provides thematic unity to a poem that laments the futility of contemporary life. Critic Raymond H. Thompson has noted that the Grail theme is frequently utilized in works that highlight the condition of the human heart or an individual's attempts to reach beyond the material world. As such, works like *The Waste Land* use the typically barren landscapes of the Grail quest as a contrasting backdrop to their characters's search for spiritual fulfillment in modern society.

Though it remains a significant thematic and allegorical device in twentieth-century literature, the Grail legend continues to be most often associated with contemporary reinterpretations of classic Arthurian legends. Charles Williams composed one of the first major poetic treatments of the Grail legend in the twentieth century, *Taliessen through Logres* (1938), and outlined the story of King Arthur and the Grail in several of his works. Other authors, such as Walker Percy, have employed the Grail as an ironic device. In *Lancelot* (1963) Percy adopts the form of the Grail quest as a paradigm for the Southern code of Stoicism in face of defeat. Barbara Tepa Lupack has argued that several twentieth-century novelists, including F. Scott Fitzgerald and Ernest Hemingway, among others, have successfully reinterpreted the Grail quest in atypical forms, employing the symbolism of the Grail in their works and personal lives. In the latter half of the twentieth century, the Grail legend continued to inspire such authors as Michael Ondaatje and Bobbie Ann Mason, both of whom have merged the traditional myth with modern-day imagery and cultural concerns. The Grail also continues to be a significant source of material and metaphor in contemporary works of science fiction and fantasy, particularly in the works of Neil Gaiman, S. P. Sumtow, and Tanith Lee.

REPRESENTATIVE WORKS

Thomas Berger
Arthur Rex (novel) 1978

Joseph Conrad
Chance (novel) 1913

T. S. Eliot
The Waste Land (poetry) 1922

F. Scott Fitzgerald
The Great Gatsby (novel) 1925

Parke Godwin
Firelord (novel) 1980

Ernest Hemingway
The Sun Also Rises (novel) 1926

Jim Hunter
Percival and the Presence of God (novel) 1978

James Joyce
Ulysses (novel) 1922

Ken Kesey
One Flew Over the Cuckoo's Nest (novel) 1962

C. S. Lewis
Arthurian Torso (novel) 1938
The Hideous Strength (novel) 1945

Arthur Machen
The Great Return (novel) 1915

Naomi Mitchison
To the Chapel Perilous (novel) 1955

Walker Percy
Lancelot (novel) 1963

Jack Spicer
The Holy Grail (novel) 1962

Alfred Tennyson
Idylls of the King (poetry) 1859

Charles Williams
War in Heaven (novel) 1930
Taliessen Through Logres (poetry) 1938

OVERVIEWS AND GENERAL STUDIES

Juliette Wood (essay date October 2000)

SOURCE: Wood, Juliette. "The Holy Grail: From Romance Motif to Modern Genre." *Folklore* 111, no. 2 (October 2000): 169-90.

[*In the following excerpted essay, Wood provides overviews of several Grail texts, beginning with a summary of Grail romances, their primary themes and motifs, and concluding with an examination of popular twentieth-century Grail-related material.*]

In his search for the Grail, Tennyson's Lancelot follows a "sweet voice singing in the topmost tower":

> . . . as in a dream I seemed to climb
> For ever: at the last I reached a door . . .
> It gave, and throe' a stormy glare, a heat
> As from a seventimes-heated furnace . . .
> And yet methought I saw the Holy Grail
> All palled in crimson samite . . .
>
> (*Idylls of the King*, 2:829-44)

Just over a century later, publishers regularly advertise Lancelot's vision of the Holy Grail with promises of new discoveries about the world of ancient Druids, Templars and assorted mystics. Books purporting to reveal the secret behind the Holy Grail literature of the Middle Ages are a widespread phenomenon of modern popular culture. Indeed so prevalent are they that any attempt at a comprehensive survey would be out of date as soon as it was printed. Nor, given the autodidactic nature of this writing, is there much point in trying to refute any of the assertions by unravelling the tortuous arguments which underpin this material. This article intends to trace the Holy Grail theme from a set of motifs in medieval romance to the modern genre of grail literature and to focus on the resulting interface between literary and popular culture.

Introduction

Suggestions put forward as to the source and meaning of the "Grail story" include Celtic myth, the Eucharistic rites of Eastern Christianity, ancient mystery religion, Jungian archetypal journeys, dualist heresies, Templar treasure, the descendants of Christ and Mary Magdalene, several actual objects, and any combination of the above. All these positions have adherents who are fierce in defence and detractors who are equally dismissive of these suggestions. The common thread which links these theories is the assumption that the grail story has a single source and that this source has a meaning which is obscured in the romances themselves. The question one might ask at this stage, from the point of view of folklore studies, is whether a series of repeated motifs necessarily implies a common tale and *a priori* source. In other words, is there a grail problem to be solved or is this simply an artefact of the methodology of grail criticism? Recent academic studies have stressed influences rather than origins and concentrated on the romances as literature rather than as repositories of secrets which the authors do not understand.[1] However, an earlier, and very influential, stream of romance criticism considered that the origin of romance was the primary question to be answered; and many modern grail studies, however eccentric the research they embody may be, still make use of such assumptions. Many current popular ideas derive from earlier grail scholarship which dates from the 1880s to the 1960s. In order to clarify why this particular story should exercise such a fascination in the popular imagination and in a particular corner of the publishing industry, it would be well to trace earlier research.

The theories discussed in this lecture developed as a by-product of renewed interest in medieval romance, and the middle ages generally, in the nineteenth century. This has to be seen in the wider context of the occult revival of this time, with its tendency to interpret Renaissance philosophy and the innovations of the Age of Enlightenment, such as masonism and Rosicrusianism, as carrying information which, while it could provide personal or cultural transformation, threatened the establishment. Many of these movements were tied in a complex way to the increasing power, and increasingly democratic interests, of the growing bourgeoisie. The appeal of the grail theme, particularly in the early part of the twentieth century, was very wide and broadly European.

Summary of the Grail Romances

One of the frustrations of this material, and a feature which has undoubtedly contributed to the increasingly bizarre theories about its origin, is the fact that no consistent "Grail story" emerges from the several romances in which material appears. However a basic story outline would be something like the following: A mysterious vessel or object which sustains life and/or provides sustenance is guarded in a castle which is difficult to find. The owner of the castle is either lame or sick and often (but not always) the surrounding land is barren. The owner can only be restored if a knight finds the castle and, after seeing a mysterious procession, asks a certain question. If he fails in this task, everything will remain as before and the search must begin again. After wanderings and adventures (many of which relate to events which the young hero fails to understand the first time), the knight returns to the castle and asks the question which cures the king and restores the land. The hero knight succeeds the wounded king (usually called the Fisher King) as guardian of the castle and its contents.

The grail episode in the relevant romances is summarised here and references to editions and translations of the romances are given in the appendix. In the text of this article references to individual romances are given in brackets using the name of the author where this is known or the identifying titles (which are themselves often a matter of convention) used in this summary. An object referred to as the grail and later as the Holy Grail occurs in a number of medieval romances written between the end of the twelfth and the end of the thirteenth century. Despite the vast antiquity for the material, its appearance in literary form occurred within a single century.

The motif first appeared in an unfinished romance *Perceval ou Le conte du Graal* by Chrétien de Troyes dated to about 1190. Chrétien's romance was written at the behest of his patron, Count Philip of Flanders, a crusader knight. The fall of Jerusalem occurred in 1187 just before the first appearance of the grail as a literary motif. The historical crusades, their effect on Europe generally and on the nobility in particular, form an important backdrop to this material, although it is equally important to distinguish between the social and economic effects of the crusades on the medieval world and the mystical speculations about Templars and such which are a part of later grail speculation.

Detail from an illuminated manuscript from 1286 showing Sir Percival, two knights, and the Holy Grail.

In Chrétien de Troyes's romance, Perceval sees the grail during a feast at a mysterious castle presided over by a lame man called the Fisher King whom he had met the day before. Chrétien calls the object simply "un graal," and its appearance is just one of the unusual events which takes place during the feast. Indeed at this time Perceval is also shown a broken sword which must be mended. The two objects together, sword and grail, are symbols of Perceval's development as a true knight.

Chrétien de Troyes died before finishing this romance, but the story was completed by other writers. *The Continuations,* as they are referred to in critical literature, expand several themes and the grail gradually acquires a more "sacramental" character. *The First Continuation* is also incomplete and the author is unknown, but it can be dated before 1200. Besides Perceval, Gawain also has a grail adventure (the womanising Gawain is the type of the perfect worldly knight and regularly forms a contrast to Perceval in these romances). During a procession which Gawain sees, the "rich grail" (as it is now called) floats about the hall and provides food for all; the bleeding lance is later identified as the Lance of Longinus (beginning the trend to see these objects as relics); and the broken sword belongs to a dead knight who is laid out on a bier. He who mends the sword will know the secrets of the grail castle (thereby strengthening the link between sword and grail). A new adventure, the Chapel of the Black Hand, is added in which a mysterious hand snuffs out the candles in the chapel.

The *Second Continuation,* written by Gauchier de Donaing (*c.* 1200), is also unfinished but pushes the story even farther into the realms of mysterious supernatural happenings. Perceval plays with a magical chess board; and a lady offers him a hunting dog and white stag's head, which he loses and has to recover before returning to the grail castle. He fails to mend the sword completely. The *Third Continuation* (*c.* 1230), written by Manessier, completes the story of Perceval and Gawain. The Fisher King explains the items in the grail procession: the spear was used by Longinus to pierce Christ's side at the Crucifixion; the cup belonged to Joseph of Arimathea; the trencher covered the cup to protect the blood; and the sword wounded both the Fisher King and his brother. Perceval undergoes the adventure of the Chapel of the Black Hand. When the sword is mended, Perceval as grail ruler heals the land. After seven years, he retires to a hermitage, and when he dies the grail, lance and dish go with him.

Unfortunately Manessier's explanation of the grail was replaced by yet another, and final, continuation of the story. The *Fourth Continuation* by Gerbert de Montreuil (*c.* 1230) has a strong moralising tone. It takes up the story after Perceval's first failure and introduces a long series of adventures before Perceval returns to the Grail castle to mend the sword.

While Chrétien's romance was the first, and remains in many ways central to developments within the tradition, other medieval writers took up the theme; as well as development, there is cross fertilisation. Between *c.* 1191-1200, the Burgundian poet, Robert de Boron, also writing at the behest of a crusader patron, the Lord of Montfaçon, produced three romances, *Joseph d'Arimathie, Merlin* (most of which is lost) and *Perceval* (which may or may not actually have been written). All these romances treat the grail theme. Robert de Boron puts the grail into the context of Christ's passion. In *Joseph d'Arimathie,* Pilate gives the cup used at the Last Supper and Crucifixion to Joseph of Arimathea who is subsequently imprisoned. Christ brings the grail to Joseph in prison where it sustains him and teaches him its secrets. Joseph is freed by the emperor Vespasian who has been cured by Veronica's veil (another mysterious relic associated with Christ's passion). Robert introduces two more characters, Joseph's sister and her husband, Hebron (Bron). Joseph establishes a second table of the grail, and Bron catches a fish which is placed on the table and separates the just from the unjust. The object is called the Holy Grail at this point and gives joy to all who sit at the table. Alain, the leader of Bron's twelve sons, goes to Britain to await the "third man" (Perceval?) who will be the permanent keeper of the grail. Bron becomes the "Rich Fisher" and journeys with the grail to Britain, while Joseph returns to Arimathea. In Robert de Boron's *Merlin,* the magician constructs the Round Table in imitation of the Grail table and adds the Siege Perilous which awaits the truest knight who will find the grail. Later Merlin helps Perceval on his grail adventures, and after Perceval becomes Grail King Merlin retires to the woods to dictate the grail story to the priest, Blaise. Whether Robert de Boron actually wrote *Perceval* is not known but the prose version based on these romances (usually called the *Roman du Graal*) established the fashion for a new format which traced the history of the grail from its origins in the biblical story of Christ's passion to its achievement by one of the knights. In effect this became a grail cycle which focused on the knights who undertook the quest for the grail rather than the courtly knights who accomplished adventures for the love of a lady and the honour of the king.

The *Didot Perceval* (*c.* 1220) is a prose romance based on Robert de Boron's lost *Perceval* and the *Second Continuation.* Here, Perceval is the son of Alain le Gros (evidence of the Joseph of Arimathea tradition). After he sits in the forbidden seat at the Round Table, the stone splits, the grail appears, and a voice announces the quest to restore order and lift the enchantments. The context is Arthur's court and the grail is absorbed into the Arthurian saga in which all the knights undertake the quest. Perceval's adventures include the loss of a stag and hound (from the *Second Continuation*), the fight with the knight of the tomb, the children in the tree, the hermit uncle and the Fisher King (from Chrétien), and an encounter with Merlin (from Robert de Boron). Perceval asks the grail questions which cure the Fisher King, repairs the stone, reveals the secret of the grail (not to the reader of course), and remains as ruler of Grail castle. Then the tale continues with Arthur as its focus.

An anonymous French prose romance, the *Perlesvaus* was written *c.* 1212-1220 for another crusader patron, Jean de Nesle. It uses elements from Chrétien and Robert de Boron. As well as the material relating to Perceval, Gawain sees the grail and lance but fails to ask the required question, and Lancelot too has a grail adventure. Perceval avenges his mother and frees the Grail Castle from the king of Castle Mortal. The romance has strong religious overtones with references to "New Law versus Old Law" and a number of violent adventures. In the thirteenth century this romance was adapted into middle Welsh as *Y Saint Graal* and about the same time grail-romance material became attached to the outlaw-knight figure Foulk fitz Warin.

Chrétien's story begins with Perceval living in the forest with his mother who is determined to keep him from the life of knightly adventure which killed her husband and her other sons. This incident is expanded in two "prologues," which are really independent romances that tell the adventures which lead up to Perceval's upbringing in the woods. Both prologues were written in the early thirteenth century. One, the *Bliocadron Prologue,* recounts the adventures of Bliocadron, Perceval's father, who is the last of twelve brothers killed in a tournament. The *Elucidation Prologue* tells the story of twelve well maidens who serve travellers. When they are raped and their golden cups stolen, the court of the Fisher King is lost, but Gawain and Perceval restore it. Castle Orguellos, another adventure which underlines the importance of the grail castle by reflecting it in reverse form, is set up and subdued by Arthur after a siege.

The German poet Wolfram von Eschenbach composed *Parzival* (c. 1200-1210) for his patron who was a crusader. *Parzival* is based on Chrétien, *The First Continuation* and the *Bliocadron Prologue,* but with much else. Wolfram prefaces his tale with the story of Kyot, the mythical Provençal poet who is his supposed source. He adds the story of Perceval's father and gives Perceval a pagan, piebald half-brother. Perceval is related to the Arthurian line through his father and to the grail family through his mother. The grail is a stone, the *lapsis exillis.* There are many eastern elements and a mystical tone. The grail family and a company of guardians guard the object. Wolfram calls them "templars" but there are women as well as men.

The thirteenth-century Welsh romance, *Peredur,* differs from the other romances in many ways. Its theme is vengeance for the death of a kinsman, not a grail quest. Peredur sojourns with his mistress, the Empress of Constantinople, for fourteen years. When he returns to Arthur's court, the loathly damsel berates him for failing to ask questions. He sees a head on a platter swimming in blood as part of a procession at a castle. Later he learns that it is the head of a cousin murdered by witches. These witches teach *Peredur* the craft of war, and subsequently he kills them.

Another romance with unusual features is *Diu Crone* written c. 1220 by Heinrich von dem Türlin. Here, Gawain wins the grail which is a reliquary with bread inside. Lancelot and another knight fall asleep, while Gawain sees the grail procession which includes both spear and grail.

The *Vulgate Cycle,* sometimes called "The Lancelot Grail," is a long cycle composed between c. 1215-1235 by different hands. Scholars suggest that the Cistercians were the principle authors and that they combined many elements in the earlier romances and further allegorised the story adding the figure of Galahad who follows the grail back to heaven and Sir Bors who returns to Arthur's court to tell the tale. The *Vulgate Cycle* is divided into five separate romances, given here in chronological order according to the development of the story, not in order of composition. *Estoire del Saint Graal* in which Joseph of Arimathea's son, Josephe, is Grail keeper followed by Alain, the first Fisher King, who places the grail in Corbennic Castle and waits for the Grail knight. In the *Estoire de Merlin,* Merlin dictates the grail story to Blaise and tells Arthur about Seige Perilous and Galahad. The *Prose Lancelot* contains the story of Galahad's birth, and the appearance of Sir Bors who joins Perceval, Gawain and Lancelot on the grail quest. The knights of the Round Table have a vision of the grail at which a voice announces the quest in *Queste del Saint Graal*. The grail here is the dish from which Jesus ate the Passover lamb. Lancelot's vision of the Grail is hindered because of his adultery with Guenevere and this reflects the emphasis on the corrupt nature of secular chivalry which is the underlying theme of the *Vulgate Cycle*. Gawain, Perceval and Bors sail to the Grail Castle in a mysterious ship. Galahad achieves the vision of Holy Grail and the two other knights return to Sarras (the grail castle on earth). Perceval becomes the grail king in this world and Bors returns to Camelot. The final romance, *Le Mort le Roi Artu,* links the success of the grail quest to the unravelling of the Arthurian world.

Two further romances should be mentioned. Henry Lovelich's *The History of the Holy Grail c.* 1450 is a translation from the French *Vulgate Cycle,* but adds the burial of Joseph at Glastonbury and stresses Merlin's role as prophet of the Holy Grail. The best known of these treatments is Thomas Malory's *Morte d'Arthur* written c. 1470 and published by Caxton in 1485. Malory uses the *Vulgate Cycle* for the adventures of the "Sangreal." He emphasises the role of Lancelot, and eventually the Grail is returned to the Holy Land.

Patterns and Themes

In many romances, the grail episode is only one among a number of adventures, and not always the obvious point of the story. The pattern in these complex texts is one of expansion and development. The writers were sometimes aware of other romances on the subject and often indicate their dependence on Chrétien or other sources. However, in assessing sources one needs to take into account medieval conventions in romance writing. References to strange sources and hidden books were used to give intensity to the act of composition, and writers did not necessarily intend an audience to take these literally. Although a grail and a procession lie at the centre of these stories, even these are not portrayed consistently. The grail can be a jewelled dish (*Chrétien*), a head floating in blood on a salver (*Peredur*), a stone (Wolfram), or a ciborium containing bread (*Diu Crone*). The grail procession includes a bleeding lance (Chrétien, Wolfram, de Boron), which is sometimes carried by a member of the procession but at other times in a lance-rest from which blood flows freely and is piped away (*First Continuation*). Often, the knight observing the procession is shown a broken or flawed sword, and an integral part of the task is to mend this weapon (*First, Second, Third Continuations*). In other versions (e.g. *Second Continuation*), a lady gives the knight a stag's head and hunting dog, which he subsequently loses and must restore before the main task can even be attempted. There is also an earthly counterpart to the grail castle, the Castle Orgellous or Castle of the Maidens (*Elucidation Prologue*), dominated by women who seem to represent the worldly aspect of chivalry. This adventure also needs to be completed before the return to the grail castle. Frequently Gawain, the embodiment of earthly chivalry, achieves this, while Perceval completes the grail task (*Third Continuation*). In some romances the knight plays chess with a self-moving magic chess board (*Second Continuation*). In another variation a corpse, together with a bleeding lance or broken sword, is laid out in a chapel or castle. In *Perlesvaus* it actually occurs as part of the grail procession. Once the Last Supper material was introduced early in the thirteenth century (Robert de Boron), the contrast between worldly chivalry and chivalry of a higher kind became sharper. The grail quest began to supersede the other quests in Arthurian literature and a new knight, Galahad (*Vulgate Cycle*), was introduced as the perfect grail knight. The figure of Merlin also became linked to the grail quest (de Boron, *Estoire de Merlin*, Lovelich, Malory).

Five Arthurian knights achieve a vision of the grail. Subsequent scholarship calls them "the Grail Knights," but this term is not found in the romances themselves. Perceval and Gawain are often paired; the latter as representatives of worldly chivalry. Gawain has a weakness for ladies and eventually wins a wife at the Castle of the Maidens. Some romances designate Perceval as the expected grail keeper whose adventures test and prepare him for his destiny and specify his relation to characters associated with the object and its castle (Chrétien, *The Continuations, Perlesvaus, Parzival, Peredur*). The other grail knights are Bors, Lancelot and Galahad. Lancelot is denied a full vision of the Grail because of his liaison with Guenevere, and it is his son, Galahad (*Vulgate Cycle*), who sits in the Siege Perilous, draws a mysterious sword from a stone, is transformed by the vision of the grail, and disappears from Sarras the earthly home of the grail. Bors sees the grail, and in the later versions (*Vulgate Cycle*) it is he who returns to Arthur's court to report on the events in Sarras.

It is worth pointing out, that the grail quest is always accomplished in medieval romances. During the tale the object may be withdrawn when its keepers prove unworthy or the knights are not yet ready, but eventually the destined knight finds it. This contrasts sharply with modern use of the term "holy grail" which implies something desired and sought, but never found. After he sees the grail, Perceval becomes ruler of the grail kingdom, while Galahad follows it into another realm. Malory incorporates the grail quest into his *Morte d'Arthur* where it supersedes the earthly quests of the Round Table fellowship and provides the catalyst for the ultimate failure of Arthur's kingdom. In Malory's source, the *Vulgate Cycle,* Lancelot's adultery with Guenevere causes the failure of the grail quest. Malory is more sympathetic to Lancelot, and the idea that immorality was at the root of the Camelot's fall is not prominent until Tennyson's revival and re-interpretation of the grail material in the nineteenth century.

Origin and Meaning

Earlier scholarly interest in this material was devoted to considering whether these episodes constituted a single narrative, and if so, what was its original meaning and purpose. On the whole, opinion favoured a myth about an otherworld talisman which medieval romance authors never fully understood yet attempted to explain. In other words, commentators assumed an original unity which became diversified subsequently by a process of corruption during transmission. However, if the texts are read in the sequence in which they were written, the grail material becomes more, not less, consistent over time. This suggests other possibilities, namely that romance writers adapted these diverse motifs into narratives whose meanings varied according to artistic purpose, and that, while the sources may be mythic, they do not have to feature in later contexts.

The grail itself is associated with sustenance, in particular the health of a wounded king. It appears at the beginning of some tales as a mysterious vision in the midst of Arthur's court and then it becomes the explicit object of the quest (*Vulgate Cycle*), and occasionally, and without the aid of human hands, it provides food and drink at a banquet in the Grail Castle (Gawain in *First Continuation*). Its major function, however, is to sustain the wounded king or kings in the mysterious castle. Robert de Boron makes it clear that the Eucharist is the sustaining food, linking the grail through Joseph of Arimathea to the Last Supper story. Chrétien de Troyes mentions "un graal" only as a jewelled dish with no aura of holiness, but even Chrétien hints that the Fisher King is sustained by sacred food. As well as the grail, the procession in Chrétien's romance includes a lance, a carved salver, several candelabra, and a sword which is shown to the hero beforehand. The table on which Perceval dines with the Fisher King is of ivory and ebony, two substances considered indestructible, and the whole passage is redolent of the kind of evocative but unspecified significance which was the stock-in-trade of medieval romances. Later a hermit describes the grail to Perceval saying that it brought food, but not a fish, to the Fisher King. This implies that "un graal" was a kind of gradulus, a large flat dish used to bring food to the table. The most likely derivation of the word grail is from Latin *gradulus,* but even if this derivation is correct, the object varies within romance tradition. Sometimes there are two dishes (*Perlesvaus*), a knight on a bier (*Continuations*), a head in a dish (*Peredur*), a stone (Wolfram), or a ciborium/reliquary (*Diu Crone*).

The Fisher King's food is mysterious in the early romances, and this may have prompted Robert de Boron to introduce the idea that the grail was the cup used at the Last Supper and the lance was the Lance of Longinus which pierced Christ's side and drew the last of his blood. In some romances, the sword seems to become identified with the sword which beheaded John the Baptist (*Vulgate Cycle, Diu Crone*). A number of factors which do not involve complex conspiracies to hide heretical secrets might have influenced this increasingly religious interpretation. One such development, for example, was the rise of popular piety movements and the increasing popularity of the Eucharist service among the laity (Gillett 1935, 95-110). Another might be that, since the Crusades had been going badly for the Europeans, there might have been increased interest in this kind of material (several of the romance writers' patrons were themselves crusaders). Again, the alleged discovery of Arthurian antiquities at Glastonbury, which occurred in 1191, might have increased interest in relics associated with biblical events located in the Holy Land. It is interesting that, although a number of relics purporting to be associated with the story of Christ's Passion (the True Cross, the Lance of Longinus, Veronica's Veil, the Holy Shroud) were brought into Europe at this period, there are no objects which claimed to be the Holy Grail. Such "grails" as exist are post-medieval. Whatever the source, Robert de Boron's verse romance written about 1210, placed the grail story on a new and fruitful track. Joseph of Arimathea and the Glastonbury connection (the latter is not clearly mentioned by de Boron) have proved just as durable as the grail, and indeed the two meld at many points (Treharne 1967, chap 2; Lewis 1955, 13-24). Labyrinthine arguments about Templars and eastern mysteries are part of the modern grail interpretation, but it is well to note that the Albigensian Crusade took place at the beginning of the thirteenth century (Sumption 1999, 77-88) and the Templars were suppressed in 1307 (Seward 1974, 197-213)

by which time the grail narratives were already well established. . . .

In 1888 Alfred Nutt published *The Holy Grail with Especial Reference to its Celtic Origin* under the aegis of the Folklore Society. This seminal work examined material in Irish, Welsh and Scots Gaelic relating to Otherworld vessels which had magic properties. These, together with vengeance tales and stories of heroes seeking supernatural objects and/or Otherworld women, were put forward as the ultimate source for the grail story. Nutt was not the first scholar to explore Celtic food-producing vessels as a source for this material. The earliest suggestion came from a neo-druid writer, Nash Williams, who noted the similarity between the grail and an object included among the Arthurian regalia in traditional Welsh lists. The relationship between the grail story and Celtic tradition was placed in a folklore context by Sabine Baring-Gould in 1878 (Baring-Gould 1976, 16-22). Ten years later Alfred Nutt published his study of the grail legend detailing the argument for a Celtic origin. He compared material in medieval romances with analogous motifs in medieval Irish and Welsh texts and with modern folklore material (Nutt 1888). Both in this work and in his subsequent writing on the subject, Nutt drew on and acknowledged a number of sources. Among them were newly edited texts from noted Irish scholars like Kuno Meyer, a substantial amount of recently collected folk narrative from collectors such as Douglas Hyde, Campbell of Islay and Paul Sébillot (Nutt 1889a; 1891; 1899; 1902a) and the *Mabinogion* tales from Charlotte Guest's translation which he re-published with his own commentary (Nutt 1902b).

All this fitted neatly into the theory that Celtic tradition had survived since pagan times and that Christianity had provided a force for preserving that tradition while introducing significant transformations and adaptations. Initially Nutt accepted J. G. Frazer's theories about a myth concerning the death and rebirth of a vegetation god, and Nutt felt that such a myth was central to Celtic mythology. Although he did not pursue this notion, it became essential to the grail theories of a scholar whom he encouraged to edit and publish Arthurian romance, namely Jessie Weston (Weston 1894; 1897; 1904; 1906-9; 1920). For Nutt, the real meaning of the grail lay in the original Celtic myths, while the romances preserved this meaning to a lesser degree. The noted French scholar Gaston Paris came to much the same conclusion quite independently, but Nutt used the then-current theories of folklore to substantiate his theory. For him, as for so many of his contemporaries, human intellect, while progressive, never left the past entirely behind but always retained "distinct marks of the ruder simpler stage out of which [it] emerged" (Nutt 1889b, 88). The Celts seemed the ideal embodiment of this. Their lively "pagan" imagination was fashionable thanks to such writers as Matthew Arnold, and was about to become more so in the next decade under the spur of W. B. Yeats's romantic ideas about Celtic culture (Yeats 1959). In addition, the prevailing view about the contact between the Celts and Christianity provided a mechanism for the transformation (and inevitable distortion) of myth. Thus the, often quite dramatic, inconsistencies between early Celtic tradition and themes in the medieval romances which incorporate grail material could be accounted for by the distorting effects of oral transmission and the adaptation of pagan myths to the context of Christian doctrine.

Nutt's folklore analysis of the grail has had an enormous influence. One hundred and twenty years later the idea that the original meaning of these romances lies in the distant past outside the romances themselves is still a basic assumption among popular writers. Through the work of R. S. Loomis it continued to be a major concern among medievalists into the 1960s when Loomis's linguistic assumptions began to be questioned; even now there is still a trickle of books which see medieval literature as a distortion of mythic material. In a volume for his "Mythology and Folklore" series produced for the general public, Nutt called the grail romances "the happy hunting ground of mystical enthusiasts" (Nutt 1902a, iv); his own rigorous studies were an attempt to redress this.

More than a hundred years later, even if attitudes to sources and subject have changed, many of his perceptions are still worth considering and any serious study of the grail material must begin with his scholarship. Although he himself never learned any Celtic languages, translations were supplied by noted specialists such as Kuno Meyer, Julius Pokorny, John Rhys and Eleanor Hull, while Jessie Weston provided continental material from medieval French, German and Dutch romances. A number of interesting studies followed his lead: Dorothy Kempe's *The Legend of the Grail* (1905); A. C. L. Brown's *The Origin of the Grail Legend* (1943); Helaine Newstead's *Bran the Blessed* (1939); and, most influential of all, the work of R. S. Loomis ([1927] 1935; 1949; 1956; 1959; 1963). Julius Pokorny's study *Der Graal in Irland und die mythischen Grundlage de Graalsage* (Pokorny 1918) is interesting, both because of the early date and because it represents the Celtic theory in a German language work (not perhaps very surprising, considering that Pokorny was a Celtic language specialist).

Later Lewis Spence was to combine the idea of Celtic origin with a suggestion in Nutt's early work. This set a mythic food-producing vessel at the centre of a Celtic agricultural myth (of the type Frazer had created). Spence's interest in shamanism and ancestor cults led him back to the neo-druidic speculations of the eighteenth century (which Nutt had rejected), especially speculations on druidism as proto-Christianity. The result is a Celtic Christian mystery religion which centres on the grail as a mystic experience (Spence 1995). In addition Spence distinguished between the benevolent occult arts and black magic. His attitude to Germanic tradition during the war was coloured by this, and he certainly contributed to the idea of a black magic conspiracy at the heart of the Nazi hierarchy (Spence 1944). In his defence Spence's ideas, particularly when he called for the revival of Celtic religion as a bulwark against the corruption of modern world, have more to do with Nietzsche than the excesses of Celtic romanticism, and there is no evidence of his involvement with the Order of the Golden Dawn or any other occult body. He created a Celtic religion out of a magpie collection of Scottish folklore, snippets of Celtic texts (always in translation), fragments of Alfred Nutt's theories, hints of George Freidrich Neitzche and oddments of Native American lore. The proposed link between the grail episode and early Celtic myth was not the only suggestion put forward to explain the grail.

Early Grail Scholarship: Alternative Origin Theories

In the 1890s, about the time that Nutt was taking a serious look at the Celtic ramifications, others began to look at the grail as a symbolic experience. Rudolf Steiner was among the first to suggest that the Grail Quest was actually a personal initiation experience coded into a narrative (Steiner 1963). Rudolf Steiner's intuitions about the grail as a symbol were taken up by W. J. Stein who put forward the idea that "grail experiences" began to be important in Charlemagne's court in the eighth and ninth centuries and then again in the twelfth. He identified the grail guardians with Charlemagne's "heirs." Stein suggested that the grail material, especially in Wolfram's romance could be interpreted as real, although hidden, history (Stein 1988). Jessie Weston's eccentric work on the "mystery rituals" allegedly behind these romances is an excellent example of the neo-Fraserian approach. Weston saw in the romances the sexual initiation of the knights which was a survival of ancient mystery religions which had to be disguised to escape the notice of Christianity (Grayson 1992).

The Meaning of the Grail in Popular Theory

Spence's strongest influence seems to be on modern Celticism, particularly the idea of Celtic Christianity and its relation to the grail. Writers like John Matthews clearly owe a great deal to his work (Matthews 1997). The theme of quest as initiation into some kind of mystery has also proved very fruitful. British occult interpretations like those of A. E. Waite, G. R. S. Mead and Jessie Weston proliferated (Wood 1998, 15-24; 1999, 3-12). The idea of quest as personal initiation, too, figures prominently in the new Celticism (Matthews 1997); and Steiner's interpretation has proved very fruitful. Rudolf Steiner himself has been suggested as the embodiment of the grail as part of an elaborate conspiracy theory linked to the theft of a relic alleged to be the Lance of Longinus from the Habsburg treasury in Vienna and involving occultism at the heart of the Nazi hierarchy (Ravenscroft 1973).

A link between the grail and the Crusades has also been seen as significant. Eastern Christian rites in which a lance-like knife is used to cut the bread at the Eucharist service have been put forward as a possible source for the grail (Holmes and Klenke 1959), although the grail procession as a whole bears little resemblance to these rites. As early as 1909 a more general eastern context was suggested and an origin in Persian tradition ultimately leading back to the followers of Ghenghis Khan in Iran (Jung/Franz 1998, 106-9; Iselin 1909, 7-12 and 61-75). Though Ghenghis Khan seems an unlikely Grail hero, the idea has been reworked recently by applying Dumézil's Indo-European theories to all Arthurian literature. A recent, and rather contentious, article in *Folklore* applied this idea to a group of Sarmatian mercenaries who settled in northern Britain in the second century. While it is difficult to accept that a small group of mercenaries would dominate a larger culture group rather than be absorbed, it is at least worth pointing out that the Roman leader of this band was a man named Lucius Artorius Castor (Wadge 1987, 204-15).

The grail episodes in romances have also been said to contain traces of alchemical and hermetic lore (Kahane 1965). Jungian analysts link the grail with alchemical and hermetic interpretations so that the Quest becomes an initiation, or "integration" in Jungian terms. The most complete and most intelligently written of these studies is that by Emma Jung, completed after her death by Marie Louise von Franz (Jung/Franz 1998). Another archetypal approach is Helen Adolf's study *Visio Pacis* which considers the grail theme in the medieval romances and in subsequent literature. She treats contemporary events such as the Crusades as a possible background for the grail romances (rather than a source for mysterious themes) and suggests the Templars might have been a model for the grail knight and his devotion to a higher chivalry (Adolf 1960).

Another grail theory favours the Templars over the Celts, and centres on the town of Rennes-le-Chateau in southern France. The ideas, which were published in the 1970s, have spawned an entire industry (Baigent et al 1984). Here, alleged links between the Holy Grail, the Templars and the Cathars go back to gnosticism, and the medieval legend concerning Christ and Mary Magdalene is added for good measure. The claim that there is a continuous dualist alternative which challenges the prevailing orthodox Christian view is a study in itself (Wood 1998, 15-24). The suggestion here is that the "grail" is a person rather than a thing, a lost royal heir. The idea owes much to Stein's ideas, presented in the 1930s, that the Grail is linked to Charlemagne and his successors. Stein's work forms the background to the assumptions made in *The Holy Blood and The Holy Grail* (Baigent et al. 1984) which links the Capetian king Dagobert and the Merovingians to a legend in Jacobus de Voragine's *The Golden Legend* in which Christ married Mary Magdalene and had children. According to this theory, the descendants of Christ are the heirs of Dagobert, one of whom was interviewed for the book. The assumptions underlying this study have been questioned in a recent BBC documentary, but they illustrate two essential features of much of this writing. These are, detective story analysis in which similarities are taken as proof of influence and connection, and an increasing tendency to refer to other popular works on the subject rather than to original source material. The Holy Blood theory has blossomed in recent years. Claims about occult geometrical patterns in certain classical paintings have been applied to the landscape around Rennes-le-Chateau (Fanthorpe 1991) to "locate" the tomb of Christ and to link the Roslyn Chapel "grail" in Scotland with buildings constructed by "Templars" in Nova Scotia (Sinclair 1992). The pattern of an explicit or an implicit group of guardians, a theme introduced in Wolfram's *Parzival*, now links Isaac Asimov's *Foundation Trilogy*, Tolkien's *Lord of the Rings*, and perhaps most intriguingly (or bizarrely) Umberto Eco's novel *Foucault's Pendulum* which was written as a satire on this very theory (Fanthorpe 1991).

In most of these romances the grail is a cup used at the Last Supper and there are several actual vessels that claim to be the Holy Grail. The earliest is an "emerald" vessel, the *sacro cratino* associated with Genoa. A sixteenth-century chronicle calls it "Saint Grail" and associates it with Christ or with King Arthur, which suggests this refers to the romances themselves rather than their sources (Jung/Franz 1998, 164). The *sacro cratino* was allegedly taken back to France by Napoleon and found to be green glass. Napoleon functions as a generic villain in many of these stories (his theft of the Templar records, for example) in providing a good excuse why something has gone missing. Two objects called confusingly the "Antioch Cup" and the "Cup of Antioch" were suggested as candidates for the grail in the 1930s. The former is a magnificent silver eucharist cup (now dated several centuries later) which is held by the Metropolitan Museum of Art in New York. The other is a glass krater, probably near-eastern glass, brought back from the crusades and fitted with a leather case to protect it some time during the Middle Ages (Cackett 1935, 7 and 23-7). There is supposedly a "grail" in Russia, and there is certainly a stone chalice in Valencia cathedral.

The beginning of this century was a peak period for grail objects. The mystic Tudor de la Pole who was much involved in transforming Glastonbury into a centre for Arthurian/Grail/Christian activity had an experience which led him to "discover" a blue glass bowl which he believed to be the grail and to expect a "third chosen one" as grail guardian. The object is still at the Chalice Gardens in Glastonbury (Villiers 1968, 26-9; Lehmann 1979, 13-24). The Powells of Nanteos, outside Aberystwyth, possessed a healing cup, recently identified as a fourteenth-century mazer bowl. The Powell family owned the site of Strata Florida Abbey and in 1905 this cup, which had been used locally since the 1880s as a healing object, suddenly acquired the title "Holy Grail."[2] Another candidate is a Roman alabaster cup in the possession of the Vernon family of Hawkstone manor. The alleged trail leads back through a medieval Welsh poem included in the story of Fulk le fitz Warin, a romance entitled "La Folie de Perceval" in B.N. Ms. 12577 (a compendium of French grail romance material) and a reference in the fifth-century by a Greek historian to the grail being taken to Britain for safety (Phillips 1995). Alas, there is no Welsh poem in the Anglo-Norman romance which tells the story of the outlaw knight, Fulk. There is no such romance as "La Folie de Perceval" in this particular French manuscript, nor is there a reference to the grail in the writings of the fifth-century Greek historian, Olympiadorus. But this work, like so many others is full of mysteries, codes and exciting "discoveries" overlooked by establishment historians and academics.

CONCLUSION

This lecture posed two initial questions—whether a series of repeated motifs necessarily implies a common tale and a prior source, and whether the "grail problem" is an artefact of the methodology of grail criticism.

It has been suggested recently that early medieval Irish culture had an awareness of ancient heritage and to some extent of the transition between oral and written (Nagy 1997). Whether the writers of medieval romance working in the context of Norman culture had the same perception we do not know. Some of them refer to earlier sources, such as Wolfram von Eschenbach's Kyot or the book given to Chrétien by his patron. These sources are likely to be literary conceits which need to be seen in the more general context in which writing was validated by an appeal to authority rather than by claims of uniqueness. Nevertheless, this certainly suggests that writers of romance recognised this material as an inheritance of some kind. Many of the motifs do resonate with earlier material such as Celtic food-producing vessels, although it is difficult to determine which, if any, myths concerned this material in earlier Celtic cultures; certainly to see the material as the survival of an important cult ritual goes beyond the evidence. The structure of the romances is broadly similar to the structure of *Märchen* in that both focus on the actions of a character who undergoes a series of adventures leading to an ultimate achievement. Here, traditional material has no doubt had an impact on a literary form, but one must caution against interpreting the formal logical structure shared by both folktale and romance as a secret code. The romances themselves show too much variation to be reduced to a single set of events and any attempt to reconstruct a coherent narrative at an earlier stage involves too many of the survivalist fallacies which folklore methodology has, quite sensibly, rejected.

The answer to the second question depends on the definition of "grail problem." The methodology used in many popular works is an eccentric application of ideas which were once current in academic circles, but the process itself is interesting from a folklore point of view as a way of reclaiming the past. Secret codes link the past with future hopes. They imply that aspects of the present which are disturbing can be overcome by reinstating a past Utopia. Such theories are now worked out in the arena of mass media, in publishing, newspaper and television. They manifest the characteristics of a real living tradition in their ability to attract material and to keep re-forming it in ever more intricate variations.

Notes

1. The focus of this article is to examine the stream of popular grail material rather than academic grail scholarship as such. This is covered in medieval and specialist Arthurian bibliographies. There are, however, a number of useful general sources which survey the material without arguing for any particular theory. For example, there are: a number of relevant articles and bibliographical references in Norris J. Lacey's *The New Arthurian Encyclopaedia* (1986); excerpts and commentary in *King Arthur in Legend and History*, edited by Richard White (1997); Richard Cavendish's *King Arthur and the Grail* (1978, 125-83 and 209-11) is still a balanced survey and introduction to the material; as are Charles Williams's and C. S. Lewis's study *Arthurian Torso* (1948). Arthurian web sites focus on the concerns of the popular grail genre, although they change too often to be listed. One such can be accessed at http://dc.smu.edu/Arthuriana.

2. The Nanteos Cup and other "holy grail" objects are the subject of an extended chapter in Nanteos edited by Gerald Morgan, forthcoming in spring 2000. Also see Evans 1937.

REPRESENTATIVE EDITIONS AND TRANSLATIONS
OF THE GRAIL ROMANCES

Perceval/Le conte du graal

Arthurian Romances of Chrétien de Troyes. Translated by William W. Kibler. Harmondsworth: Penguin, 1991.

Continuations

Perceval: The Story of the Grail. Translated by N. Bryant. In *Arthurian Studies,* no. 5, ed. D. S. Brewer. Cambridge: D. S. Brewer, 1982. Contains: *The First Perceval Continuation, The Second Perceval Continuation*; Gerbert De Montreuil, *Perceval Continuation* [the third continuation]; Manessier, *Perceval Continuation*

Robert de Boron

Le Roman de l'Estoire dou Graal. Edited by William Nitze. Paris: Champion, 1927.

Didot Perceval

The Didot Perceval. Edited by William Roach. Philadelphia: University of Pennsylvania Press, 1941 (this edition was translated by D. Skeeles and published by University of Washington Press in 1966).

Prologues

The Elucidation: A Prologue to the Conte del Graal. Edited by A. Thompson. New York: Publications of the Institute of French Studies, 1931.

Perlesvaus

Perlesvaus: or The High Book of the Grail. Translated by N. Bryant. Ipswich: Brewer, 1978.

Peredur

"Peredur." In *Mabinogion.* Translated by Gwyn Jones and Thomas Jones. London: Dent, 1949; revised ed. 1989.

Parzival

Parzival. Translated by A. T. Hatto. Harmondsworth: Penguin, 1980.

The Vulgate Cycle

The Vulgate Version of the Arthurian Romances. Edited by H. O. Sommer. 8 vols. Washington: Carnegie Institution, 1909-16; reprint New York: Carnegie Institution, 1979.

The Quest of the Holy Grail. Edited and translated by P. M. Matarasso. Harmondsworth: Penguin, 1969.

Diu Crone

The Crown (*Diu Crone*) by Heinrich von dem Türlin. Translated by J. W. Thomas. Lincoln: University of Nebraska Press, 1989.

Lovelich

The History of the Holy Grail. Edited by F. J. Furnivall. 4 vols. London: Trübner, 1874-1905.

Malory

The Works of Sir Thomas Malory. Edited by Eugène Vinaver. 3 vols. Oxford: Clarendon Press, 1954.

OTHER REFERENCES CITED

Adolf, Helen. *Visio Pacis: Holy City and Grail.* Harrisburg: Pennsylvania State University Press, 1960.

Baigent, Michael, Richard Leigh and Henry Lincoln. *The Holy Blood and The Holy Grail.* London: Corgi, 1984.

Barber, Richard. *King Arthur Hero and Legend.* Woodbridge: The Boydell Press, 1992.

Baring-Gould, Sabine. *The Holy Grail.* 1878; reprint Llanfynydd: Unicorn Press, 1976.

Brown, A. C. L. *The Origin of the Grail Legend.* Cambridge, MA: Harvard University Press, 1943.

Cackett, S. W. Gentle. *The Antioch Cup.* London: Palestine and Bible Lands Exhibition, 1935.

Cavendish, Richard. *King Arthur and the Grail.* London: Wiedenfeld and Nicolson, 1978.

Currer-Briggs, Noel. *The Shroud and the Grail.* New York: St Martin's Press, 1987.

Evans, George Eyre. 'Cwpan Nanteos'. *Cardiganshire Antiquarian Transactions,* no. 12 (1937): 29-30 and 58.

Fanthorpe, Lionel and Patricia. *Rennes-Le-Chateau: Its Mysteries and Secrets.* Middlesex: BelleVue Books, 1991.

Gillett, H. M. *The Story of the Relics of the Passion.* Oxford: Basil Blackwell, 1935.

Godwin, Malcolm. *The Holy Grail: Its Origins, Secrets and Meaning Revealed.* London: Labyrinth Books, 1994.

Goetinck, Glenys. *Peredur: A Study of Welsh Tradition in the Grail Legends.* Cardiff: University of Wales Press, 1975.

Grayson, Janet. "In Quest of Jessie Weston." In *Arthurian Literature XI,* ed. Richard Barber. 1-80. Cambridge: Boydell and Brewer, 1992.

Holmes, Urban T. and Amelia Klenke. *Chrétien de Troyes and the Grail.* Chapel Hill: University of North Carolina Press, 1959.

Hopkins, Andrea, ed. *Chronicles of King Arthur.* London: Collins and Brown, 1995.

Iselin, L. E. *Der morgenländische Ursprung der Grallegende.* Halle, 1909.

Jung, Emma and Marie-Louise von Franz. *The Grail Legend.* 1960. 2nd edn. Translated by Andrea Dykes. Princeton, New Jersey: Princeton University Press, 1998.

Kahane, Henry and Renee. *The Krater and the Grail.* Urbana: University of Illinois Press, 1965.

Kempe, Dorothy. *The Legend of the Holy Grail.* London: K. Paul, Trübner and Co, 1905.

Lacey, Norris J. *The New Arthurian Encyclopaedia.* New York: Peter Bedrick Books, 1986.

Lehmann, Rosamund. *My Dear Alexias: Letters from Wellesley Tudor Pole to Rosamund Lehmann.* Sudbury: Neville Spearman, 1979.

Lewis, Revd Lionel Smithett. *St. Joseph of Arimathea at Glastonbury.* London: James Clarke and Co., 1955.

Loomis, Roger Sherman. *Celtic Myth and Arthurian Romance.* New York: Columbia Press 1927; revised edn 1935.

Loomis, Roger Sherman. *Arthurian Tradition and Chrétien de Troyes.* New York: Columbia University Press, 1949.

Loomis, Roger Sherman. *Wales and the Arthurian Legend.* Cardiff: University of Wales Press, 1956.

Loomis, Roger Sherman. *The Grail: From Celtic Myth to Christian Symbol.* Cardiff: University of Wales Press, 1959.

Loomis, Roger Sherman, ed. *Arthurian Literature in the Middle Ages.* Oxford: Clarendon Press, 1959.

Map, Walter. *De Nugis Curialiam: Courtiers Trifles.* Edited and translated by M. R. James; revised by C. N. L. Brooke and R. A. B. Mynors. Oxford: Oxford University Press, 1983.

Markale, Jean. *Le Graal.* Paris: Retz, 1982.

Marx, Jean. *La Légende Arthurienne et le Graal.* Paris: Presses Universitaires de France, 1952.

Matthews, John. *The Mystic Grail: The Challenge of the Arthurian Quest.* London: Thorsens, 1997.

Michell, John F. *The Flying Saucer Vision: The Holy Grail Restored.* London: Sidgewick and Jackson, 1967.

Nagy, Joseph Falaky. *Conversing with Angels and Ancients.* Dublin: Four Courts Press, 1997.

Newstead, Helaine. *Bran the Blessed in Arthurian Romance.* New York: Columbia University Press, 1939.

Nitze, W. A. *Perceval and the Legend of the Holy Grail,* 1952.

Nutt, Alfred. *Studies in the Legend of the Holy Grail: With Especial Reference to the Hypothesis of its Celtic Origin.* Folk-Lore Society Publications, no. 23. London: David Nutt, 1888.

Nutt, Alfred. "The Legend of the Buddha's Alms Dish and the Legend of the Holy Grail." *Archaeological Review* 3 (1889): 267-71. (1889a).

Nutt, Alfred. "Recent Archaeological Research. II: Folk-Lore." *Archaeological Review* 3 (1889):75-88. (1889b).

Nutt, Alfred. "Les derniers travaux allemands sur la légende du Saint Graal." *Folk-Lore* 2 (1891):i-xlviii.

Nutt, Alfred. *The Influence of Celtic upon Medieval Romance.* Popular Studies in Mythology, Romance and Folklore, no. 1. London: David Nutt, 1899.

Nutt, Alfred. *The Legends of the Holy Grail.* Popular Studies in Mythology Romance and Folklore, no. 14. London: David Nutt, 1902. (1902a)

Nutt, Alfred. Notes to Lady Charlotte Guest's, *The Mabinogion: Mediaeval Welsh Romances.* London: David Nutt, 1902. (1902b).

Peebles, Rose Jeffries. *The Legend of Longinus in Ecclesiastical Tradition and in English Literature, and Its Connection with the Holy Grail.* Baltimore: Bryn Mawr College Monographs, vol. 9, 1911.

Pokorny, Julius. *Der Graal in Irland und die mythischen Grundlage de Graalsage.* Vienna: Anthropolog Gesellshaft, 1918.

Phillips, Graham. *The Search for the Grail.* London: Century, 1995.

Ravenscroft, Trevor. *The Spear of Destiny.* London: Sphere Books, 1973.

Seward, Desmond. *The Monks of War.* Paladin: St Albans, 1974.

Sinclair, Andrew. *The Sword and the Grail.* New York: Crown, 1992.

Spence, Lewis. *Will Europe Follow Atlantis?* London: Rider Press, 1944.

Spence, Lewis. *The Magic Arts in Celtic Britain.* London: Constable, 1995.

Stein, W. J. *The Ninth Century and the Holy Grail.* London: Temple Lodge Press, 1988.

Steiner, Rudolf. *Christ and the Spiritual World and The Search for the Holy Grail.* London: Rudolf Steiner Press, 1963.

Sumption, Jonathan. *The Albigensian Crusade.* London: Faber and Faber, 1999.

Tennyson, Lord Alfred. *Idylls of the King* (1859-91). London: Penguin, 1988.

Treharne, R. F. *The Glastonbury Legends, Joseph of Arimathea, the Holy Grail and King Arthur.* London: The Cresset Press, 1967.

Villiers, Oliver G. *Wellesley Tudor Pole: Appreciation and Valuation.* Canterbury: Hardcastle, 1968.

Vinaver, Eugène. *The Rise of Romance.* Oxford: Clarendon Press, 1941.

Wadge, Richard. "King Arthur: A British or Sarmartian Hero." *Folklore* 98 (1987): 204-15.

Waite, A. E. *The Hidden Church of the Holy Grail.* London: Rider, 1909.

Weston, Jessie Laidley. *The Legend of Sir Gawain: Studies upon its Original Scope and Significance.* The Grimm Library, no. 7. London: David Nutt, 1897.

Weston, Jessie Laidley. *Sir Gawain at the Grail Castle.* Arthurian Romances, no. 6. London: David Nutt, 1904.

Weston, Jessie Laidley. *King Arthur and his Knights: A Survey of Arthurian Romance.* Popular Studies in Romance, Folklore and Mythology, no. 4. London: David Nutt, 1905.

Weston, Jessie Laidley. *The Legend of Sir Perceval: Studies upon its Origin, Development, and Position in the Arthurian Cycle.* The Grimm Library, nos. 17 and 19. London: David Nutt, 1906-1909.

Weston, Jessie Laidley. *From Ritual to Romance.* 1920; reprint Princeton: Princeton University Press, 1993.

Weston, Jessie Laidley. Obituary for Alfred Nutt (1856-1910). *Folklore* 21 (1910): 512-14.

Weston, Jessie Laidley, trans. Wolfram *von Eschenbach's Parzival.* 2 vols. London: David Nutt, 1894.

White, Richard, ed. *King Arthur in Legend and History.* London: Dent, 1997.

Williams, Charles and C. S. Lewis. *Arthurian Torso.* Oxford: Clarendon Press, 1948.

Wood, Juliette. "The Celtic Tarot and the Secret Tradition: A Study on Modern Legend Making." *Folklore* 109 (1998): 15-24.

Wood, Juliette. "Folklore Studies at the Celtic Dawn: The Role of Alfred Nutt as Publisher and Scholar." *Folklore* 110 (1999): 3-12.

Yeats, W. B. *Irish Folk Stories and Fairytales.* New York: Grosset and Dunlop, 1959.

Raymond H. Thompson (essay date 2000)

SOURCE: Thompson, Raymond H. "The Grail in Modern Fiction: Sacred Symbol in a Secular Age." In *The Grail: A Casebook,* edited by Dhira B. Mahoney, pp. 545-60. New York: Garland Publishing Inc., 2000.

[*In the following essay, Thompson discusses the use of the Grail motif in modern fiction, including a brief analysis of four twentieth-century novels.*]

As in medieval accounts, modern treatments of the Grail legend offer two distinct ranges of possibility: it may be more or less Christian, and it may be more or less linked to Arthur's realm. At its first appearance in the *Perceval* of Chrétien de Troyes, the Grail is undoubtedly mysterious, but not particularly holy. It was left to Robert de Boron to identify it as the vessel of the Last Supper used by Joseph of Arimathea to catch Christ's blood after the Crucifixion. To the voluminous medieval romances on the Grail, later scholars have added learned commentary upon its nature and origins. Modern authors, thus, may perceive it as either pagan or Christian, endowed in either case with a rich history that precedes its manifestation to the Round Table. Moreover, despite the claim in the Vulgate *Queste del Saint Graal* and Sir Thomas Malory's *Morte Darthur* that the Grail was removed from this sinful world forever, it has returned in the pages of modern fiction more often than even King Arthur himself.[1] Indeed, interest in the Grail has quickened in the 1990s with the publication of several anthologies of short stories.[2]

At times, this interest may amount to no more than the borrowing of isolated elements of the legend in works with other interests. The Grail is transferred to a new guardian in Marion Zimmer Bradley's "Chalice of Tears, or I Didn't Want That Damned Grail Anyway" (1992). The Siege Perilous transports the hero of Andre Norton's *Witch World* (1963) to a magical otherworld. Parsifal tests the valor of the protagonist in *Bring Me the Head of Prince Charming* (1991) by Roger Zelazny and Robert Sheckley; and as Peredur he is one of the mythic figures who haunt a magical forest in Robert Holdstock's *Mythago Wood* (1984). The motif of the maimed Fisher King and the resultant wasteland appear in Darrell Schweitzer's "The Faces of Midnight" (1981, revised and published the same year as "Midnight, Moonlight, and the Secrets of the Sea"), Gael Baudino's Dragonsword series (1991-92), *The Grail and the Ring* (1994) by Teresa Edgerton, and *Merlin's Bones* (1995) by Fred Saberhagen. These characters and elements are undeveloped, however: they remain convenient plot devices in those works where they appear.

These are all fantasies, but elements of the Grail story turn up in "realistic" fiction also.[3] Among those in a contemporary setting are a handful of mystery and suspense novels.[4] In *The Grail Tree* (1979) by Jonathan Gash, for example, murder is committed to gain possession not of the battered pewter cup reputed to be the Grail, but of the ornate silver casket in which it is placed. While there is no suggestion of spiritual values in the novel, that the thieves should be punished for their materialism is not inappropriate to the Grail theme.

More frequently, however, elements of the legend are introduced into a realistic contemporary setting by the process of transposition. Suggestive parallels are created rather than features actually borrowed. The figure of the Fisher King is evoked in Richard Chizmar's short story "The Sinner King" (1994); in Tony Cosier's as yet unpublished novel *Perceval,* of which six excerpts have appeared in various magazines since 1983; in Nicole St. John's *Guinever's Gift* (1977), which recreates the Arthur-Guenevere-Lancelot love triangle; in *The Paper Grail* (1991) by James P. Blaylock, where the Grail is a nineteenth-century Japanese sketch that was once folded into the shape of a cup and used to gather blood; in *The Fisher King* (1991), a novel by Leonore Fleischer based on the motion picture; in Tim Power's *Last Call* (1992), in which the renewal of the reign of the goddess-queen and her consort, the young king who replaces his predecessor, is reenacted among a group of gamblers in Las Vegas; and in *The Green Knight* (1993) by Iris Murdoch, which loosely transposes not only the account of Gawain's encounter with the Green Knight, but also the motifs of the Castle of Marvels and the Holy Fool, as well as the Fisher King, from Grail legend.

The figure of Perceval, the Holy Fool, who appears with the Fisher King in several of the above-mentioned works, is an equally popular borrowing among novels that transpose parts of the Grail legend. His Grail Quest is used by J. H. Shorthouse to condemn women committed to socialism in *Sir Perceval* (1886); by John Cowper Powys to assert the power of mysticism in a material world in *A Glastonbury Romance* (1933); by Bernard Malamud to recount the career of a gifted baseball player in *The Natural* (1952); by Raja Rao in the structure of *The Serpent and the Rope* (1960); by David Lodge to mock the idiosyncrasies of the academic conference circuit in *Small World* (1984); by John Crowley to reveal the scholarly fascination with research in *Ægypt* (1987); and by Katherine Patterson to explore the anguish of a young boy's search for information about his father who died in Vietnam in *Park's Quest* (1988).

By contrast, Galahad is transposed in only one very short story, "The Christmas of Sir Galahad" (1871) by Elizabeth Stuart Phelps, where he remains faithful to a very trying wife, although he does turn up as a reincarnation in both Theodore Sturgeon's "Excalibur and the Atom" (1951) and *The Forever King* (1992) by Molly Cochran and Warren Murphy. Lancelot's Quest is hardly more popular, but his pursuit of the "Unholy Grail"—to expose the corruption that lies behind the glittering facade of modern America in general and Hollywood in particular—in Walker Percy's *Lancelot* (1978) marks one of the most impressive achievements in modern Grail fiction. The Grail sought in *The Grail: A Novel* (1963) by Babs H. Deal is an unbeaten football season which the team's quarterback, Lance, only just fails to pull off. It also turns up as the mischievously named Platter of Plenty in *The Lyre of Orpheus* (1988), Robertson Davies's novel about staging an Arthurian opera.

These works offer only tantalizing fragments and echoes of Grail tradition. A far larger number actually send their characters on a Quest for the Grail itself; or sometimes have them stumble across it unawares, as did Perceval on his first visit to the Grail Castle. The experience may take place in a future portrayed by science fiction: in David Bischoff's *Star Spring* (1982), the search takes place in a computer-generated fantasy world; in Andre Norton's "That Which Overfloweth" (1992), it happens in a distant future of a waning earth; in John Gregory Betancourt's "Dogs Questing" (1992), it is conducted by dogs seeking to restore their ancient bond with mankind; in Patricia Kennealy-Morrison's Keltiad series (1984-), it is for one of the Thirteen Treasures of a Celtic race that has taken its customs into space. Or it may take place in an alternate universe imagined in fantasy: one in which Hitler won the war, as in Brad Linaweaver's "Under an Appalling Sky" (1992); or one even more crassly commercial than our own, as in Adam-Troy Castro's "Jesus Used a Paper Cup" (1994).

More commonly, however, the Quest for the Grail takes place in a contemporary setting. In one group of short stories, all published in 1992, this involves time travel: in Neil Gaiman's "Chivalry," Galaad comes forward in time to bargain with an old-age pensioner who bought the Holy Grail in an Oxfam shop; in "The Steel American" by S. P. Somtow and "That Way Lies Camelot" by Jenny Wurts, it is Perceval's turn to make the trip; in "Greggie's Cup" by Rick Wilber, the fabric of time is torn aside when a modern boy meets Lancelot. Conversely, people in the modern world attempt to retrieve the Grail from the past in "A Knyght There Was" (1963) by Robert F. Young, and *The Fetch* (1991) by Robert Holdstock. The Grail is also found by a Canadian teenager who is transported first to the world of Nwm, then to her own world's Arthurian past, in *The Third Magic* (1988) by Welwyn Wilton Katz. There she discovers that she herself is none other than Morgan le Fay.

In many of the modern Grail Quests, the heroes find themselves in competition with evil-doers who scheme to wield the power of the Grail for their own destructive ends. In *The Sleepers* (1968) by Jane Curry (where the Grail is one of the Thirteen Treasures of Britain), Sanders Anne Laubenthal's *Excalibur* (1973), and *The Return of Merlin* (1995) by Deepak Chopra, these foes are traditional Arthurian figures like Morgan Le Fay, Morgause of Orkney, and Mordred. They are religious cults in Sherard Vines's *Return, Belphegor!* (1932); evil magicians in both *A Wheel of Stars* (1989) by Laura Gilmour Bennett and *The Forever King* (1992) by Cochran and Murphy; Nazis in *Indiana Jones and the Last Crusade* (1989), a novel adapted by Rob MacGregor from the film screenplay; neo-Nazis in Jerry and Sharon Ahern's "Siege Perilous" (1992); and criminals in Jack C. Haldeman II's "Ashes to Ashes" (1992). In Charles

Williams's *War in Heaven* (1930) and Susan Cooper's Dark Is Rising series (1968-77), the heroes must struggle against the supernatural force of evil itself.

Traditional figures or their modern equivalents appear not only as foes, however. Spiritual successors to the Fisher King appear in C. S. Lewis's *That Hideous Strength* (1945) as Ransom, the Pendragon and leader of the struggle of good against evil; and in *The Column of Dust* (1909) by Evelyn Underhill, where he turns over guardianship of the Holy Grail to a woman. Edwin Casson-Perceval, the naive narrator and friend of Hitler in *The Ring Master* (1987) by David Gurr, desperately excavates various sites in a misguided search for the Grail amidst the wasteland of wartorn Europe. Like Perceval, modern protagonists fail to ask the vital question in two short stories, "A Deal with God" by Pat Cadigan and "Storyville, Tennessee" by Richard Gilliam, both published in 1992. Arthur Machen develops the contrast between the spiritual and material worlds in *The Great Return* (1915) and in *The Secret Glory* (1922) where the hero's high-minded impracticality compares favorably with the cruelty and hypocrisy of the world in which he lives. As in the latter novel, modern characters are inspired by the Grail to lead better lives in *The Sparrow Child* (1958) by Meriol Trevor, *The Flowering Thorn* (1961) by Elizabeth Yunge-Bateman,[5] Nancy Holder's "To Leave If You Can," and Lawrence Watt-Evans's "Visions" (both 1992).

The Grail is sought and/or found not only in the modern period, but in earlier ones also: the nineteenth century in Lee Hoffman's "Water" (1992), in which a cowboy's discovery of it breaks a drought in the American West, and in Karl Edward Wagner's "One Paris Night" (1992), in which two adventurers melt it down for silver bullets to shoot a werewolf; the High Middle Ages in *The Hidden Treasure of Glaston* (1946) by Eleanore M. Jewett and *Kingdom of the Grail* (1992) by A. A. Attanasio (in both of which it performs miracles), "Castle of Maidens" (1992) by Richard Lee Byers and *Merlin's Destiny* (1993) by Sigmund Brouwer (in both of which it turns up in unlikely places); and the years shortly after the battle of Camlann in Christopher Webb's *Eusebius the Phoenician* (1969).

Most Grail Quests (or encounters) in modern fiction do, however, take place in King Arthur's day. Many of the historical novels are set in post-Roman Britain during the Dark Ages, but in keeping with the attempts to create a sense of authenticity, they demystify the Grail. In Victor Canning's Crimson Chalice Trilogy (1976-80), the traditions linked with the chalice are recounted, but it comes into the possession of Arturo's mother who passes it on to her son as a cherished talisman, rather than the object of a Quest. It is one of the ancient Treasures of Britain sought in both Thomas Clare's *King Arthur and the Riders of Rheged* (1992) and Mary Stewart's Arthurian novels (1970-). In *The Prince and the Pilgrim* (1995), however, Stewart's most recent addition to the series, she introduces another, more Christian Grail, brought over to Britain by a royal Merovingian refugee. In some novels, the Grail exercises a negative influence upon characters and events: in *The Emperor Arthur* (1967) by Godfrey Turton, Galahad's credulity is exploited by an ambitious Church; in George Finkel's *Twilight Province* (1967, published in the United States as *Watch Fires to the North,* 1968), Glahad [sic] becomes a religious fanatic; in *The Pendragon* (1978) by Catherine Christian, the Grail seems to be no more than a delusion resulting from the madness of Peredur. Others, however, present it in more positive terms: in *Excalibur!* (1980) by Gil Kane and John Jakes, it is the land of Britain itself; in Parke Godwin's *Firelord* (1980), it is a battered cup of uncertain authenticity that challenges people's faith; in *Guinevere: The Legend in Autumn* (1991), the conclusion to Persia Woolley's Guinevere trilogy (1987-91), it means many things to many people. Alone among these historical novels in a Dark Age setting, Jim Hunter's *Percival and the Presence of God* (1978) focuses upon the Grail Quest rather than includes it as but one episode in the course of Arthur's career.

Also set in the Dark Ages are six fantasies: in *The Mists of Avalon* (1982) by Marion Zimmer Bradley, the cup, dish, and spear are relics sacred to the worship of the Mother Goddess; in Sharan Newman's *Guinevere Evermore* (1985), the Quest follows that in Malory except that Palomides replaces Bors; in *Arthur* (1989) and again in *Pendragon* (1994), both by Stephen R. Lawhead, the mortally wounded Arthur goes for healing by the Grail to the Fisher King's palace in Avallon, though only in the latter novel does he return; in "The Cup and the Cauldron" (1992) by Mercedes Lackey, a follower of the Goddess and a Christian nun must overcome their religious prejudices before they can become Grail Maidens; in Judith Tarr's "Silver, Stone, and Steel" (1995), Merlin dreams of the coming of the Grail to Britain and into the custody of three queen-goddesses. Like these, *The City of Sarras* (1887) by U. Ashworth Taylor and Michael L. Nelson's "Perceval and the Holy Grail" (1979), two works set in the High Middle Ages, invoke the mystical aspects of the Grail, but whereas the first six stress the oneness of all worship, the latter pair emphasize its Christian identity.

More commonly, however, fiction set in the High Middle Ages explores character rather than mystical experience. Although he is sometimes overshadowed by others, Galahad is important to Mary Southworth's *Galahad, Knight Errant* (1907), John Erskine's *Galahad: Enough of His Life to Explain His Reputation* (1926), and Gwendolyn Bowers's *Brother to Galahad* (1963). Gawin's [sic] confusion and Perceval single-mindedness are examined in Dorothy James Roberts's

Kinsmen of the Grail (1963); Aglovale's struggle with a strict conscience in *The Life of Sir Aglovale de Galis* (1905) by Clemence Housman; the sins and final repentance of Kundry and Amfortas in *The Grail of Hearts* (1992) by Susan Shwartz; the religious fanaticism of Mador in "Sir Mador Seeks the Grail" (1987) and the perplexity of Lancelot in "Prelude to the Quest" (1989), two stories by David Gareth from a projected collection dealing with the Quest for the Grail. T. H. White offers penetrating insights into Gawaine, Lionel, Aglovale, and Lancelot, each of whom relates the adventures he encountered on his Quest in *The Ill-Made Knight* (1940, later incorporated into *The Once and Future King*, 1958). Two novels depart from tradition to celebrate the steadfastness of women who achieve the Grail: in *A Lady of King Arthur's Court* (1909) by Sara Hawks Sterling, it is one of Guenever's damsels, disguised as a monk; in *The King's Damosel* (1976) by Vera Chapman, it is ever-adventurous Lynett.

The last group consists of ironic fiction. This too is set in the High Middle Ages, but it measures the gap between expectations and results, rather than heroic achievements. Some of these make use of the Grail legend to condemn human failings: Robert Nye's *Merlin* (1978), Richard Monaco's Grail series (1977-85), and Erin Caine's erotic novel *Knights of Pleasure* (1992; reissued in 1994 as *Avalon Nights* by Sophie Danson, another pseudonym) describe, in graphic detail, the depravity of humanity; Monaco's *Broken Stone* (1985) and "The Unholy" (1994) by Doug Murray unfold plans to wield an evil counterpart of the Holy Grail; Tanith Lee's "Exalted Hearts" (1994) reveals that more is lost than gained by the Quest.

Others, by contrast, react to our follies with affectionate laughter: the uncertain nature of the Grail generates humor in *A Connecticut Yankee in King Arthur's Court* (1889) by Mark Twain, *To the Chapel Perilous* (1955) by Naomi Mitchison, and Thomas Berger's *Arthur Rex* (1978); in "Maureen Birnbaum and the Saint Graal" (1993) by George Alec Effinger and in Tom Holt's *Grailblazers* (1994), where the object of the Quest is a berry bowl and a washing-up bowl respectively; and in "The Awful Truth in Arthur's Barrow" (1992) by Lionel Fenn, where it turns out to be a "hideously gorgeous woman" named Holy Gail. The Grail questers themselves are the source of comedy in Matt Cohen's *Too Bad Galahad* (1972) and in "The Power in Penance" (1994) by Edward E. Kramer, where the Holy Grail consumes in flames all who try to drink from it save only the bishop's cat named Percy.

This rapid survey of modern fiction reveals significant developments in Grail tradition. Some authors have been influenced by scholars who argue that the Grail evolved from the Cauldron of Plenty in Celtic legend: Katz takes her description of the Grail from that of the cauldron in the ancient Welsh poem *The Spoils of Annwfn*; Clare, Curry, and Kennealy-Morrison include it among the Thirteen Treasures of Britain; Stewart and Bradley link it with sword, spear, and dish as ancient relics of power. Bradley and Mitchison, among others, make it sacred to the worship of the Mother Goddess.

Most authors who make this identification are women, and they, along with others, not only pay closer attention to female characters like Elaine of Corbenic, Kundry, and successive Grail maidens, but also expand the role of women in the Grail story. Both Katz and Bradley make Morgan le Fay the Grail bearer; Underhill, Norton, and Bradley (in her short story) have guardianship of the Grail transferred to women; Chapman, Kennealy-Morrison, Mitchison, and Sterling send women to quest for the Grail; and girls are among the group of young people who seek it in the juvenile novels of Cooper, Trevor, and Yunge-Batemen.

Among the figures from Grail legend, Perceval and the Fisher King have exercised the strongest fascination for modern authors. The Waste Land has also manifested itself in an intriguing variety of ways, from drought in the otherworld of fantasy, to the desolation of modern, post-industrial cities. Evil is sometimes identified with contemporary manifestations like religious cults and the Nazis. The attempts of such evildoers to use the power of the Grail for selfish ends are a departure from medieval tradition that insists upon its purity. Perhaps aware of this, some authors have invented an Unholy Grail.

Another departure from tradition is the use of irony. While the composers of medieval romances were ready to parody the conventions of the genre, they were much more respectful in their treatment of Grail legend, whether out of Christian belief or fear of Church censure. Irony does appear in Chrétien's *Perceval* and the fourteenth-century English verse *Sir Perceval of Galles*, but the former predates identification of the Grail with the cup used at the Last Supper, while the latter omits the Grail altogether. By contrast, modern authors are ready not only to laugh at the impracticalities of the Grail Quest, but even to condemn an often intolerant Church for exploiting it. It is one measure of how the Church's authority has waned in the twentieth century.

I wish now to examine more closely four of these novels, chosen partly for their representative nature, but mainly for their success in dealing with the Grail legend.[6] The first is Parke Godwin's *Firelord*, which shows how it has been integrated into an account of Arthur's full career in a Dark Age setting.[7] Since the novels set in the Dark Ages are concerned with verisimilitude, many choose either to omit all reference to the Grail, dismissing it as a legend that attached itself to Arthur as tales of his achievements spread, or else to rationalize it. *Firelord* falls into the latter category.

Here the Grail found by Peredur in the well at the foot of Wyrral Tor turns out to be "An ordinary shallow bowl of pitted bronze" (359). To those who see it for the first time, it is a disappointment, "not what we thought" (357), but as Peredur points out, "It's the reaching, the hope and the faith that really count. How can any reality shine like the dream of it?" (360). In this respect, the Grail mirrors a central theme of the novel, the inspiration provided by the vision of "bright tomorrows you carved out of wishes and painted with dreams" (7).

The integration of the Grail legend into the structure of the novel is demonstrated by a scrutiny of the conclusion. As Arthur lies dying, he has a dream in which he is visited in succession by various figures who have been important in his life. First comes Merlin, here a projection of Arthur himself, with his dream of a brighter world, like that offered by the Grail itself. Then comes Ambrosius, who insists "I've got to save *some* of you for the historians" (392). His commitment to Roman logic is matched by that of Peredur in his search for the Grail, as Arthur recognizes: "His faith might have sent him down into the well, but a keen, critical mind led him there" (361). Peredur even retains an element of skepticism about his find: "if there was a Grail, it would look like nothing so much as this" (360).

The next visitors to the dying Arthur are Trystan and Geraint, who sweep him off into legend "that will endure as long as men dream" (392-93). Because the Grail is equally inspiring, the faithful pray at the bier of Peredur who "touched an enduring need in their hearts" (361). Trystan and Geraint are followed by Guenevere, her mind full of political concerns. These too are an important dimension in Godwin's Grail story. From the outset Arthur must learn to cope with the religious intolerance of the Grail's most fervent believers. The skill with which he masters the lesson is demonstrated when he uses the Grail to help reconcile the rebels led by Guenevere and Lancelot.

If this performance reveals Arthur's political astuteness, his final visitor, Morgana, releases "the last and best" part of him (395). She it was who taught him to love, and this is the quality that makes him such a beloved leader. It also brings him the Grail, for out of love for his old friend he allows Peredur to seek the holy vessel when policy might argue more secure restraint for so valuable a captive. "Someone who heeded fallen sparrows," he prays, "might take a moment for Peredur" (352). The Quest for the Grail is thus freely adapted by Godwin to fit into his vision of a leader worthy of the legend that has reverberated down through the ages.

Like *Firelord*, Jim Hunter's *Percival and the Presence of God* is a first-person narrative set in the Dark Ages (though there is a timeless quality about this world).[8]

Whereas the Grail Quest is but a minor episode in the former, however, it dominates the latter which is told from Percival's point of view. Despite temptations to abandon his heroic quest, first for Arthur's court, then for the castle of the fisher-lord, Percival stubbornly persists. To it, he dedicates his life.

Yet his search for Arthur's course leads him only to a gutted castle and a ruined chapel within which he is trapped by a fallen beam. As he lies, "dying in an absurdity" (133), the only pattern he can discern in events is "either of an immense and grand cruelty, or of a vast indifference. Percival was simply not of interest to God" (125). The castle, he later learns, belonged not to Arthur but to a king named Poel, though the stories told about him were similar. Nor is his search for the castle of the fisher-lord, where he failed to ask the vital question during his first visit, any more successful. Hope of a quick return gradually fades.

What Percival undergoes is a "slow and baffled" (141) learning journey:

> I think I do now accept that either things are truly arbitrary, an utter haphazardness of God, or their direction is likely to be too difficult for us to understand, so that they appear arbitrary though they are not so.
>
> To some this is cynicism, and to others it is faith.
>
> (138)

Nor does his persistence bring consolation: "To address God is to address a remoteness. God doesn't blaze and touch me now, as in my adolescence, and possibly will never do so again" (139). He does not, however, yield to despair, rather to "a gentler counterpart: disappointment, and acquiescence" (137). As the novel ends, Percival confesses, "I no longer believe in Arthur, it being all I can manage to believe in God. . . . Remote one, stay within reach of my mind" (140-41).

While medieval questers may reject worldly for spiritual values, they never wonder whether Arthur's court and its ideals actually exist; and while they may doubt their worthiness to find the Grail, they never question God's purpose and concern with mankind. Hunter has transformed the legend from a medieval journey toward faith into a modern exploration of Christian existentialism: "self-sacrifice is not harder but easier, when there is no certainty of meaning. In a blank windless world, without confident directions of our own, we are most free to respond to needs outside ourselves" (138-39). His is a Grail Quest for a less spiritually confident age.

Thomas Berger's *Arthur Rex* is set, not in the Dark Ages, but in the High Middle Ages.[9] Like *Firelord*, however, it deals with the entire career of Arthur, and so the Quest for the Grail occupies but a small part of the novel, made even smaller because most adventures are not reported in detail. Berger integrates the stories of both Percival and Galahad, but it is the former who achieves a vision of the Holy Grail and who heals the maimed King Pelles. Thereafter, he and Galahad die with the rest of Arthur's knights in the last battle against Mordred.

These changes are necessary to Berger's ironic purpose. Since so spiritual an undertaking offers limited opportunities for humor, the Quest is moved largely into the background, so that attention may focus on those elements with most comic potential: Galahad's conception, Perceval's naïveté, and the obscure nature of the Grail so assiduously sought. The first two, however, are largely detached from the Grail Quest, for Galahad does not actually go on the Quest, and most of the comic scenes involving Percival occur before he starts his.

Most of the humor is thus directed at the dubiousness of the undertaking: "Methinks it is strange that an hundred knights are questing for that which they do not even know the look of," observes Arthur when Leodegrance explains the absence of his knights, to which that monarch replies, "The very mystery of it is a lure" (73). This, however, is only part of its fascination. When Percival later marvels that the Grail should be found so close to Camelot after he and others have searched far and wide, Galahad points out, "But if you had known where it was immediately, would you have had so many interesting adventures?" (450). This question brings Percival to an important realization: "I think I was happy in not finding it straightway. For all I ever wanted was to be a knight and to have adventures" (450).

Since the Grail "can not be seen except by him who is perfectly pure and without sin altogether" (73), it really is unattainable. Even Percival, who is "almost perfect" (424), is granted but a brief glimpse of the Grail. What is important, for Percival and all the other knights, is to pursue the vision, for only by striving may we improve ourselves, whatever our shortcomings. This is in keeping with a central theme of the novel for, as the ghost of Gawaine reminds his uncle, "though man be eternally contemptible, he should not be contemptuous of that which he can achieve" (483). This explains why Percival's completion of the Grail Quest is so anticlimactic. It is the Quest itself that is important, not the fleeting glory of an incomplete achievement. Just as the Grail maiden tells Percival, "Do not despair, for wert thou not as good a man as thou art, thou shouldst not see it at all" (424), so Arthur comforts Bedivere, "Do not weep. . . . Rather thank God in joy that for a little while we were able to make an interregnum in the human cycle of barbarism and decadence" (495).

In Naomi Mitchison's *To the Chapel Perilous,* the Grail Quest is central once again.[10] Although set in the High Middle Ages, it anachronistically introduces a press with modern standards, struggling to deal with conflicting stories on the one hand and political manipulation on the other. The result is a fascinating combination of delightful irony and thoughtful insight.

The problem for Lienors and Dalyn, the reporters waiting outside the Perilous Chapel, is that more than one Grail is found: Gawain finds a cauldron of plenty, Lancelot a cup and a lance that drips blood, Peredur/Perceval a stone that spills forth gold coins, Bors the dish of the Last Supper, Galahad a cup full of blood that "threw a curious illumination through his fingers" (19). Other knights find other things. When Dalyn wonders, "we always supposed—there was only one Grail," the hermit responds, "Yes, indeed . . . and each knight won it" (15).

Yet they cannot simply report this fact. There are too many interests to take into consideration: sub-editors trying to angle the stories, publishers anxious to placate advertisers, readers with expectations they want fulfilled, influential figures like Elayne and Guinevere, and powerful institutions like the Court and an increasingly intolerant Church. Since none of these wants a multiplicity of Grails, it becomes necessary to choose one. It is the Church that finally wins the day, endorsing Galahad's as the true Grail and condemning any pagan associations in reports of the other finds: "they had very clear ideas of what it ought to be like, so it was quite easy for them to do it out of their heads or else to consult those who had recently had visions" (89).

Mitchison's approach offers valuable insights into both Grail tradition and the modern news media. Since she is not forced to adhere to one particular version of the legend, she is able to include as much material as she chooses. Thus she recalls the devils that take on the guise of beautiful women to tempt questers when Bors mistakes Lienors for just such a "temptation" (70); and she explores the more primitive aspects of the Perceval story by having him revert to his pagan roots in the Foret Sauvage where he is known as Peredur. Kundrie, the loathly damsel who reproaches Perceval for not asking the appropriate question of the Fisher King, is linked with the Flower Bride of Celtic tradition by a reporter from the Cymric People. The modern skepticism of the reporters provides rich opportunity for irony.

Yet the modern world has its own failings, as is revealed by how news stories are shaped. Where the Cymric People gives extensive coverage to Peredur/Perceval, the Northern Pict shows more interest in Gawain, each appealing to national and regional preoccupations. Lancelot's encounter with Elayne of Corbyn "had been a marvellous story, but they'd had to kill it. You couldn't risk a row with the Round Table attaches over a Court release" (19). Reports of more than one Grail displease Lord Horny, the newspaper publisher: "people . . .

might all start off questing and who'd be left to read the advertisements?" (21). He worries, "it might set people thinking. We couldn't have that" (55). To gain the release of Lienors, the Camelot Chronicle publishes the unconfirmed and highly suspect story of Galahad's experiences in Sarras provided by the Church.

The trouble is that many patterns can be discerned in life, and each is represented by a different Grail.

> And each pattern uncovers a different aspect of the heart: a different means of wisdom. . . . And each pattern is dangerous to the other patterns and must seem hateful to their followers. . . . Most people are much too frightened to be tolerant. And at any one time and place there's always one pattern on top.
>
> (159)

Since "truth" may be distorted, we must look for the underlying pattern: "the wound is healed, the secret told, the riddle becomes plain, the reconciliation is made between man and what surrounds him" (170). To achieve this, we, like Lienors and Dalyn, must abandon our detachment from life and each seek our own Grail: "It would be sad beyond all telling if the finding of the Grail were to happen once for all. Because then it could not happen again for anyone" (171). Only thus can we find our own pattern, discover what is important to us, not just to those who exercise power for their own advantage.

What all four novels offer is insight into the human heart and, through it, a glimpse of the eternal. The yearning for a better world than that in which we live drives the knights to seek the Grail, however formidable the obstacles, great the sacrifice, and uncertain (perhaps doomed) the outcome. Thus the Grail may be seen as a more refined and spiritual image of the whole Arthurian world, the dream of which continues to lure us down through the ages.

Significantly, though, this spiritual Quest is one that, by and large, takes place without the mediation of the Church. Whereas priests and hermits offer valuable guidance in most medieval Grail romances, the Church is more of a hindrance than a help in these four novels: because of the abbot's advice, Hunter's Percival keeps silent in the castle of the fisher-lord; despite the Christian principles of Arthur and his knights in Berger's novel, the bishops of the Church are characterized as corrupt "caitiffs" (34); the Church and its most fervent supporters are power hungry and intolerant in the novels of Godwin and Mitchison. Mitchison's hermit alone is estimable, but he seems to have few links with the Church and his answers to questions are enigmatic. He prefers to leave people to make their own decisions.

The predominantly negative portrayal of organized religion in all four novels reflects a widespread attitude throughout modern Arthurian fiction. The Church's intolerance and craving for power are frequently criticized. Even more important, however, is its frequent exclusion from the deepest mysteries of the Grail. The Grail Quest is a spiritual journey that must, in the final analysis, be taken alone, for we are each responsible for our own salvation. The authors and readers of modern fiction are clearly warier of external authorities than were our medieval ancestors. We have, after all, been witness to the cruelty and oppression perpetrated on others in the name of organized religion, not only down the centuries, but still today.

Amidst the sterile wasteland of a materialistic world driven by greed, self-interest, and the lust for power over others, our thirst for spiritual sustenance is fiercer than ever. It may only be slaked, however, by undertaking the Quest for our own Grail. It will not be easy, for we must struggle against our own obstinately recalcitrant nature, against the temptation to neglect our wider responsibilities, and against the efforts of others to exploit our good intentions for base purposes. Yet the rewards are beyond all reckoning. And if modern fiction is a guide to what we may expect to find, then the Grail that awaits us is love, compassion, forgiveness—love of God, compassion for others, forgiveness of ourselves. Whether we shall ever find it, or recognize it if we do, is uncertain. But the Quest itself is a more glorious endeavor than any other we might choose, and that in itself may prove enough in this broken world.

Notes

1. For bibliographical information on the fiction discussed in this article, see individual author entries in *The New Arthurian Encyclopedia,* ed. Norris J. Lacy et al., Updated Paperback Edition (New York: Garland, 1996); for a summary of the evolution of the Grail in both medieval literature and modern scholarship, see particularly the entries by Richard O'Gorman (pp. 212-13) and Marylyn Parins (pp. 406-09); for a discussion of the motif of Arthur's return, see Geoffrey Ashe's entry (pp. 381-82) and *King Arthur's Modern Return,* ed. Debra N. Mancoff (New York: Garland, 1998).

2. First published in two limited editions as *Grails: Quests, Visitations, and Other Occurrences,* ed. Richard Gilliam, Martin H. Greenberg, and Edward E. Kramer (Atlanta: Unnameable, 1992), this anthology was augmented with additional stories and reissued as two separate volumes: *Grails: Quests of the Dawn* and *Grails: Visitations of the Night,* both published in New York by Roc/Penguin, 1994.

3. These works are realistic in their approach to the Grail material rather than to such elements as plot and character. For a fuller discussion of the rationale for the categories of fiction that I adopt, as

well as many of the novels mentioned, see Raymond H. Thompson, *The Return from Avalon: A Study of the Arthurian Legend in Modern Fiction* (Westport, CT: Greenwood, 1985). Several works mentioned in this article might be placed in more than the one category I have chosen for ease of discussion.

Many of the novels are also discussed by Beverly Taylor and Elisabeth Brewer, *The Return of King Arthur: British and American Literature since 1800* (Woodbridge, Eng.: Boydell and Brewer; Totowa, NJ: Barnes and Noble, 1983); and by Maureen Fries, "Trends in the Modern Arthurian Novel," in *King Arthur Through the Ages,* ed. Valerie M. Lagorio and Mildred Leake Day, 2 vols. (New York: Garland, 1990), II, 207-22.

4. For a discussion of Mystery and Suspense Fiction, see Daniel Nastali's entry in *The New Arthurian Encyclopedia,* pp. 339-40.

5. For a fuller discussion of the Grail quest in these two novels, as well as those by Jewett and Webb below, see Raymond H. Thompson, "From Inspiration to Warning: the Changing Role of Arthurian Legend in Fiction for Younger Readers," *Bulletin of the John Rylands University Library of Manchester,* 76, No. 3 (Autumn 1994), 238.

6. Among the novels that might have been explored further are those by White and Percy. For a discussion of the Grail quest in the former, see John Crane, *T. H. White* (New York: Twayne, 1974); Martin Kellman, *T. H. White and the Matter of Britain* (Lewiston, NY: Mellen, 1988); and Elisabeth Brewer, *T. H. White's The Once and Future King* (Woodbridge, Eng.: Brewer, 1993). For a discussion of the Grail quest in Percy, see J. Donald Crowley and Sue Mitchell Crowley, "Walker Percy's Grail," Chapter 17 in this anthology; and John Bugge, "Arthurian Myth Devalued in Walker Percy's *Lancelot,*" in *The Arthurian Tradition: Essays in Convergence,* ed. Mary Flowers Braswell and John Bugge (Tuscaloosa: University of Alabama, 1988), pp. 175-87.

7. Although the author describes the novel as a fantasy in the Acknowledgements, he does try to preserve what he calls "the bone of historical fact," based upon studies like *The Age of Arthur* (1973) by John Morris. All quotations are from the first edition (Garden City, NY: Doubleday, 1980), and are cited parenthetically in the text.

8. (London: Faber and Faber, 1978). Quotations are cited parenthetically in the text.

9. *Arthur Rex: A Legendary Novel* (New York: Delacorte, 1978). Quotations are cited parenthetically in the text. For a discussion of the role of Galahad, see Jay Ruud, "Thomas Berger's *Arthur Rex*: Galahad and Earthly Power," *Critique,* 25 (1984), 92-100.

10. (London: Allen and Unwin, 1955). Quotations are cited parenthetically in the text. See also Marilyn K. Nellis, "Anachronistic Humor in Two Arthurian Romances of Education: *To the Chapel Perilous* and *The Sword in the Stone,*" *Studies in Medievalism,* 2, No. 4 (1983), 57-77.

MAJOR WORKS

Paul B. Newman (essay date 1962)

SOURCE: Newman, Paul B. "Hemingway's Grail Quest." *University of Kansas City Review* 28 (1962): 295-303.

[*In the following essay, Newman remarks on the influence of T. S. Eliot and Jessie Weston on Ernest Hemingway, pointing out that Hemingway's writing reflected contemporary concerns over the breakdown of individualism that was often addressed by an interest in and the use of the Holy Grail theme.*]

"All of Eliot's poems are perfect," Hemingway wrote in 1925, "and there are very few of them. He has a very fine talent and he is very careful of it. He never takes chances with it and it is doing very well thank you."

In the early twenties Hemingway was a good friend of Ezra Pound, at a time when the latter had just finished editing "The Waste Land." Eliot himself was an occasional visitor to Paris and the story of the Fisher King may well have been a topic of discussion in the evenings of Gertrude Stein. The influence of Eliot's work on Hemingway is perhaps deeper than has been generally appreciated. Beneath the surface of *The Sun Also Rises* runs a current of symbolic overtones which seems to owe much to the concepts of Eliot and to the work of Jessie Weston. It will be my purpose to call attention to these influences, as well as to suggest an affinity between the current interest in the breakdown of individualism and the preoccupation of a number of writers with the legend of the Holy Grail.

The Sun Also Rises opens with a description of Robert Cohn, who serves as Hemingway's exemplar of the modern neurotic man, or, to use David Riesman's famous term, the other-directed man. "If he were in a crowd nothing he said stood out," Jake Barnes says, making the comparison clear enough; and the first book of *The Sun Also Rises* may be seen as an attempt to place Robert in his proper setting. We soon learn that Robert is suffering from a literary malaise: a desire to go to South America which he has contracted through reading W. H. Hudson's romantic novel, *The Purple Land*. Jake, who ought perhaps to sympathize, refuses to encourage him. Jake is planning a trip to Spain. He is prepared to go to British East Africa to hunt. He and Robert are both expatriates—both romantics in some degree—but in Jake's attitude we can sense the beginning of an attempt to make a careful distinction between the other and himself: a process which is not ended until the book's conclusion.

> "All my life I've wanted to go on a trip like that," Robert says. "I'll be too old before I can ever do it."
>
> "Don't be a fool," Jake answers. "You can go anywhere you want. You've got plenty of money."
>
> "I know. But I can't get started."

Robert's motivation, coming from without, lacks passionate justification. He refuses to seek involvement, as the existentialists would say, and his inability to make a creative decision is perhaps the natural consequence.

Jake perceives clearly enough Robert's desire to escape is a kind of vanity. Suspecting that his dislike of Paris has been gained from reading H. L. Mencken, he tells him, "Going to another country doesn't make any difference. I've tried all that. You can't get away from yourself by moving from one place to another. There's nothing to that."

The romantic quest will fail for the other-directed man, this remark strongly suggests, for the reason that for him it is an escape from selfhood; and Jake foreshadows at once the climax of the story and the defeat of Robert's romantic aspirations in the remark he makes for solace: "Nobody ever lives their life all the way up except bullfighters."

Writing at a time when the neoclassical movement had been spurred by the evident breakdown of individualism in World War I, Hemingway apparently wished to clarify the status of the romantic individual by approaching romanticism in the spirit of classical strictness and discipline. Robert Cohn may be seen as his vision of the collapsed Byronian romantic at a time when individualism, if it was to be preserved, had to be stripped of all emphasis on abstract will.

Replying with seeming casualness to Robert's fears that (like J. Alfred Prufrock) he is growing old without having lived, Jake tells Robert to begin living his life in Paris. His advice is apt and friendly, but Robert refuses to be comforted. Falling in love with Brett, Robert dismisses his former mistress, and his "affair with a lady of title" replaces South America as the locus of his Byronian struggle for romantic self-assertion. But precisely this love-affair with Brett serves to deepen and arouse Jake's antagonism, intensifying the struggle within Jake to separate the genuine romantic from the false; and it is this dynamic struggle which makes up the central conflict of the book.

We can see this conflict taking shape in Chapter IV, when Harvey Stone asks Robert in Jake's presence:

> "Tell us right off. Don't think. What would you rather do if you could do anything you wanted?"
>
> Cohn started to consider.
>
> "Don't think. Bring it right out."

But Robert cannot bring it right out. He has lost his "Unity of Being," in W. B. Yeats' terms, and his will, separated from passion, has become abstract. Harvey leaves and Robert's former mistress, Frances Clyne, appears. Her vengeful sarcasm makes Harvey's remarks seem relatively mild, but it serves the same purpose. As Frances smilingly insults Robert, Jake wonders:

> "I do not know how people could say such terrible things to Robert Cohn. There are people to whom you could not say insulting things. They give you a feeling that the world would be destroyed, would actually be destroyed before your eyes, if you said certain things. But here was Cohn taking it all."

In Yeats' terms the state of unity of being is achieved through the pursuit of a dramatic "mask"; but Robert is incapable of following such a mask, for, under the destructive pressure of Frances' analysis, he is unable to defend himself, and any vision of a higher self which he might possess is too weak to rally his energies in this crisis.

The effect of this scene on Jake is to heighten his ironic sense of the consequences of an abuse of romantic will. In the above quotation he is perhaps comparing Robert with a man of genuine unity of being (which Robert most emphatically is not), but the point of the whole scene must be that Robert is failing to recognize his true condition. He is continuing in the pursuit of the romantic mask without fulfilling the preliminary requirement of self-recognition.

In the other Parisian scenes Jake meets a series of characters who suffer from some form of physical or psychic impotence (including nymphomania): Brett, the prostitute Georgette, and a group of homosexuals. In the midst of a scene in which the prostitute dances with the homosexuals, Jake is introduced to a literary man, a Chicagoan with an English accent. Jake becomes angry with him and finds the other admiring his anger in the abstract. "Oh, how charmingly you get angry," this objective figure tells him. "I wish I had that faculty."

The important point, that we must note here, is that Jake *in his total being* is actually less impotent than the other man, in spite of the fact that Jake's impotence is physical while the other is only suffering from psychological maladjustment. In this connection, it is interesting to note that Hemingway has recently pointed out that Jake has not been castrated, and that his wound has left him capable of a full range of desires and passions.[1] As the book continues, Jake's need to distinguish between his own physical impotence and the psychic impotence of the other characters develops into a subtle study of the breakdown of individualism, of which the loss of sexual potency is an identifying symbol. Ultimately Jake's understanding of the causes of this breakdown leads to tragic self-recognition.

For the present it is enough to note that the characters of the first book of *The Sun Also Rises* have all been wounded in one way or another, and their scars are symbols of a progression toward a passive state of mind in which the unity of thought and passion has been lost. Robert Cohn's flattened nose, the Count Mippipopolous' arrow wounds, Brett Ashley's nymphomania, Mike Campbell's alcoholism are all indicative of impotence in this sense of shattered faith. Jake is the Fisher King of a Waste Land whose inhabitants are in the same disastrous condition as himself. As Yeats says, "True Unity of Being, where all the nature murmurs in response if but a single note be touched, is found emotionally, instinctively, by the rejection of all experience not of the right quality, and by the limitation of its quantity."

The characters of *The Sun Also Rises* have lost this instinctive discipline. They have allowed themselves to range too widely in a spirit of romantic freedom—smashing through the crumbling tradition of an "objective"[2] era. The result has been their scars: the outward symbols of their romantic revolt and the signs of an inner loss of unity.

A number of critics have already pointed out that Jake Barnes is Hemingway's Fisher King and that postwar Paris is his Waste Land. It remains to show in more detail how Jake's story parallels the Grail Quest.

In the second book of *The Sun Also Rises,* Jake and Bill Gorton board a train which carries seven carloads of pilgrims to Rome and Lourdes. Their encounter with these good Catholics from Dayton, Ohio, is not an accident but an integral part of the novel's design, for they themselves are pilgrims. Jake's hesitant Catholicism, his prayers in the cathedral at Pamplona, are further indications of the nature of his journey. If the first book of *The Sun Also Rises* shows us Hemingway's Waste Land, the second shows us Jake's quest for faith.

"Let no man be ashamed to kneel here in the great out-of-doors," Bill says while he and Jake are fishing in the Spanish mountains. "Remember the woods were God's first temples." His mockery hints at the religious implications of the fishing scenes. In both pagan and Christian myths, fishing symbolizes a search for faith. This overlapping of pagan and Christian references is typical of Hemingway's method throughout the novel. Bill's mockery also hints at those complex and ironic reservations toward romanticism which Hemingway has already begun to develop in the early scenes involving the Count Mippipopolous and Robert Cohn. In Hemingway's view, the romantic quest demands not the denial but the acceptance of any tradition which manifests itself in the living selfhood of the individual. The natural and the traditional, in this sense, are one, and Christianity, as in the legend of the Grail, may not entirely forsake its roots in paganism.

As Jessie Weston points out, the Cup and the Spear in the Grail legend are phallic, and the discovery of their meaning is one step in an initiation ceremony which symbolizes the rebirth of faith. Based on certain ancient fertility rites, this ceremony allegorically heals the impotent Fisher King and leads to the restoration of the Waste Land. In this sense, the Grail and Spear are symbols of unity of being. Furthermore, the Grail and the Spear unite the pagan worship of the body with the Christian worship of the spirit, for, in addition to their pagan meaning, they represent Christ's cup at the last supper and the spear which pierced his side. They thus serve as a link between the body and the spirit, and the discovery of their dual meaning symbolizes the recovery of faith and spiritual love through sublimation of sexual passion.

Hemingway's interest in the phallic origin of faith is illustrated in the scene of the uncaging of the bulls, where the contrast between the bulls and steers quickly develops into an ironic study of Robert Cohn's relationship to the group of *goyim*. In this scene the struggle between passion and abstract conscience is beautifully symbolized by the conflict between the bulls and steers. Passion overthrows faithless conscience as the bulls gore the steers and Mike baits Robert Cohn. But the outcome is ironic, for the result is impotence. If Robert Cohn represents a man in whom conscience has become abstract (i.e., divorced from passion), then Mike represents a man in whom conscience has been overthrown by passion. As Robert is an ironic steer, so Mike is an ironic bull. In both of them unity of being has been destroyed.

The dangers of the Grail quest have been noted by Jessie Weston, who associates "the horrors of physical death" with the first phases of the Mystery ritual in which the Grail legends have their source. She suggests "that the Mystery ritual comprised a double initiation, the Lower, into the mysteries of generation, *i.e.,* of physical Life; the Higher, in the Spiritual Divine Life, where man is made one with God." The ironic significance of the wounds of Hemingway's characters would seem to be that they have never passed beyond the first phase of the initiation. Their impotence results from an inability to achieve the sublimation of their passion into faith, and this failure results either from lack of control, in characters like Mike Campbell and the Count Mippipopolous, or over-control in characters like Robert Cohn and the Chicagoan with the English accent. Unity of being, the perfect fusion of passion and control, is beyond their reach, for the reason that they are trapped by their own vanity.

The scene of the uncaging of the bulls also dramatizes the ironic view of impotence which, as we have already seen, has been gradually forming in Jake's mind. This view consists in part at least in the intuitive perception that puritanism (e.g., the war spirit of Wilsonian idealism) is a force which destroys man's phallic being, leaving him to guide his actions by abstract will. In order to understand Jake's feelings, we must see how Robert's actions affect the others. Entering the group of *goyim,* Robert disrupts its inner harmony, opening the wounds which constitute the personal disaster of each of its members and in some curious way upsetting them as did the war. The chief understanding within the group is that Brett is Mike's woman. Challenging this, Robert upsets and excites them all, disturbing their balance, arousing their jealousy and anger. Brett herself becomes disturbed. The sickness within each of them is deepened and intensified.

It is as though the sexual conflict had now replaced the battlefield and yet maintained some connection with it in the balance and interplay of ideas. And Jake notes later as they all sit down to dinner: "It was like certain dinners I remember from the war. There was much wine, an ignored tension, and a feeling of things coming that you could not prevent happening." The connection of the war with the antagonism toward Robert Cohn is subtly drawn and has an important effect on Jake's development.

To see this connection, we note again that Robert is an outsider, a Jew, and that he has suffered badly from discrimination at Princeton. Jake tells us that he attempted to compensate for his sense of inferiority there by becoming the university middleweight boxing champion. But the point that Jake seems to make is that this aggressive self-assertion did not wipe out Robert's inner sense of psychic defeat; rather, it heightened it. Because of his false romanticism he is a perpetual outsider, exaggerating the beatitudes of groups to which he can never belong; and it is this failure of self-recognition which makes him an other-directed man.

We have now come to one of Hemingway's major points: that self-assertion in a state of abstraction is in reality a form of phallic self-destruction. Recognizing this, we are prepared to seek a further unity in the story and to look for a relationship among the characters which further establishes the web of implications that holds the book together. For we can now see that the others have been guilty of a form of self-destruction similar to that of Robert Cohn. They too have been guilty of aggressive self-assertion in a situation in which they had not established their identity, and the result has been the same discontinuity or deracination from their inner selves. The sense of shame, the loss of individuality occasioned by submission to the war's impersonal goals in which the individual felt no involvement, constituted a step backward in the psychic evolution of their personalities. The result of participation in the war was really a lessened capacity for self-assertion, made up for by hysteria.

This hysteria is the quality which Robert has aroused and which Jake refers to in his comment on the war. The others are really aware of Robert's weakness, and they sense it within themselves. They know that Robert's kind of self-assertion is a substitute for psychic self-control, yet they cannot withstand the vicious impulses which he arouses. This is the tragedy of Mike, who while condemning Robert as a steer cannot resist the destructive force of sadism which is tearing him apart within.

As regimentation in mass war destroys one's manhood, corrupting one's integrity through a false romanticism, so the breakdown of tradition in an objective time betrays the individual through his own vanity, leading him to deny his own being through perversions of the will leading finally to impotence. Loss of unity of being serves as an ultimate pole of reference in the novel, as it does in the work of Conrad.

Hemingway's truths are related to the fact that man is limited. The individual has a center of being which he must protect, even though it is finite—even though it leads him into error. Robert Cohn has disregarded his own center of being, and his identity has been crushed as a result. The same process has begun to happen to the other characters of the novel.

The stage is now set for the climax. Accusing Jake of acting as a pimp, Robert attacks him, knocks Mike down, and goes in search of Brett. He finds her with Pedro Romero, the bullfighter. He beats Romero but cannot defeat him. Brett gives Robert a tongue-lashing and he breaks down and cries. The climax has now passed. Robert's romanticism stands exposed for what it is: the outcome of vanity, not love. The bullfighter with his more integrated selfhood is capable of actual hatred as he is capable of actual love. He refuses to accept Robert's apology, hits him in the face and tells him he will kill him unless he gets out of town by morning.

Examining Robert's action, we can see clearly that an individual's self-assertion should not exceed his empathy, or the result will be hysteria. The balance, the unity must be maintained, or one has lost his contact with reality. The result of Robert's outbreak is a personal disaster. "He [the bullfighter] ruined Cohn," Mike says. "You know I don't think Cohn will ever want to knock people about again." Robert will go back to France, Jake surmises.

Jake comes into Robert's room. As the latter lies there despairing over the loss of Brett—the woman whom Jake has also lost—the difference between the two men comes to us quite simply as a difference in awareness. For Jake is facing self-recognition while Robert, blinded by vanity, is undergoing self-defeat.

On the following day Jake watches the bullfighter throwing off the effects of Robert's violence:

> During Romero's first bull his hurt face had been very noticeable. Everything he did showed it. All the concentration of the awkwardly delicate working with the bull that could not see well brought it out. The fight with Cohn had not touched his spirit but his face had been smashed and his body hurt. He was wiping all that out now. Each thing that he did with this bull wiped that out a little cleaner.

In these words Jake implies his own efforts to overcome the effects of Robert's hysteria. We can see how Pedro creates an image for Jake, drawing him toward a faith in man's ability to discipline his passions and to choose his own identity. To some extent, the realization toward which Jake is groping parallels the ideas of Sartre:

> When we say that man chooses his own self, we mean that everyone of us does likewise; but we also mean by that that in making this choice he also chooses all men. In fact, in creating the man that we want to be, there is not a single one of our acts which does not at the same time create an image of man as we think he ought to be. To choose to be this or that is to affirm at the same time the value of what we choose.

The bull which Pedro Romero kills, presenting the ear to Brett, is the same animal which killed a peasant in the uncontrolled violence of the morning. Through killing it with style, Pedro helps to restore the image of heroic man which has been lost in the two deterministic incidents which preceded the bullfight: the death of the peasant and the outbreak of Robert Cohn.

Thus above all others in the novel, in Jake's eyes, Pedro Romero is a man of tragic stature, transcending the determinism of hysteria (over-control) and undisciplined passion (lack of control) through the maximum of free will: the maximum of style. Pedro's importance to the story would seem to be fully understood only if we refer again to Yeats. In Yeats' terms an individual or a nation reaches unity through imitation of a leader who embodies an anti-self:

> Nations, races and individual men are unified by an image, or bundle of related images, symbolical or evocative of the state of mind, which is of all states of mind not impossible, the most difficult to that man, race, or nation; because only the greatest obstacle that can be contemplated without despair rouses the will to full intensity.

Through watching Pedro, Jake is freed of the conscientious anxiety which is his link with Robert. He is strengthened in his struggle toward what unity of being he can still achieve.

Hemingway's view would seem to be that sublimation is not the same thing as the self-emasculating process of abstract will. And Jake's wound is ironic or not, depending upon the view one takes of it.

A similar implication may be seen in Hemingway's story, "God Rest You Merry Gentlemen," in which a boy wounds himself on Christmas Day precisely as Jake is wounded, mutilating himself out of sexual guilt. At first sight the story would seem to be merely an ironic comment on the crucifixion, but as one considers it, it seems to have a deeper meaning which might be expressed as follows. Phallic being exists most fully not in the sexual act itself but in some mystery—some act of faith—which is accomplished by a sublimation of sensual into spiritual desire. Thus Jake's quest (like that of Yeats himself) is a search for "Unity of Being," which can be recovered through an initiation into the hidden significance which inheres in the phallic symbols of the Grail and Spear (or the corollary symbols of the Tuatha de Danann).[3]

Jake's search for a release from impotence is thus answered by all the events of the novel. The story is an initiation which reaches its climax when Pedro takes Brett at the summit of the pagan-Christian festival of San Fermin, destroying Robert (who thus fails to pass the test) but permitting Jake to enter into the order of the initiate. The further significance of the initiation is perceived by Jake during the bullfight the following morning. At this bullfight the matador's sword would seem to serve as an adequate representation of the Spear, while the bull's ear as the award for the ability to wear the "mask" in the face of "the greatest obstacle that can be contemplated without despair" is the symbol of the highest unity of being, and hence an adequate correlative for the Grail. And, furthermore, as we have already seen, Pedro presents the ear to Brett in honor of the fact that she has become his mistress.

As the man who possesses the most unity of being in the novel, Pedro wins Brett and takes her with him to Madrid. But her unworthiness is suggested by the fact that she leaves the bull's ear in a drawer among a litter of cigarette stubs, where Jake later finds it.

Shortly afterward, Jake leaves Pamplona and spends a few days along the border between France and Spain. In the difference between the two countries he finds further support for his view that impotence is a consequence of abstract will: "Everything is on such a clear financial basis in France. It is the simplest country to live in. No one makes things complicated by becoming your friend for any obscure reason. If you want people to like you you have only to spend a little money." In Jake's decision to return to Spain we feel that he has achieved some clarification of feeling which has yet to be confirmed by a final gesture of renunciation.

Brett now gives up the bullfighter. She calls Jake to her once again; but his love toward her has been purified of vanity by the experience of Robert Cohn. He is through with vain regrets, as he is through with false romanticism; and to her tender reminder of the good time they could have had together he only answers, "Yes, isn't it pretty to think so." Brett in giving up the bullfighter has rediscovered her own version of control, and so, in giving up Brett, has he. His progress toward the second phase of the Grail initiation is now, perhaps, ready to begin.

Notes

1. See the interview with Hemingway in the *Paris Review,* Spring, 1958, pp. 76-77.

2. I am using this word in the sense in which Yeats uses it in his *Autobiographies* to describe President Wilson.

3. Cup, Lance, Dish and Sword.

Linda Ray Pratt (essay date winter 1973)

SOURCE: Pratt, Linda Ray. "The Holy Grail: Subversion and Revival of a Tradition in Tennyson and T. S. Eliot." *Victorian Poetry* 11, no. 4 (winter 1973): 307-21.

[*In the following essay, Pratt compares the use of the Grail myth in Alfred Tennyson's* Idylls of the King *and T. S. Eliot's* The Waste Land, *contending that both authors have significant differences in the way they view the legend—for Eliot, the Grail is representative of individual salvation, while for Tennyson, the quest for the Grail is an act that deflects man from the responsibilities he must assume in the real world.*]

The modern writer's need for myth is acute in a society which lacks any cohesive belief or coherent design of its own. In portraying just such a society in their long poems, *Idylls of the King* and *The Waste Land,* both Tennyson and T. S. Eliot employ the mythic structure inherent in the grail legends. Tennyson uses the popular

Photograph of T. S. Eliot.

and largely traditional literary versions of Arthurian legend, while Eliot uses the older, more purely archetypal versions of the Fisher King. Yet Tennyson's use of the familiar Arthurian legend took a radical direction. Numerous critics have observed that Tennyson's grail quest is a destructive force which contributes to the fall of Camelot.[1] As J. Philip Eggers shows, "For all but Tennyson, and perhaps Arnold, however, Arthurian legend remains what it had been in the Romantic period—a glorification of nature and fantasy" (*Eggers,* p. 105). Eliot's use of the grail material is a telling contrast, for despite his less traditional version, he interprets the material in a wholly traditional way. In Eliot's wasteland, the grail offers spiritual salvation and an escape from a meaningless worldly existence, the conventional meaning of the myth. In Tennyson's Camelot, however, the grail inspires moral irresponsibility which destroys a utopian possibility, a decidedly unconventional attitude about the grail in the nineteenth century.

Each poet's interpretation of the myth indicates his conclusions about the possibilities of secular life, conclusions obscured by the poet's ironic contrast of the myth with its setting. The struggle is between secularism and transcendence, the earthly versus the spiritual domain. The ancient grail tradition supports Eliot's desire for a mystical escape beyond the secular modern world to a "still point" of eternity, but the same mythic tradition undermines Tennyson's confidence that man has any "heavenly city" outside the new one he daily constructs in the secular world. Eliot's use of the grail legend in its full Christian-pagan associations is a throwback to a much earlier and more conventionally Neoplatonic tradition than that found in recent centuries. In contrast, Tennyson's rejection of the same grail tradition frees him to celebrate a new reliance on man as his own salvation and the earth as his proper sphere. The "modern" landscape of *The Waste Land* belies the traditional grail values of the poem, while Tennyson's medieval setting of Arthurian romance disguises a fundamentally secular and modern vision of man becoming his own god.

The landscapes in both poems share the usual grail imagery, though the grail itself becomes a major cause for the fall of Camelot. A careful reader might have noted, however, that the countryside outside Camelot was always marred by yawning chasms, bleaching bone, bats, and creeping mists. Arthur finds "the land of Cameliard . . . waste, / Thick with wet woods" ("The Coming of Arthur," ll. 20-21), not unlike Eliot's Thames scene where "the last fingers of leaf / Clutch and sink into the wet bank."[2] Cameliard is the domain of wild dogs, wolf, bear, and boar. It is, as Arthur says, a "dead world" (l. 93). The town where Geraint finds Enid, for example, is as desolate as rat's alley:

> And thither came Geraint, and underneath
> Beheld the long street of a little town
> In a long valley, on one side whereof,
> White from the mason's hand, a fortress rose;
> And on one side a castle in decay,
> Beyond a bridge that spanned a dry ravine:
> And out of town and valley came a noise
> As of a broad brook o'er a shingly bed
> Brawling, or like a clamour of the rooks
> At distance, ere they settle for the night.
>
> ("The Marriage of Geraint," ll. 241-250)

This medieval "urban scene"[3] is "ruinous" with "broken stones" and "shattered archway":

> His charger trampling many a prickly star
> Of sprouted thistle on the broken stones.
> He looked and saw that all was ruinous.
> Here stood a shattered archway plumed with fern;
> And here had fallen a great part of a tower,
> Whole, like a crag that tumbles from the cliff,
> And like a crag was gay with wilding flowers:
> And high above a piece of turret stair,
> Worn by the feet that now were silent, wound
> Bare to the sun, and monstrous ivy-stems
> Claspt the gray walls with hairy-fibred arms,
> And sucked the joining of the stones, and looked
> A knot, beneath, of snakes, aloft, a grove.
>
> (ll. 313-325)

Decay invades every corner of the kingdom after the fatal grail quest. In such traditional versions of the myth as Eliot's, this wasted condition usually initiates a quest. Tennyson's ironic use of the myth is perpetuated when the wounded Arthur assumes the posture, not only of Fisher King,[4] but also of the dead knight of the Chapel Perilous. He is placed in

> a chapel nigh the field,
> A broken chancel with a broken cross,
> That stood on a dark strait of barren land.
>
> ("The Passing of Arthur," ll. 176-178)

The passing of Arthur out of the secular world occasions profound agony for a deserted land:

> And, as it were one voice, an agony
> Of lamentation, like a wind that shrills
> All night in a waste land, where no one comes,
> Or hath come, since the making of the world.
>
> (ll. 368-371)

Tennyson's unrelenting concern for "the world" is underscored by the rationale Arthur offers for his death, "'The old order changeth, yielding place to new, / . . . Lest one good custom should corrupt the world'" (ll. 408-409). Even the promise of hope in the face of Arthur's death points back to the secular world: "'He comes again'" (l. 451).

In *The Waste Land*, of course, the absence of the grail and the values it symbolizes seems to be the cause of the desolation. The landscape is stony rubbish:

> What are the roots that clutch, what branches grow
> Out of this stony rubbish? Son of man,
> You cannot say, or guess, for you know only
> A heap of broken images, where the sun beats,
> And the dead tree gives no shelter, the cricket no relief,
> And the dry stone no sound of water. Only
> There is shadow under this red rock,
> (Come in under the shadow of this red rock),
> . . . . .
> I will show you fear in a handful of dust.
>
> (ll. 19-30)

The scene repeats the images of stone, ruin, sun, and branches used by Tennyson, but for reasons totally different. Waste overtakes Tennyson's landscapes when the knights abandon their moral responsibility to the society. The knights who choose to follow the grail necessarily neglect their duty to the earthly order. The quest leads them off in pursuit of "wandering fires" which eventually consume both men and kingdom. Only Arthur dedicates himself to chasing local bandits and honoring a peculiarly Victorian sense of civic duty and law and order. Yet the civic role is the true quest, for it is the only way a man makes his utopian vision a reality. Eliot's utopia is not of this world, and in his poem a preoccupation with secular life leads to a nihilistic materialism destructive of both spiritual and humanistic values. In a rigid dualism of Reality and shadow, Eliot seeks complete escape from his secular society through the traditional promise of heavenly transfiguration in the grail.

The questers in both poems are destined to fail the sick king who must, according to the Fisher King myths, depend on them for healing. True to the pattern, Eliot's impotent Fisher King sits in anticipation of a grail visitation and wonders, "Shall I at least set my lands in order?" Arthur, who opposed the grail quest from the first, warns that the grail is "A sign to maim this Order which I made" ("The Holy Grail," l. 297). Clyde de L. Ryals observes the ironic use of "maim" because of the earlier suggestions that the grail brings health,[5] but even a "successful" quest will further maim Arthur. The grail quest, which may traditionally heal the sick king, in Arthur's case only advances the illness. Traditionally, if the knights fail in the quest, the king is doomed. Arthur knows that his knights follow "wandering fires / Lost in the quagmire" (ll. 319-320) while the "chance of noble deeds will come and go / Unchallenged" (ll. 318-319). Even those like Galahad who succeed in finding the grail are lost to Arthur and contribute to his death. As Charles Moorman notes, the quest opposes the goals of "chivalry":

> Certainly, Tennyson thinks that the Grail is only for the devout few and that the great majority of knights are following a mistaken zeal and vision that are essentially alien to the expressed aims of chivalry. I think it is possible to say, therefore, that the Grail reaches a position in Tennyson almost wholly opposite in meaning and emphasis from that which it had held in the work of Chrétien.
>
> (Moorman, p. 34)

Tennyson's opposition to the grail actually goes beyond that indicated by Moorman, for even "the devout few" constitute a liability to the well-being of other men.

The quest is destined to failure because the knights choose the quester's role for unholy reasons; escapism and guilt account for more vows than does the desire to heal the kingdom or seek God's grace. The grail itself, although often combining the usual aspects of spiritual and vegetative regeneration, is more phallic than religious. All "rose-red with beatings" or

> Blood-red, and sliding down the blackened marsh
> Blood-red, and on the naked mountain top
> Blood-red, and in the sleeping mere below
> Blood-red,
>
> (ll. 473-476)

the grail is the manifestation of the knights' sexual preoccupation. The vow to follow the grail originates with the sublimated sexual yearnings of the little nun who sought the convent when her own human passions were unfulfilled:

> A holy maid; though never maiden glowed,
> But that was in her earlier maidenhood,
> With such a fervent flame of human love,
> Which being rudely blunted, glanced and shot
> Only to holy things.
>
> (ll. 72-76)

With her passion "rudely blunted" somehow, she turns to prayer and fasting in behalf of the adulterous Guinevere. When that will no longer satisfy her, she fixes her imagination on the grail, which subsequently appears in a phallic vision:

> And down the long beam stole the Holy Grail,
> Rose-red with beatings in it, as if alive,
> Till all the white walls of my cell were dyed
> With rosy colours leaping on the wall;
> And then the music faded, and the Grail
> Past, and the beam decayed, and from the walls
> The rosy quiverings died into the night.
>
> (ll. 117-123)

Inspired by this mystical orgasm, she sets about exciting others to seek her "vision." She inspirits her own passion into Galahad, handsome and also virgin, and makes from her own hair a silken sword belt for his sword. She speaks to him as to a lover:

> My knight, my love, my knight of heaven,
> O thou, my love, whose love is one with mine,
> I, maiden, round thee, maiden, bind my belt.
>
> . . . . .
>
> and as she spake
> She sent the deathless passion in her eyes
> Through him, and made him hers, and laid her mind
> On him, and he believed in her belief.
>
> (ll. 157-165)

Galahad wishes to lose himself to save himself, and the other knights, fired by the sudden abundance of miracles, and knowing that they have more need of being saved than Galahad, join in the swearing. Tradition says that the holy cup will heal anyone who can touch it, and the knights, losing their proper perspective on "use and name and fame," hope not so much to cure the kingdom as to cure themselves. Hugh Kenner says that Tennyson's grail quest partakes of a "depraved religiosity," and that "the cup . . . never succeeds in being more than the reward of a refined and sublimated erotic impulse."[6] Perhaps Arthur understands the questers' sublimated need to escape sexual thoughts inspired by Guinevere's infidelity when he describes their quest as following "wandering fires"; "ye have seen what ye have seen" (l. 915) he tells them when they return, for each knight has found in the quest only that vision of Camelot which he had had before.[7]

The absence of the grail and the apathy of the questers are major causes for the meaningless existence in Eliot's wasteland. Had Arthur's knights disavowed the false quest they might have truly saved the kingdom, but Eliot's wasteland is doomed precisely because all the questers decline the search for the grail. The companion of the hyacinth girl turns away in silence and the carbuncular clerk "gropes his way, finding the stairs unlit." The Chapel Perilous is empty and the grail has abandoned the land:

> In this decayed hole among the mountains
> In the faint moonlight, the grass is singing
> Over tumbled graves, about the chapel
> There is the empty chapel, only the wind's home.
> It has no windows, and the door swings,
> Dry bones harm no one.
>
> (ll. 386-391)

According to tradition, if the Chapel were not empty, the quester could expect to be healed on the next day. Missing the grail, however, the land remains in decay. Instead of the sacramental foot washing and *"ces voix d'enfants, chantant dans la couple,"* one hears only the obscene lyrics about Mrs. Porter and her daughter who wash their "feet" in soda water. The return of the grail could bring to the land, the questers, and the Chapel Perilous the traditional renewal of their original meaning.

While the desolate scene of Eliot's ruined chapel indicates the urgent need for a fruitful grail quest, the nightmare quests of the knights of Arthur's court suggest the waste and delusion in their journey. Lancelot's and Percivale's accounts of their quest are a paradigm of the grail's effect on the Order. "Every evil word," "every evil thought," and "every evil deed" goad Percivale, who finds himself "alone, and in a land of sand and thorns" (l. 376). His conscience says, "This Quest is not for thee" (l. 378), but he rides on to encounter a series of symbolic scenes which fall into dust when he tries to touch them. The apple trees by the brook fall into dust before he can quench his burning thirst; the baby held out to him is dead. Couched in ironic imagery of the Nativity, this promise of life arrives stillborn, and both mother and babe fall "into dust and nothing."[8] Camelot itself is suggested in the pinnacled city:

> And I rode on and found a mighty hill,
> And on the top, a city walled: the spires
> Pricked with incredible pinnacles into heaven.
> And by the gateway stirred a crowd; and these
> Cried to me climbing, "Welcome, Percivale!"
>
> . . . . .
>
> but [I] found at top
> No man, nor any voice. And thence I past
> Far through a ruinous city, and I saw
> That man had once dwelt there; but there I found
> Only one man of an exceeding age.
> "Where is that goodly company," said I,
> "That so cried out upon me?" and he had
> Scarce any voice to answer, and yet gasped,
> "Whence and what art thou?" and even as he spoke
> Fell into dust, and disappeared, and I
> Was left alone once more, and cried in grief,
> "Lo, if I find the Holy Grail itself
> And touch it, it will crumble into dust."
>
> (ll. 421-439)

This ruined city and its old man with "scarce any voice" project a vision of Camelot which will greet the knights on their return home. The imagined city of the grail quest is thus an image of the real city that will be destroyed because of the quest.

The wasteland visions of Lancelot complete the desolation as Arthur's "finest" knight wanders in confusion. His quest was wracked by madness and terror:

> My madness came upon me as of old,
> And whipt me into waste fields far away;
>
> . . . . .
>
> and then I came
> All in my folly to the naked shore,
> Wide flats, where nothing but coarse grasses grew;
> But such a blast, my King, began to blow,
> So loud a blast along the shore and sea,
> Ye could not hear the waters for the blast,
> Though heapt in mounds and ridges all the sea
> Drove like a cataract, and all the sand
> Swept like a river, and the clouded heavens
> Were shaken with the motion and the sound.
>
> (ll. 784-798)

Lancelot personally shares the ill effects of the grail quest; instead of healing the warring emotions within his soul, the quest distorts them and reduces him to madness. As Ryals says, the grail quest does not separate the wholesome flower of his being from the poisonous one; it only "leaves the flowers entwined and splits *him* apart" (Ryals, p. 175). The effect on the kingdom is the same; the quest heals no sins, leaves responsible deeds undone, and wastes completely all but a tithe of the questers.

Eliot's and Tennyson's use of light and water imagery in *The Waste Land* and the *Idylls* supports the opposing values attached to the grail. In Tennyson's poem, the grail is a "blood-red" distortion of refracted light, while the "pure" light of perfection shines from Arthur's mortal head. Even the "eternal deep" is connected with temporal history. In Eliot's poem, the waters which promise fertility and salvation have disappeared from a dying earth, and the light only bakes men into a meaningless death frieze. Water, as Jerome Buckley explains, "is Tennyson's perpetual and ambiguous symbol of changeless change . . . the token both of man's mutability and of the infinite amorphous oneness of nature which mocks the transient human being."[9] Arthur's birth out of a great wave intimately links him to the mysterious deep:

> And then the two [Belys and Merlin]
> Dropt to the cove, and watched the great sea fall,
> Wave after wave, each mightier than the last,
> Till last, a ninth one, gathering half the deep
> And full of voices, slowly rose and plunged
> Roaring, and all the wave was in a flame.
>
> ("The Coming of Arthur," ll. 376-381)

Though the horizon is "in heaven," the babe thrown up out of this wave of flame is real and mortal. The link between the human Arthur and the supernatural waters is clearest in his relationship to the mystical Lady of the Lake. She represents not only the divine powers of the deep, but also the eternal calm beyond the reach of external storms, or as Buckley says, "changeless change." The moaning of the phantom sea during Arthur's last battle seems the chorus of sea-voices which announced his birth and now mourn his earthly death. The sea images provide a continuum of time and eternal mystery out of which all the life and values of Camelot eventually merge and emerge. In the figure of Arthur, the mortal child of the immortal sea, Tennyson fuses secular and temporal values with eternal and divine ones.

In *The Waste Land* the waters of the earth are stagnant, and the waters that might bring rebirth are, like the grail, absent and beyond our reach. The sea, instead of being full of voices, is as desolate and empty as the land: *"Oed' und leer das Meer."* The reader is told to fear death by water, and the poet reveals to us the bones of Phlebas as a warning. Only from the fishermen in Lower Thames Street and from the "pearl eyes" of the drowned sailor are there any hints that the sea might contain life and mystery. The fishermen are in a public bar, though, and the pearl eyes a mere memory. Elsewhere, the rivers are polluted, the canals dull with sunken waters. Rain, when it does come, must be avoided by taking shelter in closed cars and the colonnade. The fear of rain is the fear of living. Rain stirs the "dull roots" which threaten to quicken into feelings more painful than lethargy. But the rain itself is a tease and a mockery, for when the desire for water outweighs the fear of it, there is no water. Water can be the source of salvation both for the land and the soul, but too often water brings death, or nothing at all. The waters actually present in Eliot's wasteland, such as the canal, the Thames, and the deep sea currents, become part of the burden of life, and the life-giving waters that are withheld belong to the distant realm of the Thunder.

In contrast to the way in which Tennyson blends pure light with light on the earth, Eliot retains a strict separation of the living "heart of light" (his symbol for Absolute Reality) and the deadening sun of this world. Tennyson's use of light more nearly follows the Neoplatonic concept of levels of emanation from a center of pure light, as seen in the example of golden-curled Arthur, born in a wave of flame, who "lightens" the dead world to make it live. He brings order to the darkened land by "letting in the sun" and wedding the woman who seems to be all the glory of May mornings.[10] In the earliest days of Arthur's reign, Camelot is "a city all on fire / With sun and cloth of gold" ("The Coming of Arthur," ll. 478-479). The knights are in turn touched, too, by the force of light in swearing their vows to Arthur:

> That when they rose, knighted from kneeling, some
> Were pale as at the passing of a ghost,
> Some flushed, and others dazed, as one who wakes
> Half-blinded at the coming of a light.
>
> (ll. 262-265)

This light represents what Guinevere calls "the highest." It symbolizes godliness and truth with the attendant qualities of life, order, authority, and purpose. She calls it "that fine air, / That pure severity of perfect light." Arthur believes visible light is not "light," but vision:

> Let visions of the night or of the day
> Come, as they will; and many a time they come,
> Until this earth he walks on seems not earth,
> This light that strikes his eyeball is not light,
> This air that smites his forehead is not air
> But vision.
>
> ("The Holy Grail," ll. 906-911)

This "vision" of God's design on earth is what Arthur had hoped to make real. Men's eyes are "dense and dim," however, and although Arthur could see God "in the shining of the stars," he strove in vain "to work His will." As Arthur loses his moral authority and clarity of purpose, he loses the quality of light which had shone from him in the beginning.[11] Receding into the fog, he grays into a colorless shadow:

> and more and more
> The moony vapour rolling round the King,
> Who seemed the phantom of a Giant in it,
> Enwound him fold by fold, and made him gray
> And grayer, till himself became a mist
> Before her, moving ghostlike to his doom.
>
> ("Guinevere," ll. 596-601)

In contrast to Arthur's "light" is the perverted light of the grail. The "blood-red" grail is a perversion of the divine light because the knights who follow its "fires" leave "His work" undone. Vivien links such light to lust, this "fire of heaven, / This old sun-worship," that will rise and destroy the kingdom. Guinevere, too, prefers the impure, refracted light of the "low sun." Only the light in Arthur's eyes suggests the best in humanity. The true light is the essence of good, the rule of order, the authority of truth. And it, too, resides in man.

No similar mixture of light imagery occurs in *The Waste Land* where the separation of earth and heaven is maintained. The Neoplatonic "heart of light" is the central image of the "still point of the turning world" in *Four Quartets,* but the light over the wasteland is not a true grail light. "Where the sun beats," the barrenness of dry stone and hot sand increases. Shade from this sun would be a relief, but that, too, is impossible. "The sun's last rays" dry the "combinations" of the typist, and the "sad light" in Belladonna's room comes from "the flames of sevenbranched candelabra" reflected in the glitter of her jewels and vials. In this subdued and flickering light, only the silly Cupidon is golden. Even the sea-wood burns green and orange. The flame in the heart is lust, as "The Fire Sermon" ends with its lesson: "Burning burning burning burning." The "flash of lightning" (which must come out of "the heart of light") is the one suggestion of power and meaning. But the dazzle does not really seem to be for our eyes, and the lightning is at best an intimation, not a vision. The images of light, like those of water, remain negative in their associations with the earth.

Confusion over true and false grail bearers troubles the questers in both poems. The grail does not appear in *The Waste Land* in part because the true grail bearers are rejected while the false grail bearers (the nymphs, the typist) embrace in a decadent parody of the holy ritual. In the *Idylls,* the knights confuse the true grail bearers, such as Enid, with the false ones, such as Guinevere. In Eliot's poem, it is the man who fails the hyacinth girl, but in Tennyson's poem, "the hyacinth girl" herself turns out to be a fraud.

Eliot's hyacinth girl makes the one clear offer of love and fertility in the wasteland. She stands with her arms full, presumably with that flower symbolizing sexual fertility, and her hair wet with life-giving waters:

> "You gave me hyacinths first a year ago;
> They called me the hyacinth girl."
> —Yet when we came back, late, from the Hyacinth garden,
> Your arms full, and your hair wet, I could not
> Speak, and my eyes failed, I was neither
> Living nor dead, and I knew nothing,
> Looking into the heart of light, the silence.
> *Oed' und Leer das Meer*"
>
> (ll. 35-42)

Her companion had given her hyacinths, but the gesture was one only of form. When the time came to act on the promise in the gift, he could not speak. The hyacinth girl is the very "heart of light," but her gift is rejected by one who cannot bear the reality of life or pure light. He prefers to know "nothing" and finds his ease with one who expects nothing, resents nothing. The hyacinth girl is Eliot's only attractive figure in *The Waste Land.* Her springlike beauty and promise of love stand in contrast to the mean and vulgar lives of all the other inhabitants.

The "hyacinth girl" in the *Idylls* is Guinevere, who is linked with that flower. By associating the hyacinth with her love for Lancelot, however, she corrupts the meaning of her sexual love. In "Balin and Balan" Guinevere tells her lover:

> 'Sweeter to me' she said 'this garden rose
> Deep-hued and many-folded! sweeter still
> The wild-wood hyacinth and the bloom of May.'
>
> (ll. 264-266)

After she is in hiding at the nunnery, she remembers when she and Lancelot

> Rode under groves that looked a paradise
> Of blossom, over sheets of hyacinth
> That seemed the heavens upbreaking through the earth.
>
> ("Guinevere," ll. 386-388)

Arthur believes Guinevere "the fairest under heaven" with whom he might join to "live together as one life" and bring rebirth to the "dead land." He conceives of her as a grail bearer, and when he "felt the light of her eyes," he did not turn away unable to speak. He turns his bare face to her and allows her "light" to pass into his life. Guinevere, however, prefers the darker, less pure colors of the "low sun": "For who loves me must have a touch of earth," she claims in backhanded praise of Lancelot. When Guinevere rejects her husband and her role as grail bearer, the promise of life ends in death, the promise of fulfillment in sterility. Instead of life-giver, Arthur is forced into the role of Fisher King. "Sick" with a "grievous wound," he acknowledges his weakness when denied a true union with his wife:

> Woe is me!
> Authority forgets a dying king,
> Laid widowed of the power in his eye
> That bowed the will.
>
> ("The Passing of Arthur," ll. 288-291)

In the *Idylls* true healing power lies not in the mysterious grail, but in the real women who offer love to the questers. Their gift of healing love parallels that of Eliot's hyacinth girl, and they are, in fact, the true bearers of the grail's powers.[12] Enid, for example, is more nearly a real grail bearer than those women of deeper enchantments. Her love saves her foolish husband and heals him of his physical and mental wounds. Enid eventually joins her life with Geraint's in ruling a peaceful, just realm.

Percivale also encounters one true grail bearer in his misdirected quest. He spurns her, though, believing that she will ruin his life and purpose. The journey takes him to the castle of the only woman "who had ever / Made my heart leap." She offers him what the hyacinth girl in *The Waste Land* had offered her companion:

> one fair morn,
> I walking to and fro beside a stream

> That flashed across her orchard underneath
> Her castle-walls, she stole upon my walk,
> And calling me the greatest of all knights,
> Embraced me, and so kissed me the first time,
> And gave herself and all her wealth to me.
>
> ("The Holy Grail," ll. 590-596)

Percivale thinks his love for her the "wandering fires" of which Arthur warned. Hating himself and all but her, he flees from this gift of love and life to follow the grail with Galahad. As a result Percivale suffers the spiritual deadness which stopped the companion of Eliot's hyacinth girl:

> Then after I was joined with Galahad
> Cared not for her, nor anything upon earth.
>
> (ll. 610-611)

The irony of the idyll is that in rejecting a true grail bearer in order to pursue the false quest for the holy vessel, Percivale acquires the spiritual sickness which the grail was meant to cure.

Nowhere in the *Idylls* does Tennyson approve the desire to forget earth's cares in exchange for heaven's peace. His interest in God is in doing His work in this world, not in joining him in another. The asceticism Eliot admires is to Tennyson a profound evil. The escapist grail quest is as much, perhaps more, of a sin than the adultery. Arthur assesses the damage done the Order by the grail, revealing at the close virtual scorn for Percivale and an amazing casualness about the ascendency of Galahad:

> Was I too dark a prophet when I said
> To those who went upon the Holy Quest,
> That most of them would follow wandering fires,
> Lost in the quagmire?—lost to me and gone,
> And left me gazing at a barren board,
> And a lean Order—scarce returned a tithe—
> And out of those to whom the vision came
> My greatest hardly will believe he saw;
> Another hath beheld it afar off,
> And leaving human wrongs to right themselves,
> Cares but to pass into the silent life.
> And one hath had the vision face to face,
> And now his chair desires him here in vain,
> However they may crown him otherwise.
>
> ("The Holy Grail," ll. 885-898)

Merlin, too, had been lost when he "by misadvertence" sat in the chair called "The Siege perilous."[13] Tennyson glossed this line, "The perilous seat which stands for the spiritual imagination" (Ricks, p. 1666n) Throughout the *Idylls,* Tennyson has viewed "the spiritual imagination" as "perilous" to one's responsible acceptance of life. The results to both Merlin and Galahad, who later sits in the same chair, suggest that the grail is another escape from one's proper role in this world. The only legitimate vision for man seems to be "this earth he walks on" transfigured till it seems not earth but heaven; the best love is not that for holy relics but of man for woman; the best life is not that spent in silent meditation, but in striving to right human wrongs. Tennyson has given us in the *Idylls* the very values which are anathema to Eliot: the secularization of the mystical.

Of course Eliot's secular world has "reeled back into the beast" already, but the values which he longs to see restored are not really those which Tennyson embodies in a utopian Camelot. Both poets desire spiritual and physical vitality in man but for different reasons. Although given to mystical trances himself and comforted by the conception of some benign spiritual force, Tennyson is essentially concerned with reforming and revitalizing this world. Eliot, however, essentially longs to escape it. "Not here / Not here the darkness, in this twittering world," he writes in the later poem that expressly reveals his yearning "to become renewed, transfigured, in another pattern." Thus, the holy grail is for Eliot a mystic vessel through which he may find "the still point of the turning world." Those whose lives are spent in "prayer, observance, discipline, thought and action": seeking "the moment in and out of time" would, of course, create a society on this earth of "ardour and selflessness and self-surrender," but that society is only incidental to making "the impossible union" "actual" ("The Dry Salvages"). Eliot admires the "eastern and western asceticism" of Buddha and St. Augustine (his footnote to *The Waste Land*), and his best use for this world is that it allows men the solitude "to purify the soul."

For Tennyson, the grail threatens to do the very thing which Eliot longs for it to do: to take men out of the world, or turn their attention toward some form of "eastern and western asceticism." In tracing the meaning of the grail legend through literature down to Tennyson, Charles Moorman observes:

> The progress of the Grail would seem to originate in Chrétien's Christian mysticism, then to move, still retaining its devoutly religious tone, into the context of the Arthurian story in the French *Queste*. From there, the story progresses into a slightly more secularized version in Malory, and finally into a position where it represents a wrong attitude, a mistaken zeal. The Grail thus diminishes in thematic importance as it comes down in the tradition, and in this process loses entirely its original mystical tone.
>
> (Moorman, p. 34)

Tennyson long hesitated to write the grail idyll because "I doubt whether such a subject could be handled in these days, without incurring a charge of irreverence."[14] His tone is not so much that of irreverence as of repudiation, however, as the grail becomes a distraction which men who live in a dangerous and complex society could well do without. Eliot himself once observed that Tennyson's "desire for immortality never is quite the desire for Eternal Life; his concern is for the loss of man rather than for the gain of God."[15] This distinction is the key to each poet's use of the grail material. The grail in the *Idylls* is evil because "the gain of God" comes at the expense of society's loss of man. The grail in *The Waste Land,* however, would mean "the gain of God" *through* the loss of man. Not until *Four Quartets* did Eliot realize in poetry the elimination of self and secularism which the grail traditionally promised to the successful quester. Eliot's medieval longing to escape the secular world is fundamentally anti-modern, anti-life, and in his case, finally anti-poetic. Tennyson's attitude toward the grail legend is a significant break with the past as his repudiation of a traditional Christian fetish opens the way toward a more existentialist reliance on man as his own salvation and upon "this earth" not as earth, but as "vision."

Notes

1. Among the several critics making this interpretation are Charles Moorman, *Arthurian Triptych* (Univ. of California Press, 1960); F. E. L. Priestley, "Tennyson's Idylls," *UTQ* 19 (1949), 35-49; W. R. Brashear, *The Living Will: A Study of Tennyson and Nineteenth-Century Subjectivism* (The Hague, 1969); and J. Philip Eggers, *King Arthur's Laureate* (New York Univ. Press, 1971).

2. All quotations from Tennyson's poetry are from *The Poems of Tennyson,* ed. Christopher Ricks (London, 1969). All quotations from Eliot's poetry are from *The Complete Poems and Plays 1909-1950* (New York, 1952).

3. Helen Gardner uses this term in her article, "The Landscapes of Eliot's Poetry," *CritQ,* 10 (1968), 313-329.

4. Eggers says that "Tennyson omitted the magical elements of the bleeding lance and the fisher king from the story of the grail" (p. 160). Arthur is, as I suggest, the Fisher King, and one could argue that Lancelot represents the traditional phallic lance, which is sometimes also the instrument for wounding the king.

5. *From the Great Deep: Essays on Idylls of the King* (Ohio Univ. Press, 1967), p. 170

6. *The Invisible Poet* (New York, 1959), p. 170.

7. In a somewhat different context, Eggers sees the grail as "primarily a test" which only brings out in each knight "what is already within him" (pp. 159-162).

8. Brashear comments on Percivale's struggle, "As long as he attempts to 'discover' or find the Grail, as his own self, his quest is futile, for all objects disintegrate on penetration by the self's own forms of intuition into nothingness" (p. 147).

9. *Tennyson: The Growth of A Poet* (1960; rpt. Boston, 1965), p. 113.

10. Eggers further notes that "there is a general darkening of the landscape accompanying the loss of Arthur's ideal in Camelot" (p. 186).

11. Eggers connects the failure of light in Arthur with an analogous failure of his formerly keen eyesight (p. 187).

12. Grover Smith, *T. S. Eliot's Poetry and Plays* (Univ. of Chicago Press, 1956), identified the hyacinth girl as a grail-bearer (p. 74).

13. In the "Merlin and Vivien" idyll Tennyson presents a different version of Merlin's loss. In that idyll Vivien tricks him out of his secret wisdom and then uses it against him to capture him forever in a tree trunk.

14. Hallam, Lord Tennyson, *Alfred Lord Tennyson: A Memoir* (New York, 1897), I, 456.

15. Eliot, *Essays Ancient and Modern* (New York, 1936), p. 197.

Julie M. Johnson (essay date 1981)

SOURCE: Johnson, Julie M. "The Damsel and Her Knights: The Goddess and the Grail in Conrad's *Chance*." *Conradiana* 13, no. 3 (1981): 221-28.

[*In the following essay, Johnson studies the parallels between the Grail legend and Joseph Conrad's novel,* Chance.]

Joseph Conrad's novel, *Chance,* is divided into two parts, the first entitled "The Damsel," the second entitled "The Knight." These allusions to the chivalric tradition have been understood to be a reference to Captain Anthony's sacrificial, celibate marriage to Flora de Barral, a marriage which embodies the romantic ideal of his father's poetry.[1] It also has been argued that the subtitles are intentionally ironic, that Conrad adopted them to belie any accusation that he failed to realize "how over-simplified and falsely romantic is his treatment of [Flora's] plight."[2] However, it is my conviction that the subtitles are neither superficial nor, finally, ironic. Rather, they signify the underlying structure of the novel, which is that of the separate quests of three knights for one damsel. The "damsel," Flora de Barral, embodies the dual nature of Christian Grail-symbol and pagan fertility goddess—a conjunction which is characteristic of much quest literature in the Arthurian tradition. The three knights—Anthony, Powell, and Marlow—have their counterparts in Galahad, Percivale, and Bors, the three knights who traveled together during part of their respective quests for the Holy Grail, and whose quests were all successful, though in different ways.

In the late nineteenth-century, perhaps the best known sources for the Grail material were Malory's version in "The Tale of the Sankgreal," and Tennyson's *Idylls of the King*. However, the Arthurian material could be found in various other works, and therefore either Malory or Tennyson, or both, or neither, may have been Conrad's primary source. Malory had adapted and developed his sources; Tennyson adapted and developed Malory; Conrad, in turn, used only that which suited his purpose, and the borrowing was minimal—simply the skeleton of the final events: Anthony, like Galahad, dies after his quest is completed; like Percivale, Powell sees the Grail only after the death of Anthony-Galahad, and then retires to a hermitage; Marlow, like Bors, returns to tell the tale to an eager listener.[3] Whatever Conrad's source or sources may have been, the parallels between the essential facts and Conrad's novel are uncanny if not intentional.

Flora de Barral is the focus of *Chance*; Conrad tells us that "this novel relates the story of her life."[4] She is the obsessive object of interest of every character in the novel, including Marlow himself. Further, as critics have pointed out, the reaction of each character to Flora's vulnerability is a measure of his "humanity."[5] It is through Flora that the theme of "emotional isolation" is most powerfully expressed,[6] and we judge each character in light of the degree to which he either increases or decreases that isolation, whether he attempts to rescue her from her entrapment or to ensnare her further.

Flora, a maiden captive to a selfish and tyrannical father, is named after the Roman fertility goddess. Through the connotations of this imagery she is linked to the fertility aspect of the Grail legends, and Marlow even refers to her at one point as a "vessel" (119), making the relationship between sexuality and the Grail imagistically explicit. Both Damsel and Grail are quest objects in romance literature, and are, in that context, often interchangeable, as mythologists, cultural anthropologists, and analytical psychologists have long pointed out.[7] In *Chance,* the conjoined sexual and Christian symbolism of fertility goddess and Grail come together in the pagan-Christian figure of the damsel, a union which is reinforced on one level by images of her dwellings. To begin with, Flora's mother was raised in a "vicarage" (70) because Flora's grandfather was a churchwarden as well as a sea-captain; Flora herself lived in a country house called "The Priory" (73) until her mother's death. Later, aboard the "Ferndale," she is isolated in another kind of sanctuary, the captain's cabin. This room has been "shut off" (300) from the rest of the ship and refitted like a "palace," with appointments that "glitter" and "gleam" (349). The cabin is separated into two parts: one side houses Flora and her hovering, manipulative father; Anthony lives alone in the other half. This unnatural temple is divided by a heavy curtain which creates a "solid wall" (415) between the goddess and her worshipper, like the rood screen in a medieval church. After her father's death, the screen is removed and the cabin becomes the more natural temple of a fertility goddess in a "fern-dale." Finally, when Anthony dies, Flora leaves the cabin to settle under "blue sky," and surrounded by a "dreamless peace" (442). There Flora is served by a votary, "'an unobtrusive, even an indistinct, middle-aged person in black'" (443).

In addition to providing the Grail-Goddess with visible temples, Marlow also depicts her as a temple in herself. Recounting the governess's attack upon the young Flora, Marlow says that Flora's "'unconsciousness was about to be broken into with profane violence, with desecrating circumstances like a temple violated by a mad, vengeful impiety'" (99). Later he returns to this simile, merging the spiritual and sexual in one figure:

> "A young girl . . . is something like a temple. You pass by and wonder what mysterious rites are going on in there, what prayer, what visions? The privileged man, the lover, the husband, who are given the key of the sanctuary do not always know how to use it. For myself, without claim, without merit, simply by chance I had been allowed to look through the half-opened door and I had seen the saddest possible desecration, the withered brightness of youth. . . ."
>
> (311)

This image is developed in its spiritual dimension by the allusion to Flora as "as saint, an angel with white wings" (302), and by reference to Powell's sense of "'a sort of divinity hedging in a captain's wife'" (289).

The symbol which most completely merges Christian and pagan, sexuality and spirituality, the goddess and the Grail, is Flora's remarkable blue eyes—eyes which enchant Marlow (201, 215, 231), captivate Anthony (227), and are stoutly affirmed by Powell in the face of the obtuse observation that they are black. Eyes have long been traditional symbols of the soul, and Flora's eyes bespeak both mystery and sensuality. "Enigmatic" (180), "like blue gleams of fire" (217), they both mystify and attract. For Marlow they produced "'a night effect when you seem to see vague shapes and don't know what reality you may come upon at anytime'" (215); for Anthony they were like the "blue unfathomable sea" into which he "plunged" (332) and which held him helpless. At the same time, their blueness suggests Flora's Christian aspect, for blue is the color of the Virgin. Finally, Flora's name and the color of her eyes come together in the symbol of the blue flower, which J. E. Cirlot, in *A Dictionary of Symbols,* defines as "an allusion to the 'mystic Center' as represented by the Grail and other such symbols."[8]

The symbolism of the damsel as a fertility goddess and Grail-figure is completed by the imagery of the questing knights. It has been said that one of the thematic threads of *Chance* is the inherent danger in "modern knight errantry."[9] Certainly this is true, for Anthony, Powell and Marlow all must work at their quests; the Grail is not easily obtained. Furthermore, each quest presents different difficulties, for each quester stands in a different relationship to the Grail-Goddess who is the object of the quests.

Conrad's knights share certain characteristics as questers (aside from their affinity for those marvellous blue eyes): All, like their prototypes, are "pure of heart and firm of faith."[10] Both Anthony and Powell are dependent on permission from Flora to act upon their love; both are martyrs to their love, though each in his own way (Anthony gives up sex, Powell the sea); and both are highly idealistic and imbued with a chivalric view of love. All three men are equally unrelenting in their quests, although, again each in his own way; and, finally, it is only in relationship to these questers that Flora is drawn out of isolation and into community. At this point resemblances end.

Anthony is the embodiment of the romantic idealism of his poet-father whose poetry was, ironically, in direct opposition to his practice. Carleon Anthony—whose given name is that of the legendary site of the Round Table—left his son a legacy of idealism which "'grew to the size of a passion filling with inward sobs the big form of the man who had never in his life read a single one of those famous sonnets singing of the most highly civilized, chivalrous love'" (332). Captain Anthony's forgivable "vanity" was that he refused to do anything which might be construed as taking advantage of a girl who, Mr. Fyne solemnly informed him, did not love him, yet needed him (331-33). Consequently he settles upon the idea of a magnanimous renunciation of his conjugal rights, together with an equally magnanimous acceptance of responsibility for "the great de Barral's" last years. It never occurs to Anthony that Fyne is incorrect in his assessment of Flora's feelings, nor does it occur to him to challenge this assessment with the same passion with which he had pursued their betrothal. He simply accepts Fyne's construction of her feelings and channels sexual passion into idealistic fervor, seeing in his sacrifice "something as incredible as the fulfillment of an amazing and startling dream in which he could take the world in his arms—all the suffering world—not to possess its pathetic fairness but to console and cherish its sorrow" (348). However, this magnanimity, which is rooted in every good and chivalrous intention, is, for the damsel who cannot believe that anyone could love her "in that way," a "new perfidity of life," leaving her bereft of the "moral support" she had come in such a short time to count on: "'the sustaining whirlwind had let her down, to stumble on again'" (227, 336, 428).

Anthony's passion is obviously sexual, but at the same time he perceives in Flora something that is incorporeal and incompatible with physicality. In his frustration over her refusal to come to terms with his passion and his proposal, he cries: "You white-faced wisp, you wreath of mist, you little ghost of all the sorrow in the world. . . . Some rough wind will blow you away altogether. You have no holding on this earth" (226). This wisp of the unreal—this mysteriously recalcitrant fertility goddess—remains elusive, although Anthony believes "that if only he could get hold of her, no woman would belong to him so completely as this woman" (224). The quest mires in misunderstanding until Anthony, provoked by de Barral's attempt to poison him, acts like Galahad once acted: he deliberately tempts fate. Galahad sat in Merlin's fatal seat, but did not die. Instead, he had a sudden and unexpected vision of the Holy Grail.[11] Analagously, Anthony tempts fate by telling Flora that he is releasing her from their marriage, and he, like Galahad, is immediately rewarded by a vision of the object of his desire: Flora throws her arms about his neck and declares her love for him. His quest now over, he sets aside his "delicacy" (435) once and for all, and wastes no time consummating his marriage.

Anthony and Flora live together happily aboard the "Ferndale" for several years until Anthony, like Galahad, dies.[12] Flora then retreats to her cottage, where she is visited by the second knight, Percivale-Powell. Powell, who served on the "Ferndale" the entire time Flora was married to Anthony, had been devoted to his captain, as was Percivale to Galahad. Therefore, his pursuit of Anthony's widow, though rigorous, is worshipful and honorable. Never thinking to press his suit, he gives up the sea to spend the rest of his days making chaste pilgrimages to the little cottage on the marsh. These pilgrimages are humorously reminiscent of the traditional approach to the Chapel Perilous in that they involve a marked degree, if not of difficulty, at least of nuisance. Powell must navigate his small, shallow-bottomed boat up a "narrow tidal creek" at high tide, and then is firmly aground until the next high tide—a knight without a horse, so to speak. Once docked, he must cross a "dark, still marsh" in an "oppressive stillness one-and-one-half miles to Flora's home (258-61). He always surrounds this undertaking with great secrecy, leading Marlow, who is going to equally much trouble to follow him, to remark: "'I don't think he ever wanted to avoid me. But it is a fact that he used to disappear out of the river in a very mysterious manner sometimes'" (253).

Powell's worship of Flora is of a different nature than Anthony's was, for whereas Anthony was a passionate solitary, Powell is a child-like "enthusiast" (426). Nevertheless, Powell's chivalric sense has always been as idealistic as Anthony's. He once berated a steward who had implied that Flora was less than a dutiful wife, and this, Marlow said, "'established Powell as a champion of Mrs. Anthony. Nothing more bearing on the question was ever said before him'" (39). Powell's sense of the chivalric proprieties is so strong that, when Marlow ultimately suggests that he mention his "enthusiasm" to Flora, he is astounded at Marlow's "audacity"—his "'almost *sacrilegious* hint'" that the goddess be approached in her temple. Then, realizing that no one could have overheard this impious suggestion, Powell "'allowed a gleam to light up his eyes, like the reflection of some inward fire tended in the sanctuary of his heart by a devotion as pure as that of any vestal'" (441; italics mine). Powell's quest is rewarded by possession of the Grail-Goddess only through the happy intervention of Marlow's suggestion, whispered in the ear of both parties, that each reveal his (her) feelings to the other. Marlow's action is prompted by his frustration with what he considers to be an unnatural relationship, for in his own brand of romantic idealism, the only fit conclusion to any romantic quest is union: "'Pairing off is the fate of mankind,'" he argues. "'And if two beings thrown together, mutually attracted, resist the necessity, fail in understanding and voluntarily stop short of the— the embrace, in the noblest meaning of the word, then they are committing a sin against life, the call of which is simple. Perhaps sacred'" (427). Happily for Marlow, Powell and Flora answer the "sacred call" and marry. At that time, Powell retires to Flora's lonely cottage—a Percivale to the hermitage.[13]

This romantic who could not bear to watch a quest unconsummated is Conrad's version of Sir Bors, the knight who finally returned to King Arthur to relate the stories of the Grail quests of his fellow-knights.[14] As the story-teller, Marlow remains detached from the quests of Anthony and Powell—"the expert in the psychological wilderness," as the first-person narrator describes him (311). His attitude toward their quests reflects incredulity that such purity of soul and action could exist—that one man would surrender his conjugal rights and another his career to pursue a damsel.[15] However, Marlow is not immune to the compelling charm of this fertility goddess. Once, when Flora had raised her eyes to his, she had done so "'with extraordinary effect. It was like catching sight of a piece of blue sky, or a stretch of open water. And for a moment [Marlow] understood the desire of that man to whom the sea and sky of his solitary life had appeared suddenly incomplete without that glance which seemed to belong to them both'" (231).

In the orbit of Flora's attraction, Marlow the story-teller becomes Marlow the quester, pursuing the damsel across the space of many years with all the avidity of a knight seeking the Grail. Marlow wants to possess the story of Flora de Barral even as Anthony and Powell want to possess the woman herself, and to this end he goes to absurd lengths—procuring a boat and devoting long periods of time—to track Powell and his "mystery" through the shallow tidal waters of the Thames. Then, after learning the story of Flora's life, and unraveling its secrets, Marlow, like his prototype, recounts his story to a fascinated listener, the first-person narrator.

It is significant that Marlow does not tell us Flora's story directly, but relates it to another. It is this listener, the narrator, who picks up on the quest imagery which Marlow has used to describe the relationships between Anthony, Powell, and Flora, and it is he who assigns the subtitles. Anthony and Powell do not perceive themselves as knights on a quest; nor does Flora see herself as a fertility goddess and Grail-figure. Marlow sees them in this light. The narrator, in turn, recognizes Marlow as yet another knight on the same quest, although Marlow himself is oblivious to his knighthood.

Critics usually react negatively to Anthony's death and the marriage of Flora and Powell, taking the position that everything subsequent to the crisis in the ship's cabin is anti-climatic. The ending has been called "arbitrary and wanton,"[16] the "major weakness of the novel,"[17] and "not quite true."[18] However, the ending, albeit trite, can be justified in terms of the tripartite quest structure of the novel. The damsel, like the Grail, must be pursued and possessed, in some manner, by all three knights. Without Anthony's death, Powell's quest could not be completed; and only upon the completion of Powell's quest can Marlow tell his tale.

Notes

1. See, for example, Frederick R. Karl, *A Reader's Guide to Joseph Conrad* (New York: H. Wolff, 1960), p. 241.

2. Douglas Hewitt, *Conrad: A Reassessment* (Cambridge: Bowes and Bowes, 1952), p. 90. Hewitt argues that *Chance* marks the beginning of the so-called decline in Conrad's fiction.

3. All of this information about the three knights is found at the end of Malory's last chapter of "The Tale of the Sankgreal," "The Miracle of Galahad."

Conrad is closer to Malory, for in Tennyson's version, unlike Malory's, both Bors and Percivale return to Arthur's court, and only afterward does Percivale enter the monastery. Also, whereas Malory tells us that Bors related the story of the Grail quests at some length, according to Tennyson he refused to discuss what he has seen, saying, "'Ask me not, for I may not speak of it / I saw it . . .'" (Alfred, Lord Tennyson, *Idylls of the King* [Philadelphia: Henry Altemus, 1889], p. 262). Tennyson had not originally intended to include Bors, and he does not treat Bors as fully as does Malory (J. Philip Eggers, *King Arthur's Laureate: A Study of Tennyson's "Idylls of the King"* [New York: New York University Press, 1971], pp. 156-57).

4. Joseph Conrad, "Author's Notes," *Chance*, vol. 14 of *Collected Works of Joseph Conrad* (Garden City: Doubleday, Page and Co., 1925), p. xiii. *Chance* was originally published in 1914. Subsequent references to this work will be noted in the text by page number.

5. Mary Geddes, "The Structure of Sympathy: Conrad and the *Chance* that Wasn't," *English Language in Transition,* 12 (1969), 176-77.

6. Jocelyn Baines, *Joseph Conrad: A Critical Biography* (New York: McGraw-Hill, 1960), p. 387.

7. See, for example, Jessie L. Weston's *From Ritual to Romance* and Joseph Campbell's *Creative Mythology* (vol. 4 of *The Masks of God*).

8. J. E. Cirlot, *A Dictionary of Symbols* (New York: Philosophical Library, 1962), p. 105.

9. J. I. M. Stewart, "Conrad," *Eight Modern Writers*, vol. 12 of *The Oxford History of English Literature*, edited by F. P. Wilson and Bonamy Dobrée (Oxford: Clarendon Press, 1963), p. 216.

10. Henry C. Walsh, Intro., *Idylls of the King*, p. viii.

11. "The Departure" in "The Tale of the Sankgreal," *The Works of Sir Thomas Malory,* ed. by Eugène Vinaver (London: Oxford University Press, n. d.), p. 631.

12. According to both sources, Percivale sees the Grail only after Galahad's death: Tennyson's Galahad tells Percivale, "'thou shalt see the vision when I go,'" and he does (pp. 254-55); in Malory, the Grail is seen as the soul of Galahad is borne upward by angels (pp. 739-40).

13. "Sir Percivale yelded hym to an ermytayge out of the cité" (Malory, p. 740).

14. Bors returns to tell Arthur "of the hyghe aventures of the Sankgreal." These stories, together with those of Launcelot, were "made in grete bookes and put up in almeryes at Salysbury" (p. 740).

15. John R. Reed has argued that "'The Holy Grail' transforms purity, embodied in Galahad, to the next world or [embodied in Percivale,] confines it in a cloister." Although Reed is speaking specifically of Tennyson's poem, the statement applies to *Chance* as well, for only the realist—Marlow-Bors—returns to the so-called real world. *Perception and Design in Tennyson's "Idylls of the King"* (Athens: Ohio University Press, 1969), p. 90.

16. Hewitt, p. 98.

17. David McGrail, "The Narrator in the Fiction of Joseph Conrad," Unpubl. Ph.D. diss., University of Pennsylvania, 1971, p. 240.

18. Hugh Walpole, "Introduction," *Chance,* p. viii.

J. Donald Crowley and Sue Mitchell Crowley (essay date 1990)

SOURCE: Crowley, J. Donald, and Sue Mitchell Crowley. "Walker Percy's Grail." In *King Arthur Through the Ages,* edited by Valerie M. Lagorio and Mildred Leake Day, pp. 255-75. New York: Garland Publishing Inc., 1990.

[*In the following essay, the Crowleys expound on Percy's Christian vision as it is expressed in his fiction and nonfiction, noting that the author often used Arthurian motifs in his writing to embody a Southern code of Stoicism. The critics also point out that despite Percy's theological stance, he did not shy away from using the Grail quest to parody the chivalric code associated with the South.*]

> In the concept of the Second Coming the motif of Withdrawal-and-Return attains its deepest spiritual meaning. . . . In the myth of the Second Coming of Arthur, . . . the vanquished Britons consoled themselves for the failure of the historic Arthur to avert the ultimate victory of the English barbarian invaders.
>
> —Arnold Toynbee

>   I think
>   that we
> Shall never more, at any future time,
> Delight our souls with talk of knightly deeds,
> Walking about the gardens and the halls
> Of Camelot, as in the days that were.
> I perish by this people which I made,—
> Tho' Merlin swore that I should come again . . .
>
> —Tennyson, "Morte D'Arthur"

Since Walker Percy has characterized himself as a Catholic existentialist,[1] it is not surprising that his fictional heroes are questers, that each is *homo viator*,[2] a sovereign wayfarer. Nor is it surprising that both the way and the goal of these spiritual travelers inheres in sacrament. Insofar as Percy's "knights" inhabit a postmodern world, they suffer and confront both the internal monsters of Kierkegaardian dread and despair and the Heideggerian malaise of everydayness, endemic with its external monsters of a desacralized culture. This double trajectory—a fiction that projects philosophical and theological understandings and values and, at the same time, criticizes the civilization that has lost those values—has marked Percy's work since his first novel, *The Moviegoer*.[3] How, he seems always to have asked, does one speak to a secular culture? How does one begin, particularly in America (and, to be sure, as a Catholic), to begin again, to make a "new earth" or, more properly, renew the old, old one. Possessed of a prophetic-apocalyptic quality in plot and tone, conceived in the complexly linear time structure of the Judaeo-Christian tradition, Percy's works as fictional critique ponder the past and present and thrust forward into an increasingly uncertain future. Binx Bolling of *The Moviegoer* (1961) and Will Barrett of *The Last Gentleman* (1966) are on horizontal searches for faith; Dr. Tom More, a fallen version of his namesake (Percy's own knight of faith—that eminently practical saint who stood against the adultery of his king and tried to save the old church in England, Sir Thomas More), is in *Love in the Ruins: The Adventures of a Bad Catholic at a Time Near the End of the World* (1971) and *The Thanatos Syndrome* (1987) struggling against a wasteland of secularism in which science and sex, both exclusively genital now, reign supreme.

As Percy's theologically based critical commentary has evolved, his readers have become growingly aware that it is born out of a broad sweeping mythical-historical vision. Percy is in his historical understanding greatly indebted to Arnold Toynbee's *Study of History*,[4] particularly to Toynbee's views on the endurance of the Jews in history, and the Incarnation, the god-man, as the ultimate and only lasting conception of withdrawal and return. Though their own religious convictions are quite disparate, Percy is, no less than Toynbee, fascinated with the manner in which the thought of the Mediterranean world was a crucible of Christianity. He is concerned, too, with the negative as well as positive influence of Greek and Roman philosophy on later Christian thought. This long view is personalized in all Percy's fiction because of his overriding need, in the light of his own conversion to Roman Catholicism, to work through what he calls the southern Stoicism of his own ancestors, especially of William Alexander Percy, the man of letters who raised him.

In a 1956 *Commonweal* essay, "Stoicism in the South," Percy makes the connections that will frequently inform his later fiction: preeminent among those ideas are Roman Stoicism, the southern tradition, and the Arthurian legends:

> The greatness of the South, like the greatness of the English squirearchy, had always a stronger Greek flavor than it ever had a Christian. Its nobility and graciousness was the nobility and graciousness of the old Stoa.... If the Stoic way was remarkably suited to the Empire of the first century, it was quite as remarkably suited to the agrarian South of the last century.... It was a far nobler relationship than what usually passes under the name of paternalism. The nobility of Sartoris ... was the nobility of the natural perfection of the Stoics, the stern inner summons to man's full estate, to duty, to honor, to generosity toward his fellowmen and above all to his inferiors—not because they were made in the image of God and were therefore lovable in themselves, but because to do them an injustice would be to defile the inner fortress which was oneself.... For the Southern Stoic the day has been lost and lost for good.... Southern society was above all a society of manners, an incredible triumph of manners, and a twilight of manners seems a twilight of the world. For the Stoic there is no real hope. His finest hour is to sit tight-lipped and ironic while the world comes crashing down around him.
>
> It must be otherwise with the Christian. The urban plebs is not the mass which is to be abandoned to its own barbaric devices, but the lump to be leavened. The Christian is optimistic precisely where the Stoic is pessimistic.... We in the South can no longer afford the luxury of maintaining the Stoa beside the Christian edifice. In the past we managed the remarkable feat of keeping both, one for living in, the other for dying in. But the Church is no longer content to perform rites of passage; she has entered the arena of the living and must be reckoned with.[5]

Arthurian motifs occur often in the densely allusive texture of Percy's fiction: they serve regularly as paradigms for the southern code of Stoicism in the face of defeat. Where Percy employs the Arthurian legends he does so with two very completely interrelated intentions. On the one hand, he parodies the chivalric code which he associates with the Stoicism of the ante- and post-bellum South; on the other hand, he discovers an antidote for that Stoa, that Roman inheritance of aristocratic paternalism, absolute reliance on reason, and heroic resignation before the dictates of fate, in a conception of the human being as incarnate creature, participating both in the fall and its many consequences—most pointedly in a quest, both individual and communal, for the Grail, not as provocative literary and legendary symbol but in its ultimate incarnational meaning as sacrament.

Percy's earliest fictional embodiment of southern Stoicism is Binx Bolling's Aunt Emily Cutrer (a portrait, in fact, of his "Uncle" Will Percy) in *The Moviegoer*. If Binx is the Kierkegaardian aesthete, Emily is the ethical dowager who values manners and doing "the right thing." Certain of Binx's ancestors, like Percy's own, have been well-known military men. Emily's brother Alex, the one with "the Rupert Brooke-Galahad sort of face," (24) died in the Argonne a hero's death held "as fitting since the original Alex Bolling was killed with Roberdaux Wheat in the Hood breakthrough at Gaines Mills in 1862" (24-25). And so, when Binx's little brother dies his aunt explains that he must "act like a soldier" (4). Emily, the darling of her brothers, sees herself as "the female sport of a fierce old warrior gens" (26). After a career in volunteer public service which culminated in Red Cross service in the Spanish Civil War, she has married a well-to-do Creole and settled in the Garden District to become "as handsome and formidable as her brothers, soldierly in both look and outlook, ... at sixty-five still the young prince" (27). Her husband Jules, participating, if more passively, in her chivalric code, can describe a Tulane goal-line stand against LSU as "King Arthur standing fast in the blood-red sunset against Sir Modred and the traitors" (30). So goes one of Percy's anticly postmodern transmogrifications of Arthurian materials.

Emily regards herself as "an Episcopalian by emotion, a Greek by nature and a Buddhist by choice" (23). A patron of good causes and the arts and possessed of a Socratic manner, she is strongly individualistic, philosophical, serene, and self-righteous. Like the Roman Stoics and Arthur in his defeat, she fears that "the fabric is dissolving" (54) but, adds Percy, "for her even the dissolving makes sense. She understands the chaos to come." She sees the "barbarians at the inner gate" (133) with no one to defend the West, and the future as her own "Dover Beach" of "the going under of the evening land" (54). The world itself is "an insignificant cinder spinning away in a dark corner of the universe," and the reason for human existence "a secret which the high gods have not confided" to her (54). She is the embodiment of William Alexander Percy's devotion to the resignation of Marcus Aurelius. She is less than resigned, however, when she suspects that Binx has betrayed her code by sexually compromising her stepdaughter Kate; Emily, "as erect and handsome as the Black Prince," (221) accuses him of breaking his trust. In fact, Binx and Kate's failed sexual encounter on the train to Chicago is the outward sign of that inner grace which permits their mutual discovery of a deeper intimacy as creatures in despair on a common journey, as co-questers in the religious mode.

Percy symbolizes Emily's moral rectitude and lack of a supernatural religious understanding with a distinctly Arthurian metaphor. As she confronts Binx on his return from Chicago, they both gaze at a letter opener, a small Excalibur, the "soft iron sword she has withdrawn from the grasp of the helmeted figure on the inkstand" (221). Emily realizes that the tip of the blade is bent, and Binx, ever the existential questioner, is acutely conscious now that, years before, he himself had bent it in trying to open a drawer. Emily, relentless Stoic, now accuses him of breaking "sacred trust" that involves the common assumptions of "gentlefolk" who share "a native instinct for behavior, a natural piety or grace," a certain kind of "class," over against the "common" people, who have "enshrined mediocrity" as a national ideal. Emily "raises the sword to Prytania Street" (222-24) and explains that she has tried to "save" him: "More than anything I wanted to pass on to you the one heritage of the men of our family, a certain quality of spirit, a gaiety, a sense of duty, a nobility worn lightly, a sweetness, a gentleness with women—the only good things the South ever had and the only things that really matter in this life" (224). However, Binx will find his Grail, not in an idealized past but rather in the present of the communal feast of fish with his mother and her family, in the Mass they attend together, in his handicapped and holy brother Lonnie's devotion to sacramental Penance and his request for the last rites, and, finally, in his love for and marriage to Kate.

If Percy has given us Binx as his Kierkegaardian "knight of faith," in the "knight" of his fourth novel, *Lancelot*,[6] the reader is confronted with a complete antihero in search of an Unholy Grail. This "grail" Lancelot Andrewes Lamar will define as sin and, then more precisely, as sexual sin. He relives his quest as he makes a deeply perverse anticonfession to an old friend and failed priest-psychiatrist, whom long years ago in his youth he had begun to call "Percival." His unconscious self-revelation continues for 257 pages and forms the basis of the very complex structure of the novel. Lance tells the priest:

> I don't know why I want to talk to you or what I need to tell you or need to hear from you. . . . I have to tell you in order to know what I already know. . . . Perhaps I talk to you because of your silence.
>
> (85)

The confessor with his "hooded look" speaks only in the last two pages of the novel and then, like the knight of the Wasteland, to infer a question and to imply, cryptically, that there is an answer. At the same time, however, Percy controls Lancelot's narrative in such a way that Percival—who, as much as his Arthurian prototype, has had a life of relentless difficulty and uncertainty in defining his true vocation—becomes extraordinarily present as a character, and the reader begins to understand that, for him as well, "there is something wrong." For Percival will come to know the nature of his own quest only when he hears the story of Lance's antithetical one. As the medieval friends Lancelot and Percival sought each other during their Grail quests, so these two twentieth-century souls are deeply interdependent and, in Percy's word, potentially "intersubjective." They share a story fraught with Arthurian names, symbols and situations, and give that story two possible endings, not totally unlike the divergent destinies of their paradigms. Percy's parodic art leaves little doubt that there are also in *Lancelot* echoes and correspondences to the homecoming of Odysseus, but these are by no means as dominant as the parallels to Arthurian materials in his scheme here of employing myth to illustrate history.

The legendary Launcelot understood his singleminded passion for Guinevere as a guilty love. For a time he wandered in the forest, driven mad by public scorn and personal shame. Though he struggled to tear his two loves asunder in his heart, his one poisonous sin was inextricably bound to his quest, and he was doomed to follow wandering fires to the end of his days. On the other hand, Percival was characterized as "The Pure," that is, possessed, not only of chastity but of purity of intention, purity of heart. All his other endeavors turned to dust because he was destined for a single quest. Readers of Malory will recall that after Launcelot has been sent from "the holy place" where the knight was healed, he curses the day of his birth and comprehends that it is his adultery with the queen and his betrayal of his king that have prevented him from an actual vision of the Sangreal. Then, coming upon a hermitage and a hermit, Launcelot "prayed him for charity for to hear his life" (XI, 190).[7] The hermit, a man of great good will, marvels that the knight looks so "abashed," and he senses somehow that God must love him. The hermit warns Launcelot that, though he is the greatest knight in the world, he has been deeply presumptuous in seeking to be "where His flesh and His blood was" while still unshriven of his "lechery." Though Launcelot makes his confession and is enjoined to do penance, he is nonetheless never free of his love of Guinevere and forgets "the promise and the perfection that he made in the quest."[8]

Percy's Lance has as his hermitage a New Orleans "Center for Aberrant Behavior" following the explosion of his ancestral home, Belle Isle, in which the bodies of his wife and three others are found, and it is only late in the course of the novel that the reader knows that Lance has been incarcerated for having wreaked his vengeance by multiple murder violent and obscene. From the cell Lance and, later, Percival as well look down on both "Lafayette Cemetery," suggestive of both revolutionary chivalry and death, and "Annunciation Street," evocative of new, redemptive life in the Incarnation. This dual view points directly to the opposing choices open to Lance and his old friend at the end of the novel.

Lance sees Percival, in his J. C. (a singular but typical Percy wordplay) Penney pantsuit, standing in the graveyard with a woman who is scrubbing the white New Orleans tombs and who apparently asks the priest to pray for the dead. It is All Souls' Day, a feast that (like Christmas) would permit Father John to say three masses, but he apparently refuses the request. Percy seems to be indicating that the priest considers himself unworthy because he himself knows that he suffers from the "sickness unto death." Lance, too, suffers from despair and has a shock of recognition; at the sight of Percival he feels he is "overtaken by the past" and is seeing himself. Lance, however, suffers from what Kierkegaard calls the despair of defiance, truly demonic despair, so what he encounters in Percival is a former self or the self he might have been. Lance invites Percival to "Come into my cell" (3). These two deconstructed—or reconstructed—Arthurian knights then re-enact in a radically postmodern and desacralized setting essential elements of the relationship between their literary/legendary ancestors.

In earlier days when he lived at Northumberland near Belle Isle, Percival, though he was not pugnacious but brilliant, obscure and withdrawn, bore the misnomer Harry Hotspur. He was built "like Pius XII" but called Prince Hal because he seemed happy only in whorehouses. "Also," Percy writes in an emphatic fragment—"as Percival and Parsifal, who found the Grail and brought life to a dead land" (10). Now he is Father John, either because he is a loner like the Baptist, or because he loved much like the Evangelist. Like Percival, Lance was part of the gone-to-pot Anglo-Saxon aristocracy which inhabited the River Road, called "the English Coast" since it was an enclave of British gentry united by a crazy-quilt dislike both of Catholics and the Longs. Unlike the Creoles who have mastered the secret of living ordinary lives well, making money and "making" Mardi Gras, their "honorable" families "lived from one great event to another, tragic events, triumphant events, with years of melancholy in between. They lost at Vicksburg and Shiloh, "fought duels, defied Huey Long, and were bored to death between times" (23-24). In contrast to the River Road, Percy characterizes New Orleans proper as a Catholic city, not really part of the South, a city which has had no heroes in three hundred years and has its cathedral set in the Vieux Carré in a concentration of sin.

The Anglo-Saxon backgrounds shared by Lancelot and Percival have, however, resulted in strikingly different careers. Percival, perhaps because the men in his family are prone to depression and early suicide, has found Louisiana "not good enough for him" and chosen to work in Biafra. Lance, whose life peaked in college when he became a Rhodes scholar, had become a nonpracticing lawyer and a liberal gone sour, devoted on the one hand to rather paternalistic civil rights endeavors and, on the other, to publishing nostalgic essays on Civil War skirmishes in the *Louisiana Historical Journal*. In all this he had rather forlornly repeated the same dilettante efforts of his own father without knowing it. And he had done so because, being one of Percy's seemingly incurable romantics who puts his most cherished ideals just out of his reach, he is drawn, like his father (and, to be sure, Nick Carraway besides), inexorably into the past. That father, Maury, had been poet-laureate of Feliciana Parish, busying himself with publishing vignettes of historical events and non-Roman churches. His library was filled with romantic English poetry, the Waverley novels, Episcopal Church history, southern history and biographies of Robert E. Lee. He loved Lee "the way Catholics love St. Francis" (116): the Confederate hero had become for him "as legendary and mythical as King Arthur and the Round Table." The books indicate the reasons for the name given him by his father:

> Do you think I was named Lancelot for nothing? The Andrewes was tacked on by him to give it Episcopal sanction, but what he really had in mind . . . was that old nonexistent Catholic brawler and adulterer, Lancelot du Lac, King Ban of Benwick's son, knight of the

Round Table and—here was the part he could never get over [or, it seems, get right]—one of only two knights to see the Grail (you, Percival, the other); and above all the extraordinariness of those chaste and incorrupt little Anglican chapels set down in this violent and corrupt land besieged on all sides by savage Indians, superstitious Romans, mealy-mouthed Baptists, howling Holy Rollers.

(116)

"What's in a name?" all Percy's work would seem to ask. In this novel and in Lance's name there are, clearly, genes and destiny, the maddened living and killing, and the need both to tell and hear of it, the re-living of the whole after the fact.

Whether Lance's father and mother saw themselves in this romantic light, or Lance chooses to recall them in this way is unclear. But the romance dissolved in each case as the young Lance made his first discoveries of evil. The first took the form of an ill-gotten $10,000 found under the argyle socks in Maury's drawer. Lance recalls his sense of delight as his eyes devoured the money, "the sweet shameful heart of something, the secret." The reader has an early clue to his later quest: "There is no secret in honor. If one could but discover the secret at the heart of dishonor" (213). While his father had been tending to such business, Lance's mother Lily had been having a kind of courtly love relationship with "Uncle" Harry Wills, a Mardi Gras krewe knight in a Duke's costume, who gives Lance gifts of a glass pistol with candy inside and a Swiss army knife. Thus, Maury, a cuckold, a sorrily trivialized Arthur, became a sort of role model for his son, precursor of Lance's own cuckolding. And Lily, a clear parody of the maid of Astolat, was "like a lovebird. She lived for love. Literally. Unless she was loved, she withered and died" (212). In this mix love seems to join money as twin bitch goddesses in Percy's postmodern American culture.

It is Lance's mysterious Cousin Callie who, appearing from out of the hurricane at the end of the novel, wearing an out-of-season camellia, like Dumas' Camille, pinned to her shoulder, provides us with Lance's reminiscence of Lily. In fact, Lance begins to confuse the two, perceiving them both as fallen women. He remembers Lily in a picture of a VMI military wedding, prankishly "proffering an unsheathed sword" to the photographer (225): "The sword is upright, the blade held in her hands, the hand guard making a cross." There he sees her as a Joan of Arc, but his ultimate mental picture of Lily has her with Uncle Harry "in the linoleum-cold gas-heat-hot tourist cabin" (216). Are these two his mother and father? The reader, with Lance, wonders. With all his rich heritage of names, Lance literally—and spiritually—does not know, cannot know whence he sprang. He must question his own paternity as he will later that of his daughter.

Continually within the point of view of his gnostic—even Manichean—hero's memory and current consciousness, Percy complicates these pictures of human evil with one of surd evil. Lancelot recalls that he was "in love" with Lucy Cobb. As a Louisiana football hero, from a state in which people valued fistfights and cockfights, Lance met the Georgian Lucy in Highlands, North Carolina, where the easy decorous manners of the eastern South prevailed. They were married, moved to Belle Isle and had two children. "Then," Lance says, "she died." Of Elaine, the Lily Maid of Astolet, who simply ceases breathing and dies of her love for Lancelot, Tennyson writes:

> She grew so cheerful that they deem'd her death
> Was rather in the fantasy than the blood.[9]

In Lucy the cause is leukemia and the fantasy in the mind and character of her husband, as Percy creates another, radically different version of the romantic Lily Maid.

Lance himself is unromantically discharged from the army, "not bloody and victorious and battered by Sir Turquine but with persistent diarrhea" (28). In the second generation Lance has witnessed not only the end of heroism but the decay of courtly love. The antithesis of the pure knight of the Grail, his son is no Galahad—consummate finder of the real grail—but bisexual and living in an old streetcar. And this Galahad has a sister seduced by a lesbian.

If Lucy was Lance's romantic past, Margot, his second wife, despite her infatuation with the crafts, the artifacts of the past, becomes his present. Belle Isle, fallen on hard times, opens its doors to tourists on the Azalea Trail, and Margot, from Texas with ten million, has become a "belle." Though it is impossible for new money to participate in the Comus ball, the Azalea Festival is a uniting of the oil rich and old, broke River Road gentry, the very same "rare royal betrothal" Margot and Lance will make. Less coy than Scarlett, Margot, Percy tells us, met the master of Belle Isle and promptly doffed her ante-bellum costume in order to become its mistress: "Damned if the hoop skirt didn't work like chaps" (75). Margot has a Morgan le Faye-like gift for transformations.

Now, in his cell, Lance feels that he himself was transformed by Margot. He ponders what love is and speaks to Percival: "For by your dear sweet Jesus I did love her there for her droll mercenariness and between her sweet legs and in her mouth . . ." (81). The "there," where he first made love to Margot, is the pigeonnier of Belle Isle. Along with the hospital cell, the pigeonnier is a critically important place of discovery in the novel, at once the Oriel of Launcelot and Guinevere and the Chapel Perilous of a question to be answered. It is there that Lance and Percival had first read *Ulysses* and discovered sex and the anger of an Odyssean hero whose wife has other suitors.[10] Margot can (or could), however, be like Morgan, both helpful and malicious in her crafts. Lance describes how this "Texas magician" transformed Belle Isle with its Carrara mantelpiece, English antiques and slave chairs, back to its original state. In addition, she turned the pigeonnier into a kind of "hunting lodge"-office for Lance. But, Lance explains, when she was finished with Belle Isle, she was finished with him.

Margot's new project involves a film crew at work on the new enchantment, twentieth-century cinematic magic, which will employ Belle Isle as well as a miniature steamboat on False River as settings. Margot has only a bit part and acts as girl Friday to Merlin, the Hemingwayesque director; Lance, in the background off-stage, is adviser on matters of southern history. Margot, having transformed the ancestral home to a celluloid stage-set, has her future sights set on playing Nora in "A Doll's House" for Janos Jacoby, co-director and alter-Merlin, who seems actually to be in charge.

It is during the filming that Lance makes his great "discovery." He is in the pigeonnier where he first made love to Margot and will later have his vision of the Lady of the Camellias. What Lance discovered, in glancing at his daughter Siobhan's camp application, and now remembers so vividly, is the letter "O" (significantly grailshaped) in her blood type, which indicates that she cannot be both his and Margot's daughter. Old bills and a bit of figuring confirm that she was in Texas with Merlin during the time Siobhan would have been conceived. He has discovered his wife's infidelity. And it is at this point that the nature of the quest he is reliving with Percival becomes explicit. If "the greatest good," Lance says, "is to be found in love, so is the greatest evil" (139). Armed with this new knowledge, the gnostic Lancelot seems restored to health. No longer a victim of the malaise, he quits drinking and with a virtually insidious lucidity develops his plan to seek the ultimate sin. Margot had been his "absolute," his "infinite," his "feast," his grail: "That was my communion, Father—no offense intended, that sweet dark sanctuary guarded by the heavy gold columns of her thighs, the ark of her covenant" (171). Now he would seek sin in the same place. As he tells it, "So Sir Lancelot set out, looking for something rarer than the Grail. A sin" (140).

His decision has caused Lance to take a hard look at himself in the mirror. What he saw was a man gone to seed: "Do you remember the picture of Lancelot disgraced, discovered in adultery with the queen, banished, living in the woods, stretched out on a rock, chin cupped in both hands, bloodshot eyes staring straight ahead, yellow hair growing down over his brows? But it's a bad comparison. My bloodshot eyes were staring too but it was not so much the case of my screwing the queen as the queen getting screwed by somebody else" (64). He engages Elgin, a black MIT engineering senior and liveried tour guide at Belle Isle, to "watch" and to film the sexual encounters of the film crew at the motel. When Lance views Elgin's flawed films he sees tiny reddish figures in a Dantesque hell, with tiny Pentecostal flames flickering over each head. Percy readers will recognize in the delta shape of the Margot-Merlin-Jacoby *menage à trois* and the "rough swastikaed triangle" (192) of Raine Robinette and Troy Dana, the film's stars, and Lucy, Lance's daughter by his first wife, a ghastly parody in which perverted sex becomes the horrible inversion of Percy's own intersubjective theory of symbol which he describes in his essay, "The Delta Factor."[11] With his suspicions empirically validated, he devises his own plot—a marplot whose events, in initiating life's evils, totally outstrip them in their killing cruelty—by which the crew will move into Belle Isle and be blown up by leaking methane gas from the well upon which the old mansion sits. He sends away both his daughters as well as Merlin, with whom he shares a sense of perverse fellowship as cuckold. Ironically, it is the Christmas season, the tree is lighted in the living room, and the traditional bonfires are burning on the levee to celebrate the Incarnation. At the same time Lance is planning his elaborately staged destruction, a great hurricane is threatening the coast. Percy, a lover of puns and word games and jokes, names the hurricane "Marie." Raine, whose name may signify "rein" or "reign" or "raines," the fabric of Guinevere's shroud, insists that they take "champagne" up to the belvedere atop Belle Isle and "have a party named 'Goodbye movie, hello Marie'" (204).

As he relives the events with Percival, he recalls for the first time how he performed their old Bowie knife test, sticking the blade, supposed to have belonged to Jim Bowie himself, into the cypress wall and trying to withdraw it. The Excalibur of their youth would become Lancelot's instrument of an act by which he discovers, beyond envy and revenge, no secret but only the nothingness at the heart of evil.

Knowing understood as a gnostic grasp of esoteric fact and "knowing" in the biblical sense become one in his dark ritual; both are essential to Lance's plan as he visits the bedrooms of Belle Isle, where Elgin's concealed cameras convert living into mere acting, home into cinematic stage-set, and sex into sheer obscenity. In Raine's room, Troy Dana—the "faggot" as Lance calls him—lies stoned on the far side of the bed. Lance, seeing his daughter Lucy's sorority ring on Raine's hand, sodomizes the willing actress in order to discover her "secret." Then he finds Margot and Janos Jacoby in the great Calhoun bed whose design, complete with its buttresses, gargoyles and altar screen, resembles a Gothic cathedral. Lance the new knight sees the two as the new beast and squeezes them more tightly together: "Mashed together, the two were never more apart, never more themselves" (240). Then all three seem to float in the methane-filled air. They, in fact, replicate Dante's Paola and Francesca, destined to be inseparable and driven forever by the winds of the Inferno. Their sin?—their adultery, of course, which resulted from their having read the story of Lancelot and Guinevere.

Lancelot consummates his nihilistic quest in wreaking vengeful judgment on the new barbarians. He slits Jacoby's throat with his Bowie knife, given him years before by that ambiguously fallen woman, the Lady of the Camellias, his Lady of the Lake. After the explosion in which Lance is blown free, he returns to the ruins, not to find the four bodies but to retrieve the knife. Later judged incompetent to stand trial, he will be freed when he is declared sane. Although guilt is not seen to be an issue for either the law or Lance, Percy's reader, like Percival, knows that this unholy knight's unholy grail is in himself.

And so a year later he carries on his curiously compulsive monologue with Father John, who makes him feel that he is overtaken by his past, by his self. Lance, having confessed to Percival, the hooded knight, senses that Percival still has a question: "Do you love?" Lance has an answer ready, though it is hardly the one Percival has in mind. Because he cannot stand the world as he finds it, Lance has been developing a Utopian vision of a new order and a theory of sexual love by which to defend himself against the barbarism and start the world over. Behavior will be based, he insists manically, not on Catholicism or any other ism but on a stern new code for "gentlemen," who will hold a "gentleness toward women and an intolerance of swinishness, a counsel kept, and above all a readiness to act, and act alone if necessary" (157). This third revolution will take place in Virginia and follow the other two—that of 1776, won because the British were stupid, and the second, in 1861, which failed because, as Lance says, "we got stuck with the Negro thing and it was our fault" (157). His new knight will look like the Virginian, with his gun across his shoulders standing on the Blue Ridge, a perfect reembodiment of the broad sword tradition.

Lance explains that such new men would "have felt at home at Mont-Saint-Michel, the Mount of the Archangel with the flowing sword, or with Richard Cocur-de Lion at Acre. They believed in a God who said he came not to bring peace but the sword" (157). As opposed to Christian *caritas,* Lance's code involves a "stern rectitude," a "tight-lipped courtesy toward men," and "chivalry toward women," who "must be saved from the whoredom they have chosen" (158). Women, for their part, will be either virgins or whores.

Lance's abstracted history of sex relates directly, if unbeknownst to him, to his own biographical revelations. First, there was the romantic period in which he "fell in love" with Lucy, the figure of light in the Paradiso, whom he insists was a virgin. The current period, represented by Margot and the film company, is like a "baboon colony" or a "soap opera." The third stage he insistently predicts will be a clarification by way of catastrophe, a living death, when everything will become desert. This phase and the "new earth" that it will for him ensure is symbolized by the third woman in Lance's life, Anna, a young woman made autistic as a result of gang-rape with whom he communicates by tapping in Morse Code on the cell wall. From Lance's skewed perception, she is both whore, as a victim of rape, and virgin in that she is now like a ten-year-old. He will take her to Virginia and build a log cabin and they will be the New Adam and Eve of the third revolution—still another attempt, stupidly and self-righteously Utopian, to redefine a gnostically solipsistic Grail.

The film story within the novel depicts Lancelot's second phase, or the current state of sex in America. In addition, the film and its stars, in turn, constitute Percy's comic indictment of a particular scholarly work on the Grail legend. Perhaps the most fascinating parody related to Arthurian materials in *Lancelot* is the one Percy works on Jessie Weston's *From Ritual to Romance.*[12] Merlin believes, and rightly so, that he has "created" Troy Dana, whose name evokes both paganism and the heroic code of the Homeric epics. In himself Troy is "nothing, a perfect cipher," but with his helmet of golden hair he is perceived in the film as a "creature of light," (147) with a temperature "around 101. He actually glows." Everyone else in the film is "hung up" and, therefore, dead. Not only is Troy free in this universe of cinematic glare, he offers resurrection; he frees others, if only pathetically, for that false world. "Perhaps he is a god. At least he is a kind of Christ-type" (148). He frees Sarah, the librarian-initiate, played by Margot, in the stacks. "It is not just screwing," Merlin explains, "but a kind of sacrament and celebration of life. He could be a high priest of Mithras [in Weston, responsible for the initiation of women]."[13] Merlin expounds in postmodern doublespeak that the film will not treat love but be content with "the erotic which in any form at all, is always life-enhancing." The sharecropper of the vegetation-ritual film finds his celluloid Beatrice in the aristocratic girl. Jacoby explains: "'It is the aristocrat in this case who has the life-embracing principle and not the sharecropper, as is usually the case, since he is usually shown as coming from the dirt.' 'Soil,' said Margot" (114).

If indeed the Grail legends, as Weston believes, have their kernel, their sole origin, in the Vegetation Ritual, the Life-Cult, what, Percy seems to ask, has become of the fertility ritual in the twentieth century? While Percy is, on the one hand, pronouncing judgment on the gnosticism, which Weston associates with the cults of Mithra and Attis, and the violence of his hero, much of Lance's critique of the American scene is the author's own—gone crazy, as the author knows. Percy would believe that the sort of Grail conception which is Weston's—divorced as it is from the source of the Grail, Christ—results in the very infertility that announces the true Wasteland of our time. Albeit through his unreliable narrator, he has provided a novel full of examples of desacralized sex so that the fiction may itself be read as a statement on Weston's theory: the discovery of the adulterous female symbol as sign of fertility in the letter "O," the ultimate impotence of both Merlin and Lancelot; the unerotically perverted sex of the film crew; the unspeakable rape of Anna; and, finally, the parodic rape in the film which takes place in the pigeonnier-Oriel of Belle Isle. *Lancelot* is Percy's fullest fictional dramatization of those conditions describing the character of postmodern American sexuality as seen by the noted American psychiatrist quoted by Percy: "In Harry Stack Sullivan's words, the mark of success in the culture is how much one can do to another's genitals without risking one's self-esteem unduly."[14] Joyous Gard or Camelot, clearly, Percy says, lies in a world elsewhere. Merlin's film satirizes Weston's pre-Christian ideas directly, as does Lance's own post-Christian story. In both love is divorced from spiritual as well as physical fertility and, therefore, from the source of love and life alike. Clearly, Lance has no genuine conception of authentic love, of caritas. His chauvinistic new chivalry is very old and very false, and it will not recreate a lost civilization. The role of Percival in the novel is to hold and transmit the secret that will.

For Percy, the existentialist, the question which still hangs in the air of this Chapel Perilous should not find its answer in an abstracted definition of love but in an act. What is the Grail? Whom shall it serve? The seeming ambiguity of the structure and, in particular, of the open-endedness of the novel almost hides Percy's answers. In the first sentence of the novel Lancelot has said to Percival: "Come into my cell. Make yourself at home."[15] As the priest's visits go on, Percy, in the manner of Flannery O' Connor, has Lance address him by what might almost be termed "taking the name of the Lord in vain," in a coincidence of opposites. "Jesus, come in and sit down" (84). Lance has referred to Father John as one "obsessed with God" (216), as one who chose "the time-place god" (31). Twice the priest looks like Isaiah's "man of sorrows" (53:3) and, thus Percy implies, he must himself be "acquainted with infirmity." Lance sees Percival's sadness as nothing more than a "tolerant Catholic world-weariness" (131) which loses all distinctions and loves everything. But his cynical statement is precisely Percy's ironic affirmation of Percival as incarnate creature and of the need for participation in both the fall and the healing Incarnation. Percy has conceived of Percival, as Malory did, as one of the very few people who "believed in our Lord Jesus Christ . . . who believed in God perfectly."[16]

In his final visit, Percival wears what Lance calls his "priest uniform" (163). Lance asks if he is "girding for battle or dressed up like Lee for surrender" (163). In Lance's scheme the priest might join the third revolution or retain the old Stoicism, but Percival has his own ideas of spiritual battle and surrender, closer perhaps to the dark night of the soul and that surrender to the love of God described by the mystics. The time is still November, the month of All Souls, when the last meeting occurs, and Father John has now begun to pray for the dead, for himself and Lance, those knights whose wounds are secret. Lance will soon be leaving and he will stroll down Annunciation Street. Will there be a fullness of message for him, an annunciation of incarnation, in what has been the only partially seen billboard sign from the "little view" from his cell?

The question for this knight of the Unholy Grail may well have been formulated at the very beginning of the novel when Lance points out the fragmented "message":

Free &
  Ma
    B

The gnostic Lance has missed the significance of the phonetic hieroglyph that would tell him what Percival "knows," that each of them—and Percy's reader as well—is free and may *be*; to "be," for Walker Percy, is both to become and to believe. But Lance, feeling very cold, complains: "Why did I discover nothing at the heart of evil? There was no 'secret' after all. . . . There is no question. There is no unholy grail as there was no Holy Grail" (253). Percival gazes at him with his same steady sadness, and Lancelot once again formulates the priest's perennial question: "Do I think I can ever love anyone?" (254). Each knight must make a decision and a new beginning, because there is a secret.

Lance refuses to live in the world he sees as Sodom and seems perched to create his own world with Anna in Virginia, even if it takes an apocalyptic sword to protect his Utopia. Yet Percy's endings always leave his characters open to possibility, and in this novel Lancelot seems willing to "wait" and give Percival's God "time," as he says. Curiously, it is Lance who jocularly describes Percival's grail: "So you plan to take a little church in Alabama, Father, preach the gospel, turn bread into flesh, forgive the sins of Buick dealers, administer communion to suburban housewives?" (256). Then, as if he is only now realizing what he must do, Percival looks straight at Lancelot. Under that gaze of the hooded knight, Lance says, "You know something you think I don't know, and you want to tell me but you hesitate" (256). Then Percival, speaking for the first time in the novel, says simply, "Yes." And his continued affirmations, his "yeses" (he says "yes" twelve times in this final scene, "no" just once), project into the future, they stand over against the "no's," the deep negations of Lancelot that have been the structure of the past, of his unholy quest. The Grail question still remains in the final lines. Lancelot: "Is there anything you wish to tell me before I leave?" Percival utters the novel's final word: "Yes." Unlike his paradigmatic predecessor, Lancelot has not done penance and he does not love, but he is free and he "may," because in Percy's grace-filled, redeemed world, anything may "happen." Percival, who will find the Grail, knows that secret.

. . . . .

It is in Tennyson's and then again Toynbee's understanding of the failure of the Arthurian myth before the onslaught of the barbarians that Percy finds sanctions for his attack on Stoicism and the chivalric codes of courtly love and the broad sword as they have developed in the 1970's in America. As the concept of a second coming of Arthur was completely inadequate to the Britons before the onslaught of the barbarians, so are those Arthurian values inadequate to the barbarism of sexual abuse and modern violence which define the postmodern world of Lancelot Andrewes Lamar.

Arthur's Christian realm was destroyed by the barbarians within—the adultery and resultant blood feuds—as much as by Modred and the barbarians without. When his knights departed on their separate quests, Arthur sorrowed that he would not see many of them again and realized that the Round Table and its code were at an end. Percy, like Malory and Tennyson, is deeply concerned with "decline and fall"[17] and the available alternatives to that decline and fall. One is what Will Percy called "the unassailable wintry kingdom of Marcus Aurelius"; still another is Lance's apocalyptic third revolution of individualistic conservatism; the third is implicit in all Percy's work: "Compared to the fatalism of his artistocratic Uncle Will, and the messianism of Lancelot, Percy says he has much more hope. 'I'm a Catholic, and I believe that with all the difficulty it is having, the Judaeo-Christian tradition is the last best hope of sustaining democracies.'"[18] In that tradition Percy sees the world as full of signs: words (even on billboards), events, people, sacraments. Each work ends with sacrament, Walker Percy's Grail. In *The Moviegoer* Binx follows the Mardi Gras of his life with the penitential understanding of Ash Wednesday. Like Chrétien's Percival on Good Friday, he then has the potential to see the Grail. He can reject the "knowing" Stoicism of his Aunt Emily and begin to "do" the works of faith, to love and marry Kate, to care for his brothers and sisters, whom he has hitherto thought of only as his "half-brothers and -sisters." *The Last Gentleman* ends with a baptism in Santa Fe, *Love in the Ruins* with a Christmas Mass. *The Second Coming,* the novel which follows *Lancelot,* is as much about life as *Lancelot* is about death. It offers an answer to both the malaise and the old and new adulteration of love in the truly life-enhancing coming together and marriage of Will Barret and Allie, herself a sacrament for Will. The "Space Odyssey," the last chapter of *Lost in the Cosmos,* concludes with the ancient Abbot Liebowitz offering Mass for an extraordinarily ecumenical group of survivors as the world begins over again after the nuclear holocaust of the obscene year 2069. *The Thanatos Syndrome,* Percy's most recent fiction, concludes with a Mass of the Epiphany, the feast which celebrates Christ's being shown forth to the world. Walker Percy's grail is, quite simply, what it has always been in the Christian tradition, the cup of the last supper and the blood of the crucified Christ. Percy, both piously and parodically a new Joseph of Arimathea, would save it for the wasteland of the postmodern world.

Notes

1. Zoltán Abádi-Nagy, "A Talk with Walker Percy," (1973), *Conversations with Walker Percy,* eds. Lewis A. Lawson and Victor A. Kramer (Jackson, 1985), 73.

2. Percy adopts this Thomistic term from Gabriel Marcel's title. Marcel's work, like that of Søren Kierkegaard and Martin Heidegger, has been a definitive influence in Percy's thought.

3. Walker Percy, *The Moviegoer* (New York, 1967) (cited by page numbers hereafter within the text). The novel was first published by Alfred A. Knopf in 1961 and won the 1962 National Book Award.

4. The epigraph to this essay is from D. C. Somervell's abridgement of Toynbee's multivolume work (New York, 1947) 1, 223.

5. Walker Percy, "Stoicism in the South," *Commonweal* 64, 14 (July 6, 1956), 343-44.

6. Walker Percy, *Lancelot* (New York, 1977) (cited by page numbers hereafter within the text).

7. Sir Thomas Malory, *Le Morte D'Arthur* (London, 1906) 2, 190-91. Percy is clearly familiar with Malory and Tennyson, but any critic who knows his thoroughgoing habit of research may well imagine he has read older texts as well.

8. Malory, 2, 271.

9. *Idylls of the King,* in *The Works of Tennyson,* ed. Hallam Lord Tennyson (New York, 1931), 406.

10. "Personified by the driven-to-murder Lancelot is 'what my Uncle Will used to call the broad-sword tradition, that goes back to Ulysses taking revenge

on all the suitors who were hanging around his house when he got back from his long voyage to Troy. He doesn't just throw them out. He kills them all, you know. If somebody offends you, you kill them.'" (Percy in a 1977 interview with William Delaney in "A Southern Novelist Whose CB Crackles with Kierkegaard," *Conversations with Walker Percy,* eds. Lewis A. Lawson and Victor A. Kramer [Jackson, 1985], 154).

11. Walker Percy, *The Message in the Bottle* (New York, 1954).

12. Jessie L. Weston, *From Ritual to Romance* (New York: Peter Smith, 1941). See also John Edward Hardy, *The Fiction of Walker Percy* (Urbana: University of Illinois Press, 1987), 146-49.

13. Weston, quoting Cumont, describes Mithra as "le génie de la lumière céleste," 156.

14. *The Message in the Bottle,* 100.

15. The verb "come" resonates in Percy's fiction in the title of the novel that follows *Lancelot, The Second Coming*; in the final words of *Lost in the Cosmos,* "Come back." In his essay on faith, "The Message in the Bottle," Percy explains that the apostle who delivers the good news may, when "everyone is saying, 'Come!,' when radio and television say nothing else but 'Come!,'" find that "the best way to say 'Come!' is to remain silent." *The Message in the Bottle,* 148.

16. Malory, 2, 198.

17. Delaney interview, 152.

18. Delaney interview, 157.

Theresa O'Connor (essay date 1992)

SOURCE: O'Connor, Theresa. "Demythologizing Nationalism: Joyce's Dialogized Grail Myth." In *Joyce in Context,* edited by Vincent J. Cheng and Timothy Martin, pp. 100-21. Cambridge, Great Britain: Cambridge University Press, 1992.

[*In the following essay, O'Connor proposes that throughout* Ulysses, *James Joyce juxtaposes the quest for regeneration via male sacrifice with a search for regeneration through maternal love.*]

> Hot fresh blood they prescribe for decline. Blood always needed. Insidious.
>
> (*U* [*Ulysses*] 8.729 30)

"For many centuries," Conor Cruise O'Brien observed in a recent article on nationalist ideology, "the grand legitimizer of hatred in our culture was called Religion. Then after the great surfeit of the Wars of Religion, the power of religion to legitimize war and persecution began to fade and the cult of Nationalism took its place . . . Henceforward, it was in the name of the nation that men would be most likely to feel it legitimate to hate and kill other men, and women and children" (27). Linking nationalism with religion, O'Brien argues that both creeds serve to legitimize war and bloodshed because both are rooted in the perverse notion that renewal comes through blood sacrifice. It is precisely this belief that Joyce sets out to decode in *Ulysses*. Like O'Brien, he was convinced that as he himself put it—nationality "must find its reason for being rooted in something that surpasses and transcends and informs changing things like blood and the human word" (*CW* [*The Critical Writings of James Joyce*] 166). In *Ulysses* he sets out to demythologize the discourse of Irish nationalism, a discourse rooted in what is undoubtedly the most powerful narrative script embodying the doctrine of sacrificial renewal in the history of Western culture, the legend of the Holy Grail. To do this, he confronts the hegemonic nationalist myth with the Celtic myth in which it had its origins. Joyce's revisionary Grail myth slowly takes on form by means of a continuous series of dialogic encounters between antithetical Grails.

The chief architect of the Irish nationalist discourse was William Butler Yeats. For Yeats, as John Hutchinson points out, "Irish culture was seen in essentially a passive role as material to be moulded by an artistic elite who would create the authentic Irish nation . . . in the pagan Celtic archetype. His heroes and heroines were mystical aristocrats who, by sacrificing themselves, were able to redeem a fallen people" (135). As early as 1891 Yeats had begun to combine his mythic, nationalist and occult interests in an attempt to awaken "ancient fires," and forge a new post-colonial consciousness for the Irish race (Ellmann, *Masks* 86-134). Influenced by Wagner's *Parsifal,* by Celtic mythology, and by the French Order of the Rosy Cross of the Temple and of the Grail, he imagined a new Irish system which would have as its focal point a "symbolic fabric" centering on the four sacred talismans of the Tuatha Dé Danann ("The People of the Goddess Danu"), chief of which is the "cauldron" of the Goddess, the Celtic prototype for the Grail (Yeats, *Memoirs* 125; Raine 177-246). "A time will come for [the Tuatha Dé Danann] also," Yeats declares in "Rosa Alchemica," "but they cannot build their temples again till there have been martyrdoms and victories" (*Mythologies* 281). Precisely the same body of Celtic myth that supplied the central images for Yeats's work provided the framework for the amalgam of tales that came to be known in twelfth-century France as the Grail myth. In both mythic systems the symbolism of the Celtic quest myth is inverted. In fact, both systems are palimpsests in which are inscribed two radically divergent cultural scripts: one, the conceptualizing discourse of logos, the Word made flesh, and the other, the occulted discourse of motherhood, the flesh made word. The process of narrative colonization functions in different ways in each myth. Whereas in the christianized Grail myth the Celtic concept of female sacrality is repressed and male blood and violence are canonized as the primary source of life, in Yeats's *Cathleen Ni Houlihan,* a central political text in neocolonial Ireland (Deane 147), the female image is retained, and used to provide legitimization for the nationalist ideology of cultural paternity. A harbinger of violence and destruction, Yeats's Cathleen demands blood-sacrifice for the rebirth of the Motherland.

Like thirst-ravaged vampires, Joyce's parodic Cathleens, the sinister sisterhood of the "Gaptoothed Kathleen" (*U* 9.36-7), and their cohorts, the brotherhood of the "bloodfadder" (*FW* [*Finnegans Wake*] 496.26), stalk through the pages of *Ulysses* in quest of blood. In "Circe" one sister inquires, "(with expectation) Is he bleeding!" (*U* 15.4778). This quest for regeneration through sacrificial male blood is juxtaposed throughout *Ulysses* with a quest for regeneration through maternal love: "*Amor matris,* subjective and objective genitive . . . the only true thing in life" (*U* 9.842-3). The endless oscillation between these two quests in *Ulysses* deprivileges the canonical nationalist myth and enables us to view the Grail as at once the sacrificial blood of a male victim and savior and as the regenerative blood of the mother. The fault line, as it were, around which this revisionary Grail myth is constructed occupies scarcely two lines in *Ulysses*:

> *On the altarstone Mrs Mina Purefoy, goddess of unreason, lies, naked, fettered, a chalice resting on her swollen belly.*
>
> (*U* 15.4691-3)

The dialogized chalice, represented here by an amalgam of the Eucharistic chalice and the womb-chalice of Mina, also serves as a parergon, or enclosing frame, for Joyce's text.[1] Mulligan's shaving bowl, a parodic Eucharistic chalice, frames the opening consecration in "Telemachus," and Molly's womb, her "chalice" of menstrual blood, dominates "Penelope." "Telemachus" begins an immense pivoting so that its subtext, the occulted voice of the old Celtic Goddess (the milkwoman who speaks not a word of her own language) dominates "Penelope." In other words, Joyce's dialogized Grail myth has a dynamic and reversible structure. Viewed from the perspective of the canonical (masculinist) Grail myth, it reinforces the structure of Western patriarchy, but turned on its head, as it were, and viewed from the perspective of the occulted Celtic myth, it subverts that same structure.[2]

If we are to uncover the subversive force of Joyce's dialogized Grail myth in *Ulysses,* we need first to uncover the occulted discourse it sets out to retrieve. Thus, before it reaches its subject, my discussion here will require a brief preamble: a review of the main lines of interconnection between the christianized Grail myth and—to use Joyce's words—the "matt*her* of Erryn" (emphasis added), those "grandest gynecollege histories" (*FW* 389.6-9).[3] As Arthur C. L. Brown points out in *The Origins of the Grail Legend,* the work of Chrétien, the French poet who wrote one of the first christianized versions of the Grail myth in the twelfth century, draws heavily on Celtic mythic motifs. Chrétien's story of Perceval's parentage and boyhood deeds (*Perceval le gallois ou Le Conte du graal*), he claims, had its remote origins in the *Machníomhartha Finn* (*The Boyhood Deeds of Fionn*). Precisely the same theme, the quest for a mysterious cauldron of regeneration, is central to both tales; however, the form this vessel takes differs radically in each version of the myth. Whereas Chrétien's Perceval journeys out in search of the "graal" (Barber 5), Fionn mac Cumhaill (represented here as a descendant of Bran-Nuadu, the chief god of the Tuatha Dé Danann) searches for the crane bag (*corrbolg*), a strange vessel of poetic inspiration made from crane skin. The pedigree of Fionn's mysterious bag, which James MacKillop links with "the beginnings of the insular alphabet, ogham" (21), is given in "The Crane Bag," a brief poem which appears in the *Duanaire Finn* (*The Book of the Lays of Fionn*). In answer to the question "to whom did the good Crane-bag belong that Cumhall son of Tréanmhór had?," the poet is told that the bag belonged to Manannán Mac Lir (Mac Neill 119). The Irish literary journal *The Crane Bag* summarizes the story as follows:

> Mananaan the god of the sea . . . wishing to punish his wife Aoife, transformed her into a crane. She retaliated by ensuring that his secret alphabet of wisdom, which he treasured, would be shared with the populace. Consequently, whenever cranes are in flight they form images in the sky of the secret alphabet for all to read.
>
> (5)

After Aoife's death, Mananaan apparently made the crane bag (*corrbolg*) of her skin, and in it he kept "every precious thing" he owned (Mac Neill 119). When Jessie Weston—Joyce's "Westend Woman" (*FW* 292.6)—dismissed the theory of the Celtic origins of the Grail legend, she was obviously unaware of the legend of the crane bag. The Celtic cauldron, she argues, is merely "a food providing" vessel, whereas the Christian Grail, in contrast, is surrounded by an atmosphere of "sanctity" befitting the holiest of relics (73). But the crane bag of Fionn mac Cumhaill and the Fianna is much more than a mere "food providing" vessel. Made from the skin of a woman, symbol of fertility and regeneration, source of language and poetic wisdom, it is a feminine pre-Christian counterpart for the Christian Grail chalice.

The old Celtic voyage tales (*Immrama*), which tell of a series of journeys to the Otherworld, a mysterious Land of Women (*Tír na m-Ban*) where, as Brown observes, "sex is no sin," served as the basis for the marvelous adventures of Iwain in Chrétien's work (Brown 3-7). Bran Mac Febail, closely related to "Bran the Blessed" ("god of the sacred cauldron") in Welsh mythology, is the hero of the oldest of the voyage tales, *The Voyage of Bran*.[4] He apparently acquired his sacred cauldron on his voyage to the Land of Women. This otherworld is given a variety of names and assumes a variety of different forms in Celtic myth. Representing, on one level, a submerged state of consciousness (akin, in some senses, to Julia Kristeva's semiotic *chora*), it is almost always situated in distant islands, beneath the sea, or beneath the mounds of the *Sid*. As Proinsias Mac Cana notes, it may be reached through a mist, or through a cave, or "simply through the granting of a sudden insight" (125). In some myths, as Mac Cana points out, it appears as a revolving wheel or castle symbolic of the turning world; in others, it is represented as a tower of glass (*turris vitrea*) or a fortress of glass (*Caer Wydyr*) (129). In others still, it is *Tír na n-óg,* the land of the dead and the land of the ever young. Ultimately, whatever form or name it takes, the Celtic Otherworld—"Tear-nan-Ogre," as Joyce puts it in *Finnegans Wake* (479.2)—is, in its very essence, the opening "tear" to otherness, difference, alterity.

The apple, sacred symbol of Venus, figures largely in the Celtic myths of the otherworld. In fact, Avalon, the Otherworld of Arthurian mythology, is, quite literally, the "Apple-Land" of immortality (Walker 479). In *The Voyage of Bran,* as in many of the Celtic voyage myths, a woman bearing a golden apple bough guides the hero to the Otherworld. Other symbols frequently associated with the Celtic Goddess are blood and milk. As several critics have remarked, Medb of Cruachain, "Naif Cruachan" (*FW* 526.20), the fertility goddess/heroine of the ancient Irish epic *Táin Bó Cuailnge* (*The Cattle Raid of Cuailnge*), was quite possibly the only woman to menstruate in Irish literature before Molly Bloom. Medb's blood, which flows to form a river at the end of the great cattle raid, is a vivid symbol of female creative power. Significantly, it is Medb's daughter Finnabair who served as the prototype for Guinevere in the Arthurian legends. Milk is one of the chief symbols of the goddess Brigid (one of the prototypes for Biddy the hen in *Finnegans Wake*) in her role as Cow Goddess. The milk of the sacred cow, as Mary Condren points out, was "one of the earliest sacred foods throughout the world, equivalent to our present day communion" (58). Indeed, so powerful was the symbolism associated with the Cow Goddess in ancient Ireland that it was not until the Synod of Cashel in 1172 that the use of milk in baptism was finally banned (Condren 177).

The final set of mythic symbols I will consider here are drawn from the central tales in *Lebor Gabala* (*The Book of Invasions*): the battles of Mag Tuired. These battles were fought between Nuadu, king of the Tuatha Dé Danann, and the Fomorians for possession of a queen, Ériu, and for her four sacred talismans: spear, stone, sword, and cauldron. Because it was *geis* (taboo) for a man with a physical or psychological blemish to rule the country, Nuadu, who lost an arm in the first battle of Mag Tuired, is forced to relinquish his kingship to Bres, his Fomorian enemy. Bres, however, lacks *fír flaitheman* (which Mac Cana translates as "truth of the ruler"); thus the land becomes a Waste Land, and the queen (a personification of the land) grows ugly and haggard. The Waste Land is redeemed only when the Goddess is reunited sexually with a spiritually and physically worthy spouse. In fact, sexuality plays a major role in the inauguration rite, known as the *banfheis rígi* (the wife feast of kingship) of the sacral king. This ceremony involves two ritual acts: the female offers a golden cup containing a red drink to her chosen spouse, and this symbolic offering is then followed by sexual intercourse between the king and the "sovereignty" (Mac Cana 114-21). In the Arthurian myths, only one of Nuadu's aspects, that of reigning king, is transferred to King Arthur. His second aspect, that of a wounded (or impotent) god kept alive by the magic talismans of the Goddess, is represented by the Fisher King.

In almost every instance, the motifs and symbols which appear in the "matther of Erryn" correspond closely with those which appear in the later christianized versions of the myth. There is, however, one glaring exception. Whereas in Celtic myth the cauldron belongs to the Goddess, the Christian Grail has a decidedly masculine lineage; in fact, no woman may even hear of it (Weston 137). In the christianized versions of the myth a new world vision is constructed in which all generativity and creativity fall to God, the spiritual father, rather than to the female. With the same masterful stroke, sexuality, now projected onto the female, is assigned to the realm of the sinful. Whereas the quest for a woman's love is a central feature in the mythology of the Celts, we hear no mention of such love in Robert de Boron's *Roman de l'estoire dou graal*, a work which appeared almost contemporaneously with Chrétien's *Perceval*. In de Boron's work—which links the *matière de Bretagne* with the legend of Joseph of Arimathea—the Grail is represented as the cup used to collect the redeeming blood, the *sang real,* which flowed from the wounds of the crucified Christ. The cup is brought by Joseph of Arimathea to Glastonbury in England (the reputed burial place of Arthur and Guinevere), and, thereafter, it becomes the object of knightly quests that can be achieved only by those who are chaste.[5]

In the "Matter of Brettaine," which Joyce links with "brut fierce" in *Finnegans Wake* (292.34), male friendship receives priority. Malory's fifteenth-century version of the Grail myth, *Morte d'Arthur,* presents a world dominated by battles, civil wars and tournaments. Here, love is a subordinate interest, and the comitatus, the fraternal bond between man and man, replaces the bond between man and woman. Several hundred years later, in *Parsifal*, Richard Wagner's operatic rerendering of the German poet Wolfram von Eschenbach's work, celibacy is again exalted, and the Grail is once again linked with the blood-filled chalice of the Eucharist. Apparently, Wagner's work so influenced Adolf Hitler that he adopted as his insignum the swastika, the age-old symbol of renewal in the Thule Grail mysteries (Whitmont 161).[6]

Beginning in the mists of Celtic prehistory and moving inexorably forward through Chrétien's *Perceval*, Robert de Boron's *Roman de L'estoire dou graal*, Gottfried von Strassburg's *Tristan and Isolde*, Wolfram von Eschenbach's *Parzival*, Sir Thomas Malory's *Morte d'Arthur*, Alfred Tennyson's *Idylls of the King*, and Richard Wagner's *Parsifal* and *Tristan und Isolde* (to name but a few versions of the myth), the language, symbolism, and ideology of the Grail myth has had a profound influence on our civilization and culture. In Yeats's *Cathleen Ni Houlihan*, the Grail myth came full circle. Here the powerful Celtic mother figure, the original bearer of the Grail, is de-sexualized and harnessed to the service of an ideology that has at its center not the life-giving blood of the mother, but the sacrificial blood of a male victim-savior. So, by a "commodius vicus of recirculation" (*FW* 3.2), we return now to Joyce's work, where we find ourselves confronted with a dialogized Grail and a decentered nationalist vision. Pervading the entire text we find almost all of the symbols and motifs from the Celtic Grail myth: the Waste Land, the Grail Castle (the Crystal Palace), the otherworldly Apple Land, the wounded Fisher King, the Loathly Lady, the Gold Cup, and the questing Knight.

Ulysses's Ireland is a Waste Land (*U* 14.476-83). The fields are barren, the cattle are diseased, and women, disparagingly referred to as "cowflesh" (*U* 14.807), have difficulty giving birth (*U* 14.114-17). The actual drought in June 1904 is reflected in the spiritual paralysis of the people, a paralysis manifestly evident in "Oxen of the Sun" where the agony of Mina (Joyce's everywoman) in "that allhardest of woman hour" is counterpointed by the raucous laughter of Buck Mulligan and his cronies. "I shudder to think of the future of a race," the young "learningknight" Dixon states, "where the seeds of such malice have been sown and where no right reverence is rendered to mother and maid in house of Horne" (*U* 14.832-4). The attitude of the callous "medicals," whose discussion centers around such topics as abortion, contraception, their sexual triumphs with women, and their losses in the Gold Cup Race, is explicitly contrasted with the reverential treatment of the mother in Celtic society (*U* 14.33-49). We are reminded of the Waste Land theme in Celtic myth, and, indeed, in Chrétien's *Perceval*, where the desecration of the Grail country is caused by the violation of the Grail maiden and the theft of her gold cup (the gold cup, as Weston points out, is yet another name for the Grail chalice). Significantly, references to a gold cup echo like a Wagnerian leitmotif throughout *Ulysses*. Represented in the parodic framework of the Gold Cup Race at Ascot, Joyce's "gold cup" theme, like that of Chrétien, is closely associated with the idea of the betrayal of love.

In an ironic inversion of the symbolism of the Christian Grail myth, the Eucharistic chalice emerges in *Ulysses* as one of the major emblems of the Waste Land. In "Telemachus," the blood-filled chalice—a key symbol in the rhetoric of Irish nationalism—is explicitly linked with war and death. Here, Mulligan stands on the gunrest of a tower built for defense in time of war, as he holds aloft his "chalice," a shaving bowl, in an age-old gesture of ritual appeasement. "For this, O dearly beloved," he declares, "is the genuine christine: body and soul and blood and ouns" (*U* 1.21-2). A tissue of allusions links Malachi, whose "plump shadowed face and sullen oval jowl recalled a prelate, patron of the arts in the middle ages" (*U* 1.31-3), with St. Malachy, the celibate Cistercian monk who died in the arms of his friend and biographer St. Bernard, the spiritual father of the Knights Templars (the original Grail Knights). Malachy was responsible for the introduction of Roman ecclesiastical discipline into the Irish Church, thus effectively bringing an end to Celtic Christianity (a system more closely aligned with Gnosticism than with Pauline and Latin Christianity). In thus threatening the power of the British crown in Ireland, he was also in part responsible for the papal bull entitled *Laudabiliter* by which the Englishman, Pope Adrian IV, granted Ireland to Henry II of England in 1155. Thus, it was Malachy—whose greatest enemy was, significantly, King Stephen of England—and not, as the misogynistic Deasy suggests, "a faithless woman," who was responsible for bringing "strangers" to Ireland's shores. As a result of the profound changes introduced by St. Malachy into the Irish Church, the Celtic Mother Goddess was dispossessed of her spiritual power, and her womb/chalice of life-giving blood was framed by the blood-filled chalice of the Father.

St. Malachy's triumph over the Celtic Cow Goddess is mirrored in "Telemachus," where Mulligan dismisses the old milkwoman's can as a urinal: "Can you recall, brother," he asks Stephen, "is mother Grogan's tea and water pot spoken of in the Mabinogion or is it in the Upanishads?" (*U* 1.370-1). Mulligan's "omphalos" (*U* 1.544), a Martello tower rented from the secretary of state for war, serves as a type of phallic parergon for *Dumha na Bó* (the Mound of the Cow), the "omphalos" of the Celtic Mother Goddess at *Teamhair* (pronounced "tower") (Condren 58). Indeed, *Ulysses* is rife with examples of such displacement. In Mulligan's world, a world where "hot fresh blood" is "prescribe[d] for decline" (*U* 8.729), and dying martyrs have spectacular erections, a world, moreover, where "commodious milkjugs" are "destined to receive the most precious blood of the most precious victim" (*U* 12.623-4), the once venerated Cow Goddess is reduced to "a wandering crone, lowly form of an immortal serving her conqueror and her gay betrayer" (*U* 1.404-5). Whereas the Celtic Cow Goddess Brigid was patron of *filidecht* (poetry), this milkwoman does not even recognize her own language; her milk—a traditional symbol of female wisdom—is "not hers" (*U* 1.398). Her usurpers, all key exponents of linguistic and cultural nationalism, all "Pretenders" (*U* 3.313) to the throne of Cathleen, and all, in one sense or another, "bloodfadders," invariably take on the life-centered imagery of the "milkmudder" (*FW* 496.26). In "Circe," Mananaan Mac Lir (alias the "sacrificial butter" [9.64]: the dairy expert, and nationalist sympathizer, A.E.), vehemently and somewhat incongruously insists that he is "the dreamery creamery butter" (*U* 15.2275-6). Not to be outdone, Malachi Mulligan weeps "tears of molten butter" (*U* 15.4179), and, with imperial hauteur, his cohort Haines, the Gaelic-speaking Oxonian, the "Britisher" who shares the citizen's goal of bringing "once more into honour among mortal men the winged speech of the seadivided Gael" (*U* 12.1188-9), demands to know if the milk in his tea is "real Irish cream." "I don't want to be imposed on," he adds (*U* 10.1094-5). The irony is telling.

In many early Celtic myths, the Waste Land is redeemed only by a quest into the otherworldly Apple Land of Women. In *Ulysses,* a text where almost everything contains "two thinks at a time" (*FW* 583.7), no such singular solutions are forthcoming. Here even the apple, the traditional passport to the Otherworld, is dialogized. Joyce's "Applewoman" makes her first appearance in "Lestrygonians" where she hawks her imported "glazed" wares "Two for a penny!" (*U* 8.69-70). She reappears in "Circe" as a supporter of the nationalist cause. In a parody of the traditional role of the Celtic Goddess as emissary to the Otherworld, she joins the chorus of voices urging Bloom to assume his role as successor to Parnell, hero-martyr for the motherland: "He's a man like Ireland wants," she says (*U* 15.1540). Although it is impossible to determine whether the Apple-woman calls Bloom to a Christian hell or a pagan heaven, her counterpart, Old Gummy Granny, who propositions Stephen in "Circe," places her bid for sacrifice in an explicitly Christian context: "At 8.35 a.m.," she promises, "you will be in heaven and Ireland will be free" (*U* 15.4737-8). Joyce's intertextual layering of Christian and Celtic motifs here points to an aporia or double-bind in nationalist rhetoric. In the ancient Irish myths from which the nationalists took their myth of origin—myths where, as Stephen discovered, there is "no trace of hell," where the "moral idea seems lacking, the sense of destiny, of retribution" (*U* 10.1082-4)—the apple is the passport to eternal life. In the Christian myth from which their doctrine of sacrificial renewal derives, however, the apple is the forbidden fruit, the cause of the fall, and the emblem of (woman's) original sin: our "grandam," as Stephen puts it—drawing, appropriately enough, on the work of St. Bernard and St. Augustine—"sold us all, seed, breed and generation, for a penny pippin" (*U* 14.300-1). The Applewoman's wares in *Ulysses,* the fruit at once of redemption and damnation, straddle, as it were, the strategic fault-line between two antithetical narrative paradigms. The result is a dialogism that mocks simultaneously the nationalist concept of a monological voice of culture, and the Christian concept of an authoritative narrative of origin.

Like the apples of wisdom, Joyce's parodic Otherworld, his *Caer Wydyr* (crystal palace), is hopelessly convoluted and divided. There is some irony in the fact that the crystal palace makes its first appearance in the "Cyclops" episode, an episode resonant with references to blood-sacrifice—"a genuinely instructive treat" (*U* 12.551)—cattle-disease, pornography, and, significantly, misinformation with regard to the winner of the "gold cup" (*U* 12.1898). The irony is compounded by the fact that the episode is presided over by the misogynistic, xenophobic "Citizen," the self-styled champion of "Kathleen ni Houlihan" (*U* 12.1375), for whom woman is, paradoxically, one of the chief representatives of cultural "otherness." "A dishonoured wife," he states, "that's what's the cause of all our misfortunes" (*U* 12.1163-4). His obsessive catch cry is *"Sinn Fein . . . Sinn Fein amhain"* (*U* 12.523). In a text where the axis of otherness is constantly being displaced, his doctrine of political and cultural separatism is constantly being mocked. Consider, for example, the paragraph in which the crystal palace appears:

> In Inisfail the fair there lies a land, the land of holy Michan. There rises a watchtower beheld of men afar. There sleep the mighty dead as in life they slept, warriors and princes of high renown . . . Lovely maidens sit in close proximity to the roots of the lovely trees singing the most lovely songs . . . And heroes voyage from afar to woo them . . . princes, the sons of kings. And there rises a shining palace whose crystal glittering roof is seen by mariners who traverse the extensive sea in barks built expressly for that purpose . . .
>
> (*U* 12.68-89)

The passage evokes the romantic imagery typical of nationalist rhetoric; however, the crystal palace-Inisfail-questing hero complex of images, which gives it its distinctly Celtic resonance, is framed by an imperialist context. As Weldon Thornton observes, the paragraph almost certainly derives from James Clarence Mangan's translation of "Prince Alfred's Itinerary through Ireland" (257). Joyce's intertextual dialogism here unsettles the idealist quest for meaning (selfhood) that belong to "Sinn Fein," Ourselves Alone. Indeed, even the crystal palace reference itself is a type of Trojan horse. In the context of the Celtic myth, it represents the Otherworld, but it might also refer to the British Crystal Palace, the icon of imperialism erected in Hyde Park, London, for the Great Exhibition in 1851 (Thornton 258). The connotation of the word Inisfail (a traditional name for Ireland) is also open to question, since the stone from which it derives its name, the *Lia Fáil* (the Stone of Fál or "stone of destiny," one of the four sacred symbols of the Tuatha Dé Danann), is itself colonized. Apparently the "Liam Fail"—as Joyce puts it in *Finnegans Wake*—now rests under the Coronation throne in "Westmunster" Abbey (*FW* 131.10-11). The blurred demarcations between the self and the other, the carefully controlled counterpoint between antithetical (imperial and Celtic) motifs and quest myths, here exemplify Joyce's dialogic practice in destabilizing hegemonic nationalist and, moreover, imperialist, narrative forms.

Let us turn our attention now to Joyce's two potential knights, the two "Seekers on the great quest . . . East of the sun, west of the moon: *Tír na n-óg*" (*U* 9.411-13). Both Sir Leopold, "bedight in sable armour" (*U* 12.215), and—to use Biddy the Clap's words—"yon sable knight" (*U* 15.4636) Stephen Dedalus are cast in two quest myths simultaneously. One of the structuring features of Joyce's dialogized Grail myth, as I suggested earlier, is the opposition of blood-filled chalice and the womb. As we trace the threads of this theme as it relates to Stephen through *Ulysses,* we see a new pattern emerging, one in which both chalice and womb are equated as purveyors of death. If the bloody "cup" offered to him by Cathleen Ni Houlihan, alias Old Gummy Granny (*U* 15.4736), represents for Stephen the nightmare of Irish history from which he is trying to escape, the mother is the "Womb of sin" (*U* 3.44), the "allwombing tomb" (*U* 3.402); to both he says "*Non serviam!*" (*U* 15.4228).

In Joyce's treatment of Stephen's relationship with his mother, we find a recapitulation of themes and motifs from a number of Grail myths, particularly Chrétien's *Perceval*. Stephen's quest, like that of Perceval, revolves around the motif of the question, and like Perceval too, he is obsessed with guilt at the plight of his sister and the death of his mother: "They say I killed you, mother," he screams, "choking with fright, remorse and horror" in "Circe." "Cancer did it," he pleads, "not I. Destiny" (*U* 15.4186-7). As Emma Jung and Marie-Louise von Franz have remarked, the failure of Perceval's quest in Chrétien's work is due to an offence against the emotional, spiritual side of the self represented by the mother. Perceval, they state, "did not attend to his mother and he did not ask about the Grail—and the latter offence is actually described as a consequence of the former." "As its primal image," they add, "the Grail takes the place of the mother" (181). In *Ulysses* too, Stephen's quest and his neglect of the mother are inextricably intertwined. In fact, the question which haunts him throughout *Ulysses* is posed directly to the mother: "Tell me the word, mother," he begs at the climax of the novel in "Circe," "if you know now. The word known to all men" (*U* 15.4192-3). Significantly, no answer is forthcoming. The motif of the unanswered question (a motif found in a number of Grail myths) is closely bound up with the notion that "meaning" cannot be imposed by an external authority. Rather, it must be sought within the self. Stephen's quest for the word of the mother, then, is both an inversion and an interiorization of his quest for the Word of the Father. Whereas the nationalist (and Christian) quest myth centers around a quest for a defined "good"—the rejuvenation of a political abstraction called Cathleen Ni Houlihan—and the attendant defeat of an "evil" other, these polar oppositions are interiorized in the quest which centers around the mother. In his drunken state in "Circe," Stephen is dimly aware of the fact that it is in his own consciousness that he must kill the scapegoated other: "the priest and the king" (*U* 15.4437). It is in himself too, as the reader discovers in "Scylla and Charybdis," that Stephen has buried the Grail of love (the repressed "woid" of the mother) that will heal the Waste Land of the spirit (*U* 9.429-30).

That the Celtic quest myth is, in its very essence, a narrative detailing the growth of individual consciousness is evident from the fact that in several versions of the myth the Otherworld may be reached "simply through the granting of a sudden insight" (MacCana 125). In *A Portrait of the Artist as a Young Man,* Stephen, the fledgling poet, had a fleeting vision of this hidden world: he heard "a voice from beyond the world" (*P* [*A Portrait of the Artist as a Young Man*] 167) and saw a woman, a "strange and beautiful seabird" with legs "delicate as a crane's" (*P* 171). "Her eyes had called to him," but he turned away from her and dedicated himself to the "old father, old artificer" whose name he bore. This link between the would-be poet and the crane woman is particularly significant since, as I have already pointed out, the Grail of Fionn, the poet of the Fianna, is a mysterious bag of poetic wisdom made from the skin of the crane woman, Aoife. In rejecting the visionary woman for the Father, Stephen rejected the Grail he so desperately sought, committing himself instead to the very paralysis he struggles to escape from in *Ulysses*. Trapped in a selfish aestheticism, fearful of death and the fluidity of the feminine, he remains at the end of *Ulysses* "the eternal son and ever virgin" (*U* 14.342-3). The meaning of love, like the apples of wisdom and self-knowledge (*U* 3.432), remains for him a "bitter mystery" (*U* 15.4190).

Like Stephen Dedalus, Bloom, the would-be architect of "Bloomusalem," an otherworldly New Jerusalem "with crystal roof" (*U* 15.1548), is cast in two quest myths simultaneously: he is at once Joyce's Christian Fisher of men and his pagan Fisher King. The "cod-eyed" Bloom (*U* 15.1871), the "last sardine of summer" (*U* 11.1220-1), whose nickname, by the way, is "Mackerel" (*U* 8.405), is, as the Citizen so eloquently puts it, "[a] fellow that's neither fish nor flesh" (*U* 12.1055-6). Sex, the key to renewal in the pagan quest myth and an impediment to renewal in the Christian quest myth, is the aporia on which Bloom's dialogized Grail quest rests. He may be "the very truest knight of the world one that ever did minion service to lady" (*U* 14.184-5), yet, from the perspective of his wife, his "service" leaves something to be desired. Molly resents the fact that she has been cast in the role of the Loathly Lady: "its a wonder Im not an old shrivelled hag before my time," she complains, "living with him so cold never embracing me except sometimes when hes asleep the wrong end of me" (*U* 18.1399-1401). This "new apostle to the gentiles" (*U* 12.1489), who has not had sexual intercourse with Molly since the death of their only son almost eleven years before, is, it seems, a celibate (of sorts). Appropriately enough, he assumes the role of the chaste redeemer in "Circe" where, wearing "a seamless garment marked I.H.S.," he burns "amid phoenix flames" (*U* 15.1935-6). Bloom's credentials as a Christian redeemer, however, are somewhat sullied by the fact that, like the Fisher King of the Grail castle, his celibacy is due to impotence (of a sort). Fearful of the feminine, which he associates with death and corruption, this middle-aged Tristan looks to virgins for consolation, to "Green apples" (*U* 13.1086), and to the cold curves of stone "goddesses" (*U* 8.922). In "Lestrygonians," he imagines these plaster virgins as immortals drinking nectar from "golden dishes" (*U* 8.925-6). Conscious of his own mortality, he envies them their fleshless state. The icons in Bloom's *salle aux images,* the statue of Venus in the National Gallery (*U* 8.1180-1), the various pornographic "Venus in Furs" figures that populate his daydreams, the disgruntled nymph framed over his bed, the immature Gerty MacDowell, the mysterious Martha Clifford, and, most importantly, Cathleen Ni Houlihan—the sterile icon of the militant nationalist group he is reputed to have been instrumental in founding—are the psychological equivalent of the condom he carries in his pocketbook. They enable him to indulge his erotic desires, yet, at the same time, they shield him from the (for him) horrors of female fecundity, and its corollary, death.

Nationalist, freemason, Jew, Christ figure, advocate of universal love, and self-cuckolded lover, Bloom is the personification of Joyce's indeterminacy principle. Although he has apparently immersed himself in a new type of fatherhood, the regenerative fatherhood of Sinn Féin (*U* 18.1227-9), he, nevertheless, rejects the nationalist ethic of justice and domination in favor of an ethic of care and responsibility. "Force, hatred, history, all that," he argues, offers no "life for men and women."

"And everybody knows," he points out, "that it's the very opposite of that that is really life" (*U* 12.1481-5): Love. Throughout *Ulysses,* Bloom searches ceaselessly for "that other world" (*U* 13.1262-3). His quest, which begins in what might be described as the "Perilous Chapel" in "Hades" and ends in Molly's "Perilous bed," "a lair or ambush of lust or adders" (*U* 17.2116-18), in "Penelope," reaches its climax in "Circe." In this dreamworld of dissolving identities and blurred boundaries, the dual-gendered Bello/Bella serves as his guide on his journey to the otherworldly "womancity" (*U* 15.1327). "For such favours," she claims, "knights of old laid down their lives" (*U* 15.3080-1). Here, Bloom comes face to face with all the debased images of women that have appeared throughout *Ulysses.* He unveils the virginal nymph who "flees from him unveiled, her plaster cracking, a cloud of stench escaping from the cracks" (*U* 15.3469-70). Gummy Granny in her role as the blood-thirsty Cathleen is also banished. Finally, in the Black Mass scene at the end of "Circe," the diffuse thematic pattern of this postmodernist Grail myth reaches its climax. Bloom has a vision of the dialogized Grail:

> *On an eminence, the centre of the earth, rises the field-altar of Saint Barbara. Black candles rise from its gospel and epistle horns . . . On the altarstone Mrs Mina Purefoy, goddess of unreason, lies, naked, fettered, a chalice resting on her swollen belly.*
>
> (*U* 15.4688-93)

In German legend, as Jung and von Franz point out, the "round mountain of St. Barbara" is the home of the Knight of the Swan (Lohengrin). Here, it is said, "Venus lives in the Grail" (121).

If *Ulysses* begins with an image of a colonized "Mother Ireland," "Silk of the kine and poor old woman" (*U* 1.403), it ends, like Yeats's *Cathleen Ni Houlihan,* with an image of a revivified Mother Goddess. Whereas Yeats's Cathleen is rejuvenated by heroic sacrifice, we find no mention of sacrificial martyrdom in "Penelope"; whereas the maternal embodiment of the nation in the discourse of Irish nationalism was rigorously chaste and virginal, Joyce's "Gea Tellus" is a sexually active woman. Molly Bloom has no patience with the "trash and nonsense" (*U* 18.384) of "Sinner Fein or the freemasons" (*U* 18.1227). In the place of dogmatic nationalism, she offers 'plurabilities'; in the place of sacrificial death, she offers a vision of cyclical life.

The two powerful female icons Molly tries to transcend in *Ulysses* are the sexless Cathleen, the Grail of the Nationalists, and the Virgin Mother, the chaste icon of the Templars, the first Christian Grail Knights.[7] Appropriately enough, Molly, the daughter of a Templar, shares both the name and the birthday of the Virgin. Yet, although she is herself a bereaved mother famous for her stirring rendition of Rossini's *Stabat Mater,* Molly

Bloom recalls not the Christian *Mater dolorosa,* but Isis, the Sacred Moon Cow, the prototype not only for the Virgin Mother but also for the Celtic Cow Goddess, Brigid. According to the Isis myth (possibly the earliest version of the Grail story) the origins of life are not male but female. Isis was originally the mother/wife of Osiris, the earliest resurrected god. The pagan myth, Barbara Walker notes, was copied by Christianity, "except for one vital point: the agent of Osiris's resurrection was not the heavenly father," but the mother (216).

A rejuvenated Sacred Cow Goddess, "Marion of the bountiful bosoms" (*U* 12.1006-7), presides over Joyce's otherworldly "Apple Land" in "Penelope." Her blood-filled commode is, significantly, "totally covered by square cretonne cutting, apple design" (*U* 17.2102-3). Molly is, as she herself puts it, "a mixture of plum and apple" (*U* 18.1535). The proliferation of O's in her language points to the Irish *ubhal* (apple), a word which, Harold Bayley—the Scottish scholar of symbolism whose work influenced Yeats—points out, "resolves itself into iabel, the 'orb of god,' oko, 'the great O'" (303). Furthermore, Molly's curiosity about the "capital initial of the name of a city in Canada, Quebec" (*U* 17.679-80), an interest linked to her fascination with Irish "hieroglyphics," points to the Q the letter of the *Quert* (apple) in the Oghamic tree alphabet. In the "penelopean patience" of "Penelope," as Anna Livia observes in *Finnegans Wake,* the "feminine libido" is represented by "those interbranching ogham sex upandinsweeps" (*FW* 123.4-9).

The final passages in "Penelope" are awash with images of fertility and regeneration. Blazes Boylan, Bloom's rival for the affections of Molly, has lost his bet on the Gold Cup Race, and he has also lost the affections of Molly. In spite of the size of his "tremendous big red brute of a thing" (*U* 18.144), Boylan, it seems, lacks *fír flaitheman.* Molly is convinced that Bloom "has more spunk in him" (*U* 18.168); she believes, moreover, that "he understood or felt what a woman is" (*U* 18.1578-9). Bloom did not, of course, place a bet on the Gold Cup Race, he is no "winner"; yet, as Molly observes, "if anyone asked could he ride the steeplechase for the gold cup hed say yes" (*U* 18.955-6). In her "snakespiral" (*U* 17.2116) bed, her omphalos—a symbol of the mystery of nonduality—Molly is planning to initiate Bloom into the life-empowering mysteries of love; she is planning what is, in effect, a *banfheis rígi.* Yes, she will give him "one more chance" (*U* 18.1498). "I suppose hed like my nice cream too" (*U* 18.1506), she thinks, as she plans her early morning shopping trip to her local crystal palace (the Dublin fruit and vegetable market). She will "throw him up his tea" in an imitation Crown Derby cup, and she will serve him eggs (the sacred symbol of Isis) while he sits in bed "like the king of the country" (*U* 18.931).

Although the title of the final illustration in Sebastian Evans's translation of *The High History of the Holy Graal* (one of Joyce's main sources for the Grail theme) is "Perceval Winneth the Golden Cup," the final chapter in *Ulysses* offers no such Telos; here "nought nowhere [is] never reached" (*U* 17.1068-9). Even as Molly determines to effect changes in her relationship with Bloom, her "new womanly man" is asleep at "the wrong end" of her; in short, Bloom still views the feminine from an inverted perspective. His dilemma, like that of all Grail knights—Bran-Nuadu, Arthur, Perceval, Gawain—when faced with *la vieille ogresse,* the "old shrivelled hag" (*U* 18.1399), who embodies the ever-revolving cycle of life-in-death and death-in-life, centers on the question of vision. As long as he fears death—which he projects onto the feminine—he will reject Molly, and the Waste Land will prevail. But if he can accept her as she is, if he can restore the phallic spear (as in Wagner's *Parsifal*) to her Grail/womb, he will—in mythopoeic terminology—achieve kingship in her timeless realm, and the Waste Land will be fruitful once more.

In the introduction to this essay I suggested that Joyce sets out in *Ulysses* to decenter the nationalist myth of sacrificial renewal by confronting it with an opposing voice. This type of "ideological decentering," as Bakhtin points out, will occur only when a national culture, or a national myth is dialogized: when it "loses its sealed-off and self-sufficient character, when it becomes conscious of itself as only one among *other* cultures and languages" (370). In *Ulysses,* Joyce achieves his purpose by initiating a dialogic exchange between the hegemonic nationalist Grail myth and its *own* occulted Celtic prototype. Thus, in the place of a monological myth of origin in *Ulysses,* we find two versions of the same myth—to use Bakhtin's words—"mutually animating one another." In the earlier myth, a moral and humanitarian principle of love, represented symbolically by *"Amor matris"* (*U* 9.842-3), is represented as the source of life, spiritual and physical; in its successor, patriotic martyrdoms and war take the place of love. In one myth, dualism is emphasized; in the other, we find a recognition of the positive values of otherness and difference that have been suppressed by the hegemony of logos. The endless oscillations between these two Grails in *Ulysses* ensure that meaning is never final but is in a constant process of metamorphosis. Here, there are no "winners," but only the constant whirling of antithetical impulses. As Joyce puts it in *Finnegans Wake,*

> there are two signs to turn to, the yest and the ist, the wright side and the wronged side . . . It is a sot of a swigswag, systomy, dystomy, which everabody you ever anywhere at all doze. Why? Such me.
>
> (597.10-22)

Notes

1. The word "parergon" is used here and elsewhere in the essay in the Kantian/Derridian sense of the term. For an interesting discussion of "parergonal logic"—to use Derrida's term—see Barbara Johnson's "The Frame of Reference: Poe, Lacan, Derrida" (Young 225-43).

2. Richard Ellmann's catalogue of Joyce's library in *The Consciousness of Joyce* provides ample evidence of Joyce's interest in the Grail myth while writing *Ulysses*. The library includes such works as Sebastian Evans's translation of *The High History of the Holy Graal* (112), Lady Charlotte Guest's translation of the Welsh *Mabinogion* (118)—described as the "Welsh Greal" in the introduction to Evans's work—a heavily annotated copy of Francis Hueffer's *The Troubadours: A History of Provençal Life and Literature in the Middle Ages* (112), Joseph Bédier's *Le Roman de Tristan et Iseut* (101), several of Richard Wagner's works, and an assortment of titles on Celtic themes by various members of the Irish Literary Renaissance.

   One of the earliest studies of the Celtic roots of the Grail legend to which Joyce had access in Dublin was a summary of A. C. L. Brown's *Iwain: A Study of the Origin of Arthurian Romance*, which appeared in the November December 1903 issue of *Celtia* (the journal of the St. Stephen's Green Celtic Association). Contrary to popular opinion, Joyce's access to Celtic manuscript materials was in no sense restricted when he left Ireland. In fact, during both of his sojourns in Paris (1902-3 and 1920-39), he had access not only to the Celtic materials in the Bibliothèque Nationale but also to the extensive holdings in the library of the Ecole Pratique des Hautes Etudes of the Sorbonne. The materials in the Sorbonne library range from relatively obscure journals such as *Celtia*, to facsimile copies of rare manuscripts such as *The Book of Ballymote* (this contains several hundred Ogham cipher-alphabets), to translations of old Irish poetry like the *Duanaire Finn*. The library also contains a comprehensive collection of scholarly works on Celtic mythology, history, religion, and the Celtic languages, including to name but a few—Alfred Nutt's *Studies in the Legend of the Holy Grail*, Kuno Meyer and Nutt's *The Voyage of Bran* (the latter includes an interesting discussion of the relationship between the Greek and Celtic doctrines of metempsychosis), John Rhys's *Lectures on the Origin and Growth of Religion as Illustrated by Celtic Heathendom*, and Eugene O'Curry's *Lectures on the Manuscript Materials of Ancient Irish History*. Both Rhys's and O'Curry's works provide extensive background information on all aspects of Celtic culture, history, and literature, and both touch on such Grail-related motifs and topics as the voyage theme, the apple motif, the stone of Fál, and the Otherworld of women.

3. The Grail myth, the creation of centuries of accretion of religious and mythological themes, contains elements from several different traditions, including Celtic mythology, Anglo-Saxon and French courtly traditions, Christian iconography, alchemical lore, classical myth, Arabic poetry, and Sufi teaching (Whitmont 153). Symbols and motifs from several of these traditions are threaded throughout *Ulysses, Finnegans Wake,* and Joyce's earlier works as well. A discussion of the significance of the Grail myth for the entire Joycean œuvre—a topic well beyond the scope of this essay—is the subject of a book-length work in progress.

4. For a brief, yet comprehensive survey of the various cycles of Celtic myth discussed here, see Mac Cana.

5. For a chronological list of Arthurian literature since 1800, see Taylor and Brewer 324-60.

6. Hitler is quoted in the work of the German historian Wilfried Daim as having said:

   > You ought to understand Parzifal differently from the way it is generally interpreted. Behind the trivial Christian dressing of the external story, with its Good Friday magic, this profound drama has a quite different content. It is not a Christian, Schopenhauerian religion of compassion, but the pure, aristocratic blood that is glorified . . . The eternal life that is the gift of the Grail is only for the truly pure and noble . . . How is one to stop racial decay? Politically we have acted: no equality no democracy. But what about the masses of the People? . . . Should we form an elect group of real initiates? An order of templars around the grail of the pure blood?

   (Daim 140; quoted in Whitmont 162-3)

   Hitler found in the Grail myth a justification for one of the most horrific bloodbaths in human history. Although the goals of the Nazi "templars" were in no sense analogous to those of Yeats and the Irish nationalists, it is significant that many of the same mechanisms they exploited to incite Germany's collective madness in the Jewish holocaust were used to unify the emerging nationalist movement in Ireland. Both systems were marked by a union of religious and military force; both were predicated on the deliberate manipulation of an alienated people through the exploitation of the archetypes of universal history contained in the Grail myth; in both systems the mother archetype (represented by Ostara in Germany, Cathleen in

Ireland) was coopted by a patriarchal system hostile to women and nature; and, finally, in both systems this mother archetype was virginized.

7. The link between the Templars, the Grail, and the cult of the Virgin can be traced back to "Bernardus" (biographer and friend of St. Malachy), the authority on Christian doctrine to whom Stephen refers in "Oxen of the Sun" when he points to the apple, Eve's "penny pippin," as the emblem of the fall (*U* 14.299-301). St. Bernard was not only personally responsible for the phenomenal increase in the popularity of the cult of the Virgin which took place in the twelfth century, but, primarily, through his eighty-six sermons on Solomon's "Song of Songs" (*U* 17.729-30), he lent doctrinal authority to the beliefs put forward by one of the leaders of the First Crusade—the Muslim Prester John (*U* 12.190)—beliefs that linked the Temple of Solomon with the Grail. "Salmonson," as Joyce puts it in *Finnegans Wake,* "set his seel on a hexengown" (297.3-4). Bernard himself preached the Second Crusade and wrote the rule of the Order of the Templars, commending the celibate warrior Knights (who took their name from the Temple of Solomon) to the protection of the Virgin in their bloody quest for the New Jerusalem, the *Visio Pacis* flowing with milk and honey. The last depository of the Templar tradition in the twentieth century, as Arthur Edward Waite points out, is the Masonic order, an all male sect (to which Bloom, it seems, also belongs) whose avowed vocation it is to use mathematics to rebuild Solomon's Temple of the soul (235-9). In fact, it is precisely here, in this Faustian quest to control nature and create a New Jerusalem of the spirit, that Molly's two male protectors, her Templar father and her Mason husband, find common ground.

On St. Bernard's influence on the Grail legend see Cleland 39-61. On St. Bernard and the cult of the Virgin, see Julia Kristeva's "Stabat Mater" in *The Kristeva Reader.*

Works Cited

Bakhtin, M. M. *The Dialogic Imagination.* Trans. Caryl Emerson and Michael Holquist. Ed. Michael Holquist. Austin: University of Texas Press, 1981.

Barber, Richard. *The Arthurian Legends.* New York: Bedrick, 1979.

Bayley, Harold. *The Lost Language of Symbolism.* Secaucus, N.J.: Citadel, 1988.

Brown, Arthur C. L. *The Origin of the Grail Legend.* 1943. Rpt. New York: Russell, 1966.

Celtia: A Pan Celtic Monthly Magazine. [Dublin.] 111:8 (October 1903).

Cleland, John. "Bernardian Ideas in Wolfram's *Parzival* about Christian War and Human Development." *The Chimera of His Age: Studies on Bernard of Clairvaux.* Cistercian Studies Series 63. Kalamazoo, Mich.: Cistercian, 1980.

Condren, Mary. *The Serpent and the Goddess: Women, Religion, and Power in Celtic Ireland.* San Francisco: Harper, 1989.

The Crane Bag 4.1 (1980).

Daim, Wilfried. *Der Mann, der Hitler die Ideen gab.* Vienna: Institut für politische Psychologie, 1958.

Deane, Seamus. *A Short History of Irish Literature.* London: Hutchinson, 1986.

Ellmann, Richard. *The Consciousness of Joyce.* London: Faber, 1977.

———. *Yeats: The Man and the Masks.* 1948. New York: Dutton, 1958.

Evans, Sebastian, trans. *The High History of the Holy Graal.* London: Dent, 1910.

Hutchinson, John. *The Dynamics of Cultural Nationalism: The Gaelic Revival and the Creation of the Irish Nation State.* London: Allen, 1987.

Joyce, James. *The Critical Writings of James Joyce.* Ed. Ellsworth Mason and Richard Ellmann. New York: Viking, 1959.

———. *Finnegans Wake.* New York: Viking, 1939.

———. *"A Portrait of the Artist as a Young Man": Text, Criticism, and Notes.* Ed. Chester G. Anderson. New York: Viking, 1968.

———. *Ulysses: The Corrected Text.* Ed. Hans Walter Gabler et al. New York: Random, 1986.

Jung, Emma, and Marie-Louise von Franz. *The Grail Legend.* 2nd edn. Trans. Andrea Dykes. Boston: Sigo, 1986.

Kristeva, Julia. *The Kristeva Reader.* Ed. Toril Moi. Oxford: Blackwell, 1986.

Mac Cana, Proinsias. *Celtic Mythology.* Harmondsworth: Newnes, 1983.

MacKillop, James. *Fionn mac Cumhaill: Celtic Myth in English Literature.* Syracuse, N.Y.: Syracuse University Press, 1986.

Mac Mathúna, Séamus. *Immram Brain: Bran's Journey to the Otherworld.* Tübingen: Niemeyer, 1983.

Mac Neill, Eoin, ed. and trans. *Duanaire Finn I: The Book of the Lays of Fionn.* Irish Texts Society 7. London: Nutt, 1908.

Meyer, Kuno, and Alfred Nutt. *The Voyage of Bran.* 2 vols. Grimm Library Series. London: Nutt, 1895-7.

Nutt, Alfred. *Studies in the Legend of the Holy Grail.* London: Nutt, 1897.

O'Brien, Conor Cruise. "A Lost Chance to Save the Jews." *New York Review of Books* 27 April 1989: 27+.

O'Curry, Eugene. *Lectures on the Manuscript Materials of Ancient Irish History.* 1873. Rpt. *Celtic Review* 1 (1904-5).

Raine, Kathleen. *Yeats the Initiate: Essays on Certain Themes in the Work of W. B. Yeats.* London: Allen, 1986.

Rhys, John. *Lectures on the Origin and Growth of Religion as Illustrated by Celtic Heathendom: The Hibbert Lectures for 1886.* London: Williams, 1888.

Taylor, Beverly, and Elisabeth Brewer. *The Return of King Arthur: British and American Arthurian Literature since 1900.* Totowa, N.J.: Barnes, 1983.

Thornton, Weldon. *Allusions in "Ulysses": An Annotated List.* Chapel Hill: University of North Carolina Press, 1968.

Waite, Arthur Edward. *A New Encyclopaedia of Freemasonry.* London: Rider, 1921.

Walker, Barbara G. *The Woman's Dictionary of Symbols and Sacred Objects.* San Francisco: Harper, 1988.

Weston, Jessie L. *From Ritual to Romance.* Garden City, N.Y.: Doubleday, 1957.

Whitmont, Edward C. *The Return of the Goddess.* New York: Crossroad, 1987.

Yeats, William Butler. *Memoirs.* Ed. Denis Donoghue. London: Macmillan, 1972.

———. *Mythologies.* London: Macmillan, 1959.

Young, Robert, ed. *Untying the Text: A Post-Structuralist Reader.* Boston: Routledge, 1981.

ABBREVIATIONS

Quotations from the following works are cited in the text, parenthetically:

CW Joyce, James. *The Critical Writings of James Joyce.* Ed. Ellsworth Mason and Richard Ellmann. New York: Viking, 1959.

FW Joyce, James. *Finnegans Wake.* New York: Viking, 1939.

P Joyce, James. *A Portrait of the Artist as a Young Man.* New York: Viking, 1964.

Joyce, James. *"A Portrait of the Artist as a Young Man": Text, Criticism, and Notes.* Ed. Chester G. Anderson. New York: Viking, 1968.

U Joyce, James. *Ulysses: A Critical and Synoptic Edition.* Ed. Hans Walter Gabler with Wolfhard Steppe and Claus Melchior. 3 vols. New York: Garland, 1986.

Joyce, James. *Ulysses: The Corrected Text.* Ed. Hans Walter Gabler with Wolfhard Steppe and Claus Melchior. New York: Random; London: Bodley Head; Harmondsworth: Penguin, 1986

Passages from *Ulysses,* following its editor's suggestion, are identified by episode and line number. Sections of *Finnegans Wake* are identified by book (roman numeral) and chapter (arabic), as in "II.4." Quotations from the *Wake* are identified by page and line number—"313.21-35"—except that lines in footnotes in II.2 are numbered separately. Thus, "*FW* 279fn.21" designates the twenty-first line of footnoted material on page 279 of *Finnegans Wake. The James Joyce Archive* and the *Letters of James Joyce* are cited by volume and page number.

These conventions follow, with minor exceptions, the format prescribed by the *James Joyce Quarterly.*

Raymond M. Olderman (essay date 1992)

SOURCE: Olderman, Raymond M. "The Grail Knight Arrives: Ken Kesey, *One Flew Over the Cuckoo's Nest.*" In *A Casebook on Ken Kesey's 'One Flew Over the Cuckoo's Nest,'* edited by George J. Searles, pp. 67-79. Albuquerque: University of New Mexico Press, 1992.

[*In the following essay, Olderman examines Ken Kesey's novel as a "brilliant version of our contemporary wasteland and a successful Grail Knight" who frees both the Fisher King and the human spirit in an act of affirmation and release.*]

Randle Patrick McMurphy sweeps into the asylum wasteland of Ken Kesey's *One Flew Over the Cuckoo's Nest* like April coming to T. S. Eliot's wasteland: "mixing / Memory and desire, stirring / Dull roots with spring rain." He literally drags the unwilling asylum wastelanders out of the tranquilized fog that protects them—a fog that is forever "snowing down cold and white all over,"[1] where they try to hide "in forgetful snow, feeding / A little life with dried tubers." And, by dragging them from their retreat, he cures the Fisher King, Chief Bromden—a six-foot-eight-inch giant from a tribe of "fish Injuns," who is wounded, like all other wastelanders, in his manhood. The cure takes hold most dramatically on a fishing trip when McMurphy supplies the Chief and eleven other disciples with drink for their thirst, a woman for their desires, stimulation for their memories, and some badly needed self-respect for their shriveled souls—and all this despite the fact that the Chief "fears death by water." ("Afraid I'd step in over my head and drown, be sucked off down the drain and clean out to sea. I used to be real brave around water when I was a kid" [p. 169].) The silent Chief's voice is restored and he becomes the prophet who narrates the tale, while the false prophet—the enemy, the Big Nurse, Madam Sosostris, who has the "movement of a tarot-card reader in a glass arcade case" (p. 188)—is deprived of her voice in the last moments of the book.

The tale takes place in the ward of an insane asylum where an iron-minded, frost-hearted nurse rules by means of one twentieth-century version of brutality—mental and spiritual debilitation. Her patients are hopeless "Chronics" and "Vegetables," or they are "Acutes" who do not, according to McMurphy, seem "any crazier than the average asshole on the street" (p. 63). McMurphy comes to the asylum from a prison work farm. He has been a logger, a war hero, a gambler, and generally a happy, heavily muscled, self-made drifter and tough guy. A contest develops between McMurphy (whose initials, R. P. M., urge us to note his power) and the Big Nurse (whose name, Ratched, tips us off about her mechanical nature as well as her offensive function as a "ball-cutter"). The implications of the contest deepen; it becomes a battle pitting the individual against all those things that make up the modern wasteland, for the Nurse represents singly what the institution and its rules really are. The drama of the battle is intense, and the action seesaws as McMurphy gradually discovers he must give his strength to others in order to pry loose the Big Nurse's hold on their manhood. As they gain in health, McMurphy weakens, and his ultimate victory over the Big Nurse is a mixed one. He is lobotomized, a "castration of the frontal lobes," but he gives his lifeblood to Chief Bromden who breaks free and leaves behind in the Nurse and the Institution not a destroyed power, but a shrunken, silent, and temporarily short-circuited one. Beautifully structured, the novel provides us with both a brilliant version of our contemporary wasteland and a successful Grail Knight, who frees the Fisher King and the human spirit for a single symbolic and transcendent moment of affirmation.

The world of this wasteland is mechanically controlled from a central panel, as the narrator sees it, so that everything in it is run by tiny electrical wires or installed machinery. People are often robots or are made of electric tubing and wiring and springs, as the "adjusted" ones seem to be. The Big Nurse is only one agent of a "Combine" which rules all things, including time and the heart and mind of man. *Combine,* as the word implies, is not just an organization; it is a mechanism, a machine that threshes and levels; its ends are Efficiency and Adjustment. According to Chief Bromden, the Combine had gone a long way in doing things to gain total control,

> *things like, for example—a* train *stopping at a station and laying a string of full-grown men in mirrored suits and machine hats, laying them like a hatch of identical insects, half-life things coming pht-pht-pht out of the last car, then hooting its electric whistle and moving on down the spoiled land to deposit another hatch.*
>
> (p. 227-28)

Those are the adjusted ones. The ones who cannot adjust are sent to the asylum to have things installed so that the Combine can keep them in line.

> *The ward is a factory for the Combine. It's for fixing up mistakes made in the neighborhoods and in the schools and the churches, the hospital is. When a completed product goes back out into society, all fixed up good as new,* better *than new sometimes, it brings joy to the Big Nurse's heart; something that came in all twisted different is now a functioning, adjusted component, a credit to the whole outfit and a marvel to behold. Watch him sliding across the land with a welded grin, fitting into some nice little neighborhood.*
>
> (p. 38)

He is a "Dismissal," spiritually and morally empty, but "happy" and adjusted. If you do not fit, you are a malfunctioning machine—

> *machines with flaws inside that can't be repaired, flaws born in, or flaws beat in over so many years of the guy running head-on into solid things that by the time the hospital found him he was bleeding rust in some vacant lot.*
>
> (p. 4)

That is what is called a "Chronic." Some people do escape in a way. People like McMurphy who keep moving, and people like Pete Bancini who are just too simple, are missed by the Combine, and if they are lucky, they can get hidden and stay missed.

All this is only the view of the narrator, a paranoid Indian. But there is enough evidence in the way the world around Chief Bromden runs to make his terms more and more acceptable as the novel progresses. Among the few characters on the "Outside" that Kesey takes the time to describe is one of the insulting loafers who taunt the patients while they wait to board their boat for the fishing trip. The man is described as having "purple under his eyes," the same kind of purple that appears under the eyes of all the ward's finished, lobotomized products. There is, at least for a moment, a frightening suggestion that the Combine's inmates may truly be everywhere. For Chief Bromden, it is no madman's logic—after seeing the actual persecution of his father, family, and tribe by the U.S. Department of the Interior—to posit a large central organization that seeks the doom of all things different.

The wasteland of the asylum is characterized not only by mechanization and efficiency but by sterility, hopelessness, fear, and guilt. The inmates are aimless, alienated, and bored; they long for escape; they "can connect / Nothing with Nothing," not even picture puzzles; they are enervated and emasculated; their dignity is reduced to something less than human. Most of all, they are run as the asylum is run—by women; it is a "matriarchy," and behind almost every ruined man is a grasping, castrating female whose big bosom belies her sterility but reveals a smothering momism. So, McMurphy perceives almost immediately that Big Nurse Ratched is pecking at their "everlovin' balls." But the same has been true of Harding's wife, and Chief Bromden's mother, and Billy Bibbit's mother—and these are just about the only women we see in the novel, except a couple of sweet whores named Candy and Sandy. However, what is more startling about this terrible world is its leveling sense of order and its rules. In one incident McMurphy wants to brush his teeth before the proper teeth-brushing time. He is told that the toothpaste is locked up. After questioning the aide about what possible harm anyone could do with a tube of toothpaste, he is advised that the toothpaste is locked up because it is the rule, and rules are rules. After all, what would happen if everyone just started brushing his teeth whenever he had a mind to. Kesey's point by this time is clear; the true madness, the real dry root of the wasteland is not the patient's irrationality, but the deadly order, system, and rationality of the institution. What is normal is perverted, and reason becomes madness, while some small hope for salvation lies in the nonrational if not the downright irrational.

The institution's general significance and its effect on humanity come together in the single person of the Big Nurse, who causes the patients' hopelessness, their inadequacy, fear, anxiety, and alienation. She is the institution itself, the wasteland personified. White and starched stiff, she suggests Melville's plunge into the dreadful ambiguity and possible evil that could live in the heart of what is white. (McMurphy wears fancy shorts with jumping white whales on them, given to him by an Oregon State coed who called him a "symbol.") But with the Big Nurse the ambiguity is only superficial and thrives only on the name of respectability—her real villainy is clear. She is the enemy, the "Belladonna," obstacle to the Grail Knight. She enervates her patients by playing upon their fears, guilts, and inadequacies. She and all other castrators are

> people who try to make you weak so they can get you to toe the line, to follow their rules, to live like they want you to. And the best way to do this, to get you to knuckle under, is to weaken you by gettin' you where it hurts the worst.
>
> (p. 58)

She is relentless in her crippling pity and capable of using any weapon in order to preserve her control. She has handpicked her aides, three shadowy and sadistic black men who are hooked to her by electrical impulses of hate. They have been twisted by white brutality, and their response is savage. As weapons in the Big Nurse's arsenal, they serve as symbols of the force of guilt, which she uses to torment her patients. Guilt and the black man twine identities in the white mind to cut deeper into its already vitiated self-respect.

The Big Nurse is continually pictured in images of frost or machinery, or as a crouching, swelling beast. She is described as a collection of inert materials: plastic, porcelain—any of modern America's favorite respectable synthetics.

> *Her face is smooth, calculated, and precision-made, like an expensive baby doll, skin like flesh-colored enamel, blend of white and cream and baby-blue eyes, small nose, pink little nostrils—everything working together except the color on her lips and fingernails, and the size of her bosom.*
>
> (p. 5)

She is sexless and cold enough to halt McMurphy's lecture on how a man can always win out over a woman; she is "impregnable" in almost every sense, even by so vaunted a "whambam" as McMurphy.

> *What she dreams of there in the center of those wires is a world of precision efficiency and tidiness like a pocket watch with a glass back, a place where the schedule is unbreakable and all the patients who aren't Outside, obedient under her beam, are wheelchair Chronics with catheter tubes run direct from every pant-leg to the sewer under the floor.*
>
> (p. 17)

She controls clock time, has all the rules on her side, and uses insinuation like a torture rack. Fear, cowardice, and timidity are all she sees in man. She sums up all that is debilitating to the individual about a modern world of massive institutions. In wasteland terms, she is the keeper of the keys, the false prophet; for not only is she the cause of enervation and division, but she also perverts the holy words that are the key to coping with the wasteland. When she gives, she emasculates; when she sympathizes, she reduces; and when she controls, she destroys. McMurphy, the Grail Knight, the savior, not only must contest her power, but must listen to, learn how to live by, and restore the true meaning of the holy words from "What the Thunder Said": Give, Sympathize, Control.

The narrative movement of the novel is built around McMurphy's growth in knowledge and his progress toward curing Chief Bromden. As he learns to give and to sympathize, he moves toward death while the Chief moves toward rebirth, "blown-up" to full size by McMurphy's sacrifice and gift of self-control. At the beginning we are given two images foreshadowing McMurphy's fate: Ellis, the patient who stands like an empty Christ, arms outstretched in tortured crucifixion, fixed that way by an electric shock machine used as a weapon of the institution; and Ruckly, blanked of all but mindless, obscene answers and beaten by the trump card of the institution—lobotomy—beaten as a means of dealing with his rebellion. McMurphy will also be personally beaten, crucified, and lobotomized, because there is no final victory over the Big Nurse and her wasteland; she will continue just as Eliot's wasteland continues after the rain that falls.

> *She's too big to be beaten. She covers one whole side of the room like a Jap statue. There's no moving her and no help against her. She's lost a little battle here today, but it's a minor battle in a big war that she's been winning and that she'll go on winning . . . just like the Combine, because she has all the power of the Combine behind her.*
>
> (p. 109)

But the little battle she loses is enough to cure the Chief and bring a little rain to a parched land.

Ironically, McMurphy enters the asylum supposedly on a request for "transfer" to get "new blood" for his poker games, but from that very entrance, as he laughs, winks, and goes around shaking limp hands, it is he that does the transferring and the giving of blood. The first foretelling of his effect on Chief Bromden comes as McMurphy seizes the Chief's hand.

> *That palm made a scuffing sound against my hand. I remember the fingers were thick and strong closing over mine, and my hand commenced to feel peculiar and went to swelling up out there on my stick of an arm, like he was transmitting his own blood into it. It rang with blood and power. It blowed up near as big as his.*
>
> (pp. 23-24)

He brings contact, the human touch, to a place sterilized of all but inverted relationships. His giving and his sacrifice are not, however, a continuous unbroken process, but are correlated to his learning. He launches into full battle with the Big Nurse and begins pulling the patients out of their tranquilized fog. His first assault reaches its peak in the contest over TV privileges.

McMurphy strengthens the other men enough to rebel in unison against the Big Nurse, and he does it by the symbolic gesture of attempting to lift a massive "control panel." It is a symbol of his resistance and willingness to keep trying even when he is going to be beaten, even when he *knows* he is going to be beaten. The strain on him is balanced by his effect on the men and on Chief Bromden in particular. The Chief asserts himself for the first time. He raises his hand to join the vote against the Big Nurse and recognizes that no external power is controlling him—he himself has lifted his own arm expressing his own decision. This first sign of self-control, inspired by McMurphy's struggle with the control panel, leads the Chief out of his fog and out of his safety; he ceases to be the blind, impotent Tiresias and begins literally to see again. Waking up late at night, he looks out a window and sees clearly, without hallucination—something he has been unable to do since he has been in the asylum. What he sees, on another level, is that McMurphy has succeeded in being himself, that it is possible to be yourself without hiding and without the Combine getting you. But just as the Chief makes this discovery, McMurphy learns what it really means to be "committed" in this asylum, and he faces the temptation that is hazard to any Grail Knight—the temptation to quit.

Learning that most of the patients are "voluntary," that he is one of the few "committed," and that the duration of his commitment is to be determined by the Big Nurse, McMurphy becomes "cagey" (an ominous word in this mechanized world). He promptly ceases giving and ceases sympathizing. The immediate result is an assertion of the wasteland—Cheswick, one of the patients dependent on McMurphy, drowns himself. Without resistance from the Grail Knight, the wasteland perverts water, the symbol of fertility, into the medium of death.

But the demands made on McMurphy by the weaker inmates determine his return to battle, for the weak are driven to the wasteland by "Guilt. Shame. Fear. Self-belittlement" (p. 294), while the strong are driven by the needs of the weak. As the Chief ultimately realizes, McMurphy is driven by the inmates, and this drive

> *had been making him go on for weeks, keeping him standing long after his feet and legs had given out, weeks of making him wink and grin and laugh and go on with his act long after his humor had been parched dry between two electrodes.*
>
> (pp. 304-5)

To signal his renewed challenge to the institution and his acceptance of commitment, McMurphy stands up at what looks like the Big Nurse's decisive victory, strides mightily across the ward, "the iron in his bootheels cracking lightning out of the tile," and runs his fist through the Big Nurse's enormous glass window, shattering her dry hold as "the glass comes apart like water splashing" (p. 190). McMurphy knows where his gesture will lead; he was told in the very beginning that making trouble—breaking windows and similar actions—will lead him to crucifixion on the shock table and destruction by lobotomy.

What McMurphy has learned is the secret of "What the Thunder Said," for, as one critic of Eliot's poem explained it:

> *If we can learn to give of ourselves and to live in sympathetic identification with others, perhaps we may also learn the art of self-control and thereby prepare ourselves to take on the most difficult of responsibilities: that of giving directions ourselves, of controlling our destinies and perhaps those of others, as an expert helmsman controls a ship.*[2]

McMurphy, as helmsman, leads his twelve followers, including Chief Bromden, aboard a ship and on a fishing trip where, through his active sympathy, he gives them the gift of life so that they may gain control of their own destinies. The fishing trip—considering that fish are traditional mystical symbols of fertility—is the central incident in McMurphy's challenge to the wasteland. What he gives to the men is drained from his own lifeblood, and the path of his descent to weariness is crossed by Chief Bromden "pumped up" to full size, the cured Fisher King. And at that point, we are told "the wind was blowing a few drops of rain" (p. 294). "*Damyata:* The boat responded / Gaily, to the hand expert with sail and oar."

McMurphy gives the men not only self-confidence and a renewed sense of virility, but also what Kesey sees as man's only weapon against the wasteland—laughter. There has been no laughter in the asylum; McMurphy notices that immediately and comments, "when you lose your laugh you lose your *footing*" (p. 68). By the end of the fishing trip McMurphy has everyone laughing "because he knows you have to laugh at the things that hurt you just to keep yourself in balance, just to keep the world from running you plumb crazy" (pp. 237-38). In effect, he teaches the men to be black humorists, and it is the vision and the balance of black humor that Kesey attempts to employ as a stay against the wasteland. To Kesey, being human and having control means being able to laugh, for the rational, ordered world has done us in, and only an insurgence of energy from the irrational can break through the fear and sterility that have, paradoxically, made the world go mad. It is ultimately their laughter that the men cram down the Big Nurse's maw in their brief moment of victory.

In the final section of the book, McMurphy works with growing fatigue and resignation toward his inevitable sacrifice. He battles with the Nurse's aides, gets repeated shock treatments, has a chance to capitulate to the Big Nurse and refuses, returns from the cruelty of the shock table to the ward where he is faced with the charge of mixed and ulterior motives, and finally holds his mad vigil in the upside-down world of the Chapel Perilous. But madness here is antiorder, and so a sign of health. The scene is the night of Billy Bibbit's lost virginity. McMurphy and his followers run wild, completely subverting the order of the Big Nurse's ward and violating the sanctity of all rules. Billy's entrance into manhood symbolizes the inmates' initiation into the final mysteries of life and fertility. All this is as it should be during and following a vigil in the Chapel Perilous. But, as we already know, you cannot beat the Big Nurse. She regains her power by cowing Billy with shame and forcing him to betray his deliverer. Billy, broken again, slits his throat, and the Big Nurse attempts one last time to turn guilt against McMurphy. His response is the ultimate sacrificial gesture; he rips open her dress, exposing her mountainous and smothering breasts, and chokes her—not able to kill her, but only to weaken and silence her. The contest ends in violence, the individual's last offense against the immensities that oppress him. Kesey, like John Hawkes, finds something ultimately necessary and cleansing about violence.

At McMurphy's fall,

> *he gave a cry. At the last, falling backward, his face appearing to us for a second upside down before he was smothered on the floor by a pile of white uniforms, he let himself cry out: a sound of cornered-animal fear and hate and surrender and defiance.*
>
> (p. 305)

It was the only sound and the only sign that "he might be anything other than a sane willful, dogged man performing a hard duty" (p. 305). His madness is all the salvation the twentieth century can muster, for to give and to sympathize in our kind of wasteland is itself a sign of madness. McMurphy is lobotomized, and in the final moments of the book, Chief Bromden snuffs out the life of the body connected to that already dead spirit and, with his gift of life, seizes the huge "control panel" McMurphy had blown him up to lift, then spins it through the asylum window. "The glass splashed out in the moon, like a bright cold water baptizing the sleeping earth" (p. 310). The Fisher King is free. Although the wasteland remains, McMurphy, the redheaded Grail Knight, has symbolically transcended it through his gesture of sacrifice, and at least allowed others to "come in under the shadow of this red rock."

One Flew Over the Cuckoo's Nest is a modern fable that pits a fabulous use of many of the traditional devices of American romance. For example, the novel emphasizes plot and action (not character), and it employs myth, allegory, and symbol. There are equally obvious points of contact between the themes of Kesey's book and traditional American themes, such as the rebellion against old orders and old hierarchies, and the need for communal effort in the face of an alien and overwhelmingly negative force. *Cuckoo's Nest* is closely tied to American tradition, yet there is much in it that offers a paradigm for what is different about the characteristic vision in the American novel of the 1960s. It does not return to the past, gaze toward the future, or travel to the unknown to get its "romance" setting. The setting is the static institution which sums up both the preoccupation of our age with the mystery of power, and the substitution of an image of the wasteland for the image of a journey between Eden and Utopia. It is shot through with the vitality of its use of the here and now. We are constantly shocked into discovering how the book is really tied to the recognizable, not to the distant or strange, but to our very own world—to the technology we know, the clichés we use, the atmosphere possible only in the atomic tension of our times. Just as no one can confidently say who is mad and who is not in Kesey's novel, no one can say in what sense his story is real and in what sense it is fiction. The narrator sounds a note that echoes everywhere in the sixties:

> *You think this is too horrible to have really happened, this is too awful to be the truth! But please. It's still hard for me to have a clear mind thinking on it. But it's the truth even if it didn't happen.*
>
> (p. 8)

The romance elements in the book are not based on devices that whisk us away to some "theatre, a little removed from the highway of ordinary travel,"[3] and then whisk us back fueled up with truth. We suspect with horror that what we are seeing very possibly *is* our highway of ordinary travel, fantastic as it may seem.

The romance elements in *One Flew Over the Cuckoo's Nest* are inspired by a world vision which questions the sanity of fact. It is a cartoon and comic-strip world—where a man's muscles can be "blown-up" like Popeye's arms after a taste of spinach—"a cartoon world, where the figures are flat and outlined in black, jerking through some kind of goofy story that might be real funny if it weren't for the cartoon figures being real guys" (p. 31). Not only is this a good image of Kesey's world, but it supplies the pattern for his character development. The movement from being a cartoon figure to becoming a painfully real guy is exemplified by Billy Bibbit. His name and his personality are reminiscent of comic-strip character Billy Batson, a little crippled kid, weak and helpless, who could say "Shazam" and turn into Captain Marvel. And just when Billy Bibbit stops being a little crippled kid, after the comic-book fun of his tumble with Candy, just when his "Whambam" Shazam should turn him into this big, powerful, unbeatable Captain Marvel, the Big Nurse turns him into a real guy—a Judas, in fact, who proceeds from betrayal to slitting his very real throat.[4] While Kesey attempts to employ the mode of black humor, and while he does see the value of laughter in coping with the wasteland, one suspects that he is more pained and embittered by the "real guy" than a black humorist can afford to be. His humor often loses that fine edge between pain and laughter that we see in Elkin, Vonnegut, Barth, and Pynchon, while his "flat" portrayal of women and of blacks is more stereotypic and uncomfortable than funny or appropriate to his cartoon-character pattern. It borders too much on the simplistic.

The romance elements also revolve around our new version of mystery. Though we may certainly be tempted to call it paranoia, it is definitely a part of the equipment of our times, and it is undoubtedly malevolent. The Big Nurse, the Combine, the asylum—all three seem to symbolize that immense power that reduces us, and that seems to be mysteriously unlocatable. Kesey is one of those writers of the sixties who explore some mystery about fact itself that portends mostly defeat for man. This sense of mystery adds complexity to the paradoxes of what is mad and sane, real and unreal, for it drives us to seek its heart in some huge force conspiring against us. Although it arises in connection with the image of the wasteland, this mystery is the antipathy of Eliot's hoped-for God. It is only a further cause of divisive fear.

The mystery is best represented, to Kesey, by the asylum itself, but he leaves us with two possible locations of the mystery's source. It could be located somewhere external to us, as Chief Bromden sees it, or, as McMurphy tries to explain, maybe blaming it on a Combine is "just passing the buck." It may really be our own "deep-down hang-up that's causing the gripes" (p. 181). Perhaps there is some big bad wolf—and then perhaps there is only us. In the past, the essential shock in American fictional experience has been a character's discovery that deep down he too is capable of evil; the shock in the sixties is the character's discovery that deep down he may be a source of unrelenting insanity. Down there, perhaps, that unknowable and seemingly immense power against us comes into being and then mounts to become a world gone mad. Against or within that shock, the writer, the prophet, sees new paradoxes of reason and irrationality, fact and mystery, and writes his novels no longer sure of what is fact or fiction, nor whether malevolence lies within or without. His only possible rationale is this one, voiced by a Kesey character:

> *These things don't happen.... These things are fantasies you lie awake at night dreaming up and then are afraid to tell your analyst. You're not* really *here. That wine isn't real;* none *of this exists. Now, let's go on from there.*
>
> (p. 285)

Notes

Originally published in *Beyond the Waste Land: The American Novel in the Nineteen-Sixties* (Yale University Press, 1972), pp. 35-51. Copyright 1972, Yale University, New Haven, CT 06520.

1. Ken Kesey, *One Flew Over the Cuckoo's Nest* (New York: Viking, 1962), p. 7. All subsequent references are to this edition, and are parenthesized within the text.

2. Kimon Friar and John Malcolm Brinin, eds., *Modern Poetry* (New York: Appleton-Century-Crofts, 1951), p. 472.

3. Nathaniel Hawthorne, "Preface" to *Blithedale Romance* (New York: Norton, 1958), p. 27.

4. Kesey actually refers directly to the "Captain Marvel" comic strip in a long discussion in his second novel *Sometimes a Great Notion* (New York: Viking, 1964), p. 142-43.

Bibliography

In compiling this bibliography, I have consulted the *MLA International Bibliography* for the years 1962-1989, along with the following:

Bischoff, Joan. "Views and Reviews: An Annotated Bibliography." *Lex et Scientia: The International Journal of Law and Science.* Perspectives on a Cuckoo's Nest: A Special Symposium Issue on Ken Kesey, edited by Peter G. Beidler and John W. Hunt. 13.1-2 (1977): 93-103.

Carnes, Bruce. "Selected Bibliography." In *Ken Kesey,* 47-50. Boise State University Western Writers Series, 12. Boise, ID: Boise State University, 1974.

Frank, Robert. "Ken Kesey." In *Fifty Western Writers: A Bio-Bibliographical Sourcebook,* edited by Fred Erisman and Richard Etulain, 246-56. Westport, CT: Greenwood Press, 1982.

Leeds, Barry H. "Bibliography." In *Ken Kesey,* 125-27. Modern Literature Series. New York: Ungar, 1981.

Tanner, Stephen L. "Selected Bibliography." In *Ken Kesey,* 150-54. Twayne's United States Authors Series. Boston: Twayne, 1983.

Weixlmann, Joseph. "Ken Kesey: A Bibliography." *Western American Literature* 10 (1975): 219-31.

———. "Selected Bibliography." In *One Flew Over the Cuckoo's Nest: Text and Criticism,* edited by John C. Pratt, 559-67. The Viking Critical Library. New York: Viking, 1976.

I have omitted interviews, biographical studies, reviews, articles in popular periodicals, unpublished doctoral dissertations, and treatments of Kesey's works other than *One Flew Over the Cuckoo's Nest.* I have also excluded the pieces reprinted in this volume. To the best of my knowledge, however, this bibliography is complete with respect to other scholarly articles and book chapters.

By necessity, the individual entries repeatedly refer to Kesey and to his books and characters. For the sake of simplicity, I have abbreviated those references as follows: Kesey is K, McMurphy is M, Chief Bromden is B, Nurse Ratched is R; *One Flew Over the Cuckoo's Nest* is *CN*, *Sometimes a Great Notion* is *SGN*, and *Kesey's Garage Sale* is *GS*.

D. G. Kehl and Allene Cooper (essay date 1993)

SOURCE: Kehl, D. G., and Allene Cooper. "Sangria in the Sangreal: *The Great Gatsby* as Grail Quest." *Rocky Mountain Review of Language and Literature* 47, no. 4 (1993): 203-17.

[*In the following essay, Kehl and Cooper explore F. Scott Fitzgerald's fascination with Arthurian myths, focusing on his use of the Grail legend in* The Great Gatsby *in particular.*]

Near the end of Fitzgerald's *This Side of Paradise*, Amory Blaine, returning to Princeton after his disillusioning sojourn in Atlantic City, concludes that he knows one thing: "If living isn't a seeking for the grail it may be a damned amusing game" (278). For Fitzgerald, by the time he wrote *The Great Gatsby* five years later, living had become both a quest for the grail and "a damned amusing game," with emphasis sometimes on the quest and sometimes on the game. It took Fitzgerald another eleven years and a "crack-up" to verbalize the paradox: "The test of a first-rate intelligence is the ability to hold two opposed ideas in the mind at the same time, and still retain the ability to function" (*The Crack Up* 69). Jay Gatsby "found that he had committed himself to the following of a grail" (149). The grail, personified in Daisy Buchanan, is paradoxically beautiful and romantic but also, like the cut-glass bowl in Fitzgerald's 1920 story with that title, hard, empty, and, at least for Nick, "easy to see through" (*Flappers and Philosophers* 97).

Fitzgerald's interest in the quest tale has been noted. For example, James E. Miller has discussed *This Side of Paradise* as a "quest book" (16-22), and Edwin M. Moseley has commented on *Gatsby* as "a prose 'Waste Land'" with Nick as "modern quester" (31). Several other studies have made passing references to the grail motif in *Gatsby*, perhaps the most pertinent being K. G. Probert's limited discussion in "Nick Carraway and the Romance of Art." Probert, however, failing to grasp Fitzgerald's paradox, faults both Gatsby and Nick, the former for transforming "highminded romance impulses into mere gangsterism" and the latter for voyeuristically "distort[ing] the story of Gatsby in order to affirm his own unrealistic and childish nostalgia" (204, 206). Fitzgerald's early and lasting fascination with the Arthurian romance, perhaps surpassed among modern American writers only by that of John Steinbeck, is little recognized, nor has the ambivalent function of the grail quest in *The Great Gatsby* been examined.

"Did you ever read The Passing of Arthur?" Josephine asks Mr. Bailey in Fitzgerald's "A Snobbish Story" (*The Basil and Josephine Stories,* 253). The reference to *Idylls of the King*, in which Tennyson first included the Grail story in 1869, is perhaps the best clue to Fitzgerald's source of the Grail Quest story. Of the many versions composed between the 8th and early 20th centuries, those most familiar include Chrétien de Troyes's story of Perceval in *Li Contes del Grail* (1160-1185), Malory's *The Tale of the Sankgreal* (1460-1470), and Wolfram von Eschenbach's *Parzival* (1200-1207). Other possible sources include those versions made available by the resurgence of interest in medieval lore in the 19th century that prompted Tennyson and Wagner to write their works on the Grail (Loomis 3).

It is unlikely that Fitzgerald was familiar with Chrétien de Troyes because his *Perceval* was not available in

Photograph of F. Scott Fitzgerald.

English until 1952 (Linker vii). Although Vinaver's 1954 edition of Caxton's Malory is the definitive text today, it is most likely that Fitzgerald knew one of the popular editions of the late 19th and early 20th centuries. Larry Benson, in his review of Malory editions, holds that Pollard's abridged 1900 edition was probably the most popular version from 1900 to 1947 and that "for the last third of the nineteenth century [the reader] will have to consult Strachey's bowdlerized version" (89-90).

Wolfram's German grail legend may have been available to Fitzgerald in the only English translation at the time, Jessie L. Weston's 1894 edition (Zeydel vii). Fitzgerald may also have been acquainted with Wagner's *Parsifal,* his last opera, completed in 1882. Most likely, though, Fitzgerald knew the grail quest story from Tennyson's *Idylls,* likely reading material for him as a student. He may have been introduced to the story by *The Boy's King Arthur,* edited by Sidney Lanier, published in 1880.

That Fitzgerald himself identified with the grail quest knights is clear in a Notebook entry: "As a novelist I reach out to the end of all man's variance, all man's villainy—as a man I do not go that far. I cannot claim honor—but even the knights of the Holy Grail were only striving for it, as I remember" (Bruccoli 324). In reaching out, in questing, for the extremities of the human condition—both the negative, villainy, and the positive, honor—Fitzgerald identified with the quest knights and manifested his ability "to hold two opposed ideas in his mind at the same time and still retain the ability to function." For him, striving, questing, is all.

In addition to the polarities of striving/achieving and negative/positive, the entry presents those of person/artist in worlds of mundane reality/romantic magic. These dichotomies appear in a 1921 story that anticipates *Gatsby* in significant ways—"'O Russet Witch,'" Fitzgerald's second fictional work (after *This Side of Paradise*) to allude to the Arthurian romance. In its reference to the Arthurian tale and its other parallels, this story relates to *Gatsby* in ways perhaps as striking as those noted between "Absolution" and the novel. Appearing originally as "His Russet Witch" in *Metropolitan Magazine* and included the following year in *Tales of the Jazz Age,* the story is about a young man employed by the Moonlight Quill Bookshop in Manhattan, Merlin Grainger, and his "romantic yearning" for the Daisyesque *femme fatale,* Alicia Dare, whose luxurious apartment faces the single window of Merlin's single room. Captivated by her beauty, Merlin watches her through the window, like the prototypical Midwestern boy outside the ballroom with his nose to the glass, and constructs an elaborate romance. One day when she walks into the bookshop, he has "the sense of a breathless second hanging suspended in Time" (*Six Tales* 94). If Daisy's voice was "indiscreet" and "full of money" (*Gatsby* 120) it also conveyed a "warm human magic" (109), a point usually overlooked. Similarly, Alicia's "voice was rich and full of sorcery" (94). As Gatsby watches the green light across the bay, Merlin draws from Alicia's presence a "dazzling essence of light" (96). Then for a week after her visit "her lights failed to go on" (100), in the same way that "when curiosity about Gatsby was at its highest . . . the lights in his house failed to go on" (*Gatsby* 113). Unlike Gatsby, Merlin settles for the plain, mundane Olive Masters, marries her, and fathers a son, fittingly named Arthur. Six years later, in a crowd of people exiting churches on "a radiant, flowerful Easter morning" (108), Merlin catches a glimpse of Alicia, no daisy but "an orchid rising from the black bouquet" of her surroundings (108). Some thirty years later, at sixty-five, he sees her one last time in the Moonlight Quill—"an old woman remarkably preserved, unusually handsome, unusually erect, but still an old woman" (114)—"her voice no more than the echo of a forgotten dream" (116). Unlike Gatsby, Merlin accepts that he cannot repeat the past: "He had angered Providence by resisting too many temptations. There was nothing left but heaven, where he would meet only those who, like him, had wasted earth" (119). Merlin, unlike Gatsby, seeks the magic of romance in books; rather than pursuing the elusive grail, he settles for what Fitzgerald elsewhere calls "the cracked plate" ("Handle with Care," *The Crack Up* 75).

Merlin begets Arthur, but Arthur, too, is "a cracked plate." "Young Arthur was gone into Wall Street to sell bonds [a profession for which Fitzgerald had special disdain], as all young men seemed to be doing in that day. This, of course, was as it should be. Let old Merlin get what magic he could from his books—the place of young King Arthur was in the countinghouse" (*Six Tales* 111). King Arthur in the countinghouse! Where has the Arthurian romance been subjected to such burlesque since Twain's *Connecticut Yankee in King Arthur's Court* (1889)? (In another Notebook entry, Fitzgerald added this postscript to a "bread and butter" letter: "If you called that thing a cocktail then listerine is the Holy Grail" [Bruccoli 270].) Beyond simple burlesque, however, Fitzgerald, in his typical "double vision" manner, presents two aspects of himself and perhaps of the American self: Merlin seeking his magical dream in fantasy but wasting opportunities and settling for the mundane, Arthur seeking a modern desacralized grail of worldly success.

However, Merlin, a nonquester who settles for the mundane, is revived in the character of Jay Gatsby, who is perhaps a composite of King Arthur and Bors/Galahad/Perceval. Gatsby will not accept mundane reality, nor can he accept Nick's insistence that one cannot repeat the past. "'Can't repeat the past?' he cried incredulously. 'Why of course you can!'" (111).[1] It is Nick, of course, who goes East to "learn the bond business" (3), but it is Gatsby who, like Arthur in the story, commits himself to "the service of a vast, vulgar, and meretricious beauty" (99).

It is clear, then, that Fitzgerald had been keenly interested in the Arthurian and grail quest romance for at least six years before he wrote *The Great Gatsby*. Examining the novel in terms of the typical grail quest story illuminates some obscure passages and clarifies some misunderstandings.

In an essay on "The Quest Hero," devoted largely to a discussion of J. R. R. Tolkien's *The Lord of the Rings*, W. H. Auden specified six essential elements of the typical quest story, all of which appear in *Gatsby*:

> 1) A precious Object and/or Person to be found and possessed or married;
>
> 2) A long journey to find it, for its whereabouts are not originally known to the seekers;
>
> 3) A hero. The precious Object cannot be found by anybody, but only by the one person who possesses the right qualities of breeding or character;
>
> 4) A Test or series of Tests by which the unworthy are screened out, and the hero revealed;
>
> 5) The Guardians of the Object who must be overcome before it can be won. They may be simply a further test of the hero's *arete*, or they may be malignant in themselves;
>
> 6) The Helpers who who with their knowledge and magical powers assist the hero and but for whom he would never succeed.
>
> (83)

The precious object or person Gatsby seeks to find, possess, *and* marry is Daisy Buchanan nee Daisy Fay. Her maiden surname invests Daisy with ambiguity: "fay," from Middle English *fai*, means fairy (a cognate of "fate"), in some legends a fairy who lives in a lake among precious treasures; in Arthurian legend the name suggests Morgan le Fay, King Arthur's evil fairy half sister who seeks every opportunity to do him ill. But the name Fay, from Middle English *fei*, means "faith," reminiscent, at least in her ambiguity, of Hawthorne's Faith Brown whose pink ribbons are a combination of passion's scarlet and purity's whiteness.

"High in a white palace [Daisy is] the king's daughter, the golden girl" (120). Even the metonymic green light at the end of her dock becomes one of Gatsby's "enchanted objects" (94). Gatsby "knew that Daisy was extraordinary" (149), the epitome of his romantic ideal, and

> he wanted nothing less of Daisy than that she should go to Tom and say 'I never loved you.' After she had obliterated four years with that sentence they could decide upon the more practical measures to be taken. One of them was that after she was free, they were to go back to Louisville and be married from her house. . . .
>
> (111)

In Celtic tradition the grail as vessel also represented the Female principle of reproductive energy, as the lance or spear represented the Male (Weston, *Ritual* 75). The personification of the grail as Daisy, a woman, to be possessed or married thus fits the legend.

The medieval grail held special properties. Various writers of Fitzgerald's time, perhaps most notably Jessie L. Weston in *The Quest of the Holy Grail* (1913) and Alfred Nutt in *The Legends of the Holy Grail* (1902), both accessible to Fitzgerald at Princeton, and later Weston in *From Ritual to Romance* (1920), describe those properties Fitzgerald included in his own quest tale. "To the romance writers the Grail was something secret, mysterious and awful" (Weston, *Ritual* 138). When Gatsby first visited Daisy in Louisville, "there was a ripe mystery" about her and her house, "an air of breathless intensity," a hint of romances (148).

The Grail was also known for its exquisite beauty and captivating charm, whether a stone as in Wolfram, the gleaming chalice used at the Last Supper, or a silver cup, vase, or dish in which Joseph of Arimathea captured the blood flowing from the wounds of Jesus on the cross. Daisy, too, "[gleams] like silver, safe and proud above the hot struggles of the poor" (150). Her voice, Nick says, carried an "inexhaustible charm that rose and fell in it, the jingle of it, the cymbals' song of it" (120). The paradox of Daisy as grail is suggested here by two words: *jingle,* whose connotation is more pejorative than honorific—the sound of metal against metal, the sound of money; and *cymbals' song,* again a variety of metallic sounds, themselves hardly "songs," produced by percussion instruments. Perhaps significant to Daisy's paradoxical identity with the holy chalice is the derivation of *cymbal* from the Latin *cymbalum,* the hollow of a bowl or vessel. Daisy's voice has at once the meretricious sound of lucre and the mellifluous song of the grail. For Gatsby, "that voice held him most, with its fluctuating, feverish warmth, because it couldn't be over-dreamed—that voice was a deathless song" (*Gatsby* 97).

Perhaps most significantly, the grail was said to have mystical qualities as a talisman, possessing magical powers of healing and life-restoration. According to one version, the grail was a food-supplying vessel that sustained Joseph of Arimathea in forty years of solitary captivity. Similarly, Gatsby is sustained by his dream, during "five years of unwavering devotion" (110), to possess his grail. One autumn night five years earlier, as he walked with Daisy, "Gatsby saw that the blocks of the sidewalks really formed a ladder and mounted to a secret place above the trees—he could climb to it, if he climbed alone, and once there he could suck on the pap of life, gulp down the incomparable milk of wonder" (112). Again, the imagery is ambiguous: the ladder is at once a child's access to a tree house and a Dantesque/Eliotesque Ladder to the transcendent. "Pap," or nipple, is a conceit, as in Song of Solomon and in Edward Taylor's *Meditation 150,* representing spiritual sustenance. Thus the grail represents the higher secret of the Mystery of Life, regeneration, and spiritual fulfillment. Daisy, of course, hardly measures up, for, as Nick says, she and Tom "were careless people . . . [who] smashed up things and creatures and then retreated back into their money or their vast carelessness . . . and let other people clean up the mess" (180-181). In fact, Daisy, rather than healing or restoring life, is responsible for the death of Myrtle Wilson and, because of her callous insensitivity, for the death of Gatsby as well. Yet, paradoxically, Gatsby's quest for his grail does lead to a form of spiritual transformation.

Gatsby's quest requires a long journey both in space—Louisville to Long Island via Europe and three times around the continent with Dan Cody (101)—and in time. The journey commenced with a kiss five years earlier, just as Perceval wandered five years. "Then he kissed her. At his lips' touch she blossomed for him like a flower and the incarnation was complete" (112). Underlying the novel are not merely four incarnations, as Probert has noted (203), but seven, suggesting the symbolic, and perhaps anagogic, layering of much of Fitzgerald's fiction. Basic to all is the prototype/archetype from Fitzgerald's Catholic theology: "the Word made flesh." On a national level, the Dutch sailors incarnate their idealistic visions in the "fresh, green breast of the new world" (182). James Gatz of North Dakota incarnates his "Platonic conception of himself" (99) in Jay Gatsby of West Egg. Nick Carraway, bond salesman from St. Paul, incarnates his romantic ideals in Gatsby, even though he "represented everything for which [Nick had] an unaffected scorn" (2). Aesthetically, Fitzgerald incarnates his own ideals in the novel and invites universal reader response: "So *we* beat on, boats against the current" (182, emphasis added).

Shortly after their incarnating kiss, Gatsby and Daisy are separated by Gatsby's military tour of duty in Europe. The "grail" subsequently falls into the hands of the crude, materialistic monster, Tom Buchanan. Gatsby commits himself to finding his Blancheflor avatar, whose whereabouts are unknown to him, and to possessing her despite overwhelming odds.

Initially Gatsby's quest took the form of reading the Chicago newspapers for years "just on the chance of catching a glimpse of Daisy's name" (80). Then, as Jordan tells Nick, he bought the house "so that Daisy would be just across the bay. . . . He had waited five years and bought a mansion where he dispensed starlight to casual moths—so that he could 'come over' some afternoon to a stranger's garden" (79, 80). He gave extravagant parties in hopes that Daisy would wander in some evening.

Gatsby's efforts are endowed with ritualism, a ceremonialism that renders his quest beatific. "The Grail story," Weston writes, "is not . . . the product of imagination, literary or popular. At its root lies the record, more or less distorted, of an ancient Ritual, having for its ultimate object the entrance into the secret of the sources of Life, physical and spiritual" (*Ritual* 203). In a ritualistic gesture, Fitzgerald first presents Gatsby through Nick's eyes: "—He stretched out his arms toward the dark water in a curious way, and, far as I was from him, I could have sworn he was trembling. Involuntarily I glanced seaward—and distinguished nothing except a single green light, minute and far away, that might have been the end of a dock" (22). The scene is reminiscent of the experience of Gawain, who, having ridden "all day through a land waste and desolate . . . at nightfall comes to the seashore; he sees a causeway, arched over by trees, leading out into the water, and washed over by waves; at the end glimmers a light" (Weston, *Quest* 34).

Gatsby's raising of his arms toward the green light, a beatific gesture of veneration and supplication, is only the first in a series of such ritualistic gestures which are part of his quest. The second occurs, significantly, as one of Gatsby's lavish parties is breaking up:

> The caterwauling horns had reached a crescendo and I turned away and cut across the lawn toward home. I glanced back once. *A wafer* of a moon was shining over Gatsby's house, making the night fine as before, and surviving the laughter and the sound of his still glowing garden. A sudden emptiness seemed to flow now from the windows and the great doors, endowing the *figure of the host,* who stood on the porch, *his hand up in a formal gesture of farewell.*
>
> (56, emphasis added)

Perhaps not since Crane's *The Red Badge of Courage,* in which "the sun was pasted in the sky like a wafer," has a fictional scene been so fraught with mystical overtones. "The host" steps to his balcony and raises his hand in a pontifical gesture of consecration. By the gesture, Gatsby wishes to transubstantiate the hollow laughter and empty frivolity of his parties into his precious prize.

A third ritualistic gesture occurs when Gatsby stands vigil outside Daisy's house after the accident that killed Myrtle Wilson: "*He put his hands in his coat pockets,* and turned back eagerly to the scrutiny of the house, as though my presence marred the *sacredness of the vigil.* So I walked away and left him standing there in the moonlight—*watching over nothing*" (146, emphasis added). Here the gesture is one of accommodation, of self-immolation, for Gatsby, in not revealing Daisy as the driver of the "death-car," has chivalrously sacrificed his life for her. Paradoxically, though, he sacrifices himself for and conducts a sacred vigil over—nothing.

Gatsby tells Nick of a fourth gesture, one of desperation which occurred when he returned after the war to Louisville, while Tom and Daisy were still on their wedding trip:

> The track curved and now it was going away from the sun, which, as it sank lower, seemed to spread itself in benediction over the vanishing city where she had drawn her breath. *He stretched out his hand, desperately* as if to snatch only a wisp of air, to save a fragment of the spot that she had made lovely for him. But it was all going by so fast now for his blurred eyes and he knew that he had lost that part of it, the freshest and the best, forever.
>
> (153, emphasis added)

Here the sun, like the moon in the earlier passage, offers benediction, a blessing, ironically over the conspicuous absence of the precious object. Or, viewed from another perspective, the consecrated Host, Gatsby, is exposed in a monstrance for blessing and adoration.

The novel ends with the sixth ritualistic gesture, a universal one of anticipation, of expectation. "Gatsby believed in the green light," Nick concludes, "the orgiastic [Fitzgerald's original *orgastic* has been restored since 1988] future which year by year recedes before us. It eluded us then, but that's no matter—tomorrow we will run faster, *stretch out our arms farther.* . . . And one fine morning—" (182, emphasis added). Fitzgerald nationalizes, even universalizes, the quest. As Auden notes, each of the elements of the quest story corresponds to "an aspect of our subjective experience" (83).

Gatsby is a true quest hero not because he possesses special qualities of breeding and aristocratic stature; on the contrary, he begins as "a penniless young man without a past" (149). In typically American fashion—like Ben Franklin, James J. Hill, and P. T. Barnum—Gatsby *acquires* "the right qualities" to win his "grail"—money, a mansion, material possessions, power and mystique of the nouveau riche—through association with Dan Cody and Meyer Wolfsheim, but he remains uncorrupted by mammon. It is, after all, the *love* of money which St. Paul said was "the root of all evil," not money itself or its possession. Accordingly, someone without a dime could be corrupted by love of money and someone like Gatsby, with ill-gotten wealth, could remain uncorrupted. Gatsby, Nick tells us, valued "everything in his house according to the measure of response it drew from [Daisy's] well-loved eyes" (92). He remained aloof from his own parties. And his beautiful shirts are, as Marius Bewley has correctly noted, "sacramentals," and he shows them "neither in vanity nor in pride, but with a reverential humility in the presence of some inner vision he cannot consciously grasp, but toward which he desperately struggles in the only way he knows" (271).

According to Alfred Nutt, the quest hero is "a shadowy perfection, a bloodless and unreal creature . . . [removed] from a world in which he has neither part nor share," his romance being characterized "by the fervour of its sacramental symbolism" (37). Gatsby, *in* the world of corruption but not *of* it, measures up to this description.

Rather than being simply "childish" as some commentators suggest—manifesting negative characteristics of childhood: self-centeredness, impatience, lack of self-control, naivete—Gatsby is largely "childlike"—manifesting positive characteristics of childhood: an uncorrupted innocence, a sense of wonder and awe, a romantic sense of hope.

Auden specifies two types of Quest hero: "One resembles the hero of Epic; his superior *arete* is manifest to all. . . . The other type, so common in fairy tales, is the hero whose *arete* is concealed" (84). Gatsby is of the second type, yet his *arete,* though concealed even to some critics, is considerable. The Greek term means "virtue," "goodness," or "good quality of any kind." Wolfram's Perceval is "one who suffers and sins, but who also loves and endures, is staunch and true, and who, purified by the discipline of suffering, attains at last the summit of usefulness" (Nutt 96-97). Gatsby remains faithful to "his incorruptible dream" (155); he "turned out all right at the end," Nick concludes (2). The "summit of usefulness" he attains is his self-immolation and his model for Nick. According to St. John, "greater love has no person than this, that one lay down his/her life for a friend," but what of the love which motivates one to sacrifice life for a selfish, insensitive person like Daisy?

Those who argue that Gatsby is not "great," that his life and death are a pathetic waste, fail to make a crucial distinction, one which Robert Penn Warren's Murray Guilfort in *Meet Me in the Green Glen* learns and verbalizes: *"The dream is a lie, but the dreaming is truth"* (370). So it is with Gatsby: Daisy, his dream, is a lie—superficial, manipulative, selfish, insensitive, materialistic—but his dreaming is truth. To Nick, Gatsby is truly "great" because of his "heightened sensitivity to the promises of life" (2), his "romantic readiness" (2), his commitment to his grail, and his faithful singleness of purpose in making the quest.

The quest hero must pass certain tests—physical, psychological, spiritual—to prove his worthiness. The tests vary from one version to another: surviving a terrible storm; passing a night in the Chapel Perilous where a Black Hand snuffs out the light; confronting a Head, then the Devil in full form. Frequently he is required to weld a broken lance or sword; failing to do so will prevent him from achievement. In several texts, Perceval fails to ask the right question of the grail. According to Weston, "The test here demanded of the Quester is that he shall ask concerning the nature and use of the mysterious vessel" (*Quest* 91). To ask would have effected the healing of the king and his lands. Instead the quest hero falls asleep and subsequently wanders for five years without thinking of God.

Gatsby is subject to various tests, most notably remaining faithful to his dream, staying uncorrupted by mammon, and being willing to sacrifice himself for his "grail." The tea party with Daisy at Nick's house is a major test for Gatsby. Because he was not wealthy, Daisy had not waited for Gatsby to return from Europe to marry her. At the tea party and in the subsequent events, Gatsby attempts to retake the test he could not pass five years earlier.

To prove himself worthy, Gatsby dresses in his "white flannel suit, silver shirt, and gold-colored tie" (84-85). He attempts to be "the gold-hatted, high-bouncing lover," of the novel's epigraph, to bounce high enough to win the king's daughter, the golden girl, high in her white palace (120). Later he invites Daisy to tour the splendors of his mansion. All he possesses—his collection of imported shirts, his toilet seat of pure gold, his swimming pool and hydroplane—are calculated to alter in Daisy's eyes the deficiency of his past. He passes this test but fails to restore the king and the waste land, perhaps because he does not ask the right question of the grail. He asks not what it is but whom or what it serves, and is thus doomed from the beginning by devotion to an unexamined ideal. But perhaps his quest is as pure as his grail is not. If the grail legend is, as Weston has said, "the story of an initiation . . . carried out on the astral plane, and reacting with fatal results upon the physical" (*Ritual* 182), Gatsby poignantly dramatizes both the initiation and the fatal consummation.

The "fatal result," Gatsby's loss of his dream and his death, results from his inevitable conflict with the Guardians of the grail, who are a further test of the hero's *arete* and, in some ways, malignant in themselves. According to one account, after Joseph of Arimathea's death, the grail passed into the keeping of his kin, from whom were descended Perceval's father and the Fisher King, who was wounded supposedly for his presumption in approaching too near the Holy Grail or for sleeping in the Castle Corbenic. In Wolfram, the grail was guarded by a sacred order of knights, the Templeisen. Some versions mention three grail-keepers (believed by some to symbolize the Trinity): Joseph, Brons, and the grandson of Brons. In other versions, there are only two—father and son or uncle and nephew. Weston notes that "Chrétien and Wolfram know of two kings: the lord of the Grail Castle in their versions uniting the characters of Fisher, and Maimed, King. . . . The title of 'Fisher' King [is] applied to the Guardians of the Grail" (*Quest* 93, 94). It remains a mystery how the grail-keepers fell from their high estate and how Pelles, the last of them, became wounded and his lands laid waste. Weston concludes that the "Guardian would represent the Life-Principle" and "the Maimed King would correspond closely with the Dead, or Wounded, God" (*Quest* 94). Viewed with these legends as a backdrop, several of the novel's characters take on added meaning.

The most obvious guardian of Gatsby's "grail" is the unmistakably malevolent Tom Buchanan. Nick describes him with such words as "supercilious," "arrogant," "aggressive," "hard," "gruff," and "cruel" (7). He displays "contempt" and "fractiousness" (7), cheats on his wife, breaks his mistress's nose with his open palm, spouts racist views, and investigates Gatsby's background with the intention of ruining him. According to Nick, "'Jay Gatsby' had broken up like glass against Tom's hard malice" (148).

If Tom is the fallen, malignant guardian, Doctor T. J. Eckleberg, whose "persistent stare" presides over the "waste land" (24), is the Maimed King who corresponds to the Dead or Wounded God. In his grotesque deformity, retinas that "look out of no face, but, instead, from a pair of enormous yellow spectacles which pass over a non-existent nose" (23), this god of the Waste Land reflects the ruin of his lands. "This is a valley of ashes—a fantastic farm where ashes grow like wheat into ridges and hills and grotesque gardens" (23). Eckleberg, along with his walking extensions, George Wilson and Owl-Eyes, is a maimed agrarian deity presiding over a wasted land, once fertile and fructuous, once the "fresh, green breast of the new world" (182) that held such promise for the Dutch sailors. Had the grail quest been successful, the Waste Land would have been restored and its people liberated from the evil spell of a devastated social order.

Gatsby attempts to break the spell on the lost generation by creating his own new world, and at times Nick sees a vision of what Gatsby can create. At Gatsby's party, "the scene . . . [changes] before [Nick's] eyes into something significant, elemental, and profound" (47). With Gatsby in New York, Nick feels that "anything can happen . . . anything at all," and he sees the city filled with "wild promise of all the mystery and the beauty in the world" (69). Fitzgerald's ambivalence, his trust and doubt in America, is soon manifested as Nick's hope-filled visions of beauty and order dissipate. Gatsby's charmed guests turn into "highly indignant wives" and "sheepish" husbands (52). New York's promise of beauty is marred by "a dead man" in a hearse and by the "ferocious" eating habits of the gangster Wolfsheim (71). Gatsby's new world of wealth and a mansion full of interesting people do nothing to restore the wasted land of the lost generation. Gatsby's hopes, like those of Tennyson's Arthur, are disappointed:

> And when King Arthur made
> His Table Round . . . surely he had thought
> That now the Holy Grail would come again;
> But sin broke out. Ah, Christ, that it would come,
> And heal the world of all their wickedness!
>
> (115)

As noted above, however, Gatsby does not heal the Fisher King or restore the Waste Land. He cannot revive an American Dream turned profanely meretricious, but he does at least set his own lands in order. He learns and demonstrates the Words of the Thunder: "Be disciplined"; "Have compassion"; and "Give."

The sixth element of the typical Quest story is "Helpers who with their knowledge and magical powers assist the hero and but for whom he would never succeed" (Auden 83). In the Perceval romances, the hero is given wise counsel by his mother. In the accounts of Chrétien and Wolfram, "the hero, after leaving Arthur's court, finds his way to the castle of an old knight, who receives him kindly, and, shocked at his lack of knightly breeding and accomplishments, does his best to impart to him a measure of skill in arms and courtesy of manner" (Weston, *Quest* 42-43). After leaving the old knight, the hero is given shelter in the castle of his late host's niece and subsequently in the hall of another castle, where he is presented with a mysterious sword. One of the main features of the Gawain quest is the presence, outside the grail chamber, of twelve weeping maidens who offer prayers and orisons.

Gatsby's helpers are Nick Carraway and Jordan Baker, who arrange the tea party so Gatsby and Daisy can be reunited. Gatsby's childlikeness and his trepidation because "he's waited so long" (80) are reminiscent of Perceval's naivete and fear. Nick and Jordan are able to help Gatsby because they, like the traditional quest helpers, possess knowledge which Gatsby lacks. Nick, like the old knight, is astounded at Gatsby's seeming naivete, especially about repeating the past.

Nick offers psychological and spiritual support of Gatsby as well; he goes far beyond mere assistance to approbation and even identification. "They're a rotten crowd," he shouts to Gatsby across the lawn; "you're worth the whole damn bunch put together" (154). "I found myself on Gatsby's side, and alone," he says later (165). "I began to have a feeling of defiance, of scornful solidarity between Gatsby and me against them all" (166). The night before he returns to the Midwest, Nick erases an obscene word from the white steps of Gatsby's house (181), a key symbolic act, especially because of the earlier descriptions of Gatsby in "his gorgeous pink rag of a suit [making] a bright spot of color against the white steps" (154). Nick's admiration of Gatsby and his romantic dream can hardly be labeled "tawdry," "voyeuristic," or "scatological" (Probert 204). Rather than a "childish nostalgia," it is a childlike *Sehnsucht,* a profound, bittersweet longing. Gatsby as grail quest knight is an archetype of fidelity to the ideal in a paradoxical world. With his "extraordinary gift for hope," his "heightened sensitivity to the promises of life" (2), and "the colossal vitality of his illusions" (97), Gatsby illustrates Fitzgerald's paradoxical view that such dreaming, though never to be fulfilled, greatly enriches life.

Note

1. In a real sense, as Karen C. Way has pointed out (123), Gatsby *does* repeat the past: having won and lost Daisy previously, he does so again, just as Nick also repeats the past in words, including his warning to Gatsby that the task is impossible, and just as Fitzgerald repeats the past—as artists regularly *do*.

Works Cited

Auden, W. H. "The Quest Hero." *Texas Quarterly* 4 (1961): 81-93.

Benson, Larry. "Editions of Malory." *Critical Approaches to Six Major English Works: Beowulf Through Paradise Lost*. Eds. R. Lumiansky and Hershel Baker. Philadelphia: University of Pennsylvania Press, 1968.

Bewley, Marius. "Scott Fitzgerald and the Collapse of the American Dream." *The Eccentric Design: Form in the Classic American Novel*. New York: Columbia University Press, 1963.

Bruccoli, Matthew J., ed. *The Notebooks of F. Scott Fitzgerald*. New York: Harcourt Brace Jovanovich, 1978.

Chrétien de Troyes. *Arthurian Romances*. Trans. W. W. Comfort. London: Everyman, 1984.

Fitzgerald, F. Scott. *This Side of Paradise*. New York: Macmillan, 1986.

———. *The Great Gatsby*. New York: Macmillan, 1986.

———. *Six Tales of the Jazz Age and Other Stories*. New York: Scribner's, 1960.

———. *The Basil and Josephine Stories*. New York: Macmillan, 1973.

———. *Flappers and Philosophers*. New York: Macmillan, 1987.

———. *The Crack Up*. Ed. Edmund Wilson. New York: New Directions, 1956.

Linker, Robert White, trans. *Chrétien de Troyes: The Story of the Grail*. Chapel Hill: University of North Carolina Press, 1952.

Loomis, Roger Sherman. *The Grail: From Celtic Myth to Christian Symbol*. New York: University of Wales Press, 1963.

Miller, James E. *F. Scott Fitzgerald: His Art and Technique*. New York: New York University Press, 1964.

Moseley, Edwin M. *F. Scott Fitzgerald*. Grand Rapids: Eerdmans, 1967.

Nutt, Alfred. *The Legends of the Holy Grail*. London: David Nutt, 1902.

Probert, K. G. "Nick Carraway and the Romance of Art." *English Studies in Canada* 10 (1984): 188-208.

Tennyson, Alfred Lord. *Idylls of the King*. Ed. Willis Boughton. Boston: Ginn and Co., 1913.

Warren, Robert Penn. *Meet Me in the Green Glen*. New York: Random House, 1971.

Way, Karen C. "'So We Beat On': Quest and Ennui in Fitzgerald's *The Great Gatsby*." *West Virginia Philological Papers* 28 (1982): 119-126.

Weston, Jessie L. *From Ritual to Romance*. Garden City, NY: Doubleday, 1957.

———. *The Quest of the Holy Grail*. London: G. Bell and Sons, 1913.

Wolfram Von Eschenbach. *Parzival*. Trans. Helen M. Mustard and Charles E. Passage. New York: Vintage, 1961.

Zeydel, Edwin H. *The Parzival of Wolfram von Eschenbach*. Chapel Hill: University of North Carolina Press, 1951.

Barbara Tepa Lupack (essay date winter 1994)

SOURCE: Lupack, Barbara Tepa. "F. Scott Fitzgerald's 'Following of a Grail'." *Arthuriana* 4, no. 4 (winter 1994): 324-47.

[*In the following essay, Lupack chronicles the inclusion of Arthurian motifs, the wasteland, and the Grail quest in many of F. Scott Fitzgerald's works, remarking that the author's interest in these stories also carried over into his personal life.*]

The Arthurian legends appealed not only to T. S. Eliot, Edwin Arlington Robinson, and other American poets of the early twentieth century but also to some of the most prominent American novelists as well. F. Scott Fitzgerald, the great chronicler of the Jazz Age, found special vitality and contemporaneity in the legends and incorporated aspects of them into much of his best work. Like his contemporary Ernest Hemingway, who (in *The Sun Also Rises* and in several of the Nick Adams tales in *In Our Time*) used the story of the Fisher King as an analogue for the moral sterility and ethical impotence of his age, Fitzgerald was drawn to traditional elements of Arthurian mythology, especially the wasteland and the Grail quest; but, in his fiction, he reinterpreted those elements in untraditional and distinctly American ways. The wasteland, for instance—a concept popularized by Eliot in *The Waste Land* (1922)—afforded Fitzgerald a powerful image for the deterioration of social values and the resulting emphasis on materialism and gaudy excess in the first half of the century, particularly the years between the two world wars. The Grail quest, a related and recurring image, became a paradigm for contemporary man's search for honor—though, in both Fitzgerald's shorter fiction and his novels, his characters generally failed to fulfill their quests because they abandoned their ideals or perverted and debased the notion of the Grail itself.

Fitzgerald's fascination with medievalism, particularly with Arthurian myth and the romance of chivalry, began early. As a child, he imagined himself to be the son not of his parents but 'of a king, a king who ruled the whole world' (Fitzgerald, 'Author's House,' cited in Turnbull 28). Even his own family's snobbery had its origins in a nostalgia for the romantic values of a by-gone era threatened by the encroaching materialism of the twentieth century (a theme which—recast—becomes prominent in *The Great Gatsby* [1925], his most significant work). Fitzgerald's forebears, after all, were patrician. His ancestors included Francis Scott Key, for whom Fitzgerald was named; and, as André Le Vot demonstrates, their 'moral heritage, reviewed and revised by [F. Scott's] romantic imagination, can be summed up as an idealistic attitude contrasting with America's postwar materialism—the Southern aristocracy's traditional panache, inherited from the English Cavaliers and sharply different from the down-to-earth mercantilism of the Puritans' descendants' (6). It is therefore unsurprising that Fitzgerald admired his father's distinctly Southern courtesy, courtliness and romantic love of the past or that, even after the elder Fitzgerald's financial failure adversely affected the family's social standing, Scott still found him to be a sympathetic figure ('of tired stock' perhaps, but nevertheless 'his [son's] moral guide' [Piper 9, II], like Reverend Diver in *The Beautiful and Damned*.)[1]

Fitzgerald's whole life had romantic overtones. It was, as Matthew J. Bruccoli observed, 'a quest for heroism' (Bruccoli *Grandeur* xx); and Fitzgerald's commitment to and sense of a personal chivalric code continued even as his own life and behavior grew increasingly more unheroic. 'I feel very strongly about you doing [your] duty' (*Letters* 15), he wrote to his young daughter Scottie; and he urged her to establish certain resolves (similar to the 'General Resolves' outlined by Gatsby as a young man) which would encourage her to pay attention to scholarship, to her ability to understand and get along with people, and to her own body as 'a useful instrument.' Such a basic code of behavior was important, he explained with paternal concern, because 'My generation of the radicals and the breakers-down never found anything to take the place of the old virtues of work and courage and the old graces of courtesy and politeness' (*Letters* 50).

Fitzgerald was acutely aware of his own breaches of that code, as his voluminous correspondence with family and friends reveals. After one of his wife Zelda's numerous hospitalizations, he wrote to Dr. Carroll, her physician, that—despite his recent 'slip off the wagon'—he recognized his responsibility to help Zelda stabilize her health. At the same time, he explained in familiar chivalric terms that any real reconciliation with her would constitute an impossible quest. 'There is simply too much of the past between us. When that mist falls . . . no knight errant can traverse its immense distance' (*Correspondence* 487). In a note written shortly before his death to his mistress Sheilah Graham, he apologizes for yet another episode of rude and drunken behavior. His unfitness 'for any human relations' was, he contends, in marked contrast to her conduct, which he praised as 'fine and chivalrous' (Graham 300-301). This awareness and acknowledgement of chivalric conduct served to inform his fictional characters as well, who, as Sy Kahn observed, are variously undone by an idealism much like Fitzgerald's own, an idealism 'bravely asserted but doomed' (47); and such conduct became one significant measure of his code hero, much the way that 'grace under pressure' did for Hemingway's code hero.

Fitzgerald's interest in the medieval was also evident in other aspects of his life. As a boy, he read *Scottish Chiefs, Ivanhoe,* and action-based historical stories for young men, and by high school he progressed to Tennyson, Chesterton, and Twain. Fitzgerald's earliest writings, according to his *Ledger* entry for June, 1909, included an imitation of *Ivanhoe* called 'Elavo' and 'a complicated story of some knights,' both unfinished (Bruccoli *Grandeur* 20, 28; Kuehl 17).

Years later, in an epilogue to Bruccoli's biography of Fitzgerald, Scottie Fitzgerald recalled her father's 'annoyance when I kept falling asleep during his detailed background briefings on *Ivanhoe*.' She remembered, too, the charts of the Middle Ages and other 'Histomaps' which hung on the walls of his workroom in Baltimore and his collections of miniature soldiers, 'which he deployed on marches around our Christmas trees' (Scottie Fitzgerald Smith in Bruccoli *Grandeur* 496). Scottie herself played 'Knights of the Round Table' with paper dolls which had been elaborately painted by Zelda (Bruccoli *Grandeur* 262) in a dollhouse described by Fitzgerald in 'Outside the Cabinet-Maker's.' (In that poignant story, written when the Fitzgeralds were living at Ellerslie in Wilmington and Scottie was six, a father buys an expensive doll's house for his young daughter. Though he knows it is only a costly piece of cabinet-making and not a fairy's castle, he imagines for her mysteries 'whose luster and texture he could never see or touch any more himself' [140].)

It was during Fitzgerald's years at Princeton University (1913-17) that his fascination with the medieval deepened and his vision of the questing romantic hero, which became the basis for all of his fictional characters, crystallized. The Gothic splendor of the campus provided a fertile environment for the young Fitzgerald's preoccupation with chivalric tradition: at the time he attended, Princeton was not simply a top-ranked college but an academic and social community so organized that it resembled an order of chivalry, with its various heroes, ceremonies and cults (Le Vot 42, 46). The very architecture of the venerable institution evoked in him 'a deep and almost reverent liking for the gray walls and gothic peaks and all they symbolized in the store of the ages of antiquity' ('The Spire and the Gargoyle' 106). As he rambled down the shadowy lanes whose names he later recited with devotion in his stories and novels or as he explored the imposing buildings on the campus, Fitzgerald felt that he had crossed into a different world and time. And he viewed it all with the awe of the outsider who is offered a privileged glance into the secrets of the aristocracy, which he later drew on thematically in some of his best fiction.

Among the most important of Princeton's cults was the football team: they were champions, in the medieval sense, defending the community's prestige and honor in perilous tournaments. Fitzgerald—who revered the football players for their skill, intelligence and prowess—considered them to be modern-day knights; in 'The Bowl,' he described them as questing heroes, 'bewitched figures in another world, strange and infinitely romantic, . . . consecrated and unreachable—vaguely holy' (97). Hobey Baker, captain of the football team during Fitzgerald's freshman year, was one of the greatest athletes in Princeton's history; Bruccoli notes that to Fitzgerald and his classmates Baker seemed like 'a Galahad figure on and off the field' (Bruccoli *Grandeur* 44).

Although Fitzgerald himself failed to qualify for the team—a disappointment matched only by his inability a few years later to see action during World War I—he followed Princeton football fervently throughout his college years and beyond; at the time of his fatal heart attack in 1940, in fact, he was readying an article about the current football season for the *Princeton Alumni Weekly*. His interest in the game which he termed symbolic of the 'essential and beautiful' ('Princeton' in *Afternoon of an Author* 72) persisted because he saw football in chivalric terms—as an act of faith, intensely personal, on the one hand; an expression of communion, ritually collective, on the other. Even in his fiction, football assumed a critical place, as a romantic longing for all that is best in youth and idealism, in much the same way that sports like bullfighting and baseball did in Hemingway's code work.[2] In *The Great Gatsby*, for example, Tom Buchanan's only real personal claim to fame—apart from his family's money—is that he used to be 'one of the most powerful ends that ever played football at New Haven—a national figure.' But Tom betrayed that promise and became an arrogant, supercilious man with 'a cruel body,' a man who, having reached such 'an acute limited excellence at twenty-one that everything afterward savors of anticlimax,' wistfully drifts on forever seeking 'the dramatic turbulence of some irrecoverable football game' (*GG The Great Gatsby* 6).

As he later did with his fictional characters, Fitzgerald cast himself in the role of romantic hero. The various honors and successes which he achieved at Princeton—making the prestigious Cottage Club, becoming president of Triangle Club, and holding other offices—were, to him, 'badges of pride, medals' (Milford 29, citing Fitzgerald). With those tokens he hoped to earn the admiration of his peers and, perhaps even more importantly at the time, to prove himself worthy of his first love, a rich and wildly popular young woman from Chicago with the almost improbably Arthurian name of Ginevra King. But, just as Daisy left Gatsby for Tom, the moneyed scion of a prominent Midwestern family, Ginevra eventually terminated her relationship with Fitzgerald and married another man, William Mitchell, 'the current catch of Chicago' and heir to an extremely wealthy family associated with Chicago banking (Lehan 67).[3] Fitzgerald was crushed by the break-up. As Andrew Turnbull writes, 'Ginevra had been the princess for whom he sought fame and honors at Princeton in the spirit of the knight errant' (72),[4] and he never really got over losing her. In fact, his longing for Ginevra, the rich, beautiful girl he could never possess, finds its way into much of his work, especially in Gatsby's expressions of his undying love for Daisy.

But the loss of Ginevra was only one of many setbacks which Fitzgerald suffered during and soon after his Princeton years. A malaria-like illness forced him to move back temporarily to the Midwest, and a record of undistinguished academic achievement upon his return to college required him to repeat a year; eventually he left altogether without graduating. By then the war was being fought in Europe, and Fitzgerald managed to get a commission as an infantry 2nd lieutenant. Envisioning himself a 'hero in the field' (Turnbull 80), he expected to be posted overseas; instead, he was sent to Kansas and afterwards to Alabama, where he met and courted Zelda Sayre, the popular Montgomery belle whose wit and antic behavior he later appropriated as the stuff of his fiction.

After several months of courtship, however, Zelda grew 'nervous' about Fitzgerald's elusive career success (as Daisy later reacts to the young Gatsby's), broke off their engagement, and returned to the gay world of parties and dances. The episode reminded Scott of the failure of his quest for Ginevra, and he recorded his disappointment in his *Ledger* in typically romantic fashion: 'Failure. I used to wonder why they locked princesses in towers' (Milford 45; Le Vot 69). He repeated that sentiment in at least six letters to Zelda, who finally replied that she had heard enough from him about towers. Later, plagiarizing their lives as Fitzgerald so often did, Zelda included the episode in her autobiographical novel, *Save Me the Waltz* (1932). David Knight, the male protagonist obviously based on Fitzgerald, writes to his beloved Alabama: 'Oh, my dear, you are my princess and I'd like to shut you up forever in an ivory tower for my private delectation' (55). And the self-assured Alabama replies that she does not want him to mention the tower ever again.

Back again, and alone, in Saint Louis, Fitzgerald—still trying to prove his worthiness to Zelda and her parents—returned to a manuscript which had earlier been rejected for publication. Revised and expanded, the novel was soon published to considerable acclaim. A history of Amory Blaine, a 'romantic egotist,' from his indulged childhood with his eccentric mother through prep school and Princeton, *This Side of Paradise* (1920) culminates in an unhappy love affair and a 'renewed quest for values upon which to erect a fulfilling life' (Bruccoli *Grandeur* 124). Concluding that he is 'capable of infinite expansion for good or evil' (*TSP This Side of Paradise* 18), Amory—a projection of the youthful Fitzgerald—formulates 'a code to live by . . . a sort of aristocratic egotism' (as Gatsby, another romantic dreamer, would later do as well) and undertakes a regimen of self-improvement, part of which includes the reading of certain biographical novels which he christens 'quest books,' books about heroes who 'set off in life armed with the best weapons' but who discover that 'there might be a more magnificent use' for their talents than simply pushing 'selfishly and blindly' ahead (*TSP* 120).

In the course of Fitzgerald's first novel, Amory acts much as the questing heroes he reads about do: pushing ahead, at first selfishly and finally a little less blindly, he comes of age and begins to metamorphose.[5] Sergio Perosa likens this period of Amory's development, of his preparation for the new trials to come, as 'typical [of] Celtic heroes from Parsifal to Tristan' (Perosa 20). Amory leaves behind some of his earlier egotism and tries to reshape himself as a man 'spiritually unmarried [who] continually seeks for new systems that will control or counteract human nature' (*TSP* 272).

By novel's end, he has not yet become that 'personage' to which he aspires, but at least he has attained the ground from which he may begin to work. As Robert Sklar notes, Amory 'has given up a passive but secure place in the social order for an active and problematic role in creating constructive social change. He has turned his back on a system of values which exalts the individual will in theory but in practice constricts it. Now he must make a direct confrontation with the capacity of his will to create values for himself' (Sklar 56).

In a point of view for the first time distinctly his own, Amory starts to free himself from both genteel social conventions and the extremes of romantic despair. A quest hero of sorts, he is left to embark on a new quest. 'Even if, deep in my heart, I thought we were all blind atoms in a world as limited as a stroke of a pendulum,' he admits, 'I and my sort would struggle against tradition; try, at least, to displace old cants with new ones . . . faith is difficult. One thing I know. *If life isn't a seeking for the grail it may be a damned amusing game.*'[6]

That important line about life as a seeking for the grail provides perhaps the best explanation for the earlier self-directed and sometimes silly behavior of Amory and of the other characters in Fitzgerald's novels: without noble aspirations (epitomized by 'a seeking of the grail'), they lead purposeless lives, at best amusing, but at worst fatuous and despairing. In *The Beautiful and Damned* (1922), for instance, Gloria and Anthony Patch become, as their name suggests, little more than a colorful swatch on the fabric of American social life in the decade between 1910 and 1920.[7] Anthony—obsessed with 'a self-absorption with no comfort, a demand for expression with no outlet, a sense of time rushing by, ceaselessly and wastefully . . . assuaged only by that conviction that there was nothing to waste, because all efforts and attainments were equally valueless' (*BD The Beautiful and Damned* 93)—is no more than a pathetic dilettante who rationalizes his indolence, a wastelander with little hope of ameliorating his sorry plight. His beautiful, manipulative wife Gloria provides him with some distraction and occasionally some direction, but their climb up the social ladder is followed by their inexorable slide into depression, alcoholism, and madness. From the beginning, theirs is no noble quest; and in the end, even the inheritance from Anthony's grandfather which they have coveted for years cannot obliterate their unhappiness. Ultimately, their good financial fortune affords them a more lavish lifestyle but no escape from the inherent meaninglessness of their lives. Similarly, in *Tender Is the Night* (1934), Dick and Nicole Diver are the stuff of a Jazz Age wasteland, hollow people in a hollow land, whose very name echoes their declining fortunes.

It is in Fitzgerald's third and best-known novel *The Great Gatsby*, though, that both the idea of life as a seeking for the Grail and the whole quest motif find their fullest expression. Gatsby, the novel's title character, is a more developed questing hero than the romantic and egotistical Amory Blaine, or the spiritually spent Anthony Patch, or even the broken Dick Diver (though, as 'brother' to those other protagonists, he wins sympathy because he clings to a romantic, Platonic image of himself in spite of his disillusioning pilgrimage [Kahn 47]). Gatsby is, in fact, a contemporary Grail knight who undergoes numerous trials in order to become worthy of the precious object he desires. That object is the 'excitingly desirable' (*GG* 148) Daisy Fay Buchanan, a woman with such extraordinary 'star-shine' (which Fitzgerald describes as a 'bought luxury' of the affluent [*GG* 149]) that she blinds others to her irresolute carelessness and facile cynicism. From their first meeting five years earlier, Gatsby had 'felt married to her, that was all.' And so, with the unattainable Daisy ever drawing him on, over the years 'he found that he committed himself to the following of a grail' (*GG* 149).

To earn Daisy's love, he observes a regimen as disciplined and purposeful as any knight errant's, transforming himself into what he believes she wants him to be. Earnest Jimmy Gatz, a young army officer so poor that he must borrow a uniform in order to go courting, becomes handsome, mysterious Jay Gatsby, a man so affluent that he can afford to hold his own court on the shore of West Egg. But, despite his best efforts to ingratiate himself, he remains an outsider to Daisy's world, a parvenu whose lack of social standing distinguishes him from the careless rich across the bay.[8]

As the story of a contemporary romantic questing knight errant who has journeyed east from his home in North Dakota in search of a larger experience of life, Gatsby's tale takes on a special—and mythic—significance which, at least initially, reverses the old formulas of west and east in American fiction and ultimately reexamines the notion of the American dream. The once limitless western horizon which attracted Gatsby's mentor Dan Cody and other pioneering entrepreneurs had, by Gatsby's generation, been circumscribed by the 'bored, sprawling, swollen towns beyond the Ohio, with their interminable inquisitions which spared only the children and the very old' (*GG* 177); the locus of opportunity had shifted from a once glamorous and golden West, now a dull and settled land of conformist, respectable towns,[9] to the big cities of the East. For those reasons, after some nomadism immediately following their marriage, the Buchanans settle 'permanently' on Long Island because Tom would be 'a God damned fool to live anywhere else' (*GG* 10); Nick, for whom the Middle West 'seemed like the ragged edge of the universe' (*GG* 3), heads for New York with a dozen volumes on finance which promise 'to unfold the shining secrets that only Midas, Morgan and Maecenas knew' (4); and even the green light on which Gatsby fixates shines in just one direction—from the East across the continent, beckoning him to its coast; from the East across the bay to his mansion in West Egg, beckoning him to Daisy. Only those too deeply mired in the wasteland to make any movement—George Wilson, who wants to 'go West' (*GG* 123) to start a new life with his wife, and Myrtle Wilson, who expects to divorce George, marry Tom, and go 'West for a while until it blows over' (*GG* 34)—still find promise in the West.

For Fitzgerald, though, the lure of the East was false and represented 'a profound displacement of the American dream, a turning back upon itself of the historic pilgrimage towards the frontier which had, in fact, created and sustained that dream' (Ornstein 63).[10] That dream, after all, had once been, as Milton Stern suggests, a dream of self 'at the golden moment of emergence from wanting greatness to being great' (166, 190)—a dream shared by all of Fitzgerald's characters beginning with Amory Blaine—but it had deteriorated into the irresponsible actuality of American wealth, complete with the deceit and superficiality of its appearances. Promising an 'orgiastic future,' it had instead 'borne back' (*GG* 182) the transcendent expectations of Gatsby and other youthful dreamers. Thus, only the irresponsible, perpetually adolescent Buchanans eventually resettle in the East. A more sober and mature Nick, fed up with the artificiality of New York society, instead returns to the Midwest. And Gatsby dies, destroyed as much by the provincial squeamishness which makes all Westerners in the novel 'unadaptable to Eastern life' (*GG* 177) as by his own 'small-time notions of virtue and chivalry' (Ornstein 65).

In portraying the limitations of the orgiastic future inherent in the new American dream, *The Great Gatsby* mourns the emptiness and hollowness of America in the Jazz Age. Implicating America itself, which measures its heroes not by their morality but by their material success (Whitley 18), Fitzgerald expresses a certain disenchantment with the post-World-War-I era in which ideals are corrupted and love, like faith, is impossible. But, while in its portrait of contemporary life *Gatsby* is a singularly American romance, in its imagery and its structure it harks back to earlier romantic tradition. As Jerome Mandel notes, there are numerous similarities between 'the Arthurian—[and] the American—Way of Life' (547), beginning with Fitzgerald's depiction of the aristocratic class in American society as a modern version of the medieval nobility, presided over by powerful lords like Tom Buchanan in 'white palaces' (*GG* 5-6); privileged ladies like Daisy Fay, 'the king's daughter, the golden girl' (*GG* 120), safely distant from the struggling poor; and noble knights like Nick Carraway, whose family is 'descended from the Dukes of Buccleuch' (*GG* 2). Fitzgerald himself recognized the similarities: he characterized the New York society of the Buchanans as 'a silly, pretentious, vicious mockery of a defunct feudal regime . . . [with] violently selfish and unchivalric standards' (Fitzgerald, *F. Scott Fitzgerald in His Own Time* 190).

In telling his very contemporary romance, Fitzgerald borrows various important elements from medieval romance, such as the existence of two distinct worlds in which the action occurs—one public, a world of political concerns and accepted laws, where the ordinary rules of proper behavior normally prevail; the other private, a lovers' world inhabited by only two, where the ordinary rules that govern society are suspended in the service of courtly love (Mandel 547). In *Gatsby,* the public world is typified by the lavish parties which Gatsby throws, parties to which come all manner of socially pretentious and sycophantic guests with names like Leech, Civet, Beaver, Fishguard, Whitebait, Beluga, Catlip, Belcher, Smirke.'' Each weekend, Gatsby's lawn is manicured by an extra crew of gardeners; his house is lit up like 'a Christmas tree'; his Rolls-Royce becomes an omnibus, bearing guests to and from the city; and his station wagon 'scampers like a little yellow bug to meet all trains' (*GG* 39). With fruiterers and caterers abounding, the parties resemble medieval banquets: 'On buffet tables, garnished with glistening hors-d'oeuvre, spiced baked hams crowded against salads of harlequin designs and pastry pigs and turkeys bewitched to a dark gold' (*GG* 39-40).

But once Daisy makes clear her distaste for such spectroscopic affairs, Gatsby abandons them, deferring, as a courtly lover would, to the wishes of his beloved. His 'elaborate road-house' (*GG* 64) becomes a bower of bliss, a private world in which the servants are sent away; the house goes dark; and 'Daisy comes over quite often—in the afternoons' (*GG* 114). Even in more extreme circumstances, as Mandel suggests, the lovers attempt to recreate their own private world (548). For instance, as partying guests take over his mansion one weekend, Gatsby steals away for half an hour with Daisy; ignoring the noise and distractions of the revelers, they take refuge together on the steps of Nick's cottage as Nick stands guard in the garden. And on the trip to New York, to which the summer-weary Buchanans and their friends escape for the day, Daisy and Gatsby create another private moment for themselves by arranging to drive alone in Tom's coupé.

Nick senses the lovers' intimacy almost immediately. After facilitating Gatsby and Daisy's first meeting in his home, he feels so much like an intruder in their private world that he runs off and sits on the lawn gazing in the rain at the architecture of the sprawling white mansion next door. When he returns a half hour later, he tries loudly to announce his presence. 'But I don't believe they heard a sound,' he says. 'They were sitting at either end of the couch, looking at each other as if some question had been asked, or was in the air, and every vestige of embarrassment was gone' (*GG* 90).

Tom Buchanan and his mistress Myrtle Wilson have also established a private lovers' world of sorts; they keep an apartment in New York, at a safe remove from the garage apartment Myrtle shares with her husband, George. But Tom and Myrtle's carnal, violent relationship, which provides a worldly foil to Gatsby's more idealized and spiritual love for Daisy, perverts any notion of courtly love; and even their apartment reflects the perversion. It is garish and grotesque, the oversized furniture decorated with large tapestries of palatial scenes from Versailles. Moreover, instead of being private (as Gatsby's house becomes after he and Daisy become lovers), it is public: Myrtle invites her neighbors and her sister in for a party which becomes so raucous that it ends in a fight during which Tom breaks Myrtle's nose, a foreshadowing of the deadly violence—also at Tom's hands (albeit more indirectly)—that soon claims Myrtle's life. As Mandel notes, 'the idealized values and spiritual concerns of medieval authors never exist in Tom and Myrtle's private world, which is characterized by increasingly drunken conversations about people and feet and appendicitis' (548). In fact, the apartment scene in the second chapter is almost a parody of the private, idyllic Cave of Lovers to which Iseult, Tristan, and the handsome hound Hudein retreat. Tom and Myrtle's place is a perverse cave into which they bring a mongrel dog, purchased for the exorbitant sum of $10 from a street vendor who bears 'an absurd resemblance to John D. Rockefeller' (*GG* 27).

The most enduring of the lovers' worlds in *Gatsby*, however, is neither Tom and Myrtle's nor Gatsby and Daisy's; it is the Buchanans'. Bound together in their disregard of the consequences of their actions, Tom and Daisy are 'careless people . . . [who] smashed up things and people and then retreated back into their money or their vast carelessness, or whatever it was that kept them together, and let other people clean up the mess they had made' (*GG* 180-81). The night of Myrtle's death, as Gatsby the Grail knight watches over Daisy's home with 'the sacredness of a vigil,' Nick spies the Buchanans at their kitchen table, holding hands and talking earnestly over cold chicken and ale. 'There was,' Nick remarks, 'an unmistakable air of natural intimacy about the picture, and anybody would have said that they were conspiring together' (*GG* 146). The next day, when Nick calls to tell Daisy of Gatsby's death, he learns the nature and extent of that conspiracy: she and Tom had gone away earlier that afternoon. They had taken baggage but left no word of where they were heading or when they would return, withdrawing into the protected world of money and lack of conscience in which they were so inutterably wed. Indeed, Nick realizes, Gatsby had been 'watching over nothing' (*GG* 146); the Grail he had followed for so long and held so sacred was a mere illusion.

If the various lovers' private worlds provide, at least for a time, some solace and consolation from the vicissitudes of the outside world, there is one place which provides no solace or consolation whatsoever: the wasteland which Fitzgerald calls the Valley of the Ashes. Located between the privileged world of the Long Island Eggs and the corrupt world of New York, the valley is a 'fantastic farm where ashes grow like wheat into ridges and hills and grotesque gardens; where ashes take the form of houses and chimneys and rising smoke and . . . ash-gray men who move dimly and already crumbling through the powdery air' (*GG* 23). It is a place whose physical deterioration mirrors the moral despair of its few remaining inhabitants, who are bereft not only of hope but also of vitality. Like Eliot's wasteland, it is an 'arid plane,' a 'dead land' strewn with 'dry bones' (*WL The Waste Land* ll. 425, 2, 391).

The valley is presided over by the eyes of Dr. Eckleburg, an oculist long since gone from the borough. Peering down from a solitary signpost, those huge eyes, simultaneously unseeing and all-seeing, mock the misery of the wastelanders below and serve as a reminder that God, too, has turned a blind eye to their suffering. Letha Audhuy, who draws extensive parallels between *The Waste Land* and *The Great Gatsby,* suggests that, in the wasteland of Gatsby's world, Eckleburg is himself a godlike figure, the false new god of 'commercialism or materialism . . . in America in the 1920's.' She points to 'the line from "Gerontion" (a poem so closely related to *The Waste Land* that Eliot wanted to use it for a prologue): "Signs are taken for wonders," and concludes that in *Gatsby* 'Fitzgerald's joke is to make an actual sign (board) into a wonder' (43). Similarly, John W. Bicknell, who sees in the grotesque image of Eckleburg 'a symbol of what God has become in the modern world . . . indifferent, faceless, blank,' draws the comparison to the lines from *The Waste Land,* which he notes Fitzgerald 'knew by heart': 'What are the roots that clutch, what branches grow / Out of this stony rubbish? Son of man, / You cannot say, or guess, for you know only / A heap of broken images, where the sun beats / And the dead tree gives no shelter . . .' (Bicknell 68).

No one in Eckleburg's view seems to suffer more than George Wilson, owner of a grimy garage, one of only two shops left on 'a small block of yellow brick sitting on the edge of the waste land' (*GG* 24). A blond, faintly handsome man, George is as spiritless as his surroundings. When he appears in the door of his office to greet Tom and Nick, he is 'wiping his hands on a piece of waste' (*GG* 25). So poor that he had to borrow a suit in which to wed Myrtle (just as Gatsby had to borrow clothing in which to court Daisy in Louisville), George wants only to please his wife, who—unbeknownst to him—is smitten with Tom and who prefers Tom's brand of vulgarity.

There is, to be sure, a certain symmetry in the fact that both George and Gatsby die in the service of the women they love, women who are taken from them in a kind of *droit de seigneur* by Tom.[12] Both men, moreover, are condemned as cowards for their inability to hold on to the objects of their desire; and both die oblivious to the actual forces which destroy their illusions and their lives. When Daisy, driving Gatsby's yellow Rolls-Royce through the Valley of the Ashes, kills Myrtle, Gatsby assumes the blame, a gesture he as chivalrous lover gladly makes to protect his beloved. After keeping a vigil outside her window that evening, the next day he dies awaiting word from her, unaware that she has betrayed him, and, by her betrayal, conspired in his death.

Similarly, incited by Tom to avenge what he believes to be Gatsby's gutlessness and carelessness (a revenge Tom is not courageous enough to exact directly), the griefstricken George kills Gatsby and then turns the gun on himself. Tom is thus as complicitous in George's death as he is in Gatsby's. Milton Stern summarizes the major plot action even more succinctly: 'Tom,' he writes, 'cuckolds Wilson, indirectly causes Myrtle's and Gatsby's death; Daisy betrays Gatsby, directly causes Myrtle's and indirectly causes Gatsby's death' (240).

Daisy is herself amoral and adulterous; she shares Tom's moral corruptness, as is apparent in her encouraging of promiscuity between Nick and her close friend Jordan, a golf champion who cheats to win and who, like the Buchanans, drives recklessly (a metaphor in the novel for other careless behaviors). Inherently insincere, Daisy merely plays with Gatsby's affections, perhaps out of her own romantic nostalgia, perhaps as retribution for Tom's infidelities, perhaps—as Bicknell suggests—more 'as a relief from boredom' (Bicknell 69); and she even repudiates Tom briefly, until her fear of possible reprisals for her criminal actions sends her back to him, and to the protection of his good family name.

Only Nick, the novel's true moral center, fully grasps both Buchanans' duplicity. Feeling as uncomfortable in their home as he does initially at Gatsby's parties, he chooses after Gatsby's death to return to the Middle West, whose fertile wheatfields contrast sharply with the valley's aridness and barrenness and the spiritual emptiness of the neighboring Eggs. Interestingly, Nick's final act before leaving New York is to visit Jordan. Wanting 'to leave things in order and not just trust that obliging sea to sweep my refuse away,' Nick confronts her about her carelessness and hypocrisy; it is something he must do, he claims, because 'I'm . . . too old to lie to myself and call it honor' (*GG* 178-79). His deliberate gesture is as diametrically opposed to the Buchanan's careless 'smash[ing] up' of things and letting 'other people clean up the mess they made' (*GG* 180-81) as the natural fecundity of the Midwest is to the artificial splendor of East Egg.

If Nick is able to see realistically, Gatsby sees only romantically. And, like earlier romantic heroes, particularly the heroes of medieval romance, Gatsby appears to be unbound by time.[13] (By contrast, most of the other characters, like Eliot's aimless and sterile wastelanders, feel restricted by or unable to handle chronological time: Daisy, for instance, wearily repeats the question, 'What'll we do with ourselves this afternoon . . . and the day after that, and the next thirty years?' [*GG* 118], much the way Eliot's lady asks 'What shall we do tomorrow? What shall we ever do?') Convinced that he can adjust time or at least set it askew by simply erasing the last five years, Gatsby insists that Daisy admit that she never really loved Tom, not even on their wedding day—an admission Daisy makes but quickly retracts. By pushing Daisy to repudiate Tom, Gatsby tries to legitimate his own unsacramental 'marriage' to her, which in his eyes invalidates her subsequent marriage to Tom. And when Daisy responds that she did, at one time, love her husband, Gatsby dismisses those feelings as 'just personal,' thus distinguishing Tom and Daisy's affection from his own spiritual and ideal love.

Likewise, Gatsby replies with astonishment to Nick's observation that one cannot repeat the past: 'Why of course you can!' And that is what he proceeds to try to do, beginning with his intention to take Daisy, 'after she was free, . . . back to Louisville and be married from her house—just as if it were five years ago' (*GG* 111). Significantly, at Nick's home during his first encounter with Daisy, Gatsby leans against the mantelpiece upon which rests a clock, old and defunct but nonetheless dangerous as it tilts at his head. 'I'm sorry about the clock' (*GG* 87), he says, oblivious to the irony. But only Nick makes the connection: later, after Tom denounces Gatsby as a common thug and exposes his vulnerability, Nick realizes that Gatsby 'was running down like an overwound clock' (93).

In his disregard of chronological time, Gatsby is reminiscent of the hero of medieval romance, who exists outside of time. Moreover, as Jerome Mandel (554) notes, he is also like Parzifal, who fails to ask the questions at the Grail castle and then searches again for the castle to rectify the original error. Unlike Parzifal, however, Gatsby merely repeats his error as he singlemindedly attempts to recreate his month of love with Daisy, the only idyllic part of his youth. Whereas Gatsby's humble origins prevented him from winning Daisy's hand years before, the ignoble past which haunts him again ruins his effort to claim her. The wealth he acquired through bootlegging and other illicit enterprises, rather than obliterating his low birth, gives him a history which Tom exploits, a history which Gatsby cannot ultimately explain or wish away, as he does with the five years of lost time apart from Daisy.

But if Gatsby's unconventional background makes him a less heroic Grail seeker, Daisy, in turn, is an even less worthy Grail. Unlike the priceless cup which justifies and completes the seeker's quest, she proves to be more like 'a loving cup that goes hand to hand' (*BD* 182), an image which Gloria uses to describe herself in *The Beautiful and Damned*. Common dross, Daisy eventually tarnishes Gatsby and most of those around her. Superficial and remorseless—all gilt and no guilt—she lives in an 'artificial world redolent of orchids and pleasant, cheerful snobbery and orchestras which set the rhythm of the year, summing up the sadness and suggestiveness of life in new tunes,' a world in which 'a hundred pairs of golden and silver slippers shuffled the shining dust' (*GG* 151)—a dust which, despite its shine, originates in the wasteland.

While Gatsby professes not to comprehend what compelled Daisy to marry Tom, he in fact is overwhelmingly aware of 'the youth and mystery that wealth imprisons and preserves, of the freshness of many clothes, and of Daisy, gleaming like silver, safe and proud above the hot struggles of the poor' (*GG* 150). That is why, in order to reclaim her affection, he knows he must amass a fortune more considerable than Tom's. But that fortune is important to Gatsby only as a means to an end; for him, it is but one more test of worthiness in the pursuit of his personal Grail, one more proof of his courtly love. As Gatsby takes Daisy through his estate for the first time, Nick observes that 'Gatsby revalued everything in his house according to the measure of response it drew from her well-loved eyes'; it was 'as though in her actual and astounding presence none of it was any longer real' (*GG* 92).

But, for Daisy, what matters is precisely the reality of it; unlike Gatsby, who lives for the seeking, she delights in the having. That is why, when faced with the choice between a letter of love from Gatsby, who is absent and whose future is uncertain, and the three-hundred-and-fifty-thousand dollar pearl necklace from Tom, who is very much present and whose future is lavishly certain (Stern 245), she opts not for Gatsby's vision but for Tom's money. At West Egg, Daisy admires 'with enchanting murmurs . . . this aspect or that of the feudal silhouette [of Gatsby's ostentatious home] against the sky' (*GG* 92), but the towered mansion becomes tangible to her only when she can actually handle its pricey contents. After seeing in Gatsby's bedroom 'the toilet set of pure dull gold,' she grabs the brush 'with great delight' (*GG* 93), and, as if to confirm that it is real, strokes her own hair—a scene which Mandel likens to Lancelot's finding Guinevere's comb in *Le Chevalier de la Charrette* and the medieval tradition of holding sacred the hair of a lover.[14] Later, in another scene with possible medieval and Arthurian analogues,[15] Daisy is moved to tears by the amplitude of Gatsby's closets. Lost in the rich heaps of his expensive silk, linen and soft flannel shirts, she begins to sob and 'to cry stormily' (*GG* 93). It is during this orgiastic emptying of Gatsby's closets that the two achieve their greatest intimacy. Occurring in the bedroom of the great castle-like home he has purchased and maintained for her, this strange consummation of their relationship involves no actual lovemaking—fittingly so, perhaps, since Daisy represents for Gatsby a spiritual, not a physical ideal, and Gatsby represents for Daisy not the satisfaction of any sexual need but rather of her lust for material excess.

Virtually every description of Daisy, even those unwittingly provided by Gatsby, hint at her vulgarity. Daisy's voice, though it sings to him 'a deathless song' (*GG*

97), is nonetheless 'full of money' (*GG* 120). Even her name, Daisy, suggests not an exotic hothouse orchid but a common, almost weedlike flower—as common as Myrtle, the rival whom she eventually destroys. Just as the daisy's white petals sometimes obscure its golden center, Daisy uses her genteel manners and expensive tastes to mask her baseness. It is with some irony, therefore, that she, herself so skilled in duplicity, fails to appreciate the unspoiled sentimentality which underlies Gatsby's occasional coarseness and unsavory associations. But she survives, even thrives, while Gatsby dies precisely because of her reluctance to look below the surface; her lack of sentimentality becomes part of the 'hard malice' which not only drives her but also saves her from engagement and accountability.

Daisy is every bit as false, or fey, as her maiden name suggests. But that name, Fay, hints at more than her duplicity: it also suggests her kinship to another Fay, Morgan Le Fay, the evil enchantress of Arthurian myth. Daisy's magic is as powerful, and as malicious, as her namesake's. The 'enchanting murmurs' (*GG* 92) of Daisy's whispery voice cast spells on those around her. To Nick, she boasts of her sophistication. But 'the instant her voice broke off,' Nick remembers, 'ceasing to compel my attention, my belief, I felt the basic insincerity of what she had said. It made me uneasy, as though the whole evening had been a trick of some sort . . .' (18). Even Nick's first impression of Daisy suggests a certain witchcraft: her dress is rippled and fluttery as if she 'had just been blown back in after a short flight around the house' (*GG* 8), and she herself seems to be floating above her living room couch. For Gatsby, Daisy works the strongest magic of all: she creates an illusion of innocent beauty which endures virtually until his death. The bewitched Gatsby includes Daisy in his 'count of enchanted objects' (*GG* 94); and his last thoughts are of 'the pale magic of her face' (*GG* 153).

Despite Daisy's repeated abuses of his devotion, he remains captive to that magic and to his wishful remembrance of past affection. In the Plaza Hotel suite parlor, where he is humiliated first by Tom and then by Daisy, Gatsby still continues to cling to the 'colossal vitality of his illusion' (*GG* 97). He does not realize, as Nick already has intuited, that his happiness is doomed. In a fine bit of foreshadowing which also underscores the contrast between Nick's realism and Gatsby's romanticism, Gatsby completely ignores the portent upon which Nick comments: en route to New York City, Nick recalls, 'a dead man passed us in a hearse.' The juxtaposition of gaiety and sorrow makes Nick aware that 'anything can happen now that we've slid over this bridge' (*GG* 69).

Only Gatsby's 'romantic readiness' and 'extraordinary gift for hope' (*GG* 2), writes Fitzgerald, kept his dream of Daisy alive as long as it did; and in the end Gatsby 'paid a high price for living too long with a single dream' (*GG* 162). The 'shining dust' of silver and gold slippers from Daisy's world which Gatsby so admired and by which he was so entranced becomes the 'foul dust float[ing] in the wake of his dreams' (*GG* 2) and extinguishes his quest for the life-affirming Grail, for the green light at the end of the dock which suggests promise and vitality, for the 'fresh green breast of the new world' in which Gatsby so fervently believed. After Gatsby's death, even his palatial home—'a huge incoherent failure' (*GG* 181), now overgrown and empty, an obscenity scrawled on its white steps—begins to resemble the wasteland from which the foul dust emanates. As surely as Daisy tarnishes Gatsby's ideals, the dust of the wasteland sullies his dreams and reverberates in a number of finely-honed images throughout the novel, from the conspiratorially silent careless world of the Buchanans, whose actions are reminiscent of the rote movements of the lovers in Eliot's poem, to the sly corruption of Jordan Baker and Meyer Wolfsheim, Jordan's practices being only superficially more genteel than Meyer's while ethically just as culpable.

Drawing his inspiration for the wastelands of *Gatsby* from Eliot, whom Fitzgerald regarded, with profound admiration, as 'the greatest living poet in any language' (*Letters* 221) and in whose vision of deadening decadence and cultural malaise he found a theme which, while universal, was especially topical and symbolically appropriate to the material excesses and the spiritual paucity of his time, Fitzgerald explored that theme not only in *Gatsby* (published a mere three years after Eliot's poem) but also in his other novels. The wasteland is evident in the parched European beaches, places which his well-heeled characters in *The Beautiful and Damned* 'invented' and 'perverted to the tastes of the tasteless' (*BD* 280), and to which they retreat to escape their shallow lives; in the 'waste acres' (*BD* 175) of the suburbs outside New York City, which the Patches visit; in the physical illnesses which mirror spiritual malaise; in the mechanical lovemaking and the disintegrating marriages; in the incessant bickering and abominable drunken sprees which 'decay and coarsen' (*BD* 424). From the 'smothery' rooms (*BD* 150) in which Anthony hides to avoid the ghastly sounds of 'the business of life' below him to the insane asylums in *Tender is the Night,* where the inmates are saner than their doctors, Fitzgerald chronicles 'the drought in the marrow of his [characters'] bones' (*TN* [*Tender is the Night*] 190). Even in his unfinished novel *The Last Tycoon,* the theme recurs. Monroe Stahr, 'the last of the princes' (*LT* [*The Last Tycoon*[27), a man more 'royal' (*LT* 65)—and powerful—than most kings, whose crashing death is a metaphor for the fates of many of Fitzgerald's protagonists and of the Fitzgeralds themselves, for a time rules Hollywood, a place so barren and soulless that it is perhaps the biggest wasteland of all. A land of 'jerky hopes and graceful rogueries and awkward sorrows' (*LT* 20), it not only thrives on the superficial but it creates the artifice by which men and women gauge the hollowness of their lives.

The image of the wasteland also occurs in many of Fitzgerald's short stories, from 'One Trip Abroad' and 'The Swimmer' to 'The Ice Palace' and 'The Diamond as Big as the Ritz'; and it finds particularly rich expression in probably Fitzgerald's best and most frequently anthologized short story 'Babylon Revisited' (1931). Charlie Wales, haunted by his dissolute past in the postwar wasteland and his youthful carelessness which contributed to the death of his wife and to the loss of custody of their daughter, returns to Paris. But, unsuccessful in his attempt to regain 'Honoria,' Charlie is left to ponder his fate at the Ritz Bar, the scene of some of his earlier debauches; his resulting sense of personal loss is part of a larger loss—of values, of honor, of meaning—in his society and his culture. For Fitzgerald, honor was an especially appropriate if not always attainable quest. In his *Notebooks,* he observed: 'As a novelist I reach out to the end of all man's variance, all man's villainy—as a man I do not go that far. I cannot claim honor—but even the knights of the Holy Grail were only striving for it, as I remember' (*Notebooks* 324).

While the Grail and the wasteland are the predominant Arthurian images in Fitzgerald's work, others appear as well. The Lady of Shalott, for example, figures prominently in the story, 'The Spire and the Gargoyle' (later incorporated as a chapter in *This Side of Paradise*)—both implicitly, in the tower of one of the Princeton buildings which becomes for the protagonist 'the symbol of his perception' ('There was something terribly pure in the slope of the chaste stone, something which led and directed and called' [106]); and more explicitly (in the description of his college preceptor, a 'gargoyle' among the hallowed spires because he cannot appreciate the magnificence which surrounds him or the intelligence of his young charges, a man whose view is so distorted that he sees only through his 'two "Mirrors of Shallot"' [110]).

Even more important is the character of Merlin, whom Fitzgerald makes the subject of an entire story, 'O Russet Witch!,' one of the contemporary 'fantasies' in *Tales of the Jazz Age.* In the story, originally entitled 'His Russet Witch,' a modest bookstore clerk, Merlin Grainger, becomes infatuated with a beautiful, mysterious young woman, Alicia Dare ('all is a dare' [Lehan *Short Stories* 9]), an enchantress whose voice is 'full of sorcery' (*ORW* ['O Russet Witch!'] 239). But rather than succumb to her magic, Merlin assumes domestic responsibilities and settles for a drab, mundane life with his wife, appropriately named Olive, and their ungrateful son, Arthur. He sacrifices for them, putting their interests above his own; but, in the end, he realizes that both 'used him for their blind purposes' (*ORW* 272). Olive had nagged and coerced him into ignoring Alicia's attractive presence over the years and Arthur, showing no interest in his father's business, had chosen instead to sell bonds on Wall Street. 'Let Old Merlin get what magic he could from his books,' Merlin scornfully remarked; 'the place of young King Arthur was in the counting house' (*ORW* 262).

When, at the end of the story, Merlin again sees the 'russet witch'—now a grandmother—who, for four decades, had embodied his 'romantic yearning' for the beautiful, he realizes that she was never possessed of any special magic; it was only Merlin's imagination which had turned a flamboyant, silly socialite into such a bewitching figure. Left with no illusions, 'He knew now that he had always been a fool . . . But it was too late. He had angered Providence by resisting too many temptations' (*ORW* 272).

The tale is not one of Fitzgerald's most successful ones, but in it he uses elements of Arthurian myth to suggest that fantasy, though it inevitably disrupts solid middle class respectability, is necessary to give color to drab lives (Sklar 90). He had expressed a similar sentiment while writing *Gatsby,* which shares some plot similarities to 'O Russet Witch!': 'That's the whole burden of [*The Great Gatsby*],' Fitzgerald noted to a friend, 'the loss of those illusions that give such color to the world so you don't care whether things are true or false as long as they partake of the magical glory' (Stern 165).

At the same time, however, in 'O Russet Witch!' Fitzgerald appears to be utilizing the framework of the Arthurian story to comment in some ways favorably on the Jazz Age, a period during which people flouted conventional notions of respectability and protested stupid laws like Prohibition by breaking them. Merlin, locked so solidly into his marriage and his position in the bookshop, fails to avail himself of the kinds of distractions which might have brought an element of pleasure to his life. For example, he notices 'Alicia' dancing atop a round table in a restaurant but tries not to glance her way because it would upset Olive. Such distractions may ultimately prove fleeting; but Merlin's failure to risk or to dream proves even more debilitating. In the end, Merlin's life is a flimsy construct, less real and substantive than the fantasies in which he refused to indulge.

From his early short stories on, Fitzgerald demonstrated an interest in the medieval and in medievalism which persisted throughout his lifetime. ('Tarquin of Cheepside' [1917], for instance, makes repeated mention of the legend of Britomartis in *The Faerie Queene*; a later story, 'Six of One—' [1931], contrasts over the course of a decade a half dozen poor boys with the sons of wealth, six 'young knights' and 'six young princes in velvet.') In fact, among the projects which Fitzgerald had outlined for himself shortly before his death was a continuation of 'The Count of Darkness,' a series begun in 1934 about a medieval knight named Phillipe—modeled on Hemingway, but not recognizably so—whose life spanned the founding of France as a nation and the consolidation of the feudal system. Those stories, which Scottie Fitzgerald called his 'most abysmal failure' (Bruccoli *Grandeur* 496) but which Max Perkins thought profitable enough to consider publishing, had originally been planned to be part of *The Castle,* a novel set entirely in medieval times. And in his best work, most notably *The Great Gatsby,* Fitzgerald used specifically Arthurian themes and motifs, which he reinterpreted in topical and distinctly American ways. His literary career would therefore indicate that, like the characters about whom he wrote, F. Scott Fitzgerald had indeed 'committed himself to the following of a grail.'

Notes

1. Piper quotes from Fitzgerald's fragmentary manuscript, 'The Death of My Father' (1931). That handwritten manuscript is reproduced on pp. 177-82 of *The Apprentice Fiction of F. Scott Fitzgerald.*

2. Bruccoli (*Grandeur* 228) notes that the second story which Fitzgerald ever wrote, 'Reade, Substitute Right Half,' published in the February 1910 *Now and Then,* was 'a perfect example of fiction as wish-fulfillment . . . a small boy comes off the bench to lead his football team to victory.'

   Fitzgerald's interest in football persisted throughout his lifetime. In numerous letters to Scottie (for instance, November 2, 1940, in *Letters* 114), Fitzgerald writes that he is listening to Princeton football games on the radio. His companion Sheilah Graham remembers that he would often doodle football plays in her books (*The Real F. Scott Fitzgerald* 147)

   And Turnbull (*Scott Fitzgerald* 211-12) recalls playing football with Fitzgerald, who gave him football books and introduced him to the *Football Annual.* Fitzgerald also took the young Turnbull to a Navy game at Princeton. Turnbull was 'struck by his uncanny familiarity with the Princeton team. He knew so many details about each player that I suspected him of having memorized the programs of previous contests.'

3. 'The current catch of Chicago' is how Fitzgerald described Gordon Tinsley in 'A Woman with a Past,' one of the Josephine stories based on Ginevra King. (Ginevra later married another wealthy Midwesterner, John Pirie.)

4. Turnbull also comments upon Fitzgerald's sense of 'corruption in the rich': 'That was always my experience,' he wrote near the end of his life, '—a poor boy in a rich town; a poor boy in a rich boy's school; a poor boy in a rich man's club at Princeton. . . . I have never been able to forgive the rich for being rich, and it has colored my entire life and works.' He told a friend that 'the whole idea of Gatsby is the unfairness of a poor young man not being able to marry a girl with money. This theme comes up again and again because I lived it' (150).

5. Bruccoli (*Grandeur* 51) notes that, in this instance, fiction certainly imitated life. 'The strongest influences' on Fitzgerald as a young man, notes Bruccoli, 'were the novels he called "quest books."'

6. The emphasis in the quote is mine, not Fitzgerald's. In *The Beautiful and Damned* (305), Fitzgerald expressed a similar sentiment: 'If living was not purposeful it was, at any rate, essentially romantic!'

7. Like Fitzgerald's other novels, *The Beautiful and Damned* contains various medieval images and allusions. For instance, Anthony expresses his intention to write 'a history of the Middle Ages' (15); he speaks of creating a character called the Chevalier, a sentimentalist and romantic who was exiled 'in the late days of chivalry' (89); and he refers to the need for a chivalric code ('a clear code of honor' [226]).

8. Bruccoli (*Grandeur* 25) observed that Fitzgerald was very self-conscious about his own breeding. 'If I were elected King of Scotland tomorrow after graduating from Eton, Magdalene the Guards with an embryonic history which tied me to the Plantagonets,' Fitzgerald wrote, 'I would still be a *parvenue.*'

9. Milton R. Stern (151-288) analyzes at some length Fitzgerald's use of East and West as symbols in *The Great Gatsby.* (See especially 191, 198-213, 241-250.)

10. Stern adds that 'The West had become a dull and settled place, and the Middle West had, by 1925, come to represent Babbitt on Main Street in his repressive Winesburg, Ohio' (198).

11. Ironically, even Tom Buchanan recognizes the animalistic, atavistic tendencies of Gatsby's invited and uninvited guests, which reflect on the nature of his own society. 'I suppose,' utters Tom to Gatsby, 'you've got to make your house into a pigsty in order to have any friends—in the modern world' (*GG* 131).

12. In 'Handle with Care,' one of the three articles that Edmund Wilson edited as *The Crack-Up,* Fitzgerald wrote of how his own love for Zelda

was almost 'doomed for lack of money': 'The man with the jingle of money in his pocket who married the girl a year later would always cherish an abiding distrust, an animosity toward the leisure class—not the conviction of a revolutionist but the smouldering hatred of a peasant. In the years since then I have never been able to stop wondering where my friends' money came from, nor to stop thinking that at one time a sort of *droit de seigneur* might have been exercised to give one of them my girl' (Stern 164).

13. It is interesting to note that the brewer who built the house in West Egg which Gatsby purchases felt, in odd ways, similarly unbound by time. Fitzgerald writes that, in a sort of throwback to feudal times, 'he'd agreed to pay five years' taxes on all the neighboring cottages if the owners would have their roofs thatched with straw.' When they refused, the brewer went into 'an immediate decline' and—ominously for Gatsby—'his children sold his house with the black wreath still on the door' (*GG* 89).

14. Mandel (554) writes: 'the hair of the beloved is sacred to the medieval lover. Soredamors sews a strand of her own hair into a shirt that Guenevere gives to Alexander; when he discovers the secret of the shirt, "all night he presses the shirt in his arms, and when he looks at the golden hair, he feels like the lord of the whole wide world." When Lancelot in *Le Chevalier de la Charrette* finds Guenevere's comb on a stone, he discovers a few "strands of the Queen's hair . . . clinging in the teeth of the comb." He removes the hair "so carefully that he tears none of it" and "lays [it] in his bosom near his heart . . . He would not exchange [it] for a cartload of emeralds."'

15. Mandel (547 n. 10) notes that medieval romance is flush with splendid descriptions of gorgeous clothes. 'Erec's coronation robes, Isolde's clinging robe when she enters the judgment hall in Ireland, Culhwch's clothes on his spectacular ride to Arthur's court are only among the most obvious examples of this medieval love of splendor and display.' He concludes that 'they may well be the folkloric source of Gatsby's splendid display of shirts.'

Works Cited

Audhuy, Letha. 'The Waste Land Myth and Symbols in *The Great Gatsby*.' *Etudes Anglaises* 33 (1980): 41-54.

Bicknell, John W. 'The Waste Land of F. Scott Fitzgerald.' *Virginia Quarterly Review* 30 (Autumn 1954): 556-72. Rpt. in Eble 67-80.

Bruccoli, Matthew J. *Some Sort of Epic Grandeur: The Life of F. Scott Fitzgerald.* New York: Harcourt Brace Jovanovich, 1981.

Bryer, Jackson R., ed. *The Short Stories of F. Scott Fitzgerald: New Approaches in Criticism.* Madison: U of Wisconsin P, 1982.

Eble, Kenneth E., ed. *F. Scott Fitzgerald: A Collection of Criticism.* New York: McGraw-Hill, 1973.

Eliot, T. S. *The Waste Land.* New York: Boni & Liveright, 1922.

Fitzgerald, F. Scott. *Afternoon of an Author: A Selection of Uncollected Stories and Essays.* Ed. Arthur Mizener. New York: Scribner's, 1957.

———. 'Babylon Revisited.' In *The Short Stories of F. Scott Fitzgerald: A New Collection.* New York: Scribner's, 1989. 616-33.

———. *The Beautiful and Damned.* 1922. New York: Scribner's, 1950.

———. 'The Bowl.' *The Saturday Evening Post.* January 21, 1928. 6-7, 93-94, 97, 100.

———. *Correspondence of F. Scott Fitzgerald.* Ed. Matthew J. Bruccoli and Margaret M. Duggan, with the assistance of Susan Walker. New York: Random House, 1980.

———. *F. Scott Fitzgerald in His Own Time: A Miscellany.* Ed. Matthew J. Bruccoli and Jackson R. Bryer. Kent: Kent State UP, 1971.

———. *The Great Gatsby.* 1925. New York: Scribner's, 1953.

———. *The Last Tycoon: An Unfinished Novel. Together with The Great Gatsby.* 1925, 1941. New York: Scribner's, 1951.

———. *The Letters of F. Scott Fitzgerald.* Ed. Andrew Turnbull. 1963. New York: Laurel, 1966.

———. *The Notebooks of F. Scott Fitzgerald.* Ed. Matthew J. Bruccoli. New York: Harcourt Brace Jovanovich, 1978.

———. 'O Russet Witch!' *Tales of the Jazz Age.* New York: Scribner's, 1922. 234-72.

———. 'Outside the Cabinet-Maker's.' *Afternoon of an Author.* 137-41.

———. 'Six of One—.' *The Short Stories of F. Scott Fitzgerald: A New Collection.* Ed. Matthew J. Bruccoli. New York: Scribner's, 1989. 667-69.

———. 'The Spire and the Gargoyle.' *The Apprentice Fiction of F. Scott Fitzgerald: 1909-1917.* Ed. John Kuehl. New Brunswick: Rutgers UP, 1965. 105-14.

———. *Tales of the Jazz Age.* New York: Scribner's, 1922.

———. 'Tarquin of Cheepside.' *The Apprentice Fiction of F. Scott Fitzgerald: 1909-1917.* Ed. John Kuehl. New Brunswick: Rutgers UP, 1965. 118-23.

———. *Tender Is the Night.* 1933. New York: Scribner's, 1962.

———. *This Side of Paradise.* 1920. New York: Scribner's, 1948.

Fitzgerald, Zelda. *Save Me the Waltz.* 1932. London: The Grey Walls Press, 1953.

Graham, Sheilah. *The Real F. Scott Fitzgerald: Thirty-Five Years Later.* New York: Warner Books, 1976.

Graham, Sheilah and Gerold Frank. *Beloved Infidel: The Education of a Woman.* New York: Henry Holt, 1958.

Kahn, Sy. '*This Side of Paradise*: The Pageantry of Disillusion.' *The Midwest Quarterly* 7 (January 1966), 177-194. Rpt. in Eble 34-47.

Kazin, Alfred. *F. Scott Fitzgerald: The Man and His Work.* 1951. New York: Collier, 1962.

Lehan, Richard D. *F. Scott Fitzgerald and the Craft of Fiction.* Carbondale: Southern Illinois UP, 1966. 91-102, 122-23. Rpt. as '*The Great Gatsby* and Its Sources.' *Critical Essays on The Great Gatsby.* Ed. Scott Donaldson. Boston: G. K. Hall, 1984. 66-74.

———. 'The Romantic Self and the Uses of Place in the Stories of F. Scott Fitzgerald.' In Bryer 3-21.

Le Vot, André. *F. Scott Fitzgerald: A Biography.* 1979. New York: Warner Books, 1983.

Mandel, Jerome. 'The Grotesque Rose: Medieval Romance and *The Great Gatsby*.' *Modern Fiction Studies* 34.4 (Winter 1988): 541-58.

Milford, Nancy. *Zelda: A Biography.* New York: Harper & Row, 1970.

Ornstein, Robert. 'Scott Fitzgerald's Fable of East and West.' *College English* 18 (1956): 139-43. Rpt. in Eble 60-66.

Piper, Henry Dan. *F. Scott Fitzgerald: A Critical Portrait.* New York: Holt, Rinehart and Winston, 1965.

Sklar, Robert. *F. Scott Fitzgerald: The Last Laocoön.* New York: Oxford UP, 1967.

Smith, Scottie Fitzgerald. 'The Colonial Ancestors of Francis Scott Key Fitzgerald. In Bruccoli, *Some Sort of Epic Grandeur.* 496-509.

Stern, Milton R. *The Golden Moment: The Novels of F. Scott Fitzgerald.* Urbana: U of Illinois P, 1970.

Turnbull, Andrew. *Scott Fitzgerald.* New York: Scribner's, 1962.

Weir, Charles, Jr. '"An Invite with Gilded Edges": A Study of F. Scott Fitzgerald.' *The Virginia Quarterly Review.* Rpt. in Kazin. 133-146.

Whitley, John S. *F. Scott Fitzgerald: The Great Gatsby.* London: Edward Arnold, 1976.

Charles Moorman (essay date 2000)

SOURCE: Moorman, Charles. "T. S. Eliot." In *The Grail: A Casebook,* edited by Dhira P. Mahoney, pp. 505-23. New York: Garland Publishing Inc., 2000.

[*In the following essay, Moorman analyses T. S. Eliot's literary and philosophical development, specifically his ideas on the creation of literary myths and use of the Grail legend in his poetry. Moorman contends that Eliot's spiritual viewpoint was central to his writing, and in* The Waste Land *the legend of the grail assumes a position of vital importance because of its connections with images of religious fertility.*]

So much has been written about T. S. Eliot's literary and philosophical development that it would seem unnecessary to comment further on these matters. But although critics have made much of Eliot's swing from restless poetic innovation and fierce social and religious criticism to metrical formality and acceptance of a tradition-bound society and church, little has been said concerning the basic attitude, present in Eliot's work from the beginning, which underlies and in a sense motivates these seemingly irresponsible changes. Since this attitude has a great deal to do with Eliot's use of myth, it will be necessary to attempt a definition of this prevailing point of view.

I have already attempted to define the sort of mentality involved in the creation of literary myth. Basically, the mythmaker is a primitive; he sees no division between himself and the nature that exists outside himself. To quote again from Henri Frankfort:

> The world appears to primitive man neither inanimate nor empty, but redundant with life; and life has individuality, in man and beast and plant, and in every phenomenon which confronts man—the thunderclap, the sudden shadow, the eerie and unknown clearing in the wood, the stone which suddenly hurts him when he stumbles on a hunting trip. Any phenomenon may at any time face him, not as "It," but as "Thou." In this confrontation, "Thou" reveals its individuality, its qualities, its will. "Thou" is not contemplated with intellectual detachment; it is experienced as life confronting life, involving every faculty of man in a reciprocal relationship.[1]

A modern version of this same attitude, it seems to me, is contained in Eliot's famous description of the unified sensibility:

> When a poet's mind is perfectly equipped for its work, it is constantly amalgamating disparate experience; the ordinary man's experience is chaotic, irregular, frag-

mentary. The latter falls in love, or reads Spinoza, and these two experiences have nothing to do with each other, or with the noise of the typewriter or the smell of cooking; in the mind of the poet these experiences are always forming new wholes.[2]

In both instances, primitive man and modern poet, we have a point of view suggested which regards the universe as a reconcilable and unified, if not thoroughly systematic, whole. The principles of identity and reconciliation are present in both statements and represent a quality that is common to and necessary for both the mythmaker and, in Eliot's view, the poet.

This identification of mythmaker and poet seems to me to throw a good deal of light on Eliot's basic attitude toward poetry and toward the world. This point of view, which I call "sacramental," seems to me to underlie all of Eliot's work. Basically, the sacramentalist, like primitive man, can see no difference between himself and the world of natural things which surrounds him; he has, in Eliot's phrase, a "unified sensibility" that enables him to see all experience, however disparate it may first appear, as a whole and unified complex of meaning, unified because it is interpreted in terms of its relation to the whole milieu of experience by a mind that is not only cognizant of those relations, but ready and able to interpret them as they relate to one another and to his own personality. In short, the "odour of a rose," in Eliot's view, becomes a total part of Donne's experience and personality;[3] Donne unites that odor with the total complex of his experience, seen under the aspects of both time and space, of which it is a part. *Sub specie aeternitatis,* therefore, Donne is of no more importance in the total experience than is the rose that originally started the chain of reaction; they exist as equal parts of a total experience.

In addition to seeing no difference between the "I" of self and the "It" of nature, the sacramentalist also constantly identifies symbol and object. To use again the most obvious nonliterary example, there is no essential difference to a communicant who accepts the doctrine of the Real Presence in the "reality" of the actual Body and Blood of Christ and the wafer of unleavened bread and cup of wine which symbolize that Body and that Blood. No matter how the particular relationship of symbol and object is defined, whether as transubstantiation or consubstantiation, the main point, grasped and adhered to certainly by an act of faith, is that that symbol and object do exist in some sort of unity, which though certainly undefinable is nevertheless "real." Because of this, reason and thus definition cannot be used to explain the phenomenon; it is only properly felt and believed by a mentality unaccustomed, whether unconsciously or consciously, to analysis and unused to the separation of man and nature, self and nonself. This is, of course, precisely the same habit of thinking that primitive man employs when he blames the stone that he kicked for hurting him. Thus it is that the poetry of Charles Williams admits no difference in kind between the modern world and the Arthurian myth that he uses as its symbol. Thus it is that Donne is able to compare his ailing body to a map[4] and Marvell the progress of his love to a set of geometrical equations[5] with no sense of insecurity, or of unreality, or of ineptness. These poets and primitives see man and nature, seen and unseen, object and symbol as parts of a total experience, unified in spite of itself by their sacramental points of view. To them the word is made flesh at all times and on an infinite number of levels.

These two aspects of the sacramental point of view—the fusion of man and nature and of symbol and object—seem to me to underlie all of Eliot's career from "The Love Song of J. Alfred Prufrock" through "Little Gidding"; they are demonstrable in his poetry long before his conversion to Anglo-Catholicism. That he has continued them in his later religious poetry is obvious, since Eliot's current belief in the Incarnation as the unifier of all experience ("Here the impossible union / Of spheres of existence is actual")[6] has led him further from the analytical abstracting of the scientific mind than did his early theory of the dissociation of sensibility, which is primarily a matter of literary history. But even before *For Launcelot Andrewes,* the sacramental viewpoint was there, exhibiting itself in a form totally unlike that of any poet (with the possible exceptions of Coleridge and Hopkins) since the metaphysicals. This is nowhere so graphically illustrated as in the mythopoetic method of *The Waste Land.*

It is a commonplace that the secret to any interpretation of *The Waste Land* lies in an analysis of Eliot's use of myth in that poem. But more often than not this fact is singled out for scorn rather than for praise. At first glance, the poem appears chaotic, disunified; the profusion of references to myth and literature and the lack of transitional statements between the swift changes in scene give the poem a cluttered appearance. Because of this, some critics have claimed that the poem lacks any sort of unity, except perhaps for a purely artificial and mechanical unity of method and for an over-all unity of effect based on the shaky principle of imitative form.[7] This so-called "fallacy of imitative form" we can, I think, safely ignore since it is concerned only with partial effect and is not therefore really connected with any principle of total unity. The question of artificial unity of method, on the other hand, comes closer to the truth of the matter.

The mechanical unity of the poem is said to lie in Eliot's trick of setting a scene from myth or literature and a contemporary scene in close proximity and then settling back to watch the immediate effect of that comparison.[8] A good example of this method appears in the use of Tiresias in the seduction scene of "The Fire Sermon."⁹ Eliot in his notes to the poem quotes a section of the *Metamorphoses* which explains two essential facts about the Greek seer—(1) he has been both man and woman, and (2) he is able to know the future. Both of these miraculous qualities, moreover, are caused by his having been involved in situations involving sexual relations. He was condemned to live for seven years as a woman because he interfered with the mating of two snakes; he was privileged to see the future as compensation for the blindness imposed on him by Juno when he judged against her on a question of sexual pleasure. Thus, Tiresias "though blind, throbbing between two lives, / Old man with wrinkled female breasts, can see" and judge the sordid affair between the callous "typist home at teatime" and the vain carbuncular clerk. Passages involving Tiresias occur three times during the scene—(1) in the short introductory passage I have quoted, (2) just before the entrance of the clerk when it is said that Tiresias "perceived the scene, and foretold the rest," and (3) at the moment of intercourse when he says that he has "foresuffered all / Enacted on this same divan or bed," he who has "sat by Thebes below the wall / And walked among the lowest of the dead." Here then is a mythological figure, both man and woman, seer and prophet, set beside a cheap, effortless and mechanical seduction, the most striking quality of which is its obvious triviality. The effect of the comparison is, to me at least, immediate and overwhelming. Here is Tiresias, representing the world of myth, who knows the sexual act both as a man knows it and as a woman knows it, who has been condemned and honored for interference in sexual situations, who has been involved in the great tragedy of Oedipus, who has held communion with the tragic living and "walked among the lowest of the dead"—here is Tiresias, in whose life the sexual act has been of tremendous meaning and importance, forced to watch with disgust a sexual act that is wholly mechanical and totally void of meaning. Sexual intercourse, which in past time has driven men to war, murder, and poetry and for which men once lost the world and thought the world well lost, has become, in the contemporary waste land, a matter of routine, as mechanical as combing one's hair or placing a record on the phonograph. In short, the waste land itself is by implication devoid of meaning.

The conclusion of the scene between the typist and the clerk affords another instance of Eliot's general method. As an example of a past world in which love had meaning, Eliot here uses a scrap of a song in Goldsmith's *The Vicar of Wakefeld*.¹⁰ After the clerk has gone, the typist remarks that she is "glad it's over," and at this point appear the lines:

> When lovely lady stoops to folly and
> Paces about her room again, alone,
> She smooths her hair with automatic hand,
> And puts a record on the gramophone.
>
> (11. 253-256)

The lines from *The Vicar of Wakefield* which Eliot is parodying begin:

> When lovely woman stoops to folly,
> And finds too late that men betray,
> What charm can soothe her melancholy?
> What art can wash her guilt away?

and conclude with the observation that the only "art her guilt to cover" is "to die." Again the contrast is immediate and overwhelming. Eliot's ironic use of this eighteenth-century lyric, and especially of the sexual connotations of "to die," expresses directly and forcefully a contrast between modern sexual ennui and an older concept of romantic honor by suggesting, in the twisting of Goldsmith's lyric, the difference between two civilizations.

I bring forward these interpretations in demonstration of a kind of unity which underlies the poem and which can be clearly demonstrated by an analysis of Eliot's method at any point in the poem. Yet it is manifestly a mechanical unity, imposed from without by an intellect extremely conscious of the trick it is using. An organic unity must, by definition, come from within the poem's elementary structure, guiding and shaping the tenor and structure of the whole poem rather than of the parts. Two comments on organic structure, in specific application to Eliot and *The Waste Land,* come immediately to mind. The first is: This organic unity must proceed out of what I have previously called a sacramental point of view that, as I have defined it, either will not or cannot see that the compared and contrasted items, no matter from where in time or space they may be drawn, are of any essential difference in kind. In short, just as Donne's comparison of the body and map or of the lovers and compass is perfectly natural to a mind used to this sort of mythopoetic thought, so must the presence of Tiresias in the room of the typist proceed not from a conscious trick of methodology but from a mind, like Donne's, which sees neither strangeness nor trickery in the comparison.

The existence of such an attitude is manifestly undemonstrable except perhaps by the method I have previously suggested, i.e., that the poet is able to work with equal ease with either set of terms involved in the comparison. Unfortunately, the comparisons introduced in *The Waste Land* are too limited in duration to allow this method. But the presence of the sacramental point of view may also be indicated by the nature of the images used by Eliot in the poem; with this matter I wish to deal in the second of these two general comments on organic unity in *The Waste Land*. The objections of those critics who give to *The Waste Land* mechanical but not organic unity may be reduced, it seems to me, to a single statement—*The Waste Land* consists of too great a variety of comparisons to have any one organically unifying principle. These critics have a point; *The Waste Land* is on first glance a hodgepodge. Yet the varying images and seemingly disconnected comparisons of *The Waste Land* may be shown to be variations of one image and one comparison, a fact that would seem to point to the presence of the sacramental point of view. That basic metaphor involves the waste land of the Arthurian myth.

Eliot's introductory note to the poem states that "not only the title, but the plan and a good deal of the incidental symbolism of the poem were suggested by Miss Jessie L. Weston's book on the Grail legend: *From Ritual to Romance*." It is almost certain, judging from Eliot's note, that he came to know the myth from Miss Weston's book. He thus saw the myth primarily from her ritualist and Celticist point of view and accepted her interpretation of the major symbols. The Fisher King-waste-land myth, according to Miss Weston's interpretation, is primarily sexual in conception and function. The Fisher King is interpreted as a symbolic representative of the life principle whose maimed condition indicates a failure in his virility; his traditional wound in the thigh becomes a symbolic castration. This wounding of the Fisher King's virility, moreover, is reflected in the blight visited upon his land. Having quoted a passage from the *Sone de Nansai* which lists among the blights that strike the waste land the facts that

> Ne enfes d'omme n'e nasqui
> Ne puchielle n'i ot mari
> Ne arbres fueille n'i porta
> Ne nus pres n'i reverdia,
> Ne nus oysiaus n'i ot naon
> Ne se n'i ot beste faon. . . .[11]

Miss Weston says concerning this passage:

> Now there can be no possible doubt here, the condition of the King is sympathetically reflected on the land, the loss of virility in the one brings about a suspension of the reproductive processes of Nature on the other.[12]

According to Miss Weston, this legend, which has its roots in fertility rituals, becomes associated in the Middle Ages with the growing body of the Arthurian materials, and the cup and lance of the older legend (both of which are patently sexual in origin in Miss Weston's view) become the Grail and Bleeding Lance of the Christian story.

I have already quoted in connection with Charles Williams, Eliot's remarks on a poet's method of operation. The gist of those remarks is that the poet is, by nature, a man of "unified sensibility," who sees all experience, however disparate, as potential material for art. The theory of the "objective correlative," moreover, assumes that emotional states are transmitted not by abstractions, but by these disparate poetic concretions that serve in turn to evoke like states of mind in the reader. It seems to me that Eliot finds in Miss Weston's discussion of the Fisher King-waste-land legend a perfect objective correlative to his own generalized emotion toward contemporary society. To Eliot, the modern world *is* a waste land, devastated by moral and spiritual wounds that have affected its reproductive organs and creative functions. The modern world cannot create, cannot reproduce; it is, in essence, a dead land. In the myth, as it exists in Miss Weston's reading, this death is intimately connected with sterility, and it is my contention that this central image of sexual sterility forms the underlying foundation of all the supposedly varied and disunified metaphorical allusions in the poem. My case for organic unity, and hence for the sacramental point of view in *The Waste Land*, therefore, lies in Eliot's use of the sterility image of the Fisher King-waste-land myth as it comes to him from Jessie Weston's *From Ritual to Romance*.

One need only glance at the wealth of exegetical studies of *The Waste Land* to realize that every detail of the poem has already been interpreted in the light of its possible connections with myth generally and with the Grail myth in particular. Grover Smith states in prefacing a complete examination of the text that "*The Waste Land* summarizes the Grail legend, not precisely in the usual order, but retaining the principal incidents and adapting them to a modern setting."[13] There is thus no need for my explicating the poem in detail. The Grail myth can be seen to underlie the poem at every point, either in images that refer directly to the myth (the protagonist's "fishing in the dull canal," the journey to the Chapel Perilous) or indirectly to the sexual sterility that, in Miss Weston's interpretation, is a vital part of the myth (the frustrated women of "A Game of Chess," the homosexual Mr. Eugenides).

The use of the Grail myth as a unifying image thus allows for the presence of the sacramental point of view in that the myth provides a kind of matrix out of which and about which all of Eliot's images, drawn from wherever or whenever, may evolve and cluster. The Arthurian myth establishes for Eliot by means of its own inclusiveness and unity the artistic equivalent of Charles Williams' "co-inherence of souls." Just as the concept of the co-inherence allows Williams to mix magical and commonplace, living and dead, so Eliot's over-all waste-land myth allows him to fuse Marvell's "Coy Mistress," Day's goddess Diana, and the exfighter Apeneck Sweeney into a single image that contains within itself the opposites of attraction and repulsion, past and present, mythical and modern and *is* itself a sacramental fusing of image and idea.

A few examples from the poem should demonstrate how the Grail myth serves to permit Eliot's sacramentalism to operate in *The Waste Land*.

The poem begins with a section "identifying the class and character of the protagonist."[14] Yet the first seven lines of the poem serve also to introduce the general theme of sexual sterility which underlies the poem, and thus prepare us for the introduction of the myth. April is generally associated with the regeneration of the earth and thus with love and birth. But in Eliot's poem, April is "cruel": "the dull roots" are stirred by the rain; the lilacs are simply "bred" out of a "dead soil" (ll. 1-7). Birth is an uncomfortable process; winter with its "forgetful snow" and "dried tubers" was sterile, yet safer than this birth-giving April. It is in this context that we first see the waste land itself:

> A heap of broken images, where the sun beats,
> And the dead tree gives no shelter, the cricket no relief,
> And the dry stone no sound of water.
>
> (ll. 22-24)

But even in the midst of this desert lies a hope:

> There is shadow under this red rock,
> (Come in under the shadow of this red rock).
>
> (ll. 25-26)

Under this "rock," then, exists some kind of regeneration; there is "shadow" here. The symbol of the rock is here ambivalent, referring as it does to Christ ("the shadow of a great rock in a weary land"), to the Grail itself (in Wolfram's *Parzifal*, "the Grail is said to be a stone, and those who are called to its quiet are said to be called as children and to grow up under its shadow")[15] and to Chrétien's castle of ladies, "la roche de Sanguin."[16] Thus, in the midst of images of sterility, the Grail itself is present to remind us of a kind of religious fertility and order which may revitalize the waste land.

There follow immediately in the poem two other sets of symbols referring again to this pattern of sexual sterility and demonstrating the presence of the sacramental point of view (ll. 31-42). The hopeful cry of the sailor accompanying Isolde to Cornwall and its answer, the dismal report of the shepherd who watches the empty sea for Isolde's return, are used to frame the protagonist's encounter with the hyacinth girl. The hyacinth girl, "arms full and hair wet," obviously a symbol of sexual fertility, is greeted by her lover (to Grover Smith, the Grail quester himself), who, neither "living nor dead," cannot in any way partake of her sexuality and is stunned by her vibrant life; he "knew nothing, / Looking into the heart of light, the silence." Thus, in this opening description of the waste land, Eliot presents in rapid succession an image (the red rock) which refers directly to the Grail legend and, in the Isolde and hyacinth girl sections, images that refer indirectly to the sterility-fertility dichotomy that underlies the Grail myth. This opening passage, moreover, indicates quite clearly the type of methodology and the kind of poetic mentality which pervade the poem; an image of great potential fertility drawn from whatever source (the seaman's song, the hyacinth girl) is presented and then immediately fused with a contrary image or with a denial of the original image in its own terms (the shepherd's song, the protagonist's refusal to accept the girl). The sacramental point of view, stemming from the unified sensibility, thus allows Eliot to "amalgamate disparate experience" in images that unite oppositions in time, place, and attitude.

Other images show the same process at work. In Eliot's presentation of Madame Sosostris, the fortuneteller (ll. 43-59), the Tarot deck of cards, which once played a part in ancient fertility rituals, is here seen as a mere fortunetelling device used, significantly, by a society fortuneteller who has a "cold," which is generally in Eliot a sterility symbol.[17] The characters as they appear on the cards also become symbols connected with the basic fertility-sterility image pattern that dominates the poem. The "drowned Phoenician sailor" is later connected with the Phoenician merchant who suffers "death by water" and so becomes, as Brooks suggests, a "type of the fertility god whose image was thrown into the sea annually. . . ."[18] "Belladonna [symbolically a modern poisoning of the image of the Blessed Virgin], the Lady of the Rocks" is a denial of Divine Motherhood, hence motherhood itself, in terms of the waste land. She has become simply the "lady of situations," a phrase that would seem to carry connotations of illicit sexual relationships. The "man with three staves" is associated by Eliot himself with the maimed Fisher King; the one-eyed merchant later becomes associated with the homosexual Mr. Eugenides, who represents another kind of sexual sterility; the Hanged Man of the Tarot deck is associated by Eliot with Frazer's Hanged God and so directly with Christ and indirectly with the Grail. Thus again, the emphasis of the scene is directed to the principal themes and symbols of the Fisher King myth—sexual sterility and the saving power of the Grail.

One could go on demonstrating the same point in almost every line. The fusion of the passionate fertility of myth (Cleopatra, Dido, Eve) with the frustration and sterility of modern society in "A Game of Chess," the intermingling of the various river scenes in "The Fire Sermon," the journey to the Chapel Perilous and the final images of fragmentation in "What the Thunder Said"—all of these images indicate clearly the use of the Grail myth as objective correlative and as matrix.

It should be clear also that this fusing of images within the organic unity of the poem differs from the simple mechanical unity obtained by setting past and present side by side. This latter device corresponds to the "illustrative" use of metaphor; it is a comparative device, and from this point of view the image of Tiresias in "The Fire Sermon" is simply compared with the image of clerk and typist. However, by means of the sacramental point of view the images are not compared, but identified, and in the seduction scene it will be noted that Tiresias is physically present and that he both sees the scene before him and feels (by means of his "foresuffering") the emotions of both (because of his dual sexuality) typist and clerk. Tiresias, in the poem, is not compared with the modern lovers; he is identified with them in terms of the sterility-fertility myth of which they are both a part. Eliot himself reinforces in the notes to the poem this notion of the kind of unity exhibited in the poem by stating that "just as the one-eyed merchant, seller of currants, melts into the Phoenician Sailor, and the latter is not wholly distinct from Ferdinand Prince of Naples, so all the women are one woman, and the two sexes meet in Tiresias."[19]

So in Eliot's poem, all literature and all myth become aspects of one literature and one myth. The poem's much discussed contrasts between Elizabethan England and modern England, Eastern religion and Western secular thought, fertility and sterility all exist within the context of the poem as parts and aspects of a legend and symbol that Eliot uses to control the material that goes into the making of his vision of his own time.

This use of the sacramental point of view to suggest by means of allusion whole structures and attitudes, moreover, is seen throughout Eliot's work. In four well known lines from "Sweeney among the Nightingales," Eliot alludes in passing to four myths:

> The nightingales are singing near
> The Convent of the Sacred Heart,
> And sang within the bloody wood
> When Agamemnon cried aloud.

The reader, perhaps unfairly, is expected to enlarge upon each of these allusions, bringing to bear on the poem the whole weight of the full situation that each allusion suggests. He must know that the legends concerning the rape of Philomel, the Crucifixion of Christ, the murder of the priest in the sacred wood at Nemi, and the murder of Agamemnon by Aegisthus and Clytemnestra are all basically concerned with high crimes involving murder, sex, violence, and treachery. The reader must also apply this information to the text of the whole of Eliot's poem in order to understand the contrast that Eliot is enforcing, a contrast between these ancient crimes, all of which involve violence and meaning and purpose, and the proposed murder of Sweeney, which is confused and most obviously meaningless and purposeless. But, to repeat, the whole force and impact of the poem depend upon the reader's ability to supply the full meaning of the mythical situations to which Eliot merely alludes. This method is typical of Eliot's general handling of myth. A name, a place, an allusion is enough to suggest the whole situation from which the key word comes. Thus it is that in *The Waste Land* the twisted lines from Marvell and Day suggest the whole poems from which they are taken as well as the total milieu and cultural situation which produced those poems.

This reliance on myth and on the sacramental point of view may well be, as I have suggested earlier, the unifying thread that binds all of Eliot's work together. Grover Smith points out, quite conclusively it seems to me, that the mythical pattern of death and rebirth underlies almost all of Eliot's creative work,[20] and I would maintain that the sacramental method is the means whereby this pattern is presented in terms and symbols which, though they shift from work to work, are nevertheless consistent in that they constantly reflect that pattern, and that it is also the means whereby Eliot's works acquire organic unity.

Certainly, from one point of view, the earlier poems can be seen as quests, if not for the specifically Christian Grail of the Arthurian myth, then at least for the fertility and purpose and vision which the Grail symbolizes. Though it is perhaps an error to see specific allusions to the Grail myth in poems such as "The Love Song of J. Alfred Prufrock," "Mr. Apollinax," and "Gerontion," there is nevertheless demonstrated in these poems the same sacramental use of myth which determines the form and meaning of *The Waste Land*.

"Prufrock" fuses into a series of images two worlds, the world Prufrock envisions (the redeemed and fertile waste land) and the world as it is (the waste land itself). Thus the famous image of "the evening . . . spread out against the sky / Like a patient etherised upon a table" fuses Prufrock's romantic expectation (he expects the evening to be "spread out" in a magnificent fashion) with his actual perception (the etherized patient). And the same sacramental fusion is present in the images drawn from myth and literature. The socialite, culture-conscious "women" of Prufrock's own society and Michelangelo (here representing the most vigorously masculine and fertile creativity) are fused into a single image. Prufrock is ironically compared, again by means of this same kind of image, with Hamlet, with Lazarus, with John the Baptist, with Marvell's lover, and through the epigraph to the poem, with Guido de Montefeltro, all of whom represent the fertile, active, decisive life for which Prufrock is searching.

This same technique is perceptible in other early poems of Eliot. In "Mr. Apollinax," the hero, a "charming man," is sharply ridiculed by images in which he is linked, and so ironically compared, with Priapus, the old man of the sea, and the centaur. "Gerontion" defines the sterility and ineffectualness of the modern waste land by fusing images of modern sterility (the old man's house, his blindness, the sneezing woman, the hazy international set of lines 23-29, the distorted images of history, the final fragments) with images of fertility (Thermopylae, the pirates, the goat, Christ the tiger, May, passion). In "Sweeney Erect," Apeneck Sweeney, here awakening in a brothel, is identified with Polyphemus and the "epileptic on the bed" with Nausicäa. In each of these poems, the sacramental method controls both meaning and structure by yoking items of "disparate experience," all of which ultimately stem from the central image of the failure of the quest for fertile life in the midst of a sterile world.

The sacramental fusion of images is even more readily apparent in the poems, and incidentally the plays, following *The Waste Land,* though here specifically Christian images, drawn principally from Dante, St. John of the Cross, and the liturgy, take the place of the older pagan symbols. In these poems, the "still point," the point of fusion of time and timelessness, matter and spirit, man and God comes more and more to fill Eliot's mind and to dominate and so give organic unity to his poems. The image of the still point, or in specifically Christian terms the Incarnation, which appears in *Four Quartets* and in *The Family Reunion* and *Murder in the Cathedral* is itself the supreme image of the sacramental consciousness:

> Here the impossible union
> Of spheres of existence is actual,
> Here the past and future
> Are conquered and reconciled. . . .
>
> ("The Dry Salvages")

It is toward this "impossible union" that Eliot continually strives in his later work. Hence one finds in these poems an even greater clustering and fusing of images drawn from myth and literature, images that again are determined by the constant pervading and unifying influence of the death-rebirth pattern. In "Journey of the Magi," ordinary temporality is ignored as the wise men encounter images of the crucifixion ("three trees on the low sky," "six hands at an open door dicing for pieces of silver") as they approach Bethlehem. Once there, they find the "birth" to be "hard and bitter agony for [them], like Death." In "Ash Wednesday," images taken from *The Divine Comedy,* St. John of the Cross, Shakespeare's sonnets, the bestiaries, the Scriptures, the liturgy, Grimm's fairy tales, and Guido Cavalcanti flow together with perfect ease to form a single unified image of penitence. Grover Smith finds in sixty lines of the "second movement" of "Little Gidding" possible allusions to Kipling, Tourneur, Shakespeare, Mallarmé, Milton, Swift, Ford, Yeats, Johnson, and Dante fused into an image "showing past time as simultaneously alive";[21] and almost any given section of *Four Quarters* would, I expect, yield similar fruit.

One might be disposed to treat such a use of allusion as mere virtuosity, a delight in erudition and obscurity for their own sakes. But it can also be seen as Eliot's attempt to make his poetry itself an image of the "impossible union / Of spheres of existence," to create within his poetry a single concentrated image of life, seen *sub specie aeternitatis,* an image distilled out of time and space by means of the sacramental point of view.

But specifically how and why does Eliot use the Arthurian myth in *The Waste Land*? It is obvious, first of all, that I cannot say as I did concerning C. S. Lewis that Eliot selects and uses parts of the myth to suggest the whole meaning of the myth. Neither can I say as I did of Charles Williams that what we have in *The Waste Land* is a complete recreation of the whole legend. On the other hand, it is perfectly clear that the symbols of the Fisher King and the waste land dominate and control the movement of the poem. One solution I would suggest is this: Eliot finds in these two symbols almost perfect objective correlatives by which he can express the emotion he feels toward the modern world. Here in the legend are symbols that express Eliot's own disillusion (this is in spite of Eliot's statements that he was never disillusioned) and disgust—the maimed ruler and the sterile land. The advantage of this particular myth lies then in the fact that it at once focuses and interprets Eliot's general feeling toward his own age. Thus, the myth Eliot adopts in *The Waste Land* becomes the sort of image to which he can transfer his emotion and by which he can express it in art.

Eliot's own remark on myth is probably the best single statement of the point of view I am attempting to define in this study. This statement may be used, furthermore, to help define Eliot's own use of the Arthurian myth in *The Waste Land*. Myth, in Eliot's terms, becomes a "way of controlling, of ordering, of giving a shape and a significance to the immense panorama of futility and anarchy which is modern history."[22] That *The Waste Land* involves as its major theme "the futility and anarchy of modern history" no one will doubt. And I have tried to show that the Fisher King-waste-land myth "is a way of controlling, of ordering, of giving a shape and a significance" to Eliot's vision. Certainly, at any rate, if this single myth and image along with the images of sterility which it naturally implies can be traced throughout the poem, then this part of the myth does in a very real sense order and control *The Waste Land*. If, however, it is objected that it is foolish to cry "order and control" in the face of such a manifestly chaotic poem as *The Waste Land,* let me retort that Eliot's own statement on myth is made apropos of what seems superficially to be one of the most obviously chaotic novels of our time—Joyce's *Ulysses*. The point is, I think, that superficial eccentricities and difficulties do not necessarily point to a central disunity. There is no "fallacy of imitative form" actually present in *The Waste Land;* there are merely superficial difficulties engendered by the difficulty of writing a poem based on many facets of a single myth and by Eliot's notion that since "our civilization comprehends great variety and complexity," the poet must seek a central order in a surface disorder, thus producing a poetry that, in Eliot's opinion, "must be difficult."[23] But in *The Waste Land,* as in *Ulysses,* the surface variants of the basic myth (the Fisher King-waste-land theme in Eliot, the Ulysses search theme in Joyce) always point inward to the central unity. All the images, like all the characters, of *The Waste Land* are in essence one image, and this single myth, embracing as it does all the variant myths of the poem, does give order, shape, and significance to Eliot's picture of modern society.

But why, again, does Eliot pick this particular myth? One answer I have already suggested; the Fisher King-waste-land myth involves not simply fertility and sterility, but more particularly religious fertility and secular sterility, a concept implicit, though undeveloped, in Chrétien, the Vulgate Cycle, and Malory. The Fisher King, at least in the later versions that connect the whole Arthurian myth with the Grail material, is the keeper of the Grail. His only cure in these legends lies in a re-sanctification of his person and his mission. He awaits the coming of the pure hero who can win the Grail and use it to cure him. Thus, the waste land itself becomes an image of secularism and the Fisher King an image of the failure of religion. Significantly, and this fact must have been obvious to Eliot at the time, the only cure possible for the modern world, as well as for the waste land, is religious in nature. In spite of Miss Weston's protestations, this section of the Arthurian myth is principally a homily on the destructiveness of complete secularism. Eliot himself, of course, has since said the same thing; from 1934 onward, it has become his principal text:

> If you do away with this struggle, and maintain that by tolerance, benevolence, inoffensiveness, and a redistribution or increase of purchasing power, combined with a devotion, on the part of an elite, to Art, the world will be as good as anyone could require, then you must expect human beings to become more and more vaporous.[24]
>
> . . . the struggle of our time [is] to concentrate, not to dissipate; to renew our association with traditional wisdom; to re-establish a vital connexion between the individual and the race; the struggle [is], in a word, against Liberalism. . . .[25]

Thus although we find Eliot preaching no direct sermons in *The Waste Land,* it is sure that the very image, the myth that guides and controls the poem, preaches the required sermon by implication. To the general reader, as to the student of Miss Weston, the Grail myth has to do first of all with religion. Talk of mystery rites is apt and pertinent (and we have no evidence that Eliot did not accept Miss Weston's theory), but the myth at heart is religious, and by virtue of this fact *The Waste Land* is a religious poem.

It will be helpful, I think, to approach this problem of myth and unity from another vantage point. The difficulties of the poem occur not, as some critics maintain, from Eliot's failure to unite the various cultures he draws upon, but from a misunderstanding of Eliot's attitude toward the whole problem of unification. Eliot's purpose is certainly not to foster a belief in the various myths he uses. Although the great variety of myths involved hinders a superficial reading of the poem, it does not negate the possibility that the poem has unity or that it represents more than a chaos of unassimilated knowledge and impression. Myth is in itself a way of ordering knowledge, of stating precisely what the poet feels to be the state of modern society, and it is altogether possible that this "way of ordering knowledge" becomes not only the principal device of the poem, but one of its major themes as well. As in "Sweeney among the Nightingales," Eliot is involved in contrasting both the modern world in which nothing has meaning with a world where all actions have meaning and, at the same time, the secular viewpoint that sees no meaning in action with his own sacramental point of view that sees meaning in all things. Thus, the myths in *The Waste Land* may very well have a double function; they may serve not only to contrast the fertile religious order of the past with the sterile secular chaos of the present, but also to contrast the modern dissociation of matter and form with the poet's own viewpoint that asserts the inseparability of matter and form. *The Waste Land* not only opposes spiritual life-in-death with secular death-in-life, but also a sacramental habit of thought with a dissociated sensibility that forbids any assimilation of experience. Seen in this light, Eliot's own attitude toward the poem becomes clear. The myths themselves may be of less importance in the poem than the attitude toward myth which unites them; Eliot everywhere suggests through his use of myth a consistent world viewpoint capable of uniting these mythical elements of the poem in contrast to a modern world view that sees all experience as disjunctive. There are thus two sets of contrasts in *The Waste Land*: a contrast of order and chaos and a contrast of the sacramental and whole world view with the secularized and partial world view.

The sacramental point of view that can equate evening and etherized patient in "The Love Song of J. Alfred Prufrock" can be seen identifying the fire and the rose in "Little Gidding"; Eliot's sacramental viewpoint orders and controls his poetry throughout his career. *The Waste Land,* moreover, would seem to be a *locus classi-*

cus of this particular sort of method and mentality. Here, Eliot, beginning with a single myth and a single image, is able to expand that myth and that image in all directions, seeing applications of the basic principle in many times and literatures, yet never losing the single thread of imagery which controls and unifies all the subsidiary imagery of the poem. The Fisher King-waste-land section of the Arthurian myth, involving as it does religious fertility and secular sterility, thus becomes the center of Eliot's poem. In a sense, then, the Arthurian myth assumes in Eliot, just as it does in Williams and Lewis, a position of central importance.

Notes

Reprinted with permission from *Arthurian Triptych: Mythic Materials in Charles Williams, C. S. Lewis, and T. S. Eliot* (Berkeley and Los Angeles: University of California Press, 1960). Chapter 5, "T. S. Eliot," pp. 127-48 and Notes, pp. 162-63.

1. *The Intellectual Adventure of Ancient Man* (Chicago: University of Chicago Press, 1946), p. 6.
2. "The Metaphysical Poets," *Selected Essays: 1917-1932* (New York: Harcourt, Brace, 1932), p. 247.
3. *Ibid.*
4. In *A Hymn to God, My God, in My Sickness.*
5. In *The Definition of Love.*
6. "The Dry Salvages," *Four Quartets* (New York: Harcourt, Brace, 1943), p. 27.
7. See especially Yvor Winters' condemnation of this theory in connection with Eliot that "modern art must be chaotic in order to express chaos." According to Winters, who denies any unity to *The Waste Land,* imitative form in the poem results only in confusion (*The Anatomy of Nonsense* [Norfolk: New Directions, 1943], pp. 163-165).
8. This opinion is upheld most effectively by Edmund Wilson, who finds in Eliot's apparent fragmentariness a certain proportion and order (*Axel's Castle* [New York: Scribner, 1931], p. 112). Although Cleanth Brooks in his excellent analysis (*Modern Poetry and the Tradition* [Chapel Hill: University of North Carolina Press, 1939], pp. 136-172) treats the problem of unity only by implication, he would seem to find some unity in the poet's use of irony and "the obverse of irony" as reflected in Eliot's method of contrasting myth and contemporary reality. Other critics (see note 7 above on Yvor Winters) find that Eliot's poetic method has not even mechanical unity. Stephen Spender complains that Eliot's greatest weakness is his "fragmentariness" (*The Destructive Element* [Boston: Houghton Mifflin, 1936], p. 154). F. R. Leavis finds that the "comprehensiveness" of *The Waste Land* has been achieved at the "cost of structure" (*New Bearings in English Poetry* [London: Chatto and Windus, 1932], p. 112). This same criticism lies at the base of Richard Chase's comment that Eliot's prose statement that myth is an ordering device "is constantly belied by his use of myth in his own poems" (*Quest for Myth* [Baton Rouge: Louisiana State University Press, 1949], pp. v-vi).
9. All the quotations from Eliot's poetry other than *Four Quartets* are taken from the American edition of the *Collected Poems, 1909-1935* (New York: Harcourt, Brace, 1936). As far as I know, none of the materials that I have used in explication are original with me, nor can I always be sure from what commentaries they are taken. The fullest explications of *The Waste Land* are those of F. O. Matthiessen in *The Achievement of T. S. Eliot* (New York: Oxford University Press, 1947), Cleanth Brooks in *Modern Poetry and the Tradition,* and Grover Smith, Jr. in *T. S. Eliot's Poetry and Plays* (Chicago: University of Chicago Press, 1956). Smith's notes contain a full bibliography of the important commentaries on the poem.
10. Although in *The Waste Land,* Eliot's point of reference to past glories includes both literary and mythological allusions, it is clear that they fulfill exactly the same function in that both are used to suggest total situations or milieus that can be compared to the modern waste land.
11. Nor was any child of man born there,
    Nor was any maiden married there,
    Nor did the trees there bear leaves,
    Nor any meadow blossom,
    Nor did any birds bear young,
    Nor any beast faun.
12. *From Ritual to Romance* (Cambridge: Cambridge University Press, 1920), p. 21.
13. *Op. cit.,* p. 70.
14. Brooks, *op. cit.,* p. 139.
15. Maynard Mack et al., *Modern Poetry,* "English Masterpieces" Series (New York: Prentice-Hall, 1950), p. 124.
16. Smith, *op. cit.,* p. 73.
17. See "Gerontion": "The goat coughs at night in the field overhead." The goat is normally a fertility symbol.
18. *Op. cit.,* p. 142.
19. *Collected Poems,* p. 94.

20. *Op. cit., passim.*

21. *Op. cit.,* p. 284.

22. "'Ulysses,' Order, and Myth," *Dial,* LXXV, 5 (Nov., 1923), 483.

23. "The Metaphysical Poets," p. 248.

24. *After Strange Gods* (New York: Harcourt, Brace, 1934), p. 46.

25. *Ibid.,* p. 53.

FURTHER READING

Criticism

Abdoo, Sherlyn. "Woman as Grail in T. S. Eliot's *The Wasteland.*" *Centennial Review* 28, no. 1 (winter 1984): 48-60.

Explores the image of woman as being the very object of the Grail quest in T. S. Eliot's *The Waste Land.*

Cleeve, Brian. "The World's Need." In *At the Table of the Grail: Magic and the Use of Imagination,* edited by John Matthews, pp. 129-44. London: Routledge and Kegan Paul, 1984.

Debates the nature of the Grail, contending that the Grail serves humans only as they serve the Grail.

Cormier, Raymond J. "Rohmer's Grail Story: Anatomy of a French Flop." *Stanford French Review* 5, no. 3 (winter 1981): 391-96.

Offers an account of Sax Rohmer's treatment of the Grail legend in his film *Perceval and the Grail.*

Fledderus, Bill. "'The English Patient Reposed in His Bed Like a [Fisher] King': Elements of Grail Romance in Ondaatje's *The English Patient.*" *Studies in Canadian Literature* 22, no. 1 (1997): 19-54.

Maintains that Ondaatje's novel is informed by the work of Jessie Weston in the field of romance criticism, and that there are many covert references to the Grail legend in this story that assist in developing an increased sense of aesthetic and critical judgement of this work.

Froula, Christine. "Eliot's Grail Quest, or The Lover, the Police, and *The Waste Land.*" *Yale Review* 78, no. 2 (winter 1989): 235-53.

Examines the Grail motif in *The Waste Land* as a reflection of T. S. Eliot's own struggle with his sexuality, noting that the poem was reflective of a failed quest toward female identification.

Goldfarb, Clare. "An Archetypal Reading of *The Golden Bowl*: Maggie Verver as Questor." *American Literary Realism* 14, no. 1 (spring 1981): 52-61.

Interprets the character of Maggie Verver as a Questor whose primary mission in the book becomes a search for the identity of her father instead of a meaningful relationship with her husband.

Hoffman, Donald L. "A Darker Shade of Grail: Questing at the Crossroads in Ishmael Reed's *Mumbo Jumbo.*" *Callaloo* 17, no. 4 (fall 1994): 1245-56.

Claims that in his novel *Mumbo Jumbo,* often praised as one of Ishmael Reed's greatest works, the author revisions the Grail legend in order to redefine Euro-centric interpretations of myth and civilization.

Pierce, Carol. "A Fellowship in Time: Durrell, Eliot, and the Quest of the Grail." In *Lawrence Durrell: Comprehending the Whole,* edited by Julius Rowan Raper, Melody L. Enscore, and Paige Matthey Bynum, pp. 70-81. Columbia: University of Missouri Press, 1995.

Compares the influence Lawerence Durrell and T. S. Eliot had on each other as writers, focusing on the impact Eliot's *The Waste Land* and his use of the Grail myth in that work had on Durrell's writing.

Riley, Peter. "The Narratives of *The Holy Grail.*" *boundary 2* 6, no. 1 (fall 1977): 163-90.

Detailed overview of Jack Spicer's *The Holy Grail.*

Stich, Klaus P. "The Grail Is a *Rum Thing*: Robertson Davies' Cornish Trilogy." *Canadian Literature* 164 (spring 2000): 116-35.

Studies Robertson Davies's notion of the Grail as it is represented in his Cornish trilogy, characterizing it as an "over-all presence" in all three books.

Coverage on Arthurian Literature is contained in the following source published by the Gale Group: *Classical and Medieval Literature Criticism,* **Vol. 10; for coverage of Arthurian Revival, see** *Nineteenth-Century Literature Criticism,* **Vol. 36.**

Literary Expressionism

The following entry presents criticism on authors and works of literary Expressionism.

INTRODUCTION

Generally dated by scholars as ranging from 1910 to 1925, the Expressionist movement rejected previous concepts of artistic form, subordinated representation to emotional and visionary experience, and exhibited a profound disillusionment with the modern world that often led to political activism. Most of the writers and artists associated with the movement lived in the northern part of Europe—Germany, the Scandinavian countries, the Netherlands, and northern Belgium. Though there were marked differences in their individual styles and philosophies, the Expressionists shared a common vision that emphasized passion, independence, and a desire to reach beyond the superficial to the essential aspect of all things. As artist Paul Klee wrote, the object of the Expressionists was "to make visible that which is not ordinarily revealed to the senses."

Rooted in German Romantic philosophy, particularly the ideals of Friedrich Schlegel and the poetry of Novalis, Expressionists also embraced the writings of Arthur Schopenhauer, Friedrich Nietzsche, and composer Richard Wagner, all of whom commented on the dichotomy between the real world and the inner world of the artist, asserting that the artist's duty is to dramatize his or her inner world. Literary forerunners of the Expressionists included Stéphane Mallarmè, Arthur Rimbaud, Charles Baudelaire, Edgar Allan Poe, and Walt Whitman—writers who passionately lived and wrote against the grain of conventional society. Caricaturists like Frank Wedekind and Carl Sternheim also influenced the Expressionists, contributing elements of satire, the grotesque, and linguistic playfulness to the movement. With Berlin as the center of their activity, the Expressionists gathered as a group around Herwarth Walder's periodical *Der Sturm,* which started publication in 1910. Their common goal was to protest against the reigning literary, academic, and social establishment, insisting on artistic and personal liberty, integrity, and spiritual self-expression. Poetry and drama proved to be particularly suited to showcasing their emotionally charged, often leftist or revolutionary sentiments, and such writers as August Stramm, Ernst Toller, Georg Trakl, Franz Werfel, and Oscar Kokoschka enjoyed widespread popularity. Expressionist writers are also noted for their versatility: for example, Kokoschka excelled as a playwright and as a painter, and Ernst Barlach was as successful sculptor, essayist, and playwright.

The works of the Expressionist writers were well-known and largely admired by their contemporaries, but they were banned by Adolf Hitler from the mid-1930s to the mid-1940s due to what Hitler regarded as their decadent and artificial subject material. The works of the Expressionists were rediscovered in Germany and elsewhere after the war, but it was not until the 1970s that scholarly interest in the movement began to flourish. Since then, there have been many critical evaluations of literary Expressionism, especially of the cultural and political atmosphere in which it developed. Commentators have also explored the international aspects of the movement, as well its influence on writers in the United States and England. The question of whether Expressionism can be referred to as a movement or whether it is more accurate to describe it as a style continues to be debated, though scholars generally agree that the intensity of Expressionist writings is their chief distinguishing characteristic. Richard Brinkmann has written, "Hardly any other period in the history of German literature has wrestled with language with such passion and abandon."

REPRESENTATIVE WORKS

Hugo Ball
Gesamelte Gedichte (poetry) 1963

Ernst Barlach
Der arme Vetter (play) 1919
Die Sündflut (play) 1924
Der blaue Boll (play) 1926

Johannes R. Becher
Erde (novel) 1912

Bertolt Brecht
Tremmeln in der Nacht (play) 1922
Mann ist Mann (play) 1926

Theodor Däubler
Der neue Standpunkt (essays) 1916

Reinhold Goering
Seeschlacht (play) 1918

Friedrich Gundelfinger
George (criticism) 1920

Hermann Hesse
Der Steppenwolf [*Steppenwolf*] (novel) 1927

Georg Kaiser
Von morgens bis mitternachts (play) 1917

Wassily Kandinsky
Der Blaue Reiter [editor, with Franz Marc] (almanac) 1912
Uber der Geistige in der Kunst [*The Art of Spiritual Harmony*] (criticism) 1912

Oscar Kokoschka
Mörder, Hoffnung der Frauen [*Murderer, Hope of Women*] (play) 1907
Hiob (play) 1917

Georg Lukács
Deutsche Literatur im Zeitalter des Imperialismus: Eine Übersicht ihrer Hauptströmungen (essays) 1945

Thomas Mann
Betrachtungen eines Unpolitischen [*Reflections of a Nonpolitical Man*] (essay) 1918

Robert Musil
Der Mann ohne Eigenschaften. 3 vols. (novel) 1930-33, 1943

Kurt Pinthus
Menschheitsdämmerung (poetry) 1920

Rainer Maria Rilke
Die Anfzeichnungen der Malte Laurids Brigge [*The Note-Books of Malte Laurids Brigge*] (novel) 1910

Arnold Schoenberg
Erwartung (monodrama) 1909
Die glueckliche Hand (libretto) 1910-13

Reinhard Sorge
Der Bettler (play) 1917

Carl Sternheim
Die Hose: Ein Bürgerliches Lustspiel [*The Underpants: A Middle-Class Comedy*] (play) 1911

August Stramm
Die Liebesgedichte (poetry) 1915

Ernst Toller
Masse Mensch (play) 1920
Die Maschinenstürmer (play) 1922

Georg Trakl
Gedichte (poetry) 1913

Herwarth Walder
Der Sturm [editor] (journal) 1910-32

Frank Wedekind
Die Büchse der Pandora: Tragödie in drei Aufzügen [*Pandora's Box*] (play) 1904

Franz Werfel
Spiegelmensch (play) 1920

Wilhelm Worringer
Abstraktion und Einfühlung [*Abstraction and Empathy*] (philosophy) 1908

OVERVIEWS AND GENERAL STUDIES

Ulrich Weisstein (essay date winter 1967)

SOURCE: Weisstein, Ulrich. "Expressionism: Style or Weltanschauung?" *Criticism: A Quarterly for Literature and the Arts* 9, no. 1 (winter 1967): 42-62.

[*In the following essay, Weisstein considers the question of whether scholars should evaluate Expressionism primarily as a literary style, or whether they need to take into account its social and political dimensions as well.*]

"No matter how things turn out, one will have to admit that Expressionism was the last common, general, and conscious attempt of a whole generation to instill new life into art, music, and literature."[1] I think that this holds true even though, geographically speaking, Expressionism was more or less restricted to the Teutonic part of Europe: Germany, Scandinavia, and the Netherlands, including the northern, Flemish part of Belgium (James Ensor). Although, except in the theater—where Tairoff and Meyerhold helped in shaping the physiognomy of "Revolutionary Romanticism"—Russia did not substantially contribute to this general *Aufbruch*, inspiration for many German Expressionistic writers (such as Franz Werfel and, later, Hermann Hesse) came from Dostoievsky, just as some of the Activists were fond of Tolstoi. And in painting, the spirit of Russian mysticism strongly pervaded the esthetic thinking of the *Blaue Reiter*.

It is not generally known that the latter group, apart from its whip Kandinsky, counted a considerable number of Russians among its members, as did its predecessor, the *Neue Künstlervereinigung*. Wladimir Bechtejeff, the brothers Burliuk, Axel von Jawlensky, Moissej Kogan, and Marianne von Werefkin are perhaps the most prominent of these. As a curiosity it might be mentioned that one of the *Blaue Reiter* was the American Albert Bloch, who subsequently became Professor of Art at the University of Kansas.

On the whole, Expressionism had little immediate impact on the Anglo-Saxon world, however. John Marin and the cubistically inclined Lyonel Feininger (who spent the decisive years of his career in Germany) embraced the cause; and shortly before World War I Wyndham Lewis and Henri Gaudier-Brzeska briefly raised the Vorticist flag in London.[2] The plays of Georg Kaiser, Franz Werfel, and Ernst Toller, performed on the New York stage around 1920, gave impetus to playwrights like Eugene O'Neill, Elmer Rice and, later, Thornton Wilder; and the English Group Theatre of Auden and Isherwood, including T. S. Eliot's Aristophanic minstrel show *Sweeney Agonistes,* was not unaffected by the German model.

Yet it is no secret that, until fairly recently, the Busch-Reisinger Museum at Harvard University owned the only representative collection of paintings by members of the *Brücke* group to be found anywhere in the United States. But now the graphic and pictorial work of these artists is suddenly in great demand, and Peter Selz' monumental study of *German Expressionist Painting* offers the most authoritative analysis of their art.[3] German Expressionist literature, on the other hand, is still unfamiliar and poorly understood in America and England. At least a few anthologies of plays and poetry in translation are now available: Hamburger and Middleton's *German Poetry 1910-1960* and Sokel's *An Anthology of German Expressionist Drama*, absurdly subtitled "A Prelude to the Absurd."[4] And one critical monograph in English, Sokel's *The Writer in Extremis*, has been published, albeit its predominantly thematic orientation reduces its value for those who seek to define the Expressionistic *style*.[5] But, after all: As Expressionism had first to be discovered in England and America, it had to be rediscovered in post-war Germany. For Adolf Hitler had consigned it to esthetic Limbo when he labelled all art that failed to live up to the naturalistic standards of Franz Leibl "entartet."

The Latin countries found Expressionism uncongenial to their way of thinking and feeling. Being classicists at heart, the French prefer an art that seeks to depict objectively verifiable and measurable formal beauty. The father of Cubism was a Frenchman, Paul Cézanne; but it was a Dutchman, Piet Mondrian, who lifted the quasi-abstract art of Braque and Picasso into the untroubled realm of what he called Pure Plastic Art. For the true Expressionist, however, Classicism was the very establishment whose foundations he sought to undermine, his *Weltgefühl* being admittedly closer to that of the Romantics. Gottfried Benn's introduction to the collection *Lyrik des expressionistischen Jahrzehnts*—which is a revised version of an essay in defense of Expressionism published, courageously, in 1933—culminates in the rhetorical assertion: "[Expressionism] rose, fought its battles on the Catalonian fields, and was defeated. It raised its flag on the Bastille, the Kreml, and at Golgatha, but never reached Mount Olympus and other classical terrain."[6]

Apart from Georges Rouault's neo-medieval stained-glass technique, the only kind of Expressionism France produced was the decorative "Ausdruckskunst" of *Les Fauves*: the wild beasts André Derain, Maurice Vlaminck, and Henri Matisse in their paintings executed between 1905 and 1910. Like the members of *Die Brücke* in the Dresden of those years, the Fauves developed a sudden, intense interest in primitive art, which had hitherto lingered away in ethnographic museums. But their Gallic *esprit* kept them from getting too fiercely involved in the quest for a revival of the barbaric spirit. Standing at the crossroads between Cubism and Expressionism, Picasso created his "Demoiselles d'Avignon" (1908), but then moved on to an art that was less contorted and more serene.

Italy witnessed the spectacular rise of the proto-Fascist movement known as Futurism: a violent action art which sought, like Dadaism, to destroy the past with its burdensome heritage. The Futurists indulged in a blind worship of speed and the machine, preferably when used as a means of warfare. In literature, they sought, in the words of Filippo Marinetti's *Technical Manifesto*, to free language by releasing it from the fetters of Latin grammar: "It is an urgent necessity to liberate the words by dragging them out of the cage of Latin syntax."[7] Their recipes were used by some of the radical German Expressionists: Johannes R. Becher, the late Minister of Culture in the German Democratic Republic, but then one of the most violent makers of word cascades, and Alfred Döblin, author of *Die Ermordung einer Butterblume* and *Die drei Sprünge des Wang-Lun*.

Spain, to complete our rapid survey of the international situation, remained quite unaffected by Expressionism, even though the naturalized Toledan Domenico Theotocopuli, better known as El Greco, was, like Matthias Grünewald, regarded as one of the spiritual godfathers of Germany's twentieth century "Stürmer und Dränger." In his autobiography, Salvador Dali reports that when he entered the Madrid Academy his teachers had just begun to notice that shadows weren't black and were duly shocked when he blithely proceeded to demonstrate Cubist techniques of painting. Spain, perhaps partly on account of its Moorish background, soon afterwards came under the spell of French Surrealism.

Kurt Pinthus' statement was not invalidated by the birth of Surrealism in 1924, i. e. at a time when Expressionism had spent its force. True, Surrealism—due, most likely, to its Freudian underpinning—gained far more universal recognition than was ever bestowed on its German counterpart. But as a movement it was originally tied to poetry, painting being formally introduced only after Dali's arrival in Paris, when André Breton decided that an extension of the Surrealist esthetic to the plastic arts was feasible. However, the movement, as was inevitable, produced a wealth of artistically inferior works due to the underlying assumption that art must rely on chance, and that the automatic transcription of subliminal experiences is a valid form of expression. At least in the first, experimental phase, the Surrealists wished nothing better than to be *appareils enregistreurs,* just as the Impressionists had shown themselves satisfied with being "nothing but eyes," to use a phrase coined by Cézanne and aimed at Monet.

Surrealism altogether eschews the volitional element in art, the intention or what Wilhelm Worringer calls the *Kunstwollen.* Precisely this aspect prevails in Expressionistic art, where it predicates a total involvement of the artist, thereby precluding any sort of playful experimentation or automatism. No doubt: a lot of Expressionistic art, both poetry and painting, has also dated on account of its pronounced stylistic mannerisms; but enough literary and pictorial works of sound value remain to make Expressionism a vital and enduring force in modern European culture.

What renders Expressionism doubly interesting to students of contemporary art is the fact that its gospel spread to all the arts, thereby encouraging the formation and cultivation of *Doppelbegabungen.* Which is hardly surprising if one keeps in mind that what mattered to the Expressionists was not so much the formal perfection of the finished product, i. e., the craft and technical skill (Worringer's *Können*) as the intensity of the artistic drive. As Ernst Stadler puts it in a poem that has often been called programmatic:

> Form und Riegel mussten erst zerspringen,
> Welt durch aufgeschlossne Röhren dringen:
> Form ist Wollust, Friede, himmlisches Genügen,
> Doch mich reisst es, Ackerschollen umzupflügen.
> Form will mich verschnüren und verengen,
> Doch ich will mein Sein in alle Weiten drängen.

"Form wants to oppress and stifle me, but I desire a vast expansion of my being"; such is the message to which many artists of that generation harkened. Oskar Kokoschka is not only a painter but also the author of boldly experimental plays like *Mörder Hoffnung der Frauen,* a prototype of the Expressionistic *Schreidrama.*

Arnold Schönberg was a composer, a dramatist (he wrote the texts for several of his operas) and a painter. Indeed, some of his paintings were included in the first exhibition of the *Blaue Reiter.* Ernst Barlach, finally, was a sculptor and graphic artist as well as novelist and playwright, a man who expressed himself with equal force in several media. Barlach, who hated to be classed with any group or movement, was perhaps the most genuine Expressionist, an Expressionist "beyond fashion and full of necessity."[8] One of his basic themes was resurrection; and he treated it most poignantly in those comedies (*Der arme Vetter* and *Der blaue Boll*) where transcendence is achieved in a thoroughly earthy setting delineated with the utmost realism. Barlach was greatly shocked when he discovered that, at the Berlin *Staatstheater,* his characters were portrayed with Expressionistic onesidedness.[9]

Following Kurt Pinthus, I have, so far, carefully avoided calling Expressionism a movement. For viewed as a historical phenomenon in its totality, it cannot be properly regarded as such. The term *movement,* that is to say, should be reserved for groups of contemporaries having a common goal and subscribing to a formulated program. To be sure, in painting we have *Die Brücke,* a true *Künstlergemeinschaft* until 1913 when Ernst Ludwig Kirchner's chronicle met with the disapproval of his fellow painters. The *Blaue Reiter,* on the other hand, showed relatively little artistic coherence. In literature, the situation was even more chaotic; and, with the exception of the clique gathered around Herwarth Walden's periodical *Der Sturm,* programs were written and theories developed only after the fact by critics, editors, anthologists and other "outsiders."

In the introduction to his pamphlet *Über neue Prosa* (which forms part of the well-known series *Tribüne der Kunst und Zeit*), Max Krell observes that Expressionism is a collective term used to refer to a complex of views and feelings ("Sammelwort eines Gefühls- und Anschauungskomplexes") but that the individual Expressionist prefers *Lösung* (creative freedom or independence) to *Bindung* (adherence to a common cause).[10] However, as Krell points out, there are the Activists, a group of writers associated with publications like *Das Ziel, Die Aktion,* and René Schickele's far less virulent *Die weissen Blätter.* The Activists, of whom Heinrich Mann was the most prominent, had specific goals and shared a *Weltanschauung,* the term being here used in the narrower, socio-political sense. Perhaps they actually were, as on writer puts it, thwarted humanists who had discovered that the world in which they lived did not measure up to the ideal glowingly painted by their teachers.[11]

The literary output of the Activists was infused with a rigorously ethical spirit; for what they had in common with their Expressionistic brethren was a craving for the

Renaissance of man. Their idol was Friedrich Schiller, whom Nietzsche, in an unforgettable phrase, had dubbed the "Moraltrompeter von Säckingen." These *Zivilisationsliteraten,* as Thomas Mann calls them in his autobiographical *Betrachtungen eines Unpolitischen,* were invariably Pacifists, but, unlike the Dadaists, constructive ones. Many of them actively participated in setting up local and regional governments during the revolution of 1918-1919. The lines of distinction between Expressionism and Activism have been admirably drawn in a book by Wolfgang Paulsen.[12]

What, however, makes it possible for us to discuss the Expressionists as a group, if there is no such thing as an Expressionistic program or manifesto? And can we, in spite of the apparent incoherence of views and styles, find some common denominator for all their efforts? I think most of the writers and painters whom we now regard as Expressionists would have agreed that they were primarily concerned with capturing the essence of things rather than their external appearance. They found nothing more contemptible than the Naturalistic "slice of life" and its Impressionist variant. "Mensch werde wesentlich," the clarion call sounded by the Baroque epigrammatist Angelus Silesius, was their motto. The essence or core of things, however, can be reached only by resolutely piercing the various layers of social, political, and psychological reality. This thrust, this plunging into depth, i. e. into a realm forbidden to the senses, presupposes a quasi-religious fervor, an urge to bring about a total *Vergeistigung* (spiritualization) of life and art. In the works of Expressionism, man is, therefore, directly confronted with eternity. Art, for these writers and painters, was not a substitute for religion; it was religion itself. And their principal line of communication, like that of the Mystics, was not a horizontal but a vertical one. This, naturally, poses an entirely new problem of communication on the human plane.

Even before World War I, a number of critics conversant with the current trends sought to isolate certain traits in order to gain valid criteria for analyzing contemporary works of art. They did so almost invariably in terms of style, not content. For even if one concedes that certain themes—such as the father-son conflict, the struggle between duty and conviction, the *Aufbruch* from one mode of existence to another—occur frequently in Expressionistic literature, the thematic approach is doomed to failure when it comes to judging the plastic arts or comparing poetic with pictorial works. Kurt Pinthus, who singled out "intensity" as the principal feature of Expressionism, himself succumbed to the thematic fallacy—which he rejected in theory—when arranging the contents of his anthology.

In his collection of essays *Der neue Standpunkt,* one of the first and most eloquent apologies for the new art, Theodor Däubler—the man whom Barlach seems to have used as a model for *Der blaue Boll*[13]—lists "speed, simultaneity, and extreme intensity in the telescopic view of the world" as traits characteristic of a style which, in his as yet undifferentiated view, comprises Cubism, Futurism, and Expressionism.[14] "When a man is hanged, he relives his entire life over again in a final moment" is another way in which Däubler expresses the same idea.[15] Viewed historically, such a description would seem to be more applicable to paintings like Chagall's proto-Surrealistic "I and the Village" (1917) or Gino Severini's "Dynamic Hieroglyphic of the Bal Tabarin" (1912) than to any Expressionistic work, except perhaps of the type represented by Franz Marc's "Tierschicksale" (1913).

Däubler also refers to Expressionistic art as that of a highly concentrated vision: "A vision seeks to manifest itself with extreme succinctness in the realm of mannered simplicity: that is Expressionism in every style."[16] With regard to literature, Kasimir Edschmid, another pioneer of Expressionism in both theory and practice, claims that "the rhythmic construction of the sentences is different. They serve the same intention, the same spiritual urge which renders only the essential."[17] The sentences "link peak with peak, are telescoped into each other, and have ceased to be connected by the buffers of logical transition or the external plaster of psychology."[18]

An excellent illustration of this technique occurs in Georg Kaiser's play *Von morgens bis mitternachts,* when the protagonist—a bank clerk who has absconded with a large sum of money and is now trying to reap the fruits of his *Aufbruch*—describes the effect of the climactic moment of a tandem race upon the already frenzied audience: "This is the utmost concentration of fact. Here it does the impossible. A fusion of all galleries. The utter dissolution of the individual leads to the formation of a dense core: passion."[19] And later, when the waiter of a restaurant enters the *chambre separée* to inquire what he wants to eat, the clerk replies: "Peaks, peaks, from beginning to end. Peaks are the utmost concentrations in everything."[20] It is this passion for intensity which explains, among other things, the telegram style of the Expressionistic *Schrei-Drama,* as exemplified by Reinhard Goering's famous *Seeschlacht.* This telegram style is the very opposite of the Naturalistic *Sekundenstil,* which forms the literary equivalent of the "slice of life."

Phrases such as "Höhe des Gefühls," "Spitzen des Gefühls," "Berge des Herzens" (this latter coined by Rilke) abound in Expressionistic literature, indicating that its mysticism is dynamic. Indeed, nothing could be further from the Expressionist than to imitate the saints in the First Duino Elegy who, experiencing levitation, "knieten, Unmögliche, weiter und achtetens nicht." Perhaps the word most frequently uttered by Expressionistic protagonists is *Aufbruch* which, untranslatable into English, suggests a complete desertion of the past, a burning of bridges, a progress beyond the point of no return. *Aufbruch* is the catchword of a generation which, following Faust's example, seeks "auf neuer Bahn den Äther zu durchdringen / Zu neuen Sphären reiner Tätigkeit." Such an awakening may occur either in the form of a sudden, volcanic eruption or, as in the *Stationendrama* of Strindbergian provenience, in a number of stages leading to some sort of spiritual catharsis, as in the protagonist's contrived *Ecce Homo* pose at the end of *Von morgens bis mitternachts*.

The "Weltgefühl" which animates the Expressionistic writers is captured in the titles of the numerous magazines, books, series, and anthologies issued between 1910 and 1920: *Erhebung, Anbruch, Verkündigung, Botschaft, Entfaltung, Das neue Pathos, Der jüngste Tag,* whereas the Activist publications carry names like *Kameraden der Menschheit* or *Gemeinschaft. Menschheitsdämmerung,* patterned after Wagner's *Götterdämmerung* and Nietzsche's *Götzendämmerung,* points both to the end (dusk) of an epoch and to the beginning (dawn) of a new era. By far the most influential of all these periodicals was *Der Sturm,* not only because in its pages literature, painting, and the graphic arts found themselves united—for that was a feature common to many publications of the time—but also because its editor, Herwarth Walden, solidified his own views on modern art by extracting a literary theory from the poems of August Stramm and by founding and supporting institutions like the *Sturmschule* and the *Sturmbühne*.

The title of this essay must seem paradoxical to those who believe that, whether directly or indirectly, style must be a reflection of *Weltanschauung, Weltanschauung* being the sum total of intellectual views and emotional attitudes embraced by a given individual. No such paradox applies to those artistic movements which aim at reproducing tangible reality by means of imitation. If Realism, which is the most moderate and commonsensical of these movements, can be defined, with Vivian de Sola Pinto, as "that art which gives a truthful impression of actuality as it appears to the normal consciousness,"[21] then the "advance" of Naturalism or Impressionism can be measured as a deviation from that norm, as a shift of accent or change in emphasis effected by a Courbet or Monet, a Verlaine or Zola.

Realists, Naturalists and Impressionists, in their different ways, wish to portray solely that which is visible, audible, etc., not only to themselves but to everybody else as well. They fight their pitched battles uniformly in the name of objectivity. With the Expressionists—as, by the way, also with the Surrealists—the matter is radically different. In their opinion, the function of art is not to reproduce the visible but, in Paul Klee's words ("Kunst gibt nicht das Sichtbare wieder, sondern macht sichtbar"),[22] to make visible that which is not ordinarily revealed to the senses. "The world exists already," says Kasimir Edschmid. "It would be useless to repeat it."[23] Unlike the Surrealists, however, the Expressionists realized that before one can make the invisible visible one must experience a vision.

As Proust points out in *Du Coté de chez Swann,* this externalization of the internal is natural enough to the writer, who enjoys the inestimable advantage of being able to place himself and his readers inside the characters he has created, whereas in real life we cannot intuit other people's soul states:

> A real person, profoundly as we may sympathise with him, is in a great measure perceptible only through our senses, that is to say, he remains opaque, offers a dead weight which our sensibilities have not the strength to lift. . . . The novelist's happy discovery was to think of substituting for those opaque sections, impenetrable by the human spirit, their equivalent in immaterial sections, things, that is, which the spirit can assimilate to itself.[24]

But how is the painter to accomplish a similar feat? How can he, being so closely tied to the world of ordinary sense perception, break through the shell in order to reveal what it hides from view, i. e., our inmost thoughts and feelings? The answer furnished by the Expressionists is simple: *through style;* style meaning primarily shapes and colors representing an order of things that is different from the natural one. Seen from the mimetic point of view, however, this signifies abstraction or, at least, some sort of more or less violent distortion. Unlike mere stylization, as we find it, say, in Mannerism or *Art Nouveau (Jugendstil),* style is not constituted by a mild, gradual, decorative abstraction from organic form, resulting in a kind of arabesque. In the most radical instances of Expressionistic style, the beholder, unless he prefers to ignore intentions by concentrating on formal values, is thus faced with the grim task of reuniting "abstract" compositions with their underlying *Weltanschauung*.

The arguments I have used are partly taken from Wilhelm Worringer's book *Abstraktion und Einfühlung* which, originally published in 1908, was the esthetic Bible of Expressionism, especially of the *Blaue Reiter.* Worringer contends that the urge for abstraction (*Abstraktionsdrang*) arises on two different stages of man's spiritual evolution: a) at the primitive stage when, numinously overwhelmed by the supernatural forces which he thinks inherent in nature, man fashions objects which, being geometric and regular, i. e. *unnatural,* give him a sense of superiority and, hence, security; and b) at a highly sophisticated stage when the world of matter becomes indifferent and transcendence is, once more, desired. This latter phase produces the abstract, spiritualized and highly ornamental art of the Orient.

Worringer and his British disciple T. E. Hulme—the man who laid the theoretical foundations for Vorticism—scorned the realistic stage which intervenes between a and b. They spoke contemptuously of the classical art of Greece, of the Renaissance, and of the positivistic nineteenth century. Inspiring the Expressionists, Worringer singled out the Gothic and the Baroque as the only two ages which, due to their spiritual unrest and mystical aspiration, ought to be admired by the moderns. He himself preferred the Gothic to the Baroque, because the latter, by intensifying the sensual until it became suprasensual,[25] had chosen a devious way toward spiritualization, whereas in the Gothic cathedral man's urge toward spiritual transcendence (*Vergeistigung*) was directly embodied.

In Worringer's and Hulme's opinion, all classical art, grown out of a harmonious relationship between man and nature, signals an abdication of the will. *Kunstwollen* (artistic volition), however, to their mind, was the agent which assured man's ascendancy over his environment. Empathy and imitation are the cornerstones of an esthetic formed by weaklings. They were now to be deposed, and alienation and abstraction crowned in their place.

The two leading German schools of Expressionistic art may serve to illustrate the two levels of abstraction named by Worringer: the *Brücke* group representing the neo-primitive phase, and the *Blaue Reiter* the oriental. As Hermann Bahr states in his book *Expressionismus,* "Just as primitive man, frightened by nature, hides within himself, we moderns flee a civilization that devours man's soul."[26] How the members of *Die Brücke* saved their souls was recently demonstrated by the exhibition "Das Ursprüngliche und die Moderne," which was held at the West Berlin *Akademie der Künste.* Here the primitive objects owned by the Berlin and Dresden ethnographic museums were shown side by side with the paintings and sculptures they had inspired.

Following in the footsteps of Paul Gauguin, Emil Nolde and Max Pechstein separately visited the South Sea Islands in 1913 and 1914. Both returned imbued with the "savage" spirit. Pechstein's Credo in the volume *Schöpferische Konfession* begins with exclamations like "Work. Frenzy. Crush the brain. Chew. Devour. Gulp. Squash. Blissful pains of delivery. The brush cracks and should like to pierce the canvas. Trample on the paint tubes . . . Paint. Roll in paints, wallow in chords. In the thick of chaos."[27] At approximately the same time, Stravinsky reincarnated the savage state in his *Sacre du Printemps,* and O'Neill followed suit with his *Emperor Jones.*

The neo-primitives of the *Brücke* group were at their best in the graphic arts, especially in the woodcut. Wyndham Lewis found their work to be "African, in that it is sturdy, cutting through . . . to the monotonous wall of space, and intense yet hale; permeated by eternity—an atmosphere in which only the black core of life rises and is silhouetted." For him, the woodcut was "a miniature sculpture where the black nervous fluid of existence in flood forms into hard stagnant masses."[28] What appealed to the Expressionists in this medium, as used by the German primitives of the fifteenth century, was its imperviousness to psychological finesse, as well as its harsh angularity.—In the field of sculpture, Amedeo Modigliani in France (with his Caryatids) and Henri Gaudier-Brzeska in England came perhaps closest to reaching this Vorticist-Expressionist ideal, whereas Germany, Barlach excepted, produced no major Expressionistic sculptor, even though Lehmbruck's elongated figures are often drawn into the discussion.

The works of several *Blaue Reiter,* on the other hand, breathe the spirit of Worringer's post-empathetic phase. Franz Marc looked at his own art in much the same light, as it shown by his remark: "Our European urge for abstract form is nothing but our hyperconscious, superactive reaction to, and triumph over, the sentimental spirit. Primitive man, however, had not met the latter when he loved abstraction."[29] August Macke, reaching, at least experimentally, the stage of pure abstraction in 1907, wrote to his fiancée: "Just now all my bliss derives from pure colors. Last week I placed colors side by side on a wooden board without thinking of any object, such as men or trees, as in crochetry."[30] Kandinsky and Adolf Hoelzel—Nolde's and Baumeister's teacher—broke the barrier around 1910, and Franz Marc, with his "Fighting Forms," four years later. Of the members of *Die Brücke,* Ernst Ludwig Kirchner was probably the only one to grope his way toward abstraction in his colored woodcut illustrations to *Peter Schlemihl.*

We have reached the crucial point in any discussion of Expressionism in literature or painting; for whoever wishes to make his peace with that style has to know where to draw the line between so-called non-objective and representational art. In statement after statement, the Expressionists professed that it was their aim to mate the abstract with the concrete, soul with body, and spirit with matter—just as the Surrealists wished to reconcile the world of dreams with that of waking, the subconscious with the conscious. Walter von Hollander, for example, calls Paul Kornfeld's drama *Die Verführung* Expressionistic in so far as, in it, the soul finds an outlet through the body.[31] And Kasimir Edschmid bluntly states: "We want the flesh, but in sharpened suprasensual pleasures."[32]

As the chief apologist for Expressionistic literature, Edschmid fought the notion that a school of pure abstraction might develop within its framework. "The urge for abstraction no longer knows any limits, no longer realizes how subtle the balance of content and creative form. Exceeding the boundaries of the sensuous, it creates pure theory."[33] Edschmid was undoubtedly shocked by Däubler's definition of the new style as "color without a name, line without definition," but "rhythmically placed nouns without attributes"[34] must have been more to his taste. Still, Edschmid must have rejected the extreme views pushed by the artists of the *Sturm* circle: Rudolf Blümner's use of abstract word formations and Lothar Schreyer's theory of the Expressionistic *Gesamtkunstwerk* composed of pure words, sounds, forms, colors, and rhythms.

Indeed, "Abstract Expressionism" is a logical absurdity unless we can somehow salvage Kandinsky's concept of art as based on the principle of inner necessity. Kandinsky himself would not have called his works abstractions, since, for him, form was always the expression of a content.[35] Thus, as far as the underlying intentions are concerned, his Impressions, Improvisations and Compositions are polar opposites of the serene abstractions of *De Stijl* and the stark geometries of Malevich's Suprematism.

Kandinsky's esthetic issues from the conviction that art is a vehicle of communication between the artist and his audience. In his programmatic treatise *Über das Geistige in der Kunst,* he uses the piano to show that art is "purposive playing with the human soul." With the aid of color and form, the feelings of the beholders of his pictures are to be manipulated in such a way that "[color] is the keyboard, the eyes are the hammers, the soul is the piano with many strings, [and] the artist is the hand that plays, touching one key or another purposively, to cause vibration in the soul."[36]

To this end all of Kandinsky's efforts were directed. Ideally, he wanted the beholder to be compelled to "wander around" in the finished picture,[37] just as Paul Klee, writing in *Schöpferische Konfession,* invites us to take a little journey.[38] What Kandinsky hoped to achieve was, paradoxically enough, a sort of "empathy through abstraction." But how is this empathy to be brought about? For assuming even that one sincerely believes in the veracity of the feelings an artist claims to have channelled into his work, it is, and always will be, quite impossible to extract such feelings from their visual record on the canvas. Of course we may rely on intuition, which found so strong an advocate in Henri Bergson. But intuition is an unreliable guide and difficult to translate into the language of ordinary logic. Thus Kandinsky's paintings after 1910, to quote Däubler's beautifully turned phrases, are "Blue manifestations of a decision before their embodiment in action; Mongolianisms which mistily invade us, creating chaos through the mystical use of color or [generating] a cosmos."[39]

Arnold Schönberg, the inventor of the "method of composition with twelve tones which are related only with one another," broke resolutely with the musical past by completing a process that had begun with Wagner's chromaticism and continued via Debussy's experiments to the full emancipation of dissonance in Stravinsky's *Sacre*. Similarly, Kandinsky broke with the tradition of representational art by pushing to the limit the implications of a statement with which van Gogh, writing from Arles to his brother Theo, had announced the emancipation of pictorial dissonance:

> Because instead of trying to reproduce exactly what I have before my eyes, I use color more arbitrarily so as to express myself more forcefully. Well, let that be as a matter of theory, but I am going to give you an example of what I mean.
>
> I should like to paint the portrait of an artist friend, a man who dreams great dreams, who works as the nightingale sings, because it is his nature. He'll be a fair man. I want to put into the picture my appreciation, the love that I have for him. So I paint him as he is, as faithfully as I can, to begin with.
>
> But the picture is not finished yet. To finish it I am now going to be the arbitrary colorist. I exaggerate the fairness of the hair, I get to orange tones, chromes and pale lemon yellow.
>
> Beyond the head, instead of painting the ordinary wall of the mean room, I paint infinity, a plain background of the richest, intensest blue that I can contrive, and by this simple combination the bright head illuminated against a rich blue background acquires a mysterious effect, like the star in the depths of an azure sky.[40]

I do not think that the Expressionistic theory of art in general, and of portrait painting in particular, has ever been more clearly articulated. The painter's statement helps to resolve the dichotomy posed by our contention that the Expressionists wanted to show the essence of things (their *Wesen*) and Herbert Read's definition of the style as one which seeks to reproduce "not the objective reality of the world, but the subjective reality of the feelings which objects and events arouse in us."[41] For the finished product, as indicated by van Gogh, was to embody both the sitter's personality and the artist's estimation thereof, i.e., a perfect blend of the objective (not conceived in a superficial, realistic way) and the subjective.

With the coming of Expressionism, the focus of attention was, once again, shifted from physical to human nature. Indeed, the Expressionists are among the greatest portrait painters of all time. They invariably show their sitters *en face*, never in profile, because the eyes "are the windows of the soul."[42] It is precisely the soul, however—especially the soul in writing anguish—which the Expressionists desired to project.

Edvard Munch, many of whose paintings are, in Däubler's words, "highly erotic but not sensual,"[43] reflects this anguish in his pictorial allegory of the

"Scream," which seems to illustrate Hermann Bahr's puzzling statement: "Impressionism treated the eye like an ear, Expressionism like a mouth. The ear is dumb, and Impressionism bade the soul be silent. The mouth is deaf, and the Expressionist cannot hear the world."[44] Paula Modersohn-Becker's portrait of Rainer Maria Rilke (1906) represents one of the earliest stages in the Expressionistic search for the pictorial equivalent of soul states; and Oskar Kokoschka's masterful Self-Portrait of 1917 reveals the "ghost" of the painter through the enormously dilated pale blue eyes and the twisted hands that look like caterpillars. According to Edschmid, a literary parallel to this phenomenon is found in the work of Alfred Döblin, "who so fabulously permeates and irradiates the flesh with injections of spirit that the ghost (a different thing from the skeleton) becomes solely visible."[45] Edschmid credits August Strindberg—we think of his *Ghost Sonata*—with having done the same thing in drama.

Unlike Munch, Modersohn-Becker, and Kokoschka, certain Expressionists sought to plumb the depth of the souls of animals. According to August Macke, "the senses are a bridge connecting the visible and the invisible. To look at plants and animals means to feel their secret."[46] Thus Franz Marc, the Expressionistic animal painter par excellence, sought to portray the world of beasts not as we see it but as the eagle, the horse, the cow, or the tiger see it. Every animal thus becomes, in Däubler's words, "the incarnation of its cosmic rhythm."[47]

Moving still further down the Great Chain of Being, other Expressionists breathed a soul even into inanimate things, not in order to reveal their inner geometry (for that was what the Cubists aimed at doing) but with the intention of demonstrating their latent dynamism. Speaking of Robert Delaunay, Däubler calls him the first Expressionist on account of his "portraits" of the Eiffel Tower. In fact, that tower is "scaffold and skeleton of the future . . . [It] is the first Expressionist . . . [it] has a soul . . . [it] is an artist . . . It is also the father of Delaunay."[48] Thus Wilhelm Worringer hits the mark when, surveying Expressionism in a retrospective essay, he credits it with having theomorphized the world in its drive for total spiritualization.[49] Impressionism having run its course, landscape, too—in the words of Kurt Pinthus—was no longer "copied, described, glorified . . . but wholly humanized."[50] Such an interpretation could well be placed on El Greco's "View of Toledo" or van Gogh's "Starry Night."

On the pictorial plane, such spiritualization is invariably manifested as distortion. Distortion of form or color is, in fact, the very hallmark of Expressionistic art. But how about Expressionistic literature? I believe that even in this respect a perfect parallelism exists between the two media. A few hints may suffice in the present context. The immediate forerunners of German literary Expressionism were Frank Wedekind and Carl Sternheim, whose tools were caricature, the grotesque, and satire; in other words: techniques which invariably involve distortion. When Thomas Mann defined Expressionism in the *Betrachtungen,* he singled out these very traits to show how totally writers like his brother Heinrich had lost touch with contemporary life and political reality.

The syntactical distortions which occur in Expressionistic poetry are nowhere more prominent than in Gottfried Benn's "Karyatide," which contains the difficult lines "Bespei die Säulensucht: toderschlagene / Greisige Hände bebten sie / Verhangenen Himmeln zu," which Michael Hamburger renders clumsily as "Spit on this column mania: done to death / mere senile hands they trembled / towards cloud-covered heavens," and Lohner / Corman more appropriately "Spit on this passion for pillars: the death-dealing / hoary hands trembled them / to overhanging heaven."[51]

To be sure, in the realm of language it seems particularly bold to strive for the kind of simplification and foreshortening found in the woodcuts of the *Brücke* group or the kind of abstraction familiar from Kandinsky. Nevertheless, such tendencies made themselves felt in the poetry of August Stramm and other, more radical exponents of *Sturm* art. Herwarth Walden demanded that the poet should use words and rhythm in the same way in which the painter uses color and form, and the composer sound and rhythm. Stramm, who was not a theoretician, transformed *Dichtung* (poetry) into *Wortkunst,* as in the poem "Schwermut," which reads:

> Schreiten Streben
> Leben sehnt
> Schauern Stehen
> Blicke suchen
> Sterben wächst
> Das Kommen
> Schreit!
> Tief
> Stummen
> Wir.

Under the aegis of Rudolf Blümner, the level of pure abstraction was reached shortly afterwards in the *Lautkunst* of poems like "Ango Laina," which opens with the cryptic line "Oiaí laéla oía ssísialu" and ends with what sounds like a parody of Stramm's one-word lines: "gádse / ina / leíola / kbáo / sagór / kadó." Blümner took the matter very seriously and would have been offended had anybody told him about the curious resemblance between "Ango Laina" and certain Dadaist nonsense poems. Like the experiments with abstract rhythms which Edith Sitwell undertook in *Façade, Lautkunst* entails a complete breakdown of communication of the level on which language commonly operates. For how are we to extract any sort of meaning from Blümner's African-sounding word formations? Benn, who was fascinated by what he called "das südliche Wort," and who dreamed of realizing the purely formal art which Gustave Flaubert envisaged when he stood on the Acropolis, wisely refrained from putting his theory into practice. So did Ezra Pound, a great admirer of Kandinsky, who wished to rid poetry of all literary values (as Verlaine had proclaimed in "Art Poétique") and who, at least in the Imagist-Vorticist phase of his career, championed an art devoid of meaning. For while the general public has, at long last, been reconciled with abstraction in the pictorial arts, abstraction in literature, or even a private, synthetic language of the kind employed in *Finnegans Wake,* is not likely ever to be fashionable.

As a term, Expressionism, which had been launched by the French painter Julien-Auguste Harvé in 1901, found general acceptance in 1911 when a number of German art critics applied it to the Fauvist paintings included in an exhibition of the Berlin *Sezession.* Worringer gave his blessing when, writing in *Der Sturm,* he spoke of the "Pariser Synthetisten und Expressionisten: Cézanne, van Gogh, Matisse." No transfer to literature was attempted until several years later, probably 1914 or 1915; and as early as 1918 Kasimir Edschmid spoke of literary Expressionism as a fad embraced by a horde of imitators. Four years later, Kurt Pinthus, asked to prepare a new edition of his anthology, decided to leave *Menschheitsdämmerung* untouched. For he felt that "after the completion of this lyrical symphony, no poetry has been written that inalienably belongs to it."[52]

Those were the years of transition from Expressionism to *Neue Sachlichkeit* (New Objectivity). Soon the *Bauhaus* was to be the most influential force in the fine and applied arts, and sobriety began to reassert itself in literature and music. Expressionism was an impulse quickly spent. The *Weltanschauung* at its root, and the style to which it gave rise, were those of youthful enthusiasts who overreached themselves or slid back into more conventional channels of expression. "Let the young," said Rudolf Kurtz in a phrase that applies to the Storm and Stress as well as to Expressionism, "stay young even to the point of catastrophe. Immaturity is the most powerful yeast of history."[53]

The title of our essay posed the question as to whether Expressionism should be viewed primarily as a stylistic phenomenon or as a *Weltanschauung,* i. e., whether it should be judged by esthetic or extra-esthetic criteria. We pointed out that, luckily, the socio-political aspect can be subsumed by the term Activism. If, excluding this aspect, one defines the term broadly enough to include man's attitude toward himself, his fellow-beings and the world at large, one can defend the use of *Weltanschauung* in the sense of a sharp rejection of previously embraced views on the part of an entire generation. This is what the Expressionists meant by *Aufbruch,* by their concentration on soul states, by their determination to make the invisible visible. Hence the intensity, the spiritual unrest, the emotionally charged atmosphere of their products. Indeed, one cannot imagine an Expressionist work to be conceived rationally and in cold blood.

Although, as critics and historians of art, we prefer to approach Expressionism inductively (through an analysis of stylistic devices), we see nothing wrong with the deductive method, provided that it leads to tangible results and comes to grips with specific problems. We object, however, to the thematic treatment proffered in *The Writer in Extremis.* For as is shown by the unrepresentativeness of the examples adduced by Sokel, what mattered to the Expressionists was not the *what*—or, for that matter, the *why*—but only the *how* of a given phenomenon. They simply did not care whether the *Aufbruch* they sought to portray occurred in the life of a son, a bank teller, or an artist.

Notes

1. *Menschheitsdämmerung: Ein Dokument des Expressionismus* (Hamburg, 1959), p. 16. All translations used in this essay are my own.

2. For a discussion of Vorticism see my article "Vorticism: Expressionism English Style" in the *Yearbook of Comparative and General Literature,* XIII (1964), 28-40.

3. Peter Selz, *German Expressionist Painting* (Berkeley, 1957).

4. Michael Hamburger and Christopher Middleton, *German Poetry 1910-1960* (New York, 1962); Walter H. Sokel, ed., *An Anthology of German Expressionist Drama* (New York, 1963).

5. Walter H. Sokel, *The Writer in Extremis* (Stanford, 1959).

6. *Lyrik des expressionistischen Jahrzehnts* (Munich, 1962), p. 16. The essay "Expressionismus" appears in Benn's *Gesammelte Werke,* ed. Dieter Wellershoff (Wiesbaden, 1959), I, 240-256.

7. Filippo Marinetti, "Manifesto Tecnico della letteratura futurista" in *I Poeti Futuristi* (Milano, 1912), p. 12 f.

8. From Julius Bab's *Chronik des deutschen Dramas* (Berlin, 1922), iv, 106, as quoted in *Expressionismus: Literatur und Kunst 1910-1923* (Munich, 1960), p. 312.

9. See Barlach's letter to his brother Karl of October 18, 1924.

10. *Über neue Prosa* (Berlin, 1919), p. 11.

11. "Die Expressionisten waren enttäuschte Humanisten, da die Wirklichkeit, in der sie lebten, nichts gemein hatte mit jener, die der Humanist der Gymnasien und Universitäten lehrte" (Pinthus in *Menschheitsdämmerung*, p. 15).

12. *Aktivismus und Expressionismus: Eine typologische Untersuchung* (Bern/Leipzig, 1935).

13. In 1913, Barlach wrote to his publisher, Reinhard Piper: "[Der blaue Boll] ist ein schönes Modell, aber schwer. Man denkt: so viel Fleisch und Bein soll und will überwunden werden."

14. "Schnelligkeit, Simultaneität, höchste Anspannung um die Ineinandergehörigkeit des Geschauten" *Der neue Standpunkt* (Dresden-Hellerau, 1916), p. 179.

15. "Wenn einer gehängt wird, so erlebt er im letzten Augenblick sein ganzes Leben nochmals" *Ibid*.

16. "Eine Vision will sich in letzter Knappheit im Bezirk verstiegener Vereinfachung kundgeben: das ist Expressionismus in jedem Stil" *Ibid*.

17. "Die Sätze [liegen] im Rhythmus anders gefaltet als gewohnt. Sie unterstehen der gleichen Absicht, demselben Strom des Geistes, der nur das Eigentliche gibt." *Über den Expressionismus in der Literatur und die neue Dichtung* (Berlin, 1919), p. 65.

18. "(Sie) binden Spitze an Spitze, sie schnellen ineinander, nicht mehr verbunden durch Puffer logischer Überleitung, nicht mehr durch den federnden äusserlichen Kitt der Psychologie" *Ibid.*, p. 66.

19. "Das ist die letzte Ballung des Tatsächlichen. Hier schwingt es sich zu seiner schwindelhaften Leistung auf. Vom ersten Rang bis in die Galerie Verschmelzung. Aus siedender Auflösung des einzelnen geballt der Kern: Leidenschaft!" *Deutsches Theater des Expressionismus,* ed. Joachim Schondorff (Munich, n. d. [1963]), p. 217.

20. "Spitzen, Spitzen . . . Von Anfang bis zu Ende nur Spitzen . . . Spitzen sind letzte Ballungen in allen Dingen" *Ibid.*, p. 220 f.

21. "Realism in English Poetry," *Essays and Studies by Members of the English Association,* XXV (1939), 81-101.

22. *Schöpferische Konfession* (Berlin, 1920), p. 28.

23. *Op. cit.,* p. 56.

24. *Swann's Way,* tr. C. K. Scott Moncrieff (New York, n. d.), p. 118 f.

25. "Only twice [in the history of Western art] a large scale attempt was made to broaden the narrow frame of the relationship [between individualism and sensualism] and to reach out for God by creating a supernatural and suprapersonal, spiritualized art. In the age of the Baroque, this was done covertly, in Expressionism overtly, i. e., in the former through the exaggeration of the sensualistic, in the latter through the exaggeration of the individualistic component of this relationship." *Fragen und Gegenfragen* (Munich, 1956), p. 97 f.

26. *Expressionismus* (Munich, 1920), p. 115.

27. "Arbeiten! Rausch! Gehirn zerschmettern! Kauen, fressen, schlingen, zerwühlen! Wonnevolle Schmerzen des Gebärens! Krachen des Pinsels, am liebsten Durchstossen der Leinwände. Zertrampeln der Farbtuben . . . Malen! Wühlen in Farben, Wälzen in Klängen! Im Brei des Chaos!" *Schöpferische Konfession,* p. 19.

28. *Wyndham Lewis, the Artist* (London, 1939), p. 109.

29. "Unser europäischer Wille zur abstrakten Form ist ja nichts anderes als unsre höchst bewusste, tatenheisse Erwiderung und Überwindung des sentimentalen Geistes. Jener frühe Mensch aber war dem Sentimentalen noch nicht begegnet, als er das Abstrakte liebte." Quoted from *Briefe, Aufzeichnungen und Aphorismen* (Berlin, 1920) in Will Grohmann, *Bildende Kunst und Architektur* [zwischen den beiden Kriegen] (Frankfurt a. M., 1953), p. 411.

30. "Meine ganze Seligkeit suche ich jetzt fast nur in reinen Farben. Vorige Woche habe ich auf einem Brett versucht, Farben zusammenzusetzen, ohne an irgendwelche Gegenstände, wie Menschen oder Bäume, zu denken, ähnlich wie bei der Stickerei." The letter, dating May 16, 1907, is quoted in the catalogue of the exhibition *Der Blaue Reiter* held in 1963 in the Städtische Galerie, Munich. It appears opposite the illustration No. 46.

31. Quoted from *Die Neue Rundschau* in *Expressionismus: Literature und Kunst 1910-1923*, p. 304.

32. "Wir wollen das Fleisch, aber in gehobenen Übersinnslüsten." From the essay "Döblin und die Futuristen" in *Die doppelköpfige Nymphe* (Berlin, 1920), p. 133.

33. *Über den dichterischen Expressionismus . . .* , p. 73.

34. "Farbe ohne Bezeichnung, Zeichnung und kein Erklären . . . im Rhythmus festgesetztes Hauptwort ohne Attribut" *Der neue Standpunkt,* p. 179.

35. "Since form is merely the expression of a content, and the content differs with different artists, it is obvious that several equally valid forms may exist at the same time." Quoted from the essay "Über

die Formfrage" (*Der Blaue Reiter*, p. 75) in the exhibition catalogue opposite the illustration No. 25. The *Blaue Reiter* has been newly edited by Klaus Lankheit (Munich, 1965).

36. *Concerning the Spiritual in Art* (New York, 1947), p. 47.

37. "For many years, I have tried to find a way of making the viewer walk around in my pictures, of forcing him to forget himself in the act of contemplation" Exhibition catalogue *Der Blaue Reiter*, opposite the illustration No. 20.

38. "Let us make a little trip into the land of greater insight, with the help of a topographic plan" *Schöpferische Konfession*, p. 29.

39. "Blaue Kundgebungen des Beschlusses vor ihren Einkörperungen in Taten" or "Mongoleien" which "farbenmystisch chaotisierend oder einen Kosmos ergrenzend, zu uns hereinwolken" *Der neue Standpunkt*, p. 183 f.

40. The letter, written in mid-August, 1888, appears in *The Letters of Vincent van Gogh* (New York, 1963), p. 276 ff.

41. *The Philosophy of Modern Art* (New York, 1955), p. 51.

42. For a discussion of this problem see Karen Machover, *Personality Projection in the Drawing of the Human Figure* (Springfield, Ill., 1949), p. 47 ff.

43. *Der neue Standpunkt*, p. 86.

44. "Hat der Impressionismus das Auge zum blossen Ohr gemacht, so macht es der Expressionismus zum blossen Mund. Das Ohr ist stumm; der Impressionist liess die Seele schweigen. Der Mund ist taub; der Expressionist kann die Welt nicht hören." *Op. cit.*, p. 116.

45. ". . . der das Fleisch mit Geistinjektionen so fabelhaft durchwühlt und durchschimmert, dass nur das Gespenst (was eine andere Geschichte ist als das Skelett) entsteht." *Die doppelköpfige Nymphe*, p. 133.

46. Quoted from August Macke's essay "Die Masken" (*Der Blaue Reiter*, p. 21) in the exhibition catalogue, opposite illustration No. 48.

47. *Der neue Standpunkt*, p. 138.

48. *Ibid.*, p. 181 f.

49. *Fragen und Gegenfragen*, p. 89.

50. *Menschheitsdämmerung*, p. 29.

51. Hamburger's translation appears in Hamburger, Middleton, *German Poetry 1910-1960*, the Lohner Corman version in *Origin*, VII (Autumn, 1952), 144.

52. *Menschheitsdämmerung*, p. 33.

53. From Kurtz' introduction to *Die neue Kunst*, a bimonthly publication edited by F. S. Bachmair, I/1 (1913-14), as quoted on p. 67 of *Expressionismus: Literatur und Kunst 1910-1923*.

Ralph Freedman (essay date winter 1969)

SOURCE: Freedman, Ralph. "Refractory Visions: The Contours of Literary Expressionism." *Contemporary Literature* 10, no. 1 (winter 1969): 54-74.

[*In the following essay, Freedman discusses the Expressionist technique of blurring the contours of ordinary objects in order to explore the relationship between human consciousness and the real world.*]

I

If it is at all true that artists express the needs and values of their culture, it follows that they also reflect its impasse. In our time, they have sought to isolate this crucial recognition by distorting the world around them—their own features, and ours, as well as those "classical" forms we still intuitively accept as our standards. We want to determine what these modern distortions mean in our cultural history—whether they suggest a height of artistic power, as most of us now think, or whether, as the old term "decadence" implies, they are symptoms of decline. These are odd questions to ask in the late nineteen-sixties, nearly a century after "Le Bâteau Ivre," more than half a century after the first serious impact of Ezra Pound and James Joyce, after Franz Kafka and Hermann Broch, after the imagists, the surrealists, the expressionists, the *nouveau roman*, and the theater of the absurd. And yet they remain persistent questions, for though individual forms have changed and yesterday's avant-garde today seems very old-fashioned, "distortion" has remained as a symptom, at times acting as a subversive undercurrent, at other times emerging as a dominant style in painting and music, poetry and prose.

In what sense, then, does "modernism" express a uniquely contemporary impasse? Radical distortions may be produced by a vision of "higher" truths at variance with an inadequate "real" world, a vision derived from private insights otherwise incommunicable. Or distortions may reflect despair, an awareness of a loss of coherence, the need to portray incoherence precisely. Or they may reflect our rejection of contemporary values, our assertion that in an enslaved and enslaving world man is free only in a realm of the imagination he creates for himself. Naturally, each of these motives has governed artists at one point or another during the past century's history of peculiarly "modern" distortions.

But perhaps it is also true that none of these common explanations is quite sufficient, that the motives for the most intense distortions may lie deeper, that they may be rooted in our growing obsession with the conditions of our awareness, with the way in which we self-consciously relate ourselves to our modes of thinking and feeling, with a questioning not so much of appearances and values themselves as of our sense of appearances and values by which we have been conditioned.

The work of Franz Kafka and Hermann Broch may, briefly, serve as an example to point out two different modes of distortion which have dominated the modern sensibility. One way, Kafka's, we may associate with a "realistic" sense of distortion, a manner of analyzing the relations between consciousness and objects. The other way, which is made remarkably clear in Broch's *Death of Virgil*, suggests an internal exploration of consciousness, a widening of eyesight into visionary experience. Most of the novel is suspended between the poet's window and his bed, the figures of life and death, of waking and dreaming experience, of present and past, merging with one another as the outer eye is joined with the inner. The distortions which result from this juxtaposition suggest one manner of rendering reality that seems to be peculiarly "modern." Things are absorbed by the mind which transforms their images into visions: a mirroring of life and death in various layers of consciousness.

The other source of distortion, which can be found in Kafka, results from the *encounter* between minds and objects. If in Broch's *Death of Virgil* the outer world is absorbed by the sensibility, in Kafka's work it remains independent, functioning as an antagonist of the self. The dislocations of "The Metamorphosis" or *The Trial* emerge from the hero's self-conscious encounter with a significantly rearranged reality (the world of the beetle; the transformed world of the Trial). Reminiscent of grotesques, or satires like Swift's, these shifts in reality are used to reveal essential characteristics of objects and conditions in relation to minds. Distortions, then, may occur not because an imaginative, hallucinatory, or symbolic sensibility is at work, but because minds have observed certain essential characteristics in the outside world which they may wish to reveal more succinctly.

The reciprocal impact upon one another of mind and object (or consciousness and reality) has emerged as the artist's accommodation of a philosophical and literary realism to the twentieth century "atmosphere of the mind." Kafka's dislocations of the world suggest one such way. Another would be Rainer Maria Rilke's manner of endowing objects with semblances of human consciousness. For even in some of Rilke's most descriptive work, like *New Poems,* we can discern a tendency to project the self into things rather than absorbing things into the mind. The following passage from one of Rilke's essays on Rodin may serve as an example. Describing his master's reading, Rilke relates how objects can be seen:

> He [Rodin] read Dante's *Divine Comedy* for the first time. It was a revelation. He saw the suffering bodies of another generation, beyond all the days of his life, a century whose garments had been torn off, saw the great unforgettable judgment which a poet had passed on his time. There were images which justified his judgment, and when he read of the weeping feet of Nicholas III, he already knew that there was such a thing as weeping feet, that there is one great weeping that was everywhere, all over the entire person, which poured from all pores.[1]

This passage seems indeed to convey a fresh picture of reality—of a world whose contours had been subtly changed by a painter's and a poet's consciousness: Dante, Rodin, Rilke, apprehending universal tears pouring from all things as an emblem of man's state. Objects are infused with recognitions that bend them out of focus so that there can be such a thing as weeping feet to convey a meaningful statement about the world. Rilke's style, then, suggests yet another way in which the modern concern with mind has been utilized to render a clearer picture of things, of life and history, and of the spiritual and social reality in which we live. It also describes one of the most conspicuous methods used by a movement until recently far too neglected: literary expressionism—a movement which was concerned precisely with the meaning of the object in relation to minds and which has used this concern in its creation of a new style.

II

The contours of modern expressionism are vague, indeed. In its widest sense, the term may be used to describe any expressive language, or any "expression" as opposed to a "communication" theory of art. As a special kind of expressiveness, it has been traced to Baudelaire, Rimbaud, or George. Its vision of man has been seen prefigured in Kierkegaard, Nietzsche, Dostoevsky, Strindberg. But as a specific contribution to literature, the term might be limited to a particular historical situation, a particular way of conceiving reality as an infusion of the world by minds, which was especially favored by a movement that radiated outward from German-speaking countries between 1910 and 1933, when, ecstatically, a new style was created.

New moments of stylistic creation are exciting points in literary and intellectual history. Accompanied by manifestos and appropriate slogans, at the very least they give insight into the sensibility of a generation; at best they shed light on a new phase in the development of several literatures. Such was the case with literary expressionism. Although many of its practitioners are either not yet or no longer widely known, expressionism defined that new way of looking at reality which the modern drive towards the clarification of its values had revealed: a solution of that awkward discrepancy between self and thing. At the same time, the movement itself was bafflingly diversified (composed of political activists, religious mystics, or didactic artists of the most various shades), although deeply united in an angry protest against the literary, academic, and social establishment. The chief point of agreement between them was found in the use of language, a particular style in both poetry and prose which paralleled the motions and dislocations of form found in expressionistic painting.[2]

Our first question, then, concerns the unity of the expressionistic movement in relation to its style. What common ground is there between the following selections from Johannes R. Becher's "Wannsee" (1917), Franz Werfel's morality play *Spiegelmensch* (*Mirror Man,* 1920), and Georg Heym's poem "Der Gott der Stadt" ("The God of the City," 1910), except a similar stylistic principle? Becher's early poem, squarely within his "expressionistic period," is acidulous social criticism as it describes sunbathers at the beach of the *Wannsee* near Berlin:

> Zinnobrer Tag! Im dürren Paradiese,
> Ein Mosaik im Abrutsch schaukelnder Kabinen,
> Vor deren Gärten farbene Huren blühen.
> Azurene Fläche sich aus deren Mündern giesst.
>
> Vermillion day. In the desiccated paradise,
> A mosaic of swaying cabins sliding downward,
> With gardens before which blossom colorful whores.
> Azure surfaces out of their mouths pouring.[3]

In content and lyrical mood, the following lines spoken by Mirror Man ("soul"), appearing as Seductive Woman, to the hero, Thamal (representing Man), seem to be a striking contrast:

> Weisst du denn nicht? Noch warten goldene Zonen,
> Das Südlicht rollt durch Palmen-Avenuen.
> Du wirst mit mir in grellen Häusern wohnen,
> Lust-Scheiterhaufen, die uns nie verglühn.
> Wenn schlaff wir ruhn auf flutenden Terrassen,
> Wird sich Orchesterwonne niederlassen,
> Wie Tiefsee-Fische schlafen wir im Grund
> Der Weltmusik, befriedigt, schwebend, bunt!
>
> Do you not know then? Golden zones still await us.
> The southern light rolls down palmtree avenues.
> You will reside with me in homes that glare with brightness,
> Burning stakes of lust that for us will never dim.
> When, limp, we shall recline on flooding terraces,
> Orchestral bliss will settle down, and
> Like deep-sea fish we shall slumber at the bottom
> Of the world's music—sated, floating, multi-colored![4]

Or, to provide yet another contrast, lines taken from Georg Heym's interesting poem about the city show modern urban life against the destructive image of itself personified as a latter-day Baal:

> Vom Abend glänzt der rote Bauch dem Baal,
> Die grossen Städte knien um ihn her.
> Der Kirchenglocken ungeheure Zahl
> Wogt auf zu ihm aus schwarzer Türme Meer.
>
> Toward evening-time the red belly glows on Baal
> And the large cities kneel all about him.
> Massed church bells in enormous numbers
> Surge up to him from the black-towered sea.[5]

In each case, we note an animation of reality. However divergent the purpose—to shock, to teach, to describe—the poet appears to be concerned with extracting a peculiarly meaningful relation between his own vision (and that of the beholder) and the world of things on which he focused. To be sure, we find here varying degrees of distortion, but no symbolic refashioning of life, nor even symbolic references to a world of experience suppressed and evoked by the poem's language. When Becher writes "Azure surfaces out of [the whores'] mouths pouring," he creates a series of images which are supposed to express a moral point: the open mouths, the azure of water and sky, the aggressive outpouring are telescoped and, together, reveal the meaning not of the metaphoric whores, but of the whole lascivious business of sunbathing as a bourgeois enterprise. Yet there is no transformation into symbol, aesthetic or psychological. It is the distortion of an existing visual pattern which makes the point with disarming directness. Similarly, the passage from Werfel is a bold attempt to suggest the sexual act, whose vision of Seductive Woman flashes before Thamal's eyes to suggest it in its totality, its drama, its universal arrogance, without ever leaving the framework of described objects or without forcing the objects to stand for anything but themselves. Attention is focused on the *object*; by animating reality, the poet affirms the conditions in terms of which alone the object can exist: its relevance to *persons* or to ideas meaningful to persons.

Expressionistic style, then, is more than expressive language; it is a particular kind of expressive language. Indeed, it exists as a pivot between two phases of style which had emerged from the nineteenth century. One is the "underground" style of heightened romanticism: Baudelaire's carcass, Rimbaud's drunken boat, which culminated in Mallarmé's pure, self-denying order, and Valéry's geometrical world of light, or in psychological or mystical visions, the internal imagery of Cocteau or Eluard. The other is the style of naturalism, i.e., a heightening of realistic depiction, in which the poet is suppressed. Expressionism partook of both these styles, and worlds, at once. Not only concerned with the self's "remarkable visions," refusing to absorb objects into dream but intensifying them by dream, the expressionistic style focused attention on the world of things. Distortions were not to lead to formations of symbols; sensations were not to be frozen into golden birds of heraldic significance. Rather, the world of objects was distorted to reveal its essential meaning. And "essential" is a value term imparted by people. Expressionism, therefore, described the relations between man and object; it commanded engagement.

III

One of the striking features of expressionistic language is its way of suggesting thematic meanings (political or metaphysical) while resolutely remaining itself. The engagement, i.e., the concealed meaning within the object, is built into the very description. The following lines from Ernst Stadler's poem, "Fahrt über die Kölner Rheinbrücke bei Nacht" ("Journey Across the Rhine River Bridge at Cologne by Night") may illustrate this point:

> Der Schnellzug tastet sich
>   und stösst die Dunkelheit entlang.
> Kein Stern will vor. Die ganze Welt ist nur ein enger
>   nachtumschienter Minengang.
> Darein zuweilen Förderstellen
>   blauen Lichtes jähe Horizonte reissen: Feuerkreis
> Von Kugellampen, Dächern, Schloten,
>   dampfend, strömend . . . nur sekundenweis . . .
> Und alles wieder schwarz,
>   Als führen wir ins Eingeweid der Nacht zur
> Schicht.

> The express train gropes
>   and pushes along the darkness ahead.
> No star will come forward. The entire world is but a
> narrow
>   night-tracked mine-shaft,
> Wherein at times way stations
>   of blue light tear off sudden horizons: fiery circle
> Of bowl lamps, roofs, smokestacks,
>   steaming, streaming . . . only for seconds . . .
> And all is black again,
>   As if we were riding to our shift through the innards of
>   the night.

Most of the comparisons in this poem are absorbed into the language itself. For example, the untranslatable phrase "nachtumschienter Minengang" represents a complex telescoping of different images and allusions. The basic image alluded to is "nachtumschienen," already forced but referring to "shone upon by night" or even "suffused by the absence of light, by night." "Schienen," however, are railroad tracks pushing through the mine-shaft at night. The image obviously means: the trip across the bridge at night is like travelling through a mine-shaft; the mine-shaft suffused by night, is also like a mine-shaft imprisoned by tracks, telescoping the negative light of night and the tracks into a single abbreviated expression. Indeed, expressionistic language, which among its drearier practitioners so often reverts to mere animation, can be made fresh and exciting by images of this sort. The simile of riding into the night as if penetrating the innards of the night is more direct. Yet neither creates that new metaphoric level which we have come to expect from the symbolist experiment. In the last lines of the poem, the human point is extracted from the dark landscape:

> Und dann die langen Einsamkeiten. Nackte Ufer.
>   Stille. Nacht. Besinnung. Einkehr. Kommunion.
> Und Glut und Drang
> Zum Letzten, Segnenden. Zum Zeugungsfest.
> Zur Wollust. Zum Gebet. Zum Meer.
> Zum Untergang.

> And then the long stretches of loneliness. Naked
> banks.
>   Silence. Night. Concentration. Contemplation.
> Communion.
>   And Passion and urge,
> To the last one, to him who bestows blessings. To the
> feast of
>   procreation.

> To lust. To prayer. To the sea.
> To doom.[6]

This ending is not really defensible, even if the poem itself is linguistically striking. There is too much *Götterdämmerung*; too many identifications of lust, sex, prayer, and death are extracted from this simple trip across the Rhine in an express train to make the image work. But it does illustrate the expressionistic method of extraction: the abstract statement of the conclusion literally forces itself upon the text. More technically, what we may perhaps find disturbing is that the language is "straight" both ways: the distorted vision of the object as well as the linguistic utterance are given without being pressed into a combining metaphor. But this very fact forms part of the dramatic, declamatory method of expressionism—in content as well as in style. The picture is retained (the sounds of the utterance continue to imitate the moving train and so force the listener to remain within the framework of the initial situation); but the meaning is also stated.

These considerations lead to the conclusion that both in its history and in its technical achievement, expressionistic writing achieved a heightening of rather than, as its practitioners thought, a counter-statement to naturalism. Indeed, if most of the expressionists rejected naturalism, they did so not because it was aesthetically unsatisfying, but because, in a very special sense, it was ideologically unsatisfying. If the romantic imagination produced an extension of the poet's vision and knowledge, the naturalist's imagination had been equivalent to the world itself. As Zola pointed out in the *Roman expérimental,* the ideal poet-author, being detached, is by definition noncommittal, unengaged. He may be seized by rage at the conditions he describes, but officially at least he does not take a stand. Ideally, his attitude is scientific, his analysis detached. The expressionist, on the other hand, took a stand. The external world, in fact, had no meaning, no *raison d'être* by itself. *Die*

Welt ist da. (So wrote the theoretician Kasimir Edschmid.) *Es wäre sinnlos sie zu wiederholen.* ("The world exists. It would be senseless to repeat it.") Presenting "a pure, unfalsified picture of the world," the expressionist seeks to create it anew. For the world is relevant only insofar as consciousness reshapes it and makes it meaningful to people, as it conveys an "essence."[7]

In this latter sense, the expressionistic poets we have examined thought of themselves as diametrically opposed to naturalism. They refused to accept the "objective" conception of reality. They equally rejected the pure analysis of the soul, cultivated in symbolist writing. Rather, the world must be distorted to reveal its inner meaning. As the eyes of hungry children, for example, are shown large on the prints of Käthe Kollwitz, so in expressionist literature men and women, psychologically motivated plots, and poetic imagery are equally stylized to illuminate their relevance to people. This involvement of expressionist poets in human fate, whether political or religious, lends a specific moral weight to their sometimes overwrought images and plots, and leads to their formation of their own language. For instance, Becher's prose description of wounded German soldiers returning from the lines in World War I, exaggerates and wrenches out of focus the underlying naturalistic description:

> There comes, hurrying across the field—immensely heightened—a procession of soldiers whose intestines are breaking out of their bodies. Swirling foam. Around their necks they are wearing (like amulets) white placards with mysterious signs on them: certifying the fact that they were wounded. A great wind roars and blows billows of smoke like powdery dust. Riders dance in the distance. They have smoked out a small Galician village; girls, charred, hang in the windows. Earth is darkening. . . .[8]

Partly we respond to the sense of speed and animation in an otherwise static situation: swirling foam, roaring wind, dancing riders, darkening earth. Partly, however, we discern the exaggerated realism, its deliberate push from the horror of the given towards the irrational to make the thematic point. Becher's passage, of course, is programmatic. But Gottfried Benn's terrifying poem, "Schöne Jugend" ("Beautiful Youth"), taken from his early *Morgue* poems, pursues a similar course without an evident programmatic intention, to reveal, one might suppose, the hideousness and terror of both man and world.

> Der Mund eines Mädchens, das lange im Schilf gelegen hatte,
> Sah so angeknabbert aus.
> Als man die Brust aufbrach war die Speiseröhre
> so löcherig.
> Schliesslich in einer Laube unter dem Zerchfell
> fand man ein Nest von jungen Ratten.
>
>   . . . . .

> The mouth of a girl who had long lain in the reeds
> Looked sort of gnawed on.
> When they opened her chest, the esophagus was sort of
> punctured.
> Finally, in a bower under the diaphragm
> they found a nest of young rats.[9]
>
>   . . . . .

A further tendency in naturalism is to view the self as being helplessly acted upon, oppressed by an external world it cannot control, by a fate it is powerless to prevent. Expressionist poets shared this image of the passive, suffering self, because, unlike many other avant-gardists of their time, they could not view the poet's imaginative consciousness as sufficiently powerful in itself to liberate the enslaved self from the bondage of time, place, and milieu. For example, surrealistic poetry, coinciding with the self's inner vision, with Rimbaud's deliberately disordered dream, can retain the poet's mind as a principal motive power—unconscious dream absorbs and transforms outer reality. Similarly, Mallarmé and Stefan George both acted as high priests whose magic could convert the limiting world of the senses into liberating art. But the expressionists—bent upon rendering the drama of human suffering and redemption—had to recognize that once the confrontation between "mind" and "thing" is accepted, the exposed self is continuously assailed by powers in reality evidently superior to itself. Again, it may be Rilke among the great poets of this rich period who pointed the way to the expressionist experiment, not only in his heightened language, his preoccupation with things, his difficult syntax, but especially in his projection of the self as a passive image, of the poet as sufferer, as the man who endures. Whatever may have been his ultimate purpose in the loose poetic novel, *The Note-Books of Malte Laurids Brigge* (1910), for example, its hero is Job and the Suffering Servant, assailed by things and by the vision of God before he is turned into the Prodigal Son. However different from naturalistic writing in its lyrical tone (though not wholly divorced from it in its descriptions of city landscapes, of horror and dread), in its subjective mood and its heraldic imagery this novel may be, it does project clearly an image of the poet as the enduring self. And it is this image which the expressionists, too, had evolved from naturalism before turning it in the bizarre, contorted light of their particular perspective.

The expressionist poet, then, like the hero of expressionist fiction and drama, endures. In the works of social protest, he endures injustice inflicted upon him by society. In the religious and mystical works, he is destined to suffer before redemption is possible, like Thamal in Werfel's morality play *Spiegelmensch* (*Mirror Man*). In both cases, the naturalistic premise that man and the world are defined by causality was heightened and distorted by the peculiar concerns of the expressionists. It was reshaped by ideas and artistic purposes alike. For if the hero of expressionist literature with a revolutionary or social message suffered because of pressure from a threatening, mechanistic society, the hero of the religious literature did so because suffering is a Christian condition. Suffering thus becomes a way not only of presenting reality but also of reaching the idea: in the first instance because the endurance of wrongs is a step towards the revolution, in the second instance because it is a step towards redemption. And both, in their intensely stylized way, aim towards a definition of man, who, like Kafka's K., helplessly struggles among an overpowering, if contorted, world of things.

This tendency is equally marked in the pure lyric. For example, the early Werfel's handling of anxiety and depression, with all their oppressive and redemptive qualities, exaggerates the action of objects upon the poet's consciousness as he gives himself to their power. Thus, the first stanza of his "Ballade von Wahn und Tod" ("Ballad of Delusion and Death"):

> Im grossen Raum des Tags,—
> Die Stadt ging hohl, Novembermeer, und schallte schwer
> Wie Sinai schallt. Vom Turm geballt
> Die Wolke fiel.—Erstickten Schlags
> Mein Ohr die Stunde traf,
> Als ich gebeugt sass über mich zu sehr.
> Und ich entfiel mir, rollte hin, und schwankte da auf einem Schlaf.
>
> In the grand expanse of day,—
> The city walked hollow, November sea, and sounded hard
> The way Sinai sounds. Clenched to a ball by the tower
> The cloud fell down.—With muffled blow
> My ear hit the hour,
> As, too far bent over myself, I sat.
> And fell from myself, rolled off, and swayed upon a sleep.[10]

In addition to the poet's passive role, moreover, we also discern the taut rendering of a consciousness suspended between dream-like perception and death-like sleep, seeking to determine objects through its awareness while itself being determined by them. The strained language starkly mirrors these relations.

Finally, the inversion of the naturalistic premise, the heightening of naturalistic effect, while lending expressionism its striking, paradoxical character, is only part of its definition. Distortions, as we have seen, do not necessarily concern themselves with horrible or ugly subjects. Rather, the point of expressionism is to show that distortion *per se* becomes a means of revealing the mutual relations between mind and thing through the infusion of an idea. Hence, poets, novelists, or dramatists may indeed distort any situation, even a landscape, to bare its hidden, essential significance. In his beautiful poem "Geburt" ("Birth"), whose expressionistic traits are clearly marked, Georg Trakl, for example, discerns interweaving relations between a mountain landscape, and its hunting men, and the birth of a child, which he telescopes and renders as a single imagistic expression.

> Gebirge: Schwärze, Schweigen und Schnee.
> Rot vom Wald niedersteigt die Jagd;
> O, die moosigen Blicke des Wilds.
>
> Stille der Mutter; unter schwarzen Tannen
> Öffnen sich die schlafenden Hände,
> Wenn verfallen der kalte Mond erscheint.
>   . . . . .
> Weh, der Gebärenden Schrei. Mit schwarzem Flügel
> Rührt die Knabenschläfe die Nacht,
> Schnee, der leise aus purpurner Wolke sinkt.
>
> Mountain ranges: blackness, silence, and snow.
> Red, the hunters descend from the forest;
> Oh, the mossy glances of the deer.
>
> The mother's silence; under the black fir trees
> Sleeping hands open
> When the cold moon appears, withered.
>   . . . . .
> Woe, the screams of her who gives birth. With its black wing
> Night fans the boys' temples,
> Snow, gently drifting down from its purple cloud.[11]

The animation of the world, and the motion discernible in the diction transferring the drama of birth to the landscape and letting both partake of an image of man's fate—all of these are distinctly expressionistic. But we note especially how the act of birth and the mountain landscape, the hunters, the children of Man, are all distorted by the poet's consciousness holding them together in a single sustained yet moving image.

In prose, too, the projection of any idea, whether ideological or mystical, can transform the diction and the imagery of concrete objects without seeming to be in any way derived from naturalistic distortion. The following passage, for example, is taken from the opening pages of Johannnes R. Becher's first novel, *Erde* (*Earth*; 1912), an as yet unpolitical book, in which sexuality becomes religion and religion relentlessly sexual:

> The night began with the song of bells. The wind rustled in the trees. Thus he hung in the death of the room, an unclear height, given over to pious contemplation: the Savior, the dear Lord, the humanly sacrificed. Arms given over to the night, five wounds of the grossest colors of urgent red. . . . The gentle force of the darkness robbed the bright star of its child-like pleasure. So relentlessly reigned Black. Only near the distant hills did Mildness hover: the great festive roar, moving towards the sea, the eternal sea.[12]

The poet, whatever his subject, sought to convey neither mind nor object by itself, but the meaning which emerged from a relation between them both, a rational or political, irrational or nihilistic, religious or mystically ecstatic meaning. Evidently, the type of diction with which Heym described the confluence of City and Baal, or Trakl that of landscape and birth, can also communicate the idea of delusion and death, or the intermingling of redemptive themes both sexual and religious.

IV

Stylistic distortion to render the meaning-relation existing between subject and thing naturally received its first formulation, as well as rationale, through painting. Although the term "expressionism" was first applied to painters like Cézanne, Van Gogh, and Matisse, and was later extended to all Fauvist painters, it soon emerged as a more specific self-conscious phenomenon.[13] Directly and indirectly, we discern a tendency towards statement: in Ernst Barlach, for example, who also wrote plays and prose, in Oskar Kokoschka, who was both painter and playwright, in Käthe Kollwitz, who portrayed social themes; but also, among many others, in much of Franz Marc and Paul Klee. These artists, like the more programmatic literary expressionists, eroded and often expanded contours, changed and animated their lines, to reach an essential meaning of the thing. But they did not dissolve the external form, i.e., they neither refashioned the form as an abstract design nor did they dissolve it into mental imagery. In painting, as in literature, the artist discerns the meaning (i.e., the idea) in the object and communicates it to the audience. The expressionistic artist thus confronts a dual situation. On the one hand, his beliefs are lodged in the aesthetic object, and the artist makes the object express these beliefs (by rearranging reality accordingly). *Expressiveness* is heightened. On the other hand, he communicates these beliefs to the audience by means of the object. *Communication* is enhanced.

This double action, implied in the didactic nature of expressionistic literature, draws the contours of both language and literary forms. Drama, of course, is most suitable for this purpose, since through its action the interplay between person and world can be made visually accessible. Plays in which these relationships are developed for political purposes include such well-known landmarks of the revolutionary era following World War I as Ernst Toller's *Masse Mensch* (*Mass Man*; 1920) or *Maschinenstürmer* (*Machine Breakers*; 1922) or Georg Kaiser's *Gas* plays (1917-25). Reality in these plays is generalized through a stylization of realistic form. Characters are turned into types; action is declamatory, approaching the starkest forms of classical tragedy. But expressionism also developed new forms in spheres other than those of social involvement, as its language focused on mystical and religious themes as well. Beginning as early as Reinhard Sorge's "first drama of expressionism" *Der Bettler* (*The Beggar*; 1912), the drama, like lyrical poetry, started out with highly allusive, ecstatic language that sought to infuse the world with an animating consciousness. It also evolved towards forms like the mystery plays and allegories, while retaining the directness of the stylized statement. Such plays may include Fritz von Unruh's *Ein Geschlecht* (*A Generation*; 1916), a one-act tragedy about the consequences of murder, or Oskar Kokoschka's short play *Hiob* (*Job*; 1917). Pointedly, perhaps, the expressionistic style has also produced iconoclastic statements of sexual and religious rebellion like Hans Henny Jahnn's *Pastor Ephraim Magnus* (1919), a drama in which the decision to go the way of the world is rewarded by murder and death, but the decision to shoulder Christ's sacrifice by an eternal sentence to labor in the grave without peace, without being able to decompose. Yet, like the social drama of the expressionists, so their spiritual forms turned more and more towards a new ritualism. Werfel's morality play *Spiegelmensch,* from which we cited, is a fair example of this trend which, by turning the realism implied in expressionistic imagery towards ritual, also approached the allegorical. There is no meaning to Thamar's plight, which is surprisingly like Faust's, if it did not point beyond him. Similarly, Ernst Barlach's shattering play, *Die Sündflut* (*The Deluge*; 1924), a play in five parts about that crucial episode in *Genesis*, is clearly ritual allegory, and the existential horror that emerges when devil, leper, and handless angel die in the slime of the Flood becomes an apocalyptic vision of reality. "Noah's God," shouts the devil, "is as fierce as I used to be, and I am scared of his divinity." But these images do not function through symbolic transformations; rather, they obtain their horror, and their meaning as a whole, through a pointed reshaping of the external world.

In expressionistic prose, the double action of expressiveness and communication we noted in other genres is also evident, although after a time it seems to have followed an almost separate development. Johannes R. Becher's first novel, *Erde,* with its ecstatic identification of carnal and spiritual love, naturally accompanied its author's preoccupation with the language of lyrical poetry. But as we look toward and into the nineteen-twenties, expressionistic prose began to evolve a style of its own. Indeed, the principles governing the movement's theory of language, while ostensibly pertinent to all literary diction and style, and to all genres, became particularly suitable for prose which seemed to respond most fully to the expressionistic penchant for direct statement. A few sentences from an erotic novella in overwrought prose, *Die Fürstin* (*The Princess*; 1916) by the movement's theoretician Kasimir Edschmid may show the beginning of this development: "The sails' bellies bowed deeper and brushed across the colorless water and emerged once more, raised, into the red sun"—as a description of sailing at dusk. Animation occurs through the verbs which lend the object the semblance of human activity. Hence this description of the sky: "Coolly arched stands our sky, still blossoming antiquely." Or, a sentence from a description of the author's visit to the zoo with his mistress:

> Peacocks sprang into the trees and, menacingly, turned unheard-of wheels towards the reddened west and screamed with longing. Towards the bars, white bears grew out of their cages, roared as if crucified and, under the steadily waxing moon, bit into the iron.[14]

The word, Edschmid wrote a year later in his theoretical manifesto (1917), must become an arrow; it must hit the core of the object and reveal its soul. But we have already seen how this "interior" or essential core suggests the presence of mind—of the relevance of the object to consciousness and hence their engagement in poetry and now particularly in prose. "The personal grows into the general," wrote Edschmid. "All things will be built back towards their essential being: the simple, the universal, the essential."[15]

Expressionistic narrative, developing from these linguistic principles, emphasized a close relationship between the essential or general aspects of language and the precise particularity of objects. It used the erosion of contours, stylization, the rendering of reality as ritual, clearly reminiscent of poetic technique, within the medium of consecutive narration. It therefore emphasized even further both intensity and speed of diction. Intensity is clearly revealed in a tragic narrative like von Unruh's *Opfergang* (*Sacrificial Pilgrimage*; 1919) which deals with the debacle of Verdun. In a later work, Klabund's *Pjotr* (1923), short, abrupt strokes of intensely penetrating, swiftly moving language seek to capture the essential "core" of Peter the Great and his historical stature. Gradually, however, further forms distilled themselves. For example, Alfred Döblin's expressionistic prose changed and radicalized both the strength and the tempo of its distortions from his early *Drei Sprünge des Wang-Lun* (*The Three Leaps of Wang-Lun*; 1915) to his final and best known expressionistic novel, *Berlin-Alexanderplatz* (1929), where the external reality of the city and the internal reality of the confused criminal Franz Biberkopf are juxtaposed in violent and often interlocking encounters. Or Hermann Hesse's work of his so-called "expressionistic period" of the mid-nineteen-twenties—work that culminated in his *Steppenwolf* (1927)—matches the violent reality of the urban and mechanized present with a hallucinatory eternity produced by a heightened consciousness that telescopes both in a single image.

The experimentations in lyrical poetry, then, bore fruit for the novel in an increasingly rich manner as a new prose style emerged, flourished, and, even in declining, left clear imprints upon modern fiction. It was a style supple enough to render the thing as it is and its meaning (or "essence") simultaneously. Or, as Wilhelm Emrich suggests in his book on Kafka, expressionism could, as could no other style, develop a metaphysical level of existence without abandoning the physical level. Indeed, it is this element in Kafka's seemingly realistic prose which lends it a further dimension of meaning—the sense that the clearest object is at once never itself and fully itself. This "absolutely new element in Kafka's work," wrote Emrich, is the use of figurative language, even imagery, which is beyond allegory and symbol, as all things are endowed with a particular significance while resolutely remaining themselves. Expressionism has made possible this type of reference with its "dualistic metaphorical language."[16] It is in this sense that in the narratives of Kafka, expressionistic prose achieved its most refined and impressive dimension.

V

Our analyses, first of expressionistic language, then of expressionistic forms, have distilled for us the relationships which expressionism as an artistic style has striven to define. Describing this style epistemologically, we might say that expressionistic distortion—in poetry, the drama, and in narrative prose—is based, in various ways, on the distinction between consciousness and objects. Although there is a tendency to rearrange the world in a hallucinatory, dream-like way or to lend language a verve that seems inspired by the movements of consciousness, neither language nor things are purified out of existence, nor are they made exclusively part of the poet's mental furniture or his internal landscape. The vivacity, the horror, the spiritual meaning exist through linguistic rearrangements designed to reveal a point—didactic, political, religious, existential—which determines the relationship between self and thing, or their paradoxical contraction.

For this reason, expressionistic technique has produced strained, if interesting, diction and imagery in lyrical poetry, but it has excelled particularly in those genres which *display* the interaction between consciousness and world. Therefore, painting where the artist must relate himself to the object; the drama where man and world interact demonstrably; or fiction where consciousness projects itself into and among the things of reality, have all developed peculiar techniques which have intensified and enlarged the artistic discoveries of the expressionists. Moreover, their concern with the dualisms of consciousness and object, and of didactic communication and expressiveness, obviously had to extend far beyond their specifically German artistic climate to make them part of the general European avant-garde. The futurists, as Philippo Marinetti's *Manifesto* (1909) makes clear, celebrated dynamism as an end in itself.

And although, as we noted, surrealism in many ways represented a pole opposite to that of expressionism, its techniques recur in expressionistic language as well. Indeed, the lines often blur, and some of the artists of the time, like René Schickele and Hans Arp, were active in both movements. But in its effect, too, the expressionistic manner of distorting reality left clear imprints on other literatures, especially in the drama. The familiar indebtedness to expressionism of the American stage of the 'twenties and 'thirties is a case in point. Distortion and erosion of contours favor satire and social comedies, like Kaufmann's and Connely's *Beggar on Horseback* or Elmer Rice's *The Adding Machine,* but they also extend to serious social drama of the 'thirties, that ritualistic enactment of reality which we note, for example, in Odets and which has now become a common dramatic form.

Whether in their relevance to other genres or in their meaning to the international avant-garde, the principles that have defined expressionism are mostly succinctly rendered in its language. Although, as we had occasion to discover, the expressionistic lyric remained exaggeratedly strained, it still gave us our first clue to the direction the movement was to take. Such a clue may also be given to us by E. E. Cummings, especially in his poetry of the nineteen-twenties, which suggests a similar didactic streamlining of the self's encounters and a similar projection of a consciousness into the object. A few lines from an early poem by Cummings may illustrate this relationship:

> in making marjorie god hurried
> a boy's body on unsuspicious
> legs of a girl, his left hand quarried
> the quartz-like face, his right slapped
> the amusing big vital vicious
> vegetable of her mouth.[17]

This poem seems indeed to return us to the linguistic point with which we began. For these lines emerge as a statement. Although at first glance the language appears strained, it soon turns out to be simple and direct. The image of the person, Marjorie, is described through God's action in creating her, in composing her "picture." And the imposition of this action upon the parts of Marjorie's face and body creates a sense of distortion, an apparent rearrangement through the unexpected movements we see God perform—*hurrying* one form upon another, one hand *quarrying,* the other *slapping,* etc. But clearly this distortion is produced by statement rather than through any transformation of reality into symbol; it is part of a direct address to the audience. And if we compare these lines to Gottfried Benn's poem about the rats found in the girl's corpse—"Schöne Jugend"—we note a similar heightening of realistic detail and a similar manner of rendering this detail through direct activity. Distortion is produced in both poems to reveal the meaning of existence, both of mind and of thing.

This way of fashioning reality lends itself to Gothic distortion—not the Gothic of the romantic tale or even of Poe where distortion symbolizes an internal state, but the Gothic in its earlier, preromantic character—as a presentation of a deliberately rearranged reality superficially at least as an end in itself. Romantic writers, in exploiting Gothic distortions and fairy-tale devices, often lost the sense that reality can be changed to reveal purpose or purposelessness *in itself.* (Horror may exist, as Ingmar Bergmann has shown, as a state of the soul.) But expressionism has led to another way of viewing the Gothic, and of using Gothic devices and motifs, a way which has since come to life in Ernst Jünger and in Beckett: the sense that reality—though deeply relevant to human beings—must be distorted *qua* reality to reveal meaning or meaninglessness as the case may be. Eschewing the symbolic transformations we know well from Coleridge, or Novalis, or Baudelaire, expressionism states its point through a purposive reformulation of its world.

Romantic and symbolist poets, and the heroes they created, were visionaries for whom the world was ultimately an extension of themselves. Expressionism, at first a less respectable and recalcitrant offshoot of this tradition, concerned itself with the object of the vision, with the world as it is revealed by the vision and infused by it. The theater of Jean-Paul Sartre and Bertolt Brecht, as well as those sharp, traumatic encounters between man and world in "existentialist" fiction, have enlarged these premises of the expressionist generation. For its unique way of distorting reality not to produce symbolism *per se* but to develop a moral point, its offbeat, ecstatic way of seeing the world, its strange identification of the carnal and divine, and its mixtures of the material and the mystical—all of these point, in the inter-war period and beyond, to a further alternative to the post-romantic involvement in the mind. Thus expressionism has functioned as a poetry of statement and as a literature of objects, portraying the intense encounter between the modern consciousness and the realities of its world. It may, in all these respects, correspond to a new "baroque," drawing those "refractory visions" in life and art which have shaped the modern sensibility.

Notes

1. *Sämtliche Werke* (Frankfurt, 1965), V, 152.

2. Walter H. Sokel's *The Writer in Extremis: Expressionism in Twentieth-Century German Literature* (Stanford, 1959), which develops different points from those pursued in this essay, remains one of the fullest recent surveys of the subject in English.

3. *Ausgewählte Gedichte: 1911-18* (Berlin/Weimar, 1965), p. 328.

4. Part III ("Fenster"), Scene 5. *Die Dramen* (Frankfurt, 1959), p. 328.

5. *Dichtungen und Schriften,* ed. Karl Ludwig Schneider (Hamburg, 1964), I (*Lyrik*), 192.

6. *Dichtungen,* ed. Karl Ludwig Schneider (Hamburg, n.d.), I, 161-62. Cited, with particular attention to expressionistic "animation," by Richard Samuel and R. Hinton Thomas, *Expressionism in German Life, Literature, and the Theater* (Cambridge, 1939), p. 176.

7. Kasimir Edschmid, "Uber den dichterischen Expressionismus" (Autumn 1917), *Frühe Manifeste* (Hamburg, 1957), pp. 32, 34.

8. Cited from Helmut Uhlig, "Johannes R. Becher" in *Expressionismus. Gestalten einer literarischen Bewegung,* ed. Hermann Friedmann and Otto Mann (Heidelberg, 1956), p. 188. For the relationship between expressionism and naturalism, see "Introduction."

9. *Gesammelte Gedichte* (Zürich, 1956), p. 18.

10. *Das Lyrische Werk,* ed. Adolf Klarmann (Frankfurt, 1967), p. 199.

11. *Die Dichtungen* (Salzburg, 1938), p. 136.

12. *Erde* (Berlin, 1912), p. 6.

13. *Expressionism* as a term was first introduced in painting, in an exhibition in 1901 at the *Salon des indépendants* by Julien-Auguste Hervé. In 1911 Wilhelm Worringer applied it to Cézanne, Matisse, and others.

14. *Die Fürstin* (München, 1916), pp. 6-7, 23. For the "double action" as part of the shift from naturalism to expressionism in prose, see Erich V. Kahler, "Die Prosa des Expressionismus," *Der deutsche Expressionismus,* ed. Hans Steffen (Göttingen, 1965), pp. 159 ff.

15. *Ibid.,* pp. 38-39.

16. *Franz Kafka* (Bonn, 1958), pp. 74-91 *et passim*. See also Walter Muschg, *Von Trakl zu Brecht. Dichter des Expressionismus* (München, 1962), pp. 149-173.

17. *Poems 1923-1954* (New York, 1954), p. 114.

Christopher Waller (essay date 1986)

SOURCE: Waller, Christopher. "The Criticisms." In *Expressionist Poetry and Its Critics*, pp. 10-23. London: Institute of Germanic Studies, University of London, 1986.

[*In the following excerpt, Waller comments on criticism leveled against Expressionist writers by five contemporary critics: R. M. Rilke, Thomas Mann, Georg Lukács, Stefan George (through Friedrich Gundolf), and Robert Musil.*]

> Literary criticism ought to be a history of man's ideas and imaginings in the setting of the conditions which have shaped them.[1]

This book takes as its starting-point, and will use as a framework, a series of criticisms of Expressionism by contemporary writers, who have something pertinent and incisive to say about the movement. There are two principal bands of criticism, the formal and the thematic. Rilke and George, who focus their attention on formal considerations, regard Expressionism as a cult of formlessness, whereas Lukács and Thomas Mann argue that Expressionism claims a vital involvement in the political and social spheres, but has no insight into the practical responsibilities which are the inevitable concomitants of such involvement. It is rare for a critic to object to Expressionism on both counts, although it is certainly possible to see the objection of formal irresponsibility as analogous to that of political irresponsibility: indeed, by 1930, Thomas Mann, who makes his original criticism of Expressionism in 1918, is deeply aware of the analogy. The five writers, whose reservations are recorded here, are not some kind of unimpeachable critical idols. Issue will be taken with their criticism; they are, after all, very much part of the same literary and social ambience from which Expressionism emerged, and the charges which they level at Expressionism can frequently be turned round and directed at their own work. What is particularly interesting is that, from an early date, these writers demur to be swept along by the fervour of the latest literary fashion; they resist it, they raise important objections to it, and, no matter how loosely they may voice their objections, they offer potentially fruitful ways to approach Expressionist writing.

(A) R. M. Rilke

> . . . this salutary antagonism . . . there must be not only a partnership, but a union; an interpenetration of passion and of will, of spontaneous impulse and of voluntary purpose.[2]

Rilke's life represents one long repudiation of the political branch of Expressionism known as activism. Where he interprets any commitment to his own age or to philanthropic goals merely as a source of inauthenticity and as a potentially fatal impoverishment of his uncompromising view of his poetic mission, the activist Expressionist writers derive their literary sustenance and existential justification from a feeling of commitment and responsibility. In his memoirs, Erich Mühsam, an activist Expressionist, recounts how he was once chided by Wedekind for dissipating his time and energies, for dividing his efforts, for seeking to play two roles in life—that of a 'Caféhausliterat' and that of a fighter for proletarian rights:

'You are standing on the back of two horses straining in different directions; they will rip your legs apart'.

'If I let one go,' I replied, 'I shall lose my balance and break my neck'.[3]

Against this determination to 'ride two horses' Rilke sets the example of Rodin and the image of 'the mighty course of the river which refuses to divide into two branches'.[4] This image appears in a letter written in 1903, but it could easily have been written in 1913 or 1923 (though not with reference to Rodin) as a counter-example to the likes of Mühsam, Pinthus, Pfemfert, Rubiner and Hiller. Expressionism's will-to-diffuseness, which Rilke regards as fissiparous and wastefully arrogant, is offset by his monumental will-to-be-all-of-a-piece, will-to-create-whatever-one-is. His rejection both of political activism and of the whole movement of Expressionism is contained in one particular letter, written on 12 September 1919. The actress Anni Mewes had sent him a 'carefully and beautifully sealed little parcel'. In it was a pamphlet entitled *Die Silbergäule* written by Heinrich Vogeler, a painter, whom Rilke had visited in Worpswede in 1900. In his reply to Anni, Rilke sharply dismisses the pamphlet and its message of Expressionist love for all mankind. His use of the image of the train leaping off the rails soon indicates that his main objection to Expressionism is going to be concerned with poetic form. Expressionism, according to him, is uncontrolled and undisciplined, it takes an appearance of intensity to be the actual quality of intensity, it is a premature outer manifestation of inner dynamism, and Rilke dismisses Vogeler's grandiose philanthropic project as a paradigm of just this sort of wilful scattering of inner resources. It is not fortuitous or self-contradictory that four years earlier, in his warm praise of the early Expressionist poet Georg Trakl,[5] Rilke should use such words as 'Zäune' (fences), 'eingezäunt' (fenced in) and 'Einfriedungen' (enclosures) to signal the kind of control which characterizes Trakl's best work. Rilke's criticism of the Expressionist poet is founded in precisely the same objections as those which he levels against Vogeler and other activists:

> The Expressionist, this explosive spirit pouring its boiling lava over all things and insisting that the arbitrary form into which the crusts harden is the new, the future, the veritable outline of being,—is a desperate soul . . .
>
> (12 September 1919)

Expressionism, Rilke argues, is like an erupting volcano and is an example of that 'imageless act' ('Tun ohne Bild') in the Ninth Elegy, activity without necessary intellectual curb and concomitant mental picture. The Expressionist poet, like the volcano, may indeed by overwhelmed by a kind of inner necessity to gush forth, but the whole point is, Rilke implies, that he should *not* be like a volcano. By patience and craftsmanship he should shape his inspiration (which Rilke does not for a moment deny him) and should eliminate all arbitrariness and adventitiousness—these are the qualities which Rilke repudiates above all in Expressionist poetry. It is a question of finding Coleridge's 'salutary antagonism', of matching deeply felt emotion with painstakingly sought form and coherence.

The appropriateness of Rilke's criticism of Expressionist form can be gauged from the fact that Expressionist writers continually avail themselves of the same image of the volcano when they define their attitude to poetic form. Max Deri, for example, in a 1918 article entitled 'Expressionismus und Idealismus', explains how intensity of feeling is a value in itself in Expressionist poetry: 'all the dams of Classical restraint are burst asunder. Dynamic feeling seeks an outlet, "expression" in an upsurge of almost unchecked ecstasy. Anything which does not course down from the peaks with an incandescent glow has no worth'.[6] Yet Rilke's repudiation of Expressionist form should not be accepted uncritically. Given that Expressionist poets do write in the way Rilke portrays in his image of the volcano, why should that self-evidently make their poetry into a 'bad thing'? The genesis of a poem tells us nothing about the quality of the poem as artifact. What of the *Elegies,* for instance? Arriving with whirlwind force in January 1912, finished in what reads by Rilke's own account like an excess of Expressionist fervour almost exactly ten years later, do they not represent a powerful counter-argument to Rilke's criticism of Expressionist poetry? Is there not something intensely Expressionistic about their genesis, something of Expressionism's intensity about them? The answer is plainly yes and no: they did pour forth, but they had, after all, 'fermented' for ten years, ten years of single-minded concentration and strenuousness. There is no question in them of a sort of inspirational slopping-over, of what Rilke in his poem 'Doute' calls a 'premature exaltation', or of settling for the first stammering, faltering words which adventitiously enter the poet's mind and of which Valéry, a great contemporary poet and an important influence on Rilke's thought, warns:

> Il faut prendre garde aux premiers mots qui prononcent une question dans notre esprit. Une question nouvelle est d'abord à l'état d'enfance en nous; elle balbutie: elle ne trouve que des termes étrangers, tout chargés de valeurs et d'associations accidentelles; elle est obligée de les emprunter.[7]

Only the trance-like act of hearkening to and recording the dictates of inspiration bears the hallmark of Expressionism, as Rilke defines it. Like all his work from the *Neue Gedichte* onwards, the *Elegies* are 'a fully matured configuration, pervaded by the glow of the poet's inspiration'.[8] To which Expressionist poems can one apply a similar description? To those of Heym and Trakl, to some poems by Werfel, to all the poems of Stramm (whose work Rilke did not know), and to very few others. Rilke's criticism of Expressionism is all of a piece with his general views on poetry *and* with his own poetic practice. This criticism can be interpreted as a corrective to those among the Expressionist poets who believed that immediacy of inspiration and heedless intensity *of themselves* produced a good poem. As a contemporary poet who felt that such a corrective was needed, Rilke renders the same kind of service to twentieth-century German poetry as Eliot does to twentieth-century English poetry—the same kind, but not to the same degree. Eliot with his conviction that 'the "greatness", the intensity, of the emotions, the components are not what counts, but the intensity of the artistic process, the pressure under which the fusion takes place' provided precisely the sort of stabilizing influence and corrective to excesses which twentieth-century German poetry lacks—in spite of the example and achievement of Rilke. And in the famous lines from the fifth section of 'Little Gidding', '. . . every word is at home, / Taking its place to support the others . . .', Eliot underlines the very qualities which Rilke misses in Expressionist poetry: an indissoluble harmony between felt emotion and articulated word, balance, symmetry and proportion—all antitheses to the arbitrariness and luxuriance of 'the Expressionist, this explosive spirit . . .'

(B) THOMAS MANN

Only reality, though certainly not every reality—but a selected reality.[9]

Reality—, Europe's demonic concept.[10]

Thomas Mann, on the later of the two principal occasions in *Betrachtungen eines Unpolitischen* (1918) where he discusses Expressionism, reiterates part of Rilke's description of the Expressionist poet:

> Expressionism . . . is that artistic trend which, in violent contrast to the passivity, the meekly receptive and reproductive methods of Impressionism, has the utmost scorn for any attempt to imitate reality and, resolutely repudiating any obligation to reality, places in its stead the sovereign, explosive, heedlessly creative authority of the intellect/spirit ('Geist').[11]

Even more categorically than Rilke, Mann rejects the movement: his parody of the Expressionist poets, as represented by Daniel Zur Höhe in *Doktor Faustus,* is blatant and crude. Unlike Rilke, however, Mann's criticism offers metaphysics instead of concrete insight, generalization instead of detail, rhetorical bluster instead of conveyed understanding. Nevertheless it should be borne in mind that Mann's reservations about Expressionism are voiced as early as 1918 (that is, at a time when many were still rallying to its banner) and also that his criticism yields two categories—those of 'reality' and 'responsibility'—which are central to any understanding of Expressionism and consequently need further elaboration.

Mann uses the protean term 'reality' twice in the quoted extract. He is certainly right to insist that Expressionism, if it means anything at all, is a rejection of the mimetic approach in art. Expressionist writers are intent on destroying the prestige of empirical reality; they scorn any idea of merely reproducing the visible world and indeed regard reality and art as mutually exclusive—'the era of modern art is founded in the burgeoning insight that reality and art are not dependent on or conditioned by each other: on the contrary, they are incompatible'.[12] What does Pinthus mean here by 'reality'? What does Mann mean by 'reality'? Mann is clearly using the word in the conventional, quotidian sense which Pinthus defines on another occasion, in 'Rede für die Zukunft' (1920), an unwitting retort to Mann's charge and an endeavour to demonstrate how 'responsible' Expressionism is to 'reality'. Pinthus writes:

> Reality means to man everything which is and has been outside him, around him, in front of him. Reality is nature and all manifestations of nature, the form and workings of which he perceives through the exhilarating and yet wretched apparatus of his senses—perceives and takes to be true. Reality means man's past and man's history, and, at any given time, he regards himself as the last link in that history. When man talks of reality he means all those associations and institutions which he created for himself (state, economic system, social order) in order to relieve the agony of living and which, subsequently, dominated him as if they were his god.[13]

This, or something like this, is what Thomas Mann understands by the 'reality' for which the Expressionist writer is denying all responsibility. It is, moreover, precisely this 'reality' which Expressionist writers dismiss as . . . 'unreal'. Pinthus in 'Rede für die Zukunft' provides an example of the Expressionist polemicist's habit of setting up a series of alleged dialectical opposites from which he then derives a kind of intense, emotional momentum. On one side there is Mann's 'reality' which is dismissed variously (by Pinthus and other Expressionist writers) as 'so-called', 'infinitely inferior to the reality created by the poet', 'bogus', 'chimaerical', 'a mistake', 'non-existent', as the tedious old world of the senses with its wearisome 'social conditions', fit only to be destroyed or to be 'the plaything of the poet's grotesque games'. On the other side is the Expressionist writer's view of 'reality'—'real reality', 'inner reality', abstract, timeless, higher, ethical, new. These stereotyped oppositions are rehearsed again and again by Expressionist writers, who hedge the word 'reality' round with a series of qualifying adjectives intended to underline its otherness.

As for the second category to which Mann introduces us—'responsibility'—Expressionist writers, too, talk of 'responsibility to reality'. Pinthus, for example, in 'Rede für die Zukunft', enjoins the artist to 'acknowledge his task and responsibility', and Rubiner expatiates on the artist's 'personal responsibility to his fellow-men'.¹⁴ A contemporary of Thomas Mann, Max Weber, illuminates this elusive word 'responsibility'. In his 1918/19 essay 'Politik als Beruf' Weber establishes a nice difference between 'gesinnungsethisch' which represents a category of uncompromising, chiliastic idealism and 'verantwortungsethisch' which amounts to a much more pragmatic and rational kind of idealism. Weber argues that, whilst passion is an integral part of any good politician's character, it must be tempered by such qualities as a sense of proportion ('Augenmaß') and a sense of responsibility ('Verantwortungsgefühl') which, in turn, are sustained by objectivity and distance.¹⁵ It is true that Weber is writing about politics, and that Mann is writing about literature and art, but the whole point is that for the Expressionist/activist writer any dividing-line between politics and art is erased. In a quite definite way, Weber's depiction of the 'responsible politician' recalls Rilke's poetic criteria and Coleridge's 'salutary antagonism'. Weber could well have Expressionist writers in mind when he discusses politics and politicians:

> For the problem is precisely this: how can ardent passion and cool judgement be harnessed together in the same cause? The politician must use his head, not other parts of his body or soul. And yet devotion to politics, if it is to be a genuinely human activity and not some frivolous intellectual game, must be born of passion and sustained by passion. That powerful taming of the soul which distinguishes the passionate politician and differentiates him from the merely 'sterile sensationalism' of the political dilettante can be achieved only if an attitude of detachment is adopted.
>
> (p. 436)

'Tamed passion' as against 'sterile amateurish sensationalism'—this is the kind of opposition which Rilke's criticism of Expressionism sets up, and Rilke's emphasis on craftsmanship, patience and scrupulous work is paralleled by Weber's 'Politics is a steady, slow drilling of hard planks, using passion and a sense of proportion at the same time' (p. 450) and by his 'Politics is a difficult business, and anyone who takes it upon himself to interfere with the spokes of the wheel of the political development of his country must not be so sentimental that he cannot practise earthly politics'.¹⁶

Mann's categories of 'responsibility' and 'reality' are extremely helpful, even though he provides little elaboration of them. Weber offers valuable insights into the concept of political responsibility, and Expressionist writers define, even if they do not make altogether clear, what *they* mean by 'reality'. What remains to be examined is the extent to which Expressionist theorizing about 'reality' is distilled in the poetry—in other words, the extent to which Expressionist poets take issue with reality in the conventional sense and keep faith with their professed intention of concentrating on a 'superior' reality. As far as 'responsibility' is concerned, this is essentially a nebulous, extra-literary concept and becomes a vital factor only because the Expressionist poets were keen to make it so by arrogating all kinds of poetical, ethical and moral responsibilities to themselves and thus unhesitatingly making their literature available to the political sphere. By 1944 the Expressionist writer's impetuous arrogation of responsibility has issued, in at least one instance, into a penitential *mea culpa*. Franz Werfel unambiguously acknowledges the responsibility which he and his generation bear for the greatest catastrophe of all:

> I have come to know many kinds of arrogance, in myself and in others. Yet there is no more consuming, more brazen, more disdainful, more diabolical arrogance than that of the avant-garde artists and radical intellectuals, bursting with the vain passion to be profound and obscure and difficult, and to cause pain: all this I can confirm from my own experience, since in my youth I myself was of that company for a while. Mocked in amused indignation by a few philistines, we inconsiderable men were the first to bring fuel to the hell-fire in which mankind is now roasting.¹⁷

Where Werfel speaks of his generation's 'bringing fuel to the hell-fire in which mankind is now roasting', Thomas Mann in his 1930 speech 'Deutsche Ansprache' writes that extra-political causes have assisted National Socialism, that it has been sustained by 'succour from intellectual/spiritual sources'. Mann elaborates on what these sources might be. In fact, he concentrates on one source, namely the economic decline of the middle class and the intensely anti-bourgeois attitude of those who in pre-war Germany had proclaimed 'a new spiritual situation for all mankind'. This proclamation, this revolt against all that the bourgeoisie stood for, found its artistic voice in 'the Expressionist soul-scream'.¹⁸ Mann's undefined charge of 'irresponsibility to reality' has, by 1930, sharpened into an altogether more incisive and pertinent accusation, for by that date he has come to see Expressionism as a precipitate of all that was worst in Romanticism, as a powerful force for irrationalism and as an accomplice of National Socialism.

(C) GEORG LUKÁCS

> Expressionism offered the revolutionary gesture, the upraised arm, the clenched fist in papier-mâché.¹⁹

Marxist literary theory has always looked at Expressionism from one angle—as an ideological phenomenon. However much individual insights and judgements of Expressionism may differ, the method of regarding Expressionism as a political and ideological phenomenon has persisted. Georg Lukács's 1934 essay '"Größe und Verfall" des Expressionismus' triggered a series of assenting and dissenting articles which were printed in the pages of the periodical *Das Wort* in 1937 and 1938. Lukács's essay, in spite of the expectations raised by its title, is primarily a work of demolition, and, as if to reinforce his 1934 essay, Lukács repeats many of the same points four years later in his contribution to the 'Expressionismus-Debatte', namely an essay called 'Es geht um den Realismus', and in his much later *Deutsche Literatur im Zeitalter des Imperialismus* (1950).

He founds his whole case against Expressionism in what he sees as the latter's defective response to reality. It is an anaemic, solipsistic 'abstracting away from reality'. Transferred to the political sphere, Expressionism represents the literary form of the USP ideology in all its subjective idealism, has no authentic point of contact with the proletariat, offers only abstract and Bohemian opposition to the bourgeoisie and, because it is under the sway of some 'mystic objective idealism' or 'a subjective idealism', it has no grasp at all of social, historical, economic and political forces. Lukács quotes Lenin to the effect that any search for that Expressionist ideal, 'the pure essence' (devoid of a socio-politico-economical context) is bound to be futile. He might also have quoted from that section called 'German, or "True", Socialism' towards the end of the *Manifesto of the Communist Party*, where Marx and Engels inveigh against the abstract German Socialism of the 1840s which emphasizes 'not true requirements, but the requirements of truth' and 'not the interests of the proletariat, but the interests of Human Nature, of Man in general, who belongs to no class, has no reality, who exists only in the misty realm of philosophical fantasy'. Expressionism, Lukács argues in the manifesto, is an epigonal manifestation of this kind of Utopian Socialism, a seam in what Marx and Engels describe as 'the robe of speculative cobwebs, embroidered with flowers of rhetoric, steeped in the dew of sickly sentiment, this extravagant robe in which German Socialists wrapped their sorry "eternal truths", all skin and bone'.

Expressionism, Lukács maintains, is parasitic upon the bourgeoisie, it flees the battle-field of the class-struggle, it distends and distorts all contemporary questions into eternal abstractions. Its fight against the war and the bourgeoisie is a cheap masquerade, because it is a fight against War and the Bourgeoisie. Lukács sets up a litany of arraignment in which phrases like 'abstracting poverty of content', 'extraordinary meagreness of substance' and 'abstract distortion of basic questions' are continually rehearsed. In denying causality and logic, and in aiming for totality, the Expressionist writer leaves out a living context: his resort to simultaneism in an effort to replace that context is a desperate and futile manoeuvre. The end-result of all his manoeuvres is that Expressionism assists in the growth of Fascism: Expressionism is 'without doubt one of the numerous bourgeois-ideological currents which subsequently issue into Fascism, and the part it plays in preparing the way for Fascist ideology is no greater—and no smaller—than that played by many other contemporary currents'.[20]

And Expressionist form? It is 'arbitrary' and 'subjective'; detached from empirical reality, devoid of substance, the Expressionist scream amounts to no more than 'an empty aggregate of emotional effusions', 'the hysterical distillation of inflated images and symbols which jostle haphazardly together and lack all intrinsic coherence'. Seizing upon Nietzsche's interpretation of 'style de décadence' in the seventh section of *Der Fall Wagner*, in which stylistic decadence is seen to arise when the word is made sovereign at the expense of the whole, Lukács turns his attack on Herwarth Walden, the editor of the Expressionist magazine *Der Sturm*. He belabours Expressionist writers for neglecting the 'living context' of the sentence—in the same way as he has belaboured them for ignoring a living social and political context. Here, once again, as with the Rilke-Weber-Mann criticism of Expressionism, the movement's formal irresponsibility is set on a parallel course with its political irresponsibility. The papier-mâché poetry of Expressionism is, according to Lukács, a faithful reflection of the whole movement's catchpenny response to political issues and social problems: the poetry, heavy with apocalyptic promise, proves to be as nugatory as the political opposition to capitalism and imperialism.

The following points ought to be made in answer to Lukács; his criticism represents the habitual charge of any literary-critical conservatism against any poetic revolution; in castigating Expressionism for being 'abstract' and 'timeless', he employs many of the epithets which Expressionist writers *liked* to use of themselves (Pinthus, for example, in his 1915 essay 'Zur jüngsten Dichtung', repudiates as 'the hotchpotch of our social, cultural, political, economic relations and institutions' precisely that 'reality' for which Lukács searches in vain in Expressionism); there is nothing in Lukács's formulations that could not be turned round and used against him and his literary-metaphysical jargon; his assertion that Expressionism was 'one of the bourgeois ideological currents which subsequently issue into Fascism' should be weighed against the fact that the Communists disrupted Weimar no less than the National Socialists with whom they were allied in 1932. Lukács's criticism of Expressionism is, moreover, clothed in the same kind of abstract language which he finds so objectionable in Expressionist writing: this is partly because he, like Expressionist writers, relies on the terminology of idealism to do his work for him and partly because he gleans almost all his material from diffuse Expressionist theoreticians. Consider the following glaireous slab which contains the nub of his criticism:

> This abstracting impoverishment of content is not only an indication of Expressionism's line of development

and, thus, of its fate, it is from the very beginning Expressionism's fundamental, insurmountable stylistic problem, for the extraordinary meagerness of content which is the direct result stands in screaming contrast to the pretentious claims of the delivery.²¹

How can it be '*Ver*armung' 'from the very beginning' when the German prefix 'ver-' implies gradual, subsequent deterioration? Why the portentousness of 'fate' when all he means is 'development'? Why, of all words, '*screaming* contrast' without a hint of irony and humour? This is exaggerated, pretentious, and . . . Expressionist stuff. So why bother with it? First, because Marxist criticism (of which Lukács is the leading practitioner) represents a major, influential dissenting voice and secondly, as with Thomas Mann's criticism, crucial and productive critical categories come to the surface—for example, the invertebrate and abstract quality of Expressionism's political involvement.

(D) Stefan George/Friedrich Gundolf

> Man screams—not for the sake of screaming, but in order to rouse himself and his fellow human beings into offering help.²²

Stefan George never belonged to the artistic avant-garde, yet he was a close observer of the contemporary literary scene. His career ran parallel with that of Expressionism, and many Expressionist writers admired George and were fascinated by him. Edschmid, in his 1918 speech 'Expressionismus in der Dichtung', asserts that 'after George it could not be forgotten that a great form was indispensable to a work of art', Benn's 1934 speech, 'Rede auf Stefan George', is emphatically pro-George, and Heym once tried to join the George circle. The implicit *and* explicit reverence felt by some Expressionist writers for George the poet and exemplary teacher is not reciprocated, for he despised and dismissed all Expressionist poetry wholesale. His repudiation of Expressionism is succinctly recorded by Edgar Salin: 'Expressionism as it was called also appeared to represent [between 1918-23] . . . a genuine resurgence of art—the disciples were strongly influenced by it. George listened to them patiently, scrutinized many Expressionist poems and rejected the lot'.²³ Early in his career George declares that 'art cannot concern itself with world reform and dreams of universal happiness which, at the present time according to some people in this country, contain the seed of everything new and yet, however attractive they may indeed be, belong to a different realm from that of poetry'²⁴ and subsequently remains faithful to this credo for much of his life. And as a poet who is concerned with transforming experience in the medium of art and with *in*direct expression of that experience by specific artistic means, he is set on a collision course with a political, activist movement which enthusiastically makes art available to a social purpose and, moreover, seeks to cast feelings, immediately and unmediated, into poetic form. A short piece of prose which George wrote in 1896 contains ante facto his critique of Expressionism. He takes it up again in 1903 and, with more relevance to our theme, in 1933 when clearly, in republishing it, he may have been casting a retrospective glance at Expressionism. It is called 'Über Kraft':

> One should be on one's guard against excessively violent eruptions of power in a work of art . . . behind such eruptions there is often no trace at all of authentic, deep feeling, but only festering immaturity or the strenuous effort to persuade oneself by means of one's own screams of something which is not present. True power is demonstrated if these eruptions are controlled . . . art is not pain, nor is it sensual pleasure, it is the triumph over the former and the transfiguration of the latter . . .²⁵

In this quotation many of the threads of Expressionist criticism and of general poetic theory which we have used come together: Coleridge's 'interpenetration of spontaneous impulse and of voluntary purpose', Rilke's image of the volcano, Eliot's emphasis on due proportions and harmony, Weber's appeal for 'tamed passion', and the whole Valéryan ethos of maturity and his admonition that 'il faut prendre garde aux premiers mots . . .'.

Durzak, in his excellent book²⁶ on George, does not doubt that 'Über Kraft' contains George's critique of Expressionism. He is probably right. What is certain is that Friedrich Gundolf in *his* fierce condemnation of Expressionism is representing Stefan George's view of Expressionist poetry. That condemnation is to be found in the first chapter of Gundolf's *George* (Berlin, 1920). In this first chapter Gundolf is concerned to achieve three objectives: to eulogize the poetry of his master, to level a broadside at Expressionism, and to play down (or to unmask as a misunderstanding) the influence which George had on certain Expressionist writers. Gundolf's assault is vituperative. He draws up an inventory of Expressionism's sins—'fanatical humanitarianism and overblown compassion', 'the demolition of all forms in a spiritual or material pulp', 'a lack of restraint, moderation and nucleus', 'luxuriating narcissism', 'abstract, all-inclusive philanthropy', 'repudiation of all standards' etc. etc. and the Expressionist writers themselves are 'puffed-up, second-rate schoolmasters', 'demented priests', 'ranting charlatans' etc. etc. Their characteristic noise is the scream. Then he continues:

> The scream is at one and the same time an animal reaction, a political social programme and spiritual tension. They are screaming for the unattainable, for utopia, because the act of screaming itself is already an unburdening, a release, no matter what is being screamed for. Language is shattered into its illogical, sightless components, its prespiritual infantine babble because this very act of shattering is an expression of something.²⁷

This is the conventional picture of the Expressionist poet—straining at the leash, pent-up passion bursting forth, yearning for unrealizable dreams, screaming for the sake of it, bestial, primitive, purely destructive, wreaking all sorts of havoc on language. It is the conventional picture in 1920 and the one arrived at and propagated ten years later in a seminal National Socialist work—

> The freakish excrescence called Expressionism—a whole generation screamed for expression and found it no longer had anything to express. It called for beauty and had no ideal of beauty any more. In a new creative spirit it sought to thrust its way into life and had lost all real power to create. So expression became mannerism; no new power, no new style was evolved; instead, the process of atomisation was continued. Rootless, emotionally adrift, people devoured 'primitive art' . . .[28]

It is neither fortuitous nor arbitrary that the names of Gundolf/George and Rosenberg, set up by Hitler as the official National Socialist philosopher/historian, should be linked in the same context: Gundolf and George, courted without ultimate success by the National Socialists, who with characteristic eclecticism took from everywhere whatever could be made to serve their purpose, *and* Rosenberg, representing that wing of National Socialism which saw Expressionism as an integral part of degenerate modern art, come together in endorsing the standard image of the Expressionist poet. The names of Gundolf and Goebbels (much less hostile than Rosenberg to Expressionism) had already been linked in 1920/21 when Goebbels was working on his dissertation ('The Dramatist Wilhelm von Schütz. A Contribution to the History of the Romantic Drama') under Gundolf's direction in Heidelberg.

(E) Robert Musil

> Let us avoid big words; we have too frequently seen such words in league with vile deeds: let us not conjure the unconjurable![29]

Musil's antipathy toward Expressionism is total and culminates, in *Der Mann ohne Eigenschaften,* in the figure of the young poet Friedel Feuermaul,[30] an amusing parody of the activist philanthropic branch of Expressionism in general and of Werfel in particular. Feuermaul is 'gifted, young, immature'. He is also a pathetic figure, 'a little lambkin running to fat before its time', a careerist for ever mouthing 'Man is good' and other bromides, a Messiah, a 'man of feeling' not concerned to explain anything by rational argument or reasoned debate, an 'exponent of the spirit of the times', a champion of revolutionary views ('only so long as it doesn't actually come to any sort of revolution'), a man motivated by a profound 'sentiment towards "the old country" and its mission to mankind'—a sentiment, Musil adds caustically, 'that would as easily have turned to bringing back the obsolete omnibus with its three-horse team as to propaganda for Viennese porcelain'. Musil's satire is acrimonious and pertinent, for he believes that Feuermaul and poets like him are dangerous. Feuermaul raises huge expectations and claims all sorts of powers, yet, in practice, does nothing except add to universal moral chaos and to what Musil calls 'the general rubble of futile feelings'. Ultimately, when it matters, when a stand has to be taken, he and the message he brings are useless: he pales beside other characters in the novel, for example the fiercely pragmatic and hard-headed Bremshuber. Through another character, Arnheim, Musil speaks of 'modern youth's craving for stability and leadership': Feuermaul arrogates to himself the reins of moral, political and poetic leadership and, in his very small way, joins the ranks of those 'intellectual dictators' who Musil, in the 1930s, retrospectively believes have played a disproportionately large and fateful role in Germany's history: 'Long before the dictators our age brought forth a veneration for intellectual dictators. Think of George, Kraus and Freud, Adler and Jung. Add Klages and Heidegger to the list. The common factor here is probably a need for domination and leadership, for the essential characteristics of the saviour'.[31]

In a series of articles, reviews and essays written between 1912 and 1920, Musil is for ever taking the side of the intellect and rational thinking against passion and emotion. For example, in his 1912 essay 'Das Geistliche, der Modernismus und die Metaphysik', he writes scathingly of 'the soul's attempt to erupt' and of 'a shapeless excess of feeling from whose gelatinous mess modernism, too, draws its sustenance'. He reserves his real venom for those 'sceptics and reformers who dispense with precise thinking and then, with the help of an alleged "emotional intuition", invent a universal spirit or a cosmic soul or a god to satisfy their temperament or to achieve the "necessary" harmony or to round off their theory of life'. He believes that modern artists have not only renounced precise thinking, but have ceased to think altogether. In a 1913 review entitled 'Pilgrimage into the Interior'[32] he expresses anxiety about the modern writer's preoccupation with metaphysics and mysticism—the review begins 'Metaphysics is on the increase; woe to anyone who offers shelter to metaphysics! Quest by writers everywhere for God . . .'. People, he argues, are peculiarly vulnerable at this time ('. . . blithe defencelessness in the face of purveyors of doctrines of salvation'), the hawkers of pseudo-mystical panaceas are not accountable to anyone, and feeling is all. In Margarete Susmann's *Vom Sinn der Liebe,* one of the two books under review, the question 'Do you love me?' has been ousted by 'Do you love?', the stability of a belief in God by 'the dispossessed, consistently religious feeling in search of a new Lord'. A great deal of raw and fervent emotion is waiting, homeless and expectant, for the right strong cause.

Musil, like Thomas Mann, regards Expressionism as a force for irrationalism and unchecked emotionality. Expressionism, according to him, feeds into, and is in turn nourished by, the reservoir of hectically expectant public feeling and is symptomatic of what, in *Der Mann ohne Eigenschaften,* is characterized as 'the new generation's attack on objectivity. intellectual responsibility and the balanced personality' (p. 405). Its humanistic-philanthropic attitudes amount to little more than a pathetic gesture, exemplified by the fiasco of the 1918 revolution ('it lacked even the seriousness with which people turned out to watch the fire-brigade'; p. 630). Musil's particular scorn is reserved for Werfel: his diaries, essays and aphorisms are littered with more or less snide remarks about Werfel whom he regards as a charlatan. Yet, for a time he is at least outwardly close to early Expressionism because of his work on the Leipzig-based periodical *Der lose Vogel.* His recorded comments on Expressionism are without exception hostile and very dependent on Thomas Mann. There is, however, at least one occasion when Musil writes at length and in his own voice about Expressionism, in a 1921 essay entitled 'Geist und Erfahrung. Anmerkungen für Leser, welche dem "Untergang des Abendlandes" entronnen sind' (*Tagebücher, Aphorismen* . . . , pp. 651-67). Having completed a diagnosis of his age and rehearsed some of the themes which had appeared in his pre-war reviews, he turns to Expressionism:

> This age, to give another example of it, has combined with Expressionism to vulgarize and dilute one of art's basic insights because those who sought to introduce spirit ('Geist') into poetry were not capable of thinking. They were not capable of it because they think in empty slogans ('Luftworte') which lack content, the restraint imposed by empiricism. Naturalism offered reality without spirit, Expressionism spirit without reality: both are un-spirit ('Ungeist').
>
> (p. 666)

Lack of true content, lack of regard for practical experience, opposition to Naturalism—these are familiar comments, though they are strikingly well stated. Defective thinking, a fondness for heady bombast, and the primacy given to 'Geist'—these charges are certainly implied in the four other principal criticisms, but not with Musil's force. What is 'Geist'? Whole chapters have been devoted to skirmishing with the word's accretions and contradictions,[33] but Musil himself is in no doubt—at least, on the evidence of a letter to Adolf Frisé in January 1931, he is in no doubt that it is composed of reason and feeling and amounts to a mutual interpenetration of both. But for the Expressionist writers it has a mystical, all-purpose, incantatory quality which resides partly in its elusiveness and indefinability as its meaning distends to include irrationality, intuition, spirit, subconscious, passion *and* intellect, rationality, mind etc . . . The fundamental credo of Expressionism is that empirical reality is inferior to 'geistig' reality, but Musil, too, shares the same credo. He may disapprove of the *kind* of metaphysics practised by the Expressionist writers, he may come to voice his reservations about contemporary reverence for 'geistig' dictators, but he himself is involved in a spiritual quest, a search for some all-embracing 'geistig' reality (note how in the above extract, he rejects both Naturalism and Expressionism as 'Ungeist') composed of mysticism and reason, punctiliousness and soul, ratio and emotion—a reality which is as difficult to envisage as all the Expressionist blather about 'essence' ('Wesen'). There is very little trace in his *Verwirrungen des Zöglings Törless* or in *Der Mann ohne Eigenschaften* of a stringent condemnation of the fastidiously 'geistig' protagonists. The Expressionist credo, at all events, culminates in Hiller's loudly proclaimed project of founding a 'Bund der Geistigen' in 1918. Various seminal Expressionist works parade the word: Heinrich Mann's *Geist und Tat* (1910), Kandinsky's *Über das Geistige in der Kunst* (1912) and Hiller's *Tätiger Geist* (1917/18) are obvious examples. Ironically, Musil, by employing 'Geist' in his critique of Expressionism, is echoing one of the most popular slogans (i.e. 'Luftworte') of the day,[34] popular not only with Expressionist writers and artists, but also part of the common currency amongst intellectuals like Henry Pachter who, looking back in 1971 to the stance he and people like him adopted in the 1920s, *still* resorts to this mysterious and untranslatable talisman:

> We too were Romantics about the state; we too agreed that the Republic had no Geist; we too lacked real contact with the masses; we too saw ourselves as members of the elite; we too ridiculed the Republic as an ugly thing. We agreed: The Republic had no style.[35]

It remains to determine whether it is merely another Expressionist 'Luftwort' or can stand as a useful and fruitful critical category in any consideration of the movement.

The criticisms assembled in the preceding pages also embrace the principal charges which have been levelled at Expressionism by commentators other than those quoted. Without exception, the criticisms are either directly or indirectly adverse and cast in general terms. The fact that on occasions they can be turned round and directed at the critic's own work or that profound reservations may be expressed about their tone or their terminology does not necessarily diminish their validity or importance. The critical categories can be distilled to: formal arbitrariness and adventitiousness, political irresponsibility culminating in some kind of complicity in the rise of National Socialism, thematic insubstantiality, irrationalism, excessive emotionality, syntactical iconoclasm and heady rhetorical effluvium.

Notes

1. E. Wilson, *Axel's Castle* (London, 1964), dedication.

2. S. T. Coleridge, *Biographia Literaria*, edited by J. Shawcross, 2 vols (Oxford, 1973), II, 49-50.

3. E. Mühsam, *Unpolitische Erinnerungen* (Berlin, 1961), p. 12.

4. Letter to Lou Andreas-Salomé, 8 August 1903; *Briefe aus den Jahren 1892-1904* (Leipzig, 1939), p. 380.

5. See the letter to Ficker of 8 February 1915; *Briefe aus den Jahren 1914-1921* (Leipzig, 1938), pp. 33-35.

6. Quoted in: E. Kolinsky, *Engagierter Expressionismus* (Stuttgart, 1970), p. 78.

7. Paul Valéry, *Variété V* (Paris, 1945), p. 131.

8. Rilke (1903-04), quoted in: P. Zech, *Rainer Maria Rilke: Der Mensch und das Werk* (Dresden, 1930), pp. 113-14.

9. F. Nietzsche, *Menschliches, Allzumenschliches II*; *Nietzsche Werke: Kritische Gesamtausgabe*, edited by G. Colli and M. Montinari, 30 vols (Berlin, 1967-), IV/3, 62. Unless otherwise stated, all quotations from Nietzsche's work will be taken from this edition.

10. G. Benn, 'Expressionismus'; *Gesammelte Werke*, I (1959), 246.

11. Thomas Mann, *Gesammelte Werke*, 13 vols (Frankfurt a.M., 1974), XII, 564.

12. K. Pinthus, 'Zur jüngsten Dichtung', *Die Weißen Blätter*, 2, Heft 12 (July-September 1915), 1503.

13. K. Pinthus, 'Rede für die Zukunft', *Die Erhebung*, 1 (Berlin, 1920), 411.

14. L. Rubiner (ed.), *Kameraden der Menschheit* (Potsdam, 1919), p. 173.

15. Max Weber, *Gesammelte Politische Schriften* (Munich, 1921), p. 435.

16. Quoted by G. Hufnagel, *Kritik als Beruf. Der kritische Gehalt im Werke Max Webers* (Frankfurt a.M., 1971), p. 121.

17. F. Werfel, *Zwischen oben und unten* (Stockholm, 1946), pp. 361-62. Note this passage is quoted by Joachim Fest in his brilliant *Das Gesicht des Dritten Reiches* (Munich, 1963), p. 353, to clinch his argument that culture played a part in its own destruction and in the rise of National Socialism.

18. For all these quotations from Mann's 'Deutsche Ansprache' see *Gesammelte Werke*, XI, 876-77.

19. W. Benjamin, 'Linke Melancholie', in: *Lesezeichen*, edited by G. Seidel (Leipzig, 1970), p. 255.

20. Georg Lukács, '"Größe und Verfall" des Expressionismus'; *Werke*, 17 vols (Neuwied and Berlin, 1962-75), IV (1971), 121.

21. '"Größe und Verfall"'; *Werke*, IV, 121.

22. K. Pinthus, 'Rede für die Zukunft', p. 419.

23. E. Salin, *Um Stefan George* (Munich and Düsseldorf, 1954), p. 216.

24. S. George, *Blätter für die Kunst*, Preface to first series, 1 (1892).

25. *Werke*, 2 vols (Munich and Düsseldorf, 1958), I, 531-32.

26. M. Durzak, *Zwischen Symbolismus und Expressionismus: Stefan George* (Stuttgart, Berlin, Cologne and Mainz, 1974).

27. F. Gundolf, *George* (Berlin, 1920), p. 20.

28. A. Rosenberg, *Der Mythus des zwanzigsten Jahrhunderts* (Munich, 1930), p. 284.

29. H. Carossa, *Ungleiche Welten*, in: *Sämtliche Werke*, 2 vols (Frankfurt a.M., 1962), II, 838.

30. See chapters 36, 37 and 38 of Book 2, third part.

31. R. Musil (1934-37), *Tagebücher, Aphorismen, Essays und Reden* (Hamburg, 1955), p. 398.

32. To be found in: *Die Neue Rundschau*, 24 (1913), vol. 1, 588.

33. For a discussion of the word, see Pascal, *From Naturalism . . .*, pp. 297-305.

34. Thomas Mann uses the word in his critique of Expressionism, and note how the article from which Musil's critique is extracted is headed 'Geist und Erfahrung . . .'.

35. Quoted in: R. G. L. Waite, *The Psychopathic God Adolf Hitler* (New York, 1977), p. 320.

Peter Vergo (essay date 1993)

SOURCE: Vergo, Peter. "The Origins of Expressionism and the Notion of *Gesamtkunstwerk*." In *Expressionism Reassessed*, edited by Shulamith Behr, David Fanning, and Douglas Jarman, pp. 11-9. Manchester, England: Manchester University Press, 1993.

[*In the following essay, Vergo explores how Richard Wagner's notion of* Gesamtkunstwerk *(total work of art) influenced the Expressionists' view of the dichotomy between the external and internal meaning of a work of art.*]

Over the past several decades, a number of writers—among them Carl Schorske, Donald Gordon, and Reinhold Heller[1]—have underlined the importance of the Idealist tradition in nineteenth-century German philosophy for any understanding of the genesis of Expressionism, pointing especially to the works of philosophers such as Schopenhauer and Nietzsche. It is also invariably the case that somewhere along the line, in any discussion of the philosophical antecedents of Expressionism, another major influence is mentioned—that of Wagner; but these seemingly obligatory allusions are usually unaccompanied by any more detailed discussion. For while it is true that a very great deal has been written about 'Wagnerism' and its influence on the Symbolist generation, as well as its wider cultural and political influence,[2] Wagner's significance for the 1900s and after, especially in the domain of the visual arts, has by comparison gone largely unexamined. I therefore propose to consider in this paper the influence exerted by Wagnerian theory and practice, in particular the Wagnerian notion of the *Gesamtkunstwerk* (total work of art), on the artists of the expressionist generation.

In discussing Wagnerian theory, it should perhaps be observed at the outset that the composer's ideas would, at least in the opinion of the present writer, have had relatively little impact had it not been for the power of his music. Even Wagner himself, in the preface to the second edition of his treatise *Opera and Drama*, referred to what he called the 'obduracy' of his ideas; and since then author after author has pointed to the composer's convoluted language and the turgidity of his rhetoric. Michael Tanner, for example, in his contribution to that well-known anthology, *The Wagner Companion*, describes Wagner's writings as 'full of special pleading and, except when he is being practical or hits the odd inspired phrase, lacking in the astonishing energy and resource of both the man and his art'.[3] Rather, what happened—and this can be clearly demonstrated in the case of the French Symbolists, for example—was that artists working in other media (writers, poets, painters) from the 1870s onwards were simply bowled over by the musical and dramatic effect of Wagner's operas; and then, having picked themselves up, they turned to his theoretical writings, which are of course voluminous, in search of a key which might unlock the mystery of the Wagnerian magic.

Unfortunately, Wagner's writings do not in themselves provide a very good key. His meaning is sometimes obscure and his arguments are often rambling and inconsistent, which is perhaps why so many subsequent admirers picked on the one notion that seemed relatively easy to comprehend: that of the *Gesamtkunstwerk*. Not only did they pick on it; they distorted it in ways scarcely credible, given that, in this instance at least, Wagner's own intentions were quite unambiguous. It is none the less the case that during the years around 1900, the term *Gesamtkunstwerk* was hurled around like a kind of verbal projectile, being applied to things that Wagner himself would never have conceived of, and certainly would never have sanctioned: book design and typography, interior decor and furnishing, architecture and design. The first editor of the Viennese periodical *Ver Sacrum*, Wilhelm Schölermann, described the relationship between typography and illustration, the layout of graphic material on the printed page, as creating a 'kind of *Gesamtkunstwerk*', while other writers found the same term equally appropriate in discussing, for example, the architecture and interiors of the Scottish art nouveau architect Charles Rennie Mackintosh—improbable though such a usage might seem.

Ironically, Wagner himself does not actually put that much stress on the *term Gesamtkunstwerk,* preferring, typically, more convoluted formulations such as 'Gesamtvolkskunst' or 'das Kunstwerk des Gesamtvolkes'—the 'work of art of an entire people'. He also refers repeatedly to 'das gemeinsame Kunstwerk', another term difficult to translate and which might perhaps best be rendered as 'communal art', or even 'the common artistic endeavour', the purpose of which was the expression of what Wagner calls 'der künstlerische Mensch'—artistic man:

> Artistic man can be wholly satisfied only by the unification of all forms of art in the service of the common artistic endeavour; any fragmentation of his artistic sensibilities limits his freedom, prevents him from being fully that which he is capable of being. The highest form of communal art is drama; it can exist in its full entirety only if it embraces every variety of art . . . only when eye and ear mutually reinforce the impressions each receives, only then is artistic man present in all his completeness.[4]

As so often, the language used in this particular passage is somewhat opaque, but the thrust of Wagner's argument generally is quite clear. What he means by 'das gemeinsame Kunstwerk' is a new kind of art which will express the identity, the character, the cultural and mythic aspirations of an entire people, while uniting them in a common ritualistic and—in Wagner's eyes at least—religious experience. At the same time, the 'gemeinsame Kunstwerk' was to unite the different *forms* of art—the arts with a small 'a'—in the service of a higher idea, subordinating them to the overall *dramatic* purpose which, in his early writings at least, Wagner believed ruled supreme, taking precedence even over the purely musical element (hence his subsequent elaboration of the notion of 'music drama'). Fortunately, his reading of Schopenhauer at the critical moment, between his completion of the text for his tetralogy *The Ring of the Nibelung* and the composition of the music, convinced him—we might say 'just in time'—of the intrinsic supremacy of music over all other forms of art as vehicle of pure expression.

Wagner, of course, was notorious for not always practising what he preached—or rather, he rarely practised what he preached. In the case of his own operas he never actually applied the principle of the *Gesamtkunstwerk* in the kind of additive or accretive way he himself described—the piling of one art form upon another, as if the more varied the different kinds of art combined at the same time on the operatic stage, the greater would be the impact. Moreover, though he minutely specified the scenic effects he wished to achieve on the stage, he found himself obliged to leave their actual realisation in the hands of others, so that, even at Bayreuth, the scenic aspect of the staging of his operas continued as before to be left to professional stage designers. Wagner himself, in any case, had little real sensitivity to the visual arts, which perhaps goes some way towards explaining the coarse naturalism of the early Bayreuth productions—grandiose visions that were long on imagination and short on practicality and which were the frequent butt of critics and satirists.[5] Even Wagner's admirers are frequently led to confess that they perceive a strain of vulgarity, not in his music, but in his dramatic conceptions. For whatever reason, the naturalist tradition continued to dominate the Wagnerian stage throughout the remainder of the nineteenth century, and it not until well after 1900 that we encounter anywhere in Europe anything which, as regards its visual aspect, deviates in any significant way from the early Munich and Bayreuth productions.

An article such as this hardly permits further exploration of the history of the Wagnerian stage, fascinating though that subject is. What I do want to examine is the way in which the Wagnerian notion of the *Gesamtkunstwerk* was creatively *mis*interpreted by the generation of artists who came to maturity during the years after 1900—how it was subjected, as it were, to a series of fruitful misunderstandings. Of these misunderstandings two, in particular, were to be of profound consequence for the theory and practice of Expressionism.

First, during the early years of this century, Wagner's authority was frequently invoked in support of the idea that the various arts were growing ever closer together, that they even sprang from the same common root, and that the distinctions between them were becoming more and more irrelevant, of merely 'external' significance—a quintessentially expressionist view. In reality, Wagner had believed almost exactly the opposite: that both the character and purpose of the various forms of art were quite different. That did not bother the expressionist artists. They believed—and here once again the influence of Schopenhauerian philosophy is clearly seen—that the task of art was to give voice to an *inner* world, and that the inner experience of the artist and the inner nature of the world itself were in essence the same. Hence their disdain for everything external since it was the internal, not the external aspect of art that was important. The material differences between the different art forms were merely external; it was the inner message that was of crucial significance, and all that mattered was to choose the external form most appropriate to the inner message which it was the task of art to convey. And since 'skill' in the manipulation of a given medium was likewise a merely external attribute, the artist was at liberty to range freely from painting to poetry to musical composition—or all at the same time—no matter in which (if any) of these fields his or her formal training might have been.

In practice, what is striking is just how many expressionist artists in fact 'crossed the boundaries' which had previously divided one art form from another. Kokoschka, in addition to his pictorial work, wrote poems, plays and essays; Barlach was active both as sculptor and playwright; Kandinsky made paintings, graphics, poems, plays. His stage works afford a particularly interesting example, not least for their point of contact with the exactly contemporary experiments of Schoenberg. Kandinsky, admittedly, having little musical competence, turned to a professional composer, his compatriot Thomas von Hartmann, for the music for his play *The Yellow Sound*—just as Wagner, having no competence in the visual arts, had relied on professional stage designers. But for *The Yellow Sound* and his other dramatic experiments—'stage compositions', he called them—Kandinsky wrote his own texts, visualised both sets and costumes, and wrote down meticulous directions not only for the visual aspect of the staging, but also gesture, movement, expression etc. Indeed, in some dozen pages of the text of *The Yellow Sound* there are to be found no more than fifteen lines of spoken or sung dialogue. In this we may detect another obvious point of resemblance with Wagner's operas, where the obsessively detailed stage directions often rival in length the actual lines given to the dramatis personae.

There are, however, not only striking similarities between these early expressionist stage works and their Wagnerian antecedents, but also a number of important differences—differences that spring, at least in part, from a second misunderstanding of Wagner's ideas. Wagner, as we have seen, had been content to leave at least some aspects of the staging of his music-dramas in the hands of others. Regarding music-drama generally, he even stated quite specifically that the composer and the librettist, for example, need not be one and the same person (though in reality he invariably wrote the libretto for his own operas, evidently attaching great importance to every detail of the poetic and verse forms which he, in many cases, more or less invented—another instance of the frequent discrepancies between what he said and his actual practice). By contrast, if we look at the dramatic experiments created by a number of expressionist artists during the early years of the twentieth century, we find the author or composer frequently assuming a kind of tyrannical role, almost a cross between artistic dictator and master of ceremonies. The fact that such artists sought to apply what they considered to be Wagnerian ideas in a way that is actually far more literal than Wagner himself intended or practised—taking, for example, every detail of costume and decor and choreography, as well as music and libretto, into their own hands—constitutes the second of those 'fruitful misunderstandings' referred to earlier.

To focus briefly on two particular examples, the early stage works of Schoenberg—his monodrama *Erwartung,* and the opera *Die glückliche Hand*—are a case in point. For *Erwartung,* while Schoenberg himself provided a whole succession of very detailed sketches for the staging, he in fact drew on a text by an amateur writer called Marie Pappenheim, whose portrait he also painted. But in the case of *Die glückliche Hand,* usually translated as *The Lucky Hand,* Schoenberg followed what he must have regarded as Wagnerian precedent with almost slavish loyalty,[6] creating not merely the music but also the text and the set and costume designs with his own hands. Without doubt, *The Lucky Hand* is, in any case, by far the most Wagnerian of all Schoenberg's stage works and contains a number of quite specific Wagnerian borrowings, most notably the moment at which the sword-brandishing hero (or anti-hero), observing workers forging diadems, seizes a hammer which he brings down with a mighty blow on an anvil which then splits in two—an undisguised allusion to the forging scene in Act I of *Siegfried,* mixed with a dash of the enslaved Nibelungen from *Rheingold* for good measure. Schoenberg's use of the chorus in *Die glückliche Hand,* six men and six women who comment mordantly on the drama, also echoes Wagner's notions concerning the role of the chorus in Greek tragedy—however misguided those may have been.

There is, however, one major point of divergence compared with Wagner's operas—a divergence which has to do with the apparent lack of stage action and virtual anonymity of the characters in Schoenberg's operatic works. *Erwartung,* in particular, is strikingly devoid of action—or does it, indeed, all happen in the mind? All we know, or are told, is that an unnamed woman is found wandering alone in a forest at night. Approximately one third of the way through this drama—if 'drama' it can be called—she stumbles across the dead body of her lover. The remaining two thirds of the work pass in a kind of waking nightmare, in which the woman reproaches the corpse for its alleged infidelities—though whether these grievances are real or imagined it is impossible to tell. And that is all: nothing else happens, merely the unbridled expression of naked emotion of the most sinister kind by an anonymous female figure, alone, somewhere in a forest, in the middle of the night.

Die glückliche Hand has, it is true, somewhat more in the way of narrative than *Erwartung,* centering as it does around a triangular relationship between a woman and two men, but their roles are no further defined than simply by their sex, and we are told nothing about their identity nor indeed about their relationship to each other, save in terms of their mutual attraction, jealousy and desire. And in both these early Schoenberg stage works, external actions and events pale into insignificance by comparison with that which they in a sense symbolise: states of mind, fears and aspirations, love, jealousy, hatred—in other words, psychological states. It is by no means coincidental that *Erwartung* has often been seen as the archetype, as well as one of the earliest examples, of pure psycho-drama. Nor is it any coincidence that in other expressionist stage works, too (Kandinsky's *The Yellow Sound,* Kokoschka's *Murderer, Hope of Women*) we find the same lack of specificity, the same disdain for merely external narrative—characters identified merely as 'giants' or 'people in flowing garb', 'warriors' or 'maidens', without any indication of the relationship between them or indeed where or when the action might be taking place; all these 'external' details are stripped away in order to allow the inner message of the drama to sound forth more powerfully, more clearly, more unequivocally.

All this contrasts dramatically—or at least appears to do so—with Wagner's stage works, which are not only rich in both musical and visual symbolism but are also heavily dependent on narrative, in the sense that at almost every moment something quite specific is happening on the stage. We are also told in almost excessive detail about the relationship between characters, about their identities and respective roles, even their subterfuges—Wotan in the guise of the Wanderer, Freia the bringer of eternal youth, Hagen being Alberich's son and so on. This, indeed, was the burden of the criticisms levelled at Wagner by the expressionist generation, no matter how much they owed him: that his operas, with their convoluted plot and intricate symbolism, tended to remain on the level of 'merely external narrative'. Kandinsky, in his essay 'On Stage Composition' published in the epoch-making *Blaue Reiter Almanach* of 1912,[7] alludes specifically to Wagner in a not very flattering way, complaining at some length about what he sees as the composer's excessively materialistic manner of identifying the principal characters, as well as individual symbols such as sword, ring and so on, by means of the famous Wagnerian device of the *Leitmotiv.* He also caricatures what he calls the 'crude parallelism' which he sees as the dominant characteristic of Wagner's operas (heightened emotion, for example, being invariably accompanied by a crescendo in the orchestral writing) contrasting this with his own practice whereby, in order to highlight what he calls events of an *inner* character, a particular climactic moment may be 'externally' at odds with the musical or scenic material, a 'crescendo' of stage lighting being accompanied by a diminuendo in the orchestra, and so forth.

But in reality, has not Kandinsky here failed to grasp something absolutely crucial in Wagner—the disjunction between verbal and musical content? Despite the vagueness of many of Wagner's more general utterances about art, in describing his own operatic practice he made it perfectly clear that he envisaged a fundamental difference, a difference in kind between the verbal messages carried by the singing voice and the more abstract emotive content embodied in the purely orchestral writing. 'The particular genius of the human voice', wrote Wagner, 'is that it is circumscribed in character, but also specific and clear . . . it represents the human heart in all its delimitable, individual emotion.' 'In the instruments,' on the other hand, 'the primal organs of creation and nature are represented. What they articulate can never be clearly determined or stipulated because they render primal feeling itself, emergent from the chaos of the first creation when there might even have been no human beings to take it into their hearts.'[8] In other words (to paraphrase Wagner's somewhat lurid prose) while the characters are singing their hearts out on stage, the orchestra is actually carrying on its own extremely complex, convoluted and in many ways independent musical argument, unseen in the darkness of the orchestra pit.

We ourselves might add, of course, that the orchestra deals neither in concepts nor in images, but works upon our deeper emotions by means of the resources peculiar to music itself. The Wagnerian invention of the *Leitmotiv*, which Kandinsky disdainfully likened to the 'all-too-familar label on the accustomed wine bottle',[9] in fact put into the composer's hands an extraordinarily subtle and flexible means of conveying *thought*—not conscious, rational thought, but the most secret purposes and repressed emotions of which the characters themselves are at times partly unaware. Indeed, it is striking that, more than half a century before the expressionist artists launched their battle cry, their call for a new art, Wagner in his writings of the early 1850s had already clearly articulated this crucial distinction between the external and internal meanings inherent in the work of dramatic art, between conceptual reasoning and the communication of emotional states, between the rational and deductive on the one hand and the irrational, the inspirational on the other. In so doing he foreshadowed, however unwittingly, a dichotomy central to expressionist thinking as to the nature and purpose of art.

Notes

1. See Schorske, *Fin-de-Siècle Vienna*; Gordon, *Expressionism: Art and Idea*; R. Heller, *Brücke: German Expressionist Prints from the Granvil and Marcia Specks Collection,* Evanston, 1988, and the same author's *Art in Germany, 1909-1936*.

2. See D. Large and W. Weber (eds), *Wagnerism in European Culture and Politics,* London, 1984.

3. 'The Total Work of Art', in P. Burbidge and R. Sutton (eds), *The Wagner Companion,* Boston and London 1979, p. 148.

4. 'Das Kunstwerk der Zukunft', in W. Golther (ed.), *Richard Wagner: Gesammelte Schriften und Dichtungen in zehn Bänden,* Berlin and Leipzig, III, p. 105 (author's translation).

5. See E. Kreowski and E. Fuchs, *Richard Wagner in der Karikatur,* Berlin, 1907.

6. For an English translation of *The Lucky Hand* see Kandinsky and Schoenberg, *Letters, Pictures and Documents,* pp. 91-8.

7. Translated in Kandinsky, *Complete Writings on Art,* pp. 257-65. See also, Kandinsky and Schoenberg, *Letters, Pictures and Documents,* pp. 111-17.

8. Cited after Bryan Magee, *Aspects of Wagner,* London, 1972, p. 56.

9. Kandinsky, *Complete Writings on Art,* p. 261.

Peter Nicholls (essay date 1995)

SOURCE: Nicholls, Peter. "Cruel Structures: The Development of Expressionism." In *Modernisms: A Literary Guide,* pp. 136-64. London, England: Macmillan, 1995.

[*In the following excerpt, Nicholls focuses on the elements of linguistic and sexual violence in the poetry and drama of the Expressionist period.*]

In previous chapters we have seen Paris emerge as a magnetic cultural centre, as the very hub of European modernist activity. Here a sense of energy and dynamism brought art and metropolitan life into powerful association—the Paris of Delaunay was preeminently the city of light, colour, and movement, the city where expanding consumerism had acquired an exciting erotic aura. If that sense of erotic modernity was connected, *via* the new painting, with an attack on forms of representation, it was above all because the Symbolist preoccupation with desire as the response to *loss* was now being called into question by the sense of modernity as an experience of plenitude and abundance. In this respect, dynamism and simultaneity expressed what the Russian writers referred to as the 'self-sufficiency' of the medium, be it paint, stone, or language. Delaunay's vision of Paris caught exactly that sense of self-sufficiency in its association of non-figurative forms with a vividly coloured expression of energy and confidence.

Yet not all visitors to Paris saw it like this. In a partly autobiographical novel published in 1910, the Austrian poet Rainer Maria Rilke has his narrator begin with a strikingly gloomy question: 'People come here, then, to live? I should have thought that they came here to die.'[1] For Rilke's protagonist Malte Laurids Brigge, Paris is a city of poverty and disease—'I have been out, and I saw hospitals,' he continues. Malte's view of modernity has more in common with that of Huysmans's Des Esseintes than it does with the erotic fantasies of Cendrars and Apollinaire. For him, the new is threatening and invasive—'The electric street-cars rage through my room with ringing fury. Automobiles race over me' (4)—and where this interpenetration of inner and outer spaces might put us in mind of Futurist images like Umberto Boccioni's vibrant *The Street Enters the House* (1911), for Malte the permeability of self and other is a source of real terror. Not only does this Paris connote the mortality of the body rather than its pleasures, but Malte's isolated existence shows him cut adrift from others. 'I belonged among the outcasts,' he concludes, with the sick of the Salpêtrière and with those who, like the man he sees afflicted with St Vitus Dance, experience life as some sort of terrible invasion of the self.

This novel shows no trace of those unanimist fantasies of disembodiment and loss of self in the crowd; Malte finds himself confronting not an exciting future but an exhausted past. Rilke sets his story against the declining fortunes of his protagonist's aristocratic family—Malte is, like Des Esseintes, its last scion—and the complex mood of the novel reminds us that German-language modernism is much less sanguine about the loss of narrative and genealogical continuities than its French and Russian counterparts. As Malte's *Notebook* shows, the family retains its hold and the new tensions and mutations within it provide the most sensitive register of the condition which is modernity. The family may now be seen as 'decayed', as Hanno puts it in Thomas Mann's *Buddenbrooks* (1901),[2] but it remains the matrix of the conflicting economies which structure the present. In Germany and the Austro-Hungarian Empire, the Futurist sense of *rupture* with the past did not figure in the same way, even though by 1914 Germany had become the greatest industrial nation in Europe. The cultural effects of modernisation were felt differently here, as an unstable interpenetration of old and new, with the sentimental, semi-feudal past of conservative and military values drawn into alliance with the brutal realism of new capitalist power. Within German-language modernism, then, there was little libidinal investment in fantasies of technology and urbanism, even though the structures of patriarchal authority which persisted were often felt to be repressive and inhuman.

This was to be the world of Expressionism, and its underlying tension is predicted in Malte's *Notebook,* where the narrator recalls being comforted by his mother: 'we remained like this, weeping tenderly and kissing one another, until we felt that Father was there and that we must separate' (91). A moment of emotional unity is shattered by the arrival of the Father, but in line with the form of the Oedipal drama the moment retains its intensity, thus ensuring 'the unending reality of my childhood' (188).[3] For Rilke, as for the Expressionists, any dream of a future uncontaminated by the past will be undermined by the narrative frame which attaches to experience: Malte, for example, realises that if 'I persisted in thinking that my childhood was past, then in that same moment my whole future also vanished' (188). What is most characteristic of this particular modernism is the way in which this sense of tension between past and present produces a parallel opposition between the social and the aesthetic. Where the French modernists had derived new art-forms from the novel world around them, the German-language writers tended to value a radical aesthetic for its capacity to bring release from a claustrophobic social environment.

The tension is pronounced in Rilke's work, where we find a constant preoccupation with death as the ultimate horizon of the aesthetic. From this perspective, the family is regarded as a powerful nexus of desires and interests which always stands over against the autonomy and inwardness of the art-work. This is the moral of Rilke's version of the story of the Prodigal Son which closes Malte's *Notebook,* a parable which is here re-shaped to become 'the legend of one who did not want to be loved' (235). The love of others always changes or 'consumes' the one who is loved, such is the text of Rilke's version; and if the Son is able to return after a long absence it is because he has realised that the members of his family do not really know him, for all their protestations of love: 'What did they know of him? He was now terribly difficult to love, and he felt that One alone was capable of loving him. But he was not yet willing' (243).

Rilke's preoccupation with the idea of 'a well-finished death' (8), which consummates the death we carry within us 'as a fruit bears its kernel' (9), links a major decadent theme to a new way of identifying art with death. With the decline of Christianity, the only authentic existence seems to be one which grasps death not just as part of the totality which is life, but as the final objectification of that absence of desire as self-interest which is, for Rilke, the condition of the greatest art. Like other modernists, he finds models for writing in the visual arts—Rodin and Cézanne, in this case—but where Cubism had been drawn to forms of exteriorisation, here the emphasis is very different. In the first *Rodin-Book* (1902), for example, Rilke explains that 'This distinguishing characteristic of things, complete self-absorption, was what gave to plastic art its calm; it must have no desire nor expectation beyond itself, nor bear any reference to what lies beyond, nor be aware of anything outside itself.'[4] Rodin's objects seem to Rilke to embody 'this turning-inward-upon-oneself, this tense listening to inner depths'[5] which connote freedom from all desire, 'the great calm of objects which know no urge'[6]. Yet something more than just the interiorisation of elements of the external world is involved here: for while, as Malte knows, 'even the unheard-of must become an inward thing' (70), this becoming-inward allows things to retain their own shape because it is not motivated by desire or possessiveness. In another early piece on Rodin, Rilke imagines occasions

> when a bird-call in the open and in his inner consciousness were one, when it did not, as it were, break on the barrier of his body, but gathered both together into an undivided space, in which there was only one region of the purest, deepest consciousness, mysteriously protected.[7]

In contrast to Futurist fantasies of absolute presence, Rilke's 'undivided space' is marked by absence, as it maps the passage from outer to inner. This is the principal paradox which lies behind his development from the impressionism of the early poems of *The Book of Hours* (1905) and *The Book of Pictures* (1902, 1906) to the *New Poems* of 1907 and 1908. The 'new objectivity' of 'thing-poems' (*Ding-Gedichte*) such as 'The Panther' and 'Archaic Torso of Apollo' requires an attention not merely to the things themselves, but to the patterns of association which enable the mind to draw objects inward without interfering with them. The effect Rilke pursues here is akin to something he admires in Cézanne's still-life painting: the fruits with which the painter so often worked 'cease to be edible altogether', Rilke observes, 'that's how thinglike and real they become, how simply indestructible in their stubborn thereness'.[8] We might contrast the similar-sounding sense of 'thereness' in Cendrars's work (his emphasis on 'reality itself'), for in Rilke's case it is not a matter of remarking how the presentness of things eludes language but rather of seeing how that 'thereness' can be grasped only in the absence of all desire.[9]

This is the train of thought which will issue in the warning against 'that hidden, guilty river-god of the blood' in the Third of the *Duino Elegies* (written in Paris in 1913), prompting us to ask, perhaps, whether too high a price does not have to be paid for this type of aesthetic perception. Is there not a kind of ultimate cruelty precisely in the withholding of all desire? This is the poet who boasts that 'I have no beloved, no house, no place where I live',[10] the advocate of 'possessionless love' and one who shares Malte's confused ideas about the poor ('I know that if one tried to love them, they would weigh upon one' [201]). Rilke, however, seems to confront the issue in a poem of 1914 called 'Turning-Point':

> Work of the eyes is done, now
> go and do heart-work
> on all the images imprisoned within you; for you
> overpowered them: but even now you don't know them.[11]

In the great Elegies of the early twenties, this 'heart-work' is closely allied to the idea of praising the world, of transforming things into words. In the famous Ninth Elegy, inwardness is elided with the celebratory, not to say hymnic, function of language: 'For when the traveler returns from the mountain-slopes into the valley, / he brings, not a handful of earth, unsayable to others, but instead / some word he has gained, some pure word, the yellow and blue / gentian.'[12]

The Elegies thus exist in tension with a modernity increasingly tied to modes of objectification—'Earth, isn't this what you want: to arise within us, / *invisible*? Isn't it your dream / to be wholly invisible someday?' The question is asked because language seems increasingly to lack its former intimacy with things; as Rilke put it in a letter to his Polish translator, 'The lived and living things, the things that share our thoughts, these are on the decline and can no more be replaced.'[13] This is an effect of modernity and, more specifically perhaps, of 'the unexperienced nature of technology', as Heidegger puts it in his discussion of Rilke,[14] a condition in which 'empty indifferent things . . . counterfeit things' can only be restored to intimacy through making them 'invisible' within the human medium of language.

. . . . .

Rilke's work cannot be subsumed under the rubric of Expressionism, though it shares with that strand of German-language modernism a preoccupation with themes of inwardness, loss, death, and the family. Like Rilke, the Expressionists were also closely concerned with the interrelation of writing and the visual arts. 'Painterly' questions were thus very much to the fore, and it was with the XXII Berliner Sezession of April 1911 that the term 'Expressionist' came into general use; 1911 was also the year in which Reinhard Sorge's play *The Beggar* was first performed, an occasion which is sometimes taken to mark the beginning of literary Expressionism. As usual, though, we can detect precedents for the movement which was to take shape. A group of Dresden painters known collectively from 1905 as the 'Bridge' (*Die Brücke*), and including Ernst Kirchner, Otto Mueller and Erich Heckel, had explored aggressive effects of colour and a kind of 'savage' simplicity of form derived from Gauguin and Van Gogh. The Bridge painters felt a powerful affinity with all types of primitive art, placing a strong emphasis on self-expression through a vigorous use of line and a thematic and emotional association of the sensual and the spiritual.

In Munich, a second group, calling itself the 'Blue Rider', took shape in 1911 around the painters Franz Marc and Wassily Kandinsky. This group was also interested in primitive art, but largely at Kandinsky's instigation the work of the Blue Rider was to move in the direction of abstraction and angularity of form (Kandinsky painted what may be the first completely abstract canvas in 1911). The second group also had more to say about the theory behind their painting, and *The Blue Rider Almanac* (1912) provided an intriguing cross-section of a modernism as eclectic as it was internationally focused. Contributors to the *Almanac* were keen to stress that their new art would inaugurate a spiritual age no longer tainted by nineteenth-century materialism, and that their modernism would thus renew connections with the art of earlier epochs. So, for example, Franz Marc illustrated his essay on 'Spiritual Treasures' with images drawn from a wide range of traditions (they include German woodcuts, Chinese painting, Bavarian Mirror Painting, Picasso's *Woman with Mandolin at the Piano,* and two drawings by children). This eclecticism is both helpful and unhelpful when it comes to unravelling the complicated origins of Expressionism. On the one hand, it points to a grandness of purpose which situates this avant-garde within a broad Romantic tradition; on the other, it places an emphasis on what Kandinsky calls 'form', the outward manifestation of 'inner need', as he puts it in his most influential essay, *Concerning the Spiritual in Art* (1911).[15] For the artist to move away from 'mere representation' was, for Kandinsky, to discover—or to re-discover—a spiritual dimension obscured by contemporary materialism.

There was always a danger, of course, that Expressionism might be equated with mere expressivity, since, as one critic puts it, what the new art 'seeks to render visible . . . are soul states and the violent emotions welling up from the innermost recesses of the subconscious'.[16] There are several reasons for the Expressionists' preoccupation with *violent* emotion, first among which was their generally shared view of modernity as a condition of servitude from which humanity must break free. In contrast to the Futurists, these writers and artists were obsessed with the infernal nature of the city, with its subordination of the individual to the mechanistic environments of tenement and factory. In Hermann Bahr's words, Expressionism was a product of 'the strenuous battle between the soul and the machine for the possession of man'.[17] Subjective emotion seemed to suffer a constant repression, and in its boldness and grandiosity Expressionist art sought to direct that emotion as a transformative energy against social constraints. In practice, Expressionism veered between an often decadent preoccupation with types of spiritual 'sickness' and an attempt to harness liberated emotion to this project of social renewal; humanity might thus be regenerated, bourgeois individualism might yield to an active sense of spiritual community, the dawn of the 'New Man' may be in sight.

These large-scale objectives led on the aesthetic front to a fundamental opposition of Expressionism to earlier forms of Naturalism and Impressionism. For these writers and artists, Impressionism simply reflected humanity's servitude, projecting the passive image of 'man lowered to the position of a gramophone record of the outer world', as Hermann Bahr put it in one of the most famous manifestos of the new movement.[18] Like the Cubists, the Expressionists were interested in arriving at unfamiliar images of the world through calculated modes of distortion, but where the French artists sought some kind of analytic distance and detachment from the objects to which they alluded, the Expressionist emphasis was always on an intensity of perception secured by infusing the world with violent emotion.

For painters like Kandinsky and Marc, colour was a measure of 'spiritual' intensity and had little or nothing to do with actual objects, which provided merely a starting-point. As another spokesman for Expressionism put it:

> The world is here, it would be meaningless to reproduce it. To seek it out in its last convulsions, its intrinsic essence and to create it anew—that is the greatest meaning of art.[19]

We may note the apocalyptic implications here and the 'convulsive' energies associated with new creation. Expressionism is, characteristically, committed to an exploration of 'essence', penetrating beneath the veil of matter. The result is an art which takes pride in its 'self-sufficiency', grasping the outward world as merely 'a stimulus to improvise in colour and form', as Arnold Schönberg noted of Kandinsky and Oskar Kokoschka.[20] At the same time, though, the Expressionist painters stressed the importance of 'inner meaning', to use Kandinsky's phrase, a meaning which expressed spiritual intensity and thereby avoided the 'trap' of Cubist formalism. While the changing styles of Picasso and Braque would develop in the general direction of mastery and analysis, the Expressionists used primitive and naive forms as models for an art which sought a return to origin, to the instinctual and ostensibly 'innocent' springs of expression.

This trope of a 'return' reminds us once again of Expressionism's divergence from the main preoccupations of Futurism, a divergence all the more surprising in view of Marinetti's apparent success in promoting the movement in Germany. Two exhibitions including Italian painting were in fact held in 1912, the second attracting particular attention as it made its way from Berlin to Cologne, Munich, Karlsruhe and Dresden. Six Futurist manifestos were published in *Der Sturm* between March 1912 and March 1913, and Marinetti—here nicknamed 'Marionetti'—gave a reading of his work in Berlin in the Spring of 1913.[21] Yet for all this exposure (even a volume of Marinetti's poems appeared in German), few writers joined the Futurist camp. The anti-humanist thrust of the Italian movement was fundamentally at odds with the psychological and political preoccupations of Expressionism, and if the two avant-gardes had any common ground it amounted to little more than a shared fascination with art as an expression of energy (one contemporary American critic spoke aptly of German 'explosionism'[22]).

Of the Expressionist poets, only August Stramm sought to develop Marinetti's words-in-freedom as a kind of 'telegram style' based on a concatenation of nouns. In Stramm's hands, though, the technique yielded rather different results, with 'clenched' strings of participles and nouns creating moments of macabre intensity. Poems like 'Melancholy', for example, which register Stramm's wartime experience, record a world for which previous maps, syntactical and otherwise, are painfully obsolete:

>   Striding striving
>   living longs
>   shuddering standing
>   glances look for
>   dying grows
>   the coming
>   screams!
>   Deeply
>   we
>   dumb.[23]

Of the Expressionist poets, Stramm was, however, the only one to carry experimentalism so far, and for the most part the violence of the new writing was more a matter of imagery and content than of linguistic 'distortion'. One of the first poems of the Expressionist wave, Jakob van Hoddis's 'End of the World' (1911), set the tone for much that was to follow. The first stanza evokes great winds and rising waters, and in the second, concluding one, we read:

>   The storm has come, the seas run wild and skip
>   Landwards, to squash big jetties there.
>   Most people have a cold, their noses drip.
>   Trains tumble from the bridges everywhere.[24]

The form is regular enough, and, as Michael Hamburger notes, the novelty of the poem resides mainly in its shifting viewpoint and its collaging of disparate elements.[25] The tone has a quality of lugubrious excitement which is typical of Expressionist writing and which colours the urban landscapes of so many of these poems. Depravity lurks everywhere in the Expressionist city, peopled as it is by beggars, prostitutes and murderers. The mood of urban degeneration and apocalypse can lead, as in the poems of Georg Heym, to feelings of despair and doom, or, as in some of Ernst Stadler's work, to a sense of a new beginning.[26] What is common to the early Expressionist poets, though, is the sense of cultural emergency which makes personal anguish invest the larger scene. The loudness of such writing—both literal and figurative—constantly stresses the need for a return to that which is primal in humanity, a shedding of cultural inhibition in the name of the naked 'cry' (*Schrei*) rather than the 'intellectual' word. Such poetry is perhaps best taken in small doses, partly because of the strain imposed by its favourite devices of exclamation and repetition, but also because its cosmic ambitions lead to a calculated abstractness of theme. The subject headings of the principal anthology of Expressionist verse, Karl Pinthus's *The Twilight of Humanity* (1920), are revealing in this respect: 'decline and cry', 'the awakening of hearts', 'proclamation and revolt', 'the love of humanity'.[27] Published in 1920, the anthology encapsulates the two main phases of Expressionism: the first, running from 1911 to 1914, when the central concern is with themes of death and decline, and the second, from 1914 through to 1920, charting the phase of political or messianic Expressionism, which was finally wrecked on the failure of the November Revolution of 1918.

The major poetry of the movement was produced in the first phase, with many of its most significant talents—Stadler, Georg Heym, Alfred Lichtenstein, and Georg Trakl—perishing in the War. Of these, the Austrian poet Georg Trakl was the most important, as he was the most equivocal, figure. Pinthus published ten of his poems in the *Twilight* anthology, though Trakl's work is altogether quieter and ostensibly more passive in tone than the familiar declamatory mode of Expressionist writing. Trakl's poem called 'Occident' is thus somewhat unusual in the apocalyptic imagery of its final stanza ('Gruesome sunset red / is breeding fear / in the thunderclouds. / You dying peoples!'[28]); more customary is the gloomy landscape elsewhere in the poem, with its imagery of the 'rocky path', the 'evening pond' and 'nocturnal shadows'—a landscape haunted by a mythical figure called Elis. The motif of decline is everywhere in Trakl's verse, though it is generally evoked through a psychic landscape rather than being voiced rhetorically. The quality of inwardness in these poems is arguably more extreme than any we have looked at so far, though in contrast to mainstream Expressionism it is not the product of overt emotional pressure, of the exterior world distorted by a projected intensity. Trakl's poems disturb, rather, because any sense of a shared external reality seems to have been lost.

The characteristic mood is an autumnal one, the present tense of the poem poised between fading memories of an idyllic past and intimations of darkness and decay to come. The loud Expressionist 'I' is rarely in evidence—in fact Trakl described his work as an attempt 'to subordinate myself unconditionally to the object to be represented'[29]—and the burden of emotion resides almost wholly in a repertoire of recurring images. 'Evening Song' will provide an example:

> Walking along dark paths in the evening,
> Our pale shapes appear before us.
>
> When we are thirsty,
> We drink the white waters of the pool,
> The sweetness of our mournful childhood.
>
> Dead, we rest beneath the elder bushes,
> Watching the grey gulls.
>
> Spring clouds rise over the dark city
> Silenced by monks of nobler times.
>
> When I took your slender hands
> You opened your soft round eyes.
> That was a long time ago.
>
> Yet when a darker melody visits the soul,
> You appear, white, in your friend's autumn landscape.[30]

The poem is striking partly on account of its shifting perspectives. The two 'friends' appear first as 'pale forms', which may suggest either a trick of the evening light or that they are ghosts. With the third stanza we are told that they are dead (*erstorbene*), and the perspective then changes again to give an image of Spring against the 'dark city', which could be either regenerative or destructive. The tense now shifts to the past, linking a moment of shared emotion with 'the monks of nobler times'. The final stanza, with its suggestion that the friend (the 'white' one associated still with childhood) will reappear whenever a 'dark' (or 'gloomy', *dunkler*) 'harmony haunts the soul', makes another temporal shift, implying that the present tense of the opening lines is that of fantasy.

The combination of dark and light imagery in association with these ideas of childhood suggests that the perception of the past is somehow double, ambivalent. Trakl's work returns obsessively to a moment of loss which is generally understood in terms of his incestuous desire for his sister; 'Evening Song' was in fact part of a textual complex later refashioned as the long poem 'Helion', a work which connects the poet's 'madness' with the loss of his sister to marriage with an older man ('A pale angel / The son steps into the empty house of his fathers / The sisters have gone far away to white old men'[31]). The poems pull constantly into the past of remembered experience, back to the 'dark stillness of childhood'[32], though the contrasting imagery of whiteness and paleness, associated with the conjoint figure of 'a dying youth, the sister',[33] suggests that behind this lies what Heidegger, in his account of Trakl, calls 'the earliness of stiller childhood'.[34] This seems to be the burden of the prose poem 'Dream and Derangement', where the narrator's childhood is recalled as 'full of sickness, dread and sullen darkness'. Yet running through this text are intermittent references to 'the white form of an angel' and to 'the starry face of purity' which contrast with the 'dark rooms' of the guilt-laden family tradition ('O blighted race, accursed genealogy').

These images refer to an impossible time before guilt, a time before the crime which seems to initiate an Oedipal history ('when in the flourishing summer garden he raped the quiet child, and reflected in the afterglow, saw that profound darkness, his own face'[35]). This moment of violence, real or imagined, inaugurates the rule of sexual difference, and the insistent figures of decline and descent in the poems, associated even as they are with evening and autumn, evoke a return to some primal oneness. In 'Western Song', for example:

> O the bitter hour of decline,
> When we regard a stony face in black waters.
> But radiant the lovers raise their silver eyelids:
> One kin. From rosy pillows incense pours
> And the sweet canticle of the bodies resurrected.[36]

'Ein Geschlecht': 'one kin', but the word has a range of interconnected meanings, 'sex, genre, family, state, race, lineage, generation'.[37] As Heidegger observes, a weight of emphasis attaches to 'one' in these lines, evoking 'The force which marks the tribes of mankind as the simple oneness of "*one* generation," and thus restores them and mankind to the stiller childhood', to 'the stiller onefold simplicity of childhood [in which] is hidden also the kindred twofoldness of mankind'.[38]

. . . . .

The full articulation of this theme in Trakl's work is too complex to be pursued here, but his fantasy of a 'stiller childhood' which does not yet know the 'curse' of genealogy and sexual difference is one which also governed the development of Expressionist theatre. In fact the play usually taken to inaugurate Expressionist drama, Kokoschka's *Murderer, Hope of Women* (1907), is a macabre exploration of the negative power of sexuality, here understood in terms of a violent struggle of man against woman.[39] When Kokoschka's play was first performed in 1909, at a small outdoor theatre in Vienna, there were riotous scenes as soldiers fought with members of the audience. While these violent confrontations may have had no direct relation to the play, they accorded well enough with the electric atmosphere Kokoschka was trying to create. The players' faces bore heavily made-up mask-like expressions, while veins and muscles were vividly painted on their arms and legs. The stage-setting itself was at once starkly simple and dramatically coloured:

> Night sky. Tower with large red grille as door; torches the only light; black ground, rising to the tower in such a way that all the figures appear in relief.

As the play opens, a warlord enters, followed by a group of men; almost immediately a woman appears with her female attendants. The Woman is transfixed by sexual desire: 'Why do you bind me, man, with your gaze?', she cries, 'Devouring life overpowers me. O take away my terrible hope—and may torment overpower you.' The Man's response is to order his attendants to brand her as his possession—an old man steps forward, tears open her dress and marks her with a hot iron. In her pain and fury the Woman springs at the Man, wounding him in the side with her knife. It seems that the wound will be fatal, for the Man is placed in a coffin behind the bars of the tower. But while the rival factions of men and women now begin to sport in the shadows, the Woman is inconsolable. 'She creeps around the cage like a panther', trying to awaken the Man (she 'prods his wound, hissing maliciously, like an adder'). Suddenly, though, there is a crowing of cocks, and the Man seems to revive. In a bizarre tableau, the 'Woman covers him entirely with her body; separated by the grille, to which she clings high up in the air like a monkey'. A terrible struggle now takes place, the Man finally draining the Woman's strength ('you vampire, piecemeal you feed on me, weaken me'). With a 'slowly diminishing scream' she expires, leaving the Man to wreak havoc on the male and female attendants.

CHORUS:

> The devil! Tame him, save yourselves, save yourselves if you can—all is lost!
>
> *He walks straight towards them. Kills them like mosquitoes and leaves red behind. From very far away, crowing of cocks.*

Perhaps not surprisingly, this curiously ugly play—or, more precisely, theatrical event (it runs to only a few pages of text)—is often regarded as a forerunner of Expressionist drama, and its subsequent 'revivals' show that it continued to occupy a place in the later repertoire.[40] Even my brief sketch of the play's action should indicate its proto-Expressionist qualities. Naturalistic psychology is jettisoned in favour of an extreme stylisation, and Kokoschka builds the play around a sequence of emotional intensities rather than according to a clear narrative logic. These intensities are coupled with a primitivism of setting and emotion which gives this conflict of the sexes the quality of a primal scene. As if to reinforce this sense of the primitive and its displacement of social by sexual conflict, the play foregrounds non-textual effects of gesture and *mise en scène*. The acting style demanded by the play prefigures that 'convulsive equation of body and soul'[41] which was to become the mark of Expressionist performance and which produced the notorious staccato sound-effects of 'scream-theatre' [*Schreidrama*]. In *Murderer,* there is a high-pitched lyricism which approximates to 'singing higher and higher, soaring';[42] indeed, the primacy of sound over meaning becomes the very mark of the violence and excessiveness of desire.

This connection between sexual violence and a kind of formal 'excess' epitomises that aspect of Expressionism which would prove least assimilable to Anglo-American notions of modernism. T. S. Eliot's idea of an 'objective correlative' is a useful way of gauging the difference, especially since the term derives from a consideration of a dramatic work, Shakespeare's *Hamlet*. The famous definition is as follows:

> The only way of expressing emotion in the form of art is by finding an 'objective correlative'; in other words, a set of objects, a chain of events, which shall be the formula of that particular emotion.[43]

It is this 'correlative' which *Hamlet* apparently lacks, the play failing to ensure the 'complete adequacy of the external to the emotion'. On closer scrutiny we find that Eliot's idea that the play 'is like the sonnets, full of some stuff that the writer could not drag to light, contemplate, or manipulate into art' is closely bound up with an anxiety about the feminine as fundamentally intractable to representation.[44] Eliot's commitment to 'objectification' points up the dissociation between inner and outer, subjective and objective, which is central to his conception of art's power to transmute the primitive 'stuff' of emotion. In producing a 'formula' for the emotion, art is able to constrain that 'bodily' affect which he tends to associate with a kind of pathology.[45]

Now, as the example of Kokoschka's *Murderer* will show, the priorities of Expressionist drama are very different from those which govern Eliot's reading of *Hamlet*. In this new theatre we find that narrative indeterminacy and the hyperbolic pitch of emotion conspire to unsettle and exceed representation. Where, for Eliot, sexuality seems to threaten a moment of pure self-presence which blocks Oedipal resolution and escapes formulation in the differential medium of language (sound is dangerously privileged over meaning), in Expressionist drama a certain negativity attaches to sexuality, not because it is intractable to the 'chain' of representation but *because it is already bound by it*. To put it another way, sexuality here always exists within a structure, whether it be one of violent opposition or the Oedipal triangle itself.

So we find in *Murderer* a kind of imbalance between the perennial 'battle of the sexes'—a structure determined above all by narrative and repetition—and a countervailing use of dramatic effects to *elide* distinctions between inner and outer, self and other, so as to dissolve the symbolic in moments of pure 'bodily' affect. Eliot's representational 'chain' of objects and events is, in fact, precisely what the excessive modes of Expressionist drama seek to disrupt, for to be bound by this 'chain' is to be bound by the law of secondariness—a law which the new theatre constantly strives to violate in its struggle to establish itself as pure 'event' rather than as narrative, as 'scream' rather than speech. The difficulty we may have in interpreting *Murderer* thus stems mainly from the way in which Kokoschka employs a range of formal intensities which are deliberately (in Eliot's phrase) 'in excess of the facts'. Light, sound, gesture, a strangely overdetermined symbolism—these elements create a slippage of meaning which substitutes spectacle for narrative. Are we, for example, to explain the ugliness of the play in terms of that misogyny which seems to pervade Expressionist writing, or is narrative indeterminacy a clue to subtler contradictions of attitude?

There are few close interpretations of *Murderer*, but even these are divided by some fundamental disagreements. Perhaps the most straightforward reading of the play is that given by Frank Whitford: 'the male, threatened by the woman's sexual desire, regains his strength by killing her'.[46] But if the play expresses a triumphant misogyny, why does it end, as two other critics have observed, on a note of pessimism and foreboding?[47] And to make matters worse, Kokoschka's own comments on the play tend to complicate rather than resolve problems of interpretation. In a letter of 1931, for example, he refers to *Murderer* as 'my expressionistic dawn chorus, sung in honour of an anonymous Penthesilea',[48] and in an essay of 1935 ('On Experience') he describes the play as striking 'a blow against the thoughtlessness of our male civilization with my fundamental notion that man is mortal and woman immortal, and that only the murderer tries to reverse this basic fact in the modern world'.[49] In his autobiography, however, Kokoschka describes the famous poster advertising the play in rather different terms: 'The man is blood-red, the colour of life. But he is lying in the lap of a woman who is white, the colour of death.'[50]

These apparent contradictions arise because *Murderer* actually focuses less on gender oppositions than on something violent and contradictory which undercuts them and appears as sexuality itself. This at any rate seems to be the implication of other remarks in the autobiography, where sexual conflict is linked with those 'Greek ideas of Eros and Thanatos' which are 'the counterparts of progress and enlightenment', ideas which, according to Kokoschka, he derived from the work of J. J. Bachofen and Robert Briffault:

> one thing was certain: the instinct for self-preservation which begins with the first movement in the womb and ends in death. . . . Fear makes for inactivity, but behind that shadow of Thanatos, which had dogged me from my childhood onwards, there lurked the ever more enticing abyss of Eros. Here, in this new existence to which I began to seek the key, is perhaps the secret of my first stage play, *Mörder, Hoffnung der Frauen*.[51]

In contrast to the superficially similar polemics of Italian Futurism against the 'feminine', Kokoschka locates a certain irredeemable negativity within sexuality itself (Eros is inextricably intertwined with Thanatos).

This line of thought clearly has its place in that view of 'the deathly hatred of the sexes'[52] which had already received definitive expression in the work of Schopenhauer and Nietzsche, but it does not solve completely the problem of the play's title. Why should Man as Murderer be the '*hope* of Women'? To conclude simply that *Murderer* ends with 'the victorious male passing through all who stand in his way'[53] is not only to miss the final association of Man with death, but also to underestimate the extent to which the flamboyant experimentalism of the play is, at one level, an effect of 'excessive' female desire.

One solution lies in Otto Weininger's *Sex and Character*, first published in 1903 and a work with which Kokoschka was almost certainly familiar. In this hugely influential book (twelve editions were published between May 1903 and May 1910), Weininger combined cultural evaluation with pseudo-science to create a sprawling monument to misogyny and antisemitism. Woman, for Weininger, is 'nothing but sexuality . . . she is sexuality itself'.[54] In attempting to argue this case, Weininger assembles the main elements of traditional misogyny but gives them a polemical twist of his own: if woman's inferiority results from her failure to 'overcome the sexuality that binds her' (279), she can only be raised from her lowly status by the intervention of man, who, by denying her sexual fulfilment, will open for her the way to a new transcendence. Wagner's Kundry is, for Weininger, 'probably the most perfect representation of woman in art' (319) because she submits to the redemptive force of 'a sinless, immaculate man—Parsifal' (344).

Not surprisingly, perhaps, it has been suggested that *Sex and Character* can be read almost as an early Expressionist manifesto,[55] not least because of its habit of linking violence with regeneration. 'Love', says Weininger, 'is murder. The sexual impulse destroys the body and mind of the woman, and the psychical eroticism destroys her psychical existence' (249). But if 'sexual union . . . is allied to murder' (248), the act of desired 'regeneration' is also linked to death: 'she must certainly be destroyed, as woman; but only to be raised again from the ashes' (345). Weininger's unpleasant but influential fantasies may thus explain Kokoschka's title and the withholding of sexuality, which is the play's major theme, but questions still remain to be answered. Woman, for Weininger, is incapable of conceptual thought or self-knowledge. She lives an 'unconnected, discontinous' life and represents 'negation, the opposite pole of Godhead' (146). Throughout the book, Weininger categorises the feminine as the realm of the body and the unconscious, and it is this aspect of his polemic which is directed at the 'feminised' and decadent art of the Secession, an art which, in privileging the 'material' values of sound and ornament, allegedly obstructs the conceptual clarity of male thought.[56] 'A being like the female, without the power of making concepts, is unable to make judgments. In her "mind" subjective and objective are not separated' (194); 'It is the conception which brings freedom from the eternally subjective' (192).

Here we can begin to see just how equivocal Weininger's influence was for the Expressionists, for their whole project was founded on a revaluation of subjectivity and its 'visionary' capabilities. An early essay by Kokoschka, for example, 'On the Nature of Visions', directly opposes any Weiningerian claims for 'logic': 'The consciousness of visions is not a mode of perceiving and understanding existing objects. It is a condition in which we experience the visions themselves.'[57] Kokoschka goes on to claim that

> This consciousness of visions has a life which derives power from itself. This power freely organizes visions whether complete or barely perceptible irrespective of how they relate to each other, and in complete independence of temporal or spatial logic.
>
> (98)

As that last phrase suggests, verbal expression operates here according to very different criteria from those of Weininger:

> Thus we have to listen with complete attention to our inner voice in order to get past the shadows of words to their very source. 'The Word became flesh and dwelt among us.' And then the inner source frees itself, sometimes vigorously, sometimes feebly, from the words within which it lives like a charm.
>
> (99)

To experience 'visions' is '[t]o be possessed', and Kokoschka uses a striking analogy to describe its effect: 'Suddenly an image will take shape for us, like the first look, like the first shriek of a child, newborn, coming from its mother's womb' (100).

Kokoschka's essay demonstrates the way in which Expressionism could assimilate Weininger's negative view of sexuality while at the same time exploiting those very non-conceptual qualities which he had derided as 'feminine' and anti-modern. An explanation for this lies in the essay's vocabulary of 'source' and 'origin', which points back towards primal intensities which pre-exist a modern sexuality contaminated by repetition and commodification; for early Expressionism is indelibly marked by the *fin de siècle* fascination with the figure of the prostitute and by that '"mechanistic" and sadistic imagination which separates love from a modern eroticism without aura'.[58] Kokoschka's reference to childbirth suggests a contrasting network of associations, linking the new and visionary with the pre-discursive and pre-Oedipal in a movement which seeks to rediscover the lost aura within artistic form itself. The connection with the maternal and (in Lacan's sense) the Imaginary not only runs counter to Weiningerian 'logic', but also suggests a domain which is unavailable to linguistic expression and which exists prior to structures of gender and family.

From this point of view it is perhaps not fortuitous that the earliest exponents of an Expressionist theatre, Kokoschka and Wassily Kandinsky, were both painters. Kokoschka's association of the visionary with a fantasy of uterine return certainly informs much painterly theory in this period, as we can see from the *Blue Rider Almanac* and the writings of artist Paul Klee. This is how Klee puts it in *On Modern Art*:

> Chosen are those artists who penetrate to that secret place where primeval power nurtures all evolution. There, where the powerhouse of all time and space—call it brain or heart of creation—activates every function; who is the artist who would not dwell there? In the womb of nature, at the source of creation, where the secret key to all lies guarded.[59]

For the dramatist, Klee's 'secret place' might arguably be the point at which narrative structure suddenly yields to dramatic event, the point at which theatre seems to attain an 'impossible' freedom from the trace of externality.

Yet as we can see from the late plays of Strindberg, commonly regarded as the precursors of Expressionism proper, this fantasy of origin and presence is constantly threatened by the transcendental pull of theatricality itself, a structure of re-presentation working tirelessly to absorb affective intensity and the movement of desire. Strindberg, too, was a keen admirer of Weininger, but the impact of *Sex and Character* on his theatre prefigured the Expressionist twist later given to this set of ideas: for while he fully endorsed Weininger's anti-feminism, the dream-like structure of his own 'station-dramas' [*Stationendramen*] had a surprising affinity with Weininger's contemptuous description of woman's life as 'discrete, unconnected, discontinuous, swayed by the perceptions of the moment instead of dominating them' (146).[60]

In a well-known preface to *A Dream Play* (1901), Strindberg outlines the technique at work here and in the earlier *To Damascus* (Parts I and II 1898):

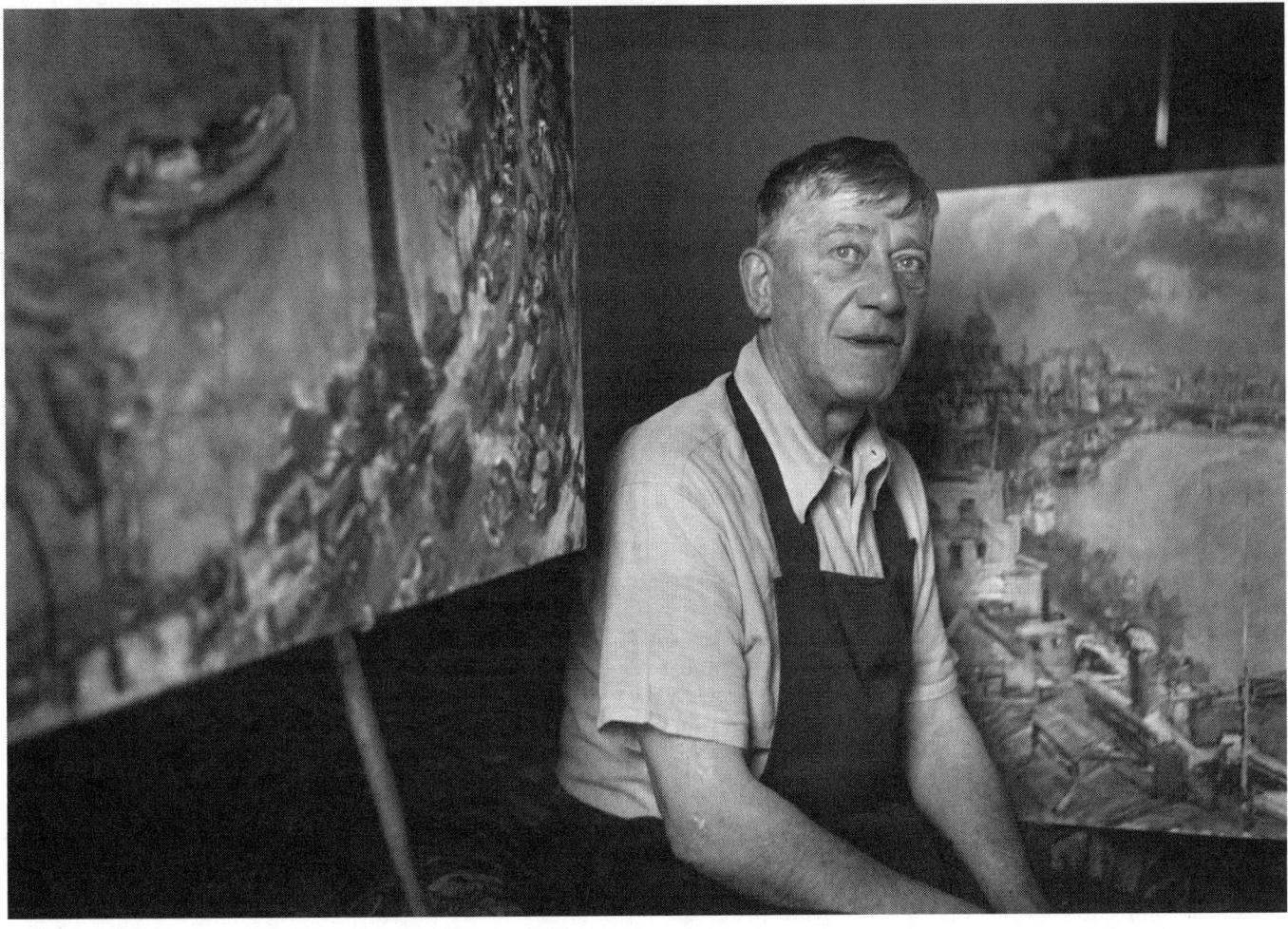

Photograph of Oscar Kokoschka.

Everything can happen, everything is possible and probable. Time and place do not exist; on an insignificant basis of reality the imagination spins, weaving new patterns; a mixture of memories, experiences, free fancies, incongruities and improvisations. The characters split, double, multiply, evaporate, condense, disperse, assemble.[61]

Yet Strindberg's description, which bears a strong resemblance to Freud's later account of the 'primary process',[62] is in marked contrast to one of the major themes of *To Damascus* (and, indeed, of *A Dream Play* and *Ghost Sonata*), the theme of *repetition*. 'Why does everything recur?' asks the Stranger at the beginning of Part I, and as the plays unfold it becomes increasingly clear that sexuality and its domestic scene (the 'inferno' of Strindberg's life and art) are marked by interminable struggle. The Lady and the Stranger endlessly torment each other, as Strindberg evokes what is described in *A Dream Play* as 'the fairest of things, which is the bitterest: love, a wife and a home; the best thing, and the worst' (584). This drama is ultimately less a matter of 'weaving *new* patterns' than of concluding that, in the words of the Advocate, 'We must torture each other, then. What makes one happy, torments the other' (588). Sexuality here becomes 'the worst thing', standing as 'Repetition. Repeating the pattern' (606).

While there is a kind of heroism ultimately claimed in the knowledge that, as the Daughter concludes in *A Dream Play,* 'Strife between opposites generates power, just as fire and water generate steam' (629), the only real but intermittent hope lies elsewhere. In *To Damascus,* for example, the Stranger awakens in the Lady 'a feeling of motherhood which I had never known before' (201), and he confesses that 'I longed to sleep at a mother's breast' (204), a wish momentarily granted later in the play ('Come, my child, and I will repay the debt I owe you. On my lap I shall rock you to peace' [224]). It is therefore not by chance that this desire to return to the mother, to an original plenitude which precedes all repetitive strife, is articulated in a dramatic form in which the 'spinning' play of imagination and improvisation seeks to undermine the structure of representation. Indeed, this seems a decisive clue to some of the concerns of early Expressionism, opposing sexuality, as structure and repetition, to the 'timeless', non-sexual love of mother and child. If the episodic, dreamlike form of Strindberg's late plays offers a model for a modernist drama, it is perhaps because it strives to couple the non-representational with a fantasy of fullness not predicated upon a lack or absence. In dramatic terms, then, the dream of the Mother is also the dream of a theatre with no 'outside', a theatre sufficient to itself and freed from the tyranny of both external reality and textual authority.

Kokoschka's *Murderer* seems to engage directly with these ideas and in so doing to test the limits of the dramatic medium itself. As several critics have observed, and as Kokoschka himself made clear in his autobiography, a decisive influence on his early work was J. J. Bachofen's *Mother Right* (1861).[63] The importance of Bachofen's thesis—it had a strong impact on writers as diverse as Nietzsche, Hauptmann, Klages, Rilke, Mann and Kafka[64]—lay in its imaginative account of three main phases of human development: the 'hetaerist-aphroditic' phase, characterised by female promiscuity and symbolised by the wild vegetation of the swamp; the Demetrian phase of mother-love and a settled, agricultural society; and finally the phase of father-right, of individual property and the division of labour. Bachofen concluded that 'Matriarchy is followed by patriarchy and preceded by unregulated hetaerism.'[65]

This evolutionary process might lie behind the attenuated narrative of *Murderer,* though Kokoschka hardly shares Bachofen's optimistic view of '[t]he progress from the maternal to the paternal conception of man'.[66] If Eros precedes or lies *behind* Thanatos, as Kokoschka suggests in his autobiography, the Man's final victory seems to represent the triumph of the deathly principle of patriarchal law, a principle governing desire and external to it. In the 'A text' of *Murderer,* the moment when the Woman covers the Man with her body is initially one of maternal affection—'Who nourishes me?' the Man cries, 'Who suckles me with blood? I devour your melting flesh'[67]—but as the lurid allusions to vampirism indicate, the 'iron chains' of male desire can no longer be resisted. In the ensuing massacre, Kokoschka again hints through the sound of the cock-crow (the sign that Peter will betray Christ) that we have entered the age of theology and transcendence.

In the echo of that symbolic cock-crow, *Murderer* seems to perform a complex interrogation of the dramatic medium, its prefiguring of Expressionist modes bound up with a desire for the pre-figurative which defines an impossible and absolute theatricality. Indeed, the association here of closure with some form of patriarchal law recalls Jacques Derrida's rather similar sense of a theatrical 'evolution':

> The origin of theater, such as it must be restored, is the hand lifted against the abusive wielder of the logos, against the father, against the God of a stage subjected to the power of speech and the text.[68]

Derrida analyses Antonin Artaud's 'theatre of cruelty' as an attempt to escape repetition and the law of representation. Artaud's 'writing of the body', an ideal 'language without trace' (175), seeks to evade the absent authority of 'a primary logos which does not belong to the theatrical site and governs it from a distance' (235).

Artaud's is an 'impossible' theatre, founded, as Derrida observes, not only on an ideal of linguistic 'non-difference' but on a related fantasy of pure self-presence which abolishes Oedipal structure:

> Restored to its absolute and terrifying proximity, the stage of cruelty will thus return me to the autarchic immediacy of my birth, my body and my speech. Where has Artaud better defined the stage of cruelty than in *Here Lies,* outside any apparent reference to the theater: 'I, Antonin Artaud, am my son / my father, my mother / and myself'?
>
> (190)

Artaud may be the best-known exponent of these claims for an 'absolute' theatre, but the Expressionists, too, dreamed of a drama which might be said to 'shelter an indestructible desire for full presence, for nondifference: simultaneously life and death' (194). Yet the theatre is, as Derrida observes, an exemplary instance of the general rule by which 'all destructive discourses . . . must inhabit the structures they demolish' (194).

That parodoxical condition, endlessly affirming difference and exteriority, is the object of ritual confrontation in Expressionist drama, a confrontation staged (as we see in *Murderer*) between two theatrical limits: on the one hand, there is a theatre prefiguring the ideal of Artaud in its search for an immediate, pre-discursive reality; on the other, there is a drama endlessly preoccupied with Oedipal structure and with an ideal of transcending it (the theme of the 'New Man' which figures so prominently in the later theatre of Expressionism). That we should find few pure instances of either type both supports Derrida's case and reflects the peculiarly hybrid nature of so many Expressionist plays.

Of the first form of Expressionist theatre Kandinsky's *The Yellow Sound* (1909) is almost the only 'pure' example.[69] This brief dramatic event comprises six scenes or 'Pictures' (*Bilder*), as Kandinsky calls them. As that term suggests, the text of the play is not so much a script as a series of directions for movements, coloured lighting and musical effects. We are given few clues to the meaning of the 'characters' here (they comprise Five Giants, Vague Creatures, a Child, a Man, People in Flowing Robes, People in Tights, a Chorus, and a Tenor (backstage). There seems to be some sort of progression from the indeterminate to the human, with timeless space giving way to recognisable objects, and it may be that the play has a utopian theme linked to Kandinsky's concept of spiritual form: 'This white ray leads to evolution, to elevation. Behind matter, within matter, the creative spirit is hidden.'[70] Ultimately, though, the play claims our attention less on account of some hidden narrative than for its radical break with the conventions of nineteenth-century drama, condemned by Kandinsky for remaining 'under the spell of external events'.[71] In contrast, *The Yellow Sound,* he suggests, 'finally consists of the complex of inner experiences (soul = vibrations) of the audience'.[72]

Kandinsky's play was, in fact, never performed, and perhaps for that reason the text published in the *Blaue Reiter Almanac* came to represent an extreme of experimentalism. It was an extreme, however, which subsequent Expressionist drama would only fitfully explore, for Kandinsky had moved far toward that apparently pre-linguistic 'ground' (*Urgrund*) of experience where all structure seemed about to dissolve in a play of purely physical effects:

> The word, independent or in sentences, was used to create a certain 'atmosphere' that frees the soul and makes it receptive. The sound of the human voice was also used pure, i.e., without being obscured by words, or by the meaning of words.[73]

Colour was therefore of primary importance to this project, producing 'irrational pictorial spaces' which allowed a kind of 'spiritual' or psychic mobility, a freedom from determinate social and psychic structures.[74]

If Kandinsky's play in some sense anticipates what André Green has termed in another context a post-Freudian theatre,[75] the major plays of fully-fledged Expressionism are dominated by the imperatives of structure, and specifically by the binding forms of the Oedipal plot. Not only does sexuality imply ineluctable repetition, as in Strindberg and Kokoschka, but its controlling network of desires is deeply embedded within the family narrative. Here the Father returns to exercise control, governing theatrical expression either directly or 'at a distance', and while plays of filial rebellion, such as Walter Hasenclever's *The Son* (1914), strive to create a final, liberating sense of independence, this amounts in practice to little more than a familiar avant-garde fantasy of self-authoring.

Although critics have tended to disregard the determinism of psychological structure in Expressionist theatre,[76] it is not just the sensational cases like Sorge's *The Beggar,* Hasenclever's *The Son* or Arnolt Bronnen's *Parricide* (1915) which bring to the fore the Oedipal conflict between father and son. Bronnen's play, in which the son kills his father and is then wooed by his naked mother, may provide the most luridly memorable handling of the theme, but the family narrative is, in fact, everywhere in Expressionist theatre, working its effects in plays as diverse as Hanns Johst's *The Young Man* (1916), Fritz von Unruh's *A Family* (1916), and Georg Kaiser's *From Morning to Midnight* (1916).

One reason why critics have tended to underestimate the determining power of the Oedipal plot is that the recurring motifs of rebellion and parricide gesture towards a new independence, a freedom from the constraints of the past and the family, and accession to the status of 'new man'. This utopian attempt to refigure masculinity in terms of a transcendence of social roles caught in the Oedipal net is clearly expressed in an influential manifesto by Kasimir Edschmid:

> Each person is no longer simply an individual bound by duty, morality, society and family. In this art, each becomes the most elevated and the most deplorable of things: *becomes a human being.*[77]

Such, then, is the dream of a new beginning (*Aufbruch*) which animates Expressionist drama, a recreation of the self which aims to purge it of any contact with the past, and, specifically, with the Father. For in these plays the force of repetition is derived from the law of the Father, and freedom can be found only in a regeneration equivalent to Artaud's idea of self-birth. The attempt to free theatre from mimesis is thus inextricably bound up with the generational struggle against paternity: representation is at once a theatrical mode which disastrously situates repetition at the heart of performance *and* that genealogical chain by which a son is bound to represent his father. Yet, as Richard Sheppard has shown in a discussion of four of these plays, 'the iron law that sons must succeed their fathers' is one which, finally, it is impossible to break. Each of these plays is, he concludes, 'caught in the classic double bind of castration by a yet secret dependence upon a more or less sadistic but absent Father'.[78]

As for the theme of salvation so much emphasised in readings of these plays (and, for example, in Hasenclever's description of *The Son* as 'the revolt of the spirit against reality'[79]), Sheppard concludes that

> No sooner does an 'anoedipal' drive manifest itself in the plays, than it is assimilated into the Oedipal chain of lack and dependence, rendered harmless by being allowed to exhaust itself in aggression against part-objects or turned into a regressive flight to the mother.
>
> (376)

The importance which Sheppard attaches to the 'closed circuit of the Oedipal drama' certainly accords with what we have already seen of the relation between sexuality and structure in early Expressionism. Yet, as Kokoschka's *Murderer* shows, the tendency to 'excess' in Expressionism means that its drama is never quite as diagrammatic as this 'circuit' suggests. Sheppard argues that 'the *Ich-Dramen* cannot envisage an essential drive in the human personality which . . . can produce free individuals' (377), thereby leaving us with 'a loss that can never be made good' (378). It is the ideal of self-presence which is complicated here: on the one hand, it exists at the thematic level, as the desired escape from structure which, expressed in the familiar rhetoric of Expressionism, is ultimately re-contained in a discursive, Oedipal order; on the other hand, though, the curiously uneven, hybrid quality of these plays arises because this thematic 'circuit' is, as it were, broken by its production as dramatic event.

Much Expressionist drama is, like Kokoschka's *Murderer,* governed by this fundamental tension between a narrative structure always already contaminated by sexuality and the Oedipal chain, and a displacement of libidinal energy into a form whose ecstatic 'bodily' rhythms strive to defer the return of the Father. To stress the compensatory effects of that form is not simply to engage in conventional critical pieties about performance values; for the tension between narrative and event, between sexuality and unstructured affect, is actually interiorised in the acting-style of Expressionism—interiorised, that is, as *strain* (at the level of voice, diaphragm, musculature) and a *straining after* the condition of 'pure', non-discursive theatricality.[80]

. . . . .

That quality of strain is something we now readily associate with Expressionism, but to follow the later mutations of its dramatic style is to see how such tension was increasingly resolved at the level of rhetoric. By 1920, the Oedipal theme was commonplace; as the Secretary puts it in Georg Kaiser's *The Coral* (1920), 'Father and son are drawn in opposite directions. It is always a life and death struggle.'[81] Yet while the opening phase had been characterised by acts of filial rebellion, plays of the twenties, like Franz Werfel's *Mirror-Man* (1920), focused increasingly on what Peter Gay has called the 'Revenge of the Father'.[82] In this changed climate the work of Ernst Toller affirmed the radical potential of theatre, but it did so through a political vision which transferred attention from the individual to the group. In *Transfiguration* (1919), for example, the way towards a 'true humanity' is seen to lie through the rejection of sexual love ('Can't you see that love and goodness are eternally separated by a hopeless gulf?'[83]), and Toller's search for a 'collectively valid subjectivity' led in his next play to the proposition that 'Only the Masses are holy.'[84] Toller thus offered one path out of what the Marxist critic Georg Lukács would soon be calling the 'self-trumpeting emotionalism' of subjective Expressionism.[85] Toller was a revolutionary (he spent five years in prison as a result of the part he played in the November Revolution of 1918), and he was able to transcend the Oedipal narrative in favour of larger social and economic themes. Yet it was precisely the largeness of such themes which ultimately proved difficult to handle, and with the exception of *The Machine-Wreckers* (1922), most of Toller's work drifted too easily towards the purely didactic and allegorical.

By 1925, in fact, the whole Expressionist experiment had begun to seem dated and out of step with modernity. An exhibition held at the Mannheim Kunsthalle in the middle of that year gave a name to a very different tendency in the arts: *Die Neue Sachlichkeit,* the new objectivity. The principal artists contributing to the show—Otto Dix, George Grosz, Max Beckmann among them—announced a return to figurative painting and to a hard-edged style of social criticism. The second half of the decade would now see a swing against the subjectivism of Expressionist art and towards a new quality of formal control and cynical detachment which ran parallel to a fascination with technology and urban capitalism (America became in several senses a cultural lodestone during this period).[86]

The collision of these two very different artistic tendencies can be seen in the early, pre-Marxist theatre of Bertolt Brecht. In *Baal* (1922), for example, Brecht depicts a wandering poet whose hedonism and flouting of social convention deliberately parody the grand humanist aspirations of later Expressionist drama (at the literary dinner which opens the play, Baal gets outrageously drunk while a young lady reads her Expressionist verse: 'The new world / Exterminating the world of pain, / Island of rapturous humanity', etc.[87]). Baal rejects all moral constraints and dedicates himself to the pursuit of pleasure. Where Expressionist theatre had struggled with the deterministic thrust of narrative, Brecht's play, with its brief, loosely articulated scenes, enacts what one critic has called 'a dream of transience accepted, of conflict enjoyed and of contradiction sustained with equanimity'.[88] This 'acceptance' of contradiction produces a nihilistic tone in the early plays which couples a cynical realism with an indifference to political struggle. The best example is *Drums in the Night* (1922), in which the protagonist Kragler deliberately turns against revolution in order to win back his fiancée. Brecht later remarked that 'It seems just about the shabbiest possible solution, particularly as there is a faint suspicion of approval on the part of the author',[89] but the element of 'approval' is motivated by a deep distrust of communal relationships and the rhetoric in which they had been celebrated in much Expressionist drama.

In rejecting didactic and allegorical modes at this point in his career, Brecht was also formulating a scepticism about the tortured modes of 'deep' subjectivity which had recently dominated the stage. With *In the Jungle of Cities* (1924) and *A Man's a Man* (1927), his drama became harder and more 'objective', mingling elements from farce with a darkly pessimistic sense of oppression. In the 'jungle of the big city', supposedly Chicago in 1912, an 'inexplicable' struggle takes place between two men.[90] In his prologue to the play, Brecht warned his audience: 'Don't worry your heads about the motives for the fight, concentrate on the stakes.' As is clear from the play's opening scene, what is at stake is nothing less than the possibility of personal freedom: when the timber merchant Shlink meets the younger Garga, a bookseller, he requests his opinion of a book and then asks: 'Is that your personal opinion? I'll buy your opinion. Is ten dollars enough?' Shlink thus begins a series of challenges to Garga's sense of the inviolability of his personal life—if his literary opinions can be bought for cash, so perhaps can his private fantasies of a bohemian existence in Tahiti.

The 'fight' that ensues forges a powerful sadomasochistic bond between the two men, and Brecht seems to imply that, in contrast to the ineluctable and predetermined Oedipal struggles of the Expressionist theatre, the conflict between Garga and Shlink is *chosen* by them as the only authentic medium of social contact—at the very end of the play, after the death of Shlink, Garga concludes: 'It's a good thing to be alone. The chaos is spent. That was the best time.'[91] Here and in *A Man's a Man*, farce and dramatic irony destroy psychological depth, reducing social life to exploitative trickery and mechanical gestures. Brecht commented on the later play that 'Every single scene of the comedy is so far removed from the problem-play or the psychological type of play that any naive actor would be bound to be able to reproduce it simply from memory.'[92] So, in *A Man's a Man*, a completely new identity is forged for Galy Gay—as the Widow Begbeck puts it in her 'Interjection':

> Mister Brecht appends this item to the bill:
> You can do with a human being what you will.
> Take him apart like a car, rebuild him bit by bit—
> As you will see, he has nothing to lose by it.[93]

Brecht gave a similar account of the play in an interview in 1926: 'It's about a man being taken to pieces and rebuilt as someone else for a particular purpose.'[94] Brecht was on the verge of discovering Marxism, but the sardonic humour of *A Man's a Man* is already enough to make us feel that the tortured humanism of Expressionist theatre belongs to another time.

Notes

1. Rainer Maria Rilke, *The Notebook of Malte Laurids Brigge*, p. 3 Further references will be given in the text.
2. Thomas Mann, *Buddenbrooks*, p. 574. In 'Thomas Mann's "Buddenbrooks"' (1901), Rilke remarked that 'even a few years ago a modern writer would have found it sufficient to portray the last stages of this decline, the last scion, who dies of his own and his forefathers' illness' (quoted in Judith Ryan, *The Vanishing Subject*, p. 58).
3. The emotional and temporal complexity of this moment is registered similarly in Arthur Schnitzler's *The Road into the Open* (1908), p. 215: 'And it seemed to him like a vague and sweet dream, as if he lay as a boy at the feet of his mother, and this moment was already a memory, remote and painful, as he was experiencing it.'
4. Rainer Maria Rilke, *Rodin and Other Prose Pieces*, p. 15.
5. Ibid., p. 17.
6. Ibid., p. 46.
7. Ibid., p. 112.
8. Rainer Maria Rilke, *Letters on Cézanne*, pp. 32-3.
9. See also Rainer Maria Rilke, *Selected Letters*, p. 123: 'Looking is such a marvellous thing, of which we know but little; through it, we are turned absolutely towards the Outside, but when we are most of all so, things happen in us that have waited longingly to be observed, and while they reach completion in us, intact and curiously anonymous, *without our aid*,—their significance grows up in the object outside.'
10. 'Der Dichter', quoted in Patricia Pollock Brodsky, *Rainer Maria Rilke*, p. 103.
11. Rainer Maria Rilke, *Selected Poetry*, p. 135.
12. Ibid., p. 199.
13. Rilke, *Selected Letters*, p. 394.
14. Martin Heidegger, *Poetry, Language, Thought*, p. 113.
15. Wassily Kandinsky, *Concerning the Spiritual in Art*, p. 26.
16. Ulrich Weisstein, 'Introduction' to *Expressionism as an International Phenomenon*, p. 23.
17. Hermann Bahr, *Expressionism* (1916), p. 83.
18. Ibid., p. 85.
19. Kasimir Edschmid, 'Concerning Poetic Experience' (1917), quoted in Mardi Valgemae, *Accelerated Grimace*, p. 4.
20. Arnold Schönberg, 'The Relationship of the Text', in Wassily Kandinsky and Franz Marc (eds), *The Blaue Reiter Almanac*, p. 102.
21. See Ulrich Weisstein, 'Futurism in Germany and England: Two Flashes in the Pan?', p. 471; Lionel Richard, 'Futurisme et Expressionisme en

Allemagne', pp. 193-8; Hanne Bergius, 'Contribution à la réception du futurisme en Allemagne', in Giovanni Lista (ed.), *Marinetti et le futurisme*, pp. 171-4.

22. Herman George Scheffauer, *The New Vision in the German Arts* (1924), pp. 26-7.
23. August Stramm, 'Melancholy', trans. in Michael Hamburger (ed.), *German Poetry 1910-1975*, p. 9.
24. Ibid., p. 83.
25. Ibid., p. xxv.
26. See Michael Hamburger, *The Truth of Poetry*, pp. 176-80.
27. Karl Pinthus (ed.), *Menschheitsdämmerung*.
28. Georg Trakl, *Georg Trakl: A Profile*, ed. Frank Graziano, p. 59.
29. Quoted in Herbert Lindenberger, *Georg Trakl*, p. 42.
30. Georg Trakl, *Autumn Sonata: Selected Poems of Georg Trakl*, p. 57. See also the commentary in Francis Michael Sharp, *The Poet's Madness*, pp. 106-9.
31. *Georg Trakl: A Profile*, p. 31.
32. Quoted from 'Year', in Martin Heidegger, *On the Way to Language*, p. 176.
33. 'Dream and Derangement', *Georg Trakl: A Profile*, p. 80.
34. Heidegger, *On the Way to Language*, p. 177.
35. *Georg Trakl: A Profile*, p. 77.
36. Ibid., p. 52.
37. Noted in Jacques Derrida, 'Geschlecht: Sexual Difference, Ontological Difference', *A Derrida Reader*, p. 385.
38. Heidegger, *On the Way to Language*, pp. 195, 185. See also, Sharp, *The Poet's Madness*, p. 159, on 'Dream and Degeneration': 'The guiltless recognition of the tie between siblings undermines the incest taboo and anticipates the destruction of the family.'
39. For German texts of the play, see Oskar Kokoschka, *Dichtungen und Dramen*, pp. 33-51. The translation quoted is by Michael Hamburger, from Walter H. Sokel (ed.), *Anthology of German Expressionist Drama*, pp. 17-21. There are four versions of the play (hereafter referred to as *Murderer*); an account of textual variations is given in Horst Denkler, 'Die Druckfassungen der Dramen Oskar Kokoschkas', pp. 90-108. Carol Diethe, *Aspects of Distorted Sexual Attitudes in German Expressionist Drama*, pp. 130-5, divides the main variants to produce an 'A text' and a 'B text'. Sokel translates the 'A text', while the other available English version, in *Seven Expressionist Plays*, trans. J. M. Ritchie and H. F. Garten, pp. 25-32, uses the later 'B text'. Confusingly, neither Ritchie nor Sokel indicates which version is the one translated.
40. See Michael Patterson, *The Revolution in German Theatre*, pp. 194, 196.
41. Roger Cardinal, *Expressionism*, p. 96.
42. *Murderer*, in Sokel, *Anthology*, p. 20.
43. T. S. Eliot, *Selected Essays*, p. 145.
44. See Jacqueline Rose, *Sexuality in the Field of Vision*, pp. 123-40.
45. See Andrew Ross, *The Failure of Modernism*, p. 22.
46. Frank Whitford, *Oskar Kokoschka: A Life*, p. 37.
47. Peter Vergo and Yvonne Modlin, '*Murderer Hope of Women*', p. 31.
48. Quoted in ibid., p. 29.
49. Quoted in ibid., p. 31, n. 61.
50. Oskar Kokoschka, *My Life*, p. 26.
51. Ibid., pp. 26, 27.
52. Nietzsche's description of the theme of Strindberg's *The Father*, quoted in Raymond Williams, *The Politics of Modernism*, p. 50.
53. J. M. Ritchie, *German Expressionist Drama*, p. 45.
54. Otto Weininger, *Sex and Character*, p. 92; further references will be given in the text. This idea is a recurrent one in the obsessive preoccupation with prostitution in German literature; in Wedekind's *Pandora's Box* (1904), for example, it is said of Lulu that 'she can't make a living out of love because love is her life'.
55. See Jacques Le Rider, *Le Cas Otto Weininger*, p. 221.
56. See Jacques Le Rider, 'Modernisme-Féminisme/Modernité-Virilité', pp. 5-20.
57. Oskar Kokoschka, 'On the Nature of Visions', in V. H. Miesel (ed.), *Voices of German Expressionism*, p. 98. Further references will be given in the text.
58. Christine Buci-Glucksman, *La Raison baroque*, p. 214. See also, the discussion of woman as commodity in Wedekind's drama in Gail Finney, *Women in Modern Drama*, pp. 79-101.

59. Paul Klee, *On Modern Art*, p. 45.
60. Strindberg's *Stationen* are 'stages in the central character's journey toward spiritual renewal' (Henry L. Schvey, *Oskar Kokoschka*, p. 24).
61. August Strindberg, *The Plays*, vol. 2, p. 555. Further references will be given in the text.
62. See Sigmund Freud, 'The Unconscious' (1915), *Pelican Freud Library*, vol. 11, pp. 190-1.
63. Noted by Vergo and Modlin, and by Donald E. Gordon, 'Oskar Kokoschka and the Visionary Tradition', in Gerald Chappel and Hans H. Schulte (eds), *The Turn of the Century*, pp. 23-52.
64. See, for example, Le Rider, *Le Cas Otto Weininger*, p. 127, and the discussion of the Cosmic Circle in Martin Green, *The Von Richthofen Sisters*.
65. J. J. Bachofen, *Myth, Religion, and Mother Right*, p. 93.
66. Ibid., p. 109.
67. Sokel, *Anthology*, p. 21. In the 'B text' the references to vampirism disappear and the Woman claims to be the Man's wife.
68. Jacques Derrida, *Writing and Difference*, p. 239. Further references will be given in the text.
69. On Kandinsky's other related experiments, see Peg Weiss, *Kandinsky and Munich*, p. 92. The translation of *The Yellow Sound* used here is from the *Blaue Reiter Almanac*, pp. 207-25.
70. *Blaue Reiter Almanac*, p. 147.
71. Ibid., p. 194, n. 4.
72. Ibid., p. 205.
73. Ibid., p. 206.
74. Paul Vogt, *The Blue Rider*, p. 81. Peg Weiss, *Kandinsky and Munich*, p. 99, notes the importance of the Shadow-play theatre (founded in 1907) in suggesting 'mystical or psychic spaces beyond the limits of conventional perspective'. The idea of an alternative spatial dimension might be compared with Robert Delaunay's concept of 'depth', an important reference point for early Expressionist art.
75. See André Green, *The Tragic Effect*, p. 16.
76. Sokel, *Anthology*, p. xvi, remarks that 'Expressionist drama is theme-centered rather than plot- or conflict-centered', and Carl E. Schorske, 'Generational Conflict and Social Change', in Gerald Chapple and Hans H. Schulte (eds), *The Turn of the Century*, p. 428, concludes that 'Musil and the Expressionist generation totally dismissed the Oedipal problem by subsuming it under a historical reality proclaimed dead.'
77. Quoted in Peter Szondi, *Theory of the Modern Drama*, p. 65.
78. Richard Sheppard, 'Unholy Families', p. 363. Further references will be given in the text.
79. Quoted in Ritchie, *German Expressionist Drama*, p. 70.
80. On dramatic technique, see, for example, Mel Gordon, 'German Expressionist Acting', pp. 34-50.
81. Georg Kaiser, *Five Plays*, pp. 168-9.
82. Peter Gay, *Weimar Culture*, pp. 102-18.
83. Ernst Toller, *Seven Plays*, p. 102.
84. Ernst Toller, 'My Works', p. 222; *Masses and Man* (1920), in *Seven Plays*, p. 150.
85. Georg Lukács, 'Expressionism: Its Significance and Decline' (1934), in *Essays on Realism*, p. 110.
86. For an account of the *Neue Sachlichkeit*, see John Willett, *The New Sobriety*.
87. Brecht, *Baal*, in *Collected Plays*, vol. 1, 6.
88. Ronald Speirs, *Brecht's Early Plays*, p. 20.
89. Bertolt Brecht, *Collected Plays*, vol. 1, p. 406.
90. Ibid., vol. 1, p. 118.
91. Ibid., vol. 1, p. 178.
92. Quoted in Ronald Speirs, *Brecht's Early Plays*, p. 131. As Peter Brooker notes in *Bertolt Brecht*, p. 110, Brecht's poetry during the twenties is also much concerned with 'the theme of the loss of self'.
93. Bertolt Brecht, *A Man's a Man*, in *Seven Plays*, p. 103.
94. Quoted in Willett, *The New Sobriety*, p. 153.

List of Abbreviations

AA Antonin Artaud, *Selected Writings*, ed. Susan Sontag (Berkeley and Los Angeles: University of California Press, 1988).

AOA Apollinaire on Art: Essays and Reviews, 1902-1918, ed. Leroy C. Breunig (New York: Viking Press, 1972).

BSW Baudelaire: Selected Writings on Art and Artists, trans. P. E. Charvet (Harmondsworth: Penguin Books, 1972).

F Marinetti: Selected Writings, trans. R. W. Flint (London: Secker & Warburg, 1972).

FM Futurist Manifestos, ed. Umbro Apollonio (London: Thames and Hudson, 1973).

I William Carlos Williams, *Imaginations,* ed. Webster Schott (New York: New Directions, 1971).

LMN Gertrude Stein, *Look at Me Now and Here I Am: Writings and Lectures 1909-45,* ed. Patricia Meyerowitz (Harmondsworth: Penguin Books, 1971).

MFT Modern French Theater: The Avant-Garde, Dada and Surrealism, trans. George Wellwarth and Michael Benedikt (New York: Dutton, 1966).

MS André Breton, *Manifestos of Surrealism,* trans. Richard Seaver and Helen R. Lane (Ann Arbor: University of Michigan Press, 1972).

MSP Mallarmé: Selected Prose Poems, Essays, and Letters, trans. Bradford Cook (Baltimore: Johns Hopkins University Press, 1956).

NS Pierre Reverdy, *Nord-Sud, Self-Defence et autres écrits sur l'art et la poésie (1917-1926)* (Paris: Flammarion, 1975).

NT Ezra Pound and Ernest Fenollosa, *The Classic Noh Theatre of Japan* (New York: New Directions, 1959).

PL Poems of Jules Laforgue, trans. Peter Dale (London: Anvil Press, 1986).

RFM Russian Futurism through its Manifestos, 1912-1928, trans. Anna Lawton and Herbert Eagle (Ithaca and London: Cornell University Press, 1988).

RP Arthur Rimbaud: Collected Poems, trans. Oliver Bernard (Harmondsworth: Penguin Books, 1987).

THEMES IN LITERARY EXPRESSIONISM

Egbert Krispyn (essay date 1964)

SOURCE: Krispyn, Egbert. "The Pattern of Pathos." In *Style and Society in German Literary Expressionism,* pp. 44-52. Gainesville: University of Florida Press, 1964.

[*In the following excerpt, Krispyn examines the trait of pathos, or the desire to awaken an emotional response in the reader, as one of the main characteristics of Expressionist literature.*]

The definition of the three main types of expressionist writing is inadequate for evaluating how closely work of other periods may be stylistically related to expressionism. A criterion must be sought which is independent of such themes and topics as hatred of Wilhelmian Germany or faith in a communist paradise. The negativistic, socio-political, and anarchic-humanistic subdivisions in the body of expressionist writing do, to be sure, represent abstractions from the multifarious ways in which the authors gave literary expression to their emotions and opinions concerning the human condition. Nevertheless, the literary categories thus obtained are still largely determined by the substance of the texts concerned, and are therefore still closely linked to the authors' ideas and intentions.

Now the purely structural elements in the definitions of the three variants of expressionism must be abstracted from those involving the substance, and a common denominator found. In the foregoing, the knowledge that the expressionists' world view conformed to one of three types helped to reduce the almost unlimited diversity of expressionist writing to three basic patterns. Similarly the socio-psychological facts serve to illuminate the question of the collective stylistic formula which combines the essential structural features of the three variants of expressionism. The different attitudes of mind of the expressionists were variants of one fundamental, Nietzsche-influenced reaction to their outsidership. They wanted to overcome their isolation, at the same time redeeming mankind by destroying the old order and establishing a better mode of life. They might conceive the objects of their hatred and hope in individual, social, or cosmic terms, but no matter in what particular embodiment or shape the social realities and ideals were perceived by the individual, he always rejected something and longed for something else.

Couched in these purposely vague terms, the basic mental outlook can be used to reconstruct the basic expressionist stylistic principle which unifies the three corresponding kinds of writing. This purely structural common denominator of all literature traditionally and unambiguously classed as expressionist is thus revealed to lie in its antithetic character. This antithesis, moreover, is not static, but dynamic, in the sense that the tension between the poles must inevitably lead to the destruction of one, while the other becomes absolute. The structure of expressionist writing thus indicates that the situation it deals with is not stable, but that a force is at work which will resolve the existing polarity. The given antithesis is, however, not going to disappear in a Hegelian synthesis of the opposing poles, but in the complete ascendancy of one pole over the other.

Apart from these characteristics, all expressionist literature, as has been pointed out, is further marked by a rhetorical attitude. Although the latter cannot be satisfactorily reduced to specific linguistic and stylistic usages, nevertheless it must in some way be evident in the structure of the works.

Herewith it becomes possible to identify three fundamental structural aspects, which together constitute a stylistic criterion of literary expressionism. *The expressionist style is antithetic, dynamic, and rhetorical.* For the purpose of placing expressionism in a wider perspective, it is of interest to determine whether the combination of the structural elements of antithesis, dynamism, and rhetoric can be translated into the traditional terminology of poetics. It seems opportune to approach this question by investigating the style of expressionism to see whether it corresponds to the stylistic concept of pathos. The word "pathos" played a very prominent part in the terminology of the expressionists themselves. Thus Rudolf Leonhard in 1916 published an essay *Vom Pathos*; Franz Werfel's first collection of poetry *Der Weltfreund* includes a poem entitled *An mein Pathos*; the Neue Club established in the year 1911 the Neopathetische Cabaret in which a new pathos was proclaimed; and in 1913 Paul Zech and others started publishing a periodical called *Das Neue Pathos,* for which Stefan Zweig wrote a declaration of editorial principles under the same title.

Subsequent commentators have also used this word without, however, defining it adequately. Still, its frequent occurrence in secondary sources does reveal a general, if imprecise, awareness of the movement's distinguishing stylistic traits. In this context Fritz Martini may be mentioned, for he explicitly ascribes an exalted pathos to all expressionistic writing.[1] Wolfgang Paulsen also writes about pathos and "eine Art neuer Pathetik" as characteristic elements of expressionist literature.[2] Wilhelmina Stuyver calls pathos the "Lebensgrundstimmung . . . der Ausdruckskünstler."[3] Of the individual authors, to give some examples, such dissimilar figures as Becher, Rubiner, Hasenclever, Heym, and Werfel are credited with pathos.[4]

In order to determine whether this frequently used term is really applicable to the common, unifying stylistic qualities of the writings usually classified as expressionistic, it is necessary—against the custom which has hitherto prevailed in secondary works on this subject—to define its meaning objectively.

In the history of German literature the word "pathos" occurs in several contexts. It may refer to the moral-ethical substance of a work. This is the view represented by Schiller, who stressed that pathos illuminates the spiritual freedom of mankind by demonstrating the superiority of reason (Vernunft) over nature. Man must, through his intellect, conquer the sorrows to which as a sentient creature he is subjected. The essence of Schillerian pathos is that the will successfully resists the emotions. "Das *Sinnenwesen* muss tief und heftig *leiden*; Pathos muss da sein, damit das Vernunftwesen seine Unabhängigkeit kundtun und sich handelnd darstellen könne."[5]

It is clear that for most expressionists pathos in this sense does not play any role. In Heym's case, for instance, there is no question of humanity having any spiritual freedom: it is absolutely subjected to nature, and must defenselessly suffer everything fate inflicts on it. In the world of Heym's writings, man invariably suffers, but, lacking all will power or intellect, he has to endure passively, thereby manifesting his utter helplessness in the face of forces beyond his control.

This amounts to a complete reversal of Schiller's ideas. No other expressionist appears to conform to them either. In no case is there any suggestion that mankind could overcome its sufferings by voluntarily accepting them. The cause of its sorrow—usually specified as the social organization—has to be removed or eliminated before happiness can be found.

If pathos in Schiller's moral-ethical sense is thus irreconcilable with the expressionists' outlook on life, this may be at least partly due to their reaction to one specific aspect of their upbringing. It has been pointed out that the older generations exploited the educational process as a means of defending the status quo against the rebellious tendencies of their children. Since these conservative tendencies were not justifiable from any rational viewpoint, they were reinforced by hollow idealism. Besides the classical authors of antiquity, Schiller was most intensively misused to distort the world image of youth in the interest of the Establishment. The result was that these adolescents, insofar as they were aware of the falsity of the officially propounded views, grew up with a profound mistrust of everything idealistic. This skepticism extended, of course, to the typically idealistic concept of moral freedom and its main embodiment in the writings of Friedrich Schiller.[6]

In this way the inflation of spurious idealism in the education and the public moral codex of Wilhelmian Germany tended to devaluate also the worthwhile aspects of this attitude of mind. The younger intellectuals, from whom the expressionists were recruited, had therewith inevitably become impervious to the idealistic side of the moral-ethical pathos concept. It is symptomatic that Kurt Hiller in the opening address of the Neopathetische Cabaret attacked the "geschmähte Schillerische" pathos.[7]

There is, however, a different side to pathos, which in Schiller's theoretical writing on the subject fails to receive its due attention. Schiller's bias towards the moral-ethical facet of pathos was a consequence of his philosophical position. As a Kantian thinker—his differences with the Königsberg philosopher are not relevant in the present context—his central idea was the autonomy of the human mind. It was this preoccupation which inevitably caused him to interpret pathos in terms of mankind's capacity for overcoming the suffering imposed by nature through a morally positive, voluntary acceptance of it. The framework in which man's freedom as a rational being manifested itself was the existing discrepancy between reality and ideal, the static presentation of which thus formed an essential part of pathos in Schiller's sense.

His views in this respect are most clearly expressed when he classifies pathos as a variant of satire, and defines the latter as the style which has for a subject the representation of the disparity of actuality and ideal.[8] Though this approach was entirely consistent with Schiller's philosophical tenets, it seems to be somewhat too narrow to do full justice to the historically evolved meaning of the term "pathos." Ernst Elster therefore disagrees with Schiller and makes the point that in pathos the creative mind is not directed towards the incompatibility of reality and ideal, but towards the idea itself, in whose future realization or approximation the writer believes.[9]

Emil Staiger represents a similar view, which in his formulation reveals itself to be much less concerned with the substance of the literature concerned than Schiller's pathos-concept. "Es ist eine unmittelbare Bewegung, die sich selbst in ihrer Herkunft und Richtung nicht zu verstehen braucht. Im Unterschied zur lyrischen Bewegung aber hat sie beides, eine Herkunft und ein Ziel."[10] The definition of this style as a "direct movement" between two unspecified poles refers to the identical structural characteristics which in the foregoing pages, with reference to expressionism, were designated as antithesis and dynamism.

The "pathetic" artist has to convey his own dynamic impulse to his public, if ever the antithesis is to be resolved—and those whose resistance cannot be turned into cooperation through rhetorical persuasion must be destroyed so as not to endanger progress. This is also recognized by Staiger: "Der Dichter tut [dem Publikum] Gewalt an; und er will ihm Gewalt antun. Damit ist bereits gesagt, dass die pathetische Rede, abermals im Gegensatz zur lyrischen Sprache, ein Gegenüber voraussetzt, ein Gegenüber aber, das sie nicht, wie die epische, anerkennt, sondern aufzuheben trachtet, sei es so, dass der Redner den Hörer gewinnt, oder so, dass der Hörer von der Gewalt der Rede vernichtet wird."[11]

Thus Emil Staiger's remarks confirm that pathos in the traditional sense is defined by the same three qualities of antithesis, dynamism, and rhetoric that were found in the preceding pages to constitute the common denominator of expressionist style. In other words, *the stylistic criterion of expressionism can be designated as pathos.*

With this conclusion, the aim of defining the structural pattern of expressionist literature in terms derived from the theory of poetics has been achieved.

. . . . .

The complexity of the expressionist movement and the diversity of its literary manifestations prohibited the formulation of a definition which fixes technical or stylistic details. To find a unifying element of style it was necessary to resort to abstraction and generalization of the literary data. The lowest common denominator of the non-substantial characteristics of expressionist writing was found to pertain to the level of general structural patterns. Thus the criterion of expressionist style inevitably lacks more specific factors than those contained in the notions of antithesis, dynamism, and rhetoric, in the meaning of these terms developed in the preceding pages. This circumstance naturally affects the precision and exclusiveness of the definition which may, and does in fact, also apply to certain other works. The practical usefulness is not, however, affected by this, because it does not fit the literature of any period close enough in time to the expressionist era to cause any confusion. It may in this context be reiterated that the present study approaches the problem under discussion from a practical viewpoint. The stylistic definition of expressionism now arrived at is not intended to be "der Weisheit letzter Schluss" or a substitute for common sense. No matter how perfectly it may apply to a certain text, a work written by Goethe or one dating from the seventeenth century should not be regarded as expressionist.

But the broadness of the definition does not only leave its pragmatic value unimpaired; the broadness is actually an advantage. The reduction of expressionism to a general structural pattern, described in terms flexible enough to be applicable to works of other centuries dealing with different topics, opens up a historical perspective. The definition which, because of its abstract character, could be interpreted in terms of traditional poetic theory, therewith not only yields a convenient summarizing "label," but also illuminates certain aspects of the relationship between expressionism and the German literary heritage. It can serve, for instance, to reduce to correct proportions the affiliation between expressionism and baroque, which has been overemphasized by such commentators as Ferdinand Josef Schneider and Wolfgang Paulsen. The latter in particular continually equates the two movements and calls expressionism an "Aufleben der Barockkunst des 17. Jahrhunderts."[12]

On the basis of the foregoing findings concerning the substance and structure of expressionism, both it and the baroque can be classified as temporally defined realizations of the abstract stylistic conception of pathos. What is denoted by the term "baroque" is the unique form, determined by a unique complex of political, sociological, psychological, and literary-historical factors, in which pathos was embodied during the seventeenth century. The baroque employs pathos to deal with the relationship between man and God. Expressionism, on the other hand, is a realization of the stylistic principle of pathos which, shaped by the conditions prevailing in Wilhelmian Germany, is concerned primarily with the relations between man and man.

The recognition of traditional pathos as the stylistic substratum of expressionist writing also throws some light on certain developments and differences within the movement. Since pathos aims at affecting the audience, it is a point of some interest in what way and through which human faculties this is to be achieved. In traditional pathos the answer to this question is quite clear: the audience is to be swayed or shattered *via* its emotional susceptibility. This appears from Willi Flemming's interpretation of a remark by Martin Opitz on the highly "pathetic" baroque tragedy. "Der barocke Tragiker will sein Publikum aufwühlen und überwältigen. Bezeichnend schreibt Opitz in der Trostschrift: 'Ein grosses Betrübnis lässt sich von sanften Worten nicht abweisen: Es will mit *Kräfften* überwunden seyn / und ist wie eine Nessel / welche, wann man sie stark angreifft nachgiebt / hergegen wann man gelinde mit ihr umbgeht zu brennen pflegt.' Wegen dieser seiner Kunsttendenz zielt der Dramatiker nicht auf die kühlen Bezirke des Hirns, sondern auf die warmen Ströme des Gefühles, ja der Leidenschaft, kurz: sein Drama ruht auf der Schicht des Emotionalen."[13]

Flemming's opinion that the effect of pathos was the excitation of the passions and emotions rather than the stimulation of the intellect is confirmed by other commentators. Emil Staiger defines pathos as a mode of expression which "die Leidenschaften erregt."[14] Heinrich Wölfflin declares that the baroque "will packen mit der Gewalt des Affekts, unmittelbar, überwältigend. Was er gibt, ist nicht gleichmässige Belebung, sondern Aufregung, Ekstase, Berauschung."[15] Among the seventeenth century authorities on poetics the same insight into the nature of the baroque style prevailed; Augustus Buchner saw it as the task of the poet to induce in the reader a "beständige Bewegung durch Bewunderung."[16]

Whereas rhetorical pathos in the traditional sense thus aims at affecting the public by stirring its passions, the expressionist movement in some of its manifestations deviated slightly from the tradition in this particular aspect of "pathetic" style. Expressionism underwent a development whose early phases are represented by the views on this subject prevailing in the Neue Club. These were expounded by Erwin Loewenson, on the occasion of the first performance of the Neopathetische Cabaret, in a manifesto which has remained unpublished; however, its substance can be deduced from later essays by its author.[17]

According to Loewenson, mankind should recognize the integral essence of the world behind the apparent chaos. This mystic aim could only be achieved if all spiritual forces were engaged harmoniously in the process of living. The decisive part in the propagation of this doctrine was assigned to the writers who, consciously or unconsciously, should express it in their works. Loewenson's ideas, which represented those of the majority of the Neue Club members, had been substantially influenced by the impression which the personality and physical appearance of Georg Heym had made on them. Even before Heym joined their society, around New Year, 1910, they had subscribed to a vitalistic-metaphysical conception of life and art. The intuitive force which they claimed to discern in Heym's personality as well as in his work seemed to confirm their ideas, and in this way caused them to attempt to expand their thoughts into a comprehensive philosophical system.

The president of the club, Kurt Hiller, and a few others had too cerebral an attitude to be able to endorse these views, and this difference of opinion contributed to the schism in the Neue Club in the spring of 1911. Yet Hiller was in substantial agreement with Erwin Loewenson about the point which in the present context is the most vital one. For him, too, pathos concerned the entire personality or the totality of the mental faculties. He succinctly defined it as "erhöhte psychische Temperatur."[18]

This deviation in the Neue Club from the orthodox conception of pathos as an excitement of the passions only, was probably connected with the influence of the French symbolists. It is significant that Heym greatly admired Baudelaire, whom he felt akin to and whom he ranked first among his literary gods.[19] It is particularly important to note that Baudelaire absorbed the poetic theories of Edgar Allan Poe and partly translated his essays into French. In this way the American's theses became known in Germany.[20] Poe maintained that the effect of a poem should be an "intensive and pure elevation of the soul and not of intellect or heart." The satisfaction of the rational faculties and the appeal to the heart could, of course, also be introduced in a poem, but only in "proper subservience to the predominant aim" of elevating the soul.[21] Poe's theory remains somewhat obscure because it is not entirely clear what he meant by an elevation of the soul. Hugo Friedrich interprets it as "eine umfassende Gestimmtheit."[22] This interpretation accentuates the similarity between the ideas of Poe which were transmitted by Beaudelaire and the attitude exemplified by Loewenson's philosophy.

Apart from him and his fellow members of the early and short-lived Neue Club, however, the expressionists, in agreement with the orthodox "pathetic" attitude on this point, chose to concentrate on stirring the passions of their public. This approach was explicitly represented by the periodical *Das Neue Pathos* which Paul Zech founded in 1913. In the second issue Stefan Zweig published a salient essay which left no doubt about the orthodoxy of the pathos promoted by this journal. "Wieder wie einst scheint heute der lyrische Dichter befähigt, wenn nicht der geistige Führer der Zeit, so doch der Bändiger und Erreger ihrer Leidenschaften zu werden, der Rhapsode, der Anrufende, Befeuernde, der Entfachende des heiligen Feuers: der Energie."[23] Rudolf Leonhard expressed a similar traditional conception of pathos when he concisely defined it as the "leidenschaftliche Bewusstheit eines Zustands."[24]

Notes

1. *Was war Expressionismus?* p. 33.

2. *Expressionismus und Aktivismus. Eine typologische Untersuchung* (Bern, 1935).

3. *Die deutsche expressionistische Dichtung im Lichte der Philosophie der Gegenwart* (Amsterdam, 1939), p. 133.

4. See, respectively, Friedmann and Mann, pp. 183, 67, 96; Fritz Martini, *Deutsche Literaturgeschichte*, p. 515; Friedmann and Mann, p. 96.

5. Schiller, "Über das Pathetische," *Sämtliche Werke*, V (München, 1959), 512.

6. Cf. Friedrich Kummer, *Deutsche Literaturgeschichte des 19. und 20. Jahrhunderts*, 17-20th eds. (Dresden, 1924), I, 61: "Nicht zum wenigsten hat auch jahrzehntelang die deutsche Schule mit ihren entsetzlichen Erklärungen und Zergliederungen Schillerscher Balladen und Dramen die Jugend zum Widerspruch förmlich gezwungen."

7. *Die Weisheit der Langenweile*, Vol. I, p. 238.

8. Cf. Ernst Elster, *Prinzipien der Literaturwissenschaft*, Vol. II: *Stilistik* (Halle a/S, 1911), p. 48.

9. Elster, pp. 48, 51.

10. *Grundbegriffe der Poetik*, 2nd ed. (Zürich, 1951), p. 155.

11. *Ibid.*, p. 153.

12. Schneider, *Der expressive Mensch*, pp. 59-60; Paulsen, *Expressionismus und Aktivismus*, p. 132.

13. Flemming, *Barockdrama, Deutsche Literatur in Entwicklungsreihen, Reihe Barock*, Vol. I (Leipzig, 1930), p. 16.

14. *Grundbegriffe der Poetik*, p. 151.

15. Quoted in Friedmann and Mann, p. 21.

16. Quoted in De Boor and Newald, *Geschichte der deutschen Literatur*, V (München, 1951), 21.

17. "Bemerkungen über das 'Neopathos'" in Georg Heym, *Gesammelte Gedichte*, ed. Carl Seelig, pp. 243 ff; "Jakob van Hoddis. Erinnerungen mit Lebensdaten," in Jakob van Hoddis, *Weltende. Gesammelte Gedichte*, ed. Paul Pörtner (Zürich, 1958), pp. 96 ff; *Georg Heym oder vom Geist des Schicksals* (Hamburg, München, 1962).

18. *Die Weisheit der Langenweile*, I, 237.

19. See his diary entry of 11.5.1910.

20. See Otto Pick's article on the German translation of Baudelaire's works, in *Die Aktion*, May 1, 1912.

21. Poe, "The Philosophy of Composition," in *The Complete Works*, (New York, 1902), I, 292-93.

22. *Die Struktur der modernen Lyrik* (Hamburg, 1956), p. 26.

23. Quoted on p. 47 of Catalogue No. 7 *Expressionismus. Literatur und Kunst 1910-1923* of the Schiller-Nationalmuseum, Marbach a.N.

24. *Vom Pathos. Aus Aeonen des Fegefeuers* (Berlin, 1916), quoted by Paul Pörtner, *Literaturrevolution 1910-1925. Dokumente. Manifeste. Programme.* Vol. I: *Zur Aesthetik und Poetik*, Vol. XIII in "die mainzer reihe" (Neuwied, 1960), p. 143.

Raymond Furness (essay date 1993)

SOURCE: Furness, Raymond. "The Religious Element in Expressionist Theatre." In *Expressionism Reassessed*, edited by Shulamith Behr, David Fanning, and Douglas Jarman, pp. 163-73. Manchester, England: Manchester University Press, 1993.

[*In the following essay, Furness presents an overview of Expressionist drama and its treatment of religion, noting that its main theme may be summed up as "the revolt of the spirit against reality."*]

In Reinhard Sorge's *The Beggar*, a play written in 1910 and performed some five years later, a discussion between various *literati* in the obligatory coffee-house turns upon a recent dramatic work which is regarded as trivial, typical of an age whose writers lack, 'the intense confirmation from the Beyond' and 'the Spiritual'; the third critic puts forward the following categorical statement: 'We are waiting for someone to interpret our destiny anew—this is a dramatist whom I would call truly great. Our Haupt-Mann, you see, is impressive as an artist, but limited as a prophet.'[1] What is needed, the critic believes, is one to interpret the symbols, a seer and prophet, instrument of mantological divination. And the protagonist of this play, 'the Poet' himself, as incarnation of pure feeling, will stride through various stations and experiences in his attempt to speak through symbols of eternity: imperious visions will alternate with fervent humiliation in this quest. We have in this exemplary play the rejection of art as mimesis or as entertainment and a fusion of art and theology, a heady synthesis indeed, made even more perfervid when millennial utopias are added.

It will be my intention to look at certain expressionist plays in an attempt to understand the predilection of authors commonly accepted as having been Expressionists at some time in their lives for topoi, symbols, figures and situations which have a religious dimension: whatever else Expressionism was, it was not such a radical break with the past as has hitherto been suggested, and it frequently betrays symbolist, neo-romantic or indeed romantic elements. With hindsight it may appear that it was naturalism which was a jejune *impasse*: with its insistence upon versimilitude, plausibility and tactile impressionism it could not for long satisfy those who sought to portray transcendental realities, the inner life, the visionary and the ecstatic. Heirs to the Romantics the Expressionists may be, not necessarily neurotic and terminally violent as a recent study has argued,[2] but certainly intense, subjective and fervent. We remember that John Willett's book on Expressionism had as its cover a detail from Matthias Grünewald's *Crucifixion*:[3] the twisted agony of distortion and the intensity of religious expressiveness are here an appropriate emblem.

A good starting point for discussion would be the revival of mysticism in the late nineteenth century, the rejection of materialism and of a one-sided, mechanistic portrayal of the universe. Wagner's *Parsifal* is paradigmatic here, a work whose sultry religiosity appealed greatly to the decadents but which prepared the way for the consecration plays of Stefan George (*The Acceptance into the Order*, for example), the mystery of plays of Rudolf Steiner (*The Portals of Consecration*, 1907; *The Testing of the Soul*, 1911; *The Guardian of the Door*, 1912; and *The Soul's Awakening*, all performed in Munich) and the soul-dramas of a writer like Alfred Mombert (*Aeon*). Wagner's essay 'Religion und Kunst', published in the *Bayreuther Blätter* in October 1880 argued that it was the duty of art to come to the rescue of religion when the latter had ceased to have meaning for the populace, since art was able, through the manipulation of redolent symbols, to communicate an aura of mystery and wonder. Hermann Bahr's acute analysis of modernism in the *Studies towards a Critique of Modernism*, 1894, stressed above all the 'powerful movement away from superficial, crude naturalism' and the 'febrile search for the mystical', the need to 'exprimer l'inexprimable' and 'saisir l'insaisissable': the new writers were 'not by chance Wagnerians'.[4] The movement towards what may be called neo-romanticism is transparent here, but our concern is with Expressionism: the links, however, are close, and writers not normally associated with the latter movement may well have prepared the way (we think of Hofmannsthal's *Everyman*) for the more strident eructations to follow. The theatre as temple—this *Bayreuth-Idee* was adumbrated in *The Beggar*—or as podium for the proclamation of some kind of 'world-redemptive vision' (political? ideological?) would increasingly usurp the theatre as mere representation or recreation. This will become manifestly apparent.

We have mentioned Wagner; Nietzsche is of equal importance here. Sorge's fusion of visionary fervour and ruthless idealism is reminiscent of the work of Ludwig Derleth. Like Derleth he was overwhelmed by Nietzsche's ecstatic dithyrambs and composed his own *Zarathustra* in 1911, a dramatic 'impression' in which the writer arrogates to himself the right to create and destroy at will. (*Odysseus,* a 'dramatische Phantasie' of the same year, is dedicated to 'the prophet of the Eternal Recurrence, Friedrich Nietzsche'.) Another 'dramatische Dichtung', *Antichrist,* quotes Nietzsche's last utterance as a motto: 'Do you understand me? Dionysus against the crucified'. *Guntwar, a Becoming,* also of 1911, continues the portrayal of mystical *Entselbstung* (voiding of self) combined with a Nietzschean arrogance—this fusion of Zarathustra and Christ is a concept which fascinated many German writers at this time and is even attempted by the eponymous hero of Joseph Goebbels's novel *Michael*. It may be argued that any cosmogony or mythopoeic vision composed after Nietzsche's masterpiece must needs have felt the centripetal pull of that powerful creation; such was the force of Nietzsche's language that his imagery was indelibly imprinted upon the poetry of the following three decades. The declamatory and pseudo-biblical style of *Also sprach Zarathustra* will reverberate through literature and music before the First World War—the god-destroyer is also the god-seeker, and German expressionist theatre will provide many examples of vatic afflatus, frequently febrile. Sorge believed there was something Christ-like about Nietzsche's agony despite the latter's furious tirades against orthodox Christianity; to those starved of symbols and lacking the sustaining power of religious faith Nietzsche's own fusion of poetry, myth and cosmic vision offered a stimulating and awe-inspiring substitute. Dionysus-Christ-Zarathustra uplifted and challenged the imagination of many who found no fulfilment in the contemplation of drab social issues. After *The Beggar* Sorge's Catholicism became paramount: *The Birth of the Soul* and *Metanoeite* (the latter term being taken from Matthew, Chapter Three, verses 1-2 and meaning 'repent ye') are works of Christian apologetics couched in the form of Christian dialogues. Sorge prepared himself for the priesthood, but was killed at the battle of the Somme in 1916.

Important for Sorge and for many other expressionist playwrights was the influence of Strindberg. Strindberg had undergone a crisis when living alone in Paris and occupied himself with alchemical and occult studies: this crisis is described in *Inferno,* 1897. The period of reorientation which ensued, and the study of Swedenborg (the metaphysical play *Beyond* by Hasenclever, written in 1919, also owes much to the Swedish mystic) found expression in the plays *Advent,* 1899, *Easter,* 1900, and above all *To Damascus,* 1898-1901; subsequent plays which portray a mystical process of self-discovery include *Ghost Sonata,* 1907, and *The Great Highway,* 1909. I have written elsewhere of Strindberg's great importance in any enquiry into the roots of the anti-naturalistic tendency in the theatre;[5] between 1913 and 1915 there were one thousand and thirty-five performances of twenty-four different plays by Strindberg in Germany alone, and it was in Germany that Strindberg's expressionistic direction was to be developed and modified. *To Damascus* portrays the soul's struggle to find and transcend itself, the 'characters' being mere emanations from that soul, symbolising powers with whom the Unknown One is in combat. The canons of naturalism—the demand for plausibility and inner logic—are totally ignored, and an intense subjectivity prevails. The beggar, the woman, the doctor and the madman all represent aspects of the Unknown One's psyche, and they move before him on his journey of self-exploration. They can be called symbols—the beggar is that degradation which the protagonist fears and yet which is necessary for his rebirth; he is the embodiment of the Unknown One's repressed thoughts, the reminder of the possibility of an existence towards which the hero must move (we find a similar process in the scene with the penitents at the end of Georg Kaiser's *From Morning till Midnight*). The woman would be the link with life, a fusion of the sexual and the sublime which torments and inspires; the doctor represents the Unknown One's arrogance and pride (he is, incidentally, based upon Nietzsche, with whom Strindberg had briefly corresponded at the time of the former's mental collapse).

The concept of life as a great highway (Strindberg's *Stora Landsvagen*), along which a wanderer passes through various stages of martyrdom, represents frequently a secularised mystery-play, and Georg Kaiser comes forcibly to mind, a playwright whose work dominated the German theatre between the years 1917 and 1923. In Kaiser the idea of social reform is only of secondary importance—a Nietzschean self-overcoming, a spiritual regeneration must come first before society can be changed. *The Citizens of Calais* was first performed at the Neues Theater, Frankfurt am Main, in January 1917. This closely-argued condemnation of war culminates in a final tableau which, assisted by the lighting, emphasises the Christ-like sublimity of the moral victor and points at resurrection and ascension. Kaiser's most famous play, *From Morning till Midnight,* received its première three months later in Munich. It is a *Stationendrama* à la Strindberg, and with each 'station' the grotesque element becomes increasingly apparent. Symbols of death accompany the bank-clerk's frenzied course; betrayed by the Salvation Army girl he shoots himself before a crucifix, and his dying words sound like 'Ecce Homo'. The blasts on the trumpet which intersperse his final peroration seem to herald a last judgement. In *Hell Way Earth,* which was put on simultaneously in Berlin and Munich on 5 December 1919, we find a *Spazierer* (Wanderer) who passes through the various stages of capitalist society to found a new utopia; a bridge is crossed and the people, bathed in 'a radiant light', are transfigured in a luminous effulgence. At this point in Kaiser's work there is much talk of 'Transformation', 'Breakthrough', 'Renewal', 'Conversion', 'Awakening': the New Man, whatever else he may be, is a vision of some sort of spiritual regeneration, diffuse but intense. Kaiser is not alone here—the work of Pär Lagerkvist (*The Difficult Hour,* 1918, and *The Secret of Heaven,* 1919) shares a kindred preoccupation. And Paul Kornfeld's *Heaven and Hell,* 1919—the title is derived from Strindberg's *Legender,* where the latter speaks of Swedenborg's *De coelo et inferno*—has as its epilogue the Count's wanderings through the wilderness in search of Redemption. Kornfeld's essay 'The soul-inspired and the psychological man', a manifesto published in *Das junge Deutschland* in 1918, insists on an abstraction from reality and an emphasis on essential, that is, spiritual essences. A great gulf emerges between 'Here' and 'the Beyond'; and the belief that, to quote Georg Kaiser, 'Ultimate value lies beyond human affairs'[6] becomes part of the stock-in-trade of many dramatists of this time.

Strindberg died in 1912. In that same year the German sculptor and dramatist Ernst Barlach wrote his first play, the ghostly *The Dead Day.* Barlach had settled in the small town of Güstrow in Mecklenburg in 1910. He was not an avid theatre-goer but had read his Strindberg and greatly admired Hauptmann's 'Traumdichtung', *Little Hannah's Ascension* (he had come across a performance, quite by chance, in the Residenz Theater in Dresden in 1894). Goethe's *Faust* had always overwhelmed him, particularly Part Two: Max Reinhardt had staged the complete work in the Deutsches Theater, Berlin, in 1905 and had, incidentally, been most effective in the realisation of the plays of Strindberg, successfully touring Sweden in 1911 and again in 1917. The fusion of the real and the visionary in Hauptmann's play impressed Barlach deeply; a letter refers to the sense of intoxication he experienced after seeing it, and the sensation of feeling like a spirit that has stripped off its earthly raiment, flying now on free wings above the earth. *The Dead Day* has six characters—three humans, and three gnome-like figures, one of whom is invisible. The action takes place in darkness or semi-darkness. The dramatic exploration of the interaction of supernatural forces, some grotesque and menacing, others benign, culminates in the knowledge of The Son that his longing for the Father-principle is a longing for transcendence. Although he perishes, the gnome Steissbart proclaims that God is the Father of Man. The next play, *The Poor Cousin* of 1918 (originally called *The Easter-People*) gives a very plausible picture of an Easter outing on the banks of the Lower Elbe, but also exemplifies Barlach's concept of 'the growing excarnation of essential Man'. Fräulein Isenbarn becomes transfigured as the 'handmaiden of a higher Master', realism having given way to mystery and ultimate redemption. *The Dead Day* equates the Mother with earth and the Father with spirit; *The Poor Cousin* talks of Easter and resurrection, a tension between 'Here' and 'Beyond' in an overtly Christian manner. The sculptures of Barlach are similar in their portrayal of heavy, earthbound figures who nevertheless aspire towards visionary awareness: *Der Ekstatiker* is a good example here. *The Dead Day*, with the clash of the generations (here mother/son) is very much of its time, but in this play the conflict is sublimated into a religious dichotomy. And although Barlach is convinced of man's higher derivation there is a unity of the physical and the spiritual in his work which saves it from whimsy and bizarre eccentricity. Reality, even if it is only 'a fart of the Lord', is 'still a part of Him'.[7]

It is not only in times of crisis that religious awareness is quickened: we have seen this tendency emerge long before the First World War. But the years of conflict, suffering and collapse necessarily meant an intensification. Wolfgang Rothe, in an excellent article entitled 'Man before God: Expressionism and Theology',[8] discusses what he calls 'Weltfrömmigkeit' (world-piety) and the debasement of such words as 'Heart', 'Soul', 'Sun', 'Light', in both the poets and the dramatists in the years during and immediately after the First World War. Old Testament themes and figures are found in Friedrich Wolf, Arno Nadel and Stefan Zweig—the year 1917 saw Wolf's *The Lion of God*, Nadel's *Adam* and Stefan Zweig's *Jeremias: A Dramatic Poem in Nine Scenes*.

Another element, one which might be called the 'existentialist-ecstatic', with an emphasis on the I/Thou relationship, not merely with sexual but also religious overtones, is seen in Kokoschka's *The Burning Bush*, performed in 1917, and also in August Stramm's *Happened*, with its 'He', a blind wanderer who comes from somewhere beyond the stars and who dies in the arms of 'She': the final tableau (where 'She' stammers 'I Thou You Me . . . We!') is meant to represent a *pietà*, as is the ending of Kokoschka's play. Hasenclever's *Beyond*, performed in Leipzig in 1920, is little more than a staccato, passionate interchange between two symbolic characters surrounded by hallucinatory effects (dissolving walls, trees growing into windows and looming shadows) and involved in a mystical, nebulous presentation of life and death. An interest in Jewish themes was awakened after the war by the writings of Martin Buber; Karl Barth's rigorous theology similarly brought Christian themes to the fore. But the collapse of Germany in November 1918, the establishment of the Weimar Republic, the turmoil of violence unleashed upon the streets during the fighting between extremist factions, the fervent and hectic optimism and the strident cry for brotherhood, created an atmosphere in which utopias, dystopias and chiliastic visions met in zymogenous confusion. It is a convention that earlier Expressionism gave way at this time to a more active, political attitude, but it would be unsubtle to claim that politics ousted everything—if the new republic was meant to introduce a Heaven on Earth, then priests, prophets and god-seekers were not so easily exorcised.

Ernst Toller's *The Transformation*, 1918, is an exemplary *Stationendrama*, which reverberates with Nietzschean imagery and culminates, Zarathustra-like, in the market place where a vision is preached of universal love; religious ecstasy triumphs, for it is the God in Man that must be redeemed for a new millennium to dawn. Most remarkable is Johannes R. Becher's play *Workers Peasants Soldiers*, 1921. The title leads the audience or readers to expect 'Agitprop' theatre, but the subtitle 'A People's Breakthrough to God', and the fact that the play (or *Festspiel*) was meant to belong to a trilogy *Um Gott* gives the work an extra dimension, 'Wandlung', 'Licht', 'Ekstase'—these familiar topoi provide yet further examples of 'O Gott' (rather than 'O Mensch') drama—or, better, an uncomfortable fusion of humanity and divinity prevails at this time. Werfel's *Mirror Man* trilogy of 1920 implies that expressionistic idealism could merely be a monstrous self-delusion or self-obsession; the second part very skilfully portrays the chaos of beliefs associated with the expressionist years—religious longing, according to Werfel, was fused with political activism, primitivism, quietism, Buddhism and theosophy.

Ludwig Rubiner's *The Powerless Ones*, 1919, is again shot through with light symbolism, as is Fritz von Unruh's *Platz*, 1920. The Manichean division of the world into Light and Darkness will undeniably assume a political flavour; it is the fervour with which the new age was greeted which, almost of necessity, took on a religious atmosphere of hope and transcendental expectation. But the subjectivity, mysticism, and what may be called a religious concern for the soul of man struggling to free itself not only from the bonds of capitalism but even from life itself, could not be maintained at white heat and fever pitch for long—the collapse into bathos was perhaps inevitable, and the cosmic element receded as the years of crisis gave way to a more stable form of government. *Aktuelles Theater*—Toller's *Such is Life!* of 1927 is a good example—offered a satirical and flippant view of society in the Weimar Republic, an equivalent of the *Neue Sachlichkeit* of G. F. Hartlaub; Hasenclever's lively comedy *Marriages are made in Heaven* is eight years and as many light years away from *Be-*

yond. Where are the *Gottsucher* now, the visionaries, the prophets of the imminent excarnation of essential man? Would they survive the trauma of 1933 to greet the '1000-year Reich' as the new Millennium?

Sorge had, as has been stated, been killed at the battle of the Somme in 1916; Georg Kaiser fled Nazi Germany and died in Switzerland in 1945; Barlach died in isolation and obscurity in 1938 (his sculptures were exhibited in the *Entartete Kunst* [Degenerate Art] exhibition of 1937); Hasenclever fled to France where he committed suicide in 1940; Kornfeld was transported from Prague to Lodz were he died in 1942; Toller went into exile and committed suicide in 1939; Arno Nadel was murdered in Auschwitz in 1943; Stefan Zweig committed suicide in 1942. Rubiner had died in 1920; Friedrich Wolf survived the Third Reich and returned to East Germany to work in the theatre before his death in 1953. It appears that the rise of Nazism was the death knell of Expressionism, but we must be more subtle here. The Jewish element was of course, reviled, as was the left-wing utopianism, but Expressionism is a complex phenomenon and the links between it and Nazism should not be overlooked. The hero of Joseph Goebbels's *Michael* had argued that 'We men of today are all expressionists, men who wish to mould the outer world from within. The expressionist builds a new world within himself. It is fervour which is his secret and his power.'[9] The rejection of stultifying intellectualism, the praise of Van Gogh and Dostoevsky, the worship of energy and the use of images derived from *Also sprach Zarathustra* display obvious expressionist features. Goebbels had also written a drama *Heinrich Kampfert* and left parts of a religious play *Judas Iscariot*.

A dramatist who acted as a bridge between Expressionism and National Socialism is Hanns Johst. Johst had been very much of his time with his expressionist plays *The Youthful One: An ecstatic Scenario* of 1916 and the Grabbe play *The Lonely One: The fall of a Man* of the following year. Johst's *Schlageter*, performed on Hitler's birthday in 1933 and dedicated to him in 'loving veneration and unswerving loyalty' is blatantly propagandistic in the idealisation of the title-figure; expressionist elements are still present in the final scene of the tableau-like setting, the hyperbole and the emotional intensity; *Thomas Paine*, 1927, had also betrayed exaggerated and visionary elements. But of greater importance for our argument is the role of mystery plays in the theatre of Nazi Germany, *Thingspiele* whose cultic, festive quality owes much to earlier models (Gottfried Keller's remarkable essay 'Am Mythenstein', written after a visit to the *Schillerfest am Mythenstein*, called for a new, national, festive theatre, the resuscitation of ancient myths and legends). Some may feel it inappropriate, indeed blasphemous, to imply that any aspect of Nazism could be called 'religious', but totalitarian regimes have a pseudo-devotional aura about them, some cosmic reference which prefers mythology to history. The following statement is attributed to Adolf Hitler: 'I create my religion out of *Parsifal*. Worship in a solemn form. One can only serve God in the robes of a hero.'[10]

Richard Euringer's *German Passion*, 1933, originally a *Hörspiel* (or *Hörwerk*), combines the tradition of the open-air stage with choric recitation, fanfares, circus-effects and mystical 'Devotion'. Euringer conceived of the theatre as a 'Theatre of Nature', embracing fire, earth, water and air, the constellations and spirits of tribal deities: the people were to see presented before them an enactment of their chthonic origins. If the theatre of Weimar had concerned itself merely with ladies' underwear, sex, drunkenness, mental illness, decadence and materialism (I am grateful to J. M. Ritchie for Johst's comments here),[11] then the new Reich was to project cosmic, cultic verities. The characters of Euringer's play include 'the Unknown Soldier', 'Worker', 'Hag', 'War Invalid', 'Girl', 'Children' and 'Mother'. The German people, undermined by bolshevism and international Jewry, will nevertheless be saved: the unknown Soldier rises from his grave, a crown of barbed wire upon his head. He ascends into heaven, and the Evil Spirit is overthrown.

Kurt Eggers's *Play of Job the German* is a similar work, where 'the Lord of Hosts' promises 'the Evil Spirit' domination over the earth if he could succeed in tempting Job the German to renounce his belief in Him: war, plague, poverty, sickness and despair test the faithful Teuton who nevertheless triumphs and is chosen by 'the Lord of Lords' to rule over the earth.

One further example of a quasi-religious experience is E. W. Möller's *The Dice Game of Frankenburg* of 1936 which, although it is based on an incident from the seventeenth century, portrays trial and atonement in the manner of Georg Kaiser (*The Citizens of Calais*). J. M. Ritchie has well described the première at the time of the Berlin Olympic Games.[12] To return to Euringer: his *Totentanz*, 1934, harks back to the 'Walpurgisnacht' scene of Goethe's *Faust* in the rhythmical, dynamic alternation of pithy stichomythia: it describes the cleansing of 'Nihilists', 'Pacifists', 'Pimps', 'Bank robbers' from the temple of life, and the triumph of Nordic man.

Let us pause here. To what extent may these choric mystery-plays-cum-oratorios be called 'expressionist'? If Expressionism is a movement towards abstraction, towards the typical and the essential rather than the personal and the individual; if it exemplifies a predilection for ecstasy and despair, and hence a tendency towards the inflated and the grotesque; if it turns towards a mystic element with apocalyptic overtones; if the urgent sense of the here and now is seen not from any naturalistic standpoint, but *sub specie aeternitatis*; if there is a revolutionary fervour in it, an aspect of the atavistic, the passionate and the radical—then *Thingtheater* must surely lay claim to inclusion in the history of expressionist theatre.

Echoing Richard Wagner, Alfred Rosenberg claimed that 'it is only in Europe that art becomes a true medium of transcendence, a religion in itself'.[13] When art and religion interlock, then there indeed are some very strange hybrids. The use of massed choruses, marching, music and declamation produced a form of *Gesamtkunstwerk* which aimed at an all-embracing experience, a sense of communion and ritual. What was new, of course, was the nationalistic element, the fatherland elevated to mythological status, and the belief in the mysterious supremacy of Nordic man. The international, left-wing aspects of Expressionism belong, it seems, in a different category altogether. If Expressionism is the eruption of the most general emotions, passions and virtues, with love of humanity, brotherliness and willingness for self-sacrifice to the fore, then the *Thingspiele*, in their mystical nationalism, stand at one remove—no 'O Mensch' pathos, but 'O deutscher Mensch'.

Expressionism may be defined as the revolt of the spirit against reality. The soul under stress, racked and burning in some fearful incandescence, or longing for some nebulous excarnation, are its most striking hallmarks. Sorge's young hero longed for an ultimate vision beyond reality; Hasenclever strove to portray a 'Beyond'; Kaiser described the quest for some transcendental awareness, his heroes moving through stages of martyrdom; Kornfeld insisted on *der beseelte Mensch* (the soul-endowed man); Barlach sought Easter and Resurrection; Becher and others conceived of a new age with its deification of man; the Third Reich was portrayed by some in terms more appropriate to a medieval mystery play. And Bayreuth and Dornach, *Thingspiel* and ritual *Festspiel*, and *Faust II* provide a fascinating counterpoint. It is very much removed from our own time which is attracted above all by the (frequently aberrant) sexual daring of much expressionist writing, also by the cult of violence in many of the plays. But the god-seekers should not be forgotten, however singular the epiphanies they sought, for it is they who give to modern German literature its most distinctive voice.

Notes

1. R. Sorge, *Werke in 3 Bänden,* Nuremberg, 1964, II, p. 23.
2. C. Walker, *Expressionist Poetry and its Critics,* London, 1986, p. 167.
3. Willett, *Expressionism.*
4. H. Bahr, in *Literarische Manifeste der Jahrhundertwende,* E. Ruprecht and D. Bänsch (eds), Stuttgart 1970, p. 191.
5. R. Furness, *Expressionism,* London, 1973, pp. 5-7.
6. Quoted in B. Kenworthy, *Georg Kaiser,* Oxford, 1957, p. 101.
7. J. H. Reid, 'The Halves and the Whole: Another look at Ernst Barlach's *Der arme Vetter, The Modern Language Review,* LXXII, 1977, p. 626.
8. In W. Rothe (ed.), *Expressionismus als Literatur,* Berne and Munich, 1969, pp. 37-66.
9. J. Goebbels, *Michael: Ein deutsches Schicksal in Tagebuchblättern,* Munich 1933, p. 42.
10. Quoted in J. Fest, *Hitler,* Frankfurt am Main, 1973, p. 683.
11. J. Ritchie, *German Literature under National Socialism,* London, 1983, p. 101.
12. *Ibid.,* p. 106.
13. Quoted in U. Ketelsen, *Von heroischem Sein und völkischem Tod,* Bonn, 1970, p. 43.

Richard Murphy (essay date 1998)

SOURCE: Murphy, Richard. "Re-Writing the Discursive World: Revolution and the Expressionist Avant-Garde." In *Theorizing the Avant-Garde: Modernism, Expressionism, and the Problem of Postmodernity,* pp. 49-73. Cambridge, England: Cambridge University Press, 1998.

[*In the following excerpt, Murphy explores the revolutionary tendency of many Expressionist poets, citing their use of such techniques as irony, skepticism, and manipulation of the signifier in language.*]

"Death to the Moonlight!"

(Futurist slogan)

The heterogeneous and frequently vague nature of the many manifestoes and programmatic statements produced by the numerous writers of the expressionist movement has made it a notoriously difficult phenomenon to pin down to any clear ideological line.[1] The great variety of political and religious groupings which many of its prominent associates went on to join after its official demise, such as the various socialist and communist factions, the National-Socialists, Christians and radical Zionists, may be an indication that a breadth of opinion already existed within its ranks which made the attempt at anything more than a broad and very fleeting affiliation of like-minded thinkers virtually impossible.[2]

The question of expressionism's impact as a revolutionary event in a social and ideological sense is made even more difficult to answer by the fact that any genuinely radical political agendas proposed in the literary or programmatic writings of the movement are invariably obscured or "overdetermined" by factors apparently extraneous to the issues at stake. For besides fulfilling the intellectual's need to overcome the social and spiritual isolation through engagement within the community,[3] the notion of a revolution often appears to offer the possibility merely of curing the self vicariously through the attempt to heal the world.[4] Alternatively, the ideal of revolution frequently seems to have been embraced as part of a more general desire for spiritual renewal or even as a criminal and destructive act offering a stimulating experiential "rush" or "Lebenssteigerung."[5]

It is undeniable of course that the expressionist avant-garde's "programmatic" texts present a powerful criticism of the ideological and institutional foundations of Wilhelmine bourgeois society and its culture of affirmation. It is also no coincidence that besides the shorter literary forms of the poem, novella and the one-act play, much expressionist thought was mediated via the more direct and powerful polemical forms, such as their manifestoes and pamphlets,[6] while as a generic form the expressionist broadsheet, with its shocking, terse and excessive statements had a wide-ranging influence on the movement, constituting one of the major factors behind the belligerent and provocative tone characteristic of its "expressiveness." However it is the very diversity and vagueness of the revolutionary programs, their refusal to be fixed to a determinate set of social goals and ideologies, or to adopt a single-minded sense of direction, which may turn out, paradoxically, to offer a means of understanding the revolutionary nature of expressionism as an avant-garde literary movement. As I shall show in this [essay] (with reference mainly to the poetic and programmatic texts of the movement), the particular ideological tendency of any overt intentions or stated political goals of the expressionists is ultimately much less significant for their consideration as an avant-garde[7] than the oppositional edge they give to the iconoclastic poetics they develop.[8]

More important for expressionism as an avant-garde literary movement is that a "revolutionary" impulse is inscribed into its poetics of representation which ensures that the first premise of its construction of the real is the constant interrogation of all ideological and epistemological foundations, all inherited models of reality and all established structures of perception and experience: in short as an avant-garde it questions those dominant social discourses supported by the institution of art, and creates in their place a set of oppositional discourses. Hence the truly revolutionary element of these texts is their constant overturning of the inherited world and its images, so that the final aim appears to lie in the very act of revolution itself as a constant and ongoing process.

Dominant Social Discourse: The Prison-House of Language

For many expressionists the subversion of the inherited world is perceived in part as the active participation in, and continuation of an anomic process which has already been set in motion.[9] The expressionist writer (and later dadaist) Hugo Ball documents a typical revolutionary response of expressionism to what was perceived as the acute crisis of modernity:

> God is dead. A world broke apart . . . Religion, science, morals—phenomena which emerged from the anxieties of primitive peoples. A world breaks apart. A millenial culture breaks apart. There are no more pillars and supports, no foundations that would not have been shattered. Churches have become castles in the air. Convictions prejudices . . . The meaning of the world faded away . . . Chaos broke out . . . Man lost his heavenly face, became matter, chance, conglomerate, animal, the product of insanity, of abrupt, inadequate and convulsive thoughts. Man lost his special position, which reason had vouchsafed for him.[10]

This crisis is the experience of an epoch in which all meaning seems to have disappeared from the world, leaving a mere chaos of fragmented myths and cosmologies. The text registers the onset of chaos firstly as a decisive break in the continuity of religious and philosophical thought ("There are no more pillars and supports, no foundations") and of normative values. And as with the writing of the important predecessor of the expressionist poets and thinkers, Friedrich Nietzsche, the system's breakdown, ("the death of God") also has an important ideology-critical function: the break-up of a millennial culture is seen as bringing with it not just chaos but, more positively, the possibility of release from the constraints of conventional interpretative and orienting systems. It allows the possibility of seeing through ideologies, the reified forms of thought which have been established as objective truths ("Convictions [have become] prejudices"), and which have been set up as the foundations of meaning: "the principles of logic, of centrality, unity and reason are revealed as the postulates of a domineering theology" says Ball later in the text.[11]

The prevalence in this period of such iconoclastic and revolutionary sentiments suggests that towards the end of the nineteenth century the pervasive experience of crisis, moral chaos and discontinuity documented here by Ball emerges as the symptom of a deeper and fundamental epistemological fracture. For at precisely this time a series of Copernican revolutions shake the foundations of Western thought. In particular the work of Nietzsche, but also of Mach, Vaihinger and Freud has the effect of subjecting conventional social discourse to a rigorous re-examination of its most cherished notions.[12]

The writing of these thinkers functions as a form of "ideology-critique" and "Fiktionskritik" ("critique of fictions"). Their general effect is to show that no systems of thought regarding man and social reality are anchored by any "natural law" but possess the status merely of instruments of reflection and meaning, as mere hypotheses or "useful fictions": they are patterns of meaning postulated by man which are imposed upon the phenomenal world in order to formulate it and bring it under his control. If the function of all "transcendental signifieds" (Derrida), such as those cited in the text by Ball ("Reason," "Man," "Religion") is thus to anchor those systems of meaning which are imposed upon the world of experience, then it is these that are now increasingly exposed to skepticism.

Such systems are created by a semantic activity which formulates experience and encapsulates a world by the use of fictions and language. As Nietzsche's famous aphorism has it, "What then is Truth? A mobile army of metaphors, metonymies, anthropomorphisms, in short the sum of human relations."[13] This semantic activity has the primary function then of creating a set of representational codes and ideological formations which present reality as an eminently *discursive* construction.

Now the growing awareness in this period of the discursive nature of realities—an awareness, as we have seen, that is dialectically related to the experience of their break-up—has important consequences. Firstly, it leads to the sense that, as a centering system, discourse may serve as a self-contained and all-embracing machinery which encloses the subject within itself, separating off any other modalities of experience: the "prison-house of language" was Nietzsche's expression for this phenomenon. This awareness of being enclosed within an ideological system of fictions placing limitations on experience brings with it the pervasive sense of alienation from a more "genuine" realm of being, an alternative dimension of experience[14] which the expressionists can only gesture towards, and which they hope to attain through the pursuit of what they term "spirit," "essence" or "power" ("Geist," "Wesen"[15] or "Kraft").

Secondly, since all points of orientation are seen simply as discursive fictions which have merely been postulated, not consolidated, all values appear as relative—"There is no perspective left in the moral world. Up is down, down is up." writes Ball.[16] With the proclamation of the death of God a full-scale interrogation of the discourse of reality begins, a questioning of the fictional nature of all those "essences" (the "pillars and supports" as Ball says) which anchor systems of meaning.

Epistemological Skepticism

The literary text of this period is consequently forced to a degree to undergo a functional transformation ("Funktionswandel") if it is to respond to these changed circumstances. As a result it becomes a common practice among the Expressionist writers to create the kinds of "counter-discourse" which foreground precisely the disjunction between, on the one hand, the world of fictions and discursive orders and on the other, the reality of the referential object. The more progressive literature of the movement consequently draws attention to the mediate nature of all discursive images of the world—such as the epistemological and ideological universes which man inhabits—and simultaneously to the contingency and instability of the (fictional) concepts which underpin them.

There are several texts, drawn from the field of expressionist poetry, which we can cite briefly as typifying this skeptical consciousness of the times. Many thematize directly the shortcomings of such fictions and the individual's inability to come to terms with the world from inside the discursive system in which he is enclosed. Gustav Sack's poem "The World" is an unusually explicit presentation of this "Erkenntniskritik" or skeptical attitude towards epistemology: ". . . it's all imagery, / which so colorfully places itself before our senses, / an X, from which the veil never falls, / yes, our senses themselves are paintings, / the world, the thing, causality, time and space / everything's a difficult and puzzling dream. / And today they scream out loudly on all the streets: / no, there it is, it's concrete reality—."[17] In conceding that the world which one experiences is actually only "imagery" or the result of "painting" ("Bilderei," or "Malerei") Sack points to the discursive and fictional nature of that "dream" one might otherwise take for "concrete reality." But his attack is not simply a logical, Kantian form of cognitive criticism. In fact, it has much in common with expressionism's resistance to such rationalism.[18] For as in the works of Benn and Döblin which I will examine in chapter 3 its real targets are precisely the logical categories underpinning the dominant discourse of rationalism upon which this counterfeit world of "images" and "veils" is constructed, such as the categories cited by Sack, namely "causality, time and space."

From a similar epistemological standpoint Ernst Stadler too warns against the danger of being convinced by simple meanings and explanations, and consequently of taking appearances for essences:

> And when I . . .
> Lift up to myself appearances, lies, and games instead of the essence,
> If I pleasingly lie to myself with easy meanings,
> As if dark were clear, as if life didn't carry a thousand wildly bolted
> gates.[19]

Again, what the text typifies is a historical sense of the danger which lies in wait for those who do not practice some form of epistemological skepticism with regard to what are, in effect, discursive fictions. The implication is that when these fictions ultimately evaporate, the individual will be abandoned to the experience of nothingness. From this same historical perspective Brecht writes: "And when the fallacies are all worn out? The last one keeping us company / sitting right across from us / is nothingness"[20]

THE EXPRESSIONIST AVANT-GARDE: THE CYNICAL SUBLATION OF ART AND LIFE

With this critical shift towards an attitude of skepticism the realization grows that since there is no longer any single ideological constellation which can have an ultimate claim on the truth, alternative discourses may be created to displace the dominant ideological constructs. It becomes a widely held belief among the expressionists, for example, that if meaning and order are no longer already "given" in the world, these must be imposed by an act of will on the part of the subject: as Kurt Pinthus says, "Everything else outside of ourselves is unreal and first becomes reality, when we turn it into reality by virtue of the power of the mind."[21] Pinthus' stance here is paradigmatic for the expressionist urge to create the world anew. It also bears a similarity to that characteristically "animistic" attitude of the Expressionist poets and playwrights who create in their texts an alternative world of selfhood in which figures and events are meaningful only as essences[22] or as correlatives of consciousness,[23] and in which "the mind forms reality according to the idea."[24]

The urge to create an alternative reality of discourse thus becomes a powerful revolutionary drive in the expressionist movement. This new discursive heterocosm serves both to displace a previous reality (which is now perceived as having lost its legitimacy) and to open up new meanings to the individual as well as an altered relationship to experience based on the imposition of an intensely personal version of world. Lothar Schreyer, echoing Pinthus writes, "In us the old world shatters. The new world arises within."[25]

One of the primary means by which this alternative discursive reality is created is through a strategy linked intimately to the avant-garde's program of creating a set of oppositional discourses marked by desublimation, de-aestheticization and the distortion of organic form. It involves a massive re-coding of what had previously been accepted as "nature": the world is now re-interpreted and re-constituted in terms of a new discourse which liberates both the object and its perception from the conditions pertaining to the given. Rather than creating the kind of literary work which reproduces the natural world and which thus attempts—like the conventions of organic art that Bürger critiques—to erase the marks of its artificiality in order to assimilate itself as closely as possible to nature, the expressionist text adopts one of the central strategies of the avant-garde, the procedure embodied preeminently in the montage: it foregrounds its own artifice and constructedness.[26] Thus, far from emulating the organic—and thereby implicitly substantiating the referential realm of the determinate and the given—it appears instead to valorize the "artificial" world of human creativity, the realm of the signifier, and the sovereign autonomy of consciousness.

Now since the perspective by which nature had previously been perceived was strongly influenced and "aestheticized" by the mediation of conventional, idealist and romantic topoi (such as stars and heaven, meadow and brook), the expressionist recoding of nature takes the form of a direct onslaught on such sublimating myths. Alfred Lichtenstein writes:

> The sky is like a blue *jellyfish.*
> And all around are fields, green meadow hills—
> Peaceful world, you great *mouse trap.*
>
> The earth is like a fat *Sunday roast,*
> Nicely dipped in sweet sun-sauce.[27]

Ernst Blass describes another conventionalized topos, the moon, as like "a slime / On an enormous velour of the falling night. / The stars quiver tenderly like embryos."[28] Similarly the poet Klabund describes the "evening clouds" as "like a procession of grey tattered vagabonds / swaying threateningly like drunken coffins."[29]

Significantly, the title of the latter poem, "Ironic Landscape" ("Ironische Landschaft") points to the expressionist avant-garde's oppositional strategy in creating such pointedly desublimated and de-aestheticized tropes. Traditional poetic codes—the dominant conventions of the aesthetic discourse in which tradition (and the institution of art) have imprisoned perception—are exploded by the ironic treatment they receive at the hands of the expressionist poets. This serves both to defamiliarize vision and to unlock conventionalized constructions, while encouraging the reader towards a free-play of associations and a mode of intellectual reflection quite at odds with the traditional "empathetic" reception demanded by previous schools of nature poetry, as well as by other affirmative and sublimating forms of art: rather than diverting attention away from reality towards an idealized and aestheticized realm of the sublime beyond, the avant-garde's aesthetics of "desublimation" enforces a close examination of the world and its image.

The revolutionary function of this iconoclasm lies also in its gesture of clearing the way for a radical reinterpretation of nature. For in important respects, the expressionist avant-garde's aesthetics of desublimation corresponds at the figural level to the process of cynical re-interpretation occurring at the level of ideology and discourse: in a sense, it is as if the expressionists indeed respond to the break-up of the old cosmological fictions, the "facade of the totality," in the manner that Ernst Bloch suggests, namely "by ripping it open even further."[30] If it retains any meaning at all, the organic world is now frequently reduced merely to a set of signs pointing to humankind's spiritual abandonment and "transcendental homelessness" (Lukacs).

The common eschatological orientation of the poems is also important here, since natural phenomena now take on significance not as uplifting terrestrial manifestations of a sublime, redemptive ideal world beyond but in terms of a coming catastrophe or a failure of redemption. Van Hoddis' poem "End of the World" ("Weltende") and Heym's "Umbra Vitae"—the two texts which open Pinthus' important collection of expressionist poetry *Menschheitsdämmerung* (*Dawn of Humanity*)—are outstanding examples of this tendency. The "natural" presentiments of disaster are for example storms: "And along the coasts—the paper says—the tide is rising. / The storm is here, the wild seas are hopping / Ashore . . .";[31] or alternatively foreboding presents itself in the form of an uncannily becalmed sea: "The seas stagnate. In the waves / the ships hang mouldering and sullen . . .";[32] meanwhile humankind's state of spiritual excommunication may be read in the skies: although many search the heavens for a positive sign, "all of heaven's gates are closed shut."[33]

Even in those poems in which the negative reinterpretation of nature is not foregrounded quite as obviously as in these examples, the emphasis is still frequently upon its re-reading not as an entity which constitutes an end in itself or even a source of spiritual comfort and balm, but as a mere correlative or icon for man's troubled existence in a world of pain and anxiety. For van Hoddis, birdsong for example becomes an expression of pain: "The sparrows scream" ("Die Spatzen schrein").[34] For Lichtenstein nature is frequently a sign of disease or death, and his images are of "Bloodless trees" ("Blutlose Bäume"), "the swollen night" ("die aufgeschwollne Nacht"), and "the poisonous moon, the fat fog-spider" ("Der giftge Mond, die fette Nebelspinne").[35] Such purposefully "unnatural" uses of the organic image become a central characteristic of the expressionist poem's cynical sublation of art and life by means of desublimation: through expressionism's de-aestheticization of poetry, as well as its re-writing of the world, nature is made to undergo a reductive transformation, through which it is instrumentalized as a sign, or marginalized as a mere function of human consciousness.

Typical of the revolutionary and avant-garde impulse within expressionism is that it not only reverses traditional hierarchies but subverts those conventional values associated with nature, such as the monumental and sublime, which appear to be held in place by nature's unarguable "givenness." As nature's human counterpart, the body too is subject to a similar re-coding. Whereas the lyrical poetry of a former period had upheld the idea of the body as a criterion of beauty, with the expressionists what had been the temple of the spirit often becomes a mere heap of decaying flesh, a token of a latterday version of baroque "Vergänglichkeit" or "transience." Benn's poetry of the dissection table in the "Morgue" collection is typical of this direction in the new poetry.

Here it is again the provocative and blatant re-coding of traditional romantic themes which is prominent. Benn's poem "Schöne Jugend" for example focuses on the image of the mouth of a young girl. This is not, however, because it figures as the romantic object of a lover's desire, but rather because it "looked so gnawed-at" ("sah so angeknabbert aus") on account of the rats which found an arbor ("Laube") in her body after she drowned.[36] Typically the hierarchical relationship between humanity and the spirit on the one hand, and bestiality and materiality on the other is reversed. The avant-garde's defining feature of a "cynical sublation" of art and reality is important here: if the poem reduces the differences between art and life, then instead of elevating life to the sublime level of art in an aestheticized image (or reconstituting life in a formulation whose aesthetic necessity "masters" the horror of the real) it now joins the two by descending with art to the circle of the unredeemable: the earthly, the ugly and the profane. The "lovely childhood" ("schöne Jugend") of the title turns out to refer not to the human subject, but to the life of the young rodents. Thus the girl appears merely as an object, a store of flesh for the young rats, rather than as a vessel of the spirit. In this manner the romantic Ophelia-motif of the drowned lover is evoked but then inverted, so that any remaining idealist notions of an autonomous human subject necessarily suffer a re-interpretation, as the individual becomes mere matter, a corpse tossed carelessly onto a slab.

With this revolutionary re-coding of nature, of the body, of conventional poetic topoi and of cognitive fictions, several new perspectives are opened up. Firstly an anachronistic "Weltbild" (or "image of the world") is displaced. The subversion of those traditional "transcendental signifieds," such as God (whose heaven is now repeatedly described as "empty")[37] and the subject (now a "dissociated" entity, a "fragmented" corpse) is accomplished by their being replaced by autonomous and indeterminate signifiers. This means that the reality which these ideological "centers" had formerly anchored, together with the codes and myths which they had legitimized and held in place, are necessarily liberated.

Secondly, besides marking the break-up of the inherited world of continuity and belief, the subversion of the natural world and the linked tendencies towards dehumanization and the re-coding of the body have a further specific target: they offer a release from the values associated with the Romantic tradition of an order close to nature and retaining a precious conception of selfhood based on an anachronistic sense of "Innerlichkeit" (or "interiority").[38]

Thirdly, it is evident that other strategies of reversal similar to the re-coding of nature are common practice in expressionist texts: for example the resurrection of the socially marginal, such as madmen, prostitutes and other outcasts, and their valorization as the new prophets, saints and heroes of the age. However, this procedure is seldom utilized with any concretely political goal in mind, such as an egalitarian class revolution. Instead, by exposing the contingency of the hierarchy within such ideologies the system's boundaries and its mechanisms of exclusion *per se* are called into question. As an onslaught on the familiar, bringing with it a de-automatizing renewal of vision, the real revolutionary goal becomes the act of reversal itself: it brings about the epistemological critique of those institutionalized codes of representation which had held the concepts of the "natural" and the "organic" so firmly in place.

There are several other means by which this radical strategy of recoding is carried over into the poetics of the expressionist text, and it is to these that we now turn.

Forms of Counter-Discourse: The Avant-garde Poetics of Representation as Re-Writing

The new discursive orders which the expressionists create should not necessarily be thought of merely as a means of creating a new orderliness and fixity to replace the old. For their function is not the banishment of chaos. Chaos is often valorized by these writers for its apparent resistance to being instrumentalized by ideology and is even embraced by the strong-willed of the expressionist generation for its radical and anti-systematic character. As Huelsenbeck suggests, writing on the expressionist theme of the "New Man," this figure "recognizes no system for the living, he welcomes chaos as a friend, since he bears order in his soul."[39] Rather than the establishment of a new dominant order we may assume then that it is the destruction of inherited cosmologies and illusions of meaning that assumes the greater importance. Again, the practice of revolution itself—as a provocative and life-enhancing activity in its own right—becomes the aim, rather than the pragmatic goal of the establishment through revolution of a new social order.

In an article published in June 1915 in a journal affiliated with the expressionists, *Die weißen Blätter,* Rudolf Leonhard addresses this notion of a continuous revolutionary momentum, describing the poet as bound to a perpetual oppositional activity with a permanently rebellious and anti-ideological function: although capable of becoming happily intoxicated with the ideals of the revolution he is still quite likely to turn towards his comrades on the barricade and stick out his tongue at them, "for he is the revolutionary in every camp, the one who is dissatisfied with every situation . . ."[40] Far from being expelled from the Platonic state for this destabilizing and subversive political stance, Leonhard argues that the poet should be retained precisely on account of his function as an ideological "gadfly." His role is to oppose the perennial danger of stasis: "This is where the poet can have a counter-effect. The state cannot get by without him. It needs the stimulation of agitation in its machinery. It should hire revolutionaries, the ambiguous ones, who rebel despairingly against all sides."[41]

It is clear that through this constant revolutionary agitation and subversion a particular form of epistemological and ideological critique emerges which is characteristic of expressionism as an avant-garde movement. It produces a form of insight both into alterity—the possibility of alternative ideologies—and consequently into the discursive status of reality. As a result an ideologically informed awareness is produced that opposes dogma and fixity of the kind which might pose the danger of becoming the "center" of any new order. It is for this reason that the expressionists attempt to inscribe this chaos and openness into their texts—in ways that extend far beyond the principle of montage as analyzed by Bürger—in order to acknowledge the provisional and fictional status of the heterocosms they create.

Now it is precisely the insistence upon this unavailability to closure and fixity of the discursive reality and upon the necessarily "inorganic" and "unnatural" status of all ideological universes which constitutes a key element of the way that the poetics of expressionism functions as an avant-garde. This is evident in the attitude to mimesis. The expressionists' immediate literary-historical predecessors—the writers of the naturalist movement—typically believed that their modes of formulating and representing reality bore a necessary correspondence to the phenomenal world. Clearly this position can no longer be upheld against the historical breakdown in discursive fictions of order, and such uncomplicated attitudes towards representation in the previous generation give way to a profound skepticism with regard to mimesis amongst the expressionists. They, by contrast, reject any naive mimetic stance which would re-present its object by attempting to make the literary discourse mediating it disappear. That is, they are opposed to the kind of text which, like the organic work of art or "classic realist text," erases the marks of the enunciation and, by thus effacing the indications of its own fictionality attempts to become a transparent window on the world.

Instead, as we have seen, the new generation of expressionist writers around 1910 adopts certain practices—for example the re-coding of nature and of the body, the subversion of traditional topoi, or the reversal of conventional hierarchies of value (such as placing the sublime over the marginal, the natural over the artificial)—which "re-write" the world as a construction of human consciousness, thereby liberating it from inherited values and perceptions. By emphasizing the artificial and constructed nature of their texts and the contingency of its images *vis-à-vis* the notional object of representation they foreground the inherent fictionality and perspectivism in any form of representation. Thus they draw attention away from the referential object as such and redirect it towards the materiality and mediated nature of the text and of its signs. In this way the balance in the representational relationship is shifted: rather than emphasizing the referent, the text is itself foregrounded first and foremost as a signifier.

This autonomy of the signifier and its liberation from the realm of the referential is linked to the purely "expressive" function of these texts. As we shall see in chapter 4 (on expressionist melodrama), the hysteria and the hyperbole characteristic of the movement underline this expressivity. Rather than striving like aestheticism for purity of the aesthetic image, or like classic realism for transparency of the representation (with the aim of forming the image as an authentic reflection of the referential object), expressionism concentrates only on developing an explosive force which will tear away surface appearances. As Pinthus says,

> Art for art's sake and the aesthetic were never so disrespected as in that poetry referred to as the "new" or as "expressionist," which is all eruption, explosion, intensity—and which has to be so in order to break open the malignant crust [around reality]. That is why it avoids the naturalistic description of reality as a descriptive means . . .[42]

The emphasis is now on the medium itself as "Ausdruckskunst." Yet not in the sense of producing the refined and self-sufficient formal consciousness characteristic of aestheticism. The "aesthetic" criteria have changed in this de-aestheticized art:

> For this reason one should not ask about the quality of this art, but about its intensity. The intensity is what constitutes its value. For it is not a matter of artistic accomplishment, but of the will . . . This art will blow apart the aesthetic, if one conceives of the aesthetic as the pleasurable formation of the given . . .[43]

In expressionism it is now the directness and "intensity" of expression offered in the image which count, not the sublations of form or the "artistic accomplishment" ("Kunstfertigkeit"). And this "intensity" frequently comes to mean that the signifiers free themselves from a prior, denotative relationship to the referent and its details in order to become the "unmediated" reflex of the "will" or of a more essential personal vision or realm of consciousness.

We can observe this connection between the intensity of the vision and the growing autonomy of the signifier in the pointedly arbitrary and idiosyncratic uses of metaphor in expressionist poetry. In examining the discursive re-coding of nature and the body we have already seen that this strategy often targets existing thematic conventions, for example the language and imagery through which the world is articulated and perceived within a certain tradition. An important aspect of this poetic re-orientation involved an assault upon traditional modes of perception and experience, and hence an attack upon dominant codes of representation. As an iconoclastic gesture such onslaughts foreground the fact that the perception of phenomena rests on a fiction, a metaphor imposed upon the world. Now this same foregrounding of fictionality through the violence of an imposed image may be seen again in the rather contorted and daring comparisons of which the expressionist poets were fond. To take some brief examples from the poetry of Lichtenstein: "The sky is grey wrapping paper / Onto which the sun is glued—a butter stain"[44]; or "The sun, a buttercup, balances / On a smokestack, its thin stalk."[45]

Clearly such images work by producing a clash between very different contexts which thereby creates a profoundly bathetic effect. More specifically however, it is the strategy of de-aestheticization common to the avant-garde and its "cynical sublation" of art and life which is responsible for this provocative effect. For by calling up a conventional romantic or sublime topos (the heavens, the sun) only to thrust it down into the context of the all too mundane and earthly is to produce an anti-aesthetics: a reversal of conventional aesthetic values which "shocks the bourgeois," frustrates his or her institutionally nurtured expectations and offends his or her sense of cultural propriety.

Such de-aestheticized images and idiosyncratic comparisons have their roots in the fundamental expressionist aesthetic which dictates that the images need not be "realistic," but rather should derive their validity from other criteria, such as the "power" they display, or from the assertion of "Wille"—sheer willpower. In this they are related to the painter Franz Marc's famous blue horses,[46] or to the personal color coding in Trakl's poems where the very contingency of the choice of epithet is in the forefront.[47]

The apparent arbitrariness of the epithet is crucial. Not only does it underline the rebellion against conventional modes of seeing and representing, but in emphasizing the necessarily fictional nature of the constructed image, it presents its message as merely one possible mode of perception among many. In the case of Trakl's poetry the choice of color or metaphor may be either completely contingent, or—as in the case of an important predecessor in the development of expressionist aesthetics, namely van Gogh—highly personal.[48] But in either case the function is the same, as we shall see.

Firstly, to take the example of Marc's blue horses, the painted body of the horse is turned into a mere function of its color, and with its shocking lack of "authenticity," the color is now by far the more striking component. In a similar way, with the examples from Lichtenstein above, the referent of the poem becomes a mere vehicle for the metaphor, so that the traditional rhetorical hierarchy between the two elements is overturned. Secondly, the subversion of the referent and of its naturalistic detail re-directs the recipient away from a distracting concern with the mere particulars of the appearance towards a more essential or conceptual level of the phenomenon.

Thirdly, and perhaps most importantly, besides allowing the presented image to be understood thus as one of the many "manifestations of the concept 'horse',"[49] it is as if the deliberate "distortion," the contingency of the choice of color or epithet, serves as the attempt to place this particular manifestation "under erasure" (Derrida), or as if the artist were both using and then crossing through a term which could only be employed with caution. By invoking but simultaneously suspending the signifier the artist appears in other words only to gesture towards an entity which is either unrepresentable as such or which would only be falsified by succumbing to a concrete and "representable" form. Thus the violent discrepancy created by the shocking color or epithet emphasizes the provisional nature of the particular concretization of "das Wesen" which has emerged, insisting on the impossibility of final closure.

Furthermore, to the extent that the image is used under erasure it is also freed from any direct subservience to a referent, and can emerge as a liberated signifier.[50] Like all such terms used under erasure these signifiers can only be thought of as being grasped or comprehended in a very provisional sense, since, as their foregrounding as fictions or metaphors makes clear, they are involved in a permanent process of slippage and displacement by other possible metaphors. It is in this vital sense that the expressionist text must be understood as aiming at a permanent revolution: where the signifiers of the text are inscribed in a differential chain of signification they are constantly being effaced and so are resistant to any attempt to reduce them to a fixable meaning. This permanent denial of stability and fixity to fictions (whether aesthetic or epistemological), the constant overturning of reified or "naturalized" ideological codes and unquestioned epistemological premises defines expressionism's participation in the historical avant-garde and constitutes precisely the sense of the "expressionist revolution."

FUNCTIONAL AND STYLISTIC TRANSFORMATIONS

In conclusion we can now draw together certain perspectives developed in the foregoing analyses regarding the nature of this revolution. It should now be clear that the frequent reluctance shown by many expressionists to pin themselves down to particular ideological tendencies or to state their goals in precise political terms does not mean that one must write off their revolutionary intentions as the vague rebellious aspirations of a band of adolescent literati who were either unwilling to abandon the protection offered by a conventionalized form of aesthetic autonomy, or who were unable to give this aesthetic autonomy a purposefully ideological edge.[51] Rather one must place these aims in a different category, on an ideological and epistemological level rather than in the realm of genuine social praxis.[52]

As we have seen, it is not through concrete social plans that the expressionists present their revolutionary agenda but through a vision which, in its extremism, in its pointed artificiality or subjectivism, may even appear at first glance quite unrelated to the concrete conditions prevailing in the social world.[53] Correspondingly, it is not through an accurate mimetic representation of the status quo that their critical standpoint is achieved. Rather, as with Peter Bürger's category of the montage or non-organic work, it is paradoxically through the distortions, through the pointed constructedness and artificiality of the image that this impulse towards change comes to the fore.

The comparison with the strategies of the naturalist movement is again instructive in this respect. From a socio-historical perspective one might advance the general proposition that new literary movements are frequently subject to a kind of "cultural lag" (Ogburn) in their response to a changed social and ideological situation.[54] They often display a discrepancy between the "functional transformation" ('Funktionswandel'), that is, the new critical functions accruing to their texts as they negotiate their response to the changed set of conditions and problematics pertaining to a new historical period, and the "stylistic transformations" ("Stilwandel") or stylistic means developed to mediate the innovation and so account formally for this socio-historical change. Now it appears to be just such a cultural lag which frequently produces within the naturalist text the kind of contradiction between progressive "tendency" and conservative "technique" which Benjamin ascribes to a failure to comprehend the institutionalized cultural codes. For although the discourse of naturalist drama for example is progressive, encouraging social change and rebellion against the constraints of determinism and milieu, its dramatic form, even down to the very props it employs on stage, are so solid, and its verisimilitude so precise and uncompromising, that against its own intentions it overwhelms us with an impression of the unchangeable fixity and immovable determinacy of the world and its appearance.[55]

The importance of expressionism's revolutionary iconoclasm and avant-garde innovations in this regard is that they resolve many of the literary-historical deficits and contradictions bequeathed by its main predecessor, naturalism. For example by contrast with the solidity of naturalist verisimilitude, what the expressionist text attempts to do is to undermine appearances in order firstly to shock the audience and undermine both the inherent conservatism and the sense of reassurance it derives from recognizing the familiar, and secondly to destroy the audience's comforting illusion of having conceptually mastered or "fixed" reality.

But there is a further important dimension to this avant-garde assault on aesthetic convention. If the "real" in art is an effect produced by the use of certain culturally-privileged codes of representation, then through the forceful re-writing of old codes expressionism militates against this semiotic hegemony. It is in breaking decisively with these old ways of seeing, that it rebels against the real. For by constructing its images through forms which are tentative or "under erasure," by foregrounding their fictionality and by presenting them as pure constructions it succeeds in inscribing a revolutionary openness and resistance to closure into the texts. In this it fulfills a primary goal of the avant-garde: it loosens the grip of dominant cultural codes (and thus of the institution of art) upon the construction of the real by holding open the possibility of alternative constructions, and by demonstrating the infinite re-writability of the real. Through this two-fold openness expressionism's message of dissent is made to correspond to its means.

Finally, if expressionism is to be seen primarily as a conceptual art full of anthropomorphosed concepts and concretized ideas—in Jost Hermand's words, as a "poetic formulation of definitions" of a "purely epistemological kind" ("definitorische Dichtung," "rein erkenntnismäßiger Natur")[56]—then it must be conceded that its revolutionary function is of the same order: it operates on the theoretical level of an ideological and epistemological rethinking, in other words as a form of "Ideologie-" and "Erkenntniskritik" which challenges not only conventional views of the world but also the orienting concepts which support them, in order to reveal their fictionality, their arbitrary nature, and thus their fundamental susceptibility to change.

A talk given in 1917 by Robert Müller describes this attack on conventional "Weltbilder" (or "images of the world") in terms of a revolutionary displacement of old regimes and systems of meaning, and as an assault precisely on the fixity and closure which they prescribe:

> We are going over to the elastic systems. The rigid classical systems are a *cas limite* and are only occasionally satisfying . . .
>
> The picture of the new painter is independent of those moments of rigidity through which we reify our daily visual impressions . . . The picture of the new painter rocks the boat. Rock with it, give up your own rigidity—that is expressionism.[57]

From this it is clear that the task of the expressionist artist is to displace the fixity of the old systems with a new "elasticity"—a quality directly comparable, in terms of our discussion above, to the "openness" always inscribed into the texts of the expressionist avant-garde.[58] Through this new "elasticity" a picture is created which unsettles and "rocks" ("schaukelt") the recipient's everyday fixed images and rigid systems. Thus rather than confirming the reader's positioning within the inherited cosmology, as an avant-garde movement expressionism breaks up the stiff ideologies and fixed images on which the individual relies. This is a widespread practice within the movement, even embracing the sober poetics of Franz Kafka and his view that the text should serve as an axe "for the frozen sea within us" provoking and forcing the reader out of conventional attitudes and modes of behaviour.[59]

More than simply shocking the burgher ("épater le bourgeois"), such strategies as this "schaukeln" destabilize the social and discursive conventions by which he is protected. By thus revealing their own fictional nature the effect of such avant-garde texts is to *decenter* the reader, that is, to force the subject out of any habitual positioning by these systems and to offer not simply an alternative (and consequently equally fixed) ideological position, but rather a multiplicity of alternatives—even if these appear only tentative and "under erasure."[60]

In 1910 at the outset of the movement, in the first edition of one of the most influential expressionist journals, *Der Sturm*, Rudolf Kurtz offers a warning to the audience about this revolutionary and decentering function of expressionism: "We don't want to entertain them. We want to demolish their comfortable, serious and noble view of life artfully."[61] Given the ongoing nature of the revolution prescribed by Expressionism and the shockwaves which it has sent out in the intervening years throughout the modern and postmodern world, it is a warning which must still be taken seriously.[62]

Notes

1. A broad selection of these writings are collected in Anz and Stark (eds.), *Manifeste und Dokumente* in the section "Literatur und Politik," (especially

"Expressionismus und Revolution," 326-353). See also the collection by Paul Pörtner (ed.), *Literaturrevolution 1910-1925. Dokumente, Manifeste, Programme,* 2 vols. (Luchterhand: Neuwied, 1960). Parts of the present chapter were originally published in *German Quarterly* 64.4 (1991): 464-74.

2. The variety of affiliations taken up by former expressionists may also be indicative of their need, long postponed, for a spiritual or ideological community. See Walter H. Sokel, *The Writer in Extremis,* 228.

3. See the discussion and collection of texts on this theme in Anz and Stark (eds.), *Manifeste und Dokumente,* in the section "Soziale Entfremdung und Gemeinschaft," 247-250.

4. Sokel, *The Writer in Extremis,* 218.

5. Richard Hamann and Jost Hermand, *Expressionismus* (Munich: Nymphenberger Verlagshandlung, 1976), 114.

6. It is worth noting for example that the dadaist manifestations and "happenings" which Bürger cites as typically avant-gardistic forms (through which art is "confronted" directly with life and with the shocked reactions of the audience) took as their precedent the expressionists' provocative and often shocking "literary cabarets," in which their fantastic stories, dissonant poetry, and often grotesque one-act plays were read or performed.

7. Edgar Lohner observes that it is important to build upon Peter Bürger's theoretical analysis of the historical avant-garde by examining concretely the artists' own conceptualizations of their progressive mission. See Lohner, "Die Problematik des Begriffes der Avantgarde," 124.

8. In a similar vein Wolfgang Paulsen writes "no matter how revolutionary Expressionism seemed to be, it was not a political, nor even in any sense a socially oriented movement. At best it could be deemed a literary movement with larger political and social implications." In "Expressionism and the Tradition of Revolt" *Expressionism Reconsidered,* Houston German Studies vol. 1, ed. G. B. Pickar and K. E. Webb (Munich: Fink, 1979), 8. This is not to deny, however, the genuine engagement and political praxis of many individual expressionist (and dadaist) writers, especially those associated with the November revolution such as Toller. On this question see Frank Trommler, *Sozialistische Literatur in Deutschland. Ein historischer Überblick* (Stuttgart: Kröner, 1976) in particular the section "Schriftsteller und Revolution," 412-442; Wolfgang Frühwald, "Kunst als Tat und Leben. Über den Anteil deutscher Schriftsteller an der Revolution in München 1918/1919," *Sprache und Bekenntnis. Festschrift für Hermann Kunisch,* ed. Wolfgang Frühwald and Günter Niggl (Berlin: Dinker, 1971); Hans Meyer, "Expressionismus und Novemberrevolution," *Spuren* 5 (1978): 10-13.

9. This function of actively extending a destructive process which has already been set in motion is valorized by Ernst Bloch in his defence of expressionism over and against Lukacs' charge that these poets merely participated naively in "the ideological demise of the imperialist bourgeoisie" ("den ideologischen Verfall der imperialistischen Bourgeoisie"). As we have seen in the previous chapter, Bloch asks provocatively whether it would have been better "if they had patched up the surface of reality instead of tearing it even further apart" ("wenn sie den Oberflächenzusammenhang wieder geflickt hätten . . . statt ihn immer weiter aufzureißen?"). He thereby circumscribes the ideology-critical function of the literary movement. See Bloch, "Diskussionen über Expressionismus," *Expressionismusdebatte,* 187.

10. "Gott ist tot. Eine Welt brach zusammen . . . Religion, Wissenschaft, Moral—Phänomene, die aus Angstzuständen primitiver Völker entstanden sind. Eine Welt bricht zusammen. Eine tausendjährige Kultur bricht zusammen. Es gibt keine Pfeiler und Stützen, keine Fundamente mehr, die nicht zersprengt worden wären. Kirchen sind Luftschlösser geworden. Überzeugungen Vorurteile . . . Der Sinn der Welt schwand . . . Chaos brach hervor . . . Der Mensch verlor sein himmlisches Gesicht, wurde Materie, Zufall, Konglomerat, Tier, Wahnsinnsprodukt abrupt und unzulänglicher zuckender Gedanken. Der Mensch verlor seine Sonderstellung, die ihm die Vernunft gewährt hatte." Hugo Ball, "Kandinsky." Lecture held in Galerie Dada, Zürich, April 7, 1917. *Manifeste und Dokumente,* 124.

11. "Die Prinzipien der Logik, des Zentrums, Einheit und Vernunft wurden als Postulate einer herrschsüchtigen Theologie durchschaut."

12. The nihilism and critique of fictions and ideology which were prominent at the turn of the century and which played such an important role in expressionism are dealt with extensively by Silvio Vietta and Hans-Georg Kemper in *Expressionismus,* (Munich: UTB, 1975), 134-152.

13. "Was ist also Wahrheit? Ein bewegliches Heer von Metaphern, Metonymien, Anthropomorphismen, kurz eine Summe von menschlichen Relationen." Friedrich Nietzsche, "Über Wahrheit und Lüge im außermoralischen Sinne," *Werke III* (Frankfurt: Ullstein 1969), 1022. [Schlechta edition, vol. III, 314].

14. An example of this widespread tendency is expressed by the expressionist painter Franz Marc. He articulates his generation's search for this undefined (and undefinable) source of alterity: "Wherever we saw a crack in the crust of convention, that's what we pointed to: only there, for we hoped for a power beneath which would one day come to light" ("Wo wir einen Riß in der Kruste der Konvention sahen, da deuteten wir hin; nur dahin, da wir darunter eine Kraft erhofften, die eines Tages ans Licht kommen würde"). Franz Marc, "Der Blaue Reiter" (1914), rpt. in *Manifeste Manifeste. 1905-1933,* ed. Diether Schmidt (Dresden: Verlag der Kunst, 1956), 56.

15. See Kurt Pinthus, "Rede für die Zukunft," *Die Erhebung* (1919), cited below.

16. "[E]s gibt keine Perspektive mehr in der moralischen Welt. Oben ist unten, unten ist oben." Hugo Ball, "Kandinsky." *Manifeste und Dokumente,* 124.

17. ". . . es ist alles Bilderei, / was sich so bunt vor unsre Sinne stellt, / ein X, von dem niemals der Schleier fällt, / ja unsre Sinne selbst sind Malerei, / die Welt, das Ding, die Folge, Zeit und Raum / alles ein schwerer, rätselwirrer Traum. / Und heute schreit man laut auf allen Gassen: / nein, sie ist da, ist harte Wirklichkeit . . ." Gustav Sack, "Die Welt," *Lyrik des Expressionismus* (Tübingen, 1976), 203.

18. On this theme, see Vietta and Kemper, *Expressionismus,* esp. 144-176.

19. "Und wenn ich . . . / Schein, Lug und Spiel zu mir anstatt des Wesens hebe, / Wenn ich gefällig mich mit raschem Sinn belüge, / Als wäre Dunkles klar, als wenn nicht Leben tausend / wild verschloßne Tore trüge." Stadler, "Der Spruch," *Menschheitsdämmerung* (hereafter MHD), ed. Kurt Pinthus (Hamburg: Rowohlt, 1963), 196. Wherever possible I have used the translation (hereafter *MHD-DH*) *Menschheitsdämmerung: Dawn of Humanity. A Document of Expressionism,* trs. J. M. Ratych, R. Ley, R. C. Conard (Columbia S.C.: Camden House 1994). Klemm's poem "Philosophie" shares this same epistemological caution: "We do not know what light is / Nor what the ether and its oscillations are—/ . . . Hidden from us is what the stars signify / And the solemn march of time . . . / We do not know what God is!" *MHD-DH,* 94 ("Wir wissen nicht was das Licht ist / Noch was der Äther und seine Schwingungen—. . . Fremd ist uns, was die Sterne bedeuten / Und der Feiergang der Zeit. / . . . Wir wissen nicht was Gott ist!" *Lyrik des Expressionismus,* 202).

20. "Wenn die Irrtümer verbraucht sind? Sitzt als letzter Gesellschafter / Uns das Nichts gegenüber." Brecht, "Der Nachgeborene," *Lyrik des Expressionismus,* 249.

21. "[A]lles andere außer uns ist unwirklich und wird erst zur Wirklichkeit, wenn wir kraft der Kraft des Geistes es zur Wirklichkeit machen." Kurt Pinthus, "Rede für die Zukunft" in *Die Erhebung. Jahrbuch für neue Dichtung und Wertung,* ed. A. Wolfenstein (Berlin: Fischer 1919), 414.

22. Gottfried Benn for example explains that he has to write in this "essential" manner, "since I never see people but only the 'I', and never events, but only existence . . ." ("da ich nie Personen sehe, sondern immer nur das Ich, und nie Geschehnisse, sondern immer nur das Dasein. . . .") See "Schöpferische Konfession" *Gesammelte Werke,* vol. 4, ed. Dieter Wellershoff (Limes: Wiesbaden, 1958), 189.

23. Examples of this attitude would be the "Ich-" and "Stationendramen", the doubling and splitting of characters throughout the texts of the movement.

24. "der Geist formt die Wirklichkeit nach der Idee." Pinthus, "Rede für die Zukunft," 413.

25. "In uns zerbricht die alte Welt. Die neue Welt ersteht in uns." Lothar Schreyer, "Der neue Mensch." *Manifeste und Dokumente,* 140.

26. For example one might cite the foregrounded artificiality of the common expressionist forms of montage or "Telegrammstil," or again the artificial and seemingly purely conceptual nature of figures in the dramas and in many of the prose texts (Einstein's "Bebuquin," Kafka's "Beschreibung eines Kampfes" etc.).

27. "Der Himmel ist wie eine blaue *Qualle.* / Und rings sind Felder, grüne Wiesenhügel—/ Friedliche Welt, du große *Mausefalle.* . . . / Die Erde ist wie ein fetter *Sonntagsbraten,* / Hübsch eingetunkt in süße Sonnensauce." Lichtenstein, "Sommerfrische," *MHD* 63 (my emphasis).

28. "ein Schleim / Auf ungeheuer nachtendem Velours. / Die Sterne zucken zart wie Embryos." *Lyrik des Expressionismus,* 48.

29. "Gleich einem Zug grau zerlumpter Strolche, / Bedrohlich schwankend wie betrunkne Särge." Klabund, "Ironische Landschaft," *Lyrik des Expressionismus,* 208.

30. See Bloch, "Diskussionen über Expressionismus," *Expressionismusdebatte,* 187.

31. *MHD-DH* 61. "Und an den Küsten—liest man—steigt die Flut. / Der Sturm ist da, die wilden Meere hupfen / An Land. . . ." Van Hoddis, "Weltende," *MHD,* 39.

32. "Die Meere aber stocken. In den Wogen / Die Schiffe hängen modernd und verdrossen . . ." Heym, "Umbra Vitae," *MHD,* 39.

33. "Und aller Himmel Höfe sind verschlossen." Heym, "Umbra Vitae," *MHD,* 39.

34. Jakob v. Hoddis, "Morgens," *MHD,* 168.

35. Lichtenstein, "Nebel," *MHD,* 59.

36. Gottfried Benn, *Gesammelte Werke,* vol. 3, 8.

37. On this theme see the poems in the section "Gott ist tot—Gespräche mit Gott" in Vietta's collection *Lyrik des Expressionismus,* 155-179. For example Oskar Loerke writes: "The house of heaven pales into uncertainty" ("Ins Ungewisse bleicht das Himmelshaus" in "Die Ebene," 159); Alfred Lichtenstein: "And over everything hangs an old rag—/ The heavens . . . heathenish and without sense" "Und über allem hängt ein alter Lappen—/ Der Himmel . . . heidenhaft und ohne Sinn" in "Die Fahrt nach der Irrenanstalt I" ("Journey to the Insane-Asylum I"), 166.

38. For an analysis of this tendency towards dehumanization and "denaturization," see Jost Hermand, "Expressionismus als Revolution," *Von Mainz nach Weimar* (Stuttgart: Luchterhand 1969), 342-343.

39. "er kennt kein System für Lebendes, Chaos ist ihm willkommen als Freund, weil er die Ordnung in seiner Seele trägt." Richard Huelsenbeck, "Der neue Mensch," *Neue Jugend* 1 (May 23, 1917), 2-3. Rpt. *Manifeste und Dokumente,* 132.

40. "Denn er ist der Revolutionär in allen Lagern, der Unzufriedene mit allen Zuständen . . ." R. Leonhard, "Die Politik der Dichter," *Die weißen Blätter* 2, 6 (June 1915), 814-816. Rpt. *Manifeste und Dokumente* 364.

41. "Hier kann der Dichter gegenwirken; der Staat kann ohne ihn nicht auskommen. Er braucht die treibende Unruhe im Getriebe, er sollte Revolutionäre anstellen, zweideutige, die verzweifelt gegen alle Seiten sich empören." Leonhard, "Die Politik der Dichter." *Manifeste und Dokumente,* 365.

42. "Niemals war das Ästhetische und das l'art pour l'art so mißachtet wie in dieser Dichtung, die man die 'jüngste' oder 'expressionistische' nennt, weil sie ganz Eruption, Explosion, Intensität ist—sein muß um jene feindliche Krüste zu sprengen. Deshalb meidet sie die naturalistische Schilderung der Realität als Darstellungsmittel . . ." Pinthus, "Zuvor," Preface to *MHD* (1920). Rpt. *Manifeste und Dokumente,* 58.

43. "Deshalb frage man nicht nach der Qualität dieser Kunst, sondern nach ihrer Intensität. Die Intensität macht ihren Wert aus. Denn es geht nicht um die Kunstfertigkeit, sondern um den Willen . . . Diese Kunst wird allenthalben das Ästhetische zersprengen, wenn man das Ästhetische als wohlgefällige Formung des Gegebenen auffaßt." Kurt Pinthus, "Rede für die Zukunft" *Die Erhebung* (1919), 420. Rpt. W. Rothe (ed.), *Der Aktivismus 1915-20,* 132.

44. "Der Himmel ist ein graues Packpapier / Auf dem die Sonne klebt—ein Butterfleck." Lichtenstein, "Landschaft," *Lyrik des Expressionismus,* 209.

45. "Die Sonne, eine Butterblume, wiegt sich / Auf einem Schornstein, ihrem schlanken Stiele." Lichtenstein, "Nachmittag, Felder und Fabrik," *Lyrik des Expressionismus,* 73.

46. Franz Marc, *Turm der blauen Pferde,* 1914.

47. See especially Trakl's "Elis" and "An den Knaben Elis," *MHD,* 100, 101.

48. In a letter to his brother Theo of August 1888, Vincent van Gogh writes, "instead of trying to produce exactly what I have before my eyes, I use color more arbitrarily so as to express myself more forcefully." *The Letters of Vincent van Gogh* (New York, 1963), 276. John Willett also describes the influence of van Gogh's aesthetics in *Expressionism* (London: Weidenfeld, 1970), *passim.*

49. Hamann and Hermand, *Expressionismus,* 133.

50. Further evidence of the growing autonomy of the signifier may be seen for example in such diverse forms as the "Lautgedicht" or "sound poem" of Stramm and Ball, where the "materiality" of the medium itself is emphasized. It may also be traced, as we have seen in chapter one, in the many Expressionist narratives and dramas whose figures become increasingly free of the representational concerns of identity, plot and causality, and who tend instead to become free-floating symbols or "objective correlatives" (Sokel) rather than "realistic" characters. This independence is also related—as in the montage-structure—to a growing sense of autonomy of the various parts *within* the work, as for example in the conceptions of the "epic" in Brecht and Döblin.

51. For a commentary and extensive bibliography on the political commitment and active participation of many expressionists in revolutionary activity such as the November revolution. See *Manifeste und Dokumente,* 326-332.

52. The question of political engagement is often parried in the programmatic statements, frequently in a manner which does not so much sidestep a clear ideological commitment, as refuse to acknowledge the dichotomy between art and reality implied by such questions. Typically the dichotomy is itself subverted by the introduction of a third term, no-

tably "Geist" ("spirit," or "soul"): "art is not a flight from reality,—but rather a flight into the reality of the spirit. It is not a form of balm, but rather of agitation . . ." ("Die Kunst ist nicht Flucht aus der Wirklichkeit,—sondern Flucht in die Wirklichkeit des Geistes. Sie ist nicht Beruhigung, sondern Erregung . . .") writes Kurt Pinthus in "Rede für die Zukunft," *Die Erhebung* (1919) 415. Similarly Kurt Hiller sees the task of activism as "politicizing the spirit" ("den Geist zu politisieren"). In *Das Ziel* Jb. III, 1. Halbband, (Leipzig: Wolff, 1919). Quoted in *Manifeste und Dokumente,* 326.

53. See Sokel, *The Writer in Extremis,* 161.

54. According to Ogburn's famous thesis, a "cultural lag occurs when one of two parts of culture which are correlated changes before or in greater degree than the other part does . . ." See William F. Ogburn, "Cultural Lag as Theory" (1957) *On Culture and Social Change* (Chicago: University of Chicago Press, 1964), 86.

55. In his *Literary Theory* (Oxford: Blackwell, 1983) Terry Eagleton makes this point in a discussion of Raymond Williams' theory of drama (187).

56. Hermand, "Expressionismus als Revolution," 337.

57. "Wir gehen zu den elastischen Systemen über. Die klassischen starren Systeme sind Grenzfall und befriedigen nur fallweise . . . Das Bild des neuen Malers ist unabhängig von jenen Starrheitsmomenten, auf die hin wir unsere täglichen optischen Eindrücke versteifen . . . Das Bild des Malers schaukelt. Schaukeln Sie mit, geben Sie Ihre eigene Starre auf—das ist Expressionismus." Robert Müller, "Die Zeitrasse." In *Der Anbruch* 1 (1917/18). Rpt. *Manifeste und Dokumente,* 137.

58. As we shall see in the chapter on the poetics of expressionism, this openness is precisely what distinguishes the work of the avant-garde writers from the "monological" texts of the "naive" expressionists.

59. Franz Kafka, *Briefe 1902-1924,* ed. Max Brod (Frankfurt: Fischer, 1975), 28.

60. Thus expressionism's mode of liberation may occasionally take the paradoxical form of making the reader aware that the real world which he or she inhabits is a fiction which simultaneously serves as a prison or labyrinth preventing him from gaining access to "genuine" experience. The work of Franz Kafka with his thematization of the labyrinthine nature of truth ("Gesetz") and his sceptical attitude towards interpretation as a mere "expression of despair" must be seen in this expressionist context.

61. "Wir wollen sie nicht unterhalten. Wir wollen ihr bequemes ernst-erhabenes Weltbild tückisch demolieren." Rudolf Kurtz, "Programmatisches," *Der Sturm* 1 (3 March 1910), 2-3. Rpt. *Manifeste und Dokumente,* 515.

62. An anonymous reviewer of an earlier version of this chapter (published as an article in *German Quarterly*) quite rightly pointed to the seemingly conservative features in what I describe as the "revolutionary" make-up of expressionism, and in particular to the "religious and prophetic" tendencies which respond to the death of God by "resurrecting such essentials as 'Geist'." I would account for this apparently conciliatory moment however by maintaining firstly that an important feature of the expressionists' proclamation of these "essentials" is that such values remain, like "Geist" or the "new Man" ("neuer Mensch"), amorphous and provocatively obscure, as if the goal were the iconoclastic act of proclaiming an impossible new order, rather than the more difficult and pedestrian task (more characteristic of the earlier utopian and "idealist" avant-garde) of defining its "center," and so fixing the new order to a single position. Secondly, it should be observed that there is a self-critical tendency within expressionism—embodied precisely by its genuinely avant-garde wing rather than its idealist faction—which comes to the fore especially in the later period of its "recoil" from such prophetic excesses (Sokel), and which eschews even such vague proclamations and subjects them to parody. This recoil has its counterpart in dada's later onslaughts on the expressionists' prophetic excesses, where the very name of the group "dada" itself becomes an empty signifier parodying the often repeated watchword of the idealists within expressionism: "Geist" (i.e. "spirit," "mind" or "soul"). This central term, like the name "dada" itself, could be thought of as a hollow vessel, and one which is receptive for any new contents one cares to fill it with.

Bibliography

Anz, Thomas, and Michael Stark, eds. *Expressionismus: Manifeste und Dokumente zur deutschen Literatur 1910-1920.* Stuttgart: Metzler, 1981.

Ball, Hugo. "Kandinsky." Lecture held in Galerie Dada, Zürich, 7 April 1917. Rpt. Anz and Stark, *Manifeste und Dokumente.* 124-127.

Benn, Gottfried. "Schöpferische Konfession." *Gesammelte Werke.* Vol. 4. Ed. Dieter Wellershoff. Wiesbaden: Limes, 1958.

———. *Gehirne.* Stuttgart: Reclam, 1974.

Bloch, Ernst. "Diskussionen über Expressionismus." Schmitt, ed., *Expressionismusdebatte*. 180-191.

Brecht, Bertolt. *Schriften zum Theater*. Vol. 3. Frankfurt: Suhrkamp, 1963. "Der Nachgeborene." *Lyrik des Expressionismus*. 249.

Bürger, Peter. *Theory of the Avant-Garde*. Trans. Michael Shaw. Mineapolis: University of Minnesota Press, 1984. Trans. of *Theorie der Avantgarde*. Frankfurt: Suhrkamp, 1974.

"The Significance of the Avant-Garde for Contemporary Aesthetics: A Reply to Jürgen Habermas." *New German Critique* 8.1 (1981): 19-22.

Eagleton, Terry. *Literary Theory*. Oxford: Blackwell, 1983.

———. "Capitalism, Modernism and Postmodernism." *New Left Review* 52 (1985): 60-73.

Frühwald, Wolfgang. "Kunst als Tat und Leben. Über den Anteil deutscher Schriftsteller an der Revolution in München 1918/1919." *Sprache und Bekenntnis. Festschrift für Hermann Kunisch*. Ed. Wolfgang

———. Frühwald and Günter Niggl. Berlin: Dinker, 1971.

Hamann, Richard and Jost Hermand. *Expressionismus*. Munich: Nymphenberger Verlagshandlung, 1976.

Hermand, Jost. "Expressionismus als Revolution." *Von Mainz nach Weimar*. Stuttgart: Luchterhand, 1969. 298-355.

Heym, George. "Umbra Vitae." Pinthus, ed. *Menschheitsdämmerung*. 39-40.

———. "Der Irre." Rpt. Fritz Martini, ed. *Prosa des Expressionismus*. Stuttgart: Reclam, 1970. 140-155.

Hirst, Paul Q. "Althusser's Theory of Ideology." *Economy and Society* 5.4 (Nov. 1976): 385-412.

Hoddis, Jakob van. "Morgens." Pinthus, ed. *Menschheitsdämmerung*. 168.

Huelsenbeck, Richard, ed. *Dada. Eine literarische Dokumentation*. Hamburg: Rowohlt, 1984.

Kafka, Franz. *Briefe 1902-1924*. Ed. Max Brod. Frankfurt-on-Maine: Fischer, 1975.

———. *Gesammelte Werke*. Ed. Max Brod. Frankfurt: Fischer, 1983.

Klabund. "Ironische Landschaft." *Lyrik des Expressionismus*. 208.

Kurtz, Rudolf. "Programmatisches." *Der Sturm* 1 (3 March 1910): 2-3.

Rpt. Anz and Stark, eds. *Manifeste und Dokumente*. 515-518

Leonhard, Rudolf. "Die Politik der Dichter." *Die weißen Blätter* 2.6 (1915): 814-816. Rept. Anz and Stark, eds. *Manifeste und Dokumente*. 363-365.

Lichtenstein, Alfred. "Sommerfrische." Rpt. Pinthus, ed. *Menschheitsdämmerung*. 63.

———. "Nebel." Rpt. Pinthus, ed. *Menschheitsdämmerung*. 59.

———. "Landschaft." *Lyrik des Expressionismus*. 209.

———. "Nachmittag, Felder und Fabrik." *Lyrik des Expressionismus*. 73.

———. "Die Fahrt nach der Irrenanstalt I." *Lyrik des Expressionismus*. 166

Lohner, Edgar. "Die Problematik des Begriffes der Avantgarde." Hardt, ed. *Literarische Avantgarden*. 113-127.

Lukacs, Georg. "Es geht um den Realismus." Schmitt, ed. *Expressionismusdebatte*. 192-230.

———. "Franz Kafka oder Thomas Mann?" (in section "Die Gegenwartsbedeutung des kritischen Realismus.") *Werke IV*. Neuwied: Luchterhand, 1971. 500-550.

———. "Die weltanschaulichen Grundlagen des Avantgardeismus." *Werke IV*. 467-499.

Marc, Franz. "Der Blaue Reiter." (1914). Rpt. *Manifeste Manifeste. 1905-1933*. Ed. Diether Schmidt. Dresden: Verlag der Kunst, 1956.

Müller, Robert. "Die Zeitrasse." *Der Anbruch* 1. 1-2 (1917/18). Rpt. Anz and Stark, eds. *Manifeste und Dokumente*. 135-38.

Nietzsche Friedrich. *Werke*. Frankfurt: Ullstein 1969.

Ogburn, William F. "Cultural Lag as Theory" (1957). *On Culture and Social Change*. Chicago: University of Chicago Press, 1964.

Paulsen, Wolfgang. *Expressionismus und Aktivismus, eine typologische Untersuchung*. Bern and Leipzig: Gotthelf, 1935.

———. "Expressionism and the Tradition of Revolt" *Expressionism Reconsidered*. Houston German Studies Vol. 1. Ed. G. B. Pickar and K. E. Webb. Munich: Fink, 1979.

Pickar, G. B. and K. E. Webb, eds. *Expressionism Reconsidered*. Houston German Studies Vol. 1. Munich: Fink, 1979.

Pinthus, Kurt. "Versuch eines zukünftigen Dramas." *Schaubühne* 10.14 (2 April 1914): 391-394. Rpt. Anz and Stark, eds. *Manifeste und Dokumente*. 680-683.

———. "Rede für die Zukunft." *Die Erhebung. Jahrbuch für neue Dichtung und Wertung*. Ed. A. Wolfenstein. Berlin: Fischer 1919. Rpt. Rothe, ed. *Der Aktivismus*. 116-133.

Pinthus, Kurt, ed. *Menschheitsdämmerung. Ein Dokument des Expressionismus.* Reinbek: Rowohlt, 1983.

Pörtner, Paul ed. *Literaturrevolution 1910-1925. Dokumente, Manifeste, Programme.* 2 vols. Luchterhand: Neuwied, 1960.

Rothe, Wolfgang. *Der Aktivismus.* Munich: DTV, 1969.

Schreyer, Lothar. "Der neue Mensch." Rpt. Anz and Stark, eds. *Manifeste und Dokumente.* 140.

Sokel, Walter. *The Writer in Extremis; Expressionism in Twentieth-Century German Literature.* Stanford: Stanford University Press, 1959.

Stadler, Ernst. "Der Spruch," Pinthus, ed. *Menschheitsdämmerung.* 196.

Trakl, Georg. "Elis" and "An den Knaben Elis." Rpt. Pinthus, ed. *Menschheitsdämmerung.* 100, 101.

Trommler, Frank. *Sozialistische Literatur in Deutschland. Ein historischer Überblick.* Stuttgart: Kröner, 1976.

Vietta, Silvio, and Hans-Georg Kemper. *Expressionismus.* Munich: W. Fink, 1975.

Vietta, Silvio, ed. *Lyrik des Expressionismus.* Tübingen: Deutscher Taschenbuch-Verlag, 1976.

Willett, John. *Expressionism.* London: Weidenfeld and Nicolson, 1970.

EXPRESSIONISM IN GERMANY

Egbert Krispyn (essay date 1964)

SOURCE: Krispyn, Egbert. "Expressionists and Expressionism." In *Style and Society in German Literary Expressionism,* pp. 25-43. Gainesville: University of Florida Press, 1964.

[*In the following excerpt, Krispyn presents an overview of "expressionist" writers in Germany, emphasizing that their goals and style diverged too widely to fit under the umbrella of Expressionism.*]

The ambivalent feelings with which the expressionists from their position on the periphery of society regarded their fellow citizens determined the expressionist world view. Their feeling of hostility towards the community from which they were excluded, and whose values they had recognized as spurious, accounts for the critical outlook which became their most striking common characteristic. As Fritz Martini declares, "Die alles aufregende, noch heute keineswegs nur historisch gewordene Wirkung der expressionistischen Bewegung lag darin, dass sie rücksichtslos alles Gegebene, Bestehende, Überlieferte in Frage stellte, alle verbürgten, scheinbar endgültigen Ordnungen umwarf und durchstrich."[1]

At the same time, however, the positive side of their ambivalent feelings concerning society and the natural reaction to their loneliness and torturing isolation caused them to go beyond a purely negative attitude toward the existing state of affairs. Opposition to the status quo was not their only aim; they were also—at least potentially—inspired by some view or concept of a better world which was to take the place of the Wilhelmian reality they rejected.

These two notions gave the expressionists the urge to destroy symbolically the world and authority of the "fathers," not as a nihilistic end in itself, but in order to pave the way for a better, higher form of life. The desired destruction of the existing order was, in other words, a purgatory act with which the messianic expressionist wanted to prepare mankind for the advent of a superior pattern of existence. With reference to the inter-generation tension in which the position of the expressionists generally manifested itself, it could be said that they did not just want to kill their fathers to be rid of them; they wanted to raise them to a higher plane of humanity. The expressionists were not nihilists, but wanted the authority to which they were subjected to be worthy of their respect and reverence.

Among the expressionists there were, however, vast differences in the relative importance which they assigned to the destruction of the old world and to the creation of a new one. At one end of the scale there were those who really had no clear conception of what should replace the existing pattern of life. They were almost completely engrossed by the idea of the prerequisite demolition of the established order, and what lay beyond it occurred to them at best in occasional, almost fleeting prospects of undefined and unspecified serenity or felicity. An extreme instance of this negative outlook is that of Georg Heym, as appears from such well-known diary entries as "Warum ermordet man nicht den Kaiser oder den Zaren? Man lässt sie ruhig weiter schädlich sein. Warum macht man keine Revolution? . . . Würden einmal wieder Barrikaden gebaut. Ich wäre der erste, der sich darauf stellte, ich wollte noch mit der Kugel im Herzen den Rausch der Begeisterung spüren."[2]

In contrast to such predominantly "negative" expressionists there were those who acknowledged the need of overthrowing the Establishment as an inevitable preparatory step, but focused their attention mainly on the new world they wanted to establish on the ruins of the old.

These writers can be divided into two major categories depending upon the nature of their ideal world image. First, there were those who envisaged the future in terms of a society reorganized along definite political lines, invariably based on a communist or socialist ideology. Ernst Toller provides an example of this type of expressionist who saw the salvation of mankind in the replacement of the existing social order by a different one. A brief survey of his activities during the latter part of the war and the subsequent revolutionary days reads, "Organisiert mit Kurt Eisner den Widerstand gegen den Krieg. Beteiligt am Streik der Munitionsarbeiter in München 1918. Verhaftet, im November freigelassen. Vorsitzender der Arbeiter-, Bauern- und Soldatenräte in München. Spielte eine führende Rolle in der bayerischen Räterepublik 1919. Im Juni 1919 verhaftet, zu 5 Jahren Festung verurteilt."[3]

Second, there was a group that pinned its hopes, not on a reorganization of society, but on the intrinsic qualities of the human soul. These writers were convinced of mankind's innate goodness, which they considered to be restrained and prevented from asserting itself by the strait jacket of objectionable social codes and conventions into which the individual was forced. They visualized the redemption of man as a liberation of the elemental forces which he harbored in his soul. If the social compulsion which kept these potential spiritual powers in bondage could in any way whatever be overcome, all mankind would be united in universal love. A feeling of brotherhood would draw all men into one happy community without barriers or discriminations. Any social organization whatever would, of course, constitute a serious obstacle on the road toward such a blissful state of humane anarchy.

Those who embraced as their ideal the establishment of a new world founded solely on the hypothesis that man is basically good tended therefore to deviate somewhat from the other types of expressionist in their attitude towards the Establishment. Whereas both the negativistic and the political expressionists opposed the specific form of social organization found in Middle Europe at the beginning of the modern technological age, the "anarchists" were inclined to reject the idea of society as such, thereby rising to some extent above the very subjective and limited perspective of the others. René Schickele exemplifies the type of expressionist who passionately believes that man is good, when, with an allusion to Novalis, (which in itself is significant) he associates the emergence of a new, liberated humanity with the unveiling of the statue of Sais. "Ein Gesicht erscheint im Atmosphärenwust der Angst und Lüge: das Gesicht des Menschen. Das Gesicht einer Kreatur, überirdisch glänzend."[4]

In spite of their divergent formulations of the basic expressionist attitude *against* the old order and in *favor* of a new ideal, expressionist writers from all three groups shared one fundamental desire. They all wanted to bring about certain changes in the world which would make it conform to their own standards, so that they might be delivered from their outsidership and be integrated in the community. And this reformation of reality was to be achieved by means of their writing; their creative activity was intended to bring about the downfall of the old and the establishment of a new pattern of existence.

Their writing was not to be a record of their private ideas, not the immediate embodiment of mental processes based on the poet's emotional experience in a symbolic form which requires the reader's sympathetic understanding and initiative in order to be intelligible. The expressionists wanted to break through their isolation and establish contact with their fellows; they were driven by the desire to affect them and their outlook on the world. Therefore they addressed their work to a public which was to be forcefully called to attention and influenced.

This rhetorical approach manifested itself in general in the large number of periodicals and broadsheets published by the expressionists and in the activities of the numerous cabarets. Among the latter the Neopathetische Cabaret in Berlin played a particularly important part in the emergence of the early expressionist movement. It was an enterprise of the equally important Neue Club, founded in March, 1909, by Kurt Hiller, which counted Georg Heym, Jakob van Hoddis, and Ernst Blass among its most creatively gifted members.[5]

The expressionists' tendency to use their creative talent to gain the ear of their fellow citizens and, above all, influence them in their ideas and their way of living is programmatically expressed in the opening lines of Johannes R. Becher's *Vorbereitung*:

> Der Dichter meidet strahlende Akkorde.
> Er stösst durch Tuben, peitscht die Trommel schrill.
> Er reisst das Volk auf mit gehackten Sätzen.[6]

Even more explicit in this respect is the speech with which Kurt Hiller, in October, 1912, introduced his literary Cabaret Gnu:

> Meine Herren, meine Damen!
>
> Sie erwarten jetzt Sätze zu hören über den sogenannten Zweck dieses Cabarets. Mit dem, was Sie sich selber sagen können, möchte ich Sie nicht langweilen: nämlich damit, dass hier eine junge Gruppe von Litteraten durch Gesprochnes die Wirkung verstärken will, die ihr das bloss Geschriebne, infolge der Schlechtigkeit oder Abhängigkeit fast aller Journale, in nur schwachem Grade bietet. . . . Verlogen oder sehr dumm ist ein Künstler, stellt er in Abrede, dass sein Tun, das blosse Kunst-Schaffen, bereits ein Mittel sei, Macht über Gemüter (und nicht nur über Gemüter!) zu gewinnen.[7]

Otto Mann summarizes the aspirations of the expressionists when he describes their attitude in the words:

"Es soll wieder eine wirkungsmächtigere Kunst geschaffen werden."[8]

Thus it is clear that the expressionists strove for persuasive, efficacious literary expression of their unhappy outsidership and consequent ambivalent attitude towards society. Their world image's fundamental polarity, with Establishment and ideal as the respective objects of their hatred and yearning, appeared on the individual level either as all-absorbing hostility toward established values and concepts, or as preoccupation with the new world which was to rise out of the ruins of the old. The positive ideal could either be of a sociopolitical nature, or be envisaged as a state of happy anarchy based only on man's supposed inherent goodness.

The three types of attitude found among the expressionists are reflected in expressionist writing, which can be analogously divided into three groups. Depending upon the peculiar nature of the individual talents, each of these subdivisions in itself includes a variety of techniques and approaches. In spite of such differences in execution, all literature which is traditionally regarded as undoubtedly expressionist displays one of three possible attitudes. Corresponding to the three types of mental attitude, expressionist writing either fanatically attacks the status quo, giving only incidental and unspecified glimpses of a better world, or it evokes visions of an ideal community without dwelling on the necessity to overcome the old order first. The ideal itself can be a new social organization, or an anarchic brotherhood of men based only on mutual love.

It should perhaps be stressed that the three types and the three literary patterns so described are theoretical constructions representing the extremes of a sliding scale. "Pure" types are rare; it is the predominance of traits belonging to one type over those pertaining to others which is decisive. Even with the latter reservation, one can ascribe a type only to individual pieces of writing, not collectively to the work of an author who may change his mind or be subject to emotions which temporarily color his views. In most cases there is likely to be a large degree of consistency in the writings of one person, especially over a limited period of time; however, the exceptions are too numerous to ignore.

For the following interpretations which will demonstrate the three patterns of expressionist writing, texts have been selected which, each in its own way, are unambiguously representative of a particular trend. First those works are to be considered in which negative, destructive criticism of the existing state of affairs is the predominant feature, while positive aspects play a minimal role and are represented only in isolated, unspecific allusions to a better world. In the general objurgatory atmosphere which by their very nature pervades such writings, the idealistic elements are very frequently couched in an ironical tone. Often, too, the unattainability of the ideal is implied, thus strengthening the pessimistic portent of the work, or else the author did no more than introduce a fleeting vision of serenity into an otherwise ugly and repulsive scene. In spite of such qualifying circumstances, the presence of positive traits, no matter how slight or in what context, hints at the existence of the possibility of an ideal.

Among exponents of this current, one could mention Gustav Sack, for instance in his poem *Bagatelle* which gives a very negative picture of the big city as the epitome of the beginning technological era.

> In eine neue Bude zog ich ein!
> Ein schiefer Tisch, ein krummer Stuhl,
> eines wackligen Bettes Unzuchtpfuhl—
> in diese Bude zog ich ein.
>
> Garküchen unter mir und Kegelbahnen,
> mir gegenüber 'ne verdreckte Wand
> und über mir ein kleines blaues Band
> mit feinen weissen Wolkenfahnen.
>
> Was soll ich hier? Was will, was kann ich hier?
> Doch so war's immer schon:
> Armut und Dreck und wie zum Hohn
> leuchtet ein Fetzen Himmel mir.[9]

In this poem the references to the blue sky, which relieve the sordidness of the work, symbolize the polarity of the author's world view. A similar antithesis is sometimes introduced by Georg Heym, in whose work the positive elements also play a very minor, but by no means negligible, role. His poetic technique for attacking the established order is, however, very different from Sack's references in *Bagatelle* to the less savory aspects of the big city.

In Heym's work the prevailing concept of life is denied and contradicted through the postulation of a viewpoint which differs radically from the generally accepted anthropocentric one. Heym created a universe in which man is not the supreme force whose rational powers can subjugate and use the whole of nature for his own purpose, i.e., progress in the materialistic sense. In his works a de-animated humanity, reduced to utter insignificance in the cosmic order, is the passive victim of a cruel and inexorable fate. This reversal of the current conception of the world can be traced throughout Heym's entire work, including poetry, drama, and prose.[10] It may here be illustrated with the aid of his best known poem *Der Krieg*. It describes the emergence of the demon of war out of his subterranean realm and his devastating progress over the earth, in the course of which the vulnerability and helplessness of humanity reveal themselves in its blind panic and unheroic, collective suffering and death. In the second and third stanzas of the poem, Heym depicts the shadow thrown ahead by the approaching catastrophe and shows how it casts a spell over the people, halting their movements and arousing fear and uncertainty in them.

> In den Abendlärm der Städte fällt es weit,
> Frost und Schatten einer fremden Dunkelheit.
> Und der Märkte runder Wirbel stockt zu Eis.
> Es wird still. Sie sehn sich um. Und keiner weiss.
>
> In den Gassen fasst es ihre Schulter leicht.
> Eine Frage. Keine Antwort. Ein Gesicht erbleicht.
> In der Ferne zittert ein Geläute dünn,
> Und die Bärte zittern um ihr spitzes Kinn.

The next quatrain begins with the lines:

> Auf den Bergen hebt er schon zu tanzen an,
> Und er schreit: "Ihr Krieger alle, auf und an!"

This summons to the warriors stresses the crucial fact about Heym's treatment of the subject matter: war is represented, not as an inter-human, but as a super-human phenomenon; it presses mankind into its service; man does not "make" war for his own purposes. The fate of those enlisted under the banners of war is death.

> Wo der Tag flieht, sind die Ströme schon voll Blut.
> Zahllos sind die Leichen schon im Schilf gestreckt,
> Von des Todes starken Vögeln weiss bedeckt.

No better lot than the warriors meet with awaits the fleeing civilians.

> Und was unten auf den Strassen wimmelnd flieht,
> Stösst er in die Feuerwälder, wo die Flamme brausend zieht.

That there is no direct mention of the people, but only the derogatory reference to their swarming flight, is a characteristic indication of the wretched, victimized anonymity of these human lives. These visions of passive human suffering reach a climax in the next to last quatrain, with the collective annihilation of mankind in the collapsing, burning city.

> Eine grosse Stadt versank in gelbem Rauch,
> Warf sich lautlos in des Abgrunds Bauch.

The utter negativism and pessimism of Heym's world view as exemplified in this poem is, however, in a few cases relieved through the introduction of a final vision of serenity and beauty which seems to hold some hope for mankind by implying that there must be some escape from its plight. An example of this is the stanza which ends a depressing and dehumanized depiction of a *Laubenfest*:

> Im blauen Abend steht Gewölke weit,
> Delphinen mit den rosa Flossen gleich,
> Die schlafen in der Meere Einsamkeit.

The ideal which is only wistfully and indirectly alluded to in this category of expressionist literature forms the main theme of the other patterns of expressionism, in which the criticism and the poetic destruction of the existing world are an essential but subordinate preparation for the postulation of a utopian world image. As pointed out, in many cases the expressionist sees the salvation of mankind in the establishment of a new social order. The better world which these writers look forward to is seen as something to be consciously conceived and organized by themselves and their friends. The authors concerned play the parts of messianic agitators and reformers.

The first half of Reinhard Sorge's *Der Bettler,* one of the earliest dramas of the expressionist era, illustrates the pattern.[11] In this lyrical drama the denunciation of the status quo in its artistic and moral aspects takes place in the early scenes with the critics and prostitutes. Yet it amounts to a distortion of the facts when the play is characterized as an unmasking of the "Entartung des Gesellschafts- und Kulturlebens."[12]

This critical element forms by no means the substance of the work, but is merely a preparation for the visions of a new world. One of these stems from the young poet himself; the other from his insane father. The relationship between these two figures is a very important factor in the play. Although there is mention of the fact that the poet is unhappy at home, Otto Mann misses the point when he states, "In Sorge's *Bettler* revoltiert der junge Dichter gegen ein bedrückendes Milieu."[13] Under the circumstances, the young poet's unhappiness about his environment is quite natural, and it only serves to motivate the Maecenas' offer of a stipend, the refusal of which leads the poet on to expound his utopian vision.

Far from posing a generation problem in the customary expressionist manner, the figure of the father introduces a variation on the son's theme of a better world to come. Each sees himself as the chosen redeemer of mankind, and takes upon himself the task of bringing about an improvement in the lot of humanity. This is very clearly expressed in the poet's words. "Ich will die Welt auf meine Schultern nehmen / Und sie mit Lobgesang zur Sonne tragen."

Walter Sokel points out the similarity which in this respect exists between father and son. "The Father constitutes a musical variation of the Messiah theme in *The Beggar*. His megalomaniacal Messianic dream functions as a counterpoint to the Son's search for meaning and salvation." But this commentator overemphasizes the father's materialism. "In contrast to the Son's idealism, the Father represents the materialistic counterpoint in the composition. He misinterprets the Messianic theme materialistically as technical progress and enrichment."[14]

That the father's vision goes beyond such narrow-minded materialism is indicated by his comparison of the sailing ships with doves. "Das sind die Tauben, die ich liebe." What he says about the bridges also shows that technical progress and riches are not his sole aim. "Oh Segen! Breite / Bruderbrücken binden Ufer und Ufer! / Ja, brüderlich!" In this context it is relevant that his vision concludes with the words: "Alle Wunder! Alle Wunder!" But the father's aim is best characterized by the striking similarity between his grandiose dream and the parts of *Faust II* in which the scene of Faust's final activities is described. The motifs of the canals which mean happiness, the ports, the ships, and the emphasis on the fertility of the transformed world, all occur in *Faust* in speeches by Philemon and Baucis,[15] Lynceus der Türmer,[16] and Faust himself.[17] The connection between the two works even extends to *der Weisheit letzter Schluss*: Faust's stress on the fact that man has to be diligent and brave in order to deserve the good life on his land, expressed in terms such as "kühnemsig" and "tüchtig," is echoed in the father's line: "Ja, Segen! Brot und Mark schwankt in den Lüften." The same motifs occur in the young poet's vision. "Hungernde Mädchen, / Die um ihr unecht Kind sich mager mühen, / Sollen dort Brot finden." And somewhat later, "Männer aber / Sollen die Stirnen härten an Leid und Lust."

The difference between the two visions is one of accent only; the father concentrates on the development of the earth's resources as the source of the blessed, marvelous state of mankind his dream evokes, while the son hopes to achieve the same end through his own theater, which is to be "Das Herz der Kunst: aus allen Ländern strömen / Die Menschen alle an die heilige Stätte / Zur Heiligung, nicht nur ein kleines Häuflein / Erlesener!" This vision of a classless and international audience, which may well have been inspired by Wagner's original intentions for Bayreuth, provides the most specific socio-political symbol of Sorge's ideal of a better world to be found in this play.

Other authors in the socio-politically inclined form of expressionism had a more practical and realistic conception of the forces which shape society. An example may be found in Ernst Wilhelm Lotz' well known poem *Aufbruch der Jugend*. The first five stanzas conjure up visions of revolutionary turmoil and the forceful overthrow of the established order. The final quatrain then reads:

> Beglänzt von Morgen, wir sind die verheissnen Erhellten,
> Von jungen Messiaskronen das Haupthaar umzackt,
> Aus unsern Stirnen springen leuchtende, neue Welten,
> Erfüllung und Künftiges, Tage, sturmüberflaggt!

In these verses the poet represents the tradition of the self-proclaimed redeemer, which in this period was widely revived because of the authors' personal situation. Nailed on the cross by the world they lived in, they tried to comfort themselves by equating their fate with that of Christ. "The crucified is also the savior. Persecuted at present, he will inherit the kingdom of the elect. Those who scorn him now will one day throng to the theaters and museums to worship him."[18]

The drops of blood which the crown of thorns draws from their foreheads are the new worlds of the future, in which their ideas have found fulfillment. This last image indicates not only the cerebral approach of the poet, but also the fact that he regards himself as the originator of a new order. In its extreme forms the approach represented by Lotz could lead to a disregard of artistic quality for the sake of political agitation, as can be observed in the works of such writers as Johannes R. Becher and Ludwig Rubiner.

Besides the negativistic and the socio-political trends, a third basic category is distinguishable in the realizations of the central expressionistic constellation of negative and positive concepts. It also emphasizes the latter, introducing destructive criticism of the established values and institutions only as a preliminary step to the establishment of a better society. This pattern presents the view that the faults inherent in the old order are to be overcome, not by organizing life in a new and better way, but by simply letting man's basic instincts guide him in a social vacuum. The writers stress the essential goodness of mankind, which, if only the influence of the existing order could be eliminated or overcome, would bring all men together in harmony and mutual love.

One such work is Carl Hauptmann's *Krieg. Ein Tedeum*, which depicts the total destruction of established civilization and society in a war organized by the great powers and international finance. Afterwards, out of ruins and holes the cripples emerge, who, at first hesitantly, establish a relationship of mutual trust in spite of their national origin and social status in the old world. This new tentative atmosphere of universal brotherhood is subsequently confirmed in the emotional upsurge caused by the birth of the new man.[19]

The basic attitude from which these works sprang could also express itself in an entirely different manner. Thus a similar confidence in the essential goodness of mankind motivates Carl Sternheim's satirical play *Die Hose*.[20] In this so-called comedy the faults of the bourgeois world are illuminated through the contrast between those who have undergone its corroding influence on their personalities and the primitively vital Maske, who under the cloak of outward conformity has asserted his independence of the stifling code. Sternheim, in attacking the middle-class world, shows that basically the bourgeois is a person of estimable qualities which are prevented from coming to the surface because of the unpropitious spirit of the age.

This interpretation of *Die Hose* deviates from the view held by Carol Petersen, who sees in the comedy an ironically exaggerated exposé of the bourgeois vices as embodied in Maske. "In diesem Stück gab ein offenbar fanatischer Entlarver seinen Figuren etwas von seiner Kälte mit. . . . Der Dichter hatte sie stilisiert, liess ein Netz über sie werfen, in dem sie alle verzweifelt zappelten, ohne aus ihrer Umgarnung herauszukommen. Theobald Maske hiess der Mann, der dies Netz am gestreckten Arm hielt, selber eine überdimensionale Emanation niederer Begierden. Emporkommen, unbekümmert um Tränen und Opfer Getretener, schien der einzige Sinn seiner einträglichen Beatmung [sic]."[21]

This viewpoint oversimplifies the interrelationship of the characters; Maske's main counterpart Scarron, for instance, is not caught up in a net held by the other, but in his own "impotence of the heart."[22] When Luise offers herself to him, Theobald intervenes neither in the flesh nor in the spirit, and Scarron fails for no other reason than that love to him is only a word, not an emotion. Walter Sokel's opinion of *Die Hose* does take this circumstance into account, and avoids the error of seeing Maske as the ruthless Untermensch who demoniacally terrorizes the other characters. This commentator thus arrives at a more differentiated judgment on the bourgeois husband. "Crude and egotistical though he is, Maske can love. In contrast to the poet, who promises much and gives so little, the bourgeois promises little but accomplishes much."[23]

Scarron's reluctant admiration for the primitive manliness of Maske is, no doubt justifiably, interpreted by Sokel as an expression of Sternheim's own sentiments. Yet it appears that in the final assessment of the play Sokel, too, subscribes to the view that Sternheim's main aim is an attack on the figure of the middle-class citizen represented by Theobald Maske. "He secretly admires him while overtly attacking him."[24]

Apart from the fact that there is actually nothing secret about the admiration expressed for Maske in the play, the validity of this interpretation is further limited by the absence of any real criticism directed against him. Mandelstam and Scarron are not qualified to judge him, and their attacks against him end in their total defeat, while Gertrud Deuter, whose name is indicative of her function in this respect, radically changes her initially negative opinion of him after they have together examined the view from his bedroom window.

Sternheim's intentions with *Die Hose* have apparently always been subject to misunderstandings of this nature, for in the Foreword to the second edition he tried to correct them. According to Sternheim's own interpretation, borne out by the text, it is wrong to regard *Die Hose* as an ironical attack against the figure of Theobald Maske. The latter is not intended as a personification of the negative aspects of middle-class society. He is, on the contrary, an example with which the author intended to open the eyes of his bourgeois audience to their own fundamental virtues. Maske's basic qualities, such as the urges for self-preservation and for self-sufficiency which make him disregard literature and philosophy, are demonstrated to make him superior to the erudite Scarron and the latter's cheaper pendant Mandelstam.

These two are the main exponents of the bourgeois ideology in its various aspects; the barber, for instance, through his boundless admiration for the music of Wagner, who, at least in Sternheim's opinion, epitomized the worst aspects of the Zeitgeist.[25] As Mandelstam reveals himself through his enthusiasm for this composer, so does Scarron through the opinions he voices in the debate with Maske. The crassest example is his reaction when Theobald refers to the role of the heart. "Das Herz ist ein Muskel, Maske." It is Scarron, not Maske, who adheres to the pedestrian materialism which pervaded the mental atmosphere of Wilhelmian Germany. In his other utterances Scarron indulges in empty phraseology which is intended to sound profound, but really only covers up his unwillingness to face the concrete facts of life, such facts as "dass Frauen ein Herz haben, Kinder zur Welt kommen."

Another character who deliberately shuts out the world is the scholar Stengelhöh, who is usually disregarded in interpretations of *Die Hose*. He tries to arrange his life in such a way that he need not be reminded of the basic facts of sexuality, or of the existence of any living creatures such as small children, canaries, dogs, and cats. Maske, on the other hand, refuses to bother with the realms of science and the arts, and limits himself to the instinctual level of life. That level includes food and sex, but also an awareness of the nature of love and the ability to bring some happiness into the lives of his fellows.

The text of *Die Hose* thus justifies Sternheim's claims that he wanted to awaken the bourgeois' "Mut zu seiner menschlichen Ursprünglichkeit," by demolishing the "Wall verabredeter Ideologien, Gaswolken von Apotheosen, Schützengräbern von Metaphern" behind which the middle class pursued its petty money-making.[26] The portrayal of Maske serves to show the vast resources of vitality which the bourgeois unleashes in himself if he refuses to pay homage to the artistic, philosophical, and scholarly sacred cows of his environment and time, and discards professional ambitions. But this lonely rebellion against the prevailing system is only possible under the cover of outward conformism—hence Maske's name and his concern about the central incident of the play, which might have resulted in the loss of his protective anonymity. He says, "Meine Unscheinbarkeit ist die Tarnkappe, unter der ich meinen Neigungen, meiner innersten Natur frönen darf."

In the field of poetry the absolute belief in the essential goodness of human nature is represented, among others, by Iwan Goll. The first version of Goll's poem *Der Panamakanal* (1912) describes the emergence of a harmonious brotherhood of men out of the ruins of the old world. In the first section, subtitled *DieArbeit*, the towns with their palaces and hovels and all other man-made evidence of inequality and suppression are razed. But the tenacity of the old order is shown in the laborers' inability to overcome the barriers between them of nationality and religion. Only when the canal is finally completed, and the connection between the oceans made, does the new world rise out of the chaos. There will be no hostility, but only love.

> Und wenn diese Tore sich öffnen werden,
> Wenn zwei feindliche Ozeane mit Gejubel sich küssen—
> Oh, dann müssen
> Alle Völker weinen auf Erden.

In the second part of the work, *Die Weihe*, this universal fraternization is symbolized in a number of images and is shown in its effect on the life of the people. The barriers of language, color, and custom have disappeared, and in the atmosphere of freedom which has replaced the old restrictive order even differences in individual temperament are overcome by the feeling of love and brotherhood which now unites all mankind.

Sentiments such as these inevitably led to the poetic invocation of the God who is Love, and therewith to the ecstatic religious tone of many works by Werfel, Unruh, Heynicke, the post-*Bettler* Sorge, and others. In them the problems and sorrows of human existence are an incomprehensible part of a higher plan, and are left to Him to solve by His divine grace which He imparts to all mankind.

> erwacht zu schöpferischen Glücksaufschwüngen,
> schiesst Gottes Blut, das einmal schon vergeblich rann,
> durch aller Menschen Herzen in Kometensprüngen. . . .[27]

The development of a religious attitude out of a simply human boundless love for all mankind and faith in its essential goodness, no matter how obscured and perverted through a hypocritical and evil social organization, can be demonstrated most clearly in the case of Franz Werfel. He was no less violently opposed to the existing order than poets like Sack and Heym, but his confidence in the basic qualities of his fellow men was so great that he yearned to be one with them, regardless of the unpleasant features which the established pattern of life may have given them. He did not concentrate on the evocation of destructive visions, as Heym did, but envisaged a universal brotherhood which would reduce the barriers of status, religious organization, race, and all others to utter insignificance.

His fundamental attitude is expressed in the opening line of the poem *An den Leser*. "Mein einziger Wunsch ist, dir, o Mensch verwandt zu sein!" It appears, however, that his own desire, his own will power are inadequate to the task of establishing the longed-for intimate relationship with all men against the resistance of the existing order. Thus the poem ends with an implied admission of defeat in the subjunctive mood of the verses: "O, könnte es einmal geschehen, / Dass wir uns, Bruder, in die Arme fallen!"

The realization that mere good intentions are impotent led Werfel to the invocation of a superior power, through whose intermediary he hoped to achieve his aim of identifying himself with the whole of humanity. This approach inevitably resulted in work of a predominantly religious nature. Werfel's writings include a number of poems which represent this turn to God as a way of overcoming his human isolation. A case in point is his poem entitled *Ich bin ja noch ein Kind*. In contrast to his statement in *An den Leser* "ich habe alle Schicksale durchgemacht," the poet here disclaims all familiarity with the fate of those less naïve and fortunate than he.

> Ich bin gesund,
> Und weiss noch nicht, wie Greise rosten.
> Ich hielt mich nie an groben Pfosten,
> Wie Frauen in der schweren Stund'.

Subsequent stanzas serve to illustrate the writer's incapability of identifying himself with any human being in any walk of life. His unfulfilled desire for identification, however, extends much farther than the human realm to which *An den Leser* is limited. In *Ich bin ja noch ein Kind* the poet also laments the fact that he does not know and share the fate of animals and things, cats, horses, lamps, hats, and even the wind. Hereby he makes it clear that in his work he deals with the question of individuation in an absolute sense, far beyond the effect of a specific social organization on the existence of certain groups of people, although in details the poem has pronounced social-critical aspects. "Nie war ich ein Kind, zermalmt in den Fabriken / Dieser elenden Zeit, mit Ärmchen, ganz benarbt!"

God is regarded in this poem as being present in all suffering things—the omnipresence for which the poet himself yearns.

> Du aber, Herr, stiegst nieder, auch zu mir.
> Und hast die tausendfache Qual gefunden,
> Du hast in jedem Weib entbunden,
> Und starbst im Kot, in jedem Stück Papier,
> In jedem Zirkusseehund wurdest Du geschunden,
> Und Hure warst Du manchem Kavalier!

The poet beseeches this omnipresent God to grant him the same universality in the repeated exclamation "O Herr, zerreisse mich!" When he, too, dies in every

"Lumpen," "Katze," "Gaul," and "Soldat," and is dispersed in the wind, existing in all things, even in smoke, then the words "Wir sind," which so far he has used intuitively, will really become a concrete and meaningful expression of the unity of all Creation.

Ich bin ja noch ein Kind is but one of several poems in which Werfel manifests this attitude and calls upon God to end his painful isolation from the rest of the world. Very typical in this respect is his adaptation of the traditional Pentecostal motif *Veni Creator Spiritus,* the first stanza of which concisely summarizes the despair at the fact of his individuation and the object of his profoundest desire.

> Komm, heiliger Geist, Du schöpferisch!
> Den Marmor unsrer Form zerbrich!
> Dass nicht mehr Mauer krank und hart
> Den Brunnen dieser Welt umstarrt,
> Dass wir gemeinsam und nach oben
> Wie Flammen ineinander toben!

The yearning for cosmic unification in God reaches a climax with the lines:

> Dass alle wir in Küssens Überflüssen
> Nur Deine reine heilige Lippe küssen!

This poem thus marks the extreme in the development of that type of expressionistic writing which has an almost desperate recourse to religious postulates in an endeavor to substantiate its faith in the basic, potential qualities of mankind.

The foregoing interpretations have, with the aid of specific texts, shown that expressionist writings fall into three broad categories, depending on the emphasis that is placed on the destruction of the old order, and, where applicable, the nature of the evoked ideal. Even the few examples considered demonstrate the wide variety of methods, determined by talent and genre, with which each of the three basic patterns can be realized. This diversity may make it difficult to recognize at first glance the relationship between works belonging to one group, as, for instance, Sternheim's *Die Hose* and Goll's *Der Panamakanal.* The decisive point is, however, that beyond such questions of specific execution, the writings concerned manifest the same attitude as regards the postulated ideal and the rejection of the status quo. It may be said that to be regarded as part of the body of expressionist writing, a work should either *contain a violent attack on the existing order,* which is contrasted only by implication or in vague allusions with an unspecified ideal; *or take the destruction of the status quo more or less for granted to dwell on visions of a sociopolitical, or, alternately, of a humanistic-anarchic nature.*

In addition to displaying characteristics conforming to any of these three extreme types, or a possible intermediate position between them, *an expressionist work,* because of the writers' desire to gain concrete results with it, *is rhetorical.* In fact, most of the attempts to define a typical pattern of linguistic usage seem to be based mainly on the rhetorical elements in expressionism. There are, however, many often mutually contradictory ways in which a piece of writing can clamor for attention and attempt to influence the public, while, moreover, the rhetorical effect often depends at least as much on the actual vocabulary used as on the linguistic and syntactic devices employed.

A survey of the works, which in the foregoing have been interpreted from another viewpoint, shows the multitude of rhetorical devices employed even in such a limited number of examples. In Gustav Sack's poem the most obvious of these devices are the exclamatory tone and the repetition of the first line; the "rhetorical" questions introducing the third stanza; unlyrical and crude expressions designed to shock the sense of propriety of the bourgeois, such as "Dreck," "verdreckt," "Unzuchtpfuhl," and a tendency towards colloquial, popular turns of phrase such as "Bude" and "'ne" instead of "eine."

In Georg Heym's poem *Der Krieg* the will to reach and affect an audience is manifest mainly in the heavy monotony of the metre. Each line rolls on with the irresistible finality of fate itself; the verses mercilessly pound on the reader's or hearer's mind with terrifying force and regularity.

Both *Die Hose* by Carl Sternheim and Reinhard Sorge's *Der Bettler,* as plays written to be performed before an audience, show that they seek an effect and a resonance by the very fact that they are dramas. The rhetorical tendency inherent in the genre is further heightened, in the case of Sternheim, through the liberal use of irony and satire, and in Sorge's work through shockingly grotesque scenes such as that in which the father for lack of red ink pierces a bird with his compasses.

In Iwan Goll's *Der Panamakanal* the devices of enumeration and accumulation are in evidence, while the frequent repetition of such words as "alle," "jeder," "jenes" also plays a role in the present context. Typical for Werfel's poems *An den Leser, Ich bin ja noch ein Kind,* and *Veni Creator Spiritus* are the vocative and exclamatory tone of many verses, while in Ernst Wilhelm Lotz' *Aufbruch der Jugend* the rhetorical attitude is clear in the use of "wir," the violent vocabulary and the vehement rhythm.

As these few instances indicate, the many ways in which a rhetorical effect can be achieved make it quite impracticable to formulate a rule defining this aspect of expressionism.[28] Moreover, the rhetorical appeal to the audience is by no means restricted to expressionism—in a sense it is even inherent in certain literary genres such as the drama. The rhetorical quality of a work can therefore not be used as a criterion to determine whether a given work should be considered part of the expressionist movement. On the other hand, the *absence* of a rhetorical attitude in writing which otherwise does fit into one of the three expressionist patterns would indicate the work concerned does not spring from the fundamental expressionist experience of reluctant outsidership and consequent ambivalence towards society. Such a work should therefore not be assigned to the movement.

In practice, the question whether a certain piece of writing does or does not belong to expressionism itself will only occur in the case of temporally closely related or contemporaneous work. Of greater significance than such problems of "labeling" specific works is the matter of determining the expressionist influence on later literature—not in an ideological, but in a formal sense. Practically every treatise on present-day authors finds occasion to claim such connections between them and the expressionists.[29]

Notes

1. *Was war Expressionismus?* p. 23.
2. *Dichtungen und Schriften,* III, 135, 139.
3. Catalogue No. 7, *Expressionismus. Literatur und Kunst 1910-1923,* of the Schiller-Nationalmuseum, Marbach a.N., published by Bernhard Zeller for the Deutsche Schillergesellschaft on the occasion of the "Sonderausstellung" from May 8 till October 31, 1960, p. 314.
4. Quoted in Soergel and Hohoff, p. 127.
5. In June, 1910, the Neopathetische Cabaret presented the first of its programs, which consisted of recitations, lectures on philosophical, political, and other themes, and performances of contemporary music. Unfortunately, less than one year after its inception, the development of this most significant venture was halted prematurely when a schism occurred in the Neue Club, and left it bereft of its organizer and key figure Kurt Hiller. The death of Georg Heym in January, 1912, dealt a fatal blow to both organizations, which dissolved soon afterwards. For a detailed account of the rise and fall of the Neue Club and the Neopathetische Cabaret, see my article, "Georg Heym und der Neue Club," *Revista de Letras* (Assis), IV (1963), 262-71.
6. Unless otherwise specified, all quotations of expressionist poetry are from *Menschheitsdämmerung,* with the exception of Georg Heym's poems, which are quoted after *Gesammelte Gedichte,* ed. Carl Seelig (Zürich, 1947).
7. Hiller, *Die Weisheit der Langenweile, eine Zeit- und Streitschrift* (Leipzig, 1913), I, 239-40.
8. Friedmann and Mann, p. 23.
9. *Gedichte. Die drei Reiter* (Hamburg, München, 1958), p. 39.
10. See my article, "Georg Heyms *Der Dieb*—ein Novellenbuch?" in *Levende Talen,* No. 215 (June, 1962), pp. 352 ff; also my forthcoming book on Heym.
11. Berlin, 1928.
12. Friedmann and Mann, p. 221.
13. Friedmann and Mann, p. 220.
14. *The Writer in Extremis,* p. 37.
15. Act V, "Offene Gegend."
16. Act V, "Palast."
17. Act V, "Grosser Vorhof des Palasts."
18. *The Writer in Extremis,* p. 63.
19. Text in Karl Otten, *Schrei und Bekenntnis,* pp. 126 ff.
20. *Die Hose. Ein bürgerliches Lustspiel,* 3rd ed. (München, 1920).
21. "Carl Sternheim," in Friedmann and Mann, pp. 282-83.
22. Cf. Sokel, *Writer in Extremis,* Chapter 5: "The Impotence of the Heart," pp. 119 ff.
23. *Ibid.,* p. 123.
24. *Ibid.*
25. In *Berlin oder Juste Milieu* (München, 1920), pp. 36-37, he wrote: "Der Sachse Richard Wagner, von höheren Fügungen in seiner Weltanschauung überhaupt absehend, brachte anstatt des christlichen Himmels das alte Walhall mit seinen Bewohnern dem Publikum wieder nah, nach ihrer Kleidung und sonstigen Ansprüchen ungezwungene Wesen, in deren Götterhall es aber derart skandalös und spiessbürgerlich herging, dass der gewöhnliche Sterbliche sich vollends überzeugte, wo Leben der Himmlischen so erbärmlich beschränkt und abhängig sei, könne er wirklich mit seiner Preussisch-Berliner Freiheit zufrieden sein, und mit vollem Recht von einem Fortschritt durch Jahrhunderte trotzalledem sprechen."
26. *Juste Milieu,* pp. 50-51.
27. Paul Zech, *Die neue Bergpredigt.*
28. See Introduction.

29. See, for instance, Duwe; Soergel and Hohoff; Fritz Martini, *Deutsche Literaturgeschichte von den Anfängen bis zur Gegenwart* (Stuttgart, 1948 and later).

Ulrich Weisstein (essay date May 1981)

SOURCE: Weisstein, Ulrich. "German Literary Expressionism: An Anatomy." *German Quarterly* 54, no. 3 (May 1981): 262-83.

[*In the following essay, Weisstein describes some of the significant differences and dichotomies inherent in the various strands of German Expressionism.*]

I

Any attempt to analyze the most striking and characteristic features of a complex entity like Expressionism, which some regard as a *typisch deutscher Gegenstand*,[1] must be prefaced by some methodological observations. As I have come to realize after ploughing through the vast amount of scholarship on the subject, the crux of the matter is the use, or abuse, of criteria of selection and evaluation. The complexity and diffuseness of the phenomenon under consideration compel us to conduct our investigation with special rigor. Unfortunately, Expressionism in some important ways resembles international Symbolism more closely than it does, say, Naturalism or Futurism[2]—movements that can be rather narrowly circumscribed and reduced to a relatively small body of common denominators. Hence the need for pondering several approaches and strategies capable of enlightening us about its true nature.

The easiest but surely most superficial line of attack would proceed from the methodologically questionable assumption that only those features should be dealt with under a given heading which were consciously developed at the time and to which the appropriate label was attached by the proponents of a given doctrine. This is an example of what may be called the nominalist fallacy. In actual practice, any attempt to write an authoritative history of German literary Expressionism based on this premise would fail rather abysmally, if only because a list of writers, works and techniques compiled in this mechanical way would be marred by doubtful inclusions and flagrant exclusions from the canon. What is more, a survey of Expressionism executed in that manner would be truly meaningful only if it were possible to extract a system of norms or a *Poetik*, binding for most of the adherents, from manifestoes, programs or similar declarations of intention. However, as Max Krell and other early critics have pointed out, the Expressionists *qua* Expressionists generally preferred *Lösung* (liberation, emancipation) to *Bindung* (obligation).[3]

And while it was widely—and perhaps justly—believed that these artists shared a common world view (*Weltgefühl*), they can hardly be said to have uniformly subscribed to a distinct ideology (*Weltanschauung*), such as that evidenced by their brothers-in-arms, the more highly organized Activists. The Expressionists also lacked a leader comparable to Franz Pfemfert (*Die Aktion*) or Kurt Hiller (*Das Ziel*). For even though Herwarth Walden, the founder/editor of *Der Sturm*, gradually emerged as a feared and respected kingmaker, his circle, no matter how tightly knit, represented only one aspect of the total complex.[4]

Since, as Kasimir Edschmid explained to Scandinavian audiences in the spring of 1918, the artists of the new generation engaged in producing what was then frequently called *die jüngste Dichtung* were rather indifferent toward the formal aspects of their art and generally spurned the theoretic approach,[5] even a comprehensive anthology like Paul Pörtner's two-volume *Literatur-Revolution 1910-1925: Dokumente, Manifeste, Programme* offers relatively few documents—among them the pronouncements of the Zenitists, the Aeternists and some scattered individual utterances of a normative kind—comparable to Marinetti's *Manifesto tecnico della letteratura futurista*.[6] A notable exception to the rule is, once again, constituted by the *Sturm* group and its evolving theories of *Wortkunst* and *Lautkunst*, which were taken to have paradigmatic value.[7] Much more symptomatic of loosely constituted Expressionism are the statements, partly emotive and partly meditative, gathered in the volume *Schöpferische Konfession*, one of a handful of sources, contemporary or near-contemporary, which the student ought to consult.[8] A minimal list, by the way, should also include Edschmid's lecture "Über den dichterischen Expressionismus" (perhaps the single most important text), Max Krell's pamphlet *Über moderne Prosa*, Theodor Däubler's volume of essays *Der neue Standpunkt*,[9] Otto Flake's essay "Von der jüngsten Literatur,"[10] the preface to Pinthus' anthology *Menschheitsdämmerung*, a number of polemical pieces by Carl Sternheim,[11] Bernhard Diebold's book *Anarchie im Drama*[12] and, naturally, the most crucial theoretical disquisitions by the members of the *Sturm* group, such as Herwarth Walden's *Expressionismus—Die Kunstwende*,[13] Rudolf Blümner's *Der Geist des Kubismus und die Künste*[14] and certain essays by Lothar Schreyer[15] and William Wauer.[16] (The student of Expressionism as an interdisciplinary subject must also read Wilhelm Worringer's *Abstraktion und Einfühlung*,[17] Kandinsky's *Über das Geistige in der Kunst*[18] and *Der Blaue Reiter*, the almanac published in 1912 under the joint editorship of Franz Marc and Kandinsky.)[19]

Turning now to the *Selbstverständnis* of German literary Expressionism as evinced by its champions and sympathetic contemporaries, I should like to demonstrate what difficulties the scholar is likely to encounter by briefly dissecting a famous *pièce de résistance*. An "innocent" wishing to inform himself about poetic Expressionism would most likely turn to *Menschheitsdämmerung*, a collection widely, and perhaps justly, reputed to be the *locus classicus* and chief storehouse of relevant texts. If such an uninitiated reader were to start out by reading Kurt Pinthus' preface, he would undoubtedly be struck by the editor's refusal to use the label Expressionism in his preface.[20] Moreover, the observer untainted by a little knowledge of literary historiography, which is a dangerous thing, may well regard this sheaf of poems as neither more nor less than a *florilegium* of pieces written by twenty-three different individuals whose birthdates are separated by a whole generation (Else Lasker-Schüler was born in 1869 and Johannes R. Becher, Iwan Goll and Kurt Heynicke as late as 1891). Will he find them to be stylistically or thematically unified? I don't think so. What, then, is the underlying pattern discerned by Pinthus?

Slightly embarrassed by his own preferences, Pinthus admits that in making his selection he was largely guided by intuition—bolstered, to be sure, by his vast experience as a reader (*Lektor*) for the Rowohlt-Verlag in Leipzig. The editor is equally candid in acknowledging that, in the final analysis, the poems he selected have little in common except their intensity.[21] As it turns out, things are not quite so bad, however, insofar as several other hallmarks are mentioned in the course of the prefatory argument. Thus Pinthus notes an overriding concern with the human condition (universally rather than existentially conceived)[22] and is struck by the steadfast rejection of realism, as of all mimetic modes.[23] But even if we take into account his somewhat halfhearted grouping of the poems according to motifs linked with soul states ("Sturz und Schrei," "Erweckung des Herzens," "Aufruf und Empörung," "Liebe den Menschen"), the gap, both stylistic and thematic, which sunders Georg Trakl and Else Lasker-Schüler from August Stramm and Johannes R. Becher is formidable. Actually, when viewing *Menschheitsdämmerung* in the context of the European avant-garde (as Hugo Friedrich has done, albeit in a rather limited way[24]), one might well incline toward regarding certain aspects of Trakl's poetry, for example, as exemplifying, rather, a kind of Surrealism *avant la lettre*.[25] The same shift of emphasis might seem warranted with regard to the writings of Kubin, Kafka and the so-called "Prague Expressionists," Gustav Meyrink and Hanns Heinz Ewers, none of whom has a stake in Expressionism.[26]

In the historically oriented *Expressionismus-Forschung* of recent vintage, the nominalist fallacy that concerns us presently has produced a number of hardy variants. An especially resistant strain is that represented by the "Preliminary Inventory" at the end of Armin Arnold's monograph *Prosa des Expressionismus: Herkunft, Analyse, Inventar.*[27] Believing, as he does, that it would be futile to try to characterize a novel, a novella, etc., as Expressionist on stylistic grounds, Arnold cuts the Gordian knot by simply listing the prose writings of all writers known as, or presumed to be, Expressionists.[28] His lengthy catalogue (pp. 167-88), accordingly, includes such items as Heinrich Mann's *Im Schlaraffenland* (1900), Robert Walser's *Der Gehülfe* (1908) and Kafka's "Die Verwandlung" (1912). Needless to say, there is no justification for this practice. Compounding the dilemma he has created for himself, Arnold, caught in a logical short circuit of his own making, tacitly assumes that all writings produced at any time by the reputedly Expressionist authors are, *ipso facto,* Expressionistic. Hence the appearance in his catalogue of works like Werfel's *Verdi: Roman der Oper* (1924) and Georg Kaiser's late novel *Villa Aurea* (1940).[29] Conversely, by the same token, Arnold had to refrain from listing Expressionist works created by "non-Expressionists." For instance, Rilke's "Marienlieder," *Duino Elegies* and *Sonnets to Orpheus* (which, in the opinion of at least one perceptive scholar, might well deserve a place in this constellation[30]) would have had to be discarded.

The lesson to be learned from these blunders is simple enough: that, while it is possible (and customary) to write literary history according to authors stereotyped as paragons of a movement or period style, this approach is extremely risky and methodologically unsound. In my view, the history of Expressionism, like that of any artistic movement, can, for better or worse, only be the history of those works which, partly or wholly, embody a set of norms and display features which, on the basis of his acquaintance with the material and his own preconceived notions (note the inevitable and embarrassing hermeneutic circle involved in the delicate operation!), the scholar finds to be symptomatic.

Given my own knowledge and bias, for example, I would—somewhat reluctantly—exclude proto-Expressionistic pieces such as Wedekind's *Der Marquis von Keith,*[31] certain poems by Heym and Stadler and most of the prose works on which the label "Expressionist" is so often generously bestowed.[32] I would propose a canon comprising, in addition to the most striking examples of *Sturm* art (August Stramm, Rudolf Blümner and Lothar Schreyer), specific plays by Oskar Kokoschka (*Mörder Hoffnung der Frauen*), Ernst Barlach (*Die Sündflut* and *Der arme Vetter*),[33] Georg Kaiser (*Von morgens bis mitternachts*), Reinhold Goering (*Seeschlacht*) and Hans Henny Jahnn (*Medea*),[34] poems by Becher ("Vorbereitung"), Benn ("Karyatide"), Paul Zech and possibly Werfel ("Veni Creator Spiritus"), and a number of stories by Sternheim,[35] Edschmid, Benn and perhaps Schickele.³⁶ If I were charged with compiling it, this rock-bottom list would not include a single fullblown novel, at least not in its entirety.³⁷

Changing my line of attack, I note with considerable apprehension, that the historian of literature, wishing to delimit and circumscribe a period or movement style must, willy-nilly, aim at creating a spatio-temporal framework within which to contrast and compare the particular body of works which strike his fancy with those products of the imagination which do not fit into the picture. The first step in this direction, accordingly, would be to make it clear beyond the shadow of a doubt that, if it is to be properly understood and savored, Expressionism must be seen as something belonging fairly and squarely to the twentieth century, rather than being a recurrent and thus ultimately timeless phenomenon. This note of caution must be sounded if only because some propagators of Expressionism—whether or not they used that label—were in the habit of speaking precisely in the latter terms. Such is certainly true of *Abstraktion und Einfühlung,* Worringer's immensely influential dissertation, which leaves no room for doubt that as far as its author is concerned, the immediate future belongs to an art prolonging a rhythmic sequence of anti-classical and anti-realistic styles or *Abstraktionsstile* extending from the art of the primitives by way of Egyptian art through the Middle Ages (Gothic art) to the Baroque and Romanticism,³⁸ whose literary equivalent would be the chain linking Medieval mysticism with the Baroque, the Storm and Stress and, again, Romanticism. The alternate sequence, historically enmeshed with it, would comprise the Greco-Roman period in its classical phases, the Renaissance, seventeenth- and eighteenth-century Classicism/Neo-Classicism and nineteenth-century Realism/Naturalism. Today, this view of Expressionism as part of a Viconian cycle is of little more than historical interest, except insofar as it provides us with a set of precursors whom the Expressionists found to be congenial to their way of thinking and feeling: Jakob Boehme, Angelus Silesius, Gryphius, Lenz, Novalis, Kleist (*Penthesilea*), Grabbe and Büchner among them.

Much more meaningful, because temporally circumscribed, is that perspective on literary Expressionism which regards it as a distinct period style and, in light of this assumption, operates with such chronological units as *expressionistisches Jahrzehnt* (1910-1920 plus).³⁹ Such a view, if held dogmatically, rests on the conviction that Expressionism dominated the decade to the point of overshadowing all other trends or tendencies. But no matter how long or short we take the specific time segment to be, what we inevitably overlook is the circumstance that while literary Expressionism was clearly in the ascendant by 1910 and was ideologically and aesthetically the leading trend during World War I, other, more conservative modes continued to be practiced by writers refusing to "join the chorus." After all, the teens of our century witnessed the creation and publication of such traditional, or downright conservative, works as Thomas Mann's "Der Tod in Venedig," Hofmannsthal's *Der Rosenkavalier,* Stefan George's *Der Stern des Bundes* and Gerhart Hauptmann's play *Der Bogen des Odysseus.* That Expressionism was not merely *en vogue* but something to be very seriously coped with (though not necessarily to be absorbed) by the literary institutions is demonstrated by the fact that an establishment journal like *Die Neue Rundschau* saw fit to publish Edschmid's lecture "Expressionismus in der Dichtung," but not without supplying a cautionary editorial note:

> Wir bringen den Aufsatz Edschmids aus keinem andern Grunde, als um dem Leser eine Probe zu geben, wie ein Dichter der jüngeren Generation sich seine Auffassung expressionistischer Ziele definiert und seine historischen und zeitgenössischen Urteile bildet. Wir brauchen nicht zu betonen, daß eine programmatische Bindung in dieser Zeitschrift damit nicht nur nicht gegeben ist, sondern daß wir die ästhetische und literarhistorische Rangordnung der Werte, soweit sie sich auf die Produktion der letzten dreißig Jahre bezieht, durchaus ablehnen.⁴⁰

When Edschmid wrote his lecture in December 1917, he was already convinced that Expressionism had spent much of its force and had passed into the hands of popularizers and imitators.⁴¹ By 1919, the year in which Worringer published his essay "Kritische Gedanken zur neuen Kunst,"⁴² only the most stubborn proponents of the Expressionistic creed could still maintain that it had vitality. Thus, in the preface to the second edition of *Menschheitsdämmerung* (redacted in April 1922), Pinthus confessed: "Klar herausgesagt: es ist, nach Abschluß dieser lyrischen Symphonie, nichts gedichtet worden, was zwingenderweise noch in sie hätte eingefügt werden müssen."⁴³ We have every reason, then, for refusing to extend the era of Expressionism too far into the twenties, the timespan often loosely labelled *das neusachliche Jahrzehnt.*

Having dispelled the deeply rooted myth of an Expressionistic period, the scholarly anatomist must address himself next to the even more explosive issue pertaining to the status of German literary Expressionism as a movement. To be sure, the German noun *Bewegung,* although equivalent to the English "movement," is more flexible in its meaning and could easily be stretched to accommodate an entire *Zeit-* and *Kunstwende*—two terms popular with those champions of Expressionism who wished to prove its all-encompassing nature. (In this regard, the favored use of apocalyptic, messianic and utopian titles such as *Menschheitsdämmerung, Der jüngste Tag, Verkündigung, Der Anbruch* speaks for itself.)

But this general mood of *Aufbruch,* implying a burning of all bridges and the projection into a future fashioned and dominated by the proverbial New Man, is not what concerns me here. What matters to me as a literary critic and historian is, rather, the much more narrowly conceived meaning of *movement* in the strictly literary sense. René Wellek has noted that, if it is to serve as a useful vocable in scholarly discourse, *movement* as a *terminus technicus* must be limited in its application to those self-conscious and, for the most part, theoretically based attempts on the part of a certain number of likeminded contemporaries (usually flocking around one or several leaders) to broadcast a new conception of art, usually implying a wholesale repudiation of accepted values. Marinetti's Futurism and Breton's Surrealism offer splendid examples of this kind of crystallization. By contrast, Expressionism lacks a solid core and single point of reference: "Wir sind Einzelne, die sich hier in gleichem Streben zusammentun, um doch Einzelne zu bleiben."[44]

Emulating A. O. Lovejoy's treatment of Romanticism, we might do well, in fact, to posit the existence of diverse Expressionisms loosely linked by a common *Weltgefühl,* a fluctuating pattern of individuals and groups with shifting—and even conflicting—loyalties, and with preoccupations ranging from the almost strictly esthetic[45] to the almost purely socio-political.[46] In addition to such centers of gravity as were constituted by specific individuals, periodicals or publishers (Kurt Wolff,[47] Ernst Rowohlt, Erich Reiss), there were artists like Kokoschka and Ernst Barlach who got quickly tired of cenacle-dom or refused, from the very beginning, to be drawn into the maelstrom. Thus, seen with the requisite historical detachment, no one group or confraternity can typify Expressionism as a whole.[48]

Since we are bent on demolishing a convenient but ill-conceived myth, we might as well add some remarks concerning the allegedly monolithic stance of certain key journals usually cited in general surveys of Expressionism. Thus, after reading all of *Der Sturm* or *Die Aktion,* one will conclude that it would be foolish to seek to reduce their varied contents to a common denominator. Initially, *Der Sturm,* for example, was a publication bathing in the glow of Karl Kraus's satirical spirit. For several years it offered no coherent aesthetic program of its own and acted primarily as a mediator of Cubism and Futurism in Germany.[49] And although a strong interest in *das neue Pathos* evolved as early as 1910 (i.e., in the very first volume) in connection with the matinees of the Neopathetisches Kabarett,[50] literature did not come into its own until the discovery of August Stramm, the *poeta dolorosus* of lyrical *Sturmkunst*. As for *Die Aktion,* it had, at least in its burgeoning years, no set literary program but was well satisfied with being "ein Organ des ehrlichen Radikalismus."[51]

Even on the personal level, the fiction of an Expressionist confraternity can be unmasked, almost in a trice. The fierce infighting which went on among individuals and groups is usually glossed over by the literary historians, who are inclined to smoothe out wrinkles and ignore conflicts that would force them to break up the "even flow" of their narratives. Thus, as a perusal of the editorial matter of *Der Sturm* reveals, Herwarth Walden displayed an extremely partisan, and often hostile, attitude toward many writers and critics now generally considered to be representative of Expressionism or Activism—among them Pfemfert, Becher, Werfel and Arnold Schönberg.[52] In several cases, he ended up by casting aspersions on individuals whose views and convictions he had originally shared, thus acting like a true autocrat in the editor's chair.[53]

II

So far I have concerned myself mostly with issues related to the historiography of German literary Expressionism. Now I move on to explore its generic dimension and, subsequently, its philosophical and psychological bases. The question I ask myself, at the outset, concerns the major literary types (poetry, drama, prose) and genres, it being my aim to ascertain whether these forms were basically retained by those writers a substantial portion of whose *oeuvre* would seem to merit the designation "Expressionistic," or whether—and to what extent—they were discarded, modified or supplanted. Since, as we have had occasion to note, it would be futile to look for a generally applicable, descriptive or prescriptive *Poetik* of Expressionism, I will proceed inductively by screening the vast body of works and cautiously evaluating the scattered—at times parochial or blatantly eccentric—theoretical utterances collected by Pörtner or buried in contemporary periodicals, almanacs and anthologies (prefatory matter).

What strikes me immediately is not so much an implied indifference toward generic problems as a strong distaste for dealing with the issue of poetic form. Put differently, it was felt that, art being an expression of soul states, the outward appearance of the end product mattered little, as long as a perfect correlation existed between the underlying feelings and their concrete manifestation. Like Surrealism (and, for that matter, Naturalism), Expressionism was decidedly content-oriented—so much so, in fact, that, paradoxically, content was even seen to be the overriding concern in Kandinsky's "abstract" Impressions, Improvisations and Compositions.[54] As Kandinsky himself observes in *Der Blaue Reiter*: "Da die Form nur ein Ausdruck des Inhaltes ist und der Inhalt bei verschiedenen Künstlern verschieden ist, so ist es klar, daß es zu derselben Zeit viel verschiedene Formen geben kann, die gleich gut sind."[55] Thus Abstract Expressionism—to use a familiar term which, though puzzling and seemingly paradoxical, makes perfect sense in this particular context—is invariably characterized by an underlying intention (more often unconscious than conscious) whose true nature may not be apparent in the finished product. Unlike Walden and the members of his inner circle,[56] Kandinsky was very much concerned with problems of communication and would have resented the allegation that the "purposive vibration of the human soul" which he aimed at was little more than a wild goose chase. Nevertheless, as far as intention is concerned, his brand of Expressionism must not be confused with Matisse's purely decorative variant or Benn's formal *Ausdruckskunst* as rooted in Flaubert's *Poetik*.[57]

On the whole, the Expressionist, the elusive creature I am stalking, made no concerted effort to destroy the prevailing forms: "Die drei Grundarten dichterischen Schaffens, das lyrische, das dramatische und das epische Schaffen, sind von der Kunstwende nicht zerstört worden."[58] But neither was he specifically interested in preserving them. Rather, he tended to bend and reshape them in order to make them more perfect vehicles of expression. In the case of the *Sturm* poets and playwrights, this meant a reduction of each type to its bare essentials, resulting in the creation of the pure *Wortkunstwerk, Lautkunstwerk, Farbkunstwerk, Tonkunstwerk*, etc.[59] In the case of non-*Sturm* Expressionism, on the other hand, we may discern a general loosening of metrical form in poetry (Stadler's "Form und Riegel mußten erst zerspringen, / Welt durch aufgeschlossne Röhren dringen"[60]) and of coherence or structual unity in the drama (the *Stationendrama* of Strindbergian provenience).

Generalizing, as we must, we can say without too many qualms that lyrical poetry[61] and the drama were by far the most prominent types, the former because it is, traditionally, a direct channel for the expression of feelings, moods and emotions, and the latter because it objectifies and humanizes spiritual conflicts within the Self (*Aufsplitterungen des Ich*), and between the Self and society, by projecting them onto a three-dimensional stage.[62] As for narrative prose, its role was clearly subordinate, although it, too, had its champions among the self-styled Expressionists. The reasons for this neglect are easy to grasp. After all, the novel, being firmly entrenched in the realistic nineteenth century, is much more closely tied to convention, at least in the linguistic sphere. Thus it takes exceptional courage for the *romancier* to undertake radical experiments with form and language and to dispense altogether with psychology. Hence the numerous paradoxes and ambiguities encountered to this day in the scholarly treatment of the subject.[63] One way in which prose can partake in the spirit of Expressionism would seem to be that chosen by writers of satire and the grotesque—techniques which lend themselves more readily to experimentation and a breaking up of the familiar mold. Yet it would be wrong to use Expressionism and *Grotesksatire* as synonyms, as Thomas Mann, debunking his brother's satirical novel *Der Untertan*, did in a remarkable passage of his *Betrachtungen eines Unpolitischen*.[64]

A word need also be said, in this connection, about the inclusion of extra-literary components in the works exemplifying German literary Expressionism. Let us not forget, for instance, that Expressionism had its roots in the visual arts (from Grünewald and El Greco to Van Gogh and Munch) and that, its chief goal being expressiveness, it displayed a marked affinity with music. It is no accident that the age produced such a disproportionately large number of *Doppelbegabungen* (Kokoschka being a writing painter, Barlach a writing sculptor and Schönberg a painting composer) and that there was a constant crossing of artistic borderlines. Quite a few of the Expressionist writers, in fact, thought of language as a barrier and did their level best to transcend it.[65] Thus Kokoschka's *Mörder Hoffnung der Frauen* is not so much a piece of dramatic literature in the ordinary sense as a congeries of movements, gestures, colors and sounds fused in a turbulent unity of emotion; and Rudolf Blümner, going beyond August Stramm, experimented with "abstract" poetry of sound.

It is thus in keeping with this spirit that the Expressionists in various quarters tended to regard the *Gesamtkunstwerk* as the fulfillment of their artistic dream. Thus Lothar Schreyer, founder and director of the *Sturmbühne*, registered the claim: "Das Bühnenkunstwerk ist eine künstlerische Einheit. Es ist durch Intuition empfangen, in Konzentration gereift, als Organismus geboren. Es ist gebildet aus den künstlerischen Ausdrucksmitteln Form, Farbe, Bewegung und Ton. Es ist ein selbständiges Kunstwerk, wirkend in Raum und Zeit."[66] And Kandinsky, in his essay "Über Bühnenkomposition," affirmed with equal conviction that the drama of his choice was a "Komplex der inneren Erlebnisse (Seelenvibrationen) des Zuschauers" as mirrored in the three contributing elements, "musikalischer Ton," "körperlich-seelischer Klang und seine Bewegung durch Menschen und Gegenstände ausgedrückt" and "farbiger Ton und seine Bewegung."[67] Also in *Der Blaue Reiter*, L. Sabanjew, analyzing Scriabin's tone poem *Prometheus*, proclaimed: "Es ist die Zeit der Wiedervereinigung dieser sämtlichen zerstreuten Künste gekommen."[68]

As we lay bare the skeleton of German literary Expressionism, we are likely to be faced, sooner or later, with the strategic question whether that phenomenon should be preferably approached from the angle of world view, style or thematics. As I have stated in my essay "Expressionism: Style or *Weltanschauung*?", proceeding along thematic lines without first settling the issue on philosophical/poetological grounds would be like putting the cart before the horse. Themes, after all, are concrete reflections or embodiments of a general outlook on life. Moreover, even though the Expressionist considered his art to be thoroughly content-oriented, he was not, in principle, interested in matters of plot and characterization. Thus, while there is no harm in speaking of favorite Expressionist motifs (*Aufbruch,* the New Man, etc.), it is hazardous to dwell on specific preferential themes. While one is still on relatively safe ground, for example, when calling the generational conflict a characteristic motif,[69] the Impotence of the Heart "theme" singled out by Sokel as being an overriding concern leads us (and him) rather far afield and aground.[70]

As for the Expressionist "world view," it was perhaps best epitomized by Edschmid when he stated: "Der Blick geht auf die Ewigkeit."[71] In other words, the Expressionists, more or less ignoring historical truth, wished to pierce the outer shell of ordinary reality and to descend from surface to depth, from appearance to essence (*Wesen,*[72] *Kern*[73]), with the intention of subsequently projecting that core, in a highly condensed and concentrated form (*Ballung, Spitzen*[74]) and with the utmost intensity, back into external reality, causing the latter to be—or at least to appear—distorted. (Thus beauty and all other aesthetic criteria based on objectively verifiable standards of judgment fell victim to the principle of inner necessity asserted by Kandinsky.) In the case of what, for lack of a better term, we might call the spiritualized (not intellectualized[75]) variant, represented by Marc and his fellow Blaue Reiter, violent projection is replaced by a visionary experience and its translation into the language of art.[76] This substitution of *Gesichte* (visions) for *Gesichter* (faces) lies also at the heart of Walden's more secularized aesthetics.

In all instances, immediacy is called for and intuition is exalted over ratiocination. In glaring contrast with the passive dream art of the Surrealists, who, initially at least, thought of themselves as mere *appareils enregistreurs,*[77] Expressionist art is decidedly volitional. This does not and, in fact, cannot mean that its practitioners wished to exert conscious control over their material but, rather, that they were driven by a dynamic force welling up from the unconscious.[78] What we have, in fact, is not so much the *Kunstwollen* Worringer substituted for *Kunstkönnen* as what might be designated as *Kunstmüssen.* Like the Dadaists and Surrealists, but for entirely different reasons, the Expressionists rejected any form of intervention between feeling and expression[79] and wanted altogether to dispense with logic[80] and causality[81] on the giving, and with meaning[82] on the receiving, end. This does not mean, however, that they indulged in the cult of unintelligibility; they merely wished to stress the inadequacy of interpretation and analysis.

III

What makes it so difficult to give Expressionism its due is the fact that, as its very heart, it was beset by problems arising out of a series of dichotomies, and that, consequently, it was caught in the vise of a dialectic from which it could not properly extricate itself. Inevitably—or so it seems—the Expressionist work of art is suspended between two poles, the realistic and the idealistic. Thus while, on the one hand, it is rabidly anti-mimetic, on the other it shies away from pure abstraction. Depending on the talent or inclination of the individual writer, painter, composer, etc., it moves in one or the other direction, neither succumbing to the extremes nor reconciling the opposites. In the following pages I shall briefly seek to identify the most glaring paradoxes of which the student of Expressionism must be cognizant.

One of the accusations most frequently hurled at the Expressionists is that their art is unabashedly and unashamedly subjective. A typical expression of this sentiment is Julius Bab's attack on Fritz von Unruh: "Jener 'Expressionismus' aber, der das wüste Herausschreien einer von keiner Welthingabe geklärten subjektiven Erregung bedeutet, ist das Ende aller Kunst.'[83] Similarly Herbert Read, in his influential book *The Philosophy of Modern Art,* one-sidedly defines Expressionism as that art which seeks to reproduce "not the objective reality of the world, but the subjective reality of the feelings which objects and events arouse in us."[84] This notion would seem to be corroborated by the following paragraph from a letter by Van Gogh which may be regarded as one of the most significant documents anent the Expressionist theory of art:

> Because instead of trying to reproduce exactly what I have before my eyes, I use color more arbitrarily so as to express myself more forcefully. . . . I should like to paint the portrait of an artist friend. . . . He'll be a fair man. I want to put into the picture my appreciation, the love that I have for him. I paint him as he is, faithfully as I can, to begin with. But the picture is not finished yet. To finish it I am now going to be the arbitrary colorist. I exaggerate the fairness of the hair, I get to orange tones, chromes and pale lemon yellow.[85]

So far, so good. But this shift from the objective to the subjective is, contrary to Read's belief, only the beginning of a process that leads to a second change of direction. For Van Gogh's letter continues in the true, universalizing spirit of Expressionism that leads to a higher, transcendent reality:

> Beyond the head, instead of painting the ordinary wall of the mean room, I paint infinity, a plain background of the richest, intensest blue that I can contrive, and by this simple combination the bright head illuminated against a rich blue background acquires a mysterious effect, like the star in the depths of an azure sky.

The very gist of the matter is contained in a statement by Edward Wadsworth which forms part of that Vorticist painter's contribution to the first issue of *Blast*: "In short, the effect of inner necessity on the development of art is a progressive expression of the eternally objective within the temporarily subjective. Or otherwise the subjugation of the subjective by the objective."[86]

In literature, the same desire to overcome the limitations of contingent individuality finds expression in two different but, from a higher perspective, complementary ways: in the breaking up of linguistic patterns and in the substitution of types for individuals. This mode of presentation, which involves a deliberate suppression of all idiosyncrasies, i.e., those features which make each person distinctly *sui generis,* presupposes a casting out of psychology. In fact, Edschmid and many of his *confrères* took this uprooting of an established analytical science to be the veritable secret of Expressionism.[87] In order to stave off confusion, it should be pointed out, however, that the type figures (which are often quasi-allegorical *Aufsplitterungen des Ich*[88]) of Expressionist drama have little in common with the social types encountered in Balzac's *Comédie humaine,* where each character, meant to represent a profession, sex, age group, "race" or social class, is partly or wholly dependent on the Tainian triad of *race, moment* and *milieu*. In Balzac, as in the entire Realistic tradition, which the Expressionists so heartily despised, the individual is firmly anchored in a socio-historical context, whereas in Germany's *jüngster Dichtung* "das Sekundäre verschwindet, der Apparat, das Milieu [. . .] nur angedeutet und mit kurzem Umriss der glühenden Masse des Seelischen einverschmolzen [bleibt]."[89]

To our expanding list of inherently Expressionistic dichotomies, we must add the dialectic constituted by the interrelation and interpenetration of representational and non-representational (concrete and abstract) elements in art and literature. As I have indicated, outright mimesis is taboo in Expressionism and almost automatically disqualifies a work from fitting into that context. In the words of Paul Klee: "Kunst gibt nicht das Sichtbare wieder, sondern macht sichtbar."[90] On the other hand, pure abstraction—what used to be ambiguously called non-objective art—was shunned, at least outside of the *Sturm* circle, because, in spite of Kandinsky's protestations, it sacrifices content to form, ignores the human element and undercuts the productive tensions on which truly Expressionist art must thrive. Thus Edschmid, in an implied critique of Kandinsky's theories, postulates: "Das abstrakte Wollen aber sieht keine Grenze mehr. Erkennt nicht mehr, welch ausbalanciertes Vermögen besteht zwischen dem Gegenstand und der schaffenden Form. Die Grenzen des Sinnlichen durchbrechend schafft sie lauter Theorie. Da ist kein Ding mehr, das gestaltet, umgeformt, aufgesucht wird, da ist, den Kampfplatz verlassend, nur öde Abstraktion."[91]

I asserted that pure abstraction was generally shunned except in the *Sturm* circle. For Walden and his group, the word was, indeed, "das Material der Dichtung"[92] which could be used both for its own sake and as a vehicle for meaning. Thus, whereas Stramm dispensed with syntax but stuck to the lexicon (not without juggling the vocabulary),[93] Blümner abandoned the lexicon with a vengeance: "Aber selbst diese expressionistische Dichtung (Stramm, Walden, Schreyer, Behrens, Allwohn, Liebmann, Heynicke) setzte meiner künstlerischen Freiheit die Grenzen der gegebenen Wörter, ihrer Konsonanten und Vokale."[94]

The fifth dichotomy arises from the dialectic of body and spirit, or *Stoff* and *Geist*. Once again we are faced with two contrasting but collateral tendencies, the urge for spiritualizing matter and the wish to embody soul states. Thus, clearly, the aesthetic of the *Blaue Reiter* was based on the yearning for *Entstofflichung* (dematerialization), as reflected in the following passage from Marc's "creative confession": "Der uralte Glaube an die Farbe wird durch die Entsinnlichung und Überwindung des Stoffes an extatischer [sic!] Glut zunehmen, wie einst der Gottesglaube durch die Verneinung der Götzenbilder. Die Farbe wird, vom Stoff erlöst, ein immanentes Leben führen nach unserem Willen."[95] In literature, a similar position was taken by several critics and theoreticians who denigrated that "stofflichste und daher unkünstlerischste aller Künste."[96] But except for Blümner's *Lautkunst,* what was upheld in theory was never realized in practice. More typical, on the whole, is the compromise struck by Edschmid in his essay "Döblin und die Futuristen": "Wir wollen das Fleisch, aber in gehobeneren Übersinnslüsten. Döblin macht es nun so, daß er das Fleisch mit Geistinjektionen so fabelhaft durchwühlt und durchschimmert, daß nur das Gespenst (was eine andere Geschichte ist als das Skelett) entsteht."[97] The complementary tendency—that of embodying soul states—seems to have prevailed among the Expressionists. It certainly was the one that many contemporary critics singled out. Thus Walther von Hollander, reviewing Kornfeld's *Die Verführung,* defined Expressionism as "Seele, die sich ohne Scham im Körperlichen entschleiert" and spoke of the drama itself as "rein expressionistisch auf Körperlichkeit gestellte Seele, die sich im Körper zur Schau stellt."[98]

If, as we have reason to believe, the style characteristic of German Expressionist literature is an outgrowth of the world view which I have tried to anatomize in the preceding pages, the linguistic habits developed and cultivated by the Expressionists must be a logical extension to technique (in grammar, syntax and vocabulary) of a philosophy at whose center lies the desire to substitute *Wesen* for *Schein* or even *Sein*.[99] Indeed, the theoretical statements available to us agree in demanding that language, too, must reflect the *Wirklichkeitszertrümmerung* without which all efforts to reach the core are vain. The means suited to that end were inevitably *verfremdend,* causing a more or less radical deviation from normal usage through distortion, omission, reduction and condensation (the famous *Telegrammstil*[100]). Sternheim, who was exceptionally language-conscious, presents the whole issue in a nutshell:

> [Es] ist selbstverständlich für den heute—nicht von uns sondern unseren Kritikern—Expressionismus genannten Sprachstil charakteristisch, daß er nur Hauptsachen und durchaus keine Nebensachen mehr gibt, das heißt überall da, wo Wort an sich ohne Artikel, Adjektiv und Attribut der schärfer definierende Begriff wird, aus monumentaler Kahlheit sein verloren gegangenes Essentielles für Welt wieder gerettet und überflüssige, klischierte und teils schon blödsinnige Zutat, die nur allmählich für kapierendes, bequemes Verständnis des Durchschnittslesers mitgeschleppt wurde, entfernt wird.[101]

The application of this dogma to the specifics of syntax was made, properly enough, by our star witness Kasimir Edschmid, who pontificates:

> Die Sätze liegen im Rhythmus anders gefaltet als gewohnt. Sie unterstehen der gleichen Absicht, demselben Strom des Geistes, der nur das Eigentliche gibt.... Sie binden Spitze an Spitze, sie schnellen ineinander, nicht mehr verbunden durch Puffer logischer Überleitung, nicht mehr durch den federnden äußerlichen Kitt der Psychologie.[102]

Gottfried Benn, writing about his "Vermessungsdirigent" Pameelen, declared with rhetorical pomp: "Einstürzt jede Fragestellung, die mit Erkenntnis rechnet, denn die Syntax läuft über in das Du, und der Kausalsatz herrscht in der Holunderlaube, in der sich abends was begibt."[103] And J. R. Becher defended "die neue Syntax" in a letter addressed to a critic of the *Frankfurter Zeitung*:

> Alogische Bomben unterminieren den traditionellen akademischen Satzbau der bürgerlichen Spracharchitektur. Rhythmik, Melodie, Metaphorik schwankt; die Sprache selbst produziert, unabhängig von ihrem Schöpfer, scheinbar unlösbare, eigengesetzlich gegeneinander sich bewegende, anarchisch gegenseitig explosivartig sich pressende Verknotungen.[104]

As for the poets gathered around Herwarth Walden, they, too, did away with all the *Nebensachen* and replaced the wonted syntactical structure by various kinds of *Wortreihen* (word sequences) fashioned according to rhythmic, tonal or visual requirements.[105]

Vocabulary, like syntax, underwent rough treatment at the hands of the Expressionists, partly under the influence of Marinetti's theories. Says Edschmid:

> Auch das Wort erhält andere Gewalt. Das beschreibende, das umschürfende hört auf. Dafür ist kein Platz mehr. Es wird Pfeil. Trifft in das Innere des Gegenstands und wird von ihm beseelt. Es wird kristallisch, das eigentliche Bild des Dinges. Dann fallen die Füllwörter.[106]

Up to this point, I surmise, his fellow Expressionists would have gone along with Edschmid. However, opinions differed with regard to the word class or classes to be preferentially used. Most writers clearly exalted the noun (in the case of Marinetti's disciple Becher even the *Hauptwortkette* [noun string or chain] cherished by the poets of the German Baroque); but Franz Werfel steadfastly maintained: "In der Poesie ist der Träger der Betonung das Verbum."[107] In the light of the *Sturm* poets' indifference toward such matters, Werner Rittich was probably right in declaring that it is "verlockend, aber gefährlich, den Expressionismus auf Verwendung bestimmter Wortarten abzustempeln."[108]

Finally, in accordance with their suspicion of the *ratio* and its interpretative, analytical and reductive urges, the Expressionists, both in theory and practice, disbarred those rhetorical devices and figures of speech which "by indirection seek direction out." While the hyperbole may well be regarded as a hallmark of their style (except, of course, in the chaster products of *Sturm* art), allegory,[109] symbol, metaphor,[110] and even the harmless simile[111] were all found to be wanting.

Anatomizing my anatomy, I should like to reaffirm, by way of conclusion, that, in spite of the many difficulties presenting themselves to the scholar bent upon finding some degree of unity in the diversity of phenomena subsumed under the label "German literary Expressionism," there is no reason for despair. As long as one remembers that Expressionism is no organic whole but that, like moons or satellites circling around a planet, its varied, paradoxical and sometimes contradictory elements are ultimately centered in a common core of *Weltgefühl,* one is fairly safe in treating it as a cluster, provided that in the matter of ascription one casts aside all chronological and biographical misconceptions. And while there is plenty of room for individual preferences on the part of the researcher, it is by no means impossible to agree on a list of works (and parts of works) that deserve to be labelled Expressionistic, not because the contemporaries or posterity called them so, but because they display features one has come to regard as symptomatic. Forbidding at first sight, the burden is greatly alleviated by the fact that within the vast Milky Way of Expressionism there are identifiable constellations, such as the *Sturm* group, Activism and *Der Blaue Reiter,* which can be arranged in a meaningful pattern on the celestial map.

Notes

1. This is hardly the place to review the vast, and qualitatively uneven, literature on Expressionism in general and German literary Expressionism in particular. Great profit is, naturally, to be derived from the two *Forschungsberichte* which Richard Brinkmann prepared for the *Deutsche Vierteljahr-*

esschrift (Stuttgart: Metzler, 1961 and 1980). To the best of my knowledge, there still is no first-rate book-length scholarly survey in English. Walter Sokel's well-known *The Writer in Extremis* (Stanford, 1959) has done its duty, that of stimulating discussion; given the present state of research, it can hardly be regarded as authoritative. The book I personally would recommend is John Willett's *Expressionism* (New York, 1970), which is primarily gauged to the visual arts. Much can be learned from the rather specialized study of Geoffrey Perkins, *Contemporary Theory of Expressionism* (Bern, 1974). The best essay on the subject, in my opinion, is Adolf Klarmann's "Expressionism in German Literature: A Retrospect" (*Modern Language Quarterly,* 26 [1965], pp. 62-92, to which Stefan H. Schultz's article "German Expressionism 1910-1925" (*Chicago Review,* 13 [1959], pp. 8-24) and the chapter entitled "1912" in Michael Hamburger's *Reason and Energy* (New York, 1961) might be added.

2. The interrelation and cross-fertilization of the various European avant-gardes of the period 1910-1925 have only recently begun to be seriously studied. An early attempt in English at placing Expressionism in a truly international context was made in my essay "Expressionism: Style or Weltanschauung?" (*Criticism,* 9 [1967], pp. 42-62). A more concerted and collaborative effort, undertaken a few years later, resulted in the publication of the volume *Expressionism as an International Literary Phenomenon* (Budapest/Paris, 1973) which I edited on behalf of the ICLA for its Comparative History of Literatures in European Languages. Expressionism will be assigned its proper place in the two-volume set on the European avant-gardes, now ready in manuscript, which Jean Weisgerber from the Free University of Brussels is preparing for the same series. Given the breadth of its scope, the lucidity of the presentation and the sophistication of its structure, this venture is likely to complement, and in numerous ways supercede, such earlier attempts as Guillermo de Torre's *Historia de las literaturas de vanguardia* (1925; earlier version 1925). Hugo Friedrich's *Struktur der modernen Lyrik* (Hamburg, 1956) and Renato Poggioli's *Theory of the Avant-Garde* (Cambridge, Mass., 1968; original Italian version, 1962) which, no matter how valuable in themselves, tend, by and large, to underrate or misrepresent the Germanic contribution to twentieth-century experimental literature.

3. In the introduction to his pamphlet *Über moderne Prosa* (Berlin: Reiss, 1919), Max Krell calls Expressionism a "Sammelwort eines Gefühls- und Anschauungskomplexes."

4. An advertisement circulated by Walden in 1918 proudly spoke of *Der Sturm* as "das führende Organ der Expressionisten." That this view was rather enviously shared by some Expressionists who did not belong to his circle is shown by an autobiographical observation of Rudolf Leonhard: "Manche Kritiker, soweit sie sich der Mühe unterzogen, halten mich für einen Expressionisten; ich vermute, daß Herwarth Walden, der doch ein Monopol darauf hat, mich nicht dafür hält . . ." Both references are culled from the invaluable catalogue of the Marbach exhibition, *Expressionismus: Literatur und Kunst 1910-1923,* eds. Paul Raabe and H. L. Greve (Munich: Langen/Müller, 1960), pp. 144 and 216 respectively.

5. "Nicht Kampf gegen schon Stürzendes verbindet, wo wir doch, toleranter, duldsamer als Vorangegangene, auf Formales geringsten Wert legen, wo künstlerische Fragen, im Äußeren nur ruhend, uns gleichgültig abgewendet sehen, vielmehr bedacht auf die Gesinnung." From the lecture "Über die dichterische deutsche Jugend" in *Über den Expressionismus . . . ,* p. 11. Similarly, Arnold Schönberg, writing in *Schöpferische Konfession,* ed. K. Edschmid (Berlin: Reiss, 1920), confesses: "Mehr kann ich von meinem Schaffen nicht sagen, weniger eher; auch ich könnte ein expressionistisches Programm aufstellen. Besser aber noch eines bloß für andere" (p. 75).

6. The Aeternist manifesto appears in II, 190-92, the Zenitist manifesto, redacted by Iwan Goll, *ibid.,* pp. 580f. Among the "technical" manifestoes included in the anthology we find Werfel's treatise "Substantiv und Verbum" (II, 182-88) and J. R. Becher's programmatic poem "Die neue Syntax" (II, 247-48).

7. See Werner Rittich's important monograph *Kunsttheorie, Wortkunsttheorie und lyrische Wortkunst im "Sturm"* (Greifswald, 1933).

8. The book contains autobiographical and/or programmatic statements by thirteen painters and writers, among them Benn, Unruh, Toller, Becher, Kaiser, Schickele, Beckmann, Klee, Marc, but also Schönberg.

9. Dresden-Hellerau: Hellerauer Verlag, 1916. Some of the essays here collected were originally published in *Die Neue Rundschau.*

10. *Die Neue Rundschau,* 25 (1915), pt. 2, pp. 1276-87.

11. See especially "Kampf der Metapher," "Expressionismus und Sprachgewissen" and "Brief an Kasimir Edschmid" in Sternheim's *Gesamtwerk,* ed. Wilhelm Emrich (Neuwied: Luchterhand), VI (1966).

12. Frankfurt: Frankfurter Verlags-Anstalt, 1921.

13. Berlin: Verlag Der Sturm, n.d. This is a collection of essays originally published in *Der Sturm*. Most of the pieces were authored by Walden and the members of his inner circle, but Marc and Kandinsky are also represented.

14. Berlin: Verlag Der Sturm, 1921.

15. One of the best sources for an understanding of Schreyer's doctrine is his book *Expressionistisches Theater: Aus meinen Erinnerungen* (Hamburg: Toth, 1948).

16. As early as 1911 (#74 of *Der Sturm*), Wauer published his essay "Die Inscenierung," which contains the characteristic sentence: "Worte können nur bedeutungsvoll sein, ausdrucksvoll ist nur der Tonfall, der Klang, das Mienenspiel, die Gebärde—kurz alles, was als Form und Inhalt identisch ist, wenn es vollendet erscheint."

17. Originally published by Piper in Munich (1908). An English version by Michael Bullock appeared in 1953 under the title *Abstraction and Empathy*.

18. Originally published by Piper in Munich (1912). Several English versions were made, the latest one bearing the title *Concerning the Spiritual in Art*.

19. A reprint edition with scholarly apparatus was edited by Klaus Lankheit (Munich: Piper, 1965).

20. On p. 29 of the new edition of *Menschheitsdämmerung* (Hamburg: Rowohlt, 1959), Pinthus rather coyly refers to "Dichtung, die man die 'jüngste' oder 'expressionistische' nennt."

21. "Diese Gemeinsamkeit ist die Intensität und der Radikalismus des Gefühls, der Gesinnung, des Ausdrucks, der Form." *Ibid.*, p. 23. This sentiment was echoed by many contemporaries, including Ludwig Rubiner, who stated: "Ich weiß, daß es nur ein sittliches Lebensziel gibt: Intensität, Feuerschweife der Intensität, ihr Bersten, Aufsplittern, ihre Sprengungen." From *Der Mensch in der Mitte* (Berlin, 1917) as quoted in Pörtner I, 71.

22. "Die ganze Welt und Gott bekommen Menschenangesicht" (*Menschheitsdämmerung*, p. 28), and "Die Landschaft wird niemals hingemalt, geschildert, besungen; sondern sie ist ganz vermenscht" (*ibid.*, p. 27).

23. "Man begann, die Um-Wirklichkeit zur Un-Wirklichkeit aufzulösen" (*ibid.*, p. 26) and "Der wirkliche Kampf gegen die Wirklichkeit hatte begonnen" (*ibid.*, p. 27).

24. *Die Strukter der modernen Lyrik* (Hamburg: Rowohlt, 1956). As a specialist in Romance literature, Friedrich slights the German contribution to the European avant-garde.

25. Klarmann (*op. cit.*, p. 76) also notes the Surrealist elements in the works of certain "Expressionists."

26. Except for some very early pieces, Kafka's works show no stylistic affinity with Expressionism. Kafka himself disliked the mannerisms displayed by writers like Else Lasker-Schüler, whose poetry he found repulsive.

27. "Die folgende Liste ist keinswegs als Kanon der expressionistischen Prosa gemeint. Wie wir gesehen haben, ist es unmöglich, expressionistische Prosa (stilistisch) als solche zu charakterisieren. Deshalb ist das Verzeichnis nicht 'Inventar expressionistischer Prosa,' sondern 'Prosa der Expressionisten' überschrieben. Wer nämlich als 'Expressionist' bezeichnet werden kann—das läßt sich leichter feststellen, als wer expressionistische Prosa geschrieben hat." *Prosa des Expressionismus* (Stuttgart: Kohlhammer, 1972), p. 166.

28. This is more or less common practice among bibliographers. Thus *The Drama of German Expressionism: A German-English Bibliography* by Claude Hill and Ralph Ley (Chapel Hill: University of North Carolina Press, 1960) has sections devoted to Bertolt Brecht and Sternheim.

29. Anthologists, too, are fond of this facile solution, which saves them a lot of headaches. Thus Fritz Martini's collection *Prosa des Expressionismus* (Stuttgart: Reclam, 1970) contains a number of works which could not stand the stylistic test. Similarly, Werfel's drama *Spiegelmensch,* which is, at times, a parody of Expressionism, is frequently listed as Expressionistic.

30. See Christa Saas's Indiana University dissertation "Rilkes Expressionismus" (1967).

31. In Wedekind as well as in Sternheim, the proto-Expressionistic *Aufbruch* is typically presented as a breaking into—rather than out of—society.

32. Among these, I should like to single out Alfred Döblin's story "Die Ermordung einer Butterblume," which is widely acknowledged as a masterpiece of Expressionism but which, upon close scrutiny, reveals few, if any, of the traits delineated in my essay. A parallel case is constituted by Heinrich Mann's novella "Kobes," which, Expressionistic in certain stylistic peculiarities, should definitely be read as a spoof of Expressionism.

33. Barlach himself rejected the label, even when applied to a work like *Die Sündflut*. Discussing the first production of that drama at the Landestheater Stuttgart, he wrote to his cousin: "da stehen denn zwischen expressionistischen Stilisierungen ganz natürliche Menschen und ahnen offenbar nicht, wie schlecht sie dahin gehören . . . aber nun frage

ich, was sollen so spezialisierte Individuen zwischen expressionistischen Einseitigkeiten." *Briefe,* ed. Friedrich Dross (Munich: Piper, 1968), I, 737.

34. Such lists are, naturally, selective and, for that reason, somewhat arbitrary. The present one, for instance, might well include Kornfeld's *Die Verführung* and dramas by Toller. On the other hand, I purposely exclude Sorge and Hasenclever, whose "Expressionist" plays—*Der Bettler* and *Der Sohn* respectively—are experimental in a structural, Strindbergian sense but are not stylistically prototypical. I hasten to add that many of Kaiser's widely anthologized plays (from *Die Bürger von Calais* to *Die Koralle* and *Gas,* Part Two) are much too intellectualized to qualify for inclusion in the Expressionistic pantheon I am presently erecting.

35. The case of Sternheim is a particularly touchy one, since that author's intentions have often been misunderstood—at least until Wilhelm Emrich made it plausible that his plays *Aus dem bürgerlichen Heldenleben* were actually meant as glorifications of the *entfesselte Bürger.* And while there can be no doubt that works like *Die Hose* and *Bürger Schippel* are to a certain extent stylistic *tours de force,* their underlying *Weltanschauung* is "conservative."

36. Schickele's *Benkal, der Frauentöter,* which was enthusiastically received by many contemporaneous critics and is often cited as a paradigm, fails to strike me as being in any way Expressionistic.

37. Nevertheless, the serious student of German literary Expressionism would be foolish not to take note of Döblin's *Die drei Sprünge des Wang-lun, Wadzeks Kampf mit der Dampfturbine* (if only to measure Marinetti's impact) and, naturally, *Berlin Alexanderplatz.*

38. Since *Abstraktion und Einfühlung* was written in 1906, the term "Expressionism" does not figure there. It was not applied to literature until, roughly, 1914. For a list of various discussions of the history of that term in its artistic and literary application, see pp. 331f. of *Expressionism . . .* (see note 2).

39. *Lyrik des expressionistischen Jahrzehnts* is the title of an anthology compiled by Max Niedermayer (Wiesbaden: Limes-Verlag, 1955) for which Benn provided a preface.

40. *Die Neue Rundschau,* 29 (1918), p. 359. As is well known, in the years following its foundation by Otto Brahm, the journal fervently embraced the cause of Naturalism.

41. "Nur innere Gerechtigkeit bringt bei so hohem Ziel das Radikale. Schon wird das, was Ausbruch war, Mode. Schon schleicht übler Geist herein. Nachläuferisches aufzudecken, Fehler bloßzulegen, Ungenügendes zu betonen bleibt die Aufgabe des Ehrlichen, soweit es klarliegt und schon erkennbar ist." *Über den Expressionismus . . . ,* p. 71. In his essay "Stand des Expressionismus" (originally published in the *Frankfurter Zeitung* of June 10, 1920), Edschmid calls the Expressionist generation *ausgekernt.* See p. 207 of his *Frühe Schriften,* ed. Ernst Johann (Neuwied: Luchterhand, 1970).

42. Reprinted in *Fragen und Gegenfragen: Schriften zum Kunstproblem* (Munich: Piper, 1956).

43. P. 33 of the reprint edition referred to in note 20.

44. From Rudolf Leonhard's essay "Über Gruppenbildung in der Literatur," *Das neue Pathos,* 1 (1913), No. 1, S. 31, as reprinted in Pörtner, II, 159-63.

45. "Im *Sturm* enthielt der Begriff Expressionismus keine weltanschaulichen, sondern rein stilistische Forderungen. Man vertrat im *Sturm* selten einen weltanschaulichen Standpunkt." Werner Rittich on p. 92 of his book (see note 7 above).

46. Thus Franz Pfemfert's declaration in the first issue of *Die Aktion* (February 20, 1911) opens with the sentence: "*Die Aktion* tritt, ohne sich auf den Boden einer bestimmten politischen Partei zu stellen, für die Idee der Großen Deutschen Linken ein."

47. In later years, Wolff consistently denied having been the champion of Expressionism or, for that matter, of any particular clique or movement. See the quotation from a radio address quoted on p. xxvi of *Briefwechsel eines Verlegers 1911-1963,* eds. B. Zeller and E. Otten (Frankfurt: Scheffler, 1966).

48. Thus Otto Flake commits a pardonable perspectivist error when prognosticating: "Die Historiker werden einst *Die Aktion* durchforschen, um die Geschichte der Stammelnden zu schreiben." *Die Neue Rundschau,* 25 (1915), pt. 2, p. 1282.

49. Thus, as late as 1920, Friedrich Markus Huebner, an influential critic, wrote: "*Der Sturm* neigt hauptsächlich dem Kubismus und Futurismus zu." From *Europas neue Kunst und Dichtung* (Berlin, 1920), as quoted in Pörtner II, 366.

50. Number 44 of *Der Sturm* contains Kurt Hiller's "Rede zur Eröffnung des neopathetischen Kabaretts" and, as part thereof, the characteristic sentence, "Das Geistige [ist] eine Flamme, von der die Seele ständig geheizt ist."

51. "In den Dingen der Kunst und der Literatur sucht *Die Aktion* ein Gegengewicht zu bilden zu der traurigen Gewohnheit der pseudoliberalen Presse,

neue Regungen lediglich vom Geschäftsstandpunkt aus zu bewerten, also sie totzuschweigen. Bei vollkommener Unabhängigkeit von Rechts und von Links ist *Die Aktion* eine Tribüne, von der aus jede Persönlichkeit, die Sagenswertes zu sagen hat, ungehindert sprechen kann. *Die Aktion* hat den Ehrgeiz, ein Organ des ehrlichen Radikalismus zu sein." From the manifesto referred to in note 46.

52. See also the footnote on p. 67 of Rudolf Blümner's *Der Geist des Kubismus und die Künste,* where Hasenclever, Werfel, Becher, Georg Kaiser, Sternheim, Edschmid "und die ganze dazu gehörige Gefolgschaft" are scorned as "impressionistische Dichter, die Ahnungslose für Expressionisten halten." And Kurt Hiller, responding to Sternheim's essay "Kampf der Metapher" in the *Berlinger Tageblatt* of July 25, 1917, refers to *Der Sturm* as a "Bilderböglein." The article is quoted in Sternheim's *Gesamtwerk* (see note 11), VI, 501ff.

53. A good case in point is that of Adolf Behne.

54. In Kandinsky's *Concerning the Spiritual in Art* (New York: Wittenborn & Schultz, 1947), p. 77, these three types of "symphonic composition" are said to "represent three different sources of inspiration."

55. From the essay "Über die Formfrage" in *Der Blaue Reiter* (p. 139 of the reprint edition referred to in note 19). The same point is made, more paradoxically—and even absurdly—by Lothar Schreyer, who boldly declares "daß das Wesen der abstrakten Malerei der abstrakte Inhalt ist." From his essay "Herwarth Waldens Werk" in *Der Sturm: Ein Erinnerungsbuch an Herwarth Walden und die Künstler aus dem Sturmkreis,* eds. Nell Walden and Lothar Schreyer (Baden-Baden: Klein, 1954), p. 138.

56. Thus Lothar Schreyer says of the poet: "Ihn zwingt eine innere Notwendigkeit zu sprechen, und es ist ihm gleichgültig, ob er gehört wird." From Schreyer's essay "Die neue Kunst," as quoted by Rittich, p. 33.

57. "What I am after, above all, is expression. . . . Expression to my way of thinking does not consist of the passion mirrored upon a human face or betrayed by a violent gesture. The whole arrangement of my picture is expressive." From Matisse's "Notes of a Painter" (1908) as translated by Alfred H. Barr, Jr., and reprinted in Herschel B. Chipp, ed., *Theories of Modern Art: A Source Book by Artists and Critics* (Berkeley/Los Angeles: University of California Press, 1968), pp. 131f. Benn's notions about *Ausdruckskunst* are most cogently presented in his "Rede auf Heinrich Mann" (1931) in *Werke,* ed. Dieter Wellershoff (Wiesbaden: Limes-Verlag, 1961), IV, 974ff. In his contribution to the volume *Schöpferische Konfession* (see note 5), Benn confesses: "Mich sensationiert eben das Wort ohne jede Rücksicht auf seinen beschreibenden Charakter rein als assoziatives Motiv."

58. Quoted from Schreyer's essay "Herwarth Waldens Werk" (see note 55), p. 148.

59. There is a strong—and hardly accidental—resemblance between this view and the Imagist/Vorticist emphasis on the "primary pigment" as found in the writings of Ezra Pound and Wyndham Lewis around 1913/14.

60. These are the opening lines of Stadler's poem "From ist Wollust," which Pinthus included in *Menschheitsdämmerung.*

61. *Vide* the exceptionally large number of lyrical anthologies listed and described in Paul Raabe, *Die Zeitschriften und Sammlungen des literarischen Expressionismus 1910-1921* (Stuttgart: Metzler, 1964).

62. In his *Anarchie im Drama* (see note 23), Diebold distinguishes *Ich-Dramen* from *Schrei-Dramen* and *Pflichtdramen* and discusses at length Strindberg's role as a precursor of Expressionist drama.

63. See, for instance, Walter Sokel's contribution to the volume *Expressionismus als Literatur,* ed. Wolfgang Rothe (Berne: Francke, 1969), where Döblin's theory of the novel with its objectivizing tendency, "die sich von Flaubert, Spielhagen und Henry James herleitet" (p. 155), is regarded as Expressionistic. By contrast, Erich von Kahler's presentation in the essay "Die Prosa des Expressionismus" (*Der deutsche Expressionismus: Formen und Gestalten,* ed. H. Steffen [Göttingen: Vandenhoeck & Ruprecht, 1965] is much more balanced.

64. Frankfurt a. M.: S. Fischer, 1956, p. 556.

65. Carl Einstein, for instance, finds "daß die sprachliche Darstellung eben nur unreine Kunst sei, gemessen an der Musik" (from *Bebuquin oder die Dilettanten des Wunders* [Berlin, 1912], as quoted in Pörtner I, 281). Martin Buber (quoted *ibid.,* pp. 167f.) bemoans the fact that "auch das innerlichste Erlebnis . . . vor dem Triebe zur Veräußerung nicht bewahrt bleibt" and, in a truly mystical spirit, observes: "Ich glaube an die Ekstasen, die nie ein Laut berührte, an ein unsichtbares Heiligtum der Menschheit. Die Dokumente derer, die in Worten mündeten, liegen vor mir. . . . Sobald sie [the ecstatic individuals] sprachen, waren sie schon in den Grenzen."

66. From the essay "Das Drama" in the August 1916 issue of *Der Sturm,* partly reprinted in *Expressionistisches Theater: Aus meinen Erinnerungen* (see note 15).

67. *Der Blaue Reiter,* pp. 206f.

68. *Ibid.,* p. 110.

69. The conflict is equally prominent in the drama of the Storm and Stress, which explains, in part, the Expressionists' admiration for these plays.

70. See especially the arguments offered on pp. 118ff. of *The Writer in Extremis,* where both Heinrich Mann's novella "Pippo Spano" and Hofmansthal's lyrical playlet *Der Tor und der Tod* are considered in that context, as is Franz Kafka.

71. *Die doppelköpfige Nymphe,* p. 17.

72. *Wesen* is so crucial a word in the jargon of Expressionism that it is impossible to list even the most poignant examples of its use. Ernst Stadler's reference to Angelus Silesius's famous motto "Mensch, werde wesentlich!" in the concluding line of his poem "Der Spruch" (*Menschheitsdämmerung,* p. 196) is only one case in point. Speaking in the same vein, Klee calls for a "Verwesentlichung des Zufälligen" (*Schöpferische Konfession,* p. 35) and Walden aims at the "geistige Quintessenz eines Erlebnisses."

73. Max Krell (*Über moderne Prosa,* p. 14) speaks of the desired "Entschälung der Dinge"; and Georg Kaiser's drama *Von morgens bis mitternachts* offers the sentence, "Aus siedender Auflösung des einzelnen geballt: der Kern: Leidenschaft."

74. Thus in *Von morgens bis mitternachts* reference is made to the "letzte Ballung des Tatsächlichen"; at one crucial point, the protagonist asks for "Spitzen, Spitzen. . . . Von Anfang bis zu Ende nur Spitzen. . . . Spitzen sind die letzten Ballungen in allen Dingen."

75. The terms most frequently used are *Seele* and *Geist.* Marc's contribution to the almanac *Der Blaue Reiter* is appropriately entitled "Geistige Güter," and Kandinsky's treatise is called *Über das Geistige in der Kunst. Geist* was preferred because it lacks religious overtones.

76. Theodor Däubler (*Der neue Standpunkt,* p. 179) argues: "Eine Vision will sich in letzter Knappheit im Bezirk verstiegener Vereinfachung kundgeben: das ist Expressionismus in jedem Stil." And Franz Marc refers to the "mystisch-innerliche Konstruktion, die das große Problem der heutigen Generation ist" (*Der Blaue Reiter,* p. 23).

77. Thus Frank Thiess's assertion that "der Traum . . . das expressionistische Kunstwerk par excellence [ist]" (from his essay "Der Traum als Kunstwerk," as reprinted in Pörtner I, 298) must be categorically rejected.

78. The dynamism was so strong that, pananthropomorphically, it tended to spill over into the non-human realms, both organic and inorganic (Marc's animals and Delaunay's Eiffel Tower, according to Däubler). In this light, Worringer's predilection for Gothic art becomes sensible: "Diese Unruhe, dieses Suchen hat kein organisches Leben . . . aber Leben ist da. . . . Also auf anorganischer Grundlage eine gesteigerte Bewegung, ein gesteigerter Ausdruck. . . . Das Einfühlungsbedürfnis dieser disharmonischen Völker nimmt nicht den nächstliegenden Weg zum Organischen . . . sondern braucht jenes unheimliche Pathos, das der Verlebendigung des Anorganischen anhaftet." *Abstraktion und Einfühlung,* reprint (Munich: Piper, 1948), pp. 87f.

79. Hence the Expressionists' fascination with primitive art (not to be confused with the Cubists' analogous preoccupation, although the two are jointly expressed in a hybrid painting like Picasso's "Demoiselles d'Avignon"). F. M. Huebner, in an essay entitled "Krieg und Expressionismus," states that "die neue Bewegung entstand, weil das Gemälde, das Gedicht, das Drama nicht der Dinge Letztes brachte, sondern weil stets zwischen den Eindruck und die Wiedergabe zurechtstutzend das Denken . . . trat. Hier [in the art of the primitives], so schien es, war nichts, das die seelische Erregung abschnitt von ihrem Ergebnis, dem bildnerischen Können." See Pörtner II, 178f.

80. Carl Einstein voices the characteristic complaint: "Der Fehler des Logischen ist, daß es noch nicht einmal symbolisch gelten kann. Man muß einsehen, ihr Dummköpfe, daß Logik nur Stil werden darf, ohne je eine Wirklichkeit zu berühren. . . . Wir müssen einsehen, daß das Phantastischste die Logik ist." From *Bebuquin oder die Dilettanten des Wunders* (Pörtner I, 280). And Sternheim, addressing Kasimir Edschmid, states: "Ich weiß, Sie zerschlagen mit mir . . . die borniere Rinde des Begriffs und bringen ihn von innen zu einer zweiten Explosion." *Gesamtwerk* IV, 103.

81. The destruction of causality leads to a destruction of chronology as an orderly sequence as well. Thus, as Däubler asserted repeatedly, Expressionist art is characterized by a kaleidoscopic blending of successive states, a kind of dynamic simultaneity which more closely resembles the Futurist *simultaneità* than its Cubist counterpart, the static *collage.* In a passage of his essay "An Romanautoren und ihre Kritiker," Alfred Döblin offers his own solution to the problem: "Die Darstellung erfordert bei der ungeheuren Menge des Geformten

einen Kinostil. In höchster Gedrängtheit und Präsion hat die Fülle der Gesichte vorbeizuziehen." See Pörtner I, 285.

82. Kandinsky (*Concerning the Spiritual in Art*, p. 70) resented the fact that "spectators are too accustomed to look for a 'meaning' in a picture, i.e., some external relation in its various elements." He, accordingly, opted for the viewer who places himself "in front of a picture and lets it speak for itself." And in his essay "Über die Formfrage" (*Der Blaue Reiter*, p. 164) he observed: "Die Theoretiker, die, von der Analyse der schon dagewesenen Formen ausgehend, ein Werk tadeln oder loben, sind die schädlichsten Irreführer, die zwischen dem Werk und dem naiven Beschauer eine Mauer bilden. Von diesem Standpunkte aus . . . ist die Kunstkritik der schlimmste Feind der Kunst. Der ideale Kunstkritiker wäre also . . . der Kritiker . . . , welcher zu fühlen suchen würde, wie diese oder jene Form innerlich wirkt, und dann sein Gesamterlebnis dem Publikum ausdrucksvoll mitteilen würde."

83. From Part IV of Bab's *Die Chronik des deutschen Dramas*, as quoted in the catalogue of the Marbach exhibition (see note 5), p. 309.

84. New York: Meridian Books, 1955, p. 51.

85. *The Letters of Vincent van Gogh*, ed. Mark Roskill (New York: Atheneum, 1963), p. 276ff. The letter is quoted by Read.

86. *Blast*, Volume I (1914), p. 120. This is a comment by Wadsworth on extracts from Kandinsky's *Concerning the Spiritual in Art*.

87. "Diese Menschen sind unverbildet. Sie reflektieren nicht. Sie erleben nicht in Kreisen, nicht durch Echos. Sie erleben direkt. Das ist das größte Geheimnis dieser Kunst: sie ist ohne gewohnte Psychologie." *Über den Expressionismus in der Literatur . . .*, p. 60. The Expressionists clearly were closer to Jung than to Freud.

88. As Kurt Pinthus puts it in his review of Hasenclever's *Der Sohn*, "Der Sohn ist im Stück ganz und gar das Wesentliche; zu ihm, nur zu ihm strahlt alles; alles, was andre tun und sprechen, geschieht mit Rücksicht auf ihn allein" (from *Die Schaubühne*, 10 [1914], as quoted in Pörtner I, 345). Hasenclever himself, writing in the *Neue Blätter für Kunst und Dichtung*, observes: "Der Versuch, das Gegenspiel der Figuren in demselben Darsteller zu verkörpern, würde die Einheit des Ganzen erläutern; ein Zuschauer, der dem Parkett und der Bühne entsagend, außerhalb stände, würde erkennen, daß alles, was hier geschieht, nur verschieden ist als Ausdruck des einen gleichen Gedankens." Quoted *ibid.*, p. 358.

89. Edschmid, *Über den Expressionismus in der Literatur . . .*, pp. 62f.

90. Similarly, Edschmid declares, "Die Welt ist da. Es wäre sinnlos, sie zu wiederholen" (*ibid.*, p. 56); and Walden proclaims, "Kunst ist Gabe und nicht Wiedergabe" (from his "Vorrede zum Ersten Deutschen Herbstsalon 1913," as quoted in Pörtner II, 158).

91. *Über den Expressionismus in der Literatur . . .*, pp. 73f.

92. From Walden's essay "Das Begriffliche in der Dichtung," originally published in *Der Sturm*, 9 (1918), pp. 66f. and reprinted in the book *Expressionismus: Die Kunstwende, pp. 30-38*.

93. "Wir haben keine Worte für unsere Begriffe. Wir Werdenden! Oder besser: wir Werder. Der Ister ist ein Lügner, nur der Werder weht, wahr in wahrem." From a letter to Herwarth and Nell Walden dated March 21, 1915, and quoted in Pörtner I, 54.

94. Blümner, "Die absolute Dichtung," originally published in *Der Sturm*, 12 (1921), and reprinted in Pörtner I, 446ff.

95. *Schöpferische Konfession*, p. 94.

96. Hugo Kersten, "Über Kunst, Künstler und Idioten," a series of excerpts from *Die Aktion*, 4 (1914), reproduced in Pörtner I, 131ff.

97. *Die doppelköpfige Nymphe*, p. 134.

98. From the essay "Expressionismus des Schauspielers" in *Die Neue Rundschau*, 28 (1917), pt. 1, p. 575.

99. Strangely enough, the stylistics of Expressionist literature (especially poetry) has not received its due in the secondary literature. Heinz Peter Dürsteler's book *Sprachliche Neuschöpfungen im Expressionismus* (Bern: "Wir jungen Schweizer," 1954) is a notable exception. The poetic technique of the *Sturm* poets has been studied by Werner Rittich (see note 7), and Karl-Ludwig Schneider's monograph *Der bildhafte Ausdruck in den Dichtungen Georg Heyms, Georg Trakls und Ernst Stadlers* (Heidelberg: Schneider, 1954) is a mine of information about the style not only of these three proto-Expressionists but of Expressionist poetry in general.

100. The term occurs in Döblin's essay "Futuristische Worttechnik: Offener Brief an F. T. Marinetti," originally published in *Der Sturm* (number 150/151) and reprinted in Pörtner II, 63ff. It is used derogatorily.

101. "Expressionismus und Sprachgewissen" in *Gesamtwerk*, IV, 108.

102. *Über den dichterischen Expressionismus* . . . , p. 65f.

103. *Der Vermessungsdirigent: Erkenntnistheoretisches Drama* (Berlin, 1919), p. 3, an excerpt reprinted in Pörtner I, 104. The concluding phrase refers to the overwhelming power of the life force which sweeps away rationality and, with it, causality.

104. "Brief an die Feuilletonredaktion der Frankfurter Zeitung," as reprinted in *Theorie der modernen Lyrik,* ed. Walter Höllerer (Hamburg: Rowohlt, 1965), pp. 283ff.

105. In his book *Kunsttheorie, Wortkunsttheorie und lyrische Wortkunst im "Sturm"* (see note 7), Rittich, summarizing the theory of *Wortkunst,* states: "Das Material des Wortkunstwerkes ist das Wort. Die Gestaltung erfolgt direkt mit sinnlichen Mitteln. Die sinnlichen Mittel sind klanglich, rhythmisch und bildlich. Sie vereinen die Wörter zu Wortreihen" (p. 54).

106. *Über den Expressionismus in der Literatur* . . . , p. 66.

107. Werfel's essay "Substantiv und Verbum" appeared in *Die Aktion,* 6 (1917), pp. 4-8. It is reprinted in Pörtner I, 182-88. The quoted phrase occurs on p. 183.

108. *Op. cit.,* p. 107 (footnote 153).

109. The similarity between a morality play like *Everyman* and Hasenclever's *Der Sohn* (or, for that matter, Strindberg's *Road to Damascus*) is superficial, though real.

110. Sternheim uses the phrase "Kampf der Metapher" in his programmatic review of Benn's *Fleisch* and *Gehirne.* See his *Gesamtwerk,* VI, 32.

111. Rittich's observation that "die Verwerfung des Vergleichs . . . der wesentliche Punkt [ist], in dem die Sturmtheorie mit dem Dichtungsprogramm des lit. Futurismus im Einklang steht" (*Kunsttheorie* . . . , p. 105, footnote 126) can be extended to cover the whole of literary Expressionismus.

FURTHER READING

Criticism

Allen, Roy F. "Expressionism in Berlin." In *Literary Life in German Expressionism and the Berlin Circles,* pp. 118-47. Göppingen, Germany: Verlag Alfred Kümmerle, 1972.
Discusses Berlin as the reigning capitol of Expressionism, focusing on the various literary, artistic, and philosophical currents that contributed to the flourishing of the movement.

Brinkmann, Richard. "Abstract Lyrics of Expressionism: End or Transformation of the Symbol?" In *Literary Symbolism: A Symposium,* edited by Helmut Rehder, pp. 109-36. Austin: University of Texas Press, 1965.
Outlines and discusses some of the main features of Expressionist poetry, emphasizing its tendency toward the abstract.

Bronner, Stephen Eric. *Passion and Rebellion: The Expressionist Heritage,* edited by Stephen Eric Bronner and Douglas Kellner. New York: Universe Books, 1983, 468 p.
Collection of essays reassessing Expressionism, with sections on society and politics, literature and theater, painting, music and dance, film, and aesthetic and social implications.

Furness, R. S. *Expressionism.* London: Methuen & Co. Ltd, 1973, 105 p.
Survey of Expressionism, including its origins, innovations, situation in Germany, and influence.

Gordon, Donald E. *Expressionism: Art and Idea.* New Haven, Conn.: Yale University Press, 1987, 263 p.
Discusses the intellectual background, art, and style of Expressionism.

Redlich, Fritz. "German Literary Expressionism and Its Publishers." *Harvard Library Bulletin* 17 (1969): 143-68.
Traces the relationship between German Expressionists and their publishers, with reference to both the literature and the economics of the time.

Rumold, Rainer, and O. K. Werckmeister, editors. *The Ideological Crisis of Expressionism: The Literary and Artistic German War Colony in Belgium 1914-1918.* Columbia, S.C.: Camden House, 1990, 299 p.
Explores the ideology and political predicament of a group of German Expressionist writers and artists living in Belgium during World War I.

Sheppard, Richard, editor. *Expressionism in Focus: Proceedings of the First UEA Symposium on German Studies.* New Alyth, Scotland: Lochee Publications Ltd., 1987, 211 p.
Collection of essays on various Expressionist themes and figures.

Sokel, Walter H. *The Writer in Extremis: Expressionism in Twentieth-Century German Literature.* Stanford, Calif.: Stanford University Press, 1959, 251 p.
Thematically-arranged overview of Expressionism in German literature.

Washton Long, Rose-Carol, editor. *German Expressionism: Documents from the End of the Wilhelmine Empire to the Rise of National Socialism.* New York: G. K. Hall & Co., 1993, 349 p.

Collection of seminal contemporary writings relevant to Expressionism.

Weisstein, Ulrich, editor. *Expressionism as an International Literary Phenomenon.* Paris: Didier and Akadémiai Kiadó, 1973, 360 p.

Explores the international dimension of Expressionism, including influences on the movement and the impact of the movement in various countries.

Coverage on German Expressionism is contained in the following source published by the Gale Group: *Twentieth-Century Literary Criticism,* **Vol. 34.**

Southern Gothic Literature

The following entry discusses twentieth-century Southern Gothic literature.

INTRODUCTION

Gothic literature—so called because many examples of the genre were set during the late-medieval, or Gothic, period—proliferated in England, Germany, and the United States during the late eighteenth and early nineteenth centuries. Critics date its inception to 1764, when English statesman and writer Horace Walpoe published *The Castle of Otranto: A Gothic Story*. Set against the majestic backgrounds of mysterious castles and aging palaces, many nineteenth-century English gothic novels used such bleak landscapes to create an atmosphere of horror and suspense. In particular, gothic literature found a home with writers of the American South, who used the crumbling landscape of the antebellum era as the backdrop for their tales of fantasy and the grotesque. Major twentieth-century American authors often identified with this genre include Flannery O'Connor, Cormac McCarthy, William Faulkner, Truman Capote, and to a lesser extent, Eudora Welty.

Defined by Francis Russell Hart as "fiction evocative of a sublime and picturesque landscape . . . depict(ing) a world in ruins," the gothic novel presents readers with an opportunity to vicariously experience horrifying realities. By creating worlds where tragedy and repressed behaviors come to the forefront, gothic writers explore the psychology of human existence on several unique levels, notes critic Elizabeth M. Kerr. Common elements of the gothic novel include explorations of the subconscious through dreams, a good versus evil polarity in the characters, and the use of setting and atmosphere to evoke a vivid emotional response in the reader. While English Gothicism closely paralleled the Romantic movement in literature, frequently focusing on issues of love, sexuality, and the place of reason in human existence, Southern Gothic fiction focuses largely on themes of terror, death, and social interaction.

Some commentators have argued that the adaptation of the gothic format was particularly suited to the American South because the plantation world of the antebellum period provided writers with an analogy to the medieval settings available to English gothic writers. The images of the plantation houses—representative of a quasi-feudal order in times of prosperity—contrasted with their eventual decay were evocative of the ruined castles of nineteenth-century Gothic romances, with both symbolically signalling the end of an era. However, Southern Gothic fiction also embodies an immediacy and poignancy that derives from the personal and community experiences of its authors. Kerr explains this intensity as, "the cult of the past in the South, as symbolized in its ruins, its preserved glories displayed in spring pilgrimages, its monuments and graveyards, owes less to cultural climate and imagination than to remembered history." This emphasis on history is vital to Southern Gothic fiction, which not only draws on the stylistic characteristics of nineteenth-century gothic fiction, but also finds inspiration from novels of the American past. Certain scholars—such as Leslie Fiedler in *Love and Death in the American Novel* (1960)—have identified specifically national concerns apparent in Southern Gothic fiction, particularly the relationships between races and genders. Other academics have been dismissive towards twentieth-century Southern Gothic novels, referring to the movement as a sub-genre of serious fiction and criticizing the works for their sometimes formulaic and sentimental storylines.

REPRESENTATIVE WORKS

Truman Capote
Other Voices, Other Rooms (novel) 1948
A Tree of Night, and Other Stories (short stories) 1949
The Glass Harp (novel) 1951

William Faulkner
A Rose for Emily (novel) 1924
The Sound and the Fury (novel) 1929
As I Lay Dying (novel) 1930
Light in August (novel) 1932
Absalom, Absalom! (novel) 1936

Leslie Fiedler
Love and Death in the American Novel (criticism) 1960

Zora Neale Hurston
Their Eyes Were Watching God (novel) 1937

Cormac McCarthy
The Orchard Keeper (novel) 1965
Outer Dark (novel) 1968
Child of God (novel) 1974
Suttree (novel) 1979

Flannery O'Connor
Wise Blood (novel) 1952
A Good Man Is Hard to Find (short stories) 1955; also published as *The Artificial Nigger and Other Tales*, 1957
The Violent Bear It Away (novel) 1960
Everything that Rises Must Converge (short stories) 1965
Mystery and Manners: Occasional Prose (prose) 1969
The Complete Stories of Flannery O'Connor (short stories) 1974

William Styron
Set This House On Fire (novel) 1963

Eudora Welty
A Curtain of Green and Other Stories (short stories) 1941
The Wide Net and Other Stories (short stories) 1943
The Golden Apples (short stories) 1949
The Optimist's Daughter (novel) 1972

OVERVIEWS AND GENERAL STUDIES

Margie Burns (essay date 1991)

SOURCE: Burns, Margie. "A Good Rose Is Hard to Find: Southern Gothic as Signs of Social Dislocation in Faulkner and O'Connor." In *Image and Ideology in Modern/Postmodern Discourse,* edited by David B. Browning and Susan Bazargan, pp. 105-23. Albany: State University of New York Press, 1991.

[*In the following essay, Burns contends that Southern Gothic is a literary technique that both represents and hides the dehumanization of the South into perceived stereotypes. The critic analyzes works by Flannery O'Connor and William Faulkner as examples of this technique.*]

> Between the simple backward look
> and the simple progressive thrust
> there is room for long argument but
> none for enlightenment.
>
> —Raymond Williams, *The Country and the City*

The topic of images of the South in the literature and media of the nation as a whole is rich in possibilities for cultural studies, for analysis of the processes of production, reception, and consumption of such images as they come to be formed and through which they are put to use. As anyone might recognize, cultural stereotypes about the American South are frequently projected as representations of objective reality; indeed, there exists an unanalytic habit, on the part both of the media and of canonical writers, to characterize the South through figural reification. In novels (both popular and canonical), in plays, film, and television, in periodicals, and in advertisements, versions of the same stereotypes recur, with a persistence both of form and of effect which suggests their organization by utility if not by intent. I would argue that these stereotypes both corroborate a deep-lying perception in the general consciousness, and solace an even deeper-lying doubt; without essential validity, they nevertheless fall into place with comforting neatness, to reaffirm the inferiority of the Other into which the American South has been transformed in the national consciousness. An enhanced critical consciousness, however, would perceive the political consequences of the ideological differences constituted by the various elements of the "Southern" image.

In general, the stereotypical perception of the South is organized around, literally, two *classes* of image: antebellum/magnolia/*GWTW* mythology, and cotton row/tobacco road/*Baby Doll* grotesquerie.[1] These two stereotypes embody what have been called the two greatest bourgeois perceptions of threat, the dichotomized but connected fears of a decaying "aristocracy" on one hand, and of a rebellious, primitive, "earthy" peasantry on the other.[2] The seeming triviality of these stereotypes, rather than serving to invalidate them, disguises their genuine utility—and destructiveness—in American culture. In my view, what is most illuminating about this polarized image is not the spurious distinction between its two terms but the underlying common denominators which provide the basis for the polarized image and sustain it. In this polarized construction, which is obviously a class construction and just as obviously a projection from the "central," missing term of the self-identified "middle class," the two categories correspond to two classes—upper and lower—a version of aristocracy and a version of peasantry. Furthermore, the two classes have, in these representations, three identifying characteristics in common: both are white (ironically), static, and unproductive. The gentleman of sorts lives in privileged idleness, and the redneck inhabits a Lower Slobbovia of equal idleness (although characterized as laziness rather than privilege). Both imagistic strata—the magnolia crowd and the tobacco-juice crowd—are primarily static—*stuck*—in the boonies, in ignorance, in prejudice, etc., with degenerate histories miring them down; neither group is "going anywhere," except to proceed further downward in some melodrama of degeneracy. In the typically polarized picture of the Deep South, in short, there are virtually no figures of upward mobility, no successful or productive efforts either of individual or of collectivity—there is in this regard only a glaring void waiting to be filled by the faster-moving observer from whose perspective the picture is generated. Such a perspective fulfills the formulation of Pierre Bourdieu, that for the spectator even an observed *activity* becomes

Photograph of a plantation house in Convent, Louisana, 1938.

an object; the South as spectacle/object, whose people all apparently sit still, presents an intensification of the phenomenon.

Hence the chief point of the characterization is surely to assert a contrast to the non-South nation, where all the action is; the characterization of static versus mobile, stagnation versus dynamism, corroborates a self-legitimating view of the *haute bourgeois* as the ideal mean, a mediating principle between the too-high and the too-low to work, industrious as well as industrial—with the latter as evidence of the former. It is the vision of the Connecticut Yankee, Hank the Boss, without the ironic awareness of a Clemens behind it. The putative absence of productivity (symbolized by an absence of mobility), in other words, gives the image its social and economic usefulness—and a fairly complex and multivalent usefulness at that—in the historical actuality which surrounds the image. Indeed, the usefulness of the image, far more than any mimetic relation to social reality, has kept it alive; and its uses have been social and economic, beyond the scope of this essay to cover.

The typical discourse on the South as object at least partly resembles colonial production, a nativist discourse dictated by essentially colonialist interests, but it is also more broadly constitutive of ideological differences along class lines.[3] Just as the trivialized stereotypes of Southern Women intensify a polarization projected onto women in general (good/sexually innocent versus bad/sexually experienced), so the sharply polarized image of two social strata in the South intensifies—crudely—its dichotomous inversion: the wish, projected from the missing term, the middle class, to lampoon or to obliterate an awareness of genuine class difference.

In other words, the view of the South self-identified as the "national" or "American" view is basically a colonial romance, with the rest of the nation identified with the forces of light and the South with the forces of darkness. And this romance shares a salient characteristic of virtually all post-Romantic romance: in it, the polarization of social highs and lows in actuality metamorphoses into a polarization of psychological highs and lows as the source of conflict in the literary representations and other representations. Thus the haute bourgeois middle term is, of course, even more thoroughly obscured. The image of dark loci which map the terrain of the South in the popular imagination (and in the scholarly imagination) directly serves the ideology which produced it.

Nowhere is the ideology-constitutive character of this image more apparent than in the literary mode known as "southern gothic."[4] In this essay on the southern gothic—a term in widespread use, but one which almost nobody attempts to scrutinize—I consider two famous short stories by William Faulkner and Flannery O'Connor and argue that the southern gothic is a literary technique which both enacts and conceals the dehumanization of response *to* the South, by representing it as a dehumanization of response *in* the South.[5] Needless to say, imaginative literature has played only one part in the construction of the South as an ideological Other for the nation as a whole. "Serious" imaginative literature has played an even smaller part; but the staggering blatancy with which these two works pursue their part in the construction justifies their analysis in postmodern critical practice.

II

Even the most casual survey of the literary mode called "southern gothic" would turn up Faulkner's "A Rose for Emily" (1924) and O'Connor's "A Good Man Is Hard to Find" (1954) as premier examples. "A Rose for Emily" presents Emily through languorous, external flashbacks which leave her own consciousness opaque but gradually reveal that she poisoned her jilting lover and cohabited for decades with his corpse. In "A Good Man Is Hard to Find," a worthless, déclassé southern family goes on a vacation, has a car wreck, and is thrown into the hands of a homicidal maniac (also southern) who kills everyone. The narrative presents the family's slaughter, moreover, as the result chiefly of its own idiocy and venality. Both short stories achieve their full horror through intense comedy, a black humor which largely accounts for the place of "southern" relative to "gothic"; if it happened anywhere else, it wouldn't be as funny. I contend that these narratives show how the consistent techniques of southern gothic mark the sites of *social* dislocations—phenomena conventionally regarded as nonliterary. In simplest terms, the *gothic* operates as a distancing: it mystifies the matter presented, removing it into an atmosphere detached from social actuality and engineering a response alienated and unsympathetic. This mystification has had consequences both within and outside the literature.

In the narratives discussed here, the most significant movements are concealment and entrapment. "A Rose for Emily" begins,

> When Miss Emily Grierson died, our whole town went to her funeral: the men through a sort of respectful affection for a fallen monument, the women mostly out of curiosity to see the inside of her house.
>
> (489)

This single, wonderfully economical sentence immediately sets up the demarcation between a crypto-military context for men and a setting of house interiors for women, which is sustained throughout the narrative. It also establishes a progression—death, morbidity, a monument, and concealment behind a wall or facade—typical of southern gothic, in which the luridness of the terms distracts attention away from their true relationship. Here, the outside-inside demarcation becomes perversely conflated—a "monument," which both blazons and conceals what it contains.[6] Any awareness stimulated by the hint of very real violence, however, is displaced—trivialized—into typically "gothic" suspense and a (feminine) morbid curiosity.

Repeatedly the narrative describes/erects some wall or facade which simultaneously blazons and conceals. In one stunning example, the generation previous to Miss Emily's produced the "edict that no Negro woman should appear on the streets without an apron" (489); I shall discuss this below. Similarly, the women whisper about Emily's sexual activities "behind their hands; rustling of craned silk and satin behind jalousies closed upon the sun of Sunday afternoon" (495). The facades thus erected ornament both persons and places with a dissolutely baroque prose; the Grierson house itself is

> a big, squarish frame house that had once been white, decorated with cupolas and spires and scrolled balconies in the heavily lightsome style of the seventies, . . . lifting up its stubborn and coquettish decay above the cotton wagons and the gasoline pumps—an eyesore among eyesores.
>
> (489)

Obviously, the old house is identified with Miss Emily (and perhaps with femaleness in general);[7] the phrases "heavily lightsome" and "coquettish decay," among others, anthropomorphize it, turning it into an old "eyesore" like Emily herself and suggesting a threatening, veiled sexuality in both edifices.

In a rich, curious paradox of combined limpidity and occlusion, each such verbal flourish throughout the story signals a social dislocation, an injustice. Examples abound:

> And now Miss Emily had gone to join the representatives of those august names where they lay in the cedar-bemused cemetery among the ranked and anonymous graves of Union and Confederate soldiers who fell at the battle of Jefferson.
>
> (489)

Here the nostalgic, antiquarian intrigue—"cedar-bemused" itself—obscures the deaths of nameless, ordinary soldiers. Other examples concerning Emily herself arise frequently; at an early point, Emily writes:

> a note on paper of an archaic shape, in a thin, flowing calligraphy in faded ink, to the effect that she no longer went out at all. The tax notice was also enclosed, without comment.
>
> (490)

The successful mystification of the town—a successful mystification, in more than one sense—allows Emily to escape, *seriatim,* from both death and taxes:

> So she vanquished them, horse and foot, just as she had vanquished their fathers thirty years before about the smell.
>
> (492)

But while Faulkner's submerged joke on death and taxes gives some structure to the story, it also trivializes the fundamental conflict between Emily and the men—"horse and foot"—of the town. In repetitive detail, Emily is incessantly associated with the past, with the Civil War, with the *burdens* of history devoid of any understanding of history. Always, the odor of history is mystified, through her, either decayed into a stink or misperceived as the aura of nostalgia.[8] And this diffuse mystification has a highly specific use; it transforms "history" into an intimidation serving the interests of a privileged class.

> A deputation waited upon her, knocked at the door through which no visitor had passed since she ceased giving chinapainting lessons eight or ten years earlier. They were admitted by the Old Negro into a dim hall from which a stairway mounted into still more shadow. It smelled of dust and disuse—a close, dank smell. The Negro led them into the parlor. It was furnished in heavy, leather-covered furniture. When the Negro opened the blinds of one window, they could see that the leather was cracked; and when they sat down, a faint dust rose sluggishly about their thighs, spinning with slow motes in the single sun-ray. On a tarnished gilt easel before the fireplace stood a crayon portrait of Miss Emily's father.
>
> (490)

In such an atmosphere of more than adequate oppressiveness, it is hardly surprising that the men should fail in their mission to exact money from Miss Emily, or that they should be vanquished by the single, cryptic utterance: "'See Colonel Sartoris.' (Colonel Sartoris had been dead almost ten years)" (491).

Since some vague concept of "history" is often associated with outmoded ornamentation—forgetting the spareness or angularity of any artistic styles before the "modern"—the same mystification which works on Faulkner's characters has often worked on his readers. It is easy, reading Faulkner's gothic labyrinthine prose, to get lost in the style. The tremendous artistic achievement represented by this phenomenon has invited more than its share of critical commentary in strictly literary terms; Warren and Wellek might say that the outer form of the narrative corresponds to its inner form (140, 241); metacriticism would emphasize the self-reflexivity which connects plot and style. What I wish to emphasize, however, is how the narrative both blazons and conceals its mystification of history, outside the story and in it; these are lush imaginary gardens with real structures of privilege in them.

Like an X-marks-the-spot, each high-Victorian decaying narrative curlicue instances a form (literally) of concealment, partly because the ornateness of the language distances the reader, but partly because the action presented is Byzantine:

> Colonel Sartoris invented an involved tale to the effect that Miss Emily's father had loaned money to the town, which the town, as a matter of business, preferred this way of repaying. Only a man of Colonel Sartoris' generation and thought could have invented it, and only a woman could have believed it.
>
> (490)

What might be called "gothic finance" here instances Emily's exemption from paying taxes—a privilege of her class; simultaneously, however, it also marks her inability to understand or to control her business affairs, the limitation of her sex. Emily's life includes no option of financial self-sufficiency; hence the fate worse than death when Homer Barron disappoints her and, earlier, the sense of betrayal when her father died and "it got about that the house was all that was left to her" (489). Even the rather detached narrator makes the betrayal explicit:

> We remembered all the young men her father had driven away, and we knew that with nothing left, she would have to cling to that which had robbed her, as people will.
>
> (489)

The decorative flourish, which is a neat synecdoche, signals Emily's economic limitation in that she tries to earn an income by giving lessons in chinapainting.

The preeminent flourish in the narrative, however (aside from its title), occurs at the ending, in the lavish descriptive decay of the room which contains the corpse:

> A thin, acrid pall as of the tomb seemed to lie everywhere upon this room decked and furnished as for a bridal: upon the valence curtains of faded rose color, upon the rose-shaded lights, upon the dressing table, upon the delicate array of crystal and the man's toilet things backed with tarnished silver, silver so tarnished that the monograph was obscured.
>
> (500)

Fulfilling previous images which identified the house with Emily, the rose-colored curtains and rose-shaded lights (these are the only roses in the story, unless one counts "they rose when she entered") create a stereotypically "Freudian" image of female enclosure. The dusty vulva, the "bridal" chamber—like Marvell's "fine and private place" the tomb's savage travesty of the womb (or the travesty of the latter on the former, in more misogynistic perspective)—reveals the bitter turning to dust of all the camp swampiness and swampy campness of Faulkner's other ever-prevalent allusions to feminine loci of forsythia/magnolia/genitalia. "Rose, thou art sick. . . ." The symbolically enclosed rose or *hortus conclusus* turned to desert rounds off the period of the story; as the title says, it *is* the story; and the story as an ironic rose, presented with a bow and a flourish to Emily, both advertises and dissimulates what it does to Emily Grierson and to all the other Emilys, egregiously pretending not to do exactly what it does: "'Dammit, sir,' Judge Stevens said, 'will you accuse a lady to her face of smelling bad?'" (492).

With humorous, self-disclosing hypocrisy, the fondly superficial narrator presents Emily's image: "thus she passed from generation to generation—dear, inescapable, impervious, tranquil, and perverse" (499). The word "inescapable" provides the operative hint on Emily's status; at her death—which begins the story—the narrator says, "alive, Miss Emily had been a tradition, a duty, and a care; a sort of hereditary obligation upon the town" (489).

In simplest terms, Emily resembles a curse—a war debt imposed by the Civil War on the surviving South, sphinx-like creature into whose house people go and either don't escape or barely escape, the labor pursuing original sin. A selective gyneolatry projected around her image suggests the quasi-theological:

> a window that had been dark was lighted and Miss Emily sat in it, the light behind her, and her upright torso motionless as that of an idol.
>
> (493)

> When we saw her again, her hair was cut short, making her look like a girl, with a vague resemblance to those angels in colored church windows—sort of tragic and serene.
>
> (494)

> She fitted up a studio . . . where the daughters and granddaughters of Colonel Sartoris' contemporaries were sent to her with the same regularity and in the same spirit that they were sent to church on Sundays with a twenty-five cent piece for the collection plate.
>
> (498)

> Now and then we would see her in one of the downstairs windows . . . like the carven torso of an idol in a niche, looking or not looking at us, we could never tell which.
>
> (499)

On one hand, this cluster of images suggests a quasi-deification of Emily—the projection of a stiffnecked people who have deified class privilege. From another perspective, however, it should make apparent Emily's rigid isolation, her loneliness—the punishment of her sex. Emily's strenuous repulsion of intruders forms a refrain in the story—when she repels various deputations concerning her father, her courtship, "the smell," her taxes, a mailbox, etc. But this centrifugal force, generated by a male author and a male narrator, actually conceals its dialectical opposite—the men's desire to escape the enclosure which Emily represents. Emily repels, but the men run, "vanquished": her father dies, the Baptist minister wilts, Homer Barron jilts her, deputations fade away. And when Emily herself dies,

> The Negro met the first of the ladies at the front door and let them in, . . . and then he disappeared. He walked right through the house and out the back and was not seen again.
>
> (499)

Obviously, the alternate intrusion-and-repulsion of one perspective has a sexual rhythm, culminating in a grisly climax when the town forces open Emily's room. In another perspective, a deeper pattern emerges: Emily does not get out, and the men do not get in (and survive); ultimately, the narrative prohibits any exchange between outside and inside, for a woman. Men possess the outside world and women the interior, and sex privilege separates the two in sempiternity.

Only one man partly breaks the rule and survives repeated entry into Emily's house: Emily's black manservant. And the exception, of course, proves the rule—or in this case reveals its deeper structure—because one function of race privilege, reflected with staggering honesty in Faulkner's narrative, is to triangulate class privilege and gender privilege. Only a Negro man can mediate between Emily, signifier of class privilege, and the men of the town, signifiers of gender privilege, as though he somehow combines attributes acceptable to both. A single incident recapitulates the pattern of the whole story. When Emily purchases arsenic, the druggist asks why she wants it:

> Miss Emily just stared at him, her head tilted back in order to look him eye of eye, until he looked away and went and got the arsenic and wrapped it up. The Negro delivery boy brought her the package; the druggist didn't come back.
>
> (496)

A black man provides the escape valve, allowing the white man to evade overt responsibility for the murder—and to evade an emotional confrontation with a woman. Thus race privilege allows class and gender privilege to coexist, despite all their potential conflicts, cementing them in a lasting, necrophiliac embrace.

Predictably, the object of all three operations, the person who receives their brunt, is what might be called the fourth-box case, the missing term, the character who does not appear in this story: the black woman.

> Colonel Sartoris, the mayor, . . . fathered the edict that no Negro woman should appear on the streets without an apron.
>
> (489)

The edict keeps the woman of color indoors by referring her ceaselessly to her labor: if you take your apron off, you must stay indoors (the narrative does not mention church services, holidays, etc.); if you stay indoors, you can take your apron off (cf. Pip's sister in *Great Expectations*). But any suggestion of repose indoors is spurious, because the woman's work occurs indoors anyway. Again the narrative thrusts forward a dual advertisement and obfuscation, penning the black woman behind her apron and behind walls (incidentally falsely implying, in its insistence that she *must* work, that white women do *not* have to work).

In this series of dual facades, a key signifier appears in the description of Homer Barron, whose brief characterization presents him as the embodiment of masculine vitality and the antithesis of Emily: a foreman named Homer Barron, a Yankee—a big, dark, ready man, with a big voice and eyes lighter than his face (494).

It was this detail of eyes lighter than the face, employed in both "A Rose for Emily" and "A Good Man Is Hard to Find," which first drew my attention to the connections between the two stories. The highly particularized detail (one of very few in Barron's description) of eyes lighter than his face suggests in Homer Barron an element of complexity—whether in the man himself or in his situation. Another discrepancy, it marks the intersection and thus the potential conflict of race and class privilege: Barron was not born dark; he just got that way because he works outdoors. The shadow, so to speak, rests only on the surface of this carpetbagger. Compare Emily, who looks

> bloated, like a body long submerged in motionless water, and of the pallid hue. Her eyes, lost in the fatty ridges of her face, looked like two small pieces of coal pressed into a lump of dough.
>
> (491)

Notwithstanding this reassurance—as hinted by the occasion for reassurance—the eyes-lighter-than-skin image can be sinister. It suggests a hidden energy (= power) and vision (= knowledge), a knowledge or power shadowed and unreadable, behind a facade.⁹ Clearly, black skin conveys something of the same threat; so does Emily's black dress:

> They rose when she entered—a small, fat woman in black, with a thin gold chain descending to her waist and vanishing into her belt. . . . She did not ask them to sit. She just stood in the door and listened quietly until the spokesman came to a stumbling halt. Then they could hear the invisible watch ticking at the end of the gold chain.
>
> (491)

Perhaps the humor involved in this intimidation of the townsmen—conveyed in details such as the unutterably sinister "invisible watch"—comes partly from a sympathy for Emily, on the part of the narrator. But always the covering darkness itself, the shadowed vantage concealing a watchful gaze, is sinister—as with the whispering behind jalousies, or The Misfit's sighting the car wreck from off the highway, etc. It suggests a consciousness hidden, on the other side of a wall, which can know (you) but not be known; and of this darkness, the light eyes set in dark skin constitute a physical sign: if those eyes were closed, one might be safer in some sense—but one might also be fooled. The threat of eyes lighter than skin conveys reassurance, but the reassurance also conveys a threat, along lines of class and race conflict, resolvable only on the high ground of gender privilege: Barron is a "real man." However, the conflicts between gender and race privilege are not as effectually cemented over as those between class and gender privilege. Barron, who works like a black man, still has many of the privileges of the white, but the manhood of a black man would not be equal protection from the operations of privilege, nor would the race of a poor white woman.

III

Sadly enough, the successful real-life operations of privilege in Faulkner's era—successful in producing the South of thirty years later—can be read in O'Connor's writing. Arrestingly, O'Connor's "A Good Man Is Hard to Find" employs the same sign noted above in Faulkner: Sammy Red Butts's wife, hard at work in the roadside food joint, is described as "a tall burnt-brown woman with hair and eyes lighter than her skin" (762). Like a hinge, this motif of eyes lighter than the skin connects the two narratives, separated by World War II. But the terrain has changed significantly since Faulkner, and so has the image under discussion. Barron's tan shows that although he labors, he has mobility: he can go outdoors, with the privilege of his gender. In contrast, Emily's dead-white skin, accentuated by her dark eyes, shows that her class privilege of exemption from labor only partly compensates for her gender oppression, being kept indoors. O'Connor's signifier, however, exhibits two differences from Faulkner's, and both differences achieve the same effect: in O'Connor's narrative, the character described is a woman, and she has not only eyes but also hair lighter than her skin. Like Homer Barron, Sammy Red Butts's wife works—and is in consequence "burnt brown"—but unlike him, she cannot fool anyone, and she cannot get away. Where the detail of light eyes in a dark face, alone, would suggest mystery, exoticism, the hint of ancestral Crusader in the face of a Turk, the added detail of light hair just suggests a cracker.

Uneasy in conflict, the different forms of privilege wish ultimately to bond into one indistinguishable upper-class- and white- and male-oriented force. And here the two narratives display a definite progression (of sorts): where the Faulkner narrative shows the different forms of oppression still, to some extent, in conflict, the O'Connor narrative shows oppression successful and beyond conflict, lifted to the level of an omniscient narrator and an infallible taste, with conflict confined to poor whites. Black adults of either sex are absent; whites of both sexes labor; the author herself is a woman; and class privilege has been subsumed into the monolithic gaze of the invisible, impersonal narrator—and thus foisted off onto the reader.

Thus while the narrative explicitly refers to economic pressures, and the grandmother even links them explicitly to race—"Little niggers in the country don't have things like we do" (761)—they are no longer a first, conscious, concern, "the old thrill and the old despair of a penny more or less" as in Faulkner's narrative (489). In the thirty years separating the South of the two stories, amenities purchasable by poorer white families increased: the sports section, baby food in jars, *Queen for a Day* (television), cars, comic books, peanut butter, olives, Coca-Cola, tap dancing lessons, vacations, and Hawaiian sports shirts—as memorialized unlovingly by O'Connor. It is one of the paradoxes of southern gothic literature that such accurate details—accurate in reflecting social actuality, or parts of it—serve not to bring the reader closer to the characters, but to alienate the reader further from the characters. We don't even want to *see* these people, except from the safe distance of an interstate highway (compare Mayor Koch's comments about Georgia). Indeed, such details tend rather to validate and to justify what happens to these people: the minor indulgences exemplify the characters' inability to defer gratification on the road to success. Nor does the narrative explore causality sufficiently to question why such indulgences should be offered to poor families when larger benefits, such as education, have clearly not been offered.

In short, O'Connor displaces the marks of class privilege so that they are less perceivable in differences of income or of possessions and fully perceivable only in differences of *taste*.[10] Faulkner's narrator, whose taste certainly distances him from much that he describes, nevertheless manifests his taste only within the limits of his persona, a Ratliff-like observer, modestly situated in the town—though perhaps representative of a modest collective ("we"). O'Connor's narrator controls a third-person universe, subsuming the reader's perspective in an alienation beyond which the reader is powerless to envision. So the story asks the reader to acquiesce in the family's deaths—gothic rather than tragic—basically because good taste demands these killings, from the instant of learning that the mother had "a face as broad and innocent as a cabbage" (760), or that the children are named John Wesley and June Star.

Taste particularly demands alienation and a privileging of the narrator/reader above those two examples of debased gentility—most threatening to entrenched taste in their own pretensions to the same quality—the grandmother and The Misfit:

> the grandmother had on a navy blue straw sailor hat with a bunch of white violets on the brim and a navy blue dress with a small white dot in the print. Her collars and cuffs were white organdy trimmed with lace and at her neckline she had pinned a purple spray of cloth violets containing a sachet. In case of an accident, anyone seeing her dead on the highway would know at once that she was a lady.
>
> (761)

> He was an older man than the other two. His hair was just beginning to gray and he wore silver-rimmed spectacles that gave him a scholarly look.
>
> (765)

Only the grandmother and The Misfit express any pretensions to intellectual curiosity:

> "You all ought to take them somewhere else for a change so they would see different parts of the world and be broad. They never have been to East Tennessee."
>
> (760)

> "My daddy said I was a different breed of dog from my brothers and sisters. 'you know,' Daddy said, 'it's some that can live their whole life out without asking about it and it's others has to know why it is, and this boy is one of the latters. He's going to be into everything.'"
>
> (766)

But such pretensions only obviate the possibility of genuine intellection among the characters.

Situating the reader behind the gaze of supercilious taste, O'Connor's narrative places the reader in an invidious position. But in so doing, it conforms to a respectable modernist aesthetic, transferring the dynamics of the story from the characters' experiences to the reader's, and bringing the reader closer to the narrator than to the characters. While such a perspective can heighten the sense of social actuality in the literary work—Ambrose Bierce's "The Boarded Window" touches a stunning note of realism on "pioneer history"—it more often results in alienation. Only once in "A Good Man Is Hard to Find" does the narrator seem detached from the matter described:

> She pointed out interesting details of the scenery: Stone Mountain; the blue granite that in some places came up to both sides of the highway; the brilliant red clay banks slightly streaked with purple; and the various crops that made rows of green lace-work on the ground. The trees were full of silver-white sunlight and the meanest of them sparkled.
>
> (761)

Not the meanest nor even the most superior of these characters sparkles, however; even the briefly painterly description quoted here just reinforces the impression of a place where every prospect pleases and only man is vile. Predictably, therefore, the landscape itself metamorphoses, as though in a Gresham's Law of debased values: "Behind them the line of woods gaped like a dark open mouth" (765). The landscape itself turns gothic; anthropomorphized only to become monstrous, more human only to be more alien, it reverses the pathetic fallacy, neither extending nor allowing human sympathy. In short, it "tells the story" itself, synecdoche for the terrain of the narrative; like the characters and the South—both in literature and in the mass media—it neither extends nor invites human response.[11]

In a humorous bit of self-parody, O'Connor has her characters learn about The Misfit by reading a newspaper, and the naturalism and detached perspective of the narrative resemble newspaper accounts. Again, however, characteristics which might heighten the realism of the writing just distance the incidents and characters further (that's-the-way-things-happen-down-there). Familial and social pressures, emotional discorders, and violence are all engineered to prevent sympathy and to produce distaste and detachment instead.

Hence the prevalence of certain loci in southern gothic settings—all secretive enclosures: darkened rooms with drawn blinds and wisteria crawling over their windows, New Orleans-style wrought-iron grillwork sheltering yet-undescribed Creole mysteries, shadowy verandas and backyards behind massed azaleas, distant woods at the edges of fields of stubble, and so forth. These loci, darkened little inner rooms of the psyche, actually signify their dialectical reverse, turned like a chevril glove inside out: what they actually express is not something "interior," but an *exteriorization*—a pushing away, a shunning, in which the pain and horror of real events are dislocated into imaginary gardens. Like the invisibility of Emily's consciousness in her story, what looks like seclusion represents an actuality of repudiation. So the southern gothic narratives here discussed reflect an actual social phenomenon of human response boxed off from human events; the forbidding closed doors and gingerbread decades signify barriers of Other-ness, the unthinkable exile of human beings to the unprestigious hinterlands of Dixie.

What is being discussed here is the production of a mystique, and a tenet of this essay is that the mystique has uses which help explain its production (like other mystiques). At least three historical uses can be posited for the mystique behind Southern gothic: (1) as an atmosphere of bemused languor projected onto the South, it rationalizes the bustling shopping malls and "strips" of exploitation by real-estate developers and others; (2) as a canny stance for some southern authors, selling the South—in effect—it discourages poaching on home preserves by non-Southern authors; and (3) as a seemingly nonpolitical and therefore safe treatment of southern history, it perpetuates oppression and the sufferance of oppression. This paper deals with the third point.

In both Faulkner's short story and O'Connor's, the single figure of an elderly woman characterizes the whole terrain of the story. Economically dependent and superfluous and personally objectionable, each "lady" is charged with the demoralization of her society and then dispatched (although not soon enough). Underscoring the suggestion of things put away, Emily and the grandmother *should* be put away; the poor old women are closet killers—indirectly in O'Connor's story, with its subliminal references to an "old cat" and the like. Incidentally, despite the submerged references to *The Mikado*—the cat named Pitty Sing; making "the punishment fit the crime" and making both "a source of innocent merriment"—I think the allusions constitute a tribute less to Gilbert and Sullivan than to Dorothy Sayers, another woman Catholic writer, also master of submerged puns, whose work also contains frequent references to Gilbert and Sullivan.[12] In displacing a situational problem onto two destructive but personally ineffectual individuals, the narratives hint at something destructive and ineffectual in their general context, a *hidden motive force* only too pertinent to the terrain they cover. This hidden motive force must have to do with race privilege. The old flowers of decayed femininity in these two stories, characterized as an eternally "feminine" essence without any sign of fruitfulness, surely signify the authors' recognition of a draining problem we have always with us, its causes only partly examined even by the literature which exploits it as a motive force.

The very concept of examining causes, however, introduces what I feel—borrowing Balmary's luminous formulation—to be the most important distinction between Faulkner's narrative and O'Connor's: where the Faulkner short story deals at least partly with *causes*, O'Connor's deals only with *mechanisms*. Whatever one thinks of an "Electra complex" as theory,[13] Faulkner at least uses it to provide Emily with a somewhat understandable motivation—understandable by inference: Emily's compulsive possessiveness has its source in her father's.[14] What lies behind the deaths in the O'Connor narrative is chiefly a Rube Goldberg sequence: kid kicks basket, cat leaps out, car goes into ditch.

This example could be multiplied a number of times. Where Faulkner's characters "*know* the old thrill and the old despair of a penny more or less," O'Connor's characters maunder about far-distant monomyths:

> He and the grandmother discussed better times. The old lady said that in her opinion Europe was entirely to blame for the way things were now. She said the way Europe acted you would think we were made of money and Red Sam said it was no use talking about it, she was exactly right.
>
> (763)

Where Faulkner's narrative refers to the burden of history, O'Connor's includes history only as nostalgia: "Gone With the Wind. Ha. Ha" (761). And the nostalgia is only cliché, imperfectly implied, at that—cliché already mocked in Faulkner's earlier narrative: "the very old men—some in their brushed Confederate uniforms . . . talking of Miss Emily . . . believing that they had danced with her and courted her perhaps" (499). One wonders what the old gentlemen said about their putative closeness to Emily when the dreadful bedroom is opened up. Where the Faulkner narrative deals with the problems and ironies connected to upholding tradition, the O'Connor characters sustain only debased traditions which they cheapen even in synthesizing them, such as the treasure hunt for the nonexistent secret hiding place and its Confederate riches.

These differences between the two narratives are all homologous with the main difference: while each narrative places in the foreground a character who proves more symptom than cause—Emily and the grandmother—at least the earlier narrative goes back one generation farther. That is, "A Rose for Emily" partly scrutinizes patriarchy, where "A Good Man Is Hard to Find" does not (despite its title); and the best way to turn scrutiny away from patriarchy, as Balmary illustrates, is to turn it toward "Oedipal" conflicts. Thus the O'Connor story relies on several touches of Oedipal conflict. The father in the story is the father only of small children, less a father than the grandmother's son; helpless when confronted with The Misfit, he travesties authoritarian fatherhood, any genuine authority leached out of him by the generations of "progress" culminating in his Hawaiian shirt. The grandmother herself has no parent mentioned (nothing explains how she got that way), but The Misfit had, as mentioned four times:

> It was a head-doctor at the penitentiary said what I had done was kill my daddy but I known that for a lie. My daddy died in nineteen ought nineteen of the epidemic flu and I never had a thing to do with it.
>
> (767)

At precisely the moment when, in a travesty of human contact, the grandmother identifies The Misfit as her son and reaches out to touch him, he shoots her.

"A Rose for Emily" could almost have been written to post-Lacanian specifications or to specifications for susceptibility to postmodern analysis; in it, old sins have long shadows. Its hidden fault results in defensive gestures—in both the plot of the narrative and the stylistic flourishes of its prose—which "protect and encrypt the site of incorporation" (Balmary 174), thus ensuring an ignorance of their sources. The reader looks in vain for the ordinary names in the cemetery; the townspeople might look in vain for Emily's sources of support; Emily herself might look in vain for any explanation of her own emotional state. With regard to Emily's father, to her dead lover, to Emily herself, and to racial privilege in the South, a spectral remnant of a loved object is preserved, but "only at the price of self-division" (Balmary xix). Perhaps obviously, Emily partly embodies the South, reflecting historical processes in which the South has often been projected as an American "Other," homologous with the town's projections of Emily. "We propose the following formulation: The dominated carries out the repressed of the dominant," says Lacan, following Freud (Balmary 34); "one's desire is always the desire of the Other" (Balmary 1). Homer Barron comes carpetbagging and is devoured; Emily's dead father's possessiveness metamorphoses into a ghoulish, mystified disrelish for Emily by later generations; the history of slavery fetters the South. Throughout the narrative runs the trope of a fault, a hidden history with long shadows, which manifests itself in modern dislocations which simultaneously proclaim and conceal it in postmodern criticism.

In O'Connor, the sins are still there, but their shadows are missing; there is no way to track them to their sources. In the vein of pop horror films and sensationalist journalism, the roots of The Misfit's evil (and of the family's ignorance) remain unexplored. While the history beyond Faulkner's narrative may be partly objectified by the narrative into a personalized and consciously psychological "love-hate," the history in O'Connor's narrative is even more irrevocably objectivized—as "atmosphere," lost history, inaccessible history—by fearful loathing and gallows humor. What series of forces and influences contributed to the effects visible in the grandmother's family? We never know, because they have been subsumed in the glaring synchronicity of the omniscient narrator's gaze. Thus the difference between the two stories extends to their narrative voices. Where Faulkner uses a man for his narrative persona, O'Connor does *not* use a woman or indeed any identifiable individual; any personal circuit between reader and narrative is completed only in the invisible glare of taste. Even this limited circuit is broken by the car accident, which ambushes the reader almost as thoroughly as it does the family. The film-like limpidity of O'Connor's prose, the silent void surrounding the grandmother, the absence of names for the mother and grandmother all create a shock different in degree and kind from that shared by the narrator in Faulkner's story. The sudden shock, the reader's alienation from the characters, the strict linearity of the plot which excludes any participation in reconstruction by the reader—all contribute to reduce the reader's sense of control. The absence of fathers, sources, history, and narrators creates a disembodied power of taste, floating in a kind of papal immunity from any purposeful scrutiny.

Despite all the humor in Faulkner's narrative, I think that "A Rose for Emily" still remains more of a yarn, a story, than "A Good Man Is Hard to Find"; O'Connor's narrative more resembles a joke, and a joke whose punch line is eschatological: "'She would of been a good woman,' The Misfit said, 'if it had been somebody there to shoot her every minute of her life'" (768). In this line, the most famous in the story and one of the most famous in O'Connor's writing, the narrative calls attention with a stunning limpidity to what it does, demonstrating the short-circuiting of any potential examination of causes by a subsummation into eschatology (as in the several christological allusions scattered throughout). On more than one level, and perhaps in some ways unintentionally, "A Good Man Is Hard to Find" demonstrates short cuts that don't work out. The refusal to defer gratification which contributes to—and characterizes—the family's social status; the wrong road taken, leading to an imaginary buried treasure and the family's deaths; The Misfit's version of ethics—all these are intentional illustrations of misdirected short cuts, like the grandmother's implicit valorization of class above life: "in case of an accident, anyone seeing her dead on the highway would know at once that she was a lady" (761).

So, too, is the earlier anecdote of the watermelon, as narrated by the grandmother:

> she had been courted by a Mr. Edgar Atkins Teagarden from Jasper, Georgia. She said he was a very good-looking man and a gentleman and that he brought her a watermelon every Saturday afternoon with his initials cut in it, E. A. T. Well, one Saturday, she said, Mr. Teagarden brought the watermelon and there was nobody at home and he left it on the front porch and returned in his buggy to Jasper, but she never got the watermelon, she said, because a nigger boy ate it when he saw the initials, E. A. T.!
>
> (761-62)

The ignorance and greed which snatch at immediate gratification constitute a *joke* in O'Connor's narrative, the joke in both The Misfit's line and the child's eating the watermelon, according to the grandmother: an ignorance of any transcendental signification in what is offered them or in what they do. A larger and less-funny twist in and beyond the narrative, however, suggests that transcendence itself might be another inadequate short cut, away from genuine analysis and genuine history. The imaginary gardens provide no escape from real oppression and pain, because they offer no real change: "'Shut up, Bobby Lee,' The Misfit said. 'It's no real pleasure in life'" (768).

Notes

1. For further discussion on the plethoric stereotypes/myths surrounding the image of the South, see the *Encyclopedia of Southern Culture,* ed. Charles R. Wilson and William Ferris (U of North Carolina P, 1989), especially the section titled "Mythic South," 1097-1145, by George B. Tindall.

2. This argument—my own reduction of the stereotypes to a fundamental schema of two (upper and lower)—is part of the thesis of a book-length study in progress, tentatively titled *Insignificant Other: Representations of the American South in American Media and Literature.*

3. The perspective on colonial production in this essay has been influenced by the work of Gayatri Chakravorty Spivak and Edward Said, among others. Unusual though it might seem to apply the concept of colonial production to the American South, the mode of analysis is broadly that of, and logically proceeds from, cultural studies, as in the work of Stuart Hall.

4. I am using the term *southern gothic* in the readily recognized sense in which it is understood in the *Encyclopedia of Southern Culture,* especially 1125-1127; see also 876 (on Erskine Caldwell), 917-918 (on Tennessee Williams); cf. "hogwallow politics and abnormal neuroticism." See also *The History of Southern Literature,* ed. Louis D. Rubin, Jr. (Louisiana State UP, 1985), especially 442, 475, 484, 487, and 532; also *Columbia Literary History of the United States,* ed. Emory Elliot (Columbia UP, 1988), 1139-1140; also *Fifty Southern Writers after 1900: A Bio-Bibliographical Sourcebook,* ed. Joseph M. Flora, and Robert Bain (Greenwood P, 1987), 102.

Surprisingly, given the relatively widespread currency of the phrase (and concept) "southern gothic," the concept itself has received remarkable little direct scrutiny. There are no works of literary criticism currently in print on southern gothic fiction (despite the existence of many works on southern writers, southern writing, and the gothic novel in general); "southern gothic" is not in use as a Library of Congress subject index term; there is neither a book nor an article, so far as I know, on the "southern gothic" in its across-the-board applications in both popular fiction, film, and television, and canonical literature. This lacuna indicates that few literary critics writing today have drawn extensively on abundant materials available

5. The psychological process identified here is, obviously, Freud's "projection." The application of psychoanalytic terms to the activities engaged in by a society, or by the dominant mode of scrutiny within that society, is among the tools of analysis used by Michel Foucault, Jacques Lacan, and Marie Balmary.

6. This dual movement or signification of both blazoning and concealing is discussed by Balmary in a very different context, with a partly Lacanian orientation to the analysis; it becomes relevant to Faulkner's writing in many more passages than discussed here.

7. Space prevents any detailed listing of items in a continuing tradition of the "room" as symbolic of woman; this story represents in some ways a final joke, grotesquely inverted, on the room-of-one's own continuum.

8. The relationship between, or antithesis of genuine history and a commodified "nostalgia" prevalent in the mass media has been discussed by, among others, Adrienne Rich, in a lecture at Delta State University, Cleveland, Mississippi, April, 1982.

9. See John D. MacDonald's Travis McGee, whose strangely light eyes belie the apparent simplicity suggested by his beach-bum tan. Precisely this image of light eyes in a blackened face is employed by *Time,* in a cover story (with special section) called "The Curse of Violent Crime," March 23, 1981; illustrations 17, 19. The illustration features a black-face map of the continental United States looking outward through two white, eye-shaped gaps; the effect, intentionally or otherwise, is certainly racist.

10. The historical uses of "taste," barely touched on here, were suggested to me first in a seminar conducted by Gayatri Chakravorty Spivak at the Teaching Institute, University of Illinois at Urbana-Champaign, summer, 1983.

11. Fully to document the stereotypicality of the "southern" would require a booklength study, at least. Citing only relatively modern examples, however, one might include almost any mention of the South in popular novels from *Tobacco Road* (Erskine Caldwell, 1932) to *Women's Work* (Anne T. Wallach, 1982); in plays from—of course—Tennessee Williams on; and in notable films such as *Easy Rider* (1969) and *Deliverance* (1972). For testimony to the longevity of the destructive-old-southern-lady motif, see Andrew Hacker's article on the E. R. A. in the resurrection issue of *Harper's Magazine*; also the popular two-actor play, *Greater Tuna.*

12. Interestingly, Sayers also has her chief female character (Harriet Vane) speculate, on the grounds of Oxford University, about possible modes of partnership between Catholicism and Freudian psychoanalysis, a synthesis which O'Connor also toys with in this story and others.

13. The idea of a pure "Electra complex" is, of course, Freudian analysis oversimplified; Freud conjectured about the possibility but never developed or applied it as extensively as the Oedipus complex, and subsequently arrived at the belief that children of *both* sexes form an early attachment to the mother, which they must later overcome.

14. The important contrast here, as developed in the discussion, is not a contrast between an "Electra complex" and an "Oedipus complex," but a contrast between a willingness to scrutinize the position of the father and a refusal to do so, as discussed in another context by Balmary, following (in part) Lacan.

Works Cited

Balmary, Marie. *Homme aux statues.* Tr. Engl. *Psychoanalyzing Psychoanalysis: Freud and the Hidden Fault of the Father.* Tr. N. Lukacher. Baltimore: Johns Hopkins UP, 1982.

Faulkner, William. "A Rose for Emily." *The Portable Faulkner.* Ed. Malcolm Cowley. New York: Viking, 1946.

O'Connor, Flannery. "A Good Man Is Hard to Find." *Fiction 100: An Anthology of Short Stories.* Ed. James H. Pickering. New York: MacMillan, 1978.

Wellek, Rene and Warren, Austin. *Theory of Literature.* New York: Harcourt, Brace, 1956.

MAJOR AUTHORS IN SOUTHERN GOTHIC LITERATURE

Alfred Appel Jr. (essay date 1965)

SOURCE: Appel, Alfred, Jr. "The Grotesque and the Gothic." In *A Season of Dreams: The Fiction of Eudora Welty,* pp. 73-103. Baton Rouge: Louisiana State University Press, 1965.

[*In the following essay, Appel distinguishes between grotesque and gothic elements in American fiction, using the works of Eudora Welty as examples of an au-*

thor who successfully uses the grotesque to expound on themes of social and individual displacement while instilling a sense of compassion and hope in the reader.]

The grotesque and Gothic have always been major modes in American fiction and popular culture, from Brockden Brown to Paul Bowles, from frontier humor to W. C. Fields. Perhaps the grotesque is so persistent an American genre because of the peculiarly American belief that happiness is the *norm* of existence—a belief that is accompanied by an almost fanatical resistance to any suggestions to the contrary. It is not surprising that many American writers have felt the need to use the grotesque or Gothic, as though only through distortion and exaggeration could they begin to suggest the complexity of reality—and its tragicomic implications—to an audience thoroughly committed to the "optimistic." As Flannery O'Connor said in *The Living Novel* (1957), "to the hard of hearing you shout, and for the almost blind you draw large and startling figures."

The Gothic and the grotesque may be congruent in a single work, but in recent years the terms have often been used interchangeably, which has proved confusing. Some distinctions should be made.[1] The term "Gothic" originally referred to the prose genre that was popular in Europe in the eighteenth and nineteenth centuries. Heralding the imminent shift of sensibility to Romanticism, the Gothic writers in Germany and England concerned themselves with things inexplicable, violent, grotesque, horrifying, and supernatural. The setting was often in the medieval past, in a dark forest, castle, convent, or tomb; enchantments, ghosts, hauntings, mirrors that gave back unexpected reflections, and paintings and statues that smiled or shed tears were standard Gothic fare. Despite its tendency toward horror pornography, European Gothicism sometimes managed to suggest, however crudely, the irrational aspects of life, the mysteries of the unconscious, and the destructive potential of the sex drive. But often the Gothic writers do not convince us that they are dealing with models of significant reality, and the Gothic effects remain gratuitous. Edgar Allan Poe popularized the Gothic genre in America, where it has been utilized by writers far superior to their European precursors.[2]

The grotesque is characterized by the distortion of the external world, by the description of human beings in nonhuman terms, and by the displacement we associate with dreams. The infinite possibilities of the dream inform the grotesque at every turn, suspending the laws of proportion and symmetry; our deepest promptings are projected into the details of the scene—inscape as landscape. Because the grotesque replaces supernaturalism with hallucination, it expresses the reality of the unconscious life—the formative source which the Gothic writer, in his romantic flights, may never tap. The grotesque is a heightened realism, reminiscent of caricature, but going beyond it to create a fantastic realism or realistic fantasy that evokes pathos and terror, and what Marlow, in Conrad's *Heart of Darkness* (1898), calls "that commingling of absurdity, surprise, and bewilderment in a tremor of struggling revolt, that notion of being captured by the incredible which is the very essence of dreams"—and of the grotesque. Characters seen grotesquely may be "flat"—not likely to develop or change much during the course of the action—but because they have been pushed to extremes, they become representative, objectifying the complex fears and compulsions that constrict the heart. In grotesque comedy one confronts these fears, and through laughter is released from them.

If artists and writers of the grotesque often render human beings in animal-like form or, like Kafka, *as* animals or insects, it is because too often our status seems subhuman, our lives shaped by dehumanizing forces beyond our control. It is the animal's eye view of things to look up and see the world looming above, menacing, dreadful, and confusing; thus writers of the grotesque often use the point of view of a child, animal, or dwarf, or the "lowest" perspective of all, a view from "underground." Although it has flourished in other ages, the grotesque is most compatible with the modern sensibility; perhaps the grotesque vision *is* the modern world view. Joyce, Proust, Mann, and Conrad all employ the grotesque intermittently; it is central to the aesthetic of Kafka, Faulkner, West, Nabokov, John Hawkes and Eudora Welty. These writers rarely invoke the traditional Gothic trappings;[3] instead, they use the technique of the grotesque, which involves the fusion of incongruous forms drawn from *external* reality (this point will be developed later). The impact of the grotesque depends on a sense of the familiar, for what Nathanael West called the "truly monstrous" resides not in the supernatural and the bizarre, but in our ordinary, everyday lives; "Gothic" is a term to be reserved for "special effects."

The prevalence of the grotesque in Miss Welty's fiction became immediately apparent with the publication of *A Curtain of Green*. Louise Bogan's enthusiastic review in the *Nation* was misleadingly entitled "The Gothic South," because only one story, "Clytie," could properly be called Gothic.[4] Clinically minded *Time* noted that "of seventeen pieces . . . only two report states of experience which could be called normal,"[5] and Miss Welty was accused of showing "too great a preoccupation with the abnormal and grotesque."[6] But her use of the grotesque and Gothic can be justified, for the meaning of a story never lies solely in its horror or violence; the distortions intensify the pathos of a situation and express psychological and moral truths. Miss Welty herself has provided a rejoinder to such charges by stating in *Place in Fiction* that "life *is* strange. Stories hardly make it more so; with all they are able to tell and surmise, they make it more believably, more inevitably so."

Whereas Miss Welty often employs the grotesque, the Gothic appears in only three stories, "The Purple Hat," "Clytie," and "The Burning," and none of these is as horrifying as Faulkner's "A Rose for Emily," Tennessee Williams' "Desire and the Black Masseur," or almost any one of Paul Bowles's stories. Yet in spite of these distinctions, Miss Welty is often thought of as a Gothic writer. This misconception is the result of a kind of guilt by association, for it has become a critical commonplace to characterize all Southern writers as Gothic.[7] Many reviewers and readers will group Miss Welty with any Southern writer who may come to mind, thus denying her work its virtues. The critics who force such comparisons do not distinguish between the Gothic and grotesque, nor between those writers who have used the two modes with artistic distinction and those who have exploited them. The atmosphere and symbolism in Truman Capote's fiction ultimately seem nearer to the methods of Edgar Allan Poe than to the accuracy of specification of either Faulkner or Miss Welty. Capote's South and Paul Bowles's North Africa represent a romantic symbolism in which the symbols rarely yield more than their own uniqueness. Moreover, Carson McCullers, Williams, Capote, and Flannery O'Connor far exceed Miss Welty in regard to the amount of perversion, violence, and Gothicism in their writing—and none of them has quite Miss Welty's variegated comic spirit. Unlike hers, their humor is almost always allied with horror. And in Mrs. McCullers' work, the loneliness is never relieved by any other mood.

The Gothic elements in "Clytie" and "The Purple Hat" are not a romantic symbolism, for they communicate a sense of social and individual distortion. "The Purple Hat," however, poses several problems, and to a lesser extent, so does "Clytie." "The Purple Hat" is Miss Welty's most obscure story. Here she closely approaches the traditional Gothic mode—with its violent, supernatural, and inexplicable happenings. The setting is a New Orleans bar, "a quiet little hole in the wall. It was four o'clock in the afternoon" and raining outside (WN [*The Wide Net and Other Stories*], 141). An affable fat man tells a story to the bartender and to a thin, unshaven young alcoholic with shaking hands. There is some kind of significance in the way the scene is "staged": "the two customers had chosen very particularly the knobs [seats] they would sit on. They had come in separately out of the wet, and had each chosen an end stool, and now sat with the length of the little bar between them" (141). The intense young man is somehow involved in the story that is to be unfolded.

The fat man is the armed guard who patrols the little catwalk beneath the dome of a huge New Orleans gambling casino, "The Palace of Pleasure." His little hands, "really helpless looking . . . for so large a man," are emblematic of his combination of weakness and impassive cruelty. From his unique position as the "man that everyone knows to be watching, at all they do" (145), he has been able to observe the strange activities of a certain woman:

> "In thirty years she has not changed," said the fat man. "Neither has she changed her hat. Dear God, how the moths must have hungered for that hat. But she has kept it in full bloom on her head, that monstrosity—purple, too, as if she were beautiful in the bargain. She has not aged, but keeps her middle-age."
>
> (144)

Using her "outrageous hat" as a lure, she has for thirty years picked up a different young man "at the dice table every afternoon, rain or shine, at five o'clock, and gambles till midnight and tells him goodbye" (144). She not only leads them on to no purpose, but also engages them in a strange sexual ritual. Late in the evening she takes off her hat, which the young man watches hungrily.

> He is enamoured of her ancient, battered, outrageous hat with the awful plush flowers. She lays it down below the level of the table there, on her shabby old lap, and he caresses it. . . . Well, I suppose in this town there are stranger forms of love than that, and who are any of us to say what ways people may not find to love? She seems perfectly satisfied with it.
>
> (147-48)

Noticeable only from above or when she takes off the hat is

> a little glass vial with a plunger [which] helps decorate the crown . . . [when] she . . . lays [the hat] carefully in her lap, under the table . . . you might notice the little vial, and be attracted to it and wish to take it out and examine it at your pleasure off in the washroom—to admire the handle, for instance, which is red glass, like the petal of an artificial flower.
>
> (148-49)

There is also a ten- or twelve-inch long jeweled hat pin; the bartender purses his lips as the fat man describes how "she sticks the pin back through" after taking off the hat. But these suggestively obscene details are not to be taken too literally. The fat man announces that the woman is a ghost because "to my belief she has been murdered twice" (146): the first time she had been shot by one of her pick-ups; the second time another "young lover" killed her with the symbol of her lurking, criminal passions; "no one saw it done . . . except for me, naturally." Yet she returned to the casino within a month after each "murder" and resumed her activities.

The hat's grotesque phallic overtones are obvious; their meaning, however, is not. The "flashing needle" piercing the "great, wide deep hat" (147) and the little "vial" that is best examined in the washroom have unpleasant enough symbolic connotations, suggesting that the story told by the fat man is some kind of terrible onanistic fantasy; it is *his* fantasy, after all—or is it? We can't be sure. Although the events narrated by the fat man are fantastic, Miss Welty has been careful to give the story a realistic frame; "fantasy itself must touch ground with at least one toe, and ghost stories must have one foot, so to speak, in the grave," she says in *Place in Fiction*. Thus, the story about the purple hat is more than believable to the young man: the fat man says that "New Orleans . . . is the birthplace of ready-made victims," and the young man, who has been listening with fascination—"as if there were something hypnotic and irresistible" about the fat man (148)—seems to have been already victimized by "this old and disgusting creature in her purple hat" (146). At five o'clock—the woman's hour of arrival—the young man had suddenly disappeared. The fat man gets up and pays for all the drinks, including the young man's. "Is she a real ghost?" the bartender asks confidentially, "in a real whisper." "I'll let you know tomorrow," answers the fat man. She is to be murdered for the third time that very night, and the young man is going to do it. Both he and the fat man have seemingly known it all along. At the beginning of the story the fat man said, "almost dreamily," but without taking his eyes from the young man, "'Oh, the hat she wears is a creation,' . . . It was strange that he did not once regard the bartender, who after all had done him the courtesy of asking a polite question or two" (143). Later, the fat man cried, "'I can never finish telling you about the hat!' . . . and there was a little sigh somewhere in the room, very young, like a child's" (150). The story thus has a very definite realistic level; the above mentioned "toe" is placed solidly on the ground.

In spite of the Gothicism, the woman is a recognizable type—a fantastic version of "one of those thousands of middle-aged women who come every day to the Palace, would not be kept away by anything on earth" (143). Her loneliness has assumed a terrible form. One might say—as Poe did in the Preface to *Tales of the Grotesque and Arabesque* (1840)—that the story's "terror is not of Germany but of the soul." Yet the story's admixture of realism and fantasy creates a *trompe l'oeil* effect, making its meaning extremely—if not excessively—obscure. The confusion arises from Miss Welty's relatively unsuccessful application of the methods by which she achieves her finest stories.

"The Purple Hat" can be read as a loosely allegorical story. Trying to escape boredom and find some exotic and secret pleasure, young men are drawn to the fantasy world of the "Palace of Pleasure." Once there they fall in love with the tawdry image of beauty, the hat, and especially with the mysterious vial in its crown. But the young men are left frustrated—their dreams are as empty as the vial. They try to destroy the temptress but she eludes them, for, as Ruth Vande Kieft suggests, she is "as deathless as is man's pursuit of pleasure."[8]

The fat man shows off his ruby ring and says that from up above, the casino's red carpet "changes and gives off light between the worn criss-crossing of the aisles like the facets of a well-cut ruby" (145). As a miniature of the "Palace," the ring symbolizes his singular position on the catwalk, and the omnipotence which affords him so clear a view of the most terrible aspects of the human comedy.

> "Life in the ruby. And yet somehow all that people do is clear and lucid and authentic there, as if it were magnified in the red lens, not made smaller. I can see everything in the world from my catwalk. You mustn't think I brag. . . ." He looked all at once from his ring straight at the young man's face, which was as drained and white as ever.
>
> (146)

What he "sees" is expressed in the "allegory" of the woman with the purple hat. He has a first-hand knowledge and understanding of the darkest of human aberrations, in the way that a prostitute might: "'But I can never finish telling you about the hat!' the fat man cried" (150). He is a grotesque version of the compassionate young man in "The Key," who intuitively understood the plight of the deaf and dumb couple and did what he could to help them. But the fat man's sense of power—"up on the catwalk you get the feeling now and then that you could put out your finger and make a change in the universe" (152)—is unaccompanied by any sense of sympathy. Since he somehow knows that the pathetic young alcoholic has succumbed to the lures of "The Purple Hat," his telling of the story becomes cruel. In spite of his superior knowledge he doesn't care what happens to the young man—or to anyone. He even enjoys the spectacle provided by his plight and that of all the others who pass beneath him in their futile pursuit of pleasure.

But even in his heightened awareness, he is not unlike others. After describing the second "murder," he tells the bartender, "If you had ever been to the Palace of Pleasure, you'd know it all went completely as usual—people at the tables never turn around" (151). The fat man luxuriates in his intuitive powers, "lifting his little finger like a pianist" (143), gazing fondly at his ring, but he will never lift that finger to help another, even though he is by profession a guard. His impassive and perverse curiosity is all too familiar; the terror in the story is produced not so much by the supernatural happenings as by our recognition that the fat man's passivity may well be our own.

The problem in "Clytie" is not one of obscurity but of a surfeit of Gothicism and a literary influence that is all too apparent. Clytie Farr is an old maid who lives in

Farr's Gin, a tiny town named after her once-prominent family. All her life she has been isolated from others because of a family pride ("the Farrs were too good to associate with other people" [CG (*A Cutain of Green*), 159]) that is now pathetic and ironic; she spends all her time taking care of her blind and paralyzed father, half-crazed sister, and drunken brother (whose wife left him shortly after their marriage because "he had threatened time and again to shoot her . . . he had pointed the gun against her breast. She had not understood" [167]). Another brother has committed suicide. Even Miss Welty's most ardent admirers must feel uneasy about the Farrs, who together form a virtual museum of Southern Gothic. Inside the Farrs' house,

> it was very dark and bare. The only light was falling on the white sheet which covered the solitary piece of furniture, an organ. The red curtains over the parlor door, held back by ivory hands, were still as tree trunks in the airless house. Every window was closed, and every shade was down, though behind them the rain could still be heard.
>
> Clytie took a match and advanced to the stair post, where the bronze cast of Hermes was holding up a gas fixture; and at once above this, lighted up, but quite still, like one of the unmovable relics of the house, Octavia [her sister] stood waiting on the stairs.
>
> (160-61)

This kind of musty, Gothic interior is almost academic in Southern writing; Miss Welty makes fun of it in "Old Mr. Marblehall" and "Asphodel." Clytie's mansion recalls Sutpen's Hundred in Faulkner's *Absalom, Absalom!* or Miss Emily's house in "A Rose for Emily," whereas the drunken brooding of Clytie's brother may remind one of Bayard Sartoris in *Sartoris*. But as the story unfolds, the resemblances to Faulkner become less important, and, whenever the focus shifts from the setting to Clytie herself, the story assumes a life of its own. And it is told with a tenderness and compassion that is absent from "A Rose for Emily." Miss Welty writes, "on some level all stories are stories of search . . . when Miss Brill [in Katherine Mansfield's story of that name] sits in the park we feel an old key try at an old lock again—she too is looking. Our most ancient dreams help to convince us that her timid Sunday afternoon is the adventure of her life, and measure for us her defeat."⁹ The emphasis in "Clytie" falls not on the grotesque facts of her life but on her search for love.

As the story opens, it is raining in Farr's Gin. Everyone has gone under cover, except for Miss Clytie Farr, who stands still in the middle of the road, "peering ahead in her near-sighted way, as wet as the little birds" which are scurrying across her path. She finally clenches her hands and draws them "up under her armpits, and sticking out her elbows like hen wings," she runs out of the street.

When the scene shifts indoors the perspective changes: the reader enters Clytie's mind and discovers that, mad or not, there is purpose in her grotesque antics; the nature of her search is revealed:

> In the street she had been thinking about the face of a child she had just seen . . . [who] had looked at her with such an open, serene, trusting expression as she passed by! With this small, peaceful face still in her mind . . . like an inspiration which drives all other thoughts away, Clytie had forgotten herself.
>
> (162)

Obsessed with the mystery of identity, Clytie has for a long time been inspecting the faces of people on the street; she has a deep, almost religious respect for the uniqueness, the inviolability of others: "The most profound, the most moving sight in the whole world must be a face. Was it possible to comprehend the eyes and the mouths of other people, which concealed she knew not what, and secretly asked for still another unknown thing?" She tries desperately to escape from her inner world; her reservoir of tenderness and wonder transforms reality. Even the idiot who calls himself "Mr. Tom Bate's Boy" seems fabulous to her: she observes grains of sand in his old eyes; "he might have come out of a desert, like an Egyptian" (163).

Clytie is searching for a specific face. "It was purely for a resemblance to a vision that she examined the secret, mysterious, unrepeated faces she met in the street of Farr's Gin." She had seen that face long ago, but "now it was hard to remember the way it looked, or the time when she had seen it first. It must have been when she was young. Yes, in a sort of arbor, hadn't she laughed, leaned forward . . . and that vision of a face—which was a little like all the other faces . . . and yet different . . . this face had been very close to hers, almost familiar, almost accessible." But her terrifying family situation separates her from this vision. "Their faces came between her face and another. It was their faces which had come pushing in between, long ago, to hide some face that had looked back at her" (168). Like the beauty that she saw in the face of the trusting child, this face is beyond Clytie's "reach." But another face comes within distance of her actual reach.

Mr. Bobo, the nervous town barber who "was short and had never been anything but proud of it, until he had started coming to this house once a week," and who is frightened of all the Farrs, comes into the old house to shave Clytie's bedridden father. Clytie looks at "his pitiful, greedy, small face—how very mournful it was. . . . What was it that this greedy little thing was so desperately needing?" (175). All of her desperation and loneliness erupt, and "with breathtaking gentleness" she touches his face.

> Then both of them uttered a despairing cry. Mr. Bobo turned and fled. . . . Clytie, pale as a ghost, stumbled against the railing . . . the horrible moist scratch of an

invisible beard, the dense, popping green eyes—what had she got hold of with her hand! She could hardly bear it—the thought of that face.

(176)

She runs out to the old rain barrel. She "suddenly felt that this object, now, was her friend, just in time, and her arms almost circled it with impatient gratitude." As she looks into the water, she sees a face: "It was the face she had been looking for, and from which she had been separated." It is ugly and distended, and "everything about [it] frightened and shocked her with its signs of waiting, of suffering. . . . Too late, she recognized the face. She stood there completely sick at heart, as though the poor, half-remembered vision had finally betrayed her" (177). Clytie is devastated by the realization that the face she had been looking for all along had been her own and that this lost self can never be recaptured. In that one instant, she recognizes the contrast between the vision of the laughing child of the past and the mirror image of the ugly and maddened adult of the present. Clytie submits to the terrible knowledge that the only kind of love possible for her is narcissistic love and that life for her has therefore become a living death. She "did the only thing she could think of to do." She thrust her body and head down

> into the barrel, under the water, through its glittering surface into the kind, featureless depth, and held it there.
>
> When Old Lethy found her, she had fallen forward into the barrel, with her poor ladylike black-stockinged legs up-ended and hung apart like a pair of tongs.

(178)

The final image of her legs complements the inanimate, almost antiseptic quality of a lonely and loveless existence. The grotesque image expresses all the horror of Clytie Farr's unbearable discovery.

By virtue of its genuine pathos and psychological incisiveness, "Clytie" manages to transcend its Gothicism and resemblance to "A Rose for Emily." But it should not be surprising if Faulkner has exerted an influence on his fellow Mississippian; Miss Welty has called him "the most astonishingly powered and passionate writer we have."[10] When Miss Welty began her career, Faulkner had already completed the best work in his "parable or legend of all the Deep South." If the young Southern writer chooses to write about his region, he must inevitably face the question of how to avoid rewriting Faulkner. With the possible exceptions of "Clytie" and "The Burning," Miss Welty has solved this problem.

In *Love and Death in the American Novel* (1960), Leslie Fiedler deprecatingly refers to Miss Welty as one of the "feminizing Faulknerians," yet the sounds of Faulkner's rhetoric are much more audible throughout the fiction of such "masculine Faulknerians" as Robert Penn Warren, William Styron, and Andrew Lytle. Excerpts from their work might be intermingled with passages from Faulkner and many readers would be hard put to tell them apart. Except for some passages from the first version of "The Burning" and one from "Moon Lake" (GA [*The Golden Apples*], 100), this could not be done with Miss Welty's fiction because the qualities of her language and style are her own. Faulkner's emblem of the Southern experience informs Miss Welty's sense of her region's history and his example helped her to discover the raw materials of her own art. But the influence of his specific works is negligible, for Miss Welty's fiction abounds in characters, settings, and speech rhythms which only she could have created.

"Asphodel" is one of those stories which only Miss Welty could have written. Three old maids—Cora, Phoebe, and Irene—go on a picnic the day after the funeral of a certain Miss Sabina. They climb a hill and picnic near the ruins of Asphodel, an old mansion that had belonged to Miss Sabina's husband, Mr. Don McInnis. One of the old maids says that "he is dead too." Although "her funeral was yesterday, and we've cried our eyes dry," Miss Sabina's death seems a welcomed event: after dipping "their narrow maiden feet" in a stream, they laugh "freely all at once" (97), and then unpack a lavish lunch.

In the first part of the story, they reminisce about Miss Sabina, reconstructing the events of her life. Robert Penn Warren, otherwise one of Miss Welty's most sympathetic critics, describes the story as a "failure," deploring its "hocus-pocus" and "strain for atmosphere."[11] Perhaps it should not be dismissed so quickly. It is an unusual, if sometimes puzzling, combination of disparate elements, including fantasy, mythology, and parody. Its success depends on how the reader reacts to Miss Sabina's history, which is grotesque and highly melodramatic. In the fashion of a Greek chorus, the old maids "tell over Miss Sabina's story, their voices serene and alike: how she looked, the legend of her beauty when she was young" (98), her house, her family, her marriage to Mr. Don, his infidelities, his immense popularity, their three children (all of whom died), how "she drove Mr. Don out of the house . . . with a whip, in the broad daylight" (103) and then "gratified" herself by burning Asphodel, how "she laid down the law that the name of Don McInnis and . . . of Asphodel were not to cross our lips again" (104), how in her madness she ruled the town, and how she died grotesquely in the post office. The reader is unable to accept these events as literal because the "plot" constructed by the old maids is a cataloging of the kind of clichés rampant in Southern romance fiction. I find it hard to believe that

Miss Welty intended us to take them all seriously. For example, Phoebe related her part of the narration, the deaths of Miss Sabina's children, as follows:

> There was Minerva and she was drowned—before her wedding day. There was Theo, coming out from the university in his gown of the law, and killed in a fall off the wild horse he was bound to ride. And there was Lucian the youngest, shooting himself publicly on the courthouse steps, drunk in the broad daylight.
>
> "Who can tell what will happen in this world!" said Phoebe, and she looked placidly up into the featured sky overhead.
>
> (101)

But these events did not discourage Miss Sabina: "she was born grand, with a will to impose" (101). "Asphodel" may be seen as Miss Welty's oblique attack on the old ruling class and the ineffectuality of its descendants—a parody of the romantic view of Southern gentility as perpetrated by Margaret Mitchell's *Gone With the Wind* (1936) and a hundred other novels. Several passages suggest this. Cora talks about Miss Sabina's house and her wedding:

> Inside, the house was all wood . . . carved and fluted . . . even mahogany roses in the ceilings. . . . The house was a labyrinth set with statues—Venus, Hermes, Demeter, and with singing ocean shells on draped pedestals.
>
> Miss Sabina's father came bringing Mr. Don McInnis home, and proposed the marriage to him. She was no longer young for suitors. . . . We were there. The presents were vases of gold, gold cups, statues of Diana. . . . It was spring, the flowers in the basket were purple hyacinths and white lilies that wilted in the heat and showed their blue veins. Ladies fainted from the scent . . .
>
> (98-99)

Irene continues the description of Mr. Don. Her narration is delivered in a style parodying cheap fiction:

> A great, profane man like all the McInnis men of Asphodel, Mr. Don McInnis. He was the last of his own, just as she was the last of hers. The hope was in him, and he knew it. He had a sudden way of laughter, like a rage. . . . That night he stood astride . . . astride the rooms, the guests, the flowers, the tapers, the bride and her father with his purple face. . . . He was a McInnis, a man that would be like a torch carried into a house.
>
> (100)

The exaggeration and hyperbole of these passages are certainly suggestive of parody. In its extravagance the mansion becomes absurd, the legendary Southern "gentlemen were without exception drunk," and the usually dashing hero is animalistic—"profane." The beautiful, desirable heroine of Southern romance fiction is transformed into Miss Sabina, and courting procedures are reversed: her father proposes to her suitor and "she was instructed to submit"—she is an *anti*heroine. Miss Welty seems to level Scarlett O'Hara, Rhett Butler, and the mansion of Tara with a few well-chosen words. Perhaps it is no coincidence that the sharpest, most insensitive, and surprisingly personal attack upon Miss Welty's work is found in a review by the late Margaret Mitchell.[12]

Miss Sabina and Mr. Don are thus parodied versions of those staple, stock characters in historical fiction, the tempestuous Southern lovers. But Miss Welty's couple also represent basic contrasting forces. The story told by the old maids was "like an old song they carried in their memory, the story of the two houses separated by a long, winding, difficult, untravelled road—a curve of the old Natchez Trace—but actually situated almost back to back on the ring of hills, while completely hidden from each other, like the reliefs on the opposite sides of a vase" (98). The "two houses" are literally Asphodel and Miss Sabina's house, which are contrasted symbolically by Asphodel's "mounds of wild roses" and "the mahogany roses in the ceilings" of Sabina's house—just as Mr. Don represents the sensual, pagan, life-giving force, and Miss Sabina is a manifestation of the opposing and ultimately destructive urge to control and suppress others. The two "houses" finally suggest Eros and Thanatos.

After she has driven Mr. Don away and he has supposedly died, "all her will was turned upon the population" (104).

> Her law was laid over us, her riches were distributed upon us . . . [she] set the times of weddings and funerals, even for births . . . named the children [and] moved people from one place to another in town, brought them together or drove them apart, with the mystical and rigorous devotion of a priestess in a story; and she prophesied all the things beforehand. She foretold disaster . . .
>
> (105)

One cannot take this literally. The details of Miss Sabina's life become increasingly fantastic and grotesque. Her downfall can be read as a kind of allegory of the decline of the old South. Miss Sabina represents the survivors of the "old order," with their manic attempts to maintain control and to guard against change, and their hostility to all spontaneity: "At the May Festival when she passed by, all the maypoles become hopelessly tangled, one by one" (105).

The end results of Miss Sabina's efforts to sustain an illusion are ludicrous, grotesque, and psychically crippling: she staggers along under the weight of a large black wig and heavy brocades, and suffers a terrible death in the post office—the "one door where Miss Sabina had never entered." Because it is the element of modern life beyond her control, "she acted as if the post office had no existence in the world," and "all the hate she had left in her when she was old went out to [the] little four-posted white-washed building.... For there we might still be apart in a dream, and she did not know what it was" (106). But in the end, she enters the post office: "'It was as if the place of the smallest and the longest-permitted indulgence, the little common green, were to be invaded when the time came for the tyrant to die,' said Phoebe" (107). In a horrifying sequence she first demands her letters—although she never got any—and then attacks the post office "with her bare hands," ripping everything apart.

> She was possessed ... she raged. She rocked from side to side, she danced. Miss Sabina's arms moved like a harvester's in the field, to destroy all that was in the little room. In her frenzy she tore all the letters to pieces, and even put bits in her mouth and appeared to eat them.
>
> Then she stood still in the little room. She had finished. We had not yet moved when she lay toppled on the floor, her wig fallen from her head and *her face awry like a mask* [italics mine].
>
> 'A stroke.' That is what we said, because we did not know how to put a name to the end of her life ...
>
> (108)

Since it is impossible to regulate *every* aspect of life, the fanatic's will to control is finally self-destructive: Miss Sabina is her own victim, and death reveals her impotency—the wig has fallen from her head. Miss Sabina's story is over, but the story about the three old maids is not.

They present a contrast to the violent and grotesque scene which they have just recalled, considering it happened only a few days before:

> Here in the bright sun where the three old maids sat beside their little feast, Miss Sabina's was an old story, closed and complete.... Now they lay stretched on their sides on the ground, their summer dresses spread out, *little smiles forming on their mouths, their eyes half-closed.... Above them like a dream rested the bright columns of Asphodel, a dream like the other side of their lamentations.* [italics mine]
>
> (109)

Their idyllic repose is suddenly interrupted by a bearded and naked Pan-like figure who steps out from the vines growing up among the columns and stares at the three spinsters. Terrified, they make "a soft little chorus of screams," and flee from the scene (109).

"Southern summer is nostalgic," Miss Welty once wrote, "because even when it happens it's dream-like. Find the shade of the biggest tree; in it your hammock is dreaming already, like a boat on the stream."[13] The summer atmosphere and the story's opening images of the surrealistic ruins place the action deep within a "season of dreams." With the completion of the story-within-a-story, the controlling image returns, "above them like a dream." They "did not know how to put a name" to her death, and, after narrating the children's death, Phoebe—who is undoubtedly named after Phoebus, the god of prophecy—looks "into the featureless sky" and exclaims: "Who can tell what will happen in this world!" Their narration has a decided improvisatory quality. It seems almost to be part of their consciousness—"an old song they carried in their memory." The "narrative was only part of memory now, and its beginning and ending might seem mingled and freed in the blue air of the hill" (100). They recall the day Miss Sabina drove Mr. Don from home: "It was a day like this, in summer—I remember the magnolias that made the air so heavy and full of sleep. It was just after dinner time and all the population came out and stood helpless to see, as if in a dream" (103). The old maids have related Miss Sabina's story as "in some intoxication of the time and the place," suggesting that most of the events which they have described may *never* have happened and that the three old maids, lost in their fantasy world—heightened and encouraged by the heat—choose to render Miss Sabina's life in the terms of Southern romance fiction, a set of fantasies equivalent to the unreality of their own lives. The elements of allegory and parody in their narration are thus presented in a psychological context, embodied in the characterizations of the three old maids. The parody is not forced upon the story, but grows organically out of its form: "The grapes they held upon their palms were transparent in the light, so that the little black seeds showed within" (107); this describes how Miss Sabina's story reveals the nature of the spinsters' lives. The powerful Miss Sabina was undoubtedly a real enough town eccentric, but her "story" has probably been manufactured by the old maids over a period of years as a legend in keeping with the extravagance of Miss Sabina's actual eccentricities and as a fantasy-projection of their own retreat from reality ("a dream like the other side of their lamentations"). Miss Sabina's highly grotesque death may be the only "real" event of her story. Its violence may symbolize their own suppressed anguish. Unlike Clytie Farr, they are not destroyed by their obsessions. By re-creating Miss Sabina's "life" and grotesque death—her virtual rape of the post office—they may be said to be activating and releasing their own inhibitions: Miss Sabina's story finished, "they lay stretched on their sides ... little smiles forming on their mouths ... eyes half-closed." Their contentment is short-lived.

In "Asphodel," Miss Welty uses the grotesque as both a tragic and a comic mask. When Miss Sabina died, "her wig [had] fallen ... and her face [was] awry like a mask." But the real "masks" in the story belong to Phoebe, Cora, and Irene. What is pathetic, if not tragic, in "Asphodel" is not Miss Sabina's story, but what her "story" has revealed about the three old maids. The full extent of their condition is not apparent until the appearance of the naked man. He represents the first intrusion of reality into the story. After "escaping" from him they stop. The bearded man has not moved. "That was Mr. Don McInnis," says Cora. "It was not," Irene says. "It was a vine in the wind" (110). In that one sentence of dialogue Miss Welty shows the depth of the dream world in which the old maid has immersed herself. It is one of those moments, frequent in her fiction, when she manages to squeeze meaning from the detail which, in ordinary realistic fiction, might be passed over. The reader may wonder, *is* it Mr. Don, or not? It doesn't matter; what is important is that it is a *man,* and how the three react to him.

> "He was buck-naked," said Cora. "He was as naked as an old goat. He must be as old as the hills."
>
> "I didn't look," declared Phoebe. But there at one side she stood bowed and trembling as if from a fateful encounter.
>
> "No need to cry about it, Phoebe," said Cora.
>
> (110)

Miss Welty may be reversing the Freudian method by projecting in broad daylight sexual nightmares that are in reality social symbols. The fantasy-like quality of the spinsters' lives in "Asphodel" is Miss Welty's expression of their tragic refusal to face the present and the failure of their minds to function in terms other than those of the past. Moreover, in creating a "past" for Miss Sabina, they spin fantasies out of clichés; Miss Welty thereby parodies the whole myth about that past, unmasking the myth, just as Sabina herself was unmasked at her death.

In "Asphodel," Miss Welty has maintained a tough-minded and detached attitude toward the *idea* of the South, in spite of her attachment to her Mississippi "place." This is in part due to the fact that Miss Welty is a first generation Mississippian whose parents did not come from the deep South; her mother is from West Virginia, and her father was from Ohio; they moved to Jackson in 1904, five years before Miss Welty's birth. She has humorously said that she did not suffer as a child, "except from my father's being . . . a Yankee"[14]—and her lack of antebellum ancestors has undoubtedly contributed to her sense of perspective and her independent view of Southern tradition. She has never belonged to a literary or political group, and, although many of her early stories appeared in the *Southern Review,* she never involved herself in regionalist theorizing. Unlike several Southern writers, she does not entertain any nostalgia for the grace and innocence of past Confederate days. Nor does she rail against the defilement of the "old order" by the new, commercial order; one cannot imagine Miss Welty as a contributor to *I'll Take My Stand* (1930). She offers no defense of the Old South, a fact made evident by "Asphodel," "The Burning," and the stories about the descendants of the Southern aristocracy. In "A Curtain of Green," the town is named after Mrs. Larkin's father-in-law; the town in "Clytie" is also named for the family; and much is made of old Mr. Marblehall's descent from an old family. The lives of these well-born characters are more circumscribed by fantasy than any of Miss Welty's other characters, suggesting a critical view of the old families' abilities to cope with the vagaries of reality on both a personal and social level.

Suggestions of meaning are multiplied by consideration of the title of the story. The dictionary defines "asphodel" as "any of a genus of plants of the lily family." The present-day ruins of Asphodel hardly suggest any such beauty and the past was no better; at Miss Sabina's wedding the "lilies wilted and showed their blue veins. Ladies fainted from the scent." The three old maids, casting their dreams in Asphodel's shadow, are "wilted" women, existing as "weeds" in an emotional wasteland. The lily is the flower of mourning and, as such, it is an appropriate emblem for the three ladies. The ruins of Asphodel symbolize their physical and imaginative sterility.

The asphodel is also the traditional flower of immortality. In the *Odyssey,* it covers the meadows in the Elysian fields when Ulysses meets the great dead.[15] Miss Welty makes uncommon use of her mythic material. Contemporary writers often utilize mythology in a solemn and pretentious way, but in "Asphodel" the classical correspondences are grotesque, humorous, and ironic. In the figures of Miss Sabina and Mr. Don, Miss Welty light-heartedly invokes Nietzsche's distinction between the Apollonian and Dionysian forces; the naked and bearded Mr. Don is her most explicitly Dionysian character: he steps out from among vines, looks like an "old goat," and is remembered as having "had the wildness we all worshipped" (101). Throughout the story, Miss Welty has fun at the expense of the Old South's identification with a Golden Age; the ruins of "Asphodel" point to that grand anachronism in the history of American style, "the classic revival." At Sabina's wedding, "the presents were vases of gold, gold cups, statues of Diana." She later wielded a "stick mounted with the gold head of a lion," and, when Mr. Don appears before the spinsters, he was "golden as a lion." At the end of the story, Phoebe calls it a "golden day." But instead of the immortal dead, one meets the three old maids and hears about Miss Sabina. She is a Southern Sabine who, though taken against her will, did *not* submit to her "conqueror," the Dionysian Mr. Don. Her children include "Minerva" and "Lucian the youngest." The spinsters serve as a Greek chorus; Cassandra-like, they were the first to inform Sabina of Mr. Don's unfaithfulness: Cora says, "We told the news.... We went in a body up the hill and into the house, weeping and wailing, hardly daring to name the name or the deed" (101). The old maids describe Asphodel as a Greek temple and recall that Miss Sabina's house had statues of the Seasons and of the gods—Venus, Hermes, and Demeter. Miss Welty keynotes the absurdity of the spinsters' "dream" by juxtaposing comical, almost slapstick action against the "classical" setting. Near the end of the story, as they gaze at the ruins of Asphodel, "a number of goats appeared between the columns . . . and with a little leap started down the hill." It is fitting that the satyr-like Mr. Don should be living among goats. As if at his command, the goats pour out of Asphodel—like comic versions of the Eumenides emerging from a debased temple of Dionysus—and chase the women: "Into the buggy!" screams one of the ladies. "Tails up, the goats leapt the fence as if there was nothing they would rather do. . . . There were billy-goats and nanny-goats, old goats and young, a whole thriving herd. Their little beards all blew playfully to the side in the wind of their advancement" (111). The ladies throw biscuits to the closely pursuing goats to appease them, but it does not stop them. Miss Welty utilizes her mythology in the spirit of Mack Sennett rather than Sir James Frazer. "Cora was standing up in the open buggy, driving it like a chariot. 'Give them the little baked hen, then,' she said, and they threw it. . . . The little goats stopped . . . and then their horns met over the prize" (112). Routing the forces of order and control which Miss Sabina had exemplified, the chasing goats mock the old maids and their absurd "tender dreams" of the past.

After making their escape, Irene and Cora give thanks that "Miss Sabina did not live to see us then." But in a surprise turn, Phoebe laughed aloud. As the story ends, "her voice was soft, and she seemed to be still in a tender dream and an unconscious celebration—as though the picnic were not already set rudely in the past, but were the enduring and intoxicating present . . . the golden day" (113). Phoebe seems to have enjoyed the triumph of the goats and Mr. Don, thus belying her namesake Phoebus Apollo. Perhaps all along she was secretly on the side of the Dionysian rather than Apollonian forces. With its elements of humor, fantasy, and grotesquery, "Asphodel" is a story about the South that could not have been written by any Southerner *except* Eudora Welty.

Miss Welty's most brilliant use of the grotesque occurs in "Petrified Man." It seems to be her most popular story, for it has been reprinted more often than any other (fourteen times). It is a tightly controlled, ruthlessly objective study of vulgarity of spirit, a vulgarity so absolute that it appears chemically pure, exposed in its final subhuman form. The characters in "Petrified Man" are the ultimate spiritual embodiments of the grotesque bathers of "A Memory," and the story is Miss Welty's "Waste Land."

"Petrified Man" is set in a cheap beauty parlor. Its setting and manner resemble Ring Lardner's "Haircut," although Miss Welty treats human callousness and meanness in a more complicated way than Lardner. She does not allow the reader and the writer just behind the persona such an easy sense of moral superiority.

"Petrified Man" is unfolded in two scenes, each one week apart, in which Leota, the beauty parlor attendant, and Mrs. Fletcher, her customer, converse at great length. The story's impact is almost completely dependent upon Miss Welty's ear, her gift for rendering all kinds of dialogue. Leota serves as an effaced narrator. She tells Mrs. Fletcher about her adventures with a friend from New Orleans, Mrs. Pike, thereby providing the story with its main theme. Their dialogue exposes their bitterness, rancor, self-pity, and baseness. Miss Welty's satire cuts through these levels of human weakness with unfailing sharpness.

Although there are few descriptive passages in "Petrified Man," Miss Welty selects details which add to the story's scalding humor. Like Gogol, Miss Welty opens the doors and observes the setting, describing it closely, but never cataloging; each detail increases the story's sense of an overwhelming vulgarity. The setting itself affords an ironic comment; the intense revelation of vulgarity occurs in a place whose purpose is to "beautify" at least the exterior of the female. Instead, the *inner* ugliness of the women is revealed in a "den of curling fluid and henna packs" (32), where apparatus—wave pinchers, dryers, permanent wave machines, cold wet towels, and thick fluids—is utilized with a brutal vigor suggestive of a torture chamber: customers get "yanked up by the back locks" and thick wave fluid drips down their necks and into their eyes; "you cooked me fourteen minutes," complains a customer, and Leota, with her "strong red-nailed fingers," digs both hands into Mrs. Fletcher's scalp (33). Miss Welty utilizes her painter's eye: the beauty parlor—and every implement therein, including the combs—is lavender, a particularly vulgar color. There are rows of Coca-Cola bottles along the mirror. A drugstore rental book, *Life Is Like That, Screen Secrets,* and *Startling G-Man Tales* provide the customers and the beauticians with reading material. The story begins and ends with a handful of stale peanuts ("goobers"). As for sanitary conditions, Billy Boy, Mrs. Pike's child, plays on the beauty parlor floor, "making tents with aluminum wave pinchers . . . under the sink" (36). Then there are the women themselves: Mrs. Fletcher looked "expectantly at the black part in Leota's yellow curls as she bent"; Leota "flicked an ash into the basket of dirty towels." Leota runs a comb through Mrs. Fletcher's hair, and the "hair floated out of the lavender teeth like a small storm-cloud" (33).

When Mrs. Fletcher asks, "Is it any dandruff in it?" she frowns, her "hair-line eyebrows diving down toward her nose, and her wrinkled, beady-lashed eyelids batting with concentration" (34). The mention of brand names contributes to the tone. The pregnant Mrs. Fletcher talks about buying "Stork-A-Lure" maternity clothes, and the chauvinistic Leota says she drinks only "Jax Beer" because "that's the beer that Mrs. Pike says is made right in N.O." (37). These small details combine to project a grotesque image of humanity.

The dialogue between Leota and Mrs. Fletcher abounds in phrases and passages intended to chill the reader by virtue of their grotesque insensitivity. Too stingy to send Billy Boy to a nursery, Mrs. Pike deposits him with Leota each day. "Only three years old," Leota says, "and already nuts about the beauty-parlor business" (36). Because Mrs. Fletcher does not like children she finds her pregnancy disgusting and is trying to keep it a secret. She hasn't told her husband yet because she is contemplating an abortion. Leota tells Mrs. Fletcher about Mrs. Montjoy of the Trojan Garden Club, a customer who, already in labor, stopped at the shop on the way to the maternity ward because she "wanted to look pretty while she was havin' her baby, is all" (48). And of the woman's labor pains, Leota says, "Yeah man! She was a-yellin'. Just like when I give her a perm'net" (48). The grotesque incongruities embody the baseness of the beauty-parlor women.

The grim comedy reaches its most horrifying level when Leota tells Mrs. Fletcher about the traveling freak show which she and Mrs. Pike visited. "Well, honey," says Leota, "talkin' about bein' pregnant an' all, you ought to see those twins in a bottle, you really owe it to yourself" (39).

> "Born joined plumb together—dead a course." Leota dropped her voice into a soft lyrical hum. "They was about this long—pardon—must of been full time, all right, wouldn't you say?—an' they had these two heads an' two faces an' four arms an' four legs, all kind of joined *here*. See, this face looked this-a-way, over their shoulder, see. Kinda pathetic."

From the bottled Siamese twins, Leota moves on to describe the pygmies:

> "You know, the teeniest men in the universe? Well, honey, they can just rest back on their little bohunkus an' roll around an' you can't hardly tell if they're sittin' or standin'. . . . They're about forty-two years old. Just suppose it was your husband!"
>
> "Well, Mr. Fletcher is five foot nine and one half," said Mrs. Fletcher quickly.
>
> (40)

Though the pygmies "are not bad-lookin' for what they are," Leota and Mrs. Pike preferred another "freak"—the petrified man: "ever-thing ever since he was nine years old, when it goes through his digestion, see, somehow Mrs. Pike says it goes to his joints and has been turning to stone" (41). The women not only show no compassion for the petrified man, but, by continuing to talk about themselves and the "freaks" in the same breath, they ironically fail to distinguish between "freaks" and supposedly "normal" people. Leota says,

> "He's turnin' to stone. How'd you like to be married to a guy like that? All he can do, he can move his head just a quarter of an inch. A course he *looks* just *terrible*."
>
> "I should think he would," said Mrs. Fletcher frostily. "Mr. Fletcher takes bending exercises every night of the world. I make him. . . ."
>
> "Did Mrs. Pike like the petrified man?" asked Mrs. Fletcher.
>
> "Not as much as she did the others," said Leota deprecatingly. "And then she likes a man to be a good dresser, and all that."
>
> "Is Mr. Pike a good dresser?" asked Mrs. Fletcher sceptically.
>
> (42)

After dropping the petrified man from their conversation, Leota and Mrs. Fletcher discuss love and marriage. In "Petrified Man," life between the sexes is repugnant, to put it mildly: "Dandruff, dandruff. I couldn't of caught a thing like that from Mr. Fletcher, could I?" (34). Mrs. Pike married a man fourteen years her senior. She has always sought advice from fortune tellers; "She ast Lady Evangeline about him" (42). The fortune teller advised Mrs. Pike to marry because Mr. Pike was due an inheritance, and Leota admits, "me an' Fred, we met in a rumble seat eight months ago and we was practically on what you might call the way to the altar inside of half an hour" (45).

In the second scene, a week later, Leota no longer considers Mrs. Pike a "friend." Mrs. Pike had recognized the petrified man's photo in Leota's copy of *Startling G-Man Tales*—he was wanted for raping four women in California. "Did it under his real name—Mr. Petrie" [a logical name] (53). He had lived in the apartment next to the Pikes's in New Orleans for six weeks. The reward was five hundred dollars, which Mrs. Pike collected after the police had arrested the no-longer petrified man. Leota is virtually sick over losing the reward, begrudges Mrs. Pike the money—"it was my magazine"—and says, regarding the rape victims: "Four women. I guess those women didn't have the faintest notion at the time they'd be worth a hundred an' twenty-five bucks a piece some day to Mrs. Pike" (54).

The story ends on a savage note: the two women take out their wrath on Mrs. Pike's child and spank Billy Boy viciously. It is no coincidence that Billy Boy is the only male physically present in the story. At the beginning of "Petrified Man," when Leota says, "So we rented [our extra room] to Mrs. Pike. And Mr. Pike," she inaugurates a theme that is dominant throughout the story (33): like all the other men mentioned in the story, Mr. Pike is reduced to a subordinate position. In the passages concerning pregnancy the women deny their own femininity as well as attack their husbands' sexuality. Their attitude toward the men is exemplified in Leota's first remark to Billy Boy, "Billy Boy, hon, mustn't bother nice ladies" (36). Men must know and keep their place in the world of Leota, Mrs. Pike, and Mrs. Fletcher. "Fred's five foot ten," says Leota, "but I tell him he's still a shrimp, account of I'm so tall" (41). Mrs. Fletcher says that if her husband "so much as raises his voice against me, he knows good and well I'll have one of my sick headaches, and then I'm just not fit to live with" (37). Mr. Montjoy, whose wife stopped by the beauty parlor during her labor, waited in their car but "kep' comin' in here, scared-like, but couldn't do nothin' with her a course" (47). As for his wife's yelling, Mrs. Fletcher thinks that

> "Her husband ought to make her behave. Don't it seem that way to you? . . . He ought to put his foot down."
>
> "Ha," said Leota. "A lot he could do. Maybe some women is soft."
>
> "Oh, you mistake me, I don't mean for her to get soft—far from it! Women have to stand up for themselves, or there's just no telling."
>
> (48)

It is no wonder that at best, Leota's husband Fred can "lay around the house an' bull . . . with that good-for-nothin' Mr. Pike. He says if he goes who'll cook" (49). Mr. Pike has been unemployed for six months, and Fred is virtually immobile.

The men seem to be well on their way to being figuratively "petrified" by the debilitating effects of their wives' domination; Leota suggests as much with a vivid juxtaposition: "'All Fred does is lay around the house like a rug. I wouldn't be surprised if he woke up some day and couldn't move. The petrified man just sat there moving his quarter of an inch though,' said Leota reminiscently" (42). Significantly, Mr. Pike does not want to call the police about Mr. Petrie—"Said he kinda liked that ole bird and said he was real nice. . . . But Mrs. Pike simply tole him he could just go to hell" (53); perhaps he recognized a kindred soul in the petrified man. He may have raped four women, but Mrs. Pike, who several times served him breakfast in bed, went unharmed. She either did not appeal to him—or else frightened him. Miss Welty is not morally interested in the rapes. Although the petrified man is sexually warped, he still *acts* and asserts himself—whereas the other men have been unsexed—"Mr. Fletcher can't do a thing with me" (37). They are at the complete mercy of their wives: "Mr. Fletcher takes bending exercises every night of the world. I make him" (42), and Leota has her husband work in Vicksburg because the fortune teller suggested it ("Said my lover was goin' to work in Vicksburg, so I don't know who she could mean, unless she meant Fred" [49]).

With the arrest of the petrified man the women seem to have succeeded in subjugating the only free man in the story—but not quite, for Billy Boy remains to be vanquished. He has been told to "behave" at intervals throughout the story. When they catch him eating the last of the stale peanuts, his simple boyish act is seen as a major gesture of male defiance. "'You come here to me!' screamed Leota, recklessly flinging down the comb, which scattered a whole ashtray full of bobby pins and knocked down a row of Coca-Cola bottles. 'This is the last straw!'" Mrs. Fletcher holds him while Leota paddles him with the brush, the scene becoming a communal rite of female vengeance: "From everywhere ladies began to gather round to watch the paddling" (55). As the three-year-old leaves the beauty parlor he yells, "If you're so smart, why ain't you rich?" Although he remains unconquered, he is as gross as the adults. But his taunting question is well taken, for as materialistic as they are, the women have nothing *except* their vulgarity and viciousness. Miss Welty succeeds in combining elements of the grotesque that are simultaneously comic and saddening. As Ratliff says of Snopesism in Faulkner's *The Town* (1957), "soon as you set down to laugh at it, you find out it aint funny a-tall."

The petrified man symbolizes all the ultimately destructive possibilities of a life between the sexes that has been distorted by grossness of spirit. He symbolizes the hypocrisy, pettiness, and sexual barrenness in the lives of the three women and, though less directly, in the lives of their men as well—lives that can only find "fulfillment" in vicious, idle gossiping or in somnolent loafing. The petrified man had pretended to be turning to stone and was ultimately exposed as "alive." The three women, however, are the real "pretenders" in the story because they are the ones who, figuratively, are turning to stone. That stone is their death-in-life. While their husbands have been "petrified" by female domination, the women are "petrified" because they are incapable of any human feeling; symbolically, they are as dead as the bottled Siamese twins which enthralled Leota.[16] Mrs. Pike, Leota, and Mrs. Fletcher belong to Petrified Man—that vast family whose numberless members share a similar corruption of spirit and who are, in their condition, isolated from the human race. Significantly, Miss Welty dropped the article when she entitled her story, "Petrified Man." The meaning thus moves from the particular to the general.

The elements of the grotesque and Gothic in Miss Welty's stories are artistically justifiable, for unlike Poe, she has never conjured up scenes of horror for their own sake. As Katherine Anne Porter says, in writing of "Petrified Man," "her use of this material raises the quite awfully sordid . . . tale to a level above its natural habitat, and its realism seems almost to have the quality of caricature, as complete realism so often does. Yet, as painters of the grotesque make only detailed reports of actual living types observed more keenly than the average eye is capable of observing, so Miss Welty's little human monsters are not really caricatures at all, but individuals exactly and clearly presented."[17]

As Miss Porter implies, there is a community of feeling shared by artists and writers of the grotesque. The overrun garden in "A Curtain of Green" points to the origin of the word *grotesque* in late fifteenth-century Italy. It initially referred to a style of ornamental wall painting comprised of monstrous and convoluted foliage.[18] The disquieting jungles in the paintings of the surrealist Max Ernst are the nearest modern equivalent to the ornamental grotesque. When Miss Welty "clamps" the sun on one side of the "polished sky" in "A Curtain of Green," she is echoing Ernst's series on the "Sun and Forest" motif. His paintings "The Joy of Living" and "A Moment of Calm" are remarkably accurate visual analogues to Mrs. Larkin's garden.[19]

Miss Welty's techniques recall the works of artists of the grotesque ranging from Bosch to Goya to Leonard Baskin. "Men with hawklike faces" aim their cameras at Howard in "Flowers for Marjorie." When the girl in "A Memory" finally identifies the terrible laugh she has been hearing unconsciously and focuses on "the motionless open pouched mouth of the woman," she could be looking at Edvard Munch's "The Shriek." The intense white and red make-up caked on Miss Baby Marie's face in "Livvie" and the faces of the bathers in "A Memory"—"metallic, with painted smiles in the sun"—recall the masked and menacing carnival figures in James Ensor's "The Intrigue." Mrs. Larkin's eyes are "puckered"; "her mouth was a sharp line"; Mr. Marblehall's "other wife" looks like "a woodcut of a Bavarian witch, forefinger pointing, with scratches in the air all around her"—these put-upon women are drawn with a striking clarity worthy of Callot or Goya; Miss Welty is compiling her own *Caprichos*. The affable fat guard in "The Purple Hat," who has "rather small, mournful lips . . . [a] vague smile," and a "look a little cosy and prosperous," might have been drawn by George Grosz: he "put his elbow on the counter, and rested his cheek on his hand, where he could see all the way down the bar. For a moment his eyes seemed dancing there, above one of those hands so short and so plump that you are always counting the fingers." The silent bartender's "mouth and eyes curved downward from the divide of his baby-pink nose, as if he had combed them down, like his hair." Miss Welty here anticipates the methods of contemporary artists such as Francis Bacon, who blur the edges of modeled forms in their still-wet canvases or thin their pigments with turpentine, allowing separate painted areas to run together in order to achieve visual forms that express corresponding psychic states. In "A Memory," the grotesque object of the narrator's revulsion is described in a manner that again anticipates important modern painters: the fat on the woman's arms is "like an arrested earthslide on a hill" and then her breasts themselves seem to turn to sand. The girl is experiencing something akin to the excremental vision of Jean Dubuffet, who paints his nudes with impasto pigments that are mixed with sand and pebbles, or of Willem de Kooning, whose monumental "Women" are painted in swirling and slashing brown, gray, and black strokes.[20]

Although it sometimes resembles caricature—the bartender's "enormous sad black eyebrows raised, like hoods on baby-carriages, and showed his round eyes"—Miss Welty's technique of the grotesque is essentially different from it. Caricature distorts and exaggerates the human physiognomy, but it leaves the form intact and never destroys it. But in the grotesque, as in a dream, a dimension of humanity may be displaced, missing, or replaced by an incongruous form; one detail may be stressed to the absolute exclusion of all others. In the Radio City melee of "Flowers for Marjorie," Howard stands close to a "large woman with feathery furs and a small brown wire over one tooth." Instead of a face we have the inanimate detail, in place of a body, the furs; the sense of lifeless anonymity defines Howard's crisis, his state of flux. In "The Purple Hat" our attention is continually drawn to the guard's plump little hands; they seem to have a life of their own. In a sense, he *is* his hands; they project his weakness and the absurdity of his being the Law.

The concentration on dissociated parts of the body is central to the grotesque vision: the body serves as the microcosm of a universal disorder—the lawless fragments threaten to disintegrate. In "A Memory," "fat hung upon [the woman's] upper arms like an arrested earthslide on a hill. With the first motion she might make, I was afraid that she would slide down upon herself into a terrifying heap. . . . The younger girl . . . was curled tensely upon herself. She wore a bright green bathing suit like a bottle from which she might, I felt, burst in a rage of churning smoke" (153). The "confusion of vulgarity and hatred which twined among them all like a wreath of steam rising from the wet sand" (154) is almost as self-annihilating as the spontaneous combustion which consumes Krook and his Rag and Bottle Shop in Dickens' *Bleak House*. Existence is so oppressive to some of Miss Welty's characters that they literally seem to fall apart. When the Camp Fire Girl concludes her visit of charity by leaning over the old woman and asking for her age, the old face on the pillow "slowly gathered and collapsed." In her death throes, Miss Sabina all but comes apart at the seams, and, according to the fat man, when the woman with the purple hat was "murdered" with her hat pin, it "entered between the ribs and pierced the heart . . . [and] the old creature . . . simply folded all softly in on herself, like a circus tent being taken down after the show" (151).

Sometimes Miss Welty's technique of the grotesque involves the pathetic fallacy, the projection of human characteristics into the inanimate; the roses which Howard carries through the street—his "Flowers for Marjorie"—nod "like heads in his arms." Her basic technique, however, is to describe the human in nonhuman terms: animal, vegetable, or mineral. Because the young girl in "A Memory" perceives them as virtual avatars of chaos, the bathers embody all of these possibilities. The woman's "breasts hung heavy and widening like pears"—and later seem to turn into sand—"her legs lay prone one on the other like shadowed bulwarks, uneven and deserted," and her arms are a protoplasmic landslide. The man smiles "the way panting dogs seem to be smiling" and piles the sand higher and higher on her legs, "like the teasing threat of oblivion." The family rehearses a sequence of transformations that seem to transport them from a higher order to a lower order, and from a lower order into nothingness.

Miss Welty draws upon all the details of speech, dress, and setting to fashion grotesque analogies within the various orders; the animate and inanimate share each other's properties in startling and unsettling ways. The torpor of the traveling salesman in "The Hitch-Hikers" is reflected in the old dog that moves "stiffly, like a table walking." When the delirious and dying R. J. Bowman of "Death of a Traveling Salesman" remembers the congruent drabness of his sex life and his various living quarters, instead of an individual woman, he sees the "furniture of that room." As Mrs. Marblehall walks among the crowded "old things" in her house, she "looks like funny furniture—an unornamented stair post." And by the time the narrator projects the "other little boy's" view of his mother's incipient hysteria, she seems to have metamorphosed into furniture: "for a long time he supposed that his mother was totally solid, down to her thick separated ankles." Adversity creates automata: Mrs. Marblehall "rolls back into the house as if she had been on a little wheel all this time"; Mrs. Larkin works as tirelessly as a machine; and when Miss Eckhart, the piano teacher in "June Recital," stands over the grave of the man she loved from afar, she expresses her mute grief by rocking back and forth like the prized metronome which dominates most of her waking hours. In a rare moment, Miss Eckhart plays for herself, her body swaying ecstatically from side to side, "like a tree trunk." Clytie Farr's big straw hat sags down on each side with the rain, "until it looked even more absurd and done for, like an old bonnet on a horse." Caught out in the rain with the hens and chickens, she runs down the street with "her elbows out like hen wings." In death, Clytie's legs hang apart "like a pair of tongs." To the audience, Powerhouse looks like a monkey, has banana-like fingers, and eyes that are "horny like a lizard's"; the reader sees beyond the grotesque parts. In "A Visit of Charity," the first sound the girl hears is "like a sheep bleating." The old woman has "a bunchy white forehead and red eyes like a sheep," "claws," and a "square smile" that forces her old face "dangerously awry." She speaks in a "foggy" voice, for the damp and cold place is more like an ice box than an Old Ladies' Home. When her hand reaches over to the girl, "it felt like a petunia leaf, clinging and just a little sticky."

Plant imagery figures prominently in these virtual transformations. When the orphan Easter is pulled up from the muddy bottom of Moon Lake after almost drowning, "she was arm to arm and leg to leg in a long fold, wrong-colored and pressed together as unopen leaves are"; her wet hair "lay over her face in long fern shapes"; "her side fell slack as a dead rabbit's in the woods"; the whites of her eyes "showed under the lids pale and slick as watermelon seeds" (GA, 128). In "The Whistle," Jason Morton lies under his quilt "in a long shape like a bean," and when the frost threatens their crop, the Mortons undress and lay all their clothes over the *plants*. Because her overalls are stained green, Mrs. Larkin sometimes blends in with her garden. So complete is her victimization that when she swoons under the rain, her surrender to the absurd is orgasmic: "A wind of deep wet fragrance beat against her . . . as if it had swelled and broken over a daily levee, tenderness tore and spun through her." She sinks back into the plants, "with her hair beaten away from her forehead and her open eyes closing at once when the rain touched them. Slowly her lips began to part" (219). The widowed Mrs. Larkin submits to the falling rain as if to a man; it is the ultimate grotesque conversion. Because they have been treated like things, these characters seem to have been reduced to "thinghood," and the grotesque is a protest against their brutalization and abandonment. The grotesque configurations of each physiognomy reveal the price of consciousness.

The grotesque in Eudora Welty's fiction is not nihilistic, for it continually evokes our compassion and affirms the human worth of the individual. Mrs. Larkin's grotesque appearance—her mansized overalls rolled up at the trousers and sleeves, and her wild, uncombed hair—underscores her suffering. The grotesque literally gives way to pathos when she lifts the hoe to strike Jamey: her clumsy sleeves both fall back, "exposing the thin, unsunburned whiteness of her arms, the shocking fact of their youth." Although Miss Welty's use of the grotesque sometimes precludes a sympathetic response, her intentions seem implicitly moral. Like Swift, Miss Welty might say that she hopes "to mend the world" through the grotesque satire of a story like "Petrified Man" or "A Memory." She exaggerates the ugliness of the bathers, isolating and "magnifying" it as a trauma, because she does not want her readers, like the bathers, to be "resigned to [human] ugliness"—to grossness and corruption and hatred.

Notes

1. I am presently undertaking a full-length study of the grotesque in modern literature. The remarks I will have to limit myself to here are intended only as working definitions appropriate to the subject at hand.

2. Classic nineteenth-century American writing abounds in Gothic trappings: the obsessive image of the mirror in Hawthorne's work, the letter *A* written in the heavens in *The Scarlet Letter*, and Chillingworth, who is among other things a version of that Gothic staple, the mad medico; all the supernatural portents of the river world in *Huckleberry Finn*, and the grave robberies throughout Twain's work; the ghosts and gloomy interiors of James's *The Jolly Corner* and *The Turn of the Screw*; in *Moby Dick*, the baptism in blood, the mysterious appearance of the Parsee, Queequeg's coffin, and the flames in the try-works.

3. The most withering pejorative which Vladimir Nabokov can direct at an earlier master of the grotesque, Dostoevsky, is that of "Gothic novelist."

4. Louise Bogan, "The Gothic South," *Nation*, CLIII (December 6, 1941), 572.

5. "New Writer," *Time*, XXXVIII (November 24, 1941), 110.

6. Rose Feld, "New Novels and Short Stories of America," New York *Herald Tribune Books*, November 16, 1941, p. 10.

7. A notably confused passage in Robert E. Spiller, *et al.*, (eds.), *The Literary History of the United States* (New York, 1953), furthers the assumption that all contemporary Southern writers are working in the same "Gothic" vein. See the remarks on the "Mississippi Delta School" in "Postscript at Mid-Century," 1401.

8. Vande Kieft, *Eudora Welty*, 89-90.

9. Welty, "The Reading and Writing of Short Stories," in William Van O'Connor (ed.), *Modern Prose: Form and Style* (New York, 1959), 437.

10. *Ibid.*, 441.

11. Warren, "The Love and Separateness in Miss Welty," 258.

12. Margaret Mitchell, "Notes by the Way," *Nation*, CLXIX (September 10, 1949), 256.

13. Welty, "The Abode of Summer," *Harper's Bazaar*, No. 2887 (June, 1952), 115.

14. "Eudora Welty," *Wilson Library Bulletin*, XVI (February, 1942), 410.

15. See Homer *The Odyssey* xi. 1. 543; trans. Robert Fitzgerald (Garden City, 1961), 214.

16. The bottled twins recall Sherwood Anderson's story "The Egg." As symbols, the twins are analogous to the malformed baby chicks which are similarly bottled and displayed for all to see on a shelf in the restaurant run by the narrator's parents. In both stories, the grotesqueness of the main characters is mirrored in the bottled specimens. Another parallel to "Petrified Man" is found in the macabre comedy of life and death in Charles Dickens' *Martin Chuzzlewit*: "'Which Mr. Chuzzlewit,' said Mrs. Gamp, 'is well-known to Mrs. Harris as has one sweet infant (tho she do not wish it known) in her own family by the mother's side, kep in spirits in a bottle; and that sweet babe she see at Greenwich Fair, a travelling in company with the pink eyed lady Prooshan dwarf, and livin skelinton, which judge her feeling when the barrel organ played and she was showed her own dear sister's child . . .'" (chap. LII). Like Dickens, Miss Welty cannot abide egregious piety toward the dead and toward children; witness Billy Boy and Shirley T. ("Why I Live at the P. O."), and the comedy of Bonnie Dee's death and funeral (*The Ponder Heart*).

17. Porter, Introduction, *Selected Stories of Eudora Welty*, xxi.

18. For a similar usage in literature, see Milton on the Garden of Eden, *Paradise Lost* IV.1.136. Mrs. Larkin's frantic planting may perhaps be seen as a terrifying attempt to duplicate that first garden.

19. See illustrations in William S. Lieberman (ed.), *Max Ernst* (New York, 1961), 32, 38, 39, 40.

20. See the reproductions of paintings by Bacon, de Kooning, and Dubuffet in Peter Selz, *New Images of Man* (New York, 1959).

Works Cited

By Eudora Welty

Books

The Bride of the Innisfallen. New York: Harcourt, Brace, 1955.

A Curtain of Green and Other Stories. Introduction by Katherine Anne Porter. New York: Doubleday, Doran, 1941.

Delta Wedding. New York: Harcourt, Brace, 1946.

The Golden Apples. New York: Harcourt, Brace, 1949.

Music From Spain. Greenville, Miss.: The Levee Press, 1948.

Place in Fiction. New York: House of Books, 1957. Unpaged. An edition limited to three hundred copies signed by the author. Originally published in *South Atlantic Quarterly*, LV (January, 1956), 57-72.

The Ponder Heart. New York: Harcourt, Brace, 1954.

The Robber Bridegroom. New York: Doubleday, Doran, 1942.

The Wide Net and Other Stories. New York: Harcourt, Brace, 1943.

UNCOLLECTED WORK

"The Abode of Summer," *Harper's Bazaar*, No. 2887 (June, 1952), 50, 115.

"The Burning" [first version], in Robert Gorham Davis (ed.), *Ten Modern Masters.* New York: Harcourt, Brace, 1953. Pp. 462-76.

"The Doll," *The Tanager* (Grinnell College, Grinnell, Iowa), XI (June, 1936), 11-14.

"A Flock of Guinea Hens Seen From a Car," *The New Yorker*, XXXIII (April 20, 1957), 35.

"Hello and Good-Bye," *Atlantic Monthly*, CLXXX (July, 1947), 37-40.

"Henry Green. A Novelist of the Imagination," *Texas Quarterly*, IV (Autumn, 1961), 246-56.

"How I Write," *Virginia Quarterly Review*, XXXI (Spring, 1955), 240-51. Reprinted in Cleanth Brooks and Robert Penn Warren (eds.). *Understanding Fiction.* 2nd. ed. New York: Appleton-Century-Crofts, 1959. Pp. 545-53.

"Ida M'Toy," Accent, II (Summer, 1942), 214-22. Reprinted in Joshua McClennen (ed.). *Masters and Masterpieces of the Short Story.* New York: Holt, 1957. Pp. 221-25.

"In Yoknapatawpha," *Hudson Review*, I (Winter, 1949), 596-98. Review of William Faulkner's *Intruder in the Dust.*

"José de Creeft," *Magazine of Art*, XXXVII (February, 1944), 42-47.

"Life's Impact is Oblique," *New York Times Book Review* (April 2, 1961), 5. Review of book on Henry Green.

"Literature and the Lens," *Vogue*, CIV (August 1, 1944), 102-103.

"Pageant of Birds," *New Republic*, CIX (October 25, 1943), 565-67.

"The Reading and Writing of Short Stories," *Atlantic Monthly*, CLXXXII (February, 1949), 54-58, and (March, 1949), 46-49. Reprinted in William Van O'Connor (ed.). *Modern Prose: Form and Style.* New York: Crowell, 1959. Pp. 427-43.

"Retreat," *River*, I (March, 1937), 10-12.

"A Sketching Trip," *Atlantic Monthly*, CLXXV (June, 1945), 62-70.

"Some Notes on River Country," *Harper's Bazaar*, No. 2786 (February, 1944), 85-87, 150-56.

"A Sweet Devouring," *Mademoiselle*, XLVI (December, 1957), 49, 114-16.

"The Teaching and Study of Writing," *Western Review*, XIV (Spring, 1950), 167-68.

"Time and Place—and Suspense," *New York Times Book Review* (June 30, 1963), 5, 27. Review of *The Stories of William Sansom.*

"A Touch That's Magic," *New York Times Book Review* (November 3, 1957), 5. Review of Isak Dineson's *Last Tales.*

"Where Is the Voice Coming From?" *The New Yorker*, XXXIX (July 6, 1963), 24-25.

Max Putzel (essay date fall 1971)

SOURCE: Putzel, Max. "What Is Gothic about *Absalom, Absalom!*" *Southern Literary Journal* 4, no. 1 (fall 1971): 3-19.

[*In the following essay, Putzel presents an overview of* Absalom, Absalom! *examining several gothic elements in the work as techniques used by Faulkner to create a vision of the American past that conveys decay and decline while also providing the reader with a sense of lost greatness.*]

1.

During the second World War, when he was just setting out to build Faulkner's reputation into the national monument it has since become, Malcolm Cowley placed *Absalom, Absalom!* "in the realm of Gothic romances, with Sutpen's Hundred taking the place of the haunted castle on the Rhine, with Colonel Sutpen as Faust and Charles Bon as Manfred."[1] By now one is aware of so many louder literary echoes, so many prototypes and conventions Faulker assimilated into his ambitious novel, that one hesitates to single out the Gothic vein once again. What if Leslie Fiedler does call it "the most gothic of Faulkner's books"? He has found a Goth hiding under the bed of practically every virgin in American literature, and I cannot agree with him that it is the Gothic form "that has been most fruitful in the hands of our best writers."[2]

Rather I tend to share Cleanth Brooks's annoyance when he calls this Faulkner's greatest work and insists it is a great deal more than "Gothic sauce to spice up our preconceptions about the history of American society." He cites as a typical misreading one preface that starts off, "It is a terrible Gothic sequence of events, a brooding tragic fable. . . ."[3]

Undaunted by these strictures critics nevertheless go on using the epithet without defining it or explaining why it seems to them important. Thus Michael Millgate, considering *Absalom* more like *Jane Eyre* than *Moby-Dick*, finds that Faulkner has resumed the Gothic tradition from "European sources," without saying what these are, what they signify, or how Faulkner came by them.[4] As Millgate observes, both Faulkner's and Charlotte Bronte's plots are set in great houses which harbor secret inmates and are set on fire by desperate females, who go up in flames. The *Pequod* and the House of Usher also harbor secret inmates and go down in water, though the *Pequod* is without desperate females. Are these significant likenesses—or distinctions? The question might rather be whether these are stately tragic endings or just melodramatic and contrived. Insofar as they may be "Gothic," is it a virtue or a flaw?

Concluding his essay "Revaluation of the Gothic Novel" with an unusually warped summary of the "diseased and disgusting" world depicted in *Sanctuary*, Robert D. Hume decides it is indeed Gothic, hence "offers no conclusions." "It emphasizes psychological reaction to evil," he writes, "and leads into a tangle of moral ambiguity for which no meaningful answers can be found."[5] To counter such a self-defeating and pointless conclusion one must both redefine the Gothic and give some regard to the corpus of Faulkner's work. For this purpose I think *Absalom* a more promising starting point than *Sanctuary* if only because the segment of Faulkner's world it transects is more comprehensive with respect to human and literary history than *Sanctuary* taken by itself. Here I propose to test Brooks's conclusion and some others against my own reading and to give the Gothic element no more than its due in accounting for the book's triumphs and its shortcomings.

2.

Any examination of a book with such a singular title must pause to consider the relevance of that title to the author's intention. Faulkner could have picked one alluding to the house of Sutpen or even the house of Compson. Just as the title of the favorite earlier work which introduced Quentin recalls the disintegration and despair of Macbeth, so the title of this sequel evokes the anguish of David in his Pyrrhic victory over his rebellious son. In each case the hero's soliloquy summarizes the despair that comes over him as his ambitious career passes in review before his eyes and he sees himself diminished by the punishment it has invited. What distinguishes Sutpen from David is that he founds no line and has no prophet like Nathan to point out the enormity of his transgressions. Starting from humble, country-bred obscurity, both do achieve epic renown. We can believe what Faulkner told his questioners at Charlottesville, that "the old man was himself a little too big for people no greater in stature than Quentin and Miss Rosa and Mr. Compson to see all at once."[6]

To scale him down to the dimensions of a Montoni or Schedoni would render the whole saga trivial. His demonic traits and mysterious origin may be products of Miss Rosa's reading, or simply her ignorance and frustration. The only friend he had, General Compson, was impressed with his innocence. At any rate, Faulkner saw him in a loftier, more compassionate perspective, and the last thing he had in mind was to create another Melmoth. His narrators constantly liken Sutpen not only to David, but often as well to the Homeric Agamemnon and to Bayard, the latter-day French chevalier who was without fear and without reproach. All the analogies are significant and reinforce Ilse Dusoir Lind's recognition that it was Faulkner's intention "to create, through utilization of all the resources of fiction, a grand tragic vision of historic dimension."[7]

The other myths are brought in not because Faulkner means to borrow their plots but rather to suggest connotations that are enriching and mutually revealing. Where Joyce had borrowed a structural plan from the Odyssey and Eugene O'Neill had rifled the Oresteia to find a plot for his Civil War trilogy, Faulkner had a different motive and method. To determine these we have only to look at the structure of *Absalom*.

It falls into two nearly equal parts divided into nine chapters. The first five recount what young Quentin hears from Miss Rosa Coldfield and his father on the afternoon and evening in September 1909 that end with his driving Miss Rosa out to the Sutpen domain and returning, much shaken, to his naked bed. The narrative is reflected in Quentin's bored, half listening, divided consciousness and recollection of previous tedious retellings of the same matter, the mysterious rise and fall of Thomas Sutpen. After meeting Clytemnestra and Henry Sutpen and seeing the witless black Jim Bond that night, Quentin's boredom gives way to avid, anxious concern. Only in the last four chapters do we see why. These amplify the same fable, as Quentin and his

Harvard roommate Shrevlin McCannon try to reconstruct and interpret what Quentin had learned, sitting in their dormitory rooms on a bitter cold night the following January. The mystery has come to have a bearing on Quentin's life. Analogies between *his* heritage and those of Henry Sutpen and his elegant but somehow tainted brother Charles Bon seem to circumscribe and thwart him, so that he has an obsessive need to discover and order the details of a disaster in which he has become an unwilling participant. During the four months that have elapsed he has come to identify first with one, then with all the Sutpen children, black as well as white. Into his conversations with Shreve he has interpolated more information, some of it acquired prior to his séance with Miss Rosa, some of it pieced together subsequently, and an important item of it lying on the study table on an open book between the two boys. It is a letter from his father postmarked Jefferson, Miss., 10 January 1910, reporting Miss Rosa's death following a second visit to Sutpen's Hundred, probably on Christmas Day, which resulted in the firing of the great ruined house and the deaths of Clytie and Henry in the holocaust.[8] The second part of *Absalom* begins with a fragment of that letter and ends a few lines after the rest of that fragment describing the old lady's funeral and speculating on the lasting power of her hatred for her brother-in-law. Chapter seven (the second in part two) introduces crucial information derived from General Compson's reminiscences of Sutpen's own account of his beginnings, how he formed his design, and where it went wrong. It also contains the reflections of Wash Jones, his poor-white tenant, his worshiper, and at last his infuriated murderer. The Jones episode is especially revealing since much of it is retold verbatim from a story Faulkner published two years before the novel. Thus it betrays the germ of the entire myth.[9]

Apart from Bon's letter, one bit of primary evidence, the narrative emerges out of hearsay and garbled recollections, all of them biased by the feelings of the narrators, yet all tending to magnify its central character. Sutpen's domain of a hundred square miles of virgin wilderness is really too big to fit within the county, just as he himself is too big for the community. Memory might well be called the theme of the book—not just the fallible memory of mankind reverberating with historic facts beclouded and expanded into myths that impose their imperative on each generation as it looks back through the eye or listens through the ear of the gossiping eye witness, the historian, the skald—down the corridors of time. The past is alive, the present dying in this fable with so brief a present and no discernible future. No Solomon, Orestes or Fortinbras will enter to pick up the pieces.

So the symbolic pattern is more important than the literal or the chronological and impregnates the structure. It is here that we should expect to find the Gothic elements. The first half of the book is saturated with the heat and odors of subtropical summer, the second being distanced, "attenuated" by the iron cold of a Massachusetts winter. There is constant interplay, one set of symbols implying life in death, the other death in life, and there is ghostly interplay also between the living dead and the feebly living. To Quentin on his way to Harvard in 1909 the South is "dead since 1865 and peopled with garrulous outraged baffled ghosts" (p. 9).[10] But the apparitions here belong in nature, not in the supernatural purlieus of Gothic novels. The paralyzing effect on Quentin and us of their unexplained acts, beliefs, and delusions is the more terrifying for their natural reality. The same misremembered past impinges on us as on Quentin. At the outset "still too young to be a ghost" (9), only four months later he tells Shreve he is "older at twenty than a lot of people who have died" (377).

However we try to dissociate this book from *The Sound and the Fury* we cannot forget that Quentin will be dead, too, within months. Faulkner makes no mention of his suicide when he dates the boy's death in his appendix. But the time symbols which obtrude from the first sentence of *Absalom* ("From a little after two o'clock until almost sundown . . .") ominously recall those of the author's favorite earlier work. As *Absalom* ends we hear the chimes in Harvard Yard dying away "into the icy air delicate and faint and musical as struck glass" (374) and recall Quentin shattering the crystal of his father's watch and breaking off its hands as the spring semester ends. Symbols of time mate with symbols of death, latticed yellow slashes of sun on dust motes like dead old paint, the coffin-smelling gloom inside Miss Rosa's house mixing with the perfume of twice-blooming wisteria, the wisteria recalling the summer of 1859 and anticipating the imagined remembrance of that odor Quentin sniffs when the letter reaches him in Cambridge fifty years later. So much could be said of those heady symbols, blending the past into the present, none remotely Gothic. Most eloquent of all is the scythe rusting beside Wash Jones's door ready to his hand when, in a moment of shattering recognition, he reaches for it to kill his master. The image of Wash brandishing that weapon of Time personified, reeling to his own death at the hands of the posse, is carried over from the short story, whence even this crazy tableau is overshadowed by that of the man on horseback, finally arrested by the scythe.

Here at last we come to what is Gothic in Faulkner. Medieval chivalry bulks large in every retelling of Sutpen's story as it did in the imagery of *Sartoris* before and would in *The Unvanquished*, right after *Absalom*. Miss Rosa can hardly think of her brother-in-law and his insulting offer of a trial marriage, apart from his horse. For her he is "Man-horse-demon," and she makes Quentin visualize him in statuesque tableau: "Immobile, bearded and hand palm-lifted the horseman sat . . ."—

which Quentin likens to Jehovah the Creator. Sutpen had first appeared in 1833 "with a horse and two pistols and a name nobody ever heard before" (14) and later turned his wife's drive to church each Sunday into a horse race and wrestled half naked with his slaves in a stable. When Rosa's sister, his wife Ellen, rushes in to reclaim her children a spectator mistakes her for a horse. Mr. Compson likewise visualizes Sutpen materializing "on a big hard-ridden roan horse, man and beast looking as if they had been created out of thin air" (32), and always reappearing on the roan till he rides off to war beside Colonel Sartoris "on the black stallion named out of Scott" (80)—named Rob Roy in the story "Wash." Quentin's grandfather General Compson likewise remembered his horsemanship, recalling how he would canter round a sapling with those two pistols "and put both bullets into a playing card fastened to the tree" (33), so that all these centaur images become etched on Quentin's mind. Driving Miss Rosa out to Sutpen's Hundred he fancies he "might even hear the galloping hoofs; might even see at any moment now the black stallion and the rider rush across the road before them and gallop on . . ." (363).

Such emblems serve to identify Sutpen with the chivalric culture he has tried to emulate. The living reality of the tradition is a far cry from the "old headless horseman Ichabod Crane" Eula Varner invokes to rescue her from the lecherous schoolmaster. Sutpen's stallion has the smell and snort of a real horse, unlike the black charger of Poe's "Metzengerstein" or Til Eulenspiegel's steed whose hoofprint one fingered on the parapet of a castle one visited as a child. In the fumbling imagination of his happy worshiper Wash Jones, Thomas Sutpen is indeed a god, a very Christ. Wash thinks him capable of miracles and cheerfully offers up his granddaughter Milly as a human sacrifice to the "proud galloping image" passing across the years "without weariness or progress, forever and forever immortal beneath the brandished saber and the shot-torn flags rushing down a sky in color like thunder" after tasting of "the bitter cup in the Book" which the Yankees held to his lips (287-88). The vision derives word for word from the short story and so does the instant shattering of the godhead. Milly bears Sutpen a daughter and Wash overhears Sutpen liken mother and girl child with contemptuous disparagement to the mare which that morning had dropped a male foal. It is Sutpen's unconscious, bestial contempt for humanity that unmasks him, demolishing instantly Wash's faith in him whose condescension had bestowed dignity and a spark of hope on his drab life. What Sutpen's words have blasted is belief not only in Sutpen himself but in all "the gallant, the proud, the brave; the acknowledged and chosen best among them all" (290). At this Wash sees "his whole life shredded from him and shrivel away like a dried shuck thrown into the fire" (290-91)—and takes his revenge.

3.

In one sense *Absalom* is a meditation on memory, the historical imperative that narrows the bounds of human aspiration and choice, behaving like captious Fate. Time has run out for chivalry, and what brushes the scales from Wash's eyes is part of a collective insight telling his whole generation and kind that the day of knights, damsels, vassals and slaves is ended. The day of Wash ends, too, but the day of the Snopes is at hand. Similarly Quentin penetrating the mysteries of the past can now sense the indignities Sutpen and his like have heaped on their descendants, black as well as white. It is an insight Faulkner himself achieved between writing *The Sound and the Fury* and conceiving *Absalom*. In the first Quentin goes home for Christmas, and in Virginia his railside exchange of banter with a country Negro on a mule tells him, "You are home again." In *Absalom* he can't go home again but he can read and remember Clytie and Jim Bond—and Bon. The scales have fallen from his eyes, too.

Conspiring with history-as-fate, Sutpen's moral blindness or insensitivity derives from a weakness like David's, perhaps inseparable from the heroic genius. He can feel compassion only for his own bewildered boyhood self, and so conspires in his own destruction and that of his line. Just as David's crime against Uriah and Bathsheba led his son Ammon to debauch Absalom's sister, led Absalom to rebel, and possibly led Joab to defy the King and murder Absalom, so Sutpen's crimes against his wives and slaves lead his children into crimes against one another. And so Wash is led to ignore his last command: "Stand back, Wash."

"I am telling the same story over and over, which is myself and the world," Faulkner told Cowley in a letter about *Absalom*. The moving things being "eternal in man's history," he is forever "trying to put all mankind's history in one sentence." Rightly understood that letter explains many traits including some evident defects in his style.[11] The intent to horrify in the manner of "Monk" Lewis, to mystify and explain in the manner of Mrs. Radcliffe, to berate human folly in the ranting manner of Maturin is not among them.

But in another sense *Absalom* discusses the three separate literary traditions that produced it. It was no accident that Sutpen's stallion was "named out of Scott" for Sutpen must have read *Rob Roy*. Each version of his story is couched in a separate literary manner. Miss Rosa's fevered vision of her maidenly dignity menaced by a demon is conveyed in the overheated rhetoric of a "poetess laureate" who doubtless borrowed from Scott and Shelley, perhaps too from Maturin. Mr. Compson echoes phrases culled from the *Yellow Book, Reedy's Mirror*, and the like. Handing Quentin Charles Bon's letter to Judith, he hazards the opinion Bon had loved her "after his fashion" (108). He visualizes Bon's mistress visiting his grave as "a garden scene by the Irish poet, Wilde" illustrated by "the artist Beardsley," the lady ("in a soft flowing gown designed . . . to dress some interlude of slumbrous and fatal insatiation,") followed by a "bright gigantic negress carrying a silk cushion and leading by the hand the little boy Beardsley might not only have dressed but drawn" (193). Similarly, as the two boys at Harvard seek to edit the saga, the mocking voice of Shreve recalls Buck Mulligan baiting the embittered idealist Stephen Dedalus. Shreve, a plump sentimentalist like Buck, piles up Pre-Raphaelite visions of chivalry in the South, "because it's something my people haven't got. Or if we have it, it all happened long ago across the water" (361). Imagining Judith awaiting her brother and lover returning from the war, "Jesus," Shreve exclaims, "who to know what she saw . . . what prayer, what maiden dream ridden up out of whatever fabulous land . . . the silken and tragic Lancelot" (320). Cynical or sentimental, he always gets things slightly skewed.

If all these voices do not emerge in the distinct accents of Gothic or romance, decadence or naturalism, it is because all are filtered through the troubled consciousness of Quentin. Just as we have to depend on Mr. Compson's recollection for the accents of General Compson and Wash, so we receive his own and Miss Rosa's reminiscences through Quentin's divided awareness, first doped by heat and boredom, later frozen with perplexity as the wrecked lives of Sutpen's children merge with his own unspoken anguish. Thus the style tends to monotony, and there is a trace of justice in Clifton Fadiman's scathing remark that "everybody talks the same language, a kind of Dixie Gongorism."[12] The rhetorical excesses of the narrators are blurred by Quentin's confused desires, incestuous fancies, perhaps even by an impulse to love yet detest his brother; who knows what all?

Which elements then are Gothic? Certainly Miss Rosa's idea of Sutpen as demonic knight and satanic upstart. Her "light-blinded bat-like image of his own torment" (171) may mimic the verbose diatribes of Maturin or Shelley—or Lewis, who influenced both. "Pure Gothic nonsense," John Lewis Longley rightly calls her spate of words.[13] Both the emblematic horseman and the recurrence of allusions to ancient French style and manner—to Bayard and Carcassonne—link this legend to the medieval past. One recalls Faulkner accepting the rosette of the Legion of Honor "*avec humilité*" and knows what it signifies to lure a French architect, even to kidnap one, to build one's mansion. It may not be a Gothic mansion, but its ruined state connotes awe and perhaps deep nostalgia for a Gothic past. And what of terror?

4.

One effect of all the several Gothic revivals was to domesticate the past and make it uniquely our own—whatever ownership might claim it. In England and then in Germany that past was felt to be distinct from the mysterious lost perfection of Greece or Rome. Its crumbling, ivied ruins betokened authority overcome and mouldering decay, lost greatness and failing powers. I think that Faulkner's impression of his American past is an accelerated panorama of similar decay and decline. He sees Southern chivalry as a belated but genuine survival of medieval values and faith. It arose as the product of a noble dream and perished in the nightmare of civil war, victim of mercenary force and sterile philistinism. There is a dreamlike quality to the sequence of disclosure in *Absalom*. We perceive through the medium of Quentin's meandering, helpless search—the dreamer's agony in bondage to that with which he has no strength to cope.

The spiral movement in *Absalom* is one of relentless acceleration and mounting excitement and suspense. The book moves at first with deadly, clockwise slowness around the periphery of its legend. Quentin's reluctance to accompany Miss Rosa to Sutpen's Hundred is akin to his boredom with her chatter, yet also edged with dread. Her theory that there was a "fatality and a curse" on her family and the South has to be as heavily discounted as any other part of her indignation. It is absurd to think that her pious shopkeeper father (whatever her grounds for despising him) deserves affliction at the hands of a Sutpen who is less man than demon. To call her veracity in question is not, however, to imply that her delusions carry no weight in the society to which she belongs. Her very detachment from reality is a part of Quentin's reality, for it brackets her with his mother as she appears in *The Sound and the Fury*. She is in fact a surrogate for that self-centered neurotic. In his penetrating interpretation of *The Sound and the Fury* Brooks explains in detail how Mrs. Compson's inadequacies led to the disintegration of her husband and children. She supplies the essential ingredient for understanding Mr. Compson's cynical alcoholism, Jason's harsh materialism, Caddy's promiscuity, and the incestuous yearnings that led to Quentin's suicide.[14] In *Absalom* Miss Rosa's tiresome complaints and fevered accusations echo his mother and mobilize in Quentin the same confused feelings. Pondering the imagined sacrifice Henry Sutpen had made to save his sister's and his family's honor, Quentin could hardly fail to recall the humiliation he had felt that very summer on learning that one of her lovers had got Caddy with child and on finding himself helpless to take revenge on Dalton Ames. Nothing of the sort is mentioned in *Absalom*, yet the repressed memories are dramatized in his hypothetical reconstruction of the Sutpen story.

On the drive out to Sutpen's place Quentin's attention drifts off until suddenly arrested by Miss Rosa's fury on recalling the news of Thomas Sutpen's death. "'Dead?' I cried. 'Dead? You? You lie; you're not dead . . .' But Quentin was not listening, because there was something which he too could not pass—that door, the running feet on the stairs . . ." (172). Quentin is not thinking of Sutpen's death but of Charles Bon's. He is imagining Henry bringing Judith word that he has killed Bon so soon after she at last received Bon's offer of marriage. From this point on he reads into the account of that tragedy tacit feelings about his hypochondriac mother, who arranged Caddy's impending marriage. We next hear Shreve's voice four months later, mimicking Miss Rosa, and we learn no more of Quentin's visit to Sutpen's Hundred until the end of that January evening.

Meanwhile, if Quentin is to discover what brought about the tragedy which so poignantly recalls his own loss and defeat he must summon up all he knows about Thomas Sutpen. Meditating while Shreve prattles, he recalls the Sutpen graveyard, where he and his father once paused to wait out a shower while quail hunting. Contemplating the extravagance of those tombstones, two imported from Italy midway through the war and three that Judith bought with the pitiful remains of her father's wealth, Mr. Compson muses on the "beautiful lives" women lead. The elaborate make-believe practiced by all these ladies serves to intensify the horror and savagery of the world inhabited by their men. Faulkner's insight into the grotesquely sex-divided world of men and women is strikingly like Joseph Conrad's, and what follows is reminiscent of *Heart of Darkness* and the sanctimonious gentility Marlow attributes to the two ladies—his aunt and Kurtz's Intended in the "Sepulchral City"—both scrupulously shielded from all knowledge of the blackened lives of white men in the jungle.[15]

"Yes," says Mr. Compson. "They lead beautiful lives—women. Lives not only divorced from, but irrevocably excommunicated from, all reality" (191). An episode in Sutpen's education to which too little attention has been paid is the reality of Haiti, which becomes the heart of Quentin's darkness as he relates it to the spectre of unending injustice and suffering he met face to face on his visit to the rotting gray mansion.

Born in the primitive mountain fastness of western Virginia, Sutpen had discovered the American caste system only when his family moved to the Tidewater plantation country. After a traumatic confrontation with the liveried black servant of a planter helped him formulate a scheme to avenge this boyhood humiliation, Sutpen made his way to Haiti, where he learned French and Creole, made his first fortune, and married the woman who would become Charles Bon's mother.

The year Faulkner published "Wash" Haiti was cut loose after twenty years' occupation by the United States Marine Corps. This event brought to mind its long history of genocide: how the island first found and ruled by Columbus languished under Spanish misrule, the entire Indian population of 300,000 being exterminated in the first century; how the French after acquiring it by treaty brought in black slaves to make it prosper through the earlier eighteenth century, until the Revolution inspired the blacks to rise up and exterminate the whole white population. That reign of terror in Haiti had been conducted with a mutual barbarity beside which the bloody events in Paris shone in morning innocence. A yellow fever epidemic and three gifted black rulers helped keep Napoleon from realizing his projected conquest of North America from that base, but all three died violently, and the land was plunged again in racial turmoil. There were no more white inhabitants when Sutpen came, though a few French business men were allowed to stop there, officially and privately despoiled, and covertly encouraged to beget bastards whose skin would be lighter than their mothers'. The palest of Haiti's colored people, according to a trustworthy account written about the time of Sutpen's arrival, "having but an untraceable tinge of African blood . . . were uproariously indignant if . . . accused of having any at all."[16]

Sutpen was innocent in the sense of being uninitiated in the ways of Grandfather Compson's world. He was innocent indeed by the standards of Haiti—

> a spot of earth which might have been created and set aside by Heaven itself, Grandfather said, as a theater for violence and injustice and bloodshed and all the satanic lusts of human greed and cruelty, for the last despairing fury of all the pariah-interdict and all the doomed—a little island set in a smiling and fury-lurked and incredible indigo sea, which was the halfway point between what we call the jungle and what we call civilization, halfway between the dark inscrutable continent from which the black blood, the black bones and flesh and thinking and remembering and hopes and desires, was ravished by violence, and the cold known land to which it was doomed. . . . And he overseeing it, riding peacefully about on his horse, . . . not knowing that what he rode upon was a volcano, hearing the air tremble and throb at night with the drums and the chanting and not knowing that it was the heart of the earth itself he heard, who believed (Grandfather said) that earth was kind and gentle and that darkness was merely something you saw, or could not see in . . .
>
> (250-51)

Sutpen married and put aside his wife in a land where polygamy was commonplace but where marriage of any kind was the exception rather than the rule. It was a land where sadistic tyranny seemed the only alternative to violent anarchy.

It is the insights into Sutpen's experience that derive solely from the reminiscences of General Compson and the conjectured musings of Wash Jones that bring Quentin to some appreciation of the quality of Sutpen's tragedy. We, too, come to understand as he acts to avenge himself the baffled little boy turned away from the mansion door by the haughty black servant. We understand how such conditioning could teach the man to turn away the tainted, almost forgotten son who comes to his own door to be recognized. But the concluding chapter coming after these disclosures conveys a new sense of desolation and horror.

It is one thing to encounter a tragic hero in fable or history, quite another to walk into his house and meet his victims face to face, to touch one of them, picking her up "like a handful of sticks concealed in a rag bundle, so light she was" (370), addressing the other in the shuttered bedroom where he lay, "the wasted yellow face with closed almost transparent eyelids on the pillow, the wasted hands crossed on the breast as if he were already a corpse . . ." (373). It is with more than a delicate shudder that one forces oneself to realize one has participated in the catastrophe of a great tragedy, been an accomplice before the fact to the last deed of malice visited on the children and the children's children of the hero, that one has ridden with the Eumenides. The old house Quentin sees so briefly seems "to reek in slow and protracted violence with a smell of desolation and decap as if the mood of which it was built were flesh" (366). Now it goes up in smoke and flame and Quentin sees the face at the window, hears the bellows of a human voice, the two fellow creatures burning alive, the hapless orphan orphaned once again. These are no ghosts to fear but pitiful victims, known by their timeless suffering.

If the Gothic tale is intended to make us shiver deliciously at some imagined horror, that is certainly not what we feel as Quentin lies shaking bone-chilled in his dormitory bed. What we do share peering with him into the inscrutable darkness of the past is a most frightening vision of humanity. But we get it in wandering after-image, in remembered sights, and in overheard whispers. We get no facts about his meeting with Henry or even most of the words of his father's letter. Quentin's incoherent nightmare has become our own, constantly broken in on by Shreve's sardonic and willful misunderstanding, the voice of sophomoric realism that will not be still, which finally almost by accident puts into words the half-said thing that has lurked all along behind the troubled dream: "I think in time the Jim Bonds are going to conquer the western hemisphere" (378). It is a cryptic prophecy like Benito Cereno's last words: "The Negro." When Shreve goes on to accuse Quentin of hating the South, he has fallen once more into error. Led into the heart of the South's darkness by Miss Rosa tottering after her revenge on Sutpen, Quentin has seen unrolled the endless scroll of man's injustice and folly and the compounding of these not in the South only, but in the whole fabric of the misremembered past. Himself a victim and an heir, he can neither love nor hate. He can only revert to his fearless passion for extinction—he who loved death best of all.

Surely Quentin's terror is not of Germany, but of the soul.

Notes

1. "William Faulkner's Legend of the South," *Sewanee Review*, LIII (Summer 1945), 343-61, especially p. 348. While Cowley made the suggestion, its context is important. The following sentence reads, "Then slowly it dawns on you that most of the characters and incidents have a double meaning; that besides their place in the story, they also serve as symbols or metaphors with a general application." Reviewing *The Hamlet* five years earlier, Cowley had compared Faulkner's books to "Gothic ruins, impressive only by moonlight," an error he now sought to correct.

2. *Love and Death in the American Novel*. (New York: Criterion Books, 1960), p. 325 and p. xxiii, respectively. See also pp. 395-98 and 443-45.

3. *William Faulkner: The Yoknapatawpha Country* (New Haven and London: Yale Univ. Press, 1963), pp. 295-96. The cited passage is from Harvey Breit's introduction to the 1953 Modern Library edition.

4. *The Achievement of William Faulkner* (London: Constable, 1966), pp. 162-63.

5. "Gothic Versus Romantic: A Revaluation of the Gothic Novel," *PMLA*, LXXXIV (1969), 282-90, especially, p. 288. See also, Robert L. Platzner, "'Gothic Versus Romantic': A Rejoinder," *PMLA*, LXXXVI (1971), 286-88.

6. Frederick L. Gwynn and Joseph L. Blotner, eds., *Faulkner in the University* (Charlottesville: Univ. of Virginia Press, 1959), p. 274.

7. "The Design and Meaning of *Absalom, Absalom!*" in Frederick J. Hoffman and Olga Vickery, eds. *William Faulkner: Three Decades of Criticism* (N.p.: Michigan State Univ. Press, 1960), p. 278. Reprinted from *PMLA* LXX (December 1955), pp. 887-912.

8. The discrepancy between the facts given in *The Sound and the Fury* and *Absalom, Absalom!* should be noted, though one need attach no great significance to it. In the earlier novel Quentin travels by train to Jefferson for his Christmas holidays, while in the later novel he could not have done so without being aware of the burning of Sutpen's Hundred and the fatal illness of Miss Rosa which ensued. In *Absalom* Faulkner does not

quite preclude the possibility of such a trip, but skirts the facts in accordance with a clear artistic purpose, to concentrate attention on the Sutpen plot and omit the Compson one.

9. "Wash: A Story," *Harper's*, CLXVII (February 1934), 258-66, was not the first germ of *Absalom* but marked its transition from a modern to an historic setting. The genesis of Sutpen's design as of Popeye will be found in the unpublished short story "The Big Shot," which obviously antedates the first setting copy of *Sanctuary*, May 1929. See typescript, Box 25, Ser. II B, item 2, at University of Virginia, Charlottesville, and Millgate, *Achievement of William Faulkner*, pp. 159-61.

10. This and subsequent citations are taken from The Modern Library edition (New York: Random House, 1951), and page references are given parenthetically.

11. Faulkner to Cowley, early November, 1944. See Malcolm Cowley, *The Faulkner-Cowley File* (London: Chatto & Windus, 1966), pp. 14-17.

12. "Faulkner, Extra-Special, Double-Distilled," condensed from *The New Yorker*, October 31, 1936, in *Faulkner: A Collection of Critical Essays*, ed. Robert Penn Warren, in Twentieth Century Views. (Englewood Cliffs, N. J.: Prentice-Hall, 1966), p. 289.

13. *The Tragic Mask: A Study of Faulkner's Heroes* (Chapel Hill: Univ. of North Carolina Press, 1963), pp. 210-11, and cf. p. 217, where he speaks of Miss Rosa's "absurd Gothic demonism."

14. Brooks, *Yoknapatawpha Country*, pp. 333-42. On p. 341 he concludes that "the downfall of the house of Compson is the kind of degeneration which can occur, and has occurred, anywhere at any time."

15. For an inspired discussion of the similarities between Conrad's and Faulkner's attitudes and the fundamental differences in their ethics see Joseph X. Brennan and Seymour L. Gross, "The Problem of Moral Values in Conrad and Faulkner," *The Personalist*, 41 (Winter 1960), pp. 60-70. In *The Limits of Metaphor: A Study of Melville, Conrad, and Faulkner* (Ithaca: Cornell Univ. Press, 1967), James Guetti makes a detailed study of stylistic elements, the struggle between language and the ineffable, with reference mainly to *Moby-Dick*, "Heart of Darkness," and *Absalom*.

16. My impressionistic thumbnail sketch of those aspects of Haiti's social history to which Faulkner makes no direct reference or specific allusion derives from a pioneer socio-historic study, James G. Leyburn, *The Haitian People* (New Haven: Yale Univ. Press, 1941), which sums up all data that could have been available to Faulkner. Leyburn quotes on p. 82 from Dr. Jonathan Brown's *The History and Present Condition of St. Domingo*, (Philadelphia, 1837), which Leyburn praises in his annotated bibliography.

Bill Christophersen (essay date summer 1982)

SOURCE: Christophersen, Bill. "'Jean-ah Poquelin': Cable's Place in Southern Gothic." *South Dakota Review* 20, no. 2 (summer 1982): 55-66.

[*In the following essay, Christophersen praises Cable for the success with which he appropriates the English gothic tradition to an American landscape, noting that he grounds the grotesquery of his story in the realism of the socio-economic reality of his country.*]

Ernest Stone, in his article entitled "Usher, Poquelin, Miss Emily: The Progress of Southern Gothic,"[1] renders a previous comparison between Poe's "The Fall of the House of Usher" and Faulkner's "A Rose For Emily"[2] suddenly meaningful by broadening it to include George W. Cable's story "Jean-ah Poquelin." Faulkner's story, by virtue of its plot alone, resembles Cable's story much more than it does Poe's. Cable's story and Faulkner's are, in fact, suspiciously similar.[3] Stone compares the two in detail, noting, finally, that both stories present

> . . . a central conflict between a proud and doomed, but indomitable last representative of an important family of a bygone era of the South and the progress of an encroaching and usurping civilization. Both Emily Grierson and Jean Marie Poquelin perpetuate their pristine importance by immuring themselves in a massive, impregnable, outmoded house; and both successfully and secretly conceal in that house until their death a human ghoul who is all that is left to them, the success of concealment itself recording the triumph of a figure whom time and progress have otherwise relegated to ridiculousness.[4]

For Stone, however, the parallels disappear beyond the boundaries of plot and approximate characterization.

While not wishing to dispute Faulkner's masterpiece, I believe the two stories share more than a common plot structure and range of characters. Furthermore, I think Stone exaggerates the gap between the fictional mentalities of Cable and Faulkner even as he fails to appreciate the considerable gulf in orientation between Cable and Poe—all to Cable's detriment. I believe the "characteristic modernity" Stone sees as distinguishing Faulkner from his predecessors is too protean and ambiguous a criterion for differentiation. My sympathies lie with the critic who contends that "[Cable's] subject matter, his attitudes, and his method look forward to the literary renascence of the twentieth century."[5]

Stone begins with the cogent observation that "unlike 'Usher,' Cable's and Faulkner's are stories not only of horror, but everywhere of time and place." This observation, which touches on one of Cable's important contributions, might well have served to extenuate Cable's achievement. Stone, however, forfeits the implications of his insight: he finds this time and place orientation important only in justifying the tone and the plot, which concerns the expropriation of an old Creole's land by the first influx of Americans into Louisiana. Stone writes:

> . . . merely a decade or two later, during the flood of immigration into New Orleans, Poquelin's interview with the governor would have been pathetic, rather than dramatic; and even a decade earlier, there would have been no need for it (the purchase of Louisiana in 1803 being ultimately responsible for Poquelin's desperate situation).[6]

Continuing his comparison between Poe's fiction and Cable's, Stone writes: "What distinguishes 'Jean-ah Poquelin' from the works of Poe and his Germanic predecessors is the successful mixture with Gothicism of truly local color and characterization."[7] The superficial appeal of local color, however, constitutes relatively small merit in and of itself. To relegate Cable's importance to the realm of local color, or to see him simply as one who ornamented the somber tone of the Gothic with a touch of the quaint or exotic is to overlook the ways in which he transcends the limits of 'local color,' and, finally, to overlook his more crucial contribution to the Gothic romance: namely, his Americanization of the genre.

Leslie Fiedler, in *Love and Death in the American Novel,* traces the development of the Gothic from its roots in the European novel, focusing on the socio-historical tradition out of which the Gothic novel sprung—a tradition which, serving ostensibly as backdrop, actually renders the tale significant. This tradition is embodied, typically, in the decaying castle or abbey. "Symbols of authority," writes Fiedler, "secular or ecclesiastic, in ruin—memorials of a decaying past—such crumbling edifices project the world of collapsed ego-ideals through which . . . man was groping his terrified way."[8]

One often-remarked problem faced by early American authors was the absence of an identifiable past, a ground against which our literature could be set. Those who chose the Gothic mode generally borrowed the European historical context as well, or else wrested the Gothic props and figures from their context altogether. Thus Charles Brockden Brown, in *Wieland,* imports not only his setting and accoutrements of horror, but also his characters and, more significantly, their original crimes and inherited guilts from Europe.[9] Poe, on the other hand, concerned exclusively with the individual's emotions, tends to borrow the texture of horror and rarefy the context almost out of existence. Even Poe, however, on those occasions when referents of time and place become necessary to his tale, has recourse, either implicitly or explicitly, to medieval Europe. Thus "The Fall of the House of Usher" derives from "remote feudal times," and is situated, by implication, somewhere in Europe.

Cable, on the contrary, takes great pains to set his tale, both socially and historically, in America.[10] The "old, colonial plantation house, half in ruin"[11] embodies a social system—colonial aristocracy—and a past which, at the time of the story, is still in the process of disintegrating. This disintegration must have been only the more widespread in the decades following the Civil War, during which Cable penned most of his stories. Furthermore, the memory of this disintegration lingers, on a still wider scale, in the American South of the early twentieth century—the time during which Faulkner's story is set.

Here, then, is Cable's first and, perhaps, most important contribution to the Gothic genre: he has appropriated it to the Southern milieu and made it reflect the traumas of a changing American South. Cable has rendered Poe's distilled horror as the outgrowth of a particular socio-historical situation. This socio-historical ground, in turn, fertilizes the tale, invests it with meaning. Cable has, in short—and this is the significance Stone overlooks—transplanted Poe's ethereal flower to appropriate native soil, securing for it an environment in which it can bloom to full potential.

Cable's tale transpires during the time "when the Anglo-American flood that was presently to burst in a crevasse of immigration upon the delta had thus far been felt only as slippery seepage which made the Creole tremble for his footing." Cable goes on to describe the plantation house half in ruin, which "stood aloft from civilization, the tracts that had once been its indigo fields given over to their first noxious wildness, and grown up into one of the horridest marshes within a circuit of fifty miles."[12] Cable thus sets his story at a time in which the Creole aristocracy, having propagated itself for years in a virtual vacuum, isolated from the inroads of civilization,[13] is suddenly beginning to crumble.

The house, we are told, is "grim, solid, and spiritless, its massive build a strong reminder of days still earlier, when every man had been his own peace officer and the insurrection of the blacks a daily contingency." It looks "like a giant ammunition wagon stuck in the mud and abandoned by some retreating army."[14] This further characterization of the mansion suggests a crucial sub-theme and source of guilt in the story—the blight of slavery. Cable's simile, meanwhile, depicts a beleaguered class, already a relic in its own time, brought to a halt, though not yet disarmed and dismantled.[15]

In his portrait of a Creole mansion housing two surviving half-brothers and their sole remaining manservant, Cable captures the ambience of the traditional South: an inbred, patriarchal plantation aristocracy, built on and haunted by a racist ethic, besieged by civilization and democracy, and, ultimately, defeated—as much by its own intransigence as by external forces. Faulkner employs this same myth later on in "A Rose For Emily," embodying it tacitly in the mansion and personalizing it in Emily Grierson herself. Perhaps Faulkner's most deft depiction of this passing patriarchal aristocracy occurs in the tableau the narrator imagines, in which Emily's father occupies the foreground, holding a horsewhip, and Emily is "a slender figure in white in the background," the two framed by the mansion's door.[16]

"For the most striking evidence," continues Stone, "of the wide gulf that yawns between Faulkner and his Southern precursor Cable in horror fiction, . . . we must turn to the relationships of the two protagonists with their own dead (or living dead) . . ." Stone finds the relationship in "Jean-ah Poquelin" to be, in a word, "conventional."[17] This relationship is crucial to the story and bears closer scrutiny.

Cable's tale involves two men, Jean Marie Poquelin and Jacque Poquelin. Jacques is "the gentle, young half-brother, more than thirty years his [Jean's] junior." The two half-brothers are united, however, by a bond which exceeds ordinary fraternal or even paternal affection:

> There was no trait in Jean Marie Poquelin, said the old gossips, for which he was so well known among his few friends as his apparent fondness for his "little brother." "Jacques said this" and "Jacques said that"; he "would leave this or that or anything to Jacques," for "Jacques was a scholar," and "Jacques was good," or "wise," or "just," or "far-sighted."

"They had seemed to live so happily in each other's love," we are told. "No father, mother, wife to either . . ."[18]

Their kinship notwithstanding, the two half-brothers suggest a classic homosexual pair. In addition to their complementary personalities (Jean is a "bold, frank, impetuous, chivalric adventurer," Jacques a "gentle, studious, book-loving recluse"), the two exhibit an inordinate dependence on each other, Jean deferring habitually to Jacques' judgment (in absentia, of course), and Jacques cleaving to Jean like a wife, resolving to go with Jean rather than suffer his absence when Jean proposes a voyage to Africa. In this latter scene, Cable's language infuses the relationship with an almost desperate tenor:

> Jacques had begged him hard for many days not to go, but he laughed him off, and finally said, kissing him: "Adieu, 'tit frere." . . . "No," said Jacques, "I shall go with you."[19]

In light of an earlier remark concerning Jean's "circle of exclusively male acquaintances,"[20] we are tempted to read significance into the man's name itself, Jean *Marie* Poquelin.[21] Cable's imagery reinforces the ambiguous nature of the relationship: "They lived upon the ancestral estate," we are told, "like mated birds, one always on the wing, the other always in the nest."[22]

This relationship scarcely seems "conventional." It is, on the contrary, a highly idiosyncratic portrayal that captures the inbred and isolated nature of this patriarchy whose survivors cleave to each other for emotional sustenance as their tradition becomes increasingly obsolete. If the characterization carries overtones of perversity, it can and should be seen as the reflection of a social situation (the anomalous persistence of colonial aristocracy) that, no doubt, had come to seem unnatural and perverse. Faulkner, of course, uses an elaborately perverse relationship—Emily's necrophilic attachment to Homer Barron—to dramatize his protagonist's peculiar plight.

Cable's male relationship is rendered even more significant by the story's racial overtones. Jean Poquelin is a slaver and slavetrader. Having gambled his slaves away one by one, the "generous gentleman" goes off in search of "larger profits in the African slave trade."[23] It is in light of this fact that his half-brother's fate assumes the proportions of poetic justice: the trip to Africa that was to result in a livelihood for Jean bequeaths upon Jacques a fate worse than death; an enterprise calculated to result in profits from black skin nets, instead, a devastating personal loss, dramatized by the snow-white skin of Jacques, the leper. Cable has created a myth in which, figuratively speaking, the sins of the father are visited on the son (remembering that the brothers are a full thirty years apart). This myth has obvious relevance for the post-war South, and it recurs, though the emphasis is modified, in Faulkner's portrait of Miss Emily.[24]

Even considering these aspects, I'm still not sure the depths of Cable's portrait have been plumbed. Fiedler contends that incest is the archetypal erotic theme of the American Gothic romance, even as slavery is its archetypal sociological concern.[25] Cable's portrait of two half-brothers who love each other exclusively and who live together "like mated birds" may well constitute an incest theme within a patriarchal context—thereby adding an element of decadence to the portrait and introducing, incidentally, a strange hybrid of the more familiar Gothic motif of brother-sister incest.

Much of Stone's dissatisfaction with "Jean-ah Poquelin" stems from his perceiving it as melodrama. Whether or not the story is melodrama is a moot question. Cable does indulge in melodrama in certain other stories in *Old Creole Days*, most notably in "Belles Demoiselles Plantation,"[26] in which an entire mansion collapses into the Mississippi River, killing seven frolicking girls within. However, at least one critic finds "Jean-ah Poquelin" a notable exception to this tendency.[27]

For Stone, the term "melodrama" seems to connote, in particular, a tendency toward one-dimensional characterization and subjective narration. He points out that, in Cable's story, "primarily and consistently we sympathize with Poquelin and his heroic, if baffling, resistance . . ." and contrasts Cable with Faulkner, who "impassively maintains his (and our) distance, sympathizing with and reproving, in turn, Emily and her adversary, the town."[28]

If Cable's attitude was so blatantly sympathetic toward his characters, why, we must ask, did the Creole population so disclaim the protagonist?[29] Cable's characterization is, I think, far subtler than either of these appraisals suggests. While we sympathize with Jean Poquelin, the valiant, yet kind-hearted warrior, we do not sympathize with Jean Poquelin, profiteer, smuggler, and slave-trader. While we sympathize with an old man hounded by children and adults alike, we do not especially sympathize with a hermit whose bitterness causes him to curse any child who mocks him in play. Nor are the townsfolk portrayed as all bad. Poquelin's adversary, the governor, for instance, is genial enough to Jean: when their conversation had reached an impasse, we are told he "took a quill and wrote a line to a city official, introducing Mr. Poquelin, and asking for him every possible courtesy."[30]

Even Little White, secretary to the "Building and Improvement Company" that wishes to use Poquelin's land, acts out of mixed motives that render his subsequent stance of "devil's advocate" in a more complex light. White agrees to "look into the matter"—i.e., spy on Poquelin's house in hopes of discovering some illegal business for which the old man might be convicted, and thereby evicted—as a "personal favor," in response to a suggestion of one of the members of the board of directors. This implies voluntary complicity in an unethical enterprise—a position that places White's later noble actions in strange relief. As if to insure the ambiguity of White's motives, Cable ends the episode as follows: "'I tell you frankly,' he [White] privately said to the president, 'I go into this purely for reasons of my own.'"[31] Cable thus refuses either to condemn or condone his initial involvement—a far cry, needless to say, from one-dimensional characterization.

Beyond Stone's charge of melodrama, however, lies a more serious charge—one Stone states forthrightly:

> As the moralist that his century required the serious writer of fiction to be, Cable had to inculcate in his readers attitudes of censure and approbation in viewing the opposing forces of the story.[32]

That Cable was bowing to the dictates of public interest is somewhat humorous, since the bitterest irony in his story rebukes the concept of "public interest." "Public interest" is revealed to be nothing more than society's as well as the individual's rationalization for the vilest, most indefensible enterprises.[33] Irony notwithstanding, Cable does, for whatever reason, give us an ending in which a "heart of gold" surfaces. Jean Poquelin is both revealed as a hero and absolved of taint by an unexplained, if not gratuitous death—an ending that at least verges on melodrama, and that, far from indulging the complexities of characterization previously established, effectively deflates them. Although I myself find the ending more tragic than melodramatic,[34] I must agree, in certain other respects, with Stone's contention that Cable is "inculcating . . . attitudes of censure and approbation"—and this to the detriment of his story.

In inculcating a moral perspective, Cable stifles certain ambiguities in the situation he has created, and undercuts his own provocative characterizations. It is in the depiction of his protagonist and her odd relationship that Faulkner surpasses Cable, for Faulkner dispenses entirely with genteel moral imperatives and allows Miss Emily to develop uncensored.

Cable, to be more precise, aborts his story via the intrusion of Little White. Little White, commissioned by the "Building and Improvement Company," spies on Poquelin's house. While on this errand, White discovers Jean's secret—part of which is passed on to the reader: namely, the living presence of the diseased Jacques, white as a ghost and reeking of death. Little White's function, however, is not simply to further the plot and catalyze the denouement. Cable uses Little White to interpret the relationship of Jean and Jacques Poquelin and the character of Jean's behavior. Immediately after his visit to the Poquelin mansion, White becomes the unflagging champion of old Jean. After Jean's death, White again steps into the vacuum of comprehension with the following highly editorial funeral oration:

> Gentlemen . . . here come the last remains of Jean Marie Poquelin, a better man, I'm afraid, with all his sins—yes, a better, a kinder man to his blood—a man of more self-forgetful goodness—than all of you put together will ever dare to be.[35]

White constitutes a filter through which our perceptions must pass; through him, Cable imposes transparency upon an essentially opaque relationship. Were he simply to have made his revelation without Little White—and the plot need not have included him—the reader would have been forced to scrutinize the brothers' relationship in all its complexity: a relationship with overtones not only of homosexuality, but of violence (the town, it will be recalled, suspects Jean of having killed his younger brother on the trip to Africa). The ending might have lost all semblance of melodrama, and might have proved almost as provocative as that of "A Rose For Emily." Instead, Cable resolves a unique fictional situation conventionally.

Faulkner, by contrast, engages the understated themes Cable raises but leaves to the province of fantasy. Whereas Cable captures the outward signs of his protagonist's stultification (the town children's mockery of Jean, the presumptuousness of the immigrants, etc.), Faulkner internalizes the issue, spotlighting Emily's perverted mentality. In so doing, he develops to conclusion a situation that exists embryonically in the relationship between half-brothers in "Jean-ah Poquelin." But whereas Cable raises our suspicions only to soothe us with a "heart of gold" ending, Faulkner, having assuaged our suspicions throughout, horrifies us doubly with his ending.

In making his protagonist a woman, Faulkner perhaps comes even closer than Cable to creating an apposite myth: the conflict between respect for and resentment of collapsing authority that many post-War Southerners must have felt is perhaps best embodied in a father-daughter relationship. Emily Grierson's necrophilic attachment to Homer Barron recapitulates her denial of her father's death even as it repudiates her father's authority.

Both "Jean-ah Poquelin" and "A Rose For Emily" concern the passing of an order. In Cable's story, however, inquiry into character is stayed in favor of a conventional plot resolution. Stone is quite right in observing that "in centering his inquiry on the workings of the morbid mind of his character, [Faulkner] moves beyond the terms of Cable."[36] Yet Cable's story adumbrates Faulkner's at the deepest levels of theme as well as at the more superficial levels of plot and characterization.

Notes

1. Edward Stone, "Usher, Poquelin, Miss Emily: The Progress of Southern Gothic," *Georgia Review,* 14 (Winter 1960), 433-43.

2. Cleanth Brooks and Robert Penn Warren, *Understanding Fiction,* first edition (New York: Appleton-Century-Crofts, 1943), p. 412.

3. Consider the common motif of the smell emanating from the house in both stories; or Poquelin's old, mute African servant—reincarnated almost intact in the person of Emily's black "house boy" who disappears out the back door as the mystery is revealed in much the same way as Poquelin's old servant disappears without a word in Cable's story.

4. Stone, "Southern Gothic," p. 437.

5. Louis Rubin, "The Road to Yoknapatawpha: George Cable and *John March, Southerner,*" *Virginia Quarterly Review,* 35 (Winter 1959), 129.

6. Stone, "Southern Gothic," p. 438.

7. Ibid.

8. Leslie A. Fiedler, *Love and Death in the American Novel* (London: Paladin, 1970), p. 124.

9. It is in Europe that Wieland's father performs his apostasy, from which all future guilt and criminality in the story flow. Carwin too expatriates to America from Europe (Ireland), where he has committed various offenses.

10. Those writers whom Fiedler sees as having adapted the Gothic romance to American needs (i.e., C. B. Brown, in *Edgar Huntly,* Cooper, in the Leather-stocking tales, and Hawthorne, in *The Scarlet Letter*) did so by drastically reversing the role of the genre: that is, by making the tale serve as a projection of fear and guilt associated, not with the collapse of traditional authority, but with the capacity for lawlessness and anarchy. Thus, Fiedler points out, the woods or frontier and the Indians replaced the abbey or castle and the soldiers of the Inquisition as the setting and antagonists of the new, American Gothic. (Fiedler, *Love and Death,* p. 150.) Yet if form and function mutate, can the result be rightfully considered as part of the original species? Cable's adaptation of the Gothic romance in "Jean-ah Poquelin" differs from these others in that it remains truer to the original, European Gothic usage.

11. George Washington Cable, *Old Creole Days,* with a Foreword by Shirley Ann Grau (New York: New American Library, 1961; Signet), p. 131.

12. Ibid.

13. This conceit is dramatized literally in the story, as the "inroads" made by the townsfolk destroy the sanctity of old Poquelin's property and existence.

14. Cable, *Old Creole Days,* p. 131.

15. This image, drawn from the battlefield, could not have failed to suggest, in the late 1870s, a comparison with the post-bellum South.

16. William Faulkner, *The Portable Faulkner,* revised and expanded edition, edited by Malcolm Cowley (New York: Viking Press, 1946; revised ed., 1967), p. 437.

17. Stone, "Southern Gothic," pp. 439-440.

18. Cable, *Old Creole Days,* pp. 134-35.

19. Ibid., p. 135. This Gallic display of affections—the use of diminutives, the custom of kissing among males—suggests a homosexual tenor to an Anglo-

Saxon reading public. By exploiting this French custom, Cable comes close to dramatizing a homosexual bond while remaining within the bounds of genteel propriety.

20. Ibid., p. 134.

21. Allowing the middle name to partake of the French participle that is its phonetic and graphological equivalent, the name becomes an icon of the relationship of the two half-brothers.

22. Cable, *Old Creole Days,* p. 134.

23. Ibid., p. 135.

24. While Faulkner's story is not particularly concerned with the consequences of slavery, his story nonetheless does show a woman who lives under an inherited psychological burden, and whose murder and subsequent necrophilic violation of Homer Barron may be seen, in part, as an extreme response to a domineering father and to a patriarchal culture in general.

25. Fiedler, *Love and Death,* p. 384.

26. Cable, *Old Creole Days,* pp. 97-113.

27. Philip Butcher, *George W. Cable* (New York: Twayne Publications, Inc., 1962), p. 39.

28. Stone, "Southern Gothic," p. 438.

29. Shirley Ann Grau, Foreword to *Old Creole Days,* p. ix.

30. Cable, *Old Creole Days,* p. 139.

31. Ibid., p. 144.

32. Stone, "Southern Gothic," p. 438.

33. When Jean Poquelin enters the African slave trade, all responsibility and scruple is retroactively shrugged aside in the following passage:

    > What harm could he see in it? The whole people said it was vitally necessary, and to minister to a vital public necessity—good enough certainly, and so he laid up many a doubloon, that made him none the worse in the public regard.
    >
    > (Cable, *Old Creole Days,* p. 135.)

    Later on, when the "Building and Improvement Company" voices designs on Poquelin's property, one of the board justifies their attitude as follows:

    > "Mr. President, this market house project, as I take it, is not altogether a selfish one; the community is to be benefited by it. We may feel that we are working in the public interest (the board smiled knowingly), if we employ all possible means to oust this old nuisance from among us."
    >
    > (Ibid., p. 143.)

    Finally, when the drunken mob comes in the night to harass old Poquelin, their leader, Bienvenu, defends their purpose with the words, "I am ze servan' of ze publique." (Ibid., p. 150.)

34. Not only is this the story of the last survivor of a proud, old order, a man whose existence is invaded and destroyed by newcomers; it also depicts a slave-trader who, having exploited race prejudice, becomes the victim of race prejudice himself. Cable understates Poquelin's culpability somewhat, preferring to indict his society along with him (see p. 10, note 33 above); yet it is Poquelin's culpability that makes the tale tragic, and not merely pathetic.

35. Cable, *Old Creole Days,* p. 153.

36. Stone, "Southern Gothic," p. 438.

Ronald Schleifer (essay date 1993)

SOURCE: Schleifer, Ronald. "Rural Gothic: The Sublime Rhetoric of Flannery O'Connor." In *Frontier Gothic: Terror and Wonder at the Frontier in American Literature,* edited by David Moden, Scott P. Sanders, and Joanne B. Karpinski, pp. 175-86. Cranbury, N.J.: Associated University Presses, 1993.

[*In the following essay, Schliefer proposes that O'Connor effectively uses the backdrop of the rural South and combines it with elements of the supernatural to present a world of powerful possibilities in her fiction.*]

> There are two qualities that make fiction. One is the sense of mystery and the other is the sense of manners. You get manners from the texture of existence that surrounds you. The great advantage of being a Southern writer is that we don't have to go anywhere to look for manners . . . We in the South live in a society that is rich in contradiction, rich in irony, rich in contrast, and particularly rich in speech.
>
> —Flannery O'Connor

In *A Portrait of the Artist,* that most ungothic of literary works, Stephen Dedalus explains to his friend Lynch that although Aristotle had not defined pity and terror in the *Poetics,* he, Stephen, had:

> Pity is the feeling which arrests the mind in the presence of whatsoever is grave and constant in human sufferings and unites it with the human sufferer. Terror is the feeling which arrests the mind in the presence of whatsoever is grave and constant in human sufferings and unites it with the secret cause.[1]

Stephen is attempting to define tragic art, yet his definitions are useful in developing a sense of the larger movements of gothic fiction—of the serious contemplation of the supernatural in literature. The novel, I would argue, seeks to achieve some sense of Stephen's "pity," to create the texture of a social world in which we can join in sympathy with its human sufferers. What has characterized the great novelists in English—from Defoe through Fielding and George Eliot to the human comedy of *Ulysses* itself—is an abiding sense of sympathy for the human sufferer, or its opposite, a sense of irony toward him. Another way to say this is to argue that the novel seeks to hide and to erase its own origins, to present itself and its characters on their own terms within the context of "the texture of existence that surrounds" them,[2] whereas the gothic romance seeks to reveal its hidden origins. The novel deals with the middle between apocalyptic ends; it deals with ongoing life, with what William Spanos, following Kierkegaard, calls the "interesting . . . the intentionality of *inter esse* meaning '(i) "to be between," (ii) "to be a matter of concern."'"[3]

The gothic romance, on the other hand, seeks extremes; it seeks to articulate a sense—an "experience"—of the sublime, and to this end proceeds, as Peter Brooks has noted, by means of the logic of the excluded middle.[4] "It is not made from the mean average or the typical," Flannery O'Connor has written, "but from the hidden and often the most extreme" (*MM* [*Mystery and Manners: Occasional Prose*], 58); "it is the extreme situation that best reveals what we are essentially" (*MM*, 113). The gothic romance, when it is serious, seeks essences; it seeks origins—both its own and its characters'. That is, it seeks Joyce's "secret cause" and achieves, in the course of that quest, the terror Stephen talks of. Origins are always supernatural; they are always beyond what can be known in a rational, logical way. That is why Stephen talks of the "mystical estate" of fatherhood as the basis of the Catholic Church in *Ulysses*, because "it is founded, like the world, macro- and microcosm, upon the void."[5] Origins always articulate what O'Connor calls "mystery" and what the literary tradition calls the "sublime": the manifestation and apprehension of the Sacred within quotidian reality. The gothic tradition arose, Brooks argues, "at the dead end of the Age of Reason, [when] the Sacred reasserted its claim to attention, but in the most primitive possible manifestations, as taboo and interdiction . . . [The gothic tradition] reasserts the presence in the world of forces which cannot be accounted for by the daylight self and the self-sufficient mind."[6] The daylight self and the self-sufficient mind are inhabitants of novels, where union with the human sufferer is enough and supernatural origins are beside the point: we need not know Moll Flanders' real parentage and name to feel the sympathetic understanding she occasions; and although Tom Jones's parentage is of some importance, it is precisely his indifference to such questions that makes him so appealing.

The gothic novel, however, presents precisely the need to discover origins: its characters, from *The Castle of Otranto* on, seek to find (or find thrust upon themselves) their parentage and their origins. The gothic is a haunted literature (it is no accident that both Joyce and O'Connor come from a Catholic tradition that takes the presence of the supernatural seriously), and what haunts it—whether it be Count Dracula, the Frankenstein monster, or the governess's ghosts in "The Turn of the Screw"—is some supernatural origin, some inhuman silence, forces beyond the self-sufficiency of the daylight self. These forces raise the question of identity and origin for the characters of gothic romance: "who and what am I?" ask Frankenstein's monster and Lewis's Monk and Kafka's K.; "how can I discover those forces beyond myself that originate myself, my own 'secret cause'?" To put these questions in literary terms especially appropriate to Flannery O'Connor, how can we discover the origins of the power of literature, the originary force of metaphorical language? Such discoveries, as Stephen suggests, are made in terror, made in the loss of self within its secret cause. "To know oneself," O'Connor has written, "is, above all, to know what one lacks" (*MM*, 35): it is a way of exploring the self and the world in a manner different from sympathetic understanding, through terror, violence, and encounter with the supernatural. O'Connor goes on to say,

> St. Cyril of Jerusalem, in instructing catechumens, wrote: "The dragon sits by the side of the road, watching those who pass. Beware lest he devour you. We go to the Father of Souls, but it is necessary to pass the dragon." No matter what form the dragon may take, it is of this mysterious passage past him, or into his jaws, that stories of any depth will always be concerned to tell, and this being the case, it requires considerable courage at any time, in any country, not to turn away from the storyteller.
>
> (*MM*, 35)

Seeking the Father of Souls—the secret cause and origin of identity and the "rich speech" that manifests identity—the writer and the reader must pass the dragon outside; they must, as O'Connor continually insists, recognize the literal reality of the Devil, the poverty of our self-sufficiency, and the necessity of grace. Such self-knowledge is a form of agony; as O'Connor says in what I believe is her best story, "The Artificial Nigger"—a story whose plot literally repeats the plot of St. Cyril's parable, with the artificial nigger a silent figure on the side of the road—such knowledge grows "out of agony, which is not denied to any man and which is given in strange ways to children."[7] It is this "mysterious passage" that the gothic tradition offers us when it is most serious, a passage to and through origin and identity to their secret cause.

Nowhere are origins and identity more pressing problems, as Roy Male has shown,[8] than on the frontier, where one continually encounters "mysterious strangers" who raise questions about one's own as well as others' identity. One such modern frontier is O'Connor's South: it is especially a "frontier" for a Catholic writer in the predominantly fundamentalist Protestant South. Like the gothic romance Brooks describes, O'Connor seeks in her work to "reassert" the Sacred in the quotidian world, to situate her characters on the mysterious passage between the "manners" of novels and the "mystery" of union with secret causes. Tzvetan Todorov's study, *The Fantastic,* situates gothic fiction in the "frontier" between natural and supernatural understandings of experience. In fact, although he does not use it, "frontier" itself is an apt metaphor for the situation of the gothic as Todorov defines it: "the fantastic is that hesitation experienced by a person who knows only the laws of nature, confronting an apparently supernatural event."[9] This is O'Connor's "frontier," that of a fiction which is always

> pushing its own limits outward towards the limits of mystery, because . . . the meaning of a story does not begin except at a depth where adequate motivation and adequate psychology and the various determinations have been exhausted. Such a writer . . . will be interested in possibility rather than probability. He will be interested in characters who are forced out to meet evil and grace and who act on a trust beyond themselves.
>
> (*MM,* 41-42)

The gothic, that is, presents a world beyond the understandings of metaphor, a world of mysterious inhuman forces that cannot adequately be explained by the metaphors of psychology or sociology or well-meaning humanism. It is a literature of *presence* unmediated by the substitutions of language, presences which are inhuman, terrifying, secret, sublime.

Yet O'Connor's frontier is more literal than this: her constant gesture is to place her characters between the natural and the supernatural by locating them, often on a literal journey, between the cities and the rural country of the South. "What the Southern Catholic writer is apt to find, when he descends within his imagination," she notes, "is not Catholic life but the life of this region in which he is both native and alien" (*MM,* 197). Rufus Johnson in "The Lame Shall Enter First"—a character who embodies, as many of O'Connor's characters do, the *reality* of the Devil—has a history of "senseless destruction, windows smashed, city trash boxes set afire, tires slashed—the kind of thing . . . found where boys had been transplanted abruptly from the country to the city as this one had" (*CS* [*The Complete Stories of Flannery O'Connor*], 449). This is where the supernatural is most clearly and terrifyingly encountered—on those frontiers between the country and the city, faith and faithlessness, Protestant fundamentalism and cosmopolitan skepticism. Yet Rufus Johnson, as the well-meaning humanist-protagonist of the story learns, cannot be explained: he is simply a literal force, the force of the Devil, to be encountered on this "frontier." "I have found," O'Connor writes, "that anything that comes out of the South is going to be called grotesque by the Northern reader" (*MM,* 40), and she found this because the strangeness of that frontier in our culture—that location of the clashes between terror and pity—forces upon her characters confrontations with themselves and origins beyond themselves. "While the South is hardly Christ-centered," O'Connor says, "it is most certainly Christ-haunted" (*MM,* 40).

To speak of the "literal" force of characters is to speak of one particular aspect of rhetoric, of the *power* rhetoric has to make its effects as literal as events in the world. In such an examination of rhetoric the opposition between the literal and the figurative is beside the point: discourse creates *literal* effects that move us as effectively as nondiscursive events. In this understanding, discourse creates (or "occasions" or "provokes") experience,[10] and such experience is not subject to description in terms of the opposition between "literal" and "figurative" correspondence between discourse and its object. In this understanding, "rhetoric" is not the means of expressing pre-existing experiences; rather, it occasions experience.

O'Connor has precisely this concern with rhetoric. "The problem of the novelist who wishes to write about a man's encounter with this God," O'Connor has written, "is how he shall make the experience—which is both natural and supernatural—understandable, and credible, to his reader" (*MM,* 161). This is O'Connor's rhetorical problem, to make the Sacred literal in a world in which it seems at best metaphorical, originating in a mode of perception rather than in the created world. The problem of her rhetoric, then, is the problem of the gothic, the problem of the sublime.

The act of "facing oneself" is the recurrent action of O'Connor's stories, the action of gothic romance. Perhaps the most striking example of this is that of O. E. Parker in "Parker's Back," who literally "faces" his own back with a giant tattoo of Jesus, the eyes of which "continued to look at him—still, straight, all-demanding, enclosed in silence" (*CS,* 526). This is a representative gothic gesture: to make the metaphorical literal. Gothic romance does this, as Todorov and others have shown,[11] by narrating dream and nightmare as reality and projecting our deepest impulses and fears onto the landscape. The face on Parker's back—its "all-demanding" eyes—made Parker feel "that his dissatisfaction was gone, but he felt not quite like himself. It was as if he were himself but a stranger to himself, driving into a new country though everything he saw was familiar to him, even the night" (*CS,* 527). Such a feeling—a feeling that the reader is never sure Asbury achieves or not, hence the relative failure of "An Enduring Chill"—is what Freud calls the "uncanny," "That class of terrifying which leads back to something long known to us, once very familiar"; "the uncanny," Freud says, "would always be that in which one does not know where one is, as it were."[12] The uncanny is familiar and strange, just as Parker is both familiar and strange to himself with God's constant eyes literally upon him, and he is in a country in which he is both native and alien.

That country is the country of the frontier, between the familiar and strange, the natural and supernatural. One gets there in O'Connor by "facing" oneself, by seeking origins and seeing oneself, as Mr. Head does, with God's own eyes, with God's eyes *upon* one. The gothic, I have suggested, "literalizes" the metaphorical: like the more general category of the sublime, it deals in effects rather than meanings and thus is not subject to the distinction between literal and figurative description; in it, this distinction collapses in the "literalness" of experience. O'Connor effects this collapse in the highly figurative rural speech of her characters that they understand as fully literal. It is for this reason that her backwoods characters so often use country clichés in their speech: her act is to make us see the familiar as strange, to make us see literally and thus strangely what we usually don't see at all because it is so familiar. "Christ!" someone says in the pool hall when Parker reveals his tattoo (*CS*, 526), and suddenly—almost supernaturally—O'Connor creates Christ's presence, as literal as it is for Parker, by means of the cliché of astonishment. In "The River," Bevel learns of Jesus:

> He had found out this morning that he had been made by a carpenter named Jesus Christ. Before he had thought it had been a doctor named Sladewell, a fat man with a yellow mustache who gave him shots and thought his name was Herbert. . . . If he had thought about it before, he would have thought Jesus Christ was a word like "oh" or "damn" or "God," or maybe somebody who had cheated him out of something sometime. . . .
>
> (*CS*, 163)

Such a discovery is the terrifying revelation of what we already knew: "carpenter" in this context takes on the full presence of its literal meaning of a maker, and Bevel (something a carpenter makes) is faced with a terrifying prospect of seeing himself anew.

Such an "experience" of the literal—the confrontation with the literal self, its literal origin, a powerfully literal meaning—are the repeated actions in Flannery O'Connor, and they take place in what John Hawkes has called "her almost luridly bright pastoral world,"[13] on borderlines between the city and the country or between day and night. This is why so often O'Connor's stories end at sunset, as in "Revelation," when Mrs. Turpin watches her hogs as the sun goes down:

> Then like a monumental statue coming to life, she bent her head slowly and gazed, as if through the very heart of mystery, down into the pig parlour at the hogs. They had settled all in one corner around the old sow who was grunting softly. A red glow suffused them. They appeared to pant with a secret life.
>
> (*CS*, 508)

From this sight she looks up as the sun goes down and sees her vision of a vast hoard of souls going to heaven, "whole companies of white trash, clean for the first time in their lives, and bands of black niggers in white robes, and battalions of freaks and lunatics shouting and clapping and leaping like frogs" (*CS*, 508). The metaphor O'Connor uses is almost an allusion to *Otranto* with its giant statue coming to life, but the language is that of Mrs. Turpin, another in O'Connor's procession of good country people. That language informs a rural vision, Hawkes's lurid pastoral world, with a sense of supernatural force so that the whole is seen in a new light. Here again O'Connor creates the *presence* of the supernatural, of mysterious forces beyond the daylight self, in pig and sunset. "Revelation" begins with Mrs. Turpin's confrontation with a Wellesley student in a doctor's office, yet it ends with her own uncouthness—her own rural sensibility—miraculously transformed on the frontier of a secret life.

That life is Mrs. Turpin's life, but dark, unknown, strange: it is the life revealed in the college girl's fierce remark: "Go back to hell where you came from, you old wart hog" (*CS*, 500). It is the inhuman life of wart hogs from hell that, literalized, leads strangely to Mrs. Turpin's vision of heaven. Mrs. Turpin "faces" herself with the hog; she sees her own secret life in the elemental life of her farm and discovers, as Parker had, the presence of God in and beyond His creation, in and beyond the hogs, the people, the peculiar light of the setting sun.

This is the light of grace, and it appears again at another sunset situated on the urban frontier at the end of "The Artificial Nigger." There Mr. Head and his grandson, Nelson, after the small inferno of their day in Atlanta, discover in the accidental image of suffering presented by a dilapidated statue of a Negro the "action of mercy." What is powerful in O'Connor is her ability to create the *presence* of Christ and grace felt through and beyond the world of nature. How she does this is the problem and the secret of her art. It is an art that is gothic and that depends, fully, on its situation on one of the frontiers of our culture. Herman Melville wrote in *The Confidence-Man*, "it is with fiction as with religion: it should present another world, and yet one to which we feel the tie."[14] O'Connor, like Melville, presents another world of white trash, black niggers, freaks, lunatics—in a word, a world of "good country people"—which is tied to ours yet strangely literal in its very landscape and language.

That tie with our world is the tie with what she calls the "action of mercy," and in her best work it is "tied" through her metaphoric language becoming literal.[15]

Love is the burden of "The Artificial Nigger": face to face with a broken-down statue of a Negro, Mr. Head and his grandson are "faced with some great mystery, some monument to another's victory that brought them together in their common defeat" so that they "both feel it dissolving their differences *like an action of mercy*" (*CS*, 269, emphasis added). This encounter creates a sense of humility for Mr. Head until, three paragraphs later, "he stood appalled . . . while *the action of mercy* covered his pride like a flame and consumed it." In the course of these paragraphs (and in the course of Mr. Head's experience), simile is rendered as assertion until, before our eyes, grace manifests itself, the action of mercy, the secret cause, appears:

> [Mr. Head] stood appalled, judging himself with the thoroughness of God, while the action of mercy covered his pride like a flame and consumed it. He had never thought himself a great sinner before but he saw now that his true depravity had been hidden from him lest it cause him despair. He realized that he was forgiven for sins from the beginning of time, when he had conceived in his own heart the sin of Adam, until the present when he had denied poor Nelson. He saw that no sin was too monstrous for him to claim as his own, and since God loved in proportion as He forgave, he felt ready at that instant to enter Paradise.
>
> (*CS*, 269-270)

This is the "secret cause" that Joyce speaks of, a sense of God's presence and love in the heart of Mr. Head. But what is remarkable about this passage, I believe, is that we never question the fact that the realization described—its language and its theology—is simply beyond the frontier language and evangelical Christianity of Mr. Head. Head, hick that he is, believes that an inferno underlies Atlanta and fears to be sucked down the sewer: he literalizes his own metaphor (see *CS*, 259, 267). In other words, O'Connor is able, here and elsewhere, to create a sublimely literal irony. Throughout "The Artificial Nigger" the language of the narrator constantly paraphrases Mr. Head's thoughts and language in a rhetoric completely beyond his backwoods rhetoric. This paraphrase makes that language itself—its ignorance, its racism, its violence—entirely invisible.

What reveals itself here is that Catholic grace, like the Mormon's magical glasses, includes the ability to see "through" and to understand another language. Thus the narrator notes, "They stood gazing at the artificial Negro as if they were faced with some great mystery, some monument to another's victory that brought them together in their common defeat" (*CS*, 269), but Head simply breathes, "An artificial nigger!" and says "They ain't got enough real ones here. They got to have an artificial one" (*CS*, 268, 269). "Nigger" is Head's word, "Negro" the narrator's, yet O'Connor wants us to see *through* the rhetoric to the "literal" fact, wordlessly experienced by Head and narrated in a technical theological discourse far beyond Head's experience and understanding. In other words, O'Connor creates the rhetorical *effect* of godly presence by narrating in a language that implies its own transparence, implies that the literal *inhabits* the metaphorical so that, as another theological writer, Søren Kierkegaard says, "through a negation of the immediate phenomenon the essence remains identical with the phenomenon."[16]

Such an effect is created by being situated on a "frontier" between rural discourse and cosmopolitan theology. But more than this, O'Connor is *enacting* the "mystery" of grace as well. Throughout this story—as in most of her stories—O'Connor faces her cosmopolitan readers with the language and experience of rural ignorance. When Head tells Nelson that the sewers of Atlanta are literally hell, we *know* that we know more than these ignorant characters. But when the story finally presents the sure knowledge that Mr. Head, despite his racism and ignorance, can count himself among the saved—that "he was forgiven for sins from the beginning of time" and that "since God loved in proportion as He forgave, he felt ready at that instant to enter Paradise" (*CS*, 269-70)—at that moment its readers, like St. Cyril, are faced with a mystery which cannot be understood by the self-sufficient mind of humanistic intelligence. At such moments the cosmopolitan understanding of her readers is faced with a discourse whose power is beyond the comprehensions of the irony that had seemed to govern the story's narrative throughout.

This power is that of sympathy: the passage suggests that Head, like his cosmopolitan reader, can only understand the "secret cause"—here the sin of Adam—by experiencing the agony of his own egocentric denial of "poor Nelson" (or in the case of the reader, "poor" Mr. Head himself). Mr. Head is not truly a part of the world he lives in—neither is Mrs. Turpin, O. E. Parker, and most of O'Connor's protagonists—and his struggle, like that of the others and like our own, is to find some connection in a world that simply seems alien, other, without human response. It is a world, as the Misfit says in "A Good Man is Hard to Find," in which, without an answering Jesus, there's no pleasure but meanness, "no real pleasure in life" (*CS*, 133)—a world in which, as O'Connor says, we are native and alien.

How to discover a human response in such a world is the great problem: Mr. Head can, as he has done all his life, depend on himself and his ability to give "lessons" and be a "suitable guide for the young" (*CS*, 249), or he can discover, in terror or in love, but above all in humility, supernatural forces outside himself that lead him to other human sufferers who can respond to himself.

Most of O'Connor's heroes fall into terror: they find, as Parker does, the terrifying cost of God's enduring eye; or they find, as the Misfit does, the senselessness of not knowing God is there. As O'Connor herself says, "Often the nature of grace can be made plain only by describing its absence" (*MM*, 204), and such absence *is* inhuman; it leaves our world literally senseless and results in the senseless violence—the inhuman violence—of all those who do not fit: the Misfit, Rufus, Shiftlet, and all the rest. But others—Mrs. Turpin, Mr. Head, Bailey's mother—discover love amid their terror: they discover the literal language of God already in their own Southern slang. They achieve humility when they realize that they are not fully self-possessed, that their "calm understanding," in the narrator's paraphrase of Head's evaluation of himself, leaves out their own mysterious origins and leaves out forces—articulated by Head's exclamation, "An artificial nigger!"—beyond themselves.

The action of mercy, then, is the action of rhetoric that finds meaning in a senseless world, that suggests the literal in its figured values; it offers a sense of grace, a sense of the supernatural, in the world in which O'Connor characters, both native and alien, do not quite fit.

What the rural Southern frontier finally offers O'Connor is that position in the world—that situation—where the strangers you meet can be anyone, can, in fact, be supernatural: Jesus, the Devil, the Holy Ghost.

> "I can tell you my name is Tom Shiftlet and I come from Tarwater, Tennessee, but you never have seen me before: how you know I ain't lying? How you know my name ain't Aaron Sparks, lady, and I come from Singleberry, Georgia, or how you know it's not George Speeds and I come from Lucy, Alabama, or how you know I ain't Thompson Bright from Toolafalls, Mississippi?"
>
> (*CS*, 147-48)

All these names, as Roy Male has suggested, are filled with light,[17] and they set forth the action—sometimes the failed action—of O'Connor's gothic fiction: to discover or create light out of the dark frontier of rural Georgia. "I think," O'Connor wrote, "[the Catholic writer] will feel a good deal more kinship with backwoods prophets and shouting fundamentalists than he will with those politer elements for whom the supernatural is an embarrassment of sociology or culture or personality development" (*MM*, 207). That sense of supernatural force that the backwoods prophets feel in the world repeats itself in the uncanny force and presence O'Connor achieves within the cliché-ridden language of her fiction. Both acknowledge the supernatural and discover that it can be found on the edges of our culture, dark and empty as they may be, on the rural frontier.

Notes

This essay is a revised version of "Rural Gothic: The Stories of Flannery O'Connor," that originally appeared in *Modern Fiction Studies*, 28 (1982), 475-85. That essay was reprinted in *Critical Essays on Flannery O'Connor*, ed. Melvin Friedman and Beverly Clark (New York: G. K. Hall, 1985) and *Flannery O'Connor: Modern Critical Views*, ed. Harold Bloom (New York: Chelsea House, 1986). The present essay was especially revised for this collection.

1. James Joyce, *A Portrait of the Artist as a Young Man* (New York: Viking, 1969), 204.

2. Flannery O'Connor, *Mystery and Manners: Occasional Prose*, ed. Sally and Robert Fitzgerald (New York: Farrar, Straus, and Giroux, 1969), 103; future references, abbreviated *MM*, will be included parenthetically within the text.

3. William V. Spanos, "Hermeneutics and Memory: Destroying T. S. Eliot's *Four Quartets*," *Genre*, 11 (1978): 532.

4. Peter Brooks, "Virtue and Terror: *The Monk*," *ELH*, 40 (1973): 252. For a complementary treatment of the gothic tradition, see my "The Trap of the Imagination: The Gothic Tradition, Fiction, and 'The Turn of the Screw,'" *Criticism*, 22 (1980): 297-319.

5. James Joyce, *Ulysses* (New York: Random House, 1961), 207.

6. Brooks, 249.

7. *The Complete Stories of Flannery O'Connor* (New York: Modern Library, 1974), 269. Future references to O'Connor's stories will be to this edition, abbreviated *CS* and included parenthetically in the text.

8. Roy Male, *Enter, Mysterious Stranger* (Norman: University of Oklahoma Press, 1979).

9. Tzvetan Todorov, *The Fantastic*, trans. Richard Howard (Ithaca, NY: Cornell University Press, 1975), 25.

10. For a discussion of the collapsing of the distinction between literal and figurative use of language, see Ronald Schleifer, *A. J. Greimas and the Nature of Meaning* (Lincoln: University of Nebraska Press, 1987), ch. 5, esp. 201-08.

11. *The Fantastic*, treats this throughout; see also Leslie Fiedler, *Love and Death in the American Novel* (New York: Stein and Day, 1966).

12. Sigmund Freud, "The Uncanny," in *Studies in Parapsychology* (New York: Collier books, 1963), 21.

13. John Hawkes, "Flannery O'Connor's Devil," *Sewanee Review*, 70 (1962): 399.

14. Herman Melville, *The Confidence-Man* (Indianapolis: Bobbs-Merrill, 1967), 260.

15. For Blake's similar transformation of simile to metaphor, see my "Simile, Metaphor, and Vision: Blake's Narration of Prophecy in America," *Studies in English Literature,* 19 (1979): 569-588.

16. *The Concept of Irony,* trans. Lee Capel (Bloomington: Indiana University Press, 1965), 265.

17. Male, 30.

STRUCTURE AND TECHNIQUE IN SOUTHERN GOTHIC LITERATURE

Ollye Tine Snow (essay date summer 1965)

SOURCE: Snow, Ollye Tine. "The Functional Gothic of Flannery O'Connor." *Southwest Review* 50, no. 3 (summer 1965): 286-99.

[*In the following essay, Snow discusses O'Connor's use of eighteenth-century gothic devices to convey the idea that humans can overcome adversity only if they obey Divine authority.*]

With the recent posthumous publication of Flannery O'Connor's collection of short stories *Everything That Rises Must Converge*,[1] readers are impressed again with the "terrible swift sword" that cuts away at man's sin. Again in these stories as in her other collection and in her two novels, the grotesqueries of man's defiant, sometimes stupid disobedience of God carry the theme. These grotesqueries very obviously, sometimes ironically, function on the basis of biblical prototypes and images—for example, the prophecy in "Parker's Back" of Obadiah E. Parker meets as bitter and as stubborn resistance as was Edom's enmity to Israel; the Holy Ghost's descending as a dove, or in the case of "The Enduring Chill," as a "fierce bird," shows explicit awareness of a Divine Being; Mrs. May in "Greenleaf" destroys herself through building up a wrong image in her mind of the bull ("silvered in the moonlight" at one time), just as Aaron sinned by trying to make an image of Jehovah in the Egyptian form of the golden calf.

But besides the biblical configuration, some of these grotesqueries, violent and horrifying in effect, recall the Gothic devices of eighteenth-century literature. Such a connection between the Gothic and Flannery O'Connor has already been noted in her previous work, but the connection has been chiefly deprecatory. With this appearance of the volume of stories on which she was working at the time of her death, it seems necessary to clarify the function of Gothic elements in the O'Connor fiction.

Actually, the Gothic conventions she adapts, refines, and transmutes from eighteenth-century writing, in which they were used purely for effects of horror, function organically and artistically in her writing.

So far, only fleeting tribute has been paid to this aspect of Miss O'Connor's talent. One suggestion as to the function of the horrors and distortions in her fiction is offered by Robert Y. Drake, Jr., in his article, "Miss O'Connor and the Scandal of Redemption," which appeared in the Fall, 1960 issue of *Modern Age*: "Like many other contemporary Southern writers, she has consistently displayed a penchant for horrors; but unlike some of them—Tennessee Williams, for example—her distortions are always functional, serving to embody outwardly the inner horror of sin which is her principal concern. . . ." Dr. Drake sees the Gothic element as complementary to the theme of the fiction and therefore important to the success of the entire work. The opposite viewpoint, at least of *Wise Blood,* is taken by Isaac Rosenfeld. In his *New Republic* article, "To Win by Default" (July 7, 1952), Mr. Rosenfeld expresses the opinion that there is no correlation among Miss O'Connor's style, her techniques, and her statement—no linkage between the "monsters" of the narrative and her statement.

Other critics have approached the ugly and frightening creations in Miss O'Connor's fiction from both of these poles, the approving and the dissenting. Jane Hart, writing in the *Georgia Review* ("Strange Earth, the Stories of Flannery O'Connor," Summer, 1958), mentions the "literary cheating" or "opportunism" in which she says Flannery O'Connor, along with the other writers of the Southern Gothic school, indulges. Orville Prescott, in the *New York Times Book Review* for February 24, 1960, concludes that the distortions emerge to serve "no purpose except to demonstrate Miss O'Connor's determination to pile horror upon horror." Granville Hicks, in "A Writer at Home with Her Heritage" (*Saturday Review,* May 12, 1962) writes that the author herself explains the function of the grotesque in her fiction this way: ". . . In these times the most reliable path to reality, to the kind of reality that seems to her important, is by way of the grotesque. The grotesque, as she puts it, is more real than the real, and what many people regard as the real seems to her more grotesque than any of the characters she has created."

But the examination of the Gothic conventions on the basis of their function in Flannery O'Connor's fiction can be expanded beyond what the critics have written or even what the author has expressed. For example, the Gothic details of distortion in the title story of Miss O'Connor's new book cause the reader to shudder as he discovers, "One eye of Mamma, large and staring, moved slightly to the left as if it had become unmoored. The other remained fixed. . . ." The emotional effect on the reader is primarily the same as that of the detached hand and foot on the stairwell in Horace Walpole's eighteenth-century novel, *The Castle of Otranto*. But in the short story, the eyes do much more than terrify the reader: they symbolize the purblind vision of Julian's spiritually impoverished mother.

As another example, the Gothic convention of the supernatural stranger in an episode in *The Violent Bear It Away*[2] has only a minor Gothic effect. The conversation between Francis Marion Tarwater and the "stranger" is brief; yet even here the Gothic quality functions patulously and organically. The omniscient voice, detached from a body, is a compressed Gothic device that adds a sense of mystery to the plot by its Gothic ghostlike quality and by its appearance in the midst of a deserted woods-clearing. The compression of the device, part of the supernatural motif in Gothic fiction, becomes evident if it is contrasted with the many manifestations of this particular motif in Walpole's *The Castle of Otranto*—the bleeding statue, the enormous sword, and the walking portrait.

To dismiss the "stranger," the voice, as merely a participant in an interior dialogue is to lose part of its significance. Francis Marion Tarwater, a fourteen-year-old backwoods Tennessean, converses with the "stranger" when he begins to dig the grave of his deceased greatuncle, who has reared him as a potential prophet and has commissioned him to baptize an idiot cousin. Tarwater is alone in a clearing within a desolate forest, the dead man is inside the deserted shack nearby, the sun which beams straight down is "dead still, holding its breath"—this setting culminates eerily in the emergence of the voice, a detached entity. Technically the inhuman detachment is achieved by the depersonalized representation of the dialogue between the boy and the voice, in which no quotation marks are used to distinguish the spoken words from the exposition, and by the constant repetition of the identifying label, the "stranger."

The haunting detachment of the voice is meaningful in Miss O'Connor's pervasive theme of man's struggle for freedom from authority, of his calamity when he "sets himself up as God."[3] Throughout *The Violent Bear It Away*, Tarwater searches for a means to dismiss Old Tarwater's command to serve God and instead to act by his own will. "I can act," he says, and "I can make things happen." But Tarwater has no control over the voice of the "stranger"; it punctures his brooding meditation. Most important of all, it emphasizes the contrast between the entity that is unhampered by human conventions and responsibilities and the boy who cannot escape, as the abstract voice does, from the tasks which confront him. This contrast between the voice and the fully animated, very much involved boy is heightened by the swift exchange of dialogue and the quick shifts in viewpoint, and also by the actions of the boy (he slams the door, hunts the shovel, begins to dig the grave) juxtaposed with the nonexertion of the stranger. The irresponsibly daring, Gothic-like evil voice is a foil for the character of the boy. But the full artistry of the foil is apparent only after the struggle is over and Tarwater has surrendered to authority, for the contrast is echoed again and again throughout the book as Tarwater meets the salesman who seems to do what he pleases, the schoolteacher who is much freer than himself, and finally the lavender-shirted maniac who is governed by nothing, not even conventions. Thus the purpose of this Gothic device is accomplished gradually in a pattern of contrast that develops throughout the book.

Miss O'Connor's subtlety in the use of a Gothic device to establish a significant pattern is again illustrated in another episode from the same novel. This one also is a minor part of the narrative. When the Negro Buford and his wife find Tarwater digging the grave for the old man, Buford's wife wails mournfully. Standing at the edge of the old man's grave, with the corpse nearby, and with a dark, dense forest behind her, she seems to have ample motivation for feeling frightened and upset. But she reveals another reason for her wails, telling that she has seen the old man's spirit. Momentarily, the whole dark, superstitious gamut of legends and mysteries common to the Negro tradition in the South converges from the past upon the three figures. This train of meaning, prompted by the darkness of the Gothic setting and the supernatural suggestion of the transmuted Gothic "spirit," depends on the special combination of "nigger," "spirit," "dream," "grave," "raw ground," "wail," and "unrested." It functions here to set the protagonist, the little boy, for a fleeting minute back into the past, both the past of the Negro race with whom he personally shares disquietude and bondage (his greatuncle had bound his freedom) and the past of his family among whom there is "unrest." Here the past quickly vanishes, returning frequently, however, to pester the boy in his memories of the old man, in his struggle against the commandment, and in his haunting curiosity about the forest fire. The device of the "spirit," through this interpretation, becomes a symbolic, structural link.

The patterns established in the novel by the Gothic devices of the superhuman "spirit" and "stranger" blend into the larger design of the book; representations of the past and of superhuman detachment expand the theme of the human will, plagued by past guilt and conflict, striving for freedom from Authority. And Miss O'Connor's final comment on this struggle is, of course, that man will be defeated unless he does acknowledge obedience to the Supreme Authority.

Another manifestation of the supernatural—inexplicable, ethereal sounds—establishes a dominant pattern of its own in one of Miss O'Connor's short stories, "A

Circle in the Fire."[4] Sound effects are practically absent from the beginning of the story. The noise of the farm tractor and the "Uggggghhrhh!" of the demonic Sally Virginia are the only loud sounds in the first part of the narrative; in fact, the pitch of the conversations seems muted, and one of the boys who visits the Cope farm draws "his arms across his nose as if to muffle his words" when he speaks. Into the notable half-silence of the first part of the story comes the "high vicious laugh" from the hogpen, followed by a gradual rise in volume with the whooping of the boys, shouts of the women, and later the Gothic "wild high shrieks of joy" from the woods.

Mrs. Cope, whose farm has been invaded by a crew of mischievous wandering boys, has an obsessive fear of fire; even so, she is unprepared to accept the reality of the fire the boys finally set. But the fire, like the two kinds of inexplicable noises that issue from the inanimate objects, falls outside of her control. She has perpetually but unsuccessfully tried to control and order her life—by managing her hired hand, by disciplining the boys, and by taking every precaution against fire. At each attempt she fails; thus the Gothic sounds, representing the ubiquitous and the uncontrollable, economically suggest the necessity of her self-subordination and of her reliance on a power beyond herself—and, of course, Flannery O'Connor would mean a divine power.

The Gothic devices of the superhuman being and the evil sounds operate metaphorically and distinctively, then, in Miss O'Connor's fiction. Though the Gothic effect of the devices is not necessarily subtle (the "wild high shrieks" crash with a startling effect), their metaphoric function is always penetratingly so. Furthermore, their ultimate functions are fulfilled not by the devices within themselves, but by their extension beyond themselves.

The ability to extend beyond itself and to assume significance beyond its integral horror is evidenced by another type of Gothic device which appears in both of Miss O'Connor's two novels and in at least one of her short stories. This device is the modernized evil religious figure related to Father Jerome in *The Castle of Otranto*, Ambrosio in *The Monk*, and the corrupted clergy in Hawthorne's "Goodman Brown." Adaptations of this device include Onnie Jay Holy and Asa Hawks in *Wise Blood* and, on a lesser scale, the Cormodys in *The Violent Bear It Away*. Since these figures belong to the religious profession and may be considered servants of a divine authority, they are immediately related to Miss O'Connor's pervading theme of struggle against authority.

As supposedly dedicated servants of a Supreme Authority, these characters turn into grotesques because their values are the reverse of what is expected of them. Their deeds are evil, their thoughts are selfish, and their advice is usually guided by some ulterior motive. They preach self-abnegation; yet their own creed defies any authority except self. As protagonists of evil, these figures bring destruction, which is the main representation of evil in Miss O'Connor's scheme of values. But the destructive evil seems to come through them from another force—perhaps fate, certainly a great Unknown, of which all Gothic writers seem to be aware.

Asa Hawks in *Wise Blood,* a southern modernization of a Gothic device, is a symbol in the service of theme, as are his violent actions within the narrative. Hawks, a blind man with "black glasses and curious scars," travels with his daughter, Sabbath Lily, through southern towns giving out religious tracts. Hazel Motes, the war veteran who has come to Taulkinham to preach The Church Without Christ, is strangely drawn to follow them as they stand on street corners or hibernate in their tiny, stifling room. Already a doer of evil deeds, Haze ironically encounters "temptation" through the Hawkses. Even more ironically, Hawks tries to convert Haze, but his method is sinister. Soon Haze decides to seduce Sabbath Lily. During one of his frequent visits on this mission to their room, an intensely hot little region, he learns the reason for Hawks's black glasses; his blindness (supposedly from lime) is only pretense. Hawks vanishes, after this climax, but the symbolically garish result of his hypocrisy remains in the promiscuous flirtation of his daughter, ironically named Sabbath Lily, who does realize his actual self.

Asa Hawks is the ace of hypocrites, the most hawklike of predators eating human spirit, and the compressed symbol of man trying ignobly to hide his satanic scheming for self-authority behind black glasses while lime corrodes his spirit.

Gothic conventions are also important to Miss O'Connor's sense of structure, which is acute. That she enlists the Gothic conventions in the functions of unity and coherence demonstrates her ability to give practical use to what might be considered superfluous elements. She even makes their function subtle.

Such is the case with the tyrannical figure of old Tarwater, an adapted Gothic convention reminiscent of the roaring tyrants of the eighteenth-century novels (e.g., Manfred in *The Castle of Otranto*). It is because of the violence of this tyranny that the old man's influence remains so great, even after his death in the first part of the book, as to affect the whole movement of the narrative. The structure of *The Violent Bear It Away* is roughly circular, with many flashbacks spiraling within the circle. The macabre death of old Tarwater at the beginning of the book looks forward to the birth at its end, the boy's spiritual rebirth. Like the attitudes and values of this Gothic tyrant, which are reversed from the normal human outlook, the life cycle is reversed here.

And it is the center of old Tarwater's very life that becomes the center of attention in the book and a dominating motif: ". . . He didn't have but one thing on his mind. He was a one-notion man. Jesus. Jesus this and Jesus that." Throughout the book, Francis Marion Tarwater, using his Gothic sensibility and becoming involved in Gothic conventions, orbits around this center, most of the time trying to ignore it and his grandfather's commandment to baptize his cousin, trying to take judgment into his own hands. But what Flannery O'Connor has set as the structural center of the novel remains fixed, and the conclusion she creates demands that Tarwater accept his fate of moving under God's power.

The Gothic convention of the tyrant turns up also in a story, "The Comforts of Home," from Miss O'Connor's new book. The memory of the tyranny of Thomas' father drives the son to murder, even though the latter thinks he has inherited "reason without ruthlessness" from his father. Just as in the tyranny of old Tarwater, however, it works to destroy the evil blindness.

With his Gothic energy and his Gothic outlook on life, tyrannical old Tarwater serves as the delineating boundary of the *The Violent's* circular structure, which begins with one rescue and ends with another. Both of these rescues involve force, which is parallel to the coercive force of the old man's character, this being one of his typically Gothic attributes. The details of Mason Tarwater's rescue of the boy from the clutches of Rayber, who would rear him "according to his own ideas," are given in the introductory exposition of the book. At the conclusion, Tarwater is rescued from indecision by spiritual directives to find "the children of God." But the first rescue, in itself an example of Gothic tyranny, has necessarily precipitated the second rescue or else a final floundering doom, because the great-uncle's influence over young Tarwater involves him in such a quandary that he knows "something must happen," he must "find out a few things," and he must take either one path or another. The final rescue is, of course, the spiritual salvation of Tarwater when he bows to the Supreme Authority which he had been defying for so long.

Tarwater's struggles in readying himself for the final rescue constitute the emotional and psychological coils within the whole organization. There are three of these coils. During the whole time spent at Rayber's house he tries to exert his independence, but Rayber calls it a "backwoods, irrational independence" (cultivated by old Tarwater) and will not recognize the strength of the boy's wilfulness. The Gothic struggle becomes more and more complex.

When Tarwater decides the second time to act, he slips secretly away from Rayber to the service held by Lucette, the child preacher, in the tabernacle. From this action he emerges "submissive," and his fury is carrying him paradoxically nearer the "roots of his peace." The second unit, then, stretches from this point to the drowning of Bishop, which is the inadvertent baptism, and the fulfilment of old Tarwater's wishes.

The third unit, the interim of recognition, includes the last part of the book in which Tarwater finally realizes, by a "red-gold tree of fire," that his will must be bent to that of God and the "sign of the Saviour," and, incidentally, to the will of his great-uncle. Thus Miss O'Connor shows that man can overcome his own perversity by subordinating himself to the power of God.

Linking these three units and the entire structure together are the many symbols and images of fire. The fire images relate to Tarwater and the Gothic convention of his tyranny through the fury of the fire, its uncontrollable combustion, and its wide sweep in a circle of devastation of cleansing. The basic fire image is the promise which old Tarwater gives Rayber that "the prophet I raise up out of this boy will burn your eyes clean." One initial symbolic act is the burning of the house on the plot of red clay, while the terminal ones are the woods-fire and the initiation rites of the spiritual experience. Lucette preaches that the Word of God "burns the whole world." Even Meeks, the salesman, is selling copper flues, and he plays a part in bringing the fire of God a bit nearer to Tarwater. And Powderhead, the name Mason Tarwater gave his clearing, hints of explosives, perhaps related to the explosive actions of the man himself. Though the fire images obviously recall biblical connotations, they definitely support the Gothic structure in which they are placed.

As another means of linkage and as a complement to the circular structure, Miss O'Connor uses images of circles in the book. These images all relate to destructive evil and thus indirectly to the Gothic conventions and to the atmosphere of terror. These images include old Tarwater's deep grave, Rayber's vision of a round burnt spot between two chimneys, Tarwater's "scorched eyes," the geographical unit of the Powderhead clearing, and the lake at Cherokee Lodge. Also, Tarwater's trip from the country to the city and from the city back to the country is a circular movement. Old Tarwater's Gothic Tyranny and his fury reflected in fire can be traced through these images.

The circular structure of *The Violent Bear It Away* contrasts to the horizontal structure of "A Late Encounter with the Enemy," in *A Good Man Is Hard to Find*; but the structure of the latter is as much influenced by a Gothic convention as that of the former. General Sash's vision of the past is the influential convention in the story, which furnishes another example of how Miss O'Connor harmonizes plot, theme, and structure and of how she incorporates the Gothic element into the total pattern of a narrative with facility and purpose.

The form of "A Late Encounter with the Enemy" is balanced with precision and dexterity for half of the story, thus giving the same appearance of ready order as does a smooth file of troops on a battlefield. The last half is an artistic jumble that innovates a battle within itself; here the Gothic vision, the transporting of the man both back into the past and forward into death, gives meaning to the structure.

In the ten introductory paragraphs, symmetry is achieved by a regular, invariable alternation of "General Sash" paragraphs with "Sally Sash" paragraphs. The flashback about the premiere, which comes next, is balanced in contrast by the four paragraphs succeeding it which present the astringent life of the old man who has become physically fatigued but whose "heart continued persistently to beat."

With the arrival of graduation day, the structure becomes a dynamic chaos of action, dialogue, and thought, with no regular pattern. The tempo increases because of this, and the "encounter with the enemy," the General's fight against death which has already begun, now builds to a climax. The Gothic vision occurs. At this moment, words themselves fall everywhere and anywhere under the impetus of the moment's mood. Mixed together in one paragraph are "black procession," "a sword," "bone," "music," "body riddled"—all suggestive of the dark Gothic spirit and the struggle of the old man. Here in these words, representing the past, present, and future, is born a union of the ego-driven mortal and the universe.

Another example of the Gothic convention of visions or dreams is the vision Mrs. Shortley has in "The Displaced Person." This convention, which is related to Edmund's dreams in Clara Reeve's *The Old English Baron* and Melissa's dreams of the death knell in *The Asylum*, can also be recognized as an important structural element, both within its individual narrative and in the whole book of short stories. The vision comes after Mrs. Shortley has mounted an incline while wandering through a pasture. This action recalls the opening of the story, when Mrs. Shortley had climbed a hill to stand at the summit and watch the Displaced Persons arrive. At both points, her superiority is suggested—at first, because of the peacock, the Christian symbol generally recognized as the "vigilant Church," which stands "behind" her, thus supporting her; later, because of the command to prophesy, a communication she believes is from the Lord. At both of these points in the story, not only does the character stand physically alone on a peak, but her spirit also stands on a peak, revealed for what it is.

A design of "peaks" runs through the book and ties the stories together, although for the most part their subject matter is unrelated. These stories were not written as a unit, but the form of their combination gains significance, in one way, by the Gothic details and a Gothic convention. In the title story, "A Good Man Is Hard to Find," the peak comes after all the family except the grandmother have been led away to be murdered. The Grandmother, like The Misfit himself, is stripped of her conventional outlook on life and left in the grip of a grotesque realization of her own actually misdirected life: "Finally she found herself saying, 'Jesus. Jesus,' meaning, Jesus will help you, but the way she was saying it, it sounded as if she might be cursing."

In "The River," the revelation of Mr. Paradise's actual spiritual poverty comes at the very end of the story, after he has unsuccessfully tried to save the child from drowning: "Mr. Paradise's head appeared from time to time on the surface of the water. Finally, far downstream, the old man rose like some ancient water monster and stood empty-handed, staring with his dull eyes as far down the river line as he could see."

Mr. Shiftlet in "The Life You Save May Be Your Own" is so selfish that he saves only his own life, after leaving his dim-witted wife deserted and after causing a hitchhiker to jump from his car. The revelation that his own life is saved but at the same time spiritually endangered comes as he speeds toward further mobile-freedom, racing the "galloping shower into Mobile."

In "Good Country People" the complete revelation of Mrs. Freeman's evil comes after the Bible salesman has stolen Hulga's wooden leg. She unknowingly admits the difference between the boy's simple-minded perversity and her own tendency to gossip, to persecute, and to act a hypocrite: "Mrs. Freeman's gaze drove forward and just touched him before he disappeared under the hill. Then she returned her attention to the evil-smelling onion shoot she was lifting from the ground. 'Some can't be that simple,' she said. 'I know I never could.'"

In the last story in the book, these summits of character revelation culminate in Mrs. Shortley's vision and her prophecy: "'The children of wicked nations will be butchered,' she said in a loud voice. 'Legs where arms should be, foot to face, ear in the palm of hand. Who will remain whole? Who will remain whole? Who?'" The Gothic effect of Mrs. Shiftlet's question depends on the image of mutilation and distortion. The answer to the question, based on the symbolism of the stories, is that, of course, neither the grandmother, Mr. Paradise, Mr. Shiftlet, nor Mrs. Freeman will remain "whole," and neither will the Polish man at the end of "The Displaced Person." Gothic details in each of the revelations combine and symbolically lead up to Mrs. Shortley's warning of butchering. Mr. Paradise is metaphorically a "water monster" with "dull eyes." The grandmother's cursing is a grotesquerie of her usual aimless chattering. Mrs. Freeman pulls evil-smelling onion shoots from the ground, disrupting the good earth and spreading evil. Mr. Shiftlet's "stump," his distorted arm, is another Gothic detail of mutilation. The atmosphere of the ugly, the evil, and the doomed is made to seem even more real by the supernatural message Mrs. Shiftlet finally receives, which is both a warning of the future and a résumé of the past.

Likewise, "peaks" of spiritual revelation or Gothic-like visions run throughout *Everything That Rises Must Converge*: Mrs. May "had the look of a person whose sight has been suddenly restored but who finds the light unbearable"; in Sheppard's vision of himself, he realized "he had stuffed his own emptiness with good works like a glutton"; and Mrs. Turpin saw through a "visionary light" that her supposed virtues would have to be eradicated.

Flannery O'Connor's technique of putting the Gothic conventions of her fiction to practical metaphoric and structural work is paralleled by the way she uses the conventions for tonal purposes. Initial tone in *The Violent Bear It Away* is influenced by two Gothic conventions, the old house (adapted from the Gothic castle) and the pine coffin (the Gothic tomb). Both of these are described in the first part of the book and thus are instrumental in creating a tone that is to be sustained. It is in the "large and dark" kitchen that Mason Tarwater's death occurs. He sits at the breakfast table with all kinds of stuff stacked in the room as a background—sacks of feed and mash, scrap metal, woodshavings, old rope, and ladders—but on the back porch is the old man's "pine box" that he has readied for his death. These details of setting create an atmosphere of paradoxically unsystematic order: the coffin is ready for death—the man's spiritual life is ordered and prepared, but his earthly life is a conglomeration of scrap metal and woodshavings. This atmosphere pervades the entire book as the young boy pursues a course hindered by "woodshavings" but fatefully guided toward peaceful order.

The pine box (the Gothic tomb) in "Judgement Day" (published for the first time in the new book) functions in the service of tone in much the same way as that in *The Violet Bear It Away*. It establishes a level of contrast between the pathetically unfilled final wish of Tanner and the selfish, stolidly decisive action of the daughter.

In *Wise Blood* the dominant tone changes from discontent to peacefulness. Although the tone is set chiefly by the actions of Hazel Motes and by his movements from rebellion to submission, the Gothic motif of the ancestral curse represented by the "wise blood" of Enoch Emery assists in this tonal development. The history of the motif ranges from Manfred's family curse in *The Castle of Otranto* to the enduring jinx of the Pyncheons in *The House of Seven Gables*, the inevitable fall of the House of Usher, and the degeneration of the Compsons in Faulkner's Yoknapatawpha County.

The two tones in *Wise Blood* match, first of all, the two periods in Hazel Motes's progression from conflict to peace:

> 1. Discontent—Haze comes to Taulkinham, sights Asa Hawks, establishes a residence, discontentedly wanders, purchases the "ratcolored Essex," seduces Sabbath Lily, preaches spasmodically but violently.
>
> 2. Peacefulness—Haze exists in self-inflicted blindness, forsakes active evangelism, practices fasting and silence.

Matching these two tones and two periods is wise-blooded Enoch Emery in his relationship to the motif of the ancestral curse:

> 1. Discontent—Enoch meets Haze and tells of his "wise-blood" curse, expresses desire for fellowship, visits the "new jesus," the mummy in the "Museum," shows the "new jesus" to Haze, responds to his "wise-blood" urging to steal the "new jesus."
>
> 2. Peacefulness—Enoch delivers the "new jesus" to Hazel Motes and to the world, vanishes into anonymity.

Thus the varying tonality of *Wise Blood* is actually a by-product of the central figure's actions, but it is deepened by a Gothic convention which employs a grotesque symbol of the baby Christ, a John the Baptist who brings the Word in a new way, and a distorted "chosen one" who does not accept grace until after the "new jesus" is brought to him.

Reflection merely on the technique with which Miss O'Connor handles this Gothic motif of the ancestral curse, not to mention her techniques of putting to work the Gothic character types and other devices, recalls Drake's comment quoted earlier. The artistic subtlety with which Miss O'Connor controls the "wise blood" scheme, a small part of the whole set of Gothic conventions, demonstrates that the conventions are certainly important, but in a much broader way than Drake explained. The "Southern 'Gothic' mode" of the fiction, which has been cited in half-derogatory references, can now be justified as being technically and artistically functional in the work. Basically, the conventions contribute to Miss O'Connor's theme of man's ability to overcome perversity only if he becomes obedient to Divine Authority.

Notes

1. Flannery O'Connor, *Everything That Rises Must Converge,* Farrar, Straus & Giroux, New York, $4.95.

2. New York: New American Library, 1961.

3. Harold C. Gardiner, "A Tragic New Image of Man," *America,* CII (March 5, 1960), 682, quoting Caroline Gordon.

4. In *A Good Man Is Hard to Find* (New York: New American Library, 1956).

J. Douglas Perry Jr. (essay date 1973)

SOURCE: Perry, J. Douglas, Jr. "Gothic as Vortex: The Form of Horror in Capote, Faulkner, and Styron." In *The Critical Response to Truman Capote,* edited by Joseph J. Waldmeir and John C. Waldmeir, pp. 179-91. Westport, Conn: Greenwood Press, 1999.

[*In the following essay, originally published in* Modern Fiction Studies *in 1973, Perry proposes that in addition to the commonality of theme and images, American gothic fiction also uses traditional structures and techniques to create a concentric series of events, drawing the reader into an intense interaction between human communities that exist inside and outside the novel.*]

An examination of Capote, Faulkner, and Styron reveals that modern American gothic is not only a matter of theme or image, as Irving Malin suggests,[1] but of narrative form as well, that certain basic modes of rendering are traditional to gothic, and that in structure, as in theme and image, writers like Capote, Faulkner, and Styron parallel Melville and Poe, and ultimately such gothicists as "Monk" Lewis and Mary Shelley.

A convenient rule of thumb for modern American gothic might be that its structures are analogous to its images and themes. If one considers gothic to be made up of the interaction of theme, image, and structure, Malin has covered two of the three areas. He identifies the three images of American gothic as the room, the voyage, and the mirror, and the three appropriate themes as confinement, flight—really two sides of the same coin—and narcissism.[2] It is with the remaining area, the three corresponding structural principles (which I have labeled *concentricity, predetermined sequence,* and *character repetition*) that this article will deal.

One more point should be made here. The most pervasive gothic theme, the most pervasive gothic image, points to the over-all gothic structure: the fear of being drawn in and the image of the whirlpool find their expression in a structural vortex, composed of a series of rings or levels which create a kind of hierarchy of horror, like Dante's inferno.

The three structural principles are simply ways in which a whirlpool is shifted from a visual representation to the printed page. The process down the side of the whirlpool becomes the sequential experiencing of levels, a series of events, funneling into the final one. The sequence is predetermined because the whirlpool cancels free will and random motion. To move through the whirlpool is to find oneself moving in smaller and faster circles; a novel conveys this sensation by repeating its initial event or situation in more and more strident ways, creating for us a sense of concentricity. Finally, there is the matter of character repetition, the recurrence of archetypal figures, or clusters of them, throughout the various subplots of the novel, in an obsessive and stereotypical fashion. This character repetition lets us see the workings of the gothic world, for as the main characters or their proxies reappear at successive levels, they become increasingly grotesque, distorted more and more by the whirlpool's pull.

In a sense, it is arbitrary and misleading to isolate these structures this way, because they are simply facets of the same process, even as the themes express each other: the room's boundaries both promote and define one's flight, and the mirror is not only what one flees, but what one flies to. Concentricity (which implies boundaries) and sequence (which is simply flight through the concentric events) have the same interlocking relationship. As readers, we experience the spatial arrangement of the novel (its chapters or levels) as a matter of duration, as though we ourselves flee downward through the circles of the vortex. The last structural element, character repetition (which expresses narcissism), is made possible through the interaction of the other two: it is observable because a series of human communities can exist simultaneously and be experienced concentrically in the novel.

All three of the structural principles are molded into a novel which, like the half-spent suction of the Pequod's whirlpool, sucks the reader in, only to throw him back out again, like Ishmael, or Poe's Maelstrom man. George Poulet's analysis of Poe, with slight modifications, can be applied to all American gothic:

> A sort of temporal circle surrounds Poe's characters. A whirlpool envelops them, which, like that of the maelstrom, disposes its funnel by degrees from the past in which one has been caught to the future in which one will be dead. Whether it moves in the limitless eternity of dreams or the limited temporality of awakening, the work of Poe thus always presents a time that is closed.[3]

The first principle, concentricity, is far easier for a spatial form, like painting, than for novels. Nevertheless, the novel can utilize what Hillis Miller calls "the Quaker Oats effect":

> A real Quaker Oats box is fictionalized when it becomes a picture of a Quaker Oats box which bears in turn another . . . and so on indefinitely, in an endless play of imagination and reality. The imaginary copy

tends to affirm the reality of what it copies and at the same time to undermine its substantiality. To watch a play within a play is to be transformed from spectator into actor and to suspect that all the world may be a stage and the men and women merely players. To read a narration within a narration makes all the world a novel and turns the reader into a fictional character.[4]

Such an illusion becomes all the more desirable in the whirlpool world of gothic.

It is in just such a manner that Mary Shelley draws us into her tale. As we read *Frankenstein* we are, in effect, cutting across a series of interrupted and resumed narratives, drawing a straight line through the concentric circles made by her narrators. After Mary Shelley's own preface, voyager Robert Walton writes letters to his sister embodying the narrative of Dr. Frankenstein who in turn supplies the monologue of the monster. Each story teller is interrupted by the other and only allowed to finish when his interrupter has finished. One charts one's progress through the book by the level of hearsay.

A similar if more crudely manipulated concentricity occurs in *The Monk,* between Ambrosio's fall from innocence and his on-going corruption. In a hiatus of more than one hundred pages, a second plot is introduced, involving the narration of Don Raymond, who interrupts himself first for the autobiography of Marguerite and then for Agnes's capsule gothic tale. One is farthest from the surface and from a sense of reality here, for Agnes's story—the tale of the bleeding nun—is so fantastic that not even Agnes believes it until, in melodramatic fashion, Agnes and Don Raymond themselves succumb to the Bleeding Nun.

With so many tales being recounted successively, recurrence of character types is almost inevitable. It happens in *The Monk,* of course, but the classic example of this repetition occurs in the dark and fair heroes and heroines of *Wuthering Heights*. The confusion of names in *Wuthering Heights*—with so many overlapping Heathcliffes, Lintons, and Earnshaws for namesakes—becomes not merely a problem of multiple marriages and dense plotting, but the first source of disorientation in Lockwood's gothic encounter:

> In vapid listlessness I leant my head against the window, and continued spelling over Catherine Earnshaw—Heathcliffe—Linton, till my eyes closed, but they had not rested five minutes when a glare of white letters started from the dark, as vivid as spectres—the air swarmed with Catherines.[5]

Although there is no such confusion of names in *Frankenstein,* the character of the Promethean hero is central to each ring of the concentrically formed novel. His magnitude increases proportionately as one approaches the center of the book. The outermost ring is occupied by Mary Shelley herself who, despite her disclaimer that the novel was "commenced partly as a source of amusement, and partly as an expedient for exercising my untried resources of mind," provides the book with this envoi: "And now, once again, I bid my hideous progeny go forth and prosper. I have an affection for it, for it was the offspring of happy days, when death and grief were but words."[6]

At this point, the interaction of character repetition with concentricity and sequence becomes clear. The concentricity is apparent precisely because of the recurrence. At each new level, the reader finds the patterns obsessively reestablishing themselves. As a temporal experience, the growing horror is based partly on our recognition of the inevitable course of events, a sequence we have already faced in a milder form on the previous level.

Inversely, the concentricity and sequence strengthen the reader's impulse to make the analogies. For example, Robert Walton's uncompleted journey becomes much more sinister when one sees the horrible outcome of Dr. Frankenstein's idealistic quest.

I have started my discussion with these nineteenth-century examples both because the formal methods and patterns are clear, and because they are the prototypes, as Leslie Fiedler might say, in Capote, Faulkner, and Styron. In these American authors, the use of these techniques may be more elaborate, but the issues which are treated are of the same existential profundity and ambiguity as those of *Frankenstein*. *Other Voices, Other Rooms* concerns itself, as so many American novels do, with an adolescent's quest for identity. Joel Knox, like Robin Molienux before him, seeks out the fabled relatives that may give him identity and security. When he arrives at Skully's Landing, he finds only a madhouse inhabited by his long lost father (in a near catatonic state); his father's second wife in name only (Miss Amy), a Havisham-like relic of Southern womanhood; and his cousin Randolph, a homosexual and transvestite. These are Joel's role-models, the gothic family. It is cousin Randolph, Joel's ultimate alter-ego, who poses the gothic dilemma by linking the identity quest to the gothic whirlpool:

> What a subtle torture it would be to destroy all the mirrors in the world: where then could we look for reassurance of our identities? . . . Narcissus was no egotist . . . merely another of us who, in our unshatterable isolation, recognized, on seeing his reflection, the one beautiful comrade, the only inseparable love.[7]

This passage, which clearly demonstrates Malin's diagnosis of theme and image, mirror and narcissism, leads to the kind of motifs that Ishmael attaches to water in *Moby-Dick*:

Still deeper the meaning of that story of Narcissus who because he could not grasp the tormenting mild image he saw in the fountain, plunged into it and was drowned. But that same image, we ourselves see in all rivers and oceans. It is the image of the ungraspable phantom of life; and this is the key to it all.[8]

Capote's horizon is narrower than Melville's partly because it is more exclusively gothic. The circle is vicious rather than transcendental. Joel enters the whirlpool and fails to resurface. As I have been suggesting earlier, this is a formal matter as much as a thematic one. Close to the end of the book, after Joel emerges from a series of progressively more sinister levels of gothic, he enters the final delirium, the delirium that renders him fit for the Cousin Randolph's proclivities. The brief final section of the book opens with a description of the delirium as whirlpool, with Joel in his coffin at the center of a ring of grotesques—which includes every character in the novel but Joel:

> Miss Wisteria . . . leaned so far over she nearly fell into the chest: listen, she whispered . . . are the dead as lonesome as the living? Whereupon the room commenced to vibrate slightly, then more so, chairs overturned . . . a mirror cracked, . . . down went the house, down into the earth, . . . past the deepest root, into the furry arms of horned children whose bumblebee eyes withstand forests of flame.
>
> (C [*Other Voices, Other Rooms*], p. 113)

The center of the final whirlpool is Randolph's window, where Joel, on his first day at Skully's Landing, saw "the queer lady" (C, p. 40). Joel's final submergence is accomplished by means of this specter, whom he now knows to be Randolph:

> Gradually the blinding sunset drained from the glass, . . . a face trembled like a white beautiful moth, smiled. She beckoned to him, shining and silver, and he knew he must go: unafraid, not hesitating, he paused only at the garden's edge where he stopped and looked back at the bloomless descending blue, at the boy he had left behind.
>
> (C, p. 127)

Unlike Poe's "Descent into the Maelstrom," there is no corresponding ascent; Joel makes his irrevocable choice.

To see the shape of the book, the gothic vortex, is to see only the symptom. The cause and ultimate meaning lie elsewhere. The reason why Joel must accept Randolph is that Randolph becomes the self-negating way out of an untenable and omnipresent situation: a perverted and sterile sexual triangle encountered, with different participants, not less than five times in the book. Joel finds either himself or Randolph at the apex, the variable element in each of these triangles, and each time Joel experiences or witnesses it, the triangle becomes more intense, more sinister. First Joel is a pawn in the sibling rivalry of the cruel Florabelle, totally feminine but totally self-centered, and the somewhat overbearing Idabelle, who has become a tomboy to escape the pressures of sexuality. All this can be accepted as part of the mildly confusing but normative world of adolescence. Not so healthy is the successive menage à trois of Ransom, Miss Amy, and the sexually ambivalent Randolph who, like Joel, drifts alone in the middle. Joel is then put between Zoo, feminine, warm, but somehow unattainable, and Randolph who is, at this point in the story, unacceptable.

Randolph's account of Ransom's incapacitating accident reveals a far more sinister triangle: Pepe, the stud prizefighter; Dolores, who, like Florabelle, lives only for self-worship; and Randolph, attracted differently by both, satisfied by neither. After hearing this story, Joel himself becomes the middle man in a similar but odder triangle with Miss Wisteria—a Florabelle transformed into a grotesque parody of the Southern Belle—and Idabelle, Miss Wisteria's inappropriate and hapless suitor. It does not help that Miss Wisteria in turn now covets the now terrified Joel.

The character repetition of this particular sequence makes Joel's end seem not only inevitable, but almost preferable. In effect, Capote has used the structures to turn the gothic inside out. The reader comes to understand that given the gothic nature of the outside world, which ravages Zoo, Ransom, and Randolph, the bond between Randolph and Joel—as perverse as it may be—is the most affirmative situation Joel can find.

Faulkner, in *Sanctuary,* also turns the gothic inside out. One finds in *Sanctuary,* as in *Other Voices, Other Rooms,* that while the center of the pool is the most dramatic, it is at the beguilingly calm margin that the real danger lurks. Not Popeye, but Narcissa is the real source of evil in *Sanctuary.* Faulkner uses the formal principles I have described to achieve this, but in a different way from Capote. For instance, instead of the slow but steady progress from the edge to the center, Faulkner flicks us back and forth between the two extremes. The novel begins with a confrontation, over a mirror-like pool, of Horace and Popeye who are, in some ways, the alpha and omega:

> The spring welled up . . . upon a bottom of whorled and waved sand. . . . In the spring the drinking man leaned his face to the broken and myriad reflection of his own drinking. When he rose up he saw among them the shattered reflection of Popeye's straw hat.[9]

In one sense, this is a chance encounter between men from opposite poles: Horace, the respectable small town lawyer and family man; Popeye, the vicious and impotent bootlegger. Horace comes and goes at once, with no sense of participation in Popeye's world. Nevertheless, Horace first sees Popeye as an image mixed in with his own like the kaleidoscopic everyman shiftings of Joe Christmas's face when he dies. Horace is in flight from the sterile respectability of his marriage when Popeye, the social misfit, enters his life. In fact, as Olga Vickery points out, "there are certain startling similarities between these two morally antithetical figures":

> Popeye's rapt and unnatural absorption in watching Temple and Red perform an act in which he can never share is echoed by Horace's painful exclusion from the grape arbor where Little Belle casually experiments with sex. . . . Popeye's brutal act fuses with Horace's thoughts and culminates in the nightmare vision of the rape of a composite Temple-Little Belle.[10]

What Vickery notes about the men, and implies about Temple and Little Belle, is even more applicable to the antipodal figures of Narcissa and Temple. If Temple's father is a judge, the law runs rampant through the Benbow family.[11] This familial tie with the law makes both women see law as a personal convenience rather than an institution for human betterment. Both of them are concerned with the appearance of respectability. "Honest women," Ruby sneers at Temple. "Too good to have anything to do with common people. . . . Just let a man so much as look at you and you faint away because your father the judge and your four brothers might not like it" (F, p. 55). Miss Jenny has fainter but similar scorn for Narcissa: "Do you think Narcissa'd want any of her folks could know people who would do anything as natural as make love or rob or steal?" (F, p. 115). In *Sanctuary,* the gothic world is synonymous with a loveless world, and Temple and Narcissa match the impotence of Popeye and Horace with a corresponding frigidity. Because they are not looking for adult relationships, both Temple and Narcissa are drawn to Gowan, but only to a certain point, as Horace's anecdote reveals:

> "He asked Narcissa to marry him. She told him that one child was enough for her. . . . So he got mad and said he would go to Oxford, where there was a woman he was reasonably confident he would not appear ridiculous to."
>
> (F [*Sanctuary*], p. 161)

Imprisoned throughout the book, and standing as the sole exponents of the nongothic world, are Lee Goodwin and Ruby, and it is their destruction, or rather Lee's destruction and with it the meaning of Ruby's life, that finally crushes Horace.

The feeling of character repetition is heightened by the structuring of the narrative. Instead of moving from one situation to a more sinister one to a final one, Faulkner shuttles back and forth between the respectable world of Jefferson and the depraved worlds of Old Frenchman's Place and Memphis, counterpointing his landscape and characters, holding to a strict chronological sequence. A quick check of Cleanth Brooks's chronology[12] reveals that only once does Faulkner allow the two plots to slip out of synchrony; the result there is to intensify the gothic.

In chapter XXII, Horace has learned from Clarence Snopes of Temple's whereabouts, and in the next chapter, on June third, he interviews her. In chapters XXIV and XXV, Faulkner jumps ahead to June seventeenth, describing Popeye's murder of Red, Red's wake, and the departure of Popeye and Temple. Yet when the reader returns to Horace in Jefferson (XXVI), it is still June fourth: Horace is writing a letter to his wife in the aftermath of his horror over Temple's recital; Narcissa is preparing for Horace's defeat at the hands of the district attorney; and Clarence Snopes is headed for Jackson. Thus, while Popeye and Temple move beyond his reach and arrangements are made with Judge Drake and a "Memphis Jew" lawyer, Horace continues to conduct his life at a snail's pace. At the beginning of chapter XXVII, it is still only June tenth for Horace, calling to make sure that his star witness is still safely in Memphis, a fact which may comfort Horace, but not the reader. Abruptly, Faulkner brings Horace to the eve of the trial. Temple has disappeared and only reappears to give the false testimony which convicts Lee.

Faulkner manipulates time to create a doubleness, to put Horace in molasses while evil moves by him on greased skids. The result is to make physically impossible what Miss Jenny knows to be societally impossible: "You won't ever catch up with injustice, Horace." (F, p. 115)

The final gothic twist, the final concentric pattern, is provided by Popeye's own trial. Here Popeye, that most impotent of the impotent men in *Sanctuary*, finds himself being defended by the ultimate parody of Horace's idealism: "His lawyer had an ugly, eager, earnest face. He rattled on with a kind of enthusiasm. . . . A fellow policeman, a cigar clerk, a telephone girl testified, while his own lawyer rebutted in a gaunt mixture of uncouth enthusiasm and earnest ill-judgment" (F, p. 303). Like the sideshow in *Other Voices, Other Rooms,* this courtroom comedy is the final degradation of and commentary on man's desire to act meaningfully. Both Horace's idealism and his actions are seen as if through the wrong end of a telescope, leaving a searing void like the fiery vortex which engulfs Goodwin in front of Horace's outraged eyes:

> Horace couldn't hear them. He couldn't hear the man who had got burned screaming. He couldn't hear the fire, though it swirled upward, unabated, as though it were living upon itself, and soundless: a voice of fury like in a dream, roaring silently out of a peaceful void.
>
> (F, p. 289)

In a slightly different manner from Capote, Faulkner has turned the gothic inside out. Evil seems initially a bizarre and isolatable element, confined to the aberrations of Popeye and Temple. Eventually, Horace's twin battles—with the natural world which threatens his sterile existence, and with the monstrous people who threaten his client—these merge. Nature itself, in all its forms, becomes the menace, menacing even the villains who become its victims, disrupting society, the law, and the community. When one recognizes that nature is gothic from Horace's point of view, one simultaneously realizes that Horace, all of us in fact, are unnatural, that good and evil are artificial, man-made concepts. In *Sanctuary,* Faulkner stops just short of what he later says in *As I Lay Dying* or *Light in August:* that it is man, not his universe, that is out of kilter, that the sensation of gothicness is man's projective response to the absurdity of his own existence in a totally consistent, self-sufficient, and alien universe.

If one characterizes Capote's subject matter as individual in its concerns, and Faulkner's as societal, one must call Styron's interpersonal. He is less concerned with Law and the coercions of the Community because he seems largely unconvinced that communal society can exist in America. The permanence of Jefferson, Mississippi, is negated by the transience of Port Warwick, Va.:

> In America, our landmarks and our boundaries merge, shift, and change quicker than we can tell: one day we feel rooted. . . . Then . . . it is all yanked out from beneath us, and when we come down we alight on— what? The same old street, to be sure. But where it once had the solid resounding sound of Bankhead McGruder Avenue . . . now it is called Buena Vista Terrace ("It's the California influence," my father complained, "It's going to get us all in the end.")[13]

Even the name of the narrator, Peter Leverett, is invariably garbled and lost in introductions, becoming Levenson or Levitt, lending further evidence to a theory of instability: "There must be something basically unsound about the structure of my name," Peter observes (S, p. 141). For Styron, the same problem prevails that Capote and Faulkner documented: a sense of the void at the center of things, a conviction that chaos is about to rise up and swallow man's personal order. To Styron, this feeling manifests itself not among or within people, but between them, at that instant when one person tries to establish himself in terms of his relations to others. So, in *Set This House on Fire,* three major figures (and several minor ones) of distinct and somewhat antagonistic temperaments, establish a temporary equilibrium of their opposing tensions, only to lash out at each other in the end, all in the name of self-actualization. The two survivors—Cass Kinsolving and Peter Leverett, the murderer and the not-so-innocent bystander— are left with the task of rehearsing and reconstructing the significance of the triangle.

The theme of the void provides ample explanation for Styron's adaptation of gothic methods and form. In addition, because the problem is interpersonal in nature, a treatment of gothic as group dynamics, character repetition becomes a crucial and valuable structure in Styron's story. Instead of providing merely the grotesque commentary of Capote, or the suggestive analogies of *Sanctuary,* it boxes the compass of man's capacity for good and evil. Peter, Cass, and Mason, like the three somewhat similar brothers Karamazov, cover the spectrum of observing, doing, and embodying.

Yet it is not the variety of characters, but their sameness that finally emerges as important. Here again is where the gothic concentricity, the argument from character analogy plays the major part. Peter and Cass uncover their pasts by telling the history of their involvement with each other, to each other. In so doing, they also collaborate on Mason's history, piecing together motive and murderer, cause and effect, during the entire book. Gradually, the fact of their parallel pasts overshadows the sequence of events they are trying to reconstruct. All the men are nearly identical in age: Cass and Mason cross the watershed age of thirty just before the rape, murder, and apparent suicide which occur in Sambuco; Peter, a year younger, fails to confront the issues of Sambuco until after his return home, when a general kind of angst leads him to seek out Cass and the truth. Styron suggests something like Erik Eriksen's delayed identity crisis in these men. With the significant exception of Peter, accounts are given of each man's initial sexual encounter, invariably in the late teens: from Mason's *flagrante delicto* in boarding school to Saverio's rape-murder of Angelina. Thirteen years later, the mild anxiety of Peter is set over against Cass's almost classic nineteenth-century self-flagellation. Saverio murders mindlessly; Cass murders in an ecstacy of mistaken vengeance; and Mason, like Gatsby, attempts to realize himself in a grandiose self-conception, a pursuit of "the green light, the orgiastic future,"[14] only to find himself at an impotent dead end, pursued by Cass and the insatiable demands of his own unattainable fantasies.

In each man, one finds an inner compulsion, a need to establish his value by meeting the impossible standards he has set for himself. Like the overreachers in Mary Shelley's *Frankenstein,* each refuses to recognize his own human frailty, the underlying egotism of his idealism. Like Mary Shelley, Styron uses the concentricity to drive the point home. In an obsessive way, the form of the novel is a series of nightmarish self-confrontations, of gradually increasing intensity. The cosmic unfairness of it all is that, in each case, the characters confront their moment of truth at the time when they are physically and emotionally drained, and totally inadequate to the challenge.

As one might expect, the book begins with Peter who occupies the outermost circle of the vortex, who is least susceptible to the maelstrom, and whose encounter with the nightmare is the slightest. The novel is a series of descents, with the first unchronologically but appropriately Peter's descent to Carolina and Cass, by way of Port Warwick. The reader is next given, in flashback, not the main event he has come to expect, but Peter's tragi-comic arrival at Sambuco, gothic enough in Peter's near manslaughter, by car, of a half-wit Italian motorcyclist, but retrospectively mild in comparison to the novel's final outcome:

> DiLieto . . . lay face up on the road, blood trickling gently from nose and ears, and with a sort of lopsided, dreamy expression on his features, part agony, part a smile, as if in mindless repose. . . . One eye socket was pink and sunken (I thought this my doing), and with a grisly feeling I glanced around for the missing eye. . . . For what seemed like an endless time I kept trampling around the prostrate diLieto, reeling with shock.
>
> (S [*Set This House on Fire*], pp. 32-33)

Peter is given no time, at Sambuco, to regroup from the combination of the accident itself and the travel fatigue which precipitated it and, like Faulkner's Horace, never quite catches up. In fact, Peter attributes all his misfortune to an initial sleepless night on the road: "Had I been able to sleep easily that night, I might very well have been spared my trouble of the next day. Without that misadventure, I most surely would have arrived in Sambuco fresh as a buttercup: not haggard, shattered, and cursed with a sort of skittish, haunted depletion of nerves from which I never quite recovered" (S, pp. 29-30). Peter observes that such second thoughts are no good, but both his and Cass's narratives are full of them. This is the first in a series of "if onlys" where the physiological state of the character predetermines the catastrophic outcome. Once more, sequence is all. From the moment Peter barges onto the movie set at Sambuco, until his groggy mid-afternoon awakening to the news of Mason's death, hallucination and illusion are his constant companions.

Cass repeats the pattern laid out for Peter. While in Paris when he has gone to study painting, Cass experiences a drunken hallucination, an Italian pastoral fantasy. He sets out for Rome and eventually Sambuco in quest of the sun-drenched South. When he arrives in Sambuco in a state of virtual collapse, he creates such a scene that he, like Peter, winds up confronting the local functionary. Cass's travel fatigue is heightened by his fall off the wagon. It is this alcoholic arrival, and relentless, ever-deepening alcoholism of his stay there that establishes the feeling of horrifying inevitability. His lack of money, his drunken desperation, his extramarital involvement with Francesca, his acquiescence in Mason's sinister and ever growing domination over him, and his horror at Mason's rape of Francesca: all of these culminate in Cass's act of vengeance and self-liberation, the murder of Mason. Styron's vision becomes clearer at each level of the vortex. The nature of the universe is to demand more of man than he is equipped to deliver; the nature of our relations with our fellow man is to ask him to answer for our own inadequacies, to fulfill us; and the nature of our fellow man is such that he cannot do this. So each character projects his inadequacies and frustrations on the other: Peter lives vicariously through Mason's fleshed-out fantasies; Mason subjugates Peter and Cass for self-aggrandizement; Cass flees home, family, artistic responsibility, and self for an Italian Never-Never Land, an idyll with Francesca, and so unwittingly singles her out to be Mason's means of violating Cass through her. And if Francesca's hopes for herself and her family are projected on Cass, her fears are projected onto Saverio, bringing about a self-fulfilling prophecy:

> What Mason had done to her just that same evening clung to her flesh like some loathsome disease. . . . So it was that when she met Saverio in the shadows and he put out his fingers harmlessly . . . to stroke her, the intense male hand on her arm brought back, like horror made touchable, the touch and the feel and the actuality, and she found herself shrieking.
>
> (S, pp. 453-454)

She lashes out at him preemptively, and as he strikes back, she continues to scream, "unaware now that this was Saverio, or anyone, aware of nothing save that the whole earth's protruberant and insatiate masculinity had descended upon her in the space of one summer night" (S, p. 454). The half-wit kills her in self-defense, and so provides the most graphic example of the inevitably gothic dimension of all human relationships, the mutually destructive nature of people's needs for one another.

Nevertheless, the epilogue of *Set This House on Fire*, like the epilogue of *Moby-Dick,* is written by the survivors of the whirlpool, not its victims. In *Moby-Dick,* Ishmael, like Peter, is the one least involved with the cosmos of the story, and his survival is a demonstration of the difference in stature between him and Ahab. Cass is far closer to Ahab than Ishmael and suggests that Styron envisions another kind of survivor from one who returns merely to tell somewhat uncomprehendingly his tale. Cass has grown and learned, has learned that the gothic vision, with its Manichean values, its all or nothing philosophy, is out of kilter with human nature and self-actualization:

> But to be truthful, you see, I can only tell you this: that as for being and nothingness, the one thing I did know was that to choose between them was to choose being, not for the sake of being, much less the desire to be forever—but in the hope of being what I could be for a time. That would be an ecstacy. God Knows it would.
>
> (S, pp. 476-477)

The epilogue is two documents: one testifying to Cass's anticipated paternity, a reestablishment of creativity on several counts; the other Peter's reprieve in the miraculous recovery of diLieto. Only Cass emerges as the clear victor, perhaps because we are dealing once again with a kind of double gothic. Perhaps the real gothic world is Peter's, a world of twilight perceptions, evanescent pleasures, vicariousness and lost opportunities, a world where the lack of a real dark night of the soul also means the impossibility of a real redemption.

Character repetition, sequence, and concentricity are the formal means of portraying the gothic sensation of existing in time and space. As such they apply to all of the Faulkner, Styron, and Capote. The family resemblances of *Lie Down in Darkness* to *The Sound and the Fury* are only partly explained by influence, for in fundamental ways Faulkner and Styron differ at the start: Faulkner's concern with the Compsons turns on the family as microcosm of society; Styron sees the family as the most intense and glaring example of the failure of human relationships, the unendingly destructive demands of one on another. The similarities spring from Faulkner's and Styron's mutual fascination with time: with clocks and how to stop them, with existence, consciousness and its denial, with the sterile repetitiveness of family curses and familial neuroses, swirling on through time. Both writers stress subjective time, multiple narrations which substitute a series of fragmented and irreconcilable time-consciousnesses for a Greenwich stability. Capote's *In Cold Blood* is the archetypal horror machine of time, an inexorable pit and pendulum alternation, as Capote jerks the reader back and forth from Clutter farm to Kansas highway, in rigid chronological sequence and tightening geography, until the bright blue shotgun flash in the dark.

All three writers use the gothic form, with its denial of final absolute affirmation, tragic or otherwise, to capture the irony of our twentieth-century existence: the conviction that the search for self-awareness may not only be fatal, but fruitless, because it is equivalent to self-negation; that selfhood is an arbitrary but necessary construct of man's self-protective ignorance; that self-awareness and self-destruction are one and the same: "The intense concentration of self in the middle of such a heartless immensity, my God! Who can tell it?"[15]

Notes

1. Irving Malin, *New American Gothic* (Carbondale, Ill.: University of Southern Illinois Press, 1962).

2. Malin, especially pp. 79-80, 106-107, 126-128.

3. George Poulet, *Studies in Human Time* (Baltimore: Johns Hopkins Press, 1956), pp. 333-334.

4. J. Hillis Miller, *The Form of Victorian Fiction* (Notre Dame, Ind.: University of Notre Dame, 1968), p. 35.

5. Emily Bronte, *Wuthering Heights* (New York: Dodd, Mead & Co., 1942), p. 37.

6. Mary W. Shelley, *Frankenstein* (New York: Dell, 1970), pp. 8, 14.

7. Truman Capote, *Other Voices, Other Rooms* (New York: Signet, 1958), p. 78. In subsequent references to this book, page numbers will appear after the citation, in parentheses, with the author's initial: (C, p. 78).

8. Herman Melville, *Moby-Dick* (New York: Bobbs-Merrill, 1952), p. 26.

9. William Faulkner, *Sanctuary* (New York: Vintage, 1958), p. 3. See note 7.

10. Olga Vickery, "Crime and Punishment: *Sanctuary*," reprinted in *Faulkner: A Collection of Critical Essays* (Englewood Cliffs, N.J.: Prentice-Hall, 1966), p. 132.

11. Robert Kirk thinks Narcissa's father may be Judge Benbow of *Absalom, Absalom!: Faulkner's People* (Berkeley: University of California Press, 1963), p. 323. William Volpe makes the same assumption in his Sartoris family tree: *A Reader's Guide to William Faulkner* (New York: Noonday, 1964), p. 66.

12. Cleanth Brooks, *The Yoknapatawpha Country* (New Haven: Yale University Press, 1963), pp. 287-289.

13. William Styron, *Set This House on Fire* (New York: Signet, 1961), pp. 14-15. See note 7.

14. F. Scott Fitzgerald, *The Great Gatsby* (New York: Scribners, 1953), p. 182.

15. Melville, p. 529.

Susan V. Donaldson (essay date fall 1997)

SOURCE: Donaldson, Susan V. "Making a Spectacle: Welty, Faulkner, and Southern Gothic."[1] *Mississippi Quarterly* 50, no. 4 (fall 1997): 567-83.

[*In the following essay, Donaldson compares the portraits of women created by Faulkner and Welty, noting that while Faulkner's narratives reverberate with the effort to impose cultural ideas of femininity on his Southern characters, Welty's narratives present women that break out of the narrow confines of their worlds, "a carnival of gothic and grotesque heroines" who resist placement in traditional roles and themes.*]

By the time Eudora Welty published *A Curtain of Green and Other Stories* in 1941, the term "Southern Gothic" had become something very like a synonym—or a cliche—for modern Southern literature. Louise Bogan even titled her review of Welty's collection "The Gothic South."[2] Other reviewers of *A Curtain of Green* tended to use the catch-all category of Southern Gothic interchangeably with the grotesque—or in the words of the reviewer for *Time* Magazine, "the demented, the deformed, the queer" (quoted in Peterman, p. 107). No doubt these reviewers were reassured in their easy reference to the term Southern Gothic by Carson McCullers's remarks in her 1941 essay, "The Russian Realists and Southern Literature," in which she declared that Southern writers shared with nineteenth-century Russian writers a vision of "the cheapness of human life" and a strikingly similar technique for vividly evoking that vision—"a bold and outwardly callous juxtaposition of the tragic with the humorous, the immense with the trivial, the sacred with the bawdy, the whole soul of man with a materialistic detail."[3]

Considering the stereotypes and the cliches associated with Southern Gothic and the whole host of myths defining the image of "the benighted South," as George Tindall aptly calls it, I think it's quite understandable that Welty herself has often resisted being categorized as a writer of Southern Gothic. "They better not call me that!" she abruptly told Alice Walker in an interview.[4] Following her lead, Welty scholars, Ruth Weston most recently, have often argued against placing Welty in the same category of Southern Gothic as Carson McCullers or the Faulkner of "A Rose for Emily" and *As I Lay Dying*.[5]

I would like to take issue with this reluctance to couple Southern Gothic and Welty in the same breath and with our tendency, for that matter, to take those hoary old terms Southern Gothic and Southern grotesque for granted—terms, we often argue, that were all too readily applied to William Faulkner himself in the 1930s when critics found themselves perplexed with works ranging from "A Rose for Emily" to *As I Lay Dying*. Patricia Yaeger has already undertaken the task of examining versions of the grotesque in the writing of modern Southern women writers. Her series of essays on O'Connor and Welty and her forthcoming book *Dirt and Desire* promise to recast our whole conception of the grotesque in Southern literature in distinctly feminist terms. And if we take heed of the wealth of scholarship emerging on the gothic and gender in the last twenty years, we might learn in particular that the peculiar propensity of modern Southern writers to evoke the gothic, the macabre, and the grotesque might very well have a good deal to do with regional anxiety about rapidly changing gender roles in the first half of the twentieth century. Anxiety about the New Woman in the South—and the way both Faulkner and Welty responded to the implications of her presence—might also tell us a good deal about the intertextual relationship between Faulkner's frieze of gothic women in his short fiction of the 1920s and 1930s—especially "A Rose for Emily," "Dry September," "There Was a Queen," and "That Evening Sun"—and Welty's own parade of monstrous women in *A Curtain of Green*. What we discover, I think, is something like an intertextual debate on women and the disruption of tradition in the twentieth-century South. Half sympathetic toward and half horrified by the spectacle of women betwixt and between tradition and change, Faulkner creates short stories about dangerous women who serve as disrupters of male narratives and as signifiers of the breakdown of cultural narratives of traditional manhood and womanhood. Welty's gothic heroines, though, suggest not so much the fragmentation of traditional narratives as the emergence of narratives to come—female stories about hysterics whose bodies provide expression in the absence of appropriate language. The difference, ultimately, lies in the politics of spectacle and vision—issues that have long concerned the genre of the gothic.

As Susan Wolstenholme notes, the gothic has usually been characterized as having a peculiarly "visual quality" precisely because so many scenes in gothic fiction are framed as scenes and because characters often present themselves as scenes in themselves or as spectators of scenes.[6] And as a good many commentators have noted, reading a gothic novel often takes on strikingly voyeuristic connotations. After all, what Michelle Masse calls the "Ur-plot" of gothicism focuses on a suffering woman—a titillating twist on the "Richardsonian courtship narrative in which an unprotected young woman in an isolated setting uncovers a sinister secret." Not for nothing, then, does Masse pronounce the gothic novel "a peep show of terror"—one that seems to ensure the distinction between observers and the observed.[7]

More to the point, Masse argues that the gothic stages, in her words, "what Freud calls the beating fantasy, in which a spectator watches someone being hurt by a dominant other" (p. 3). In this respect, she draws from Freud's famous 1919 essay, "A Child Is Being Beaten," in which the master speculates on the stages of a childhood fantasy entertaining the scenario of a child being beaten and the peculiar pleasure accompanying that fantasy. Noel Polk has already pointed out the relevance of this essay for a host of Faulkner texts,[8] but I would like to probe the gender implications of this beating fantasy a little more deeply. For it is with a certain grim determination that Freud catalogues the slippery transformations marking the beating fantasies of little girls in particular:

> In the first and third phantasies the child who is being beaten is always someone other than the subject; in the middle it is always the child herself, in the third phase it is almost invariably only the boys who are being

beaten. The person who does the beating is from the first her father, replaced later on by a substitute taken from the class of fathers.

(p. 196)

Even the girls themselves seem to experience metamorphosis within the realm of fantasy. "Another fact, though its connection with the rest does not appear to be close," Freud adds with a certain uneasiness and obliqueness, "is that between the second and third phases the girls change their sex, for in the phantasies of the latter phase they turn into boys" (p. 196). As Masse shrewdly notes, the closer Freud looks at the mutations of the fantasy, the more it blurs and mutates, and the more Freud himself suspects the difficulty of pinning down the fantasy once and for all. "Like the voyeur," Masse declares, "Freud contemplates the scenario again and again, seemingly unsure of the source of his dis-ease, 'an uneasy suspicion that this is not a final solution to the problem'" (p. 65).

Faulkner's and Welty's versions of Southern Gothic, I would argue, evoke something of this dis-ease and suspicion in part because some of their most prominent stories, like classic gothic tales of heroines under siege, bring attention to the spectacle of a woman, in Masse's words, "being hurt by a dominant other"—sometimes by a male character, sometimes by the community at large, and sometimes, unsettlingly enough, by the audience of the story itself. Whether Nancy in "That Evening Sun" or Welty's eponymous character Clytie in "A Curtain of Green," these women find themselves in various forms of confinement and entrapment, and quite often their imprisonment is signified by the boundaries of the stories that enclose them and by the communities and readers who scrutinize them.

In some of Faulkner's most famous short stories, like "A Rose for Emily" and "That Evening Sun," explicit attention is brought to the activity of watching the suffering of confined women. We watch along with Quentin, Caddy, and Jason as they survey with interest Nancy's increasing fear, evidenced in her keening and moaning, as the black maid anticipates the return of her husband Jesus and her own murder. Similarly, the narrator of "A Rose for Emily" underscores the intense scrutiny by the town under which Emily falls and by implication the reader as well by suggesting that Emily lies trapped in the collective gaze like a fly in amber: "We had long thought of them as a tableau, Miss Emily's slender figure in white in the background, her father a spraddled silhouette in the foreground, his back to her and clutching a horsewhip, the two of them framed by the back-flung front door."[9] And we watch along with the cook Elnora in "There Was a Queen," as she scornfully meditates on the comings and goings of Narcissa Benbow Sartoris, desperate to retrieve stolen obscene letters now in the possession of a Federal agent.

These stories are uncomfortable and vaguely salacious, I would argue, because they do evoke something of Freud's beating fantasy, posing a triangular relationship between the woman who is beaten, the figure or figures who do the beating, and the spectators who stand aside and watch. But they are also uncomfortable stories precisely because they suggest a rogues gallery of women who have stepped out of line, transgressed the boundaries of their traditional roles, and served as disruptive forces in male narratives or perhaps even threatened to usurp narratives in general. It is significant, after all, that Narcissa Sartoris in "There Was a Queen" feels a certain freedom to pursue whatever course necessary to acquire those stolen letters because she lives in a world singularly empty of white male authority. With the deaths of all the Sartoris men except her own son, "the quiet was now the quiet of womenfolks" (p. 727). It is also significant that Nancy, in "That Evening Sun," is implicitly seen by her white employers as a black woman gone wrong, one who prostitutes herself to white men, demands payment due her, and elicits beatings from irate clients and angry jailers. "[I]f you'd just let white men alone," the children's father tells her (p. 295).

Such representations were reminders that even in the early twentieth-century South the roles of women were rapidly changing as the True Woman of piety, submissiveness, and purity began to give way, in Carroll Smith-Rosenberg's words, to "the single, highly educated, economically autonomous New Woman." Quite simply, the New Woman, whether the flapper of the twenties or the professional woman resisting marriage, "challenged existing gender relations and the distribution of power" and as such, Smith-Rosenberg argues, became a "sexually freighted metaphor for social disorder and protest."[10] And if this sense of threat seemed pronounced in the nation as a whole, it bore a special weight in the South, where, as Bertram Wyatt-Brown has argued, the subordination of women was required for the maintenance of a white elite culture of honor and shame, intertwining the identity of an individual white male with the esteem of the community at large. For white women to step off the pedestal, for black women to take off their aprons, was to shake the very foundation of white Southern culture.

Hence if Faulkner's short-story portraits of women being beaten in one form or another evoke the kind of imprisonment for women often associated with the gothic, it is partly because his stories suggest something of Foucault's "spectacle of the scaffold" in a culture of shame and honor. Faulkner's gothic women—characters like Nancy, Emily Grierson, Narcissa Sartoris, and Minnie Cooper in "Dry September"—undergo narrative traits uncomfortably similar to the public executions suffered by criminals before the penal reforms of the late eighteenth and nineteenth centuries. Confined in their stories and subject to the scrutiny and sometimes the brutality of other characters, their communities, and even their readers, they face ritualistic punishment: the inscription of their culture's judgment upon their bodies so that, in Foucault's words, "the sentence [would be] legible for all."[11] In a word, we watch them being punished—by being exposed, confined, and figuratively beaten (and sometimes literally)—for not being the Southern women they are supposed to be.

The problem, though, is that the cultural narratives of discipline and punishment inscribed on their bodies are not quite successful, the sentence not quite legible, in part, I think, because Faulkner himself was so profoundly ambivalent about traditional definition of Southern womanhood and manhood. Narcissa, for one, remains distinctly unrepentant for bedding the Federal agent as the price to pay for getting her letters back, and though Jenny Du Pre seems to die from the pure shock of learning what Narcissa is capable of, her death can be read as much as a pungent commentary upon the overdue demise of the Old Order as it can a condemnation of Narcissa's actions.

But more unsettling by far is the curious interweaving in "Dry September" of Minnie Cooper's gothic tale of incarceration in small-town life with the narrative of white honor and vengeance culminating in the lynching of an innocent black man. The tale begins with a male narrative—men in a barbershop arguing about how to respond to "the rumor, the story, whatever it was. Something about Miss Minnie Cooper and a Negro" (p. 169). That this is an issue crucial for defining and asserting one's manhood in public is demonstrated in the charges of unmanliness hurled at the barber who counsels caution. The momentum of this tale of offended white male honor, though, is interrupted periodically by the story of Minnie Cooper's own background—the "furious unreality" of "her idle and empty days" and her own reaction to the way the town responds to her accusations of assault (p. 175). Our last sight of her, followed by a brief vignette about one of the lynchers, is of Minnie laughing hysterically, unable to articulate what she feels but nevertheless posing a disturbing counterpoint to the tale of white male vengeance—a counterpoint, moreover, hinting that there is more than one way to tell the tale of what happened to Minnie Cooper. And that hint in turn suggests a great deal about the tentativeness and fragility of the white male narrative in which Minnie's own fragmented tale is framed.

The figure of Minnie laughing, avidly eyed by the community, unable to talk, making her body talk for her, echoes with a peculiar force throughout the whole of Welty's first collection of short stories—*A Curtain of Green*. For Welty's volume is full of figures—the poor, the black, the marginal, the deformed, but especially women—like Minnie in particular, who make spectacles of themselves, and they do so in a strikingly panoptic world defined by a merciless collective gaze surveying the odd, the bizarre, and the marvelous. Like staffage in nineteenth-century landscape painting, her observers direct our attention time and time again to the collective gaze and to the spectacles luring that gaze: Lily Daw displaying a zinnia in her mouth; sideshow attractions like the Petrified Man and Keela the Indian Maiden; a deaf couple animatedly discussing in sign language their miraculous discovery of a key; "loud, squirming, ill-assorted" bathers at a park; Clytie Farr and Mrs. Larkin, whose private agonies render them conspicuous; the farm couple that the salesman R. J. Bowman wistfully ponders; and the jazz pianist Powerhouse, avidly watched by his white audience.[12] No wonder, then, that Ruby Fisher in "A Piece of News" suddenly feels herself under scrutiny when she discovers her name in a discarded newspaper: "What eye in the world did she feel looking in on her?" the narrator asks (p. 13). No wonder, too, that Mr. Marblehall in "Old Mr. Marblehall" strolls about under a public gaze so glaring that his house windows and the candle burners of his carriage resemble nothing so much as eyes, and that Howard in "Flowers for Marjorie" feels so exposed in the public, impersonal setting of the city that he is not at all surprised to be told four times on a subway wall "God sees me" (p. 103).

Much like Welty's characters, we as readers are encouraged to scrutinize these representations of the strange and the marvelous. But we are also urged to consider those who do the scrutinizing and the act of scrutiny itself. As a result, reading *A Curtain of Green* is roughly akin to looking at an exhibit and being vaguely uneasy about the possibility of being on exhibit oneself.

Some of this uneasiness, interestingly enough, can be detected in contemporary reviews of the collection bringing attention to the horrified fascination with which one gazes upon the spectacles populating *A Curtain of Green*. Albert Devlin speculates that the volume probably caught the interest of a good many Northern reviewers precisely because the stories seemed to confirm the notion of the South as something of a spectacle itself—benighted, grotesque, peculiar.[13] In her review for *The Nation* Louise Bogan noted that the characters could have originated in "some brokendown medieval scene ruled by its obscure and decomposing laws" (quoted in Devlin, pp. 5-6). A particularly perceptive British reviewer remarked upon the book's "fondness for the afflicted in mind or body and for strange violence of behaviour" but also took note of Welty's ability to "penetrate beneath the surface of the harsh or unprepossessing spectacle with quick, passionate sympathy" (quoted in Peterman, p. 106). If, in short, Welty's Mississippians appear peculiar and strange, veritable spectacles, these reviews suggest, so too is the experience of reading about those peculiarities.

Chief among those spectacles in *A Curtain of Green* are women whose antics and words suggest that there is something peculiarly feminine about making a spectacle of oneself, and in this respect Welty's spectacles hearken back to Minnie Cooper herself. I would argue, in fact, that Welty appropriates the figure of Minnie and other gothic women in Faulkner's short stories to explore their potential for subversiveness. For like Medusa and the Sphinx in stories of Perseus and Oedipus, Minnie and Welty's women are unsettling presences because they offer threats, in Teresa de Lauretis's words, to "man's clear vision, and their power consists in their . . . 'to-be-looked at-ness' . . . , 'their luring of man's gaze into the dark continent,' as Freud put it, the enigma of femininity."[14] In traditional male narratives such monstrous spectacle-obstacles are ordinarily conquered and swept aside if the hero's story is to proceed with a clear view of the narrative ending. What happens, though, if such spectacles stubbornly resist this sort of expulsion, if they persist in making spectacles of themselves in the public gaze?

Mary Russo, for one, suggests that being too much in the public eye can be unsettling for all concerned. Looking back on her own childhood and admonitions by her mother, she observes:

> For a woman, making a spectacle out of herself had more to do with a kind
>
> of inadvertency and loss of boundaries: the possessor of large, aging, and
>
> dimpled thighs displayed at the public beach, of overly rouged cheeks, of a
>
> voice shrill in laughter, or of a sliding bra strap—a loose, dingy bra
>
> strap especially—were at once caught out by fate and blameworthy. It was
>
> my impression that these women had done something wrong, had stepped, as it
>
> were, into the limelight out of turn—too young or too old, too early or
>
> too late—and yet anyone, any woman, could make a spectacle out of herself
>
> if she was not careful.[15]

In short, going too far, stepping over clearly defined boundaries, seems to be key in making a spectacle. It's not quite enough simply to be gazed upon, for we've been taught by feminist film critics and art historians just how gender-bound the activity of looking and being looked upon are in our culture. Stepping into the spotlight suggests the possibility of stepping into a designated site of femininity, a ready-made plot for the gothic heroine, but what happens when one essentially tries to take control of the spotlight and aggressively seeks the gaze of onlookers? What happens when women's bodies in particular become conspicuous, disorderly, disruptive—and in public spaces at that? We might discover, as Russo suggests, that ". . . women and their bodies, certain bodies, in certain public framings, in certain public spaces, are always already transgressive—dangerous, and in danger" (p. 217). We might also discover the slippery world of shifting boundaries, roles, and genders that baffles and irritates Freud in "A Child Is Being Beaten"—a slipperiness that appears to be part and parcel of that fantasy and implicit in gothic and Southern Gothic texts.

It is, I think, precisely this slippery, transgressive, dangerous possibility that Welty has inherited from Faulkner and has expanded to its fullest in story after story in *A Curtain of Green*, stories in which those who are usually marginal—the poor, the deprived, the retarded, but in particular white women and blacks—make spectacles of themselves by being excessive, transgressive, odd, disturbing, disruptive. Lily Daw unsettles her three lady friends and the entire town of Victory, Mississippi, by deciding to marry a xylophone player instead of accepting a ready-made plot of allowing herself to be put away at the Ellisville Institute for the Feeble-Minded. Ellie and Albert Morgan, so used to living in the shadows, take center stage in "The Key" where they silently but eloquently discuss their lives before a mesmerized hearing audience in a train station. Little Lee Roy in "Keela, the Outcast Indian Maiden" briefly relives his career as a geek in a sideshow with the two men who visit him and thereby underscores how he has changed the life of one of them forever. The narrator of "Why I Live at the P.O." is able to turn her entire family upside-down simply through the momentum of her ever-accelerating monologue. A "common" family of bathers in a park disrupts the daydreams of the narrator of "A Memory" by virtue of their outsized and grubby physical presence. Clytie Farr in "Clytie" disturbs the small community of Farr's Gin with unaccountable vigils in the rain, cursing sessions in her garden, and a suicide in a rain barrel. The despairing and unemployed Howard in "Flowers for Marjorie" inexplicably stabs his wife and then finds himself a prizewinner for entering Radio City Music Hall as the ten millionth person. Mrs. Larkin in "A Curtain of Green" obsessively over-plants her garden until it offers "the appearance of a sort of jungle" and she herself seems an appropriate inhabitant—"over-vigorous, disreputable, and heedless" (pp. 108 and 107). And perhaps most spectacular of all is Powerhouse, the jazz musician who is "so monstrous" with his huge feet and "vast and obscene" mouth that he sends his white audience "into oblivion" (pp. 132 and 131).

These all are figures that M. M. Bakhtin would group with the folk tradition of carnival and humor, with ritual spectacles, verbal comedy, and billingsgate finding their heyday in Roman saturnalias and the Middle Ages. But in particular he would link these figures with the grotesque, with material bodies that have become, in Bakhtin's words, "grandiose, exaggerated, immeasurable." They find their exemplar in the famous Kerch terra cotta figures of laughing pregnant hags, combining "a senile, decaying and deformed flesh with the flesh of new life, conceived but as yet unformed." Such images, Bakhtin asserts, serve as "the epitome of incompleteness," and that, he adds, "is precisely the grotesque concept of the body." Perhaps even more to the point, he notes that the grotesque body does not stand apart from the rest of the world but persists in growing, expanding, and ultimately transgressing its own boundaries. "The stress is laid on those parts of the body," he remarks, "that are open to the outside world, that is, the parts through which the world enters the body or emerges from it, or through which the body itself goes out to meet the world. This means that the emphasis is on the apertures or the convexities, or on various ramifications and offshoots: the open mouth, the genital organs, the breasts, the phallus, the potbelly, the nose."[16]

For our purposes, Bakhtin's grotesque bodies have two important implications for helping us make sense of the spectacles created in story after story in *A Curtain of Green*. Precisely because Welty's grotesque bodies do make spectacles, pursue excess, and transgress the boundaries of the expected and the ordinary, they serve as potent figures of women's anger protesting constrictions and limits. As Peter Schmidt, Ruth Weston, and Albert Devlin have shrewdly observed, the stories in *A Curtain of Green* are filled with narrow, confining spaces usually associated with women—kitchens, interiors, gardens, bedrooms, beauty parlors, and even the rain barrel in which Clytie drowns herself.[17] These are settings, Schmidt emphasizes, that underscore the restrictive narrative plots available to women, what Schmidt calls "the either/or choice between conformity and madness" tormenting so many of the female characters in *A Curtain of Green* (p. 31). What better way, then, to question and undermine the boundaries of those narrow settings than with bodies that protrude, exceed, threaten to expand endlessly? We see Clytie's legs protruding from the rain barrel, Powerhouse opening his mouth as if to engulf his white audience, Mrs. Larkin, disheveled and frantically busy in her garden, the narrator of "Why I Live at the P.O." virtually drowning everyone around her in words.

Indeed, so excessive and exaggerated are Welty's own grotesque bodies that a sudden recognition of their own strangeness appears to liberate them momentarily from restricted plots and to enable them to envision alternative stories for themselves. Thus Ruby Fisher in "A Piece of News" is lifted out of the ordinary by her encounter with a newspaper article about a woman named Ruby Fisher who is shot by her husband. Suddenly she can imagine herself in alternative scenarios—a deathbed scene' for instance—and because she is able to conjure up these other stories, she and her husband are briefly transformed: "Rare and wavering, some possibility stood timidly like a stranger between them and made them hang their heads" (p. 16). Similarly, the key that Albert and Ellie Morgan discover in "The Key" makes them feel that they "were in counter-plot against the plot of those things that pressed down upon them from outside their knowledge and their ways of making themselves understood" (p. 34).

These are bodies that serve as half-formed articulation, protests that find tentative expression not in language but in the body itself. This sort of semi-articulation is akin to hysteria as Catherine Clement sees it, "the only form of contestation possible in certain types of social organization"—that is, language "not yet at the point of verbal expression restrained within the bond of the body."[18] That these bodies do struggle with the effort of articulation says a good deal about the difficulties women in particular face in finding their own voices. "Women's power under patriarchy," Helena Michie notes in *The Flesh Made Word*, "comes only at great and psychic cost; its transformation into language, as the halting lines and gaps between the words indicate, is equally painful—the gaps themselves are scars and ruptures in the text." For women's entrance into language, Michie adds, is painful precisely because such a threshold moment involves "a shattering of the silence which enshrouds women's physical presence."[19]

The struggle to articulate inscribed on the bodies populating *A Curtain of Green* suggests something of Welty's own battle to find an appropriate idiom of expression. Elizabeth Bowen's perceptive remarks about that battle in *The Golden Apples* (1949) can also be applied to Welty's first volume:

> With her, nothing comes out of stock, and it has been impossible for her to
>
> stand still. Her art is a matter of contemplation, susceptibility, and
>
> discovery, it has been necessary for her to evolve for herself a language
>
> and to arrive, each time she writes, at a new form.[20]

Welty herself once noted in an interview: "[I]n those early stories I'm sure I needed the device of what you call the 'grotesque.' That is, I hoped to differentiate character by their physical qualities as a way of showing what they were like inside—it seemed to me the most direct way to do it."[21]

Indeed, the more grotesque the bodies in *A Curtain of Green*, the more likely they are to reverberate with scarcely repressed anger seeking articulation, the kind of rage, for instance, that inspires Clytie's cursing and

Mrs. Larkin's near-act of murder—raising her hoe and almost directing it onto the head of her garden helper, Jamey—in her extravagantly overplanted garden. "Was it possible to compensate? To punish? To protest?" Mrs. Larkin asks herself, for she seemingly has no words to express the grief she feels for the death of her husband and for "the workings of accident, of life and death, of unaccountability," of her confinement in her garden and widowhood (pp. 111 and 110).

But Welty's grotesque bodies are more than inscriptions of suffering and rage. Their very outrageousness, their grotesqueness as Bakhtin would define it, blurs the boundary between those who watch and those who are being watched, between those who suffer and those who inflict the suffering, so that we are never quite sure, to return to Freud's scenario of the beating fantasy, just who is being beaten and who is doing the beating. From Bakhtin's perspective, the grotesque body, "composed of fertile depths and procreative convexities, is never clearly differentiated from the world but is transferred, merged, and fused with it. It contains, like Pantagruel's mouth, new unknown spheres." And because the grotesque body does suggest the possibility of different worlds, different orders, different perspectives, it is able to dismantle what Bakhtin calls "the confines of the apparent (false) unity of the indisputable and stable" (pp. 339 and 48).

In short, the very grotesqueness of bodies in *A Curtain of Green* brings into question the detachment usually linked with the activity of looking, an activity that at once engrosses Welty's onlookers and renders them increasingly uncertain. Like Clytie Farr in "Clytie," Welty's observers look "purely for a resemblance to a vision," and like Clytie again, they seem to discover that the more they look the less familiar everything around them is (p. 86). Those who gaze upon the strange and marvelous, like Tom Harris in "The Hitch-Hikers," anticipate the sort of certainty they feel as children: "standing still, with nothing to touch him, feeling tall and having the world come all at once into it round shape underfoot" (p. 62). What they discover, though, like Bowman in "Death of a Traveling Salesman," is an odd blurring between those who appear to look and those who are looked upon. "Now we are all visible to one another," Bowman thinks unexpectedly after Sonny returns with borrowed fire (p. 128). Even more unexpected is the deceptiveness of things to be seen, for the two farm folk Bowman studies are not an elderly mother and son, as he initially thinks, but a fairly young couple expecting a baby. Worse yet, Bowman, who originally thinks of the couple as odd and country-quaint, is himself the oddity, barred by his solitude from "the ancient communication between two people" (p. 129).

The stories of *A Curtain of Green* explore this sort of reversal between grotesque and norm, between gazers and gazed upon, again and again, and the result is a world in which the politics of the gaze and spectacle is problematized and boundaries between binary oppositions, between normal and abnormal, classic and grotesque, insider and outsider, community and outcast, are thoroughly disrupted. In story after story, the possibility of alternative gazes, alternative perspectives, alternative narratives, is raised repeatedly, often by underscoring the limitations of the collective gaze leveled upon those labeled as strange, marvelous, grotesque, and suffering. Precisely because the raptly staring crowd in the train station has no inkling of the private story of Ellie and Albert Morgan in "The Key," the third-person narrator's direct address to a second-person audience pondering the interior lives of the Morgans is especially poignant. Similarly, we're told pointedly that there is more than one way to view a sideshow attraction, like Little Lee Roy in "Keela, the Outcast Indian Maiden," and it is the mystery of multiple views that is contemplated by the baffled and horrified young man who tells the story of Little Lee Roy's rescue.

Strikingly enough, the volume's two concluding stories, "Powerhouse" and "A Worn Path," focusing on two central (and suffering) black figures, evoke the limitations of a collective gaze with the most acidity. The white audience that avidly stares at Powerhouse, watching him playing, watching him suffering in a sense, has smug assumptions about capturing the musician's very essence in its gaze—"of course you know it is with them—Negroes—bandleaders—they would play the same way giving all they've got, for an audience of one . . ." (p. 133). A similar smugness characterizes the whites who encounter Phoenix Jackson on her journey in "A Worn Path." "I know you old colored people!" a young white hunter tells her (p. 145). But the truth of the matter is, of course, that they know neither Powerhouse nor Phoenix Jackson, whose individual stories exist outside those collective gazes. And more disconcerting still is the way both Powerhouse and Phoenix Jackson look back at their white onlookers with unsettling directness. "Somebody loves me," sings Powerhouse, staring back at his audience, and adds, in a phrase erasing the boundary between spectacle and spectator, ". . . Maybe it's you!" (p. 141).

Most unsettling of all is the disruption of the spectator-spectacle relationship, and for that matter, of the beating fantasy as well, in "A Memory," the story that serves in a sense as the key to the collection. For the narrator of "A Memory" recalls an earlier sense of self when she was a highly imaginative young girl very much an artist in the making and perhaps even more to the point an obsessive watcher and judge of others who never quite seem to meet her own high standards. "When a person, or a happening," the narrator notes, "seemed to me not in keeping with my opinion, or even my hope or expectation, I was terrified by a vision of abandonment and wildness which tore my heart with a kind of sorrow" (p. 75). Nevertheless, she ponders each sight that comes before her, for she is convinced that anything she sees might reveal "a secret of life . . . for I was obsessed with notions of concealment, and from the smallest gesture of a stranger I would wrest what was to me a communication or a presentiment" (p. 76).

The sense of power she feels simply from obsessive watching is heightened, she adds, "by the fact that I was in love then for the first time: I had identified love at once" (p. 76). Never passing a word with the boy at school who is the object of her infatuation, the young girl feels, she says, "a necessity for absolute conformity to my ideas in any happening I witnessed" (p. 76). Accordingly, she sits all day in school unceasingly apprehensive, "fearing for the untoward to happen" (p. 76). When the young boy drawing her attention unexpectedly suffers a nosebleed in class, the narrator feels a genuine sense of shock and horror. Having safely categorized the young boy as a dream of perfect love, the young girl now fears that he will not measure up, that his house and his family may be "slovenly" and "shabby" (p. 76).

But it is in the park one day, by the lake beach where she often obsessively watches, framing her vision with a square made with her hands, that she suddenly finds all her judgments and observations disrupted and thoroughly unsettled. Framing her view as always, the narrator sees more than she bargains for when that "group of loud, squirming, ill-assorted people who seemed thrown together only by the most confused accident" comes before her eyes (p. 77). Watching them with her usual stern sense of judgment, the narrator sees an overweight woman in the group unexpectedly pour great globs of sand out of her bathing suit. "I felt a peak of horror," the narrator declares, "as though her breasts themselves had turned to sand as though they were of no importance at all and she did not care" (p. 79). So outsized is the moment that the narrator's framing vision is exposed for the fragile fiction that it is. Even after the group of bathers has gone, the narrator continues to lie there, "feeling victimized by the sight of the unfinished bulwark where they had piled and shaped the wet sand around the bodies, which changed the appearance of the beach like the ravages of a storm" (p. 79). It would be, she concludes, her "last morning on the beach," and the implication is that the narrator will never again be able to conjure up the power of watching and easy categorization, of sharp distinctions between the ideal and the grotesque.

Decades after writing "A Memory," Welty would write of that story in *One Writer's Beginnings* (1984): "This is not, on reaching its end, an observer's story. The tableau discovered through the young girl's framing hands is unwelcome realism. How can she accommodate the existence of this view to the dream of love, which she carried already inside her?" Rather ominously, Welty adds: "The frame only raises the question of the story."[22]

The result, I think, is a version of Southern Gothic that does indeed raise the question of the story, mark its terrain as highly contested, unsettle the politics of vision. If Faulkner's short story portraits of women reverberate with the effort—only partially successful—to inscribe cultural narratives of Southern femininity upon women's bodies, Welty's gallery of women evokes the implicit but logical conclusion of Faulkner's tales by posing scenarios of women who break out of haunted houses and narrow confines, abruptly change places with other participants in faint echoes of beating fantasies, and explore the full potential of just what it means to be a spectacle. The dis-ease we discover in Faulkner's portrait gallery of gothic women becomes in *A Curtain of Green* a full-fledged carnival of gothic and grotesque heroines running amok, resistant to placement in traditional plots and roles. Welty's women, in fact, are more often than not characters in search of stories that have yet to be articulated. And therein, perhaps, lies the crucial difference between their two versions of Southern Gothic. Faulkner may display for us sights that are at times all too painfully familiar—the frustrated spinster, the hypocritical widow, the utterly oppressed black woman—but Welty makes spectacles that are often so outrageous and boundary-breaking that we are never quite sure what we are looking at or where to place ourselves as spectators. Ultimately, if Faulkner's tales of gothic women allude uncomfortably to the spectacle of the scaffold, Welty's stories testify to nothing so much as the scaffold's dismantling.

Notes

1. A shorter version of this essay appeared as "Dangerous Women and Gothic Debates: Faulkner, Welty, and Tales of the Grotesque," in *Faulkner's Short Fiction*, ed. Hans Skei (Oslo, Norway: Solum Forlag, 1997), pp. 106-116.

2. Gina D. Peterman, "*A Curtain of Green*: Eudora Welty's Auspicious Beginning," *Mississippi Quarterly*, 47 (Winter 1992-1993), 104.

3. Carson McCullers, "The Russian Realists and Southern Literature," in *Friendship and Sympathy: Communities of Southern Women Writers*, ed. Rosemary M. Magee (Jackson: University Press of Mississippi, 1992), pp. 21-22.

4. Quoted in Alice Walker, "Eudora Welty: An Interview," in *Conversations with Eudora Welty*, ed. Peggy Whitman Prenshaw (New York: Pocket Press, 1984), p. 152.

5. Ruth Weston, *Gothic Tradition and Narrative Techniques in the Fiction of Eudora Welty* (Baton Rouge: Louisiana State University Press, 1994), p. 4.

6. Susan Wolstenholme, *Gothic (Re)Visions: Writing Women as Readers* (Baton Rouge: Louisiana State University Press, 1993), p. 6.

7. Michelle A. Masse, *In the Name of Love: Women, Masochism, and the Gothic* (Ithaca: Cornell University Press, 1992), pp. 10, 40.

8. Noel Polk, "'The Dungeon Was Mother Herself': William Faulkner: 1927-1931," in *New Directions in Faulkner Studies: Faulkner and Yoknapatawpha*, 1983, ed. Doreen Fowler and Ann J. Abadie (Jackson: University Press of Mississippi, 1983), p. 65. See in general Sigmund Freud, "'A Child Is Being Beaten': A Contribution to the Study of the Origin of Sexual Perversions (1919)," in *The Standard Edition of the Complete Psychological Works of Sigmund Freud,* vol. 17, trans. and ed. James Strachey (London: Hogarth Press, 1955), pp. 175-205.

9. William Faulkner, "A Rose for Emily," in *Collected Stories of William Faulkner* (New York: Random House, 1950), p. 123. Subsequent references to short stories in this collection will be cited parenthetically within the text.

10. Carroll Smith-Rosenberg, *Disorderly Conduct: Visions of Gender in Victorian America* (New York: Oxford University Press, 1985), pp. 245-246.

11. Kate Ferguson Ellis, *The Contested Castle: Gothic Novels and the Subversion of Domestic Ideology* (Urbana: University of Illinois Press, 1989), p. xiv. See also Michel Foucault, *Discipline and Punish: The Birth of the Prison,* trans. Alan Sheridan (New York: Random-Vintage, 1977), p. 43.

12. Eudora Welty, "A Memory," in *A Curtain of Green,* in *The Collected Stories of Eudora Welty* (1941; rpt. New York: Harcourt Brace Jovanovich, 1980), p. 77. Subsequent references to the stories in *A Curtain of Green* will be cited parenthetically within the text.

13. Albert J. Devlin, *Eudora Welty's Chronicle. A Story of Mississippi Life* (Jackson: University of Mississippi Press, 1983), pp. 5-6.

14. Teresa de Lauretis, *Alice Doesn't: Feminism, Semiotics, Cinema* (Bloomington: Indiana University Press, 1984), p. 110. For an examination of Welty's critique and inversion of the male heroic narrative, see Rebecca Mark, *The Dragon's Blood: Eudora Welty's "The Golden Apples" and Feminist Intertextuality* (Jackson: University Press of Mississippi, 1994).

15. Mary Russo, "Female Grotesques: Carnival and Theory," in *Feminist Studies/Critical Studies,* ed. Teresa de Lauretis (Madison: University of Wisconsin Press, 1986), p. 213.

16. Mikhail Bakhtin, *Rabelais and His World,* trans. Helene Iswolsky (Bloomington: Indiana University Press, 1984), pp. 5, 19, 25, and 26.

17. Peter Schmidt, *The Heart of the Story: Eudora Welty's Short Fiction* (Jackson: University Press of Mississippi, 1991), p. 4; Weston, *Gothic Traditions,* pp. 10 and 134; and Devlin, *Eudora Welty's Chronicle,* p. 16.

18. Quoted in Michele Richman, "Sex and Signs: The Language of French Feminist Criticism," in *Language and Style* 13 (Fall 1980), 69.

19. "Helena Michie, *The Flesh Made Word. Female Figures and Women's Bodies* (New York: Oxford University Press, 1987), pp. 139 and 74-75.

20. "Elizabeth Bowen, review of *The Golden Apples,* in *Books of Today* (September 1950); rpt. in Bowen, *Seven Winters: Memories of a Dublin Childhood & Afterthoughts: Pieces on Writing* (New York: Alfred A. Knopf, 1962), p. 216.

21. "Quoted in Linda Kuehl, "The Art of Fiction XLVII: Eudora Welty," in *Conversations with Eudora Welty,* p. 93.

22. Eudora Welty, *One Writer's Beginnings,* William E. Massey, Sr., *Lectures in the History of American Civilization* (Cambridge: Harvard University Press, 1983), p. 89.

THEMES IN SOUTHERN GOTHIC LITERATURE

Claire Kahane (essay date 1983)

SOURCE: Kahane, Claire. "The Maternal Legacy: The Grotesque Tradition in Flannery O'Connor's Female Gothic." In *The Female Gothic,* edited by Juliann E. Fleenor, pp. 242-56. Montreal: Eden Press, 1983.

[*In the following essay, Kahane writes that O'Connor's female characters, using the techniques of gothic fiction, profoundly articulate their sense of helplessness within and revolt against established cultural order.*]

Gothic fiction has received a good deal of critical attention in the last decade, and much of it from psychoanalytic critics, who find its easy display of fantasy in the service of fear congenial to their analyses. For the most part, these critics employ oedipal interpretive paradigms to account for the affective power of the Gothic genre. Concentrating primarily on the incestuous desires of male protagonists, they typically interpret Gothic fiction "in the light of male psychology," as at least two unabashedly admit. "The Gothic genre," write Morton Kaplan and Robert Kloss, "depicts in varying degress of explicitness the passions of the oedipal child."[1]

While it may be true that the incestuous overtones in the relations between brother and sister, father and daughter, exerted the force of a forbidden and unacknowledged fantasy in the eighteenth and nineteenth centuries, for a post-Freudian audience, this oedipal reading seems a very partial explanation of its affect. Indeed, if we look at the conventional Gothic plot, with its heroine trapped in a threatening labyrinthean structure, in the light of female psychology, the affective tension—the fear it is generically supposed to arouse—seems to reside elsewhere. Norman Holland and Leona Sherman, for example, in recording their responses to Ann Radcliffe's *The Mysteries of Udolpho,* find that their fears turn on the castle, a nighttime house which admits a variety of projections.[2] "It becomes all the possibilities of a parent or a body," they write, "a total environment in one-to-one relation with the victim, like the all-powerful mother of early childhood." As the response of these two readers implies, inside the Gothic house, the clear subject-object differentiations characteristic of oedipal relations break down and the cultural positionings instituted by the oedipal complex are destabilized. Here, the female protagonist transgresses her conventionally passive role, actively penetrating forbidden spaces, testing the potentials of an identity and a sexuality outside the father's law. While Sherman finds gratification in these transgressions, both Sherman and Holland experience fear as the heroine approaches the secret center of the Gothic labyrinth, where boundaries break down, where life and death become confused and identities unclear, where the felt presence of a spectral mother—though typically dead or absent, exerts an uncanny force.[3]

As a good many recent studies have indicated, both women and men maintain an uneasy relation to the image of the mother, an ambivalence which, promoted by women's monopoly over infancy, extends to images of all women. As Dorothy Dinnerstein first pointed out, women's exclusive rocking of the cradle has had incalculable consequences on our psyches, irrevocably linking our most archaic fantasies and fears to this magic mother.[4] Before we know where the self ends and the world begins, the mother-woman is experienced as global, all-embracing, all-powerful. Embodying in her very being the world's body and our own, the mother becomes culturally confirmed as the realm of the flesh, and is made the bearer of our ambivalence toward it. Furthermore, because the mother is invariably female, women experience that ambivalence more intimately. As Nancy Chodorow convincingly argues,[5] while boys can use their maleness to differentiate themselves from an engulfing maternal-female presence, girls are locked into a mother-daughter confusion of identity by virtue of their gender, encouraged in that confusion by the tendency of mothers to see daughters as duplicates of themselves and to reflect that vision.

It is the imaginative exploration of that confusion, the apprehensive testing of the problematic boundaries of female identity and its relation to power, sexuality and the maternal body, that makes the Female Gothic attractive to feminist criticism. In this context, the heroine's exploration of her entrapment in a Gothic house—both she and it vulnerable to potential penetration—can be read as an exploration of her relation to the maternal body which she too shares, to the femaleness of experience, with all its connotations of power over, and vulnerability to, forces within and without. As Sherman describes her identification with the Gothic heroine, "I find myself harking back to the ultimate mystery, the maternal body with its related secrets of birth and sexuality."[6]

In her remarkably suggestive study of the Female Gothic, Ellen Moers not only points to the delights of Gothic fiction, but locates its terrors by redefining Gothic fiction as any work which "gives visual form to the fear of self."[7] While conventional Gothic fiction followed Edmund Burke's prescription that terror depends on *not* seeing clearly, and thus created obscurities that allow for maximum projection of the readers' fears, Moers implies that in the modern Gothic, what is seen is more terrifying. What is seen, according to Moers, are images of self-hatred, embodied in freaks of all kinds, which lead to a grotesque tradition in the Female Gothic, an emphasis on *visual* images of deformity.

As various studies seem to agree,[8] the grotesque is dependent upon perceptual distortions which estrange us in the physical universe, which, transgressing the normal categories of experience, assault our sense of a coherent self and world. Importantly, the core of the self-image is the body-image, assembled during the first years of life by our use of hand, mouth and eyes, and confirmed by our continued relation to the mirroring world.[9] Self-hatred, then, can be understood in its most primal form as a hatred of the body-image. In a patriarchal culture which valorizes the visible phallus as the image of autonomous power, it is not surprising that women, encouraged to see themselves as congenitally impaired, would experience a disturbed sense of self, a feeling of lack or estrangement that gives them a special eye for the imagery of self-hatred, for those signifiers of negative identity—the freak, the dwarf, the cripple—that abound in the modern Female Gothic. Unlike the conventional Gothic heroine, who found confirmations as well as threats in the non-visible obscurity of the Gothic interiors, the protagonists of the grotesque-Gothic continually find physical images of the body as vulnerable and impaired.

These issues are most effectively elaborated in the fiction of Flannery O'Connor. Although O'Connor's protagonists are male as well as female, what clearly ties her fiction to the modern Female Gothic is the pervasive issue of discovering a truth in "a dark secret center" and giving it grotesque form. Insistent herself on "staring at the Unnameable," she created a gallery of freaks who stare, or are stared at, as if looking were a matter of life and death. Interestingly, she compared her fiction to the line drawings of a child, who "doesn't intend to distort but to set down exactly what he sees."[10] "What you seen?" asks Hazel Motes' mother in *Wise Blood,* and that question reverberates throughout O'Connor's fiction. What Motes has seen is a forbidden sight—a naked female body squirming in a coffin—an image which his memory later superimposes on the image of his mother in her coffin. Enoch Emory, his comic counterpart, discovers a mystery at "the dark secret center" of the city,[11] which turns out to be a mummy (pun?), a hideous shrunken man which he later gestates in his washstand and presents to Motes as a baby, the new Jesus. In both cases, O'Connor presents us with a grotesque metamorphosis of the body which occurs in a womb-tomb, a secret center into which these characters obsessively peer to discover their fate. Just as Victor Frankenstein attempts to "penetrate the secrets of Nature" and when he does, gives birth to a monster, O'Connor's characters, compelled to peep at a sideshow, ultimately confront a monstrous image of self as grotesque body.

However, it is in her portrayal of female protagonists that O'Connor gives explicitly female form to her grotesque-Gothic fiction, by exploiting images of pregnancy and procreation—those same concerns Moers addresses in her interpretation of *Frankenstein*. That women writers should find pregnancy an appropriate Gothic metaphor is not surprising. In this most definitively female of conditions potentially lie the most extreme apprehensions: about the body as subject, about bodily integrity which shapes one's sense of self. In pregnancy, the woman's very shape changes, as she begins to feel another presence inside her, growing on her flesh, feeding on her blood. Especially since pregnancy also confirms a woman's identification with her own mother, she becomes prey to a web of infantile fears and wishes relating to her mother, and can fear the fetus as an agent of retaliation.

This anxiety is strikingly fictionalized in O'Connor's "A Stroke of Good Fortune," an early story in which a literal pregnancy becomes a Gothic horror, imprisoning its reluctant victim in a biological identity with her mother which is perceived as tantamount to death. But as if O'Connor needed to distance that horror, this story presents its theme in the guise of Gothic parody, thus keeping the reader at a very un-Gothic distance from its terrifying substructure. By inundating the reader with dramatic irony, juggling puns, displacing meaning from one image to another, transforming verbal statements into perceptual forms—in short, by all those devices characteristic of dream work, O'Connor both illuminates a central figure of the Female Gothic and ridicules the ignorance of a woman who bears its burden. The plot is simple: Ruby Hill, a fat, thirty-four year old married woman, has consulted a palmist who predicts "a long illness," ending with "a stroke of good fortune."[12] Although the reader is quickly made aware that this "good fortune" is a baby, Ruby determinedly ignores that interpretation as she laboriously climbs the stairs to her apartment. A Gothic staircase indeed—a "thin black rent in the middle of the house, covered with a mole-colored carpet that looked as if it grew from the floor. They stuck straight up like steeple steps"—the sexual innuendo in this visual image arouses Ruby's repugnance and her defensive rationalization of her symptoms. Only at the story's conclusion, after she is knocked down by a neighbor's child—"Little Mister Good Fortune"—does she admit her condition, and that acknowledgment simultaneously signals her own mortality. For the child waiting to be born is perceived by her as a killer, "waiting to make his mother, only thrity-four, into an old woman," waiting, that is, to turn her into her mother. "All those children were what did her mother in—eight of them. . . . Her mother had gotten deader with every one of them." Her conception of babies as killers becomes focused on her "baby brother," Rufus, who is, as the locution implies, another analogue of her own unwanted child. Vividly recalling the horror of his birth, she reveals the locus of her own fears:

> She was the only one of the children who couldn't stand it and she walked all the way in to Melsy, in the hot sun ten miles, to the picture show to get clear of the screaming, and had sat through two westerns and a horror picture and a serial and then had walked all the way back and found it was just beginning, and she had had to listen all night.

Here we have the blood and screaming in the night, but the Gothic villain, Ruby's husband, who has "slipped up" and betrayed her, is no longer part of the drama; only the bloody consequence remains as the Gothic horror. No wonder that Ruby, feeling a pain in her chest, wants it to be "heart trouble." "They couldn't very well remove your heart," she thinks, revealing a fear of something being ripped away in childbirth. Proud of having "no teeth out, no children," Ruby discloses her fantasy of wholeness by which she defends herself against what are essentially grotesque images of mutilation and dismemberment contextually associated with childbirth. Indeed, childbirth is presented by O'Connor as a radical mutilation, a martyrdom to the species which the story reifies in Ruby's Calvary-like ascent up the stairs, her cross no less burdensome for its comic portrayal.

But significantly, it is comically portrayed. Throughout the story O'Connor plays with a discourse which insistently points to the fears of her protagonist while the play undermines the reader's apprehensions. Perhaps the most comic station of Ruby's cross is her pause to sit down on the stairs:

> She jumped up quickly, feeling something under her. She caught her breath and then pulled the thing out: it was Hartley Gilfeet's pistol. Nine inches of treacherous tin! . . . If he had been hers, she'd have worn him out so hard so many times he wouldn't know how to leave his mess on a public stair.

A sexual burlesque which parodies the Gothic danger of penetration, the nine inches of treacherous tin seem to condense the images of the male organ and the fetus into one "thing": both have invaded her, and it is both she would pull out, or expel. Thus Ruby engages in a series of metaphorical repudiations of some obscure "something" inside of her. Spitting out certain charged words which seem to her like poisonous seeds, holding her hand tightly over her mouth at the thought of pregnancy, transforming a pain which feels like "a piece of something pushing against something else" into the word "cancer," which she then mentally slashes, aborts, and excretes—she attempts to destroy or control the "thing" through verbal displacement, just as O'Connor's story attempts to control the fantasy through linguistic play. But after Little Mr. Good Fortune charges into her "with two pistols leveled," Ruby is compelled to open her mouth and speak the words which unlock for her the secret center of this Gothic comedy: "Good Fortune, Baby." In her very articulation, the words assume a life of their own as three echoes; thus language itself confirms her maternal fate.

In this final section of the story Ruby becomes both mother and daughter, as O'Connor gives us a series of Gothic images which fuse a fantasy of giving birth with a fantasy of Ruby's own birth. Pausing again to rest, she looks down into the stairwell, which looks like "a stair cavern . . . dark green and mole colored." She "wails" like a baby: "the wail sounded at the very bottom like a voice answering her." Then that answering voice becomes incarnate as "Little Mister Good Fortune" erupts from the stairwell like a child bursting from the womb. Knocked down, Ruby sits on the stair gazing "down into the dark hold, down to the very bottom where she had started up so long ago," the baby who had made her own mother that much "deader." While throughout the story she had been pinching her fat flesh to confirm herself as baby, she is doomed to become the mother, to be sacrificed in turn to the waiting child.

O'Connor's subsequent stories conjoin the idea of penetration and impregnation with vulnerability and death, leading various female protagonists to engage in a continual repudiation of their womanhood. But their flight invariably proves to be circular, nightmarishly bringing them face to face with their female fears; face to face with the body of the mother.

In O'Connor's fiction, the pervasive question "What have you seen?" repeatedly leads us to a vision of the female body as the maternal legacy, arousing fears of physical mutilation and destruction. In this context we can reinterpret certain recurrent images in O'Connor's fiction: the world "swelling up" because of overpopulation, the inner workings of a mysterious dark secret center, long black tunnels which lead through death to life, cancer and other consuming illnesses. All these seem to be fictional transformations of a woman's fascination with the hidden processes of her body, a fascination no doubt intensified by O'Connor's subjection to the physical processess of her own mysterious and debilitating illness. When these fears are obscured through displacement, the grotesque is muted; but when O'Connor visually defines the fears of the body as such—in her mutilated and dismembered protagonists, in the theft of Hulga's wooden leg ("Good Country People"), in the one-armed tramp and his retarded bride ("The Life You Save May Be Your Own")—the Gothic yields to domination by the grotesque.

There is, however, one image which recurs in O'Connor's fiction which straddles the line between Gothic and grotesque, between unseen and seen; the hermaphrodite. Moers includes the hermaphrodite in her catalogue of freaks as an image of self-hatred; but the hermaphrodite, I would argue, is a more complex signifier, and, as a trope, transcends self-hatred through its allusiveness. For the power of the hermaphrodite as a physical image derives from what is visually obscure yet demands to be seen from what is impossible but true, from what is wished for and feared. Especially in a time when the traditional boundaries of sexual identity are in flux, the hermaphrodite mirrors the infantile wish to destroy distinction and limitation and be both sexes, and the fear of that wish when it is realized as freakishness.[13]

O'Connor exploited this ambivalent significance in one of her most successful stories, "A Temple of the Holy Ghost." Indeed, the shift in metaphor—from Gothic house to Temple—is itself an emblem of the story's movement from grotesque to sublime. Told from the point of view of an ugly twelve year old who squirms uncomfortably at the burgeoning sexuality of her two cousins, the story uses images incrementally to reveal the girl's inarticulate distaste for her own femaleness, but ultimately transforms her sense of physical inadequacy into a vision of divine benediction through the image of the hermaphrodite.

The crux of the story is a conversation between the girl and her two cousins, who taunt her with their having seen something forbidden at a fair. "'There are some things,' Susan said, 'that a child of your age doesn't know,' and they both began to giggle." Their mysterious hint immediately triggers the girl's association to the mystery of birth, as her attempt to counter their secretiveness reveals. "'One time,' she said, her voice hollow-sounding in the dark, 'I saw this rabbit having rabbits.'" Her ploy effective, the cousins tell of the "freak" they have seen, a hermaphrodite who had exhibited itself saying:

> God made me this away and if you laugh, He may strike you the same way. This is the way He wanted me to be and I ain't disputing His way. I'm showing you because I got to make the best of it. . . . I never done it to myself nor had a thing to do with it, but I'm making the best of it. I don't dispute hit.

In light of the girl's sexual concerns, the spiel of the hermaphrodite suggests that she should accept her fate as a woman, a fate the image of the hermaphrodite equates with freakishness. In this sense Moers is right in calling this an image of self-hatred. But psychologically more important for the girl and for the story, is the physical fact of its androgyny. Significantly, the hermaphrodite is never directly exhibited to the reader. Even in the one allusion to its physical appearance, when the cousin states that "it was a man and woman both. It pulled up its dress and showed us. It had on a blue dress," we do not know what it is that is seen. Had O'Connor actually presented a visual description, the story would remain within the boundaries of the grotesque. But her aim is to transform the grotesque, to bring back to it the Gothic awe of the sublime, which she does by means of indirection.

The girl subsequently imagines a dialogue in which she and the hermaphrodite linguistically merge through their identification with the phrase, "I am a temple of the Holy Ghost," a phrase which has haunted the girl throughout the story. Not only does this merger suggest that the girl fantasizes that she, too, is double-sexed, so that freakishness is a sign of God's grace, but as temples of the Holy Ghost, both are identified with the Virgin Mary, who was impregnated by the Holy Ghost ("I never done it to myself not had a thing to do with it . . . God made me this away"). O'Connor confirms this association by her reference to the blue dress of the hermaphrodite, the Virgin's color.

In "A Psychoanalysis of the Holy Ghost," Ernest Jones noted that only in the Christian Trinity does the Holy Ghost replace the mother who forms the third member of all other known trinities.[14] Elucidating the significance of the change from primal mother to Holy Ghost, Jones concludes that the Holy Ghost is a composite "of the original Mother-Goddess with the creative essence (genital organs) of the Father." Although the Holy Ghost thus functions androgynously—one is reborn of it and impregnated by it—the resulting figure is conceptually male. Jones explains this reversal of sex as "the tendency of Christian myth to exalt the Father at the expense of the Mother" to counter incestuous wishes. The original Mother-Goddess is decomposed into the awesome Holy Ghost and a simple woman, the Virgin. O'Connor's story reverses this tendency, returning the primal Mother to her original position as hermaphrodeity, by restoring to the Virgin that archaic conception of divinity that resides in androgyny.

The denouement of the story obliquely conveys the hermaphroditic power of the Virgin-Mother through a succession of framing images, the structure of each analogous to the hermaphroditic image of the phallus surrounded by the vagina. From the very first image O'Connor stresses the impossibility of seeing this directly: "With her hair blowing into the ivory sun which was framed in the middle of the blue afternoon but when she pulled it away from her eyes she had to squint." At the convent, the child and her mother attend benediction in the Gothic chapel, described as "a series of springing arches that ended with the one over the altar where the priest was kneeling in front of the monstrance, bowed low." During the *Tantum Ergo,* "the priest raised the monstrance with the Host shining ivory-colored in the center of it" while the girl "was thinking of the tent at the fair that had the freak in it." The "ivory-colored" Host enclosed within the monstrance repeats the image of the ivory sun (son?) framed within the blue afternoon, both metaphors of male divinity perceived within a framing space. Pointedly, the exhibition of the monstrance with the Host in it is juxtaposed to the tent with the hermaphrodite in it. That, in turn, suggests to the girl another framing image; she remembers the freak saying, "I don't dispute hit. This is the way He wanted me to be," recalling for the reader the blue dress of the hermaphrodite (like the blue dress of the Virgin and the blue afternoon) covering the androgynous genitals, the primary framing image. Thus the sequence moves telescopically from the extended projection of the transcendant sun within sky, through a series which returns us to the most literal carnal image of genitalia from which the series seems to derive, yet in a manner that prevents us from seeing it directly. Reading this series backward gives us precisely the kind of transformation from carnal to spiritual, grotesque to sublime, which structures the story.

The conclusion of the story is dominated by the image of the Host, which, however, changes in color from ivory-white to blood-red—a change which points to the underlying reason for the story's preoccupation with the body and the question of its defilement. In the final sentence, "The sun was a huge red ball like an elevated Host drenched in blood and when it sank out of sight, it left a line in the sky like a red clay road hanging over the trees." During the exhibition of the monstrance, the girl has imaginatively incorporated the Host; here that Host is projected outward drenched in blood. We can hardly escape the inference that underlying this religious vision of the blood of Christ is a vision of her own bleeding body, more specifically, the blood of menstruation, the monthly stigmata of her femaleness, her wound, her mutilation, with its connotations of carnal violation. The physical bloodiness of this epiphany reveals what the story transforms; the curse is turned into a blessing. The fear and horror of menstruation are reversed, the girl's shame at this physical sign of impurity and freakishness transfigured by the fantasy of her body enclosing the bloody Host, and the glory of the apprehension, "God did it, this is the way He wanted me to be." The body is transcended, just as the "red clay road" transcendently hangs over the trees. In a remarkable parallel, this final image recalls Simone de Beauvoir's description of the young religieuse, which seems so appropriate not only to this story, but to an understanding of a major gratification provided by the plight of the Gothic Heroine:

> In the humiliation of God she sees with wonder the dethronement of Man: inert, passive, covered with wounds, the Crucified is the reversed image of the white, bloodstained martyr exposed to wild beasts, to daggers, to males, with whom the little girl has so often identified herself; she is overwhelmed to see that Man, Man-God, has assumed her role. She it is who is hanging on the Tree, promised the splendor of the Resurrection. . . .
>
> In the stigmata is fully achieved the mysterious alchemy that glorifies the flesh, since they are the very presence of divine love, in the form of a bloody anguish. We can readily understand why women are especially concerned with the metamorphosis of the red flow into pure golden flame. They are obsessed with this blood flowing from the side of the King of men. . . . That is the emblem which sums up the great feminine dream: from blood to glory through love.[15]

But this feminine dream can become a masochistic nightmare in which there is no transformation of blood to glory, in which the protagonist finds no escape from the physical, in which self-hatred dominates, and the grotesque conquers. This is the vision that more often shapes O'Connor's fiction, and emerges most clearly in one of her most horrifying stories, "A View of the Woods." This story focuses precisely on a girl's obsession with the flowing blood which presages her own fate, but here, entrapment in the female body means neither power, nor glory, but only mutilation and death.

Mary Fortune Pitts, a nine year old girl (her name certainly bears the freight of meaning from "A Stroke of Good Fortune") becomes enraged with her grandfather, Mr. Fortune, when he plans to sell the property in front of their house because "we won't be able to see the woods across the road. . . . We won't be able to see the view." In an attempt to fathom her recalcitrance, her grandfather spends an uncomfortable afternoon repeatedly looking at the woods. In her description of what he sees, O'Connor indicates the highly charged nature of the view that Mary Fortune wants to keep continually before her:

> The third time he got up to look at the woods, it was almost six o'clock and the gaunt trunks appeared to be raised in a pool of red light that gushed from the almost hidden sun setting behind them. The old man stared for some time, as if for a prolonged instant he were caught up out of the rattle of everything that led to the future and were held there in the midst of an uncomfortable mystery that he had not apprehended before. He saw it, in his hallucination, as if someone were wounded behind the woods and the trees were bathed in blood. . . . He returned to his bed and shut his eyes and against the closed lids hellish red trunks rose up in a black wood.

The image of the almost hidden sun bathing the woods in blood is similar to the image of the elevated Host in "A Temple of the Holy Ghost"; O'Connor had meant both to signify the Crucifixion. In this story, however, the girl's identification with the wound shadows forth her victimization by paternal power, a power with which she is initially identified by her intimate relation to her grandfather, whose dominating point of view keeps the father's role central. O'Connor's choice of the paternal perspective on this girl turns out to be not merely a strategy for distancing the horror she envisions—although it is that too—but the very source of the conflict. To the extent that the father's law establishes the terms of femininity to which the daughter accedes, O'Connor reveals how the question of the daughter's identity is complicated by its relation to the oedipal roots of paternal authority. But even though the oedipal paradigm elucidates the psychodynamics of this story, the oedipal relationship is embedded in pre-oedipal issues of identification and identity.

The story begins with a conflict between fathers. Contemptuous of the Pitts breed, Mr. Fortune has been humiliating them for years, keeping Pitts in a state of angry dependency by refusing to sell him the property on which they live. Only Mary Fortune, a fierce little duplication of himself, is free from his despite:

> She was now nine, short and broad like himself, with his very light blue eyes, his wide prominent forehead, his steady penetrating scowl and his rich florid complexion; but *she was like him on the inside too.* She had, to a singular degree, his intelligence, his strong will, and his push and drive.
>
> (italics mine)

Although Mr. Fortune would ignore her difference, Mary Fortune's odd relation to her actual father disturbingly confirms it. Whenever Pitts, "a man of nasty temper and of unreasonable resentments," is humiliated, he routinely beats his daughter, making of her a scapegoat for his own weakness. O'Connor's understanding of the daughter's role as scapegoat for male failure is matched by her awareness of the daughter's complicity:

> A look that was completely foreign to the child's face would appear on it. The old man could not define the look but it infuriated him. It was a look that was part terror and part respect and part something else, something very like cooperation. This look would appear on her face and she would get up and follow Pitts out. They would get in the truck and drive down the road out of earshot, where he would beat her.

Her very eagerness to be beaten—"she followed him, almost ran after him out the door"—uncovers to Mr. Fortune his granddaughter's indulgence in a masochistic relation to her father which signals a female posture, and which Mr. Fortune, feeling his own integrity threatened, cannot tolerate. But when he tries to make her "stand up" to Pitts, much as he attempts to keep her inviolable by not allowing "her to sit in snaky places or put her hands on bushes that might hide hornets," Mary Fortune ritually denies that her father beats her.

Yet by noting Mr. Fortune's own heightened excitement "whenever he knew the child had been beaten," O'Connor reveals the seductiveness of the posture of submission even as she alludes to its dangers. When he spies upon Pitts beating Mary Fortune, it is as if he is spying upon a sexual scene in which he feels compelled to identify with the vulnerable female: "It was as if it were *he* that Pitts was driving down the road to beat and it was as if *he* were the one submitting to it." Rebuking Mary Fortune as a Jezebel for submitting, he is in turn unmasked by her as "the whore of Babylon," and his answering roar, "A whore is a woman" syntactically reverses the theme which controls his consciousness, and which thus shapes his granddaughter's narrative destiny.

The story moves to its grotesque climax after Mary Fortune throws a tantrum about the sale of the disputed property, and Mr. Fortune decides he too must beat her:

> She respected Pitts because, even with no just cause, he beat her; and if he—with his just cause—did not beat her now, he would have nobody to blame but himself if she turned out a hellion. . . . He saw that the time had come, that he could no longer avoid whipping her.

With the phrase "he could no longer avoid whipping her," O'Connor underlines what the rhetoric has been increasingly insinuating, that Mr. Fortune has been holding himself back from that oedipal desire which is the source of paternal power and female complicity. As he drives her to the spot where he "has seen Pitts take his belt to her," it is difficult not to recall the implications of the "Stroke of Good Fortune" in the earlier story, nor to remember the sexual significance Freud attributed to beating fantasies.[16] The erotic undertones of the situation are uncannily heightened by O'Connor's sexualized description of that spot, "an ugly red bald spot surrounded by long thin pines that appeared to be gathered there to witness anything that would take place in such a clearing."

This is the dark secret center made visual, and here the obscure Gothic terror is grotesquely embodied in repugnant images. Yet characteristically, boundaries break down in Gothic confusion, for even as Mr. Fortune moves to assume the sadistic role associated with Pitts, his identification with Mary Fortune makes him simultaneously a participant in the masochistic pleasure. The very narrative structure of the climax, in which Mary Fortune and her grandfather shift roles and positions, dramatizes the indeterminacy of agent and object, of active and passive roles. Although Mary Fortune goes along passively for the ride, when Mr. Fortune announces his intention to beat her, she turns on him with an energy fueled by all the forces of repression. Identifying with her father—"I'm PURE Pitts"—she pummels her own image in Mr. Fortune, in an orgiastic frenzy which simultaneously acts out a forbidden fantasy and denies it through her furious repudiation of passivity:

> She was on him so quickly that he could not have recalled which blow he felt first, whether the weight of her whole solid body or the jabs of her feet or the pummeling of her fist on his chest.

Only when her grandfather recalls her to his separate being—"'Stop stop!' he wheezed. 'I'm your grandfather!'"—does she pause, and then make clear the source of her power, "'You been whipped by me and I'm PURE Pitts.'"

But O'Connor does not allow her the identification with the father's power. Taking advantage of this pause, Mr. Fortune reverses their positions and smashes her head against a rock in an assault which fulfills the prophecy of the view of the woods, the inevitable blood-letting. Although Mr. Fortune dubiously claims, "There's not an ounce of Pitts in me" as he looks at the body of his granddaughter, he has acted out Pitts' sadism and has caused the mutilation that ostensibly he had been trying to prevent.

In the final paragraph the uncanny mirroring results in a further circularity of punishment as Mr. Fortune, after his eruption of aggression, sinks back into that passive helplessness which presages his own death. As in a dream, Mr. Fortune feels himself drawn to an opening in the woods, "a little place where he could escape . . . a little opening where the white sky was reflected in the water." The scene evokes an orgasmic return to the womb which engulfs and obliterates him, "the whole lake opening up before him" as he realizes "he could not swim and had not brought the boat." Only the construction machine, the "huge yellow monster . . . gorging itself on clay" remains as a testament to his fate, reminding us that overseeing this oedipal drama of the father's physical—and sexual—assault on the daughter is the figure of retribution, the still more powerful devouring mother of the archaic imagination.

Although "A View of the Woods," like "A Temple of the Holy Ghost," raises the problematic issues of female identity, unlike the latter, which transforms a conflictual fantasy of physical violation into a fictional framework which allows for its resolution, "A View of the Woods" makes resolution impossible by *literally* dealing with physical violation with minimal disguise. One of O'Connor's most "Gothic" stories, "A View of the Woods" seems indeed overwhelmed by its unconscious interconnections just as Mr. Fortune is engulfed by the construction machine. Thus, while "A Temple of the Holy Ghost" defines its conflict within the discrete consciousness of the young girl, "A View of the Woods" diffuses it. The ambiguous boundaries of identity break down so that not only are Mary Fortune and her grandfather mirror-images, but Mary Fortune becomes Pitts (her father) and Mr. Fortune, in killing her, becomes Pitts trying to repudiate Pitts in a schizoid split. This very diffusion/confusion suggests that beneath the story's concern with female identity and its relation to oedipal desire lies the more primary Gothic issue of identity-confusion, of a maternal engulfment to which the final devouring image of the story points. However, this more basic fear of self-dissolution serves to intensify the story's concern with the vulnerability of the female body, of the male breaking into it, mutilating it or destroying it entirely.

The source of imaginative power in the grotesque-Gothic, then, lies in its evocation of fearful primitive fantasies which threaten the integrity of self, fantasies which the conventional Gothic also encourages, as much by its narrative obscurities and confusions as by its imprisonment of the heroine in a Gothic castle. But while the conventional Gothic allows its heroine the heroics of transgression because of her isolation from the conventions of society, the grotesque-Gothic emphasizes the limits of female identity. In moving from an identification with the mother as outscape—the castle, to an identification with the mother as inscape—the body, the Female Gothic heroine is locked into images of self which reflect deformity, fragmentation and annihilation.

Yet there is a power that the artist of the grotesque wields, and that should not be scanted in this focus on the imagery of self-hatred. It is the same kind of power that Hulga, the one-legged Ph.D. exercises in O'Connor's "Good Country People," or Mary Grace, when she contorts her ugly face in "Revelation." Indeed, O'Connor embraced images of deformity, recognizing their power to project and objectify not only self-hatred, but rage as well. By emphasizing her deformity, the self-named Hulga repudiates the entire constellation of conventional feminine behavior and appearance which her mother would impose and, instead, compels her to look at, acknowledge, and experience her daughter's condition. Similarly, through her creation of grotesque characters, O'Connor projects a distorting, disorienting mirror to her audience. Images of physical inadequacy are, like Hulga's artificial leg, meant to horrify and fascinate, but above all, to implicate her readers, making us complicit in a democracy of freaks.

But exhibitionism is as much a confession and a self-humiliation as it is an assault. Just as Hulga's aggressive projection of her defect—which she regards as the source of her special power—ultimately boomerangs when the bible salesman compels *her* to look at pornographic pictures (which typically serve to objectify and degrade female sexual difference) and then steals her artificial leg, leaving her helpless, O'Connor's disturbing grotesques, who are meant to reflect to us our spiritual impairment, also expose her own obsession with the deformed body, an obsession which she herself recognized as imposing limitations on the range of her work.[17] Yet her work effectively generalizes an important strand of the femaleness of experience. "To know oneself," she once remarked, "is, above all, to know what one lacks."[18] That knowledge has been made especially available to women writers, who have transformed a literary mode of minor repute—the Gothic—into a profound articulation of both their revolt against the cultural order and their sense of helplessness within it.

Notes

1. Morton Kaplan and Robert Kloss, "Fantasy of Paternity and the Doppelganger: Mary Shelley's *Frankenstein*," in *The Unspoken Motive* (New York: Free Press, 1963), p. 145. Also, see Devendra Varma, *The Gothic Flame* (New York: Russell & Russell, 1964); Mario Praz, *The Romantic Agony* (New York: Meridian Books, 1967); Elino Railo, *The Haunted Castle* (New York: Humanities Press, 1964).

2. "Gothic Possibilities," *New Literary History,* 8 (1976-1977), 279-294.

3. For a lengthier discussion of these points see my "Gothic Mirrors and Feminine Identity," *Centennial Review* (Winter 1980), pp. 43-64.

4. See, *The Mermaid and the Minotaur* (New York: Harper & Row, 1977).

5. See, Nancy Chodorow, "Family Structure and Feminine Personality," *Women, Culture and Soci-*

ety, ed. M. Rosaldo and L. Lamphere (Stanford: Stanford Univ. Press, 1974); *The Reproduction of Mothering* (Berkeley: Univ. of California Press, 1979).

6. Holland and Sherman, 286.

7. Ellen Moers, *Literary Women* (Garden City: Doubleday, 1976), pp. 90-110.

8. Wolfgang Kayser, in his comprehensive study, *The Grotesque in Art and Literature* (New York: McGraw-Hill, 1966), claims the grotesque expresses our disorientation in the physical universe. For a more psychoanalytic account of the grotesque, see Michael Steig, "Defining the Grotesque: An Attempt at Synthesis," *Journal of Aesthetics and Art Criticism* (Winter 1970), pp. 253-260; also, my "Comic Vibrations and Self-Construction in Grotesque Literature," *Literature and Psychology,* 29, 3 (1979), 114-119.

9. See, Phyllis Greenacre, "Early Physical Determinants in the Development of the Sense of Identity" (1958); rpt., *Emotional Growth,* (New York: I.U.P., 1971), I, 113-127.

10. *Mystery and Manners* (New York: Noonday, 1970), p. 113. O'Connor repeatedly remarked on the importance of visual imagery to her fiction: "The writer should never be ashamed of staring" (p. 84); "Everything has its testing point in the eye, and the eye is an organ that eventually involves the whole personality" (p. 91).

11. *Wise Blood* (New York: Farrar, Straus & Giroux, 1962), p. 63.

12. *The Complete Stories* (New York: Farrar, Straus & Giroux, 1971), p. 97. Subsequent references are to this edition.

13. Leslie Fiedler speaks to this response: "No category of Freaks is regarded with such ferocious ambivalence as the hermaphrodites, for none creates in us a greater tension between physical repulsion and spiritual attraction." *Freaks* (New York: Simon & Schuster, 1978), p. 179. For a psychoanalytic view of this ambivalence, and the related desire for omnipotence that androgyny suggests, see Philip Slater, *The Glory of Hera* (Boston: Beacon Press, 1968), p. 112.

14. *Essays in Applied Psychoanalysis* (London: International Psychoanalytic Press, 1923).

15. *The Second Sex* (New York: Bantam, 1961), pp. 636-637.

16. Sigmund Freud, "A Child is Being Beaten" (1919), *SE,* XVII, 177.

17. "I've been writing for eighteen years and I've reached the point where I can't do again what I know I can do well, and the larger things that I need to do now, I doubt my capacity for doing." *The Habit of Being* (New York: Farrar, Straus & Giroux, 1979), p. 518.

18. *Mystery and Manners,* p. 35.

Erik D. Curren (essay date spring 1995)

SOURCE: Curren, Erik D. "Should Their Eyes Have Been Watching God?: Hurston's Use of Religious Experience and Gothic Horror." *African American Review* 29, no. 1 (spring 1995): 17-25.

[*In the following essay, Curren proposes that Hurston uses gothic devices in* Their Eyes Were Watching God *to effectively convey the politics of the master-slave relationship, while also ratifying the vitality and nurturing nature of African religious practice.*]

The title of a literary work may be leading or misleading, but it is often a good place to start an analysis. When title words or phrases are repeated inside the text, connecting them to the specific place where they appear seems to offer the promise of a key for decoding the meaning of the whole work. *Their Eyes Were Watching God* is a suggestive but perplexing title for Hurston's Bildungsroman of a woman's self-discovery through a quest for meaningful community. Dolan Hubbard attempts to illuminate the title by relating it to the place where its words appear in the body of Hurston's text, and analyzing it within the context of sermons and religious language. It is placed in the text just when Janie and the other folk bean pickers are beginning to realize the awesome power of the storm on the Everglades, and how weak they are when faced with God's power. Hubbard finds that the title words signal a religious transcendence of white oppression:

> The storm in this, Janie's last movement toward the horizon, symbolizes the struggle the corporate black community has to come to terms with in the oppressor's negation of its image. Out of this negation, the mythic consciousness seeks a new beginning in the future by imagining an original beginning. The social implications of this religious experience enable the oppressed community to dehistoricize the oppressor's hegemonic dominance. Metaphorically, the phrase *their eyes were watching God* means the creation of a new form of humanity—one that is no longer based on the master-slave dialectic.
>
> (176)

I would argue, however, just the opposite: that the title phrase, placed in the text at this particular point, demonstrates just how dependent on the master-slave dialectic and the principle of authority the Everglades folk community really is for Hurston. The title provides a clue to the complexity of her narrative and her ambivalence concerning the possibility of truly autonomous African American folk life.

Hubbard's interpretation accords with much Hurston criticism that *Their Eyes* is an "affirmative" text, an optimistic portrayal of a vital and creative black folk world completely separate from the hierarchy-conscious Jim Crow South. To take a well-known example, Alice Walker cites Hurston as an example of black "racial health" for her refusal to dwell on the depredations of racism and white prejudice, and for focusing instead on vital and creative African American folk life. For Walker, Hurston's work presents "a sense of black people as complete, complex, undiminished human beings, a sense that is lacking in so much black writing and literature" (xii-xiii). It is certainly true that, in contrast to many "protest" novels, most notably Wright's *Native Son*, *Their Eyes* creates a space for rural black folk culture, both in Hurston's own native town of Eatonville, and in the folk community of the Florida Everglades.[1] In the first parts of the novel, these isolated black communities serve as the backdrop for the optimistic story of Janie's quest for self-discovery.

On the other hand, there is much in *Their Eyes* that is not optimistic and uplifting, but tragic and frightening, especially in the last quarter of the story, beginning with the storm on the Everglades: the "monstropolous" and menacing Lake Okeechobee, grotesque encounters with the bodies of those caught in the storm, the mad dog that bites Tea Cake and gives him rabies, the body-burying detail in Palm Beach, and, perhaps most frightening of all, the evil transformation from loving angel to homicidal devil that rabies works on Tea Cake. All these horrors accord ill with the positive tone of Janie's life before the storm and signal, I would argue, an intentional genre change on Hurston's part, a switch from optimistic quest to gothic horror. While *Their Eyes* is certainly about the creativity and vitality of the black folk community, the book is far more than a propagandistic exercise in racial "uplift." Too little critical attention has been paid to horrors in the novel and to this dramatic change of genre, and, as a result, critics have not sufficiently explained the narrative complexity of Hurston's book.[2] It is a multi-layered exploration of the real, as opposed to the imagined, independence of any black American folk community from the larger American culture, and specifically the immunity of the black folk community to the principle of hierarchy, a cornerstone of the master-slave dialectic to which Hubbard refers.

The novel's generic complexity dramatizes Hurston's ambivalence concerning the prospects for folk culture to remain (or become) truly independent of white American values. The first three-quarters of Janie's story are an optimistic quest narrative of self-discovery.

Janie finds increasingly more freedom as she moves along the steps of her journey: Nanny, Logan Killicks, Joe Starks, and, finally, Tea Cake and the egalitarian folk community of the Everglades. Here, daytime bean picking is subordinated to the real business of life, nighttime "dancing, fighting, singing, crying, laughing, winning and losing love every hour" (197). Free from white urban commercialism, the folk community also seems free of white prejudices, and Tea Cake as its representative stands in contrast to the snobbery and chauvinism of Starks. Participation in the folk community and the love of Tea Cake seem to be the fulfillment of Janie's quest.

Then comes the storm, and Janie's story is transformed in the space of a few pages into a kind of gothic horror thriller with the storm, the mad dog, and Tea Cake's murderous delusions. But however horrible the hurricane becomes, it is the immediate prelude to the storm that is key to an understanding of Hurston's purpose in transforming her story from quest to gothic horror. In the heart of the crisis, the characters display bravery and self-sacrifice. However, just before the storm, when they are subject to fear and vague threat, the bean pickers' folk consciousness is put to the test, and found wanting. The genre change from quest to gothic horror represents a trick that Hurston plays on the reader in order to dramatize the greatest threat to folk culture that Hurston finds in the United States. This threat is the complacency of those who think that their folk heritage protects them from participating in the prejudices and attachment to hierarchy associated with white America. Hurston shows that even the folk community of the Everglades in not in fact immune to prejudice and snobbery, and it is just at the point where the book changes from optimistic quest to gothic horror thriller that the admirable egalitarianism of the folk community shows the ideological cracks—racism, materialism, and a magical belief in the power and goodness of those in authority—that threaten to undermine it completely.

The coming of the storm takes the folk community completely by surprise. When an Indian explains why the Seminoles are starting to head east out of the Everglades, that they are "'going to high ground. Saw-grass bloom. Hurricane coming,'" the bean pickers are unimpressed:

> Everybody was talking about it that night. But nobody was worried. The fire dance kept up till nearly dawn. The next day, more Indians moved east, unhurried but steady. Still a blue sky and fair weather. Beans running fine and prices good, so the Indians could be, must be, wrong. You couldn't have a hurricane when you're making seven and eight dollars a day picking beans. Indians are dumb anyhow, always were.
>
> (229)

As soon as the folk community is threatened by an outside force—in this case, the power of nature—it begins to display white attitudes. The first of these is a modern dismissal of tribal lore, a short-sighted and close-minded empiricism that discounts other ways of knowing nature. Convinced of its own monopoly on the truth, this narrow empiricism verges on fanaticism or even superstition. Is it more rational to dismiss the possibility of a hurricane because bean picking still yields "seven and eight dollars a day" than it is to heed natural signs? Related to this are bigotry and materialism more typical of white America than of black folk culture. After all, the Bahamians do not share these attitudes. On the contrary, while the American blacks will not be budged, Lias the Bahamian decides to leave because he trusts the Indians' judgment, and relies like them on natural signs—"'De crow gahn up, man.'" Tea Cake disagrees: "'Dat ain't nothin'. You ain't seen de bossman go up, is yuh? Well all right now. Man, de money's too good on the muck. It's liable tuh fair off by tuhmorer. Ah wouldn't leave if Ah wuz you'" (230).

What does this response say about Tea Cake? Claire Crabtree summarizes the standard interpretation of Tea Cake as an embodiment of the open-mindedness that separates black folk culture from white America: "Above all, Tea Cake is associated with vitality and freedom and is unhampered by the orientation toward white values which is the flaw of characters like Starks, Nanny and Mrs. Turner" (60). However, when, like the rest of the American bean pickers, he dismisses the Indians' lore, Tea Cake speaks less as a follower of folklore than as an American. He is skeptical of tribal knowledge, is wedded to Mammon, and credences the authority of whites. Tea Cake decides to stay because "'de white folks ain't gone nowhere. Dey oughta know if it's dangerous'" (231). Though he is one of the leaders of the Everglades folk community, and certainly not shy about asserting control over Janie, here Tea Cake is willing to submit himself against both folk sense and common sense to white leadership. If anything, on this particular point Tea Cake seems more, not less, hampered by an orientation toward white values than Starks, who did not look to white leadership, but decided to set up shop in all-black Eatonville because he knew that, if he were ever to succeed, he would have to get out from under the control of whites.

A brief comparison between Hurston and Richard Wright may be instructive here. In contrast to "protest" writers like Wright, who sought a more rational understanding of social conditions to counteract the irrationality of racism, Hurston was skeptical of Western rationalism, and promoted an alternative to it in the form of African-derived folklore. But her justification of folklore in *Their Eyes* is framed in oddly rationalist terms: In touch with nature and aware of its awesome power for both creation and destruction, the tribal lore of the Indians and Bahamians is actually more rational than white, Western thought, since the latter is fettered with illogical racial prejudices and a magical belief that money and technology can conquer natural forces. Of course, Hurston's portrayal of isolated black folk culture as vital and creative contrasts sharply with Wright's grim focus on urban ghetto dwellers hollowed out by the effects of racism. Yet, it would be a misreading of the scenes before the hurricane to claim that the bean pickers are a good example of isolated black folk culture. The Indians and Bahamians, both more distant from white American values than are the American blacks, are far better models of folk consciousness.

The problem with Tea Cake and the rest of the American bean pickers is that they have been influenced by white culture in ways that they do not realize. Hurston sees this influence as an infection not unlike the rabies that will strike Tea Cake over a month after the dog bite during the storm: It can lie dormant for some time, but once symptoms occur, the effects are irreversible. Savagery will set in, and death may be the only cure. With rabies, early treatment is the key, and Tea Cake could have been saved if he had not been so cavalier about the dog bite. For Hurston, the cure to America's savagery of racism, chauvinism, and materialism was folklore. So it is shocking when, in her 1950 essay "What White Publishers Won't Print," Hurston discusses a kind of "folk" lore that is not vital, creative, and empowering, but the opposite—archaic, smothering, and imprisoning, in short, the world of white racial prejudice. At its center are various stereotypes about African Americans, especially the myth of "reversion to type":

> This curious doctrine has such wide acceptance that it is tragic. One has only to examine the huge literature on it to be convinced. No matter how high we seem to climb, put us under strain and we revert to type, that is, to the bush. Under a superficial layer of Western culture, the jungle drums throb in our veins.
>
> (172)

Bitterly ironic, Hurston's characterization of bigotry and white supremacy as folk belief adds another dimension to her view of the value of myth. Not all "folklore" or received popular belief is liberating, egalitarian, or life-giving like the stories collected in *Mules and Men* (1935); some myth, like the "folklore" of racism, is just superstition that prevents people from acting in their own best interests.

To return to *Their Eyes Were Watching God*, it becomes clear that Tea Cake and the Everglades bean pickers are the victims of this negative "folk" belief. Even more frightening for Hurston, the bean pickers under strain actually confirm the stereotype of "reversion to type." Just as rabies transforms Tea Cake into a monster, so the fear and uncertainty created by the approach of the storm transforms the open-minded and vital bean pickers into "savages." But, as in her use of the word *folk-*

lore to describe vulgar racism, *savagery* for Hurston here should be understood ironically, since she employs the racist stereotype only to then turn the tables on it.

In the stereotype, Western culture is good, because it restrains the natural violence, lust, and barbarity of tribal peoples. By contrast, in the novel, it is tribal culture which is life-giving and nurturing, and the bean pickers would be better off if they had more of it. Instead, they are only superficial, leisure-time participants in folkloric culture; underneath, they are essentially Americans. When their leisure is threatened, they fall back uncritically on hierarchical thinking, with its magical valuation of power and money. Rather than reverting to the African beast, as the white stereotype would have it, they revert from their black beliefs—creative, vital, egalitarian—to an inferior set of destructive white myths suitable only for truly superstitions, modern American "savages."

When the storm picks up, the bean pickers' reliance on white ways of thinking is extended into a reliance on whites themselves. Though increasingly uneasy, the American blacks do not follow the Indians and Bahamians out, but rely on the judgment of the whites: "The folks let the people do the thinking. If the castles felt themselves secure, the cabins needn't worry" (234). "Castles" and "cabins" merges images of feudalism with American plantation slavery, suggesting that the blacks' trust in the judgment of the whites is a kind of medieval (European) superstition and, further, that slaves should not look to their masters to consider their best interests. Yet the cabins decide with their masters to remain and weather the storm: "Chink up your cracks, shiver in your wet beds and wait on the mercy of the Lord," a decision followed by a surprising piece of wishful thinking—"The bossman might have the thing stopped before morning anyway" (234).

Thus, by the time the title phase appears in the text, Hurston has given the folk community a chance to contradict all the egalitarianism and attachment to folklore that it stands for. Tea Cake and the others have denigrated Indians and tribal lore in general; they have shown that they care about money more than common sense; and they have demonstrated their trust not merely in white values (materialism, skepticism of folk knowledge) but in the almost divine power, knowledge, and benevolence of whites themselves. This sets the stage for the bean pickers' awe at the power of the storm, and the religious experience that Hubbard describes. Overawed by the violent power of God/Ole Massa, the bean pickers cannot help but respect the exercise of power, even if it is directed against them. This produces a certain kind of enlightenment:

> "If you kin see de light at daybreak, you don't keer if you die at dusk. It's so many people never seen de light at all. Ah wuz fumblin' round and God opened the door." . . .

> The wind came back with triple fury, and put out the light for the last time. They sat in company with the others in other shanties, their eyes straining against crude walls and their souls asking if He meant to measure their puny might against His. They seemed to be staring at the dark, but their eyes were watching God.
>
> (236)

Hubbard argues that being suspended between life and death just before the storm represents Janie's finest hour, "a religious response born of her having to come to terms with the impenetrable majesty of the divine" (176).

If we read this passage in isolation, and in terms of orthodox Protestant theology, as Hubbard does, the image of God opening the door certainly does sound like revelation, perhaps even a kind of epiphany that might save Janie and the others. But such a reading would fail to account for earlier references to God while the storm is brewing, or to accord with Hurston's attitude toward Christian doctrine and belief in divine omnipotence.

Let me deal with Hurston's attitude toward religion first. In the section of *Dust Tracks on a Road* entitled "Religion," Hurston describes her childhood questioning of Christian tenets that seemed absurd to her at the time: that children could not play on Sunday, that God hated for Christ to die but let him do it nonetheless, that because Christ died "folks did not have to die any more." Though the angry response of her father, the Rev. John Hurston of the Missionary Baptist Church, quickly taught the young Zora to keep her questions to herself, her head remained "full of misty fumes of doubt" (268):

> As I grew, the questions went to sleep in me. I just said the words, made the motions and went on. My father being a preacher, and my mother superintendent of the Sunday School, I naturally was always having to do with religious ceremonies. I even enjoyed participation at times; I was moved, not by the spirit, but by action, more or less dramatic.
>
> (269)

What Hurston would later take from her father's church was the creativity of folk expression that the communal worship allowed, rather than any kind of attachment to Christian belief. Indeed, Hurston describes such belief as a crutch for the weak, a fiction constructed because "the great masses fear life and its consequences"; and "though the omnipotence they rely on is a creature of their own minds," they cling to it because "it gives them a feeling of security" (277-78). Concluding this section, Hurston makes it clear that such religion has no attraction for her: "It seems to me that organized creeds are collections of words around a wish. I feel no need for such" (278-79).

Though she may have rejected the beliefs of Christianity, Hurston was not closed to the possibilities of the spiritual or supernatural realm. When investigating hoodoo in New Orleans and voodoo in Haiti, she developed a profound respect for the understanding of nature displayed by these African-derived folk religions. In *Mules and Men,* she shows some reticence in describing her experiences with the supernatural while the apprentice of several hoodoo doctors in New Orleans; yet, as Hemenway explains, with careful reading, it becomes clear that "Hurston ultimately reveals her conviction that these men and women [hoodoo practitioners], considered irrationally superstitious by most observers, have discovered many of nature's secrets. Time after time she reports that her 1928 trip found hoodoo rituals to be successful" (122). She felt the same about Haitian voodoo, and was attracted to its sensuality and its understanding of the mystery of all mysteries, the source of life represented by feminine sexuality.[3] When we consider that Hurston was far more interested in African-derived folk religions and folklore than in American Protestantism, it stands to reason that she would have been more likely to see God as a character from folktales than the primum mobile of orthodox theology. Indeed, as she herself explains in *Mules and Men,* within the African American folk tradition, the character of God is often identified with the slavemaster, just as the devil is often a clever trickster who triumphs over God's superior power through wit and resourcefulness.[4]

In the context of Hurston's views on religion, references to God in the storm section of *Their Eyes* seem more sinister. If we compare the passage where the title words appear to mentions of God and the storm that immediately precede it, we find a view of God more like the slavemaster of folklore than the benevolent deity of the Church. Tea Cake ironically remembers this insight when he ascribes god-like powers to the "bossman," but he does not realize that this is a piece of magical thinking that does him no good. Likewise, the bean pickers echo the folkloric equation God = slavemaster: "Motor looked up in his angel-looking way and said, 'Big Massa draw him chair upstairs.'" But for the humor typical of folklore, Janie, seeming to speak for the others, substitutes a religious reverence for power: "'Ole Massa is doin' *His* work now. Us oughta keep quiet'" (235). Here we should remember what Janie, in her religious awe, fails to recall, namely that keeping quiet, staying put, disdaining common sense, and respectfully watching the authorities are just what put her and the others needlessly at the mercy of the storm in the first place. Thus, perhaps watching God, much like watching to see what the bossman would do, may not be in the bean pickers' best interest. If God is just another version of Ole Massa, a kind of over-bossman, then a belief in his omnipotence and goodness is misplaced, a dangerous superstition.

Because they trust in technology (the dikes that eventually fail), scorn tribal lore, and believe in the wisdom and benevolence of those in power, the Americans, both black and white, appear the most deluded and mystified. For Hurston, their eyes are, and have been for too long, watching God—the mythic principle of hierarchical power—when they should have been watching the material world, and following the example of the Indians, animals, and Bahamians who are in closer touch with nature and who know when to get out. Thus, while Hubbard is correct that the phrase *their eyes were watching God* signifies a religious experience, it is not one that allows the folk community to transcend "hegemonic dominance," but a religious experience on the order of superstition, and one that binds the folk community even closer to the very master-slave dialectic that threatens it the most.

The significance of the title for Hurston's whole narrative may be seen when we consider it in relation to the genre shift that the title phrase in the text signals. Before the storm, Janie progresses hopefully toward the horizon. In the storm, she and the others reach their lowest point of helplessness and inertia. After the storm, Janie becomes the victim of double treachery: not only Tea Cake's rabid madness, but also the denunciations of the Everglades folk against her during the murder trial. Hurston transforms the story from quest into gothic horror to allegorize the divided consciousness of African American folk culture, and its precarious independence. To return to the disease metaphor suggested by Tea Cake's rabies, folklore is always open to infection by white thinking—or, rather, superstition. Because she sees an attachment to authority as the most dangerous American superstition, Hurston turns to a genre whose historic role has been to fight superstition and debunk authority, the gothic.

Ever since the first gothic novel, Horace Walpole's *The Castle of Otranto,* was published in 1764, the genre has attacked authority, especially the institutions of Church and Aristocracy, and has shown how power is made possible by the superstitions of the powerless.[5] American literature, as Leslie Fiedler has proposed, is particularly gothic, relying heavily on violence, the macabre, and the "Faustian bargain," a typical gothic situation that informs our three greatest classics, *The Scarlet Letter, Moby Dick,* and *Huck Finn.* For Fiedler, the gothic is so important to American literature because its deal-with-the-devil accurately portrays the central contradiction of the American project: a New Start that celebrated its own innocence while at the same time engaging in the large-scale crimes of Indian war, slavery, and exploitation of the land.

Along the same lines as Fiedler, but more to the point for Hurston, Toni Morrison, herself a writer of horror and ghost stories, considers the question of gothic literature's ascendancy in the New World and hazards an answer:

Why should a young country repelled by Europe's moral and social disorder, swooning in a fit of desire and reflection, devote its talents to reproducing in its own literature the typology of diabolism it wanted to leave behind? An answer to that seems fairly obvious: one way to benefit from the lessons of earlier mistakes and past misfortune is to record them so as to prevent their repetition through exposure and inoculation.

(36)

Why indeed, we may ask along the same lines as Morrison, would Hurston devote the last quarter of *Their Eyes* to reproducing the horrors of cruelty, violence, and prejudice that Janie's quest had sought to leave behind? A suggestive parallel can be drawn between the "young country repelled by Europe's moral and social disorder" and the Harlem Renaissance in which Hurston wrote, a young literature of a relatively innocent culture (African America) repelled by white America's moral and social corruption.

This social corruption is figured in the text by Tea Cake's rabies, a metaphor for the infection of life-affirming black folk culture by the disease of deadly white prejudices—namely, the master-slave dialectic and the belief that racial hierarchy is justified by nature. It would follow here, then, that Christianity's belief in the omnipotence and goodness of the one true God is part and parcel of a hierarchical system that is dangerous to human freedom. As we have seen, a more liberating understanding of nature for Hurston would be the pluralism of African-based folk religions like hoodoo and voodoo, with their multiplicity of different loas, gods, and spirits, all in tune with different aspects of the natural world. The gothic is particularly useful for Hurston, since it allows her to turn the tables on commonly held assumptions about religion. In her work on folk religion, Hurston attempts to demonstrate that hoodoo and voodoo, reputed to be dark cults of devil worship, zombies, and curses, are actually vital and nurturing practices in touch with nature. By contrast, in *Their Eyes,* she seems to imply that Western, enlightened thought is the truly diabolic cult of mind control. Might not the real zombies, then, be those whose eyes are watching the bossman in whatever form he is presented, whether as the omnipotent God, as money, or as the white bossman himself?

I would conclude that Hurston uses the gothic to inoculate black America against the infection of white prejudices just as Hawthorne, Melville, and Twain used horror to inoculate a young America against the infection of European evils. White America had its chance to make a "fresh start," to avoid the Old World ills of hierarchy and domination, but, for Hurston no less than for Wright, history has shown that it failed. Hurston seems to hope that African American culture will have a better chance to achieve something truly new, a society that is egalitarian not only in word, but in deed. What she fears the most is that black America will simply develop along the same lines as the rest of the nation, creating a society with its own prejudices, snobberies, and self-destructive myths of power fit only for the Nannys, Mrs. Turners, and Joe Starkses. The only way Hurston sees to prevent this is to challenge African American culture to closely examine its own commitment to creating a truly different community, not one that simply talks folklore, but one that lives its democratic impulse. In this task, the old Cold War maxim—that eternal vigilance is the price of freedom—would be the best guide to defending against a stealth infection of the master-slave dialectic. Thus, though *Their Eyes* may not be the novel of "uplift" that the first part of Janie's quest implies, the book remains an affirmation of folklore, but a kind of folklore that sees its autonomy realistically and can avoid repeating the mistakes of white America.

Notes

1. The Hurston-Wright debate is found in critical statements by the two authors and, specifically, in published reviews of each other's work: See Wright's "Between Laughter and Tears" and Hurston's review of *Uncle Tom's Children*. Critics who have dealt with this debate include Jordan; Hemenway 241-42, 333-35; Gates 180-92; and Awkward 7-12.

2. *Their Eyes Were Watching God* has traditionally been read as an "affirmative" expression of the value of rural black folk life in the South, feminine self-discovery, and romantic love between equals, missing the horror that invades the end of the novel. Notable among the many articles praising the novel as expressing "racial health" and promoting folk culture and feminism are Walker, Howard, Wainwright, and Pondrom.

3. As Hemenway explains, "By stressing its religious nature, *Tell My Horse* dignifies voodoo worship, removing it from the lurid and sensational associations held by the popular mind. Voodoo's sexual content becomes a dignified component of a complex belief on the same order as the Virgin Birth" when the voodoo houngan describes the ceremony where the priestess reveals her vagina as the source of all life and the ultimate mystery (249-50).

4. In the glossary at the end of *Mules and Men,* Gates explains that "the devil is not the terror that he is in European folk-lore. He is a powerful trickster who often competes successfully with God. There is a strong suspicion that the devil is an extension of the story-makers while God is the supposedly impregnable white masters, who are nevertheless defeated by the Negroes" (248).

5. For a discussion of the aims of the Anglo-American gothic, see Punter. For theories of the American Gothic, see Fiedler, Gross, and Ringe. Frank gives an index of Gothic devices in the hundreds of American Gothic works he lists.

Works Cited

Awkward, Michael. "Introduction." *New Essays on Their Eyes Were Watching God.* Ed. Awkward. New York: Cambridge UP, 1990. 1-27.

Crabtree, Claire. "The Confluence of Folklore, Feminism and Black Self-Determination in Zora Neale Hurston's *Their Eyes Were Watching God.*" *Southern Literary Journal* 17.2 (1985): 54-66.

Fiedler, Leslie. *Love and Death in the American Novel.* New York: Criterion, 1960.

Frank, Frederick S. *Through the Pale Door: A Guide to and Through the American Gothic.* Bibliographies and Indexes in American Literature 11. New York: Greenwood, 1990.

Gates, Henry Louis, Jr. *The Signifying Monkey: A Theory of African-American Literary Criticism.* New York: Oxford UP, 1988.

Gross, Louis. *Redefining the American Gothic: From* Wieland *to* The Day of the Dead. Ann Arbor: UMI Research P, 1989.

Hemenway, Robert E. *Zora Neale Hurston: A Literary Biography.* Urbana: U of Illinois P, 1977.

Howard, Lillie P. *Zora Neale Hurston.* Boston: Twayne, 1980.

Hubbard, Dolan. "'. . . Ah said Ah'd save de text for you': Recontextualizing the Sermon to Tell (Her)story in Zora Neale Hurston's *Their Eyes Were Watching God.*" *African American Review* 27 (1993): 167-78.

Hurston, Zora Neale. *Dust Tracks on a Road.* Ed. Robert E. Hemenway. 2nd ed. Urbana: U of Illinois P, 1984.

———. *Mules and Men.* 1935. New York: Harper, 1990.

———. Rev. of *Uncle Tom's Children,* by Richard Wright. 1938. Rpt. *Richard Wright: Critical Perspectives Past and Present.* Ed. Henry Louis Gates, Jr., and Kwame Anthony Appiah. New York: Amistad, 1993. 3-4.

———. *Their Eyes Were Watching God.* 1937. Urbana: U of Illinois P, 1978.

———. "What White Publishers Won't Print." 1950. *I Love Myself When I am Laughing . . . And Then Again When I am Looking Mean and Impressive: A Zora Neale Hurston Reader.* Ed. Alice Walker. New York: Feminist P, 1979. 169-73.

Jordan, June. "Notes Toward a Balancing of Love and Hatred: On Richard Wright and Zora Neale Hurston." *Black World* 23 (Aug. 1974): 4-8.

Morrison, Toni. *Playing in the Dark: Whiteness and the Literary Imagination.* Cambridge: Harvard UP, 1992.

Pondrom, Cyrena N. "The Role of Myth in *Their Eyes Were Watching God.*" *American Literature* 58 (1986): 181-202.

Punter, David. *The Literature of Terror: A History of Gothic Fictions from 1765 to the Present Day.* New York: Longman, 1980.

Ringe, Donald. *American Gothic.* Lexington: UP of Kentucky, 1982.

Wainwright, Mary. "The Aesthetics of Community: The Insular Black Community as Theme and Focus in *Their Eyes Were Watching God.*" *The Harlem Renaissance: Revaluations.* Ed. Amritjit Singh, William S. Shiver, and Stanley Brodwin. New York: Garland, 1989. 233-43.

Walker, Alice. "Foreword." Hemenway xi-xxiii.

Wright, Richard. "Between Laughter and Tears." *New Masses* 5 Oct. 1937: 23-25.

Robert K. Martin (essay date 1998)

SOURCE: Martin, Robert K. "Haunted by Jim Crow: Gothic Fictions by Hawthorne and Faulkner." In *American Gothic: New Inventions in a National Narrative,* edited by Robert K. Martin and Eric Savoy, pp. 129-42. Iowa City: University of Iowa Press, 1998.

[*In the following essay, Martin examines the themes of gender and race in Hawthorne's* The House of the Seven Gables, *and notes that the issues raised in the novel are mirrored in Faulkner's* Absalom, Absalom! *However, Faulkner's novel, while dealing with many of the same issues, presents a more complicated picture of the world, replacing Hawthorne's happy ending with a vision that is ultimately nightmarish.*]

In his now somewhat outdated but still influential formulation, Harold Bloom argues for an agonistic relationship between the "strong poet" and his predecessors. The task for the belated writer is simultaneously to express admiration and filiation and to mark off difference. The model does not allow for collaboration and simple indebtedness, presumably the characteristic only of weak poets. More importantly, the model assumes the centrality of the heroic individual author without allowing for a larger cultural process of self-creation and citation.

I want to examine two well-known and important American gothic texts, to suggest the ways in which the later text, Faulkner's *Absalom, Absalom!* rewrites the earlier text, Hawthorne's *The House of the Seven Gables*. Of course one way of looking at them might be simply to place them both in the context of the gothic. Indeed, Faulkner's gothicism is often remarked on. As Eric Sundquist has put it, "Which of Faulkner's major works is not an American gothic?" (44). Hawthorne's gothicism, once a commonplace of criticism, is less acknowledged these days, although it is crucial to *The Marble Faun* as well as to *House*. My argument here will be that Hawthorne's drama of "class warfare," as Richard Brodhead has called it (79), conceals other, more troubling conflicts of race and gender that are expressed through gothic elements. In Leslie Fiedler's well-known words, American gothic expresses national "obsessive concerns," especially "the ambiguity of our relationship with Indian and Negro" (xxii), constantly rewriting a masterplot of cultural authority and guilt. Faulkner's reworking of this material (whether taken as a personal or as a cultural act) places into relief the submerged texts of Hawthorne and their significance for the writing of an American history.

The gothic, it seems to be generally agreed, is most often a politically conservative form that gives expression to the anxieties of a class threatened with violent dissolution. On the other hand, the gothic can allow for the voice of the culturally repressed and hence act out a resistance to the dominant culture. This function is particularly striking in African-American adaptations of the genre, where the voice of the dead slave can act as a means of insisting on the presence of history. The references to blackness in *The House of the Seven Gables* are a reminder of that which the new generation wants to forget as it moves away from the house to begin life over again. Hawthorne's gothic text works against his dominant text to recall the anxiety over race and gender in midcentury America, writing a countertext of guilt and endless expiation in the midst of a narrative of redemption.[1] Hawthorne's use of the gothic form is no mere borrowing of its trappings, although they are certainly present. Even if *The House of the Seven Gables*, with its haunted house, doomed family, mysterious lost documents, and hereditary curse, cannot help reminding us of gothic texts such as *The Fall of the House of Usher*, its tensions could suggest a reversal of Poe's famous remark, for *Gables* is distinctly about the terrors of America, if not of Germany. Indeed, it is in part the role of Hawthorne's texts in defining American history that has rendered them so susceptible to rewriting and reinterpretation, from Henry James to John Updike. Hawthorne's gothic enacts the presence of the past, even as his text seeks to deny that past. If the motif of the haunted house central to the gothic is maintained, it is now situated in the heart of commercial Salem, not in a grotesque landscape of the imagination. Among the secrets it conceals is a racial history of slavery which at least in part shifts the novel's theme away from family guilt to national guilt or uses the family as a synecdoche of the nation. The gothic is associated with the past, with the house itself, its gothicism exaggerated as a way of attempting to escape from that tradition. Hawthorne's novel attempts to reclaim the gothic wizard for a new harmonious future, but the very gothic elements he both calls upon and mocks retain a power to haunt.

What links the two texts by Hawthorne and Faulkner is the centrality of the house that stands for a fallen family, the failure of an attempt to inscribe the self in history through possession. Both houses contain a secret, the Indian deed as well as the dead Judge Pyncheon, in Hawthorne's case, and the physical body of Henry Sutpen, standing in for the entire history of forbidden desire and aggression, in Faulkner's. In both cases, the secret of the house is the secret of the family and the sign of the family's participation in a primal crime. Faulkner's reference to Ikkemotubbe, the displaced Indian king (50), makes it clear that Sutpen's claim is as flimsy as that of the Pyncheons. If Faulkner indeed thought of Hawthorne's example as he wrote *Absalom* (and it is of course not necessary to my argument that he should have), it was not, I believe, such generic similarities that would have attracted him most.[2] Rather, what Hawthorne's text reveals, as its own secret, is the story of race in America and of the power of the phallus.

Hawthorne's text was written in the midst of a national—even international—debate over the right to property: private property as opposed to communal property, the right to hold and sell slaves, and the connections between the enslavement of women and that of black Americans.[3] Although the propertyless, like Uncle Venner, are threatened by the poorhouse, *Gables* offers a view of property that suggests the need for better management rather than any radical change, indeed, for a management that can forestall revolution. Holgrave, the Fourierist, will become a wealthy man inheriting, or marrying, property and possessing the woman by a now domesticated phallic power. Although Holgrave is the successor to Hawthorne's scientist/rapist figures, Hawthorne asks us to see him as a new-tamed phallus, domesticated by his "little housewife" (136). It is not that Holgrave lacks the power of the practitioners of black magic from whom he descends but that he chooses not to use it or to accept its service of a new domestic economy. But Hawthorne's text suggests some of the ways in which this shift to a new masculinity would not be total. Hawthorne identifies only two kinds of property—that obtained by legal means, by land grant or purchase, and that obtained by labor. The Maules base their claim to the house on the original work of clearing and building (Maule has "hewn" his land "out of the primeval forest" [7]), but that claim has come to seem weak in mid-nineteenth-century America, where property is bought and sold without any claim to "natural" possession. Even the Pyncheons, rich as they are, find themselves losing out in the new economic marketplace, and the Judge, like the Colonel his ancestor, seeks to find the original land claim. The Colonel had offered to give the Maules back their house in Salem if he can repossess his lands in Maine—his willingness to do so indicates the growth of a capitalist economy in which inheritance plays an increasingly marginal role and is supplanted by colonial mercantilism. That the almost mythic lands in Maine (an "unmeasured tract of eastern lands" [18]) can be claimed only through a missing Indian deed underlines the role of national theft and genocide. These "vast," "unexplored and unmeasured" lands are what remains of the colonial dream of America, the imposition of European property rights on native peoples; they are also a fantasy of the wealth of the "East" that awaits the merchants of Salem.

It is the cultural work of the text to resolve the dilemma of the stolen land, and it does so in a way that evades the issue of the Indian lands by staging a conflict between two white families in the absence of the now dispersed and dispossessed Indians. The two modes of property holding, through labor and through abstract ownership, come together in the marriage of Phoebe and Holgrave. If Hawthorne can acknowledge that aristocracy is based on theft, he quickly moves to resolve that guilt. Marriage between the aristocratic family and the working class makes the wealth of the aristocracy guiltless, as well as provides a new phallic potency which purifies the naked aggression of the earlier patriarchs, both Pyncheon and Maule. By marrying Phoebe, Holgrave, the last of the Maules, will inherit the Pyncheon estate (that is, reassert a male line of succession, in which Phoebe as a *female* Pyncheon is disinherited, as Walter Herbert has remarked [103]) and thereby recuperate the old Maule claim. They will have little need of the house, now that they have the money, which carries no deed and no signature. Capital, not real estate, is the key to the future. The marriage that accomplishes the closure of the novel is not only an act of reconciliation, it is an imagined moment of redemption from history. Phoebe's housekeeping activities have accomplished their goal: there is no longer the grime of history in the house, thereby fulfilling Phoebe's ideological role as the exponent of a domesticity (Pfister 161) that partakes of the Gothic of neither Pyncheon nor Maule. But the light that now penetrates the Pyncheon house also reveals its secrets: by opening the shop, Hepzibah exposes the history of slavery and cannot escape its consequences. At such a moment the sharp difference between Hawthorne and Faulkner becomes visible. For Faulkner there can be no redemption from history, only the suspension of time in death. Similarly, for Faulkner there can be no successful domestication, no Phoebe to let in the sunbeams. It is as if he must insist on the burden, or the nightmare, of history precisely to argue against an American tradition that clings to the possibility of eternal renewal, even as it repeats its gestures of exclusion.

It is not as though Hawthorne were unaware of the stakes. He may misrepresent the meaning of Hepzibah's opening of the shop as "the instant of time when the patrician lady is to be transformed into the plebeian woman" (38), thereby eliding the emergence of the mercantile system and the new middle class. (Phoebe knows how to run a shop, but once she is united with Holgrave she will presumably retire from public life to become the domestic wife. The shop will be closed not, as Hepzibah would have it, to preserve an upper-class claim to the invisibility of money's origins but to prevent any intrusion of the public sphere into the private.) However, Hawthorne locates the commercial exchange at the heart of American history. Hepzibah's first customer (she refuses Holgrave's money) is Ned Higgins, of the new Irish lower middle class, whose shabby dress is "owing to his mother's carelessness"—the renewed Pyncheons and Maules will surely have better dressed children of careful domestic mothers like Phoebe. And the first transaction is the sale of a gingerbread Jim Crow.

Slavery, we know, was the mainstay of the Salem economy and the bartering of human bodies the origin of most New England wealth. Hepzibah's own appearance signals her place in the economies of sex and race. Her turbaned head is not merely a "droll parody of Oriental splendor" (Luedtke 190) but an indication of her status as slave woman, for which the turban was the accepted sign. By the time of *Gables* slavery had been abolished in Massachusetts, of course, but the fugitive slave law still required complicity from Massachusetts—it was the only thing that got Hawthorne excited in opposition to slavery (Mellow 409-410), on which he had highly conflicted views. Hepzibah's sale of Jim Crow to the voracious boy, who will move on to other exotic animals, repeats the economics of America and reveals the hidden sources of northern wealth. That it is the body of the black that is commodified is made clear by the references to Ned as a "cannibal." The effect of Hepzibah's transaction is dramatic, as Hawthorne makes clear: the exchange of money gives her a "copper stain," the indelible mark of participation in the slave economy, which for sentimental antislavery writers was inimical to the family. "The little schoolboy, aided by the impish figure of the negro dancer, had wrought an irreparable ruin" (51). The boy and the supposedly comic figure of the black serve as a return of the (national) repressed and give the lie to the claim of aristocracy, even more than the ostensible cause of financial transaction: the aristocracy rests its claims on ownership of land and on the invisibility of the origins of its gains. Selling Jim

Crow to Ned, Hepzibah is found out. She has clearly opened the wrong door to the Pyncheon house, as to New England morality and finance, the one that should always be discreetly shut. Jim Crow is presented comically in the text, as in the minstrel show tradition from which he arises, but at the same time his dance, the sign of the culture's ability to accomplish a reduction of race to the playful, acts as a reminder of that which has been concealed, of the grounding of New England wealth in the slave trade. The Jim Crow figure evoked here illustrates the presentation of the black body as a means of asserting white purity; it is consumed (physically, by Ned) by a white population in the minstrel shows that create a public space for the black and simultaneously contain that black within the confines of an agitated body.[4] The portrayal of the black body as entertainment serves to conceal the black body as labor.

The Jim Crow episode is paralleled by the scene of the street musician. Although it is commonplace to read this scene as an allegory of money or a commentary on popular art and Hawthorne's anxiety about his own declining cultural authority, such a reading, while usefully reminding us of the commercial nature of art despite claims to its purity, also effaces the way in which racial paranoia is built into the urban landscape. Like Ned Higgins, the boy musician is an immigrant set off from the world of the rival New England families, representing another, less idyllic future than that acted out at the end of the novel. Such boys, the text reminds us, "are rather a modern feature of our streets" (162), both a sign of liveliness and activity against the deadly world of the Pyncheon House and too vulgar to be taken seriously. Although it is the immigrant who produces the first level of cultural anxiety in this episode, the text simultaneously raises the stakes by linking the organ grinder and his monkey with the dancing black, Jim Crow. The monkey holds out a "small black palm" in which he receives the "copper coin," virtually the same one that Ned used to buy his Jim Crow. It is not necessary to insist on the monkey as a displaced figure of the black, since such connections were conventional in the period and long after, expressing as they did dismay over theories of evolution.[5] Hawthorne underscores this anxiety by depicting the monkey's "strangely manlike expression" and links it with a new degraded capitalism, "the grossest form of the love of money." Particularly striking about Hawthorne's account is its association of the black/monkey figure with a dangerous and disturbing masculinity, a link already common in the minstrel shows and songs. The obscene play on the monkey's tail and its "preposterous prolixity," which is "too enormous to be decently concealed under his gabardine" (164), gives expression to a fear of cultural and physical impotence (Clifford is a man of "merely delicate endowments" whose tears once again show his femininity) as well as to a possible homoerotic attraction to the phallic black alongside a panic over his possible revolt, what Lee Edelman has memorably called "the essentializing white fantasy of the black male's intensified biological potency and virility, which makes possible the racist reduction of black man to the status of genital part" (Edelman 67). It is not merely that the street musician represents the triumph of a vulgar art of the marketplace, threatening the existence of higher cultural values, but that the musician's monkey insists on the bestiality of such public art, of the display of that which should be private, not only private domestic space but private parts. The dilemma of the text is how to find a new masculinity and fertility that are not threatening. But to evoke that public world of new values and loss of class privilege is, inevitably in the American 1850s, also to evoke the specter of slave revolt imagined in terms of a panicked response to the black phallus. The scene of fascination and horror is one that is repeated throughout Hawthorne's fiction, as the delicate man (Dimmesdale, Coverdale, Owen Warland) watches a display of masculinity with desiring terror.

The gothic embedded narrative in *Gables*, Holgrave's story of Alice Pyncheon, is similarly firmly rooted in the soil of American racism and sexualized power. The story opens with a message from Gervayse Pyncheon to Matthew Maule, brought by Pyncheon's black servant, Scipio. Scipio is not simply an anonymous messenger: the importance of his race is stressed by Holgrave. Scipio speaks in black dialect and identifies himself as that stereotyped "comic" figure, the frightened "poor nigger." Above all, the text insists upon blackness as trope and on Maule's own status as black man, or magician. Scipio says to Maule, "[W]hat for do you looks so black at me?" to which Maule replies, "No matter, darkey! Do you think nobody is to look black but yourself?" (188). If Maule employs the derogatory diminutive "darkey," he also sees himself as oppressed, by class if not by race. This claim reminds us that not all whites share the privileges of the Pyncheons (although they can imagine that they could), but at a time before the abolition of slavery (passersby can see "the shining, sable face of a slave" [191] in the windows of the house) a metaphorical reading of "black," like Thoreau's metaphorical reading of "slave," seems problematic. However, the clear analogy between the traffic in slaves and the traffic in women makes the linkage appropriate. Gervayse Pyncheon sells his daughter as he would his slave, and her speech and conduct become the expression of her new mesmerizing master, a voice of the victim seeking revenge, virtually from beyond the grave.

Maule refuses the conventions of class that would have him come to the side door, not the front, and no one is more shocked by this lèse-majesté than Scipio, the servant who, we take it, comes to identify with the masters. Pyncheon himself is willing to accept the lack of manners in the carpenter if only he can obtain the secret of the house, the missing deed. To obtain this he agrees to offer his daughter Alice. The situation is of course similar to that in the main narrative: young Matthew Maule is highly, visibly phallic, with "a long pocket for his rule, the end of which protruded," and a figure that combines "comeliness, strength, and energy" (201). To the declining Pyncheons this new source of power is attractive indeed. Maule the magician can hypnotize the young Alice so that she becomes a creature of his will, just as Holgrave can mesmerize Phoebe. They can become the slaves of love. To be mesmerized is to lose one's self, that is, to be appropriated or dispossessed by a form of possession, much as the slave lost his fundamental property—himself—by being enslaved. Such relations between father and would-be son over the body of a daughter (see the triangular relations in *The Scarlet Letter* and *Blithedale*) were always a source of enormous anxiety for Hawthorne, who worried about Sophia's susceptibility in terms that mark clearly the fear of rape. Hawthorne told Sophia, "[T]he sacredness of an individual is violated by it; there would be an intrusion into the holy of holies—and the intruder would not be thy husband!" (Mellow 190). As Hawthorne's text says of Holgrave, "he could complete his mastery over Phoebe's yet free and virgin spirit" (212). These fears of suggestive power were to be echoed, and rendered more complex, in James's use of the theme in *The Bostonians,* where Selah's control over Verena is then bartered to Olive, who must in turn compete with Basil for the ability to control Verena.

The theme of the two doors, and the refusal to accept one's place, may be fundamental to all stories of class, but the specifics of this story seem clearly echoed in Faulkner's repeated and foundational text of the young Thomas Sutpen as "the boy outside the barred door," the boy who is told "by a nigger to go around to the back" (293). Faulkner attributes much lower-class white prejudice against blacks to such insults, creating a resentment in which the poor whites seek to punish the plantation owners but settle instead on their stand-ins, the servants who execute their orders. Faulkner's rewriting of this primal scene out of the Maules' story thus moves it from a simple tale of class tension by bringing out the racial implications discreetly present in Hawthorne's text. The results, though, are strikingly different: the youngest Maule will seek to marry the last Pyncheon and thus overcome the curse, while the last Sutpens can only yearn for the forbidden black bodies with whose histories they are already intertwined. Faulkner will write no marriage novel in part because the burden of guilt and anger cannot be so easily assuaged and in part because any marriage that can be imagined (Judith and Bon, Henry and Bon, Quentin and Shreve) must be forbidden. It is not that incest is absent in Hawthorne but rather that it is treated (apart from the Beatrice Cenci theme in *The Marble Faun*) in ways that attempt to defuse its power by turning it from gothic to picturesque. Clifford and Hepzibah are essentially lovers, but Hawthorne devotes such energies to mocking Hepzibah's appearance that one forgets her love for her brother. The sterility that in the gothic would be the fated consequence of sexual transgression is now a petering out of erotic energies into a comic vision of a weird couple. They cling to the house, not as the site of their passions but rather as a tomb of forgotten desires.

Although Faulkner carries the exploration of gender much further than Hawthorne, the text of *House* is frequently occupied with the question. Hawthorne rehearses what I consider to be one of his foundational myths—the decline of an artistic male personality linked to the aristocracy in the face of opposition from a more aggressive male figure, allegedly over the possession of a woman. It is Dimmesdale and Chillingworth, Coverdale and Hollingsworth, Donatello and Kenyon, and of course Clifford and Holgrave, as well as Clifford and Judge Pyncheon. In many of these instances, Hawthorne appears to be of two minds: he has a strong identification with the somewhat feminine male whose privilege is disappearing. In *House,* however, he tries to write in support of the new man, or at least of a new man formed in union with the old. The Judge, who recalls Hawthorne's Uncle Robert Manning, is a scientist and horticulturist, breeding fruit of a "rare variety" (272) in a world that links sex and science. Phoebe and Holgrave, unlike the old Pyncheons, represent a "correct" alignment of genders and the consecration of a new domesticity. Hepzibah is deprived of all sexuality, and Clifford is depicted as androgynous (Lee Person calls him "Hawthorne's most feminine male character" [95]).[6] The Malbone portrait reveals in Clifford "feminine traits, moulded inseparably with those of the other sex!" (60) such that the narrator can ask whether he was not "an early lover of Miss Hepzibah." These render him sterile and thus ensure the doom of the Pyncheons against the forces of the phallic Colonel, whose sexual energy had "worn out three wives," and his later-day relative, the Judge, whose wife "got her death-blow in the honey-moon" (123). Holgrave is imagined as a middle ground of limited masculinity who can be contained in his masculinity by the power of the domestic, his "Black Art" now tempered by Phoebe's "natural magic" (71). Phoebe's comment about the miniature quickly warns against carrying Clifford's softness too far: "it is as sweet as a man's face can be, *or ought to be*" (75, my emphasis). It is hard to be certain whether Hawthorne extended his discussion of Clifford's femininity to the concept of his sexual difference, although there is reason to suggest something of that kind. He is the "sport of boys," "insulted by the filth of the public ways, which they would fling upon him" (247-248), in terms that suggest his violent marginalization and indeed echo the fate of sexual criminals and others exposed in the stocks. There can be no room for the refined in a world where production and reproduction are the central concerns.

Faulkner carries gender and sexual difference much further. Sutpen's two "legitimate" children, Judith and Henry, reverse gender expectations, particularly in the fighting scene. Henry runs away "screaming and vomiting," while his sister looks down calmly from the loft (31, 33). This sexual difference runs throughout the text, in Henry's love for Bon and in Quentin's relationship to Shreve. The feminization of the mulatto is a part of racial stereotyping, of course; it allies the feminine Other to the racial Other. Bon is French, or "Frenchified," which is largely the same as feminized, and is seen "reclining in a flowered, almost feminised gown . . . this man handsome elegant and even catlike" (117). The fear of Judith's marriage to Bon is thus in part the fear of a doubled sexual inversion. Given the stress in the critical debate on the question whether Henry kills Bon because he will be committing incest or because he will be committing miscegenation, it is striking that both arguments assume that Henry wants to save Judith. What if we imagine that he must save Bon for himself, by killing him if necessary? As Mr. Compson puts it, "he loved Bon, who seduced him as surely as he seduced Judith" (118). Or, even more tellingly, "Bon not only loved Judith after his fashion but he loved Henry too and I believe in a deeper sense than merely after his fashion. Perhaps in his fatalism he loved Henry the better of the two, seeing perhaps in the sister merely the shadow, the woman vessel with which to consummate the love whose actual object was the youth" (133). Faulkner's insistence on his racial theme here swerves to acknowledge the bisexuality of incest and to see the possibility of reading a doomed interracial love as homosexuality.

The emphasis on stolen land and bartered bodies joins the two texts of Hawthorne and Faulkner as national narratives and originary myths that locate the gothic as a national repressed, a series of crimes that are not incidental to but rather constitutive of the nation. At the same moment in mid-nineteenth-century America Herman Melville was dealing with similar themes in *Pierre*. Here too the inherited wealth is based on an Indian deed, and this fictionality of property is directly connected to the fiction of paternity. Faulkner's reworking of Hawthorne's material not only makes Hawthorne's own themes clearer by exposing them, but it complicates the question of guilt and, above all, like *Pierre*, renders impossible the happy ending of Hawthorne's romance. If for Hawthorne national guilt can be effaced by a wedding and the provision of a sudden fortune, if the gothic can serve as a farewell to such a past and such desires, for Faulkner it is that wedding itself (whatever form it takes, between races, between classes, between genders) that is damned. For Faulkner there can be no way out of this nightmare of murder and hatred, and a rewritten novel of Hawthorne's serves to stress a will-to-unknowing that is itself criminal.

Notes

1. Sacvan Bercovitch argues that Hawthorne was undisturbed by "Southern slavery [and] Indian genocide" (236). I would argue that the text experiences these issues differently from its author.

2. Richard Chase argues that "the non-Emersonian tradition of Hawthorne and Melville prepared the way for Faulkner by introducing the strain of dark and sombre drama" (220). I would agree with this statement, while attempting to see that "tradition" in its more concrete darkness.

3. There is an excellent account of many of these issues in Walter Benn Michaels.

4. For the Jim Crow tradition, see Lott (on the black body, see 116).

5. Although Darwin did not publish *On the Origin of Species* until 1859, the ideas were already circulating.

6. I am not sure I can agree with Person's assessment that *House* is "the novel in which [Hawthorne] most thoroughly researched alternative gender identities and roles" (95), since that seems to ignore the multiple sexual possibilities of *The Blithedale Romance* and to underestimate the power of gender conservatism in *House*.

Works Cited

Bercovitch, Sacvan. *Rites of Assent*. New York: Routledge, 1993.

Bloom, Harold. *The Anxiety of Influence*. New York: Oxford UP, 1973.

Brodhead, Richard. *Hawthorne, Melville and the Novel*. 1976. Rpt. Chicago: U of Chicago P, 1982.

Chase, Richard. *The American Novel and Its Tradition*. Garden City: Doubleday, 1957.

Edelman, Lee. "The Part for the (W)hole: Baldwin, Homophobia, and the Fantasmatics of 'Race.'" *Homographesis: Essays in Gay Literary and Cultural Theory*. New York: Routledge, 1994.

Faulkner, William. *Absalom, Absalom!* New ed. New York: Random House, 1986.

Fiedler, Leslie. *Love and Death in the American Novel*. 1960. Rpt. Cleveland: World, 1962.

Hawthorne, Nathaniel. *The House of the Seven Gables*. Ed. Fredson Bowers, Centenary Ed., vol. 2. Columbus: Ohio State UP, 1965.

Herbert, T. Walter. *Dearest Beloved: The Hawthornes and the Making of the Middle-Class Family.* Berkeley: U of California P, 1993.

Lott, Eric. *Love and Theft: Blackface Minstrelsy and the American Working Class.* New York: Oxford UP, 1993.

Luedtke, Luther S. *Nathaniel Hawthorne and the Romance of the Orient.* Bloomington: Indiana UP, 1989.

Mellow, James R. *Nathaniel Hawthorne in His Times.* Boston: Houghton Mifflin, 1980.

Michaels, Walter Benn. "Romance and Real Estate." *The American Renaissance Reconsidered.* Ed. Michaels and Donald E. Pease. Baltimore: Johns Hopkins UP, 1985.

Person, Leland S. *Aesthetic Headaches: Women and a Masculine Poetics in Poe, Melville, and Hawthorne.* Athens: U of Georgia P, 1988.

Pfister, Joel. *The Production of Personal Life: Class, Gender, and the Psychological in Hawthorne's Fiction.* Stanford: Stanford UP, 1991.

Sundquist, Eric. *Faulkner: The House Divided.* Baltimore: Johns Hopkins UP, 1983.

FURTHER READING

Criticism

Baumbach, Jonathan. "The Acid of God's Grace: *Wise Blood* by Flannery O'Connor." In *The Landscape of Nightmare: Studies in the Contemporary American Novel,* pp. 87-100. New York: New York University Press, 1965.

    Reading of *Wise Blood* as a representative work by Flannery O'Connor that explores themes of human life and redemption in the context of the author's rigid religious beliefs.

Heller, Terry. "Mirrored World's and the Gothic in Faulkner's *Sanctuary.*" *Mississippi Quarterly* 42, no. 3 (summer 1989): 247-59.

    Analyzes the use of mirrors in William Faulkner's *Sanctuary,* theorizing that they are used as a device to reflect opposing characters and viewpoints.

Kahane, Claire. "Gothic Mirrors and Feminine Identity." *Centennial Review* 24, no. 1 (winter 1980): 43-64.

    Explains Gothic fiction in the context of feminist and psychoanalytical critical interpretation, using several 18th- and 19th-century texts for illustration.

Kerr, Elizabeth M. "From Otranto to Yoknapatawpha: Faulkner's Gothic Heritage." In *William Faulkner's Gothic Domain,* pp. 3-28. Port Washington, N.Y.: Kennikat Press, 1979.

    Recounts the evolution of gothic fiction during the Romantic and Victorian eras in England and its impact on the development of nineteenth- and twentieth-century gothic fiction in the United States.

Machinek, Anna. "William Faulkner and the Gothic Tradition." *Kwartalnik Neofilologiczny* 36, no. 2 (1989): 105-14.

    Outlines basic assumptions of Gothic fiction, examining William Faulkner's *Sanctuary* and *Absalom, Absalom!* in this context.

Malin, Irving. "Flannery O'Connor and the Grotesque." In *The Added Dimension: The Art and Mind of Flannery O'Connor,* edited by Melvin J. Friedman and Lewis A. Lawson, pp. 108-22. New York: Fordham University Press, 1977.

    Focuses on Flannery O'Connor's psychological awareness as expressed via the themes and images of the grotesque in her work.

Mellard, James M. "Faulkner's Miss Emily and Blake's 'Sick Rose': 'Invisible Worm,' Nachträglichkeit, and Retrospective Gothic." *Faulkner Journal* 2, no. 1 (fall 1986): 37-45.

    Proposes that William Blake's *The Sick Rose* was the inspiration for Faulkner's *A Rose for Emily,* characterizing Faulkner's work as an innovative version of the Gothic tendencies apparent in Blake's work.

Richmond-Garza, Elizabeth M. "The Vampire's Gaze: Gothic Performance in Theory and Practice." *Comparatist: Journal of the Southern Comparative Literature Association* 22 (May 1998): 91-109.

    Examines cinematic adaptations of four contemporary Gothic works, including *Dracula, Interview with the Vampire,* and *Ran.*

Additional coverage of Gothic literature is contained in the following source published by the Gale Group: *Nineteenth-Century Literature Criticism,* **Vol. 28.**

Twentieth-Century Danish Literature

The following entry presents criticism on authors and works of twentieth-century Danish literature.

INTRODUCTION

The geographical area that currently comprises the nation of Denmark was invaded by several generations of Indo-European settlers beginning sometime around 2000 B.C. Over the next several hundred years, these ethnic groups and others merged to form the ethnic population of modern-day Denmark and Scandinavia. Although Denmark has a strong history of indigenous literature and folk tales—including poetry composed in the Runic alphabet, reminiscent of other cultures influenced by Indo-European civilizations—the modern-day Danish lexicon has its roots in the Germanic family of languages. After the advent of Christianity and throughout the Middle Ages, literature in Denmark was largely dominated by ecclesiastical writers and themes. At the time, Danish literature focused heavily on stories about saints and legends concerned with expounding the Christian view of life. One well-known exception to this trend was a history of Denmark, titled *Gesta Danorum,* that was written by Saxo Grammaticus sometime in the twelfth century. This text shows evidence of both pagan and Christian influences in its tales of the lineage of Danish kings throughout the ages. In addition to such works as *Gesta Danorum,* indigenous Danish narratives were also preserved during the Middle Ages through a continuous output of folk songs and stories. The eighteenth and nineteenth centuries saw the emergence of neoclassical literature in Denmark, followed in the twentieth century with the adoption of a more realistic national prose style.

Early twentieth-century Danish literature was heavily influenced by a reaction against the naturalist movement in prose that began in the late nineteenth century. This era witnessed the advent of a fervently nationalistic Danish literature in the works of Martin Andersen Nexø. Nexø's novel *Pelle Erobreren* (1906-10) is now regarded as a seminal work of proletarian literature and has been translated into numerous languages. In addition, the early twentieth century saw the rise of regional and rural literature in Denmark, as embodied in the works of such significant Danish writers as Marie Bregendahl and Jeppe Aakjær. Critics such as Torben Brostrøm have argued that Danish poetry underwent a major thematic shift in the early twentieth century, marked by a distinct rejection of lyrical style in favor of a more symbolist style of writing. The works of such Danish poets as Johannes Jørgensen paralleled other European writers of the period in their opposition to naturalism and their focus on personal and political concerns. One of the most notable Danish symbolist poets of the era was Paul la Cour, who asserted that poetry represents a concept of existence, a unique whole where fragments come together and reveal subtle connections. Another influential Danish poet, Johannes Jensen, published the collection *Digte* in 1906, which is considered one of the most significant texts in the history of the new form of poetry in Denmark. Although Jensen's writing clearly departed from nineteenth-century lyricism, his strong impressionistic and interpretative style set him apart from other poets of his time. Jensen was awarded the Nobel Prize in Literature in 1944.

Post-war Denmark witnessed the emergence of a new kind of realistic literature—where novels, poetry, and dramas were steeped in reality and concerned with the futility of human existence. While these works were dark and pessimistic in their descriptions of ordinary life, most concluded with a vision of hope for the future. One of the most notable figures of this period was Isak Dinesen. Dinesen is regarded as a pivotal figure in the development of modern Danish literature. Many of her works have appeared in English, the most famous being *Seven Gothic Tales* (1934) and *Den Afrikanse Farm* (1937; *Out of Africa*). Following the German occupation of Denmark during World War II, Danish literature also began reflecting overtly nationalistic sentiments filled with emotional and ethical turmoil inspired by the conflict.

Modern Denmark is a largely well-educated society with a reputation for being supportive of its literary and artistic communities. Continuing this trend through the 1960s and beyond, the novel and short story continue to be popular genres with Danish readers, while the country itself is one of the leading producers of books and periodicals in the Western world.

REPRESENTATIVE WORKS

Jeppe Aakjær

Vredens Børn, Et Tyendes Saga [*Children of Wrath, a Hired-Man's Saga*] (novel) 1904
Rugens Sange [*Songs of the Rye*] (poetry) 1906

Hans Christian Branner
Legetøj (novel) 1936
Drømmen om en kvinde (novel) 1941
"Humanismens krise" (essay) 1950

Marie Bregendahl
En Dødsnat [*A Night of Death*] (novel) 1912
Billeder af Sødalsfolkens Liv. 7 vols. [*Pictures from the Life of the People of Sodal*] (short stories) 1914-23

Paul la Cour
Leviathan (poetry) 1930
This Is Our Life (poetry) 1936
Astrid Noack (poetry) 1943

Isak Dinesen
Seven Gothic Tales (short stories) 1934
Sanhedens Haevn [*The Revenge of Truth*] (play) 1936
Den Afrikanse Farm [*Out of Africa*] (autobiography) 1937
En Baaltale med 14 Aars Forsinkelse [*Bonfire Speech Fourteen Years Delayed*] (essay) 1953
Last Tales [*Sidste Fortaellinger*] (short stories) 1957
Anecdotes of Destiny [*Skaebne-Anekdoter*] (short stories) 1958

Leck Fisher
Leif den Lykkelige [*Leif the Lucky*] (novel) 1928-29
Det maa gerne blive Mandag [*Monday May as Well Come*] (novel) 1934
Barnet (play) 1936

Thorkild Hansen
Jens Munk [*North West to Hudson Bay: The Life and Times of Jens Munk*] (novel) 1965; also translated as *The Way to Hudson Bay: The Life and Times of Jens Munk*, 1970
Sidste sommer i Angmagssalik (journals) 1978

Ole Hyltoft
Tør du være fri? (essays) 1968
Hvis lille pige er du? (novel) 1970
Hjertet sidder til venstre (novel) 1973
Revolutionens fortrop (short stories) 1975
Hvem er angst for den stygge ulv? (novel) 1976
Befriede (novel) 1979
Besejrede (novel) 1979
Byggekongen (novel) 1981
Tante Isidora (short stories) 1982

Johannes Jensen
Den gotiske Renaissance (poetry) 1901
Digte (poetry) 1906
Den lange Rejse [*The Long Journey*] (novel) 1919

Johannes Jørgensen
Essays (criticism) 1906
The Legend of My Life (biography) 1928

Martin Andersen Nexø
Skygger (short stories) 1898
Muldskud (short stories) 1900
Dryss (novel) 1902
Soldage [*Days in the Sun*] (novel) 1903
*Pelle Erobreren. 4 vols. [*Pelle the Conqueror*] (novel) 1906-10
Ditte Menneskebarn. 5 vols. (novel) 1917-21

Tor Obrestad
Sauda! Streik! (novel) 1973

Klaus Rifbjerg
Under vejr med mig selv (poetry) 1956
Camouflage (poetry) 1961
Portræt (poetry) 1963
Amagerdigte (poetry) 1965
Udviklinger (play) 1965
Hvad en mand har brug for (play) 1966
Anna (jeg) Anna (novel) 1969
Dengang det var før (memoirs) 1971
Brevet til Gerda (short stories) 1972
Den syende jomfru (short stories) 1972
R. R. (novel) 1972

Hans Scherfig
Det forsømte forår [*Stolen Spring*] (novel) 1940

*This work contains *Pelle Erobreren* (1906), *Læreaar* (1907), *Den store Kamp* (1909), and *Gryet* (1910).

MAJOR WORKS

George Bisztrav (essay date winter 1976)

SOURCE: Bisztrav, George. "Documentarism and the Modern Scandinavian Novel."[1] *Scandinavian Studies* 48, no. 1 (winter 1976): 71-83.

[*In the following essay, Bisztrav analyses the development of documentarian tendencies in the modern Scandinavian novel.*]

Early in 1969, the editors of *Vinduet* initiated a symposium to elucidate particular problems of the documentary tendency in modern literature. During the discussion, the Swedish guest, Per Olov Enquist, exclaimed: "Det er litt dumt dette med betegnelsen "dokumentær" kanskje, det sentrale spørsmålet i denne sammenheng er fiction eller non-fiction."² There was hardly a more insightful remark to be heard at the symposium. Enquist raised the very problem of the traditional distinction between "literature" and "life," or between the heroic, sweet, lofty, but "fictive" sphere of existence on the one hand, and the incoherent, accidental, petty, but "authentic" everyday events on the other hand.

What about the author who claims that he shows precisely the average, accidental events, which, at first sight, "do not make sense"? The German author Alexander Kluge's *Schlachtbeschreibung*, a fictive report on the battle of Stalingrad, was published in Swedish translation in 1965. One of its reviewers, Torsten Ekbom, openly confessed that he did not find any conventional way to approach this work. "Svårigheten är," he wrote, "att värdera Kluges insats som författare." Ekbom's proposed solution was an overly convenient one: "Det är likgiltigt att bedöma "Slaget" som skönlitteratur, det räcker med att konstatera att metoden är effektiv och åskådlig på ett sätt som överträffar alla realistiska gestaltningsförsök. "Slaget" förnyar inte romanen, den visar snarare att den traditionella tendensromanen har blivit ineffektiv, föråldrad."³ Ekbom seems to indicate two problems here, without analyzing either of them.

One of the problems, distantly related to Enquist's statement at the *Vinduet* symposium, is whether or not we may call practically any written text a literary work. In the influential Anglo-American ("New Criticism") and French ("*explication de textes*") analytical approaches to the literary text, we have traditionally seen a separation of fiction from non-fiction. This separation, however, has often been carried out by literary historians in a fairly inconsistent manner. Concentrating on Scandinavian examples, we may ask why Stiernhielm's or Swedenborg's writings or Dass' *Nordlands Trompet* are considered integrated parts of Scandinavian literary history, while Hammarskjöld's memoirs or Myrdal's two report volumes about China are not? Why are *Pan, Victoria,* or *Sult* regarded as genuine literature while Hamsun's reflections on America, or even his *Paa gjengrodde stier* are hardly discussed in literature classes? Why is Strindberg renowned as dramatist and novelist, but not as author of a fascinating sociological description of the French countryside? We also frequently ignore the unique self-documentation in his memoirs in favor of the novelistic values of this work. The question seems ultimately to boil down to some specific aesthetic values which supposedly characterize only conventional fiction and no other kinds of prose writing.

A debate which took place outside Scandinavia in the early 1930's, sheds some light on these issues. A Marxist critic, Georg Lukács, and a communist writer, Ernst Ottwalt, exchanged sharp words about the latter's documentary novel on the German legal system (*Denn sie wissen, was sie tun*). While Lukács stated that a unique selection, organization, and expression of a set of experiences was the backbone and indispensable criterion of genuine prose fiction, Ottwalt maintained that facts of life "speak for themselves," without any specific organization or stylistic criteria, without any synthesis or transformation by the artistic consciousness. Both expected commitment from the writer, but while Lukács preferred an ethical and artistic form of commitment, Ottwalt defended a political-tendentious form.⁴ How this issue contributes to the present Scandinavian literary discussion, we shall see later.

The other problem Ekbom raises comes from his assumption that older forms of tendentious literature are outdated in our time. Indeed, critics and writers during the 50's and early 60's tended to regard the prose techniques of their own times as being radically new, as opposed to the "boring" tradition of the past 3000 years. Thus, the attractive sounding, yet in reality hardly new, theories of the anti-novel or the *roman nouveau* were born. Ekbom and some participants in the *Vinduet*-symposium seem to pursue the same illusion of "novelty at any price." Inflated bibliographies of documentary literature are another, less frequent, device used to ascertain the rights of a supposedly novel prose technique, by impressing the scholarly readers with the large number of "relevant" works.⁵

Yet the question is whether documentarism, rather than being merely a sensational modern movement, could help us re-define the very concept of the novel, present or past. Precisely such redefinition seems to have been Strindberg's main purpose with his introduction to the first edition of *Tjänstekvinnans son* (1886), which he wrote in the form of a fictive "interview." Answering the questions of the "interviewer," the author explained the essence of his book, which was supposedly neither a novel nor a psychological study, but an "experiment in the literature of the future." As Strindberg believed, Zola, the last great writer who wanted to save the novel as genre, had to compromise, by adjusting the novel form to the demands of modern science. Strindberg predicted, however, that the novel was about to die anyway, and that it would give place to endless numbers of detailed self-analyses of modern individuals ("Det skulle bli dokument eller hur"). It was on the issue of showing the individual consciousness that Strindberg challenged Zola most of all. He demanded more psychological documentation, more concentration on individual consciousness, and less social determinism.⁶ Though the collective novel and the observational-reporting technique are still organic parts of the documentary tradition, the great preoccupation with individual perception and consciousness is, as we shall see, a basic structural element of the recent Scandinavian documentary novel.

Even if we disregard the artistic "confessions" of modern writers like Strindberg, a new look at the documentary tradition could clear up some of the problems around the categorizing and characterizing of literary works in general. The separation of fiction and nonfiction splits the oeuvre of numerous significant writers into a genuine, creative part, and a supposedly second-rate, reminiscent, autobiographical, essayistic part. Literary critics and historians frequently feel uncomfortable when facing the question of what to do with non-literary and non-scientific forms of writing, like biographies and autobiographies, reports, travel books, sociological and ethnographic descriptions, diaries, letters, and memoirs. Following the Platonic idea of a dichotomy between literature and the practical aspects of life, some of these kinds of writing seem to be fairly "scientific," as they do not bear evidence of basic, traditional creative methods of the arts, like selectivity and a specific arrangement of experiences. Yet another trend in literary criticism has already seriously challenged the distinction between art and science. The historicism and positivism of such respected representatives of Scandinavian literary scholarship as Francis Bull, Henrik Schück, or Vilhelm Andersen made them inclined to devote considerable space to non-literary forms of writing, especially in their multi-volume histories of Norwegian, Swedish, and Danish literature, respectively. The attempt to analyze literature from the point of view of scientific principles has recently been extended also to the investigation of the creative process itself. Modelling has become a key concept borrowed from theoretical sciences. Enquist, for instance, reminds us that also in documentary writing, the author "subjectively selects" the material, then "composes" his work—which is a modified description of any modelling process.[7] Consequently, as one reviewer of *Legionärerna* quotes Enquist, "Det är naivitet att tro att faktaprosa och fiktions-prosa lyder under skilda estetiska lagar."[8]

If what Enquist says is true, documentarism should be placed somewhere between conventional fiction and a supposedly non-fictive, informative, yet not scientifically presented or organized sort of writing. Modern European literature provides enough examples to illustrate particular characteristics of this tradition. Besides the pioneering documentary dramas of Hochhuth, Weiss, and Kipphardt during the 60's, there are also numerous prose works to list. A few random titles demonstrate an international scope: France's contribution is Henri Charrière's *Papillon,* Italy's, *Bandiera bianca a Cefalonia* by Marcello Venturi; Russia's, *Baby Yar,* by A. Kuznetsov, and perhaps some of Solzhenitsyn's novels. From among the North American novels, William Burroughs' *Nova Express* occurs frequently in the Scandinavian discussions, together with Norman Mailer's works.

The tendency to consider a descriptive, empirical, reproductive, rather than "creative" literary method as a fully justified one, is not new. Literary history discusses medieval chronicles everywhere. In an essay on the mutual relations of documentarism, science, and literary tradition, Björn Håkanson found predecessors of the documentary prose in literary positivism (naturalism), the tradition of the "novel of consciousness" (especially in the French *roman nouveau*), and the report form.[9] The few existing essays on the Scandinavian collective novel clearly prove that this tradition, too, has served as an additional source for documentarism. In the view of Peter Graves, for instance, the collective novel "takes its place in literary history as the only experiment in form in the social novel between naturalism and the modern documentary novel."[10]

In a loose definition of the term, "documentarism" is as old as literature itself. Therefore, it is the relevance, not of its general use, but its use as a term for a specific kind of literature, that concerns us most. Scandinavian literature seems to occupy a unique place in European culture in this respect. Taking into consideration the major intellectual and historical movements in Scandinavia in the last thousand years, documentation in literature has been more dominant there than in any other part of Europe.

It is certainly not the existence itself, or the quality, content, or methods of the documentary production, but rather the eminent place of documentarism and its consistent, practically unbroken presence in the Northern cultural tradition, that distinguishes this tradition among the spheres of European culture. The sagas could be regarded as historical documents, and a number of scholars (like Finnur Jónsson, Knut Liestøl, or Henrik Jæger) have, indeed, interpreted them as such. Northern protestantism produced very few genuine literary works, but scores of scientific, historical, topographical, and other documentative treatises of considerable literary value (like Georg Stiernhielm's, Olaus Rudbeck's, Absalon Beyer's, or Peder Claussøn Friis' descriptions of Swedish and Norwegian micro- and macro-geography and natural life). The interest in nature, local conditions, and history was evident in the Northern enlightenment as well as in romanticism, and in the realistic and naturalistic tendencies during the "Modern Breakthrough." In the twentieth century, particularly in the 1930's, documentary tendencies appeared in Scandinavia as elsewhere on the continent and in the Americas, and manifested themselves in such remarkable works as Josef Kjellgren's *Människor kring en bro* (1935), or, in less distinct form, in particular works of Gunnar Larsen, Arthur Omre, Harry Martinson, and others.

Among more recent novelists, the Swedish especially seem to be highly influenced by the tendency of new objectivity. Per Olov Enquist's *Legionärerna,* Per Olof Sundman's *Ingenjör Andrées luftfärd* and *Ingen fruktan, intet hopp,* Sara Lidman's *Gruva,* Sven Delblanc's *Åsnebrygga* and *Åminne,* Staffan Seeberg's *Vägen genom*

Vasaparken are works often mentioned in discussions of the documentary tendency. In Norway, Tor Obrestad's *Sauda! Streik!* is a clear example of a politically committed documentary tendency. Paal-Helge Haugen has also experimented with documentary works; his *Anna* has often been mentioned as an example. We could also consider Per Hansson's highly successful semi-fictional bestsellers (*Det største spillet, Hver tiende mann måtte dø, Mamma Karasjok*). The works of a whole generation of younger Norwegian writers (like Dag Solstad, Espen Haavardsholm, Edvard Hoem) have shown signs of a conscious use of documentary devices in a fictional or poetic context. The reader can even run across parodies of the documentary style, as in the books of Tor Åge Bringsværd.[11] More recently, some publications of "Forlaget For Flere" (for instance, pieces in Erland Kiøsterud's *Sår som aldri gror*) seem to continue the naturalistic-documentary tradition.

There are problems, however, with this impressive list of Swedish and Norwegian "documentary" works. Some of their writers obviously respected the principle that, in a documentary work, verifiable characters and events should be depicted. If this principle holds true, then we may ask in what respect modern "documentary" writing differs from conventional reports or sociological surveys. Sara Lidman's *Gruva,* or Jan Myrdal's *Rapport från kinesisk by* certainly belong to this latter category, while Delblanc's *Åsnebrygga* is simply an old-fashioned travel diary.[12] On the other hand, there are works which describe fictive, non-verifiable events or psychological processes in a pseudo-scientific way, by using abbreviations, mathematical formulas, or a (presumably) directly reproduced, non-literary language. But then in what respect do these writers (like Seeberg and Haugen) differ from the Italian and Russian futurists or the German expressionists around and after World War I? It is widely remembered that Mayakovsky propagated the new "facts" of the communist transformation of Russian society in his poems, and that Alfred Döblin reproduced, among others, street signs in his *Berlin Alexanderplatz,* just to draw an authentic, "documented" milieu.

There are apparently two concepts involved here: documentary literature and the documentary novel. Documentary literature is a vast field consisting of sociological descriptions, reports, diaries, biographies and autobiographies, historical, natural, and travel accounts, and possibly some other descriptive writings which claim some verifiable authenticity. Although they all offer a notion of objectivity, we might agree with a critic of travel literature that documentary literature is tendentious, and that its artistic perception is only relatively objective, because of the observer's cultural biases.[13]

The documentary novel can be regarded as part of documentary literature, but in a specific way. There are at least three Scandinavian *novels* written in the past few years which truly deserve the term "documentary." These are Per Olof Sundman's *Ingenjör Andrées luftfärd* (1967), Per Olov Enquist's *Legionärerna* (1968),[14] and Tor Obrestad's *Sauda! Streik!* (1972). Although all three writers rely on historical events, they nevertheless take an approach which enables them to manifest their genuine creative talent. Their achievements are successful syntheses of the conventional report and the objectivistic novel of consciousness.

The author's organizing consciousness appears in the three novels in different ways. Sundman's narrator, the Norwegian Knut Fraenkel, was the only member of the Andrée-expedition who did not leave any notes behind. Thus, the first person narrative, which takes the form of a diary, is fictional: its basis is precisely Andrée's and Nils Strindberg's diaries and notes. In Enquist's novel, the author-narrator is doing historical research in order to clarify the circumstances of a forgotten event of the post-war period. The transfer to Soviet Russia of the Baltic soldiers who fought with the Germans is the event which generates a process of consciousness in the author, and the analysis of this process is one topic of the book. Finally, in Obrestad's work, a radical student from the University of Oslo tries to attain a higher political consciousness by participating in the notorious wildcat strike of 1970 at the EFP-plant in Sauda. The true existence of Obrestad's hero, Martin Anda, is most probably unverifiable, yet this model of a young radical Norwegian intellectual facing historical events gains an almost autobiographic authenticity in the process of the report-like prose description.

Because of the different narrative perspectives, the time sequence is different in the three novels. Sundman's hero is a part of the events, consequently the novel follows a fairly conventional chronological order. There are, of course, flashbacks and short excursions in individual consciousness, yet the diary form traces the actual events day by day. In Enquist's book, however, there are two distinct time perspectives: the author's own time and that of the actual events, twenty-three years apart. This chronological gap provides a much greater opportunity for Enquist to show interchanges and overlappings of the dimensions of time, which he exploits masterfully. The ethical message of the work, the analogies between old and new social problems, comes through in a sophisticated way, due to the associations generated by the two dimensions of time. Obrestad's novel is similar to Enquist's in using the same time perspective. Here, the hero does some research into the history of the EFP-factory in Sauda, and results of this research appear as retrospective setpieces in the construction of the novel.

Representation of the phenomena of modern existence in their original complexity, and the difficult yet necessary task of their individual interpretation, are the two creative goals Sundman and Enquist seem to pursue. The result is an almost relativistic realization of the fact that the number of possible interpretations is endless. At times, the authors are so successful in their "impartiality" that their own intentions become hard to recognize. Sundman, for instance, protested against the view that he had wanted to show the Promethean struggle of modern man, of the modern explorer and scientist. On the contrary, he said, what he intended to demonstrate was the futility of European megalomania and self-assurance.[15] Indeed, the last words of the first victim of the expedition, Nils Strindberg, are a question to Andrée: "Varför i helvete blev du tvingad att ge dig in på den här resan?" (p. 339). But if a critic reads the opposite of the author's intention in the work, is it not a victory of documentarism? Sundman is, paradoxically, as upset about the misinterpretation of his message as any 19th century realist.

Enquist's book shows a greater complexity on this point, too. Like some modern Theseus, he starts out with the thread of reason and commitment in his hand to find his way in the labyrinth of state archives, interviews, and newspaper articles. He soon finds that the task is more difficult than he thought. "Hur beskriver man mekaniken i en känsla? Hur beskriver man mekaniken i en känslas uppkomst, förändring, förflyttning? Hur beskriver man mekaniken i en situation som driver människan framför sig till den punkt där hon inte kan vända om?" (p. 129). The respected "objective" sciences of modern times, like statistics, do not help. It is, for instance, only a matter of interpreting the public opinion surveys to find what the majority of Swedes thought about *baltutlämningen,* since numbers yield to several possible conclusions. The experimental method does not bring much light, either. The writer starts a hunger-strike to better understand the feelings of the Baltic soldiers threatened by deportation to the Soviet Union. He finds that the really effective factors, desperation and stress, are not reproducible, and that a healthy individual can bear starvation for several days as a trifle under balanced, "normal" conditions. Finally, he writes a letter to Chairman Mao: "'Fakta är alla ting som existerar objektivt,' säger ni. Men här sitter jag på min subjektiva pottkant, och då och nu förblandas, som hägringar" (p. 337).

If there is an objective, absolute reality, why are there no absolute ethical norms?—is another question Enquist asks. While in Sundman's novel nature's contingencies—trivial, yet fatally neglected physical factors—defeat human logic, in *Legionärerna,* the man-made, but depersonalized, bureaucratic social system plays a cruel joke with human fates. The conflict between human consciousness and detached objectivity takes on an especially fascinating shape in Enquist's novel, and repeatedly raises the question: can "documentarism," that is, a literature built on documents, fulfill its function? If not, can we call this tendency "documentary" at all?

In spite of all the problems of interpretation, there are elements of outright social criticism in Enquist's book. Here the Swedes, though humanitarian and helpful, at times prove to be quite ignorant. As they think in simplified categories, the complex character of Eichfuss-Atvars, a Latvian officer and patriot, remains inaccessible to them. The Ministry of Foreign Affairs makes a decision about the lives of hundreds of Baltic soldiers casually and negligently. Anti-Nazism and anti-communism are mixed with a cautious, if not cowardly, rejection of commitment in the public mind. At their worst, Swedish public life and the state machinery appear provincial and ethnocentric.

Tor Obrestad's novel differs from the two Swedish ones in the interpretation of perceived reality and ideological commitment. At the first reading, *Sauda! Streik!* certainly strikes one as a book strictly following the propagandistic "Proletkult" reporting style of the 1920's and early 1930's in the Soviet Union and Germany. The hero, Martin Anda, does not seem to find any complexity in social existence. Rather, he strives for the reduction of the eventual complexity to make it correspond to his Leninist-Maoist ideology. He finds what he wants: that there is no reality beyond Lenin and the Little Red Book; and that he is able to commit himself to an organized cause.

The question is, however, how great a part irony plays in the message of *Sauda! Streik!* Naturally, there are enough examples of social injustice both in history and in the present world. But the habit of calling back the time of old class struggles, or identifying the Norwegian conditions with those of today's dictatorships, gives a paradoxical character to the slogans filling Anda's consciousness. Minor clashes with the police are interpreted as bloody conflicts with the henchmen of the "class-state," and the EFP-plant in Sauda becomes a symbol of American industrial colonialism.

At the same time, Anda, Kjell Sand, and others who dream of a communistic future for Norway, cannot break out of the life-style of the welfare state. In the beginning of the novel, we find Anda sitting in a sidewalk café near to Oslo's Nationaltheatret, drinking beer and reading the daily paper—which should have cost him at least ten kroner at the location indicated. In his rented room, works of Lenin and Stalin stand on the shelf next to Westerns; on the wall, chairman Mao's picture, on the recordplayer, The Rolling Stones. In Sauda the strike committee is holding its meetings at Kjell Sand's family home on one of the hills, overlooking the fjord. Here, the revolutionaries dine on fresh flounder with vegetable salad, while striving for better times for the Norwegian working class.

Beyond its elusive political simple-mindedness, Obrestad's novel is a sophisticated work, just as much as the two Swedish novels. Though the author's identification with his hero in search of a "correct" political consciousness is a possibility which cannot be discarded, it would nevertheless be hard to verify. The problem is ultimately irrelevant, however, since *Sauda! Streik!* in just a few years will most probably be read as a parody of rootless "revolutionarism," matching in its artistic effects Jean-Luc Godard's excellent, ironical semidocumentary film *La Chinoise* (1968).

Are the heroes of the documentary novel anti-heroes? Unless a conscious irony is involved, this question is irrelevant in Obrestad's case, where the hero is gaining more human coherence and value through attaining a "correct" Marxist-Leninist ideology. The case is different with the two Swedish novels. It is true that Andrée, Strindberg or Fraenkel, Eichfuss-Atvars or other Baltic soldiers, are the playthings of a faceless machinery. Yet they also carry on a Sisyphean fight until the bitter end. It is not nature, but the loss of his comrades, which makes Fraenkel swallow the lethal overdose of pills. Only one of hundreds of Baltic soldiers chooses suicide as an escape from the horrors of the Soviet revenge which, by the way, never comes. The heroes are victims, like Kafka's characters, but not vegetables, like Beckett's anti-heroes. Sundman and Enquist seem to subscribe to Blaise Pascal's view that man is a reed, but a thinking reed. Ultimately, the essential issue in the two Swedish novels boils down to a commitment to individual consciousness, and as such, gets closest to an investigation of ideologies. Returning to the Lukács-Ottwalt debate mentioned above, we may say that the political function of commitment is just as much challenged in Sundman's and Enquist's novel as is the ethical function of commitment.

The motifs employed in the three novels are somewhat unconventional, yet no longer astonishing. It is probably still unusual to read about the strength of wind "on the Beaufort scale," or to review, together with the author, long sequences of snapshots on prison-camp life. Still, they have their place and function in a documentary novel. Traditionally insignificant details of everyday life may be matters of life or death for human beings. The endless descriptions of what the three balloon-flyers eat for breakfast, lunch and dinner, indirectly refer to one of the weaknesses of the heroes: their inability to resign from a sybaritic, "civilized" way of life in the ice wilderness, in favor of their pure physical survival.

The language of the novels also shows an attempt to reproduce colloquial speech. Enquist especially operates on different levels of expression. Official and scientific jargon, dialect and literary language appear side by side, or often together, resulting in a lingual collage which complements the montage technique of the images and motifs. Tor Obrestad even lists his textual sources: books, newspaper articles, minutes, interviews with workers; while the titles of the chapters in *Sauda! Streik!* were borrowed from Lenin and from old songs of the labor movement. But again, it would be a delusion to exaggerate the novelty of such techniques: Hemingway and Dos Passos, the German expressionists and the socialist report-novels of the 1920's and 30's already exploited these opportunities.

As a whole, it seems advisable to take a cautiously appreciative view of the modern documentary tendency in Scandinavian prose. This movement grows out of the 19th century's scientific-positivistic (as Strindberg already noted) and the 20th century's relativistic outlook of life; out of modern man's hunger for facts—for "reports" rather than "stories." Still, Enquist's statement that conventional realistic fiction did not provide more than one way of interpreting the world while the documentary prose does,[16] is highly questionable. It may be suggested, first of all, that the traditional realism of the 19th and 20th centuries does not offer ready-made solutions either, and there are quite a few ways of interpreting Tolstoy's Pierre Bezukhov, Flaubert's Madame Bovary, Lie's Inger-Johanna, or Strindberg's heroes. Secondly, Enquist's reliance on the reader's own judgment is nothing but the application of Brecht's *V-Effekt* to prose. (Brecht's immense popularity in the Scandinavian countries provides solid support for this statement.)

A major criterion of the truly documentary novel is the demand that it show events which, in the author's opinion, appear historically significant or typical to secondary (not in any sense "leading," yet authentic) people, who are themselves more or less involved in the events. This seems to be a definition which separates the documentary novel from the novel of consciousness. Furthermore, rather than contrasting the documentary tendency to earlier tradition, it would be beneficial to find a proper place for documentarism, generally speaking, both in literary history and in literary theory. The specific, rather than the novel, character of the documentary technique would then be emphasized in its development through the ages. I believe that the three modern Scandinavian novels discussed in this paper could serve as appropriate models for an investigation of the various problems of the documentary tendency, even on an international level.

Notes

1. This paper is an enlarged and updated version of the one I gave at the 62nd SASS-Meeting in New York on May 6, 1972. Since I felt that I was less familiar with documentary tendencies in Danish literature, I asked professor Niels Ingwersen (University of Wisconsin—Madison) to reproduce

his valuable contribution to my paper at the New York meeting in a written form, as appendix to present article. We hope that our joint effort will encourage the publication of further collaborative studies (commented articles, symposia, etc.) in *Scandinavian Studies*.

2. "Dokumentarisk litteratur: en samtale med Olav Angell, Per Olov Enquist, Paal-Helge Haugen, Kjell Heggelund, Bjørn Nilsen," *Vinduet*, 23 (1969), 85.

3. Quoted by Björn Håkanson, "Litterär realism; dokumentarism; vetenskaplig sanning," in *Modern prosa: arbeidsbok frå eit litteraturseminar* (Oslo: Det Norske samlaget, 1968), pp. 67-68.

4. The material of the Lukács-Ottwalt debate is available in *Marxismus und Literatur*, ed. F. Raddatz (Reinbek b. Hamburg: Rowohlt, 1969), II, 150-77.

5. Cf. e.g. Marianne Thygesen's bibliography in her *Jan Myrdal og Sara Lidman: Rapport-genren i svensk 60-tals litteratur* (Århus, 1971), pp. 110-13.

6. A. Strindberg, *Samlade skrifter*, ed. J. Landquist (Stockholm: Bonniers, 1920), XVIII, 452-58.

7. "Dokumentarisk litteratur," p. 84.

8. Margareta Zetterström, "'Det finns ingen helgonlik objektivitet:' En studie i Per Olov Enquists Legionärerna," *BLM*, 39 (1970), 525.

9. Cf. "Litterär realism etc.," passim.

10. "The Collective Novel in Sweden," *Scandinavica*, 12 (1973), 113-27; quote from p. 127.

11. Cf. e.g. his "Bløtkakemannens dagbok," in *Probok* (Oslo: Gyldendal, 1968), pp. 120-135.

12. The objection that Delblanc describes events he most probably never witnessed is relevant, but only to a certain degree. Modern memoirs and diaries have less and less adhered to historical fidelity. Malraux's *Anti-Memoirs* or Charrière's *Papillon* are good examples of the constant manifestations of poetic fantasy.

13. Cf. M. H. Braaksma, *Travel and Literature* (Groningen: Wolters, 1938).

14. Both published by Norstedt, Stockholm. References in the text are from the first editions.

15. Cf. Nils G. Åsling's reference to a debate between two Swedish literary critics and Sundman, in *Per Olof Sundman: ett porträtt* (Stockholm: Larson, 1970), pp. 52-53.

16. "Dokumentarisk litteratur," p. 83.

Torben Brostrøm (essay date 1977)

SOURCE: Brostrøm, Torben. Introduction to *Contemporary Danish Poetry: An Anthology*, edited by Line Jensen, Erik Vagn Jensen, Knud Mogensen, and Alexander D. Taylor, pp. 1-10. Boston, Mass.: Twayne, 1977.

[*In the following essay, Brostrøm reviews the development of modern Danish poetry, focusing on stylistic and thematic trends particularly influential in Denmark during the first half of the twentieth century.*]

For a description of modern Danish poetry, various historical points of departure may be chosen, e.g., the nearly century-old Naturalism with its new idea of man, coinciding with the emergence of industrialism and capitalism. In many respects we are still living under similar conditions, and poetry still finds answers to the challenges they present. The language of Naturalism, however, was not primarily that of lyric poetry. The age of modern poetry was heralded in the 1890s by the so-called Symbolists, and their major figure in this respect, Sophus Claussen, has been chosen as the introductory poet of this anthology. His knowledge of the fragmentation of consciousness, which is a characteristic feature of Modernism, was comprehensive, and in several ways modern Danish poetry has been determined by his striving to subdue and yet artistically preserve that fragmentation. This selection can but suggest some of his ways toward creating a poetic cognition, a synthesis superior to that of scientific, rational knowledge. That was his Heroica. In the final words of one of his poems: "draw . . . final thoughts, filled with the motion of the Infinite." The novel element in the language of Symbolism and, hence, of Modernism is seen in his erotic poems where soul and landscape, I and thou, connect in personal, individual symbolic images. The unconscious becomes a new conscious domain for the poet. Here—and in nature as well—are the resources which are invoked to keep together a universe threatened by fragmentation.

This tension between opposing forces was not relaxed at the turn of the century or at the time of the First World War. Time and again it reappears in different shapes, but it becomes increasingly difficult to maintain the idealistic superstructure even though it is attempted through new linguistic experiments. While the geographical and political world is expanding and the means of communication are intensified, reality keeps presenting itself as an urgent problem, and almost everywhere in the Western world modernity is experienced as an internal disruption. Poetry is a series of attempts at subjective interpretation, and, in principle, the Danish answers to such challenges correspond to reactions found in other European countries. In the period before the Second World War the Danish responses were somewhat more restrained than those in Germany,

France, and England, whereas after the war they were expressed in vehemently experimental forms, i.e. under the influence of European Modernism which now really established a tradition.

The survey of modern Danish poetry in this book includes the recent years in which the poetic activity has been exceptionally intense and virtually all kinds of poetry have been written. With e.g. Dan Turèll one finds an expansive kind of poetry which assimilates almost any kind of language: the poetry of the period after the youth revolt, perhaps inspired by the enthusiastic life of beat-lyrics and by their expansion of consciousness. The components of Turèll's language may have widely different origins. The poet speaks a searching language liberated from *style* in the sense of personal coloring. It characterizes an open, productive attitude, a constant creation with new formulations and conscious use of patterns and models. Among his contemporaries one also sees this gesture of liberation from a society like the Danish which has long been fixed by bourgeois standards. Poetry is no longer a religion, rather a matter of politics, a way of speaking about things.

Another retrospect. The other introductory figure of twentieth-century Danish poetry, Johannes V. Jensen, turned with all his will, though not always with all his being, against the spirit of decadence, doubt, and fragmentation. Instead he declared himself a man of facts in the manner of Walt Whitman, whose poems he translated into Danish. However, it is evident in Jensen's "At Memphis Station" that he did not accept wholeheartedly the new world with its noisy technology, machines, and advertising which, otherwise, he praised fervently in articles and reportages. The poem records the uneasiness of the heart which is symbolized by the journey. The impatience is also a symptom of that spirit of restlessness which is inherent in the conditions of production. The poet is fascinated by the technology of a locomotive: "Look how the engine, / that mighty machine, stands there calmly seething, / wrapping itself in smoke—it is patient." Whatever else, it is mundane, it has severed any connection with God, and to do so is the poet's aspiration as well. But he does not want to remain in one of the "poster-howling buildings" whose American way of life may conceal happiness. The great engine is chuffing and snorting, preparing for the journey through the desolate, but also fertile and inspiring countryside of the fin-de-siècle mood—here the soul-corroding rain and the wet forests of the Mississippi.

There are several reasons for Johannes V. Jensen's acceptance of the industrialized, Anglo-American world—halfhearted though it is—among them a necessary approval of progress. But after the First World War Denmark was flooded by the entire mercantile advertisement world of capitalism. It was welcomed by Otto Gelsted in his poem "The Show Boat." With its level-

Photograph of Johannes Jensen.

ing of all values and its reification of all human relations, it is a world of sensations entering the twilight harbor of Denmark. In a poetic-prose form, modeled after Johannes V. Jensen, Gelsted dissociated himself from everything his idol had staked on in his youth. What, indeed, is not on board?

> Here are clinics for make-up and bureaus for suicide,
> which men in despair can consult for a suitable fee;
> here are displayed the latest stunts of the doctor's art,
> men changed into women and women into men;
> here is the ship herself with all that's in vogue:
> tennis courts and swimming pools, the church and the newspaper office
> (that prints you the whole Bible in installments);
> here is the giant gyroscope,
> whose 180,000 revolutions to the minute
> neutralize all motion
> and safeguard the passengers from seasickness.

Gelsted organized his own youth revolt in the shape of a revolutionary student sitting in a shanty with his finger on the button, ready to blow up the entire masquerade of capitalism. A crash is heard—but it did not re-echo in the world of reality which remained problematic.

The outrage of Gelsted's revolutionary dream becomes a general dream of catastrophe in Tom Kristensen's poem "Fear." Originally, it is from his novel *Havoc*, which depicts the experience of total emptiness, of fear which can be resolved only by the catastrophe. "I have longed for the final disaster / for havoc and violent death." That was the result of the expressionist worship of the chaotic beauty of modernity. The shapeless fear had been scrutinized by Søren Kierkegaard, but now it marks an era and can be found in various versions in Kafka, Hemingway, and T. S. Eliot, to mention only a few examples. Expressionism in Denmark was not excessive and pathetic as in Germany; with great precision it annulled traditional values. It was colorful and imaginative, and it was based on senses rather than ideas, as may be seen in Tom Kristensen's poem "The Execution," an extreme expression of confrontation with the absurdity of death. From new points of departure, such confrontations became frequent in the second phase of Modernism, the period after the Second World War.

If one compares "The Show Boat" by Gelsted and Tom Kristensen's poems with respect to their description of life, it will be seen that the former poem aims at objectivity in the sense of relating to socioeconomic realities, whereas Tom Kristensen is emphatically subjective. With him the world is a projection of emotional states. Until recently, the most significant Danish poems were written along these lines. The poets of the twenties and thirties contributed little to the social analysis carried out by a number of critical *prose* writers. As an example, one may mention Jens August Schade. Through all the years his poetry has been a series of surprising expressions of the meeting of souls in the thoroughly sexualized universe he has created, made up of heavenly and human bodies, of Danish landscapes and townscapes. Without really being influenced by Surrealism, his poetry constitutes a clear parallel to it in its free motion between large and small, conscious and unconscious elements, meaningful coincidences which, with the certainty of the instinct, become regularities in a liberated view of the world. By means of libido, Schade has managed to ward off the fragmentation.

The poetry of the younger Gustaf Munch-Petersen is akin to Schade's, but as a consequence of the liberation of instincts Munch-Petersen strove for a political engagement; it must be used in a revolutionary manner. During his brief productive period he managed to express essential experiences of modernism, in both human and linguistic terms. The land below, which he describes in a poem with that title, is both the liberated collective subconscious and the natural socialism of the proletariat. In the last phase of his production, the universal and, hence, abstract I became identical with the personal I in such a way that the poem became a confession and an obligation to act. In consequence of this he went to Spain and took part in the struggle against Franco in the civil war. It cost him his life. Poetry and action became one.

The Symbolist poem ranks as a linguistic act of intrinsic value. In Danish poetry this tradition was continued most overtly by Paul la Cour, especially in his postwar poems. The poems are those very moments in which inspiration pervades the expectant consciousness and the unity of all things is established. In a series of theoretical reflections, "Fragments of a Diary," he professed his views on poetry as a general concept of existence, as that which collects the fragments and reveals the untraceable connections between all that is living. Thorkild Bjørnvig reacted against this identificational view of nature and man. The object should be maintained, the borders between subject and object must be respected if a true sense of community is to be experienced. Both poets are modern, are connoisseurs of chaos and fragmentation, but regardless of their similarities, their interpretations are based on different philosophical principles. However, the objective world of which Bjørnvig speaks is still nature, rather than society, though in a series of portrait-poems he has analyzed the titanic struggle of the artist to maintain the world as is seen in e.g. Edgar Allan Poe. Bjørnvig has launched yet another shipwreck in Danish poetry, viz. "The Ballad of the 'Great Eastern,'" another description of the modernist concept of insanity, a ship of fools, a ship of death which must be scrapped.

Bjørnvig belongs to the generation of poets that appeared during the forties. They were characterized by the ideological readjustments and philosophical revisions of the postwar years. In the literary debate, the most heretical thoughts acquired a distinctly metaphysical, existentialist slant, especially with such poets as Ole Wivel and Ole Sarvig and in the periodical *Heretica* of which Bjørnvig was a cofounder. The individualistic, subjective stance found a peculiar expression in Ole Sarvig's sequence of poems, the central book of which has the title "The I-House." In the course of the sequence, the individual, anonymous "I" completes a development reflecting the entire inner history of modern man as well as the myth of man from innocence, via the fall and loneliness to a new community through love. The mystery of natural growth is a basic pattern in the fragmented metaphoric world of modernity.

If Sarvig strives to gather the severed elements of reality in a selfmade myth, Erik Knudsen and Ivan Malinovski maintain the chaotic description, at first in an internationally dominated imagery, an esthetics of fragmentation. Through an increasingly energetic disclosure of the social and political reasons for the unsatisfactory and antihuman conditions of the civilized world, the two poets gradually became more radical. The almost de-politicized atmosphere of the Cold War period gave way to an increasing awareness of the reality of social and political relations. At first as a general attitude which was termed "cultural radicalism," later in a definite socialist attitude which became the dominant tendency in the second half of the sixties. The fragmentation came to be seen as historically determined, and not as a fundamental condition of existence. For Erik Knudsen it led to a simplification and a politicizing of the poetic language, to a dialectics of two kinds of writing, the one a complex, subjective, the other an engaged satirical poetry.

Around 1960 a new generation of poets and a new protest against the reification of reality appeared. The strength of this poetry lay in its very details, in its searching among the *disjecta membra* of civilization and its mass-produced quotidian life. A pulsating, recording, confronting poetry, the hallmark of which is vitality—also in the negative description. A poetry which is often extremely personal and private in its investigation and microscopy of physical and biological as well as social and historical life. It is seldom expressed in large syntheses. Sometimes the analysis strikes upon language which is forced through atomization into a new expressiveness. In Klaus Rifbjerg clear examples may be found of the kind of confrontation which has been mentioned several times. The concept of confrontation was launched in the title of his collection of poems from 1960. The poem "Medieval Morning" is an example of the characteristic regression through the personal and those strata of cultural history that adhere to us like a feeling of queasiness. A devaluation of worthless values to an unconditional attitude whose meeting with the external world produces new aspects of both the world and the ego. But the purgative process comes first. The poem ends with the words: "I forget me."

The meeting with the external world may be extremely simple, as when Robert Corydon draws a landscape with graphic precision; or it may be fully orchestrated as when Jørgen Sonne surgically reveals the development of puberty in "The Fold-out Men" and shows the unfolding into freedom.

In general, the atomization of language mentioned above does not lead to simplification, but rather to an open style where different linguistic spheres cooperate; with Jørgen Gustava Brandt this is seen in new symbolist fusions. Double exposures and multitracked sequences may make the writing complicated, as in the richly fertile imagination of Uffe Harder. Nausea and idiosyncracies may be used provokingly as means to liberation.

In the course of the decade a characteristic change occurs in the idea of liberation. Gradually, the new poets do away with the belief that poetry is a means to a special kind of cognition. In spite of all experiments, it is possible to remain a prisoner of the intellectual tradition of language. Poetry may then be considered as "texts," as linguistic depictions of the world, valid only as "examples," not as interpretations. Connotations, therefore, are to be precluded, and metaphors and symbols are regarded with suspicion. The poem must emphasize the relation to the reader, it must not be sufficient in itself. For a new experience of community, relations *between* people must be found.

These formal considerations, which are expressed in the texts, gradually became connected with the leftist-socialist political awakening toward the end of the sixties. If the first revolutionary awareness in Danish poetry arrived in a show-boat, the second one was not unrelated to the American warships in the Gulf of Tonkin, and both were expressions of the sickness of the capitalist and industrialized world. On the arena of international politics imperialism became frighteningly visible, there was a growing feeling of language as a means of oppression.

Generally, a change can be felt from a vertical to a horizontal concept of existence. Technically, the interest was moved to words as materials, and for a while a so-called concretist poetry appeared. One of its aims was to demystify the language of poetry. The tendency is suggested in Benny Andersen, whose portraits are made up of puns and tricky ambiguities in such a way that the material aspect of the poem is emphasized. Poetry is language, not illusion. With Vagn Steen the view is programmatic, and in the works of Per Højholt the transition is accomplished from a metaphysical poetry around 1950 to a deliberately aperspectivistic mode of writing. In the theoretical treatise "Cézanne's Method" (1967), a counterpart of Paul la Cour's "Fragments of a Diary," he argued for a poetic practice consisting of the dynamic development of the linguistic material, of its inertia, or, in the words of the painter Cézanne: the idea of art as "an extension of nature into consciousness." Again and again in Højholt's poetry the automatic and random aspects of a verbal sequence are stressed as deliberate disillusionments.

In continuation of the theory and practice of Per Højholt, concretism developed into a conscious philosophy of "writing" which could renounce the illusion completely, either by using popular literature as a pattern (as in Per Kirkeby), by creating a new sensibility of simplification and commonplaces (as in Jørgen Leth), or by means of philosophical sequences far beyond fiction (as in Peter Laugesen). Hans-Jørgen Nielsen began within dogmatic concretism, but in his later works he has attempted to unite the criticism of language with an overtly Marxist criticism of society. The poems of Sten Kaalø and Lean Nielsen testify to new possibilities of formulating direct, personal, and social experience in a more traditional, yet contemporary form. And the sensual subjectivity of Henrik Nordbrandt is strangely related to the experience of a spent world from whose enigmatic remains new modes of existence may be created.

As has already been mentioned, there is a distinct tendency within Modernism toward a depersonalization of the writing subject. As we have shown, however, this does not mean that individualism has given in. Neither did the discovery of the collective unconscious prove a way toward the experience of community. The lyrical poem in which this challenge has been taken up most explicitly, and which has united a new awareness of language with an idea of community, is Inger Christensen's *It* (1969). The poem is about "all those who go on even though it is impossible." The lack of freedom is common to human beings and, therefore, they must seek freedom together. Physical and, hence, psychological reality is shared. She speaks in one place of "our intersubjective conditions, our collective psyche or psychosis, our common prison." The book is a systematic and symmetrical construction, inspired by e.g. modern linguistics. The text grows, as it were, out of language in a creation of "it," an all-encompassing word, a utopia, a dream of freedom, of being in and among people. The book is not a statement of ideas, but a function, an attempt at creating a language which does not *speak* the idea, but which *is* the relation between human beings.

It is written in an interval between an old and a new world and speaks, therefore, of the disorder which was established as a theme at the beginning of the period described here, i.e. in the views of chaos of Sophus Claussen, Tom Kristensen, and Otto Gelsted. Inger Christensen says,

> How to integrate the leveled building
> how to put writing into its place in its chaos
>
> . . . . .
>
> How to integrate a world
> which is completely and hopelessly over
>
> in a world that will not begin . . .

That is a contemporary expression of the attempt at keeping the fragments together. It is no longer a question of the consciousness of the individual, of the interior universe, but a question of the way from alienation to the freedom of the community. A community which has not been rendered impossible by the tragic conditions of existence, but which has nearly always been determined or hindered by historically specified powers.

Frank Egholm Andersen and John Weinstock (essay date 1986)

SOURCE: Andersen, Frank Egholm, and John Weinstock. "Danish Literary Criticism since 1960." In *The Nordic Mind: Current Trends in Scandinavian Literary Criticism,* pp. 1-5. Lanham, Md.: University Press of America, 1986.

[*In the following essay, Andersen presents a brief synopsis of Danish literary critical thought.*]

It has been extremely exciting to follow Danish literary criticism and research during the last two decades. Denmark is a very small country but nevertheless has a culture and a language all its own. Exactly because of this limitation in size, Danish cultural and literary debates are notably sensitive to what is happening in other, larger cultural areas: German, French, English, and American cultural trends are absorbed quickly into the Danish cultural environment. Sometimes this sensitivity causes Danish culture to be more French than the cultural debate in France, sometimes more American than that in America, but some pronounced Danish traditions are always present to change the foreign influence into something distinctly Danish.

Another peculiarity of Danish cultural life is that everything is visible, everything is accessible. The United States, for instance, always has four or five influential cultural centers, each pulling in a different direction. Thus, it is difficult if not impossible to determine exactly what is prevalent in American cultural life. The influence of, say, French structuralism can be detected in some quarters while in others no influence is visible. That is far from the case in Denmark. Every new movement, every new cultural wave abroad will, in one way or another, find its way to Denmark and become part of the Danish cultural mainstream. This makes Denmark one of the best windows to the rest of the world—at least the Western world. Our greatest and best-known philosopher, Søren Kierkegaard, was, for instance, keenly aware of what was going on in German intellectual circles during his day. There is almost nothing in Kierkegaard's thought that doesn't show the influence of the German philosopher Hegel. But Kierkegaard nevertheless remains truly Danish. Deep Danish roots can be detected in the unambiguity and underlying continuity in his work and life as the inspiration brought from European intellectual circles required a singularly Danish point of view.

Current studies of Kierkegaard are represented here by a worthy spokesman, the poet and philosopher Villy Sørenson. Discussing Kierkegaard's short novel *Gjentagelsen,* Sørenson shows that the philosophy projected in the novel is timeless and that the solutions advocated by Kierkegaard could very well be applied today. We all lose our childhood innocence, we all seek to recapture it, and we all possess the ability to compromise in this search. Kierkegaard points out that we can either recall the spontaneity, thereby losing it, or repeat it, thereby regaining it. We can fantasize about our possibilities, or we can realize them in submitting to something or someone outside of ourselves.

It is difficult to select a handful of essays to represent two decades of Danish literary criticism. Even though the chosen essays cover important areas of Danish criticism, several critics and schools of criticism have been left out. It would have been especially informative to have been able to include more than one critic from each movement. Despite its limitations, this selection of essays can be of interest to an American audience because the 1970s have been very fertile years in literary scholarship and related fields. In the wake of upheavals in the humanities following the student unrest of the sixties, extensive changes within Danish psychology, anthropology, and sociology took place. As a result, the more traditional disciplines such as literature and history were changed radically. With these changes new movements and ideas became available to enrich Danish criticism.

The Danish literary scene of today is influenced by intellectual movements: neo-Marxism as well as structuralism and its offshoot, semiotics. The popularity of both approaches in today's European culture is due to the revolt against authority that characterized the youth culture of the late 1960s. The Danish cultural milieu has not uncritically absorbed these European movements, however. Many important intellectual contributions within neo-Marxism and structuralism are in fact Danish.

The neo-Marxistic ideas in European literary criticism of the early 1970s developed a way of dealing with text called criticism of ideology. The ideology is to be understood as a layer in a structural model of society which is constantly dominated by the need of the ruling class to legitimize its oppression of the rest of society. The ideology, which is not produced exclusively by the media but is presented there, is adjusted to the demands of those in power in a very subtle and concealed way by our great authors—none excepted.

Jørgen Holmgaard analyzes one of the successful modern authors, I. P. Jacobsen, and his short story *Pesten i Bergamo*. Holmgaard shows in the analysis how Jacobsen's theme and style develop the ideal framework for formulating the main elements of the ideology of exploitation from the latter half of the nineteenth century. This is done in such a way that Jacobsen places himself firmly alongside the "oppressed masses."

Semiotics is the study of signs. The Swiss linguist Ferdinand de Saussure first defined this interdisciplinary field in the early part of this century, but a long time passed before true semiotics in the Saussurian sense was developed. Interdisciplinary semiotics is derived from structural linguistics, which includes the "Copenhagen School" with Hjelmslev, Brøndal, and others, and from practical applications in anthropology (Claude Levi-Strauss) and in mythology (Roland Barthes). After this establishing of a basis for analyzing the diverse forms of human expression with identical tools, a number of researchers, notably those associated with the French publication *Tel Quel*, started to define the limits of semiotics.

Per Aage Brandt is one of the most important Scandinavian researchers involved with this semiotics project. He has started several semiotics circles in Scandinavia, he is the editor of a semiotics publication, and he has published several important semiotic analyses in books and articles. These analyses are fascinating because of their intensity and breadth. Brandt has advocated the use of the semiotic method with all human forms of expression: architecture, music, language, novels, films, etc. In this section Brandt analyzes one of Denmark's most "American" poets, Johannes V. Jensen, and his "Ødipus i Memphis." Brandt is very concerned with intertextuality; a text continually quotes other texts. Brandt shows Jensen's dependency on Greek mythology, a dependency he links to the psychoanalytical opening of the poem. Recognizing the link between language and sex is necessary to comprehension of the poem.

Semiotics places great importance on the difference between what is said and the way it is said, or between *enonce* and *enonciacion*. Jørgen Dines Johansen works with this distinction in his analysis of Klaus Rifbjerg's writing. Dines Johansen and Brandt have worked together to encourage the semiotic movement in Denmark. This analysis, from a book-length study of Rifbjerg, shows that when one uses the distinction between *enonce* and *enonciation*, it is possible to present a reading that includes the reader as an active part of the production of the text.

As I have attempted to show in the selection of the Danish articles, there is more to Danish literary criticism than neo-Marxism and structuralism. The controversy between the biographical approach and the New Criticism that arose in the 1920s and 1930s is still the object of study in Danish literary criticism. Aage Henriksen's essay about Isak Dinesen (Karen Blixen) is a good example of this continued search. Aage Henriksen was a personal friend of Dinesen's, and much of his research and teaching is based directly on their conversations and correspondence. Art and personality in Henriksen's view are inextricably linked, and he believes that many of Dinesen's ideas were expressed more clearly in her life than in her work. This radical extension of the biographical school is inspiring and has resulted in valuable analyses of Danish authors.

Henriksen's research fills a void in the ongoing Dinesen research. It has always been hard to place Isak Dinesen in relation to common and well-defined literary movements of her time. She placed her tales and novels in the early part of the nineteenth century, where it was easier for her to put some of the values she wished to describe in perspective. She was freed by this distance between her self and her literary theme. The more aggressive sides of the phase of modernism developing in her time repelled her. Dinesen did what she could do to avoid becoming just a part of a literary movement. Henriksen shows that it is nevertheless possible to further understand her works by considering her style and themes in relation to what was happening elsewhere in European literature. By considering seriously Dinesen's personal life, Henriksen manages to show that the more fundamental theories—fate, mask, ideal—that were earlier hallmarks in Dinesen research, are double-sided and ambiguous. It is this ambiguity that places Dinesen firmly in the modernistic age.

Peter Brask is probably one of the most exciting and original literary scholars in Scandinavia today. For several years he has worked to give structuralistic readings a more stringent language. His inspiration came out of the climate arising from the renewed popularity of structural analysis of the anthropologist Claude Levi-Strauss and the text theorist Roland Barthe's study of myth. Brask's roots are firmly established in the Copenhagen school of linguistics and in the Russian formalists of the early part of this century. Peter Brask has for many years patiently criticized superficial and thoughtless use of mathematical and logical models in literary studies. He has specifically pointed out the misuse of Aristotelian logic and mathematical terminology in connection with textual analyses by the French literary researcher A. J. Greimas. In a series of excellent analyses Brask has argued for his own method of analysis in which semantical groups are central and hence the concept of symmetry is central. In the article presented here Brask deals with a number of Hans Christian Andersen's fairy tales, which he treats from a developmental perspective in a more informal way because his structuralistic method needs long and formal discussions. Andersen didn't just create the stories from the top of his head to serve as bedtime stories for the wives and children of the bourgeosie. His fiction reveals a steady preoccupation with hidden psychological and existential problems found both individually and in general in society. Andersen's work can thus clearly benefit from a more precise and closer reading of the fairy tales. Brask shows that Andersen was more an author than a teller of tales while concurrently arguing for a considerable thematic development throughout Andersen's works without getting bogged down in parallels with Andersen's own personal life.

MAJOR AUTHORS

Aage Henriksen (essay date 1952)

SOURCE: Henriksen, Aage. "Karen Blixen and Marionettes." In *Isak Dinesen: Critical Views,* edited by Olga Anastasia Pelensky and William Mishler, pp. 1-17. Athens: Ohio University Press, 1993.

[*In the following essay, originally published in* Karen Blixen og Marionetterne *in 1952, Henriksen illustrates the use of the marionette symbol in Isak Dinesen's works, including* Out of Africa *and* Seven Gothic Tales.]

Seven Gothic Tales

The qualities that have led to Karen Blixen's literary fame are the first ones to strike the readers of her stories. The exquisite and refined narrative manner and the mysterious and fantastic elements of their plots have given her readers a somewhat intimidating impression of her: Karen Blixen as the aristocrat and sybil in Danish literature, the great anachronism who manages to combine old culture with archaic unculture. But this portrait reveals only half the truth, and it suffers a bit from banality. There is much spirit in Karen Blixen's writings, but not so much witchcraft as people have tended to impute to them; she enchants without bewitching. And her aristocratic manner never outweighs her piety.

One of the chief reasons why Karen Blixen has a dazzling and disorienting effect on her readers is because they take for literary sophistication what is basically her personal viewpoint. In her tales, stories and anecdotes are arranged in layers, one on top of the other and the innermost kernel of any of her tales is never a moral principle but rather another smaller story or an image. Compositional lines never meet in a point but come together to form a figure. This is a consistent characteristic in everything she has written—including her book of memoirs, *Out of Africa.* It was in the light of an image or through a symbol that she attempted to understand her situation in Africa when she encountered adversity. This means that for her it is not the concept but rather myth and portent that are the primary spiritual entities capable of revealing humanity's basic conditions.

In her writing Blixen gives most weight to the symbol of the marionette and the biblical myth of the Fall. Historically speaking, it seems that it was the discovery of the marionette play's perspective that provided the impulse for her mature work. In 1926, almost ten years prior to any of the works for which she was to become known, she published a little play, *The Revenge of Truth.* It is a short marionette comedy that contains in essence the thoughts which later will receive much larger orchestration in her famous tales. This is not to say that the works *The Revenge of Truth* and *Seven Gothic Tales* of her second collection, *Winter's Tales,* are merely variations of the same theme. We might try to give a picture of how these three works are related to the symbol of the marionette by recalling a well-known advertisement: a picture of a little girl carrying a package of oatmeal under her arm; on her package, a picture of the same little girl; and on that package, the hint of another picture of the same little girl. Just as the smallest little girl provides the seed of the picture, so to speak, and the largest little girl the outline of the whole, so is the marionette the seed from which sprang *The Revenge of Truth.* It also forms the delimiting line for the fates depicted in *Winter's Tales.*

The marionette had been used as a symbol in literature before Karen Blixen. Heinrich von Kleist's small, marvelously witty dialog in *On the Marionette Comedy,* for example, provides good background material for reading Blixen. The narrator of this dialog relates that one day he saw a famous ballet master in the audience at a marionette theater, and he wondered how a man used to human dancers could find enjoyment in watching lifeless dolls. When he later poses this question to the ballet master, the latter answers that it is precisely the absence of soul in the marionette that constitutes its great superiority. That the puppet has no soul means that it is impossible for it to pretend to be something that it is not. Because it is purely physical it is entirely subject to mechanical laws. A simple tug on its thread makes it perform rhythmical, dancelike motions—a dance of such indescribable grace and lightness that no human dancer can compete with it. But this is possible on the sole condition that the thread be attached at the requisite point of gravity, something one can do with marionettes but not with a human being, for the point of gravity in the human dancer is the soul, and the ability to coordinate one's soul with the corresponding gravitational point in the motion was lost at the Fall. Now it is only the marionette, pure matter, and God, pure spirit, that possess absolute gracefulness.

Implicit in this profound philosophical joke is the notion that in each human being has been implanted a definition, which it is his questionable privilege to be able actively to reject. Of all beings, only the human is capable of creating himself, of remaking himself according to his own ideas. The witch in Blixen's marionette comedy expresses the same idea with the following words:

> Some people do things they don't want to do, and they forget what they themselves really are. They upset the ideas of Nature, and they make her clear springs muddy, beware of them! In the dark, all night long, the trees in the woods are growing. If there is a wind blowing, the tops of the trees sway in it. Such people as I am talking about, wake at night, become anxious, and feel ashamed when they think about it. . . . The truth is that we are all acting in a marionette comedy, and my children, what is more important than anything else in a marionette comedy is to keep the author's idea clear. It is a secret, one which I nevertheless will tell you, that this is the real happiness which people search for in other places. And so, my fellow players, keep the author's idea clear, aye, drive it to its utmost conclusion.

In *Out of Africa* there is a short essay entitled "Of Pride" that repeats this idea with fewer images:

> Pride is faith in the idea that God had, when he made us. A proud man is conscious of the idea, and aspires to realize it. He does not strive towards a happiness, or comfort, which may be irrelevant to God's idea of him. His success is the idea of God, successfully carried through, and he is in love with his destiny. As the good citizen finds his happiness in the fulfilment of his duty to the community, so does the proud man find his happiness in the fulfilment of his fate.
>
> People who have no pride are not aware of any idea of God in the making of them, and sometimes they make you doubt that there has ever been much of an idea, or else it has been lost, and who shall find it again? They have got to accept as success what others warrant to be so, and to take their happiness, and even their own selves, at the quotation of the day. They tremble, with reason, before their fate.

(p. 271)

The marionette comedy is called *The Revenge of Truth* because the witch who states its underlying idea has put a curse on the tavern where the action takes place to the effect that every lie told therein will become truth before the night has passed. Such is the irony with which Nemesis exercises justice upon bad marionettes.

Karen Blixen kept this little comedy in mind when she began writing her mature works. In "The Roads Round Pisa," the first of the *Seven Gothic Tales,* the play is performed in a puppet theater by a troupe of traveling acrobats; this occurs at a point in the story when several of the characters have a respite from their own affairs and can turn their interest elsewhere. The play holds their attention because its double theme—marionettes subject to Nemesis—shows them an image that they themselves, in larger format, are in the process of inscribing on the landscape around Pisa.

The character in the tale who follows the fresh traces of this inscription, covering in two days' time a year's worth of events and in this way making their outline visible, is Augustus von Schimmelman, a Danish count who in the year 1821 is traveling in Italy. He is a man profoundly confused about his life. He has lost or forgotten the idea God had when he made him, and now he is vainly searching for his own image. For a few days, however, in an *osteria* outside of Pisa, Augustus is temporarily relieved of his invisible burden of unsolved problems by being pressed into service as an extra in the last act of a great drama.

The year before Augustus's arrival a great scandal had occurred in Pisa; mighty passions had been stirred up and then had subsided again. But only in appearance. For a number of the implicated persons the story cannot be forgotten; they are bound to its dark core as to a riddle or a fate. And on the day when Augustus stops at the *osteria* near Pisa, the main actors in the drama are restlessly on the move on the roads surrounding the town, all of them in some way moving toward a resolution. Augustus's role begins when an old lady, Countess Carlotta di Gampocorta, is hurt when her carriage accidentally overturns outside the inn where he has just taken up residence. She is carried inside with a broken arm. Alone with Augustus, she asks him to travel to Pisa, find her granddaughter Rosina, and tell her that her grandmother has broken her right arm and is now ready to give her her blessing. To make her message comprehensible to Augustus, she tells him her story, leading him forward into the complications of a situation that can only really be understood in reverse.

Rosina is not her real granddaughter, but her husband's from his first marriage. His first wife died in childbirth. His daughter had the same fate as her mother: at age seventeen, she, too, died giving birth to a daughter. Now it is the old lady's deepest wish that her stepgranddaughter may be spared the fate of her mother and grandmother. When the old Prince Pozentiani proposed to Rosina, Carlotta did everything in her power to bring the marriage about, for she knew that this rich old man and lover of beauty was incapable, through one of nature's quirks, of being a woman's lover. Rosina, for her part, was flattered to have such a powerful suitor and agreed to the engagement. A short time later, however, she fell passionately in love with her cousin Mario and refused to marry the prince.

Carlotta, suspecting that disaster was about to strike Rosina, warned her that to mention this relationship to her fiancé would put Mario's life in danger, because of the prince's skill with a pistol. To the prince she explained Rosina's sudden reluctance as a passing whim, and thus she forced the marriage to take place. But Rosina, having set her mind on her cousin, decided to use her knowledge of the prince's impotence. Shortly after the wedding, she threatened her husband with a public divorce on the grounds that she was still a virgin and their marriage unconsummated. The prince, terrified at the thought that the bitterest secret of his life would become a topic of public gossip, began plotting against her. She on her side plotted against him. He enlisted the help of his friend, Prince Giovanni, a great lover and lady's man, offering to pay his extensive debts if on a given night he would go to Rosina's bedroom and rape her. Meanwhile Rosina, needing to speak to Mario, gave the slip to the spies whom the prince had set to watch over her by arranging that her friend Agnese come secretly to her bedroom one night and lie in her bed while she has her rendezvous with Mario. Both secret plans got carried out on the same night. A short time later Rosina successfully petitioned the pope to annul her marriage, supporting her case with medical proof of her virginity, and soon afterward she wedded Mario.

Carlotta, unaware of either intrigue, is filled with sorrow and bitterness at the news; the old prince falls down in mortal surprise; and Giovanni believes that he has been involved in a miracle. This is the enigmatic or distorted aspect that the past presents to the actors in the drama when they set out the following year to break the magic spell. Carlotta, who had vowed to bless no marriage of Rosina's other than with the prince so long as she can raise her right arm, has heard that Rosina is pregnant, and she is on her way to Pisa to forgive her and give her her blessing. On the way she breaks her right arm. The play is almost over. What God had planned as a little idyll nears its intended conclusion in Mario and Rosina's domestic happiness, but at the same time the revenge of truth is being unleashed upon the stubborn marionettes who have not kept their author's idea clear and who have forced him to make a long, complicated comedy out of an idyll.

The next afternoon, when Augustus stops at another inn outside of Pisa, he finds himself under the same roof as the two princes and the girl, Agnese, and the clock begins to chime for all of them. During a heated and cryptic conversation, Pozentiani accuses his former friend of cheating; Giovanni has nothing to reply, since he believes that God has annulled the effect of his crime. In order to conclude this maddening story he insults the mighty marksman Pozentiani and provokes him into a duel. "A conclusion can be a divine thing," says Pozentiani mildly, as this long period of stasis finally takes a turn toward renewed life and action. The following morning his remark becomes the solemn and literal truth. At the moment when the duel is about to begin, Agnese steps forward and states that she, on the night of the rape, had been lying in Rosina's bed. At once the conspirators grasp how Providence, by the secret little maneuver of tying the two intrigues together, has taken people who were criminals in a human tragedy and made them into fools in a divine comedy. The old prince gives a final outburst of protest and falls down dead; the paid rapist turns burning with repentance and love toward Agnese; and she, with a grand gesture, forgives Giovanni and walks away, leaving him standing where his passion and his circumstances have placed him.

In the last of the *Seven Gothic Tales,* "The Poet," the action is simpler; it has less the lofty, classical air of "The Roads Round Pisa" and more the gloom of psychic twilight. The double erotic triangle of "The Roads Round Pisa" is simplified to its traditional form. The action takes place around 1836 in the region of Hirscholm; Councillor Mathiesen has Pozentiani's role here but resembles him only in his ruthlessness. The old prince was a character of great magnificence and painfully narrow limitations; he took and he gave with terrible innocence until, in desperation, he overstepped his boundaries and was cast down. The councillor does nothing but take; he is a character for whom all paths lead inward. He has put himself in the role of God for the town of Hirscholm, and he has more or less lived up to it as far as the young poet Anders Kube is concerned. Anders, who is a man with a deep, wild soul that no one understands and who therefore is unable to express himself with any degree of concentrated force, allows himself to be dominated by his Maecenas.

The councillor might have had his way, his stature increasing along with Anders's reputation, had it not been for a captivating widow by the name of Fransine who happened to settle in Hirscholm. The instant she sees Anders she understands his potential, and beneath her deep gaze Anders starts to come to life. The councillor understands nothing of this, but he does grasp that dangerous powers are being unleashed in Anders that must be quickly subdued if he is to retain his position as Maecenas. He decides to keep Anders under control by having him marry the sweet and charming widow. He pursues this plan until one day he happens to discover that Fransine too hides great reserves of imagination and passion beneath her quiet, doll-like exterior. At once he changes his plans and proposes to her himself. To Anders he now assigns the role of unhappy lover as an equally good means of control. Fransine complies. She spent her youth in a ghetto and is not used to fighting. She does what people expect of her and lives her real life in dreams. But Anders, who now understands his purpose in life, resolves to drown himself on the day of her wedding. She has called him to life, and now he would rather die than go back to his former existence. Thus the councillor's second plan is doomed to failure, since its primary purpose had been to keep Anders under his control.

Meanwhile, two events occur that are about to transform fiasco into catastrophe. The first is that Fransine falls as deeply in love with Anders as he has with her; like him, she feels reborn, as if emerging from the shadows. The second event is that the councillor is composing his third plan: having played with the young couple like a pair of marionettes, he now intends to wring the utmost from them. He arranges for them to meet in a final, heartbreaking lovers' rendezvous on the night before his and Fransine's wedding. He does not, in so many words, tell them to meet, but he is do adroit at dropping subtle hints that at last they think they have come up with the plan themselves. The councillor does not so much wish to control their thoughts as to insinuate himself into their instincts. He only half succeeds. Anders and Fransine plan their rendezvous, but Anders, who has a poet's acute eye for psychic abnormality, begins to suspect whose idea it was.

Thus when Anders and Fransine meet at night at the time and place determined by the councillor, who is spying on them from his hiding place in the foliage, the scene does not unfold as the latter had intended. In insulting and hateful terms Anders rejects Fransine's love, until she tremblingly asks: "Did you not want me to come, here, to you, tonight?" "No," he replies, "if you are asking me my honest opinion, Madame Fransine, no. I should like to be by myself." Fransine turns away in despair and runs sobbing back toward her house. Anders sits quietly for a moment, then picks up his rifle. Turning around, he finds himself standing face to face with the councillor—to the amazement of the latter but not to Anders, who all the while has felt the old man's clammy fingers around their hearts. He fires his rifle into the body of the old man and disappears from the garden.

The councillor falls to the ground mortally wounded, at the same instant falling out of his godlike role. On his belly he slowly crawls in the direction of Fransine's house. As he does, he tries to find consolation in the thought that he is under a greater spirit's, a great poet's, providential care. When finally, exhausted, bloody, and filthy, he reaches his fiancée he whispers: "Sacred, Fransine, we are sacred puppets"—at the same time moving his hand along the ground until it touches her foot. After a pause, he adds: "There the moon sits up high. You and I shall never die." "You!" cries Fransine. "You poet!" and shatters his head with a stone that she has torn loose from the garden wall. In this way these two newly created people fulfill what was written about the expulsion from paradise and about the enmity placed by God between the serpent and the woman: it shall bite her heel, but she shall crush its head.

In sum, the two tales that form the frame around the *Seven Gothic Tales* are about the marionette play from above and the marionette play from below, about God and the serpent, about the rules of life and damnation.

WINTER'S TALES

In *Out of Africa* Karen Blixen includes a little story that most people probably know in a slightly different form. She calls it "The Roads of Life" and tells it in such a way that, as if on a teeter-totter, a little joke is able to lift a heavy idea up into the light. The story, which ideally ought to be accompanied by a drawing, is about a man who lives in a little round house with a little round window in a little round garden. Nearby is a lake with lots of fish in it. One night the man is awakened by a dreadful noise. He gets up and goes out to investigate the sound. Awful things happen to him. He has the misfortune of falling over a stone twice and then into three ditches, one after the other. Eventually he discovers that the dam of the lake has broken; he repairs the break and returns home exhausted. If one follows the man's steps from the house to the lake and back again, one ends by having traced a very pretty picture of a stork. Blixen's commentary to this story begins as follows:

> I am glad that I have been told this story and I will remember it in the hour of need. The man in the story was cruelly deceived, and had obstacles put in his way. He must have thought: "What ups and downs! What a run of bad luck!" He must have wondered what was

the idea of all his trials, he could not know that it was a story. But through them all he kept his purpose in view, nothing made him turn round and go home, he finished his course, he kept his faith. That man had his reward. In the morning he saw the stork. He must have laughed out loud then.

The tight place, the dark pit in which I am now lying, of what bird is it the talon? When the design of my life is completed, shall I, shall other people see a stork?

(pp. 262-63)

The man in the story maintains his purpose; he keeps the idea of the author clear, as do the young lovers in "The Roads Round Pisa" who sacrifice all personal considerations for the passion implanted in them. He is one of the good marionettes, one of those whose reward is not comfort or any great degree of happiness but a destiny, a picture worth remembering. In his case it took the form of a stork.

Now if we were to consider that the author to whose plan the man in the story is so faithful has only a limited number of themes at his disposal, and that he alternates the successful ones, making use of the same pious formulas to fashion new destinies, we would see Blixen's marionettes in a new way: as figures enacting the limited number of valid destinies that are available down through the ages. This is how she expands the significance of the marionette symbol in *Winter's Tales*.

The structure of this collection of tales is strict and significant. There are eleven tales; the first (in the Danish version), "The Sailorboy's Tale," announces the basic theme. The second and eleventh are tales about artists, and they frame the remaining eight. The first four of these give examples of how people with resolute and original natures are capable of liberating the courage in other people, of getting them to live up to their purpose and to step into a picture. Among these is "The Dreaming Child." The last four show lives that have become distorted and confused, small-scale reenactments of the Fall. "Alkmene" is one of these. "The Dreaming Child" and "Alkmene" are both about children who at the age of six are adopted into bourgeois families; in both cases their mere arrival is the stroke of the violin that causes certain musical figures to emerge.

In "The Dreaming Child" we are introduced to a prosperous shipowner's family that in the first half of the previous century inhabited one of the large houses along Bredegade. The present owners of both the firm and the house are the young couple Jacob and Emilie Vandamm. The wife, a woman with a flexible body and rigid morals, has married her husband for neither money nor love but because it was expected of her. She and Jacob are cousins and had been bethrothed to each other since childhood. Shortly before their wedding, however, there was a moment when Emilie wanted to break the family agreement, because for the first time in her life she had fallen in love. The man was a young naval officer named Charlie Dreyer. The night before departing on a long voyage he had proposed to Emilie that they spend the night together. Horrified, Emilie had fled from him, determined to uproot his image from her heart. A short time later she married Jacob, and a month after the wedding she learned that Charlie had died of fever during his voyage. However, on the night Emilie left him, Charlie had gone to another woman with the passion Emilie had awakened in his soul. The fruit of that encounter, a boy with a face like Emilie's, has, upon the death of his mother, been placed to grow up among strangers in an impoverished household in Adelgade.[1]

The boy, Jens, feels like a stranger in this home, not because of its poverty or because he knows anything about his remarkable origin, but because he is a person whose essence is dream and longing. For a while this longing becomes focused on the wealth of the great houses in Bredegade. An old seamstress, a woman who has spent her life fantasizing about the opulence of the great houses, chooses Jens as the heir to her unrealizable dreams. She tells him that his feeling of being a stranger comes from the fact that in reality he is the dearly loved child from one of the rich houses who in some mysterious way has become separated from his parents.

So when Emilie, whose marriage has been childless, finally agrees with her husband, after careful reflection, to adopt a child, and a providential chance selects Jens, the boy is eminently well prepared for a solemn and heart-warming reunion. He does not enter the great house as a meek and miraculously elevated proletarian child but as a conqueror taking his duly appointed riches into possession. We should pay careful attention to the nature of his happiness. For him, his triumph does not consist in suddenly being able to dispose of all of the wonderful things around him but rather in the fact that his dreams have been fulfilled. The new things and the new people have only scant significance for him in and of themselves but enormous significance as signs that confirm his mighty visions.

"Jens took possession of the mansion in Bredegade," the narrator tell us, "and brought it to submission neither by might nor by power, but in the quality of that fascinating and irresistible personage, perhaps the most fascinating and irresistible in the whole world: the dreamer whose dreams come true." In this he reminds us of Joseph, who had much the same experience in the house of Potiphar and Pharaoh. The special quality of the magic emanating from Jens's person is that he bring the people around him to see themselves with dreamers' eyes and smilingly forces them to live up to an ideal. Jacob and Emilie become mild and powerful divinities, and even their stingy old kitchenmaid turns into the goddess of food and pots and pans, benefactress of mortals, a Ceres with an apron and a white ruff.

After a few months in his new house, Jens finds his longing moving in search of new areas, but without success. With increasing frequency his thoughts turn to his former, impoverished house. As he loses interest in his immediate surroundings, he falls ill, and a few months after his arrival in the wealthy house, he dies. Upon his death, the house in Bredegade collapses and reverts to what it was before, one house in a row of houses, and its inhabitants go back to their dull existences. Everyone except Emilie feels a great and painful loss. For her there had always been something upsetting about Jens's poetic temperament for which everything in life was equally good and which welcomed light and dark, joy and pain "in the same spirit of gallant, debonair approval and fellowship," for she had always struggled to distinguish between good and evil, right and wrong. Jens's attitude had disturbed her so profoundly that she had found it impossible to love him. Not until several months after his death has she absorbed his nature into her own and become transformed by it. In a conversation with Jacob she says, breaking a long silence: "He was my child, mine and Charlie Dreyer's." She understands now that at the moment when, frightened and angry, she rejected her lover, she broke faith with a deeper and more essential passion than her passion for morality, and that somehow the destiny she betrayed incarnated itself in Jens's shining and fragile form. Emilie, who has always been so scrupulous in the cause of truth, begins to wish that she could believe that what has happened did not happen.

At one point in her conversation with Jacob, Emilie says, "I saw that we could not find another such as he, that there was none so wise." And then the narrator says: "She did not know that she was quoting from Scripture, any more than the old shipowner had been aware of doing so when he ordained Jens to be buried in the field of his fathers and the cave that was therein." The verses of the Bible quoted here concern Joseph. After Joseph has interpreted the dream about the seven fat and the seven lean cattle, Pharaoh says of him, "None is so wise as he"; and the old shipowner's command refers to Joseph's bones being moved from Egypt to the burial place of Abraham's family in Canaan. Here it is clear that it is not only a question of a similarity between Joseph and Jens, a literary allusion, but of a kind of identity between their situations. If one pursues this line of thought a little further, one discovers a net of fine threads that connect the small figure of Jens to the legend of Joseph. Corresponding to Joseph's cosmic dream about the sun, moon, and eleven stars is Jens's great rainbow-colored dream, and the father whom Jens gets when he moves into the rich house is named Jacob, like Joseph's father, and like him, the latter Jacob is married to the daughter of his maternal uncle. However one interprets these connections, the intention behind them must be to show that Jens's story is a repetition in small format of Joseph's—that life, as it accomplishes the destiny of the strange little boy from Copenhagen, is in reality moving in old, well-known, and deeply engrained traces.

In the second story, "Alkmene," a Jutland pastor and his wife who have no children adopt a six-year-old girl, Alkmene. The child's origins are obscure, but it is nevertheless clear that a mixture of noble and artists' blood flows in her veins. Alkmene is a strange child; she has a glow of happiness and *joie de vivre* about her. She startles and upsets with her nonchalantly self-assured behavior and with her strange mixture of virtues and failings. She balances fearlessly on the roof ridge of the house, she gives away her new clothes, and she takes whatever anyone says to her to be literally true. She loves music and dancing, and the bright glow that surrounds her when she dances shows that dancing is part of her essential nature. She trembles and grows pale at the sight of a dead bird, but she pulls grass snakes from the hedges and carries them around without flinching. It is easier to state the qualities Alkmene lacks than the ones she has; she lacks the qualities humanity acquired through the Fall: fear, knowledge of good and evil and of the necessity of death, hatred of the snake. This remarkably wild and enchanting child grows up in a Jutland parsonage permeated by the heavy spirit of bourgeois Christianity, and she is cared for by a couple whose view of life is rooted in the Fall. By "the Fall" I mean the doubling of the self or its splitting, the mental act whereby human beings step outside of themselves and, after seeing that they are naked, perceive physical nature as a mystery that arouses both anxiety and desire. The Fall is the moment that brings both sin and virtue, both the Satan of instinct and the God of duty, into existence.

Alkmene's stepmother, the pastor's wife, Gertrud, is a warm and motherly woman, hard-working and energetic, dutifully laboring under the curse uttered when mankind was driven out of paradise. She loves Alkmene with a great, demanding, possessive love. She loves her and wants to own her, dress her up, hug her, but Alkmene is shy of being touched. She is fond of her stepmother at the start but cannot reciprocate her kind of love, which eventually becomes a torture for her. Twice, once when she is nine and again when she is eleven, she tries to run away, but both times she is brought back. "Why did you run away? Why did you want to leave us?" Gertrud asks her over and over. It is also Gertrud who tries to teach Alkmene to feel fear and who, without a word of reproach, with dutiful conscientiousness, sits at home darning Alkmene's stockings when the girl comes home from a bright and carefree day. Gradually the wish to free herself from Gertrud at any cost takes shape in Alkmene's soul.

Alkmene's stepfather, Pastor Jens Jespersen, has a deeper, more fearful understanding of the special quality of the child he has taken into his house. He, too, has had a problematical past. As a young theology student he suffered a spiritual crisis, brought on by his reading about the Greek world and its gods and nature spirits, its theater and art, its glorious vision of nature. All of this represented a threat to his soul, for he saw nature as sinful. It is a well-known law that one cannot indulge in what one considers to be sinful without truly sinning. In his fantasy, therefore, as he turned away from the world of ancient Greece, he began to see himself as someone chosen by God for a great role in life, perhaps as a leader, a man of destiny. On the verge of falling victim to megalomania, he fled from Copenhagen and took refuge in a sense of duty and stern, renunciatory piety—still tempted by the glow emanating from nature and genius and forever on guard against it. Thus he allows no dancing at the parsonage—while it is precisely in dancing that Alkmene gives expression to her true essence. He begins to instruct her in the classics, and Alkmene drinks in classical learning with desire and energy; but her joy makes him suspicious and he cuts short her instruction. Thus each of her talents is met in the parsonage by an interdiction.

When Alkmene turns fifteen she receives a large inheritance, presumably from her unknown father. It makes no impression on her but a great one on her stepfather. The prospect of so much money fills him with nervous agitation. "But if it is to be, here, a trial of strength between God and Mammon, should I decline to take on the championship of the Lord?" "Indeed," he adds, "I have known from the first that through Alkmene some great task might come to me. And when I am dead, I shall live on in her good works." A short time later he dies, and thus death comes into Alkmene's house and into her heart. She understands that this was what she had wished for her stepmother.

A few months later Alkmene asks her friend Vilhelm to accompany her in secret to Copenhagen. Once they arrive in town, she tells him that she has come for the purpose of observing a public execution. "No," she replies to Vilhelm's shocked objections, "it is not an entertainment. It is a warning to the people who may be near to do the same thing themselves, and who will be warned by nothing else." Then she quotes a saying of her stepfather's: "For God alone knows all. And who can say of himself: Of this deed I could never have been guilty?" Alkmene shivers and trembles as she stands at the foot of the scaffold, and when the executioner's axe falls she nearly faints. This is Alkmene's Fall from grace. The pressure on her has built to the point where at last it has robbed her of her effortless balance of nature and instinct that had been her innocence and strength. The pastor's death had made her look with fear into her own heart. And in her confusion Alkmene found it necessary to impress upon herself the old teaching, that the wages of sin are death. Later in her life the pastor's prediction of living on in Alkmene's deeds is fulfilled. She avoids anything capable of arousing pleasure or desire and gives herself over to the permissible vice of serving Mammon. In sterility and stinginess she lives her life, falling deeper than other people because she fell fully and entirely.

A remarkable aspect of Alkmene's story is that the person who tells it, her friend Vilhelm, does not really understand it. Her life contained a mighty promise, yet it became empty and desolate. And Vilhelm's own life became impoverished and colorless once Alkmene slipped out of it. But he does not see that he was the cause of the break in Alkmene's fate—that both of their lives were robbed of their meaning because he and the pastor, the two people closest to her, were so alienated from their instincts that they had only the vaguest and dreamiest suspicion of their real purpose in life. The reader, however, can see that this is the case, thanks to the mythical traits, though half erased and almost unrecognizable, that keep appearing in their story. They hint at an ancient pattern of destiny that one can find perhaps in its clearest and most valid form in the myth of Alkmene of Thebes.

The Greek woman Alkmene was married to the soldier Amphitryon; Zeus fell in love with her, but to obtain a night in the arms of this faithful wife the god had to take on her husband's form. Afterward, when Alkmene learns who has visited her bed and whom she has mistakenly experienced with all her heart and all of her senses as Amphitryon, she falls into such a painful state of doubt about her own nature and instincts that it threatens to undo her. But she remains true to her earthly lover/husband and comes through her trial alive and intact. That is why she is able to give birth to Zeus's son, Heracles, the great slayer of monsters. The first time the pastor and Vilhelm hear Alkmene's name, the former quotes a remark of Zeus's: "Who bore me Heracles, a child staunch of heart." And Vilhelm dreams of her at night: "She met me on a path in the field, in the midst of the tall wheat, and the capital A in her name shone like silver." The shining A does not signify only Alkmene, as Vilhelm thinks, but also Amphitryon. In the myth we are told that Amphitryon, on the way home from war, wanted to send his wife a diadem with his name on it. Zeus beat him to it and sent an identical diadem but with the first letter of his name on it. Later the husband's diadem played an important role in clearing up the nocturnal intrigue, for it was with his A that Alkmene demonstrated her irreproachable fidelity. Vilhelm often has a dream in which Alkmene disappears and he, in great anxiety and despair, goes looking for her, but during the day it does not occur to him that he actually could lose her. At the root of his being, in other words, he has preserved a reminiscence of his true identity, as the pastor also has with his megalomaniac fantasies, but both men lack the requisite simplicity and instinctiveness to live their roles as Amphitryon and Zeus.

Instead, they betray Alkmene and her demands on them—they drag her down and disrupt the harmony of her being. Thus it is only in a caricatural and crippled form that she can fulfill her destiny.

In this discussion I have tried to give an idea of the plots and the coherence of these two *Winter's Tales*. For my conclusion I will attempt to shed some light on the motif of repetition that plays such an important and remarkable role in them. I will refer to an essay by Thomas Mann, which was originally written in honor of Freud's eightieth birthday. It is entitled "Freud and the Future," and is in fact a commentary on Mann's own series of Joseph novels. There is good reason to think that Karen Blixen took a different and more personal road to her theme, so I do not know if she would have accepted the extension of perspective that I am about to propose to her story.

Thomas Mann introduces the main thesis of his essay by comparing Freud's distinction between the regulating, form-giving agency of the mind, the ego, and the blind, protoplasmic force, the id, with Schopenhauer's distinction between intellect and will. Then he takes the reader into a discussion of Schopenhauer's notion of the apparent purposefulness in the destiny of individuals. In brief, he suggests that in the same way as our nocturnal dreams are formed by our will, without our awareness or conscious control, so is reality a greater dream dreamed by the ur-will in all of us. After having thus enlarged the scope of the discussion, Mann turns back to psychoanalysis to discuss an essay by an Austrian analyst. It concerns the way in which artists' biographies used to be written. The very predictable and schematic nature of these books suggests that their primary intention was to show that the life in question had unfolded according to the proper formula, that it had followed an immemorial and hence legitimate pattern. He states that in many cases it is impossible to say what is legend, what is formula, and what is specific to the life of the individual artist. This can also be the case with modern people. Not only artists' lives but every life is determined by conscious and unconscious acts of identification. We all live the life of a certain category, of a certain profession or class.

Mann ends the essay with a description of the Joseph novels. He writes that it is correct to place his work in the boundary area between the typical and the individual, and it is appropriate to apply the viewpoint of psychoanalysis to it. As an author, he says, he has moved from the depiction of the bourgeois/individual life to the mythical/typical one. When psychology moves from the individual to the type, it enters the area of myth. The typical and the mythical are the same. And the reenactment of myth is the ordering idea of the Joseph novels. He goes on to explain that with *depth psychology,* another term often used for psychoanalysis, *depth* is to be understood also in a chronological sense. To penetrate into the soul of a present-day child is at the same time to penetrate into the primitive, into the childhood of the race. Primeval time is the well where the archetypes of all the myths—the norms of life—are to be found. This is where the timeless paradigms of human life take shape that each life unconsciously reproduces as it fashions its own characteristics. Thomas Mann finds great happiness in this insight, a bright cheerfulness, *Heiterkeit.* He calls it the smiling awareness of the eternal, of the being that lasts forever, of the paradigm to which life conforms and by which it achieves validity as a repetition of eternal truths, of humanity's footsteps in deeply worn tracks. And by taking examples from history he shows how at the moment of death, the most personal moment for each of them, the great figures of antiquity triumphantly seized upon a quotation to show that finally they had consummated a life in the form of myth. Thus, of Christ's words on the cross, "My God, my God, why hast Thou forsaken me?" he says that despite their notes of despair and disappointment they are the expression of the highest degree of messianic self-awareness. For these words are not original; they are not a spontaneous outcry, but a quotation—from the Twenty-second Psalm, which from beginning to end is a prophesy about the Messiah. And the quotation means: I am the one who was awaited, I am the Messiah who lived and died as it was written. Thus out of despair and individual misery and defeat rise an unconquerable optimism and mood of mythical rejoicing.

At the conclusion of his essay he brings the entire chain of his thoughts to rest in a symbol, the marionette comedy, the Punch and Judy show in which puppets perform a fixed and familiar set of actions. As just such a theatrical fulfillment of a predetermined plot does life appear when seen in the artistic optic of myth. The premise of the Joseph novels is the moment of insight when the individual becomes aware that he is a kind of marionette character. The happiness and equanimity felt by Joseph in the novel comes from an awareness deep inside of himself that he holds the main part in an old play, that he is identical to the Egyptian god who was torn to pieces, buried, and then lifted up again. Both the misery and the triumph in his destiny are equally essential for the beauty and harmony of the play.

As for applying these theories to Karen Blixen's writing, it is appropriate to point out that Thomas Mann had achieved an artist's insight into this combined repetition and mask motif long before he had intellectually acquired the theory to support it.

Earlier I referred to Heinrich von Kleist's *On the Marionette Comedy*. The dialog ends with the witty and profound statement that only marionettes and God have absolute gracefulness, since both are beings that consist of either absolute nature or pure spirit. In a Danish context we might say that repetition is experienced only by a marionette or a Christian, and at the mention of the latter our thoughts turn to Søren Kierkegaard, author of a book entitled *Repetition*. In this concept it is possible for Søren Kierkegaard and Karen Blixen to meet, moved by the same fear of the demonic aesthete, but they meet only to move in opposite directions away from this figure and to pursue two very different forms of piety.

Note

1. In a letter of August 9, 1952, sent to me by Karen Blixen upon the publication of this essay, she wrote:

   > I would like to point out one very simple disagreement between author and critic. I had not imagined the child Jens in "The Dreaming Child" as Charley Dreyer's son.
   >
   > Professor Brix asserts the contrary opinion in his book *Karen Blixens eventyr*, substantiating it up with various dates and facts which are not really in the story, and which, taken by themselves, seem somewhat confused—For example, on p. 183, he states that Jacob marries Emilie in 1856, and that at that point she is 19 years old, and on p. 184, that the boy is born in 1850, the year when Charley left town for the West Indies—which means that Emilie, on the night Charley asks if he might spend the night with her, would have to have been 13 years old. He also says that Jacob and Emilie take Jens into their home approximately five years after their marriage, and then adds "at only six years of age, Jens is as precocious as a musical Wunderkind, life radiates within him, and he casts its glow all around him in the large lovely rooms and on the wealthy people of the capital"—which, in other words, does not fit with the stated date of Jens's birth either. But I did not want to get involved in pointing out small inaccuracies in the professor's analysis of "The Dreaming Child," since I already had to protest against a point at which he fundamentally misunderstood the plot of "Roads Round Pisa."

Ann Gossman (essay date autumn 1963)

SOURCE: Gossman, Ann. "Sacramental Imagery in Two Stories by Isak Dinesen." *Wisconsin Studies in Contemporary Literature* 4, no. 3 (autumn 1963): 319-26.

[*In the following essay, Gossman describes the use of the theme of destiny and the search for human identity in three of Isak Dinesen's short stories.*]

Many stories by Isak Dinesen explore a pattern of destiny against which the individual must search for his identity, or else abandon his hope, his risks, and his distinctive humanity. Such a theme is evident in some of the stories in Dinesen's first published collection of short stories, *Seven Gothic Tales* (1934), especially in "The Dreamers." It reappears in her next-to-last book, *Last Tales* (1957), which contains some unfinished work and a section entitled "New Gothic Tales." This same theme is of central importance in all of the stories in *Anecdotes of Destiny* (1958), Dinesen's last book.[1]

Frequently the character in search of identity is an artist. For such a person, identity is meaningful largely in terms of a relationship both to his art and to the audience which the artist requires. To express the sacred quality of this relationship and the promise of spiritual enrichment, Dinesen makes use of imagery that suggests the Communion service in two stories about artists. One of the artists is Babette, an expert French cook, who appears in "Babette's Feast" in *Anecdotes of Destiny*. The other is the opera singer Pellegrina Leoni, the heroine of "Echoes" in *Last Tales*. These stories have close affinities and lend themselves to parallel consideration because they rely upon sacramental imagery to convey their themes. In both stories a cluster of bread-stone, blood-wine images defines the artist's relationships to art and society. Underlying both stories (or at least certain key passages from them) is *Matthew*, 7:9-10:

> Or what man is there of you, whom if his son ask bread, will he give him a stone?
> Or if he ask a fish, will he give him a serpent?

One other story must be considered at least briefly in any discussion of "Echoes." Although "Echoes" is related in theme and imagery to "Babette's Feast," it is inseparable from "The Dreamers," an earlier story dealing with the same heroine, Pellegrina Leoni. Eric O. Johannesson, who has analyzed such motifs in Dinesen's fiction as the puppet, the mask, and the overt references within the stories to the art of the story, does deal with the dream image as it is used in "The Dreamers," but he does not analyze "Echoes," nor does he discuss the sacramental imagery in Dinesen. Johannesson's conclusion that "The Dreamers" supports the dream in preference to reality[2] seems questionable. In that story, the story-teller Mira Jama asserts a preference for dreams because he is spared the trouble of inventing them, but his defense is ironic, as his imagery shows: a coffee-tree with a bent taproot will put out a number of fine, delicate roots near the surface—its dreams—in order to survive for a little while, and it will flower more richly than the thriving trees that bear fruit, but it will "die by its dreams" (*Seven Gothic Tales*, 227).

One of the minor characters in "The Dreamers" abandons his futile and comic endeavors to discover and live up to his identity; he escapes finally into an undemanding existence under an assumed name. His situa-

Photograph of Isak Dinesen.

tion provides a comic parallel with the tragic situation of Pellegrina Leoni, an opera singer who has lost her voice at the time of a fire in the opera house. No longer able to exist as an artist, she wishes to commit suicide because she has lost the two things she has loved most: her identity as a singer and her relationship with her beloved audience. After a dose of opium has failed to kill her, she renounces her identity as Pellegrina Leoni and establishes in succession three temporary and rootless identities, each of which has to be abandoned when she is in danger of committing herself too far in human relationships. Each of three men loves her in one of these assumed personalities: the prostitute Olalla, the revolutionary Madame Lola, and the saintly mystic Rosalba; or each man loves his own image of her. Each suspects the mysterious Jew whom she calls "her shadow" of some villainy, and each loses her. In none of these identities does Pellegrina experience any serious emotions. Her pleasure or pain and her happiness or unhappiness do not seem to affect her. Just after the three men have compared stories and recognized that the three women are one, they see her again and begin a pursuit of her that culminates in her death.

The sinister Jew, the implication that Rosalba may be a witch, the heavy reliance upon coincidence, the melodramatic flight through the snow, and the operatic overtones (reminiscences of *Tales of Hoffman,* for instance, and possibly of *La Forza del Destino*) give the story a decidedly Gothic atmosphere; but the witty dialogues of the three men, the satirical treatment of all three of them, and the numerous ironies by which Dinesen manipulates her coincidences to resolve disparate points of view and reveal the truth—that the fugitive is Pellegrina Leoni and that the Jew is her protector and altruistic friend—all give the story a flavor that is by no means Gothic and that is in keeping with Dinesen's later work.

"Echoes," the reader is soon given to understand, deals with an episode in Pellegrina's life after her adventures as Olalla, Lola, and Rosalba, and before her death. It is therefore a kind of tragic interlude between the two portions of the earlier story, and it is a more mature and tragic reconsideration of Pellegrina's artistic identity. "Echos" and "The Dreamers," then, when first considered together, seem mutually exclusive; but it is evident that they actually supplement one another to form a kind of paradoxical truth. In "Echoes," as in "The Dreamers," there are two divisions. These are not essentially and causally related in terms of plot, but rather by theme and imagery. Here Pellegrina Leoni temporarily recovers her real identity when she regains her voice vicariously. Thus the story provides a partial resolution of Pellegrina's search for herself. The Lord, as she observes, likes a *da capo*, and Pellegrina believes that she is now repeating her life, in a way, and that she may proceed *al fine*. She is only partly right. She is also aware that episodes that appear in one light to human beings may be seen otherwise *sub specie aeternitatis*. For that reason, "One may take liberties with God which one cannot take with men" (*Last Tales,* 165).

In the first part of "Echoes" Pellegrina is the "angel" of the Lord who reinterprets Niccolo's story to make him appear worthy of salvation rather than of persecution. In the second part she herself is persecuted. The limited vision of ordinary humanity is made apparent through references to bread and stones. From the superstitious point of view both Pellegrina and Niccolo are liable to condemnation as eaters of human flesh and blood.

Pellegrina first appears in a small Italian town as a suppliant for bread. The solitary Niccolo shares a loaf with her, but he is morbidly wary of hands, and he is troubled by her reference to the resurrection of the body. Divining his secret, Pellegrina promises not to tell the villagers, who would stone him, and she suggests that he may be part of some incomprehensible pattern of the Lord's. Niccolo admits that after a shipwreck he had eaten the hand of an old chaplain, already dead, and then had been rescued. This very hand, Pellegrina assures him, may well lift him into heaven. Her subsequent discussion of God and Christ sounds so unorthodox to him, however, that he fears that she may be stoned for heresy. For instance, she regards the counsel of perfection as *pleasant*: for what artist would not be gratified to hear it?

In church Pellegrina hears in the voice of a young choir boy the echoes of her own magnificent lost voice. A divine pattern seems evident when she learns that on the same night when the shock of the fire at the opera house destroyed her voice, the boy, Emanuele, had miraculously escaped from the mountain slide which had crushed his house. To the villagers, Providence had marked the child as a potential saint and thus a source of pride to the village. To Pellegrina, the child is the young Phoenix resurrected from the ashes of her fire, and although his pure soprano voice cannot last, she will be content if she may briefly witness "that heavenly *da capo* which is also called resurrection" (*Last Tales*, 170).

The ambiguity of the teacher-pupil relationship which she establishes with the boy is suggested by an image of devouring: "I have got my talons in him" (*Last Tales*, 172). The danger is that she will be, like the villagers, unduly possessive in destroying the boy's own identity and making him a mere instrument for her. Pellegrina's real love for the child, however, makes her more generous than predatory. That he knows (through a servant's story) who she really is, it seems, signifies that they can establish a special kind of understanding. Pellegrina now sees herself as the "nursing mother" of both Niccolo and Emanuele, but at the same time she believes that Emanuele may eventually become her lover. They establish a brief moment of communication when each echoes the other's sentiments that the death of one would be the death of the other.

Pellegrina is unaware of the tension that is building up between the villagers' interpretation and her own of her relationship with Emanuele. His sister's ominous decision to become a nun in order to pray for them seems only a beautiful gesture of love, and Pellegrina's own generosity with material things seems very unimportant to Pellegrina herself, who fails to observe the resentment which it generates. The turning point comes when Pellegrina performs a curious ritual which may be interpreted in two ways. When Pellegrina pricks Emanuele's hand with her needle, she is initiating him into the stoic acceptance of pain which an artist needs, and her maternal tenderness and love cause her then to wipe his hand with her handkerchief and to kiss it through pity for him.

Ironically, this action is misread in the village as evil. The boy comes to her with a suspicious heart and many questions about her mysterious wealth and her generous friend, whom no one in the village has actually seen. The old servant's report that she is "immortal" is applied, not to her art, but to her physical existence, and the wealthy friend (really her Jewish "shadow") is taken to be the devil. Finally, the episode of the handkerchief, which is really symbolic of the communion and sacred bond between the singer and her pupil, is "proof" to Emanuele that Pellegrina is a vampire who wants to live forever by drinking his blood. Reverting to superstitious terror, he casts a stone that marks her forehead with her own blood.

Pellegrina's reaction goes through three stages: anger at the stupidity of Emanuele's cruelty, self-criticism (for she is aware that she may have been too possessive), and finally a kind of ironic resignation. Even as she pities Emanuele, she acknowledges that this very pity "sucks the marrow out of her bones," and she feels that she may have taken upon herself too much of the work of Providence in shaping the young man's future. Let him be a priest or a saint, if he can forget "*portamento* effects" in his singing.

With terrible irony Dinesen describes the villagers at church, lacking Christ but devouring the Mass. Pellegrina sees an expressionless old woman whose toothless gums are still "moving and munching a little with the consummation of the Host." The resolution is ambivalent: Pellegrina reflects that Niccolo was right when he said that one could take liberties with God that are impossible with man. It is a commentary on the sacrament of the Mass: one may eat of the Lord's flesh, but man's tabus against cannibalism are so strong that to kiss a blood-stained handkerchief is suspect. At the same time, in spite of her disappointment, Pellegrina accepts the will of God, and she knows that it is only in a society incapable of true communion with God or man that she is an outcast.

In "Babette's Feast," the other story in which Dinesen uses sacramental imagery, two irreconcilable points of view toward food and drink are played off: the strict Puritanical rejection of any enjoyment of them as luxuries, and the Epicurean enjoyment of them for their intrinsic delight. Dinesen achieves a temporary and perilous equilibrium of these two views. In a deceptively simple story with a rather complex plot she persuades us of the truth of a highly improbable situation: that a French cook, formerly of the Café Anglais of Paris, should prepare her supreme culinary achievement for the little circle of pious friends and relations of a saintly Lutheran dean in Norway.

Like Pellegrina, Babette is an artist who strives for perfection and whose only prayer is that she may be allowed to do her utmost. To the dean's daughters, luxury in food is sinful, wine is forbidden, and frugality is imperative if one is to give to the poor. Although Dinesen depicts the Lutheran sisters with affection and gentle humor, she reveals the limitations of their little world unsparingly: pettiness, prejudice, and smugness. In all of the congregation, even the sisters, a good deal of ethical blindness is evident, as none of them can perceive the egotism that underlies their charity. The elders smile happily to think, "What nabobs would not the poor simple sisters become in the next world" (*Anecdotes of Destiny*, 59).

The naiveté of the sisters is apparent as they dread the French dinner which they have reluctantly allowed Babette to pay for and cook for once—as a favor to her. They exact from their friends a promise that no one will mention food or drink at the table, and they agonize over the strange preparations for the feast. Since they are fortunately unaware that wines have names, they are reassured that Clos Vougeot and Veuve Cliquot cannot be wines. One of the sisters is frightened ahead of time at the sight of a huge live turtle in the kitchen, but she takes comfort from the words of the old hymn that paraphrases *Matthew,* 7:10: "Wouldst thou give a stone, a reptile, to thy pleading child for food?" Unsuspectingly, she later consumes delicious turtle soup and afterwards is glad that the turtle (possibly just a nightmare after all) has not appeared in any form at table.

If Dinesen gently satirizes the Puritan narrowness, she does not spare the pagans either. Her sympathies (and therefore the reader's) are largely with the artist, but the artist has ethical as well as aesthetic commitments. Although the Puritans have overstated the case, they are partly right about the selfishness of a luxury-loving aristocracy. Dinesen dramatizes these ethical implications by involving Babette in a paradoxical situation: in the French Revolution Babette sides with the oppressed, loads the guns that shoot the aristocrats, and is herself a *pétroleuse*; but in doing so she destroys, as she is aware, the only audience capable of comprehending her art. It is her subsequent request for a situation as cook for "good people" that leads to her job, not with aristocrats, but with the righteous sisters.

Through an ironic miracle at the sacramental feast which Babette prepares, the righteous "good people" are substituted for the aristocrats with results that would have been beyond the capacity of either the Puritans or the pagans alone. Babette, who does not really know the effects of her dinner, achieves her final artistic triumph and even has her artistry understood by the one worldly guest who happens to be at the party. Thus, at the end, she dies as any artist might wish to do. In turn, the Puritans are transformed by the sacrament of food and wine into the truly charitable Christians they have always considered themselves to be. By eating and drinking in what they regard as the proper spirit, they are rewarded with "the fulfillment of an ever-present hope . . . one hour of the millennium" (*Anecdotes of Destiny,* 62).

The feast itself is a sacramental image of the harmonious synthesis that might have been possible for both the sisters and the men who had once loved them, but who had departed or been banished from the dean's exclusively pious house. Philippa, in giving up the musical career and the love of the singer Achille Papin, had in turn doomed him to the artist's hell of doing his second best. Her sister, Martine, had been loved by a young officer, the man who appears at the dinner as a worldly and successful general, defeated spiritually by his own success. The singer, though not present at the feast, is the man who had sent the sisters their French cook with a letter to the effect that in Paradise Philippa will be the artist God meant her to be. The general tells Martine that he has never forgotten her and that henceforth he will always be with her in spirit.

The guests have a clue to the miracle of the feast which they do not properly appreciate. When they sit down at the table they fortify themselves with the reflection that *even* at the Wedding of Cana grace had chosen to "manifest itself there, in the very wine, as fully as anywhere" (*Anecdotes of Destiny,* 55). It is the general, intoxicated by what he considers the noblest wine in the world, who gives them the best explanation that the story affords. In it, Dinesen uses her favorite device of the echo or formal repetition which she calls a *"da capo."* The general begins with the very words which, when spoken many years previously by the dean, had caused the young officer to give up the hope of marrying Martine:

> Mercy and truth, my friends, have met together. . . .
> Righteousness and bliss shall kiss one another.
> Now the general comprehends the words as a promise of infinite grace:
> See! that which we have chosen is given us, and that
> which we have rejected is poured upon us abundantly.
>
> (*Anecdotes of Destiny,* 60)

The feast itself, then, is a kind of sacramental union of Christian righteousness with the happiness of aristic fulfillment. It is the symbol of heavenly harmony. Just as the singer had quoted a portion of the Mozart duet that had originally revealed their love to Philippa and himself, so the general quotes the Biblical passage which he had heard from the dean, and so, at the end of the story, Philippa reassures the cook with the singer's comfort to Philippa, that in Paradise she will be the great artist God had meant her to be.

Thus the title "Echoes" would be almost as appropriate to "Babette's Feast" as to the story actually bearing that title; for each story is constructed on what Dinesen calls the *da capo* principle. Dinesen's stories have the stylized elegance and deceptive simplicity of such a composer as Mozart. Some of the initial themes are apparently as simple as folk music or folk tales; then new and seemingly unrelated material is introduced; and finally the relation of all the parts to each other and to the whole is clear. The coincidences in each story are transparently obvious so that the pattern may be made evident. Each of these two stories, "Echoes" and "Babette's Feast," depicts an artist (whether singer or cook) seeking to realize herself and to struggle against seemingly adverse destiny. Each artist is ironically deprived, through the ignorance on the part of her society, of the essential communion of artist with audience which each of these artists once had. For each, the harshness of the situation is tempered: Babette triumphs in the exercise of her art and enables her guests to achieve communion with each other; and Pellegrina achieves a temporary *rapport* with each of two human beings and comes to be at peace with God and ironically reconciled to the misunderstanding of society at the end of "Echoes," before her final triumph and death in "The Dreamers."

Notes

1. References to the three stories, "The Dreamers," "Echoes," and "Babette's Feast," are taken respectively from *Seven Gothic Tales* (New York, 1934), *Last Tales* (New York, 1957), and *Anecdotes of Destiny* (New York, 1958).
2. *The World of Isak Dinesen* (Seattle, 1959), p. 79.

Sven H. Rossel (essay date winter 1983)

SOURCE: Rossel, Sven H. "Ole Hyltoft and the Neorealistic Trends in Contemporary Danish Literature." *World Literature Today* 57, no. 1 (winter 1983): 17-21.

[*In the following essay, Rossell argues that the poetry of Ole Hyltoft is marked with sharp political satire examining the ideologies of Capitalism and Marxism, and that many of the views expressed in his writing evolved during his years as a critic and journalist.*]

> *Life is so many-sided: poetic, criminal, full of love, taunting.*
>
> Ole Hyltoft

When Klaus Rifbjerg (see *BA* 49:1, pp. 25-28), the writer largely responsible for the growth of modernist poetry in Danish literature during the 1960s, published his collection *Amagerdigte* (Amager Poems) in 1965, it became evident that a reaction against this experimental and hermetic mode of writing—a mode actually introduced by Rifbjerg himself—had begun. In 1961 his controversial poem *Camouflage* had caused bewilderment and indignation. The public had fastened upon the complete lack of punctuation and overlooked the fact that the work was a grandiose, almost ecstatic yet artistically structured attempt to conquer reality through a voyage into the realm of the subconscious. Rifbjerg used an associative technique, playing with words and putting them into unexpected combinations in a fragmented syntax. With *Amagerdigte* reality, the banal monotony of the author's childhood in a suburb of Copenhagen, is rendered in a reportorial and matter-of-fact style. The critics correctly labeled the volume an example of a neorealistic or neo-simplistic trend in Danish literature.

Other lyrical poets followed suit, but it was particularly in prose writing that the reaction against exclusive modernism manifested itself. The major representatives of modernism during the late 1950s had been Villy Sørensen and Peter Seeberg. Sørensen's writings consisted of philosophical analyses of modern man's alienation and isolation. He used the form of allegorical tales inspired by Kafka and Isak Dinesen. Seeberg dealt with the same theme but employed a more absurdist and symbolic approach in the tradition of Beckett and Ionesco. During the early 1960s the French *nouveau roman,* characterized by both an absence of the traditional plot and a sharply defined distinction between the narrator and the protagonists of the text, found two major Danish representatives: Ulla Ryum and especially Svend Åge Madsen. One of the dominant themes in Ryum's writing is the unbridgeable gap between human beings, described in a language full of ambiguity and reminiscent of the mood and method found in the works of Djuna Barnes. Madsen, on the other hand, employs a deliberately monotonous and image-free language in order to explain his relativistic view of reality as a fictional creation completely dependent upon the ideas of a given author.

As had been the case with the lyrical poetry, this experimental, partly abstract prose was succeeded by a much more factual and more easily accessible style of writing after 1965. The forerunner had been Thorkild Hansen, whose first published documentaries, *Det lykkelige Arabien* (1962; translated as *Arabia Felix,* 1964) and *Jens Munk* (1965; translated as *The Way to Hudson Bay,* 1970), were based on historical material. *Arabia Felix* tells of an eighteenth-century Danish expedition to the Arabian peninsula and has as its theme the estrangement of human beings who have been torn away from their cultural milieu. *The Way to Hudson Bay* deals with a seaman and his bold but unsuccessful attempt to find the Northwest Passage to India and China. Time and again, however, Hansen oversteps the bounds of objective reporting, particularly in his subjective style and his use of inner monologue and literary leitmotivs. It is these features that raise his writing to the level of brilliant realistic fiction.

This neorealism with its more traditional narrative technique, based on Thorkild Hansen, on various Swedish models and on Mary McCarthy's novel *The Group,* not only influenced a number of already established modernist writers such as Rifbjerg, but also created a new literary school. The complete breakthrough took place with the works of Anders Bodelsen, Christian Kampmann and Henrik Stangerup. Bodelsen became the most popular and productive of the neorealist generation. His books are characterized by a detached narrative tone and considerable formal skill. These features emerge clearly in *Drivhuset* (*The Greenhouse*; 1965), whose fourteen mystery stories and detailed portrayals of the

Danish welfare state announce the two essential elements of his subsequent works. The writings of Kampmann and Stangerup are likewise composed of critical studies of the middle-class way of life, but their psychological analyses are more acute. Stangerup, in particular, focuses on the social and political problems caused by a welfare society, in which he sees threatening tendencies of guardianship and totalitarianism.

What these three authors lack, especially Bodelsen and Kampmann, is the sharp political satire which can be found in the works of a fourth and somewhat younger writer, Ole Hyltoft (b. 1940). Prior to his first novel in 1970 he had already established prominence in the public debate as a critic and journalist, the secretary to various ministers of cultural affairs and, above all, since 1970 as the influential head of the Cultural Commission of the Danish Social Democratic Party. The view of man and society which underlies Hyltoft's fictional writing was formed precisely during these years and received its initial treatment in the essay collection *Tør du være fri?* (*Do You Dare to Be Free*; 1968) and the pamphlet *Good Day Sunshine* (1969), a view further expanded in the volume *Tør du være med?* (*Do You Dare to Come Along*; 1974).

Against the backdrop of the Vietnam War, the Soviet occupation of Czechoslovakia and the international student rebellion Hyltoft analyzes the two major ideologies, Marxism and capitalism. Both are rejected as social systems which place human well-being and growth second to a constant expansion of production. Lenin and Marcuse are attacked because of their endorsement of political violence, and capitalist society is criticized for its commercialism and cutthroat competitive spirit: "Achievements give external power. Fine exams, successful businesses and a great output of work give us external status which can soothe our fear of our own inadequacy. In societies based on achievement you can buy personal security through power. But at the same time the lack of power inspires us with dread." This dread and its causes can only be eliminated in a future society, a "deeply democratic society of people with a social conscience. That is to say people who feel uncomfortable when others suffer and who do not accept inequalities which grow in a class system."[1]

An episode in Hyltoft's novel "The Vanquished" (see below) describes the Danish counterpart to the student rebellions of the late 1960s with a mixture of sarcasm and sympathy—sarcasm because the rebellion gets out of touch with reality, sympathy because here Hyltoft finds the beginnings to that peaceful revolution which eventually can bring about his own social utopia. The process which leads to a human, undogmatic socialism rests on a realization that we are all different. A common fundamental feature, however, is our need for love and affection. This trait lies at the base of Hyltoft's view of man, his emphasis upon love as a transforming and liberating force which creates a human fellowship: "To love is to give yourself to another person. And in the beloved person you include everybody else. To love is the greatest openness a human being can attain, and it constitutes the most intensive experience of man's collective situation."[2]

The artistic experience, specifically, is able to release as well as express this altruistic urge: "In modern-day life, which threatens to become monotonous, people occasionally need to move in leaps, to change dramatically. In art we find a dramatic change which can help many attain psychological balance in an everyday life which is much too trite" (*TD*, 116). A logical extension of this view is Hyltoft's attack on the over-crowded and polluted metropolis, which in spite of its crowd of people only furthers anonymity and isolation. Anticipating today's ecological movements, he conjures up a vision of a livable city which incorporates nature and is built around our need for fellowship.

> We could give our cities colorful squares, imaginative playgrounds, botanical gardens. We could turn the coastlines near our cities into green recreational areas with marinas and woods stretching down to the beach. Here we could stroll without being hindered by signs reading PRIVATE and NO ADMITTANCE, without being chased by cars and engines. Here we could make love, here we could experience the changing of the seasons, the stormy waves during the fall, the ice of the winter, and here we could swim during the summer in an ocean which is clean.

Is this vision, which emerges again in "The Vanquished," an impractical and naïve utopia when measured with the yardstick of today's reality? It is, after all, consistent with that humanist view of society which Hyltoft defends publicly both as a debater and writer. He believes that the role of the artist is to point ahead toward new possibilities. His essays—which were instrumental in bringing the social and political debate of the 1970s beyond its narrow, dogmatic Marxist orientation—not only form the necessary theoretical basis for his fictional works, but anticipate them thematically as well. Through his fiction Hyltoft's ideas take on a more tangible form, gaining the necessary credibility and cogency as they are measured against the present state of egotism, corruption and violence.

Hyltoft's first novel *Hvis lille pige er du?* (*Whose Little Girl Are You*; 1970), contains an extraordinarily stringent depiction of contemporary life in milieus ranging from the Danish State Department to embassy and architecture circles in New York. The satire thus is aimed both at segments of the American way of life, exemplified by brilliant snapshots from New York that are based on the author's observations during a study trip in 1962, and at the bourgeois milieu of government officials in

Copenhagen. At times the book can be read as a roman à clef with some indiscreet portraits of easily identifiable cabinet ministers; but basically it is a crime novel, a genre to which Hyltoft returns in later works, often in combination with elements from the international hard-boiled-spy story. An official at the State Department, Anker Karlsen, is suddenly torn from a quiet daily routine into a world of hot pursuits, assaults and attempted murder. The action starts with the theft of Karlsen's dissertation manuscript, which was to have aided his advancement in the Foreign Service. The suspect is a conceited and ambitious colleague who, like Karlsen, lives under constant pressure to advance in his career; both are victims of social constraint. This message takes priority over the development of the rather simple plot, which reaches an acceptable if not quite unexpected solution.

Hyltoft's next novel, *Hjertet sidder til venstre* (*The Heart Is Situated on the Left Side*; 1973), is more complex and contains stronger character delineation. The well-established middle-class man with vague revolutionary sympathies and the younger, lower-class girl with whom he falls in love are characters previously sketched in Hyltoft's first novel. Here they are expanded into two brilliantly executed psychological portraits and become an integral part of the book's political plot. Niels Jensen is a deputy principal and moderate left-wing pragmatist who is able to maintain a balance between progressive pedagogues and conservative officials. Ditte, a vocational-college student, on the other hand, is a revolutionary PLO activist whose heart is situated so far to the left that she places her uncompromising political commitment ahead of her love for Niels. She forces him to steal secret documents during a dangerous mission to East Germany, and when in the last chapter she emerges as a skyjacker she is even willing to sacrifice him in her fight against Israel; but she herself is killed instead. Where does Niels stand in this political battle? Is he able to follow Ditte of his own free will? Or has he allowed himself to be totally manipulated? Perhaps even Ditte is only a pawn in a bigger, impenetrable scheme. The author gives no clear answers in this simultaneously ironic and highly serious look at the conflict-filled impact of love, social roles and political activities in our lives.

With pungent wit Hyltoft records the jargon of leftwing pseudo-intellectuals, particularly the self-righteous pedagogues surrounding Niels whose deceptive emancipation only masks intolerance and pharisaism. This exposé of fashionable trends becomes the main purpose of the short-story collection *Revolutionens fortrop* (*The Vanguard of Revolution*; 1975), one of the most hilarious political satires in modern Danish literature. The volume focuses on corruption and hypocrisy among leftist intellectuals, the opportunistic yes-people as well as the more dogmatic Marxists. Both groups manipulate their surroundings. They make up "the vanguard of revolution," but they are unable to break away from their own bourgeois background, using revolutionary clichés and the working class only as false fronts for their efforts to further their own careers. A young proletarian writer, for example, expresses his—and the author's—disgust: "You probably think that all your double-dealing has a higher meaning. But do you know what that higher meaning is called? Be smart, smart, smart—and give the lower classes the shaft. That is precisely what it is called! You may be the vanguard of revolution, but I prefer to belong to the rear guard."[3]

It is crucial to be up-to-date not only in politics but also in the realm of sexuality. Hyltoft illustrates this in two subdued, semi-tragic stories dealing with the generation gap and involving the futile attempt of a middle-aged couple to live up to the sexual emancipation of their daughter. We meet these characters and others in various combinations throughout the seven texts contained in the volume. In this way Hyltoft succeeds in creating a coherent and universal picture of his own time, an age that is permeated with self-delusion and superficiality and, as a consequence, with insecurity and dread.

Insecurity—a prominent feature of Hyltoft's protagonists—also characterizes Henning in the novel *Hvem er angst for den stygge ulv?* (*Who's Afraid of the Bad Wolf*; 1976). He too comes from a middle-class milieu. Once a successful Volkswagen salesman, he now sees his position threatened by the more popular Japanese cars. However, Henning's fight for his professional career only constitutes the background for his numerous attempts at liberating himself, which is the true subject of Hyltoft's book: a liberation from his own milieu, from the conventions of society and, finally, from the great multinational firms. All these opponents are symbolized in the "bad wolf" of the title. But whereas Henning's first rebellion—an affair with a militant feminist—succeeds, his role slowly changes through a number of confrontations with the "wolves." He evolves almost imperceptibly from manipulator to manipulated in a manner similar to that seen in "The Heart Is Situated on the Left Side."

In his writings Hyltoft frequently shifts in the same volume from a local, provincial milieu—residential areas north of Copenhagen—to more cosmopolitan surroundings. The two-volume novel *De befriede* and *De besejrede* (*The Liberated*; *The Vanquished*; both 1979), on the other hand, is a poetic declaration of love for Copenhagen and constitutes a move away from pure realism toward a more visionary outlook. The city not only provides the setting of the work, but even symbolizes the mental state and spiritual development of the principal character, Kim. "The Liberated" begins in 1945 and describes the expectations of the postwar generation, its dreams and hopes for a new, changed society. However, through Kim's eyes we see how envy and the quest for power lurk behind the optimistic surface. The idealistic plans for a "new and purified Denmark" shared by a group of young artists, upper-class business students and members of the working class turn out to be illusory. This revelation is symbolized in a subplot involving the murder of one member of the group, the poet Ib, who has preached the gospel of all-encompassing love—a demand which none of the characters can live up to. Was this why Ib had to die?

The answer is in the affirmative and is demonstrated in the second part, which takes place between 1968 and 1979, the period of the Vietnam War, the student rebellion and budding feminism. Here Hyltoft once again draws on his extensive knowledge of contemporary Danish society and his impressive insight into the most typical trends. His narrative talent unfolds in both a satirical and—a new development in his writing—a highly imaginative direction. He depicts the professional success which the artists and academics of the group have now achieved, often through corruption and compromise. But true success as a human being is reached only by the outsider Kim, who abandons a promising career as a business executive in order to become a street musician. Hyltoft's entire sympathy is focused on Kim's growing doubts about the economic boom of the 1960s and his longing "to realize himself." The children of Kim and his friends have now become young revolutionaries. To some extent Kim (and therefore Hyltoft) feels solidarity with their goal of changing society, but at the same time he must warn them sternly against the same egotism and narrow-mindedness which turned their parents into "the vanquished."

Neither generation, therefore, has been able to bring about the revolution of love which is Ib's (and Hyltoft's) message. Neither economic nor political means and solutions suffice, but this revolution is nevertheless possible, as is demonstrated in one crucial scene: a festival which, characteristically enough, takes place at the Academy of Arts. Kim participates in this fantasy, an experience of love and an almost surrealistic orgy of color, sound and form which furthers his growing self-realization and his final liberation from any social attachments. Thus art and love alone comprise the forces which are able to change and ennoble man, a step toward that universal sense of humanity which was suggested in Hyltoft's previous books and here is realized not only in Kim but also in the author's vision of a new Copenhagen, a city in which all are allowed to unfold and fulfill their creative talents. Significantly, this vision, described on the final pages of the novel, will become a reality through Kim's son, who has been elected Commissioner of City Planning.

Whereas Hyltoft's two-volume 1979 novel is simultaneously an *Entwicklungsroman,* an exquisite prose hymn to Copenhagen and a glorification of art and love, his next novel, *Byggekongen* (*The Construction King*; 1981), resumes the unveiling of human corruption and hypocrisy. Although Hyltoft returns to a basically realistic technique, he also blends lyrical elements into his narration, as in his previous work. Moreover, the tenor of these passages is the same as before: reflections about art and love as life-renewing forces, symbolized by seasonal changes in a number of exquisite nature scenes. Hyltoft thereby adds a spiritual and philosophical dimension to his novel. Combining satire, character portraits and milieu descriptions, the work emerges not as a roman à clef, as suggested by most critics, but as a timeless epic about the rise and fall of human pride and vanity.

The milieu is that of wealth and big business. Frans, a social upstart, attempts through various risky transactions to rise from local contractor to head of a multinational computer empire. His success seems due in part to his wife's family connections with the world of high finance and with the Danish royal house. This ascent, however, is accompanied by an inner decline, as Frans increasingly becomes the victim of his own ruthless manipulations—a favorite theme in Hyltoft's writings. The protagonists's misanthropy peaks when finally, driven by his ambitions, he sacrifices his loyal secretary Annemette and thereby isolates himself completely. The novel is permeated with death symbols, and Hyltoft's outlook is indeed pessimistic. Yet his confidence in the positive prevails. Love, represented by Annemette, as well as art, represented by the painter Tonni, the enfant terrible of the book and a counterpart to the artists in Hyltoft's 1979 novel, are victorious.

Hyltoft's latest work, the short-story collection *Tante Isidora* (*Aunt Isidora*; 1982), again focuses on human compassion. With subtle irony a number of human follies—snobbishness, vanity and haughtiness—are unveiled, but without the satirical attacks which frequently characterize the earlier writings. Some of the texts are permeated with pure slapstick effects, but on the whole Hyltoft emerges as a master of suggestion. Together with a delicately sustained balance between the comic and the tragic, this significant feature makes several of the short stories here obvious choices for any anthology of modern Danish prose. A common trait in Hyltoft's protagonists is the fact that they have all passed the middle stage of life and are either seeking a place in today's world or attempting to live in the past. But—and this is one of the book's points—more or less visible threads connect their childhood with the present. Life cannot be split up in isolated parts but must be accepted as an entity.

In spite of their oddities and flaws Hyltoft embraces his characters with love and compassion. In its subtlety his humanism emerges more strongly than ever before. Critical yet always with positive solutions and without any kind of ideological or moral self-righteousness, Ole Hyltoft has carved out a unique position in contemporary Danish literature.

Notes

1. Ole Hyltoft, *Good Day Sunshine,* Copenhagen, 1969, pp. 16, 18. All translations are my own.

2. Ole Hyltoft, *Tør du være fri?,* Copenhagen, 1968, p. 43. Subsequent citations use the abbreviations *TD.*

3. Ole Hyltoft, *Revolutionens fortrop,* Copenhagen, Fremad, 1975, p. 108.

Faith Ingwerson and Niels Ingwerson (essay date 1984)

SOURCE: Ingwerson, Faith, and Niels Ingwerson. "Introduction: The Age, the Man, and His Vision." In *Quests for a Promised Land: The Works of Martin Andersen Nexø,* pp. 3-33. Westport, Conn.: Greenwood Press, 1984.

[*In the following essay, Faith and Niels Ingwerson trace the political and cultural climate during Martin Andersen Nexø's time, also providing overviews of his major works and themes.*]

Martin Andersen Nexø was always involved in the history of his age: he recorded it as he saw it, and he wanted to set his mark on it. His *oeuvre* is a statement that was meant to influence opinions and affect lives. A necessary delineation follows of his times, his life and career, and his artistic universe—the contours of which may be less clear-cut than they at first seem.

Aspects of Danish Social History

In 1869, at the birth of Martin Andersen, who in 1894 added Nexø to his name, the industrial revolution was transforming Danish society. Small factories and cheap new housing projects were forming a dark ring around the old city, and the inhabitants of the old neighborhoods were looking with suspicion, if not apprehension, at the new masses. In small ways labor had begun to organize; thus, a class struggle was in the offing.[1]

Although in the rural areas, where the majority of the people still lived, feudalism had supposedly been abolished, the traditional way of life—as the early parts of *Pelle the Conqueror* and *Ditte, Humanity's Child* show—continued along age-old patterns. The common peasantry, the *almue,* worked on the farms for food, lodging, and meager wages. Many, however, followed Pelle's and Ditte's example and went to the city, which seemed to offer jobs and upward mobility. Those workers were eventually to give a different face to Danish politics. Their example was followed, somewhat later, by the working classes in the other Scandinavian countries. Between 1871 and 1916, Social Democratic parties were formed in all of Scandinavia, and as a rule, those parties were closely tied to the labor unions.[2] During the same years, the political spectrum in Denmark—going from right to left—consisted of the following major parties: the Conservatives, the Liberals, the Radical Liberals, and the Social Democrats. Toward the close of the First World War, leftist splinter groups—such as the syndicalists and the anarchists—resenting what they saw as the authoritarian stance of the Social Democrats, attempted to dominate the unions. Ironically, those schisms led to the formation of the fairly doctrinaire Danish Communist Party.

The first significant stirrings of a socialistic movement were felt in 1871, when the young Louis Pio (1841-94) started a magazine that advocated the overthrow of the prevailing political order. In fact, Pio formed a section of the First International (1864-76) and wrote to Karl Marx predicting a glorious future for socialism in Denmark. The authorities took Pio seriously, for when he organized a rally in May, 1871, the police intervened and arrested its leaders. The conservative government prohibited the International, but in consequence of that repressive act more unions began to form.

The laborious process of unionizing the often timid workers continued, and by 1890, a national workers' organization was in existence. Its adversaries, the industrial employers, responded in kind; thus, both sides were readying themselves for a confrontation. The workers were simultaneously making themselves felt within the parliamentary system, for their party, that of the Social Democrats, gained three seats in the election of 1890. The party had, however, abandoned Pio's allegiance to the First International and had modeled itself—following the German example—along the non-revolutionary, reformist lines of the Second International (1889-1914). The Social Democrats could then join the bourgeois Liberal Party in opposition to the Conservatives, whose rule—without a parliamentary majority—was unconstitutional. The success of the strategy of the Social Democrats was evidenced by their having twelve members elected to parliament in 1898.

The spring of 1899 was a decisive one for the Danish workers' movement. In a major conflict between labor and management, both sides showed their muscle; quickly spreading strikes led to punitive lockouts. As the battle of wills grew more intense, fears grew that the nation was heading for an economic breakdown. Finally, after nineteen weeks of sparring, the adversaries began negotiations that resulted in a settlement, which some deemed to be a major victory for labor and which others evaluated as, at best, a preservation of the status quo. Although the victory may have been largely symbolic, such symbols were of tremendous significance; the average worker undoubtedly felt that labor had proved its ability to stand up to intimidation and to make its adversaries listen and yield. Scenes from that dramatic period make up the rousing third volume of *Pelle the Conqueror.*

One reason for the clout of the workers was that Denmark by then had become quite heavily industrialized. Stock companies, which had been rarities twenty years before, were now numerous, and foreign capital was pouring into Denmark. Thus, the country was becoming a modern capitalistic state, in which employers were becoming more and more distant and anonymous. By the same token, the private production of commodities by artisans was slowing down, since the small shops could not compete with the new technology, the specialization, and the cheap labor of industry.

Although skilled workers felt politically stronger and more secure in their jobs—as the fourth volume of *Pelle the Conqueror* reflects—they simultaneously adopted the habits and norms of the petit bourgeoisie. It was that abandonment of those workers on the lowest rungs of society which Nexø later was to portray in the heartbreaking latter part of *Ditte, Humanity's Child,* which in graphic detail captured the suffering of the very poor. That novel thus indirectly comments on a sad historical irony: as the critic Anker Gemzøe has documented, the labor settlement of 1899 had served to consolidate the power of management.[3] The strength of unions was curbed both by the agreement that compulsory arbitration should determine the outcome of future conflicts and by the ruling that management should remain in complete control of the daily process of production.

Since the leaders of labor had little tradition or theory upon which to rely, they had agreed to conditions that in the long run favored their opponents. For labor, such tangible gains as shorter hours, prohibition of child labor, better salaries, and job security seemed to be unquestionably solid steps forward. It should also be recalled that the Social Democrats, who were committed to working within the parliamentary system, had adopted the reformist idea that historical inevitability would see to the collapse of capitalism and the peaceful birth of a socialist state.

Such a commitment to strategies in behalf of an evolutionary political process was naturally anathema to revolutionary minds within the workers' movement, but the anarchists and syndicalists belonged to a distinct minority, and their protests had little effect. Actually, the Social Democrats made impressive gains in the first elections of the new century, and by 1913, their party occupied thirty-two seats in parliament. Party leaders, such as Thorvald Stauning (1873-1942) and Frederik Borgbjerg (1866-1936), negotiated favorable health insurance and unemployment benefits but tended to discourage the supposedly inflationary demands for heavy salary increases.

During the first decades of the new century, the industrial workers could take pride in a party that protected and represented their interests. Since the Social Democrats still had to cooperate with the Liberals, a party dominated by farmers, the plight of the unorganized farm workers—the rural proletariat—was largely neglected. Only the recently established party of the Radical Liberals, one that counted the radical intelligentsia among its voters, took it upon itself to represent the interests of a segment of the poorer rural population, namely, the small holders. When that party formed a minority government in 1913, a close alliance was established between it and that of the Social Democrats, and in 1916, Thorvald Stauning—who was later to become the first Social Democratic prime minister—was appointed to a ministerial post.

Although that event may seem mundane, it reflected the substantial power of the growing labor force. The Radical Liberals had needed the support of the Social Democrats, and together they adopted a policy of wage and price regulations that was intended to keep the government in control of the national economy during the chaotic years of the First World War. To the Social Democrats and Radical Liberals that policy meant, in theory, that the lower-income groups would be protected against the fluctuations of a simple liberalistic economy; to the conservative parties it meant, ominously, that a strong state would be forged to the destruction of a liberalistic society.[4]

During the war Denmark remained neutral, while prospering from its proximity to warring nations that badly needed supplies. That situation inspired extravagant economic speculation and created a special breed of profiteers who—resentful of the interventions of the government—gambled on wild investments. As Nexø's retrospective work *In an Age of Iron* shows, fortunes were quickly made and lost.

Labor, however, did not prosper. Wages were not in keeping with the rising prices, and since raw materials necessary for industry failed to arrive as the war intensified, many workers were laid off. The sense of crisis was augmented by the ascent of the Bolshevik regime in Russia, since it seemed possible that ravaged Germany, then clearly losing the war, and even discontented Denmark were ripe for revolution.

The effect of that economically motivated political tension was that Danish workers were polarized. In the press the Social Democrats, who had finally become part of the political establishment, vehemently attacked the Soviet Union, whereas the syndicalists, who opposed the strong participation of a labor party in government—since the unions would then be subject to the state—found the Soviet experiment admirable and were gaining the attention of many uneasy workers. In the year 1918, there were a number of wildcat strikes, as well as some demonstrations that ended in violence and arrests. Behind those actions of protest there were a few new, small leftist parties and organizations that advocated the overthrow of the bourgeois order. Never in modern times had Denmark seemed closer to revolution.

The Social Democrats, nevertheless, prevailed. Since management wanted peace on the postwar labor market in order to ensure stepped-up production, the workers were able to obtain significant wage increases and the eight-hour workday. In the election of 1920, the Social Democrats made considerable gains and became—with forty-two seats—the country's second largest party. Although the next government was formed by the Liberal Party, it was clear that the day of organized labor's national rule was close; in 1923, Stauning became the first Danish Social Democratic prime minister. The Social Democratic Party, which became and remained the nation's strongest party, was to be out of power for only short periods. It was instrumental in planning and establishing the modern welfare state. Although the party would often be ready to cooperate with parties to its right, especially with the Radical Liberal, it quite consistently refused to form alliances with parties to its left. As a result, those who deplored the reformist line of the Social Democrats were to find that the party constantly discredited itself by giving way to bourgeois ideology.

Nexø had sporadically favored the camp to the left of the Social Democrats, and although he had periods of reconciliation with the party, after the events of 1918 he never trusted its leaders. His fictionalized memoirs, *Morten the Red,* offer in minute detail a record of the compromises of the Social Democrats that gradually turned him against the party. Nexø, who retained his identification with the class from which he had risen, could not forgive the Social Democrats for three betrayals: (1) that in their progress they had left the very poor behind to form a new proletariat; (2) that they had turned out to be opportunistic and, in spite of their rhetoric, adopted bourgeois political measures; and eventually, (3) that they had refused to recognize the Soviet Union as the ideal socialistic state.

The remainder of Nexø's life does not need to be outlined politically but can be treated more fittingly in a biographical sketch. It suffices to add that Nexø watched the international political scene closely and wrote polemically and spoke passionately against those political forces and historical events that threatened his vision of an ideal society. He deplored the rise of fascism; he castigated the Social Democrats for their less than vigilant attitude toward the fascists; and eventually, he lashed out at Western hostility toward the Soviet Union after the Second World War.

Nexø's Life and Career

Martin Andersen Nexø had firsthand insight into the ways in which the poor—whether they lived in the country or in the city—eked out an existence.[5] He was born in a slum district of Copenhagen, and although his parents, Mathilde and Hans Jørgen Andersen, soon moved to a healthier neighborhood, the boy's early years were not easy. His father, a stonemason from the island of Bornholm,[6] was a hard worker, but one prone to spending his money in taverns; thus, Nexø's mother, an undauntedly brave woman, often had to support the family.

In 1877, the family moved to Nexø, a tiny, old-fashioned, coastal town on Bornholm. There, the family's economic circumstances improved somewhat. The internal family situation, however, remained unaltered, and as before, the three surviving children sought shelter with their mother. It is hardly surprising that Nexø praises the endurance of the hardworking women of the poor throughout his works or that such women became a symbol in his works of the best qualities within the lower classes.

Martin received some rudimentary education, but as soon as he was old enough, he had to help his father in the quarry or tend cattle in the fields. True to custom, he left home after his confirmation and started work as a farm hand. Since he was a sickly boy, the hard physical labor of farming exceeded his strength, and instead he sought to become an artisan. In 1884, he apprenticed himself to a shoemaker in Rønne, the island's largest town. Although he found the work boring and his six years in Rønne to be lonely ones, he fortunately discovered the vast world of books and a small circle of people—inspired by the Grundtvigian folk-high-school movement—in which such authors as Bjørnstjerne Bjørnson and Henrik Ibsen were eagerly debated.[7] The gifted Martin was slowly acquiring a taste for education, and in 1891, he eagerly accepted an opportunity to attend the island's rather mediocre folk high school.

In those years socialistic ideas and rumors of labor unrest reached even the backwater of Rønne, where the old artisans fearfully and helplessly saw their crafts being threatened by industrially produced goods. During a summer vacation from the school, Martin worked as a mason's helper and encountered a German glazier, who told rousing tales of battles between workers' organizations and industrialists. As the young German was about to leave, he admonished Martin never, upon becoming an author, to forget the plight of the proletariat.

That exhortation must have seemed strange to Martin, for he merely wanted to become a teacher. Having been given some financial support, he went to Askov on the Danish mainland of Jutland. Askov was the flagship of the thriving folk-high-school movement, and in a sense, it became the young man's university. Martin delighted in the excellent teaching at Askov, and although he never shared in the school's Christian idealism and even actively reacted against it, he remained forever grateful to the folk-high-school movement for the role it played in his life. In the gruff voice of the later socialist rang the rhetoric of the folk high school, and in his way, Nexø continued to work in the spirit of the movement: he saw himself as an educator who would bring light to the people.[8]

In 1893, after two years at Askov, Martin obtained a teaching position in Odense, but owing to illness—first diagnosed as pneumonia and then as tuberculosis—his life suddenly took a different direction. With financial backing from various individuals, he was able to leave for Italy in order to regain his health. He was to help earn his way by writing travel letters to Danish newspapers.[9] When at Askov he had written for the school paper, and later he not only had published an article on Bornholm and some poems but had even practiced within the genre of travel chronicles by sending to a Norwegian newspaper a false, but lively, account of a supposed trip to Australia.[10] It seems that the former farm hand and cobbler had begun to imagine having a career as a writer, and it was then that he added "Nexø" to his name.[11]

Nexø's travels in Italy and Spain—from December, 1894, to June, 1896—revived his health and spirits. Although he had to endure long waits for money from home, he was a joyful vagabond. His splendid and vivid articles indicate that his stay in southern Europe had a major impact on his life: in Spain he encountered the proletariat anew and deeply admired its stubborn optimism in the face of suffering and oppression. Nexø's first journey abroad was both a catalyst and a homecoming, for it renewed his solidarity with the classes he, as a budding author, had left behind.

From Nexø's return to Denmark until the year 1901, he held several teaching positions; then, at the age of thirty-two, he made up his mind to live by his pen alone. Since he had married by then and had a family to support, it was a rather daring decision, even though he already had some books to his credit. One of them, completed shortly after his return from Spain, was the collection of short stories *Shadows* (*Skygger*, 1898).

The stories composed at that time fluctuate in choice of style and subject matter. Some of the texts, which are in the vein of the so-called "decadent" literature of the 1890's, use Naturalistic detail to record a favorite theme: the process of mental deterioration. It is highly likely that Nexø was influenced in his own such writing by his friend and fellow writer Jakob Hansen (1868-1909), who was deeply infatuated with Nietzsche.[12] *Shadows* also contains texts, however, that amply suggest the path Nexø's mature works were to take. The famous story "The Lottery-Swede" ("Lotterisvensken"), as well as poignant glimpses into the plight of the Spanish proletariat, not only give a disturbing insight into the degradation and destructiveness of poverty but also distinctly place the blame for such conditions on the class system. Nexø, as Børge Houmann maintains, may not have analyzed and understood the nature of capitalism nor have advocated socialism as a remedy against oppression, but in *Shadows* he gave vent to both a righteous anger and a revolutionary fervor.[13]

If a common denominator can be found for *Shadows* and Nexø's following works, it is that—much like the works of the radical intelligentsia of the 1890's—they took swipes at the dictums and morality of the bourgeoisie. The young author fared better when he relied upon personal experience, rather than upon literary convention, and his two collections of short stories called *From the Earth* (*Muldskud,* 1900 and 1905) contain tersely brilliant studies of the extraordinary fates that he remembered from Bornholm.

Nexø was becoming more comfortable with his craft, and his novel *Waste* (*Dryss,* 1902) showed that he had also learned to handle the longer narrative form. *Waste* tends to be overlooked by critics, who find it decadent and relegate it to *fin-de-siècle* literature. Although *Waste* revels in the egocentricity and defeatism of the age, it is also a well composed and angry book, the sheer verbal energy of which suggests an authorial will to transcend the cultural fatigue of the radical intelligentsia.

It was to that anti-bourgeois segment of society that Nexø felt closest during his early years as an author, and it was to that group that Jakob Hansen and such socially committed young writers as Jeppe Aakjær (1866-1930) and Johan Skjoldborg (1861-1936) belonged. Although, many years later, Nexø characterized that period of his life as one of confusion, he saw *Waste* as having been a liberating transition, for "through that book on sickly individualism (egoism), I had found the common, natural being: the worker, the proletarian."[14]

A testimony to that exuviation is *Days in the Sun* (*Soldage,* 1903), in which Nexø records the journey that he and his wife took in 1902-03 to retrace the steps of his first trip abroad.[15] As Børge Houmann has pointed out, in Spain Nexø recognized and thereafter retained a heartfelt sympathy for the anarchists' deep-seated suspicion of authority, an attitude he knew well from the common peasantry of Bornholm.[16] Nexø was at last ready to confirm his solidarity with the proletariat.

The novel *Pelle the Conqueror* brought Nexø and the Social Democrats closer together. Houmann points out that, when Nexø started his ambitious tetralogy about the industrial proletariat's struggles and success, he turned his attention for the first time to the conflict between organized labor and management, the battleground of the Social Democrats.[17] The hero of the novel, Pelle, a victorious labor organizer, was a symbolic embodiment of the labor movement's hopes and dreams.

Although Nexø had declared that he wrote as a proletarian revolutionary—and although he had prophesied, after the *Potemkin* incident in 1905, that one day the red flag would fly over Europe—*Pelle the Conqueror* was not a revolutionary novel.[18] Pelle became a Social Democrat, for in spite of his anarchistic leanings, he worked within the system and shunned violence as a means of change.

Pelle the Conqueror was quite well received, and its author soon became a celebrity on the party's lecture circuit. The novel was successfully serialized in numerous Social Democratic newspapers, at first in Germany and then in Denmark. Nexø's rise to international fame had begun.

Nexø had become a Social Democrat in 1910. The party he joined was led by a generation who had modeled it along reformist lines. Although Nexø had little in common with the leaders of the party, he vested his belief in the Social Democratic masses both at home and abroad and hoped that the various workers' parties would ensure world peace. He was thus deeply disillusioned when the German Social Democrats, upon the declaration of war in 1914, became intensely nationalistic and when the editors of the famous satirical magazine *Simplicissimus* even urged him publicly to side with the German people. Nexø, who liked Germany, sadly refused; four and a half years passed before another contribution by Nexøappeared in *Simplicissimus*.[19]

Nexø nevertheless continued to visit Germany during the war, and as a loyal Social Democrat, he sent home optimistic bulletins. As the war was drawing toward its painful close, however, he grew increasingly ill at ease as a mouthpiece for the Social Democrats. His speeches never dealt with the nitty-gritty of party issues but rather painted vistas of a glorious future for the masses. The intolerance of Stauning and other Danish leaders toward those who broke with party discipline undoubtedly vexed Nexø, and in a draft for a speech in behalf of some rebels he grumbled that "respect for the law must have its limits."[20]

The events of 1918 changed Nexø's life. He was angered by the vicious attitude of the Social Democrats toward the syndicalists, and on November 19, he sent a sum of money in support of the jailed leaders of the Workers' Socialist Party. Since the act was touted in that party's paper, it called down upon him the wrath of the Social Democrats. Nexø retaliated by renouncing his membership in the party.

During those years Nexø wrote and published *Ditte, Humanity's Child*. Its vision, in comparison with that of *Pelle the Conqueror*, is a dark one, since Nexø focuses on those of the poor whom the Social Democrats had betrayed. The book's suffering protagonist is a proletarian woman, who at the age of twenty-five dies, completely worn out by inhuman toil. The novel was the second installment in Nexø's grand plan for a trilogy on the Danish worker. Pelle, the hero of *Pelle the Conqueror*, the first part of that overall trilogy, is barely mentioned in *Ditte, Humanity's Child*. When he is, he is shrugged off as a mere party loyalist by his former friend Morten, a writer of proletarian novels. Even in the earlier work there were indications, as the novel approached its joyful conclusion, that Nexø was trying to create a distance between himself and Pelle; in *Ditte, Humanity's Child* Morten is clearly intended to be Nexø's mouthpiece.

Ditte, Humanity's Child is generally recognized as being a second masterpiece. Although *Pelle the Conqueror* brought Nexø glory, *Ditte, Humanity's Child* did little to alleviate his drastically altered situation at the end of the war. He had become estranged from the Social Democrats and, more importantly, also from the people about whom he wrote. He was a successful writer and a member of the literary establishment; thus, no matter how well he served his beloved masses by his pen, he had become separated from them.[21] When one reads the third part of the planned trilogy, *Morten the Red*, which encompasses those pre- and postwar years, one gains the nagging feeling that Nexø had become a lonely man, a man with numerous acquaintances and many correspondents but few close friends. His political disappointments, feeling of isolation, and marital crises are depicted in unpleasant and unrelenting detail in *Morten the Red*. In 1913, he was divorced and remarried, but in 1924, that marriage was also dissolved. It, too, became part of Nexø's fictional memoirs.

The disillusionment with the Social Democrats that colors *Ditte, Humanity's Child* was undoubtedly a result of the events of 1918. In many ways that year was a milestone in Nexø's life: from then on, he wholeheartedly embraced the Russian Revolution and judged people and movements according to whether they were for or against the Soviet Union. His absolute faith in the Soviet Union may seem amazing, but for Nexø, the October Revolution was a realization of his—and his class's—dream of the rise of the proletariat. First and foremost Nexø let his deep solidarity with the proletariat be his guide; he wanted the lower classes to lead decent lives and to receive the value of their hard work.

That dream was hardly revolutionary and had been espoused by bourgeois political parties as well, but as far as Nexø was concerned, only communism was honestly devoted to that program. Nexø was never—as he happily admitted—a theorist, and his reading in Karl Marx was scant.[22] Therefore, he easily fell into inconsistencies and even doctrinal heresy, but he was undoubtedly more genuinely committed to the improvement of the social conditions of the masses than many a well trained Marxist. Perhaps Nexø's attitude toward the Soviet Union and the goals of communism can be most adequately summed up by suggesting—as Jørgen Aabenhus does—that, to Nexø, the Soviet Union became a symbol of everything that was supportive to peace, to joyful work, to personal happiness, to justice, and to equality.[23] The new Russia was appointed Nexø's Eden, and it was impossible for him to question the governance of that Promised Land.

When, in 1922, Nexø traveled to the Soviet Union, he found a nation in which leaders and masses were close to one another. In Lenin—and later in Stalin—Nexø saw the embodiment of the proletariat, a genius who had preserved his qualities as a member of the common people.[24] Nexø published his exuberant impressions of the new Russia in *Toward the Dawn* (*Mod Dagningen*, 1923), a book that bourgeois critics greeted coolly, for it depicted the Soviet Union as a nation in which the solutions to seemingly insurmountable problems were sought with joy and courage.

Once Nexø called Marx a prophet or seer, and it was much the same role that the author took upon himself as the years went by.[25] Although he had become a prominent member of the Workers' Socialist Party and later became involved in the struggle between various leftist parties that eventually resulted in the formation of the Danish Communist Party in 1923, he had little taste for the cumbersome details of day-to-day politics.[26]

In 1923, Nexø left Denmark for a seven-year exile in southern Germany, where he put much of his energy and money into establishing a proletarian publishing house that eventually failed.[27] He married Johanna May in 1925 and thus achieved a new stability in his life. He became fairly reconciled with the Danish Social Democrats and wrote for their press—the Communist Party's press in Denmark was then minuscule and thus hardly a forum; in fact, in 1929, the major Social Democratic newspaper arranged the celebration in honor of Nexø's sixtieth birthday.

On that same day, Nexø's new novel, *In an Age of Iron*, appeared. It was a book voicing a relentless criticism of the ruinous economic speculations on the part of the Danish farmer during the years of the First World War. Ironically, the book appeared just prior to the economic catastrophe of 1929.

In 1930, Nexø and his family returned to Denmark and to trouble. In a letter in 1924, he had told a friend:

> I feel just marvelous down here [in Germany]. The proportions are bigger, and people are bigger too. The bourgeoisie here does not treat me like rabble, even though I stand up for the revolutionary proletariat; on the contrary. And although one is not prone to megalomania, it is pleasant to be treated decently. I represent the public consciousness through my production, which expresses the greatest in the age, the movement of the lower classes. Everybody here has a sufficient sense of history not to say, like those at home: "He has written so nicely about the poor that one can't imagine his being a communist."[28]

Whether this statement reflects simple self-esteem or conceit is a moot point, but it does reflect the important fact that Nexø, who felt a proud solidarity with the international proletariat, was prone to making rather undiplomatic remarks about the Danish "duckpond." He riled the nationalistically minded and, of course, all those who remained fearful of the Soviet Union. Actually, owing to crude forms of harassment, Nexø and his family found it necessary to move to Copenhagen from the small provincial town in which they had settled initially.[29]

Although Nexø seemed to have lost a good deal of his standing with the Danish people, he was nevertheless a writer of world renown—a fact that Hitler underscored, after he took power in 1933, by blacklisting Nexø's books—and he became an untiring participant in international movements and conferences for the preservation of peace and for a resistance to fascism. He visited the Soviet Union several times, and in numerous articles and the book *Two Worlds* (*To Verdener*, 1934) he reported with relish the continued social progress in the communist world. To him, the Soviet Union was the only effective bulwark against fascist imperialism; thus, even the Moscow Trials, a part of which he witnessed, could not shake his faith in communism.[30]

In 1937, after he had visited war-torn Spain to attend an anti-fascist authors' conference, he wrote a pamphlet admonishing the Western world to wake up to the threat of a fascist usurpation of power. In his honor the Danish volunteers who enlisted to fight against Franco even called their unit "the Nexø brigade."[31]

During the 1930's, Nexø wrote his remarkable *Memoirs* (*Erindringer*, 1932-39). They were well received by bourgeois critics, who distinguished between Nexø the wonderful writer and Nexø the red politician, an irritating distinction that haunted him for the rest of his life. In 1939, when he published a strong attack on the Finnish government, which he considered to be semi-fascist, many of the admirers of his art turned against him.[32] The Winter War between Finland and Russia was on everybody's mind, and in Scandinavia, sympathy ran heavily in favor of the little nation, valiantly fighting against its gigantic neighbor.

In the torrent of recriminations following upon Nexø's criticism of Finland, he was exposed to abuse and attack. It is informative of the mood of the Danish nation and of the degree of Nexø's unpopularity that a few of the measures suggested took extreme forms. Some gentlemen of the press suggested that the book *auto-da-fé* be revived, and a few cases of burnings of Nexø's works actually took place. Furthermore, in parliament demands were made, albeit unsuccessfully, that Nexø's yearly government subvention be rescinded.[33]

Nexø was *persona non grata*; nonetheless, after Hitler's juggernaut invaded Denmark on April 9, 1940, Nexø's books were again in great demand at the libraries. In 1941, when Hitler sent his war machine against the Soviet Union, the Communists in the occupied countries were interned. Apparently, the Danish police were eager to cooperate with the Nazis and, incredible as it seems, arrested a much larger number of people than that demanded by the German authorities. Among those unwarrantedly detained was the seventy-one-year-old Nexø.[34]

Nexø protested, even to the attorney general. He met only silence. Three months later he was released, but his earlier position as *persona non grata* was then made official: it was forbidden to mention him in the press, and his works were not reissued.

The occupation of Denmark gradually grew more repressive, and when the Danish government was cursorily dismissed in August, 1943, the Gestapo arrested many prominent Danes. Although Nexø's name then figured on the internment list, he and his family managed to escape to neutral Sweden.

Late in 1944, Nexø accepted an invitation to visit the Soviet Union; from there, he returned to Denmark after its liberation in May, 1945. During those euphoric first months of peace, praise was lavished on Nexø. Tribute was paid to the old author at a mass meeting in a park in Copenhagen. Among the more than 70,000 Danes gathered were the chieftains of the Social Democratic Party, his old adversaries. Børge Houmann points out that, in that period of reconciliation, the Social Democrats and the Communists were actually cautiously contemplating unification. During those festive days, the nation had high hopes for a future of progress, cooperation, and peace.

According to Houmann, Nexø retained a healthy skepticism toward such optimism, and in his speech to his well-wishers he wryly noted that he did not love Denmark for what it was, but for what it might become.[35]

For a short time Nexø nevertheless was not only accepted but even embraced by the Danish nation. He had become a national symbol of resistance to oppression, and he was made an honorary member of the Danish Authors' Association.[36]

Since the protagonist of this idyll was Martin Andersen Nexø, it could not last. In October, 1945—a week before the first election after the Occupation—the first volume of *Morten the Red* appeared. Although it dealt with the events leading up to the First World War, it could easily be read as an indictment of the compromising spirit of the Social Democrats. Nexø's following publication in December, 1945, only made matters worse, for in *Letters to a Countryman* (*Breve til en Landsmand*) he reiterated his disapproval of the role the Social Democrats had played in the workers' movement and during the Occupation.

Once again public opinion began to turn against Nexø, and when he was awarded a life-long honorarium by the Danish state in April, 1946, protests streamed in. A prominent Danish minister observed bitterly that no Danish author had ever spoken more derogatorily about his native land than had Nexø.[37] The public mood did not improve. The Cold War estranged the Danish Communists from the majority of their countrymen, and in February, 1948, Nexø gained notoriety by defending the Soviet takeover of Czechoslovakia. Soon afterward, when the Danish Authors' Association resolved to protest the Soviet intervention, Nexø resigned from both his honorary and his regular membership in it.

In the Danish press Nexø was ridiculed as a senile old man who, having lost his artistic gifts long ago, now dishonored past public esteem by drifting about among socialist nations while continuing to accept his yearly honorarium from the Danish state. The chorus got louder when, in 1951, Nexø rented a house in Radebeul, a suburb of Dresden in East Germany. The major Danish Social Democratic newspaper hastened to rename him Martin Andersen-Radebeul; the paper intended, of course, to intimate that Nexø's choice of country was close to treason to his native nation. Børge Houmann points out, to set the record straight, that the main reason for Nexø's decision to settle abroad was his poor health and that he intended to spend the warmer seasons in Denmark.[38] In Dresden, Nexø continued to work on the third and final volume of *Morten the Red,* but he died before he could complete it, in 1954.

Nexø's friends Hans Kirk and Børge Houmann edited the unfinished manuscript and issued it under the title *Jeanette* in 1957. Finally, the trilogy that Nexø had dreamt about for years—a trilogy consisting of *Pelle the Conqueror, Ditte, Humanity's Child,* and *Morten the Red*—was completed. Unfortunately, whether one reads the last work as fiction or as memoir, it seems dispirited. Although political events are rendered in minute detail, they do not add up to a clear picture of the age, and unfortunately, the epic quality of the earlier novels is markedly lacking.

Through the years Nexø had grown increasingly furious whenever critics invoked aesthetic criteria in judging his books, but such criteria cannot be omitted—especially since Nexø himself was ready to evaluate proletarian works and the role of the writer on artistic grounds.

In 1906, Nexø wrote his colleague Johan Skjoldborg and thanked him for his most recent novel but added that it was not "artistically" on a par with his earlier production: "Here in *Sara* [1906] you give us too often that conclusion which the reader should reach on his own."[39] That sort of aesthetic advice from the author of *Pelle the Conqueror* is not surprising. Similarly, in a letter to Josef Kjellgren, written in 1944, Nexø admonished his young colleague, "let them [dramatic human destinies] work on the reader, so he in turn is also allowed to build! If you have suggested and sketched your world correctly, he will then construct it in all its details for you—and he is thankful that he is permitted to share the labor. Nothing annoys the competent reader more than being presented with a fully completed work."[40] Curiously enough, since Nexø was then composing *Morten the Red*, it was not a piece of advice that he himself followed.

Although Nexø maintained that he never worked with his style and often reiterated that he preferred practical work to that at his desk, the author's protestations must be taken with a grain of salt. If an author is criticized for allowing tendentiousness to weaken his art, he may become understandably defensive and then take the offensive by declaring himself completely indifferent to aesthetics.[41] Nexø espoused the view that the artist was not an outstanding individual, as he was assumed to be by the dying bourgeois culture, but an exponent of the constructive forces among the masses.

Despite that proclaimed attitude, Nexø was visibly irritated when critics claimed that he was influenced by other authors, such as Zola, Dostoevsky, and Gorky. Nexø emphasized that he read little, in fact, that he had to catch up on reading his supposed models.[42] His inspiration, he pointedly remarked, lay in the experiences of his own life and in that of his class; but since his articles often reveal a knowledge of both classical and contemporary social literature, it seems fair to suggest that, from quite early in his career—ever since the success of "Pelle" had allotted him a public role—Nexø was engaged in projecting an image. That image is of a proletarian who fights with his pen for the cause of his people; thus, it is an image that, although predominantly true, downplays the artist in favor of the crusader. As the years went by, Nexø's impulse increasingly to belittle art eventually became detrimental to his own art.

The name of one accomplished artist—that of Cervantes—could nonetheless have been invoked as an influence upon Nexø without stirring up his wrath. Nexø's article on Cervantes from 1904 suggests that he identified with both the author and the hero of *Don Quixote*.[43]

The impoverished Spanish nobleman knew both the plight of the poor and the reality of persecution, and in Nexø's opinion, "three hundred years ago Cervantes created with his *Don Quixote* the first social novel."[44] It is tempting to suggest that, in the roving knight who was always in quest of a cause, Nexø found a kindred anarchistic spirit. Don Quixote rejected an unsatisfactory reality, and since he was an accomplished dreamer, he fought to create a world that would fulfill those dreams, no matter how foolish they may have seemed. When chastised for setting free the inmates of a prison, he replied, "For me it was sufficient that they were suffering; I did not ask what their crimes were."[45]

For Nexø, *Don Quixote* was a portrayal of the crusading artist. Although Don Quixote might be called a fool, Nexø had nothing against being classed with those whom the establishment scorns as foolish defiers of rules and regulations. In 1934, when Nexø answered an inquiry as to how he had become an author, he cited in his reply, "Yes, how?" ("Ja, hvordan?"), his solidarity with the proletariat as the major impetus to his writing.[46]

The highlight of Nexø's reply is a brief, but marvelous, analysis of Hans Christian Andersen's "Cold Hans" ("Klods Hans," 1855). Nexø reminds his readers that the artist may often appear to be like the seemingly unintelligent child who does not absorb the learning offered by officialdom and who thus must go to a remedial class. Such children tend to find joy in life's discarded odds and ends, and thus they can actually educate themselves quite well. Andersen's Hans is such a fellow; in contrast to his utterly bourgeois brothers, who have absorbed the knowledge proper to society, he overcomes all obstacles and wins the princess. On his way to the castle, he gathers what others consider to be junk: a broken wooden shoe, a dead crow, and handfuls of mud—all of which come in handy at the castle. There, Hans's impertinent responses gain the interest of the rather bored princess, who lustily applauds him when he slings mud at the head bureaucrat.

"The one who drew the best picture of the artist was Hans Christian Andersen—with Clod Hans," stated Nexø; and thus he declared his love for those wise fools who, like Hans and Don Quixote, through their actions challenge and change a repressive society.[47] Both Cervantes and Andersen were consummate artists—as were their heroes—and Nexø identified with them. Nexø would hardly have objected if, when approaching his works, one were to keep in mind Don Quixote's idealism and Hans's irreverence.

Nexø's Vision

Many of Nexø's mature works are filled with an infectious feeling of expectancy toward life. He voiced the optimistic conviction that a healthy culture was just on the brink of replacing one that was outworn but bitterly clinging to its hegemony. Nexø intended his works to be one of the means of impelling that necessary and inevitable transition. In the preface to *Pelle the Conqueror* Nexø unequivocally expresses a simultaneously mundane and lofty vision of the future: "*Pelle the Conqueror* was to be a book about the proletarian—that is, about the human being itself—who naked, equipped only with health and appetite, enrolls in the ranks of life; about the worker's broad strides across the world in his endless, half-unaware wandering toward the light!"[48]

In an examination of the contours of, and the ideological forces behind, Nexø's vision, his choice of genres is important, for he was undoubtedly aware that the use of a given literary form—if only to transform it—was an ideological decision.[49]

Although the older Nexø may not have read much, he had periodically read voraciously in both youth and early manhood. As Houmann suggests, Nexø's acquaintanceship with works of some of the great entertainers of the nineteenth century—Eugene Sue, Fenimore Cooper, Captain Marryatt, Karl May, and Jules Verne—may have given him that sense of plot, even of melodrama, which sometimes fortunately marks and sometimes unfortunately mars his fiction.[50] Nexø's later reading in Ibsen, Bjørnson, and Strindberg may well have sharpened his sense of literature as a forum for the vigorous debate of social problems. As Nexø prepared to become a teacher, he became quite well versed in the Danish classics, and according to a former student, he was an inspiring teacher of older Danish Literature.[51] In short, the proletarian writer had a fairly solid literary ballast.

When Nexø was asked what he intended to accomplish with *Pelle the Conqueror*, he placed the book within the context of literary history as precisely as could any academic critic.[52] Nexø pointed out that most works depicting the fates of heroes had grown increasingly individualistic and pessimistic during the nineteenth century, and he declared that his novel was meant to be an antidote to that development.[53]

Although *Pelle the Conqueror* is meant to be the harbinger of a new consciousness and a new age, the form that Nexø used to present his vision was the traditional one of the nineteenth-century *Bildungsroman*.[54] Through that choice he registered his opposition to the pessimistic novel of his own era, for in the latter—in contrast to the earlier *Bildungsroman*—the hero no longer had the power to determine his own fate. Pelle, however, is still a hero who, through personal growth, finds his rightful position within society.

With *Pelle the Conqueror* Nexø thus employed and transformed a humanistic, bourgeois paradigm and created a socialistic *Bildungsroman*. The book's variance from the traditional genre is, however, noticeable and significant, for the classical *Bildungsroman* tends to be individualistic and static in its view of history, whereas Nexø's novel, with its faith in the social progress of the proletariat, promotes a dynamic view of the historical process. Although such optimism may seem less evident in Nexø's later works, most of them—whether fiction or nonfiction—officially share the same function and outlook.

The reader familiar with the tradition of the novel of *Bildung* will recall that the genre presents the view that existence is basically ordered and meaningful and that the human being who makes the correct choices during life's decisive moments will achieve harmony and fulfillment. In Nexø's *Memoirs,* he firmly asserted that, through his writing, he had tried to combat chaos.[55] Order to Nexø may appear to mean a specific political system, but his vision is based primarily upon a humanitarian and humanistic dream of social and spiritual decency. In a speech delivered in 1913, he emphasized the conviction that proletarian striving is motivated by more than economic demands, since the common people desire human dignity beyond all else.[56] For Nexø, as for such later civil-rights proponents as Mahatma Gandhi and Martin Luther King, a movement of liberation seemed meaningful only if material and spiritual values were fused.

With such lofty dreams of an ideal society, Nexø did not escape being labeled a utopian. The advent of the Soviet Union, which seemed to prove to him that utopia could be a tangible reality, supported his vision of individual and societal *Bildung*.[57] To Nexø, the development in Russia was not an example of extremism, but the natural rise of the long-suffering proletariat. In 1942, when Denmark was occupied by the Nazis, he called Marxism "the golden mean," and in *Morten the Red*, written a few years later, the protagonist informed an incredulous bourgeois radical that "Goethe was the first Marxist."[58] As Børge Houmann insists, Nexø was, at heart, a "socialist-humanist."[59]

Nexø was also a radical rationalist, for his works are a persistent and at times exasperated call to reason. Nexø saw the exploitation by both feudal and capitalistic systems as utterly unreasonable, and he believed that eventually innate reason would triumph over all ignorance and prejudice.[60] Like the educators of the Enlightenment, Nexø basically held that the human being is good by nature and is capable of growing, a belief that could be found in such disparate camps as those of the writers of the bourgeois *Bildungsroman* and writers of anarchist manifestoes.

Not only the preeminence that Nexø gives to actual experience over theory, but also the belief he vests in evolution would seem to echo the Enlightenment. As critic Johan de Mylius has ascertained, in Nexø's adamant rejection of Darwinism he did not deny the concept of evolution, but only the liberalistic version of it, which legitimized the exploitation of the masses.[61] Nexø shared the rationalist's conviction that historical development was bound to carry humanity to hitherto unknown heights of culture.

Although Nexø may be called a utopian writer, he is very firmly grounded in social reality, and his vision, even if it may strain some readers' sense of credibility, is a mundane one that is served by his Realistic technique. It is a very tangible world with very palpable problems that one encounters in Nexø's *oeuvre*. In his anti-individualism Nexø distances himself from both psychological and philosophical pondering, a tendency that may explain why, until recently, scholarship has avoided him.[62]

Such an assessment of Nexø as an author is nonetheless inadequate, since he often, more or less obviously, transcended the mimetic mode of writing. Whether one confronts one of Nexø's works of fiction, an article, or a speech, it becomes strikingly evident that he relies heavily on a mythically inspired rhetoric, sprinkled with a generous quota of metaphors. He readily admitted that, in order to exert control over his amorphous material and bring out the essence of his vision, he had to resort to a symbolic technique.[63] Although Nexø invented symbolism when it was called for, he primarily utilized the symbols that age-old traditions made available to him through oral-formulaic narrative, myth, and the Bible.[64] He was relying on the "literary" heritage of his proletarian milieu.

That usage of inherited elements should not be considered to be merely a technical strategy, for Nexø's *oeuvre* shows that he thought of the world in terms of the mythically charged figures and structures of the narratives that had been for centuries integral to the *almue's* perception of life. In much of Nexø's fiction, from the epic novels to the briefest sketches—and even in many articles and speeches—one finds striking touches of parable, fable, fabliau, and particularly of religious legend and folktale.[65]

The last genre is the embodiment of the dreams and hopes of the proletariat. Innumerable tales relate the severe hardships suffered by some poor youth who, through passing the tests of endurance and ingenuity, earns his or her right to the ultimate social reward: a royal spouse and half the kingdom. The tale captures the poor's desire to rise to incredible social heights and to obtain tangible, material rewards. That desire thus symbolizes the proletariat's dream of *lykke,* that magnificent fortune which repressive social systems had consistently denied it.[66]

Nexø seemingly found the tale quite attractive, in spite of its individualism: one person rises to the pinnacle of success but leaves his or her class behind in its former misery. That traditional view of the tale cannot be dismissed, but it warrants modification, for the final phrase of many a tale, "and then they lived happily ever after," can be seen in a dual light. *They* may refer not only to the happy prince and princess, but also to all the people of the realm, for the former pauper has liberated them from a curse. The kingdom was ruled by evil powers, and rightful authority, usually represented by an old king, was powerless. It may therefore not be farfetched to see the arrival of the protagonist as that of a mythical liberator or savior, who slays a monstrous evil, inherits the realm, and thus grants everlasting happiness to all.

Whether or not such a reading can be applied to the majority of known tales is a moot point in this context, for (as *Pelle the Conqueror,* in particular, suggests) it was Nexø's. Pelle—as well as Poor Per, the hero of several parables and articles—is a rebel with the determination to overcome suppressors.[67] To Nexø, his own tales echoed the folktales' age-old, stubborn protest against suppression.

It may seem startling that in *Pelle the Conqueror* Nexø relied both on the *Bildungs* paradigm, which was bourgeois in origin, and on the folktale, which was, he felt, proletarian in origin. Actually, however, the fusion of the two genres is quite effortless: in the final analysis, the novel of quest seems to derive from the tale of quest. Their structural similarities are striking, and although the tales tend to focus on a material reward, some of them clearly show that the protagonists may earn their material reward only if they have gained that self-knowledge which can be termed maturity.[68] Such tales imply the spiritual dimension that is central to the process of *Bildung*: the actual reward lies in finding one's identity not only as an individual, but also as a social being. Both genres imply the marvelously optimistic message that the enlightened human being is the master of his or her own fate. A similar optimism permeates many of Nexø's works, and only the most doctrinaire Social Realist would object that such mythical aspects detract from Nexø's Realism. In fact, the East German critic Erika Kosmalla praises Nexø for having used, and given a new content to, the religious symbolism of the common people. In the same vein, Georg Lukács finds that Nexø brought a new vigor to literature precisely by relying on the lore of the masses, a lore that was the vessel of their dream of *lykke*.[69]

As a Realistic writer, Nexø intended, of course, to give his readers a glimpse of a utopia—of a life blessed by good fortune—and not surprisingly, he turned to the age-old culture he had left behind. In the *almue*, the common peasantry, who for centuries had tilled the soil, Nexø found a non-individualistic culture that, nonetheless, granted the poverty-stricken individual a profound sense of meaning and satisfaction in life. Although Nexø might deplore the fatalism of that class as a direct hindrance to social progress, he realized that the ability of the poor to resign themselves patiently to hardships enabled them to endure and persevere. Fatalism and optimism were inextricably intertwined, and that union was a guarantee—as Nexø made clear in his *Memoirs*—that the spirit of the class could not be broken.[70]

As Gemzøe has argued, Nexø met modern technological development with suspicion and sought solace and inspiration in the rural past.[71] The older, seasoned protagonist of *Pelle the Conqueror* perceives the city as a monster that entraps the masses that have come to it from the countryside, so he attempts to create a model garden-city with ties to a rural way of life. Although Gemzøe emphasized the prominent role in Nexø's thinking that this culturally time-honored preference for nature over culture played, it must be added that Nexø's ideal was a reconciliation between nature and culture, that is, land tamed and made fruitful by the busy farmer. In Nexø's *Memoirs,* he wrote, "For me the most exquisite kind of activity has always been to work with pickaxe and shovel at a piece of wasteland: to crack stones, tear up thornbushes, transform it into fertile ground. . . . I know nothing more beautiful than a home that has been wrested from the rocks or the heath."[72]

The most explicitly harmonious picture of that past way of life is found in *Pelle the Conqueror*. Pelle and his father, Lasse, visit the latter's cousin, Kalle, who owns a piece of land on the rocky heath of Bornholm. Pelle and Lasse put in long, hard, unsatisfying hours at a feudally run farm, whereas Kalle, his wife, and children joyously cultivate their own land and reap the results of their labor.

It is Kalle's blind old mother-in-law who gives voice to Nexø's mythically ideal vision.[73] As she lies dying, she reminisces about her youth and marriage and, thus, conjures up a world of spontaneity, sensual beauty, and happiness. Her husband would wake her early in the mornings, and together they would delight in the daybreak and make love under the open sky. That remembrance is a testimony to an authentic relationship not only between the sexes, but also between nature and culture, for throughout their life together—in lovemaking as well as in hard, but satisfying, work—those two human beings were at one with a beautiful and bountiful nature.

Perhaps the best term to capture the special quality of those two individuals is that of *homo ludens*.[74] Both wife and husband were mature, hardworking people, but in spite of their toil, they could frolic like children and meet life with an exuberant playfulness that testified to their spiritual strength. After such a fulfilling past, the old woman faces death with complete peace of mind. She entertains no notion of an afterlife but meets the unknown without fear, longing, or sentimentality. In this mythically charged portrayal of a woman of the old culture, Nexø made concrete the ideal, but earthy, human being of his vision.

A reconciliation between nature and culture is both a physical and a spiritual ideal, and that fact is brought home by the story "Good Fortune" ("Lykken," 1907).[75] After a stonecutter meets with an accident, his family seems headed for destitution; but thanks to a newly enacted law, the stonecutter is granted economic compensation and can move from the rocky hills to a fertile valley. As the story closes, the family is happily working its fields.

In spite of the story's stark Realism, "Good Fortune" has a mythical frame of reference. In its first pages a masterful personification of death appears: he seems to be an educated, but spiteful, man who—since the poor do not fear him—harbors a deep antipathy for them and therefore attempts to break their tenacity and will. Death is associated not only with that barren landscape in which the family initially resides, but also with that fatalistic state of mind which refuses to entertain any hope for the future. The latter deadly impulse is defeated by cultural intervention through social legislation; thus, the story in a concrete manner reflects the ancient death to-rebirth pattern.

In "Good Fortune" and in many of Nexø's other works one recognizes a by-no-means unique equation between barren nature and sterile culture. Numerous metaphors suggest that, to Nexø, the wasteland also mirrored a mental and a societal reality, since senseless violence, selfish sexuality, excessive individualism, the lust for power, and the horrors of war—all are as inimical to humanistic culture as that wilderness which always lies ready to claim the cultivated land.

Nexø's depiction of nature, of even the wilderness, may nevertheless have a strongly pantheistic touch or, as Ejnar Thomsen puts it, pan-erotic overtones.[76] Although Nexø had no patience with that barrenness which is cultural in origin, he responded with a mixture of awe and fear to primordial nature, be it nature inimical to humanity, humanity's own urge to violence, or feminine sexuality's supposed tendency toward predacy. The author, who proclaimed that first and foremost his work was meant to create order, was deeply fascinated with that chaos which actually posed a threat to his vision. His ambivalence added texture and vitality to his works but unfortunately waned as the author grew older and increasingly less willing to admit to the possible existence of an insurmountable chaos.

In Nexø's movingly unpretentious introduction to his *Memoirs*, he confessed that his personal attempt at *Bildung* might not have been entirely successful: "When I look back, it seems to me that my life has been a struggle against chaos, an endless combat to shape a somewhat acceptable whole from a heap of odds and ends. . . . My own need to turn over and over various phenomena is deeply connected with my lack of harmony and peace of mind. One cross-examines phenomena in order to find a basis for a middle ground, in desperate attempts to find peace."[77]

The same restlessness and inconclusiveness can also be found in *Morten the Red*; Morten has admitted that he had "much trouble with himself in the long-lasting battle to force his sensations and his way of feeling onto a common human level and to reach that stage where he could incorporate ordinary humanity's longings, hopes, and sufferings within himself and represent them in his works. To him that seemed the highest an author could achieve, and that was exactly why at times he was subject to a feeling of having pitifully failed."[78] Passages like the above, which suggest both the author's and his fictional alter ego's personal uncertainty and even discordance, may be said to recall stages that are past, but such conflicts seem to have been intentionally dismissed, rather than overcome.[79]

In spite of Nexø's undeniable potential for soul-searching, he resisted the impulse.[80] The critics Poul Houe and Jørgen Elbek regret that the author did not live up to his early literary promise for probing into the psyche.[81] But Nexø, like his contemporaries Knut Hamsun (1859-1952) and Johannes V. Jensen (1873-1950), seemingly chose to sustain a healthy extroverted attitude that would prohibit an exploration of the self.[82] In a sense that choice enabled Nexø to create his best known works, but even in these, the limitations that such a choice imposes briefly surface. There are moments in which neither Pelle nor Ditte can deal with inner demons. Although such situations are authorially dismissed as temporary aberrations, their being so quickly glossed over seems to cause them to linger in the mind of the reader. It seems as if Nexø's staunch anti-individualism eventually became directed not only against the bourgeois world, but also against the characters within his own fiction.

Nexø's complexity, often engendered by inconsistency, has been mentioned briefly in the discussion of the nature-culture dichotomy, but his work's other complexities, springing from similar inconsistencies, also deserve attention. In 1918, the author Marie Bregendahl (1867-1940) made the astute observation that Nexø's early works contained more homicides than all Denmark had witnessed during his lifetime.[83] Nexø, who otherwise tended in his speeches to be a spokesman for the use of peaceful means in the social struggle, replied by espousing the view that "revolution means cutting to the roots; one cannot have a revolution and let the old remain."[84] In many of Nexø's short stories and intermittently in his novels, violence is viewed as both necessary and cathartic.

In Nexø's reply to Marie Bregendahl, he states that he "loves people who are absolute" and that "murder, death are merely symbols for not stopping halfway."[85] So they may be, but it is significant that homicidal acts and violent deaths are chosen as objective correlatives for the absolute spirit. Although many savage moments are expressions of social protest, in some cases it seems to be the acts themselves that count, not their results. Nexø often focuses on the kind of mind that, in its peculiar logic, has lost all connection with societal norms and that thus asserts itself through violence.

Nexø's fascination with the grotesque individual fate may call into question his frequently repeated admiration for commonplace humanity.[86] When he conjures up images of workers with their little homes, neat gardens, and happy—and very traditional—family lives, the reader can hardly object to that vision of blissful normality, but at the same time the reader cannot suppress doubts as to its validity. One well understands that an author who has known devastating poverty as well as the curse of liquor in family life might advocate a mundane utopia, yet one wonders whether Nexø, who testified to the human being's reluctance to settle for the ordinary, was not censoring his own writing. To what extent that censorship was consciously or unconsciously imposed is difficult to ascertain, but at times the implied author and the actual author seem undeniably at odds.[87]

That ambivalence is felt most strongly in Nexø's depiction of women, for female sexuality remains veiled in a haze of mystery. He describes both the child and the old woman with touching, unsentimental tenderness, but the sexually tempting woman emerges as an intriguing and an elusive figure. Even Ditte, who—though she experiences a number of sexual relationships—may seem to contradict this statement, is basically the heroine of a mythically charged legend.

Female sexuality, as mentioned earlier, is linked with beautiful, barren—even deadly—nature. Nexø, in keeping with his sense of cultural mission, had to bring such a force under control. His answer to the threat of female sexuality is, unstartlingly, the institution of marriage. That bourgeois institution tames the excessive individualism of sexual desires and gives them cultural direction. Consequently, the woman who refuses to accept the role of the traditional housewife, but who insists however dimly upon realizing her own dreams is given short shrift in Nexø's works. Once again, however, a certain inconsistency sheds an ironic light on Nexø's vision, for some of those doomed women (for example, Marie in *In an Age of Iron*) gain in their independence and frustration a stature that is denied others who gladly live life as appendices to their men. Nexø espouses the virtues of the proverbial "doll house," but the implied author knows better.

Although deciding where the borderline lies between conscious and unconscious self-irony in Nexø's works is nearly impossible, the presence of such self-ironic elements not only supports Børge Houmann's suggestion that Nexø thus gave voice to many of his own personal conflicts, but also compels one to add that many of them remained unresolved.[88] The modern reader may wish that Nexø would have permitted himself more room for an exploration of those psychological and ideological contradictions. Nonetheless, a thorough self-questioning—such as was common among the authors that preceded Nexø—very likely would have weakened not only the infectious optimism and strength of Nexø's vision, but also the epic power of his best narratives. Perhaps the combination in Nexø's works of an overriding authorial single-mindedness with an implied ambivalence is one that will attract both the reader who craves a meaningful, life-giving vision and the reader who demands an *oeuvre* of a dialectical nature.

Nexø, who so ardently wanted to destroy bourgeois myths that were detrimental to the proletariat and who spent most of his life deflating such myths, was himself a powerful mythmaker. He dissolved myths very effectively, but in that very act he created others. By necessity a vision of his scope—happiness for all humanity—requires myth. One may charge that he simultaneously preserved bourgeois—or even pre-bourgeois—myths, but as critics Anker Gemzøe and Aage Rønning have pointed out, a man who was so passionately engaged in the historical struggle of his times could hardly help being held captive by some of the contradictions of his age.[89]

Since Nexø's works are so strongly charged both politically and ideologically, proffered advice as to how he should be read may fall on deaf ears. His prejudices as well as those of his readers may well be prohibitive to an appreciation of a masterly, if flawed, body of works. Readers are nevertheless advised to approach Nexø's *oeuvre* in terms of its simultaneous demythification and mythification of the world.

Notes

1. A number of sources have been used for this section, in particular, vols. XI and XII of *Danmarkshistorie*, ed. John Danstrup and Hal Koch (Copenhagen, 1964-65); Svend Aage Hansen, *Early Industrialization in Denmark* (Copenhagen, 1970); and Gemzøe, *Pelle Erobreren*.

2. Walter Karps, "Labor Movements and Industrial Relations," in *Nordic Democracy*, ed. Erik Allardt et al. (Copenhagen, 1981), pp. 308-23.

3. Gemzøe, *Pelle Erobreren*, pp. 42-44.

4. The Danish term for what here is called Liberal is "Venstre" (left), but the historical process is now making this a right-of-center party, one quite close to the Conservative Party, which has often been its ally in coalitions.

5. Sources for this chapter are mainly the works of Børge Houmann (see the bibliography) and Nexø's memoirs; see Martin Anderson Nexø, *Erindringer*, 2 vols. (Copenhagen, 1945).

6. Bornholm is a small, rocky island (227 square miles) situated in the Baltic Sea, ninety miles from the Danish mainland.

7. A folk high school is not a high school, and it does not offer a formal education leading to a degree. The concept of the *Folkehøjskole* was originated by the theologian and poet Nicolaj Frederik Severin Grundtvig (1783-1872) to ensure youth a culturally oriented, but pragmatic, Christian education. Initially, these schools were attended by young people who would never enter a university or professional school.

8. Børge Houmann, *Martin Andersen Nexø og hans samtid, 1869-1919* (Copenhagen, 1981), pp. 110-13. This volume, the first of a planned three-volume work, will hereafter be referred to as *MAN og samtid*, I.

9. For further information, see the discussion of Nexø's memoirs in chap. 6.

10. Houmann rediscovered this item in *Illustreret Familieblad*, 21 July-29 Sept., 1894, and republished it as *Til og i Australien* (Risskov, 1966).

11. Houmann, *MAN og samtid*, I, 130.

12. Nexø and Jakob Hansen had known each other from childhood, and the latter at times played the role of the younger man's mentor. By the late 1890's, Hansen had established himself as a "decadent" writer; but in 1909, he died from tuberculosis. Nexø had worked tirelessly to raise money for his ailing friend. See Børge Houmann, *Jacob Hansens breve til Martin Andersen Nexø* (Risskov, 1981).

13. Houmann, *MAN og samtid,* I, 159, 203.

14. From an article composed for the proposed publication of a Russian edition of Nexø's works in 1951; rpt. in Houmann, *Omkring Pelle,* p. 60. Unless otherwise indicated, the translations are by the present authors.

15. Houmann, *MAN og samtid,* I, 253-61.

16. Ibid., pp. 260-61.

17. Ibid., pp 302-04.

18. "Det røde Flag," *Verdensspejlet,* No. 42 (1905), p. 658; rpt. in Martin Andersen Nexø, *Taler og Artikler,* ed. Børge Houmann, II (Copenhagen, 1954), 7-9. (If the author's name is not given in subsequent references to articles, the texts are by Nexø.) In April, 1905, the crew of the Russian battleship *Potemkin* rebelled against its officers and took over the ship; undefeated by the tsarists, the ship's crew surrendered to Rumanian authorities ten days later. The *Potemkin* incident achieved symbolic significance in the Soviet Union not only because the crew's rebellion against its oppressors was spontaneous, but also because a number of tsarist troops joined cause with the rebels.

19. Houmann, *MAN og samtid,* I, 409-10.

20. Ibid., p. 362.

21. Helge Rønning, "Martin Andersen Nexø," in vol. I of *Danske digtere i det 20. århundrede,* ed. Torben Brostrøm and Mette Winge, new ed. (Copenhagen, 1980), p. 362.

22. In 1932, Nexø admitted that "of Karl Marx I know only the Communist Manifesto." See Clara Madsen, "The Social Philosophy of Martin Andersen Nexø," *Scandinavian Studies and Notes,* 12 (1932), 9.

23. See Jørgen Aabenhus's postscript to Martin Andersen Nexø, *Vejen mod Lyset* (Copenhagen, 1979), p. 141.

24. Martin Andersen Nexø, *Breve fra Martin Andersen Nexø,* ed. Børge Houmann, III (Copenhagen, 1972), 75. Hereafter referred to as *Breve,* a three-volume work edited by Børge Houmann.

25. See Houmann's commentary in Martin Andersen Nexø, *Breve,* II (Copenhagen, 1971), 13-16.

26. "Lenin," *Land og Folk,* 21 Jan. 1949; rpt. in Martin Andersen Nexø, *Taler og Artikler,* ed. Børge Houmann, III (Copenhagen, 1955), 216-26.

27. See Houmann's commentary in *Breve,* II, 196-98.

28. Ibid., p. 166.

29. Houmann, *Drømmen,* p. 144.

30. "Central-Processen," *Arbejderbladet,* 13 Feb. 1937; rpt. in *Taler og Artikler,* II, 125-29.

31. Martin Andersen Nexø, *Spanien* (Copenhagen, 1937); rpt. in *Taler og Artikler,* III, 130-45.

32. "Omkring Finland," *Arbejderbladet,* 15 Oct. 1939; rpt. in *Taler og Artikler,* II, 183-87.

33. Houmann, *Drømmen,* pp. 66-70.

34. Børge Houmann, *Hædersgaven* (Risskov, 1971), p. 50.

35. Børge Houmann, *Den alt for korte danske sommer* (Risskov, 1978), p. 18.

36. Ibid., pp. 28-30.

37. Ibid., p. 74.

38. Børge Houmann, *Skarntyder og tidsler* (Risskov, 1979), p. 76.

39. Martin Andersen Nexø, *Breve,* ed. Børge Houmann, I (Copenhagen, 1969), 91.

40. *Breve,* III, 205-06.

41. Nexø expresses this though as early as 1906 in a letter to Henrik Pontoppidan; see *Breve,* I, 87-88.

42. "Forbillederne," *Politiken,* 27 Feb. 1905; rpt. in *Taler og Artikler,* III, 7-8.

43. "Cervantes og Don Quijote," *Det nye Aarhundrede,* 2 (1905), 213-22; rpt. in Martin Andersen Nexø, *Taler og Artikler,* ed. Børge Houmann, I (Copenhagen, 1945), 9-17.

44. "Art and the Proletariat," *St. Louis Dispatch,* 9 Dec. 1938. See Houmann, *MAN og samtid,* I, 285.

45. *Taler og Artikler,* I, 16.

46. *Berlingske Tidende. Aften-Avisen,* 30 June 1934; rpt. in *Taler og Artikler,* I, 129-34.

47. *Taler og Artikler,* I, 132.

48. Martin Andersen Nexø, *Pelle Erobreren,* I (Copenhagen, 1974), 5.

49. Lisbet Holst and Knud Wentzel, *Solidaritet og individualitet* (Copenhagen, 1975), pp. 150-95.

50. Houmann, *MAN og samtid,* I, 76-77.

51. Ibid., p. 209.

52. Interview on the Danish Radio, 28 March 1936; rpt. in Houmann, *Omkring Pelle,* pp. 52-54.

53. Ibid., p. 53.

54. Several critics have maintained that the novel structurally and ideologically is patterned on the *Bildung* paradigm. See John Fjord Jensen, "Efter-

skrift" to Nexø's *Pelle Erobreren,* II (Copenhagen, 1965), 521-29; and Aage Henriksen, *Gotisk tid* (Copenhagen, 1971), pp. 187-92.

55. Martin Andersen Nexø, *Erindringer,* I, 9. This vol. contains *Et lille Kræ* (1932) and *Under aaben Himmel* (1935).

56. 6 July 1913; printed in *Politiken* under the title "Fattigper og Fremtiden," 8 July 1913; rpt. in *Taler og Artikler,* III, 52-57.

57. "Hilsen til 21 Aars Dagen," *Arbejderbladet,* 6 Nov. 1938; rpt. in *Taler og Artikler,* I, 169-71.

58. *Breve,* III, 165; and Martin Andersen Nexø, *Morten hin Røde,* II (Copenhagen, 1948), 369.

59. See the Preface, note 9.

60. Ejnar Thomsen, "Martin Andersen Nexø," in vol. I of *Danske Digtere i det 20. Aarhundrede,* ed. Ernst Frandsen and Niels Kaas Johansen (Copenhagen, 1951), pp. 73-98.

61. Johan de Mylius, "Ideologiske mønstre i Pelle Erobreren," *Edda,* 75 (1975), 218-19.

62. Only recently have Western critics begun to subject Nexø's works to the kind of thorough analysis that they had given to authors much younger than Nexø.

63. "*Pelle Erobreren* som selvbiografisk Værk," *Social-Democraten,* 23 May 1925; rpt. in *Taler og Artikler,* III, 80-84; and Houmann, *Omkring Pelle,* pp. 49-52.

64. These genres, passed on orally from generation to generation and easily retold—since they rely on formulae: stock phrases, personae, and plot elements—constitute a rich tradition in Denmark.

65. Martin Andersen Nexø, *Fred og Samarbejde* (Copenhagen, 1936); rpt. in *Taler og Artikler,* III, 109-16. Nexø points out that the dreams of the proletariat have been contained in the folktale since the Middle Ages.

66. Nexø's view of the tale has found support in some recent studies. See Max Lüthi, *Once Upon a Time: On the Nature of Fairy Tales* (Bloomington and London, 1976); and Jack Zipes, *Breaking the Magic Spell* (Austin, 1979).

67. *Taler og Artikler,* III, 112; see note 65.

68. Rudolf J. Jensen and Niels Ingwersen, "Den onde og den gode lykke," *Meddelelser fra Dansklærerforeningen,* No. 2 (1979), pp. 129-45.

69. Erika Kosmalla, "Probleme des Übergangs vom kritischen zum sozialistischen Realismus im Schaffen Martin Andersen Nexø" (Ph.D. diss., Greifswald, 1965); and Georg Lukács, "Dichtung aus der Solidarität," *Tägliche Rundschau,* 9 April 1947; rpt. in Houmann, *Omkring Pelle,* pp. 290-94.

70. *Erindringer,* I, 131.

71. Gemzøe, *Pelle Erobreren,* p. 109.

72. Martin Andersen Nexø, *Erindringer,* II, 217. This vol. contains *For Lud og koldt Vand* (1937) and *Vejs Ende* (1939).

73. Martin Andersen Nexø, *Pelle Erobreren* (Copenhagen, 1949). This edition will be used for all further references to the novel.

74. Johan Huizinga, in *Homo Ludens: A Study of the Play Element in Culture* (New York and Evanston, 1970), used the term in his investigation of the presence of play in human behavior.

75. "Lykken," *Illustreret Tidende,* 6 Oct.-8 Dec. 1907; rpt. in Martin Andersen Nexø, *Muldskud. Anden Samling* (Copenhagen, 1924), pp. 199-238.

76. Thomsen, "Martin Andersen Nexø," p. 83.

77. *Erindringer,* I, 11.

78. Martin Andersen Nexø, *Morten hin Røde,* I (Copenhagen, 1945), 190.

79. *Erindringer,* I, 10.

80. *Erindringer,* II, 210.

81. Poul Houe, "Martin Andersen Nexøs ungdomsarbejder," *Nordisk Tidsskrift,* 45 (1969), 420; and Jørgen Elbek, "Martin Andersen Nexø og hans sammenhæng," *Kritik,* 64 (1983), 22-33.

82. As for Jensen's case, see Jørgen Elbek, *Johannes V. Jensen* (Copenhagen, 1966).

83. *Breve,* I, 306.

84. Ibid., p. 305.

85. Ibid.

86. Nexø's admiration for the commonly human is expressed in various formulations throughout his work but is sharply delineated in his review of Richard Wright's *Native Son* (1940); see "Søn af de Sorte," *Ny Dag,* 23 March 1944; rpt. in *Taler og Artikler,* III, 197-201.

87. See Wayne Booth, *The Rhetoric of Fiction* (Chicago and London, 1961). Booth points out the necessity of distinguishing between the author that the text implies and the actual author.

88. Houmann, *MAN og samtid,* I, 435.

89. Gemzøe, *Pelle Erobreren,* pp. 135-37; and Rønning, "Martin Andersen Nexø," pp. 370, 380.

Charlotte Schiander Gray (essay date 1986)

SOURCE: Gray, Charlotte Schiander. "*Lyrical Debut*" In *Klaus Rifbjerg,* pp. 3-12. New York: Greenwood Press, 1986.

[*In the following essay, Gray details Klaus Rifbjerg's life and works, focusing on* Under vejr med mig selv *his first collection of poetry.*]

BIOGRAPHICAL BACKGROUND

Rifbjerg's biography, as such, is very undramatic, but he has an almost uncanny ability for the sensuous reproduction of basic and normal life occurrences so that they continue to offer new insights. And although the available biographical facts themselves are quite limited, Rifbjerg's recollection and recreation of them seem boundless.

Rifbjerg belongs to that subjectivist tradition where the individual feels he can speak with authority only if he speaks on behalf of himself. But as Rifbjerg has pointed out on various occasions, for example in an interview with Per Øhrgaard, "If you really tell about yourself, then what you have in common with others is also bound to appear."[1]

Rifbjerg was born on 15 December 1931 to a middle-class family on Amager, a small island engulfed by suburban Copenhagen. His parents were both school teachers and, because his mother worked, the Rifbjergs had a maid who looked after the boy and whom he felt very close to. Rifbjerg was a latecomer—his parents were in their forties—with two older sisters; and he himself has observed that he had "a very strong attachment to the feminine side of the family."[2] He was also fond of his father, whom he respected greatly, but their relationship was more distant.

As a young schoolboy, Rifbjerg was somewhat sickly and therefore to a certain degree an outsider. At one point he aligned himself with the "strong guy" in class and developed a kind of friendship later reflected in his portrayal of Tore and Janus in *Den kroniske uskyld* (*The Chronic Innocence*; 1958).

World War II Rifbjerg experienced in a basically untraumatic manner partly because the German occupation of Denmark was relatively peaceful and partly because he saw the war through the eyes of a boy, to whom it mainly meant some added color to routine school life. Rifbjerg dealt with this theme in the film *Der var engang en krig* (*Once There Was a War*; 1966). Rifbjerg's school life was disrupted only slightly by the war, and to the schoolboys, school undoubtedly was more real than the war; however, as some descriptions which cover school life—for example, *The Chronic Innocence, Tak for turen* (*Thanks for the Trip*; 1975), and *Drengene* (*The Boys*; 1977), indicate, all the important experiences of the boys seem to have taken place outside of the school walls.

Rifbjerg was brought up in a progressive atmosphere permeated by Danish culture, both traditional and modern. Politically, the family was somewhat to the left of the middle: they subscribed to the Communist daily paper *Land og Folk* (*Country and People*) and the Radical-Liberal *Politiken*; in the former, Rifbjerg read contributions by the noted Communist prose writers Hans Scherfig (1905-79) and Hans Kirk (1898-1962).[3] However, to give a more thorough description of the cultural, social, and political climate in Rifbjerg's home, it would be illuminating to refer to a certain cultural movement in Denmark called *kulturradikalismen* (cultural radicalism). The line of thought and the attitudes inherent in this movement do constitute an integral part of the atmosphere in Rifbjerg's childhood home, and Rifbjerg has often pointed to its influence on him during his formative years as well as later.

The name "cultural radicalism" designates a fairly large, broadly defined movement concerned with humanistic and democratic ideas. It was the concern of the "cultural radicals" to do away with the suppression and distortion of the human being, wherefore some of the major issues came to focus on sexuality, women's rights, child psychology, and pedagogy. Rifbjerg's aunt, his father's sister Sophie Rifbjerg, was, in fact, one of the pioneers in child psychology and its application in institutions and schools.

The historical origin of the movement may be traced back to the so-called modern breakthrough in the 1870s with its anti-Victorian thrust for a less restrictive personal life. The "modern breakthrough" was a literary movement which cultivated the "freedom of the individual"—a concept well known from Henrik Ibsen's (1828-1906) plays—but its aims and discussions reached far beyond the literary Parnassus.[4]

With its revival of cultural radicalism at the end of the 1920s, the movement rested on a much stronger basis than previously because it could now draw arguments and credibility from two new and influential disciplines: psychology and the social sciences. Without aligning itself with any political party, the movement was naturally colored by its particular historical context and was therefore in distinct contrast and opposition to Nazism with its cultural program. The *kulturradikalisme* of the 1930s was launched through the periodical *Kritisk Revy* (*Critical Revue*) in 1926-28. *Kritisk Revy* was first and foremost an architectural periodical promoting functional architecture, a simple, practical architecture designed to serve people's needs without ideological trappings; the contrast to the architecture of Nazi Germany is implicit. An important intellectual contributor to *Kritisk Revy* was the writer Otto Gelsted (1888-1968), but its driving force was the sharp and witty Poul Henningsen (1894-1967).[5] Rifbjerg has often referred admiringly to Poul Henningsen, as in the publication *Denmarkings,* where he writes: "His [Henningsen's] influence may be felt everywhere in Danish culture where imaginativeness, playfulness, ingenuity, and common sense are valued."[6]

Rifbjerg's penchant for literature and theatre naturally manifested itself in gymnasium (senior high school). Some of his favorite Danish writers were the older St. St. Blicher (1782-1848); H. C. Andersen (1805-75); the major writers of the "modern breakthrough": the critic Georg Brandes (1842-1927); J. P. Jacobsen (1847-85); Henrik Pontoppidan (1857-1943); Herman Bang (1857-1912); and the younger Johannes V. Jensen (1873-1950), and Tom Kristensen (1893-1974). He was also interested in both English and American literature and enjoyed reading the modernists James Joyce and T. S. Eliot as well as the realists Ernest Hemingway, Erskine Caldwell, John Steinbeck, and Sinclair Lewis.

In high school there was a union where the always energetic and creative Rifbjerg was very active with school magazines and revues. Here Rifbjerg met several students who were later to become well known in literature and the theatre in Denmark. Villy Sørensen (b. 1929), who was soon to be established as a leading modernist prose writer and essayist, was a little older than Rifbjerg.[7] Jesper Jensen (b. 1931), who was to make a name for himself as a revue writer, was in the class above Rifbjerg, and they wrote revues together while still in high school. Niels Barfoed (b. 1931), who later succeeded Rifbjerg as editor of the literary journal *Vindrosen,* was another comtemporary and friend of Rifbjerg.

Because of his proficiency in English Rifbjerg won a scholarship to go to the United States for one year. After having passed his *studentereksamen* (examination for the school-leaving certificate, which roughly equals passing the first year of college in the United States) in 1950, he spent a year at Princeton University. Rifbjerg's stay in America was to have an impact beyond the academic one. There was the liberating effect of being on one's own and arriving from postwar Europe. The sensuous Rifbjerg was enchanted by the material abundance, but he also became aware of some of the problems, such as racial ones, of the vast, heterogeneous society.

Back in Denmark, Rifbjerg began to study English at the University of Copenhagen, but the old-fashioned, rigid study schedule could hardly have appealed to the vigorous and creative young man. Rifbjerg became a kind of free-lancer who tried out different professions, and he had the good luck that his new wife (Inge Gerner Andersen), who had just become a teacher, could support him. Rifbjerg's initial work with student revues subsequently expanded into bigger revues and drama in general. He also became involved with film and television as an assistant film director and producer at *Laterna Film.*

Finally, he wrote increasingly for the daily paper *Information* about radio, TV, film, and theatre. In 1959 he was employed permanently as a critic by *Politiken,* and from 1959 to 1963 he was coeditor of *Vindrosen* with Villy Sørensen. The collaboration with Sørensen was a significant step towards the introduction and dissemination of modernism in Denmark.

Lyrical Prelude

Klaus Rifbjerg has always shown an almost precognitive sense for what is "up" at any given time, and the warm and humorous tone of his lyrical debut in the 1950s was both innovative and in tune with a budding atmosphere of optimism in Denmark. The dominant lyrical movement at the time was an introverted postwar existentialism centered around the periodical *Heretica* (1848-53). Its major exponents were Ole Wivel (b. 1921), Thorkild Bjørnvig (b. 1918), Erik Knudsen (b. 1922), and Ole Sarvig (1921-81).[8] Rifbjerg felt distant from the spiritualism and the somewhat pompous tone of the *Heretica* poetry, but he also quite simply wanted to make his voice distinct. Rifbjerg here exhibited his flair for correct timing, and the affirmative and new vernacular struck home with Danish readers, who were enjoying a steady growth of prosperity with increased material well-being and social benefits. This atmosphere is reflected in Rifbjerg's gleeful orientation towards everyday life and physical existence.

The life-affirming tone in Rifbjerg's debut *Under vejr med mig selv* (*Getting to Know Myself;* 1956) corresponds to that of other contemporary Danish lyricists. One of them was Frank Jæger (1926-77), whose immediacy and sensuous experience of human and other nature is shared by Rifbjerg.[9] The work of Jens August Schade (1903-78) exhibits a similar enthusiasm about life—especially sexual life.[10] The most prominent common features of the three are perhaps their rejection of "problematic" ideologies, directly reflective introspection, and spiritualization of physical existence. The spontaneous acceptance of one's ordinary life in everyday, familiar surroundings also brings to mind the older Johannes V. Jensen with his early poems *Digte 1906* (*Poems* 1906). Jensen's vivid description—in prose poems—of the concrete here-and-now expresses a similar "modern" position with its materialism and pragmatic honesty. Time difference apart, Jensen's "appetite" and optimism may be viewed as a similar youthful and vital reaction to periods of seeming progress and hope.[11]

In spite of its novelty, *Getting to Know Myself* represents a continuation of much of the existing tradition—especially through the many more or less direct literary allusions with which Rifbjerg places himself among his predecessors. *Getting to Know Myself* means "to be in the process of getting to know oneself"; however, the title should not lead the reader to expect that he or she is faced with a story of development. The protagonist does not change or necessarily become more mature during the period from conception/fetus/birth till marriage. The surprising feature—in contrast to, for example, Henrik Pontoppidan's traditional biography of development—is the fact that the narrator, whether fetus or child, is endowed with the distance and knowledge of the grown-up poet.[12] He is aware of his position in a superior manner and is therefore "Poseur from the start" as he exclaims in the first line of the poem "Fødsel" ("Birth").[13] The poet feels free to assume the position he fancies, such as, for example, that of the fetus speaking in "Foster" (Fetus) from his "lodgings" in his mother's womb: "from where I watch your rising aorta / the fairest philodendron of my life."[14] The perspectives of the fetus and the newborn do not reflect a naturalistic attempt at reconstructing early experiences, but they are the outcome of a modernistic play with the subject matter. The collection may thus partly be approached as an exercise in perspective, where the most subtle flexibility in this respect testifies to the emotional and sensory capability and adaptability of its creator. This deliberately chosen stance is also very useful in that it serves as a mask or cover-up for insecurities or modesty on part of the debutant.

The core of this little semi-autobiographical collection of poems seems to be located in emotions shaped by events and institutions which constitute both our personal and communal life. How to render these banal experiences without being banal? How to avoid stereotypes in the description of the most basic common experiences? How to replace sentimentality with humor and warmth? This litte stanza from "Birth" may serve as an example:

> Brave new world
> I function!
> I shit!
> Soon the gentle moon is lit
> full and opulent over my cradle
> the lamp nudges the darkness
> and someone lovingly lays bunting
> on my damp behind.
>
> (*Selected poems*, p. 7, tr. Alexander Taylor)

The major underlying attitude of the poems may be described as a certain loving disrespect, and it is this attitude which leads to the humorous descriptions of various institutions and stages. The small kindergarten children, who are marched on the Frederiksberg streets (a borough of Copenhagen), have no knowledge of the literature of the 1890s, of spleen and loneliness, and can therefore be used to show Rifbjerg's own jovial distance from the once fashionable self-pity and Weltschmerz in "Børnehave" (Nursery School):

> Johannes Jørgensen
> we have no inkling that you were weeping
> on these villa roads
> our sorrow is not the soul's
> our knot not the Gordian
> but our shoe lace
> which is undone
> and we cannot tie.[15]
>
> (*Getting to Know Myself*, pp. 14-15)

Jack of All Literary Trades

Rifbjerg's work with film scripts and films did not result in any significant films, and its importance possibly lies in its impact on his writing, which contains many examples of film techniques. The one film that deserves mention is *Weekend* (1962). By international standards it is somewhat amateurish and unsophisticated, but it does contain a memorable portrayal of the almost ritualistic Sunday lunch, which is conveyed effectively by a slow-moving and persistent camera. Rifbjerg has many times portrayed the Danish food cult—those sumptuous Sunday luncheons, the traditional Christmas eating—as well as the whole Danish concept of coziness (*hygge*), which often serves as a substitute function or as make-believe protection from an unpredictable world. With the emergence of TV, Rifbjerg began writing TV scripts, and he has probably reached a wider audience through that popular medium than through his more "demanding" prose and poetry.

When Rifbjerg and his co-writers (mainly Jesper Jensen) began to write revues, their primary aim was to entertain and amuse.[16] However, as the revue genre soon revealed its potential for the satirical and the political, and in tune with the trends of the times, the authors were not slow in utilizing these possibilities. They endowed their revues with a more serious and committed content so that they came to stand as an alternative to empty shows of glamour or the more commercial sexual revues. To Rifbjerg at the time, student variety shows like *Gris på gaflen* (*Pork on the Fork*; 1962) represented not only an alternative to the existing revues but also a way out of the deadlock of the Danish drama in general. In his "Tanker om teatret" ("Thoughts on the Theatre"), he suggests "that there is a way from the 'unpretentious' and 'entertaining' to the 'serious drama' through the revue."[17] The drama in Denmark had, according to Rifbjerg, suffocated from a lack of contact with contemporary life, and it could now become the role of the revue to establish contact between the fictive play and so-called real life. Rifbjerg still retains his predilection for the revue, so full of potential for a writer who wants to break down barriers and communicate in a direct manner. Considering the traditional popularity of the revue as an art form in Denmark, Rifbjerg may yet have a major success with it.

The revue as an art form is, of course, fundamentally different from modernist lyrics—a fact which might lead one to overlook the underlying similarity of themes with Rifbjerg's simultaneously written modernist poems. *Camouflage* was published in 1961, *Portræt* (*Portrait*) in 1963, and *Boi-i-ing '64* in 1964. The similarity is especially obvious with the revue *Diskret ophold* (*Discreet Stay*; 1964), coauthored with Jesper Jensen, which deals with how people avoid facing up to reality and how they guard themselves behind customary behavior and clichés. *Discreet Stay* represents a different angle and not a different theme from that of *Camouflage,* where the author merely tries in a linguistically radical way to break through these same conventional and traditional barriers himself.

Udviklinger (*Developments*; 1965), which became a success on the stage, is Rifbjerg's first independently written play; however, its technique and style point to the same openness, and the "sliding" identities of the characters are similar to those in *Discreet Stay*. It differs from the revue in being less polemical and less moralizing. The structure of the play is meant to underscore how reality may be multilayered, ambiguous, and much more complicated than it seems. The plot, which deals with erotic and marital complications, is shaped from situations which alternate between the actors' private lives and their rehearsal of a play.

Developments is a drama about love and its effect, for example, its power to transform a person. Although executed with charm and vitality, the theme is somewhat unconvincing because the lack of firm identities and the unreality surrounding these identities undermine the purpose of this potential power. According to the play, love involves change and creativity, but change per se is meaningless if the playwright has given scant indication of the specific content. It may thus be said that Rifbjerg's predilection for dynamics here unfolds itself at the cost of more concrete issues; in this manner dynamics may turn into running in place.

His next play, *Hvad en mand har brug for* (*What a Man Needs*; 1966), exhibits a combination of identity problems and concern about the role of art which is characteristic of Rifbjerg. In this case a man who is in search of the meaning of his life turns to the theatre to find an answer. John has apparently obtained all that he thought would make him happy: "an education, a wife, children, a car, a mistress, a dog, success." The mere enumeration of these "objects" reveals the reification of the protagonist and the type of problem dealt with in the play. However, it is not the authors's intent to provide subtle psychological and philosophical analysis of the consumer society; rather, he seems to want merely to stage the problems and illuminate them from different angles. The subject is presented spontaneously, and the ending is left open, whereby the whole play assumes a sketch-like character. This kind of drama is, of course, very different from the traditional classic and naturalistic play with its firmly structured themes, beginning, and end—where conflicts are introduced, climax, and are resolved. Rifbjerg's play reflects the condition of modern man through its lack of a cohesive thematic structure and through its implicit assertion that our lives cannot be rendered in terms of questions that can be answered.

John does not discover a meaning, and yet, the ending provides a kind of catharsis through a lift of atmosphere where everybody winds up dancing and singing. It may be argued that the burlesque ending to the preceding "problem drama" not only leads to an underestimation of the previous conflict, but suppresses it; however, this point must not be overemphasized, as the play is meant to be lighthearted. As a "singing drama," it approaches the problems from a humorous angle, and here the theatrical presentation is instrumental in that it serves to publicize and collectivize private life and emotions, thereby establishing the distance needed for a more humorous and accepting attitude.

The theatre possesses no magic remedy for solutions, but it is functional insofar as it serves to articulate the life and conditions of Rifbjerg and his contemporaries. The basic content and substance of life cannot be changed, but its various aspects and components can be pointed out and seen in motion and interaction. Life is movement, as John finally realizes—in accordance with the insight deduced from "Frihavnen" ("The Freeport") in *Konfrontation* (*Confrontation*; 1960)—and this insight is sufficient to change his attitude from negative to positive. John's discovery and transformation fit well with the jovial revue-related genre, and the readers' or listeners' reactions will be in accordance with this particular art form. A similar problem is treated differently in the novelistic counterpart to *What a Man Needs: Operaelskeren* (*The Opera Lover*; 1966). This lyrical novel, whose web of images and connotative symbols aptly illustrates the subtlety and complexity of inner conflicts, represents an alternative to the theatre play which presents the subject in a more external manner through dialogue and mimetic presentation. It is interesting to see how essentially the same subject—"what a man needs," as the play puts it in a rather categorical manner—is transformed, through various media and approaches, into a different artistic formulation. It is not the "content" so much as the genre and the style which are the more decisive factors with regard to the final product.

Notes

1. Per Øhrgaard, *Klaus Rifbjerg* (Copenhagen: Gyldendal, 1977), p. 127.
2. Ibid., p. 104.

3. Hans Scherfig is especially known for his novel *Den forsvundne fuldmægtig* (*The Missing Clerk*; 1938) and *Det forsømte forår* (*Stolen Spring*; 1940), which are critical of society, in particular the school system, in a humorous way. Hans Kirk's best-known novel is *Fiskerne* (*The Fishermen*; 1928), a so-called collective novel about the social life and ideologies of fishermen as a group.

4. The harbinger of the "modern breakthrough" was the Danish critic Georg Brandes with his famous lectures *Main Currents in Nineteenth Century Literature*.

5. Poul Henningsen was an architect and writer best known for his satirical and political songs, many of which were from revues. Otto Gelsted was a poet and critic, one of the most important figures among the "cultural radicals," whose leaning towards socialism made him critical of modernism.

6. *Denmarkings, Danish Literature Today,* ed. Torben Brostrøm (Copenhagen: The Danish Institute, 1982), p. 4.

7. See the description of modernism in Chapter 3. Villy Sørensen made his debut in 1953 with a collection of modernist short stories, *Sære Historier* (1953, *Strange Stories* 1956). He is not only an original fiction writer but a significant critic and philosopher whose writings draw inspiration from Freud, Kierkegaard, and Marx. See translations of Sørensen in Carol L. Schroeder, *A Bibliography of Danish Literature in English Translation 1950-1980* (Copenhagen: The Danish Institute, 1979).

8. Ole Wivel's breakthrough as a poet came with *Fiskens Tegn* (*The Sign of the Fish*; 1948). As a publisher (at Gyldendal), Wivel has promoted both Danish and foreign literature. Thorkild Bjørnvig is a significant poet (debut: *Stjærnen bag Gavlen* [*The Star Behind the Gable*], 1947) who is also very influential as a humanistic critic and essayist. Erik Knudsen, whose first publication was *Dobbelte Dage* (*Double Days*; 1945), left *Heretica* and joined *Dialog*, reflecting his growing inclination towards the left and his commitment to write in a more politically relevant manner. Ole Sarvig, who made his debut with *Grønne Digte* (*Green Poems*; 1943), created poetry that was both visual (inspired by modernist painting) and metaphysical. In English: *Late Day*, tr. Sarvig and Alexander Taylor (Willimantic, Conn.: Curbstone Press, 1976).

9. Frank Jæger made his debut in 1948 with the collection *Dydige Digte* (*Virtuous Poems*), which was followed by several popular collections of poems.

10. Jens August Schade's production encompasses lyrics as well as prose and is characterized by its vitality, fantasy, and so-called cosmological Eros.

11. Johannes V. Jensen is one of the major figures in early twentieth century literature in Denmark. Classic works are *Kongens fald* (1900-1901, *Fall of the King* 1933), a lyrical, historical novel; many of his so-called *Myter* (*Myths*); and many of his poems, notably *Digte 1906* (*Poems* 1906). See Schroeder, *A Bibliography*. See also S. Rossel, *J. V. Jensen,* TWAS No. 718 (Boston: Twayne Publishers, 1984).

12. Henrik Pontoppidan's autobiography is called *Underveis til mig selv* (*Underway to Myself*; 1943). Pontoppidan is Denmark's most significant classic realist and a Nobel laureate whose major work is *Lykke-Per* (*Lucky Per*; 1898-1904). See P. M. Mitchell, *Henrik Pontoppidan,* TWAS No. 524 (Boston: Twayne Publishers, 1979).

13. Klaus Rifbjerg, *Selected Poems,* tr. Alexander Taylor and Nadia Christensen (Willimantic, Conn.: Curbstone Press, 1976), p. 6. Rifbjerg uses "poseur" not so much in the English sense of being insincere but referring to the narrator's own choice of striking stances.

14. Klaus Rifbjerg, *Under vejr med mig selv* (Copenhagen: Det Schønbergske forlag, 1956), p. 9.

15. Johannes Jørgensen (1866-1956) was one of the poets of the 1890s influenced by French symbolism. He converted to Catholicism in 1896 and became a well-known hagiographer. See W. Glyn Jones, *Johannes Jørgensen.* TWAS No. 70 (Boston: Twayne Publishers, 1969). See also Leif Sjöberg and Niels Lyhne Jensen, "Early Scandinavian Symbolism," in *The Symbolist Movement in the Literature of European Languages,* ed. Anna Balakian (Budapest: Akadémiai Kiádo, 1983), pp. 588-90.

16. Jesper Jensen has continued to be politically engaged with texts for political songs, as in the popular recording "Den første maj" (The First of May; 1971).

17. Klaus Rifbjerg, *Rif. Klaus Rifbjerg-Journalistik,* ed. Hanne Marie Svendsen (Copenhagen: Gyldendal, 1967), p. 174.

Charlotte Schiander Gray (essay date 1986)

SOURCE: Gray, Charlotte Schiander. "The Author and His Work." In *Klaus Rifbjerg,* pp. 75-90. New York: Greenwood Press, 1986.

[*In the following essay, Gray discusses Klaus Rifbjerg's experimental style in his memoirs, short stories, and novels.*]

Travelling and Maturing

Stages of crisis, and of potentially renewed insight and development, occur especially when a character is about to enter adulthood or when he is assessing his status as an adult approaching middle age. The travel descriptions follow the same biological-psychological pattern. For example, Leif in *Leif the Happy, Jr.* (1971), is confronted with a problem similar to that of Janus and Tore in *The Chronic Innocence,* while Misse, in *The Road Along Which,* shares problems with the other traveller, Anna from *Anna (I) Anna.* The schoolboys in *Thanks for the Trip* are related to those in *The Chronic Innocence.* Geographically, Leif is travelling home to Denmark from New York; mentally, he is travelling towards adulthood, and, quite concretely, he is trying to rid himself of his state of virginity. He meets the upper-middle-class girl Ulla, but the sexy-looking American girl he encounters might have been a more efficient choice for the purpose.

Travel offers opportunities, but Leif lacks initiative; and when he finally visits Ulla in Stockholm, the trip is over—not only in the geographical sense. The vitality promoted by the journey is now gone, and their relationship becomes a mere shadow of the past. The novel terminates with Leif's final observation: "She had begun to use powder. But that was probably because it was winter. Then I left."¹ Ulla is wearing a mask; she has been reduced to mere appearance—like a persona—no longer is she a full person open to change and development.

Leif's fascination with Ulla is part of his attraction to the sophisticated first class when he is himself travelling only tourist class. The whole ship is a miniature reproduction of the real social world, as Leif discovers once he ventures down into the machine room, where he is taken aback by the overpowering smells and sounds. The fight there between two workers underscores the rough physical aspect of the working class. Leif's aversion to this class is combined with a racist ambiguity towards black people. There is a tragic incident on the boat where a black person is shot by a drunken Scandinavian—again a symbolic event reflecting the society Leif is part of.

Leif's racist bent naturally emerges in his attitude towards females. He is put off by the black man because of his supposedly purely physical being; the black woman he can "accept," not because she is not physical but because she is perceived as a purely sexual object. Leif's relationship with females in general reveals on obvious dichotomy between what he sees as a lower physical and sexual sphere and a higher, more spiritual or sophisticated sphere. The relationship with Ulla is determined by this split attitude, and the novel as a whole thereby offers a new perspective on the old problem of "chronic innocence." Leif is another chronic innocent in his unrecognized fear of the physical; unfortunately, the events on the steamer home from the United States only seem to cement this fear. The journey is not a trip out into the world but a homecoming to his parents and a seemingly passion-free relationship. No wonder Leif is bothered by the connotations of his name: he himself is no true explorer.

The Author and His Reader

After yet another approach to the travel with the travelogue *Til Spanien* (*To Spain*; 1971), came *Lena Jørgensen, 4 Klintevej, 2650 Hvidovre*, which, like *The Archives,* deals with the "silent majority." However, the focus has been shifted significantly. Whereas *The Archives* stresses how the ordinary man conforms to social conventions in search of security and continuity, *Lena Jørgensen* describes an attempt to reach beyond stifling habit. Where *The Archives* shows how people build up defensive conventions, *Lena Jørgensen* is about the wish to "break through"; and, characteristically, Rifbjerg chooses a female protagonist for this purpose.

Lena, a suburban housewife of forty-five with two children, who is married to a taxi driver, is frustrated by her own inarticulateness. She tries to overcome her failure to communicate by writing a letter to a writer—the "professional communicator." Lena reads newspapers and weeklies but normally not books and only happens to read two of Kjeld Deeners' books. One of them she especially likes because it deals with ordinary people with whom she can identify. She also reads some of Deeners' newspaper articles but is irritated and disappointed by one of them because Deeners here seems superficial and opinionated. Lena has a sharp eye for clichés, and she has found Deeners too good for that. Her note of complaint finally elicits a response from the busy writer, who agrees and yet smoothly disagrees too. Lena learns that it is hard to penetrate the eloquence of a writer but accepts his invitation to a poetry reading. There they meet, and Deeners, who is attracted to his simple but authentic reader, invites her for a beer with his colleagues. In spite of the fact that Lena is an "illiterate" in Deeners' group, she still manages to assert herself, although afterwards she is furious for feeling patronized and manipulated on the one hand, but attracted to the foreign and sophisticated world of the literate on the other.

The description of Lena's milieu and the interaction between its characters is convincing with its everyday details and vernacular, its banality, and its underlying frustrations and longings. The awkward and fragile verbal communication between the characters constitutes the overriding theme, which is sustained through symbolic events. One such symbolic pattern emerges through the recurrence, in various contexts, of the word "hello." In the beginning of the novel Lena's son, Hugo, brings his new taperecorder into the living room to have his parents record on the tape. The resulting silence is awkward, and the father's helpless "hello" still more embarrassing. When the father fails to find any words, he repeats his "hello," which now becomes like a cry for communication. Afterwards, when Hugo's mother hears the two sentences she finally managed to utter, she is struck by the foreign quality of her own voice. The recording of the voices accentuates not only the poverty of communication but also a process of alienation. When a person tries to communicate, does the message undergo a change on its way between sender and receiver? And are the words he or she utters already different from what he or she wanted to express? Or is there even a clearly defined "I" to send a message? In the end, the problem of communication is closely tied to that of identity. Is there an identity if a person cannot express it? Is there an identity regardless of the verbal expression?

Lena's everyday life is profoundly shaken by two events—a structure similar to that of *The Archives,* where "normality" is also interrupted by death and the unexpected. Her best and only girl friend dies from cancer, and she discovers that her brother is a homosexual. When Lena cannot cope with the confused emotions aroused in her, her inarticulateness grows into dumbness. Even before this symbolic illness, she has found her attempt to communicate with Kjeld Deeners ludicrous and has broken off the contact; however, the novel does not end on this realistic although negative note. Lena receives a ticket to the Canary Islands—travel as a way towards change—where she bumps into Kjeld Deeners. He takes her to a bullfight, where she suddenly regains her voice, shouting "no" to the violence. Lena is here confronted with her suppressed emotions about death and sexuality and experiences a kind of catharsis reliving them. She is thus "cured" through the indirect intervention of the writer.

The bullfight scene is captivating but literary, with its manipulation of the bullfight metaphor. Lena's "cure" seems accomplished for the benefit of the writer rather than on Lena's own terms. Towards the end, Lena becomes less convincing as an autonomous protagonist, more like an aspect of the writer Deeners' own projection. She represents Deeners'—and Rifbjerg's—troubled conscience: she is the reader he is trying to reach and cannot save. The ending, in which the symbolic solution transcends realism, represents his wishful thinking.

As realistically as she is portrayed, Lena finally becomes too abstract. From the vantage point of the end, her dialogue with Kjeld Deeners also seems based more on his conflicts as a writer than on hers as a contact-seeking housewife. This vacillation between the realistic and the symbolic also manifests itself in a technical peculiarity. The narrative is predominantly one long monologue by Lena. With its limits and advantages (discussed above in connection with *The Archives*), the story is told through Lena's consciousness. The problem is that the inarticulate Lena is surprisingly eloquent. The narrative extends beyond her ability and range of expression and again points to the all-pervasive author. *Lena Jørgensen* is thus one of the many novels which, for a great part, deals with "author problematic."

Memoirs, Short Stories, and the Experimental Novel

Rifbjerg has experimented with numerous genres and continues to employ them all: plays and TV scripts, essays, short stories, novels, and a novel in cooperation with his listeners. *Dengang det var før* (*The Time When It Was Before*; 1972) is a small collection of autobiographical stories. This kind of story is very close to Rifbjerg's fictional, autobiographically oriented writing, as, for example, the novel *The Boys,* and testifies to how he is always relating to and inspired by his childhood. The stories resemble fiction, with fully developed scenes, events, and atmospheres; but the author is also clearly present as commentator. The memoirs represent an unassuming blend of pleasant and entertaining biographical material and discursive reflection.

The short stories in *Den syende jomfru* (*The Sewing Virgin*), also published in 1972, do not offer anything strikingly new, but they tie in closely with the rest of Rifbjerg's production. These stories deal with puberty and marital problems. Noteworthy are the descriptions of female frustration. Many of the stories relate to *Travellers* in that they take place in foreign countries—hence the subtitle "Ude og hjemme" ("Away and Home"). They have one prominent feature in common with *And Other Stories*: they all revolve around something missing or unsaid, or they demonstrate how an apparently normal surface covers unexpected, often explosive, subconscious content. The title may be explained from this perspective. The so-called sewing virgin, in the short story of the same name, serves as a symbol for the boys' sexual fantasies and longings; the name for the "girl friend" is the poetic expression (sublimation) of one of the boys and thus points to hidden psychological mechanisms. In reality she is a very ordinary girl who becomes conventionally engaged at the end of this long short story. In their fantasy she assumes larger-than-life proportions—she is there and she is not there.

The first short story, "Undervandsbåden" ("The Submarine"), is a marvellous description of some boys who go to see the submarine they have heard about but who instead are confronted with the nudity of one of their mothers. They never find the submarine, but they feel that in a way they did because they experienced something else still more overpowering. The nonexistence of the submarine equals the non-existence of sexual experience; as symbol and fantasy the submarine points towards psychological realities and the future of the boys. The puberty description is connected with World War II, as always in Rifbjerg's writings, and here the symbol of war coincides perfectly with the psychological and sexual one in the submarine.

In "Renovation" ("Thrash Removal") a tennis pro comes across some shit on the locker room floor. His sheltered routine is disturbed by something unfitting and dirty. As in *The Archives,* the unsuspected event breaks through the conventional and smooth surface, indicating unpleasant and repressed underlying layers. Another story, which takes place abroad, describes an alcoholic. This theme again fits the overall pattern of a surface phenomenon hiding unsolved problems.

The marriage stories all deal with developments taking place under seemingly unchanging normal appearances. "Citationstegn" ("Quotation Marks") is a black humor tale of how a wife is suddenly aroused to action by an unsuspecting husband. One night when they are having dinner out—they are on vacation in Spain—he is inspired by his abundant alcoholic intake to make a speech for the rights of wives and the integrity of women in general. He is completely taken aback when his wife suddenly takes him at his word and decides to go home alone. Just as the alcohol has loosened him, his speech in return evokes her repressed feelings and desire to act. The other two marriage stories likewise deal with women who rebel against their marital subjugation. In the context of appearance versus reality, the institution of marriage has become an obvious target.

Rifbjerg not only employs all genres, he also repeatedly tries to create new ones. *Rifbjergs lytterroman* (*Rifbjerg's Listeners' Novel*; 1972) is an experiment in writing a novel in collaboration with readers by telephone and letters: the readers provide suggestions, and the author writes the novel in selective response. The novel, in fact, is a conglomerate including selections of the readers' suggestions and comments by the author. The book is edited, and the accompanying material is therefore selective. Doubtless, the selections have been made with the intention of connecting the novel with the suggestions as closely as possible in order to create a unified, coherent work. However, judging from the overall context of Rifbjerg's works and other sources of comments and criticism, the selections seem central and representative.

The suggestions tend to focus on the content, the ideas, and the plot, while the technical aspects—language, structure, and style—are taken care of by Rifbjerg. The writing conditions have also influenced the form of the novel somewhat. A limited time was allotted on the radio, so that the novel had to be short; and the chapters tend to be fairly independent sequential units with slightly abrupt transitions. If the author of the novel is recognizable, it is obviously because Rifbjerg remains the one with the final say and responsibility. As he comments himself, if another writer had followed the same procedure, the result would have been a completely different work. The writer and not the reader creates the work, and the benefit for the reader, in this case, is mainly instructive.

The other reason that this novel basically fits into Rifbjerg's production as a whole, both thematically and technically, relates to Rifbjerg's particular manner of working as well as with his feeling for and closeness to the prevalent issues and atmosphere of the times. Rifbjerg's novels often have an air of improvisation, with tentative beginnings and open endings; and, undoubtedly, these features contributed to his successful and willing cooperation with the readers. The filmic language, visual approach, and authorial guidance to the reader, which lend the impression of reader and writer embarking on the fictional creation together, constitute a technique apparent throughout Rifbjerg's production.

Naturally, a wide range of themes was suggested, but the major directions were clear. The novel was to deal with ordinary people and comtemporary issues such as the generation gap, political compromise, use of narcotics, and women's liberation. All in all, in the suggestions there was little that was foreign to Rifbjerg, which again underscores how Rifbjerg perceives and reacts in tune with his contemporaries. This consonance, of course, also has to do with the common base of author and readers of a broad, predominantly liberal middle class in a small and very homogeneous culture.

The readers generally agreed on the wish for a happy, light content with a positive ending—possibly activist-oriented. The writing could, for example, be part of an extensive political action involving demonstrations and occupations of various institutions: a truly novel novel. Rifbjerg is sympathetic with these wishes and follows them in his novel, with the significant exception, however, of the activist happenings.

In most of his works and through his personality, Rifbjerg displays a deep-seated preference for the positive; but since he is a realistic writer, many of his novels are written in a more gloomy and problematic vein than his natural predisposition would dictate. Many readers wanted more cheerful reading. Another objection pertained to Rifbjerg's novels being too incomprehensible and inconsequential, again reflecting the gap between the readers' wish for the ideal and the shared reality depicted. As a serious artist, Rifbjerg cannot compromise with this understandable wish for clarity and solutions on the part of the reader. One last reaction—and even aversion—to Rifbjerg, as it appeared in the listeners' comments and suggestions, concerned Rifbjerg's so-called dirty language. Rifbjerg's outspokenness and occasional scatological language in previous works have annoyed and even alienated many readers. Rifbjerg did not go against this advice, even if it was not justifiable.

The plot is not unique as a story per se, but it is interesting to see how a story which naturally tended to branch out in many directions—in response to the variety of suggestions—is technically tied up by the professionally adept but almost too manipulative author in the very last chapter. Apart from this, it is not so much the novel as the composite book as a whole which is of interest to the reader in this case; the whole experiment serves pedagogical ends more than it promotes the creation of a masterpiece.

A rough résumé of the plot will bring out the similarity of theme between this novel and other Rifbjerg novels. In the first chapter, two young people have a rendezvous. Tom is quitting his newspaper job, which he finds too compromising; Dorrit, his girl friend, is also politically aware. In the second chapter, Dorrit's family is described eating dinner. The mother is the familiar worrying housewife (she resembles Solveig in *De beskedne* [*The Modest Ones*]; 1975-76), while the father, the peaceful paterfamilias, is somewhat "compromised" but with liberal inclinations; the sister is seemingly a conventional type. Dorrit and Tom have a quarrel and she reproaches him harshly for being irresolute and perhaps insincere—the strong woman versus the wishy-washy man. In the third chapter, Tom's conflict with the newspaper is brought out into the open. He wants to make a workers' paper; the editor, who is an old socialist, speaks for moderation. Dorrits's sister, Lina, has become pregnant by the doctor, Gustav, a seeming cynic who suggests an abortion. Lina reveals her Christian morality by calling it a sin. The fourth chapter describes the parents, sleepless, in their bed. As with the dining room scene, this family description resembles *The Modest Ones* in atmosphere and content. Simultaneously, Dorrit's young twin brothers are spying at night from the garage roof on the teacher, Johannes, who is on dope; the roof breaks and they come crashing down. In the fifth chapter, the alert twins go to the hospital, and a budding maturity is indicated. Dorrit seeks help from Doctor Gustav for Johannes, who suffers from withdrawal symptoms. It turns out that Lina is there; and in the ensuing conversation, the cynical Gustav reveals the egotism and immaturity of the others. In the sixth chapter, Grumstrup becomes the saving *deus ex machina*—Rifbjerg taking advantage of a character who has been mentioned but not yet fully described. He sees Dorrit and Tom on their way out of the hospital and invites them inside. Grumstrup is an old communist who is now lonely and looking for a cause. He will help Tom but on the condition that he leaves the provincial town with its petty socialism. A growing inclination for Tom by Dorrit is intimated. Lina decides to have her child alone and live as an independent person—again the feminist theme.

The whole novel is somewhat sketchy and episodic, but the separate scenes stand clearly with their convincing dialogues and far-reaching implications. The art of sparse but suggestive descriptions has always been Rifbjerg's forte; but in this case he himself is made even more aware of its usefulness and effectiveness. He returns to the subject a couple of times in his comments, expressing his amazement as to how little is needed for a story to take shape, how sketchy a characterization will suffice for the reader to continue and complete the picture. This discussion is not pursued in the commentary, but the premises for a further investigation as to how our imagination and creative powers work are laid out. The remarks as to how a pattern is set from the very beginning point to a general human tendency towards the archetypal structure. Once a pattern is indicated, people will tend to complete it in the same manner. This pattern, of course, refers to ideas and images: the linguistic completion is still through the medium of language, to a large extent dependent on more individually determined talent.

There is no doubt that the cooperation with the reader was a learning process for Rifbjerg too. He became more aware of mutuality as a prerequisite for the success of a novel; the author's creation comes into being through the acquisition of readers. In connection with this insight, Rifbjerg was able to confirm his views as to what is essential and typical for the novel as a work of art. To him a novel must be ambiguous in the positive sense that it has more than one meaning; it must be multifaceted and rich in its composition and language as compared to merely factual or theoretical writing.

THE AUTHOR AND HIS PROTAGONIST

Brevet til Gerda (*The Letter to Gerda*; 1972) is deceptively unassuming but, in fact, sophisticated and central with regard to technique and authorial questions. The novel displays an interesting blend of realism and modernism—a juxtaposition of the two which also serves as the thematic focus. On the one hand, there is imitation of a common reality, on the other the media-aware artist's writings. The realism is found in the description of ordinary Danish people and culture—somewhat nationalistically. The central figure in this banal Danish landscape is the ladies' hairdresser, Gerda. But like Lena, in *Lena Jørgensen,* she serves to illustrate the author's need to communicate: Gerda becomes the symbol of both the "ordinary" as well as the "immediate" which the author reaches for but will always be distant from because of his function as a self-conscious writer. The modernistic aspect is added by the media-and-language-aware writer who is trying to communicate with Gerda, and results in interesting double-layered language.

The novel does not have much of a plot: or rather leaves the impression of having been improvised with no preconceived idea or structure. The narrative impetus is presented as a man's desire to write and communicate with his second wife. The novel, which is in the familiar monologue form, ends when he finally succeeds in writing a letter to her.

The narrator is a travelling book salesman—the travel theme—who is trying to formulate a letter to his hairdresser wife, Gerda, and who, in his frustration, becomes an obsessional note writer. His marriage to the seemingly complicated Ruth had been unsuccessful: they did not communicate well and failed to find a mutual life style. He now has married the opposite of Ruth: an ordinary, pretty blonde who never thinks an original thought. Not surprisingly, the protagonist also has difficulty in striking the right tone with his new wife. He succeeds with the letter in the very end, but then the letter—surprisingly, but also logically—at the same time becomes a farewell note.

Gerda is one of the "silent majority," unreflective and immediate in her narrow but familiar and protected world. Anything unknown or foreign she rejects even before reflecting on it. Her limitations are obvious, but so are her strengths, most importantly in relation to her husband: her strength is his weakness. Her unperturbed calm and inner balance, her naturalness and integrity represent an unlived, wished-for world for the narrator. Psychologically speaking, she partly represents his shadow life: she is an anima figure.

Like Lena Jørgensen, Åge is attempting to communicate with his spouse. Language is the tool and language is the barrier. The whole novel is a manifestation of the use of language with all its stereotypes as well as original expressions. The point is that this self-conscious attempt to reach immediacy and naturalness through communication is self-defeating: immediacy cannot be achieved through reflection. The more the author works at his formulation, the further away from Gerda he is. Her state of being almost represents a preverbal level and thereby the innocent pre-Fall stage—Rifbjerg's familiar theme of innocence from a linguistic perspective. This is why it makes sense to write a goodbye note in the end—it's her or him. As much as Gerda and what she represents attract him, the union is a symbiosis. She can at most be his ideal contrast and his muse—the novel is a testimony to that—but the irony is that his successful communication means her exit. She has fulfilled her function, which is obliterated with the completion of the artistic product, therefore the goodbye letter.

One of the striking features of this novel is its subtlety and the wide range of implications behind a seemingly simplistic and straightforward narrative structure. The immediate impression of the novel, supported by its cover, which pictures a cannon by the strait of Øresund and a naked blonde looking out over the water, is that of a "popular" novel. But just as the picture emits symbolic massages, the novel is far from simplistic and therefore not what would be termed a popular novel. It deals with the problem of making the ordinary and popular available in artistic form. Åge's attempt to communicate with Gerda is like Rifbjerg's with his readers. The open and outgoing Rifbjerg would like to reach a large section of the populace, but often his novels are hardly "popular" enough for that purpose.

The Faustian novel *R. R.* of 1972 offers a representative description of Rifbjerg's vision of modern man, while it also displays significant aspects of his attitudes, as an author, towards his own fiction. The two subjects are intricately connected, for Rifbjerg's novels focus on the human being; and his artistic creation, therefore, necessarily depends upon his overall perception of this being.

The novel begins with the frequently employed authorial probing of the material: "Let us now have a look at R. R. Let us see if R. R. exists. If R. R. is. The jokes already begin to take shape. But it is necessary to ask if we with a certain amount of certainty can trust that R. R. exists."[2] This tentative and self-aware opening paves the way for the author's comments on aspects of his writing throughout the novel. The author's presence is obvious and important, as is his ambiguous relationship with the protagonist, which is the nucleus around which the novel is built. The author is troubled because of his intimate knowledge of the protagonist, and he feels guilty about his failing consideration for the privacy and integrity of his character. The author is a kind of God—or as it turns out in the novel, a devil—towards the fictional character who, in consequence, is a feeble mortal.

One of first images which comes to the author's mind, and from which he creates the initial descriptive scenes, is that of the protagonist as a vulnerable human the moment before and after awakening. In this sensitive state, the poor "patient" is examined and analyzed by the insensitive, doctor-like, scientific author:

> In fact, the state of ownership of R. R. is astonishing. Here he lies wrapped in an intimacy which bears resemblance to the original state of being. In the darkness under a quilt, R. R. ought to be untouchable, invulnerable, protected. But we cannot show him any consideration. We have learned only too well and will not stay behind in method for science and the politicians who, during the century, have rendered it not only possible but also rather a matter of course to examine and catalogue, analyze and evaluate people, so to speak, according to their chemical composition and unconscious reflexes.

(p. 10)

Characteristically, Rifbjerg now adds a perspective: that of the protagonist. What are his views? What would be his reaction to these cardiographs, manometers, and encephalographs? The author suggests that he would merely control his surprise (fear, disgust) in acceptance of a modern, scientific approach; most likely, the protagonist would be in agreement with the prevailing ideas of his time. However, he might react differently: he might be frustrated—there is always the possibility of the unsuspected and surprising—and make use of a revolver hidden under his pillow. The revolver, which reemerges at the end of the novel, would represent that potential sudden outburst of violence which, in fact, undermines the whole previous image of and belief in rational behavior. An inherent contradiction is hereby indicated, and the theme is explored throughout the novel through dialogue and interaction between the author (devil) and protagonist. The protagonist sees himself as a modern rational being—a "thinking being" is the term he would use. The novel tests this rationalism, its strength and range; and, as is to be expected, it shows how it is only a thin veneer over quite a different being.

The novel begins with a description of R. R. as he is washing and getting dressed one morning. Depressed by a feeling of something missing, he is overcome by the memory of an affair ten years ago with a circus artist named Linda Ritt. The relationship lasted for only three weeks, and the memory of it seems rather exaggerated and somewhat comical. Nevertheless, R. R. seems persistent in his wish to see her again, and the inner voice he is communicating with is not able to dissuade him. This other voice is that of the narrator and could also represent R. R.'s alter ego, his rational superego. Gradually the voice is turned into or is revealed as that of the devil: its owner limps and furthermore refers to a pact between the two. R. R. was once, before he met the devil, quite a different person, and the gap and dissimilarity between the two characters alone would bode later difficulties. In the contract, it was agreed that R. R. could have everything he wished for within reasonable limits. The only condition was that he would also behave within certain accepted norms, leaving a wide margin for "ordinary" excesses such as his affair with Linda Ritt. And, of course, in accordance with tradition he would have to give away his soul; but as he did not believe in it anyway, that should not present any problem.

All goes well, R. R. becomes a successful engineer with a lovely and progressive wife and two charming daughters and all kinds of fringe benefits such as twelve bottles of Léoville Los Cases 1959 stocked in his cellar. Like Helmer in *The Opera Lover* and John in *What a Man Needs,* R. R. has everything any "rational" man in contemporary Danish society can wish for: family, position, and a comfortable life. But like the other two, he feels that something is lacking and now demands that the devil help him get back Linda Ritt. On one of his trips as an engineer, he calls Linda from the ferry across the sound of Storebælt. She is naturally surprised and tells him outright that their relationship is finished and she is committed elsewhere. This is the point when R. R. begins to move in the borderland area of what is commonly considered reasonable behavior. On several occasions he now shows a progressively irrational side of himself. In a discussion with some farmers he is dealing with, he argues against joining the Common Market; and although his argumentation may contain sympathetic views, the other side comes out as the rational and pragmatic one. At a business meeting with all his colleagues, he suddenly argues for forming a collective—run according to principles of need and humanitarianism instead of economic profit. Again his views may be idealistic ones but are hardly realistic. Finally, during an evening with his revolutionary friend Jens, his conflict climaxes in a breakdown. Jens is the super-rational being with all the "right" opinions, intentions, and behavior. But ironically, he becomes inhuman in his perfectionism; and Rifbjerg chastises this "saved" type, who resembles the rational revolutionary in *Lonni and Karl*. It becomes obvious that rationality is a relative thing determined by certain social conventions. Furthermore, although so frequently praised, it is neither necessarily sympathetic nor humane. This negative characterization of the rational attitude and accepted norms serves as a counterbalance to R. R.'s headlong behavior, which thus attains a different kind of credibility and "rationality."

R. R. succeeds in finding Linda Ritt's address. She is living in a hotel on a small street in an unfashionable part of Copenhagen and is going to leave the next day for Warsaw. She is no longer a horseback rider but now performs with trained cats. In her relationship with R. R. this change may symbolize a deterioration of sexual potency into something unreliable and fickle. The description now abounds with bad omens, and R. R. is characterized as an aged man. When he enters the hotel room, Linda is out to buy tickets for the trip, and her new boyfriend throws the "old man" out after a brief conversation. The next day, R. R. follows the couple by plane and finds Linda by bribing the concierge. Face to face with Linda in her dressing room, he is overcome by emotion and embraces her, with the result that they and the surrounding furniture tumble to the floor. Linda's lover enters, grabs R. R. firmly, and drags him outside. There, having assured himself that R. R. is alone, he shoots him with the symbolic black revolver and leaves him dying by the trash cans. The scene is thereby set for the final conversation with the devil, who obviously no longer can be of any help but who, on the other hand, is forced to give R. R. back his soul. When R. R. becomes irrational, he loses his world but regains his soul. R. R. becomes a fuller human being not because of his rationality but in spite of it. The thrust of the novel is psychological; the novel is created by an author who is concerned with a whole human being—including his shadow side—not just a rational, "flat" one. There is more to a human being than his rationality; or, rather, pursuit of one-sided rationality will lead to its own undoing. Rifbjerg's novel is a reckoning with the image of man as a rational being as this image has emerged and grown popular from the time of the Renaissance.

R. R. resembles the opera lover in his confused search for "completion" and self-fulfillment. The problem is also closely related to that of Anna in that it is tied up with the past. Like Anna, R. R. has cut his ties with the past too abruptly and completely, and the wish to resume the relationship with Linda is a result of his feeling of the past's lack of connection with the present. Linda's symbolic role to R. R. and his unresolved past become obvious when Linda's hotel is placed in the same street as R. R.'s old school. Seeing the school brings back the memory of old defeats and guilt, incompetence, and insufficiency but also a certain cozyness and a feeling of belonging. The word "solidarity" comes to R. R.'s mind, and like Anna he wants to return and reconnect with the past. At this emotionally crucial point he also has the following vision:

> He sees dark and light simultaneously. He experiences the world as through smoked glass during a solar eclipse. A glowing plate floats in front of his countenance, but it is simultaneously black. His head is cleft through from crown to chin and with separate consciousnesses he sees, Janus-like, how in the one chamber dark, hot, beckoning, indescribable figures move around, while in the other light figures of common sense and matter-of-course walk around naturally, graciously, kindly and with their visor up: Ada, Dede and Lil [his wife and daughters].
>
> (pp. 123-24)

Previous to this (Jungian) vision, two words emerged from the subconscious: "fate" and "sorrow." His fate is the return of the past that he has suppressed, and his sorrow results from his sense of loss. He now realizes that he should have accepted his past for good and bad, unconditionally. His failure to do so has resulted in a one-sided, divided psyche or, to use a more metaphysical expression, the loss of his soul.

As mentioned in the beginning of the analysis, the plot also deals with the author-work relationship. R. R. is the author's creation and as such the result of his inspiration. The author is the conscious creator and therefore, to a large extent, a representative of "rationality." When R. R. first succumbs to his emotions towards Linda Ritt, the author comments on how it gives him the creeps. Hereby a distance between author and character is indicated, and when the character refuses to listen to the devil, it also shows how the character is assuming independence. As Rifbjerg commented in his listeners' novel, the character cannot be changed or manipulated after the initial, albeit sketchy, characterization. Rifbjerg uses the expression *bordet fanger* ("a bargain is a bargain") to describe how the character and events will follow their own inner logic once a basic pattern has been established. In this case, where the character represents the irrational, the conclusion must be that the conscious writing by the rational writer can be deliberate only to a certain extent: the devil can manipulate R. R. only to a certain limit. In any true work of art, intuition (or the irrational or the subconscious) will be a decisive creative force. The writer is the devil, but the writer's situation is also similar to that of R. R. in that only by recognizing the so-called irrational aspect will his endeavors be fruitful. The name R. R. could therefore be interpreted as a doubling of Rifbjerg's own initial; R. R. is Rifbjerg's double.

Notes

1. Klaus Rifbjerg, *Leif den lykkelige jun.* (Copenhagen: Gyldendal, 1971), p. 167.

2. Klaus Rifbjerg, *R. R.* (Copenhagen: Gyldendal, 1972), p. 5.

Marlene Barr (essay date 1990)

SOURCE: Barr, Marlene. "Food for Postmodern Thought: Isak Dinesen's Female Artists as Precursors to Contemporary Feminist Fabulators."[1] In *Feminism, Utopia, and Narrative,* edited by Libby Falk Jones and Sarah Webster Goodwin, pp. 21-33. Knoxville: University of Tennessee Press, 1990.

[*In the following essay, Barr theorizes on the importance of Isak Dinesen's works as precursors to postmodern feminist writing.*]

In "Postmodernism and Consumer Society," Fredric Jameson comments, "I am very far indeed from believing that any of the most significant postmodern artists—John Cage, John Ashbery, Philippe Sollers, Robert Wilson, Andy Warhol, Ishmael Reed, Michael Snow, even Samuel Beckett himself—are in any sense schizophrenics" (118). My purpose in citing Jameson is not to take issue with his statement, but rather to make a simple observation: his list of "the most significant postmodern artists" does not include female postmodern artists. As we are all aware by now, women are omitted from "most significant" lists through no fault of their own; their contributions are either trivialized or subverted. Such has been the fate of our American female creators of postmodern fiction, our contemporary "lost" women writers. It is time to announce that these "lost" writers have been found.

In order to locate female postmodern writers, we must look towards feminist speculative fiction: the science fiction, fantasy, and utopian literature created by such writers as Joanna Russ, Marion Zimmer Bradley, and Octavia Butler. Feminist speculative fiction is replete with visions which are disconcerting to the patriarchy (planets populated by lesbian separatists, for example). The patriarchal literary establishment successfully has used the term "speculative fiction" to nullify these disconcerting visions. "Speculative fiction," "fantasy," and "utopian literature" are all synonyms for "noncanonical literature." Hence, I have proposed a new term which does not bar female speculative fiction writers from assuming their rightful place in the postmodern literary canon: feminist fabulation.[2]

I define this term as a specifically feminist corollary to Robert Scholes's "structural fabulation."[3] Structural fabulation addresses man's place within the system of the universe; feminist fabulation addresses woman's place within the system of patriarchy. It modifies the tradition of speculative fiction with an awareness that patriarchy is a contrived system, a meaning-making machine which constructs and defines patriarchal fictions—myths of female inferiority—as integral aspects of human culture, and the insights of this century's waves of feminism are accepted as fictional points of departure. It is a fictional exploration of woman's inferior status, made perceptible by the implications of recent feminist theory.

Jean Baudrillard's comment about systems addresses the critical establishment's failure to articulate the juncture between feminist fabulation and postmodernism:

> Each system . . . forms a sort of ecological niche where the essential thing is to maintain a relational decor, where all the terms must continually communicate among themselves and stay in contact, informed of the respective condition of the others and of the system as a whole, where opacity, resistance or the secrecy of a single term can lead to catastrophe.
>
> (127-28)

Feminist fabulation has been ostracized from the postmodern literary niche, prevented from communicating with and as postmodernism, denied access to the canonical system. The politics of literary interpretation resists feminist fabulation and relegates the identities of female postmodern writers to the status of secrecy. This secrecy, the marginalization of an entire category of writers—James Tiptree, Jr. (Alice Sheldon), Jody Scott, Vonda McIntyre, Suzy McKee Charnas, Elizabeth A. Lynn, and Pamela Sargent, for example—is an aesthetic catastrophe.

One way to end this catastrophic silencing of feminist voices is to establish that these voices are not speaking in isolation. Towards this end, I argue that the fantastic elements in the devalued work of contemporary feminist fabulators also are present in their modern predecessors. This essay's concentration upon Isak Dinesen's portrayal of the female artist figure in "Babette's Feast," as well as my brief concluding remarks about "The Blank Page," shows that a modern woman writer reserves space for space fiction. These stories exemplify a direct relationship between modernists and feminist fabulators. They indicate that postmodern women writers' turn to speculative fiction has not been preceded by the blank page of women's silence on the subject.

Dinesen is one who laid the groundwork for contemporary feminist fabulation. In "Babette's Feast," an implied feminist utopia,[4] Dinesen's presentation of the female artist juxtaposes feminism with the fantastic and establishes her as a modernist literary mother who engenders fabulative postmodern daughters.

The story indicates that the fantastic is an appropriate mode for feminist fiction. Its beginning includes a description of "a Huldre, a female mountain spirit of Norway" (25-26). Babette is analogous to this spirit in that she is a female alien, a French woman who enters the home of two unmarried sisters residing in the Norwegian town of Berlevaag. The sisters associate her with the marvelous: "[t]hey felt that their cook's old carpetbag was made from a magic carpet; at a given moment she might mount it and be carried off, back to Paris" (38). Babette is a magical alien who soon becomes an integral part of the sisters' familial female community.

Despite the incongruity of a French maid appearing in an austere Norwegian household, Babette adapts to her new environment. The atmosphere surrounding her becomes welcoming rather than estranging: "The old Brothers and Sisters, who had first looked askance at the foreign woman in their midst, felt a happy change in their little sisters' life, rejoiced at it and benefited by it" (37). Babette's actions encourage this positive reception. After winning ten thousand francs, instead of choosing to become an image of French elegance supported by a French lottery—an action which would reestrange her from her newfound community—Babette uses the money in a feminist manner. She literally nourishes the community when she creates her feast, a work of art which at once celebrates her substantial talents and serves the needs of the group.

As the ingredients arrive, both Babette and her feast are allied to the world of the fantastic. Robert Langbaum has pointed out that the narrator alludes to witchcraft in describing Babette's work as she cooks (Langbaum 251). I would add that the story's imagery also evokes the alien and the monstrous:

> . . . Babette, like the bottled demon of the fairy tale, had swelled and grown to such dimensions that her mistresses felt small before her. They now saw the

French dinner coming upon them, a thing of incalculable nature and range. . . . In the light of the lamp it [a turtle to be cooked for dinner] looked like some greenish-black stone, but when set down on the kitchen floor it suddenly shot out a snake-like head . . . this thing was monstrous in size and terrible to behold.

(45-46)

Babette becomes a swelled unearthly demon, a gigantic monster; the dinner is an alien "thing." All the elements of a mediocre science fiction film are metaphorically present here. The dinner prepared by the monstrous Babette could be described on a movie marquee as the attack of the thing that will eventually be eaten in Berlevaag. As an art form, Babette's creation of the alien dinner is akin to the art of feminist fabulation, which produces literature whose alien ingredients are concocted by the female imagination. As the monstrous dinner must be accepted, ingested, and appreciated by the traditional Norwegian community, feminist fabulation is the monstrous genre which must be canonized by the traditional academic literary community.

The story implies that, like quilts sewn by American pioneer women, Babette's feast should be viewed as a respected and valued art form. As a master chef, Babette has taken cooking, a part of the domestic female tradition, and manipulated it successfully in the public, masculine world of Parisian gastronomy. Her dual roles as master chef and domestic cook suggest the inappropriateness of evaluating art in terms of gender classifications. Babette, a revolutionary activist, a family cook, and a chef for aristocrats, is not concerned primarily with the moral effect her work may have on any audience. Rather than focusing upon being classified as a chef or a cook, Babette wishes to create as perfect a work as she can. Her skillful execution of both her public and her domestic cooking roles emphasizes that successful nontraditional art works such as pioneers' quilts, Babette's feast, and feminist fabulation should not be undervalued. Her feast is a transcendent experience, a personal and religious communicative rebirth:

Of what happened later in the evening nothing definite can here be stated. . . . They [the guests] only knew that the rooms had been filled with a heavenly light. . . . Taciturn old people received the gift of tongues; ears that for years had been almost deaf were opened to it. Time itself had merged into eternity. Long after midnight the windows of the house shone like gold, and golden song flowed out into the winter air.

(61)

Babette's dinner coincides with a new manifestation of time, a change in the reflective properties of the window glass, and a merger of metal and art. The feast, then, is an art form initiating a world alien to the one we know, a world which defies natural laws. The event also improves the community's social relationships:

"The two old women who had once slandered each other now in their hearts went back a long way, past the evil period in which they had been stuck, to those days of their early girlhood when together they had been preparing for confirmation and hand in hand had filled the roads round Berlevaag with singing" (61). Like the feast, feminist fabulation presents the possibility of new physical worlds and new mutual social respect. Both the feast and feminist fabulation are particularly female art forms which introduce new psychic and physical spaces.

The two present new possibilities. The story's congregation, for example, enjoys the following experience: "The vain illusions of this earth had dissolved before their [the congregation's] eyes like smoke, and they had seen the universe as it really is. They had been given one hour of the millenium . . . tonight I [General Loewenhielm] have learned . . . that in this world anything is possible" (62). In feminist fabulative works, vain patriarchal illusions about women—men's constructions of reality—dissolve; space is cleared for a new female vision of the universe (which might be how the universe really is). "Babette's Feast" has established a foundation for the eventual appearance of literature depicting women's worlds (such as the stories published in Virginia Kidd's *Millenial Women*). Dinesen prepares a space for the literature that allows women and men to learn that in this world—or in other worlds—anything is possible, reality can be declared a fiction, and women's stories can inspire the construction of a nonpatriarchal society.

It is, of course, difficult to replace patriarchy with feminism. Feminists, like all artists working in noncanonical forms, and feminist art are often misunderstood and unappreciated. Despite this lack of acceptance, however, we must do our best. Langbaum points out that Babette pursues her art in the face of misunderstanding: "She had . . . to do her best even though no-one at the dinner—she did not foresee the General's appearance—would understand what she had accomplished" (Langbaum 254). Babette's artistic accomplishment is comprehended because of the unexpected appearance of a male. Ironically, because of his experience in the alien Parisian culinary world, a powerful male general is the person best equipped to understand Babette's achievement. His presence communicates a positive view of relationships between men and women, a view asserted in recent feminist utopias such as Pamela Sargent's *The Shore of Women*.[5] The novel's presentation of a woman and a man inhabiting the same space with mutual dignity implies that the sexes can step out of their respective environments. Babette and General Loewenhielm, like Sargent's protagonists, for example, experience new social worlds. Babette moves from the excessiveness of Paris to the austerity of Berlevaag; he moves from Berlevaag to Paris. They come together at the table, a particular artistic space where women and men can coexist. Sargent and some of her fellow contemporary feminist utopian writers imply that men should seat themselves at such a table.

The diners at Babette's table enjoy a "kind of celestial second childhood." They are "bodily as well as spiritually hand in hand" during a time when the "stars have come nearer" (63). In terms of feminist fabulation, this passage hints that people can attain solidarity when they come nearer to the stars, when they engage with feminist space fiction. The fantastic elements of Dinesen's dinner scene indicate that feminist fabulation is an appropriate space for feminist writers and readers. This literature of the stars is not always inferior to that of the literary mainstream.

As the title of the story's twelfth section ("The Great Artist") and Babette herself proclaim, she is in fact a great artist. Her feast validates domestic cooking as an art form and celebrates utopian goals. She indicates that feminist fabulators who use art as she does, to advocate women's utopian concerns, should also be considered great artists, not inhabitants of a female subgeneric literary ghetto. Patriarchy works against the recognition of women artists, however. Babette's repetition of a remark made by the story's musician (Monsieur Achille Papin) indirectly comments upon this fact: "'Through all the world there goes one long cry from the heart of the artist: Give me leave to do my utmost!'" (68). The politics of patriarchal interpretation seek to silence feminist fabulators by marginalizing and trivializing their work.

At the conclusion of the story, Babette's body is "like a marble monument" (68) (like one of Arthur C. Clarke's monoliths in *2001: A Space Odyssey*), a marker attesting to the location and significance of feminist art. Langbaum states that "as marble monument, Babette symbolizes Achille and art" (Langbaum 254). Such female art also is an Achilles heel of patriarchal reality—the patriarchy's vulnerable point, where alternative versions of reality can be expressed. Defining feminist fabulation as an integral part of the postmodern canon and so ending the fiction of its subgeneric status can heighten the patriarchy's vulnerability by sparking interest in creating a woman-oriented reality.

The story's concluding words signal the hope of such an occurrence: "Yet this is not the end! . . . In Paradise you [Babette] will be the great artist that God meant you to be! . . . how you will enchant the angels!" (68). In other words, the story is not the end, but rather one beginning of respect for female art forms. In Paradise, Babette will be recognized as a great artist. She will enchant the angels, who are, for instance, exemplified by the heavenly community of women in Sandi Hall's *The Godmothers*. Langbaum's interpretation of the story's conclusion complements my own. He writes, "Now she [Phillipa, one of the sisters] understands what food it is that is symbolized by Babette's food. She understands how art unites heaven and earth" (Langbaum 254). An appreciation of women's art (symbolized by Babette's feast) can infuse the earthly patriarchal society with the utopia that feminist fabulators locate in the stars.

Indeed, the stars seem to come nearer. When Babette's guests leave her dinner, stars falling to earth in the form of snow impede them: "In the street the snow was lying so deep that it had become difficult to walk. The guests . . . staggered, sat down abruptly or fell forward . . . and were covered with snow, as if they had indeed had their sins washed white as wool, and in this regained innocent attire were gamboling like little lambs" (63). This imagery implies that the human race has a new innocence, a potential for social rebirth. The sisters' father states, "'God's paths run across the sea and the snowy mountains, where man's eye sees no track'" (30). The guests cannot make tracks in their own streets. Man's eye, the patriarchal gaze, is stopped in its own tracks. It is time, as feminist fabulation tells us, to gambol upon the goddess whose paths run across the sky and the starry galaxies. It is time to try to see the goddess's path, to place feminist tracks in the new space of unearthly reality. "Babette's Feast," collected in *Shadows of Destiny,* is an anecdote about the destiny of respect for feminist art forms and feminist social structures. It is a modern literary space which anticipates the presence of postmodern feminist fabulators.

"The Blank Page," which focuses upon the potential for female artists to fill unused and/or subversive female artistic spaces with new art forms, functions similarly. A brief consideration of this story serves as an appropriate coda to my point: the juxtaposition of domestic art with the fantastic in "Babette's Feast" is a modern precursor to feminist fabulation. "The Blank Page" directly addresses the dilemma of the feminist fabulator's creation of a specifically female art form which does not coincide with traditional art. The story emphasizes that to gain power, women must behave in a manner which is alien to femininity; they must write their own stories.

Within the story, a blood-stained bridal sheet becomes female art, a painting created with body fluid. The framed, stained sheets, which attest that the virgin bride conforms to the patriarchal story of proper female behavior, exemplify women's art as signifier of patriarchal definitions. The virgin has spent her life as a powerless, sexless blank page.

Dinesen, however, also enables the blank page to serve women's needs, to symbolize woman's potential and power rather than her hopelessness and powerlessness.

The framed bloodless white sheet which appears as "snow-white from corner to corner, a blank page" (104) is a positive blank page. The bride who slept on it does not fit patriarchal stories; her sheet-as-canvas is blank rather than literally drawn from the patriarchal definition of her own blood. This blank sheet becomes an appropriate symbol for new female art forms. Feminist fabulators, for example, stand before patriarchally unsullied blank pages and fill them as they see fit. They are fettered only by the limits of their own imaginations, not by the limiting definitions constructed by patriarchal imaginations.

Feminist fabulators confront the blank pages of feminist potential, find patriarchal reality too constricting, and create fantastic tales of women's worlds. They choose to fill the space of the blank page with space fiction. Like Dinesen, they allow the word "blank" to have positive connotations for women. For Dinesen and the feminist fabulator, "blank" becomes a positive absence, freedom from patriarchal influence, freedom to be female artists who do not tell patriarchal stories. "Babette's Feast" and "The Blank Page" allow the feminist fabulator to know that she is not creating art in subgeneric isolation. Instead of being a devalued creator of inferior fiction, she is the postmodern descendant of a modern woman writer who chose to link feminism with the fantastic. The feminist fabulator, then, inherits past female artistic culture and creates present female artistic culture. She is no orphaned subcultural artistic outcast.

The feminist fabulator is freed, in Susan Gubar's words, from the "model of the pen-penis on the virgin page," a tradition which "excludes women from the creation of culture" (77):

> [W]ere the female community less sensitive to the significance of these signs [remnants of women's lives], such stained sheets would not be considered art at all. Dinesen implies that woman's use of her own body in the creation of art results in forms of expression devalued or totally invisible to eyes trained by traditional aesthetic standards. She also seems to imply that, within the life of domesticity assigned the royal princess from birth, the body is the only accessible medium for self-expression.
>
> (Gubar 78-79)

Feminist fabulation is hardly considered art at all. The critical community has only recently begun to be sensitive to its significance. Critical eyes trained to traditional aesthetic standards are blind to the importance of this literature.

Such readers fail to see that, like Dinesen's princess, the characters created by feminist fabulators also use their bodies to create art. Feminist fabulators make the female body an expansive and powerful, rather than a limiting and powerless, means of self-expression. In fact, many feminist fabulators recreate the female body in a manner which transcends biological limitations and present female protagonists who derive power from inhabiting bodies which differ from our own. For example, Russ, Tiptree, and Charnas imagine women who can reproduce without men. These writers, like Pygmalion (whose myth is cited at the start of Gubar's discussion), build their own versions of women.

Feminist fabulators are female Pygmalions who use words to sculpt new versions of the female body. They create art objects and cultures to correct the fact that "in terms of the production of culture, she [woman] is an art object . . . not the sculptor" (Gubar 74). When the literary establishment devalues feminist fabulation, it removes the scalpel from the hands of the female writer-sculptor. It denies these new female Pygmalions the power to be female artists whose words produce diverse, fantastic images of female bodies. Dinesen insists that Babette's dinner is a legitimate art form which literally and figuratively nourishes the body of her Norwegian community. The postmodern version of this insistence takes the form of the feminist fabulator providing food for feminist thought—nourishing the contemporary feminist community—by producing fantastic visions of female biology and feminist futures.

Like the princess's blank sheet, feminist fabulation tells a different, nonpatriarchal story about women. In Gubar's terms, the feminist fabulator creates "a radically new kind of art" (92) "by not writing what she is expected to write" (89). Feminist fabulation, which is presently "devalued as mere craft or service" (Gubar 90), can, like the "snow-white sheet of the nameless princess . . . promise a breakthrough into new beginnings for new stories that can soothe the wound" patriarchy inflicts upon women (Gubar 88).

Even so, instead of being respected as the valued site of new feminist stories, feminist fabulation itself has become a wound. A bloody blank appears at the space where feminist fabulation has been wrenched from the canon. Critics might soothe this wound by validating female artists who choose to write in this mode. Critics could correct the fact that, in regard to the postmodern canon, feminist fabulation is "the blank place" (Gubar 91). This place might be filled by a contemporary female art form which represents "readiness for inspiration and creation, the self conceived and dedicated to its own potential divinity" (Gubar 91).

Feminist fabulators are postmodern Babettes, female artists who treat readers to feasts of words. Yet traditional aesthetic standards restrict the consumption of these treats, define them as forbidden fruit, the female blank pages absent from the canon. Like Babette's feast, feminist fabulation—women's creation of nourishment for a feminist body of knowledge—is a viable art form. Fat is a feminist issue. So is a traditional literary diet, in which readers avoid indulging in fabulative food for postmodern thought. In the manner of Babette, feminist fabulators should be defined as respected artists, the creators of a female art form; feminist fabulation, until now a blank page in the postmodern canonical menu, should appear in all its savory and subtle variety.

Notes

1. This essay will be adapted for inclusion in my forthcoming book, *Feminist Fabulation: Women's Space/Postmodern Fiction* (University of Iowa Press). I view feminist fabulation as a postmodern, metafictional exploration of patriarchy's fictionality. When feminist fabulators use language to construct nonsexist fictional worlds, they create useful models to learn how patriarchy is constructed. Feminist fabulation is postmodern literature which facilitates an understanding of sexism as a constructed fiction that is authored by men's power to make women the protagonists of patriarchal fiction.

2. For a discussion of feminist fabulation, see my "Feminist Fabulation; Or, Playing with Patriarchy, Versus the Masculinization of Metafiction."

3. Scholes explains that "in works of structural fabulation the tradition of speculative fiction is modified by an awareness of the nature of the universe as a system of systems, a structure of structures, and the insights of the past century of science are accepted as fictional points of departure. . . . It is a fictional exploration of human situations made perceptible by the implications of recent science" (54-55).

4. Sarah Webster Goodwin's 1987 MLA presentation, "Feminism: Implicit and Explicit Utopias," first acquainted me with the notion that "Babette's Feast" can be read as an implicit feminist utopia. Her essay in this volume is a later version of that paper.

5. The following recent feminist utopias also portray positive relationships between women and men: Doris Lessing's *The Marriages Between Zones Three, Four, and Five*, Marge Piercy's *Woman On the Edge of Time*, and Joan Slonczewski's *A Door Into Ocean*.

Works Cited

Barr, Marleen S. "Feminist Fabulation; Or, Playing with Patriarchy Versus the Masculinization of Metafiction," *Women's Studies* 14 (1987):187-91.

———. *Feminist Fabulation: Women's Space/Postmodern Fiction*. Iowa City: University of Iowa Press, forthcoming.

Baudrillard, Jean. "The Ecstasy of Communication." In *The Anti-Aesthetic: Essays On Postmodern Culture*, edited by Hal Foster, pp. 126-33. Port Townsend, Wash.: Bay Press, 1983.

Clarke, Arthur C. *2001: A Space Odyssey*. New York: New American Library, 1968.

Dinesen, Isak. "Babette's Feast." In *Anecdotes of Destiny*, pp. 23-68. New York: Random House, 1958.

———. "The Blank Page." In *Last Tales*, pp. 99-105. New York: Random House, 1957.

Goodwin, Sarah Webster. "Feminism: Implicit and Explicit Utopias." In *Feminism, Utopia, and Narrative*.

Gubar, Susan. "'The Blank Page' and the Issues of Female Creativity." In *Writing and Sexual Difference*, edited by Elizabeth Abel, pp. 73-93. Chicago: University of Chicago Press, 1982.

Hall, Sandi. *The Godmothers*. London: The Women's Press, 1982.

Jameson, Fredric. "Postmodernism and Consumer Society." In *The Anti-Aesthetic: Essays On Postmodern Culture*, edited by Hal Foster, pp. 111-25. Port Townsend, Wash.: Bay Press, 1983.

Kidd, Virginia. *Millennial Women*. New York: Dell, 1978.

Langbaum, Robert. *The Gayety of Vision: A Study of Isak Dinesen's Art* New York: Random House, 1964.

Lessing, Doris. *The Marriages Between Zones Three, Four, and Five* New York: Random House, 1980.

Piercy, Marge. *Woman on the Edge of Time*. New York: Knopf, 1976.

Sargent, Pamela. *The Shore of Women*. New York: Crown, 1986.

Scholes, Robert. "The Roots of Science Fiction." In *Science Fiction: A Collection of Critical Essays*, edited by Mark Rose, pp. 46-56. Englewood Cliffs, N.J.: Prentice Hall, 1976.

Slonczewski, Joan. *A Door Into Ocean*. New York: Avon, 1986.

Mark Mussari (essay date spring 1999)

SOURCE: Mussari, Mark. "H. C. Branner and the Colors of Consciousness." *Scandinavian Studies* 71, no. 1 (spring 1999): 41-66.

[*In the following essay, Mussari studies H. C. Branner's use of pictorial language in his writings as a means to evoke images underlying human consciousness.*]

> Time past and time future
> What might have been and what has been
> Point to one end, which is always present.
>
> — T. S. Eliot

Commenting on the power of the image in his essay "Kunst og virkelighed" (1962), H. C. Branner observed that "de store forandringer viser sig altid først i kunsten, hvad der er en simpel følge af at billedet går forud for tanken" (30) [the great changes always appear first in art, a simple result of the fact that pictures precede thoughts]. In expressionistic language, Branner often struggles to capture the pictures of the multivalent dimensions of consciousness and creates antimimetic imagery that, especially in his more elaborate stream-of-consciousness, not only expresses emotions but also stretches temporal and spatial boundaries. Like pictorial expressionists, Branner relies heavily on chromaticism to convey subjective states of being.

Much has been written about H. C. Branner as a humanist or psychoanalytical writer regrettably confining him to the postwar Heretica movement or the more narrow definitions of "Freudian" or "existentialist." This pigeonholing has deflected attention from Branner's inventive stylistic devices. In *Ideologi og æstetik i H. C. Branners sene forfatterskab*, Erik Skyum-Nielsen argues cogently that the relationship between Branner's ideas and his prose style was symbiotic and that focusing only on humanist or psychoanalytic ideas is myopic. Branner's notions of humanism and psychoanalysis changed dramatically throughout his career; his visual sense, though, remained strong, manifesting itself in an image-laden prose that frequently portrayed consciousness in pictures, painterly or iconic.[1] As Skyum-Nielsen has noted, all of Branner's writing reveals "en vilje eller hang til at se billeder i alt og metaforisere oplevelsen" (*Ideologi* 190) [a will or tendency to see pictures in everything and to make metaphors out of experience].

Paralleling the horrors of war that inspired much of the distorted imagery of German expressionism, heightened emotional states serve as the catalyst to the imagery in Branner's literary cosmos. Whether fearing the impending World War II or suffering from angst over a failing marriage, a dangerous pregnancy, or a terminal illness, Branner's characters are forced onto acute levels of consciousness and are driven to a state in which images take precedence over words which, in fact, become noticeably impotent at these moments.[2]

In his essay "Humanismens krise" (1950), Branner commented on contemporary changes in the arts:

> *Maleri og skulptur har sprængt det naturalistiske virkelighedsbillede for at give farver og former frihed til at udtrykke deres egen komplementære sandhed. Prosadigtningen har forladt det naturalistiske handlingsmønster med dets tidsmæssigt fremadskridende forløb og konstante, eentydige menneskeopfattelse og søger nu at ordne dets elementer på en ny måde, som løser det menneskelige bevidsthedsliv fra tidsfølgens sammenhæng og udtrykker det tidløse, relative og mangetydige i dets væsen.*
>
> (22-3)

(Painting and sculpture have exploded the naturalistic picture of reality to give colors and forms freedom to express their own complementary truth. Prose writing has abandoned the naturalistic plot structure with its temporally progressive sequence and constant, unambiguous concept of humanity and now seeks to arrange its elements in a new manner, one that releases the life of human consciousness from the context of progressive time and that expresses the timeless, relative, and ambiguous aspects of its nature.)

In his own prose, Branner attempts the same feat with varying degrees of success: his chromatic imagery is important in expressing his view of the atemporal consciousness, which moves from image to image and ranges through past, present, and future in varying patterns. Henri Bergson has observed that the past "nous suit à tout instant: ce que nous avons senti, pensé, voulu depuis notre premiére enfance est là, penché sur le présent qui va s'y joindre, pressant contre la porte de la conscience qui voudrait le laisser dehors" (*Œuvres* 498) ["follows us at every instant; all that we have felt, thought, and willed from our earliest infancy is there, leaning over the present which is about to join it, pressing against the portals of consciousness that would fain leave it outside" (*Creative Evolution* 5)].

The most coloristic of all Branner's works, *Drømmen om en kvinde,* unites strong pictorial imagery with an elaborate stream-of-consciousness structure, both facets reflecting the interior focus driving the novel's linguistic devices.[3] Branner, who once claimed that the novel portrayed "følelser" [feelings], not characters, could not have employed a better visual element than color to convey the emotional states of his three main characters: the pregnant Merete Rude, her husband Niels, and her "uncle," the dying—and aptly named—Knud Mortimer. Their respective and intertwining life stories constitute the novel's central focus, the incestuous relationship between the inescapable forces of life and death.

Despite the novel's myriad time shifts, the *nu* of the story is 1939, shortly before the outbreak of World War II. The possibility of war arriving in "store sorte tegn: *Krigen!—Krigen et spørgsmaal om timer!—det sidste haab bristet!*" (216) [large black characters: War!—War a question of hours!—The last hope shattered!] serves as a dark counterpoint to the various characters' dilemmas and as such is not the main subject of the novel. Unlike *Rytteren, Drømmen om en kvinde* reveals no formulaic connection between the political and the psychological; as Vosmar suggests, "Forsøget på at gøre en psykologisk sandhed til en politisk sanhed må mislykkes" (168) [The attempt to turn a psychological truth into a political one must fail]. Instead, like Branner's finest short stories, *Drømmen om en kvinde* centers on the human effort—seen through the eyes of each character's variegated consciousness—to make sense of life by merely living. Inspired by Virginia Woolf's and James Joyce's innovations in narrative structure, Branner arranged the elements of his earlier works—from the collectivist *Legetøj* (1936) to the Freudian *Barnet leger ved stranden* (1937)—into a kaleidoscopic journey into the non-linear consciousness hiding behind the mask of the public and interpersonal self. Vosmar observes,

> *I de lange passager, hvor Niels og Merete forsøger at gøre sig hinandens væsen klart, er der endda næppe tale om en udformet tankerække, snarere om en parafrase over de to unges tankebilleder. I disse afsnit har Branner fundet og rendyrket en stil, som helt er hans egen.*
>
> (67)

(In the long passages in which Niels and Merete struggle to realize fully each other's nature, it really is not an issue of an elaborate train of thought but of a paraphrase of the two young persons' mental imagery. In these sections Branner has cultivated a style that is totally his own.)

That Branner would settle into a pictorial prose relying heavily on color to convey emotional states points not only to the increasingly visual nature of his writing but also to chromaticism's strong connotative and expressive qualities. This facet allows his color-laden language to function far beyond the level of a mere symbolic code that, once broken, closes the door on the novel's meaning.

Early in the novel, Branner's prose recalls another master's innovative narrative devices: William Faulkner's haunting imagery in *Light in August* (1926). Discussing the early evening light when a group of friends is playing bridge "sidst i august" [late in August], the narrator of *Drømmen om en kvinde* describes the light of the still invisible moon: "en lygte som stod derude og lyste op i det tunge, gulgrønne løv" (7) [a light outside that illuminated the heavy, yellow-green leaves]. Like *Light in August*, *Drømmen om en kvinde* features a pregnant woman—Lena Grove/Merete Rude—near childbirth who represents the life force but is surrounded by death, particularly in the figure of a misanthropic male character—Joe Christmas/Knud Mortimer. Merete calls Mortimer "onkel," but he is actually the cousin of her late father. Both women are described in fecund nature images, Lena as a cow and Merete as "en hjortekalv" [a fawn].

Whereas Faulkner's Lena is associated with the color blue—lending a religious, Madonna-like gleam to her character, Branner gives Merete a brown dress—"hjortekalv" is also the name of a soft, orange shade of brown—reinforcing her regenerative connection to nature.

> *Hun var i en brun kjole der saa ud som den var syet om af et gammelt gardin, rimpet løseligt sammen og hæftet op i den ene side med en sikkerhedsnaal, det tynde stof var flænget ud hvor naalen sad. Det var som hun fandt en hemmelig glæde i at fremhæve sit svære underliv og det store bespændte bryst. . . .*
>
> (8)

(She was in a brown dress that looked as if it was made from an old curtain, tacked loosely together and tucked up on one side with a safety pin. The thin fabric was worn out at the pin. It was as if she found joy in accentuating her swollen belly and her large distended breasts.)

Merete's brown garb also allows Branner to take her representative function a step further. The color of decaying leaves and earth, her brown dress points to the problems in Merete's pregnancy and to Branner's strong conviction that the capacity for childbirth brings women closer not only to the life-giving creative act but also to death.

The possibility of death in Merete's problematic pregnancy manifests itself in a brown portrait of fear. In one of her dreams about her unborn baby, she searches for mushrooms "i det brune solplettede mørke" [in the brown, sun-spotted darkness] of a forest. The branches around her create "et brunligt slør af døde kviste" [a brownish veil of dead twigs]; she enters a forest of brown ferns, and the eyes of a brown frog stare up at her, "et stille bedrøvet vanvid dybt inde under mosset" (130) [a silent, grieving insanity deep down under the moss]. The scene soon melts into a curvilinear, nightmarish brown forest,

> *hvor ingenting stod oprejst og ingenting var grønt— skurvede og forkrøblede stammer bugtede sig som slanger. . . . Hendes fødder blev hele tiden hildet i knortede og krogede ting. . . . Det var som træerne forsøgte at slippe jorden med deres rødder, som om de flygtede i stum og bunden rædsel for en stor fare.*
>
> (131)

(where nothing stood upright and nothing was green— scabby and stunted tree trunks meandered like snakes . . . All the time her feet became enmeshed in gnarled and crooked things . . . It was as if the trees were trying to escape the ground with their roots, as if they were fleeing in mute and bound fear of a great danger.)

Throughout this Munchesque scene, with its threatening landscape, Merete hears a child crying in the unreachable distance,[4] but she cannot move amid the brown mass of tangled roots and branches. In *Über das Geistige in der Kunst,* Kandinsky describes "das stumpfe, harte, wenig zur Bewegung fähige Braun" (101) [the insensible and hard color brown, capable of little movement]. Merete's dream finally dissipates with her first labor pain. Emil Frederiksen lauds this scene as "et af hoved-punkterne i hele H. C. Branners digtning . . . her giver digteren en af sine bedste, mest karakteristiske natur- og sjælebeskrivelser" (50-1) [one of the high points in all of H. C. Branner's writing . . . here, the author gives one of his best, most characteristic descriptions of nature and the soul].

At one point in the novel, Niels views his wife's brown dress as "en besværlig las" (146) [an onerous rag] around her; after he leaves her at the hospital, Niels, not knowing the outcome of her difficult childbirth, "stod der og saa stift ned i det brune linoleum som en lille dreng" (153) [stood there and stared hard at the brown linoleum like a little boy]. Branner uses one of his favorite iconic devices—a figure bent forward in a chair[5]—when, at the end of the novel, Niels, waiting for word on Merete's condition, stares again into the brown linoleum and sees "ansigter og dyr og figurer" (231) [faces and animals and figures] in the patterns beneath his feet. Niels's boyish quality is emphasized in his childlike ability, heightened by his angst-ridden state, to find pictures in everything. The nothingness of brown offers all possibilities: "naar man blev træt af at se en bestemt figur behøvede man bare at glippe en gang med øjnene, saa forvandlede den sig straks til noget nyt" (231) [when you became tired of looking at a certain figure, you needed only to blink your eyes once, and it changed immediately into something new]. Through his use of an emotionless brown, Branner reinforces the uncertainty of Merete's predicament. In *Colors and Their Character*, Benjamin Kouwer observes that brown, despite its relation to most other colors, "shows no definite, clearly indicated relationship with any specific color. This uncertainty and vagueness of affinity is a very important trait" (130).

The logocentric, cancer-ridden Mortimer fears Merete's pregnancy. Like Faulkner's Lena Grove, Merete at first appears slow-witted and removed ("Det er bare synd hun er lidt dum" [It's a shame she's a little dumb], comments Mortimer's wife, Charlotte). Merete seems incapable of following the bridge game that Mortimer all but orchestrates, although Branner makes it clear that she is merely worn out anticipating her husband's return from the shipyard where he works. After her father died, Merete came to live with Mortimer. Even in his memory of Merete when she was an attractive thirteen-year-old, Mortimer sees "en hjortekalv . . . i en lysning paa lange spinkle ben" (8, 12) [a fawn . . . in a glade on long slender legs]. In the present, her swollen abdomen and distended breasts constitute an affront to Mortimer reinforced by her association with deer, nature, and the color brown. He is a fading wraith playing cards next to a fecund nature sprite.

Throughout the novel, Mortimer is described as "en skygge" [a shadow] or "en abstrakt skygge" [an abstract shadow] or as being "ind i slagskyggen" [inside the shadow], an association with the color black and its connotations of death. (He eventually leaves the party wearing a long black coat.) A living shade, he is one of Branner's infamous "døde voksner" [dead grown ups][6] whose lives consist of a materialist attraction to *ting*. His attempt to explain the bridge game with numbers and black and white diagrams fails to penetrate Merete's "tomme mørke øjne" [empty dark eyes]—another deer image. Though she can only nod helplessly to his "logiske konstruktion" [logical construction], her gaze makes him feel "latterlig for sig selv, hvad nyttede hans lille matematik overfor et hundyr som skulde føde?" (9) [ridiculous to himself; what was the use of his little mathematics in the face of a female animal about to give birth?]. Kouwer notes that black and white are "'rational' colors because they appeal to reason rather than to emotion. They have neither interiority nor exteriority. They do not 'speak' but they 'posit'" (133). Black's association with logic and rationality has been noted by such artists as the painter Odilon Redon, well known for his *noirs*: "One must respect black. Nothing prostitutes it. It does not please the eye or awaken another sense. It is the agent of the mind even more than the beautiful color of the palette or the prism" (Arnheim 330). Kandinsky, fond of merging colors and sounds, describes black "wie ein Nichts ohne Möglichkeit, wie ein totes Nichts nach dem Erlöschen der Sonne, wie ein ewiges Schweigen ohen Zukunft und Hoffnung klingt innerlich das Schwarz. Es is musikalisch dargestellt wie eine vollständig abschließende Pause, nach welcher eine Fortsetzung kommt wie der Beginn einer andern Welt" (98) ["(as) a totally dead silence . . . a silence with no possibilities . . . In music it is represented by one of those profound and final pauses, after which any continuation of the melody seems the dawn of another world" (39)].

The scene in which Niels returns home on his motorcycle and stops outside to peer into the window at his wife and friends playing cards presents some of Branner's most painterly and lovely writing. Branner bathes the "augustskoven med sit hængende løv, stille og træt" (33) [August forest with its hanging leaves, silent and tired] in a dreamy moonlight ("den sejlende hvide maane") that reinforces the prose's pensive nature. He frequently employs twilight for its spectral effects: "vejen tabte sig mere og mere i et taaget tusmørke" (36) [the road disappeared more and more in a hazy twilight]. The foggy setting, a linguistic pictorial effacement of line, also serves the characters' non-linear mental peregrinations allowing them, in classic stream-of-consciousness form, to shift in and out of various time frames. The chapter's opening description is filled with chiaroscuro: "skovbrynet saa sort paa nattehimlen" [the edge of the woods so black against the night sky] and "i lysets og skyggernes flugt" (32-3) [in the light's and the shadows' flight]. As Niels approaches the house and his wife, "han lod maanen og skoven og skyggerne svinge i en stor dristig bue" (34) [he let the moon and the forest and the shadows swing in a great, bold bow]. A sense of fall permeates the late August scene, evidenced in the harvest colors he sees on the way home: "Og langsmed vejene og inde i skoven hang rønnebærrene røde og de første gule blade sejlede lydløst i mørket" (40) [And along the edge of the roads and deep in the woods the red rowan berries and the first yellow leaves fell silently in the dark]. Branner's prose takes on a tenebrific quality due not only to the night setting but also to the angst brewing inside Niels.

Seeing Mortimer's "mørke og lukkede vogn" [dark and closed car], Niels thinks of a hearse—"den var bygget til at hans høje magre figur skulde ligge ned i den" (35) [it was built so that his (Mortimer's) tall, lean figure could lie down in it]—reinforcing the association of black with Mortimer. Mortimer's presence, particularly at the time of Merete's impending childbirth, represents a threat indicated in shadowy images infringing on Niels's magical moonlight: "Den døende mands nærhed var som en skræk i naturen, en formørkelse der langsomt krøb hen over maanen" (38) [The dying man's closeness was like a fright in nature, an eclipse creeping slowly across the moon]. This threat lingers even after Mortimer has left the scene; later in the novel, Niels, in a state of angst over his wife's condition, still senses Mortimer's presence as a shadow: "Stuen var fuld af en mørk og truende stilhed efter Mortimer. . . . Han var bange for at miste hende og turde ikke tænke den tanke" (146) [The room was full of a dark and threatening stillness after Mortimer. . . . He was afraid of losing her and dared not think that thought].

The color green has a particularly negative function in *Drømmen om en kvinde*, a characteristic it possesses in a number of Branner's works, especially when it appears in a window scene. Branner avoids the positive, nature-oriented connotations of green by never writing of verdant bliss in springtime colors; instead, like a German expressionist, he uses green in a lurid manner. His green is a neon light—artificial, urban, and sickly.[7] Branner is fond of having characters view each other through windows, and he frequently makes the watched characters appear underwater like fish in an aquarium.[8] This coloring calls to mind van Gogh's unnerving green effects in *Night Café* (1888), with its central image—a lurid green billiard table,[9] or the solitary neon-green light of Edward Hopper's urban diner, *Nighthawks* (1942).

Staring in the window of his home, Niels sees the following picture:

> De sad omkring et grønt bord og spillede kort. Der var tændt en lampe med gul skærm, men alting derinde lyste grønligt som gennem vand—at staa i det abne mørke mellem trærerne og se ind til dem var som at se ind i en grotte under vandet. Spillebordets klæde var giftgrønt som en mospude og fru Fleichers kjole var grøn, og deres ansigter var blege med et grønlight genskær. . . . Mortimer sad med ryggen mod vinduet, han havde lagt sine kort frem paa en række foran sig og sad langstrakt og ubevægelig over dem, en lurende skygge paa den grønne bund. En abstrakt skygge.
>
> (41)[10]

(They sat around a green table and played cards. A light with a yellow shade had been turned on, but everything in the room appeared greenish, as through water—to stand in the open darkness between the trees and look in at them was like seeing an underwater grotto. The card table's cover was poison-green like moss, and Mrs. Fleicher's dress was green, and their faces were pale with a greenish reflection. . . . Mortimer sat with his back toward the window; he had laid his cards in a row in front of himself and sat, elongated and motionless, over them, a threatening shadow on the green ground. An abstract shadow.)

Branner, à la Fauve, has saturated the scene in green; the reader, too, cannot help but see in green. This poison green light serves two functions simultaneously: it reflects the state of what is happening within the room permeated with Mortimer's sickly presence, and it reflects Niels's perception of what is happening in the room—his sense of Mortimer and his illness as a threat to his child's impending birth. With his back to Niels, the window, and, thus, the reader, Mortimer is reduced once again to a shadow, an "abstract" cut-out presiding over a game of chance played out on a green tablecloth. In his use of the Danish word *bund* [ground]—in artistic terms denoting the color beneath the predominant color—Branner unites this sickly green with the darkness of Mortimer's presence.

The unnatural green light also reinforces the atmosphere of an aquarium, with characters compared to carp, pike, and other fish in Niels's eyes. At one point, Mortimer is decribed as "skyggen af en gedde paa en grøn søbund" (47) [the shadow of a pike on a green sea bottom]. Merete sits in a "brunlige mørke" [brownish darkness] as Mortimer struggles to pull her into the deadly green light of his card game. Niels fears that "hun var allerede næsten død, næsten udslukt og opløst" (47) [she was already almost dead, almost extinguished and dissolved]. Leaning against a tree, he enters a half-dream state in which he remembers his departure from her that morning, and then, still dreaming, sees the present: an expressionist portrait of "store fjerne træer som tegnede ubevægelige skygger henover jorden" (48) [great distant trees that sketched immovable shadows across the earth]. Finally forcing himself to awaken, the appropriately named Niels Rude bangs on the window pane thus breaking Mortimer's shadowy spell. Inside, he finds that Merete "havde rykket sin stol lidt tilbage og sad indhyllet i sit brunlige mørke" (50) [had drawn her chair back a little and sat ensconced in her brownish darkness]. Despite the threat of Mortimer's green world, Merete finds safety in her brown corner where the possibility of life for her child still exists.

Goethe's discussion in *Zur Farbenlehre* of the symbolic use of chromaticism raises an important question:

> *Hiermit ist ein anderer Gebrauch nahe verwandt, den man den allegorischen nennen könnte. Bei diesem ist mehr Zufälliges und Willkürliches, ja man kann sagen, etwas Konventionelles, indem uns erst der Sinn des Zeichens überliefert werden muß, ehe wir wissen, was es bedeuten soll, wie es sich z.B. mit der grünen Farbe verhält, die man der Hoffnung zugeteilt hat.*
>
> (520)[11]

> Another application is nearly allied to this; it might be called the allegorical application. In this there is more of accident and caprice, inasmuch as the meaning of the sign must first be communicated to us before we know what it is to signify; what idea, for instance, is attached to the green colour, which has been appropriated to hope?
>
> (351)

Green has a long, positive tradition in the history of chromaticism. Goethe believed that "unser Auge findet in derselben eine reale Befriedigung" (501) ["the eye experiences a distinctly grateful impression from this colour" (316)], and Degas bathed many of his dancers in a luminous green light. Kandinsky claims that "absolutes Grün ist die ruhigste Farbe, die es gibt" (94) ["Green is the most restful colour that exists" (38)] and views it as the link between the earthly yellow and the spiritual blue. Yet Branner seems more inclined to agree with van Gogh, who called green the color of "those terrible things, men's passions." Even when Merete tries to picture a positive green, her efforts collapse into blackness. Imagining her newborn son taking his first steps,

> *hun saa hvordan han besværligt fik rejst sig op og gik et lille stykke i græsset. Hun vilde se det klare grønne græs, men hun saa det kun som tusmørke. Nu dumpede han og forsvandt. . . . Hun laa og ventede paa han skulde komme igen, men han kom ikke igen. Græsset blev sort og opslugte ham helt.*
>
> (229)

> (she saw how with difficulty he raised himself up and walked a little bit in the grass. She wanted to see the clear green grass, but she could only see it as a twilight. Now he fell and disappeared. . . . She lay and waited for him to get up again, but he never did. The grass had become black and swallowed him completely.)

In *Drømmen om en kvinde,* Branner also associates green with Mortimer's illness. When Mortimer has a painful attack and Charlotte attempts to drive him home, he looks out the window at "et gitter af grønligt lysende stammer, striber og pletter af maanelys inde over skovbunden" (139) [a lattice of shining green trunks, stripes and spots of moonlight over the woodland floor]. Clambering out of the car to be sick, Mortimer sits down on a "grøn, frønnet træstub" [green, decaying treestump]. Later, again staring out the window of the car, he sees "hastigt gitter af grønligt glidende stammer, maanelyse trækroner som voksede og forsvandt, voksede og forsvandt" (140) [rapidly passing bars of green tree trunks gliding by, moonlit treetops that rose and disappeared, rose and disappeared]. The reader, though given no modifier for "green," cannot help but picture the bilious hue suggested by Mortimer's sickly state.

After the pervasive green of the card game, Branner paints the initial scene of the following chapter in red, appealing to the eye's natural desire for each color's complement. The autumnal element hinted at as Niels rides his motorcycle home and passes the rowan berries and the haystacks serves a primary function in Merete's haunting reverie in the beginning of Chapter 3 (Part One). Kierkegaard was especially fond of autumn, a predilection to which he gave voice in his 1846 essay "Lovtale over Eferaaret" (Praise for Autumn). Declaring autumn "farvernes tid" [the time of colors], Kierkegaard contends that "Farve er den synlige Bevægelse og Uro" (388) [color is the visible movement and restlessness]. The passions, Kierkegaard felt, come with autumn: "og med Lidenskaberne Uroen, og med Uroen Farven" (388) [and with the passions, unrest, and with unrest color]. He also saw the "mørkladne Efteraar" [darkened autumn] as "veemodigt" (388) [wistful]. Spring's constant green ("næsten som Grønt man spiser" (339) [almost like the greens one eats]) does not excite Kierkegaard; against the starkness and bareness of autumn, colors stand out. Thus, Kierkegaard calls autumn "erindringens Tid" [memory's time] and "tænkningens Tid" [thinking's time], reinforcing the connection between color and consciousness.

Waiting for Niels to reenter the house, Merete's mind shifts abruptly to a time in her youth when a man had followed her into the forest. "Det var oktober og træerne stod stille og svømmede some røde spejlbilleder i taagen, det dryppede og sivede højt oppe fra, hun vadede til anklerne i det tunge røde løv" (51) [It was October, and the trees stood silent and swam like red reflections in the mist; it dripped and oozed from high above. She waded up to her ankles in the heavy red leaves]. In her memory, Merete searches the leaf-strewn forest floor for chestnuts; the presence of so much red and Merete's bag of chestnuts conjours up fairy-tale images (cf. Little Red Riding Hood) that juxtapose a strong sexual undercurrent also conveyed in the threatening use of red. As the afternoon draws to a close, "de røde træer svømmede langsomt ind i mørkningen" (51) [the red trees swam slowly into the dusk].

Though the reader is given no indication of the identity of the man following Merete in her memory (or what may simply be a reverie illustrating her fear of death), Branner uses certain devices to connect the threatening figure with Mortimer. In the scene in which the shadowy figure grabs her arm and looks her in the eyes, Merete sees that

> *Hans ansigt var hvidt men ellers var han helt sort og ulden i tusmørket. . . . Mens de stod saadan begyndte hans pupiller langsomt at glide opefter, der kom en hvid rand frem under dem. Det saa ud som om han døde paa stedet. . . . Hun mærkede hans greb om sin arm og hans aande, der var sort som tusmørket.*
>
> (52)

(His face was white; otherwise he was completely black and unclear in the dusk. . . . While they stood like that, his pupils began slowly to glide upwards, a white rim appeared under them. It looked as if he was dying on the spot. . . . She noticed his grasp around her arm and his breath, which was black as the twilight.)

Through the use of black and white imagery, Branner compels the reader to think of Mortimer. Merete knows—senses—that the stranger would have killed her in the forest that day; she becomes "tung og død under tanken" (53) [heavy and dead under the thought]. Colorless, rational black and white, represented in the dark figure pursuing her in the twilight, constitute a threat to the life-giving red of her world.

Curiously, this recollection comes to Merete in the moment before Niels, banging on the window, breaks not only Mortimer's green spell over the other card players but also shatters Merete's deadly daydream. Waiting for him to reenter the house, she slips into another recollection, this time of her first sexual encounter with Niels; she recalls a window scene the following morning bathed in a strong, red light: "Lidt efter kom han frem i sin badekaabe og trak gardinet fra vinduet saa hele østhimlen brød ind som en rød flodbølge. Selv om hun klemte øjnene haardt til spillede det røde lys gennem hendes øjenlaag" (56) [A little while after he came out in his bathrobe and pulled the curtains from the windows, so that all the eastern sky burst in like a red tidal wave. Although she squeezed her eyes shut, the red light appeared through her eyelids]. Merete's mind then shifts to Niels's childhood, which she is capable of "seeing"; she pictures his first nocturnal emission, at the age of fourteen:

> *Hun tænkte sig han havde drømt om en brændende skov og røde heste paa flugt gennem skoven, paa hestene red kvinder med flyvende haar og hvide bryster som galionsfigurer, en gyngende glidende flod af røde hestekroppe og hvide kvindebryster ud og ind mellem flammerne.*
>
> (59-60)

(She imagined he had dreamed of a burning forest and red horses in flight through the woods, on the horses rode women with flying hair and white breasts, like figureheads, a rocking river of red horses' bodies and women's white breasts, gliding in and out among the flames.)

This red sensuality is again identified, as it is for Kierkegaard, with autumn. Merete envisions a young, autoerotic Niels running through the October forest and throwing himself "fladt ned paa maven i det dybe røde løv, han fik hænderne fyldt med det, han borede ansigtet ned i det" (60) [flat down on his stomach in the deep red leaves, he got his hands filled with them, he bore his face down into them]. Kouwer observes that "red as color of life directs itself chiefly at one aspect of life in particular: its animal aspect. Rather than representing life in general, red is seen in connection with *emotional life*. . . . This applies still more to sexuality and erotism" (106). Kouwer also takes issue with conventional psychoanalytical readings of red as "masculine": "red is not as much the masculine *per se* as the erotic relation between the sexes in general" (107). Branner has, in fact, applied red to the feminine force—Merete—in *Drømmen om en kvinde*. In Chapter 2 of the second part of the book, as she is speaking to her doctor, Clemens, Merete daydreams of holding her unborn son: "hun sad bag sit vindue i den store stue og saa ud paa en klar oktoberdag, hvor det blæste med røde blade fra skovbrynet" (188) [she sat behind her window in the large room and looked out on a clear October day, where red leaves from the forest's edge blew by].

These window scenes, seamlessly melting into one another, indicate Branner's image-driven kind of stream-of-consciousness, its pictorial quality emphasized by the framing windows.[12] In addition, the scenes reinforce the nonlinear structure of thought: Merete oberves that she "kunde aldrig se hans [Niels] liv i rækkefølge og sammenhæng, kun som løsrevne billeder der blandede og forbyttede sig mens hun saa paa dem" (65) [could never see his life in succession and coherence, only as detached pictures that merged and changed while she looked at them]. The portraits illustrate the Bergsonian notion of *durée*, the "continuity of a background" on which seemingly discontinuous states of being exist. Bergson comments on the connection between consciousness, color, and our concept of time in *Introduction à la metaphysique*:

> *Mais de même qu'une conscience à base de couleur, qui sympathiserait intérieurement avec l'orangé, au lieu de le percevoir extérieurement, se sentirait prise entre du rouge et du jaune, pressentirait même peut-être, audessous de cette dernière couleur, tout un spectre en lequel se prolonge naturellement la continuité qui va du rouge au jaune, ainsi l'intuition de notre durée, bien loin de nous laisser suspendus dans le vide comme ferait la pure analyse, nous met en contact avec toute une continuité de durées que nous devons essayer de suivre soit vers le bas, soit vers le haut.*
>
> (Œuvres 419)

> But just as a consciousness based on color, which sympathized internally with orange instead of perceiving it externally, would feel itself held between red and yellow, would even perhaps suspect beyond this last color a complete spectrum into which the continuity from red to yellow might expand naturally, so the intuition of our duration, far from leaving us suspended in the void as pure analysis would do, brings us into contact with a whole continuity of durations which we must try to follow, whether downwards or upwards.
>
> (62-3)

Merete's mental pictures, driven by a pictorial sense rather than a temporal one, move both upwards and downwards (i.e., back and forth in time); the scenes are shuffled like cards in her consciousness.

Remembering his "regnebuefarvet" [rainbow-colored] body[13] standing at the window that first morning, Merete's mind shifts to another window scene in which Niels smokes a pipe and sits in the "blindt genskær" [blind reflection] caused by the snow outside. The ashen-white light on his face reflects Niels's reaction to an accident that day at the shipyard, an explosion in which two men have died. Awakening in the middle of the night, Merete discovers Niels staring out the window: "der var ikke blod tilbage i hans ansigt, det var som en hvid gennemsigtig skal der kunde bryde sammen til støv ved en mindste berøring" (58) [there was no blood left in his face, which was like a white transparent shell that could crumble into dust at the slightest touch].

More importantly, this association of white with angst precedes its appearance as the color of Niels's worries of losing Merete in childbirth. Branner refers to Merete's impending labor as "veernes hvide lys" (145, 146) [the labor pains's white light]. He again employs a window scene, this time in the car as they are driving to the hospital, to paint a silvery portrait of Niels's fear:

> *Han saa hendes ansigt mod ruden, hendes fortabte barneansigt med den tunge lidende mund, og han vidste saadan var det: de havde altid hørt hinanden til, og han kunde ikke miste hende uden at miste sig selv. Ingenting var mere flygtig end hendes ansigt mod ruden— han saa det gennemsigtig som en spejling af sølvskæret udenfor, og han turde ikke røre sig og næppe trække vejret af frygt for at det skulde forsvinde for øjnene af ham, løbe langt ud over markerne og tabe sig i stjernernes lys, blive eet med vejtræernes kroner som fløj forbi med tynde askehvide blade, angstfuldt jagende som stød af en puls—nu—nu—nu. . . . Han saa ud gennem ruden. Men ogsaa derude stod angsten i en stor og dødelig stilhed, han saa lige ud i en grænseegn, en sølvegn hvor alting var tyndt og hvidt som aske og kun ventede paa et vindpust.*
>
> (147)
>
> (He saw her face against the window, her lost child's face with the heavy suffering mouth, and he knew that so it was: they had always belonged to each other and he could not lose her without losing himself. Nothing was more fleeting than her face against the window pane—he saw it transparent like the reflection of a silvery glow from outside, and he dared not move and could barely breathe from fear that it should disappear before his eyes, run far out over the fields and disappear in the light of the stars, become one with the passing treetops that flew by with thin ash-white leaves, full of angst, pursuing like a throbbing pulse—now—now—now. . . . He looked out of the window. But his fear was out there too in a great and deadly silence; he stared out on a borderland, a silver meadow where everything was thin and white like ashes and only waited for a breath of air.)

Earlier in the novel, Merete recalls her dead father's many discussions with her about astronomy, uniting them with the pale light of the stars. At one point she observes that Mortimer's eyes possess "det samme fjerne hvide lys" [the same distant white light] as her father's. Her dying father had shown her "alle vinterens klare stjernebilleder . . . han kendte alle deres billeder" (128-9) [all of winter's clear constellations . . . he knew all their outlines]. Just as Merete's dead father—a sign for the lost presence of a godhead—is the source of her visual sense, Niels cites Merete as the source of the power of the silvery light that falls on the world. The world around him is created by the light of her eyes and hands. Somewhere in the highly expressionistic "stumme grænseegn" [silent borderland] that appears as they drive by, she is "en hvid sten som fløj og et bladhang som sænkede sig, hendes aande skabte dette angstfulde skær som tonede fra sølv over til hvid aske" (148) [a white stone that flew (by) and foliage that descended, her spirit created the angst-filled glow that shifts tones from silver to white ashes]. Should the dreaded "breath of air" come and scatter the silver-white world Merete's weakening spirit holds in place, Niels's remaining world would become "sort i sort" (148) [black in black], the triumph of Mortimer and death.

Niels's fears have sapped the world of its color, creating an achromatic, ashen landscape. Riding along in the early morning hours, Niels sees a wide, white main road stretch before them; the city reaches out toward them in "et langt tog af biler [som] kom jagende tæt efter hinanden med gule ravøjne" (148) [a long procession of cars (that) came chasing each other closely with yellow amber-eyes]. The street lights fly by, "svævende hvide kugler" [floating white spheres]; above them the stars have gone out and the darkness closes in on both sides "tæt som en mur" [tightly, like a wall]. After leaving Merete with the doctor, Niels arrives home in the early hours of dawn: "Han kunde se langt ud over markerne og skoven, men der var ikke lys og ikke mørke til i verden. Kun et ubevægeligt askegraat skær" (153) [He could see far off over the fields and the woods, but no light or darkness existed in the world. Only an immovable, ash-gray glow]. These gray landscapes recall

Fitzgerald's "valley of ashes" in *The Great Gatsby,* "where ashes take the forms of houses and chimneys and rising smoke and, finally, with a transcendent effort, of ash-gray men who move dimly and already crumbling through the powdery air" (23).

An array of gruesome colors greets Niels as he rides his motorcycle toward the long night of waiting. The sun sets in a "gult og svidende lys" (238) [yellow and scorching light] that blinds Niels as he rides toward the horizon. As a yellow haze of burning dust, a "forrykte skær" [demented glow], rises before him, he turns off the main road to avoid the "ulidelige gule lys" [unbearable yellow light]. Moving from warm to cold tones, the yellow light gives way to a flaming red that, after a moment, dissolves into "en dis af violet . . . en taaget masse" [a haze of violet . . . a foggy mass]. The darkness that follows rises from the ground, "et ujævnt mørke som af levende sorte myrer" [an uneven darkness as of living black ants]. This living darkness rising from the ground indicates the war's imminence—its shadow reaching up over Denmark from below—but Niels's mind is preoccupied. He fears this night that follows the burning yellow light: "han havde troet den vilde blive værre end noget andet han havde mødt i sit liv" (239) [he believed it would be worse than any other he had encountered in his life]. Even the moonlight's shadows casting their nets along the road seem threatening.

The first sign of hope finally appears: "sølvlyset laa over verden igen" [the silver light lay over the world again]. In a synesthetic moment, that light reminds Niels of Merete's whistling when she rides behind him on the motorcycle; he recalls that whenever she whistles, everything around him, the light and the air, shifts tone. As the colors of the seasons pass through his memory (the blue shadows of spring, the yellow leaves of an "oktobermelodi" [October melody]), he realizes that her presence has colored his ashen world. It is through *her* mind that Niels's world takes on chromatic possibilities; his own world is the colorlessly white one. After a sleepless night on the beach, Niels feels that "der var ikke lys og ikke mørke, og der var ingen tid til, og stadigvæk ingen sky paa himlen og ingen bevægelse i luften men kun en evig venten paa noget som aldrig skulde komme" (242) [there were no light and no darkness, and no time existed, and still no cloud in the sky and no movement in the air, but only an eternal waiting for something that would never come]. Into this "farveløse gry" [colorless dawn] the silver stripe suddenly appears, separating the sky from the sea and night from day.[14] The return of Merete's silvery light serves as the final sign of hope in the novel: she and her baby will survive.

Drømmen om en kvinde features a notable absence of the color blue, which serves no major function until two parallel scenes leading to Mortimer's death and Merete's childbirth. Though there are many dreams of women in the book—Merete pictures Niels's adolescent dreams of women; Charlotte's lover Bjørndal discusses his pubescent dream of a *synderinde*; Niels dreams a number of times about Merete—Mortimer's and Merete's simultaneous dream of being in a cathedral leads to a vision of the ultimate woman: the Madonna. Nearing his final stages of consciousness, Mortimer dreams of travelling by train with his mother, as he did as a child. In images of both motion and sight, Branner's prose is oneiric throughout this scene. Outside the window, telephone poles swing up and down in partial view recalling the tree trunks in the sickly green scene following the card game; even when the steam from the train's engine obscures them, "kunde man følge de mørke parallelle linier i deres synken og stigen" (218) [you could follow the dark, parallel lines in their rise and fall]. Once the mathematical telephone poles disappear, Mortimer has nothing to occupy his thoughts until he notices and begins counting the wheels thumping on the rail joints.

He departs at a station and takes out a map with an "x" marking a tourist destination reachable only by way of many meandering streets. He soon comes upon a Gothic cathedral, which he enters: "Han gik gennem portalen og stod under krydshvælvingerne, de graa søjleknipper rejste sig omkring ham som stammer i en forstenet skov" (220) [He went through the portal and stood under the cross-arches; gray rows of columns rose around him like tree trunks in a petrified forest]. Looking up, he notices that everything in the cathedral strives upward toward "det umulige" [the impossible]. A nun moves silently among the people in the pews as she passes around her collection box; Mortimer places a coin in it and avoids her eyes. Statues of saints in "farvet tøj" [colored clothes] stand in "halvmørke nicher" [half-dark niches]. A pregnant woman goes by, and her presence repels him. Even in his dream, Mortimer's rational mind—already shown by his fascination with the black, parallel telephone poles—cannot tolerate "hele den brogede uforstaaelighed" [all the multicolored incomprehensibility] that confronts him in the cathedral everywhere he looks. For Branner, the higher, non-mimetic levels of consciousness are colored.

The particolored scene suddenly melts into a dark, oppressive one; the sounds of an organ fill the gloomy atmosphere. Looking up into the dizzying darkness, Mortimer's eyes search for something to fix on:

> *De fandt et vindue ud imod vest, et højt spidsbuet vindue hvor himmelmoderen sad med barnet paa sit skød. Hendes kjole stod uhyre stor og blaa mod den sene sol ude bag rummet, og mens han saa op paa den, var det som alting blev blaat for øjnene af ham. Orgelspillet vældede med et blaa tonemørke, og solen fra vest var som en blaa mørkesol.*

(221-2)

(They found a window out toward the west, a high, pointed window in which the heavenly mother sat with the child on her lap. Her dress was enormously big and blue, against the late sun out behind the room; and while he looked up at it, everything seemed to become blue before his eyes. Organ music gushed forth with a dark blue tone, and the sun from the west was like a dark blue sun.)

After a lifetime of black-and-white rationalism and a skepticism—we are told he was a "radikal" in his youth—Mortimer, on the threshold of death, faces a multicolored world building to a deep blue vision. He has been forced by his illness to the brink of spirituality, depicted in the very scene he has most dreaded throughout the book: a woman and her child. In the history of chromaticism, Kandinsky has been one of the most eloquent commentators on the power of blue: "Diese Vertiefungsgabe finden wir im blau und ebenso erst theoretisch in ihren physischen Bewegungen 1. vom Menschen weg und 2. zum eigenen Zentrum. . . . Die Neigung des Blau zur Vertiefung ist so groß, daß es gerade in tieferen Tönen intensiver wird und charakteristischer innerlich wirkt" (92) ["The power of profound meaning is found in blue, and first in its physical movements (1) of retreat from the spectator, (2) of turning in upon its own centre. The inclination of blue to depth is so strong that its inner appeal is stronger when its shade is deeper" (38)]. The organ music underscoring Mortimer's reverie also echoes one of Kandinsky's many observations on the musicality of color: "Musikalisch dargestellt ist helles Blau einer Flöte ähnlich, das dunkle dem Cello, immer tiefer gehend den wunderbaren Klängen der Baßgeige; in tiefer, feierlicher Form ist der Klang des Blau dem der tiefen Orgel vergleichbar" (93) ["In music a light blue is like a flute, a darker blue a cello; a still darker a thunderous double bass; and the darkest blue of all—an organ" (38)].

The spiritual blue, darkening and tightening around Mortimer in his dream, fills him with terror. He suddenly feels he is free-falling and awakens: "han laa i sin seng og den store rædsel kom fra noget blaat han kunde se ude bag vinduet—et stykke dybblaa eftermiddagshimmel højt oppe over hustagene" (222) [he lay in his bed and the great terror came from something blue he could see out past the window—a piece of deep blue afternoon sky high up over the rooftops]. His vision of the Madonna has dissipated into a patch of blue sky. Branner, using the absorbing power of blue, blurs the temporal lines between levels of consciousness. Has the vision merely melted into the blue in the window, or has the patch of blue sky inspired the blue dream within a brief state of half-consciousness?

Fading in and out of consciousness as she waits to give birth, Merete dreams of the same Gothic cathedral. Her reverie is more populated than Mortimer's; outside the cathedral, she is surrounded by an army of children, whose words she understands though they all speak in different languages. A vast flock of doves hovering over her descends in Pentecostal fashion and lights on her head, shoulders, and arms. Still, she feels compelled to leave them and enter the cathedral. Just as every line of Mortimer's cathedral strives upward toward the impossible, Merete's columns reach up "mod det uopnaaelige" [toward the unattainable]. Organ music again fills the vast space. The gray arches appear to lift before her, "som bladtaget over en skov løfter sig umærkeligt fra aar til aar" (227) [as the roof of leaves over a forest rise imperceptibly from year to year]. Her eyes eventually fix on the stained-glass image of the Madonna: "Himmelmoderen sad i det vindue med sit nyfødte barn paa skødet, og vestsolen brød i skraa støtter gennem hendes klædning og gjorde den saa lysende blaa" (227) [The heavenly mother sat in the window with her newborn child on her lap, and the western sun broke in slanting pillars through her clothes and made them so brilliantly blue]. Her increasing labor pains darken Merete's vision finally reducing it to a blue fog: she awakens to the same patch of deep-blue afternoon sky that Mortimer had seen. Though her labor pains parallel his horrible attacks, unlike Mortimer, she does not awaken in horror. The children in her dream point not only to her pregnancy but to a child-like state of receptivity still lacking in Mortimer.

In his discussion of the lost blue of the stained-glass windows in the twelfth-century cathedral at Chartres, Henry Adams describes the child-like mind-set necessary for an appreciation of the effects of the blue glass: "Any one can feel it who will only consent to feel like a child . . . feel a sense beyond the human ready to reveal a sense divine that would make that world once more intelligible, and would bring the Virgin to life again . . . any one willing to try could feel it like the child, reading new thought without end into the art he has studied a hundred times" (178). Adams hints at a sense of abandonment, a surrender to the synesthetic power of one color. Although Merete longs to yield to the blue vision, Mortimer cannot.

In both Merete's and Mortimer's descriptions, the Gothic cathedral is compared to a forest. Merete's association with nature, illustrated throughout the book in a number of forest images, is both positive and red, and negative and brown, whereas Mortimer's only scene in the woods occurs on the ghastly green night when he stops and is sick. The cathedral's columns remind both characters, though, of towering trees. In *Der Untergang des Abendlandes*, Oswald Spengler comments on the sylvan elements of the cathedral in Western culture:

> In dem Wälderhaften der Dome, der mächtigen Erhöhung des Mittelschiffs über die Seitenschiffe gegenüber der flachgedeckten Basilika, in der Verwandlung der Säulen, die durch Basis und Kapitäl als

abgeschlossene Einzeldinge in den Raum gestellt waren, zu Pfeilern und Pfeilerbündeln, die aus dem Boden wachsen und deren Äste und Linien sich über dem Scheitel im Unendlichen verteilen und verschlingen, während von den Riesenfenstern, welche die Wand aufgelöst haben, ein ungewisses Licht durch den Raum flutet, liegt die architektonische Verwirklichung eines Weltgefühls, das im Hochwald der nordischen Ebenen sein ursprünglichstes Symbol gefunden hatte. Und zwar im Laubwalde mit dem geheimnisvollen Gewirr seiner Äste und dem Raunen der ewig bewegten Blättermassen über dem Haupte des Betrachters, hoch über der Erde, von der die Wipfel durch den Stamm sich zu lösen versuchen.

(512-3)

(The character of the Faustian cathedral is that of the *forest*. The mighty elevation of the nave above the flanking aisles, in contrast to the flat roof of the basilica; the transformation of the columns, which with base and capital had been set as self-contained individuals in space, into pillars and clustered-pillars that grow up out of the earth and spread on high into an infinite subdivision and interlacing of lines and branches; the giant windows by which the wall is dissolved and the interior filled with mysterious light—these are the architectural actualizing of a world-feeling that had found the first of all its symbols in the high forest of the Northern plains, the deciduous forest with its mysterious tracery, its whispering of ever-mobile foliage over men's heads, its branches straining through the trunks to be free of earth).

(396)

In the incessant reaching upwards which appears in both Merete's and Mortimer's dreams, Spengler senses a reflection of human longing. Like Kandinsky, he also sees this longing reflected in organ music: "*Deshalb wurde die Orgel, deren tiefes und helles Brausen unsere Kirchen füllt, deren Klang . . . etwas Grenzenloses und Ungemessenes besitzt, das Organ der abendländischen Andacht. Dom und Orgel bilden eine symbolische Einheit wie Tempel und Statue*" (513-4) ["And for that reason the organ, that roars deep and high through our churches in tones which . . . seem to know neither limit nor restraint, is the instrument of instruments in Western devotions. Cathedral and organ form a symbolic unity like temple and statue" (396)].

In his final moments, Mortimer experiences an epiphany. The foolishness of his materialistic logocentricism has finally become clear, because he now faces something greater than himself: death. He accepts the irrational thought that the only life worth living exists outside of the warped image presented in the here and now:

> *Han vaagnede lidt efter lidt til en ny tanke og en ny tro. Det liv der nu skulde gaa under i døden var ikke hans liv. Det var kun en illusion, et forvrænget spejlbillede, et ynkeligt og forkrøg. Hans virkelige liv levede et helt andet sted, det levede i ufatteligt storhed og sandhed i en helt anden tid, paa et helt andet plan. Det var ikke nogen logisk eller rimelig tanke, men sandheden boede i den fordi den var nødvendig. Og nu skulde døden komme og gøre ham til eet med sit liv.*
>
> (236)

(He awakened gradually to a new thought and a new belief. The life that would now perish in death was not his life. It was only an illusion, a distorted reflection, a pathetic and stunted attempt. His real life existed in a whole other place; it lived in incomprehensible greatness and truth in a whole other time, on a whole other plane. It was not a logical or rational thought, but the truth lived in it because it was necessary. And now death was coming to make him one with his life.)

Mortimer acquires a new view of death—he finally attains the child-like imagination missing from his adult life. Awakening from the dream of mimetic reality, Mortimer becomes like a child once more: "*Døden, tænkte han, og ogsaa den tanke var ny for ham, han kaldte den ved navn som et barn der vaagner af en hæslig drøm kalder paa sin mor*" (236) [Death, he thought, and that thought was also new for him; he called it by name, as a child that awakens from a bad dream calls for its mother]. Tying together the novel's myriad window images—the frames around our image-bound consciousness—Mortimer realizes that he "*behøvede kun at have set ud ad mit vindue*" (236) [needed only to have looked out my window] to have realized the existence of something greater than himself.

. . . . .

In *Drømmen om en kvinde* Branner uses colorific language to emphasize the various levels of consciousness that comprise life. Just as colors lead Merete and Niels from one memory of each other to another, Branner's stream of consciousness fades in and out of the telling moments in each character's life. Having abandoned the formulaic writing of the collective and the psychoanalytical novel that had defined his earlier works and not yet struggling with the large political issues that propel his later novels, Branner crafts a seamless meld of image and idea in *Drømmen om en kvinde*. Though the novel is not as strictly Freudian as his previous work, Branner maintains—and continues to maintain throughout his literary career—a multi-layered sense of human consciousness.

In *Open Minded: Working Out the Logic of the Soul*, Jonathan Lear notes: "A battle may be fought over Freud, but the war is over our culture's image of the human soul. Are we to see humans as having depth—as complex psychological organisms who generate layers of meaning which lie beneath the surface of their own understanding? Or are we to take ourselves as transparent to ourselves?" (27). Branner would have surely advocated the former view. His novels and short stories reveal his search, through pictorial language, for the images lurking beneath our own understanding.

Notes

1. With its emphasis on color and light—but not line—Branner's pictorial language falls in the category of the "painterly" as defined by Heinrich Wölfflin.

2. Commenting on stream-of-consciousness in *Principles of Psychology,* William James has observed that "every definite image in the mind is steeped and dyed in the free water that flows around it" (255).

3. I have used the 1956 edition. Though Emil Frederiksen disapproves of some of Branner's abbreviations in the 1956 edition, I find the prose and the entire novel more taut. Branner also deleted some of the more heavy-handed religious dialogue, thus allowing the imagery to convey the message.

4. Cf. Branner's use of this image in his short story "Et grædende barn."

5. Cf. the widower Valdemar Skjold-Lassen in the short story "To minutters stilhed" (see Branner, *Om lidt*).

6. Cf. Gabriel in *Ingen Kender Natten.*

7. A parallel on canvas can be found in the ghastly green background of Ernst Ludwig Kirchner's *Five Women in the Street* (1913).

8. As early as "Isaksen" (1933), see Branner *Om lidt,* his third published story and the basis for his first novel *Legetøj,* Branner introduced his comparison of people to fish: the insidious office manager Feddersen is described as "en lurende gedde" (8) [a threatening pike].

9. In a letter (9 September 1888) to his brother Theo, van Gogh writes: "In my picture of the Night Café, I have tried to express the idea that the café is a place where one can destroy oneself, go mad or commit a crime. In short, I have tried, by contrasting soft pink with blood-red and wine-red, soft Louis xv-green and Veronese green with yellow-green and harsh blue-greens, all this in an atmosphere of an infernal furnace in pale sulphur, to express the powers of darkness in a common tavern" (399).

10. This use of "giftgrøn" [poison-green] is one of the few instances of Branner using a modifier on the color. Recognizing the subjective nature of each person's "view" of any color, he tends simply to write "red" or "green" and to let the context lead the reader toward a more positive or negative hue.

11. One could answer with Matisse's contention in "The Path of Colour" (1947): "It is enough to invent signs. When you have a real feeling for nature, you can create signs which are equivalents to both the artist and the spectator" (178).

12. An excellent example of this device occurs in Branner's short story "Om lidt er vi borte," in which a young man wandering the Copenhagen streets at night stops at different windows, where the portrait of a life is expressed in one fleeting scene.

13. When Charlotte returns from her tryst with her lover Carl Bjørndal, the dying Mortimer cannot escape the rainbow in his wife's eyes: "Han kunde se det regnbuefarvede lys der flimrer fra et nøgent legeme. . . . Han vilde ikke se det. Men han maatte. Han kunde ikke slippe det" (224) [He could see the rainbow-colored light that shimmers from a naked body. . . . He did not want to see it. But he had to. He could not escape it].

14. Branner uses a similar device in his novella *Angst*: After a horrible night described in the most German expressionist prose of all Branner's works, the narrator finally sees "en Stribe blaagrøn Morgenhimmel" (62) [a streak of blue-green morning sky], a thin slice of hope.

Works Cited

Adams, Henry. *Mont Saint Michel and Chartres.* Princeton: Princeton UP, 1989.

Arnheim, Rudolf. *Art and Visual Perception: A Psychology of the Creative Eye.* The New Edition. Berkeley: U California P, 1974.

Bergson, Henri. *An Introduction to Metaphysics.* Trans. T. E. Hulme. New York and London: Putnam, 1912.

———. *Creative Evolution.* Trans. Arthur Mitchell. New York: Henry Holt, 1944.

———. *Œuvres.* Paris: Presses Universitaires de France, 1959.

Branner, H. C. *Angst.* Copenhagen: Boghallen, 1947.

———. *Drømmen om en kvinde: Roman.* Copenhagen: Gyldendal, 1956.

———. *Drømmeren og andre noveller.* Frederiksberg: Fisker Schou, 1997.

———. "Et grædende barn." *Vandring langs Floden.* Copenhagen: Gyldendal, 1956. 47-58.

———. "Humanismens krise." *Mennesket i tiden* 1. Copenhagen: Hans Reitzels Forlag, 1950.

———. *Ingen kender natten.* Copenhagen: Gyldendal, 1955.

———. *Kunstens uafhængighed.* Copenhagen: Gyldendal, 1957.

———. "Kunst og virkelighed." *Louisiana Revy* (October 1962): 28-31.

———. *Legetøj*. Copenhagen: Branner, 1936.

———. *Om lidt er vi borte og To minutters stilhed*. Copenhagen: Gyldendal, 1969.

———. *Rytteren: Roman*. Copenhagen: Branner og Korch, 1949.

Faulkner, William. *Light in August*. New York: Random House, 1985.

Fitzgerald, F. Scott. *The Great Gatsby*. New York: Scribner's, 1953.

Frederiksen, Emil. *H. C. Branner: Et kritisk grundrids*. Copenhagen: Gyldendal, 1966.

Gage, John. *Color and Culture: Practice and Meaning from Antiquity to Abstraction*. Boston: Little Brown, 1993.

Goethe, Johann Wolfgang. *Zur Farbenlehre. Werke: Hamburger Ausgabe* Vol. 13. München: Deutscher Taschenbuch Verlag, 1982. 314-536; translated as *Theory of Colours*. Trans. Charles Lock Eastlake. Cambridge, MA: M.I.T. Press, 1975.

Itten, Johannes. *Kunst der Farbe: Subjektives Erleben und objektives Erkennen als Wege zur Kunst*. Ravensburg: Maier, 1961.

James, William. *The Principles of Psychology*. Vol. 1. The Works of William James. Cambridge: Harvard UP, 1983.

Kandinsky, Wassily. *Über das Geistige in der Kunst*. Bern: Benteli, 1973; translated as *Concerning the Spiritual in Art*. Trans. M. T. H. Sadler. New York: Dover, 1977.

Kierkegaard, Søren. "Lovtale over Efteraaret." *Søren Kierkegaards Papirer*. Ed. Niels Thulstrup. Vol. 7, Part 1. Copenhagen: Gyldendal, 1968. 385-90.

Kouwer, Benjamin J. *Colors and Their Character: A Psychological Study*. Trans. H. C. Bosvan Kasteel. The Hague: Martinus Nijhoff, 1949.

Lamb, Trevor, and Janine Bourriau, eds. *Colour: Art & Science*. Cambridge: Cambridge UP, 1995.

Lear, Jonathan. *Open Minded: Working Out the Logic of the Soul*. Cambridge: Harvard UP, 1998.

Matisse, Henri. *Matisse on Art*. Ed. Jack Flam. Berkeley: U California P, 1995.

Raskin, Richard. *Color: An Outline of Terms and Concepts*. Aarhus: Aarhus UP, 1986.

Riley, Charles A. *Color Codes: Modern Theories of Color in Philosophy, Painting and Architecture, Literature, Music, and Psychology*. Hanover: UP of New England, 1995.

Schmidt, Lone. *Farven og lyset: Studier i Goethes farvelære*. Risskov: Klematis, 1995.

Secher, Claus. "Humanismens sande krise: en analyse af H. C. Branners *Rytteren*." *Analyser af danske romaner* Vol. 3. Ed. Jørgen Holmgaard. Cophenhagen: Borgens, 1977. Pp. 202-34.

Shlain, Leonard. *Art & Physics: Parallel Visions in Space, Time and Light*. New York: Morrow, 1991.

Skyum-Nielsen, Erik. *Ideologi og æstetik i H. C. Branners sene forfatterskab*. Copenhagen: Gyldendal, 1980.

———. "To minutters skønhed, tredive års opbyggelighed." *Læsninger i Dansk Litteratur* 4. Eds. Povl Schmidt, Anne-Marie Mai, and Gjesing Knud Bjarne. Odense: Odense Universitetsforlag, 1997. 25-40.

Spengler, Oswald. *Der Untergang des Abendlandes: Umrisse einer Morphologie der Weltgeschichte*. Vol. 1. *Gestalt und Wirklickkeit*. München: Beck, 1922-23; translated as *The Decline of the West*. Vol. 1. *Form and Actuality*. New York: Knopf, 1926.

Steiner, Wendy. *The Colors of Rhetoric: Problems in the Relation between Modern Literature and Painting*. Chicago: U Chicago P, 1982.

van Gogh, Vincent. *The Letters of Vincent van Gogh*. Ed. Ronald de Leeuw. Trans. Arnold Pomerans. London: Penguin, 1996.

Vosmar, Jørn. *H. C. Branner*. Copenhagen: Gyldendal, 1959.

Wölfflin, Heinrich. *Kunstgeschichtliche Grundbegriffe: Das Problem der Stilentwicklung in der neueren Kunst*. München, Bruckmann, 1921.

FURTHER READING

Criticism

Gray, Charlotte Schiander. "Klaus Rifbjerg: A Contemporary Danish Writer." *Books Abroad* 49, no. 1 (winter 1975): 25-8.

    Chronicles the literary output of Danish poet and novelist Klaus Rifbjerg, characterizing him as a leading figure amongst contemporary Danish writers.

Jorgensen, Aage. "Touring the 1970's with the Solvognen in Denmark." *Drama Review* 26, no. 3(95) (fall 1982): 3-14.

    Follows the development of twentieh-century Danish theater, focusing in particular on the development of the Royal Theatre in Copenhagen.

Koefoed, H. A. "Martin Andersen Nexø—Some Viewpoints." *Scandinavica* 4, no. 1 (May 1965): 27-37.

Theorizes that Nexø's political views, often expressed strongly in his works, have tended to diminish his importance as a literary figure in Danish literature.

Mitchell, P. M. "A Need for Myth: Danish Literature After 1940." In *A History of Danish Literature,* pp. 279-301. New York: Kraus-Thomson Organization Limited, 1971.

Provides an overview of Danish literature between 1940 and the mid 1950s.

Poole, Roger. "The Unknown Kierkegaard: Twentieth-Century Receptions." In *The Cambridge Companion to Kierkegaard,* edited by Alastair Hannay and Gordon D. Marino, pp. 48-75. Cambridge, England: Cambridge University Press, 1998.

Traces Kierkegaard's development as an author and critic of major importance in twentieth-century literary studies.

How to Use This Index

The main references

> **Calvino, Italo**
> 1923-1985 .... CLC 5, 8, 11, 22, 33, 39, 73; SSC 3, 48

list all author entries in the following Gale Literary Criticism series:

AAL = *Asian American Literature*
BG = *The Beat Generation: A Gale Critical Companion*
BLC = *Black Literature Criticism*
BLCS = *Black Literature Criticism Supplement*
CLC = *Contemporary Literary Criticism*
CLR = *Children's Literature Review*
CMLC = *Classical and Medieval Literature Criticism*
DC = *Drama Criticism*
HLC = *Hispanic Literature Criticism*
HLCS = *Hispanic Literature Criticism Supplement*
HR = *Harlem Renaissance: A Gale Critical Companion*
LC = *Literature Criticism from 1400 to 1800*
NCLC = *Nineteenth-Century Literature Criticism*
NNAL = *Native North American Literature*
PC = *Poetry Criticism*
SSC = *Short Story Criticism*
TCLC = *Twentieth-Century Literary Criticism*
WLC = *World Literature Criticism, 1500 to the Present*
WLCS = *World Literature Criticism Supplement*

The cross-references

> See also CA 85-88, 116; CANR 23, 61;
> DAM NOV; DLB 196; EW 13; MTCW 1, 2;
> RGSF 2; RGWL 2; SFW 4; SSFS 12

list all author entries in the following Gale biographical and literary sources:

AAYA = *Authors & Artists for Young Adults*
AFAW = *African American Writers*
AFW = *African Writers*
AITN = *Authors in the News*
AMW = *American Writers*
AMWR = *American Writers Retrospective Supplement*
AMWS = *American Writers Supplement*
ANW = *American Nature Writers*
AW = *Ancient Writers*
BEST = *Bestsellers*
BPFB = *Beacham's Encyclopedia of Popular Fiction: Biography and Resources*
BRW = *British Writers*
BRWS = *British Writers Supplement*
BW = *Black Writers*
BYA = *Beacham's Guide to Literature for Young Adults*
CA = *Contemporary Authors*
CAAS = *Contemporary Authors Autobiography Series*
CABS = *Contemporary Authors Bibliographical Series*
CAD = *Contemporary American Dramatists*
CANR = *Contemporary Authors New Revision Series*
CAP = *Contemporary Authors Permanent Series*
CBD = *Contemporary British Dramatists*
CCA = *Contemporary Canadian Authors*
CD = *Contemporary Dramatists*
CDALB = *Concise Dictionary of American Literary Biography*
CDALBS = *Concise Dictionary of American Literary Biography Supplement*
CDBLB = *Concise Dictionary of British Literary Biography*

CMW = *St. James Guide to Crime & Mystery Writers*
CN = *Contemporary Novelists*
CP = *Contemporary Poets*
CPW = *Contemporary Popular Writers*
CSW = *Contemporary Southern Writers*
CWD = *Contemporary Women Dramatists*
CWP = *Contemporary Women Poets*
CWRI = *St. James Guide to Children's Writers*
CWW = *Contemporary World Writers*
DA = *DISCovering Authors*
DA3 = *DISCovering Authors 3.0*
DAB = *DISCovering Authors: British Edition*
DAC = *DISCovering Authors: Canadian Edition*
DAM = *DISCovering Authors: Modules*
   DRAM: *Dramatists Module;* **MST:** *Most-studied Authors Module;*
   MULT: *Multicultural Authors Module;* **NOV:** *Novelists Module;*
   POET: *Poets Module;* **POP:** *Popular Fiction and Genre Authors Module*
DFS = *Drama for Students*
DLB = *Dictionary of Literary Biography*
DLBD = *Dictionary of Literary Biography Documentary Series*
DLBY = *Dictionary of Literary Biography Yearbook*
DNFS = *Literature of Developing Nations for Students*
EFS = *Epics for Students*
EXPN = *Exploring Novels*
EXPP = *Exploring Poetry*
EXPS = *Exploring Short Stories*
EW = *European Writers*
FANT = *St. James Guide to Fantasy Writers*
FW = *Feminist Writers*
GFL = *Guide to French Literature,* Beginnings to 1789, 1798 to the Present
GLL = *Gay and Lesbian Literature*
HGG = *St. James Guide to Horror, Ghost & Gothic Writers*
HW = *Hispanic Writers*
IDFW = *International Dictionary of Films and Filmmakers: Writers and Production Artists*
IDTP = *International Dictionary of Theatre: Playwrights*
LAIT = *Literature and Its Times*
LAW = *Latin American Writers*
JRDA = *Junior DISCovering Authors*
MAICYA = *Major Authors and Illustrators for Children and Young Adults*
MAICYAS = *Major Authors and Illustrators for Children and Young Adults Supplement*
MAWW = *Modern American Women Writers*
MJW = *Modern Japanese Writers*
MTCW = *Major 20th-Century Writers*
NCFS = *Nonfiction Classics for Students*
NFS = *Novels for Students*
PAB = *Poets: American and British*
PFS = *Poetry for Students*
RGAL = *Reference Guide to American Literature*
RGEL = *Reference Guide to English Literature*
RGSF = *Reference Guide to Short Fiction*
RGWL = *Reference Guide to World Literature*
RHW = *Twentieth-Century Romance and Historical Writers*
SAAS = *Something about the Author Autobiography Series*
SATA = *Something about the Author*
SFW = *St. James Guide to Science Fiction Writers*
SSFS = *Short Stories for Students*
TCWW = *Twentieth-Century Western Writers*
WLIT = *World Literature and Its Times*
WP = *World Poets*
YABC = *Yesterday's Authors of Books for Children*
YAW = *St. James Guide to Young Adult Writers*

Literary Criticism Series
Cumulative Author Index

20/1631
See Upward, Allen

A/C Cross
See Lawrence, T(homas) E(dward)

Abasiyanik, Sait Faik 1906-1954
See Sait Faik
See also CA 123

Abbey, Edward 1927-1989 .... **CLC 36, 59**
See also AMWS 13; ANW; CA 45-48; 128; CANR 2, 41; DA3; DLB 256, 275; LATS 1; MTCW 2; TCWW 2

Abbott, Edwin A. 1838-1926 .... **TCLC 139**
See also DLB 178

Abbott, Lee K(ittredge) 1947- .... **CLC 48**
See also CA 124; CANR 51, 101; DLB 130

Abe, Kobo 1924-1993 ...... **CLC 8, 22, 53, 81; SSC 61; TCLC 131**
See also CA 65-68; 140; CANR 24, 60; DAM NOV; DFS 14; DLB 182; EWL 3; MJW; MTCW 1, 2; RGWL 3; SFW 4

Abe Kobo
See Abe, Kobo

Abelard, Peter c. 1079-c. 1142 ...... **CMLC 11**
See also DLB 115, 208

Abell, Kjeld 1901-1961 .... **CLC 15**
See also CA 191; 111; DLB 214; EWL 3

Abercrombie, Lascelles
1881-1938 .... **TCLC 141**
See also CA 112; DLB 19; RGEL 2

Abish, Walter 1931- .... **CLC 22; SSC 44**
See also CA 101; CANR 37, 114; CN 7; DLB 130, 227

Abrahams, Peter (Henry) 1919- .... **CLC 4**
See also AFW; BW 1; CA 57-60; CANR 26; CDWLB 3; CN 7; DLB 117, 225; EWL 3; MTCW 1, 2; RGEL 2; WLIT 2

Abrams, M(eyer) H(oward) 1912- ... **CLC 24**
See also CA 57-60; CANR 13, 33; DLB 67

Abse, Dannie 1923- .... **CLC 7, 29; PC 41**
See also CA 53-56; CAAS 1; CANR 4, 46, 74; CBD; CP 7; DAB; DAM POET; DLB 27, 245; MTCW 1

Abutsu 1222(?)-1283 .... **CMLC 46**
See Abutsu-ni

Abutsu-ni
See Abutsu
See also DLB 203

Achebe, (Albert) Chinua(lumogu)
1930- ...... **BLC 1; CLC 1, 3, 5, 7, 11, 26, 51, 75, 127, 152; WLC**
See also AAYA 15; AFW; BPFB 1; BRWC 2; BW 2, 3; CA 1-4R; CANR 6, 26, 47; CDWLB 3; CLR 20; CN 7; CP 7; CWRI 5; DA; DA3; DAB; DAC; DAM MST, MULT, NOV; DLB 117; DNFS 1; EWL 3; EXPN; EXPS; LAIT 2; LATS 1; MAI-CYA 1, 2; MTCW 1, 2; NFS 2; RGEL 2; RGSF 2; SATA 38, 40; SATA-Brief 38; SSFS 3, 13; TWA; WLIT 2

Acker, Kathy 1948-1997 .... **CLC 45, 111**
See also AMWS 12; CA 117; 122; 162; CANR 55; CN 7

Ackroyd, Peter 1949- .... **CLC 34, 52, 140**
See also BRWS 6; CA 123; 127; CANR 51, 74, 99; CN 7; DLB 155, 231; HGG; INT CA-127; MTCW 1; RHW; SUFW 2

Acorn, Milton 1923-1986 .... **CLC 15**
See also CA 103; CCA 1; DAC; DLB 53; INT 103

Adamov, Arthur 1908-1970 .... **CLC 4, 25**
See also CA 17-18; 25-28R; CAP 2; DAM DRAM; EWL 3; GFL 1789 to the Present; MTCW 1; RGWL 2, 3

Adams, Alice (Boyd) 1926-1999 .. **CLC 6, 13, 46; SSC 24**
See also CA 81-84; 179; CANR 26, 53, 75, 88; CN 7; CSW; DLB 234; DLBY 1986; INT CANR-26; MTCW 1, 2; SSFS 14

Adams, Andy 1859-1935 .... **TCLC 56**
See also TCWW 2; YABC 1

Adams, (Henry) Brooks
1848-1927 .... **TCLC 80**
See also CA 123; 193; DLB 47

Adams, Douglas (Noel) 1952-2001 .. **CLC 27, 60**
See also AAYA 4, 33; BEST 89:3; BYA 14; CA 106; 197; CANR 34, 64; CPW; DA3; DAM POP; DLB 261; DLBY 1983; JRDA; MTCW 1; NFS 7; SATA 116; SATA-Obit 128; SFW 4

Adams, Francis 1862-1893 .... **NCLC 33**

Adams, Henry (Brooks)
1838-1918 .... **TCLC 4, 52**
See also AMW; CA 104; 133; CANR 77; DA; DAB; DAC; DAM MST; DLB 12, 47, 189, 284; EWL 3; MTCW 1; NCFS 1; RGAL 4; TUS

Adams, John 1735-1826 .... **NCLC 106**
See also DLB 31, 183

Adams, Richard (George) 1920- ... **CLC 4, 5, 18**
See also AAYA 16; AITN 1, 2; BPFB 1; BYA 5; CA 49-52; CANR 3, 35; CLR 20; CN 7; DAM NOV; DLB 261; FANT; JRDA; LAIT 5; MAICYA 1, 2; MTCW 1, 2; NFS 11; SATA 7, 69; YAW

Adamson, Joy(-Friederike Victoria)
1910-1980 .... **CLC 17**
See also CA 69-72; 93-96; CANR 22; MTCW 1, 2; SATA 11; SATA-Obit 22

Adcock, Fleur 1934- .... **CLC 41**
See also CA 25-28R, 182; CAAE 182; CAAS 23; CANR 11, 34, 69, 101; CP 7; CWP; DLB 40; FW

Addams, Charles (Samuel)
1912-1988 .... **CLC 30**
See also CA 61-64; 126; CANR 12, 79

Addams, Jane 1860-1935 .... **TCLC 76**
See also AMWS 1; FW

Addams, (Laura) Jane 1860-1935 . **TCLC 76**
See also AMWS 1; CA 194; FW

Addison, Joseph 1672-1719 .... **LC 18**
See also BRW 3; CDBLB 1660-1789; DLB 101; RGEL 2; WLIT 3

Adler, Alfred (F.) 1870-1937 .... **TCLC 61**
See also CA 119; 159

Adler, C(arole) S(chwerdtfeger)
1932- .... **CLC 35**
See also AAYA 4, 41; CA 89-92; CANR 19, 40, 101; CLR 78; JRDA; MAICYA 1, 2; SAAS 15; SATA 26, 63, 102, 126; YAW

Adler, Renata 1938- .... **CLC 8, 31**
See also CA 49-52; CANR 95; CN 7; MTCW 1

Adorno, Theodor W(iesengrund)
1903-1969 .... **TCLC 111**
See also CA 89-92; 25-28R; CANR 89; DLB 242; EWL 3

Ady, Endre 1877-1919 .... **TCLC 11**
See also CA 107; CDWLB 4; DLB 215; EW 9; EWL 3

A.E. .... **TCLC 3, 10**
See Russell, George William
See also DLB 19

Aelfric c. 955-c. 1010 .... **CMLC 46**
See also DLB 146

Aeschines c. 390B.C.-c. 320B.C. ..... **CMLC 47**
See also DLB 176

Aeschylus 525(?)B.C.-456(?)B.C. .. **CMLC 11, 51; DC 8; WLCS**
See also AW 1; CDWLB 1; DA; DAB; DAC; DAM DRAM, MST; DFS 5, 10; DLB 176; LMFS 1; RGWL 2, 3; TWA

Aesop 620(?)B.C.-560(?)B.C. .... **CMLC 24**
See also CLR 14; MAICYA 1, 2; SATA 64

Affable Hawk
See MacCarthy, Sir (Charles Otto) Desmond

Africa, Ben
See Bosman, Herman Charles

Afton, Effie
See Harper, Frances Ellen Watkins

Agapida, Fray Antonio
See Irving, Washington

Agee, James (Rufus) 1909-1955 ...... **TCLC 1, 19**
See also AAYA 44; AITN 1; AMW; CA 108; 148; CDALB 1941-1968; DAM NOV; DLB 2, 26, 152; DLBY 1989; EWL 3; LAIT 3; LATS 1; MTCW 1; RGAL 4; TUS

Aghill, Gordon
See Silverberg, Robert
Agnon, S(hmuel) Y(osef Halevi)
1888-1970 .... **CLC 4, 8, 14; SSC 30**
See also CA 17-18; 25-28R; CANR 60, 102; CAP 2; EWL 3; MTCW 1, 2; RGSF 2; RGWL 2, 3
Agrippa von Nettesheim, Henry Cornelius
1486-1535 .... **LC 27**
Aguilera Malta, Demetrio
1909-1981 .... **HLCS 1**
See also CA 111; 124; CANR 87; DAM MULT, NOV; DLB 145; EWL 3; HW 1; RGWL 3
Agustini, Delmira 1886-1914 .... **HLCS 1**
See also CA 166; HW 1, 2; LAW
Aherne, Owen
See Cassill, R(onald) V(erlin)
Ai 1947- .... **CLC 4, 14, 69**
See also CA 85-88; CAAS 13; CANR 70; DLB 120; PFS 16
Aickman, Robert (Fordyce)
1914-1981 .... **CLC 57**
See also CA 5-8R; CANR 3, 72, 100; DLB 261; HGG; SUFW 1, 2
Aidoo, (Christina) Ama Ata
1942- .... **BLCS; CLC 177**
See also AFW; BW 1; CA 101; CANR 62; CD 5; CDWLB 3; CN 7; CWD; CWP; DLB 117; DNFS 1, 2; EWL 3; FW; WLIT 2
Aiken, Conrad (Potter) 1889-1973 .... **CLC 1, 3, 5, 10, 52; PC 26; SSC 9**
See also AMW; CA 5-8R; 45-48; CANR 4, 60; CDALB 1929-1941; DAM NOV, POET; DLB 9, 45, 102; EWL 3; EXPS; HGG; MTCW 1, 2; RGAL 4; RGSF 2; SATA 3, 30; SSFS 8; TUS
Aiken, Joan (Delano) 1924- .... **CLC 35**
See also AAYA 1, 25; CA 9-12R, 182; CAAE 182; CANR 4, 23, 34, 64, 121; CLR 1, 19, 90; DLB 161; FANT; HGG; JRDA; MAICYA 1, 2; MTCW 1; RHW; SAAS 1; SATA 2, 30, 73; SATA-Essay 109; SUFW 2; WYA; YAW
Ainsworth, William Harrison
1805-1882 .... **NCLC 13**
See also DLB 21; HGG; RGEL 2; SATA 24; SUFW 1
Aitmatov, Chingiz (Torekulovich)
1928- .... **CLC 71**
See Aytmatov, Chingiz
See also CA 103; CANR 38; MTCW 1; RGSF 2; SATA 56
Akers, Floyd
See Baum, L(yman) Frank
Akhmadulina, Bella Akhatovna
1937- .... **CLC 53; PC 43**
See also CA 65-68; CWP; CWW 2; DAM POET; EWL 3
Akhmatova, Anna 1888-1966 ..... **CLC 11, 25, 64, 126; PC 2**
See also CA 19-20; 25-28R; CANR 35; CAP 1; DA3; DAM POET; EW 10; EWL 3; MTCW 1, 2; RGWL 2, 3
Aksakov, Sergei Timofeyvich
1791-1859 .... **NCLC 2**
See also DLB 198
Aksenov, Vassily
See Aksyonov, Vassily (Pavlovich)
Akst, Daniel 1956- .... **CLC 109**
See also CA 161; CANR 110
Aksyonov, Vassily (Pavlovich)
1932- .... **CLC 22, 37, 101**
See also CA 53-56; CANR 12, 48, 77; CWW 2; EWL 3
Akutagawa Ryunosuke 1892-1927 ... **SSC 44; TCLC 16**
See also CA 117; 154; DLB 180; EWL 3; MJW; RGSF 2; RGWL 2, 3

Alabaster, William 1568-1640 .... **LC 90**
See also DLB 132; RGEL 2
Alain 1868-1951 .... **TCLC 41**
See also CA 163; EWL 3; GFL 1789 to the Present
Alain de Lille c. 1116-c. 1203 .... **CMLC 53**
See also DLB 208
Alain-Fournier .... **TCLC 6**
See Fournier, Henri-Alban
See also DLB 65; EWL 3; GFL 1789 to the Present; RGWL 2, 3
Al-Amin, Jamil Abdullah 1943- .... **BLC 1**
See also BW 1, 3; CA 112; 125; CANR 82; DAM MULT
Alanus de Insluis
See Alain de Lille
Alarcon, Pedro Antonio de
1833-1891 .... **NCLC 1; SSC 64**
Alas (y Urena), Leopoldo (Enrique Garcia)
1852-1901 .... **TCLC 29**
See also CA 113; 131; HW 1; RGSF 2
Albee, Edward (Franklin) (III)
1928- .. **CLC 1, 2, 3, 5, 9, 11, 13, 25, 53, 86, 113; DC 11; WLC**
See also AAYA 51; AITN 1; AMW; CA 5-8R; CABS 3; CAD; CANR 8, 54, 74; CD 5; CDALB 1941-1968; DA; DA3; DAB; DAC; DAM DRAM, MST; DFS 2, 3, 8, 10, 13, 14; DLB 7, 266; EWL 3; INT CANR-8; LAIT 4; LMFS 2; MTCW 1, 2; RGAL 4; TUS
Alberti, Rafael 1902-1999 .... **CLC 7**
See also CA 85-88; 185; CANR 81; DLB 108; EWL 3; HW 2; RGWL 2, 3
Albert the Great 1193(?)-1280 .... **CMLC 16**
See also DLB 115
Alcala-Galiano, Juan Valera y
See Valera y Alcala-Galiano, Juan
Alcayaga, Lucila Godoy
See Godoy Alcayaga, Lucila
Alcott, Amos Bronson 1799-1888 .... **NCLC 1**
See also DLB 1, 223
Alcott, Louisa May 1832-1888 . **NCLC 6, 58, 83; SSC 27; WLC**
See also AAYA 20; AMWS 1; BPFB 1; BYA 2; CDALB 1865-1917; CLR 1, 38; DA; DA3; DAB; DAC; DAM MST, NOV; DLB 1, 42, 79, 223, 239, 242; DLBD 14; FW; JRDA; LAIT 2; MAICYA 1, 2; NFS 12; RGAL 4; SATA 100; TUS; WCH; WYA; YABC 1; YAW
Aldanov, M. A.
See Aldanov, Mark (Alexandrovich)
Aldanov, Mark (Alexandrovich)
1886(?)-1957 .... **TCLC 23**
See also CA 118; 181
Aldington, Richard 1892-1962 .... **CLC 49**
See also CA 85-88; CANR 45; DLB 20, 36, 100, 149; LMFS 2; RGEL 2
Aldiss, Brian W(ilson) 1925- . **CLC 5, 14, 40; SSC 36**
See also AAYA 42; CA 5-8R; CAAE 190; CAAS 2; CANR 5, 28, 64, 121; CN 7; DAM NOV; DLB 14, 261, 271; MTCW 1, 2; SATA 34; SFW 4
Aldrich, Bess Streeter
1881-1954 .... **TCLC 125**
See also CLR 70
Alegria, Claribel
See Alegria, Claribel
See also DLB 145, 283
Alegria, Claribel 1924- .... **CLC 75; HLCS 1; PC 26**
See Alegria, Claribel
See also CA 131; CAAS 15; CANR 66, 94; CWW 2; DAM MULT; EWL 3; HW 1; MTCW 1

Alegria, Fernando 1918- .... **CLC 57**
See also CA 9-12R; CANR 5, 32, 72; EWL 3; HW 1, 2
Aleichem, Sholom .... **SSC 33; TCLC 1, 35**
See Rabinovitch, Sholem
See also TWA
Aleixandre, Vicente 1898-1984 .... **HLCS 1; TCLC 113**
See also CANR 81; DLB 108; EWL 3; HW 2; RGWL 2, 3
Aleman, Mateo 1547-1615(?) .... **LC 81**
Alencon, Marguerite d'
See de Navarre, Marguerite
Alepoudelis, Odysseus
See Elytis, Odysseus
See also CWW 2
Aleshkovsky, Joseph 1929-
See Aleshkovsky, Yuz
See also CA 121; 128
Aleshkovsky, Yuz .... **CLC 44**
See Aleshkovsky, Joseph
Alexander, Lloyd (Chudley) 1924- ... **CLC 35**
See also AAYA 1, 27; BPFB 1; BYA 5, 6, 7, 9, 10, 11; CA 1-4R; CANR 1, 24, 38, 55, 113; CLR 1, 5, 48; CWRI 5; DLB 52; FANT; JRDA; MAICYA 1, 2; MAICYAS 1; MTCW 1; SAAS 19; SATA 3, 49, 81, 129, 135; SUFW; TUS; WYA; YAW
Alexander, Meena 1951- .... **CLC 121**
See also CA 115; CANR 38, 70; CP 7; CWP; FW
Alexander, Samuel 1859-1938 .... **TCLC 77**
Alexie, Sherman (Joseph, Jr.)
1966- .... **CLC 96, 154; NNAL**
See also AAYA 28; BYA 15; CA 138; CANR 65, 95; DA3; DAM MULT; DLB 175, 206, 278; LATS 1; MTCW 1; NFS 17; SSFS 18
al-Farabi 870(?)-950 .... **CMLC 58**
See also DLB 115
Alfau, Felipe 1902-1999 .... **CLC 66**
See also CA 137
Alfieri, Vittorio 1749-1803 .... **NCLC 101**
See also EW 4; RGWL 2, 3
Alfred, Jean Gaston
See Ponge, Francis
Alger, Horatio, Jr. 1832-1899 .... **NCLC 8, 83**
See also CLR 87; DLB 42; LAIT 2; RGAL 4; SATA 16; TUS
Al-Ghazali, Muhammad ibn Muhammad
1058-1111 .... **CMLC 50**
See also DLB 115
Algren, Nelson 1909-1981 ..... **CLC 4, 10, 33; SSC 33**
See also AMWS 9; BPFB 1; CA 13-16R; 103; CANR 20, 61; CDALB 1941-1968; DLB 9; DLBY 1981, 1982, 2000; EWL 3; MTCW 1, 2; RGAL 4; RGSF 2
al-Hariri, al-Qasim ibn 'Ali Abu Muhammad al-Basri
1054-1122 .... **CMLC 63**
See also RGWL 3
Ali, Ahmed 1908-1998 .... **CLC 69**
See also CA 25-28R; CANR 15, 34; EWL 3
Ali, Tariq 1943- .... **CLC 173**
See also CA 25-28R; CANR 10, 99
Alighieri, Dante
See Dante
Allan, John B.
See Westlake, Donald E(dwin)
Allan, Sidney
See Hartmann, Sadakichi
Allan, Sydney
See Hartmann, Sadakichi

Allard, Janet .... **CLC 59**
Allen, Edward 1948- .... **CLC 59**
Allen, Fred 1894-1956 .... **TCLC 87**
Allen, Paula Gunn 1939- ..... **CLC 84; NNAL**
  See also AMWS 4; CA 112; 143; CANR 63; CWP; DA3; DAM MULT; DLB 175; FW; MTCW 1; RGAL 4
Allen, Roland
  See Ayckbourn, Alan
Allen, Sarah A.
  See Hopkins, Pauline Elizabeth
Allen, Sidney H.
  See Hartmann, Sadakichi
Allen, Woody 1935- .... **CLC 16, 52**
  See also AAYA 10, 51; CA 33-36R; CANR 27, 38, 63; DAM POP; DLB 44; MTCW 1
Allende, Isabel 1942- ... **CLC 39, 57, 97, 170; HLC 1; SSC 65; WLCS**
  See also AAYA 18; CA 125; 130; CANR 51, 74; CDWLB 3; CWW 2; DA3; DAM MULT, NOV; DLB 145; DNFS 1; EWL 3; FW; HW 1, 2; INT CA-130; LAIT 5; LAWS 1; LMFS 2; MTCW 1, 2; NCFS 1; NFS 6, 18; RGSF 2; RGWL 3; SSFS 11, 16; WLIT 1
Alleyn, Ellen
  See Rossetti, Christina (Georgina)
Alleyne, Carla D. .... **CLC 65**
Allingham, Margery (Louise)
  1904-1966 .... **CLC 19**
  See also CA 5-8R; 25-28R; CANR 4, 58; CMW 4; DLB 77; MSW; MTCW 1, 2
Allingham, William 1824-1889 ...... **NCLC 25**
  See also DLB 35; RGEL 2
Allison, Dorothy E. 1949- .... **CLC 78, 153**
  See also AAYA 53; CA 140; CANR 66, 107; CSW; DA3; FW; MTCW 1; NFS 11; RGAL 4
Alloula, Malek .... **CLC 65**
Allston, Washington 1779-1843 .... **NCLC 2**
  See also DLB 1, 235
Almedingen, E. M. .... **CLC 12**
  See Almedingen, Martha Edith von
  See also SATA 3
Almedingen, Martha Edith von 1898-1971
  See Almedingen, E. M.
  See also CA 1-4R; CANR 1
Almodovar, Pedro 1949(?)- .... **CLC 114; HLCS 1**
  See also CA 133; CANR 72; HW 2
Almqvist, Carl Jonas Love
  1793-1866 .... **NCLC 42**
Alonso, Damaso 1898-1990 .... **CLC 14**
  See also CA 110; 131; 130; CANR 72; DLB 108; EWL 3; HW 1, 2
Alov
  See Gogol, Nikolai (Vasilyevich)
Al Siddik
  See Rolfe, Frederick (William Serafino Austin Lewis Mary)
  See also GLL 1; RGEL 2
Alta 1942- .... **CLC 19**
  See also CA 57-60
Alter, Robert B(ernard) 1935- .... **CLC 34**
  See also CA 49-52; CANR 1, 47, 100
Alther, Lisa 1944- .... **CLC 7, 41**
  See also BPFB 1; CA 65-68; CAAS 30; CANR 12, 30, 51; CN 7; CSW; GLL 2; MTCW 1
Althusser, L.
  See Althusser, Louis
Althusser, Louis 1918-1990 .... **CLC 106**
  See also CA 131; 132; CANR 102; DLB 242
Altman, Robert 1925- .... **CLC 16, 116**
  See also CA 73-76; CANR 43

Alurista .... **HLCS 1**
  See Urista, Alberto H.
  See also DLB 82
Alvarez, A(lfred) 1929- .... **CLC 5, 13**
  See also CA 1-4R; CANR 3, 33, 63, 101; CN 7; CP 7; DLB 14, 40
Alvarez, Alejandro Rodriguez 1903-1965
  See Casona, Alejandro
  See also CA 131; 93-96; HW 1
Alvarez, Julia 1950- .... **CLC 93; HLCS 1**
  See also AAYA 25; AMWS 7; CA 147; CANR 69, 101; DA3; DLB 282; LATS 1; MTCW 1; NFS 5, 9; SATA 129; WLIT 1
Alvaro, Corrado 1896-1956 .... **TCLC 60**
  See also CA 163; DLB 264; EWL 3
Amado, Jorge 1912-2001 ... **CLC 13, 40, 106; HLC 1**
  See also CA 77-80; 201; CANR 35, 74; DAM MULT, NOV; DLB 113; EWL 3; HW 2; LAW; LAWS 1; MTCW 1, 2; RGWL 2, 3; TWA; WLIT 1
Ambler, Eric 1909-1998 .... **CLC 4, 6, 9**
  See also BRWS 4; CA 9-12R; 171; CANR 7, 38, 74; CMW 4; CN 7; DLB 77; MSW; MTCW 1, 2; TEA
Ambrose, Stephen E(dward)
  1936-2002 .... **CLC 145**
  See also AAYA 44; CA 1-4R; 209; CANR 3, 43, 57, 83, 105; NCFS 2; SATA 40, 138
Amichai, Yehuda 1924-2000 .. **CLC 9, 22, 57, 116; PC 38**
  See also CA 85-88; 189; CANR 46, 60, 99; CWW 2; EWL 3; MTCW 1
Amichai, Yehudah
  See Amichai, Yehuda
Amiel, Henri Frederic 1821-1881 .... **NCLC 4**
  See also DLB 217
Amis, Kingsley (William)
  1922-1995 ...... **CLC 1, 2, 3, 5, 8, 13, 40, 44, 129**
  See also AITN 2; BPFB 1; BRWS 2; CA 9-12R; 150; CANR 8, 28, 54; CDBLB 1945-1960; CN 7; CP 7; DA; DA3; DAB; DAC; DAM MST, NOV; DLB 15, 27, 100, 139; DLBY 1996; EWL 3; HGG; INT CANR-8; MTCW 1, 2; RGEL 2; RGSF 2; SFW 4
Amis, Martin (Louis) 1949- .... **CLC 4, 9, 38, 62, 101**
  See also BEST 90:3; BRWS 4; CA 65-68; CANR 8, 27, 54, 73, 95; CN 7; DA3; DLB 14, 194; EWL 3; INT CANR-27; MTCW 1
Ammianus Marcellinus c. 330-c. 395 .... **CMLC 60**
  See also AW 2; DLB 211
Ammons, A(rchie) R(andolph)
  1926-2001 .... **CLC 2, 3, 5, 8, 9, 25, 57, 108; PC 16**
  See also AITN 1; AMWS 7; CA 9-12R; 193; CANR 6, 36, 51, 73, 107; CP 7; CSW; DAM POET; DLB 5, 165; EWL 3; MTCW 1, 2; RGAL 4
Amo, Tauraatua i
  See Adams, Henry (Brooks)
Amory, Thomas 1691(?)-1788 .... **LC 48**
  See also DLB 39
Anand, Mulk Raj 1905- .... **CLC 23, 93**
  See also CA 65-68; CANR 32, 64; CN 7; DAM NOV; EWL 3; MTCW 1, 2; RGSF 2
Anatol
  See Schnitzler, Arthur
Anaximander c. 611B.C.-c. 546B.C. .... **CMLC 22**
Anaya, Rudolfo A(lfonso) 1937- .... **CLC 23, 148; HLC 1**
  See also AAYA 20; BYA 13; CA 45-48; CAAS 4; CANR 1, 32, 51; CN 7; DAM

MULT, NOV; DLB 82, 206, 278; HW 1; LAIT 4; MTCW 1, 2; NFS 12; RGAL 4; RGSF 2; WLIT 1
Andersen, Hans Christian
  1805-1875 .... **NCLC 7, 79; SSC 6, 56; WLC**
  See also CLR 6; DA; DA3; DAB; DAC; DAM MST, POP; EW 6; MAICYA 1, 2; RGSF 2; RGWL 2, 3; SATA 100; TWA; WCH; YABC 1
Anderson, C. Farley
  See Mencken, H(enry) L(ouis); Nathan, George Jean
Anderson, Jessica (Margaret) Queale
  1916- .... **CLC 37**
  See also CA 9-12R; CANR 4, 62; CN 7
Anderson, Jon (Victor) 1940- .... **CLC 9**
  See also CA 25-28R; CANR 20; DAM POET
Anderson, Lindsay (Gordon)
  1923-1994 .... **CLC 20**
  See also CA 125; 128; 146; CANR 77
Anderson, Maxwell 1888-1959 .... **TCLC 2**
  See also CA 105; 152; DAM DRAM; DFS 16; DLB 7, 228; MTCW 2; RGAL 4
Anderson, Poul (William)
  1926-2001 .... **CLC 15**
  See also AAYA 5, 34; BPFB 1; BYA 6, 8, 9; CA 1-4R; 181; 199; CAAE 181; CAAS 2; CANR 2, 15, 34, 64, 110; CLR 58; DLB 8; FANT; INT CANR-15; MTCW 1, 2; SATA 90; SATA-Brief 39; SATA-Essay 106; SCFW 2; SFW 4; SUFW 1, 2
Anderson, Robert (Woodruff)
  1917- .... **CLC 23**
  See also AITN 1; CA 21-24R; CANR 32; DAM DRAM; DLB 7; LAIT 5
Anderson, Roberta Joan
  See Mitchell, Joni
Anderson, Sherwood 1876-1941 .. **SSC 1, 46; TCLC 1, 10, 24, 123; WLC**
  See also AAYA 30; AMW; AMWC 2; BPFB 1; CA 104; 121; CANR 61; CDALB 1917-1929; DA; DA3; DAB; DAC; DAM MST, NOV; DLB 4, 9, 86; DLBD 1; EWL 3; EXPS; GLL 2; MTCW 1, 2; NFS 4; RGAL 4; RGSF 2; SSFS 4, 10, 11; TUS
Andier, Pierre
  See Desnos, Robert
Andouard
  See Giraudoux, Jean(-Hippolyte)
Andrade, Carlos Drummond de ...... **CLC 18**
  See Drummond de Andrade, Carlos
  See also EWL 3; RGWL 2, 3
Andrade, Mario de .... **TCLC 43**
  See de Andrade, Mario
  See also EWL 3; LAW; RGWL 2, 3; WLIT 1
Andreae, Johann V(alentin)
  1586-1654 .... **LC 32**
  See also DLB 164
Andreas Capellanus fl. c. 1185- .... **CMLC 45**
  See also DLB 208
Andreas-Salome, Lou 1861-1937 ... **TCLC 56**
  See also CA 178; DLB 66
Andreev, Leonid
  See Andreyev, Leonid (Nikolaevich)
  See also EWL 3
Andress, Lesley
  See Sanders, Lawrence
Andrewes, Lancelot 1555-1626 .... **LC 5**
  See also DLB 151, 172
Andrews, Cicily Fairfield
  See West, Rebecca
Andrews, Elton V.
  See Pohl, Frederik

Andreyev, Leonid (Nikolaevich)
1871-1919 .... **TCLC 3**
See Andreev, Leonid
See also CA 104; 185

Andric, Ivo 1892-1975 .... **CLC 8; SSC 36; TCLC 135**
See also CA 81-84; 57-60; CANR 43, 60; CDWLB 4; DLB 147; EW 11; EWL 3; MTCW 1; RGSF 2; RGWL 2, 3

Androvar
See Prado (Calvo), Pedro

Angelique, Pierre
See Bataille, Georges

Angell, Roger 1920- .... **CLC 26**
See also CA 57-60; CANR 13, 44, 70; DLB 171, 185

Angelou, Maya 1928- ... **BLC 1; CLC 12, 35, 64, 77, 155; PC 32; WLCS**
See also AAYA 7, 20; AMWS 4; BPFB 1; BW 2, 3; BYA 2; CA 65-68; CANR 19, 42, 65, 111; CDALBS; CLR 53; CP 7; CPW; CSW; CWP; DA; DA3; DAB; DAC; DAM MST, MULT, POET, POP; DLB 38; EWL 3; EXPN; EXPP; LAIT 4; MAICYA 2; MAICYAS 1; MAWW; MTCW 1, 2; NCFS 2; NFS 2; PFS 2, 3; RGAL 4; SATA 49, 136; WYA; YAW

Angouleme, Marguerite d'
See de Navarre, Marguerite

Anna Comnena 1083-1153 .... **CMLC 25**

Annensky, Innokenty (Fyodorovich)
1856-1909 .... **TCLC 14**
See also CA 110; 155; EWL 3

Annunzio, Gabriele d'
See D'Annunzio, Gabriele

Anodos
See Coleridge, Mary E(lizabeth)

Anon, Charles Robert
See Pessoa, Fernando (Antonio Nogueira)

Anouilh, Jean (Marie Lucien Pierre)
1910-1987 . **CLC 1, 3, 8, 13, 40, 50; DC 8, 21**
See also CA 17-20R; 123; CANR 32; DAM DRAM; DFS 9, 10; EW 13; EWL 3; GFL 1789 to the Present; MTCW 1, 2; RGWL 2, 3; TWA

Anthony, Florence
See Ai

Anthony, John
See Ciardi, John (Anthony)

Anthony, Peter
See Shaffer, Anthony (Joshua); Shaffer, Peter (Levin)

Anthony, Piers 1934- .... **CLC 35**
See also AAYA 11, 48; BYA 7; CA 21-24R; CAAE 200; CANR 28, 56, 73, 102; CPW; DAM POP; DLB 8; FANT; MAICYA 2; MAICYAS 1; MTCW 1, 2; SAAS 22; SATA 84; SATA-Essay 129; SFW 4; SUFW 1, 2; YAW

Anthony, Susan B(rownell)
1820-1906 .... **TCLC 84**
See also CA 211; FW

Antiphon c. 480B.C.-c. 411B.C. .... **CMLC 55**

Antoine, Marc
See Proust, (Valentin-Louis-George-Eugene) Marcel

Antoninus, Brother
See Everson, William (Oliver)

Antonioni, Michelangelo 1912- .... **CLC 20, 144**
See also CA 73-76; CANR 45, 77

Antschel, Paul 1920-1970
See Celan, Paul
See also CA 85-88; CANR 33, 61; MTCW 1

Anwar, Chairil 1922-1949 .... **TCLC 22**
See Chairil Anwar
See also CA 121; RGWL 3

Anzaldua, Gloria (Evanjelina)
1942- .... **HLCS 1**
See also CA 175; CSW; CWP; DLB 122; FW; RGAL 4

Apess, William 1798-1839(?) .... **NCLC 73; NNAL**
See also DAM MULT; DLB 175, 243

Apollinaire, Guillaume 1880-1918 .... **PC 7; TCLC 3, 8, 51**
See Kostrowitzki, Wilhelm Apollinaris de
See also CA 152; DAM POET; DLB 258; EW 9; EWL 3; GFL 1789 to the Present; MTCW 1; RGWL 2, 3; TWA; WP

Apollonius of Rhodes
See Apollonius Rhodius
See also AW 1; RGWL 2, 3

Apollonius Rhodius c. 300B.C.-c. 220B.C. .... **CMLC 28**
See Apollonius of Rhodes
See also DLB 176

Appelfeld, Aharon 1932- ... **CLC 23, 47; SSC 42**
See also CA 112; 133; CANR 86; CWW 2; EWL 3; RGSF 2

Apple, Max (Isaac) 1941- .... **CLC 9, 33; SSC 50**
See also CA 81-84; CANR 19, 54; DLB 130

Appleman, Philip (Dean) 1926- .... **CLC 51**
See also CA 13-16R; CAAS 18; CANR 6, 29, 56

Appleton, Lawrence
See Lovecraft, H(oward) P(hillips)

Apteryx
See Eliot, T(homas) S(tearns)

Apuleius, (Lucius Madaurensis)
125(?)-175(?) .... **CMLC 1**
See also AW 2; CDWLB 1; DLB 211; RGWL 2, 3; SUFW

Aquin, Hubert 1929-1977 .... **CLC 15**
See also CA 105; DLB 53; EWL 3

Aquinas, Thomas 1224(?)-1274 ..... **CMLC 33**
See also DLB 115; EW 1; TWA

Aragon, Louis 1897-1982 .... **CLC 3, 22; TCLC 123**
See also CA 69-72; 108; CANR 28, 71; DAM NOV, POET; DLB 72, 258; EW 11; EWL 3; GFL 1789 to the Present; GLL 2; LMFS 2; MTCW 1, 2; RGWL 2, 3

Arany, Janos 1817-1882 .... **NCLC 34**

Aranyos, Kakay 1847-1910
See Mikszath, Kalman

Arbuthnot, John 1667-1735 .... **LC 1**
See also DLB 101

Archer, Herbert Winslow
See Mencken, H(enry) L(ouis)

Archer, Jeffrey (Howard) 1940- .... **CLC 28**
See also AAYA 16; BEST 89:3; BPFB 1; CA 77-80; CANR 22, 52, 95; CPW; DA3; DAM POP; INT CANR-22

Archer, Jules 1915- .... **CLC 12**
See also CA 9-12R; CANR 6, 69; SAAS 5; SATA 4, 85

Archer, Lee
See Ellison, Harlan (Jay)

Archilochus c. 7th cent. B.C.- .... **CMLC 44**
See also DLB 176

Arden, John 1930- .... **CLC 6, 13, 15**
See also BRWS 2; CA 13-16R; CAAS 4; CANR 31, 65, 67; CBD; CD 5; DAM DRAM; DFS 9; DLB 13, 245; EWL 3; MTCW 1

Arenas, Reinaldo 1943-1990 .. **CLC 41; HLC 1**
See also CA 124; 128; 133; CANR 73, 106; DAM MULT; DLB 145; EWL 3; GLL 2; HW 1; LAW; LAWS 1; MTCW 1; RGSF 2; RGWL 3; WLIT 1

Arendt, Hannah 1906-1975 .... **CLC 66, 98**
See also CA 17-20R; 61-64; CANR 26, 60; DLB 242; MTCW 1, 2

Aretino, Pietro 1492-1556 .... **LC 12**
See also RGWL 2, 3

Arghezi, Tudor .... **CLC 80**
See Theodorescu, Ion N.
See also CA 167; CDWLB 4; DLB 220; EWL 3

Arguedas, Jose Maria 1911-1969 .... **CLC 10, 18; HLCS 1**
See also CA 89-92; CANR 73; DLB 113; EWL 3; HW 1; LAW; RGWL 2, 3; WLIT 1

Argueta, Manlio 1936- .... **CLC 31**
See also CA 131; CANR 73; CWW 2; DLB 145; EWL 3; HW 1; RGWL 3

Arias, Ron(ald Francis) 1941- .... **HLC 1**
See also CA 131; CANR 81; DAM MULT; DLB 82; HW 1, 2; MTCW 2

Ariosto, Ludovico 1474-1533 ... **LC 6, 87; PC 42**
See also EW 2; RGWL 2, 3

Aristides
See Epstein, Joseph

Aristophanes 450B.C.-385B.C. .... **CMLC 4, 51; DC 2; WLCS**
See also AW 1; CDWLB 1; DA; DA3; DAB; DAC; DAM DRAM, MST; DFS 10; DLB 176; LMFS 1; RGWL 2, 3; TWA

Aristotle 384B.C.-322B.C. .... **CMLC 31; WLCS**
See also AW 1; CDWLB 1; DA; DA3; DAB; DAC; DAM MST; DLB 176; RGWL 2, 3; TWA

Arlt, Roberto (Godofredo Christophersen)
1900-1942 .... **HLC 1; TCLC 29**
See also CA 123; 131; CANR 67; DAM MULT; EWL 3; HW 1, 2; LAW

Armah, Ayi Kwei 1939- . **BLC 1; CLC 5, 33, 136**
See also AFW; BW 1; CA 61-64; CANR 21, 64; CDWLB 3; CN 7; DAM MULT, POET; DLB 117; EWL 3; MTCW 1; WLIT 2

Armatrading, Joan 1950- .... **CLC 17**
See also CA 114; 186

Armitage, Frank
See Carpenter, John (Howard)

Armstrong, Jeannette (C.) 1948- .... **NNAL**
See also CA 149; CCA 1; CN 7; DAC; SATA 102

Arnette, Robert
See Silverberg, Robert

Arnim, Achim von (Ludwig Joachim von Arnim) 1781-1831 ..... **NCLC 5; SSC 29**
See also DLB 90

Arnim, Bettina von 1785-1859 ...... **NCLC 38, 123**
See also DLB 90; RGWL 2, 3

Arnold, Matthew 1822-1888 ..... **NCLC 6, 29, 89, 126; PC 5; WLC**
See also BRW 5; CDBLB 1832-1890; DA; DAB; DAC; DAM MST, POET; DLB 32, 57; EXPP; PAB; PFS 2; TEA; WP

Arnold, Thomas 1795-1842 .... **NCLC 18**
See also DLB 55

Arnow, Harriette (Louisa) Simpson
1908-1986 .... **CLC 2, 7, 18**
See also BPFB 1; CA 9-12R; 118; CANR 14; DLB 6; FW; MTCW 1, 2; RHW; SATA 42; SATA-Obit 47

Arouet, Francois-Marie
See Voltaire

Arp, Hans
See Arp, Jean

Arp, Jean 1887-1966 .... **CLC 5; TCLC 115**
See also CA 81-84; 25-28R; CANR 42, 77; EW 10

Arrabal
See Arrabal, Fernando

Arrabal, Fernando 1932- ... **CLC 2, 9, 18, 58**
See also CA 9-12R; CANR 15; EWL 3; LMFS 2

Arreola, Juan Jose 1918-2001 .... **CLC 147; HLC 1; SSC 38**
See also CA 113; 131; 200; CANR 81; DAM MULT; DLB 113; DNFS 2; EWL 3; HW 1, 2; LAW; RGSF 2

Arrian c. 89(?)-c. 155(?) .... **CMLC 43**
See also DLB 176

Arrick, Fran .... **CLC 30**
See Gaberman, Judie Angell
See also BYA 6

Arriey, Richmond
See Delany, Samuel R(ay), Jr.

Artaud, Antonin (Marie Joseph)
1896-1948 .... **DC 14; TCLC 3, 36**
See also CA 104; 149; DA3; DAM DRAM; DLB 258; EW 11; EWL 3; GFL 1789 to the Present; MTCW 1; RGWL 2, 3

Arthur, Ruth M(abel) 1905-1979 ..... **CLC 12**
See also CA 9-12R; 85-88; CANR 4; CWRI 5; SATA 7, 26

Artsybashev, Mikhail (Petrovich)
1878-1927 .... **TCLC 31**
See also CA 170

Arundel, Honor (Morfydd)
1919-1973 .... **CLC 17**
See also CA 21-22; 41-44R; CAP 2; CLR 35; CWRI 5; SATA 4; SATA-Obit 24

Arzner, Dorothy 1900-1979 .... **CLC 98**

Asch, Sholem 1880-1957 .... **TCLC 3**
See also CA 105; EWL 3; GLL 2

Ash, Shalom
See Asch, Sholem

Ashbery, John (Lawrence) 1927- .. **CLC 2, 3, 4, 6, 9, 13, 15, 25, 41, 77, 125; PC 26**
See Berry, Jonas
See also AMWS 3; CA 5-8R; CANR 9, 37, 66, 102; CP 7; DA3; DAM POET; DLB 5, 165; DLBY 1981; EWL 3; INT CANR-9; MTCW 1, 2; PAB; PFS 11; RGAL 4; WP

Ashdown, Clifford
See Freeman, R(ichard) Austin

Ashe, Gordon
See Creasey, John

Ashton-Warner, Sylvia (Constance)
1908-1984 .... **CLC 19**
See also CA 69-72; 112; CANR 29; MTCW 1, 2

Asimov, Isaac 1920-1992 ..... **CLC 1, 3, 9, 19, 26, 76, 92**
See also AAYA 13; BEST 90:2; BPFB 1; BYA 4, 6, 7, 9; CA 1-4R; 137; CANR 2, 19, 36, 60; CLR 12, 79; CMW 4; CPW; DA3; DAM POP; DLB 8; DLBY 1992; INT CANR-19; JRDA; LAIT 5; LMFS 2; MAICYA 1, 2; MTCW 1, 2; RGAL 4; SATA 1, 26, 74; SCFW 2; SFW 4; SSFS 17; TUS; YAW

Askew, Anne 1521(?)-1546 .... **LC 81**
See also DLB 136

Assis, Joaquim Maria Machado de
See Machado de Assis, Joaquim Maria

Astell, Mary 1666-1731 .... **LC 68**
See also DLB 252; FW

Astley, Thea (Beatrice May) 1925- .. **CLC 41**
See also CA 65-68; CANR 11, 43, 78; CN 7; DLB 289; EWL 3

Astley, William 1855-1911
See Warung, Price

Aston, James
See White, T(erence) H(anbury)

Asturias, Miguel Angel 1899-1974 .... **CLC 3, 8, 13; HLC 1**
See also CA 25-28; 49-52; CANR 32; CAP 2; CDWLB 3; DA3; DAM MULT, NOV; DLB 113; EWL 3; HW 1; LAW; LMFS 2; MTCW 1, 2; RGWL 2, 3; WLIT 1

Atares, Carlos Saura
See Saura (Atares), Carlos

Athanasius c. 295-c. 373 .... **CMLC 48**

Atheling, William
See Pound, Ezra (Weston Loomis)

Atheling, William, Jr.
See Blish, James (Benjamin)

Atherton, Gertrude (Franklin Horn)
1857-1948 .... **TCLC 2**
See also CA 104; 155; DLB 9, 78, 186; HGG; RGAL 4; SUFW 1; TCWW 2

Atherton, Lucius
See Masters, Edgar Lee

Atkins, Jack
See Harris, Mark

Atkinson, Kate 1951- .... **CLC 99**
See also CA 166; CANR 101; DLB 267

Attaway, William (Alexander)
1911-1986 .... **BLC 1; CLC 92**
See also BW 2, 3; CA 143; CANR 82; DAM MULT; DLB 76

Atticus
See Fleming, Ian (Lancaster); Wilson, (Thomas) Woodrow

Atwood, Margaret (Eleanor) 1939- ... **CLC 2, 3, 4, 8, 13, 15, 25, 44, 84, 135; PC 8; SSC 2, 46; WLC**
See also AAYA 12, 47; AMWS 13; BEST 89:2; BPFB 1; CA 49-52; CANR 3, 24, 33, 59, 95; CN 7; CP 7; CPW; CWP; DA; DA3; DAB; DAC; DAM MST, NOV, POET; DLB 53, 251; EWL 3; EXPN; FW; INT CANR-24; LAIT 5; MTCW 1, 2; NFS 4, 12, 13, 14; PFS 7; RGSF 2; SATA 50; SSFS 3, 13; TWA; YAW

Aubigny, Pierre d'
See Mencken, H(enry) L(ouis)

Aubin, Penelope 1685-1731(?) .... **LC 9**
See also DLB 39

Auchincloss, Louis (Stanton) 1917- .. **CLC 4, 6, 9, 18, 45; SSC 22**
See also AMWS 4; CA 1-4R; CANR 6, 29, 55, 87; CN 7; DAM NOV; DLB 2, 244; DLBY 1980; EWL 3; INT CANR-29; MTCW 1; RGAL 4

Auden, W(ystan) H(ugh) 1907-1973 . **CLC 1, 2, 3, 4, 6, 9, 11, 14, 43, 123; PC 1; WLC**
See also AAYA 18; AMWS 2; BRW 7; BRWR 1; CA 9-12R; 45-48; CANR 5, 61, 105; CDBLB 1914-1945; DA; DA3; DAB; DAC; DAM DRAM, MST, POET; DLB 10, 20; EWL 3; EXPP; MTCW 1, 2; PAB; PFS 1, 3, 4, 10; TUS; WP

Audiberti, Jacques 1900-1965 .... **CLC 38**
See also CA 25-28R; DAM DRAM; EWL 3

Audubon, John James 1785-1851 . **NCLC 47**
See also ANW; DLB 248

Auel, Jean M(arie) 1936- .... **CLC 31, 107**
See also AAYA 7, 51; BEST 90:4; BPFB 1; CA 103; CANR 21, 64, 115; CPW; DA3; DAM POP; INT CANR-21; NFS 11; RHW; SATA 91

Auerbach, Erich 1892-1957 .... **TCLC 43**
See also CA 118; 155; EWL 3

Augier, Emile 1820-1889 .... **NCLC 31**
See also DLB 192; GFL 1789 to the Present

August, John
See De Voto, Bernard (Augustine)

Augustine, St. 354-430 .... **CMLC 6; WLCS**
See also DA; DA3; DAB; DAC; DAM MST; DLB 115; EW 1; RGWL 2, 3

Aunt Belinda
See Braddon, Mary Elizabeth

Aunt Weedy
See Alcott, Louisa May

Aurelius
See Bourne, Randolph S(illiman)

Aurelius, Marcus 121-180 .... **CMLC 45**
See Marcus Aurelius
See also RGWL 2, 3

Aurobindo, Sri
See Ghose, Aurabinda

Aurobindo Ghose
See Ghose, Aurabinda

Austen, Jane 1775-1817 ...... **NCLC 1, 13, 19, 33, 51, 81, 95, 119; WLC**
See also AAYA 19; BRW 4; BRWC 1; BRWR 2; BYA 3; CDBLB 1789-1832; DA; DA3; DAB; DAC; DAM MST, NOV; DLB 116; EXPN; LAIT 2; LATS 1; LMFS 1; NFS 1, 14, 18; TEA; WLIT 3; WYAS 1

Auster, Paul 1947- .... **CLC 47, 131**
See also AMWS 12; CA 69-72; CANR 23, 52, 75; CMW 4; CN 7; DA3; DLB 227; MTCW 1; SUFW 2

Austin, Frank
See Faust, Frederick (Schiller)
See also TCWW 2

Austin, Mary (Hunter) 1868-1934 . **TCLC 25**
See Stairs, Gordon
See also ANW; CA 109; 178; DLB 9, 78, 206, 221, 275; FW; TCWW 2

Averroes 1126-1198 .... **CMLC 7**
See also DLB 115

Avicenna 980-1037 .... **CMLC 16**
See also DLB 115

Avison, Margaret 1918- .... **CLC 2, 4, 97**
See also CA 17-20R; CP 7; DAC; DAM POET; DLB 53; MTCW 1

Axton, David
See Koontz, Dean R(ay)

Ayckbourn, Alan 1939- ...... **CLC 5, 8, 18, 33, 74; DC 13**
See also BRWS 5; CA 21-24R; CANR 31, 59, 118; CBD; CD 5; DAB; DAM DRAM; DFS 7; DLB 13, 245; EWL 3; MTCW 1, 2

Aydy, Catherine
See Tennant, Emma (Christina)

Ayme, Marcel (Andre) 1902-1967 ... **CLC 11; SSC 41**
See also CA 89-92; CANR 67; CLR 25; DLB 72; EW 12; EWL 3; GFL 1789 to the Present; RGSF 2; RGWL 2, 3; SATA 91

Ayrton, Michael 1921-1975 .... **CLC 7**
See also CA 5-8R; 61-64; CANR 9, 21

Aytmatov, Chingiz
See Aitmatov, Chingiz (Torekulovich)
See also EWL 3

Azorin .... **CLC 11**
See Martinez Ruiz, Jose
See also EW 9; EWL 3

Azuela, Mariano 1873-1952 .. **HLC 1; TCLC 3**
See also CA 104; 131; CANR 81; DAM MULT; EWL 3; HW 1; LAW; MTCW 1, 2

Ba, Mariama 1929-1981 .... **BLCS**
See also AFW; BW 2; CA 141; CANR 87; DNFS 2; WLIT 2

Baastad, Babbis Friis
See Friis-Baastad, Babbis Ellinor

Bab
See Gilbert, W(illiam) S(chwenck)

Babbis, Eleanor
See Friis-Baastad, Babbis Ellinor

Babel, Isaac
See Babel, Isaak (Emmanuilovich)
See also EW 11; SSFS 10

Babel, Isaak (Emmanuilovich)
1894-1941(?) .... **SSC 16; TCLC 2, 13**
See Babel, Isaac
See also CA 104; 155; CANR 113; DLB 272; EWL 3; MTCW 1; RGSF 2; RGWL 2, 3; TWA

Babits, Mihaly 1883-1941 .... **TCLC 14**
See also CA 114; CDWLB 4; DLB 215; EWL 3

Babur 1483-1530 .... **LC 18**

Babylas 1898-1962
See Ghelderode, Michel de

Baca, Jimmy Santiago 1952- . **HLC 1; PC 41**
See also CA 131; CANR 81, 90; CP 7; DAM MULT; DLB 122; HW 1, 2

Baca, Jose Santiago
See Baca, Jimmy Santiago

Bacchelli, Riccardo 1891-1985 .... **CLC 19**
See also CA 29-32R; 117; DLB 264; EWL 3

Bach, Richard (David) 1936- .... **CLC 14**
See also AITN 1; BEST 89:2; BPFB 1; BYA 5; CA 9-12R; CANR 18, 93; CPW; DAM NOV, POP; FANT; MTCW 1; SATA 13

Bache, Benjamin Franklin
1769-1798 .... **LC 74**
See also DLB 43

Bachelard, Gaston 1884-1962 ...... **TCLC 128**
See also CA 97-100; 89-92; GFL 1789 to the Present

Bachman, Richard
See King, Stephen (Edwin)

Bachmann, Ingeborg 1926-1973 .... **CLC 69**
See also CA 93-96; 45-48; CANR 69; DLB 85; EWL 3; RGWL 2, 3

Bacon, Francis 1561-1626 .... **LC 18, 32**
See also BRW 1; CDBLB Before 1660; DLB 151, 236, 252; RGEL 2; TEA

Bacon, Roger 1214(?)-1294 .... **CMLC 14**
See also DLB 115

Bacovia, George 1881-1957 .... **TCLC 24**
See Vasiliu, Gheorghe
See also CDWLB 4; DLB 220; EWL 3

Badanes, Jerome 1937- .... **CLC 59**

Bagehot, Walter 1826-1877 .... **NCLC 10**
See also DLB 55

Bagnold, Enid 1889-1981 .... **CLC 25**
See also BYA 2; CA 5-8R; 103; CANR 5, 40; CBD; CWD; CWRI 5; DAM DRAM; DLB 13, 160, 191, 245; FW; MAICYA 1, 2; RGEL 2; SATA 1, 25

Bagritsky, Eduard .... **TCLC 60**
See Dzyubin, Eduard Georgievich

Bagrjana, Elisaveta
See Belcheva, Elisaveta Lyubomirova

Bagryana, Elisaveta .... **CLC 10**
See Belcheva, Elisaveta Lyubomirova
See also CA 178; CDWLB 4; DLB 147; EWL 3

Bailey, Paul 1937- .... **CLC 45**
See also CA 21-24R; CANR 16, 62; CN 7; DLB 14, 271; GLL 2

Baillie, Joanna 1762-1851 .... **NCLC 71**
See also DLB 93; RGEL 2

Bainbridge, Beryl (Margaret) 1934- . **CLC 4, 5, 8, 10, 14, 18, 22, 62, 130**
See also BRWS 6; CA 21-24R; CANR 24, 55, 75, 88; CN 7; DAM NOV; DLB 14, 231; EWL 3; MTCW 1, 2

Baker, Carlos (Heard)
1909-1987 .... **TCLC 119**
See also CA 5-8R; 122; CANR 3, 63; DLB 103

Baker, Elliott 1922- .... **CLC 8**
See also CA 45-48; CANR 2, 63; CN 7

Baker, Jean H. .... **TCLC 3, 10**
See Russell, George William

Baker, Nicholson 1957- .... **CLC 61, 165**
See also AMWS 13; CA 135; CANR 63, 120; CN 7; CPW; DA3; DAM POP; DLB 227

Baker, Ray Stannard 1870-1946 .... **TCLC 47**
See also CA 118

Baker, Russell (Wayne) 1925- .... **CLC 31**
See also BEST 89:4; CA 57-60; CANR 11, 41, 59; MTCW 1, 2

Bakhtin, M.
See Bakhtin, Mikhail Mikhailovich

Bakhtin, M. M.
See Bakhtin, Mikhail Mikhailovich

Bakhtin, Mikhail
See Bakhtin, Mikhail Mikhailovich

Bakhtin, Mikhail Mikhailovich
1895-1975 .... **CLC 83**
See also CA 128; 113; DLB 242; EWL 3

Bakshi, Ralph 1938(?)- .... **CLC 26**
See also CA 112; 138; IDFW 3

Bakunin, Mikhail (Alexandrovich)
1814-1876 .... **NCLC 25, 58**
See also DLB 277

Baldwin, James (Arthur) 1924-1987 . **BLC 1; CLC 1, 2, 3, 4, 5, 8, 13, 15, 17, 42, 50, 67, 90, 127; DC 1; SSC 10, 33; WLC**
See also AAYA 4, 34; AFAW 1, 2; AMWR 2; AMWS 1; BPFB 1; BW 1; CA 1-4R; 124; CABS 1; CAD; CANR 3, 24; CDALB 1941-1968; CPW; DA; DA3; DAB; DAC; DAM MST, MULT, NOV, POP; DFS 11, 15; DLB 2, 7, 33, 249, 278; DLBY 1987; EWL 3; EXPS; LAIT 5; MTCW 1, 2; NCFS 4; NFS 4; RGAL 4; RGSF 2; SATA 9; SATA-Obit 54; SSFS 2, 18; TUS

Bale, John 1495-1563 .... **LC 62**
See also DLB 132; RGEL 2; TEA

Ball, Hugo 1886-1927 .... **TCLC 104**

Ballard, J(ames) G(raham) 1930- . **CLC 3, 6, 14, 36, 137; SSC 1, 53**
See also AAYA 3, 52; BRWS 5; CA 5-8R; CANR 15, 39, 65, 107; CN 7; DA3; DAM NOV, POP; DLB 14, 207, 261; EWL 3; HGG; MTCW 1, 2; NFS 8; RGEL 2; RGSF 2; SATA 93; SFW 4

Balmont, Konstantin (Dmitriyevich)
1867-1943 .... **TCLC 11**
See also CA 109; 155; EWL 3

Baltausis, Vincas 1847-1910
See Mikszath, Kalman

Balzac, Honore de 1799-1850 ... **NCLC 5, 35, 53; SSC 5, 59; WLC**
See also DA; DA3; DAB; DAC; DAM MST, NOV; DLB 119; EW 5; GFL 1789 to the Present; LMFS 1; RGSF 2; RGWL 2, 3; SSFS 10; SUFW; TWA

Bambara, Toni Cade 1939-1995 .... **BLC 1; CLC 19, 88; SSC 35; TCLC 116; WLCS**
See also AAYA 5, 49; AFAW 2; AMWS 11; BW 2, 3; BYA 12, 14; CA 29-32R; 150; CANR 24, 49, 81; CDALBS; DA; DA3; DAC; DAM MST, MULT; DLB 38, 218; EXPS; MTCW 1, 2; NFS 8; RGAL 4; RGSF 2; SATA 112; SSFS 4, 7, 12

Bamdad, A.
See Shamlu, Ahmad

Bamdad, Alef
See Shamlu, Ahmad

Banat, D. R.
See Bradbury, Ray (Douglas)

Bancroft, Laura
See Baum, L(yman) Frank

Banim, John 1798-1842 .... **NCLC 13**
See also DLB 116, 158, 159; RGEL 2

Banim, Michael 1796-1874 .... **NCLC 13**
See also DLB 158, 159

Banjo, The
See Paterson, A(ndrew) B(arton)

Banks, Iain
See Banks, Iain M(enzies)

Banks, Iain M(enzies) 1954- .... **CLC 34**
See also CA 123; 128; CANR 61, 106; DLB 194, 261; EWL 3; HGG; INT 128; SFW 4

Banks, Lynne Reid .... **CLC 23**
See Reid Banks, Lynne
See also AAYA 6; BYA 7; CLR 86

Banks, Russell (Earl) 1940- .... **CLC 37, 72; SSC 42**
See also AAYA 45; AMWS 5; CA 65-68; CAAS 15; CANR 19, 52, 73, 118; CN 7; DLB 130, 278; EWL 3; NFS 13

Banville, John 1945- .... **CLC 46, 118**
See also CA 117; 128; CANR 104; CN 7; DLB 14, 271; INT 128

Banville, Theodore (Faullain) de
1832-1891 .... **NCLC 9**
See also DLB 217; GFL 1789 to the Present

Baraka, Amiri 1934- .... **BLC 1; CLC 1, 2, 3, 5, 10, 14, 33, 115; DC 6; PC 4; WLCS**
See Jones, LeRoi
See also AFAW 1, 2; AMWS 2; BW 2, 3; CA 21-24R; CABS 3; CAD; CANR 27, 38, 61; CD 5; CDALB 1941-1968; CP 7; CPW; DA; DA3; DAC; DAM MST, MULT, POET, POP; DFS 3, 11, 16; DLB 5, 7, 16, 38; DLBD 8; EWL 3; MTCW 1, 2; PFS 9; RGAL 4; TUS; WP

Baratynsky, Evgenii Abramovich
1800-1844 .... **NCLC 103**
See also DLB 205

Barbauld, Anna Laetitia
1743-1825 .... **NCLC 50**
See also DLB 107, 109, 142, 158; RGEL 2

Barbellion, W. N. P. .... **TCLC 24**
See Cummings, Bruce F(rederick)

Barber, Benjamin R. 1939- .... **CLC 141**
See also CA 29-32R; CANR 12, 32, 64, 119

Barbera, Jack (Vincent) 1945- .... **CLC 44**
See also CA 110; CANR 45

Barbey d'Aurevilly, Jules-Amedee
1808-1889 .... **NCLC 1; SSC 17**
See also DLB 119; GFL 1789 to the Present

Barbour, John c. 1316-1395 .... **CMLC 33**
See also DLB 146

Barbusse, Henri 1873-1935 .... **TCLC 5**
See also CA 105; 154; DLB 65; EWL 3; RGWL 2, 3

Barclay, Bill
See Moorcock, Michael (John)

Barclay, William Ewert
See Moorcock, Michael (John)

Barea, Arturo 1897-1957 .... **TCLC 14**
See also CA 111; 201

Barfoot, Joan 1946- .... **CLC 18**
See also CA 105

Barham, Richard Harris
1788-1845 .... **NCLC 77**
See also DLB 159

Baring, Maurice 1874-1945 .... **TCLC 8**
See also CA 105; 168; DLB 34; HGG

Baring-Gould, Sabine 1834-1924 ... **TCLC 88**
See also DLB 156, 190

Barker, Clive 1952- .... **CLC 52; SSC 53**
See also AAYA 10; BEST 90:3; BPFB 1; CA 121; 129; CANR 71, 111; CPW; DA3; DAM POP; DLB 261; HGG; INT 129; MTCW 1, 2; SUFW 2

Barker, George Granville
1913-1991 .... **CLC 8, 48**
See also CA 9-12R; 135; CANR 7, 38; DAM POET; DLB 20; EWL 3; MTCW 1

Barker, Harley Granville
See Granville-Barker, Harley
See also DLB 10

Barker, Howard 1946- .... **CLC 37**
See also CA 102; CBD; CD 5; DLB 13, 233

Barker, Jane 1652-1732 .... **LC 42, 82**
See also DLB 39, 131

Barker, Pat(ricia) 1943- ...... **CLC 32, 94, 146**
See also BRWS 4; CA 117; 122; CANR 50, 101; CN 7; DLB 271; INT 122

Barlach, Ernst (Heinrich)
1870-1938 .... **TCLC 84**
See also CA 178; DLB 56, 118; EWL 3

Barlow, Joel 1754-1812 .... **NCLC 23**
See also AMWS 2; DLB 37; RGAL 4

Barnard, Mary (Ethel) 1909- .... **CLC 48**
See also CA 21-22; CAP 2

Barnes, Djuna 1892-1982 .... **CLC 3, 4, 8, 11, 29, 127; SSC 3**
See Steptoe, Lydia
See also AMWS 3; CA 9-12R; 107; CAD; CANR 16, 55; CWD; DLB 4, 9, 45; EWL 3; GLL 1; MTCW 1, 2; RGAL 4; TUS

Barnes, Jim 1933- .... **NNAL**
See also CA 108, 175; CAAE 175; CAAS 28; DLB 175

Barnes, Julian (Patrick) 1946- . **CLC 42, 141**
See also BRWS 4; CA 102; CANR 19, 54, 115; CN 7; DAB; DLB 194; DLBY 1993; EWL 3; MTCW 1

Barnes, Peter 1931- .... **CLC 5, 56**
See also CA 65-68; CAAS 12; CANR 33, 34, 64, 113; CBD; CD 5; DFS 6; DLB 13, 233; MTCW 1

Barnes, William 1801-1886 .... **NCLC 75**
See also DLB 32

Baroja (y Nessi), Pio 1872-1956 .... **HLC 1; TCLC 8**
See also CA 104; EW 9

Baron, David
See Pinter, Harold

Baron Corvo
See Rolfe, Frederick (William Serafino Austin Lewis Mary)

Barondess, Sue K(aufman)
1926-1977 .... **CLC 8**
See Kaufman, Sue
See also CA 1-4R; 69-72; CANR 1

Baron de Teive
See Pessoa, Fernando (Antonio Nogueira)

Baroness Von S.
See Zangwill, Israel

Barres, (Auguste-)Maurice
1862-1923 .... **TCLC 47**
See also CA 164; DLB 123; GFL 1789 to the Present

Barreto, Afonso Henrique de Lima
See Lima Barreto, Afonso Henrique de

Barrett, Andrea 1954- .... **CLC 150**
See also CA 156; CANR 92

Barrett, Michele .... **CLC 65**

Barrett, (Roger) Syd 1946- .... **CLC 35**

Barrett, William (Christopher)
1913-1992 .... **CLC 27**
See also CA 13-16R; 139; CANR 11, 67; INT CANR-11

Barrie, J(ames) M(atthew)
1860-1937 .... **TCLC 2**
See also BRWS 3; BYA 4, 5; CA 104; 136; CANR 77; CDBLB 1890-1914; CLR 16; CWRI 5; DA3; DAB; DAM DRAM; DFS 7; DLB 10, 141, 156; EWL 3; FANT; MAICYA 1, 2; MTCW 1; SATA 100; SUFW; WCH; WLIT 4; YABC 1

Barrington, Michael
See Moorcock, Michael (John)

Barrol, Grady
See Bograd, Larry

Barry, Mike
See Malzberg, Barry N(athaniel)

Barry, Philip 1896-1949 .... **TCLC 11**
See also CA 109; 199; DFS 9; DLB 7, 228; RGAL 4

Bart, Andre Schwarz
See Schwarz-Bart, Andre

Barth, John (Simmons) 1930- ... **CLC 1, 2, 3, 5, 7, 9, 10, 14, 27, 51, 89; SSC 10**
See also AITN 1, 2; AMW; BPFB 1; CA 1-4R; CABS 1; CANR 5, 23, 49, 64, 113; CN 7; DAM NOV; DLB 2, 227; EWL 3; FANT; MTCW 1; RGAL 4; RGSF 2; RHW; SSFS 6; TUS

Barthelme, Donald 1931-1989 ... **CLC 1, 2, 3, 5, 6, 8, 13, 23, 46, 59, 115; SSC 2, 55**
See also AMWS 4; BPFB 1; CA 21-24R; 129; CANR 20, 58; DA3; DAM NOV; DLB 2, 234; DLBY 1980, 1989; EWL 3; FANT; LMFS 2; MTCW 1, 2; RGAL 4; RGSF 2; SATA 7; SATA-Obit 62; SSFS 17

Barthelme, Frederick 1943- .... **CLC 36, 117**
See also AMWS 11; CA 114; 122; CANR 77; CN 7; CSW; DLB 244; DLBY 1985; EWL 3; INT CA-122

Barthes, Roland (Gerard)
1915-1980 .... **CLC 24, 83; TCLC 135**
See also CA 130; 97-100; CANR 66; EW 13; EWL 3; GFL 1789 to the Present; MTCW 1, 2; TWA

Barzun, Jacques (Martin) 1907- ..... **CLC 51, 145**
See also CA 61-64; CANR 22, 95

Bashevis, Isaac
See Singer, Isaac Bashevis

Bashkirtseff, Marie 1859-1884 .... **NCLC 27**

Basho, Matsuo
See Matsuo Basho
See also PFS 18; RGWL 2, 3; WP

Basil of Caesaria c. 330-379 .... **CMLC 35**

Bass, Kingsley B., Jr.
See Bullins, Ed

Bass, Rick 1958- .... **CLC 79, 143; SSC 60**
See also ANW; CA 126; CANR 53, 93; CSW; DLB 212, 275

Bassani, Giorgio 1916-2000 .... **CLC 9**
See also CA 65-68; 190; CANR 33; CWW 2; DLB 128, 177; EWL 3; MTCW 1; RGWL 2, 3

Bastian, Ann .... **CLC 70**

Bastos, Augusto (Antonio) Roa
See Roa Bastos, Augusto (Antonio)

Bataille, Georges 1897-1962 .... **CLC 29**
See also CA 101; 89-92; EWL 3

Bates, H(erbert) E(rnest)
1905-1974 .... **CLC 46; SSC 10**
See also CA 93-96; 45-48; CANR 34; DA3; DAB; DAM POP; DLB 162, 191; EWL 3; EXPS; MTCW 1, 2; RGSF 2; SSFS 7

Bauchart
See Camus, Albert

Baudelaire, Charles 1821-1867 . **NCLC 6, 29, 55; PC 1; SSC 18; WLC**
See also DA; DA3; DAB; DAC; DAM MST, POET; DLB 217; EW 7; GFL 1789 to the Present; LMFS 2; RGWL 2, 3; TWA

Baudouin, Marcel
See Peguy, Charles (Pierre)

Baudouin, Pierre
See Peguy, Charles (Pierre)

Baudrillard, Jean 1929- .... **CLC 60**

Baum, L(yman) Frank 1856-1919 .. **TCLC 7, 132**
See also AAYA 46; BYA 16; CA 108; 133; CLR 15; CWRI 5; DLB 22; FANT; JRDA; MAICYA 1, 2; MTCW 1, 2; NFS 13; RGAL 4; SATA 18, 100; WCH

Baum, Louis F.
See Baum, L(yman) Frank

Baumbach, Jonathan 1933- .... **CLC 6, 23**
See also CA 13-16R; CAAS 5; CANR 12, 66; CN 7; DLBY 1980; INT CANR-12; MTCW 1

Bausch, Richard (Carl) 1945- .... **CLC 51**
See also AMWS 7; CA 101; CAAS 14; CANR 43, 61, 87; CSW; DLB 130

Baxter, Charles (Morley) 1947- . **CLC 45, 78**
See also CA 57-60; CANR 40, 64, 104; CPW; DAM POP; DLB 130; MTCW 2

Baxter, George Owen
See Faust, Frederick (Schiller)

Baxter, James K(eir) 1926-1972 .... **CLC 14**
See also CA 77-80; EWL 3

Baxter, John
See Hunt, E(verette) Howard, (Jr.)

Bayer, Sylvia
See Glassco, John

Baynton, Barbara 1857-1929 .... **TCLC 57**
See also DLB 230; RGSF 2

Beagle, Peter S(oyer) 1939- .... **CLC 7, 104**
See also AAYA 47; BPFB 1; BYA 9, 10, 16; CA 9-12R; CANR 4, 51, 73, 110; DA3; DLBY 1980; FANT; INT CANR-4; MTCW 1; SATA 60, 130; SUFW 1, 2; YAW

Bean, Normal
See Burroughs, Edgar Rice

Beard, Charles A(ustin)
1874-1948 .... **TCLC 15**
See also CA 115; 189; DLB 17; SATA 18

Beardsley, Aubrey 1872-1898 .... **NCLC 6**

Beattie, Ann 1947- ..... **CLC 8, 13, 18, 40, 63, 146; SSC 11**
See also AMWS 5; BEST 90:2; BPFB 1; CA 81-84; CANR 53, 73; CN 7; CPW; DA3; DAM NOV, POP; DLB 218, 278; DLBY 1982; EWL 3; MTCW 1, 2; RGAL 4; RGSF 2; SSFS 9; TUS

Beattie, James 1735-1803 .... **NCLC 25**
See also DLB 109

Beauchamp, Kathleen Mansfield 1888-1923
See Mansfield, Katherine
See also CA 104; 134; DA; DA3; DAC; DAM MST; MTCW 2; TEA

Beaumarchais, Pierre-Augustin Caron de
1732-1799 .... **DC 4; LC 61**
See also DAM DRAM; DFS 14, 16; EW 4; GFL Beginnings to 1789; RGWL 2, 3

Beaumont, Francis 1584(?)-1616 .. **DC 6; LC 33**
See also BRW 2; CDBLB Before 1660; DLB 58; TEA

Beauvoir, Simone (Lucie Ernestine Marie Bertrand) de 1908-1986 .... **CLC 1, 2, 4, 8, 14, 31, 44, 50, 71, 124; SSC 35; WLC**
See also BPFB 1; CA 9-12R; 118; CANR 28, 61; DA; DA3; DAB; DAC; DAM MST, NOV; DLB 72; DLBY 1986; EW 12; EWL 3; FW; GFL 1789 to the Present; LMFS 2; MTCW 1, 2; RGSF 2; RGWL 2, 3; TWA

Becker, Carl (Lotus) 1873-1945 ..... **TCLC 63**
See also CA 157; DLB 17

Becker, Jurek 1937-1997 .... **CLC 7, 19**
See also CA 85-88; 157; CANR 60, 117; CWW 2; DLB 75; EWL 3

Becker, Walter 1950- .... **CLC 26**

Beckett, Samuel (Barclay)
1906-1989 .. **CLC 1, 2, 3, 4, 6, 9, 10, 11, 14, 18, 29, 57, 59, 83; SSC 16; WLC**
See also BRWC 2; BRWR 1; BRWS 1; CA 5-8R; 130; CANR 33, 61; CBD; CDBLB 1945-1960; DA; DA3; DAB; DAC; DAM DRAM, MST, NOV; DFS 2, 7, 18; DLB

13, 15, 233; DLBY 1990; EWL 3; GFL 1789 to the Present; LATS 1; LMFS 2; MTCW 1, 2; RGSF 2; RGWL 2, 3; SSFS 15; TEA; WLIT 4

Beckford, William 1760-1844 .... **NCLC 16**
See also BRW 3; DLB 39, 213; HGG; LMFS 1; SUFW

Beckham, Barry (Earl) 1944- .... **BLC 1**
See also BW 1; CA 29-32R; CANR 26, 62; CN 7; DAM MULT; DLB 33

Beckman, Gunnel 1910- .... **CLC 26**
See also CA 33-36R; CANR 15, 114; CLR 25; MAICYA 1, 2; SAAS 9; SATA 6

Becque, Henri 1837-1899 .... **DC 21; NCLC 3**
See also DLB 192; GFL 1789 to the Present

Becquer, Gustavo Adolfo 1836-1870 .... **HLCS 1; NCLC 106**
See also DAM MULT

Beddoes, Thomas Lovell 1803-1849 .. **DC 15; NCLC 3**
See also DLB 96

Bede c. 673-735 .... **CMLC 20**
See also DLB 146; TEA

Bedford, Denton R. 1907-(?) .... **NNAL**

Bedford, Donald F.
See Fearing, Kenneth (Flexner)

Beecher, Catharine Esther 1800-1878 .... **NCLC 30**
See also DLB 1, 243

Beecher, John 1904-1980 .... **CLC 6**
See also AITN 1; CA 5-8R; 105; CANR 8

Beer, Johann 1655-1700 .... **LC 5**
See also DLB 168

Beer, Patricia 1924- .... **CLC 58**
See also CA 61-64; 183; CANR 13, 46; CP 7; CWP; DLB 40; FW

Beerbohm, Max
See Beerbohm, (Henry) Max(imilian)

Beerbohm, (Henry) Max(imilian) 1872-1956 .... **TCLC 1, 24**
See also BRWS 2; CA 104; 154; CANR 79; DLB 34, 100; FANT

Beer-Hofmann, Richard 1866-1945 .... **TCLC 60**
See also CA 160; DLB 81

Beg, Shemus
See Stephens, James

Begiebing, Robert J(ohn) 1946- .... **CLC 70**
See also CA 122; CANR 40, 88

Behan, Brendan (Francis) 1923-1964 .... **CLC 1, 8, 11, 15, 79**
See also BRWS 2; CA 73-76; CANR 33, 121; CBD; CDBLB 1945-1960; DAM DRAM; DFS 7; DLB 13, 233; EWL 3; MTCW 1, 2

Behn, Aphra 1640(?)-1689 .. **DC 4; LC 1, 30, 42; PC 13; WLC**
See also BRWS 3; DA; DA3; DAB; DAC; DAM DRAM, MST, NOV, POET; DFS 16; DLB 39, 80, 131; FW; TEA; WLIT 3

Behrman, S(amuel) N(athaniel) 1893-1973 .... **CLC 40**
See also CA 13-16; 45-48; CAD; CAP 1; DLB 7, 44; IDFW 3; RGAL 4

Belasco, David 1853-1931 .... **TCLC 3**
See also CA 104; 168; DLB 7; RGAL 4

Belcheva, Elisaveta Lyubomirova 1893-1991 .... **CLC 10**
See Bagryana, Elisaveta

Beldone, Phil "Cheech"
See Ellison, Harlan (Jay)

Beleno
See Azuela, Mariano

Belinski, Vissarion Grigoryevich 1811-1848 .... **NCLC 5**
See also DLB 198

Belitt, Ben 1911- .... **CLC 22**
See also CA 13-16R; CAAS 4; CANR 7, 77; CP 7; DLB 5

Bell, Gertrude (Margaret Lowthian) 1868-1926 .... **TCLC 67**
See also CA 167; CANR 110; DLB 174

Bell, J. Freeman
See Zangwill, Israel

Bell, James Madison 1826-1902 .... **BLC 1; TCLC 43**
See also BW 1; CA 122; 124; DAM MULT; DLB 50

Bell, Madison Smartt 1957- ...... **CLC 41, 102**
See also AMWS 10; BPFB 1; CA 111, 183; CAAE 183; CANR 28, 54, 73; CN 7; CSW; DLB 218, 278; MTCW 1

Bell, Marvin (Hartley) 1937- .... **CLC 8, 31**
See also CA 21-24R; CAAS 14; CANR 59, 102; CP 7; DAM POET; DLB 5; MTCW 1

Bell, W. L. D.
See Mencken, H(enry) L(ouis)

Bellamy, Atwood C.
See Mencken, H(enry) L(ouis)

Bellamy, Edward 1850-1898 ...... **NCLC 4, 86**
See also DLB 12; NFS 15; RGAL 4; SFW 4

Belli, Gioconda 1949- .... **HLCS 1**
See also CA 152; CWW 2; EWL 3; RGWL 3

Bellin, Edward J.
See Kuttner, Henry

Bello, Andres 1781-1865 .... **NCLC 131**
See also LAW

Belloc, (Joseph) Hilaire (Pierre Sebastien Rene Swanton) 1870-1953 .... **PC 24; TCLC 7, 18**
See also CA 106; 152; CWRI 5; DAM POET; DLB 19, 100, 141, 174; EWL 3; MTCW 1; SATA 112; WCH; YABC 1

Belloc, Joseph Peter Rene Hilaire
See Belloc, (Joseph) Hilaire (Pierre Sebastien Rene Swanton)

Belloc, Joseph Pierre Hilaire
See Belloc, (Joseph) Hilaire (Pierre Sebastien Rene Swanton)

Belloc, M. A.
See Lowndes, Marie Adelaide (Belloc)

Belloc-Lowndes, Mrs.
See Lowndes, Marie Adelaide (Belloc)

Bellow, Saul 1915- . **CLC 1, 2, 3, 6, 8, 10, 13, 15, 25, 33, 34, 63, 79; SSC 14; WLC**
See also AITN 2; AMW; AMWC 2; AMWR 2; BEST 89:3; BPFB 1; CA 5-8R; CABS 1; CANR 29, 53, 95; CDALB 1941-1968; CN 7; DA; DA3; DAB; DAC; DAM MST, NOV, POP; DLB 2, 28; DLBD 3; DLBY 1982; EWL 3; MTCW 1, 2; NFS 4, 14; RGAL 4; RGSF 2; SSFS 12; TUS

Belser, Reimond Karel Maria de 1929-
See Ruyslinck, Ward
See also CA 152

Bely, Andrey .... **PC 11; TCLC 7**
See Bugayev, Boris Nikolayevich
See also EW 9; EWL 3; MTCW 1

Belyi, Andrei
See Bugayev, Boris Nikolayevich
See also RGWL 2, 3

Bembo, Pietro 1470-1547 .... **LC 79**
See also RGWL 2, 3

Benary, Margot
See Benary-Isbert, Margot

Benary-Isbert, Margot 1889-1979 .... **CLC 12**
See also CA 5-8R; 89-92; CANR 4, 72; CLR 12; MAICYA 1, 2; SATA 2; SATA-Obit 21

Benavente (y Martinez), Jacinto 1866-1954 .... **HLCS 1; TCLC 3**
See also CA 106; 131; CANR 81; DAM DRAM, MULT; EWL 3; GLL 2; HW 1, 2; MTCW 1, 2

Benchley, Peter (Bradford) 1940- .. **CLC 4, 8**
See also AAYA 14; AITN 2; BPFB 1; CA 17-20R; CANR 12, 35, 66, 115; CPW; DAM NOV, POP; HGG; MTCW 1, 2; SATA 3, 89

Benchley, Robert (Charles) 1889-1945 .... **TCLC 1, 55**
See also CA 105; 153; DLB 11; RGAL 4

Benda, Julien 1867-1956 .... **TCLC 60**
See also CA 120; 154; GFL 1789 to the Present

Benedict, Ruth (Fulton) 1887-1948 .... **TCLC 60**
See also CA 158; DLB 246

Benedikt, Michael 1935- .... **CLC 4, 14**
See also CA 13-16R; CANR 7; CP 7; DLB 5

Benet, Juan 1927-1993 .... **CLC 28**
See also CA 143; EWL 3

Benet, Stephen Vincent 1898-1943 ... **SSC 10; TCLC 7**
See also AMWS 11; CA 104; 152; DA3; DAM POET; DLB 4, 48, 102, 249, 284; DLBY 1997; EWL 3; HGG; MTCW 1; RGAL 4; RGSF 2; SUFW; WP; YABC 1

Benet, William Rose 1886-1950 ..... **TCLC 28**
See also CA 118; 152; DAM POET; DLB 45; RGAL 4

Benford, Gregory (Albert) 1941- ..... **CLC 52**
See also BPFB 1; CA 69-72, 175; CAAE 175; CAAS 27; CANR 12, 24, 49, 95; CSW; DLBY 1982; SCFW 2; SFW 4

Bengtsson, Frans (Gunnar) 1894-1954 .... **TCLC 48**
See also CA 170; EWL 3

Benjamin, David
See Slavitt, David R(ytman)

Benjamin, Lois
See Gould, Lois

Benjamin, Walter 1892-1940 .... **TCLC 39**
See also CA 164; DLB 242; EW 11; EWL 3

Ben Jelloun, Tahar 1944-
See Jelloun, Tahar ben
See also CA 135; EWL 3; RGWL 3; WLIT 2

Benn, Gottfried 1886-1956 .. **PC 35; TCLC 3**
See also CA 106; 153; DLB 56; EWL 3; RGWL 2, 3

Bennett, Alan 1934- .... **CLC 45, 77**
See also BRWS 8; CA 103; CANR 35, 55, 106; CBD; CD 5; DAB; DAM MST; MTCW 1, 2

Bennett, (Enoch) Arnold 1867-1931 .... **TCLC 5, 20**
See also BRW 6; CA 106; 155; CDBLB 1890-1914; DLB 10, 34, 98, 135; EWL 3; MTCW 2

Bennett, Elizabeth
See Mitchell, Margaret (Munnerlyn)

Bennett, George Harold 1930-
See Bennett, Hal
See also BW 1; CA 97-100; CANR 87

Bennett, Gwendolyn B. 1902-1981 .... **HR 2**
See also BW 1; CA 125; DLB 51; WP

Bennett, Hal .... **CLC 5**
See Bennett, George Harold
See also DLB 33

Bennett, Jay 1912- .... **CLC 35**
See also AAYA 10; CA 69-72; CANR 11, 42, 79; JRDA; SAAS 4; SATA 41, 87; SATA-Brief 27; WYA; YAW

Bennett, Louise (Simone) 1919- .... **BLC 1; CLC 28**
See also BW 2, 3; CA 151; CDWLB 3; CP 7; DAM MULT; DLB 117; EWL 3

Benson, A. C. 1862-1925 .... **TCLC 123**
See also DLB 98

Benson, E(dward) F(rederic)
1867-1940 .... **TCLC 27**
See also CA 114; 157; DLB 135, 153;
HGG; SUFW 1

Benson, Jackson J. 1930- .... **CLC 34**
See also CA 25-28R; DLB 111

Benson, Sally 1900-1972 .... **CLC 17**
See also CA 19-20; 37-40R; CAP 1; SATA
1, 35; SATA-Obit 27

Benson, Stella 1892-1933 .... **TCLC 17**
See also CA 117; 154, 155; DLB 36, 162;
FANT; TEA

Bentham, Jeremy 1748-1832 .... **NCLC 38**
See also DLB 107, 158, 252

Bentley, E(dmund) C(lerihew)
1875-1956 .... **TCLC 12**
See also CA 108; DLB 70; MSW

Bentley, Eric (Russell) 1916- .... **CLC 24**
See also CA 5-8R; CAD; CANR 6, 67;
CBD; CD 5; INT CANR-6

ben Uzair, Salem
See Horne, Richard Henry Hengist

Beranger, Pierre Jean de
1780-1857 .... **NCLC 34**

Berdyaev, Nicolas
See Berdyaev, Nikolai (Aleksandrovich)

Berdyaev, Nikolai (Aleksandrovich)
1874-1948 .... **TCLC 67**
See also CA 120; 157

Berdyayev, Nikolai (Aleksandrovich)
See Berdyaev, Nikolai (Aleksandrovich)

Berendt, John (Lawrence) 1939- ...... **CLC 86**
See also CA 146; CANR 75, 93; DA3;
MTCW 1

Beresford, J(ohn) D(avys)
1873-1947 .... **TCLC 81**
See also CA 112; 155; DLB 162, 178, 197;
SFW 4; SUFW 1

Bergelson, David 1884-1952 .... **TCLC 81**
See Bergelson, Dovid

Bergelson, Dovid
See Bergelson, David
See also EWL 3

Berger, Colonel
See Malraux, (Georges-)Andre

Berger, John (Peter) 1926- .... **CLC 2, 19**
See also BRWS 4; CA 81-84; CANR 51,
78, 117; CN 7; DLB 14, 207

Berger, Melvin H. 1927- .... **CLC 12**
See also CA 5-8R; CANR 4; CLR 32;
SAAS 2; SATA 5, 88; SATA-Essay 124

Berger, Thomas (Louis) 1924- .. **CLC 3, 5, 8, 11, 18, 38**
See also BPFB 1; CA 1-4R; CANR 5, 28,
51; CN 7; DAM NOV; DLB 2; DLBY
1980; EWL 3; FANT; INT CANR-28;
MTCW 1, 2; RHW; TCWW 2

Bergman, (Ernst) Ingmar 1918- ...... **CLC 16, 72**
See also CA 81-84; CANR 33, 70; DLB
257; MTCW 2

Bergson, Henri(-Louis) 1859-1941 . **TCLC 32**
See also CA 164; EW 8; EWL 3; GFL 1789
to the Present

Bergstein, Eleanor 1938- .... **CLC 4**
See also CA 53-56; CANR 5

Berkeley, George 1685-1753 .... **LC 65**
See also DLB 31, 101, 252

Berkoff, Steven 1937- .... **CLC 56**
See also CA 104; CANR 72; CBD; CD 5

Berlin, Isaiah 1909-1997 .... **TCLC 105**
See also CA 85-88; 162

Bermant, Chaim (Icyk) 1929-1998 ... **CLC 40**
See also CA 57-60; CANR 6, 31, 57, 105;
CN 7

Bern, Victoria
See Fisher, M(ary) F(rances) K(ennedy)

Bernanos, (Paul Louis) Georges
1888-1948 .... **TCLC 3**
See also CA 104; 130; CANR 94; DLB 72;
EWL 3; GFL 1789 to the Present; RGWL
2, 3

Bernard, April 1956- .... **CLC 59**
See also CA 131

Berne, Victoria
See Fisher, M(ary) F(rances) K(ennedy)

Bernhard, Thomas 1931-1989 ..... **CLC 3, 32, 61; DC 14**
See also CA 85-88; 127; CANR 32, 57; CD-
WLB 2; DLB 85, 124; EWL 3; MTCW 1;
RGWL 2, 3

Bernhardt, Sarah (Henriette Rosine)
1844-1923 .... **TCLC 75**
See also CA 157

Bernstein, Charles 1950- .... **CLC 142**
See also CA 129; CAAS 24; CANR 90; CP
7; DLB 169

Berriault, Gina 1926-1999 .... **CLC 54, 109; SSC 30**
See also CA 116; 129; 185; CANR 66; DLB
130; SSFS 7,11

Berrigan, Daniel 1921- .... **CLC 4**
See also CA 33-36R; CAAE 187; CAAS 1;
CANR 11, 43, 78; CP 7; DLB 5

Berrigan, Edmund Joseph Michael, Jr.
1934-1983
See Berrigan, Ted
See also CA 61-64; 110; CANR 14, 102

Berrigan, Ted .... **CLC 37**
See Berrigan, Edmund Joseph Michael, Jr.
See also DLB 5, 169; WP

Berry, Charles Edward Anderson 1931-
See Berry, Chuck
See also CA 115

Berry, Chuck .... **CLC 17**
See Berry, Charles Edward Anderson

Berry, Jonas
See Ashbery, John (Lawrence)
See also GLL 1

Berry, Wendell (Erdman) 1934- ... **CLC 4, 6, 8, 27, 46; PC 28**
See also AITN 1; AMWS 10; ANW; CA
73-76; CANR 50, 73, 101; CP 7; CSW;
DAM POET; DLB 5, 6, 234, 275; MTCW
1

Berryman, John 1914-1972 ... **CLC 1, 2, 3, 4, 6, 8, 10, 13, 25, 62**
See also AMW; CA 13-16; 33-36R; CABS
2; CANR 35; CAP 1; CDALB 1941-1968;
DAM POET; DLB 48; EWL 3; MTCW 1,
2; PAB; RGAL 4; WP

Bertolucci, Bernardo 1940- .... **CLC 16, 157**
See also CA 106

Berton, Pierre (Francis Demarigny)
1920- .... **CLC 104**
See also CA 1-4R; CANR 2, 56; CPW;
DLB 68; SATA 99

Bertrand, Aloysius 1807-1841 .... **NCLC 31**
See Bertrand, Louis oAloysiusc

Bertrand, Louis oAloysiusc
See Bertrand, Aloysius
See also DLB 217

Bertran de Born c. 1140-1215 .... **CMLC 5**

Besant, Annie (Wood) 1847-1933 ..... **TCLC 9**
See also CA 105; 185

Bessie, Alvah 1904-1985 .... **CLC 23**
See also CA 5-8R; 116; CANR 2, 80; DLB
26

Bestuzhev, Aleksandr Aleksandrovich
1797-1837 .... **NCLC 131**
See also DLB 198

Bethlen, T. D.
See Silverberg, Robert

Beti, Mongo .... **BLC 1; CLC 27**
See Biyidi, Alexandre
See also AFW; CANR 79; DAM MULT;
EWL 3; WLIT 2

Betjeman, John 1906-1984 ...... **CLC 2, 6, 10, 34, 43**
See also BRW 7; CA 9-12R; 112; CANR
33, 56; CDBLB 1945-1960; DA3; DAB;
DAM MST, POET; DLB 20; DLBY 1984;
EWL 3; MTCW 1, 2

Bettelheim, Bruno 1903-1990 .... **CLC 79**
See also CA 81-84; 131; CANR 23, 61;
DA3; MTCW 1, 2

Betti, Ugo 1892-1953 .... **TCLC 5**
See also CA 104; 155; EWL 3; RGWL 2, 3

Betts, Doris (Waugh) 1932- ..... **CLC 3, 6, 28; SSC 45**
See also CA 13-16R; CANR 9, 66, 77; CN
7; CSW; DLB 218; DLBY 1982; INT
CANR-9; RGAL 4

Bevan, Alistair
See Roberts, Keith (John Kingston)

Bey, Pilaff
See Douglas, (George) Norman

Bialik, Chaim Nachman
1873-1934 .... **TCLC 25**
See also CA 170; EWL 3

Bickerstaff, Isaac
See Swift, Jonathan

Bidart, Frank 1939- .... **CLC 33**
See also CA 140; CANR 106; CP 7

Bienek, Horst 1930- .... **CLC 7, 11**
See also CA 73-76; DLB 75

Bierce, Ambrose (Gwinett)
1842-1914(?) ..... **SSC 9; TCLC 1, 7, 44; WLC**
See also AMW; BYA 11; CA 104; 139;
CANR 78; CDALB 1865-1917; DA;
DA3; DAC; DAM MST; DLB 11, 12, 23,
71, 74, 186; EWL 3; EXPS; HGG; LAIT
2; RGAL 4; RGSF 2; SSFS 9; SUFW 1

Biggers, Earl Derr 1884-1933 .... **TCLC 65**
See also CA 108; 153

Billiken, Bud
See Motley, Willard (Francis)

Billings, Josh
See Shaw, Henry Wheeler

Billington, (Lady) Rachel (Mary)
1942- .... **CLC 43**
See also AITN 2; CA 33-36R; CANR 44;
CN 7

Binchy, Maeve 1940- .... **CLC 153**
See also BEST 90:1; BPFB 1; CA 127; 134;
CANR 50, 96; CN 7; CPW; DA3; DAM
POP; INT CA-134; MTCW 1; RHW

Binyon, T(imothy) J(ohn) 1936- .... **CLC 34**
See also CA 111; CANR 28

Bion 335B.C.-245B.C. .... **CMLC 39**

Bioy Casares, Adolfo 1914-1999 ... **CLC 4, 8, 13, 88; HLC 1; SSC 17**
See Casares, Adolfo Bioy; Miranda, Javier;
Sacastru, Martin
See also CA 29-32R; 177; CANR 19, 43,
66; DAM MULT; DLB 113; EWL 3; HW
1, 2; LAW; MTCW 1, 2

Birch, Allison .... **CLC 65**

Bird, Cordwainer
See Ellison, Harlan (Jay)

Bird, Robert Montgomery
1806-1854 .... **NCLC 1**
See also DLB 202; RGAL 4

Birkerts, Sven 1951- .... **CLC 116**
See also CA 128; 133, 176; CAAE 176;
CAAS 29; INT 133

Birney, (Alfred) Earle 1904-1995 .. **CLC 1, 4, 6, 11; PC 52**
See also CA 1-4R; CANR 5, 20; CP 7;
DAC; DAM MST, POET; DLB 88;
MTCW 1; PFS 8; RGEL 2

Biruni, al 973-1048(?) .... **CMLC 28**
Bishop, Elizabeth 1911-1979 ..... **CLC 1, 4, 9, 13, 15, 32; PC 3, 34; TCLC 121**
See also AMWR 2; AMWS 1; CA 5-8R; 89-92; CABS 2; CANR 26, 61, 108; CDALB 1968-1988; DA; DA3; DAC; DAM MST, POET; DLB 5, 169; EWL 3; GLL 2; MAWW; MTCW 1, 2; PAB; PFS 6, 12; RGAL 4; SATA-Obit 24; TUS; WP
Bishop, John 1935- .... **CLC 10**
See also CA 105
Bishop, John Peale 1892-1944 ..... **TCLC 103**
See also CA 107; 155; DLB 4, 9, 45; RGAL 4
Bissett, Bill 1939- .... **CLC 18; PC 14**
See also CA 69-72; CAAS 19; CANR 15; CCA 1; CP 7; DLB 53; MTCW 1
Bissoondath, Neil (Devindra) 1955- .... **CLC 120**
See also CA 136; CANR 123; CN 7; DAC
Bitov, Andrei (Georgievich) 1937- ... **CLC 57**
See also CA 142
Biyidi, Alexandre 1932-
See Beti, Mongo
See also BW 1, 3; CA 114; 124; CANR 81; DA3; MTCW 1, 2
Bjarme, Brynjolf
See Ibsen, Henrik (Johan)
Bjoernson, Bjoernstjerne (Martinius) 1832-1910 .... **TCLC 7, 37**
See also CA 104
Black, Robert
See Holdstock, Robert P.
Blackburn, Paul 1926-1971 .... **CLC 9, 43**
See also BG 2; CA 81-84; 33-36R; CANR 34; DLB 16; DLBY 1981
Black Elk 1863-1950 .... **NNAL; TCLC 33**
See also CA 144; DAM MULT; MTCW 1; WP
Black Hawk 1767-1838 .... **NNAL**
Black Hobart
See Sanders, (James) Ed(ward)
Blacklin, Malcolm
See Chambers, Aidan
Blackmore, R(ichard) D(oddridge) 1825-1900 .... **TCLC 27**
See also CA 120; DLB 18; RGEL 2
Blackmur, R(ichard) P(almer) 1904-1965 .... **CLC 2, 24**
See also AMWS 2; CA 11-12; 25-28R; CANR 71; CAP 1; DLB 63; EWL 3
Black Tarantula
See Acker, Kathy
Blackwood, Algernon (Henry) 1869-1951 .... **TCLC 5**
See also CA 105; 150; DLB 153, 156, 178; HGG; SUFW 1
Blackwood, Caroline 1931-1996 .... **CLC 6, 9, 100**
See also BRWS 9; CA 85-88; 151; CANR 32, 61, 65; CN 7; DLB 14, 207; HGG; MTCW 1
Blade, Alexander
See Hamilton, Edmond; Silverberg, Robert
Blaga, Lucian 1895-1961 .... **CLC 75**
See also CA 157; DLB 220; EWL 3
Blair, Eric (Arthur) 1903-1950 .... **TCLC 123**
See Orwell, George
See also CA 104; 132; DA; DA3; DAB; DAC; DAM MST, NOV; MTCW 1, 2; SATA 29
Blair, Hugh 1718-1800 .... **NCLC 75**
Blais, Marie-Claire 1939- .... **CLC 2, 4, 6, 13, 22**
See also CA 21-24R; CAAS 4; CANR 38, 75, 93; DAC; DAM MST; DLB 53; EWL 3; FW; MTCW 1, 2; TWA

Blaise, Clark 1940- .... **CLC 29**
See also AITN 2; CA 53-56; CAAS 3; CANR 5, 66, 106; CN 7; DLB 53; RGSF 2
Blake, Fairley
See De Voto, Bernard (Augustine)
Blake, Nicholas
See Day Lewis, C(ecil)
See also DLB 77; MSW
Blake, Sterling
See Benford, Gregory (Albert)
Blake, William 1757-1827 . **NCLC 13, 37, 57, 127; PC 12; WLC**
See also AAYA 47; BRW 3; BRWR 1; CDBLB 1789-1832; CLR 52; DA; DA3; DAB; DAC; DAM MST, POET; DLB 93, 163; EXPP; LATS 1; LMFS 1; MAICYA 1, 2; PAB; PFS 2, 12; SATA 30; TEA; WCH; WLIT 3; WP
Blanchot, Maurice 1907-2003 .... **CLC 135**
See also CA 117; 144; 213; DLB 72; EWL 3
Blasco Ibanez, Vicente 1867-1928 . **TCLC 12**
See also BPFB 1; CA 110; 131; CANR 81; DA3; DAM NOV; EW 8; EWL 3; HW 1, 2; MTCW 1
Blatty, William Peter 1928- .... **CLC 2**
See also CA 5-8R; CANR 9; DAM POP; HGG
Bleeck, Oliver
See Thomas, Ross (Elmore)
Blessing, Lee 1949- .... **CLC 54**
See also CAD; CD 5
Blight, Rose
See Greer, Germaine
Blish, James (Benjamin) 1921-1975 . **CLC 14**
See also BPFB 1; CA 1-4R; 57-60; CANR 3; DLB 8; MTCW 1; SATA 66; SCFW 2; SFW 4
Bliss, Reginald
See Wells, H(erbert) G(eorge)
Blixen, Karen (Christentze Dinesen) 1885-1962
See Dinesen, Isak
See also CA 25-28; CANR 22, 50; CAP 2; DA3; DLB 214; LMFS 1; MTCW 1, 2; SATA 44
Bloch, Robert (Albert) 1917-1994 .... **CLC 33**
See also AAYA 29; CA 5-8R; 179; 146; CAAE 179; CAAS 20; CANR 5, 78; DA3; DLB 44; HGG; INT CANR-5; MTCW 1; SATA 12; SATA-Obit 82; SFW 4; SUFW 1, 2
Blok, Alexander (Alexandrovich) 1880-1921 .... **PC 21; TCLC 5**
See also CA 104; 183; EW 9; EWL 3; LMFS 2; RGWL 2, 3
Blom, Jan
See Breytenbach, Breyten
Bloom, Harold 1930- .... **CLC 24, 103**
See also CA 13-16R; CANR 39, 75, 92; DLB 67; EWL 3; MTCW 1; RGAL 4
Bloomfield, Aurelius
See Bourne, Randolph S(illiman)
Blount, Roy (Alton), Jr. 1941- .... **CLC 38**
See also CA 53-56; CANR 10, 28, 61; CSW; INT CANR-28; MTCW 1, 2
Blowsnake, Sam 1875-(?) .... **NNAL**
Bloy, Leon 1846-1917 .... **TCLC 22**
See also CA 121; 183; DLB 123; GFL 1789 to the Present
Blue Cloud, Peter (Aroniawenrate) 1933- .... **NNAL**
See also CA 117; CANR 40; DAM MULT
Blugagge, Oranthy
See Alcott, Louisa May

Blume, Judy (Sussman) 1938- .... **CLC 12, 30**
See also AAYA 3, 26; BYA 1, 8, 12; CA 29-32R; CANR 13, 37, 66; CLR 2, 15, 69; CPW; DA3; DAM NOV, POP; DLB 52; JRDA; MAICYA 1, 2; MAICYAS 1; MTCW 1, 2; SATA 2, 31, 79, 142; WYA; YAW
Blunden, Edmund (Charles) 1896-1974 .... **CLC 2, 56**
See also BRW 6; CA 17-18; 45-48; CANR 54; CAP 2; DLB 20, 100, 155; MTCW 1; PAB
Bly, Robert (Elwood) 1926- .... **CLC 1, 2, 5, 10, 15, 38, 128; PC 39**
See also AMWS 4; CA 5-8R; CANR 41, 73; CP 7; DA3; DAM POET; DLB 5; EWL 3; MTCW 1, 2; PFS 6, 17; RGAL 4
Boas, Franz 1858-1942 .... **TCLC 56**
See also CA 115; 181
Bobette
See Simenon, Georges (Jacques Christian)
Boccaccio, Giovanni 1313-1375 ... **CMLC 13, 57; SSC 10**
See also EW 2; RGSF 2; RGWL 2, 3; TWA
Bochco, Steven 1943- .... **CLC 35**
See also AAYA 11; CA 124; 138
Bode, Sigmund
See O'Doherty, Brian
Bodel, Jean 1167(?)-1210 .... **CMLC 28**
Bodenheim, Maxwell 1892-1954 .... **TCLC 44**
See also CA 110; 187; DLB 9, 45; RGAL 4
Bodenheimer, Maxwell
See Bodenheim, Maxwell
Bodker, Cecil 1927-
See Bodker, Cecil
Bodker, Cecil 1927- .... **CLC 21**
See also CA 73-76; CANR 13, 44, 111; CLR 23; MAICYA 1, 2; SATA 14, 133
Boell, Heinrich (Theodor) 1917-1985 ..... **CLC 2, 3, 6, 9, 11, 15, 27, 32, 72; SSC 23; WLC**
See Boll, Heinrich
See also CA 21-24R; 116; CANR 24; DA; DA3; DAB; DAC; DAM MST, NOV; DLB 69; DLBY 1985; MTCW 1, 2; TWA
Boerne, Alfred
See Doeblin, Alfred
Boethius c. 480-c. 524 .... **CMLC 15**
See also DLB 115; RGWL 2, 3
Boff, Leonardo (Genezio Darci) 1938- .... **CLC 70; HLC 1**
See also CA 150; DAM MULT; HW 2
Bogan, Louise 1897-1970 .... **CLC 4, 39, 46, 93; PC 12**
See also AMWS 3; CA 73-76; 25-28R; CANR 33, 82; DAM POET; DLB 45, 169; EWL 3; MAWW; MTCW 1, 2; RGAL 4
Bogarde, Dirk
See Van Den Bogarde, Derek Jules Gaspard Ulric Niven
See also DLB 14
Bogosian, Eric 1953- .... **CLC 45, 141**
See also CA 138; CAD; CANR 102; CD 5
Bograd, Larry 1953- .... **CLC 35**
See also CA 93-96; CANR 57; SAAS 21; SATA 33, 89; WYA
Boiardo, Matteo Maria 1441-1494 .... **LC 6**
Boileau-Despreaux, Nicolas 1636-1711 . **LC 3**
See also DLB 268; EW 3; GFL Beginnings to 1789; RGWL 2, 3
Boissard, Maurice
See Leautaud, Paul
Bojer, Johan 1872-1959 .... **TCLC 64**
See also CA 189; EWL 3
Bok, Edward W. 1863-1930 .... **TCLC 101**
See also DLB 91; DLBD 16
Boker, George Henry 1823-1890 . **NCLC 125**
See also RGAL 4

Boland, Eavan (Aisling) 1944- .. **CLC 40, 67, 113**
See also BRWS 5; CA 143; CAAE 207; CANR 61; CP 7; CWP; DAM POET; DLB 40; FW; MTCW 2; PFS 12

Boll, Heinrich
See Boell, Heinrich (Theodor)
See also BPFB 1; CDWLB 2; EW 13; EWL 3; RGSF 2; RGWL 2, 3

Bolt, Lee
See Faust, Frederick (Schiller)

Bolt, Robert (Oxton) 1924-1995 .... **CLC 14**
See also CA 17-20R; 147; CANR 35, 67; CBD; DAM DRAM; DFS 2; DLB 13, 233; EWL 3; LAIT 1; MTCW 1

Bombal, Maria Luisa 1910-1980 .... **HLCS 1; SSC 37**
See also CA 127; CANR 72; EWL 3; HW 1; LAW; RGSF 2

Bombet, Louis-Alexandre-Cesar
See Stendhal

Bomkauf
See Kaufman, Bob (Garnell)

Bonaventura .... **NCLC 35**
See also DLB 90

Bond, Edward 1934- .... **CLC 4, 6, 13, 23**
See also AAYA 50; BRWS 1; CA 25-28R; CANR 38, 67, 106; CBD; CD 5; DAM DRAM; DFS 3, 8; DLB 13; EWL 3; MTCW 1

Bonham, Frank 1914-1989 .... **CLC 12**
See also AAYA 1; BYA 1, 3; CA 9-12R; CANR 4, 36; JRDA; MAICYA 1, 2; SAAS 3; SATA 1, 49; SATA-Obit 62; TCWW 2; YAW

Bonnefoy, Yves 1923- .... **CLC 9, 15, 58**
See also CA 85-88; CANR 33, 75, 97; CWW 2; DAM MST, POET; DLB 258; EWL 3; GFL 1789 to the Present; MTCW 1, 2

Bonner, Marita .... **HR 2**
See Occomy, Marita (Odette) Bonner

Bonnin, Gertrude 1876-1938 .... **NNAL**
See Zitkala-Sa
See also CA 150; DAM MULT

Bontemps, Arna(ud Wendell)
1902-1973 .... **BLC 1; CLC 1, 18; HR 2**
See also BW 1; CA 1-4R; 41-44R; CANR 4, 35; CLR 6; CWRI 5; DA3; DAM MULT, NOV, POET; DLB 48, 51; JRDA; MAICYA 1, 2; MTCW 1, 2; SATA 2, 44; SATA-Obit 24; WCH; WP

Booth, Martin 1944- .... **CLC 13**
See also CA 93-96; CAAE 188; CAAS 2; CANR 92

Booth, Philip 1925- .... **CLC 23**
See also CA 5-8R; CANR 5, 88; CP 7; DLBY 1982

Booth, Wayne C(layson) 1921- .... **CLC 24**
See also CA 1-4R; CAAS 5; CANR 3, 43, 117; DLB 67

Borchert, Wolfgang 1921-1947 .... **TCLC 5**
See also CA 104; 188; DLB 69, 124; EWL 3

Borel, Petrus 1809-1859 .... **NCLC 41**
See also DLB 119; GFL 1789 to the Present

Borges, Jorge Luis 1899-1986 ... **CLC 1, 2, 3, 4, 6, 8, 9, 10, 13, 19, 44, 48, 83; HLC 1; PC 22, 32; SSC 4, 41; TCLC 109; WLC**
See also AAYA 26; BPFB 1; CA 21-24R; CANR 19, 33, 75, 105; CDWLB 3; DA; DA3; DAB; DAC; DAM MST, MULT; DLB 113, 283; DLBY 1986; DNFS 1, 2; EWL 3; HW 1, 2; LAW; LMFS 1; MSW; MTCW 1, 2; RGSF 2; RGWL 2, 3; SFW 4; SSFS 17; TWA; WLIT 1

Borowski, Tadeusz 1922-1951 .... **SSC 48; TCLC 9**
See also CA 106; 154; CDWLB 4; DLB 215; EWL 3; RGSF 2; RGWL 3; SSFS 13

Borrow, George (Henry)
1803-1881 .... **NCLC 9**
See also DLB 21, 55, 166

Bosch (Gavino), Juan 1909-2001 ..... **HLCS 1**
See also CA 151; 204; DAM MST, MULT; DLB 145; HW 1, 2

Bosman, Herman Charles
1905-1951 .... **TCLC 49**
See Malan, Herman
See also CA 160; DLB 225; RGSF 2

Bosschere, Jean de 1878(?)-1953 ... **TCLC 19**
See also CA 115; 186

Boswell, James 1740-1795 ... **LC 4, 50; WLC**
See also BRW 3; CDBLB 1660-1789; DA; DAB; DAC; DAM MST; DLB 104, 142; TEA; WLIT 3

Bottomley, Gordon 1874-1948 ..... **TCLC 107**
See also CA 120; 192; DLB 10

Bottoms, David 1949- .... **CLC 53**
See also CA 105; CANR 22; CSW; DLB 120; DLBY 1983

Boucicault, Dion 1820-1890 .... **NCLC 41**

Boucolon, Maryse
See Conde, Maryse

Bourget, Paul (Charles Joseph)
1852-1935 .... **TCLC 12**
See also CA 107; 196; DLB 123; GFL 1789 to the Present

Bourjaily, Vance (Nye) 1922- .... **CLC 8, 62**
See also CA 1-4R; CAAS 1; CANR 2, 72; CN 7; DLB 2, 143

Bourne, Randolph S(illiman)
1886-1918 .... **TCLC 16**
See also AMW; CA 117; 155; DLB 63

Bova, Ben(jamin William) 1932- .... **CLC 45**
See also AAYA 16; CA 5-8R; CAAS 18; CANR 11, 56, 94, 111; CLR 3; DLBY 1981; INT CANR-11; MAICYA 1, 2; MTCW 1; SATA 6, 68, 133; SFW 4

Bowen, Elizabeth (Dorothea Cole)
1899-1973 . **CLC 1, 3, 6, 11, 15, 22, 118; SSC 3, 28**
See also BRWS 2; CA 17-18; 41-44R; CANR 35, 105; CAP 2; CDBLB 1945-1960; DA3; DAM NOV; DLB 15, 162; EWL 3; EXPS; FW; HGG; MTCW 1, 2; NFS 13; RGSF 2; SSFS 5; SUFW 1; TEA; WLIT 4

Bowering, George 1935- .... **CLC 15, 47**
See also CA 21-24R; CAAS 16; CANR 10; CP 7; DLB 53

Bowering, Marilyn R(uthe) 1949- ...... **CLC 32**
See also CA 101; CANR 49; CP; CWP

Bowers, Edgar 1924-2000 .... **CLC 9**
See also CA 5-8R; 188; CANR 24; CP 7; CSW; DLB 5

Bowers, Mrs. J. Milton 1842-1914
See Bierce, Ambrose (Gwinett)

Bowie, David .... **CLC 17**
See Jones, David Robert

Bowles, Jane (Sydney) 1917-1973 ..... **CLC 3, 68**
See Bowles, Jane Auer
See also CA 19-20; 41-44R; CAP 2

Bowles, Jane Auer
See Bowles, Jane (Sydney)
See also EWL 3

Bowles, Paul (Frederick) 1910-1999 . **CLC 1, 2, 19, 53; SSC 3**
See also AMWS 4; CA 1-4R; 186; CAAS 1; CANR 1, 19, 50, 75; CN 7; DA3; DLB 5, 6, 218; EWL 3; MTCW 1, 2; RGAL 4; SSFS 17

Bowles, William Lisle 1762-1850 . **NCLC 103**
See also DLB 93

Box, Edgar
See Vidal, Gore
See also GLL 1

Boyd, James 1888-1944 .... **TCLC 115**
See also CA 186; DLB 9; DLBD 16; RGAL 4; RHW

Boyd, Nancy
See Millay, Edna St. Vincent
See also GLL 1

Boyd, Thomas (Alexander)
1898-1935 .... **TCLC 111**
See also CA 111; 183; DLB 9; DLBD 16

Boyd, William 1952- .... **CLC 28, 53, 70**
See also CA 114; 120; CANR 51, 71; CN 7; DLB 231

Boyle, Kay 1902-1992 .... **CLC 1, 5, 19, 58, 121; SSC 5**
See also CA 13-16R; 140; CAAS 1; CANR 29, 61, 110; DLB 4, 9, 48, 86; DLBY 1993; EWL 3; MTCW 1, 2; RGAL 4; RGSF 2; SSFS 10, 13, 14

Boyle, Mark
See Kienzle, William X(avier)

Boyle, Patrick 1905-1982 .... **CLC 19**
See also CA 127

Boyle, T. C.
See Boyle, T(homas) Coraghessan
See also AMWS 8

Boyle, T(homas) Coraghessan
1948- .... **CLC 36, 55, 90; SSC 16**
See Boyle, T. C.
See also AAYA 47; BEST 90:4; BPFB 1; CA 120; CANR 44, 76, 89; CN 7; CPW; DA3; DAM POP; DLB 218, 278; DLBY 1986; EWL 3; MTCW 2; SSFS 13

Boz
See Dickens, Charles (John Huffam)

Brackenridge, Hugh Henry
1748-1816 .... **NCLC 7**
See also DLB 11, 37; RGAL 4

Bradbury, Edward P.
See Moorcock, Michael (John)
See also MTCW 2

Bradbury, Malcolm (Stanley)
1932-2000 .... **CLC 32, 61**
See also CA 1-4R; CANR 1, 33, 91, 98; CN 7; DA3; DAM NOV; DLB 14, 207; EWL 3; MTCW 1, 2

Bradbury, Ray (Douglas) 1920- .... **CLC 1, 3, 10, 15, 42, 98; SSC 29, 53; WLC**
See also AAYA 15; AITN 2; AMWS 4; BPFB 1; BYA 4, 5, 11; CA 1-4R; CANR 2, 30, 75; CDALB 1968-1988; CN 7; CPW; DA; DA3; DAB; DAC; DAM MST, NOV, POP; DLB 2, 8; EXPN; EXPS; HGG; LAIT 3, 5; LATS 1; LMFS 2; MTCW 1, 2; NFS 1; RGAL 4; RGSF 2; SATA 11, 64, 123; SCFW 2; SFW 4; SSFS 1; SUFW 1, 2; TUS; YAW

Braddon, Mary Elizabeth
1837-1915 .... **TCLC 111**
See also BRWS 8; CA 108; 179; CMW 4; DLB 18, 70, 156; HGG

Bradfield, Scott (Michael) 1955- .... **SSC 65**
See also CA 147; CANR 90; HGG; SUFW 2

Bradford, Gamaliel 1863-1932 .... **TCLC 36**
See also CA 160; DLB 17

Bradford, William 1590-1657 .... **LC 64**
See also DLB 24, 30; RGAL 4

Bradley, David (Henry), Jr. 1950- .... **BLC 1; CLC 23, 118**
See also BW 1, 3; CA 104; CANR 26, 81; CN 7; DAM MULT; DLB 33

Bradley, John Ed(mund, Jr.) 1958- . **CLC 55**
See also CA 139; CANR 99; CN 7; CSW

Bradley, Marion Zimmer
1930-1999 .... **CLC 30**
See Chapman, Lee; Dexter, John; Gardner, Miriam; Ives, Morgan; Rivers, Elfrida
See also AAYA 40; BPFB 1; CA 57-60; 185; CAAS 10; CANR 7, 31, 51, 75, 107; CPW; DA3; DAM POP; DLB 8; FANT; FW; MTCW 1, 2; SATA 90, 139; SATA-Obit 116; SFW 4; SUFW 2; YAW

Bradshaw, John 1933- .... **CLC 70**
See also CA 138; CANR 61

Bradstreet, Anne 1612(?)-1672 ...... **LC 4, 30; PC 10**
See also AMWS 1; CDALB 1640-1865; DA; DA3; DAC; DAM MST, POET; DLB 24; EXPP; FW; PFS 6; RGAL 4; TUS; WP

Brady, Joan 1939- .... **CLC 86**
See also CA 141

Bragg, Melvyn 1939- .... **CLC 10**
See also BEST 89:3; CA 57-60; CANR 10, 48, 89; CN 7; DLB 14, 271; RHW

Brahe, Tycho 1546-1601 .... **LC 45**

Braine, John (Gerard) 1922-1986 . **CLC 1, 3, 41**
See also CA 1-4R; 120; CANR 1, 33; CDBLB 1945-1960; DLB 15; DLBY 1986; EWL 3; MTCW 1

Braithwaite, William Stanley (Beaumont)
1878-1962 .... **BLC 1; HR 2; PC 52**
See also BW 1; CA 125; DAM MULT; DLB 50, 54

Bramah, Ernest 1868-1942 .... **TCLC 72**
See also CA 156; CMW 4; DLB 70; FANT

Brammer, William 1930(?)-1978 ...... **CLC 31**
See also CA 77-80

Brancati, Vitaliano 1907-1954 .... **TCLC 12**
See also CA 109; DLB 264; EWL 3

Brancato, Robin F(idler) 1936- .... **CLC 35**
See also AAYA 9; BYA 6; CA 69-72; CANR 11, 45; CLR 32; JRDA; MAICYA 2; MAICYAS 1; SAAS 9; SATA 97; WYA; YAW

Brand, Max
See Faust, Frederick (Schiller)
See also BPFB 1; TCWW 2

Brand, Millen 1906-1980 .... **CLC 7**
See also CA 21-24R; 97-100; CANR 72

Branden, Barbara .... **CLC 44**
See also CA 148

Brandes, Georg (Morris Cohen)
1842-1927 .... **TCLC 10**
See also CA 105; 189

Brandys, Kazimierz 1916-2000 .... **CLC 62**
See also EWL 3

Branley, Franklyn M(ansfield)
1915-2002 .... **CLC 21**
See also CA 33-36R; 207; CANR 14, 39; CLR 13; MAICYA 1, 2; SAAS 16; SATA 4, 68, 136

Brant, Beth (E.) 1941- .... **NNAL**
See also CA 144; FW

Brathwaite, Edward Kamau
1930- .... **BLCS; CLC 11**
See also BW 2, 3; CA 25-28R; CANR 11, 26, 47, 107; CDWLB 3; CP 7; DAM POET; DLB 125; EWL 3

Brathwaite, Kamau
See Brathwaite, Edward Kamau

Brautigan, Richard (Gary)
1935-1984 .... **CLC 1, 3, 5, 9, 12, 34, 42; TCLC 133**
See also BPFB 1; CA 53-56; 113; CANR 34; DA3; DAM NOV; DLB 2, 5, 206; DLBY 1980, 1984; FANT; MTCW 1; RGAL 4; SATA 56

Brave Bird, Mary .... **NNAL**
See Crow Dog, Mary (Ellen)

Braverman, Kate 1950- .... **CLC 67**
See also CA 89-92

Brecht, (Eugen) Bertolt (Friedrich)
1898-1956 ..... **DC 3; TCLC 1, 6, 13, 35; WLC**
See also CA 104; 133; CANR 62; CDWLB 2; DA; DA3; DAB; DAC; DAM DRAM, MST; DFS 4, 5, 9; DLB 56, 124; EW 11; EWL 3; IDTP; MTCW 1, 2; RGWL 2, 3; TWA

Brecht, Eugen Berthold Friedrich
See Brecht, (Eugen) Bertolt (Friedrich)

Bremer, Fredrika 1801-1865 .... **NCLC 11**
See also DLB 254

Brennan, Christopher John
1870-1932 .... **TCLC 17**
See also CA 117; 188; DLB 230; EWL 3

Brennan, Maeve 1917-1993 ... **CLC 5; TCLC 124**
See also CA 81-84; CANR 72, 100

Brent, Linda
See Jacobs, Harriet A(nn)

Brentano, Clemens (Maria)
1778-1842 .... **NCLC 1**
See also DLB 90; RGWL 2, 3

Brent of Bin Bin
See Franklin, (Stella Maria Sarah) Miles (Lampe)

Brenton, Howard 1942- .... **CLC 31**
See also CA 69-72; CANR 33, 67; CBD; CD 5; DLB 13; MTCW 1

Breslin, James 1930-
See Breslin, Jimmy
See also CA 73-76; CANR 31, 75; DAM NOV; MTCW 1, 2

Breslin, Jimmy .... **CLC 4, 43**
See Breslin, James
See also AITN 1; DLB 185; MTCW 2

Bresson, Robert 1901(?)-1999 .... **CLC 16**
See also CA 110; 187; CANR 49

Breton, Andre 1896-1966 .. **CLC 2, 9, 15, 54; PC 15**
See also CA 19-20; 25-28R; CANR 40, 60; CAP 2; DLB 65, 258; EW 11; EWL 3; GFL 1789 to the Present; LMFS 2; MTCW 1, 2; RGWL 2, 3; TWA; WP

Breytenbach, Breyten 1939(?)- .. **CLC 23, 37, 126**
See also CA 113; 129; CANR 61, 122; CWW 2; DAM POET; DLB 225; EWL 3

Bridgers, Sue Ellen 1942- .... **CLC 26**
See also AAYA 8, 49; BYA 7, 8; CA 65-68; CANR 11, 36; CLR 18; DLB 52; JRDA; MAICYA 1, 2; SAAS 1; SATA 22, 90; SATA-Essay 109; WYA; YAW

Bridges, Robert (Seymour)
1844-1930 .... **PC 28; TCLC 1**
See also BRW 6; CA 104; 152; CDBLB 1890-1914; DAM POET; DLB 19, 98

Bridie, James .... **TCLC 3**
See Mavor, Osborne Henry
See also DLB 10; EWL 3

Brin, David 1950- .... **CLC 34**
See also AAYA 21; CA 102; CANR 24, 70; INT CANR-24; SATA 65; SCFW 2; SFW 4

Brink, Andre (Philippus) 1935- . **CLC 18, 36, 106**
See also AFW; BRWS 6; CA 104; CANR 39, 62, 109; CN 7; DLB 225; EWL 3; INT CA-103; LATS 1; MTCW 1, 2; WLIT 2

Brinsmead, H. F.
See Brinsmead, H(esba) F(ay)

Brinsmead, H. F(ay)
See Brinsmead, H(esba) F(ay)

Brinsmead, H(esba) F(ay) 1922- ...... **CLC 21**
See also CA 21-24R; CANR 10; CLR 47; CWRI 5; MAICYA 1, 2; SAAS 5; SATA 18, 78

Brittain, Vera (Mary) 1893(?)-1970 . **CLC 23**
See also CA 13-16; 25-28R; CANR 58; CAP 1; DLB 191; FW; MTCW 1, 2

Broch, Hermann 1886-1951 .... **TCLC 20**
See also CA 117; 211; CDWLB 2; DLB 85, 124; EW 10; EWL 3; RGWL 2, 3

Brock, Rose
See Hansen, Joseph
See also GLL 1

Brod, Max 1884-1968 .... **TCLC 115**
See also CA 5-8R; 25-28R; CANR 7; DLB 81; EWL 3

Brodkey, Harold (Roy) 1930-1996 .. **CLC 56; TCLC 123**
See also CA 111; 151; CANR 71; CN 7; DLB 130

Brodskii, Iosif
See Brodsky, Joseph

Brodsky, Iosif Alexandrovich 1940-1996
See Brodsky, Joseph
See also AITN 1; CA 41-44R; 151; CANR 37, 106; DA3; DAM POET; MTCW 1, 2; RGWL 2, 3

Brodsky, Joseph . **CLC 4, 6, 13, 36, 100; PC 9**
See Brodsky, Iosif Alexandrovich
See also AMWS 8; CWW 2; DLB 285; EWL 3; MTCW 1

Brodsky, Michael (Mark) 1948- .... **CLC 19**
See also CA 102; CANR 18, 41, 58; DLB 244

Brodzki, Bella ed. .... **CLC 65**

Brome, Richard 1590(?)-1652 .... **LC 61**
See also DLB 58

Bromell, Henry 1947- .... **CLC 5**
See also CA 53-56; CANR 9, 115, 116

Bromfield, Louis (Brucker)
1896-1956 .... **TCLC 11**
See also CA 107; 155; DLB 4, 9, 86; RGAL 4; RHW

Broner, E(sther) M(asserman)
1930- .... **CLC 19**
See also CA 17-20R; CANR 8, 25, 72; CN 7; DLB 28

Bronk, William (M.) 1918-1999 .... **CLC 10**
See also CA 89-92; 177; CANR 23; CP 7; DLB 165

Bronstein, Lev Davidovich
See Trotsky, Leon

Bronte, Anne 1820-1849 ..... **NCLC 4, 71, 102**
See also BRW 5; BRWR 1; DA3; DLB 21, 199; TEA

Bronte, (Patrick) Branwell
1817-1848 .... **NCLC 109**

Bronte, Charlotte 1816-1855 ...... **NCLC 3, 8, 33, 58, 105; WLC**
See also AAYA 17; BRW 5; BRWC 2; BRWR 1; BYA 2; CDBLB 1832-1890; DA; DA3; DAB; DAC; DAM MST, NOV; DLB 21, 159, 199; EXPN; LAIT 2; NFS 4; TEA; WLIT 4

Bronte, Emily (Jane) 1818-1848 ... **NCLC 16, 35; PC 8; WLC**
See also AAYA 17; BPFB 1; BRW 5; BRWC 1; BRWR 1; BYA 3; CDBLB 1832-1890; DA; DA3; DAB; DAC; DAM MST, NOV, POET; DLB 21, 32, 199; EXPN; LAIT 1; TEA; WLIT 3

Brontes
See Bronte, Anne; Bronte, Charlotte; Bronte, Emily (Jane)

Brooke, Frances 1724-1789 .... **LC 6, 48**
See also DLB 39, 99

Brooke, Henry 1703(?)-1783 .... **LC 1**
See also DLB 39

Brooke, Rupert (Chawner)
1887-1915 ..... **PC 24; TCLC 2, 7; WLC**
See also BRWS 3; CA 104; 132; CANR 61; CDBLB 1914-1945; DA; DAB; DAC; DAM MST, POET; DLB 19, 216; EXPP; GLL 2; MTCW 1, 2; PFS 7; TEA

Brooke-Haven, P.
See Wodehouse, P(elham) G(renville)

Brooke-Rose, Christine 1926(?)- ...... **CLC 40**
See also BRWS 4; CA 13-16R; CANR 58, 118; CN 7; DLB 14, 231; EWL 3; SFW 4

Brookner, Anita 1928- .. **CLC 32, 34, 51, 136**
See also BRWS 4; CA 114; CANR 37, 56, 87; CN 7; CPW; DA3; DAB; DAM POP; DLB 194; DLBY 1987; EWL 3; MTCW 1, 2; TEA

Brooks, Cleanth 1906-1994 . **CLC 24, 86, 110**
See also CA 17-20R; 145; CANR 33, 35; CSW; DLB 63; DLBY 1994; EWL 3; INT CANR-35; MTCW 1, 2

Brooks, George
See Baum, L(yman) Frank

Brooks, Gwendolyn (Elizabeth)
1917-2000 ... **BLC 1; CLC 1, 2, 4, 5, 15, 49, 125; PC 7; WLC**
See also AAYA 20; AFAW 1, 2; AITN 1; AMWS 3; BW 2, 3; CA 1-4R; 190; CANR 1, 27, 52, 75; CDALB 1941-1968; CLR 27; CP 7; CWP; DA; DA3; DAC; DAM MST, MULT, POET; DLB 5, 76, 165; EWL 3; EXPP; MAWW; MTCW 1, 2; PFS 1, 2, 4, 6; RGAL 4; SATA 6; SATA-Obit 123; TUS; WP

Brooks, Mel .... **CLC 12**
See Kaminsky, Melvin
See also AAYA 13, 48; DLB 26

Brooks, Peter (Preston) 1938- .... **CLC 34**
See also CA 45-48; CANR 1, 107

Brooks, Van Wyck 1886-1963 .... **CLC 29**
See also AMW; CA 1-4R; CANR 6; DLB 45, 63, 103; TUS

Brophy, Brigid (Antonia)
1929-1995 .... **CLC 6, 11, 29, 105**
See also CA 5-8R; 149; CAAS 4; CANR 25, 53; CBD; CN 7; CWD; DA3; DLB 14, 271; EWL 3; MTCW 1, 2

Brosman, Catharine Savage 1934- ..... **CLC 9**
See also CA 61-64; CANR 21, 46

Brossard, Nicole 1943- .... **CLC 115, 169**
See also CA 122; CAAS 16; CCA 1; CWP; CWW 2; DLB 53; EWL 3; FW; GLL 2; RGWL 3

Brother Antoninus
See Everson, William (Oliver)

The Brothers Quay
See Quay, Stephen; Quay, Timothy

Broughton, T(homas) Alan 1936- ...... **CLC 19**
See also CA 45-48; CANR 2, 23, 48, 111

Broumas, Olga 1949- .... **CLC 10, 73**
See also CA 85-88; CANR 20, 69, 110; CP 7; CWP; GLL 2

Broun, Heywood 1888-1939 .... **TCLC 104**
See also DLB 29, 171

Brown, Alan 1950- .... **CLC 99**
See also CA 156

Brown, Charles Brockden
1771-1810 .... **NCLC 22, 74, 122**
See also AMWS 1; CDALB 1640-1865; DLB 37, 59, 73; FW; HGG; LMFS 1; RGAL 4; TUS

Brown, Christy 1932-1981 .... **CLC 63**
See also BYA 13; CA 105; 104; CANR 72; DLB 14

Brown, Claude 1937-2002 ... **BLC 1; CLC 30**
See also AAYA 7; BW 1, 3; CA 73-76; 205; CANR 81; DAM MULT

Brown, Dee (Alexander)
1908-2002 .... **CLC 18, 47**
See also AAYA 30; CA 13-16R; 212; CAAS 6; CANR 11, 45, 60; CPW; CSW; DA3; DAM POP; DLBY 1980; LAIT 2; MTCW 1, 2; NCFS 5; SATA 5, 110; SATA-Obit 141; TCWW 2

Brown, George
See Wertmueller, Lina

Brown, George Douglas
1869-1902 .... **TCLC 28**
See Douglas, George
See also CA 162

Brown, George Mackay 1921-1996 ... **CLC 5, 48, 100**
See also BRWS 6; CA 21-24R; 151; CAAS 6; CANR 12, 37, 67; CN 7; CP 7; DLB 14, 27, 139, 271; MTCW 1; RGSF 2; SATA 35

Brown, (William) Larry 1951- .... **CLC 73**
See also CA 130; 134; CANR 117; CSW; DLB 234; INT 133

Brown, Moses
See Barrett, William (Christopher)

Brown, Rita Mae 1944- .... **CLC 18, 43, 79**
See also BPFB 1; CA 45-48; CANR 2, 11, 35, 62, 95; CN 7; CPW; CSW; DA3; DAM NOV, POP; FW; INT CANR-11; MTCW 1, 2; NFS 9; RGAL 4; TUS

Brown, Roderick (Langmere) Haig-
See Haig-Brown, Roderick (Langmere)

Brown, Rosellen 1939- .... **CLC 32, 170**
See also CA 77-80; CAAS 10; CANR 14, 44, 98; CN 7

Brown, Sterling Allen 1901-1989 ...... **BLC 1; CLC 1, 23, 59; HR 2**
See also AFAW 1, 2; BW 1, 3; CA 85-88; 127; CANR 26; DA3; DAM MULT, POET; DLB 48, 51, 63; MTCW 1, 2; RGAL 4; WP

Brown, Will
See Ainsworth, William Harrison

Brown, William Hill 1765-1793 .... **LC 93**
See also DLB 37

Brown, William Wells 1815-1884 ...... **BLC 1; DC 1; NCLC 2, 89**
See also DAM MULT; DLB 3, 50, 183, 248; RGAL 4

Browne, (Clyde) Jackson 1948(?)- ... **CLC 21**
See also CA 120

Browning, Elizabeth Barrett
1806-1861 ... **NCLC 1, 16, 61, 66; PC 6; WLC**
See also BRW 4; CDBLB 1832-1890; DA; DA3; DAB; DAC; DAM MST, POET; DLB 32, 199; EXPP; PAB; PFS 2, 16; TEA; WLIT 4; WP

Browning, Robert 1812-1889 . **NCLC 19, 79; PC 2; WLCS**
See also BRW 4; BRWC 2; BRWR 2; CDBLB 1832-1890; DA; DA3; DAB; DAC; DAM MST, POET; DLB 32, 163; EXPP; LATS 1; PAB; PFS 1, 15; RGEL 2; TEA; WLIT 4; WP; YABC 1

Browning, Tod 1882-1962 .... **CLC 16**
See also CA 141; 117

Brownmiller, Susan 1935- .... **CLC 159**
See also CA 103; CANR 35, 75; DAM NOV; FW; MTCW 1, 2

Brownson, Orestes Augustus
1803-1876 .... **NCLC 50**
See also DLB 1, 59, 73, 243

Bruccoli, Matthew J(oseph) 1931- ... **CLC 34**
See also CA 9-12R; CANR 7, 87; DLB 103

Bruce, Lenny .... **CLC 21**
See Schneider, Leonard Alfred

Bruchac, Joseph III 1942- .... **NNAL**
See also AAYA 19; CA 33-36R; CANR 13, 47, 75, 94; CLR 46; CWRI 5; DAM MULT; JRDA; MAICYA 2; MAICYAS 1; MTCW 1; SATA 42, 89, 131

Bruin, John
See Brutus, Dennis

Brulard, Henri
See Stendhal

Brulls, Christian
See Simenon, Georges (Jacques Christian)

Brunner, John (Kilian Houston)
1934-1995 .... **CLC 8, 10**
See also CA 1-4R; 149; CAAS 8; CANR 2, 37; CPW; DAM POP; DLB 261; MTCW 1, 2; SCFW 2; SFW 4

Bruno, Giordano 1548-1600 .... **LC 27**
See also RGWL 2, 3

Brutus, Dennis 1924- ... **BLC 1; CLC 43; PC 24**
See also AFW; BW 2, 3; CA 49-52; CAAS 14; CANR 2, 27, 42, 81; CDWLB 3; CP 7; DAM MULT, POET; DLB 117, 225; EWL 3

Bryan, C(ourtlandt) D(ixon) B(arnes)
1936- .... **CLC 29**
See also CA 73-76; CANR 13, 68; DLB 185; INT CANR-13

Bryan, Michael
See Moore, Brian
See also CCA 1

Bryan, William Jennings
1860-1925 .... **TCLC 99**

Bryant, William Cullen 1794-1878 . **NCLC 6, 46; PC 20**
See also AMWS 1; CDALB 1640-1865; DA; DAB; DAC; DAM MST, POET; DLB 3, 43, 59, 189, 250; EXPP; PAB; RGAL 4; TUS

Bryusov, Valery Yakovlevich
1873-1924 .... **TCLC 10**
See also CA 107; 155; EWL 3; SFW 4

Buchan, John 1875-1940 .... **TCLC 41**
See also CA 108; 145; CMW 4; DAB; DAM POP; DLB 34, 70, 156; HGG; MSW; MTCW 1; RGEL 2; RHW; YABC 2

Buchanan, George 1506-1582 .... **LC 4**
See also DLB 132

Buchanan, Robert 1841-1901 .... **TCLC 107**
See also CA 179; DLB 18, 35

Buchheim, Lothar-Guenther 1918- .... **CLC 6**
See also CA 85-88

Buchner, (Karl) Georg 1813-1837 . **NCLC 26**
See also CDWLB 2; DLB 133; EW 6; RGSF 2; RGWL 2, 3; TWA

Buchwald, Art(hur) 1925- .... **CLC 33**
See also AITN 1; CA 5-8R; CANR 21, 67, 107; MTCW 1, 2; SATA 10

Buck, Pearl S(ydenstricker)
1892-1973 .... **CLC 7, 11, 18, 127**
See also AAYA 42; AITN 1; AMWS 2; BPFB 1; CA 1-4R; 41-44R; CANR 1, 34; CDALBS; DA; DA3; DAB; DAC; DAM MST, NOV; DLB 9, 102; EWL 3; LAIT 3; MTCW 1, 2; RGAL 4; RHW; SATA 1, 25; TUS

Buckler, Ernest 1908-1984 .... **CLC 13**
See also CA 11-12; 114; CAP 1; CCA 1; DAC; DAM MST; DLB 68; SATA 47

Buckley, Christopher (Taylor)
1952- .... **CLC 165**
See also CA 139; CANR 119

Buckley, Vincent (Thomas)
1925-1988 .... **CLC 57**
See also CA 101; DLB 289

Buckley, William F(rank), Jr. 1925- . **CLC 7, 18, 37**
See also AITN 1; BPFB 1; CA 1-4R; CANR 1, 24, 53, 93; CMW 4; CPW; DA3; DAM POP; DLB 137; DLBY 1980; INT CANR-24; MTCW 1, 2; TUS

Buechner, (Carl) Frederick 1926- . **CLC 2, 4, 6, 9**
See also AMWS 12; BPFB 1; CA 13-16R; CANR 11, 39, 64, 114; CN 7; DAM NOV; DLBY 1980; INT CANR-11; MTCW 1, 2

Buell, John (Edward) 1927- .... **CLC 10**
See also CA 1-4R; CANR 71; DLB 53

Buero Vallejo, Antonio 1916-2000 ... **CLC 15, 46, 139; DC 18**
See also CA 106; 189; CANR 24, 49, 75; DFS 11; EWL 3; HW 1; MTCW 1, 2

Bufalino, Gesualdo 1920(?)-1990 ...... **CLC 74**
See also CWW 2; DLB 196

Bugayev, Boris Nikolayevich 1880-1934 .... **PC 11; TCLC 7**
See Bely, Andrey; Belyi, Andrei
See also CA 104; 165; MTCW 1

Bukowski, Charles 1920-1994 ... **CLC 2, 5, 9, 41, 82, 108; PC 18; SSC 45**
See also CA 17-20R; 144; CANR 40, 62, 105; CPW; DA3; DAM NOV, POET; DLB 5, 130, 169; EWL 3; MTCW 1, 2

Bulgakov, Mikhail (Afanas'evich) 1891-1940 .... **SSC 18; TCLC 2, 16**
See also BPFB 1; CA 105; 152; DAM DRAM, NOV; DLB 272; EWL 3; NFS 8; RGSF 2; RGWL 2, 3; SFW 4; TWA

Bulgya, Alexander Alexandrovich 1901-1956 .... **TCLC 53**
See Fadeev, Aleksandr Aleksandrovich; Fadeev, Alexandr Alexandrovich; Fadeyev, Alexander
See also CA 117; 181

Bullins, Ed 1935- ... **BLC 1; CLC 1, 5, 7; DC 6**
See also BW 2, 3; CA 49-52; CAAS 16; CAD; CANR 24, 46, 73; CD 5; DAM DRAM, MULT; DLB 7, 38, 249; EWL 3; MTCW 1, 2; RGAL 4

Bulosan, Carlos 1911-1956 .... **AAL**
See also CA 216; RGAL 4

Bulwer-Lytton, Edward (George Earle Lytton) 1803-1873 .... **NCLC 1, 45**
See also DLB 21; RGEL 2; SFW 4; SUFW 1; TEA

Bunin, Ivan Alexeyevich 1870-1953 ... **SSC 5; TCLC 6**
See also CA 104; EWL 3; RGSF 2; RGWL 2, 3; TWA

Bunting, Basil 1900-1985 ...... **CLC 10, 39, 47**
See also BRWS 7; CA 53-56; 115; CANR 7; DAM POET; DLB 20; EWL 3; RGEL 2

Bunuel, Luis 1900-1983 ... **CLC 16, 80; HLC 1**
See also CA 101; 110; CANR 32, 77; DAM MULT; HW 1

Bunyan, John 1628-1688 ..... **LC 4, 69; WLC**
See also BRW 2; BYA 5; CDBLB 1660-1789; DA; DAB; DAC; DAM MST; DLB 39; RGEL 2; TEA; WCH; WLIT 3

Buravsky, Alexandr .... **CLC 59**

Burckhardt, Jacob (Christoph) 1818-1897 .... **NCLC 49**
See also EW 6

Burford, Eleanor
See Hibbert, Eleanor Alice Burford

Burgess, Anthony . **CLC 1, 2, 4, 5, 8, 10, 13, 15, 22, 40, 62, 81, 94**
See Wilson, John (Anthony) Burgess
See also AAYA 25; AITN 1; BRWS 1; CDBLB 1960 to Present; DAB; DLB 14, 194, 261; DLBY 1998; EWL 3; MTCW 1; RGEL 2; RHW; SFW 4; YAW

Burke, Edmund 1729(?)-1797 .... **LC 7, 36; WLC**
See also BRW 3; DA; DA3; DAB; DAC; DAM MST; DLB 104, 252; RGEL 2; TEA

Burke, Kenneth (Duva) 1897-1993 ... **CLC 2, 24**
See also AMW; CA 5-8R; 143; CANR 39, 74; DLB 45, 63; EWL 3; MTCW 1, 2; RGAL 4

Burke, Leda
See Garnett, David

Burke, Ralph
See Silverberg, Robert

Burke, Thomas 1886-1945 .... **TCLC 63**
See also CA 113; 155; CMW 4; DLB 197

Burney, Fanny 1752-1840 .... **NCLC 12, 54, 107**
See also BRWS 3; DLB 39; NFS 16; RGEL 2; TEA

Burney, Frances
See Burney, Fanny

Burns, Robert 1759-1796 ... **LC 3, 29, 40; PC 6; WLC**
See also AAYA 51; BRW 3; CDBLB 1789-1832; DA; DA3; DAB; DAC; DAM MST, POET; DLB 109; EXPP; PAB; RGEL 2; TEA; WP

Burns, Tex
See L'Amour, Louis (Dearborn)
See also TCWW 2

Burnshaw, Stanley 1906- .... **CLC 3, 13, 44**
See also CA 9-12R; CP 7; DLB 48; DLBY 1997

Burr, Anne 1937- .... **CLC 6**
See also CA 25-28R

Burroughs, Edgar Rice 1875-1950 . **TCLC 2, 32**
See also AAYA 11; BPFB 1; BYA 4, 9; CA 104; 132; DA3; DAM NOV; DLB 8; FANT; MTCW 1, 2; RGAL 4; SATA 41; SCFW 2; SFW 4; TUS; YAW

Burroughs, William S(eward) 1914-1997 .. **CLC 1, 2, 5, 15, 22, 42, 75, 109; TCLC 121; WLC**
See Lee, William; Lee, Willy
See also AITN 2; AMWS 3; BG 2; BPFB 1; CA 9-12R; 160; CANR 20, 52, 104; CN 7; CPW; DA; DA3; DAB; DAC; DAM MST, NOV, POP; DLB 2, 8, 16, 152, 237; DLBY 1981, 1997; EWL 3; HGG; LMFS 2; MTCW 1, 2; RGAL 4; SFW 4

Burton, Sir Richard F(rancis) 1821-1890 .... **NCLC 42**
See also DLB 55, 166, 184

Burton, Robert 1577-1640 .... **LC 74**
See also DLB 151; RGEL 2

Buruma, Ian 1951- .... **CLC 163**
See also CA 128; CANR 65

Busch, Frederick 1941- ... **CLC 7, 10, 18, 47, 166**
See also CA 33-36R; CAAS 1; CANR 45, 73, 92; CN 7; DLB 6, 218

Bush, Barney (Furman) 1946- .... **NNAL**
See also CA 145

Bush, Ronald 1946- .... **CLC 34**
See also CA 136

Bustos, F(rancisco)
See Borges, Jorge Luis

Bustos Domecq, H(onorio)
See Bioy Casares, Adolfo; Borges, Jorge Luis

Butler, Octavia E(stelle) 1947- .. **BLCS; CLC 38, 121**
See also AAYA 18, 48; AFAW 2; AMWS 13; BPFB 1; BW 2, 3; CA 73-76; CANR 12, 24, 38, 73; CLR 65; CPW; DA3; DAM MULT, POP; DLB 33; LATS 1; MTCW 1, 2; NFS 8; SATA 84; SCFW 2; SFW 4; SSFS 6; YAW

Butler, Robert Olen, (Jr.) 1945- ...... **CLC 81, 162**
See also AMWS 12; BPFB 1; CA 112; CANR 66; CSW; DAM POP; DLB 173; INT CA-112; MTCW 1; SSFS 11

Butler, Samuel 1612-1680 .... **LC 16, 43**
See also DLB 101, 126; RGEL 2

Butler, Samuel 1835-1902 .... **TCLC 1, 33; WLC**
See also BRWS 2; CA 143; CDBLB 1890-1914; DA; DA3; DAB; DAC; DAM MST, NOV; DLB 18, 57, 174; RGEL 2; SFW 4; TEA

Butler, Walter C.
See Faust, Frederick (Schiller)

Butor, Michel (Marie Francois) 1926- .... **CLC 1, 3, 8, 11, 15, 161**
See also CA 9-12R; CANR 33, 66; DLB 83; EW 13; EWL 3; GFL 1789 to the Present; MTCW 1, 2

Butts, Mary 1890(?)-1937 .... **TCLC 77**
See also CA 148; DLB 240

Buxton, Ralph
See Silverstein, Alvin; Silverstein, Virginia B(arbara Opshelor)

Buzo, Alex
See Buzo, Alexander (John)
See also DLB 289

Buzo, Alexander (John) 1944- .... **CLC 61**
See also CA 97-100; CANR 17, 39, 69; CD 5

Buzzati, Dino 1906-1972 .... **CLC 36**
See also CA 160; 33-36R; DLB 177; RGWL 2, 3; SFW 4

Byars, Betsy (Cromer) 1928- .... **CLC 35**
See also AAYA 19; BYA 3; CA 33-36R, 183; CAAE 183; CANR 18, 36, 57, 102; CLR 1, 16, 72; DLB 52; INT CANR-18; JRDA; MAICYA 1, 2; MAICYAS 1; MTCW 1; SAAS 1; SATA 4, 46, 80; SATA-Essay 108; WYA; YAW

Byatt, A(ntonia) S(usan Drabble) 1936- .... **CLC 19, 65, 136**
See also BPFB 1; BRWC 2; BRWS 4; CA 13-16R; CANR 13, 33, 50, 75, 96; DA3; DAM NOV, POP; DLB 14, 194; EWL 3; MTCW 1, 2; RGSF 2; RHW; TEA

Byrne, David 1952- .... **CLC 26**
See also CA 127

Byrne, John Keyes 1926-
See Leonard, Hugh
See also CA 102; CANR 78; INT CA-102

Byron, George Gordon (Noel) 1788-1824 ..... **NCLC 2, 12, 109; PC 16; WLC**
See also BRW 4; BRWC 2; CDBLB 1789-1832; DA; DA3; DAB; DAC; DAM MST, POET; DLB 96, 110; EXPP; LMFS 1; PAB; PFS 1, 14; RGEL 2; TEA; WLIT 3; WP

Byron, Robert 1905-1941 .... **TCLC 67**
See also CA 160; DLB 195

C. 3. 3.
See Wilde, Oscar (Fingal O'Flahertie Wills)

Caballero, Fernan 1796-1877 .... **NCLC 10**

Cabell, Branch
See Cabell, James Branch

Cabell, James Branch 1879-1958 .... **TCLC 6**
See also CA 105; 152; DLB 9, 78; FANT; MTCW 1; RGAL 4; SUFW 1

Cabeza de Vaca, Alvar Nunez 1490-1557(?) .... **LC 61**

Cable, George Washington 1844-1925 .... **SSC 4; TCLC 4**
See also CA 104; 155; DLB 12, 74; DLBD 13; RGAL 4; TUS

Cabral de Melo Neto, Joao
1920-1999 .... **CLC 76**
See Melo Neto, Joao Cabral de
See also CA 151; DAM MULT; LAW; LAWS 1

Cabrera Infante, G(uillermo) 1929- . **CLC 5, 25, 45, 120; HLC 1; SSC 39**
See also CA 85-88; CANR 29, 65, 110; CDWLB 3; DA3; DAM MULT; DLB 113; EWL 3; HW 1, 2; LAW; LAWS 1; MTCW 1, 2; RGSF 2; WLIT 1

Cade, Toni
See Bambara, Toni Cade

Cadmus and Harmonia
See Buchan, John

Caedmon fl. 658-680 .... **CMLC 7**
See also DLB 146

Caeiro, Alberto
See Pessoa, Fernando (Antonio Nogueira)

Caesar, Julius .... **CMLC 47**
See Julius Caesar
See also AW 1; RGWL 2, 3

Cage, John (Milton, Jr.) 1912-1992 . **CLC 41**
See also CA 13-16R; 169; CANR 9, 78; DLB 193; INT CANR-9

Cahan, Abraham 1860-1951 .... **TCLC 71**
See also CA 108; 154; DLB 9, 25, 28; RGAL 4

Cain, G.
See Cabrera Infante, G(uillermo)

Cain, Guillermo
See Cabrera Infante, G(uillermo)

Cain, James M(allahan) 1892-1977 .. **CLC 3, 11, 28**
See also AITN 1; BPFB 1; CA 17-20R; 73-76; CANR 8, 34, 61; CMW 4; DLB 226; EWL 3; MSW; MTCW 1; RGAL 4

Caine, Hall 1853-1931 .... **TCLC 97**
See also RHW

Caine, Mark
See Raphael, Frederic (Michael)

Calasso, Roberto 1941- .... **CLC 81**
See also CA 143; CANR 89

Calderon de la Barca, Pedro
1600-1681 .... **DC 3; HLCS 1; LC 23**
See also EW 2; RGWL 2, 3; TWA

Caldwell, Erskine (Preston)
1903-1987 .... **CLC 1, 8, 14, 50, 60; SSC 19; TCLC 117**
See also AITN 1; AMW; BPFB 1; CA 1-4R; 121; CAAS 1; CANR 2, 33; DA3; DAM NOV; DLB 9, 86; EWL 3; MTCW 1, 2; RGAL 4; RGSF 2; TUS

Caldwell, (Janet Miriam) Taylor (Holland)
1900-1985 .... **CLC 2, 28, 39**
See also BPFB 1; CA 5-8R; 116; CANR 5; DA3; DAM NOV, POP; DLBD 17; RHW

Calhoun, John Caldwell
1782-1850 .... **NCLC 15**
See also DLB 3, 248

Calisher, Hortense 1911- ..... **CLC 2, 4, 8, 38, 134; SSC 15**
See also CA 1-4R; CANR 1, 22, 117; CN 7; DA3; DAM NOV; DLB 2, 218; INT CANR-22; MTCW 1, 2; RGAL 4; RGSF 2

Callaghan, Morley Edward
1903-1990 .... **CLC 3, 14, 41, 65**
See also CA 9-12R; 132; CANR 33, 73; DAC; DAM MST; DLB 68; EWL 3; MTCW 1, 2; RGEL 2; RGSF 2

Callimachus c. 305B.C.-c.
240B.C. .... **CMLC 18**
See also AW 1; DLB 176; RGWL 2, 3

Calvin, Jean
See Calvin, John
See also GFL Beginnings to 1789

Calvin, John 1509-1564 .... **LC 37**
See Calvin, Jean

Calvino, Italo 1923-1985 .... **CLC 5, 8, 11, 22, 33, 39, 73; SSC 3, 48**
See also CA 85-88; 116; CANR 23, 61; DAM NOV; DLB 196; EW 13; EWL 3; MTCW 1, 2; RGSF 2; RGWL 2, 3; SFW 4; SSFS 12

Camara Laye
See Laye, Camara
See also EWL 3

Camden, William 1551-1623 .... **LC 77**
See also DLB 172

Cameron, Carey 1952- .... **CLC 59**
See also CA 135

Cameron, Peter 1959- .... **CLC 44**
See also AMWS 12; CA 125; CANR 50, 117; DLB 234; GLL 2

Camoens, Luis Vaz de 1524(?)-1580
See Camoes, Luis de
See also EW 2

Camoes, Luis de 1524(?)-1580 . **HLCS 1; LC 62; PC 31**
See Camoens, Luis Vaz de
See also DLB 287; RGWL 2, 3

Campana, Dino 1885-1932 .... **TCLC 20**
See also CA 117; DLB 114; EWL 3

Campanella, Tommaso 1568-1639 .... **LC 32**
See also RGWL 2, 3

Campbell, John W(ood, Jr.)
1910-1971 .... **CLC 32**
See also CA 21-22; 29-32R; CANR 34; CAP 2; DLB 8; MTCW 1; SCFW; SFW 4

Campbell, Joseph 1904-1987 .... **CLC 69; TCLC 140**
See also AAYA 3; BEST 89:2; CA 1-4R; 124; CANR 3, 28, 61, 107; DA3; MTCW 1, 2

Campbell, Maria 1940- .... **CLC 85; NNAL**
See also CA 102; CANR 54; CCA 1; DAC

Campbell, (John) Ramsey 1946- ..... **CLC 42; SSC 19**
See also AAYA 51; CA 57-60; CANR 7, 102; DLB 261; HGG; INT CANR-7; SUFW 1, 2

Campbell, (Ignatius) Roy (Dunnachie)
1901-1957 .... **TCLC 5**
See also AFW; CA 104; 155; DLB 20, 225; EWL 3; MTCW 2; RGEL 2

Campbell, Thomas 1777-1844 .... **NCLC 19**
See also DLB 93, 144; RGEL 2

Campbell, Wilfred .... **TCLC 9**
See Campbell, William

Campbell, William 1858(?)-1918
See Campbell, Wilfred
See also CA 106; DLB 92

Campion, Jane 1954- .... **CLC 95**
See also AAYA 33; CA 138; CANR 87

Campion, Thomas 1567-1620 .... **LC 78**
See also CDBLB Before 1660; DAM POET; DLB 58, 172; RGEL 2

Camus, Albert 1913-1960 ...... **CLC 1, 2, 4, 9, 11, 14, 32, 63, 69, 124; DC 2; SSC 9; WLC**
See also AAYA 36; AFW; BPFB 1; CA 89-92; DA; DA3; DAB; DAC; DAM DRAM, MST, NOV; DLB 72; EW 13; EWL 3; EXPN; EXPS; GFL 1789 to the Present; LATS 1; LMFS 2; MTCW 1, 2; NFS 6, 16; RGSF 2; RGWL 2, 3; SSFS 4; TWA

Canby, Vincent 1924-2000 .... **CLC 13**
See also CA 81-84; 191

Cancale
See Desnos, Robert

Canetti, Elias 1905-1994 .. **CLC 3, 14, 25, 75, 86**
See also CA 21-24R; 146; CANR 23, 61, 79; CDWLB 2; CWW 2; DA3; DLB 85, 124; EW 12; EWL 3; MTCW 1, 2; RGWL 2, 3; TWA

Canfield, Dorothea F.
See Fisher, Dorothy (Frances) Canfield

Canfield, Dorothea Frances
See Fisher, Dorothy (Frances) Canfield

Canfield, Dorothy
See Fisher, Dorothy (Frances) Canfield

Canin, Ethan 1960- .... **CLC 55**
See also CA 131; 135

Cankar, Ivan 1876-1918 .... **TCLC 105**
See also CDWLB 4; DLB 147; EWL 3

Cannon, Curt
See Hunter, Evan

Cao, Lan 1961- .... **CLC 109**
See also CA 165

Cape, Judith
See Page, P(atricia) K(athleen)
See also CCA 1

Capek, Karel 1890-1938 .... **DC 1; SSC 36; TCLC 6, 37; WLC**
See also CA 104; 140; CDWLB 4; DA; DA3; DAB; DAC; DAM DRAM, MST, NOV; DFS 7, 11; DLB 215; EW 10; EWL 3; MTCW 1; RGSF 2; RGWL 2, 3; SCFW 2; SFW 4

Capote, Truman 1924-1984 . **CLC 1, 3, 8, 13, 19, 34, 38, 58; SSC 2, 47; WLC**
See also AMWS 3; BPFB 1; CA 5-8R; 113; CANR 18, 62; CDALB 1941-1968; CPW; DA; DA3; DAB; DAC; DAM MST, NOV, POP; DLB 2, 185, 227; DLBY 1980, 1984; EWL 3; EXPS; GLL 1; LAIT 3; MTCW 1, 2; NCFS 2; RGAL 4; RGSF 2; SATA 91; SSFS 2; TUS

Capra, Frank 1897-1991 .... **CLC 16**
See also AAYA 52; CA 61-64; 135

Caputo, Philip 1941- .... **CLC 32**
See also CA 73-76; CANR 40; YAW

Caragiale, Ion Luca 1852-1912 ...... **TCLC 76**
See also CA 157

Card, Orson Scott 1951- .... **CLC 44, 47, 50**
See also AAYA 11, 42; BPFB 1; BYA 5, 8; CA 102; CANR 27, 47, 73, 102, 106; CPW; DA3; DAM POP; FANT; INT CANR-27; MTCW 1, 2; NFS 5; SATA 83, 127; SCFW 2; SFW 4; SUFW 2; YAW

Cardenal, Ernesto 1925- .... **CLC 31, 161; HLC 1; PC 22**
See also CA 49-52; CANR 2, 32, 66; CWW 2; DAM MULT, POET; EWL 3; HW 1, 2; LAWS 1; MTCW 1, 2; RGWL 2, 3

Cardozo, Benjamin N(athan)
1870-1938 .... **TCLC 65**
See also CA 117; 164

Carducci, Giosue (Alessandro Giuseppe)
1835-1907 .... **PC 46; TCLC 32**
See also CA 163; EW 7; RGWL 2, 3

Carew, Thomas 1595(?)-1640 . **LC 13; PC 29**
See also BRW 2; DLB 126; PAB; RGEL 2

Carey, Ernestine Gilbreth 1908- .... **CLC 17**
See also CA 5-8R; CANR 71; SATA 2

Carey, Peter 1943- .... **CLC 40, 55, 96**
See also CA 123; 127; CANR 53, 76, 117; CN 7; DLB 289; EWL 3; INT CA-127; MTCW 1, 2; RGSF 2; SATA 94

Carleton, William 1794-1869 .... **NCLC 3**
See also DLB 159; RGEL 2; RGSF 2

Carlisle, Henry (Coffin) 1926- .... **CLC 33**
See also CA 13-16R; CANR 15, 85

Carlsen, Chris
See Holdstock, Robert P.

Carlson, Ron(ald F.) 1947- .... **CLC 54**
See also CA 105; CAAE 189; CANR 27; DLB 244

Carlyle, Thomas 1795-1881 ..... **NCLC 22, 70**
See also BRW 4; CDBLB 1789-1832; DA; DAB; DAC; DAM MST; DLB 55, 144, 254; RGEL 2; TEA

361

Carman, (William) Bliss 1861-1929 ... **PC 34; TCLC 7**
See also CA 104; 152; DAC; DLB 92; RGEL 2

Carnegie, Dale 1888-1955 .... **TCLC 53**

Carossa, Hans 1878-1956 .... **TCLC 48**
See also CA 170; DLB 66; EWL 3

Carpenter, Don(ald Richard) 1931-1995 .... **CLC 41**
See also CA 45-48; 149; CANR 1, 71

Carpenter, Edward 1844-1929 .... **TCLC 88**
See also CA 163; GLL 1

Carpenter, John (Howard) 1948- ... **CLC 161**
See also AAYA 2; CA 134; SATA 58

Carpenter, Johnny
See Carpenter, John (Howard)

Carpentier (y Valmont), Alejo 1904-1980 . **CLC 8, 11, 38, 110; HLC 1; SSC 35**
See also CA 65-68; 97-100; CANR 11, 70; CDWLB 3; DAM MULT; DLB 113; EWL 3; HW 1, 2; LAW; LMFS 2; RGSF 2; RGWL 2, 3; WLIT 1

Carr, Caleb 1955(?)- .... **CLC 86**
See also CA 147; CANR 73; DA3

Carr, Emily 1871-1945 .... **TCLC 32**
See also CA 159; DLB 68; FW; GLL 2

Carr, John Dickson 1906-1977 .... **CLC 3**
See Fairbairn, Roger
See also CA 49-52; 69-72; CANR 3, 33, 60; CMW 4; MSW; MTCW 1, 2

Carr, Philippa
See Hibbert, Eleanor Alice Burford

Carr, Virginia Spencer 1929- .... **CLC 34**
See also CA 61-64; DLB 111

Carrere, Emmanuel 1957- .... **CLC 89**
See also CA 200

Carrier, Roch 1937- .... **CLC 13, 78**
See also CA 130; CANR 61; CCA 1; DAC; DAM MST; DLB 53; SATA 105

Carroll, James Dennis
See Carroll, Jim

Carroll, James P. 1943(?)- .... **CLC 38**
See also CA 81-84; CANR 73; MTCW 1

Carroll, Jim 1951- .... **CLC 35, 143**
See Carroll, James Dennis
See also AAYA 17; CA 45-48; CANR 42, 115; NCFS 5

Carroll, Lewis ... **NCLC 2, 53; PC 18; WLC**
See Dodgson, Charles L(utwidge)
See also AAYA 39; BRW 5; BYA 5, 13; CDBLB 1832-1890; CLR 2, 18; DLB 18, 163, 178; DLBY 1998; EXPN; EXPP; FANT; JRDA; LAIT 1; NFS 7; PFS 11; RGEL 2; SUFW 1; TEA; WCH

Carroll, Paul Vincent 1900-1968 ...... **CLC 10**
See also CA 9-12R; 25-28R; DLB 10; EWL 3; RGEL 2

Carruth, Hayden 1921- ..... **CLC 4, 7, 10, 18, 84; PC 10**
See also CA 9-12R; CANR 4, 38, 59, 110; CP 7; DLB 5, 165; INT CANR-4; MTCW 1, 2; SATA 47

Carson, Rachel
See Carson, Rachel Louise
See also AAYA 49; DLB 275

Carson, Rachel Louise 1907-1964 .... **CLC 71**
See Carson, Rachel
See also AMWS 9; ANW; CA 77-80; CANR 35; DA3; DAM POP; FW; LAIT 4; MTCW 1, 2; NCFS 1; SATA 23

Carter, Angela (Olive) 1940-1992 ...... **CLC 5, 41, 76; SSC 13; TCLC 139**
See also BRWS 3; CA 53-56; 136; CANR 12, 36, 61, 106; DA3; DLB 14, 207, 261; EXPS; FANT; FW; MTCW 1, 2; RGSF 2; SATA 66; SATA-Obit 70; SFW 4; SSFS 4, 12; SUFW 2; WLIT 4

Carter, Nick
See Smith, Martin Cruz

Carver, Raymond 1938-1988 ..... **CLC 22, 36, 53, 55, 126; SSC 8, 51**
See also AAYA 44; AMWS 3; BPFB 1; CA 33-36R; 126; CANR 17, 34, 61, 103; CPW; DA3; DAM NOV; DLB 130; DLBY 1984, 1988; EWL 3; MTCW 1, 2; PFS 17; RGAL 4; RGSF 2; SSFS 3, 6, 12, 13; TCWW 2; TUS

Cary, Elizabeth, Lady Falkland 1585-1639 .... **LC 30**

Cary, (Arthur) Joyce (Lunel) 1888-1957 .... **TCLC 1, 29**
See also BRW 7; CA 104; 164; CDBLB 1914-1945; DLB 15, 100; EWL 3; MTCW 2; RGEL 2; TEA

Casal, Julian del 1863-1893 .... **NCLC 131**
See also DLB 283; LAW

Casanova de Seingalt, Giovanni Jacopo 1725-1798 .... **LC 13**

Casares, Adolfo Bioy
See Bioy Casares, Adolfo
See also RGSF 2

Casas, Bartolome de las 1474-1566
See Las Casas, Bartolome de
See also WLIT 1

Casely-Hayford, J(oseph) E(phraim) 1866-1903 .... **BLC 1; TCLC 24**
See also BW 2; CA 123; 152; DAM MULT

Casey, John (Dudley) 1939- .... **CLC 59**
See also BEST 90:2; CA 69-72; CANR 23, 100

Casey, Michael 1947- .... **CLC 2**
See also CA 65-68; CANR 109; DLB 5

Casey, Patrick
See Thurman, Wallace (Henry)

Casey, Warren (Peter) 1935-1988 .... **CLC 12**
See also CA 101; 127; INT 101

Casona, Alejandro .... **CLC 49**
See Alvarez, Alejandro Rodriguez
See also EWL 3

Cassavetes, John 1929-1989 .... **CLC 20**
See also CA 85-88; 127; CANR 82

Cassian, Nina 1924- .... **PC 17**
See also CWP; CWW 2

Cassill, R(onald) V(erlin) 1919-2002 .... **CLC 4, 23**
See also CA 9-12R; 208; CAAS 1; CANR 7, 45; CN 7; DLB 6, 218; DLBY 2002

Cassiodorus, Flavius Magnus c. 490(?)-c. 583(?) .... **CMLC 43**

Cassirer, Ernst 1874-1945 .... **TCLC 61**
See also CA 157

Cassity, (Allen) Turner 1929- .... **CLC 6, 42**
See also CA 17-20R; CAAS 8; CANR 11; CSW; DLB 105

Castaneda, Carlos (Cesar Aranha) 1931(?)-1998 .... **CLC 12, 119**
See also CA 25-28R; CANR 32, 66, 105; DNFS 1; HW 1; MTCW 1

Castedo, Elena 1937- .... **CLC 65**
See also CA 132

Castedo-Ellerman, Elena
See Castedo, Elena

Castellanos, Rosario 1925-1974 ..... **CLC 66; HLC 1; SSC 39**
See also CA 131; 53-56; CANR 58; CDWLB 3; DAM MULT; DLB 113; EWL 3; FW; HW 1; LAW; MTCW 1; RGSF 2; RGWL 2, 3

Castelvetro, Lodovico 1505-1571 .... **LC 12**

Castiglione, Baldassare 1478-1529 ...... **LC 12**
See Castiglione, Baldesar
See also LMFS 1; RGWL 2, 3

Castiglione, Baldesar
See Castiglione, Baldassare
See also EW 2

Castillo, Ana (Hernandez Del) 1953- .... **CLC 151**
See also AAYA 42; CA 131; CANR 51, 86; CWP; DLB 122, 227; DNFS 2; FW; HW 1

Castle, Robert
See Hamilton, Edmond

Castro (Ruz), Fidel 1926(?)- .... **HLC 1**
See also CA 110; 129; CANR 81; DAM MULT; HW 2

Castro, Guillen de 1569-1631 .... **LC 19**

Castro, Rosalia de 1837-1885 ... **NCLC 3, 78; PC 41**
See also DAM MULT

Cather, Willa (Sibert) 1873-1947 . **SSC 2, 50; TCLC 1, 11, 31, 99, 132; WLC**
See also AAYA 24; AMW; AMWC 1; AMWR 1; BPFB 1; CA 104; 128; CDALB 1865-1917; DA; DA3; DAB; DAC; DAM MST, NOV; DLB 9, 54, 78, 256; DLBD 1; EWL 3; EXPN; EXPS; LAIT 3; LATS 1; MAWW; MTCW 1, 2; NFS 2; RGAL 4; RGSF 2; RHW; SATA 30; SSFS 2, 7, 16; TCWW 2; TUS

Catherine II
See Catherine the Great
See also DLB 150

Catherine the Great 1729-1796 .... **LC 69**
See Catherine II

Cato, Marcus Porcius 234B.C.-149B.C. .... **CMLC 21**
See Cato the Elder

Cato, Marcus Porcius, the Elder
See Cato, Marcus Porcius

Cato the Elder
See Cato, Marcus Porcius
See also DLB 211

Catton, (Charles) Bruce 1899-1978 . **CLC 35**
See also AITN 1; CA 5-8R; 81-84; CANR 7, 74; DLB 17; SATA 2; SATA-Obit 24

Catullus c. 84B.C.-54B.C. .... **CMLC 18**
See also AW 2; CDWLB 1; DLB 211; RGWL 2, 3

Cauldwell, Frank
See King, Francis (Henry)

Caunitz, William J. 1933-1996 .... **CLC 34**
See also BEST 89:3; CA 125; 130; 152; CANR 73; INT 130

Causley, Charles (Stanley) 1917- .... **CLC 7**
See also CA 9-12R; CANR 5, 35, 94; CLR 30; CWRI 5; DLB 27; MTCW 1; SATA 3, 66

Caute, (John) David 1936- .... **CLC 29**
See also CA 1-4R; CAAS 4; CANR 1, 33, 64, 120; CBD; CD 5; CN 7; DAM NOV; DLB 14, 231

Cavafy, C(onstantine) P(eter) .... **PC 36; TCLC 2, 7**
See Kavafis, Konstantinos Petrou
See also CA 148; DA3; DAM POET; EW 8; EWL 3; MTCW 1; RGWL 2, 3; WP

Cavalcanti, Guido c. 1250-c. 1300 .... **CMLC 54**

Cavallo, Evelyn
See Spark, Muriel (Sarah)

Cavanna, Betty .... **CLC 12**
See Harrison, Elizabeth (Allen) Cavanna
See also JRDA; MAICYA 1; SAAS 4; SATA 1, 30

Cavendish, Margaret Lucas 1623-1673 .... **LC 30**
See also DLB 131, 252, 281; RGEL 2

Caxton, William 1421(?)-1491(?) .... **LC 17**
See also DLB 170

Cayer, D. M.
See Duffy, Maureen

Cayrol, Jean 1911- .... **CLC 11**
See also CA 89-92; DLB 83; EWL 3

Cela, Camilo Jose 1916-2002 .... **CLC 4, 13, 59, 122; HLC 1**
See also BEST 90:2; CA 21-24R; 206; CAAS 10; CANR 21, 32, 76; DAM MULT; DLBY 1989; EW 13; EWL 3; HW 1; MTCW 1, 2; RGSF 2; RGWL 2, 3

Celan, Paul .... **CLC 10, 19, 53, 82; PC 10**
See Antschel, Paul
See also CDWLB 2; DLB 69; EWL 3; RGWL 2, 3

Celine, Louis-Ferdinand .. **CLC 1, 3, 4, 7, 9, 15, 47, 124**
See Destouches, Louis-Ferdinand
See also DLB 72; EW 11; EWL 3; GFL 1789 to the Present; RGWL 2, 3

Cellini, Benvenuto 1500-1571 .... **LC 7**

Cendrars, Blaise .... **CLC 18, 106**
See Sauser-Hall, Frederic
See also DLB 258; EWL 3; GFL 1789 to the Present; RGWL 2, 3; WP

Centlivre, Susanna 1669(?)-1723 .... **LC 65**
See also DLB 84; RGEL 2

Cernuda (y Bidon), Luis 1902-1963 . **CLC 54**
See also CA 131; 89-92; DAM POET; DLB 134; EWL 3; GLL 1; HW 1; RGWL 2, 3

Cervantes, Lorna Dee 1954- ..... **HLCS 1; PC 35**
See also CA 131; CANR 80; CWP; DLB 82; EXPP; HW 1

Cervantes (Saavedra), Miguel de 1547-1616 .... **HLCS; LC 6, 23, 93; SSC 12; WLC**
See also BYA 1, 14; DA; DAB; DAC; DAM MST, NOV; EW 2; LAIT 1; LATS 1; LMFS 1; NFS 8; RGSF 2; RGWL 2, 3; TWA

Cesaire, Aime (Fernand) 1913- .... **BLC 1; CLC 19, 32, 112; PC 25**
See also BW 2, 3; CA 65-68; CANR 24, 43, 81; DA3; DAM MULT, POET; EWL 3; GFL 1789 to the Present; MTCW 1, 2; WP

Chabon, Michael 1963- ... **CLC 55, 149; SSC 59**
See also AAYA 45; AMWS 11; CA 139; CANR 57, 96; DLB 278

Chabrol, Claude 1930- .... **CLC 16**
See also CA 110

Chairil Anwar
See Anwar, Chairil
See also EWL 3

Challans, Mary 1905-1983
See Renault, Mary
See also CA 81-84; 111; CANR 74; DA3; MTCW 2; SATA 23; SATA-Obit 36; TEA

Challis, George
See Faust, Frederick (Schiller)
See also TCWW 2

Chambers, Aidan 1934- .... **CLC 35**
See also AAYA 27; CA 25-28R; CANR 12, 31, 58, 116; JRDA; MAICYA 1, 2; SAAS 12; SATA 1, 69, 108; WYA; YAW

Chambers, James 1948-
See Cliff, Jimmy
See also CA 124

Chambers, Jessie
See Lawrence, D(avid) H(erbert Richards)
See also GLL 1

Chambers, Robert W(illiam) 1865-1933 .... **TCLC 41**
See also CA 165; DLB 202; HGG; SATA 107; SUFW 1

Chambers, (David) Whittaker 1901-1961 .... **TCLC 129**
See also CA 89-92

Chamisso, Adelbert von 1781-1838 .... **NCLC 82**
See also DLB 90; RGWL 2, 3; SUFW 1

Chance, James T.
See Carpenter, John (Howard)

Chance, John T.
See Carpenter, John (Howard)

Chandler, Raymond (Thornton) 1888-1959 .... **SSC 23; TCLC 1, 7**
See also AAYA 25; AMWC 2; AMWS 4; BPFB 1; CA 104; 129; CANR 60, 107; CDALB 1929-1941; CMW 4; DA3; DLB 226, 253; DLBD 6; EWL 3; MSW; MTCW 1, 2; NFS 17; RGAL 4; TUS

Chang, Diana 1934- .... **AAL**
See also CWP; EXPP

Chang, Eileen 1921-1995 .... **AAL; SSC 28**
See Chang Ai-Ling
See also CA 166; CWW 2

Chang, Jung 1952- .... **CLC 71**
See also CA 142

Chang Ai-Ling
See Chang, Eileen
See also EWL 3

Channing, William Ellery 1780-1842 .... **NCLC 17**
See also DLB 1, 59, 235; RGAL 4

Chao, Patricia 1955- .... **CLC 119**
See also CA 163

Chaplin, Charles Spencer 1889-1977 .... **CLC 16**
See Chaplin, Charlie
See also CA 81-84; 73-76

Chaplin, Charlie
See Chaplin, Charles Spencer
See also DLB 44

Chapman, George 1559(?)-1634 . **DC 19; LC 22**
See also BRW 1; DAM DRAM; DLB 62, 121; LMFS 1; RGEL 2

Chapman, Graham 1941-1989 .... **CLC 21**
See Monty Python
See also CA 116; 129; CANR 35, 95

Chapman, John Jay 1862-1933 .... **TCLC 7**
See also CA 104; 191

Chapman, Lee
See Bradley, Marion Zimmer
See also GLL 1

Chapman, Walker
See Silverberg, Robert

Chappell, Fred (Davis) 1936- .... **CLC 40, 78, 162**
See also CA 5-8R; CAAE 198; CAAS 4; CANR 8, 33, 67, 110; CN 7; CP 7; CSW; DLB 6, 105; HGG

Char, Rene(-Emile) 1907-1988 .... **CLC 9, 11, 14, 55**
See also CA 13-16R; 124; CANR 32; DAM POET; DLB 258; EWL 3; GFL 1789 to the Present; MTCW 1, 2; RGWL 2, 3

Charby, Jay
See Ellison, Harlan (Jay)

Chardin, Pierre Teilhard de
See Teilhard de Chardin, (Marie Joseph) Pierre

Chariton fl. 1st cent. (?)- .... **CMLC 49**

Charlemagne 742-814 .... **CMLC 37**

Charles I 1600-1649 .... **LC 13**

Charriere, Isabelle de 1740-1805 .. **NCLC 66**

Chartier, Alain c. 1392-1430 .... **LC 94**
See also DLB 208

Chartier, Emile-Auguste
See Alain

Charyn, Jerome 1937- .... **CLC 5, 8, 18**
See also CA 5-8R; CAAS 1; CANR 7, 61, 101; CMW 4; CN 7; DLBY 1983; MTCW 1

Chase, Adam
See Marlowe, Stephen

Chase, Mary (Coyle) 1907-1981 .... **DC 1**
See also CA 77-80; 105; CAD; CWD; DFS 11; DLB 228; SATA 17; SATA-Obit 29

Chase, Mary Ellen 1887-1973 .... **CLC 2; TCLC 124**
See also CA 13-16; 41-44R; CAP 1; SATA 10

Chase, Nicholas
See Hyde, Anthony
See also CCA 1

Chateaubriand, Francois Rene de 1768-1848 .... **NCLC 3**
See also DLB 119; EW 5; GFL 1789 to the Present; RGWL 2, 3; TWA

Chatterje, Sarat Chandra 1876-1936(?)
See Chatterji, Saratchandra
See also CA 109

Chatterji, Bankim Chandra 1838-1894 .... **NCLC 19**

Chatterji, Saratchandra .... **TCLC 13**
See Chatterje, Sarat Chandra
See also CA 186; EWL 3

Chatterton, Thomas 1752-1770 .... **LC 3, 54**
See also DAM POET; DLB 109; RGEL 2

Chatwin, (Charles) Bruce 1940-1989 .... **CLC 28, 57, 59**
See also AAYA 4; BEST 90:1; BRWS 4; CA 85-88; 127; CPW; DAM POP; DLB 194, 204; EWL 3

Chaucer, Daniel
See Ford, Ford Madox
See also RHW

Chaucer, Geoffrey 1340(?)-1400 .. **LC 17, 56; PC 19; WLCS**
See also BRW 1; BRWC 1; BRWR 2; CD-BLB Before 1660; DA; DA3; DAB; DAC; DAM MST, POET; DLB 146; LAIT 1; PAB; PFS 14; RGEL 2; TEA; WLIT 3; WP

Chavez, Denise (Elia) 1948- .... **HLC 1**
See also CA 131; CANR 56, 81; DAM MULT; DLB 122; FW; HW 1, 2; MTCW 2

Chaviaras, Strates 1935-
See Haviaras, Stratis
See also CA 105

Chayefsky, Paddy .... **CLC 23**
See Chayefsky, Sidney
See also CAD; DLB 7, 44; DLBY 1981; RGAL 4

Chayefsky, Sidney 1923-1981
See Chayefsky, Paddy
See also CA 9-12R; 104; CANR 18; DAM DRAM

Chedid, Andree 1920- .... **CLC 47**
See also CA 145; CANR 95; EWL 3

Cheever, John 1912-1982 .... **CLC 3, 7, 8, 11, 15, 25, 64; SSC 1, 38, 57; WLC**
See also AMWS 1; BPFB 1; CA 5-8R; 106; CABS 1; CANR 5, 27, 76; CDALB 1941-1968; CPW; DA; DA3; DAB; DAC; DAM MST, NOV, POP; DLB 2, 102, 227; DLBY 1980, 1982; EWL 3; EXPS; INT CANR-5; MTCW 1, 2; RGAL 4; RGSF 2; SSFS 1, 14; TUS

Cheever, Susan 1943- .... **CLC 18, 48**
See also CA 103; CANR 27, 51, 92; DLBY 1982; INT CANR-27

Chekhonte, Antosha
See Chekhov, Anton (Pavlovich)

Chekhov, Anton (Pavlovich) 1860-1904 ...... **DC 9; SSC 2, 28, 41, 51; TCLC 3, 10, 31, 55, 96; WLC**
See also BYA 14; CA 104; 124; DA; DA3; DAB; DAC; DAM DRAM, MST; DFS 1, 5, 10, 12; DLB 277; EW 7; EWL 3; EXPS; LAIT 3; LATS 1; RGSF 2; RGWL 2, 3; SATA 90; SSFS 5, 13, 14; TWA

Cheney, Lynne V. 1941- .... **CLC 70**
See also CA 89-92; CANR 58, 117

Chernyshevsky, Nikolai Gavrilovich
See Chernyshevsky, Nikolay Gavrilovich
See also DLB 238

Chernyshevsky, Nikolay Gavrilovich
1828-1889 .... **NCLC 1**
See Chernyshevsky, Nikolai Gavrilovich
Cherry, Carolyn Janice 1942-
See Cherryh, C. J.
See also CA 65-68; CANR 10
Cherryh, C. J. .... **CLC 35**
See Cherry, Carolyn Janice
See also AAYA 24; BPFB 1; DLBY 1980; FANT; SATA 93; SCFW 2; SFW 4; YAW
Chesnutt, Charles W(addell)
1858-1932 .... **BLC 1; SSC 7, 54; TCLC 5, 39**
See also AFAW 1, 2; BW 1, 3; CA 106; 125; CANR 76; DAM MULT; DLB 12, 50, 78; EWL 3; MTCW 1, 2; RGAL 4; RGSF 2; SSFS 11
Chester, Alfred 1929(?)-1971 .... **CLC 49**
See also CA 196; 33-36R; DLB 130
Chesterton, G(ilbert) K(eith)
1874-1936 . **PC 28; SSC 1, 46; TCLC 1, 6, 64**
See also BRW 6; CA 104; 132; CANR 73; CDBLB 1914-1945; CMW 4; DAM NOV, POET; DLB 10, 19, 34, 70, 98, 149, 178; EWL 3; FANT; MSW; MTCW 1, 2; RGEL 2; RGSF 2; SATA 27; SUFW 1
Chiang, Pin-chin 1904-1986
See Ding Ling
See also CA 118
Chief Joseph 1840-1904 .... **NNAL**
See also CA 152; DA3; DAM MULT
Chief Seattle 1786(?)-1866 .... **NNAL**
See also DA3; DAM MULT
Ch'ien, Chung-shu 1910-1998 .... **CLC 22**
See also CA 130; CANR 73; MTCW 1, 2
Chikamatsu Monzaemon 1653-1724 ... **LC 66**
See also RGWL 2, 3
Child, L. Maria
See Child, Lydia Maria
Child, Lydia Maria 1802-1880 .. **NCLC 6, 73**
See also DLB 1, 74, 243; RGAL 4; SATA 67
Child, Mrs.
See Child, Lydia Maria
Child, Philip 1898-1978 .... **CLC 19, 68**
See also CA 13-14; CAP 1; DLB 68; RHW; SATA 47
Childers, (Robert) Erskine
1870-1922 .... **TCLC 65**
See also CA 113; 153; DLB 70
Childress, Alice 1920-1994 . **BLC 1; CLC 12, 15, 86, 96; DC 4; TCLC 116**
See also AAYA 8; BW 2, 3; BYA 2; CA 45-48; 146; CAD; CANR 3, 27, 50, 74; CLR 14; CWD; DA3; DAM DRAM, MULT, NOV; DFS 2, 8, 14; DLB 7, 38, 249; JRDA; LAIT 5; MAICYA 1, 2; MAICYAS 1; MTCW 1, 2; RGAL 4; SATA 7, 48, 81; TUS; WYA; YAW
Chin, Frank (Chew, Jr.) 1940- .... **CLC 135; DC 7**
See also CA 33-36R; CANR 71; CD 5; DAM MULT; DLB 206; LAIT 5; RGAL 4
Chin, Marilyn (Mei Ling) 1955- .... **PC 40**
See also CA 129; CANR 70, 113; CWP
Chislett, (Margaret) Anne 1943- ...... **CLC 34**
See also CA 151
Chitty, Thomas Willes 1926- .... **CLC 11**
See Hinde, Thomas
See also CA 5-8R; CN 7
Chivers, Thomas Holley
1809-1858 .... **NCLC 49**
See also DLB 3, 248; RGAL 4
Choi, Susan .... **CLC 119**
Chomette, Rene Lucien 1898-1981
See Clair, Rene
See also CA 103

Chomsky, (Avram) Noam 1928- ..... **CLC 132**
See also CA 17-20R; CANR 28, 62, 110; DA3; DLB 246; MTCW 1, 2
Chona, Maria 1845(?)-1936 .... **NNAL**
See also CA 144
Chopin, Kate ..... **SSC 8; TCLC 127; WLCS**
See Chopin, Katherine
See also AAYA 33; AMWR 2; AMWS 1; BYA 15; CDALB 1865-1917; DA; DAB; DLB 12, 78; EXPN; EXPS; FW; LAIT 3; MAWW; NFS 3; RGAL 4; RGSF 2; SSFS 17; TUS
Chopin, Katherine 1851-1904
See Chopin, Kate
See also CA 104; 122; DA3; DAC; DAM MST, NOV
Chretien de Troyes c. 12th cent. - . **CMLC 10**
See also DLB 208; EW 1; RGWL 2, 3; TWA
Christie
See Ichikawa, Kon
Christie, Agatha (Mary Clarissa)
1890-1976 .. **CLC 1, 6, 8, 12, 39, 48, 110**
See also AAYA 9; AITN 1, 2; BPFB 1; BRWS 2; CA 17-20R; 61-64; CANR 10, 37, 108; CBD; CDBLB 1914-1945; CMW 4; CPW; CWD; DA3; DAB; DAC; DAM NOV; DFS 2; DLB 13, 77, 245; MSW; MTCW 1, 2; NFS 8; RGEL 2; RHW; SATA 36; TEA; YAW
Christie, Philippa .... **CLC 21**
See Pearce, Philippa
See also BYA 5; CANR 109; CLR 9; DLB 161; MAICYA 1; SATA 1, 67, 129
Christine de Pizan 1365(?)-1431(?) .... **LC 9**
See also DLB 208; RGWL 2, 3
Chuang Tzu c. 369B.C.-c.
286B.C. .... **CMLC 57**
Chubb, Elmer
See Masters, Edgar Lee
Chulkov, Mikhail Dmitrievich
1743-1792 .... **LC 2**
See also DLB 150
Churchill, Caryl 1938- .... **CLC 31, 55, 157; DC 5**
See Churchill, Chick
See also BRWS 4; CA 102; CANR 22, 46, 108; CBD; CWD; DFS 12, 16; DLB 13; EWL 3; FW; MTCW 1; RGEL 2
Churchill, Charles 1731-1764 .... **LC 3**
See also DLB 109; RGEL 2
Churchill, Chick 1938-
See Churchill, Caryl
See also CD 5
Churchill, Sir Winston (Leonard Spencer)
1874-1965 .... **TCLC 113**
See also BRW 6; CA 97-100; CDBLB 1890-1914; DA3; DLB 100; DLBD 16; LAIT 4; MTCW 1, 2
Chute, Carolyn 1947- .... **CLC 39**
See also CA 123
Ciardi, John (Anthony) 1916-1986 . **CLC 10, 40, 44, 129**
See also CA 5-8R; 118; CAAS 2; CANR 5, 33; CLR 19; CWRI 5; DAM POET; DLB 5; DLBY 1986; INT CANR-5; MAICYA 1, 2; MTCW 1, 2; RGAL 4; SAAS 26; SATA 1, 65; SATA-Obit 46
Cibber, Colley 1671-1757 .... **LC 66**
See also DLB 84; RGEL 2
Cicero, Marcus Tullius
106B.C.-43B.C. .... **CMLC 3**
See also AW 1; CDWLB 1; DLB 211; RGWL 2, 3
Cimino, Michael 1943- .... **CLC 16**
See also CA 105
Cioran, E(mil) M. 1911-1995 .... **CLC 64**
See also CA 25-28R; 149; CANR 91; DLB 220; EWL 3

Cisneros, Sandra 1954- .. **CLC 69, 118; HLC 1; PC 52; SSC 32**
See also AAYA 9, 53; AMWS 7; CA 131; CANR 64, 118; CWP; DA3; DAM MULT; DLB 122, 152; EWL 3; EXPN; FW; HW 1, 2; LAIT 5; LATS 1; MAICYA 2; MTCW 2; NFS 2; RGAL 4; RGSF 2; SSFS 3, 13; WLIT 1; YAW
Cixous, Helene 1937- .... **CLC 92**
See also CA 126; CANR 55, 123; CWW 2; DLB 83, 242; EWL 3; FW; GLL 2; MTCW 1, 2; TWA
Clair, Rene .... **CLC 20**
See Chomette, Rene Lucien
Clampitt, Amy 1920-1994 .... **CLC 32; PC 19**
See also AMWS 9; CA 110; 146; CANR 29, 79; DLB 105
Clancy, Thomas L., Jr. 1947-
See Clancy, Tom
See also CA 125; 131; CANR 62, 105; DA3; INT CA-131; MTCW 1, 2
Clancy, Tom .... **CLC 45, 112**
See Clancy, Thomas L., Jr.
See also AAYA 9, 51; BEST 89:1, 90:1; BPFB 1; BYA 10, 11; CMW 4; CPW; DAM NOV, POP; DLB 227
Clare, John 1793-1864 .. **NCLC 9, 86; PC 23**
See also DAB; DAM POET; DLB 55, 96; RGEL 2
Clarin
See Alas (y Urena), Leopoldo (Enrique Garcia)
Clark, Al C.
See Goines, Donald
Clark, (Robert) Brian 1932- .... **CLC 29**
See also CA 41-44R; CANR 67; CBD; CD 5
Clark, Curt
See Westlake, Donald E(dwin)
Clark, Eleanor 1913-1996 .... **CLC 5, 19**
See also CA 9-12R; 151; CANR 41; CN 7; DLB 6
Clark, J. P.
See Clark Bekederemo, J(ohnson) P(epper)
See also CDWLB 3; DLB 117
Clark, John Pepper
See Clark Bekederemo, J(ohnson) P(epper)
See also AFW; CD 5; CP 7; RGEL 2
Clark, M. R.
See Clark, Mavis Thorpe
Clark, Mavis Thorpe 1909-1999 .... **CLC 12**
See also CA 57-60; CANR 8, 37, 107; CLR 30; CWRI 5; MAICYA 1, 2; SAAS 5; SATA 8, 74
Clark, Walter Van Tilburg
1909-1971 .... **CLC 28**
See also CA 9-12R; 33-36R; CANR 63, 113; DLB 9, 206; LAIT 2; RGAL 4; SATA 8
Clark Bekederemo, J(ohnson) P(epper)
1935- .... **BLC 1; CLC 38; DC 5**
See Clark, J. P.; Clark, John Pepper
See also BW 1; CA 65-68; CANR 16, 72; DAM DRAM, MULT; DFS 13; EWL 3; MTCW 1
Clarke, Arthur C(harles) 1917- .... **CLC 1, 4, 13, 18, 35, 136; SSC 3**
See also AAYA 4, 33; BPFB 1; BYA 13; CA 1-4R; CANR 2, 28, 55, 74; CN 7; CPW; DA3; DAM POP; DLB 261; JRDA; LAIT 5; MAICYA 1, 2; MTCW 1, 2; SATA 13, 70, 115; SCFW; SFW 4; SSFS 4, 18; YAW
Clarke, Austin 1896-1974 .... **CLC 6, 9**
See also CA 29-32; 49-52; CAP 2; DAM POET; DLB 10, 20; EWL 3; RGEL 2

Clarke, Austin C(hesterfield) 1934- .. **BLC 1; CLC 8, 53; SSC 45**
See also BW 1; CA 25-28R; CAAS 16; CANR 14, 32, 68; CN 7; DAC; DAM MULT; DLB 53, 125; DNFS 2; RGSF 2

Clarke, Gillian 1937- .... **CLC 61**
See also CA 106; CP 7; CWP; DLB 40

Clarke, Marcus (Andrew Hislop) 1846-1881 .... **NCLC 19**
See also DLB 230; RGEL 2; RGSF 2

Clarke, Shirley 1925-1997 .... **CLC 16**
See also CA 189

Clash, The
See Headon, (Nicky) Topper; Jones, Mick; Simonon, Paul; Strummer, Joe

Claudel, Paul (Louis Charles Marie) 1868-1955 .... **TCLC 2, 10**
See also CA 104; 165; DLB 192, 258; EW 8; EWL 3; GFL 1789 to the Present; RGWL 2, 3; TWA

Claudian 370(?)-404(?) .... **CMLC 46**
See also RGWL 2, 3

Claudius, Matthias 1740-1815 .... **NCLC 75**
See also DLB 97

Clavell, James (duMaresq) 1925-1994 .... **CLC 6, 25, 87**
See also BPFB 1; CA 25-28R; 146; CANR 26, 48; CPW; DA3; DAM NOV, POP; MTCW 1, 2; NFS 10; RHW

Clayman, Gregory .... **CLC 65**

Cleaver, (Leroy) Eldridge 1935-1998 .... **BLC 1; CLC 30, 119**
See also BW 1, 3; CA 21-24R; 167; CANR 16, 75; DA3; DAM MULT; MTCW 2; YAW

Cleese, John (Marwood) 1939- .... **CLC 21**
See Monty Python
See also CA 112; 116; CANR 35; MTCW 1

Cleishbotham, Jedediah
See Scott, Sir Walter

Cleland, John 1710-1789 .... **LC 2, 48**
See also DLB 39; RGEL 2

Clemens, Samuel Langhorne 1835-1910
See Twain, Mark
See also CA 104; 135; CDALB 1865-1917; DA; DA3; DAB; DAC; DAM MST, NOV; DLB 12, 23, 64, 74, 186, 189; JRDA; LMFS 1; MAICYA 1, 2; NCFS 4; SATA 100; SSFS 16; YABC 2

Clement of Alexandria 150(?)-215(?) .... **CMLC 41**

Cleophil
See Congreve, William

Clerihew, E.
See Bentley, E(dmund) C(lerihew)

Clerk, N. W.
See Lewis, C(live) S(taples)

Cliff, Jimmy .... **CLC 21**
See Chambers, James
See also CA 193

Cliff, Michelle 1946- .... **BLCS; CLC 120**
See also BW 2; CA 116; CANR 39, 72; CD-WLB 3; DLB 157; FW; GLL 2

Clifford, Lady Anne 1590-1676 .... **LC 76**
See also DLB 151

Clifton, (Thelma) Lucille 1936- .... **BLC 1; CLC 19, 66, 162; PC 17**
See also AFAW 2; BW 2, 3; CA 49-52; CANR 2, 24, 42, 76, 97; CLR 5; CP 7; CSW; CWP; CWRI 5; DA3; DAM MULT, POET; DLB 5, 41; EXPP; MAICYA 1, 2; MTCW 1, 2; PFS 1, 14; SATA 20, 69, 128; WP

Clinton, Dirk
See Silverberg, Robert

Clough, Arthur Hugh 1819-1861 ... **NCLC 27**
See also BRW 5; DLB 32; RGEL 2

Clutha, Janet Paterson Frame 1924-
See Frame, Janet
See also CA 1-4R; CANR 2, 36, 76; MTCW 1, 2; SATA 119

Clyne, Terence
See Blatty, William Peter

Cobalt, Martin
See Mayne, William (James Carter)

Cobb, Irvin S(hrewsbury) 1876-1944 .... **TCLC 77**
See also CA 175; DLB 11, 25, 86

Cobbett, William 1763-1835 .... **NCLC 49**
See also DLB 43, 107, 158; RGEL 2

Coburn, D(onald) L(ee) 1938- .... **CLC 10**
See also CA 89-92

Cocteau, Jean (Maurice Eugene Clement) 1889-1963 ...... **CLC 1, 8, 15, 16, 43; DC 17; TCLC 119; WLC**
See also CA 25-28; CANR 40; CAP 2; DA; DA3; DAB; DAC; DAM DRAM, MST, NOV; DLB 65, 258; EW 10; EWL 3; GFL 1789 to the Present; MTCW 1, 2; RGWL 2, 3; TWA

Codrescu, Andrei 1946- .... **CLC 46, 121**
See also CA 33-36R; CAAS 19; CANR 13, 34, 53, 76; DA3; DAM POET; MTCW 2

Coe, Max
See Bourne, Randolph S(illiman)

Coe, Tucker
See Westlake, Donald E(dwin)

Coen, Ethan 1958- .... **CLC 108**
See also CA 126; CANR 85

Coen, Joel 1955- .... **CLC 108**
See also CA 126; CANR 119

The Coen Brothers
See Coen, Ethan; Coen, Joel

Coetzee, J(ohn) M(axwell) 1940- ..... **CLC 23, 33, 66, 117, 161, 162**
See also AAYA 37; AFW; BRWS 6; CA 77-80; CANR 41, 54, 74, 114; CN 7; DA3; DAM NOV; DLB 225; EWL 3; LMFS 2; MTCW 1, 2; WLIT 2

Coffey, Brian
See Koontz, Dean R(ay)

Coffin, Robert P(eter) Tristram 1892-1955 .... **TCLC 95**
See also CA 123; 169; DLB 45

Cohan, George M(ichael) 1878-1942 .... **TCLC 60**
See also CA 157; DLB 249; RGAL 4

Cohen, Arthur A(llen) 1928-1986 ...... **CLC 7, 31**
See also CA 1-4R; 120; CANR 1, 17, 42; DLB 28

Cohen, Leonard (Norman) 1934- ...... **CLC 3, 38**
See also CA 21-24R; CANR 14, 69; CN 7; CP 7; DAC; DAM MST; DLB 53; EWL 3; MTCW 1

Cohen, Matt(hew) 1942-1999 .... **CLC 19**
See also CA 61-64; 187; CAAS 18; CANR 40; CN 7; DAC; DLB 53

Cohen-Solal, Annie 19(?)- .... **CLC 50**

Colegate, Isabel 1931- .... **CLC 36**
See also CA 17-20R; CANR 8, 22, 74; CN 7; DLB 14, 231; INT CANR-22; MTCW 1

Coleman, Emmett
See Reed, Ishmael

Coleridge, Hartley 1796-1849 .... **NCLC 90**
See also DLB 96

Coleridge, M. E.
See Coleridge, Mary E(lizabeth)

Coleridge, Mary E(lizabeth) 1861-1907 .... **TCLC 73**
See also CA 116; 166; DLB 19, 98

Coleridge, Samuel Taylor 1772-1834 ...... **NCLC 9, 54, 99, 111; PC 11, 39; WLC**
See also BRW 4; BRWR 2; BYA 4; CD-BLB 1789-1832; DA; DA3; DAB; DAC; DAM MST, POET; DLB 93, 107; EXPP; LATS 1; LMFS 1; PAB; PFS 4, 5; RGEL 2; TEA; WLIT 3; WP

Coleridge, Sara 1802-1852 .... **NCLC 31**
See also DLB 199

Coles, Don 1928- .... **CLC 46**
See also CA 115; CANR 38; CP 7

Coles, Robert (Martin) 1929- .... **CLC 108**
See also CA 45-48; CANR 3, 32, 66, 70; INT CANR-32; SATA 23

Colette, (Sidonie-Gabrielle) 1873-1954 .... **SSC 10; TCLC 1, 5, 16**
See Willy, Colette
See also CA 104; 131; DA3; DAM NOV; DLB 65; EW 9; EWL 3; GFL 1789 to the Present; MTCW 1, 2; RGWL 2, 3; TWA

Collett, (Jacobine) Camilla (Wergeland) 1813-1895 .... **NCLC 22**

Collier, Christopher 1930- .... **CLC 30**
See also AAYA 13; BYA 2; CA 33-36R; CANR 13, 33, 102; JRDA; MAICYA 1, 2; SATA 16, 70; WYA; YAW 1

Collier, James Lincoln 1928- .... **CLC 30**
See also AAYA 13; BYA 2; CA 9-12R; CANR 4, 33, 60, 102; CLR 3; DAM POP; JRDA; MAICYA 1, 2; SAAS 21; SATA 8, 70; WYA; YAW 1

Collier, Jeremy 1650-1726 .... **LC 6**

Collier, John 1901-1980 . **SSC 19; TCLC 127**
See also CA 65-68; 97-100; CANR 10; DLB 77, 255; FANT; SUFW 1

Collier, Mary 1690-1762 .... **LC 86**
See also DLB 95

Collingwood, R(obin) G(eorge) 1889(?)-1943 .... **TCLC 67**
See also CA 117; 155; DLB 262

Collins, Hunt
See Hunter, Evan

Collins, Linda 1931- .... **CLC 44**
See also CA 125

Collins, Tom
See Furphy, Joseph
See also RGEL 2

Collins, (William) Wilkie 1824-1889 .... **NCLC 1, 18, 93**
See also BRWS 6; CDBLB 1832-1890; CMW 4; DLB 18, 70, 159; MSW; RGEL 2; RGSF 2; SUFW 1; WLIT 4

Collins, William 1721-1759 .... **LC 4, 40**
See also BRW 3; DAM POET; DLB 109; RGEL 2

Collodi, Carlo .... **NCLC 54**
See Lorenzini, Carlo
See also CLR 5; WCH

Colman, George
See Glassco, John

Colonna, Vittoria 1492-1547 .... **LC 71**
See also RGWL 2, 3

Colt, Winchester Remington
See Hubbard, L(afayette) Ron(ald)

Colter, Cyrus J. 1910-2002 .... **CLC 58**
See also BW 1; CA 65-68; 205; CANR 10, 66; CN 7; DLB 33

Colton, James
See Hansen, Joseph
See also GLL 1

Colum, Padraic 1881-1972 .... **CLC 28**
See also BYA 4; CA 73-76; 33-36R; CANR 35; CLR 36; CWRI 5; DLB 19; MAICYA 1, 2; MTCW 1; RGEL 2; SATA 15; WCH

Colvin, James
See Moorcock, Michael (John)

Colwin, Laurie (E.) 1944-1992 .... **CLC 5, 13, 23, 84**
See also CA 89-92; 139; CANR 20, 46; DLB 218; DLBY 1980; MTCW 1

Comfort, Alex(ander) 1920-2000 .... **CLC 7**
See also CA 1-4R; 190; CANR 1, 45; CP 7; DAM POP; MTCW 1

Comfort, Montgomery
See Campbell, (John) Ramsey

Compton-Burnett, I(vy) 1892(?)-1969 .... **CLC 1, 3, 10, 15, 34**
See also BRW 7; CA 1-4R; 25-28R; CANR 4; DAM NOV; DLB 36; EWL 3; MTCW 1; RGEL 2

Comstock, Anthony 1844-1915 ...... **TCLC 13**
See also CA 110; 169

Comte, Auguste 1798-1857 .... **NCLC 54**

Conan Doyle, Arthur
See Doyle, Sir Arthur Conan
See also BPFB 1; BYA 4, 5, 11

Conde (Abellan), Carmen 1901-1996 .... **HLCS 1**
See also CA 177; DLB 108; EWL 3; HW 2

Conde, Maryse 1937- ..... **BLCS; CLC 52, 92**
See also BW 2, 3; CA 110; CAAE 190; CANR 30, 53, 76; CWW 2; DAM MULT; EWL 3; MTCW 1

Condillac, Etienne Bonnot de 1714-1780 .... **LC 26**

Condon, Richard (Thomas) 1915-1996 .... **CLC 4, 6, 8, 10, 45, 100**
See also BEST 90:3; BPFB 1; CA 1-4R; 151; CAAS 1; CANR 2, 23; CMW 4; CN 7; DAM NOV; INT CANR-23; MTCW 1, 2

Confucius 551B.C.-479B.C. .... **CMLC 19; WLCS**
See also DA; DA3; DAB; DAC; DAM MST

Congreve, William 1670-1729 ... **DC 2; LC 5, 21; WLC**
See also BRW 2; CDBLB 1660-1789; DA; DAB; DAC; DAM DRAM, MST, POET; DFS 15; DLB 39, 84; RGEL 2; WLIT 3

Conley, Robert J(ackson) 1940- .... **NNAL**
See also CA 41-44R; CANR 15, 34, 45, 96; DAM MULT

Connell, Evan S(helby), Jr. 1924- . **CLC 4, 6, 45**
See also AAYA 7; CA 1-4R; CAAS 2; CANR 2, 39, 76, 97; CN 7; DAM NOV; DLB 2; DLBY 1981; MTCW 1, 2

Connelly, Marc(us Cook) 1890-1980 . **CLC 7**
See also CA 85-88; 102; CANR 30; DFS 12; DLB 7; DLBY 1980; RGAL 4; SATA-Obit 25

Connor, Ralph .... **TCLC 31**
See Gordon, Charles William
See also DLB 92; TCWW 2

Conrad, Joseph 1857-1924 . **SSC 9; TCLC 1, 6, 13, 25, 43, 57; WLC**
See also AAYA 26; BPFB 1; BRW 6; BRWC 1; BRWR 2; BYA 2; CA 104; 131; CANR 60; CDBLB 1890-1914; DA; DA3; DAB; DAC; DAM MST, NOV; DLB 10, 34, 98, 156; EWL 3; EXPN; EXPS; LAIT 2; LATS 1; LMFS 1; MTCW 1, 2; NFS 2, 16; RGEL 2; RGSF 2; SATA 27; SSFS 1, 12; TEA; WLIT 4

Conrad, Robert Arnold
See Hart, Moss

Conroy, (Donald) Pat(rick) 1945- ... **CLC 30, 74**
See also AAYA 8, 52; AITN 1; BPFB 1; CA 85-88; CANR 24, 53; CPW; CSW; DA3; DAM NOV, POP; DLB 6; LAIT 5; MTCW 1, 2

Constant (de Rebecque), (Henri) Benjamin 1767-1830 .... **NCLC 6**
See also DLB 119; EW 4; GFL 1789 to the Present

Conway, Jill K(er) 1934- .... **CLC 152**
See also CA 130; CANR 94

Conybeare, Charles Augustus
See Eliot, T(homas) S(tearns)

Cook, Michael 1933-1994 .... **CLC 58**
See also CA 93-96; CANR 68; DLB 53

Cook, Robin 1940- .... **CLC 14**
See also AAYA 32; BEST 90:2; BPFB 1; CA 108; 111; CANR 41, 90, 109; CPW; DA3; DAM POP; HGG; INT CA-111

Cook, Roy
See Silverberg, Robert

Cooke, Elizabeth 1948- .... **CLC 55**
See also CA 129

Cooke, John Esten 1830-1886 .... **NCLC 5**
See also DLB 3, 248; RGAL 4

Cooke, John Estes
See Baum, L(yman) Frank

Cooke, M. E.
See Creasey, John

Cooke, Margaret
See Creasey, John

Cooke, Rose Terry 1827-1892 .... **NCLC 110**
See also DLB 12, 74

Cook-Lynn, Elizabeth 1930- .... **CLC 93; NNAL**
See also CA 133; DAM MULT; DLB 175

Cooney, Ray .... **CLC 62**
See also CBD

Cooper, Douglas 1960- .... **CLC 86**

Cooper, Henry St. John
See Creasey, John

Cooper, J(oan) California (?)- .... **CLC 56**
See also AAYA 12; BW 1; CA 125; CANR 55; DAM MULT; DLB 212

Cooper, James Fenimore 1789-1851 .... **NCLC 1, 27, 54**
See also AAYA 22; AMW; BPFB 1; CDALB 1640-1865; DA3; DLB 3, 183, 250, 254; LAIT 1; NFS 9; RGAL 4; SATA 19; TUS; WCH

Cooper, Susan Fenimore 1813-1894 .... **NCLC 129**
See also ANW; DLB 239, 254

Coover, Robert (Lowell) 1932- .... **CLC 3, 7, 15, 32, 46, 87, 161; SSC 15**
See also AMWS 5; BPFB 1; CA 45-48; CANR 3, 37, 58, 115; CN 7; DAM NOV; DLB 2, 227; DLBY 1981; EWL 3; MTCW 1, 2; RGAL 4; RGSF 2

Copeland, Stewart (Armstrong) 1952- .... **CLC 26**

Copernicus, Nicolaus 1473-1543 .... **LC 45**

Coppard, A(lfred) E(dgar) 1878-1957 .... **SSC 21; TCLC 5**
See also BRWS 8; CA 114; 167; DLB 162; EWL 3; HGG; RGEL 2; RGSF 2; SUFW 1; YABC 1

Coppee, Francois 1842-1908 .... **TCLC 25**
See also CA 170; DLB 217

Coppola, Francis Ford 1939- ... **CLC 16, 126**
See also AAYA 39; CA 77-80; CANR 40, 78; DLB 44

Copway, George 1818-1869 .... **NNAL**
See also DAM MULT; DLB 175, 183

Corbiere, Tristan 1845-1875 .... **NCLC 43**
See also DLB 217; GFL 1789 to the Present

Corcoran, Barbara (Asenath) 1911- .... **CLC 17**
See also AAYA 14; CA 21-24R; CAAE 191; CAAS 2; CANR 11, 28, 48; CLR 50; DLB 52; JRDA; MAICYA 2; MAICYAS 1; RHW; SAAS 20; SATA 3, 77, 125

Cordelier, Maurice
See Giraudoux, Jean(-Hippolyte)

Corelli, Marie .... **TCLC 51**
See Mackay, Mary
See also DLB 34, 156; RGEL 2; SUFW 1

Corman, Cid .... **CLC 9**
See Corman, Sidney
See also CAAS 2; DLB 5, 193

Corman, Sidney 1924-
See Corman, Cid
See also CA 85-88; CANR 44; CP 7; DAM POET

Cormier, Robert (Edmund) 1925-2000 .... **CLC 12, 30**
See also AAYA 3, 19; BYA 1, 2, 6, 8, 9; CA 1-4R; CANR 5, 23, 76, 93; CDALB 1968-1988; CLR 12, 55; DA; DAB; DAC; DAM MST, NOV; DLB 52; EXPN; INT CANR-23; JRDA; LAIT 5; MAICYA 1, 2; MTCW 1, 2; NFS 2, 18; SATA 10, 45, 83; SATA-Obit 122; WYA; YAW

Corn, Alfred (DeWitt III) 1943- .... **CLC 33**
See also CA 179; CAAE 179; CAAS 25; CANR 44; CP 7; CSW; DLB 120, 282; DLBY 1980

Corneille, Pierre 1606-1684 ... **DC 21; LC 28**
See also DAB; DAM MST; DLB 268; EW 3; GFL Beginnings to 1789; RGWL 2, 3; TWA

Cornwell, David (John Moore) 1931- .... **CLC 9, 15**
See le Carre, John
See also CA 5-8R; CANR 13, 33, 59, 107; DA3; DAM POP; MTCW 1, 2

Cornwell, Patricia (Daniels) 1956- . **CLC 155**
See also AAYA 16; BPFB 1; CA 134; CANR 53; CMW 4; CPW; CSW; DAM POP; MSW; MTCW 1

Corso, (Nunzio) Gregory 1930-2001 . **CLC 1, 11; PC 33**
See also AMWS 12; BG 2; CA 5-8R; 193; CANR 41, 76; CP 7; DA3; DLB 5, 16, 237; LMFS 2; MTCW 1, 2; WP

Cortazar, Julio 1914-1984 ... **CLC 2, 3, 5, 10, 13, 15, 33, 34, 92; HLC 1; SSC 7**
See also BPFB 1; CA 21-24R; CANR 12, 32, 81; CDWLB 3; DA3; DAM MULT, NOV; DLB 113; EWL 3; EXPS; HW 1, 2; LAW; MTCW 1, 2; RGSF 2; RGWL 2, 3; SSFS 3; TWA; WLIT 1

Cortes, Hernan 1485-1547 .... **LC 31**

Corvinus, Jakob
See Raabe, Wilhelm (Karl)

Corwin, Cecil
See Kornbluth, C(yril) M.

Cosic, Dobrica 1921- .... **CLC 14**
See also CA 122; 138; CDWLB 4; CWW 2; DLB 181; EWL 3

Costain, Thomas B(ertram) 1885-1965 .... **CLC 30**
See also BYA 3; CA 5-8R; 25-28R; DLB 9; RHW

Costantini, Humberto 1924(?)-1987 . **CLC 49**
See also CA 131; 122; EWL 3; HW 1

Costello, Elvis 1954- .... **CLC 21**
See also CA 204

Costenoble, Philostene
See Ghelderode, Michel de

Cotes, Cecil V.
See Duncan, Sara Jeannette

Cotter, Joseph Seamon Sr. 1861-1949 .... **BLC 1; TCLC 28**
See also BW 1; CA 124; DAM MULT; DLB 50

Couch, Arthur Thomas Quiller
See Quiller-Couch, Sir Arthur (Thomas)

Coulton, James
See Hansen, Joseph

Couperus, Louis (Marie Anne) 1863-1923 .... **TCLC 15**
See also CA 115; EWL 3; RGWL 2, 3

Coupland, Douglas 1961- .... **CLC 85, 133**
See also AAYA 34; CA 142; CANR 57, 90; CCA 1; CPW; DAC; DAM POP

Court, Wesli
See Turco, Lewis (Putnam)

Courtenay, Bryce 1933- .... **CLC 59**
See also CA 138; CPW

Courtney, Robert
See Ellison, Harlan (Jay)

Cousteau, Jacques-Yves 1910-1997 .. **CLC 30**
See also CA 65-68; 159; CANR 15, 67; MTCW 1; SATA 38, 98

Coventry, Francis 1725-1754 .... **LC 46**

Coverdale, Miles c. 1487-1569 .... **LC 77**
See also DLB 167

Cowan, Peter (Walkinshaw) 1914- .... **SSC 28**
See also CA 21-24R; CANR 9, 25, 50, 83; CN 7; DLB 260; RGSF 2

Coward, Noel (Peirce) 1899-1973 . **CLC 1, 9, 29, 51**
See also AITN 1; BRWS 2; CA 17-18; 41-44R; CANR 35; CAP 2; CDBLB 1914-1945; DA3; DAM DRAM; DFS 3, 6; DLB 10, 245; EWL 3; IDFW 3, 4; MTCW 1, 2; RGEL 2; TEA

Cowley, Abraham 1618-1667 .... **LC 43**
See also BRW 2; DLB 131, 151; PAB; RGEL 2

Cowley, Malcolm 1898-1989 .... **CLC 39**
See also AMWS 2; CA 5-8R; 128; CANR 3, 55; DLB 4, 48; DLBY 1981, 1989; EWL 3; MTCW 1, 2

Cowper, William 1731-1800 ..... **NCLC 8, 94; PC 40**
See also BRW 3; DA3; DAM POET; DLB 104, 109; RGEL 2

Cox, William Trevor 1928-
See Trevor, William
See also CA 9-12R; CANR 4, 37, 55, 76, 102; DAM NOV; INT CANR-37; MTCW 1, 2; TEA

Coyne, P. J.
See Masters, Hilary

Cozzens, James Gould 1903-1978 . **CLC 1, 4, 11, 92**
See also AMW; BPFB 1; CA 9-12R; 81-84; CANR 19; CDALB 1941-1968; DLB 9; DLBD 2; DLBY 1984, 1997; EWL 3; MTCW 1, 2; RGAL 4

Crabbe, George 1754-1832 .... **NCLC 26, 121**
See also BRW 3; DLB 93; RGEL 2

Crace, Jim 1946- .... **CLC 157; SSC 61**
See also CA 128; 135; CANR 55, 70, 123; CN 7; DLB 231; INT CA-135

Craddock, Charles Egbert
See Murfree, Mary Noailles

Craig, A. A.
See Anderson, Poul (William)

Craik, Mrs.
See Craik, Dinah Maria (Mulock)
See also RGEL 2

Craik, Dinah Maria (Mulock) 1826-1887 .... **NCLC 38**
See Craik, Mrs.; Mulock, Dinah Maria
See also DLB 35, 163; MAICYA 1, 2; SATA 34

Cram, Ralph Adams 1863-1942 ..... **TCLC 45**
See also CA 160

Cranch, Christopher Pearse 1813-1892 .... **NCLC 115**
See also DLB 1, 42, 243

Crane, (Harold) Hart 1899-1932 .... **PC 3; TCLC 2, 5, 80; WLC**
See also AMW; AMWR 2; CA 104; 127; CDALB 1917-1929; DA; DA3; DAB; DAC; DAM MST, POET; DLB 4, 48; EWL 3; MTCW 1, 2; RGAL 4; TUS

Crane, R(onald) S(almon) 1886-1967 .... **CLC 27**
See also CA 85-88; DLB 63

Crane, Stephen (Townley) 1871-1900 ...... **SSC 7, 56; TCLC 11, 17, 32; WLC**
See also AAYA 21; AMW; AMWC 1; BPFB 1; BYA 3; CA 109; 140; CANR 84; CDALB 1865-1917; DA; DA3; DAB; DAC; DAM MST, NOV, POET; DLB 12, 54, 78; EXPN; EXPS; LAIT 2; LMFS 2; NFS 4; PFS 9; RGAL 4; RGSF 2; SSFS 4; TUS; WYA; YABC 2

Cranmer, Thomas 1489-1556 .... **LC 95**
See also DLB 132, 213

Cranshaw, Stanley
See Fisher, Dorothy (Frances) Canfield

Crase, Douglas 1944- .... **CLC 58**
See also CA 106

Crashaw, Richard 1612(?)-1649 .... **LC 24**
See also BRW 2; DLB 126; PAB; RGEL 2

Cratinus c. 519B.C.-c. 422B.C. ...... **CMLC 54**
See also LMFS 1

Craven, Margaret 1901-1980 .... **CLC 17**
See also BYA 2; CA 103; CCA 1; DAC; LAIT 5

Crawford, F(rancis) Marion 1854-1909 .... **TCLC 10**
See also CA 107; 168; DLB 71; HGG; RGAL 4; SUFW 1

Crawford, Isabella Valancy 1850-1887 .... **NCLC 12, 127**
See also DLB 92; RGEL 2

Crayon, Geoffrey
See Irving, Washington

Creasey, John 1908-1973 .... **CLC 11**
See Marric, J. J.
See also CA 5-8R; 41-44R; CANR 8, 59; CMW 4; DLB 77; MTCW 1

Crebillon, Claude Prosper Jolyot de (fils) 1707-1777 .... **LC 1, 28**
See also GFL Beginnings to 1789

Credo
See Creasey, John

Credo, Alvaro J. de
See Prado (Calvo), Pedro

Creeley, Robert (White) 1926- .. **CLC 1, 2, 4, 8, 11, 15, 36, 78**
See also AMWS 4; CA 1-4R; CAAS 10; CANR 23, 43, 89; CP 7; DA3; DAM POET; DLB 5, 16, 169; DLBD 17; EWL 3; MTCW 1, 2; RGAL 4; WP

Crevecoeur, Hector St. John de
See Crevecoeur, Michel Guillaume Jean de
See also ANW

Crevecoeur, Michel Guillaume Jean de 1735-1813 .... **NCLC 105**
See Crevecoeur, Hector St. John de
See also AMWS 1; DLB 37

Crevel, Rene 1900-1935 .... **TCLC 112**
See also GLL 2

Crews, Harry (Eugene) 1935- ..... **CLC 6, 23, 49**
See also AITN 1; AMWS 11; BPFB 1; CA 25-28R; CANR 20, 57; CN 7; CSW; DA3; DLB 6, 143, 185; MTCW 1, 2; RGAL 4

Crichton, (John) Michael 1942- .... **CLC 2, 6, 54, 90**
See also AAYA 10, 49; AITN 2; BPFB 1; CA 25-28R; CANR 13, 40, 54, 76; CMW 4; CN 7; CPW; DA3; DAM NOV, POP; DLBY 1981; INT CANR-13; JRDA; MTCW 1, 2; SATA 9, 88; SFW 4; YAW

Crispin, Edmund .... **CLC 22**
See Montgomery, (Robert) Bruce
See also DLB 87; MSW

Cristofer, Michael 1945(?)- .... **CLC 28**
See also CA 110; 152; CAD; CD 5; DAM DRAM; DFS 15; DLB 7

Criton
See Alain

Croce, Benedetto 1866-1952 .... **TCLC 37**
See also CA 120; 155; EW 8; EWL 3

Crockett, David 1786-1836 .... **NCLC 8**
See also DLB 3, 11, 183, 248

Crockett, Davy
See Crockett, David

Crofts, Freeman Wills 1879-1957 .. **TCLC 55**
See also CA 115; 195; CMW 4; DLB 77; MSW

Croker, John Wilson 1780-1857 .... **NCLC 10**
See also DLB 110

Crommelynck, Fernand 1885-1970 .. **CLC 75**
See also CA 189; 89-92; EWL 3

Cromwell, Oliver 1599-1658 .... **LC 43**

Cronenberg, David 1943- .... **CLC 143**
See also CA 138; CCA 1

Cronin, A(rchibald) J(oseph) 1896-1981 .... **CLC 32**
See also BPFB 1; CA 1-4R; 102; CANR 5; DLB 191; SATA 47; SATA-Obit 25

Cross, Amanda
See Heilbrun, Carolyn G(old)
See also BPFB 1; CMW; CPW; MSW

Crothers, Rachel 1878-1958 .... **TCLC 19**
See also CA 113; 194; CAD; CWD; DLB 7, 266; RGAL 4

Croves, Hal
See Traven, B.

Crow Dog, Mary (Ellen) (?)- .... **CLC 93**
See Brave Bird, Mary
See also CA 154

Crowfield, Christopher
See Stowe, Harriet (Elizabeth) Beecher

Crowley, Aleister .... **TCLC 7**
See Crowley, Edward Alexander
See also GLL 1

Crowley, Edward Alexander 1875-1947
See Crowley, Aleister
See also CA 104; HGG

Crowley, John 1942- .... **CLC 57**
See also BPFB 1; CA 61-64; CANR 43, 98; DLBY 1982; SATA 65, 140; SFW 4; SUFW 2

Crud
See Crumb, R(obert)

Crumarums
See Crumb, R(obert)

Crumb, R(obert) 1943- .... **CLC 17**
See also CA 106; CANR 107

Crumbum
See Crumb, R(obert)

Crumski
See Crumb, R(obert)

Crum the Bum
See Crumb, R(obert)

Crunk
See Crumb, R(obert)

Crustt
See Crumb, R(obert)

Crutchfield, Les
See Trumbo, Dalton

Cruz, Victor Hernandez 1949- ... **HLC 1; PC 37**
See also BW 2; CA 65-68; CAAS 17; CANR 14, 32, 74; CP 7; DAM MULT, POET; DLB 41; DNFS 1; EXPP; HW 1, 2; MTCW 1; PFS 16; WP

Cryer, Gretchen (Kiger) 1935- .... **CLC 21**
See also CA 114; 123

Csath, Geza 1887-1919 .... **TCLC 13**
See also CA 111

Cudlip, David R(ockwell) 1933- .... **CLC 34**
See also CA 177

Cullen, Countee 1903-1946 .... **BLC 1; HR 2; PC 20; TCLC 4, 37; WLCS**
See also AFAW 2; AMWS 4; BW 1; CA 108; 124; CDALB 1917-1929; DA; DA3; DAC; DAM MST, MULT, POET; DLB 4, 48, 51; EWL 3; EXPP; LMFS 2; MTCW 1, 2; PFS 3; RGAL 4; SATA 18; WP

Culleton, Beatrice 1949- .... **NNAL**
See also CA 120; CANR 83; DAC

Cum, R.
See Crumb, R(obert)

Cummings, Bruce F(rederick) 1889-1919
See Barbellion, W. N. P.
See also CA 123

Cummings, E(dward) E(stlin) 1894-1962 .. **CLC 1, 3, 8, 12, 15, 68; PC 5; TCLC 137; WLC**
See also AAYA 41; AMW; CA 73-76; CANR 31; CDALB 1929-1941; DA; DA3; DAB; DAC; DAM MST, POET; DLB 4, 48; EWL 3; EXPP; MTCW 1, 2; PAB; PFS 1, 3, 12, 13; RGAL 4; TUS; WP

Cunha, Euclides (Rodrigues Pimenta) da 1866-1909 .... **TCLC 24**
See also CA 123; LAW; WLIT 1

Cunningham, E. V.
See Fast, Howard (Melvin)

Cunningham, J(ames) V(incent) 1911-1985 .... **CLC 3, 31**
See also CA 1-4R; 115; CANR 1, 72; DLB 5

Cunningham, Julia (Woolfolk) 1916- .... **CLC 12**
See also CA 9-12R; CANR 4, 19, 36; CWRI 5; JRDA; MAICYA 1, 2; SAAS 2; SATA 1, 26, 132

Cunningham, Michael 1952- .... **CLC 34**
See also CA 136; CANR 96; GLL 2

Cunninghame Graham, R. B.
See Cunninghame Graham, Robert (Gallnigad) Bontine

Cunninghame Graham, Robert (Gallnigad) Bontine 1852-1936 .... **TCLC 19**
See Graham, R(obert) B(ontine) Cunninghame
See also CA 119; 184

Curnow, (Thomas) Allen (Monro) 1911-2001 .... **PC 48**
See also CA 69-72; 202; CANR 48, 99; CP 7; EWL 3; RGEL 2

Currie, Ellen 19(?)- .... **CLC 44**

Curtin, Philip
See Lowndes, Marie Adelaide (Belloc)

Curtin, Phillip
See Lowndes, Marie Adelaide (Belloc)

Curtis, Price
See Ellison, Harlan (Jay)

Cusanus, Nicolaus 1401-1464 .... **LC 80**
See Nicholas of Cusa

Cutrate, Joe
See Spiegelman, Art

Cynewulf c. 770- .... **CMLC 23**
See also DLB 146; RGEL 2

Cyrano de Bergerac, Savinien de 1619-1655 .... **LC 65**
See also DLB 268; GFL Beginnings to 1789; RGWL 2, 3

Cyril of Alexandria c. 375-c. 430 . **CMLC 59**

Czaczkes, Shmuel Yosef Halevi
See Agnon, S(hmuel) Y(osef Halevi)

Dabrowska, Maria (Szumska) 1889-1965 .... **CLC 15**
See also CA 106; CDWLB 4; DLB 215; EWL 3

Dabydeen, David 1955- .... **CLC 34**
See also BW 1; CA 125; CANR 56, 92; CN 7; CP 7

Dacey, Philip 1939- .... **CLC 51**
See also CA 37-40R; CAAS 17; CANR 14, 32, 64; CP 7; DLB 105

Dagerman, Stig (Halvard) 1923-1954 .... **TCLC 17**
See also CA 117; 155; DLB 259; EWL 3

D'Aguiar, Fred 1960- .... **CLC 145**
See also CA 148; CANR 83, 101; CP 7; DLB 157; EWL 3

Dahl, Roald 1916-1990 .... **CLC 1, 6, 18, 79**
See also AAYA 15; BPFB 1; BRWS 4; BYA 5; CA 1-4R; 133; CANR 6, 32, 37, 62; CLR 1, 7, 41; CPW; DA3; DAB; DAC; DAM MST, NOV, POP; DLB 139, 255; HGG; JRDA; MAICYA 1, 2; MTCW 1, 2; RGSF 2; SATA 1, 26, 73; SATA-Obit 65; SSFS 4; TEA; YAW

Dahlberg, Edward 1900-1977 .. **CLC 1, 7, 14**
See also CA 9-12R; 69-72; CANR 31, 62; DLB 48; MTCW 1; RGAL 4

Daitch, Susan 1954- .... **CLC 103**
See also CA 161

Dale, Colin .... **TCLC 18**
See Lawrence, T(homas) E(dward)

Dale, George E.
See Asimov, Isaac

Dalton, Roque 1935-1975(?) ..... **HLCS 1; PC 36**
See also CA 176; DLB 283; HW 2

Daly, Elizabeth 1878-1967 .... **CLC 52**
See also CA 23-24; 25-28R; CANR 60; CAP 2; CMW 4

Daly, Mary 1928- .... **CLC 173**
See also CA 25-28R; CANR 30, 62; FW; GLL 1; MTCW 1

Daly, Maureen 1921- .... **CLC 17**
See also AAYA 5; BYA 6; CANR 37, 83, 108; JRDA; MAICYA 1, 2; SAAS 1; SATA 2, 129; WYA; YAW

Damas, Leon-Gontran 1912-1978 .... **CLC 84**
See also BW 1; CA 125; 73-76; EWL 3

Dana, Richard Henry Sr. 1787-1879 .... **NCLC 53**

Daniel, Samuel 1562(?)-1619 .... **LC 24**
See also DLB 62; RGEL 2

Daniels, Brett
See Adler, Renata

Dannay, Frederic 1905-1982 .... **CLC 11**
See Queen, Ellery
See also CA 1-4R; 107; CANR 1, 39; CMW 4; DAM POP; DLB 137; MTCW 1

D'Annunzio, Gabriele 1863-1938 ... **TCLC 6, 40**
See also CA 104; 155; EW 8; EWL 3; RGWL 2, 3; TWA

Danois, N. le
See Gourmont, Remy(-Marie-Charles) de

Dante 1265-1321 .... **CMLC 3, 18, 39; PC 21; WLCS**
See also DA; DA3; DAB; DAC; DAM MST, POET; EFS 1; EW 1; LAIT 1; RGWL 2, 3; TWA; WP

d'Antibes, Germain
See Simenon, Georges (Jacques Christian)

Danticat, Edwidge 1969- .... **CLC 94, 139**
See also AAYA 29; CA 152; CAAE 192; CANR 73; DNFS 1; EXPS; LATS 1; MTCW 1; SSFS 1; YAW

Danvers, Dennis 1947- .... **CLC 70**

Danziger, Paula 1944- .... **CLC 21**
See also AAYA 4, 36; BYA 6, 7, 14; CA 112; 115; CANR 37; CLR 20; JRDA; MAICYA 1, 2; SATA 36, 63, 102; SATA-Brief 30; WYA; YAW

Da Ponte, Lorenzo 1749-1838 .... **NCLC 50**

Dario, Ruben 1867-1916 .... **HLC 1; PC 15; TCLC 4**
See also CA 131; CANR 81; DAM MULT; EWL 3; HW 1, 2; LAW; MTCW 1, 2; RGWL 2, 3

Darley, George 1795-1846 .... **NCLC 2**
See also DLB 96; RGEL 2

Darrow, Clarence (Seward) 1857-1938 .... **TCLC 81**
See also CA 164

Darwin, Charles 1809-1882 .... **NCLC 57**
See also BRWS 7; DLB 57, 166; LATS 1; RGEL 2; TEA; WLIT 4

Darwin, Erasmus 1731-1802 .... **NCLC 106**
See also DLB 93; RGEL 2

Daryush, Elizabeth 1887-1977 .... **CLC 6, 19**
See also CA 49-52; CANR 3, 81; DLB 20

Das, Kamala 1934- .... **PC 43**
See also CA 101; CANR 27, 59; CP 7; CWP; FW

Dasgupta, Surendranath 1887-1952 .... **TCLC 81**
See also CA 157

Dashwood, Edmee Elizabeth Monica de la Pasture 1890-1943
See Delafield, E. M.
See also CA 119; 154

da Silva, Antonio Jose 1705-1739 .... **NCLC 114**

Daudet, (Louis Marie) Alphonse 1840-1897 .... **NCLC 1**
See also DLB 123; GFL 1789 to the Present; RGSF 2

Daumal, Rene 1908-1944 .... **TCLC 14**
See also CA 114; EWL 3

Davenant, William 1606-1668 .... **LC 13**
See also DLB 58, 126; RGEL 2

Davenport, Guy (Mattison, Jr.) 1927- .... **CLC 6, 14, 38; SSC 16**
See also CA 33-36R; CANR 23, 73; CN 7; CSW; DLB 130

David, Robert
See Nezval, Vitezslav

Davidson, Avram (James) 1923-1993
See Queen, Ellery
See also CA 101; 171; CANR 26; DLB 8; FANT; SFW 4; SUFW 1, 2

Davidson, Donald (Grady) 1893-1968 .... **CLC 2, 13, 19**
See also CA 5-8R; 25-28R; CANR 4, 84; DLB 45

Davidson, Hugh
See Hamilton, Edmond

Davidson, John 1857-1909 .... **TCLC 24**
See also CA 118; DLB 19; RGEL 2

Davidson, Sara 1943- .... **CLC 9**
See also CA 81-84; CANR 44, 68; DLB 185

Davie, Donald (Alfred) 1922-1995 .... **CLC 5, 8, 10, 31; PC 29**
See also BRWS 6; CA 1-4R; 149; CAAS 3; CANR 1, 44; CP 7; DLB 27; MTCW 1; RGEL 2

Davie, Elspeth 1919-1995 .... **SSC 52**
See also CA 120; 126; 150; DLB 139

Davies, Ray(mond Douglas) 1944- ... **CLC 21**
See also CA 116; CANR 92

Davies, Rhys 1901-1978 .... **CLC 23**
See also CA 9-12R; 81-84; CANR 4; DLB 139, 191

Davies, (William) Robertson 1913-1995 .... **CLC 2, 7, 13, 25, 42, 75, 91; WLC**
See Marchbanks, Samuel
See also BEST 89:2; BPFB 1; CA 33-36R; 150; CANR 17, 42, 103; CN 7; CPW; DA; DA3; DAB; DAC; DAM MST, NOV, POP; DLB 68; EWL 3; HGG; INT CANR-17; MTCW 1, 2; RGEL 2; TWA

Davies, Sir John 1569-1626 .... **LC 85**
See also DLB 172
Davies, Walter C.
See Kornbluth, C(yril) M.
Davies, William Henry 1871-1940 ... **TCLC 5**
See also CA 104; 179; DLB 19, 174; EWL 3; RGEL 2
Da Vinci, Leonardo 1452-1519 ..... **LC 12, 57, 60**
See also AAYA 40
Davis, Angela (Yvonne) 1944- .... **CLC 77**
See also BW 2, 3; CA 57-60; CANR 10, 81; CSW; DA3; DAM MULT; FW
Davis, B. Lynch
See Bioy Casares, Adolfo; Borges, Jorge Luis
Davis, Frank Marshall 1905-1987 ...... **BLC 1**
See also BW 2, 3; CA 125; 123; CANR 42, 80; DAM MULT; DLB 51
Davis, Gordon
See Hunt, E(verette) Howard, (Jr.)
Davis, H(arold) L(enoir) 1896-1960 . **CLC 49**
See also ANW; CA 178; 89-92; DLB 9, 206; SATA 114
Davis, Rebecca (Blaine) Harding
1831-1910 .... **SSC 38; TCLC 6**
See also CA 104; 179; DLB 74, 239; FW; NFS 14; RGAL 4; TUS
Davis, Richard Harding
1864-1916 .... **TCLC 24**
See also CA 114; 179; DLB 12, 23, 78, 79, 189; DLBD 13; RGAL 4
Davison, Frank Dalby 1893-1970 ..... **CLC 15**
See also CA 116; DLB 260
Davison, Lawrence H.
See Lawrence, D(avid) H(erbert Richards)
Davison, Peter (Hubert) 1928- .... **CLC 28**
See also CA 9-12R; CAAS 4; CANR 3, 43, 84; CP 7; DLB 5
Davys, Mary 1674-1732 .... **LC 1, 46**
See also DLB 39
Dawson, (Guy) Fielding (Lewis)
1930-2002 .... **CLC 6**
See also CA 85-88; 202; CANR 108; DLB 130; DLBY 2002
Dawson, Peter
See Faust, Frederick (Schiller)
See also TCWW 2, 2
Day, Clarence (Shepard, Jr.)
1874-1935 .... **TCLC 25**
See also CA 108; 199; DLB 11
Day, John 1574(?)-1640(?) .... **LC 70**
See also DLB 62, 170; RGEL 2
Day, Thomas 1748-1789 .... **LC 1**
See also DLB 39; YABC 1
Day Lewis, C(ecil) 1904-1972 . **CLC 1, 6, 10; PC 11**
See Blake, Nicholas
See also BRWS 3; CA 13-16; 33-36R; CANR 34; CAP 1; CWRI 5; DAM POET; DLB 15, 20; EWL 3; MTCW 1, 2; RGEL 2
Dazai Osamu .... **SSC 41; TCLC 11**
See Tsushima, Shuji
See also CA 164; DLB 182; EWL 3; MJW; RGSF 2; RGWL 2, 3; TWA
de Andrade, Carlos Drummond
See Drummond de Andrade, Carlos
de Andrade, Mario 1892-1945
See Andrade, Mario de
See also CA 178; HW 2
Deane, Norman
See Creasey, John
Deane, Seamus (Francis) 1940- ...... **CLC 122**
See also CA 118; CANR 42
de Beauvoir, Simone (Lucie Ernestine Marie Bertrand)
See Beauvoir, Simone (Lucie Ernestine Marie Bertrand) de

de Beer, P.
See Bosman, Herman Charles
de Brissac, Malcolm
See Dickinson, Peter (Malcolm)
de Campos, Alvaro
See Pessoa, Fernando (Antonio Nogueira)
de Chardin, Pierre Teilhard
See Teilhard de Chardin, (Marie Joseph) Pierre
Dee, John 1527-1608 .... **LC 20**
See also DLB 136, 213
Deer, Sandra 1940- .... **CLC 45**
See also CA 186
De Ferrari, Gabriella 1941- .... **CLC 65**
See also CA 146
de Filippo, Eduardo 1900-1984 ... **TCLC 127**
See also CA 132; 114; EWL 3; MTCW 1; RGWL 2, 3
Defoe, Daniel 1660(?)-1731 .. **LC 1, 42; WLC**
See also AAYA 27; BRW 3; BRWR 1; BYA 4; CDBLB 1660-1789; CLR 61; DA; DA3; DAB; DAC; DAM MST, NOV; DLB 39, 95, 101; JRDA; LAIT 1; LMFS 1; MAICYA 1, 2; NFS 9, 13; RGEL 2; SATA 22; TEA; WCH; WLIT 3
de Gourmont, Remy(-Marie-Charles)
See Gourmont, Remy(-Marie-Charles) de
de Hartog, Jan 1914-2002 .... **CLC 19**
See also CA 1-4R; 210; CANR 1; DFS 12
de Hostos, E. M.
See Hostos (y Bonilla), Eugenio Maria de
de Hostos, Eugenio M.
See Hostos (y Bonilla), Eugenio Maria de
Deighton, Len .... **CLC 4, 7, 22, 46**
See Deighton, Leonard Cyril
See also AAYA 6; BEST 89:2; BPFB 1; CDBLB 1960 to Present; CMW 4; CN 7; CPW; DLB 87
Deighton, Leonard Cyril 1929-
See Deighton, Len
See also CA 9-12R; CANR 19, 33, 68; DA3; DAM NOV, POP; MTCW 1, 2
Dekker, Thomas 1572(?)-1632 ..... **DC 12; LC 22**
See also CDBLB Before 1660; DAM DRAM; DLB 62, 172; LMFS 1; RGEL 2
de Laclos, Pierre Ambroise Franois
See Laclos, Pierre Ambroise Francois
Delafield, E. M. .... **TCLC 61**
See Dashwood, Edmee Elizabeth Monica de la Pasture
See also DLB 34; RHW
de la Mare, Walter (John)
1873-1956 . **SSC 14; TCLC 4, 53; WLC**
See also CA 163; CDBLB 1914-1945; CLR 23; CWRI 5; DA3; DAB; DAC; DAM MST, POET; DLB 19, 153, 162, 255, 284; EWL 3; EXPP; HGG; MAICYA 1, 2; MTCW 1; RGEL 2; RGSF 2; SATA 16; SUFW 1; TEA; WCH
de Lamartine, Alphonse (Marie Louis Prat)
See Lamartine, Alphonse (Marie Louis Prat) de
Delaney, Franey
See O'Hara, John (Henry)
Delaney, Shelagh 1939- .... **CLC 29**
See also CA 17-20R; CANR 30, 67; CBD; CD 5; CDBLB 1960 to Present; CWD; DAM DRAM; DFS 7; DLB 13; MTCW 1
Delany, Martin Robison
1812-1885 .... **NCLC 93**
See also DLB 50; RGAL 4
Delany, Mary (Granville Pendarves)
1700-1788 .... **LC 12**
Delany, Samuel R(ay), Jr. 1942- .... **BLC 1; CLC 8, 14, 38, 141**
See also AAYA 24; AFAW 2; BPFB 1; BW 2, 3; CA 81-84; CANR 27, 43, 115, 116; CN 7; DAM MULT; DLB 8, 33; FANT; MTCW 1, 2; RGAL 4; SATA 92; SCFW 4; SFW 4; SUFW 2

De la Ramee, Marie Louise (Ouida)
1839-1908
See Ouida
See also CA 204; SATA 20
de la Roche, Mazo 1879-1961 .... **CLC 14**
See also CA 85-88; CANR 30; DLB 68; RGEL 2; RHW; SATA 64
De La Salle, Innocent
See Hartmann, Sadakichi
de Laureamont, Comte
See Lautreamont
Delbanco, Nicholas (Franklin)
1942- .... **CLC 6, 13, 167**
See also CA 17-20R; CAAE 189; CAAS 2; CANR 29, 55, 116; DLB 6, 234
del Castillo, Michel 1933- .... **CLC 38**
See also CA 109; CANR 77
Deledda, Grazia (Cosima)
1875(?)-1936 .... **TCLC 23**
See also CA 123; 205; DLB 264; EWL 3; RGWL 2, 3
Deleuze, Gilles 1925-1995 .... **TCLC 116**
Delgado, Abelardo (Lalo) B(arrientos)
1930- .... **HLC 1**
See also CA 131; CAAS 15; CANR 90; DAM MST, MULT; DLB 82; HW 1, 2
Delibes, Miguel .... **CLC 8, 18**
See Delibes Setien, Miguel
See also EWL 3
Delibes Setien, Miguel 1920-
See Delibes, Miguel
See also CA 45-48; CANR 1, 32; HW 1; MTCW 1
DeLillo, Don 1936- ...... **CLC 8, 10, 13, 27, 39, 54, 76, 143**
See also AMWC 2; AMWS 6; BEST 89:1; BPFB 1; CA 81-84; CANR 21, 76, 92; CN 7; CPW; DA3; DAM NOV, POP; DLB 6, 173; EWL 3; MTCW 1, 2; RGAL 4; TUS
de Lisser, H. G.
See De Lisser, H(erbert) G(eorge)
See also DLB 117
De Lisser, H(erbert) G(eorge)
1878-1944 .... **TCLC 12**
See de Lisser, H. G.
See also BW 2; CA 109; 152
Deloire, Pierre
See Peguy, Charles (Pierre)
Deloney, Thomas 1543(?)-1600 .... **LC 41**
See also DLB 167; RGEL 2
Deloria, Ella (Cara) 1889-1971(?) ..... **NNAL**
See also CA 152; DAM MULT; DLB 175
Deloria, Vine (Victor), Jr. 1933- .... **CLC 21, 122; NNAL**
See also CA 53-56; CANR 5, 20, 48, 98; DAM MULT; DLB 175; MTCW 1; SATA 21
del Valle-Inclan, Ramon (Maria)
See Valle-Inclan, Ramon (Maria) del
Del Vecchio, John M(ichael) 1947- .. **CLC 29**
See also CA 110; DLBD 9
de Man, Paul (Adolph Michel)
1919-1983 .... **CLC 55**
See also CA 128; 111; CANR 61; DLB 67; MTCW 1, 2
DeMarinis, Rick 1934- .... **CLC 54**
See also CA 57-60, 184; CAAE 184; CAAS 24; CANR 9, 25, 50; DLB 218
de Maupassant, (Henri Rene Albert) Guy
See Maupassant, (Henri Rene Albert) Guy de
Dembry, R. Emmet
See Murfree, Mary Noailles
Demby, William 1922- .... **BLC 1; CLC 53**
See also BW 1, 3; CA 81-84; CANR 81; DAM MULT; DLB 33
de Menton, Francisco
See Chin, Frank (Chew, Jr.)

Demetrius of Phalerum c. 307B.C.- .... **CMLC 34**

Demijohn, Thom
See Disch, Thomas M(ichael)

De Mille, James 1833-1880 .... **NCLC 123**
See also DLB 99, 251

Deming, Richard 1915-1983
See Queen, Ellery
See also CA 9-12R; CANR 3, 94; SATA 24

Democritus c. 460B.C.-c. 370B.C. .. **CMLC 47**

de Montaigne, Michel (Eyquem)
See Montaigne, Michel (Eyquem) de

de Montherlant, Henry (Milon)
See Montherlant, Henry (Milon) de

Demosthenes 384B.C.-322B.C. .... **CMLC 13**
See also AW 1; DLB 176; RGWL 2, 3

de Musset, (Louis Charles) Alfred
See Musset, (Louis Charles) Alfred de

de Natale, Francine
See Malzberg, Barry N(athaniel)

de Navarre, Marguerite 1492-1549 ..... **LC 61**
See Marguerite d'Angouleme; Marguerite de Navarre

Denby, Edwin (Orr) 1903-1983 .... **CLC 48**
See also CA 138; 110

de Nerval, Gerard
See Nerval, Gerard de

Denham, John 1615-1669 .... **LC 73**
See also DLB 58, 126; RGEL 2

Denis, Julio
See Cortazar, Julio

Denmark, Harrison
See Zelazny, Roger (Joseph)

Dennis, John 1658-1734 .... **LC 11**
See also DLB 101; RGEL 2

Dennis, Nigel (Forbes) 1912-1989 ...... **CLC 8**
See also CA 25-28R; 129; DLB 13, 15, 233; EWL 3; MTCW 1

Dent, Lester 1904(?)-1959 .... **TCLC 72**
See also CA 112; 161; CMW 4; SFW 4

De Palma, Brian (Russell) 1940- ...... **CLC 20**
See also CA 109

De Quincey, Thomas 1785-1859 ..... **NCLC 4, 87**
See also BRW 4; CDBLB 1789-1832; DLB 110, 144; RGEL 2

Deren, Eleanora 1908(?)-1961
See Deren, Maya
See also CA 192; 111

Deren, Maya .... **CLC 16, 102**
See Deren, Eleanora

Derleth, August (William) 1909-1971 .... **CLC 31**
See also BPFB 1; BYA 9, 10; CA 1-4R; 29-32R; CANR 4; CMW 4; DLB 9; DLBD 17; HGG; SATA 5; SUFW 1

Der Nister 1884-1950 .... **TCLC 56**
See Nister, Der

de Routisie, Albert
See Aragon, Louis

Derrida, Jacques 1930- .... **CLC 24, 87**
See also CA 124; 127; CANR 76, 98; DLB 242; EWL 3; LMFS 2; MTCW 1; TWA

Derry Down Derry
See Lear, Edward

Dersonnes, Jacques
See Simenon, Georges (Jacques Christian)

Desai, Anita 1937- .... **CLC 19, 37, 97, 175**
See also BRWS 5; CA 81-84; CANR 33, 53, 95; CN 7; CWRI 5; DA3; DAB; DAM NOV; DLB 271; DNFS 2; EWL 3; FW; MTCW 1, 2; SATA 63, 126

Desai, Kiran 1971- .... **CLC 119**
See also BYA 16; CA 171

de Saint-Luc, Jean
See Glassco, John

de Saint Roman, Arnaud
See Aragon, Louis

Desbordes-Valmore, Marceline 1786-1859 .... **NCLC 97**
See also DLB 217

Descartes, Rene 1596-1650 .... **LC 20, 35**
See also DLB 268; EW 3; GFL Beginnings to 1789

De Sica, Vittorio 1901(?)-1974 .... **CLC 20**
See also CA 117

Desnos, Robert 1900-1945 .... **TCLC 22**
See also CA 121; 151; CANR 107; DLB 258; EWL 3; LMFS 2

Destouches, Louis-Ferdinand 1894-1961 .... **CLC 9, 15**
See Celine, Louis-Ferdinand
See also CA 85-88; CANR 28; MTCW 1

de Tolignac, Gaston
See Griffith, D(avid Lewelyn) W(ark)

Deutsch, Babette 1895-1982 .... **CLC 18**
See also BYA 3; CA 1-4R; 108; CANR 4, 79; DLB 45; SATA 1; SATA-Obit 33

Devenant, William 1606-1649 .... **LC 13**

Devkota, Laxmiprasad 1909-1959 . **TCLC 23**
See also CA 123

De Voto, Bernard (Augustine) 1897-1955 .... **TCLC 29**
See also CA 113; 160; DLB 9, 256

De Vries, Peter 1910-1993 ..... **CLC 1, 2, 3, 7, 10, 28, 46**
See also CA 17-20R; 142; CANR 41; DAM NOV; DLB 6; DLBY 1982; MTCW 1, 2

Dewey, John 1859-1952 .... **TCLC 95**
See also CA 114; 170; DLB 246, 270; RGAL 4

Dexter, John
See Bradley, Marion Zimmer
See also GLL 1

Dexter, Martin
See Faust, Frederick (Schiller)
See also TCWW 2

Dexter, Pete 1943- .... **CLC 34, 55**
See also BEST 89:2; CA 127; 131; CPW; DAM POP; INT 131; MTCW 1

Diamano, Silmang
See Senghor, Leopold Sedar

Diamond, Neil 1941- .... **CLC 30**
See also CA 108

Diaz del Castillo, Bernal 1496-1584 .... **HLCS 1; LC 31**
See also LAW

di Bassetto, Corno
See Shaw, George Bernard

Dick, Philip K(indred) 1928-1982 ... **CLC 10, 30, 72; SSC 57**
See also AAYA 24; BPFB 1; BYA 11; CA 49-52; 106; CANR 2, 16; CPW; DA3; DAM NOV, POP; DLB 8; MTCW 1, 2; NFS 5; SCFW; SFW 4

Dickens, Charles (John Huffam) 1812-1870 .... **NCLC 3, 8, 18, 26, 37, 50, 86, 105, 113; SSC 17, 49; WLC**
See also AAYA 23; BRW 5; BRWC 1, 2; BYA 1, 2, 3, 13, 14; CDBLB 1832-1890; CMW 4; DA; DA3; DAB; DAC; DAM MST, NOV; DLB 21, 55, 70, 159, 166; EXPN; HGG; JRDA; LAIT 1, 2; LATS 1; LMFS 1; MAICYA 1, 2; NFS 4, 5, 10, 14; RGEL 2; RGSF 2; SATA 15; SUFW 1; TEA; WCH; WLIT 4; WYA

Dickey, James (Lafayette) 1923-1997 .... **CLC 1, 2, 4, 7, 10, 15, 47, 109; PC 40**
See also AAYA 50; AITN 1, 2; AMWS 4; BPFB 1; CA 9-12R; 156; CABS 2; CANR 10, 48, 61, 105; CDALB 1968-1988; CP 7; CPW; CSW; DA3; DAM NOV, POET, POP; DLB 5, 193; DLBD 7; DLBY 1982, 1993, 1996, 1997, 1998; EWL 3; INT CANR-10; MTCW 1, 2; NFS 9; PFS 6, 11; RGAL 4; TUS

Dickey, William 1928-1994 .... **CLC 3, 28**
See also CA 9-12R; 145; CANR 24, 79; DLB 5

Dickinson, Charles 1951- .... **CLC 49**
See also CA 128

Dickinson, Emily (Elizabeth) 1830-1886 ... **NCLC 21, 77; PC 1; WLC**
See also AAYA 22; AMW; AMWR 1; CDALB 1865-1917; DA; DA3; DAB; DAC; DAM MST, POET; DLB 1, 243; EXPP; MAWW; PAB; PFS 1, 2, 3, 4, 5, 6, 8, 10, 11, 13, 16; RGAL 4; SATA 29; TUS; WP; WYA

Dickinson, Mrs. Herbert Ward
See Phelps, Elizabeth Stuart

Dickinson, Peter (Malcolm) 1927- .. **CLC 12, 35**
See also AAYA 9, 49; BYA 5; CA 41-44R; CANR 31, 58, 88; CLR 29; CMW 4; DLB 87, 161, 276; JRDA; MAICYA 1, 2; SATA 5, 62, 95; SFW 4; WYA; YAW

Dickson, Carr
See Carr, John Dickson

Dickson, Carter
See Carr, John Dickson

Diderot, Denis 1713-1784 .... **LC 26**
See also EW 4; GFL Beginnings to 1789; LMFS 1; RGWL 2, 3

Didion, Joan 1934- . **CLC 1, 3, 8, 14, 32, 129**
See also AITN 1; AMWS 4; CA 5-8R; CANR 14, 52, 76; CDALB 1968-1988; CN 7; DA3; DAM NOV; DLB 2, 173, 185; DLBY 1981, 1986; EWL 3; MAWW; MTCW 1, 2; NFS 3; RGAL 4; TCWW 2; TUS

Dietrich, Robert
See Hunt, E(verette) Howard, (Jr.)

Difusa, Pati
See Almodovar, Pedro

Dillard, Annie 1945- .... **CLC 9, 60, 115**
See also AAYA 6, 43; AMWS 6; ANW; CA 49-52; CANR 3, 43, 62, 90; DA3; DAM NOV; DLB 275, 278; DLBY 1980; LAIT 4, 5; MTCW 1, 2; NCFS 1; RGAL 4; SATA 10, 140; TUS

Dillard, R(ichard) H(enry) W(ilde) 1937- .... **CLC 5**
See also CA 21-24R; CAAS 7; CANR 10; CP 7; CSW; DLB 5, 244

Dillon, Eilis 1920-1994 .... **CLC 17**
See also CA 9-12R, 182; 147; CAAE 182; CAAS 3; CANR 4, 38, 78; CLR 26; MAI-CYA 1, 2; MAICYAS 1; SATA 2, 74; SATA-Essay 105; SATA-Obit 83; YAW

Dimont, Penelope
See Mortimer, Penelope (Ruth)

Dinesen, Isak .... **CLC 10, 29, 95; SSC 7**
See Blixen, Karen (Christentze Dinesen)
See also EW 10; EWL 3; EXPS; FW; HGG; LAIT 3; MTCW 1; NCFS 2; NFS 9; RGSF 2; RGWL 2, 3; SSFS 3, 6, 13; WLIT 2

Ding Ling .... **CLC 68**
See Chiang, Pin-chin
See also RGWL 3

Diphusa, Patty
See Almodovar, Pedro

Disch, Thomas M(ichael) 1940- ... **CLC 7, 36**
See Disch, Tom
See also AAYA 17; BPFB 1; CA 21-24R; CAAS 4; CANR 17, 36, 54, 89; CLR 18; CP 7; DA3; DLB 8; HGG; MAICYA 1, 2; MTCW 2; SAAS 15; SATA 92; SCFW; SFW 4; SUFW 2

Disch, Tom
See Disch, Thomas M(ichael)
See also DLB 282

d'Isly, Georges
See Simenon, Georges (Jacques Christian)

Disraeli, Benjamin 1804-1881 ... **NCLC 2, 39, 79**
See also BRW 4; DLB 21, 55; RGEL 2
Ditcum, Steve
See Crumb, R(obert)
Dixon, Paige
See Corcoran, Barbara (Asenath)
Dixon, Stephen 1936- .... **CLC 52; SSC 16**
See also AMWS 12; CA 89-92; CANR 17, 40, 54, 91; CN 7; DLB 130
Doak, Annie
See Dillard, Annie
Dobell, Sydney Thompson 1824-1874 .... **NCLC 43**
See also DLB 32; RGEL 2
Doblin, Alfred .... **TCLC 13**
See Doeblin, Alfred
See also CDWLB 2; EWL 3; RGWL 2, 3
Dobroliubov, Nikolai Aleksandrovich
See Dobrolyubov, Nikolai Alexandrovich
See also DLB 277
Dobrolyubov, Nikolai Alexandrovich 1836-1861 .... **NCLC 5**
See Dobroliubov, Nikolai Aleksandrovich
Dobson, Austin 1840-1921 .... **TCLC 79**
See also DLB 35, 144
Dobyns, Stephen 1941- .... **CLC 37**
See also AMWS 13; CA 45-48; CANR 2, 18, 99; CMW 4; CP 7
Doctorow, E(dgar) L(aurence) 1931- .... **CLC 6, 11, 15, 18, 37, 44, 65, 113**
See also AAYA 22; AITN 2; AMWS 4; BEST 89:3; BPFB 1; CA 45-48; CANR 2, 33, 51, 76, 97; CDALB 1968-1988; CN 7; CPW; DA3; DAM NOV, POP; DLB 2, 28, 173; DLBY 1980; EWL 3; LAIT 3; MTCW 1, 2; NFS 6; RGAL 4; RHW; TUS
Dodgson, Charles L(utwidge) 1832-1898
See Carroll, Lewis
See also CLR 2; DA; DA3; DAB; DAC; DAM MST, NOV, POET; MAICYA 1, 2; SATA 100; YABC 2
Dodson, Owen (Vincent) 1914-1983 .. **BLC 1; CLC 79**
See also BW 1; CA 65-68; 110; CANR 24; DAM MULT; DLB 76
Doeblin, Alfred 1878-1957 .... **TCLC 13**
See Doblin, Alfred
See also CA 110; 141; DLB 66
Doerr, Harriet 1910-2002 .... **CLC 34**
See also CA 117; 122; 213; CANR 47; INT CA-122; LATS 1
Domecq, H(onorio Bustos)
See Bioy Casares, Adolfo
Domecq, H(onorio) Bustos
See Bioy Casares, Adolfo; Borges, Jorge Luis
Domini, Rey
See Lorde, Audre (Geraldine)
See also GLL 1
Dominique
See Proust, (Valentin-Louis-George-Eugene) Marcel
Don, A
See Stephen, Sir Leslie
Donaldson, Stephen R(eeder) 1947- .... **CLC 46, 138**
See also AAYA 36; BPFB 1; CA 89-92; CANR 13, 55, 99; CPW; DAM POP; FANT; INT CANR-13; SATA 121; SFW 4; SUFW 1, 2
Donleavy, J(ames) P(atrick) 1926- .... **CLC 1, 4, 6, 10, 45**
See also AITN 2; BPFB 1; CA 9-12R; CANR 24, 49, 62, 80; CBD; CD 5; CN 7; DLB 6, 173; INT CANR-24; MTCW 1, 2; RGAL 4

Donnadieu, Marguerite
See Duras, Marguerite
See also CWW 2
Donne, John 1572-1631 ... **LC 10, 24, 91; PC 1, 43; WLC**
See also BRW 1; BRWC 1; BRWR 2; CDBLB Before 1660; DA; DAB; DAC; DAM MST, POET; DLB 121, 151; EXPP; PAB; PFS 2, 11; RGEL 2; TEA; WLIT 3; WP
Donnell, David 1939(?)- .... **CLC 34**
See also CA 197
Donoghue, P. S.
See Hunt, E(verette) Howard, (Jr.)
Donoso (Yanez), Jose 1924-1996 ... **CLC 4, 8, 11, 32, 99; HLC 1; SSC 34; TCLC 133**
See also CA 81-84; 155; CANR 32, 73; CDWLB 3; DAM MULT; DLB 113; EWL 3; HW 1, 2; LAW; LAWS 1; MTCW 1, 2; RGSF 2; WLIT 1
Donovan, John 1928-1992 .... **CLC 35**
See also AAYA 20; CA 97-100; 137; CLR 3; MAICYA 1, 2; SATA 72; SATA-Brief 29; YAW
Don Roberto
See Cunninghame Graham, Robert (Gallnigad) Bontine
Doolittle, Hilda 1886-1961 . **CLC 3, 8, 14, 31, 34, 73; PC 5; WLC**
See H. D.
See also AMWS 1; CA 97-100; CANR 35; DA; DAC; DAM MST, POET; DLB 4, 45; EWL 3; FW; GLL 1; LMFS 2; MAWW; MTCW 1, 2; PFS 6; RGAL 4
Doppo, Kunikida .... **TCLC 99**
See Kunikida Doppo
Dorfman, Ariel 1942- .... **CLC 48, 77; HLC 1**
See also CA 124; 130; CANR 67, 70; CWW 2; DAM MULT; DFS 4; EWL 3; HW 1, 2; INT CA-130; WLIT 1
Dorn, Edward (Merton) 1929-1999 .... **CLC 10, 18**
See also CA 93-96; 187; CANR 42, 79; CP 7; DLB 5; INT 93-96; WP
Dor-Ner, Zvi .... **CLC 70**
Dorris, Michael (Anthony) 1945-1997 .... **CLC 109; NNAL**
See also AAYA 20; BEST 90:1; BYA 12; CA 102; 157; CANR 19, 46, 75; CLR 58; DA3; DAM MULT, NOV; DLB 175; LAIT 5; MTCW 2; NFS 3; RGAL 4; SATA 75; SATA-Obit 94; TCWW 2; YAW
Dorris, Michael A.
See Dorris, Michael (Anthony)
Dorsan, Luc
See Simenon, Georges (Jacques Christian)
Dorsange, Jean
See Simenon, Georges (Jacques Christian)
Dos Passos, John (Roderigo) 1896-1970 ... **CLC 1, 4, 8, 11, 15, 25, 34, 82; WLC**
See also AMW; BPFB 1; CA 1-4R; 29-32R; CANR 3; CDALB 1929-1941; DA; DA3; DAB; DAC; DAM MST, NOV; DLB 4, 9; DLBD 1, 15, 274; DLBY 1996; EWL 3; MTCW 1, 2; NFS 14; RGAL 4; TUS
Dossage, Jean
See Simenon, Georges (Jacques Christian)
Dostoevsky, Fedor Mikhailovich 1821-1881 .. **NCLC 2, 7, 21, 33, 43, 119; SSC 2, 33, 44; WLC**
See Dostoevsky, Fyodor
See also AAYA 40; DA; DA3; DAB; DAC; DAM MST, NOV; EW 7; EXPN; NFS 3, 8; RGSF 2; RGWL 2, 3; SSFS 8; TWA
Dostoevsky, Fyodor
See Dostoevsky, Fedor Mikhailovich
See also DLB 238; LATS 1; LMFS 1, 2
Doty, M. R.
See Doty, Mark (Alan)

Doty, Mark
See Doty, Mark (Alan)
Doty, Mark (Alan) 1953(?)- .... **CLC 176**
See also AMWS 11; CA 161, 183; CAAE 183; CANR 110
Doty, Mark A.
See Doty, Mark (Alan)
Doughty, Charles M(ontagu) 1843-1926 .... **TCLC 27**
See also CA 115; 178; DLB 19, 57, 174
Douglas, Ellen .... **CLC 73**
See Haxton, Josephine Ayres; Williamson, Ellen Douglas
See also CN 7; CSW
Douglas, Gavin 1475(?)-1522 .... **LC 20**
See also DLB 132; RGEL 2
Douglas, George
See Brown, George Douglas
See also RGEL 2
Douglas, Keith (Castellain) 1920-1944 .... **TCLC 40**
See also BRW 7; CA 160; DLB 27; EWL 3; PAB; RGEL 2
Douglas, Leonard
See Bradbury, Ray (Douglas)
Douglas, Michael
See Crichton, (John) Michael
Douglas, (George) Norman 1868-1952 .... **TCLC 68**
See also BRW 6; CA 119; 157; DLB 34, 195; RGEL 2
Douglas, William
See Brown, George Douglas
Douglass, Frederick 1817(?)-1895 ..... **BLC 1; NCLC 7, 55; WLC**
See also AAYA 48; AFAW 1, 2; AMWC 1; AMWS 3; CDALB 1640-1865; DA; DA3; DAC; DAM MST, MULT; DLB 1, 43, 50, 79, 243; FW; LAIT 2; NCFS 2; RGAL 4; SATA 29
Dourado, (Waldomiro Freitas) Autran 1926- .... **CLC 23, 60**
See also CA 25-28R; 179; CANR 34, 81; DLB 145; HW 2
Dourado, Waldomiro Autran
See Dourado, (Waldomiro Freitas) Autran
See also CA 179
Dove, Rita (Frances) 1952- . **BLCS; CLC 50, 81; PC 6**
See also AAYA 46; AMWS 4; BW 2; CA 109; CAAS 19; CANR 27, 42, 68, 76, 97; CDALBS; CP 7; CSW; CWP; DA3; DAM MULT, POET; DLB 120; EWL 3; EXPP; MTCW 1; PFS 1, 15; RGAL 4
Doveglion
See Villa, Jose Garcia
Dowell, Coleman 1925-1985 .... **CLC 60**
See also CA 25-28R; 117; CANR 10; DLB 130; GLL 2
Dowson, Ernest (Christopher) 1867-1900 .... **TCLC 4**
See also CA 105; 150; DLB 19, 135; RGEL 2
Doyle, A. Conan
See Doyle, Sir Arthur Conan
Doyle, Sir Arthur Conan 1859-1930 .... **SSC 12; TCLC 7; WLC**
See Conan Doyle, Arthur
See also AAYA 14; BRWS 2; CA 104; 122; CDBLB 1890-1914; CMW 4; DA; DA3; DAB; DAC; DAM MST, NOV; DLB 18, 70, 156, 178; EXPS; HGG; LAIT 2; MSW; MTCW 1, 2; RGEL 2; RGSF 2; RHW; SATA 24; SCFW 2; SFW 4; SSFS 2; TEA; WCH; WLIT 4; WYA; YAW
Doyle, Conan
See Doyle, Sir Arthur Conan
Doyle, John
See Graves, Robert (von Ranke)

Doyle, Roddy 1958(?)- .... **CLC 81, 178**
See also AAYA 14; BRWS 5; CA 143; CANR 73; CN 7; DA3; DLB 194

Doyle, Sir A. Conan
See Doyle, Sir Arthur Conan

Dr. A
See Asimov, Isaac; Silverstein, Alvin; Silverstein, Virginia B(arbara Opshelor)

Drabble, Margaret 1939- ...... **CLC 2, 3, 5, 8, 10, 22, 53, 129**
See also BRWS 4; CA 13-16R; CANR 18, 35, 63, 112; CDBLB 1960 to Present; CN 7; CPW; DA3; DAB; DAC; DAM MST, NOV, POP; DLB 14, 155, 231; EWL 3; FW; MTCW 1, 2; RGEL 2; SATA 48; TEA

Drakulic, Slavenka 1949- .... **CLC 173**
See also CA 144; CANR 92

Drakulic-Ilic, Slavenka
See Drakulic, Slavenka

Drapier, M. B.
See Swift, Jonathan

Drayham, James
See Mencken, H(enry) L(ouis)

Drayton, Michael 1563-1631 .... **LC 8**
See also DAM POET; DLB 121; RGEL 2

Dreadstone, Carl
See Campbell, (John) Ramsey

Dreiser, Theodore (Herman Albert) 1871-1945 .... **SSC 30; TCLC 10, 18, 35, 83; WLC**
See also AMW; AMWC 2; AMWR 2; BYA 15, 16; CA 106; 132; CDALB 1865-1917; DA; DA3; DAC; DAM MST, NOV; DLB 9, 12, 102, 137; DLBD 1; EWL 3; LAIT 2; LMFS 2; MTCW 1, 2; NFS 8, 17; RGAL 4; TUS

Drexler, Rosalyn 1926- .... **CLC 2, 6**
See also CA 81-84; CAD; CANR 68; CD 5; CWD

Dreyer, Carl Theodor 1889-1968 ...... **CLC 16**
See also CA 116

Drieu la Rochelle, Pierre(-Eugene) 1893-1945 .... **TCLC 21**
See also CA 117; DLB 72; EWL 3; GFL 1789 to the Present

Drinkwater, John 1882-1937 .... **TCLC 57**
See also CA 109; 149; DLB 10, 19, 149; RGEL 2

Drop Shot
See Cable, George Washington

Droste-Hulshoff, Annette Freiin von 1797-1848 .... **NCLC 3**
See also CDWLB 2; DLB 133; RGSF 2; RGWL 2, 3

Drummond, Walter
See Silverberg, Robert

Drummond, William Henry 1854-1907 .... **TCLC 25**
See also CA 160; DLB 92

Drummond de Andrade, Carlos 1902-1987 .... **CLC 18; TCLC 139**
See Andrade, Carlos Drummond de
See also CA 132; 123; LAW

Drummond of Hawthornden, William 1585-1649 .... **LC 83**
See also DLB 121, 213; RGEL 2

Drury, Allen (Stuart) 1918-1998 .... **CLC 37**
See also CA 57-60; 170; CANR 18, 52; CN 7; INT CANR-18

Dryden, John 1631-1700 ..... **DC 3; LC 3, 21; PC 25; WLC**
See also BRW 2; CDBLB 1660-1789; DA; DAB; DAC; DAM DRAM, MST, POET; DLB 80, 101, 131; EXPP; IDTP; LMFS 1; RGEL 2; TEA; WLIT 3

du Bellay, Joachim 1524-1560 .... **LC 92**
See also GFL Beginnings to 1789; RGWL 2, 3

Duberman, Martin (Bauml) 1930- ..... **CLC 8**
See also CA 1-4R; CAD; CANR 2, 63; CD 5

Dubie, Norman (Evans) 1945- .... **CLC 36**
See also CA 69-72; CANR 12, 115; CP 7; DLB 120; PFS 12

Du Bois, W(illiam) E(dward) B(urghardt) 1868-1963 ..... **BLC 1; CLC 1, 2, 13, 64, 96; HR 2; WLC**
See also AAYA 40; AFAW 1, 2; AMWC 1; AMWS 2; BW 1, 3; CA 85-88; CANR 34, 82; CDALB 1865-1917; DA; DA3; DAC; DAM MST, MULT, NOV; DLB 47, 50, 91, 246, 284; EWL 3; EXPP; LAIT 2; LMFS 2; MTCW 1, 2; NCFS 1; PFS 13; RGAL 4; SATA 42

Dubus, Andre 1936-1999 ..... **CLC 13, 36, 97; SSC 15**
See also AMWS 7; CA 21-24R; 177; CANR 17; CN 7; CSW; DLB 130; INT CANR-17; RGAL 4; SSFS 10

Duca Minimo
See D'Annunzio, Gabriele

Ducharme, Rejean 1941- .... **CLC 74**
See also CA 165; DLB 60

Duchen, Claire .... **CLC 65**

Duclos, Charles Pinot- 1704-1772 .... **LC 1**
See also GFL Beginnings to 1789

Dudek, Louis 1918-2001 .... **CLC 11, 19**
See also CA 45-48; 215; CAAS 14; CANR 1; CP 7; DLB 88

Duerrenmatt, Friedrich 1921-1990 ... **CLC 1, 4, 8, 11, 15, 43, 102**
See Durrenmatt, Friedrich
See also CA 17-20R; CANR 33; CMW 4; DAM DRAM; DLB 69, 124; MTCW 1, 2

Duffy, Bruce 1953(?)- .... **CLC 50**
See also CA 172

Duffy, Maureen 1933- .... **CLC 37**
See also CA 25-28R; CANR 33, 68; CBD; CN 7; CP 7; CWD; CWP; DFS 15; DLB 14; FW; MTCW 1

Du Fu
See Tu Fu
See also RGWL 2, 3

Dugan, Alan 1923-2003 .... **CLC 2, 6**
See also CA 81-84; CANR 119; CP 7; DLB 5; PFS 10

du Gard, Roger Martin
See Martin du Gard, Roger

Duhamel, Georges 1884-1966 .... **CLC 8**
See also CA 81-84; 25-28R; CANR 35; DLB 65; EWL 3; GFL 1789 to the Present; MTCW 1

Dujardin, Edouard (Emile Louis) 1861-1949 .... **TCLC 13**
See also CA 109; DLB 123

Duke, Raoul
See Thompson, Hunter S(tockton)

Dulles, John Foster 1888-1959 .... **TCLC 72**
See also CA 115; 149

Dumas, Alexandre (pere) 1802-1870 .... **NCLC 11, 71; WLC**
See also AAYA 22; BYA 3; DA; DA3; DAB; DAC; DAM MST, NOV; DLB 119, 192; EW 6; GFL 1789 to the Present; LAIT 1, 2; NFS 14; RGWL 2, 3; SATA 18; TWA; WCH

Dumas, Alexandre (fils) 1824-1895 ...... **DC 1; NCLC 9**
See also DLB 192; GFL 1789 to the Present; RGWL 2, 3

Dumas, Claudine
See Malzberg, Barry N(athaniel)

Dumas, Henry L. 1934-1968 .... **CLC 6, 62**
See also BW 1; CA 85-88; DLB 41; RGAL 4

du Maurier, Daphne 1907-1989 .. **CLC 6, 11, 59; SSC 18**
See also AAYA 37; BPFB 1; BRWS 3; CA 5-8R; 128; CANR 6, 55; CMW 4; CPW; DA3; DAB; DAC; DAM MST, POP; DLB 191; HGG; LAIT 3; MSW; MTCW 1, 2; NFS 12; RGEL 2; RGSF 2; RHW; SATA 27; SATA-Obit 60; SSFS 14, 16; TEA

Du Maurier, George 1834-1896 ..... **NCLC 86**
See also DLB 153, 178; RGEL 2

Dunbar, Paul Laurence 1872-1906 ... **BLC 1; PC 5; SSC 8; TCLC 2, 12; WLC**
See also AFAW 1, 2; AMWS 2; BW 1, 3; CA 104; 124; CANR 79; CDALB 1865-1917; DA; DA3; DAC; DAM MST, MULT, POET; DLB 50, 54, 78; EXPP; RGAL 4; SATA 34

Dunbar, William 1460(?)-1520(?) .... **LC 20**
See also BRWS 8; DLB 132, 146; RGEL 2

Dunbar-Nelson, Alice .... **HR 2**
See Nelson, Alice Ruth Moore Dunbar

Duncan, Dora Angela
See Duncan, Isadora

Duncan, Isadora 1877(?)-1927 .... **TCLC 68**
See also CA 118; 149

Duncan, Lois 1934- .... **CLC 26**
See also AAYA 4, 34; BYA 6, 8; CA 1-4R; CANR 2, 23, 36, 111; CLR 29; JRDA; MAICYA 1, 2; MAICYAS 1; SAAS 2; SATA 1, 36, 75, 133, 141; WYA; YAW

Duncan, Robert (Edward) 1919-1988 .... **CLC 1, 2, 4, 7, 15, 41, 55; PC 2**
See also BG 2; CA 9-12R; 124; CANR 28, 62; DAM POET; DLB 5, 16, 193; EWL 3; MTCW 1, 2; PFS 13; RGAL 4; WP

Duncan, Sara Jeannette 1861-1922 .... **TCLC 60**
See also CA 157; DLB 92

Dunlap, William 1766-1839 .... **NCLC 2**
See also DLB 30, 37, 59; RGAL 4

Dunn, Douglas (Eaglesham) 1942- .... **CLC 6, 40**
See also CA 45-48; CANR 2, 33; CP 7; DLB 40; MTCW 1

Dunn, Katherine (Karen) 1945- .... **CLC 71**
See also CA 33-36R; CANR 72; HGG; MTCW 1

Dunn, Stephen (Elliott) 1939- .... **CLC 36**
See also AMWS 11; CA 33-36R; CANR 12, 48, 53, 105; CP 7; DLB 105

Dunne, Finley Peter 1867-1936 ...... **TCLC 28**
See also CA 108; 178; DLB 11, 23; RGAL 4

Dunne, John Gregory 1932- .... **CLC 28**
See also CA 25-28R; CANR 14, 50; CN 7; DLBY 1980

Dunsany, Lord .... **TCLC 2, 59**
See Dunsany, Edward John Moreton Drax Plunkett
See also DLB 77, 153, 156, 255; FANT; IDTP; RGEL 2; SFW 4; SUFW 1

Dunsany, Edward John Moreton Drax Plunkett 1878-1957
See Dunsany, Lord
See also CA 104; 148; DLB 10; MTCW 1

Duns Scotus, John 1266(?)-1308 ... **CMLC 59**
See also DLB 115

du Perry, Jean
See Simenon, Georges (Jacques Christian)

Durang, Christopher (Ferdinand) 1949- .... **CLC 27, 38**
See also CA 105; CAD; CANR 50, 76; CD 5; MTCW 1

Duras, Marguerite 1914-1996 . **CLC 3, 6, 11, 20, 34, 40, 68, 100; SSC 40**
See Donnadieu, Marguerite
See also BPFB 1; CA 25-28R; 151; CANR 50; CWW 2; DLB 83; EWL 3; GFL 1789 to the Present; IDFW 4; MTCW 1, 2; RGWL 2, 3; TWA

Durban, (Rosa) Pam 1947- .... **CLC 39**
See also CA 123; CANR 98; CSW

Durcan, Paul 1944- .... **CLC 43, 70**
See also CA 134; CANR 123; CP 7; DAM POET; EWL 3

Durfey, Thomas 1653-1723 .... **LC 94**
See also DLB 80; RGEL 2

Durkheim, Emile 1858-1917 .... **TCLC 55**

Durrell, Lawrence (George)
1912-1990 ..... **CLC 1, 4, 6, 8, 13, 27, 41**
See also BPFB 1; BRWS 1; CA 9-12R; 132; CANR 40, 77; CDBLB 1945-1960; DAM NOV; DLB 15, 27, 204; DLBY 1990; EWL 3; MTCW 1, 2; RGEL 2; SFW 4; TEA

Durrenmatt, Friedrich
See Duerrenmatt, Friedrich
See also CDWLB 2; EW 13; EWL 3; RGWL 2, 3

Dutt, Michael Madhusudan
1824-1873 .... **NCLC 118**

Dutt, Toru 1856-1877 .... **NCLC 29**
See also DLB 240

Dwight, Timothy 1752-1817 .... **NCLC 13**
See also DLB 37; RGAL 4

Dworkin, Andrea 1946- .... **CLC 43, 123**
See also CA 77-80; CAAS 21; CANR 16, 39, 76, 96; FW; GLL 1; INT CANR-16; MTCW 1, 2

Dwyer, Deanna
See Koontz, Dean R(ay)

Dwyer, K. R.
See Koontz, Dean R(ay)

Dybek, Stuart 1942- .... **CLC 114; SSC 55**
See also CA 97-100; CANR 39; DLB 130

Dye, Richard
See De Voto, Bernard (Augustine)

Dyer, Geoff 1958- .... **CLC 149**
See also CA 125; CANR 88

Dyer, George 1755-1841 .... **NCLC 129**
See also DLB 93

Dylan, Bob 1941- .... **CLC 3, 4, 6, 12, 77; PC 37**
See also CA 41-44R; CANR 108; CP 7; DLB 16

Dyson, John 1943- .... **CLC 70**
See also CA 144

Dzyubin, Eduard Georgievich 1895-1934
See Bagritsky, Eduard
See also CA 170

E. V. L.
See Lucas, E(dward) V(errall)

Eagleton, Terence (Francis) 1943- .. **CLC 63, 132**
See also CA 57-60; CANR 7, 23, 68, 115; DLB 242; LMFS 2; MTCW 1, 2

Eagleton, Terry
See Eagleton, Terence (Francis)

Early, Jack
See Scoppettone, Sandra
See also GLL 1

East, Michael
See West, Morris L(anglo)

Eastaway, Edward
See Thomas, (Philip) Edward

Eastlake, William (Derry)
1917-1997 .... **CLC 8**
See also CA 5-8R; 158; CAAS 1; CANR 5, 63; CN 7; DLB 6, 206; INT CANR-5; TCWW 2

Eastman, Charles A(lexander)
1858-1939 .... **NNAL; TCLC 55**
See also CA 179; CANR 91; DAM MULT; DLB 175; YABC 1

Eaton, Edith Maude 1865-1914 .... **AAL**
See Far, Sui Sin
See also CA 154; DLB 221; FW

Eaton, Winnifred 1875-1954 .... **AAL**
See also DLB 221; RGAL 4

Eberhart, Richard (Ghormley)
1904- .... **CLC 3, 11, 19, 56**
See also AMW; CA 1-4R; CANR 2; CDALB 1941-1968; CP 7; DAM POET; DLB 48; MTCW 1; RGAL 4

Eberstadt, Fernanda 1960- .... **CLC 39**
See also CA 136; CANR 69

Echegaray (y Eizaguirre), Jose (Maria Waldo) 1832-1916 .... **HLCS 1; TCLC 4**
See also CA 104; CANR 32; EWL 3; HW 1; MTCW 1

Echeverria, (Jose) Esteban (Antonino)
1805-1851 .... **NCLC 18**
See also LAW

Echo
See Proust, (Valentin-Louis-George-Eugene) Marcel

Eckert, Allan W. 1931- .... **CLC 17**
See also AAYA 18; BYA 2; CA 13-16R; CANR 14, 45; INT CANR-14; MAICYA 2; MAICYAS 1; SAAS 21; SATA 29, 91; SATA-Brief 27

Eckhart, Meister 1260(?)-1327(?) ... **CMLC 9**
See also DLB 115; LMFS 1

Eckmar, F. R.
See de Hartog, Jan

Eco, Umberto 1932- .... **CLC 28, 60, 142**
See also BEST 90:1; BPFB 1; CA 77-80; CANR 12, 33, 55, 110; CPW; CWW 2; DA3; DAM NOV, POP; DLB 196, 242; EWL 3; MSW; MTCW 1, 2; RGWL 3

Eddison, E(ric) R(ucker)
1882-1945 .... **TCLC 15**
See also CA 109; 156; DLB 255; FANT; SFW 4; SUFW 1

Eddy, Mary (Ann Morse) Baker
1821-1910 .... **TCLC 71**
See also CA 113; 174

Edel, (Joseph) Leon 1907-1997 .. **CLC 29, 34**
See also CA 1-4R; 161; CANR 1, 22, 112; DLB 103; INT CANR-22

Eden, Emily 1797-1869 .... **NCLC 10**

Edgar, David 1948- .... **CLC 42**
See also CA 57-60; CANR 12, 61, 112; CBD; CD 5; DAM DRAM; DFS 15; DLB 13, 233; MTCW 1

Edgerton, Clyde (Carlyle) 1944- ...... **CLC 39**
See also AAYA 17; CA 118; 134; CANR 64; CSW; DLB 278; INT 134; YAW

Edgeworth, Maria 1768-1849 .... **NCLC 1, 51**
See also BRWS 3; DLB 116, 159, 163; FW; RGEL 2; SATA 21; TEA; WLIT 3

Edmonds, Paul
See Kuttner, Henry

Edmonds, Walter D(umaux)
1903-1998 .... **CLC 35**
See also BYA 2; CA 5-8R; CANR 2; CWRI 5; DLB 9; LAIT 1; MAICYA 1, 2; RHW; SAAS 4; SATA 1, 27; SATA-Obit 99

Edmondson, Wallace
See Ellison, Harlan (Jay)

Edson, Russell 1935- .... **CLC 13**
See also CA 33-36R; CANR 115; DLB 244; WP

Edwards, Bronwen Elizabeth
See Rose, Wendy

Edwards, G(erald) B(asil)
1899-1976 .... **CLC 25**
See also CA 201; 110

Edwards, Gus 1939- .... **CLC 43**
See also CA 108; INT 108

Edwards, Jonathan 1703-1758 .... **LC 7, 54**
See also AMW; DA; DAC; DAM MST; DLB 24, 270; RGAL 4; TUS

Edwards, Sarah Pierpont 1710-1758 .. **LC 87**
See also DLB 200

Efron, Marina Ivanovna Tsvetaeva
See Tsvetaeva (Efron), Marina (Ivanovna)

Egoyan, Atom 1960- .... **CLC 151**
See also CA 157

Ehle, John (Marsden, Jr.) 1925- ...... **CLC 27**
See also CA 9-12R; CSW

Ehrenbourg, Ilya (Grigoryevich)
See Ehrenburg, Ilya (Grigoryevich)

Ehrenburg, Ilya (Grigoryevich)
1891-1967 .... **CLC 18, 34, 62**
See Erenburg, Il'ia Grigor'evich
See also CA 102; 25-28R; EWL 3

Ehrenburg, Ilyo (Grigoryevich)
See Ehrenburg, Ilya (Grigoryevich)

Ehrenreich, Barbara 1941- .... **CLC 110**
See also BEST 90:4; CA 73-76; CANR 16, 37, 62, 117; DLB 246; FW; MTCW 1, 2

Eich, Gunter
See Eich, Gunter
See also RGWL 2, 3

Eich, Gunter 1907-1972 .... **CLC 15**
See Eich, Gunter
See also CA 111; 93-96; DLB 69, 124; EWL 3

Eichendorff, Joseph 1788-1857 .... **NCLC 8**
See also DLB 90; RGWL 2, 3

Eigner, Larry .... **CLC 9**
See Eigner, Laurence (Joel)
See also CAAS 23; DLB 5; WP

Eigner, Laurence (Joel) 1927-1996
See Eigner, Larry
See also CA 9-12R; 151; CANR 6, 84; CP 7; DLB 193

Einhard c. 770-840 .... **CMLC 50**
See also DLB 148

Einstein, Albert 1879-1955 .... **TCLC 65**
See also CA 121; 133; MTCW 1, 2

Eiseley, Loren
See Eiseley, Loren Corey
See also DLB 275

Eiseley, Loren Corey 1907-1977 .... **CLC 7**
See Eiseley, Loren
See also AAYA 5; ANW; CA 1-4R; 73-76; CANR 6; DLBD 17

Eisenstadt, Jill 1963- .... **CLC 50**
See also CA 140

Eisenstein, Sergei (Mikhailovich)
1898-1948 .... **TCLC 57**
See also CA 114; 149

Eisner, Simon
See Kornbluth, C(yril) M.

Ekeloef, (Bengt) Gunnar
1907-1968 .... **CLC 27; PC 23**
See Ekelof, (Bengt) Gunnar
See also CA 123; 25-28R; DAM POET

Ekelof, (Bengt) Gunnar 1907-1968
See Ekeloef, (Bengt) Gunnar
See also DLB 259; EW 12; EWL 3

Ekelund, Vilhelm 1880-1949 .... **TCLC 75**
See also CA 189; EWL 3

Ekwensi, C. O. D.
See Ekwensi, Cyprian (Odiatu Duaka)

Ekwensi, Cyprian (Odiatu Duaka)
1921- .... **BLC 1; CLC 4**
See also AFW; BW 2, 3; CA 29-32R; CANR 18, 42, 74; CDWLB 3; CN 7; CWRI 5; DAM MULT; DLB 117; EWL 3; MTCW 1, 2; RGEL 2; SATA 66; WLIT 2

Elaine .... **TCLC 18**
See Leverson, Ada Esther

El Crummo
See Crumb, R(obert)

Elder, Lonne III 1931-1996 ..... **BLC 1; DC 8**
See also BW 1, 3; CA 81-84; 152; CAD; CANR 25; DAM MULT; DLB 7, 38, 44

Eleanor of Aquitaine 1122-1204 ... **CMLC 39**

Elia
See Lamb, Charles

Eliade, Mircea 1907-1986 .... **CLC 19**
See also CA 65-68; 119; CANR 30, 62; CDWLB 4; DLB 220; EWL 3; MTCW 1; RGWL 3; SFW 4

Eliot, A. D.
See Jewett, (Theodora) Sarah Orne

Eliot, Alice
See Jewett, (Theodora) Sarah Orne

Eliot, Dan
See Silverberg, Robert

Eliot, George 1819-1880 ...... **NCLC 4, 13, 23, 41, 49, 89, 118; PC 20; WLC**
See also BRW 5; BRWC 1, 2; BRWR 2; CDBLB 1832-1890; CN 7; CPW; DA; DA3; DAB; DAC; DAM MST, NOV; DLB 21, 35, 55; LATS 1; LMFS 1; NFS 17; RGEL 2; RGSF 2; SSFS 8; TEA; WLIT 3

Eliot, John 1604-1690 .... **LC 5**
See also DLB 24

Eliot, T(homas) S(tearns) 1888-1965 ...... **CLC 1, 2, 3, 6, 9, 10, 13, 15, 24, 34, 41, 55, 57, 113; PC 5, 31; WLC**
See also AAYA 28; AMW; AMWC 1; AMWR 1; BRW 7; BRWR 2; CA 5-8R; 25-28R; CANR 41; CDALB 1929-1941; DA; DA3; DAB; DAC; DAM DRAM, MST, POET; DFS 4, 13; DLB 7, 10, 45, 63, 245; DLBY 1988; EWL 3; EXPP; LAIT 3; LATS 1; LMFS 2; MTCW 1, 2; NCFS 5; PAB; PFS 1, 7; RGAL 4; RGEL 2; TUS; WLIT 4; WP

Elizabeth 1866-1941 .... **TCLC 41**

Elkin, Stanley L(awrence) 1930-1995 .. **CLC 4, 6, 9, 14, 27, 51, 91; SSC 12**
See also AMWS 6; BPFB 1; CA 9-12R; 148; CANR 8, 46; CN 7; CPW; DAM NOV, POP; DLB 2, 28, 218, 278; DLBY 1980; EWL 3; INT CANR-8; MTCW 1, 2; RGAL 4

Elledge, Scott .... **CLC 34**

Elliott, Don
See Silverberg, Robert

Elliott, George P(aul) 1918-1980 .... **CLC 2**
See also CA 1-4R; 97-100; CANR 2; DLB 244

Elliott, Janice 1931-1995 .... **CLC 47**
See also CA 13-16R; CANR 8, 29, 84; CN 7; DLB 14; SATA 119

Elliott, Sumner Locke 1917-1991 ..... **CLC 38**
See also CA 5-8R; 134; CANR 2, 21; DLB 289

Elliott, William
See Bradbury, Ray (Douglas)

Ellis, A. E. .... **CLC 7**

Ellis, Alice Thomas .... **CLC 40**
See Haycraft, Anna (Margaret)
See also DLB 194; MTCW 1

Ellis, Bret Easton 1964- ...... **CLC 39, 71, 117**
See also AAYA 2, 43; CA 118; 123; CANR 51, 74; CN 7; CPW; DA3; DAM POP; HGG; INT CA-123; MTCW 1; NFS 11

Ellis, (Henry) Havelock 1859-1939 .... **TCLC 14**
See also CA 109; 169; DLB 190

Ellis, Landon
See Ellison, Harlan (Jay)

Ellis, Trey 1962- .... **CLC 55**
See also CA 146; CANR 92

Ellison, Harlan (Jay) 1934- ... **CLC 1, 13, 42, 139; SSC 14**
See also AAYA 29; BPFB 1; BYA 14; CA 5-8R; CANR 5, 46, 115; CPW; DAM POP; DLB 8; HGG; INT CANR-5; MTCW 1, 2; SCFW 2; SFW 4; SSFS 13, 14, 15; SUFW 1, 2

Ellison, Ralph (Waldo) 1914-1994 .... **BLC 1; CLC 1, 3, 11, 54, 86, 114; SSC 26; WLC**
See also AAYA 19; AFAW 1, 2; AMWC 2; AMWR 2; AMWS 2; BPFB 1; BW 1, 3; BYA 2; CA 9-12R; 145; CANR 24, 53; CDALB 1941-1968; CSW; DA; DA3; DAB; DAC; DAM MST, MULT, NOV; DLB 2, 76, 227; DLBY 1994; EWL 3; EXPN; EXPS; LAIT 4; MTCW 1, 2; NCFS 3; NFS 2; RGAL 4; RGSF 2; SSFS 1, 11; YAW

Ellmann, Lucy (Elizabeth) 1956- ..... **CLC 61**
See also CA 128

Ellmann, Richard (David) 1918-1987 .... **CLC 50**
See also BEST 89:2; CA 1-4R; 122; CANR 2, 28, 61; DLB 103; DLBY 1987; MTCW 1, 2

Elman, Richard (Martin) 1934-1997 .... **CLC 19**
See also CA 17-20R; 163; CAAS 3; CANR 47

Elron
See Hubbard, L(afayette) Ron(ald)

Eluard, Paul .... **PC 38; TCLC 7, 41**
See Grindel, Eugene
See also EWL 3; GFL 1789 to the Present; RGWL 2, 3

Elyot, Thomas 1490(?)-1546 .... **LC 11**
See also DLB 136; RGEL 2

Elytis, Odysseus 1911-1996 .... **CLC 15, 49, 100; PC 21**
See Alepoudelis, Odysseus
See also CA 102; 151; CANR 94; CWW 2; DAM POET; EW 13; EWL 3; MTCW 1, 2; RGWL 2, 3

Emecheta, (Florence Onye) Buchi 1944- .... **BLC 2; CLC 14, 48, 128**
See also AFW; BW 2, 3; CA 81-84; CANR 27, 81; CDWLB 3; CN 7; CWRI 5; DA3; DAM MULT; DLB 117; EWL 3; FW; MTCW 1, 2; NFS 12, 14; SATA 66; WLIT 2

Emerson, Mary Moody 1774-1863 .... **NCLC 66**

Emerson, Ralph Waldo 1803-1882 . **NCLC 1, 38, 98; PC 18; WLC**
See also AMW; ANW; CDALB 1640-1865; DA; DA3; DAB; DAC; DAM MST, POET; DLB 1, 59, 73, 183, 223, 270; EXPP; LAIT 2; LMFS 1; NCFS 3; PFS 4, 17; RGAL 4; TUS; WP

Eminescu, Mihail 1850-1889 .. **NCLC 33, 131**

Empedocles 5th cent. B.C.- .... **CMLC 50**
See also DLB 176

Empson, William 1906-1984 ... **CLC 3, 8, 19, 33, 34**
See also BRWS 2; CA 17-20R; 112; CANR 31, 61; DLB 20; EWL 3; MTCW 1, 2; RGEL 2

Enchi, Fumiko (Ueda) 1905-1986 ..... **CLC 31**
See Enchi Fumiko
See also CA 129; 121; FW; MJW

Enchi Fumiko
See Enchi, Fumiko (Ueda)
See also DLB 182; EWL 3

Ende, Michael (Andreas Helmuth) 1929-1995 .... **CLC 31**
See also BYA 5; CA 118; 124; 149; CANR 36, 110; CLR 14; DLB 75; MAICYA 1, 2; MAICYAS 1; SATA 61, 130; SATA-Brief 42; SATA-Obit 86

Endo, Shusaku 1923-1996 ..... **CLC 7, 14, 19, 54, 99; SSC 48**
See Endo Shusaku
See also CA 29-32R; 153; CANR 21, 54; DA3; DAM NOV; MTCW 1, 2; RGSF 2; RGWL 2, 3

Endo Shusaku
See Endo, Shusaku
See also DLB 182; EWL 3

Engel, Marian 1933-1985 .... **CLC 36; TCLC 137**
See also CA 25-28R; CANR 12; DLB 53; FW; INT CANR-12

Engelhardt, Frederick
See Hubbard, L(afayette) Ron(ald)

Engels, Friedrich 1820-1895 .. **NCLC 85, 114**
See also DLB 129; LATS 1

Enright, D(ennis) J(oseph) 1920-2002 .... **CLC 4, 8, 31**
See also CA 1-4R; 211; CANR 1, 42, 83; CP 7; DLB 27; EWL 3; SATA 25; SATA-Obit 140

Enzensberger, Hans Magnus 1929- .... **CLC 43; PC 28**
See also CA 116; 119; CANR 103; EWL 3

Ephron, Nora 1941- .... **CLC 17, 31**
See also AAYA 35; AITN 2; CA 65-68; CANR 12, 39, 83

Epicurus 341B.C.-270B.C. .... **CMLC 21**
See also DLB 176

Epsilon
See Betjeman, John

Epstein, Daniel Mark 1948- .... **CLC 7**
See also CA 49-52; CANR 2, 53, 90

Epstein, Jacob 1956- .... **CLC 19**
See also CA 114

Epstein, Jean 1897-1953 .... **TCLC 92**

Epstein, Joseph 1937- .... **CLC 39**
See also CA 112; 119; CANR 50, 65, 117

Epstein, Leslie 1938- .... **CLC 27**
See also AMWS 12; CA 73-76; CAAE 215; CAAS 12; CANR 23, 69

Equiano, Olaudah 1745(?)-1797 . **BLC 2; LC 16**
See also AFAW 1, 2; CDWLB 3; DAM MULT; DLB 37, 50; WLIT 2

Erasmus, Desiderius 1469(?)-1536 ..... **LC 16, 93**
See also DLB 136; EW 2; LMFS 1; RGWL 2, 3; TWA

Erdman, Paul E(mil) 1932- .... **CLC 25**
See also AITN 1; CA 61-64; CANR 13, 43, 84

Erdrich, Louise 1954- .... **CLC 39, 54, 120, 176; NNAL; PC 52**
See also AAYA 10, 47; AMWS 4; BEST 89:1; BPFB 1; CA 114; CANR 41, 62, 118; CDALBS; CN 7; CP 7; CPW; CWP; DA3; DAM MULT, NOV, POP; DLB 152, 175, 206; EWL 3; EXPP; LAIT 5; LATS 1; MTCW 1; NFS 5; PFS 14; RGAL 4; SATA 94, 141; SSFS 14; TCWW 2

Erenburg, Ilya (Grigoryevich)
See Ehrenburg, Ilya (Grigoryevich)

Erickson, Stephen Michael 1950-
See Erickson, Steve
See also CA 129; SFW 4

Erickson, Steve .... **CLC 64**
See Erickson, Stephen Michael
See also CANR 60, 68; SUFW 2

Erickson, Walter
See Fast, Howard (Melvin)

Ericson, Walter
See Fast, Howard (Melvin)

Eriksson, Buntel
See Bergman, (Ernst) Ingmar

Ernaux, Annie 1940- .... **CLC 88**
See also CA 147; CANR 93; NCFS 3, 5

Erskine, John 1879-1951 .... **TCLC 84**
See also CA 112; 159; DLB 9, 102; FANT
Eschenbach, Wolfram von
See Wolfram von Eschenbach
See also RGWL 3
Eseki, Bruno
See Mphahlele, Ezekiel
Esenin, Sergei (Alexandrovich)
1895-1925 .... **TCLC 4**
See Yesenin, Sergey
See also CA 104; RGWL 2, 3
Eshleman, Clayton 1935- .... **CLC 7**
See also CA 33-36R; CAAE 212; CAAS 6;
CANR 93; CP 7; DLB 5
Espriella, Don Manuel Alvarez
See Southey, Robert
Espriu, Salvador 1913-1985 .... **CLC 9**
See also CA 154; 115; DLB 134; EWL 3
Espronceda, Jose de 1808-1842 ..... **NCLC 39**
Esquivel, Laura 1951(?)- ... **CLC 141; HLCS 1**
See also AAYA 29; CA 143; CANR 68, 113;
DA3; DNFS 2; LAIT 3; LMFS 2; MTCW
1; NFS 5; WLIT 1
Esse, James
See Stephens, James
Esterbrook, Tom
See Hubbard, L(afayette) Ron(ald)
Estleman, Loren D. 1952- .... **CLC 48**
See also AAYA 27; CA 85-88; CANR 27,
74; CMW 4; CPW; DA3; DAM NOV,
POP; DLB 226; INT CANR-27; MTCW
1, 2
Etherege, Sir George 1636-1692 .... **LC 78**
See also BRW 2; DAM DRAM; DLB 80;
PAB; RGEL 2
Euclid 306B.C.-283B.C. .... **CMLC 25**
Eugenides, Jeffrey 1960(?)- .... **CLC 81**
See also AAYA 51; CA 144; CANR 120
Euripides c. 484B.C.-406B.C. .... **CMLC 23, 51; DC 4; WLCS**
See also AW 1; CDWLB 1; DA; DA3;
DAB; DAC; DAM DRAM, MST; DFS 1,
4, 6; DLB 176; LAIT 1; LMFS 1; RGWL
2, 3
Evan, Evin
See Faust, Frederick (Schiller)
Evans, Caradoc 1878-1945 ... **SSC 43; TCLC 85**
See also DLB 162
Evans, Evan
See Faust, Frederick (Schiller)
See also TCWW 2
Evans, Marian
See Eliot, George
Evans, Mary Ann
See Eliot, George
Evarts, Esther
See Benson, Sally
Everett, Percival
See Everett, Percival L.
See also CSW
Everett, Percival L. 1956- .... **CLC 57**
See Everett, Percival
See also BW 2; CA 129; CANR 94
Everson, R(onald) G(ilmour)
1903-1992 .... **CLC 27**
See also CA 17-20R; DLB 88
Everson, William (Oliver)
1912-1994 .... **CLC 1, 5, 14**
See also BG 2; CA 9-12R; 145; CANR 20;
DLB 5, 16, 212; MTCW 1
Evtushenko, Evgenii Aleksandrovich
See Yevtushenko, Yevgeny (Alexandrovich)
See also RGWL 2, 3
Ewart, Gavin (Buchanan)
1916-1995 .... **CLC 13, 46**
See also BRWS 7; CA 89-92; 150; CANR
17, 46; CP 7; DLB 40; MTCW 1

Ewers, Hanns Heinz 1871-1943 ..... **TCLC 12**
See also CA 109; 149
Ewing, Frederick R.
See Sturgeon, Theodore (Hamilton)
Exley, Frederick (Earl) 1929-1992 .... **CLC 6, 11**
See also AITN 2; BPFB 1; CA 81-84; 138;
CANR 117; DLB 143; DLBY 1981
Eynhardt, Guillermo
See Quiroga, Horacio (Sylvestre)
Ezekiel, Nissim 1924- .... **CLC 61**
See also CA 61-64; CP 7; EWL 3
Ezekiel, Tish O'Dowd 1943- .... **CLC 34**
See also CA 129
Fadeev, Aleksandr Aleksandrovich
See Bulgya, Alexander Alexandrovich
See also DLB 272
Fadeev, Alexandr Alexandrovich
See Bulgya, Alexander Alexandrovich
See also EWL 3
Fadeyev, A.
See Bulgya, Alexander Alexandrovich
Fadeyev, Alexander .... **TCLC 53**
See Bulgya, Alexander Alexandrovich
Fagen, Donald 1948- .... **CLC 26**
Fainzilberg, Ilya Arnoldovich 1897-1937
See Ilf, Ilya
See also CA 120; 165
Fair, Ronald L. 1932- .... **CLC 18**
See also BW 1; CA 69-72; CANR 25; DLB 33
Fairbairn, Roger
See Carr, John Dickson
Fairbairns, Zoe (Ann) 1948- .... **CLC 32**
See also CA 103; CANR 21, 85; CN 7
Fairfield, Flora
See Alcott, Louisa May
Fairman, Paul W. 1916-1977
See Queen, Ellery
See also CA 114; SFW 4
Falco, Gian
See Papini, Giovanni
Falconer, James
See Kirkup, James
Falconer, Kenneth
See Kornbluth, C(yril) M.
Falkland, Samuel
See Heijermans, Herman
Fallaci, Oriana 1930- .... **CLC 11, 110**
See also CA 77-80; CANR 15, 58; FW;
MTCW 1
Faludi, Susan 1959- .... **CLC 140**
See also CA 138; FW; MTCW 1; NCFS 3
Faludy, George 1913- .... **CLC 42**
See also CA 21-24R
Faludy, Gyoergy
See Faludy, George
Fanon, Frantz 1925-1961 .... **BLC 2; CLC 74**
See also BW 1; CA 116; 89-92; DAM
MULT; LMFS 2; WLIT 2
Fanshawe, Ann 1625-1680 .... **LC 11**
Fante, John (Thomas) 1911-1983 .... **CLC 60; SSC 65**
See also AMWS 11; CA 69-72; 109; CANR
23, 104; DLB 130; DLBY 1983
Far, Sui Sin .... **SSC 62**
See Eaton, Edith Maude
See also SSFS 4
Farah, Nuruddin 1945- ...... **BLC 2; CLC 53, 137**
See also AFW; BW 2, 3; CA 106; CANR
81; CDWLB 3; CN 7; DAM MULT; DLB
125; EWL 3; WLIT 2
Fargue, Leon-Paul 1876(?)-1947 .... **TCLC 11**
See also CA 109; CANR 107; DLB 258;
EWL 3
Farigoule, Louis
See Romains, Jules

Farina, Richard 1936(?)-1966 .... **CLC 9**
See also CA 81-84; 25-28R
Farley, Walter (Lorimer)
1915-1989 .... **CLC 17**
See also BYA 14; CA 17-20R; CANR 8,
29, 84; DLB 22; JRDA; MAICYA 1, 2;
SATA 2, 43, 132; YAW
Farmer, Philip Jose 1918- .... **CLC 1, 19**
See also AAYA 28; BPFB 1; CA 1-4R;
CANR 4, 35, 111; DLB 8; MTCW 1;
SATA 93; SCFW 2; SFW 4
Farquhar, George 1677-1707 .... **LC 21**
See also BRW 2; DAM DRAM; DLB 84;
RGEL 2
Farrell, J(ames) G(ordon)
1935-1979 .... **CLC 6**
See also CA 73-76; 89-92; CANR 36; DLB
14, 271; MTCW 1; RGEL 2; RHW; WLIT 4
Farrell, James T(homas) 1904-1979 . **CLC 1, 4, 8, 11, 66; SSC 28**
See also AMW; BPFB 1; CA 5-8R; 89-92;
CANR 9, 61; DLB 4, 9, 86; DLBD 2;
EWL 3; MTCW 1, 2; RGAL 4
Farrell, Warren (Thomas) 1943- .... **CLC 70**
See also CA 146; CANR 120
Farren, Richard J.
See Betjeman, John
Farren, Richard M.
See Betjeman, John
Fassbinder, Rainer Werner
1946-1982 .... **CLC 20**
See also CA 93-96; 106; CANR 31
Fast, Howard (Melvin) 1914-2003 .. **CLC 23, 131**
See also AAYA 16; BPFB 1; CA 1-4R, 181;
214; CAAE 181; CAAS 18; CANR 1, 33,
54, 75, 98; CMW 4; CN 7; CPW; DAM
NOV; INT CANR-33; LATS 1;
MTCW 1; RHW; SATA 7; SATA-Essay
107; TCWW 2; YAW
Faulcon, Robert
See Holdstock, Robert P.
Faulkner, William (Cuthbert)
1897-1962 .... **CLC 1, 3, 6, 8, 9, 11, 14, 18, 28, 52, 68; SSC 1, 35, 42; TCLC 141; WLC**
See also AAYA 7; AMW; AMWR 1; BPFB
1; BYA 5, 15; CA 81-84; CANR 33;
CDALB 1929-1941; DA; DA3; DAB;
DAC; DAM MST, NOV; DLB 9, 11, 44,
102; DLBD 2; DLBY 1986, 1997; EWL
3; EXPN; EXPS; LAIT 2; LATS 1; LMFS
2; MTCW 1, 2; NFS 4, 8, 13; RGAL 4;
RGSF 2; SSFS 2, 5, 6, 12; TUS
Fauset, Jessie Redmon
1882(?)-1961 .. **BLC 2; CLC 19, 54; HR 2**
See also AFAW 2; BW 1; CA 109; CANR
83; DAM MULT; DLB 51; FW; LMFS 2;
MAWW
Faust, Frederick (Schiller)
1892-1944(?) .... **TCLC 49**
See Austin, Frank; Brand, Max; Challis,
George; Dawson, Peter; Dexter, Martin;
Evans, Evan; Frederick, John; Frost, Frederick; Manning, David; Silver, Nicholas
See also CA 108; 152; DAM POP; DLB
256; TUS
Faust, Irvin 1924- .... **CLC 8**
See also CA 33-36R; CANR 28, 67; CN 7;
DLB 2, 28, 218, 278; DLBY 1980
Faustino, Domingo 1811-1888 ...... **NCLC 123**
Fawkes, Guy
See Benchley, Robert (Charles)
Fearing, Kenneth (Flexner)
1902-1961 .... **CLC 51**
See also CA 93-96; CANR 59; CMW 4;
DLB 9; RGAL 4

Fecamps, Elise
See Creasey, John

Federman, Raymond 1928- .... **CLC 6, 47**
See also CA 17-20R; CAAE 208; CAAS 8; CANR 10, 43, 83, 108; CN 7; DLBY 1980

Federspiel, J(uerg) F. 1931- .... **CLC 42**
See also CA 146

Feiffer, Jules (Ralph) 1929- ...... **CLC 2, 8, 64**
See also AAYA 3; CA 17-20R; CAD; CANR 30, 59; CD 5; DAM DRAM; DLB 7, 44; INT CANR-30; MTCW 1; SATA 8, 61, 111

Feige, Hermann Albert Otto Maximilian
See Traven, B.

Feinberg, David B. 1956-1994 .... **CLC 59**
See also CA 135; 147

Feinstein, Elaine 1930- .... **CLC 36**
See also CA 69-72; CAAS 1; CANR 31, 68, 121; CN 7; CP 7; CWP; DLB 14, 40; MTCW 1

Feke, Gilbert David .... **CLC 65**

Feldman, Irving (Mordecai) 1928- ..... **CLC 7**
See also CA 1-4R; CANR 1; CP 7; DLB 169

Felix-Tchicaya, Gerald
See Tchicaya, Gerald Felix

Fellini, Federico 1920-1993 .... **CLC 16, 85**
See also CA 65-68; 143; CANR 33

Felltham, Owen 1602(?)-1668 .... **LC 92**
See also DLB 126, 151

Felsen, Henry Gregor 1916-1995 ..... **CLC 17**
See also CA 1-4R; 180; CANR 1; SAAS 2; SATA 1

Felski, Rita .... **CLC 65**

Fenno, Jack
See Calisher, Hortense

Fenollosa, Ernest (Francisco)
1853-1908 .... **TCLC 91**

Fenton, James Martin 1949- .... **CLC 32**
See also CA 102; CANR 108; CP 7; DLB 40; PFS 11

Ferber, Edna 1887-1968 .... **CLC 18, 93**
See also AITN 1; CA 5-8R; 25-28R; CANR 68, 105; DLB 9, 28, 86, 266; MTCW 1, 2; RGAL 4; RHW; SATA 7; TCWW 2

Ferdowsi, Abu'l Qasem 940-1020 . **CMLC 43**
See also RGWL 2, 3

Ferguson, Helen
See Kavan, Anna

Ferguson, Niall 1964- .... **CLC 134**
See also CA 190

Ferguson, Samuel 1810-1886 .... **NCLC 33**
See also DLB 32; RGEL 2

Fergusson, Robert 1750-1774 .... **LC 29**
See also DLB 109; RGEL 2

Ferling, Lawrence
See Ferlinghetti, Lawrence (Monsanto)

Ferlinghetti, Lawrence (Monsanto)
1919(?)- ..... **CLC 2, 6, 10, 27, 111; PC 1**
See also CA 5-8R; CANR 3, 41, 73; CDALB 1941-1968; CP 7; DA3; DAM POET; DLB 5, 16; MTCW 1, 2; RGAL 4; WP

Fern, Fanny
See Parton, Sara Payson Willis

Fernandez, Vicente Garcia Huidobro
See Huidobro Fernandez, Vicente Garcia

Fernandez-Armesto, Felipe .... **CLC 70**

Fernandez de Lizardi, Jose Joaquin
See Lizardi, Jose Joaquin Fernandez de

Ferre, Rosario 1938- ...... **CLC 139; HLCS 1; SSC 36**
See also CA 131; CANR 55, 81; CWW 2; DLB 145; EWL 3; HW 1, 2; LAWS 1; MTCW 1; WLIT 1

Ferrer, Gabriel (Francisco Victor) Miro
See Miro (Ferrer), Gabriel (Francisco Victor)

Ferrier, Susan (Edmonstone)
1782-1854 .... **NCLC 8**
See also DLB 116; RGEL 2

Ferrigno, Robert 1948(?)- .... **CLC 65**
See also CA 140

Ferron, Jacques 1921-1985 .... **CLC 94**
See also CA 117; 129; CCA 1; DAC; DLB 60; EWL 3

Feuchtwanger, Lion 1884-1958 .... **TCLC 3**
See also CA 104; 187; DLB 66; EWL 3

Feuillet, Octave 1821-1890 .... **NCLC 45**
See also DLB 192

Feydeau, Georges (Leon Jules Marie)
1862-1921 .... **TCLC 22**
See also CA 113; 152; CANR 84; DAM DRAM; DLB 192; EWL 3; GFL 1789 to the Present; RGWL 2, 3

Fichte, Johann Gottlieb
1762-1814 .... **NCLC 62**
See also DLB 90

Ficino, Marsilio 1433-1499 .... **LC 12**
See also LMFS 1

Fiedeler, Hans
See Doeblin, Alfred

Fiedler, Leslie A(aron) 1917-2003 ..... **CLC 4, 13, 24**
See also AMWS 13; CA 9-12R; 212; CANR 7, 63; CN 7; DLB 28, 67; EWL 3; MTCW 1, 2; RGAL 4; TUS

Field, Andrew 1938- .... **CLC 44**
See also CA 97-100; CANR 25

Field, Eugene 1850-1895 .... **NCLC 3**
See also DLB 23, 42, 140; DLBD 13; MAICYA 1, 2; RGAL 4; SATA 16

Field, Gans T.
See Wellman, Manly Wade

Field, Michael 1915-1971 .... **TCLC 43**
See also CA 29-32R

Field, Peter
See Hobson, Laura Z(ametkin)
See also TCWW 2

Fielding, Helen 1959(?)- .... **CLC 146**
See also CA 172; DLB 231

Fielding, Henry 1707-1754 .... **LC 1, 46, 85; WLC**
See also BRW 3; BRWR 1; CDBLB 1660-1789; DA; DA3; DAB; DAC; DAM DRAM, MST, NOV; DLB 39, 84, 101; NFS 18; RGEL 2; TEA; WLIT 3

Fielding, Sarah 1710-1768 .... **LC 1, 44**
See also DLB 39; RGEL 2; TEA

Fields, W. C. 1880-1946 .... **TCLC 80**
See also DLB 44

Fierstein, Harvey (Forbes) 1954- ..... **CLC 33**
See also CA 123; 129; CAD; CD 5; CPW; DA3; DAM DRAM, POP; DFS 6; DLB 266; GLL

Figes, Eva 1932- .... **CLC 31**
See also CA 53-56; CANR 4, 44, 83; CN 7; DLB 14, 271; FW

Filippo, Eduardo de
See de Filippo, Eduardo

Finch, Anne 1661-1720 .... **LC 3; PC 21**
See also BRWS 9; DLB 95

Finch, Robert (Duer Claydon)
1900-1995 .... **CLC 18**
See also CA 57-60; CANR 9, 24, 49; CP 7; DLB 88

Findley, Timothy (Irving Frederick)
1930-2002 .... **CLC 27, 102**
See also CA 25-28R; 206; CANR 12, 42, 69, 109; CCA 1; CN 7; DAC; DAM MST; DLB 53; FANT; RHW

Fink, William
See Mencken, H(enry) L(ouis)

Firbank, Louis 1942-
See Reed, Lou
See also CA 117

Firbank, (Arthur Annesley) Ronald
1886-1926 .... **TCLC 1**
See also BRWS 2; CA 104; 177; DLB 36; EWL 3; RGEL 2

Fish, Stanley
See Fish, Stanley Eugene

Fish, Stanley E.
See Fish, Stanley Eugene

Fish, Stanley Eugene 1938- .... **CLC 142**
See also CA 112; 132; CANR 90; DLB 67

Fisher, Dorothy (Frances) Canfield
1879-1958 .... **TCLC 87**
See also CA 114; 136; CANR 53; CLR 71; CWRI 5; DLB 9, 102, 284; MAICYA 1, 2; YABC 1

Fisher, M(ary) F(rances) K(ennedy)
1908-1992 .... **CLC 76, 87**
See also CA 77-80; 138; CANR 44; MTCW 1

Fisher, Roy 1930- .... **CLC 25**
See also CA 81-84; CAAS 10; CANR 16; CP 7; DLB 40

Fisher, Rudolph 1897-1934 .... **BLC 2; HR 2; SSC 25; TCLC 11**
See also BW 1, 3; CA 107; 124; CANR 80; DAM MULT; DLB 51, 102

Fisher, Vardis (Alvero) 1895-1968 .... **CLC 7; TCLC 140**
See also CA 5-8R; 25-28R; CANR 68; DLB 9, 206; RGAL 4; TCWW 2

Fiske, Tarleton
See Bloch, Robert (Albert)

Fitch, Clarke
See Sinclair, Upton (Beall)

Fitch, John IV
See Cormier, Robert (Edmund)

Fitzgerald, Captain Hugh
See Baum, L(yman) Frank

FitzGerald, Edward 1809-1883 .... **NCLC 9**
See also BRW 4; DLB 32; RGEL 2

Fitzgerald, F(rancis) Scott (Key)
1896-1940 ... **SSC 6, 31; TCLC 1, 6, 14, 28, 55; WLC**
See also AAYA 24; AITN 1; AMW; AMWC 2; AMWR 1; BPFB 1; CA 110; 123; CDALB 1917-1929; DA; DA3; DAB; DAC; DAM MST, NOV; DLB 4, 9, 86, 219; DLBD 1, 15, 16, 273; DLBY 1981, 1996; EWL 3; EXPN; EXPS; LAIT 3; MTCW 1, 2; NFS 2; RGAL 4; RGSF 2; SSFS 4, 15; TUS

Fitzgerald, Penelope 1916-2000 . **CLC 19, 51, 61, 143**
See also BRWS 5; CA 85-88; 190; CAAS 10; CANR 56, 86; CN 7; DLB 14, 194; EWL 3; MTCW 2

Fitzgerald, Robert (Stuart)
1910-1985 .... **CLC 39**
See also CA 1-4R; 114; CANR 1; DLBY 1980

FitzGerald, Robert D(avid)
1902-1987 .... **CLC 19**
See also CA 17-20R; DLB 260; RGEL 2

Fitzgerald, Zelda (Sayre)
1900-1948 .... **TCLC 52**
See also AMWS 9; CA 117; 126; DLBY 1984

Flanagan, Thomas (James Bonner)
1923-2002 .... **CLC 25, 52**
See also CA 108; 206; CANR 55; CN 7; DLBY 1980; INT 108; MTCW 1; RHW

Flaubert, Gustave 1821-1880 .... **NCLC 2, 10, 19, 62, 66; SSC 11, 60; WLC**
See also DA; DA3; DAB; DAC; DAM MST, NOV; DLB 119; EW 7; EXPS; GFL 1789 to the Present; LAIT 2; LMFS 1; NFS 14; RGSF 2; RGWL 2, 3; SSFS 6; TWA

Flavius Josephus
See Josephus, Flavius

Flecker, Herman Elroy
See Flecker, (Herman) James Elroy

Flecker, (Herman) James Elroy
1884-1915 .... TCLC 43
See also CA 109; 150; DLB 10, 19; RGEL 2

Fleming, Ian (Lancaster) 1908-1964 . **CLC 3, 30**
See also AAYA 26; BPFB 1; CA 5-8R; CANR 59; CDBLB 1945-1960; CMW 4; CPW; DA3; DAM POP; DLB 87, 201; MSW; MTCW 1, 2; RGEL 2; SATA 9; TEA; YAW

Fleming, Thomas (James) 1927- ...... **CLC 37**
See also CA 5-8R; CANR 10, 102; INT CANR-10; SATA 8

Fletcher, John 1579-1625 .... **DC 6; LC 33**
See also BRW 2; CDBLB Before 1660; DLB 58; RGEL 2; TEA

Fletcher, John Gould 1886-1950 .... **TCLC 35**
See also CA 107; 167; DLB 4, 45; LMFS 2; RGAL 4

Fleur, Paul
See Pohl, Frederik

Flooglebuckle, Al
See Spiegelman, Art

Flora, Fletcher 1914-1969
See Queen, Ellery
See also CA 1-4R; CANR 3, 85

Flying Officer X
See Bates, H(erbert) E(rnest)

Fo, Dario 1926- .... **CLC 32, 109; DC 10**
See also CA 116; 128; CANR 68, 114; CWW 2; DA3; DAM DRAM; DLBY 1997; EWL 3; MTCW 1, 2

Fogarty, Jonathan Titulescu Esq.
See Farrell, James T(homas)

Follett, Ken(neth Martin) 1949- .... **CLC 18**
See also AAYA 6, 50; BEST 89:4; BPFB 1; CA 81-84; CANR 13, 33, 54, 102; CMW 4; CPW; DA3; DAM NOV, POP; DLB 87; DLBY 1981; INT CANR-33; MTCW 1

Fontane, Theodor 1819-1898 .... **NCLC 26**
See also CDWLB 2; DLB 129; EW 6; RGWL 2, 3; TWA

Fontenot, Chester .... **CLC 65**

Fonvizin, Denis Ivanovich
1744(?)-1792 .... **LC 81**
See also DLB 150; RGWL 2, 3

Foote, Horton 1916- .... **CLC 51, 91**
See also CA 73-76; CAD; CANR 34, 51, 110; CD 5; CSW; DA3; DAM DRAM; DLB 26, 266; EWL 3; INT CANR-34

Foote, Mary Hallock 1847-1938 .. **TCLC 108**
See also DLB 186, 188, 202, 221

Foote, Shelby 1916- .... **CLC 75**
See also AAYA 40; CA 5-8R; CANR 3, 45, 74; CN 7; CPW; CSW; DA3; DAM NOV, POP; DLB 2, 17; MTCW 2; RHW

Forbes, Cosmo
See Lewton, Val

Forbes, Esther 1891-1967 .... **CLC 12**
See also AAYA 17; BYA 2; CA 13-14; 25-28R; CAP 1; CLR 27; DLB 22; JRDA; MAICYA 1, 2; RHW; SATA 2, 100; YAW

Forche, Carolyn (Louise) 1950- .... **CLC 25, 83, 86; PC 10**
See also CA 109; 117; CANR 50, 74; CP 7; CWP; DA3; DAM POET; DLB 5, 193; INT CA-117; MTCW 1; PFS 18; RGAL 4

Ford, Elbur
See Hibbert, Eleanor Alice Burford

Ford, Ford Madox 1873-1939 ... **TCLC 1, 15, 39, 57**
See Chaucer, Daniel
See also BRW 6; CA 104; 132; CANR 74; CDBLB 1914-1945; DA3; DAM NOV, DLB 34, 98, 162; EWL 3; MTCW 1, 2; RGEL 2; TEA

Ford, Henry 1863-1947 .... **TCLC 73**
See also CA 115; 148

Ford, Jack
See Ford, John

Ford, John 1586-1639 .... **DC 8; LC 68**
See also BRW 2; CDBLB Before 1660; DA3; DAM DRAM; DFS 7; DLB 58; IDTP; RGEL 2

Ford, John 1895-1973 .... **CLC 16**
See also CA 187; 45-48

Ford, Richard 1944- .... **CLC 46, 99**
See also AMWS 5; CA 69-72; CANR 11, 47, 86; CN 7; CSW; DLB 227; EWL 3; MTCW 1; RGAL 4; RGSF 2

Ford, Webster
See Masters, Edgar Lee

Foreman, Richard 1937- .... **CLC 50**
See also CA 65-68; CAD; CANR 32, 63; CD 5

Forester, C(ecil) S(cott) 1899-1966 ... **CLC 35**
See also CA 73-76; 25-28R; CANR 83; DLB 191; RGEL 2; RHW; SATA 13

Forez
See Mauriac, Francois (Charles)

Forman, James
See Forman, James D(ouglas)

Forman, James D(ouglas) 1932- .... **CLC 21**
See also AAYA 17; CA 9-12R; CANR 4, 19, 42; JRDA; MAICYA 1, 2; SATA 8, 70; YAW

Forman, Milos 1932- .... **CLC 164**
See also CA 109

Fornes, Maria Irene 1930- . **CLC 39, 61; DC 10; HLCS 1**
See also CA 25-28R; CAD; CANR 28, 81; CD 5; CWD; DLB 7; HW 1, 2; INT CANR-28; MTCW 1; RGAL 4

Forrest, Leon (Richard)
1937-1997 .... **BLCS; CLC 4**
See also AFAW 2; BW 2; CA 89-92; 162; CAAS 7; CANR 25, 52, 87; CN 7; DLB 33

Forster, E(dward) M(organ)
1879-1970 ...... **CLC 1, 2, 3, 4, 9, 10, 13, 15, 22, 45, 77; SSC 27; TCLC 125; WLC**
See also AAYA 2, 37; BRW 6; BRWR 2; CA 13-14; 25-28R; CANR 45; CAP 1; CDBLB 1914-1945; DA; DA3; DAB; DAC; DAM MST, NOV; DLB 34, 98, 162, 178, 195; DLBD 10; EWL 3; EXPN; LAIT 3; LMFS 1; MTCW 1, 2; NCFS 1; NFS 3, 10, 11; RGEL 2; RGSF 2; SATA 57; SUFW 1; TEA; WLIT 4

Forster, John 1812-1876 .... **NCLC 11**
See also DLB 144, 184

Forster, Margaret 1938- .... **CLC 149**
See also CA 133; CANR 62, 115; CN 7; DLB 155, 271

Forsyth, Frederick 1938- .... **CLC 2, 5, 36**
See also BEST 89:4; CA 85-88; CANR 38, 62, 115; CMW 4; CN 7; CPW; DAM NOV, POP; DLB 87; MTCW 1, 2

Forten, Charlotte L. 1837-1914 .... **BLC 2; TCLC 16**
See Grimke, Charlotte L(ottie) Forten
See also DLB 50, 239

Fortinbras
See Grieg, (Johan) Nordahl (Brun)

Foscolo, Ugo 1778-1827 .... **NCLC 8, 97**
See also EW 5

Fosse, Bob .... **CLC 20**
See Fosse, Robert Louis

Fosse, Robert Louis 1927-1987
See Fosse, Bob
See also CA 110; 123

Foster, Hannah Webster
1758-1840 .... **NCLC 99**
See also DLB 37, 200; RGAL 4

Foster, Stephen Collins
1826-1864 .... **NCLC 26**
See also RGAL 4

Foucault, Michel 1926-1984 . **CLC 31, 34, 69**
See also CA 105; 113; CANR 34; DLB 242; EW 13; EWL 3; GFL 1789 to the Present; GLL 1; LMFS 2; MTCW 1, 2; TWA

Fouque, Friedrich (Heinrich Karl) de la Motte 1777-1843 .... **NCLC 2**
See also DLB 90; RGWL 2, 3; SUFW 1

Fourier, Charles 1772-1837 .... **NCLC 51**

Fournier, Henri-Alban 1886-1914
See Alain-Fournier
See also CA 104; 179

Fournier, Pierre 1916- .... **CLC 11**
See Gascar, Pierre
See also CA 89-92; CANR 16, 40

Fowles, John (Robert) 1926- . **CLC 1, 2, 3, 4, 6, 9, 10, 15, 33, 87; SSC 33**
See also BPFB 1; BRWS 1; CA 5-8R; CANR 25, 71, 103; CDBLB 1960 to Present; CN 7; DA3; DAB; DAC; DAM MST; DLB 14, 139, 207; EWL 3; HGG; MTCW 1, 2; RGEL 2; RHW; SATA 22; TEA; WLIT 4

Fox, Paula 1923- .... **CLC 2, 8, 121**
See also AAYA 3, 37; BYA 3, 8; CA 73-76; CANR 20, 36, 62, 105; CLR 1, 44; DLB 52; JRDA; MAICYA 1, 2; MTCW 1; NFS 12; SATA 17, 60, 120; WYA; YAW

Fox, William Price (Jr.) 1926- .... **CLC 22**
See also CA 17-20R; CAAS 19; CANR 11; CSW; DLB 2; DLBY 1981

Foxe, John 1517(?)-1587 .... **LC 14**
See also DLB 132

Frame, Janet .. **CLC 2, 3, 6, 22, 66, 96; SSC 29**
See Clutha, Janet Paterson Frame
See also CN 7; CWP; EWL 3; RGEL 2; RGSF 2; TWA

France, Anatole .... **TCLC 9**
See Thibault, Jacques Anatole Francois
See also DLB 123; EWL 3; GFL 1789 to the Present; MTCW 1; RGWL 2, 3; SUFW 1

Francis, Claude .... **CLC 50**
See also CA 192

Francis, Dick 1920- .... **CLC 2, 22, 42, 102**
See also AAYA 5, 21; BEST 89:3; BPFB 1; CA 5-8R; CANR 9, 42, 68, 100; CDBLB 1960 to Present; CMW 4; CN 7; DA3; DAM POP; DLB 87; INT CANR-9; MSW; MTCW 1, 2

Francis, Robert (Churchill)
1901-1987 .... **CLC 15; PC 34**
See also AMWS 9; CA 1-4R; 123; CANR 1; EXPP; PFS 12

Francis, Lord Jeffrey
See Jeffrey, Francis
See also DLB 107

Frank, Anne(lies Marie)
1929-1945 .... **TCLC 17; WLC**
See also AAYA 12; BYA 1; CA 113; 133; CANR 68; DA; DA3; DAB; DAC; DAM MST; LAIT 4; MAICYA 2; MAICYAS 1; MTCW 1, 2; NCFS 2; SATA 87; SATA-Brief 42; WYA; YAW

Frank, Bruno 1887-1945 .... **TCLC 81**
See also CA 189; DLB 118; EWL 3

Frank, Elizabeth 1945- .... **CLC 39**
See also CA 121; 126; CANR 78; INT 126

Frankl, Viktor E(mil) 1905-1997 ...... **CLC 93**
See also CA 65-68; 161

Franklin, Benjamin
See Hasek, Jaroslav (Matej Frantisek)

Franklin, Benjamin 1706-1790 .... **LC 25; WLCS**
See also AMW; CDALB 1640-1865; DA; DA3; DAB; DAC; DAM MST; DLB 24, 43, 73, 183; LAIT 1; RGAL 4; TUS

Franklin, (Stella Maria Sarah) Miles (Lampe) 1879-1954 .... **TCLC 7**
See also CA 104; 164; DLB 230; FW; MTCW 2; RGEL 2; TWA

Fraser, Antonia (Pakenham) 1932- . **CLC 32, 107**
See also CA 85-88; CANR 44, 65, 119; CMW; DLB 276; MTCW 1, 2; SATA-Brief 32

Fraser, George MacDonald 1925- ...... **CLC 7**
See also AAYA 48; CA 45-48, 180; CAAE 180; CANR 2, 48, 74; MTCW 1; RHW

Fraser, Sylvia 1935- .... **CLC 64**
See also CA 45-48; CANR 1, 16, 60; CCA 1

Frayn, Michael 1933- . **CLC 3, 7, 31, 47, 176**
See also BRWC 2; BRWS 7; CA 5-8R; CANR 30, 69, 114; CBD; CD 5; CN 7; DAM DRAM, NOV; DLB 13, 14, 194, 245; FANT; MTCW 1, 2; SFW 4

Fraze, Candida (Merrill) 1945- .... **CLC 50**
See also CA 126

Frazer, Andrew
See Marlowe, Stephen

Frazer, J(ames) G(eorge) 1854-1941 .... **TCLC 32**
See also BRWS 3; CA 118; NCFS 5

Frazer, Robert Caine
See Creasey, John

Frazer, Sir James George
See Frazer, J(ames) G(eorge)

Frazier, Charles 1950- .... **CLC 109**
See also AAYA 34; CA 161; CSW

Frazier, Ian 1951- .... **CLC 46**
See also CA 130; CANR 54, 93

Frederic, Harold 1856-1898 .... **NCLC 10**
See also AMW; DLB 12, 23; DLBD 13; RGAL 4

Frederick, John
See Faust, Frederick (Schiller)
See also TCWW 2

Frederick the Great 1712-1786 .... **LC 14**

Fredro, Aleksander 1793-1876 .... **NCLC 8**

Freeling, Nicolas 1927- .... **CLC 38**
See also CA 49-52; CAAS 12; CANR 1, 17, 50, 84; CMW 4; CN 7; DLB 87

Freeman, Douglas Southall 1886-1953 .... **TCLC 11**
See also CA 109; 195; DLB 17; DLBD 17

Freeman, Judith 1946- .... **CLC 55**
See also CA 148; CANR 120; DLB 256

Freeman, Mary E(leanor) Wilkins 1852-1930 .... **SSC 1, 47; TCLC 9**
See also CA 106; 177; DLB 12, 78, 221; EXPS; FW; HGG; MAWW; RGAL 4; RGSF 2; SSFS 4, 8; SUFW 1; TUS

Freeman, R(ichard) Austin 1862-1943 .... **TCLC 21**
See also CA 113; CANR 84; CMW 4; DLB 70

French, Albert 1943- .... **CLC 86**
See also BW 3; CA 167

French, Antonia
See Kureishi, Hanif

French, Marilyn 1929- .. **CLC 10, 18, 60, 177**
See also BPFB 1; CA 69-72; CANR 3, 31; CN 7; CPW; DAM DRAM, NOV, POP; FW; INT CANR-31; MTCW 1, 2

French, Paul
See Asimov, Isaac

Freneau, Philip Morin 1752-1832 .. **NCLC 1, 111**
See also AMWS 2; DLB 37, 43; RGAL 4

Freud, Sigmund 1856-1939 .... **TCLC 52**
See also CA 115; 133; CANR 69; EW 8; EWL 3; LATS 1; MTCW 1, 2; NCFS 3; TWA

Freytag, Gustav 1816-1895 .... **NCLC 109**
See also DLB 129

Friedan, Betty (Naomi) 1921- .... **CLC 74**
See also CA 65-68; CANR 18, 45, 74; DLB 246; FW; MTCW 1, 2; NCFS 5

Friedlander, Saul 1932- .... **CLC 90**
See also CA 117; 130; CANR 72

Friedman, B(ernard) H(arper) 1926- .... **CLC 7**
See also CA 1-4R; CANR 3, 48

Friedman, Bruce Jay 1930- .... **CLC 3, 5, 56**
See also CA 9-12R; CAD; CANR 25, 52, 101; CD 5; CN 7; DLB 2, 28, 244; INT CANR-25; SSFS 18

Friel, Brian 1929- .... **CLC 5, 42, 59, 115; DC 8**
See also BRWS 5; CA 21-24R; CANR 33, 69; CBD; CD 5; DFS 11; DLB 13; EWL 3; MTCW 1; RGEL 2; TEA

Friis-Baastad, Babbis Ellinor 1921-1970 .... **CLC 12**
See also CA 17-20R; 134; SATA 7

Frisch, Max (Rudolf) 1911-1991 ... **CLC 3, 9, 14, 18, 32, 44; TCLC 121**
See also CA 85-88; 134; CANR 32, 74; CD-WLB 2; DAM DRAM, NOV; DLB 69, 124; EW 13; EWL 3; MTCW 1, 2; RGWL 2, 3

Fromentin, Eugene (Samuel Auguste) 1820-1876 .... **NCLC 10, 125**
See also DLB 123; GFL 1789 to the Present

Frost, Frederick
See Faust, Frederick (Schiller)
See also TCWW 2

Frost, Robert (Lee) 1874-1963 .. **CLC 1, 3, 4, 9, 10, 13, 15, 26, 34, 44; PC 1, 39; WLC**
See also AAYA 21; AMW; AMWR 1; CA 89-92; CANR 33; CDALB 1917-1929; CLR 67; DA; DA3; DAB; DAC; DAM MST, POET; DLB 54, 284; DLBD 7; EWL 3; EXPP; MTCW 1, 2; PAB; PFS 1, 2, 3, 4, 5, 6, 7, 10, 13; RGAL 4; SATA 14; TUS; WP; WYA

Froude, James Anthony 1818-1894 .... **NCLC 43**
See also DLB 18, 57, 144

Froy, Herald
See Waterhouse, Keith (Spencer)

Fry, Christopher 1907- .... **CLC 2, 10, 14**
See also BRWS 3; CA 17-20R; CAAS 23; CANR 9, 30, 74; CBD; CD 5; CP 7; DAM DRAM; DLB 13; EWL 3; MTCW 1, 2; RGEL 2; SATA 66; TEA

Frye, (Herman) Northrop 1912-1991 .... **CLC 24, 70**
See also CA 5-8R; 133; CANR 8, 37; DLB 67, 68, 246; EWL 3; MTCW 1, 2; RGAL 4; TWA

Fuchs, Daniel 1909-1993 .... **CLC 8, 22**
See also CA 81-84; 142; CAAS 5; CANR 40; DLB 9, 26, 28; DLBY 1993

Fuchs, Daniel 1934- .... **CLC 34**
See also CA 37-40R; CANR 14, 48

Fuentes, Carlos 1928- .. **CLC 3, 8, 10, 13, 22, 41, 60, 113; HLC 1; SSC 24; WLC**
See also AAYA 4, 45; AITN 2; BPFB 1; CA 69-72; CANR 10, 32, 68, 104; CD-WLB 3; CWW 2; DA; DA3; DAB; DAC; DAM MST, MULT, NOV; DLB 113; DNFS 2; EWL 3; HW 1, 2; LAIT 3; LATS 1; LAW; LAWS 1; LMFS 2; MTCW 1, 2; NFS 8; RGSF 2; RGWL 2, 3; TWA; WLIT 1

Fuentes, Gregorio Lopez y
See Lopez y Fuentes, Gregorio

Fuertes, Gloria 1918-1998 .... **PC 27**
See also CA 178; 180; DLB 108; HW 2; SATA 115

Fugard, (Harold) Athol 1932- . **CLC 5, 9, 14, 25, 40, 80; DC 3**
See also AAYA 17; AFW; CA 85-88; CANR 32, 54, 118; CD 5; DAM DRAM; DFS 3, 6, 10; DLB 225; DNFS 1, 2; EWL 3; LATS 1; MTCW 1; RGEL 2; WLIT 2

Fugard, Sheila 1932- .... **CLC 48**
See also CA 125

Fukuyama, Francis 1952- .... **CLC 131**
See also CA 140; CANR 72

Fuller, Charles (H.), (Jr.) 1939- .... **BLC 2; CLC 25; DC 1**
See also BW 2; CA 108; 112; CAD; CANR 87; CD 5; DAM DRAM, MULT; DFS 8; DLB 38, 266; EWL 3; INT CA-112; MTCW 1

Fuller, Henry Blake 1857-1929 .... **TCLC 103**
See also CA 108; 177; DLB 12; RGAL 4

Fuller, John (Leopold) 1937- .... **CLC 62**
See also CA 21-24R; CANR 9, 44; CP 7; DLB 40

Fuller, Margaret
See Ossoli, Sarah Margaret (Fuller)
See also AMWS 2; DLB 183, 223, 239

Fuller, Roy (Broadbent) 1912-1991 ... **CLC 4, 28**
See also BRWS 7; CA 5-8R; 135; CAAS 10; CANR 53, 83; CWRI 5; DLB 15, 20; EWL 3; RGEL 2; SATA 87

Fuller, Sarah Margaret
See Ossoli, Sarah Margaret (Fuller)

Fuller, Sarah Margaret
See Ossoli, Sarah Margaret (Fuller)
See also DLB 1, 59, 73

Fulton, Alice 1952- .... **CLC 52**
See also CA 116; CANR 57, 88; CP 7; CWP; DLB 193

Furphy, Joseph 1843-1912 .... **TCLC 25**
See Collins, Tom
See also CA 163; DLB 230; EWL 3; RGEL 2

Fuson, Robert H(enderson) 1927- .... **CLC 70**
See also CA 89-92; CANR 103

Fussell, Paul 1924- .... **CLC 74**
See also BEST 90:1; CA 17-20R; CANR 8, 21, 35, 69; INT CANR-21; MTCW 1, 2

Futabatei, Shimei 1864-1909 .... **TCLC 44**
See Futabatei Shimei
See also CA 162; MJW

Futabatei Shimei
See Futabatei, Shimei
See also DLB 180; EWL 3

Futrelle, Jacques 1875-1912 .... **TCLC 19**
See also CA 113; 155; CMW 4

Gaboriau, Emile 1835-1873 .... **NCLC 14**
See also CMW 4; MSW

Gadda, Carlo Emilio 1893-1973 .... **CLC 11**
See also CA 89-92; DLB 177; EWL 3

Gaddis, William 1922-1998 ... **CLC 1, 3, 6, 8, 10, 19, 43, 86**
See also AMWS 4; BPFB 1; CA 17-20R; 172; CANR 21, 48; CN 7; DLB 2, 278; EWL 3; MTCW 1, 2; RGAL 4

Gaelique, Moruen le
See Jacob, (Cyprien-)Max

Gage, Walter
See Inge, William (Motter)

Gaines, Ernest J(ames) 1933- .. **BLC 2; CLC 3, 11, 18, 86**
See also AAYA 18; AFAW 1, 2; AITN 1; BPFB 2; BW 2, 3; BYA 6; CA 9-12R; CANR 6, 24, 42, 75; CDALB 1968-1988; CLR 62; CN 7; CSW; DA3; DAM MULT; DLB 2, 33, 152; DLBY 1980; EWL 3; EXPN; LAIT 1; LATS 1; MTCW 1, 2; NFS 5, 7, 16; RGAL 4; RGSF 2; RHW; SATA 86; SSFS 5; YAW

Gaitskill, Mary 1954- .... **CLC 69**
See also CA 128; CANR 61; DLB 244

Gaius Suetonius Tranquillus c. 70-c. 130
See Suetonius

Galdos, Benito Perez
See Perez Galdos, Benito
See also EW 7

Gale, Zona 1874-1938 .... **TCLC 7**
See also CA 105; 153; CANR 84; DAM DRAM; DFS 17; DLB 9, 78, 228; RGAL 4

Galeano, Eduardo (Hughes) 1940- . **CLC 72; HLCS 1**
See also CA 29-32R; CANR 13, 32, 100; HW 1

Galiano, Juan Valera y Alcala
See Valera y Alcala-Galiano, Juan

Galilei, Galileo 1564-1642 .... **LC 45**

Gallagher, Tess 1943- .... **CLC 18, 63; PC 9**
See also CA 106; CP 7; CWP; DAM POET; DLB 120, 212, 244; PFS 16

Gallant, Mavis 1922- ..... **CLC 7, 18, 38, 172; SSC 5**
See also CA 69-72; CANR 29, 69, 117; CCA 1; CN 7; DAC; DAM MST; DLB 53; EWL 3; MTCW 1, 2; RGEL 2; RGSF 2

Gallant, Roy A(rthur) 1924- .... **CLC 17**
See also CA 5-8R; CANR 4, 29, 54, 117; CLR 30; MAICYA 1, 2; SATA 4, 68, 110

Gallico, Paul (William) 1897-1976 ..... **CLC 2**
See also AITN 1; CA 5-8R; 69-72; CANR 23; DLB 9, 171; FANT; MAICYA 1, 2; SATA 13

Gallo, Max Louis 1932- .... **CLC 95**
See also CA 85-88

Gallois, Lucien
See Desnos, Robert

Gallup, Ralph
See Whitemore, Hugh (John)

Galsworthy, John 1867-1933 .... **SSC 22; TCLC 1, 45; WLC**
See also BRW 6; CA 104; 141; CANR 75; CDBLB 1890-1914; DA; DA3; DAB; DAC; DAM DRAM, MST, NOV; DLB 10, 34, 98, 162; DLBD 16; EWL 3; MTCW 1; RGEL 2; SSFS 3; TEA

Galt, John 1779-1839 .... **NCLC 1, 110**
See also DLB 99, 116, 159; RGEL 2; RGSF 2

Galvin, James 1951- .... **CLC 38**
See also CA 108; CANR 26

Gamboa, Federico 1864-1939 .... **TCLC 36**
See also CA 167; HW 2; LAW

Gandhi, M. K.
See Gandhi, Mohandas Karamchand

Gandhi, Mahatma
See Gandhi, Mohandas Karamchand

Gandhi, Mohandas Karamchand 1869-1948 .... **TCLC 59**
See also CA 121; 132; DA3; DAM MULT; MTCW 1, 2

Gann, Ernest Kellogg 1910-1991 ..... **CLC 23**
See also AITN 1; BPFB 2; CA 1-4R; 136; CANR 1, 83; RHW

Gao Xingjian 1940- .... **CLC 167**
See Xingjian, Gao

Garber, Eric 1943(?)-
See Holleran, Andrew
See also CANR 89

Garcia, Cristina 1958- .... **CLC 76**
See also AMWS 11; CA 141; CANR 73; DNFS 1; EWL 3; HW 2

Garcia Lorca, Federico 1898-1936 ...... **DC 2; HLC 2; PC 3; TCLC 1, 7, 49; WLC**
See Lorca, Federico Garcia
See also AAYA 46; CA 104; 131; CANR 81; DA; DA3; DAB; DAC; DAM DRAM, MST, MULT, POET; DFS 4, 10; DLB 108; EWL 3; HW 1, 2; LATS 1; MTCW 1, 2; TWA

Garcia Marquez, Gabriel (Jose) 1928- .... **CLC 2, 3, 8, 10, 15, 27, 47, 55, 68, 170; HLC 1; SSC 8; WLC**
See also AAYA 3, 33; BEST 89:1, 90:4; BPFB 2; BYA 12, 16; CA 33-36R; CANR 10, 28, 50, 75, 82; CDWLB 3; CPW; DA; DA3; DAB; DAC; DAM MST, MULT, NOV, POP; DLB 113; DNFS 1, 2; EWL 3; EXPN; EXPS; HW 1, 2; LAIT 2; LATS 1; LAW; LAWS 1; LMFS 2; MTCW 1, 2; NCFS 3; NFS 1, 5, 10; RGSF 2; RGWL 2, 3; SSFS 1, 6, 16; TWA; WLIT 1

Garcilaso de la Vega, El Inca 1503-1536 .... **HLCS 1**
See also LAW

Gard, Janice
See Latham, Jean Lee

Gard, Roger Martin du
See Martin du Gard, Roger

Gardam, Jane (Mary) 1928- .... **CLC 43**
See also CA 49-52; CANR 2, 18, 33, 54, 106; CLR 12; DLB 14, 161, 231; MAICYA 1, 2; MTCW 1; SAAS 9; SATA 39, 76, 130; SATA-Brief 28; YAW

Gardner, Herb(ert) 1934- .... **CLC 44**
See also CA 149; CAD; CANR 119; CD 5; DFS 18

Gardner, John (Champlin), Jr. 1933-1982 .... **CLC 2, 3, 5, 7, 8, 10, 18, 28, 34; SSC 7**
See also AAYA 45; AITN 1; AMWS 6; BPFB 2; CA 65-68; 107; CANR 33, 73; CDALBS; CPW; DA3; DAM NOV, POP; DLB 2; DLBY 1982; EWL 3; FANT; LATS 1; MTCW 1; NFS 3; RGAL 4; RGSF 2; SATA 40; SATA-Obit 31; SSFS 8

Gardner, John (Edmund) 1926- .... **CLC 30**
See also CA 103; CANR 15, 69; CMW 4; CPW; DAM POP; MTCW 1

Gardner, Miriam
See Bradley, Marion Zimmer
See also GLL 1

Gardner, Noel
See Kuttner, Henry

Gardons, S. S.
See Snodgrass, W(illiam) D(e Witt)

Garfield, Leon 1921-1996 .... **CLC 12**
See also AAYA 8; BYA 1, 3; CA 17-20R; 152; CANR 38, 41, 78; CLR 21; DLB 161; JRDA; MAICYA 1, 2; MAICYAS 1; SATA 1, 32, 76; SATA-Obit 90; TEA; WYA; YAW

Garland, (Hannibal) Hamlin 1860-1940 .... **SSC 18; TCLC 3**
See also CA 104; DLB 12, 71, 78, 186; RGAL 4; RGSF 2; TCWW 2

Garneau, (Hector de) Saint-Denys 1912-1943 .... **TCLC 13**
See also CA 111; DLB 88

Garner, Alan 1934- .... **CLC 17**
See also AAYA 18; BYA 3, 5; CA 73-76, 178; CAAE 178; CANR 15, 64; CLR 20; CPW; DAB; DAM POP; DLB 161, 261; FANT; MAICYA 1, 2; MTCW 1, 2; SATA 18, 69; SATA-Essay 108; SUFW 1, 2; YAW

Garner, Hugh 1913-1979 .... **CLC 13**
See Warwick, Jarvis
See also CA 69-72; CANR 31; CCA 1; DLB 68

Garnett, David 1892-1981 .... **CLC 3**
See also CA 5-8R; 103; CANR 17, 79; DLB 34; FANT; MTCW 2; RGEL 2; SFW 4; SUFW 1

Garos, Stephanie
See Katz, Steve

Garrett, George (Palmer) 1929- .. **CLC 3, 11, 51; SSC 30**
See also AMWS 7; BPFB 2; CA 1-4R; CAAE 202; CAAS 5; CANR 1, 42, 67, 109; CN 7; CP 7; CSW; DLB 2, 5, 130, 152; DLBY 1983

Garrick, David 1717-1779 .... **LC 15**
See also DAM DRAM; DLB 84, 213; RGEL 2

Garrigue, Jean 1914-1972 .... **CLC 2, 8**
See also CA 5-8R; 37-40R; CANR 20

Garrison, Frederick
See Sinclair, Upton (Beall)

Garro, Elena 1920(?)-1998 .... **HLCS 1**
See also CA 131; 169; CWW 2; DLB 145; EWL 3; HW 1; LAWS 1; WLIT 1

Garth, Will
See Hamilton, Edmond; Kuttner, Henry

Garvey, Marcus (Moziah, Jr.) 1887-1940 .... **BLC 2; HR 2; TCLC 41**
See also BW 1; CA 120; 124; CANR 79; DAM MULT

Gary, Romain .... **CLC 25**
See Kacew, Romain
See also DLB 83

Gascar, Pierre .... **CLC 11**
See Fournier, Pierre
See also EWL 3

Gascoyne, David (Emery) 1916-2001 .... **CLC 45**
See also CA 65-68; 200; CANR 10, 28, 54; CP 7; DLB 20; MTCW 1; RGEL 2

Gaskell, Elizabeth Cleghorn 1810-1865 .... **NCLC 5, 70, 97; SSC 25**
See also BRW 5; CDBLB 1832-1890; DAB; DAM MST; DLB 21, 144, 159; RGEL 2; RGSF 2; TEA

Gass, William H(oward) 1924- . **CLC 1, 2, 8, 11, 15, 39, 132; SSC 12**
See also AMWS 6; CA 17-20R; CANR 30, 71, 100; CN 7; DLB 2, 227; EWL 3; MTCW 1, 2; RGAL 4

Gassendi, Pierre 1592-1655 .... **LC 54**
See also GFL Beginnings to 1789

Gasset, Jose Ortega y
See Ortega y Gasset, Jose

Gates, Henry Louis, Jr. 1950- ... **BLCS; CLC 65**
See also BW 2, 3; CA 109; CANR 25, 53, 75; CSW; DA3; DAM MULT; DLB 67; EWL 3; MTCW 1; RGAL 4

Gautier, Theophile 1811-1872 .. **NCLC 1, 59; PC 18; SSC 20**
See also DAM POET; DLB 119; EW 6; GFL 1789 to the Present; RGWL 2, 3; SUFW; TWA

Gawsworth, John
See Bates, H(erbert) E(rnest)

Gay, John 1685-1732 .... **LC 49**
See also BRW 3; DAM DRAM; DLB 84, 95; RGEL 2; WLIT 3

Gay, Oliver
See Gogarty, Oliver St. John

Gay, Peter (Jack) 1923- .... **CLC 158**
See also CA 13-16R; CANR 18, 41, 77; INT CANR-18

Gaye, Marvin (Pentz, Jr.) 1939-1984 .... **CLC 26**
See also CA 195; 112

Gebler, Carlo (Ernest) 1954- .... **CLC 39**
See also CA 119; 133; CANR 96; DLB 271
Gee, Maggie (Mary) 1948- .... **CLC 57**
See also CA 130; CN 7; DLB 207
Gee, Maurice (Gough) 1931- .... **CLC 29**
See also AAYA 42; CA 97-100; CANR 67, 123; CLR 56; CN 7; CWRI 5; EWL 3; MAICYA 2; RGSF 2; SATA 46, 101
Geiogamah, Hanay 1945- .... **NNAL**
See also CA 153; DAM MULT; DLB 175
Gelbart, Larry (Simon) 1928- .... **CLC 21, 61**
See Gelbart, Larry
See also CA 73-76; CANR 45, 94
Gelbart, Larry 1928-
See Gelbart, Larry (Simon)
See also CAD; CD 5
Gelber, Jack 1932-2003 ...... **CLC 1, 6, 14, 79**
See also CA 1-4R; 216; CAD; CANR 2; DLB 7, 228
Gellhorn, Martha (Ellis)
1908-1998 .... **CLC 14, 60**
See also CA 77-80; 164; CANR 44; CN 7; DLBY 1982, 1998
Genet, Jean 1910-1986 .. **CLC 1, 2, 5, 10, 14, 44, 46; TCLC 128**
See also CA 13-16R; CANR 18; DA3; DAM DRAM; DFS 10; DLB 72; DLBY 1986; EW 13; EWL 3; GFL 1789 to the Present; GLL 1; LMFS 1; MTCW 1, 2; RGWL 2, 3; TWA
Gent, Peter 1942- .... **CLC 29**
See also AITN 1; CA 89-92; DLBY 1982
Gentile, Giovanni 1875-1944 .... **TCLC 96**
See also CA 119
Gentlewoman in New England, A
See Bradstreet, Anne
Gentlewoman in Those Parts, A
See Bradstreet, Anne
Geoffrey of Monmouth c.
1100-1155 .... **CMLC 44**
See also DLB 146; TEA
George, Jean
See George, Jean Craighead
George, Jean Craighead 1919- .... **CLC 35**
See also AAYA 8; BYA 2, 4; CA 5-8R; CANR 25; CLR 1; 80; DLB 52; JRDA; MAICYA 1, 2; SATA 2, 68, 124; WYA; YAW
George, Stefan (Anton) 1868-1933 . **TCLC 2, 14**
See also CA 104; 193; EW 8; EWL 3
Georges, Georges Martin
See Simenon, Georges (Jacques Christian)
Gerald of Wales c. 1146-c. 1223 ... **CMLC 60**
Gerhardi, William Alexander
See Gerhardie, William Alexander
Gerhardie, William Alexander
1895-1977 .... **CLC 5**
See also CA 25-28R; 73-76; CANR 18; DLB 36; RGEL 2
Gerson, Jean 1363-1429 .... **LC 77**
See also DLB 208
Gersonides 1288-1344 .... **CMLC 49**
See also DLB 115
Gerstler, Amy 1956- .... **CLC 70**
See also CA 146; CANR 99
Gertler, T. .... **CLC 34**
See also CA 116; 121
Gertsen, Aleksandr Ivanovich
See Herzen, Aleksandr Ivanovich
Ghalib .... **NCLC 39, 78**
See Ghalib, Asadullah Khan
Ghalib, Asadullah Khan 1797-1869
See Ghalib
See also DAM POET; RGWL 2, 3
Ghelderode, Michel de 1898-1962 ..... **CLC 6, 11; DC 15**
See also CA 85-88; CANR 40, 77; DAM DRAM; EW 11; EWL 3; TWA

Ghiselin, Brewster 1903-2001 .... **CLC 23**
See also CA 13-16R; CAAS 10; CANR 13; CP 7
Ghose, Aurabinda 1872-1950 .... **TCLC 63**
See Ghose, Aurobindo
See also CA 163
Ghose, Aurobindo
See Ghose, Aurabinda
See also EWL 3
Ghose, Zulfikar 1935- .... **CLC 42**
See also CA 65-68; CANR 67; CN 7; CP 7; EWL 3
Ghosh, Amitav 1956- .... **CLC 44, 153**
See also CA 147; CANR 80; CN 7
Giacosa, Giuseppe 1847-1906 .... **TCLC 7**
See also CA 104
Gibb, Lee
See Waterhouse, Keith (Spencer)
Gibbon, Lewis Grassic .... **TCLC 4**
See Mitchell, James Leslie
See also RGEL 2
Gibbons, Kaye 1960- .... **CLC 50, 88, 145**
See also AAYA 34; AMWS 10; CA 151; CANR 75; CSW; DA3; DAM POP; MTCW 1; NFS 3; RGAL 4; SATA 117
Gibran, Kahlil 1883-1931 . **PC 9; TCLC 1, 9**
See also CA 104; 150; DA3; DAM POET, POP; EWL 3; MTCW 2
Gibran, Khalil
See Gibran, Kahlil
Gibson, William 1914- .... **CLC 23**
See also CA 9-12R; CAD 2; CANR 9, 42, 75; CD 5; DA; DAB; DAC; DAM DRAM, MST; DFS 2; DLB 7; LAIT 2; MTCW 2; SATA 66; YAW
Gibson, William (Ford) 1948- .... **CLC 39, 63; SSC 52**
See also AAYA 12; BPFB 2; CA 126; 133; CANR 52, 90, 106; CN 7; CPW; DA3; DAM POP; DLB 251; MTCW 2; SCFW 2; SFW 4
Gide, Andre (Paul Guillaume)
1869-1951 ...... **SSC 13; TCLC 5, 12, 36; WLC**
See also CA 104; 124; DA; DA3; DAB; DAC; DAM MST, NOV; DLB 65; EW 8; EWL 3; GFL 1789 to the Present; MTCW 1, 2; RGSF 2; RGWL 2, 3; TWA
Gifford, Barry (Colby) 1946- .... **CLC 34**
See also CA 65-68; CANR 9, 30, 40, 90
Gilbert, Frank
See De Voto, Bernard (Augustine)
Gilbert, W(illiam) S(chwenck)
1836-1911 .... **TCLC 3**
See also CA 104; 173; DAM DRAM, POET; RGEL 2; SATA 36
Gilbreth, Frank B(unker), Jr.
1911-2001 .... **CLC 17**
See also CA 9-12R; SATA 2
Gilchrist, Ellen (Louise) 1935- .. **CLC 34, 48, 143; SSC 14, 63**
See also BPFB 2; CA 113; 116; CANR 41, 61, 104; CN 7; CPW; CSW; DAM POP; DLB 130; EWL 3; EXPS; MTCW 1, 2; RGAL 4; RGSF 2; SSFS 9
Giles, Molly 1942- .... **CLC 39**
See also CA 126; CANR 98
Gill, Eric 1882-1940 .... **TCLC 85**
See Gill, (Arthur) Eric (Rowton Peter Joseph)
Gill, (Arthur) Eric (Rowton Peter Joseph) 1882-1940
See Gill, Eric
See also CA 120; DLB 98
Gill, Patrick
See Creasey, John

Gillette, Douglas .... **CLC 70**
Gilliam, Terry (Vance) 1940- .... **CLC 21, 141**
See Monty Python
See also AAYA 19; CA 108; 113; CANR 35; INT 113
Gillian, Jerry
See Gilliam, Terry (Vance)
Gilliatt, Penelope (Ann Douglass)
1932-1993 .... **CLC 2, 10, 13, 53**
See also AITN 2; CA 13-16R; 141; CANR 49; DLB 14
Gilman, Charlotte (Anna) Perkins (Stetson)
1860-1935 ...... **SSC 13, 62; TCLC 9, 37, 117**
See also AMWS 11; BYA 11; CA 106; 150; DLB 221; EXPS; FW; HGG; LAIT 2; MAWW; MTCW 1; RGAL 4; RGSF 2; SFW 4; SSFS 1, 18
Gilmour, David 1946- .... **CLC 35**
Gilpin, William 1724-1804 .... **NCLC 30**
Gilray, J. D.
See Mencken, H(enry) L(ouis)
Gilroy, Frank D(aniel) 1925- .... **CLC 2**
See also CA 81-84; CAD; CANR 32, 64, 86; CD 5; DFS 17; DLB 7
Gilstrap, John 1957(?)- .... **CLC 99**
See also CA 160; CANR 101
Ginsberg, Allen 1926-1997 ...... **CLC 1, 2, 3, 4, 6, 13, 36, 69, 109; PC 4, 47; TCLC 120; WLC**
See also AAYA 33; AITN 1; AMWC 1; AMWS 2; BG 2; CA 1-4R; 157; CANR 2, 41, 63, 95; CDALB 1941-1968; CP 7; DA; DA3; DAB; DAC; DAM MST, POET; DLB 5, 16, 169, 237; EWL 3; GLL 1; LMFS 2; MTCW 1, 2; PAB; PFS 5; RGAL 4; TUS; WP
Ginzburg, Eugenia .... **CLC 59**
Ginzburg, Natalia 1916-1991 .... **CLC 5, 11, 54, 70; SSC 65**
See also CA 85-88; 135; CANR 33; DFS 14; DLB 177; EW 13; EWL 3; MTCW 1, 2; RGWL 2, 3
Giono, Jean 1895-1970 .... **CLC 4, 11; TCLC 124**
See also CA 45-48; 29-32R; CANR 2, 35; DLB 72; EWL 3; GFL 1789 to the Present; MTCW 1; RGWL 2, 3
Giovanni, Nikki 1943- .... **BLC 2; CLC 2, 4, 19, 64, 117; PC 19; WLCS**
See also AAYA 22; AITN 1; BW 2, 3; CA 29-32R; CAAS 6; CANR 18, 41, 60, 91; CDALBS; CLR 6, 73; CP 7; CSW; CWP; CWRI 5; DA; DA3; DAB; DAC; DAM MST, MULT, POET; DLB 5, 41; EWL 3; EXPP; INT CANR-18; MAICYA 1, 2; MTCW 1, 2; PFS 17; RGAL 4; SATA 24, 107; TUS; YAW
Giovene, Andrea 1904-1998 .... **CLC 7**
See also CA 85-88
Gippius, Zinaida (Nikolaevna) 1869-1945
See Hippius, Zinaida
See also CA 106; 212
Giraudoux, Jean(-Hippolyte)
1882-1944 .... **TCLC 2, 7**
See also CA 104; 196; DAM DRAM; DLB 65; EW 9; EWL 3; GFL 1789 to the Present; RGWL 2, 3; TWA
Gironella, Jose Maria (Pous)
1917-2003 .... **CLC 11**
See also CA 101; 212; EWL 3; RGWL 2, 3
Gissing, George (Robert)
1857-1903 .... **SSC 37; TCLC 3, 24, 47**
See also BRW 5; CA 105; 167; DLB 18, 135, 184; RGEL 2; TEA
Giurlani, Aldo
See Palazzeschi, Aldo

Gladkov, Fedor Vasil'evich
See Gladkov, Fyodor (Vasilyevich)
See also DLB 272

Gladkov, Fyodor (Vasilyevich)
1883-1958 .... TCLC 27
See Gladkov, Fedor Vasil'evich
See also CA 170; EWL 3

Glancy, Diane 1941- .... NNAL
See also CA 136; CAAS 24; CANR 87; DLB 175

Glanville, Brian (Lester) 1931- .... CLC 6
See also CA 5-8R; CAAS 9; CANR 3, 70; CN 7; DLB 15, 139; SATA 42

Glasgow, Ellen (Anderson Gholson)
1873-1945 .... SSC 34; TCLC 2, 7
See also AMW; CA 104; 164; DLB 9, 12; MAWW; MTCW 2; RGAL 4; RHW; SSFS 9; TUS

Glaspell, Susan 1882(?)-1948 ..... DC 10; SSC 41; TCLC 55
See also AMWS 3; CA 110; 154; DFS 8, 18; DLB 7, 9, 78, 228; MAWW; RGAL 4; SSFS 3; TCWW 2; TUS; YABC 2

Glassco, John 1909-1981 .... CLC 9
See also CA 13-16R; 102; CANR 15; DLB 68

Glasscock, Amnesia
See Steinbeck, John (Ernst)

Glasser, Ronald J. 1940(?)- .... CLC 37
See also CA 209

Glassman, Joyce
See Johnson, Joyce

Gleick, James (W.) 1954- .... CLC 147
See also CA 131; 137; CANR 97; INT CA-137

Glendinning, Victoria 1937- .... CLC 50
See also CA 120; 127; CANR 59, 89; DLB 155

Glissant, Edouard (Mathieu)
1928- .... CLC 10, 68
See also CA 153; CANR 111; CWW 2; DAM MULT; EWL 3; RGWL 3

Gloag, Julian 1930- .... CLC 40
See also AITN 1; CA 65-68; CANR 10, 70; CN 7

Glowacki, Aleksander
See Prus, Boleslaw

Gluck, Louise (Elisabeth) 1943- .. CLC 7, 22, 44, 81, 160; PC 16
See also AMWS 5; CA 33-36R; CANR 40, 69, 108; CP 7; CWP; DA3; DAM POET; DLB 5; MTCW 2; PFS 5, 15; RGAL 4

Glyn, Elinor 1864-1943 .... TCLC 72
See also DLB 153; RHW

Gobineau, Joseph-Arthur
1816-1882 .... NCLC 17
See also DLB 123; GFL 1789 to the Present

Godard, Jean-Luc 1930- .... CLC 20
See also CA 93-96

Godden, (Margaret) Rumer
1907-1998 .... CLC 53
See also AAYA 6; BPFB 2; BYA 2, 5; CA 5-8R; 172; CANR 4, 27, 36, 55, 80; CLR 20; CN 7; CWRI 5; DLB 161; MAICYA 1, 2; RHW; SAAS 12; SATA 3, 36; SATA-Obit 109; TEA

Godoy Alcayaga, Lucila 1899-1957 .. HLC 2; PC 32; TCLC 2
See Mistral, Gabriela
See also BW 2; CA 104; 131; CANR 81; DAM MULT; DNFS; HW 1, 2; MTCW 1, 2

Godwin, Gail (Kathleen) 1937- ..... CLC 5, 8, 22, 31, 69, 125
See also BPFB 2; CA 29-32R; CANR 15, 43, 69; CN 7; CPW; CSW; DA3; DAM POP; DLB 6, 234; INT CANR-15; MTCW 1, 2

Godwin, William 1756-1836 .. NCLC 14, 130
See also CDBLB 1789-1832; CMW 4; DLB 39, 104, 142, 158, 163, 262; HGG; RGEL 2

Goebbels, Josef
See Goebbels, (Paul) Joseph

Goebbels, (Paul) Joseph
1897-1945 .... TCLC 68
See also CA 115; 148

Goebbels, Joseph Paul
See Goebbels, (Paul) Joseph

Goethe, Johann Wolfgang von
1749-1832 .... DC 20; NCLC 4, 22, 34, 90; PC 5; SSC 38; WLC
See also CDWLB 2; DA; DA3; DAB; DAC; DAM DRAM, MST, POET; DLB 94; EW 5; LATS 1; LMFS 1; RGWL 2, 3; TWA

Gogarty, Oliver St. John
1878-1957 .... TCLC 15
See also CA 109; 150; DLB 15, 19; RGEL 2

Gogol, Nikolai (Vasilyevich)
1809-1852 .... DC 1; NCLC 5, 15, 31; SSC 4, 29, 52; WLC
See also DA; DAB; DAC; DAM DRAM, MST; DFS 12; DLB 198; EW 6; EXPS; RGSF 2; RGWL 2, 3; SSFS 7; TWA

Goines, Donald 1937(?)-1974 ... BLC 2; CLC 80
See also AITN 1; BW 1, 3; CA 124; 114; CANR 82; CMW 4; DA3; DAM MULT, POP; DLB 33

Gold, Herbert 1924- ... CLC 4, 7, 14, 42, 152
See also CA 9-12R; CANR 17, 45; CN 7; DLB 2; DLBY 1981

Goldbarth, Albert 1948- .... CLC 5, 38
See also AMWS 12; CA 53-56; CANR 6, 40; CP 7; DLB 120

Goldberg, Anatol 1910-1982 .... CLC 34
See also CA 131; 117

Goldemberg, Isaac 1945- .... CLC 52
See also CA 69-72; CAAS 12; CANR 11, 32; EWL 3; HW 1; WLIT 1

Golding, William (Gerald)
1911-1993 ..... CLC 1, 2, 3, 8, 10, 17, 27, 58, 81; WLC
See also AAYA 5, 44; BPFB 2; BRWR 1; BRWS 1; BYA 2; CA 5-8R; 141; CANR 13, 33, 54; CDBLB 1945-1960; DA; DA3; DAB; DAC; DAM MST, NOV; DLB 15, 100, 255; EWL 3; EXPN; HGG; LAIT 4; MTCW 1, 2; NFS 2; RGEL 2; RHW; SFW 4; TEA; WLIT 4; YAW

Goldman, Emma 1869-1940 .... TCLC 13
See also CA 110; 150; DLB 221; FW; RGAL 4; TUS

Goldman, Francisco 1954- .... CLC 76
See also CA 162

Goldman, William (W.) 1931- .... CLC 1, 48
See also BPFB 2; CA 9-12R; CANR 29, 69, 106; CN 7; DLB 44; FANT; IDFW 3, 4

Goldmann, Lucien 1913-1970 .... CLC 24
See also CA 25-28; CAP 2

Goldoni, Carlo 1707-1793 .... LC 4
See also DAM DRAM; EW 4; RGWL 2, 3

Goldsberry, Steven 1949- .... CLC 34
See also CA 131

Goldsmith, Oliver 1730-1774 .... DC 8; LC 2, 48; WLC
See also BRW 3; CDBLB 1660-1789; DA; DAB; DAC; DAM DRAM, MST, NOV, POET; DFS 1; DLB 39, 89, 104, 109, 142; IDTP; RGEL 2; SATA 26; TEA; WLIT 3

Goldsmith, Peter
See Priestley, J(ohn) B(oynton)

Gombrowicz, Witold 1904-1969 .... CLC 4, 7, 11, 49
See also CA 19-20; 25-28R; CANR 105; CAP 2; CDWLB 4; DAM DRAM; DLB 215; EW 12; EWL 3; RGWL 2, 3; TWA

Gomez de Avellaneda, Gertrudis
1814-1873 .... NCLC 111
See also LAW

Gomez de la Serna, Ramon
1888-1963 .... CLC 9
See also CA 153; 116; CANR 79; EWL 3; HW 1, 2

Goncharov, Ivan Alexandrovich
1812-1891 .... NCLC 1, 63
See also DLB 238; EW 6; RGWL 2, 3

Goncourt, Edmond (Louis Antoine Huot) de
1822-1896 .... NCLC 7
See also DLB 123; EW 7; GFL 1789 to the Present; RGWL 2, 3

Goncourt, Jules (Alfred Huot) de
1830-1870 .... NCLC 7
See also DLB 123; EW 7; GFL 1789 to the Present; RGWL 2, 3

Gongora (y Argote), Luis de
1561-1627 .... LC 72
See also RGWL 2, 3

Gontier, Fernande 19(?)- .... CLC 50

Gonzalez Martinez, Enrique
1871-1952 .... TCLC 72
See also CA 166; CANR 81; EWL 3; HW 1, 2

Goodison, Lorna 1947- .... PC 36
See also CA 142; CANR 88; CP 7; CWP; DLB 157; EWL 3

Goodman, Paul 1911-1972 ..... CLC 1, 2, 4, 7
See also CA 19-20; 37-40R; CAD; CANR 34; CAP 2; DLB 130, 246; MTCW 1; RGAL 4

Googe, Barnabe 1540-1594 .... LC 94
See also DLB 132; RGEL 2

Gordimer, Nadine 1923- .... CLC 3, 5, 7, 10, 18, 33, 51, 70, 123, 160, 161; SSC 17; WLCS
See also AAYA 39; AFW; BRWS 2; CA 5-8R; CANR 3, 28, 56, 88; CN 7; DA; DA3; DAB; DAC; DAM MST, NOV; DLB 225; EWL 3; EXPS; INT CANR-28; LATS 1; MTCW 1, 2; NFS 4; RGEL 2; RGSF 2; SSFS 2, 14; TWA; WLIT 2; YAW

Gordon, Adam Lindsay
1833-1870 .... NCLC 21
See also DLB 230

Gordon, Caroline 1895-1981 . CLC 6, 13, 29, 83; SSC 15
See also AMW; CA 11-12; 103; CANR 36; CAP 1; DLB 4, 9, 102; DLBD 17; DLBY 1981; EWL 3; MTCW 1, 2; RGAL 4; RGSF 2

Gordon, Charles William 1860-1937
See Connor, Ralph
See also CA 109

Gordon, Mary (Catherine) 1949- .... CLC 13, 22, 128; SSC 59
See also AMWS 4; BPFB 2; CA 102; CANR 44, 92; CN 7; DLB 6; DLBY 1981; FW; INT CA-102; MTCW 1

Gordon, N. J.
See Bosman, Herman Charles

Gordon, Sol 1923- .... CLC 26
See also CA 53-56; CANR 4; SATA 11

Gordone, Charles 1925-1995 .. CLC 1, 4; DC 8
See also BW 1, 3; CA 93-96; 180; 150; CAAE 180; CAD; CANR 55; DAM DRAM; DLB 7; INT 93-96; MTCW 1

Gore, Catherine 1800-1861 .... NCLC 65
See also DLB 116; RGEL 2

Gorenko, Anna Andreevna
See Akhmatova, Anna
Gorky, Maxim .... **SSC 28; TCLC 8; WLC**
See Peshkov, Alexei Maximovich
See also DAB; DFS 9; EW 8; EWL 3; MTCW 2; TWA
Goryan, Sirak
See Saroyan, William
Gosse, Edmund (William)
1849-1928 .... **TCLC 28**
See also CA 117; DLB 57, 144, 184; RGEL 2
Gotlieb, Phyllis Fay (Bloom) 1926- .. **CLC 18**
See also CA 13-16R; CANR 7; DLB 88, 251; SFW 4
Gottesman, S. D.
See Kornbluth, C(yril) M.; Pohl, Frederik
Gottfried von Strassburg fl. c.
1170-1215 .... **CMLC 10**
See also CDWLB 2; DLB 138; EW 1; RGWL 2, 3
Gotthelf, Jeremias 1797-1854 .... **NCLC 117**
See also DLB 133; RGWL 2, 3
Gottschalk, Laura Riding
See Jackson, Laura (Riding)
Gould, Lois 1932(?)-2002 .... **CLC 4, 10**
See also CA 77-80; 208; CANR 29; MTCW 1
Gould, Stephen Jay 1941-2002 .... **CLC 163**
See also AAYA 26; BEST 90:2; CA 77-80; 205; CANR 10, 27, 56, 75; CPW; INT CANR-27; MTCW 1, 2
Gourmont, Remy(-Marie-Charles) de
1858-1915 .... **TCLC 17**
See also CA 109; 150; GFL 1789 to the Present; MTCW 2
Govier, Katherine 1948- .... **CLC 51**
See also CA 101; CANR 18, 40; CCA 1
Gower, John c. 1330-1408 .... **LC 76**
See also BRW 1; DLB 146; RGEL 2
Goyen, (Charles) William
1915-1983 .... **CLC 5, 8, 14, 40**
See also AITN 2; CA 5-8R; 110; CANR 6, 71; DLB 2, 218; DLBY 1983; EWL 3; INT CANR-6
Goytisolo, Juan 1931- .... **CLC 5, 10, 23, 133; HLC 1**
See also CA 85-88; CANR 32, 61; CWW 2; DAM MULT; EWL 3; GLL 2; HW 1, 2; MTCW 1, 2
Gozzano, Guido 1883-1916 .... **PC 10**
See also CA 154; DLB 114; EWL 3
Gozzi, (Conte) Carlo 1720-1806 .... **NCLC 23**
Grabbe, Christian Dietrich
1801-1836 .... **NCLC 2**
See also DLB 133; RGWL 2, 3
Grace, Patricia Frances 1937- .... **CLC 56**
See also CA 176; CANR 118; CN 7; EWL 3; RGSF 2
Gracian y Morales, Baltasar
1601-1658 .... **LC 15**
Gracq, Julien .... **CLC 11, 48**
See Poirier, Louis
See also CWW 2; DLB 83; GFL 1789 to the Present
Grade, Chaim 1910-1982 .... **CLC 10**
See also CA 93-96; 107; EWL 3
Graduate of Oxford, A
See Ruskin, John
Grafton, Garth
See Duncan, Sara Jeannette
Grafton, Sue 1940- .... **CLC 163**
See also AAYA 11, 49; BEST 90:3; CA 108; CANR 31, 55, 111; CMW 4; CPW; CSW; DA3; DAM POP; DLB 226; FW; MSW
Graham, John
See Phillips, David Graham

Graham, Jorie 1950- .... **CLC 48, 118**
See also CA 111; CANR 63, 118; CP 7; CWP; DLB 120; EWL 3; PFS 10, 17
Graham, R(obert) B(ontine) Cunninghame
See Cunninghame Graham, Robert (Gallnigad) Bontine
See also DLB 98, 135, 174; RGEL 2; RGSF 2
Graham, Robert
See Haldeman, Joe (William)
Graham, Tom
See Lewis, (Harry) Sinclair
Graham, W(illiam) S(idney)
1918-1986 .... **CLC 29**
See also BRWS 7; CA 73-76; 118; DLB 20; RGEL 2
Graham, Winston (Mawdsley)
1910-2003 .... **CLC 23**
See also CA 49-52; CANR 2, 22, 45, 66; CMW 4; CN 7; DLB 77; RHW
Grahame, Kenneth 1859-1932 ...... **TCLC 64, 136**
See also BYA 5; CA 108; 136; CANR 80; CLR 5; CWRI 5; DA3; DAB; DLB 34, 141, 178; FANT; MAICYA 1, 2; MTCW 2; RGEL 2; SATA 100; TEA; WCH; YABC 1
Granger, Darius John
See Marlowe, Stephen
Granin, Daniil .... **CLC 59**
Granovsky, Timofei Nikolaevich
1813-1855 .... **NCLC 75**
See also DLB 198
Grant, Skeeter
See Spiegelman, Art
Granville-Barker, Harley
1877-1946 .... **TCLC 2**
See Barker, Harley Granville
See also CA 104; 204; DAM DRAM; RGEL 2
Granzotto, Gianni
See Granzotto, Giovanni Battista
Granzotto, Giovanni Battista
1914-1985 .... **CLC 70**
See also CA 166
Grass, Guenter (Wilhelm) 1927- ... **CLC 1, 2, 4, 6, 11, 15, 22, 32, 49, 88; WLC**
See also BPFB 2; CA 13-16R; CANR 20, 75, 93; CDWLB 2; DA; DA3; DAB; DAC; DAM MST, NOV; DLB 75, 124; EW 13; EWL 3; MTCW 1, 2; RGWL 2, 3; TWA
Gratton, Thomas
See Hulme, T(homas) E(rnest)
Grau, Shirley Ann 1929- .... **CLC 4, 9, 146; SSC 15**
See also CA 89-92; CANR 22, 69; CN 7; CSW; DLB 2, 218; INT CA-89-92, CANR-22; MTCW 1
Gravel, Fern
See Hall, James Norman
Graver, Elizabeth 1964- .... **CLC 70**
See also CA 135; CANR 71
Graves, Richard Perceval
1895-1985 .... **CLC 44**
See also CA 65-68; CANR 9, 26, 51
Graves, Robert (von Ranke)
1895-1985 .. **CLC 1, 2, 6, 11, 39, 44, 45; PC 6**
See also BPFB 2; BRW 7; BYA 4; CA 5-8R; 117; CANR 5, 36; CDBLB 1914-1945; DA3; DAB; DAC; DAM MST, POET; DLB 20, 100, 191; DLBD 18; DLBY 1985; EWL 3; LATS 1; MTCW 1, 2; NCFS 2; RGEL 2; RHW; SATA 45; TEA
Graves, Valerie
See Bradley, Marion Zimmer

Gray, Alasdair (James) 1934- .... **CLC 41**
See also BRWS 9; CA 126; CANR 47, 69, 106; CN 7; DLB 194, 261; HGG; INT CA-126; MTCW 1, 2; RGSF 2; SUFW 2
Gray, Amlin 1946- .... **CLC 29**
See also CA 138
Gray, Francine du Plessix 1930- ...... **CLC 22, 153**
See also BEST 90:3; CA 61-64; CAAS 2; CANR 11, 33, 75, 81; DAM NOV; INT CANR-11; MTCW 1, 2
Gray, John (Henry) 1866-1934 .... **TCLC 19**
See also CA 119; 162; RGEL 2
Gray, Simon (James Holliday)
1936- .... **CLC 9, 14, 36**
See also AITN 1; CA 21-24R; CAAS 3; CANR 32, 69; CD 5; DLB 13; EWL 3; MTCW 1; RGEL 2
Gray, Spalding 1941- ...... **CLC 49, 112; DC 7**
See also CA 128; CAD; CANR 74; CD 5; CPW; DAM POP; MTCW 2
Gray, Thomas 1716-1771 .... **LC 4, 40; PC 2; WLC**
See also BRW 3; CDBLB 1660-1789; DA; DA3; DAB; DAC; DAM MST; DLB 109; EXPP; PAB; PFS 9; RGEL 2; TEA; WP
Grayson, David
See Baker, Ray Stannard
Grayson, Richard (A.) 1951- .... **CLC 38**
See also CA 85-88; CAAE 210; CANR 14, 31, 57; DLB 234
Greeley, Andrew M(oran) 1928- ...... **CLC 28**
See also BPFB 2; CA 5-8R; CAAS 7; CANR 7, 43, 69, 104; CMW 4; CPW; DA3; DAM POP; MTCW 1, 2
Green, Anna Katharine
1846-1935 .... **TCLC 63**
See also CA 112; 159; CMW 4; DLB 202, 221; MSW
Green, Brian
See Card, Orson Scott
Green, Hannah
See Greenberg, Joanne (Goldenberg)
Green, Hannah 1927(?)-1996 .... **CLC 3**
See also CA 73-76; CANR 59, 93; NFS 10
Green, Henry .... **CLC 2, 13, 97**
See Yorke, Henry Vincent
See also BRWS 2; CA 175; DLB 15; EWL 3; RGEL 2
Green, Julian (Hartridge) 1900-1998
See Green, Julien
See also CA 21-24R; 169; CANR 33, 87; DLB 4, 72; MTCW 1
Green, Julien .... **CLC 3, 11, 77**
See Green, Julian (Hartridge)
See also EWL 3; GFL 1789 to the Present; MTCW 2
Green, Paul (Eliot) 1894-1981 .... **CLC 25**
See also AITN 1; CA 5-8R; 103; CANR 3; DAM DRAM; DLB 7, 9, 249; DLBY 1981; RGAL 4
Greenaway, Peter 1942- .... **CLC 159**
See also CA 127
Greenberg, Ivan 1908-1973
See Rahv, Philip
See also CA 85-88
Greenberg, Joanne (Goldenberg)
1932- .... **CLC 7, 30**
See also AAYA 12; CA 5-8R; CANR 14, 32, 69; CN 7; SATA 25; YAW
Greenberg, Richard 1959(?)- .... **CLC 57**
See also CA 138; CAD; CD 5
Greenblatt, Stephen J(ay) 1943- .... **CLC 70**
See also CA 49-52; CANR 115
Greene, Bette 1934- .... **CLC 30**
See also AAYA 7; BYA 3; CA 53-56; CANR 4; CLR 7; CWRI 5; JRDA; LAIT 4; MAICYA 1, 2; NFS 10; SAAS 16; SATA 8, 102; WYA; YAW

Greene, Gael .... CLC 8
See also CA 13-16R; CANR 10

Greene, Graham (Henry)
1904-1991 .... **CLC 1, 3, 6, 9, 14, 18, 27, 37, 70, 72, 125; SSC 29; WLC**
See also AITN 2; BPFB 2; BRWR 2; BRWS 1; BYA 3; CA 13-16R; 133; CANR 35, 61; CBD; CDBLB 1945-1960; CMW 4; DA; DA3; DAB; DAC; DAM MST, NOV; DLB 13, 15, 77, 100, 162, 201, 204; DLBY 1991; EWL 3; MSW; MTCW 1, 2; NFS 16; RGEL 2; SATA 20; SSFS 14; TEA; WLIT 4

Greene, Robert 1558-1592 .... **LC 41**
See also BRWS 8; DLB 62, 167; IDTP; RGEL 2; TEA

Greer, Germaine 1939- .... **CLC 131**
See also AITN 1; CA 81-84; CANR 33, 70, 115; FW; MTCW 1, 2

Greer, Richard
See Silverberg, Robert

Gregor, Arthur 1923- .... **CLC 9**
See also CA 25-28R; CAAS 10; CANR 11; CP 7; SATA 36

Gregor, Lee
See Pohl, Frederik

Gregory, Lady Isabella Augusta (Persse)
1852-1932 .... **TCLC 1**
See also BRW 6; CA 104; 184; DLB 10; IDTP; RGEL 2

Gregory, J. Dennis
See Williams, John A(lfred)

Grekova, I. .... **CLC 59**

Grendon, Stephen
See Derleth, August (William)

Grenville, Kate 1950- .... **CLC 61**
See also CA 118; CANR 53, 93

Grenville, Pelham
See Wodehouse, P(elham) G(renville)

Greve, Felix Paul (Berthold Friedrich)
1879-1948
See Grove, Frederick Philip
See also CA 104; 141, 175; CANR 79; DAC; DAM MST

Greville, Fulke 1554-1628 .... **LC 79**
See also DLB 62, 172; RGEL 2

Grey, Lady Jane 1537-1554 .... **LC 93**
See also DLB 132

Grey, Zane 1872-1939 .... **TCLC 6**
See also BPFB 2; CA 104; 132; DA3; DAM POP; DLB 9, 212; MTCW 1, 2; RGAL 4; TCWW 2; TUS

Griboedov, Aleksandr Sergeevich
1795(?)-1829 .... **NCLC 129**
See also DLB 205; RGWL 2, 3

Grieg, (Johan) Nordahl (Brun)
1902-1943 .... **TCLC 10**
See also CA 107; 189; EWL 3

Grieve, C(hristopher) M(urray)
1892-1978 .... **CLC 11, 19**
See MacDiarmid, Hugh; Pteleon
See also CA 5-8R; 85-88; CANR 33, 107; DAM POET; MTCW 1; RGEL 2

Griffin, Gerald 1803-1840 .... **NCLC 7**
See also DLB 159; RGEL 2

Griffin, John Howard 1920-1980 .... **CLC 68**
See also AITN 1; CA 1-4R; 101; CANR 2

Griffin, Peter 1942- .... **CLC 39**
See also CA 136

Griffith, D(avid Lewelyn) W(ark)
1875(?)-1948 .... **TCLC 68**
See also CA 119; 150; CANR 80

Griffith, Lawrence
See Griffith, D(avid Lewelyn) W(ark)

Griffiths, Trevor 1935- .... **CLC 13, 52**
See also CA 97-100; CANR 45; CBD; CD 5; DLB 13, 245

Griggs, Sutton (Elbert)
1872-1930 .... **TCLC 77**
See also CA 123; 186; DLB 50

Grigson, Geoffrey (Edward Harvey)
1905-1985 .... **CLC 7, 39**
See also CA 25-28R; 118; CANR 20, 33; DLB 27; MTCW 1, 2

Grile, Dod
See Bierce, Ambrose (Gwinett)

Grillparzer, Franz 1791-1872 .... **DC 14; NCLC 1, 102; SSC 37**
See also CDWLB 2; DLB 133; EW 5; RGWL 2, 3; TWA

Grimble, Reverend Charles James
See Eliot, T(homas) S(tearns)

Grimke, Angelina (Emily) Weld
1880-1958 .... **HR 2**
See Weld, Angelina (Emily) Grimke
See also BW 1; CA 124; DAM POET; DLB 50, 54

Grimke, Charlotte L(ottie) Forten
1837(?)-1914
See Forten, Charlotte L.
See also BW 1; CA 117; 124; DAM MULT, POET

Grimm, Jacob Ludwig Karl
1785-1863 .... **NCLC 3, 77; SSC 36**
See also DLB 90; MAICYA 1, 2; RGSF 2; RGWL 2, 3; SATA 22; WCH

Grimm, Wilhelm Karl 1786-1859 .... **NCLC 3, 77; SSC 36**
See also CDWLB 2; DLB 90; MAICYA 1, 2; RGSF 2; RGWL 2, 3; SATA 22; WCH

Grimmelshausen, Hans Jakob Christoffel von
See Grimmelshausen, Johann Jakob Christoffel von
See also RGWL 2, 3

Grimmelshausen, Johann Jakob Christoffel von 1621-1676 .... **LC 6**
See Grimmelshausen, Hans Jakob Christoffel von
See also CDWLB 2; DLB 168

Grindel, Eugene 1895-1952
See Eluard, Paul
See also CA 104; 193; LMFS 2

Grisham, John 1955- .... **CLC 84**
See also AAYA 14, 47; BPFB 2; CA 138; CANR 47, 69, 114; CMW 4; CN 7; CPW; CSW; DA3; DAM POP; MSW; MTCW 2

Grosseteste, Robert 1175(?)-1253 . **CMLC 62**
See also DLB 115

Grossman, David 1954- .... **CLC 67**
See also CA 138; CANR 114; CWW 2; EWL 3

Grossman, Vasilii Semenovich
See Grossman, Vasily (Semenovich)
See also DLB 272

Grossman, Vasily (Semenovich)
1905-1964 .... **CLC 41**
See Grossman, Vasilii Semenovich
See also CA 124; 130; MTCW 1

Grove, Frederick Philip .... **TCLC 4**
See Greve, Felix Paul (Berthold Friedrich)
See also DLB 92; RGEL 2

Grubb
See Crumb, R(obert)

Grumbach, Doris (Isaac) 1918- . **CLC 13, 22, 64**
See also CA 5-8R; CAAS 2; CANR 9, 42, 70; CN 7; INT CANR-9; MTCW 2

Grundtvig, Nicolai Frederik Severin
1783-1872 .... **NCLC 1**

Grunge
See Crumb, R(obert)

Grunwald, Lisa 1959- .... **CLC 44**
See also CA 120

Gryphius, Andreas 1616-1664 .... **LC 89**
See also CDWLB 2; DLB 164; RGWL 2, 3

Guare, John 1938- .... **CLC 8, 14, 29, 67; DC 20**
See also CA 73-76; CAD; CANR 21, 69, 118; CD 5; DAM DRAM; DFS 8, 13; DLB 7, 249; EWL 3; MTCW 1, 2; RGAL 4

Gubar, Susan (David) 1944- .... **CLC 145**
See also CA 108; CANR 45, 70; FW; MTCW 1; RGAL 4

Gudjonsson, Halldor Kiljan 1902-1998
See Laxness, Halldor
See also CA 103; 164; CWW 2

Guenter, Erich
See Eich, Gunter

Guest, Barbara 1920- .... **CLC 34**
See also BG 2; CA 25-28R; CANR 11, 44, 84; CP 7; CWP; DLB 5, 193

Guest, Edgar A(lbert) 1881-1959 ... **TCLC 95**
See also CA 112; 168

Guest, Judith (Ann) 1936- .... **CLC 8, 30**
See also AAYA 7; CA 77-80; CANR 15, 75; DA3; DAM NOV, POP; EXPN; INT CANR-15; LAIT 5; MTCW 1, 2; NFS 1

Guevara, Che .... **CLC 87; HLC 1**
See Guevara (Serna), Ernesto

Guevara (Serna), Ernesto
1928-1967 .... **CLC 87; HLC 1**
See Guevara, Che
See also CA 127; 111; CANR 56; DAM MULT; HW 1

Guicciardini, Francesco 1483-1540 ..... **LC 49**

Guild, Nicholas M. 1944- .... **CLC 33**
See also CA 93-96

Guillemin, Jacques
See Sartre, Jean-Paul

Guillen, Jorge 1893-1984 . **CLC 11; HLCS 1; PC 35**
See also CA 89-92; 112; DAM MULT, POET; DLB 108; EWL 3; HW 1; RGWL 2, 3

Guillen, Nicolas (Cristobal)
1902-1989 .... **BLC 2; CLC 48, 79; HLC 1; PC 23**
See also BW 2; CA 116; 125; 129; CANR 84; DAM MST, MULT, POET; DLB 283; EWL 3; HW 1; LAW; RGWL 2, 3; WP

Guillen y Alvarez, Jorge
See Guillen, Jorge

Guillevic, (Eugene) 1907-1997 .... **CLC 33**
See also CA 93-96; CWW 2

Guillois
See Desnos, Robert

Guillois, Valentin
See Desnos, Robert

Guimaraes Rosa, Joao 1908-1967 .... **HLCS 2**
See also CA 175; LAW; RGSF 2; RGWL 2, 3

Guiney, Louise Imogen
1861-1920 .... **TCLC 41**
See also CA 160; DLB 54; RGAL 4

Guinizelli, Guido c. 1230-1276 .... **CMLC 49**

Guiraldes, Ricardo (Guillermo)
1886-1927 .... **TCLC 39**
See also CA 131; EWL 3; HW 1; LAW; MTCW 1

Gumilev, Nikolai (Stepanovich)
1886-1921 .... **TCLC 60**
See Gumilyov, Nikolay Stepanovich
See also CA 165

Gumilyov, Nikolay Stepanovich
See Gumilev, Nikolai (Stepanovich)
See also EWL 3

Gunesekera, Romesh 1954- .... **CLC 91**
See also CA 159; CN 7; DLB 267

Gunn, Bill .... **CLC 5**
See Gunn, William Harrison
See also DLB 38

Gunn, Thom(son William) 1929- .. **CLC 3, 6, 18, 32, 81; PC 26**
See also BRWS 4; CA 17-20R; CANR 9, 33, 116; CDBLB 1960 to Present; CP 7; DAM POET; DLB 27; INT CANR-33; MTCW 1; PFS 9; RGEL 2

Gunn, William Harrison 1934(?)-1989
See Gunn, Bill
See also AITN 1; BW 1, 3; CA 13-16R; 128; CANR 12, 25, 76

Gunn Allen, Paula
See Allen, Paula Gunn

Gunnars, Kristjana 1948- .... **CLC 69**
See also CA 113; CCA 1; CP 7; CWP; DLB 60

Gunter, Erich
See Eich, Gunter

Gurdjieff, G(eorgei) I(vanovich)
1877(?)-1949 .... **TCLC 71**
See also CA 157

Gurganus, Allan 1947- .... **CLC 70**
See also BEST 90:1; CA 135; CANR 114; CN 7; CPW; CSW; DAM POP; GLL 1

Gurney, A. R.
See Gurney, A(lbert) R(amsdell), Jr.
See also DLB 266

Gurney, A(lbert) R(amsdell), Jr.
1930- .... **CLC 32, 50, 54**
See Gurney, A. R.
See also AMWS 5; CA 77-80; CAD; CANR 32, 64, 121; CD 5; DAM DRAM; EWL 3

Gurney, Ivor (Bertie) 1890-1937 ... **TCLC 33**
See also BRW 6; CA 167; DLBY 2002; PAB; RGEL 2

Gurney, Peter
See Gurney, A(lbert) R(amsdell), Jr.

Guro, Elena 1877-1913 .... **TCLC 56**

Gustafson, James M(oody) 1925- ... **CLC 100**
See also CA 25-28R; CANR 37

Gustafson, Ralph (Barker)
1909-1995 .... **CLC 36**
See also CA 21-24R; CANR 8, 45, 84; CP 7; DLB 88; RGEL 2

Gut, Gom
See Simenon, Georges (Jacques Christian)

Guterson, David 1956- .... **CLC 91**
See also CA 132; CANR 73; MTCW 2; NFS 13

Guthrie, A(lfred) B(ertram), Jr.
1901-1991 .... **CLC 23**
See also CA 57-60; 134; CANR 24; DLB 6, 212; SATA 62; SATA-Obit 67

Guthrie, Isobel
See Grieve, C(hristopher) M(urray)

Guthrie, Woodrow Wilson 1912-1967
See Guthrie, Woody
See also CA 113; 93-96

Guthrie, Woody .... **CLC 35**
See Guthrie, Woodrow Wilson
See also LAIT 3

Gutierrez Najera, Manuel
1859-1895 .... **HLCS 2**
See also LAW

Guy, Rosa (Cuthbert) 1925- .... **CLC 26**
See also AAYA 4, 37; BW 2; CA 17-20R; CANR 14, 34, 83; CLR 13; DLB 33; DNFS 1; JRDA; MAICYA 1, 2; SATA 14, 62, 122; YAW

Gwendolyn
See Bennett, (Enoch) Arnold

H. D. .... **CLC 3, 8, 14, 31, 34, 73; PC 5**
See Doolittle, Hilda

H. de V.
See Buchan, John

Haavikko, Paavo Juhani 1931- .. **CLC 18, 34**
See also CA 106; EWL 3

Habbema, Koos
See Heijermans, Herman

Habermas, Juergen 1929- .... **CLC 104**
See also CA 109; CANR 85; DLB 242

Habermas, Jurgen
See Habermas, Juergen

Hacker, Marilyn 1942- ...... **CLC 5, 9, 23, 72, 91; PC 47**
See also CA 77-80; CANR 68; CP 7; CWP; DAM POET; DLB 120, 282; FW; GLL 2

Hadewijch of Antwerp fl. 1250- ... **CMLC 61**
See also RGWL 3

Hadrian 76-138 .... **CMLC 52**

Haeckel, Ernst Heinrich (Philipp August)
1834-1919 .... **TCLC 83**
See also CA 157

Hafiz c. 1326-1389(?) .... **CMLC 34**
See also RGWL 2, 3

Haggard, H(enry) Rider
1856-1925 .... **TCLC 11**
See also BRWS 3; BYA 4, 5; CA 108; 148; CANR 112; DLB 70, 156, 174, 178; FANT; LMFS 1; MTCW 2; RGEL 2; RHW; SATA 16; SCFW; SFW 4; SUFW 1; WLIT 4

Hagiosy, L.
See Larbaud, Valery (Nicolas)

Hagiwara, Sakutaro 1886-1942 .... **PC 18; TCLC 60**
See Hagiwara Sakutaro
See also CA 154; RGWL 3

Hagiwara Sakutaro
See Hagiwara, Sakutaro
See also EWL 3

Haig, Fenil
See Ford, Ford Madox

Haig-Brown, Roderick (Langmere)
1908-1976 .... **CLC 21**
See also CA 5-8R; 69-72; CANR 4, 38, 83; CLR 31; CWRI 5; DLB 88; MAICYA 1, 2; SATA 12

Haight, Rip
See Carpenter, John (Howard)

Hailey, Arthur 1920- .... **CLC 5**
See also AITN 2; BEST 90:3; BPFB 2; CA 1-4R; CANR 2, 36, 75; CCA 1; CN 7; CPW; DAM NOV, POP; DLB 88; DLBY 1982; MTCW 1, 2

Hailey, Elizabeth Forsythe 1938- ..... **CLC 40**
See also CA 93-96; CAAE 188; CAAS 1; CANR 15, 48; INT CANR-15

Haines, John (Meade) 1924- .... **CLC 58**
See also AMWS 12; CA 17-20R; CANR 13, 34; CSW; DLB 5, 212

Hakluyt, Richard 1552-1616 .... **LC 31**
See also DLB 136; RGEL 2

Haldeman, Joe (William) 1943- .... **CLC 61**
See Graham, Robert
See also AAYA 38; CA 53-56, 179; CAAE 179; CAAS 25; CANR 6, 70, 72; DLB 8; INT CANR-6; SCFW 2; SFW 4

Hale, Janet Campbell 1947- .... **NNAL**
See also CA 49-52; CANR 45, 75; DAM MULT; DLB 175; MTCW 2

Hale, Sarah Josepha (Buell)
1788-1879 .... **NCLC 75**
See also DLB 1, 42, 73, 243

Halevy, Elie 1870-1937 .... **TCLC 104**

Haley, Alex(ander Murray Palmer)
1921-1992 .... **BLC 2; CLC 8, 12, 76**
See also AAYA 26; BPFB 2; BW 2, 3; CA 77-80; 136; CANR 61; CDALBS; CPW; CSW; DA; DA3; DAB; DAC; DAM MST, MULT, POP; DLB 38; LAIT 5; MTCW 1, 2; NFS 9

Haliburton, Thomas Chandler
1796-1865 .... **NCLC 15**
See also DLB 11, 99; RGEL 2; RGSF 2

Hall, Donald (Andrew, Jr.) 1928- ...... **CLC 1, 13, 37, 59, 151**
See also CA 5-8R; CAAS 7; CANR 2, 44, 64, 106; CP 7; DAM POET; DLB 5; MTCW 1; RGAL 4; SATA 23, 97

Hall, Frederic Sauser
See Sauser-Hall, Frederic

Hall, James
See Kuttner, Henry

Hall, James Norman 1887-1951 ..... **TCLC 23**
See also CA 123; 173; LAIT 1; RHW 1; SATA 21

Hall, Joseph 1574-1656 .... **LC 91**
See also DLB 121, 151; RGEL 2

Hall, (Marguerite) Radclyffe
1880-1943 .... **TCLC 12**
See also BRWS 6; CA 110; 150; CANR 83; DLB 191; MTCW 2; RGEL 2; RHW

Hall, Rodney 1935- .... **CLC 51**
See also CA 109; CANR 69; CN 7; CP 7; DLB 289

Hallam, Arthur Henry
1811-1833 .... **NCLC 110**
See also DLB 32

Halleck, Fitz-Greene 1790-1867 ..... **NCLC 47**
See also DLB 3, 250; RGAL 4

Halliday, Michael
See Creasey, John

Halpern, Daniel 1945- .... **CLC 14**
See also CA 33-36R; CANR 93; CP 7

Hamburger, Michael (Peter Leopold)
1924- .... **CLC 5, 14**
See also CA 5-8R; CAAE 196; CAAS 4; CANR 2, 47; CP 7; DLB 27

Hamill, Pete 1935- .... **CLC 10**
See also CA 25-28R; CANR 18, 71

Hamilton, Alexander
1755(?)-1804 .... **NCLC 49**
See also DLB 37

Hamilton, Clive
See Lewis, C(live) S(taples)

Hamilton, Edmond 1904-1977 .... **CLC 1**
See also CA 1-4R; CANR 3, 84; DLB 8; SATA 118; SFW 4

Hamilton, Eugene (Jacob) Lee
See Lee-Hamilton, Eugene (Jacob)

Hamilton, Franklin
See Silverberg, Robert

Hamilton, Gail
See Corcoran, Barbara (Asenath)

Hamilton, Jane 1957- .... **CLC 179**
See also CA 147; CANR 85

Hamilton, Mollie
See Kaye, M(ary) M(argaret)

Hamilton, (Anthony Walter) Patrick
1904-1962 .... **CLC 51**
See also CA 176; 113; DLB 10, 191

Hamilton, Virginia (Esther)
1936-2002 .... **CLC 26**
See also AAYA 2, 21; BW 2, 3; BYA 1, 2, 8; CA 25-28R; 206; CANR 20, 37, 73; CLR 1, 11, 40; DAM MULT; DLB 33, 52; DLBY 01; INT CANR-20; JRDA; LAIT 5; MAICYA 1, 2; MAICYAS 1; MTCW 1, 2; SATA 4, 56, 79, 123; SATA-Obit 132; WYA; YAW

Hammett, (Samuel) Dashiell
1894-1961 .... **CLC 3, 5, 10, 19, 47; SSC 17**
See also AITN 1; AMWS 4; BPFB 2; CA 81-84; CANR 42; CDALB 1929-1941; CMW 4; DA3; DLB 226; DLBD 6; DLBY 1996; EWL 3; LAIT 3; MSW; MTCW 1, 2; RGAL 4; RGSF 2; TUS

Hammon, Jupiter 1720(?)-1800(?) .... **BLC 2; NCLC 5; PC 16**
See also DAM MULT, POET; DLB 31, 50

Hammond, Keith
See Kuttner, Henry

Hamner, Earl (Henry), Jr. 1923- ...... **CLC 12**
See also AITN 2; CA 73-76; DLB 6

Hampton, Christopher (James)
1946- .... **CLC 4**
See also CA 25-28R; CD 5; DLB 13;
MTCW 1

Hamsun, Knut .... **TCLC 2, 14, 49**
See Pedersen, Knut
See also EW 8; EWL 3; RGWL 2, 3

Handke, Peter 1942- .... **CLC 5, 8, 10, 15, 38, 134; DC 17**
See also CA 77-80; CANR 33, 75, 104;
CWW 2; DAM DRAM, NOV; DLB 85,
124; EWL 3; MTCW 1, 2; TWA

Handy, W(illiam) C(hristopher)
1873-1958 .... **TCLC 97**
See also BW 3; CA 121; 167

Hanley, James 1901-1985 ..... **CLC 3, 5, 8, 13**
See also CA 73-76; 117; CANR 36; CBD;
DLB 191; EWL 3; MTCW 1; RGEL 2

Hannah, Barry 1942- .... **CLC 23, 38, 90**
See also BPFB 2; CA 108; 110; CANR 43,
68, 113; CN 7; CSW; DLB 6, 234; INT
CA-110; MTCW 1; RGSF 2

Hannon, Ezra
See Hunter, Evan

Hansberry, Lorraine (Vivian)
1930-1965 ... **BLC 2; CLC 17, 62; DC 2**
See also AAYA 25; AFAW 1, 2; AMWS 4;
BW 1, 3; CA 109; 25-28R; CABS 3;
CAD; CANR 58; CDALB 1941-1968;
CWD; DA; DA3; DAB; DAC; DAM
DRAM, MST, MULT; DFS 2; DLB 7, 38;
EWL 3; FW; LAIT 4; MTCW 1, 2; RGAL
4; TUS

Hansen, Joseph 1923- .... **CLC 38**
See Brock, Rose; Colton, James
See also BPFB 2; CA 29-32R; CAAS 17;
CANR 16, 44, 66; CMW 4; DLB 226;
GLL 1; INT CANR-16

Hansen, Martin A(lfred)
1909-1955 .... **TCLC 32**
See also CA 167; DLB 214; EWL 3

Hansen and Philipson eds. .... **CLC 65**

Hanson, Kenneth O(stlin) 1922- .... **CLC 13**
See also CA 53-56; CANR 7

Hardwick, Elizabeth (Bruce) 1916- . **CLC 13**
See also AMWS 3; CA 5-8R; CANR 3, 32,
70, 100; CN 7; CSW; DA3; DAM NOV;
DLB 6; MAWW; MTCW 1, 2

Hardy, Thomas 1840-1928 .... **PC 8; SSC 2, 60; TCLC 4, 10, 18, 32, 48, 53, 72; WLC**
See also BRW 6; BRWC 1, 2; BRWR 1;
CA 104; 123; CDBLB 1890-1914; DA;
DA3; DAB; DAC; DAM MST, NOV,
POET; DLB 18, 19, 135, 284; EWL 3;
EXPN; EXPP; LAIT 2; MTCW 1, 2; NFS
3, 11, 15; PFS 3, 4, 18; RGEL 2; RGSF
2; TEA; WLIT 4

Hare, David 1947- .... **CLC 29, 58, 136**
See also BRWS 4; CA 97-100; CANR 39,
91; CBD; CD 5; DFS 4, 7, 16; DLB 13;
MTCW 1; TEA

Harewood, John
See Van Druten, John (William)

Harford, Henry
See Hudson, W(illiam) H(enry)

Hargrave, Leonie
See Disch, Thomas M(ichael)

Hariri, Al- al-Qasim ibn 'Ali Abu Muhammad al-Basri
See al-Hariri, al-Qasim ibn 'Ali Abu Muhammad al-Basri

Harjo, Joy 1951- ..... **CLC 83; NNAL; PC 27**
See also AMWS 12; CA 114; CANR 35,
67, 91; CP 7; CWP; DAM MULT; DLB
120, 175; EWL 3; MTCW 2; PFS 15;
RGAL 4

Harlan, Louis R(udolph) 1922- .... **CLC 34**
See also CA 21-24R; CANR 25, 55, 80

Harling, Robert 1951(?)- .... **CLC 53**
See also CA 147

Harmon, William (Ruth) 1938- .... **CLC 38**
See also CA 33-36R; CANR 14, 32, 35;
SATA 65

Harper, F. E. W.
See Harper, Frances Ellen Watkins

Harper, Frances E. W.
See Harper, Frances Ellen Watkins

Harper, Frances E. Watkins
See Harper, Frances Ellen Watkins

Harper, Frances Ellen
See Harper, Frances Ellen Watkins

Harper, Frances Ellen Watkins
1825-1911 ..... **BLC 2; PC 21; TCLC 14**
See also AFAW 1, 2; BW 1, 3; CA 111; 125;
CANR 79; DAM MULT, POET; DLB 50,
221; MAWW; RGAL 4

Harper, Michael S(teven) 1938- ... **CLC 7, 22**
See also AFAW 2; BW 1; CA 33-36R;
CANR 24, 108; CP 7; DLB 41; RGAL 4

Harper, Mrs. F. E. W.
See Harper, Frances Ellen Watkins

Harpur, Charles 1813-1868 .... **NCLC 114**
See also DLB 230; RGEL 2

Harris, Christie 1907-
See Harris, Christie (Lucy) Irwin

Harris, Christie (Lucy) Irwin
1907-2002 .... **CLC 12**
See also CA 5-8R; CANR 6, 83; CLR 47;
DLB 88; JRDA; MAICYA 1, 2; SAAS 10;
SATA 6, 74; SATA-Essay 116

Harris, Frank 1856-1931 .... **TCLC 24**
See also CA 109; 150; CANR 80; DLB 156,
197; RGEL 2

Harris, George Washington
1814-1869 .... **NCLC 23**
See also DLB 3, 11, 248; RGAL 4

Harris, Joel Chandler 1848-1908 ..... **SSC 19; TCLC 2**
See also CA 104; 137; CANR 80; CLR 49;
DLB 11, 23, 42, 78, 91; LAIT 2; MAICYA 1, 2; RGSF 2; SATA 100; WCH;
YABC 1

Harris, John (Wyndham Parkes Lucas) Beynon 1903-1969
See Wyndham, John
See also CA 102; 89-92; CANR 84; SATA
118; SFW 4

Harris, MacDonald .... **CLC 9**
See Heiney, Donald (William)

Harris, Mark 1922- .... **CLC 19**
See also CA 5-8R; CAAS 3; CANR 2, 55,
83; CN 7; DLB 2; DLBY 1980

Harris, Norman .... **CLC 65**

Harris, (Theodore) Wilson 1921- .... **CLC 25, 159**
See also BRWS 5; BW 2, 3; CA 65-68;
CAAS 16; CANR 11, 27, 69, 114; CDWLB 3; CN 7; CP 7; DLB 117; EWL 3;
MTCW 1; RGEL 2

Harrison, Barbara Grizzuti
1934-2002 .... **CLC 144**
See also CA 77-80; 205; CANR 15, 48; INT
CANR-15

Harrison, Elizabeth (Allen) Cavanna
1909-2001
See Cavanna, Betty
See also CA 9-12R; 200; CANR 6, 27, 85,
104, 121; MAICYA 2; SATA 142; YAW

Harrison, Harry (Max) 1925- .... **CLC 42**
See also CA 1-4R; CANR 5, 21, 84; DLB
8; SATA 4; SCFW 2; SFW 4

Harrison, James (Thomas) 1937- ...... **CLC 6, 14, 33, 66, 143; SSC 19**
See Harrison, Jim
See also CA 13-16R; CANR 8, 51, 79; CN
7; CP 7; DLBY 1982; INT CANR-8

Harrison, Jim
See Harrison, James (Thomas)
See also AMWS 8; RGAL 4; TCWW 2;
TUS

Harrison, Kathryn 1961- .... **CLC 70, 151**
See also CA 144; CANR 68, 122

Harrison, Tony 1937- .... **CLC 43, 129**
See also BRWS 5; CA 65-68; CANR 44,
98; CBD; CD 5; CP 7; DLB 40, 245;
MTCW 1; RGEL 2

Harriss, Will(ard Irvin) 1922- .... **CLC 34**
See also CA 111

Hart, Ellis
See Ellison, Harlan (Jay)

Hart, Josephine 1942(?)- .... **CLC 70**
See also CA 138; CANR 70; CPW; DAM
POP

Hart, Moss 1904-1961 .... **CLC 66**
See also CA 109; 89-92; CANR 84; DAM
DRAM; DFS 1; DLB 7, 266; RGAL 4

Harte, (Francis) Bret(t)
1836(?)-1902 ... **SSC 8, 59; TCLC 1, 25; WLC**
See also AMWS 2; CA 104; 140; CANR
80; CDALB 1865-1917; DA; DA3; DAC;
DAM MST; DLB 12, 64, 74, 79, 186;
EXPS; LAIT 2; RGAL 4; RGSF 2; SATA
26; SSFS 3; TUS

Hartley, L(eslie) P(oles) 1895-1972 ... **CLC 2, 22**
See also BRWS 7; CA 45-48; 37-40R;
CANR 33; DLB 15, 139; EWL 3; HGG;
MTCW 1, 2; RGEL 2; RGSF 2; SUFW 1

Hartman, Geoffrey H. 1929- .... **CLC 27**
See also CA 117; 125; CANR 79; DLB 67

Hartmann, Sadakichi 1869-1944 ... **TCLC 73**
See also CA 157; DLB 54

Hartmann von Aue c. 1170-c.
1210 .... **CMLC 15**
See also CDWLB 2; DLB 138; RGWL 2, 3

Hartog, Jan de
See de Hartog, Jan

Haruf, Kent 1943- .... **CLC 34**
See also AAYA 44; CA 149; CANR 91

Harvey, Gabriel 1550(?)-1631 .... **LC 88**
See also DLB 167, 213, 281

Harwood, Ronald 1934- .... **CLC 32**
See also CA 1-4R; CANR 4, 55; CBD; CD
5; DAM DRAM, MST; DLB 13

Hasegawa Tatsunosuke
See Futabatei, Shimei

Hasek, Jaroslav (Matej Frantisek)
1883-1923 .... **TCLC 4**
See also CA 104; 129; CDWLB 4; DLB
215; EW 9; EWL 3; MTCW 1, 2; RGSF
2; RGWL 2, 3

Hass, Robert 1941- ... **CLC 18, 39, 99; PC 16**
See also AMWS 6; CA 111; CANR 30, 50,
71; CP 7; DLB 105, 206; EWL 3; RGAL
4; SATA 94

Hastings, Hudson
See Kuttner, Henry

Hastings, Selina .... **CLC 44**

Hathorne, John 1641-1717 .... **LC 38**

Hatteras, Amelia
See Mencken, H(enry) L(ouis)

Hatteras, Owen .... **TCLC 18**
See Mencken, H(enry) L(ouis); Nathan,
George Jean

Hauptmann, Gerhart (Johann Robert)
1862-1946 .... **SSC 37; TCLC 4**
See also CA 104; 153; CDWLB 2; DAM
DRAM; DLB 66, 118; EW 8; EWL 3;
RGSF 2; RGWL 2, 3; TWA

Havel, Vaclav 1936- ..... **CLC 25, 58, 65, 123; DC 6**
See also CA 104; CANR 36, 63; CDWLB 4; CWW 2; DA3; DAM DRAM; DFS 10; DLB 232; EWL 3; LMFS 2; MTCW 1, 2; RGWL 3

Haviaras, Stratis .... **CLC 33**
See Chaviaras, Strates

Hawes, Stephen 1475(?)-1529(?) .... **LC 17**
See also DLB 132; RGEL 2

Hawkes, John (Clendennin Burne, Jr.) 1925-1998 .. **CLC 1, 2, 3, 4, 7, 9, 14, 15, 27, 49**
See also BPFB 2; CA 1-4R; 167; CANR 2, 47, 64; CN 7; DLB 2, 7, 227; DLBY 1980, 1998; EWL 3; MTCW 1, 2; RGAL 4

Hawking, S. W.
See Hawking, Stephen W(illiam)

Hawking, Stephen W(illiam) 1942- . **CLC 63, 105**
See also AAYA 13; BEST 89:1; CA 126; 129; CANR 48, 115; CPW; DA3; MTCW 2

Hawkins, Anthony Hope
See Hope, Anthony

Hawthorne, Julian 1846-1934 .... **TCLC 25**
See also CA 165; HGG

Hawthorne, Nathaniel 1804-1864 ... **NCLC 2, 10, 17, 23, 39, 79, 95; SSC 3, 29, 39; WLC**
See also AAYA 18; AMW; AMWC 1; AMWR 1; BPFB 2; BYA 3; CDALB 1640-1865; DA; DA3; DAB; DAC; DAM MST, NOV; DLB 1, 74, 183, 223, 269; EXPN; EXPS; HGG; LAIT 1; NFS 1; RGAL 4; RGSF 2; SSFS 1, 7, 11, 15; SUFW 1; TUS; WCH; YABC 2

Haxton, Josephine Ayres 1921-
See Douglas, Ellen
See also CA 115; CANR 41, 83

Hayaseca y Eizaguirre, Jorge
See Echegaray (y Eizaguirre), Jose (Maria Waldo)

Hayashi, Fumiko 1904-1951 .... **TCLC 27**
See Hayashi Fumiko
See also CA 161

Hayashi Fumiko
See Hayashi, Fumiko
See also DLB 180; EWL 3

Haycraft, Anna (Margaret) 1932-
See Ellis, Alice Thomas
See also CA 122; CANR 85, 90; MTCW 2

Hayden, Robert E(arl) 1913-1980 ..... **BLC 2; CLC 5, 9, 14, 37; PC 6**
See also AFAW 1, 2; AMWS 2; BW 1, 3; CA 69-72; 97-100; CABS 2; CANR 24, 75, 82; CDALB 1941-1968; DA; DAC; DAM MST, MULT, POET; DLB 5, 76; EWL 3; EXPP; MTCW 2; PFS 1; RGAL 4; SATA 19; SATA-Obit 26; WP

Hayek, F(riedrich) A(ugust von) 1899-1992 .... **TCLC 109**
See also CA 93-96; 137; CANR 20; MTCW 1, 2

Hayford, J(oseph) E(phraim) Casely
See Casely-Hayford, J(oseph) E(phraim)

Hayman, Ronald 1932- .... **CLC 44**
See also CA 25-28R; CANR 18, 50, 88; CD 5; DLB 155

Hayne, Paul Hamilton 1830-1886 . **NCLC 94**
See also DLB 3, 64, 79, 248; RGAL 4

Hays, Mary 1760-1843 .... **NCLC 114**
See also DLB 142, 158; RGEL 2

Haywood, Eliza (Fowler) 1693(?)-1756 .... **LC 1, 44**
See also DLB 39; RGEL 2

Hazlitt, William 1778-1830 ...... **NCLC 29, 82**
See also BRW 4; DLB 110, 158; RGEL 2; TEA

Hazzard, Shirley 1931- .... **CLC 18**
See also CA 9-12R; CANR 4, 70; CN 7; DLB 289; DLBY 1982; MTCW 1

Head, Bessie 1937-1986 .... **BLC 2; CLC 25, 67; SSC 52**
See also AFW; BW 2, 3; CA 29-32R; 119; CANR 25, 82; CDWLB 3; DA3; DAM MULT; DLB 117, 225; EWL 3; EXPS; FW; MTCW 1, 2; RGSF 2; SSFS 5, 13; WLIT 2

Headon, (Nicky) Topper 1956(?)- ...... **CLC 30**

Heaney, Seamus (Justin) 1939- ..... **CLC 5, 7, 14, 25, 37, 74, 91, 171; PC 18; WLCS**
See also BRWR 1; BRWS 2; CA 85-88; CANR 25, 48, 75, 91; CDBLB 1960 to Present; CP 7; DA3; DAB; DAM POET; DLB 40; DLBY 1995; EWL 3; EXPP; MTCW 1, 2; PAB; PFS 2, 5, 8, 17; RGEL 2; TEA; WLIT 4

Hearn, (Patricio) Lafcadio (Tessima Carlos) 1850-1904 .... **TCLC 9**
See also CA 105; 166; DLB 12, 78, 189; HGG; RGAL 4

Hearne, Samuel 1745-1792 .... **LC 95**
See also DLB 99

Hearne, Vicki 1946-2001 .... **CLC 56**
See also CA 139; 201

Hearon, Shelby 1931- .... **CLC 63**
See also AITN 2; AMWS 8; CA 25-28R; CANR 18, 48, 103; CSW

Heat-Moon, William Least .... **CLC 29**
See Trogdon, William (Lewis)
See also AAYA 9

Hebbel, Friedrich 1813-1863 . **DC 21; NCLC 43**
See also CDWLB 2; DAM DRAM; DLB 129; EW 6; RGWL 2, 3

Hebert, Anne 1916-2000 .... **CLC 4, 13, 29**
See also CA 85-88; 187; CANR 69; CCA 1; CWP; CWW 2; DA3; DAC; DAM MST, POET; DLB 68; EWL 3; GFL 1789 to the Present; MTCW 1, 2

Hecht, Anthony (Evan) 1923- ...... **CLC 8, 13, 19**
See also AMWS 10; CA 9-12R; CANR 6, 108; CP 7; DAM POET; DLB 5, 169; EWL 3; PFS 6; WP

Hecht, Ben 1894-1964 ..... **CLC 8; TCLC 101**
See also CA 85-88; DFS 9; DLB 7, 9, 25, 26, 28, 86; FANT; IDFW 3, 4; RGAL 4

Hedayat, Sadeq 1903-1951 .... **TCLC 21**
See also CA 120; EWL 3; RGSF 2

Hegel, Georg Wilhelm Friedrich 1770-1831 .... **NCLC 46**
See also DLB 90; TWA

Heidegger, Martin 1889-1976 .... **CLC 24**
See also CA 81-84; 65-68; CANR 34; MTCW 1, 2

Heidenstam, (Carl Gustaf) Verner von 1859-1940 .... **TCLC 5**
See also CA 104

Heidi Louise
See Erdrich, Louise

Heifner, Jack 1946- .... **CLC 11**
See also CA 105; CANR 47

Heijermans, Herman 1864-1924 .... **TCLC 24**
See also CA 123; EWL 3

Heilbrun, Carolyn G(old) 1926-2003 .... **CLC 25, 173**
See Cross, Amanda
See also CA 45-48; CANR 1, 28, 58, 94; FW

Hein, Christoph 1944- .... **CLC 154**
See also CA 158; CANR 108; CDWLB 2; CWW 2; DLB 124

Heine, Heinrich 1797-1856 .... **NCLC 4, 54; PC 25**
See also CDWLB 2; DLB 90; EW 5; RGWL 2, 3; TWA

Heinemann, Larry (Curtiss) 1944- .. **CLC 50**
See also CA 110; CAAS 21; CANR 31, 81; DLBD 9; INT CANR-31

Heiney, Donald (William) 1921-1993
See Harris, MacDonald
See also CA 1-4R; 142; CANR 3, 58; FANT

Heinlein, Robert A(nson) 1907-1988 . **CLC 1, 3, 8, 14, 26, 55; SSC 55**
See also AAYA 17; BPFB 2; BYA 4, 13; CA 1-4R; 125; CANR 1, 20, 53; CLR 75; CPW; DA3; DAM POP; DLB 8; EXPS; JRDA; LAIT 5; LMFS 2; MAICYA 1, 2; MTCW 1, 2; RGAL 4; SATA 9, 69; SATA-Obit 56; SCFW 1, 2; SFW 4; SSFS 7; YAW

Helforth, John
See Doolittle, Hilda

Heliodorus fl. 3rd cent. - .... **CMLC 52**

Hellenhofferu, Vojtech Kapristian z
See Hasek, Jaroslav (Matej Frantisek)

Heller, Joseph 1923-1999 . **CLC 1, 3, 5, 8, 11, 36, 63; TCLC 131; WLC**
See also AAYA 24; AITN 1; AMWS 4; BPFB 2; BYA 1; CA 5-8R; 187; CABS 1; CANR 8, 42, 66; CN 7; CPW; DA; DA3; DAB; DAC; DAM MST, NOV, POP; DLB 2, 28, 227; DLBY 1980, 2002; EWL 3; EXPN; INT CANR-8; LAIT 4; MTCW 1, 2; NFS 1; RGAL 4; TUS; YAW

Hellman, Lillian (Florence) 1906-1984 .. **CLC 2, 4, 8, 14, 18, 34, 44, 52; DC 1; TCLC 119**
See also AAYA 47; AITN 1, 2; AMWS 1; CA 13-16R; 112; CAD; CANR 33; CWD; DA3; DAM DRAM; DFS 1, 3, 14; DLB 7, 228; DLBY 1984; EWL 3; FW; LAIT 3; MAWW; MTCW 1, 2; RGAL 4; TUS

Helprin, Mark 1947- .... **CLC 7, 10, 22, 32**
See also CA 81-84; CANR 47, 64; CDALBS; CPW; DA3; DAM NOV, POP; DLBY 1985; FANT; MTCW 1, 2; SUFW 2

Helvetius, Claude-Adrien 1715-1771 .. **LC 26**

Helyar, Jane Penelope Josephine 1933-
See Poole, Josephine
See also CA 21-24R; CANR 10, 26; CWRI 5; SATA 82; SATA-Essay 138

Hemans, Felicia 1793-1835 .... **NCLC 29, 71**
See also DLB 96; RGEL 2

Hemingway, Ernest (Miller) 1899-1961 .... **CLC 1, 3, 6, 8, 10, 13, 19, 30, 34, 39, 41, 44, 50, 61, 80; SSC 1, 25, 36, 40, 63; TCLC 115; WLC**
See also AAYA 19; AMW; AMWC 1; AMWR 1; BPFB 2; BYA 2, 3, 13, 15; CA 77-80; CANR 34; CDALB 1917-1929; DA; DA3; DAB; DAC; DAM MST, NOV; DLB 4, 9, 102, 210; DLBD 1, 15, 16; DLBY 1981, 1987, 1996, 1998; EWL 3; EXPN; EXPS; LAIT 3, 4; LATS 1; MTCW 1, 2; NFS 1, 5, 6, 14; RGAL 4; RGSF 2; SSFS 17; TUS; WYA

Hempel, Amy 1951- .... **CLC 39**
See also CA 118; 137; CANR 70; DA3; DLB 218; EXPS; MTCW 2; SSFS 2

Henderson, F. C.
See Mencken, H(enry) L(ouis)

Henderson, Sylvia
See Ashton-Warner, Sylvia (Constance)

Henderson, Zenna (Chlarson) 1917-1983 .... **SSC 29**
See also CA 1-4R; 133; CANR 1, 84; DLB 8; SATA 5; SFW 4

Henkin, Joshua .... **CLC 119**
See also CA 161

Henley, Beth .... **CLC 23; DC 6, 14**
See Henley, Elizabeth Becker
See also CABS 3; CAD; CD 5; CSW; CWD; DFS 2; DLBY 1986; FW

Henley, Elizabeth Becker 1952-
See Henley, Beth
See also CA 107; CANR 32, 73; DA3; DAM DRAM, MST; MTCW 1, 2

Henley, William Ernest 1849-1903 .. **TCLC 8**
See also CA 105; DLB 19; RGEL 2

Hennissart, Martha
See Lathen, Emma
See also CA 85-88; CANR 64

Henry VIII 1491-1547 .... **LC 10**
See also DLB 132

Henry, O. ..... **SSC 5, 49; TCLC 1, 19; WLC**
See Porter, William Sydney
See also AAYA 41; AMWS 2; EXPS; RGAL 4; RGSF 2; SSFS 2, 18

Henry, Patrick 1736-1799 .... **LC 25**
See also LAIT 1

Henryson, Robert 1430(?)-1506(?) ...... **LC 20**
See also BRWS 7; DLB 146; RGEL 2

Henschke, Alfred
See Klabund

Henson, Lance 1944- .... **NNAL**
See also CA 146; DLB 175

Hentoff, Nat(han Irving) 1925- .... **CLC 26**
See also AAYA 4, 42; BYA 6; CA 1-4R; CAAS 6; CANR 5, 25, 77, 114; CLR 1, 52; INT CANR-25; JRDA; MAICYA 1, 2; SATA 42, 69, 133; SATA-Brief 27; WYA; YAW

Heppenstall, (John) Rayner
1911-1981 .... **CLC 10**
See also CA 1-4R; 103; CANR 29; EWL 3

Heraclitus c. 540B.C.-c. 450B.C. ... **CMLC 22**
See also DLB 176

Herbert, Frank (Patrick)
1920-1986 .... **CLC 12, 23, 35, 44, 85**
See also AAYA 21; BPFB 2; BYA 4, 14; CA 53-56; 118; CANR 5, 43; CDALBS; CPW; DAM POP; DLB 8; INT CANR-5; LAIT 5; MTCW 1, 2; NFS 17; SATA 9, 37; SATA-Obit 47; SCFW 2; SFW 4; YAW

Herbert, George 1593-1633 ...... **LC 24; PC 4**
See also BRW 2; BRWR 2; CDBLB Before 1660; DAB; DAM POET; DLB 126; EXPP; RGEL 2; TEA; WP

Herbert, Zbigniew 1924-1998 ..... **CLC 9, 43; PC 50**
See also CA 89-92; 169; CANR 36, 74; CDWLB 4; CWW 2; DAM POET; DLB 232; EWL 3; MTCW 1

Herbst, Josephine (Frey)
1897-1969 .... **CLC 34**
See also CA 5-8R; 25-28R; DLB 9

Herder, Johann Gottfried von
1744-1803 .... **NCLC 8**
See also DLB 97; EW 4; TWA

Heredia, Jose Maria 1803-1839 .... **HLCS 2**
See also LAW

Hergesheimer, Joseph 1880-1954 ... **TCLC 11**
See also CA 109; 194; DLB 102, 9; RGAL 4

Herlihy, James Leo 1927-1993 .... **CLC 6**
See also CA 1-4R; 143; CAD; CANR 2

Herman, William
See Bierce, Ambrose (Gwinett)

Hermogenes fl. c. 175- .... **CMLC 6**

Hernandez, Jose 1834-1886 .... **NCLC 17**
See also LAW; RGWL 2, 3; WLIT 1

Herodotus c. 484B.C.-c. 420B.C. .. **CMLC 17**
See also AW 1; CDWLB 1; DLB 176; RGWL 2, 3; TWA

Herrick, Robert 1591-1674 .... **LC 13; PC 9**
See also BRW 2; BRWC 2; DA; DAB; DAC; DAM MST, POP; DLB 126; EXPP; PFS 13; RGAL 2; TEA; WP

Herring, Guilles
See Somerville, Edith Oenone

Herriot, James 1916-1995 .... **CLC 12**
See Wight, James Alfred
See also AAYA 1; BPFB 2; CA 148; CANR 40; CLR 80; CPW; DAM POP; LAIT 3; MAICYA 2; MAICYAS 1; MTCW 2; SATA 86, 135; TEA; YAW

Herris, Violet
See Hunt, Violet

Herrmann, Dorothy 1941- .... **CLC 44**
See also CA 107

Herrmann, Taffy
See Herrmann, Dorothy

Hersey, John (Richard) 1914-1993 .... **CLC 1, 2, 7, 9, 40, 81, 97**
See also AAYA 29; BPFB 2; CA 17-20R; 140; CANR 33; CDALBS; CPW; DAM POP; DLB 6, 185, 278; MTCW 1, 2; SATA 25; SATA-Obit 76; TUS

Herzen, Aleksandr Ivanovich
1812-1870 .... **NCLC 10, 61**
See Herzen, Alexander

Herzen, Alexander
See Herzen, Aleksandr Ivanovich
See also DLB 277

Herzl, Theodor 1860-1904 .... **TCLC 36**
See also CA 168

Herzog, Werner 1942- .... **CLC 16**
See also CA 89-92

Hesiod c. 8th cent. B.C.- .... **CMLC 5**
See also AW 1; DLB 176; RGWL 2, 3

Hesse, Hermann 1877-1962 ... **CLC 1, 2, 3, 6, 11, 17, 25, 69; SSC 9, 49; WLC**
See also AAYA 43; BPFB 2; CA 17-18; CAP 2; CDWLB 2; DA; DA3; DAB; DAC; DAM MST, NOV; DLB 66; EW 9; EWL 3; EXPN; LAIT 1; MTCW 1, 2; NFS 6, 15; RGWL 2, 3; SATA 50; TWA

Hewes, Cady
See De Voto, Bernard (Augustine)

Heyen, William 1940- .... **CLC 13, 18**
See also CA 33-36R; CAAS 9; CANR 98; CP 7; DLB 5

Heyerdahl, Thor 1914-2002 .... **CLC 26**
See also CA 5-8R; 207; CANR 5, 22, 66, 73; LAIT 4; MTCW 1, 2; SATA 2, 52

Heym, Georg (Theodor Franz Arthur)
1887-1912 .... **TCLC 9**
See also CA 106; 181

Heym, Stefan 1913-2001 .... **CLC 41**
See also CA 9-12R; 203; CANR 4; CWW 2; DLB 69; EWL 3

Heyse, Paul (Johann Ludwig von)
1830-1914 .... **TCLC 8**
See also CA 104; 209; DLB 129

Heyward, (Edwin) DuBose
1885-1940 .... **HR 2; TCLC 59**
See also CA 108; 157; DLB 7, 9, 45, 249; SATA 21

Heywood, John 1497(?)-1580(?) .... **LC 65**
See also DLB 136; RGEL 2

Hibbert, Eleanor Alice Burford
1906-1993 .... **CLC 7**
See Holt, Victoria
See also BEST 90:4; CA 17-20R; 140; CANR 9, 28, 59; CMW 4; CPW; DAM POP; MTCW 2; RHW; SATA 2; SATA-Obit 74

Hichens, Robert (Smythe)
1864-1950 .... **TCLC 64**
See also CA 162; DLB 153; HGG; RHW; SUFW

Higgins, George V(incent)
1939-1999 .... **CLC 4, 7, 10, 18**
See also BPFB 2; CA 77-80; 186; CAAS 5; CANR 17, 51, 89, 96; CMW 4; CN 7; DLB 2; DLBY 1981, 1998; INT CANR-17; MSW; MTCW 1

Higginson, Thomas Wentworth
1823-1911 .... **TCLC 36**
See also CA 162; DLB 1, 64, 243

Higgonet, Margaret ed. .... **CLC 65**

Highet, Helen
See MacInnes, Helen (Clark)

Highsmith, (Mary) Patricia
1921-1995 .... **CLC 2, 4, 14, 42, 102**
See Morgan, Claire
See also AAYA 48; BRWS 5; CA 1-4R; 147; CANR 1, 20, 48, 62, 108; CMW 4; CPW; DA3; DAM NOV, POP; MSW; MTCW 1, 2

Highwater, Jamake (Mamake)
1942(?)-2001 .... **CLC 12**
See also AAYA 7; BPFB 2; BYA 4; CA 65-68; 199; CAAS 7; CANR 10, 34, 84; CLR 17; CWRI 5; DLB 52; DLBY 1985; JRDA; MAICYA 1, 2; SATA 32, 69; SATA-Brief 30

Highway, Tomson 1951- ...... **CLC 92; NNAL**
See also CA 151; CANR 75; CCA 1; CD 5; DAC; DAM MULT; DFS 2; MTCW 2

Hijuelos, Oscar 1951- .... **CLC 65; HLC 1**
See also AAYA 25; AMWS 8; BEST 90:1; CA 123; CANR 50, 75; CPW; DA3; DAM MULT, POP; DLB 145; HW 1, 2; MTCW 2; NFS 17; RGAL 4; WLIT 1

Hikmet, Nazim 1902(?)-1963 .... **CLC 40**
See also CA 141; 93-96; EWL 3

Hildegard von Bingen 1098-1179 . **CMLC 20**
See also DLB 148

Hildesheimer, Wolfgang 1916-1991 .. **CLC 49**
See also CA 101; 135; DLB 69, 124; EWL 3

Hill, Geoffrey (William) 1932- ...... **CLC 5, 8, 18, 45**
See also BRWS 5; CA 81-84; CANR 21, 89; CDBLB 1960 to Present; CP 7; DAM POET; DLB 40; EWL 3; MTCW 1; RGEL 2

Hill, George Roy 1921-2002 .... **CLC 26**
See also CA 110; 122; 213

Hill, John
See Koontz, Dean R(ay)

Hill, Susan (Elizabeth) 1942- ...... **CLC 4, 113**
See also CA 33-36R; CANR 29, 69; CN 7; DAB; DAM MST, NOV; DLB 14, 139; HGG; MTCW 1; RHW

Hillard, Asa G. III .... **CLC 70**

Hillerman, Tony 1925- .... **CLC 62, 170**
See also AAYA 40; BEST 89:1; BPFB 2; CA 29-32R; CANR 21, 42, 65, 97; CMW 4; CPW; DA3; DAM POP; DLB 206; MSW; RGAL 4; SATA 6; TCWW 2; YAW

Hillesum, Etty 1914-1943 .... **TCLC 49**
See also CA 137

Hilliard, Noel (Harvey) 1929-1996 ... **CLC 15**
See also CA 9-12R; CANR 7, 69; CN 7

Hillis, Rick 1956- .... **CLC 66**
See also CA 134

Hilton, James 1900-1954 .... **TCLC 21**
See also CA 108; 169; DLB 34, 77; FANT; SATA 34

Hilton, Walter (?)-1396 .... **CMLC 58**
See also DLB 146; RGEL 2

Himes, Chester (Bomar) 1909-1984 .. **BLC 2; CLC 2, 4, 7, 18, 58, 108; TCLC 139**
See also AFAW 2; BPFB 2; BW 2; CA 25-28R; 114; CANR 22, 89; CMW 4; DAM MULT; DLB 2, 76, 143, 226; EWL 3; MSW; MTCW 1, 2; RGAL 4

Hinde, Thomas .... **CLC 6, 11**
See Chitty, Thomas Willes
See also EWL 3

Hine, (William) Daryl 1936- .... **CLC 15**
See also CA 1-4R; CAAS 15; CANR 1, 20; CP 7; DLB 60

Hinkson, Katharine Tynan
See Tynan, Katharine

Hinojosa(-Smith), Rolando (R.)
1929- .... **HLC 1**
See Hinojosa-Smith, Rolando
See also CA 131; CAAS 16; CANR 62; DAM MULT; DLB 82; HW 1, 2; MTCW 2; RGAL 4

Hinton, S(usan) E(loise) 1950- .. **CLC 30, 111**
See also AAYA 2, 33; BPFB 2; BYA 2, 3; CA 81-84; CANR 32, 62, 92; CDALBS; CLR 3, 23; CPW; DA; DA3; DAB; DAC; DAM MST, NOV; JRDA; LAIT 5; MAICYA 1, 2; MTCW 1, 2; NFS 5, 9, 15, 16; SATA 19, 58, 115; WYA; YAW

Hippius, Zinaida .... **TCLC 9**
See Gippius, Zinaida (Nikolaevna)
See also EWL 3

Hiraoka, Kimitake 1925-1970
See Mishima, Yukio
See also CA 97-100; 29-32R; DA3; DAM DRAM; GLL 1; MTCW 1, 2

Hirsch, E(ric) D(onald), Jr. 1928- .... **CLC 79**
See also CA 25-28R; CANR 27, 51; DLB 67; INT CANR-27; MTCW 1

Hirsch, Edward 1950- .... **CLC 31, 50**
See also CA 104; CANR 20, 42, 102; CP 7; DLB 120

Hitchcock, Alfred (Joseph)
1899-1980 .... **CLC 16**
See also AAYA 22; CA 159; 97-100; SATA 27; SATA-Obit 24

Hitchens, Christopher (Eric)
1949- .... **CLC 157**
See also CA 152; CANR 89

Hitler, Adolf 1889-1945 .... **TCLC 53**
See also CA 117; 147

Hoagland, Edward 1932- .... **CLC 28**
See also ANW; CA 1-4R; CANR 2, 31, 57, 107; CN 7; DLB 6; SATA 51

Hoban, Russell (Conwell) 1925- ... **CLC 7, 25**
See also BPFB 2; CA 5-8R; CANR 23, 37, 66, 114; CLR 3, 69; CN 7; CWRI 5; DAM NOV; DLB 52; FANT; MAICYA 1, 2; MTCW 1, 2; SATA 1, 40, 78, 136; SFW 4; SUFW 2

Hobbes, Thomas 1588-1679 .... **LC 36**
See also DLB 151, 252, 281; RGEL 2

Hobbs, Perry
See Blackmur, R(ichard) P(almer)

Hobson, Laura Z(ametkin)
1900-1986 .... **CLC 7, 25**
See Field, Peter
See also BPFB 2; CA 17-20R; 118; CANR 55; DLB 28; SATA 52

Hoccleve, Thomas c. 1368-c. 1437 ...... **LC 75**
See also DLB 146; RGEL 2

Hoch, Edward D(entinger) 1930-
See Queen, Ellery
See also CA 29-32R; CANR 11, 27, 51, 97; CMW 4; SFW 4

Hochhuth, Rolf 1931- .... **CLC 4, 11, 18**
See also CA 5-8R; CANR 33, 75; CWW 2; DAM DRAM; DLB 124; EWL 3; MTCW 1, 2

Hochman, Sandra 1936- .... **CLC 3, 8**
See also CA 5-8R; DLB 5

Hochwaelder, Fritz 1911-1986 .... **CLC 36**
See Hochwalder, Fritz
See also CA 29-32R; 120; CANR 42; DAM DRAM; MTCW 1; RGWL 3

Hochwalder, Fritz
See Hochwaelder, Fritz
See also EWL 3; RGWL 2

Hocking, Mary (Eunice) 1921- .... **CLC 13**
See also CA 101; CANR 18, 40

Hodgins, Jack 1938- .... **CLC 23**
See also CA 93-96; CN 7; DLB 60

Hodgson, William Hope
1877(?)-1918 .... **TCLC 13**
See also CA 111; 164; CMW 4; DLB 70, 153, 156, 178; HGG; MTCW 2; SFW 4; SUFW 1

Hoeg, Peter 1957- .... **CLC 95, 156**
See also CA 151; CANR 75; CMW 4; DA3; DLB 214; EWL 3; MTCW 2; NFS 17; RGWL 3; SSFS 18

Hoffman, Alice 1952- .... **CLC 51**
See also AAYA 37; AMWS 10; CA 77-80; CANR 34, 66, 100; CN 7; CPW; DAM NOV; MTCW 1, 2

Hoffman, Daniel (Gerard) 1923- . **CLC 6, 13, 23**
See also CA 1-4R; CANR 4; CP 7; DLB 5

Hoffman, Stanley 1944- .... **CLC 5**
See also CA 77-80

Hoffman, William 1925- .... **CLC 141**
See also CA 21-24R; CANR 9, 103; CSW; DLB 234

Hoffman, William M(oses) 1939- ..... **CLC 40**
See Hoffman, William M.
See also CA 57-60; CANR 11, 71

Hoffmann, E(rnst) T(heodor) A(madeus)
1776-1822 .... **NCLC 2; SSC 13**
See also CDWLB 2; DLB 90; EW 5; RGSF 2; RGWL 2, 3; SATA 27; SUFW 1; WCH

Hofmann, Gert 1931- .... **CLC 54**
See also CA 128; EWL 3

Hofmannsthal, Hugo von 1874-1929 ... **DC 4; TCLC 11**
See also CA 106; 153; CDWLB 2; DAM DRAM; DFS 17; DLB 81, 118; EW 9; EWL 3; RGWL 2, 3

Hogan, Linda 1947- ..... **CLC 73; NNAL; PC 35**
See also AMWS 4; ANW; BYA 12; CA 120; CANR 45, 73; CWP; DAM MULT; DLB 175; SATA 132; TCWW 2

Hogarth, Charles
See Creasey, John

Hogarth, Emmett
See Polonsky, Abraham (Lincoln)

Hogg, James 1770-1835 .... **NCLC 4, 109**
See also DLB 93, 116, 159; HGG; RGEL 2; SUFW 1

Holbach, Paul Henri Thiry Baron
1723-1789 .... **LC 14**

Holberg, Ludvig 1684-1754 .... **LC 6**
See also RGWL 2, 3

Holcroft, Thomas 1745-1809 .... **NCLC 85**
See also DLB 39, 89, 158; RGEL 2

Holden, Ursula 1921- .... **CLC 18**
See also CA 101; CAAS 8; CANR 22

Holderlin, (Johann Christian) Friedrich
1770-1843 .... **NCLC 16; PC 4**
See also CDWLB 2; DLB 90; EW 5; RGWL 2, 3

Holdstock, Robert
See Holdstock, Robert P.

Holdstock, Robert P. 1948- .... **CLC 39**
See also CA 131; CANR 81; DLB 261; FANT; HGG; SFW 4; SUFW 2

Holinshed, Raphael fl. 1580- .... **LC 69**
See also DLB 167; RGEL 2

Holland, Isabelle (Christian)
1920-2002 .... **CLC 21**
See also AAYA 11; CA 21-24R, 181; 205; CAAE 181; CANR 10, 25, 47; CLR 57; CWRI 5; JRDA; LAIT 5; MAICYA 1, 2; SATA 8, 70; SATA-Essay 103; SATA-Obit 132; WYA

Holland, Marcus
See Caldwell, (Janet Miriam) Taylor (Holland)

Hollander, John 1929- .... **CLC 2, 5, 8, 14**
See also CA 1-4R; CANR 1, 52; CP 7; DLB 5; SATA 13

Hollander, Paul
See Silverberg, Robert

Holleran, Andrew 1943(?)- .... **CLC 38**
See Garber, Eric
See also CA 144; GLL 1

Holley, Marietta 1836(?)-1926 .... **TCLC 99**
See also CA 118; DLB 11

Hollinghurst, Alan 1954- .... **CLC 55, 91**
See also CA 114; CN 7; DLB 207; GLL 1

Hollis, Jim
See Summers, Hollis (Spurgeon, Jr.)

Holly, Buddy 1936-1959 .... **TCLC 65**
See also CA 213

Holmes, Gordon
See Shiel, M(atthew) P(hipps)

Holmes, John
See Souster, (Holmes) Raymond

Holmes, John Clellon 1926-1988 .... **CLC 56**
See also BG 2; CA 9-12R; 125; CANR 4; DLB 16, 237

Holmes, Oliver Wendell, Jr.
1841-1935 .... **TCLC 77**
See also CA 114; 186

Holmes, Oliver Wendell
1809-1894 .... **NCLC 14, 81**
See also AMWS 1; CDALB 1640-1865; DLB 1, 189, 235; EXPP; RGAL 4; SATA 34

Holmes, Raymond
See Souster, (Holmes) Raymond

Holt, Victoria
See Hibbert, Eleanor Alice Burford
See also BPFB 2

Holub, Miroslav 1923-1998 .... **CLC 4**
See also CA 21-24R; 169; CANR 10; CDWLB 4; CWW 2; DLB 232; EWL 3; RGWL 3

Holz, Detlev
See Benjamin, Walter

Homer c. 8th cent. B.C.- .... **CMLC 1, 16, 61; PC 23; WLCS**
See also AW 1; CDWLB 1; DA; DA3; DAB; DAC; DAM MST, POET; DLB 176; EFS 1; LAIT 1; LMFS 1; RGWL 2, 3; TWA; WP

Hongo, Garrett Kaoru 1951- .... **PC 23**
See also CA 133; CAAS 22; CP 7; DLB 120; EWL 3; EXPP; RGAL 4

Honig, Edwin 1919- .... **CLC 33**
See also CA 5-8R; CAAS 8; CANR 4, 45; CP 7; DLB 5

Hood, Hugh (John Blagdon) 1928- . **CLC 15, 28; SSC 42**
See also CA 49-52; CAAS 17; CANR 1, 33, 87; CN 7; DLB 53; RGSF 2

Hood, Thomas 1799-1845 .... **NCLC 16**
See also BRW 4; DLB 96; RGEL 2

Hooker, (Peter) Jeremy 1941- .... **CLC 43**
See also CA 77-80; CANR 22; CP 7; DLB 40

Hooker, Richard 1554-1600 .... **LC 95**
See also BRW 1; DLB 132; RGEL 2

hooks, bell
See Watkins, Gloria Jean

Hope, A(lec) D(erwent) 1907-2000 .... **CLC 3, 51**
See also BRWS 7; CA 21-24R; 188; CANR 33, 74; DLB 289; EWL 3; MTCW 1, 2; PFS 8; RGEL 2

Hope, Anthony 1863-1933 .... **TCLC 83**
See also CA 157; DLB 153, 156; RGEL 2; RHW

Hope, Brian
See Creasey, John

Hope, Christopher (David Tully)
1944- .... **CLC 52**
See also AFW; CA 106; CANR 47, 101; CN 7; DLB 225; SATA 62

Hopkins, Gerard Manley
1844-1889 .... **NCLC 17; PC 15; WLC**
See also BRW 5; BRWR 2; CDBLB 1890-1914; DA; DA3; DAB; DAC; DAM MST, POET; DLB 35, 57; EXPP; PAB; RGEL 2; TEA; WP

Hopkins, John (Richard) 1931-1998 .. **CLC 4**
See also CA 85-88; 169; CBD; CD 5

Hopkins, Pauline Elizabeth
1859-1930 .... **BLC 2; TCLC 28**
See also AFAW 2; BW 2, 3; CA 141; CANR 82; DAM MULT; DLB 50

Hopkinson, Francis 1737-1791 .... **LC 25**
See also DLB 31; RGAL 4

Hopley-Woolrich, Cornell George 1903-1968
See Woolrich, Cornell
See also CA 13-14; CANR 58; CAP 1; CMW 4; DLB 226; MTCW 2

Horace 65B.C.-8B.C. .... **CMLC 39; PC 46**
See also AW 2; CDWLB 1; DLB 211; RGWL 2, 3

Horatio
See Proust, (Valentin-Louis-George-Eugene) Marcel

Horgan, Paul (George Vincent O'Shaughnessy) 1903-1995 .. **CLC 9, 53**
See also BPFB 2; CA 13-16R; 147; CANR 9, 35; DAM NOV; DLB 102, 212; DLBY 1985; INT CANR-9; MTCW 1, 2; SATA 13; SATA-Obit 84; TCWW 2

Horkheimer, Max 1895-1973 .... **TCLC 132**
See also CA 216; 41-44R

Horn, Peter
See Kuttner, Henry

Horne, Frank (Smith) 1899-1974 .... **HR 2**
See also BW 1; CA 125; 53-56; DLB 51; WP

Horne, Richard Henry Hengist
1802(?)-1884 .... **NCLC 127**
See also DLB 32; SATA 29

Hornem, Horace Esq.
See Byron, George Gordon (Noel)

Horney, Karen (Clementine Theodore Danielsen) 1885-1952 .... **TCLC 71**
See also CA 114; 165; DLB 246; FW

Hornung, E(rnest) W(illiam)
1866-1921 .... **TCLC 59**
See also CA 108; 160; CMW 4; DLB 70

Horovitz, Israel (Arthur) 1939- .... **CLC 56**
See also CA 33-36R; CAD; CANR 46, 59; CD 5; DAM DRAM; DLB 7

Horton, George Moses
1797(?)-1883(?) .... **NCLC 87**
See also DLB 50

Horvath, odon von 1901-1938
See von Horvath, Odon
See also EWL 3

Horvath, Oedoen von -1938
See von Horvath, Odon

Horwitz, Julius 1920-1986 .... **CLC 14**
See also CA 9-12R; 119; CANR 12

Hospital, Janette Turner 1942- .... **CLC 42, 145**
See also CA 108; CANR 48; CN 7; DLBY 2002; RGSF 2

Hostos, E. M. de
See Hostos (y Bonilla), Eugenio Maria de

Hostos, Eugenio M. de
See Hostos (y Bonilla), Eugenio Maria de

Hostos, Eugenio Maria
See Hostos (y Bonilla), Eugenio Maria de

Hostos (y Bonilla), Eugenio Maria de
1839-1903 .... **TCLC 24**
See also CA 123; 131; HW 1

Houdini
See Lovecraft, H(oward) P(hillips)

Houellebecq, Michel 1958- .... **CLC 179**
See also CA 185

Hougan, Carolyn 1943- .... **CLC 34**
See also CA 139

Household, Geoffrey (Edward West)
1900-1988 .... **CLC 11**
See also CA 77-80; 126; CANR 58; CMW 4; DLB 87; SATA 14; SATA-Obit 59

Housman, A(lfred) E(dward)
1859-1936 .... **PC 2, 43; TCLC 1, 10; WLCS**
See also BRW 6; CA 104; 125; DA; DA3; DAB; DAC; DAM MST, POET; DLB 19, 284; EWL 3; EXPP; MTCW 1, 2; PAB; PFS 4, 7; RGEL 2; TEA; WP

Housman, Laurence 1865-1959 .... **TCLC 7**
See also CA 106; 155; DLB 10; FANT; RGEL 2; SATA 25

Houston, Jeanne (Toyo) Wakatsuki
1934- .... **AAL**
See also AAYA 49; CA 103; CAAS 16; CANR 29, 123; LAIT 4; SATA 78

Howard, Elizabeth Jane 1923- ..... **CLC 7, 29**
See also CA 5-8R; CANR 8, 62; CN 7

Howard, Maureen 1930- .... **CLC 5, 14, 46, 151**
See also CA 53-56; CANR 31, 75; CN 7; DLBY 1983; INT CANR-31; MTCW 1, 2

Howard, Richard 1929- .... **CLC 7, 10, 47**
See also AITN 1; CA 85-88; CANR 25, 80; CP 7; DLB 5; INT CANR-25

Howard, Robert E(rvin)
1906-1936 .... **TCLC 8**
See also BPFB 2; BYA 5; CA 105; 157; FANT; SUFW 1

Howard, Warren F.
See Pohl, Frederik

Howe, Fanny (Quincy) 1940- .... **CLC 47**
See also CA 117; CAAE 187; CAAS 27; CANR 70, 116; CP 7; CWP; SATA-Brief 52

Howe, Irving 1920-1993 .... **CLC 85**
See also AMWS 6; CA 9-12R; 141; CANR 21, 50; DLB 67; EWL 3; MTCW 1, 2

Howe, Julia Ward 1819-1910 .... **TCLC 21**
See also CA 117; 191; DLB 1, 189, 235; FW

Howe, Susan 1937- .... **CLC 72, 152**
See also AMWS 4; CA 160; CP 7; CWP; DLB 120; FW; RGAL 4

Howe, Tina 1937- .... **CLC 48**
See also CA 109; CAD; CD 5; CWD

Howell, James 1594(?)-1666 .... **LC 13**
See also DLB 151

Howells, W. D.
See Howells, William Dean

Howells, William D.
See Howells, William Dean

Howells, William Dean 1837-1920 ... **SSC 36; TCLC 7, 17, 41**
See also AMW; CA 104; 134; CDALB 1865-1917; DLB 12, 64, 74, 79, 189; LMFS 1; MTCW 2; RGAL 4; TUS

Howes, Barbara 1914-1996 .... **CLC 15**
See also CA 9-12R; 151; CAAS 3; CANR 53; CP 7; SATA 5

Hrabal, Bohumil 1914-1997 .... **CLC 13, 67**
See also CA 106; 156; CAAS 12; CANR 57; CWW 2; DLB 232; EWL 3; RGSF 2

Hrotsvit of Gandersheim c. 935-c. 1000 .... **CMLC 29**
See also DLB 148

Hsi, Chu 1130-1200 .... **CMLC 42**

Hsun, Lu
See Lu Hsun

Hubbard, L(afayette) Ron(ald)
1911-1986 .... **CLC 43**
See also CA 77-80; 118; CANR 52; CPW; DA3; DAM POP; FANT; MTCW 2; SFW 4

Huch, Ricarda (Octavia)
1864-1947 .... **TCLC 13**
See also CA 111; 189; DLB 66; EWL 3

Huddle, David 1942- .... **CLC 49**
See also CA 57-60; CAAS 20; CANR 89; DLB 130

Hudson, Jeffrey
See Crichton, (John) Michael

Hudson, W(illiam) H(enry)
1841-1922 .... **TCLC 29**
See also CA 115; 190; DLB 98, 153, 174; RGEL 2; SATA 35

Hueffer, Ford Madox
See Ford, Ford Madox

Hughart, Barry 1934- .... **CLC 39**
See also CA 137; FANT; SFW 4; SUFW 2

Hughes, Colin
See Creasey, John

Hughes, David (John) 1930- .... **CLC 48**
See also CA 116; 129; CN 7; DLB 14

Hughes, Edward James
See Hughes, Ted
See also DA3; DAM MST, POET

Hughes, (James Mercer) Langston
1902-1967 ..... **BLC 2; CLC 1, 5, 10, 15, 35, 44, 108; DC 3; HR 2; PC 1; SSC 6; WLC**
See also AAYA 12; AFAW 1, 2; AMWR 1; AMWS 1; BW 1, 3; CA 1-4R; 25-28R; CANR 1, 34, 82; CDALB 1929-1941; CLR 17; DA; DA3; DAB; DAC; DAM DRAM, MST, MULT, POET; DFS 6, 18; DLB 4, 7, 48, 51, 86, 228; EWL 3; EXPP; EXPS; JRDA; LAIT 3; LMFS 2; MAI-CYA 1, 2; MTCW 1, 2; PAB; PFS 1, 3, 6, 10, 15; RGAL 4; RGSF 2; SATA 4, 33; SSFS 4, 7; TUS; WCH; WP; YAW

Hughes, Richard (Arthur Warren)
1900-1976 .... **CLC 1, 11**
See also CA 5-8R; 65-68; CANR 4; DAM NOV; DLB 15, 161; EWL 3; MTCW 1; RGEL 2; SATA 8; SATA-Obit 25

Hughes, Ted 1930-1998 . **CLC 2, 4, 9, 14, 37, 119; PC 7**
See Hughes, Edward James
See also BRWC 2; BRWR 2; BRWS 1; CA 1-4R; 171; CANR 1, 33, 66, 108; CLR 3; CP 7; DAB; DAC; DLB 40, 161; EWL 3; EXPP; MAICYA 1, 2; MTCW 1, 2; PAB; PFS 4; RGEL 2; SATA 49; SATA-Brief 27; SATA-Obit 107; TEA; YAW

Hugo, Richard
See Huch, Ricarda (Octavia)

Hugo, Richard F(ranklin)
1923-1982 .... **CLC 6, 18, 32**
See also AMWS 6; CA 49-52; 108; CANR 3; DAM POET; DLB 5, 206; EWL 3; PFS 17; RGAL 4

Hugo, Victor (Marie) 1802-1885 .... **NCLC 3, 10, 21; PC 17; WLC**
See also AAYA 28; DA; DA3; DAB; DAC; DAM DRAM, MST, NOV, POET; DLB 119, 192, 217; EFS 2; EW 6; EXPN; GFL 1789 to the Present; LAIT 1, 2; NFS 5; RGWL 2, 3; SATA 47; TWA

Huidobro, Vicente
See Huidobro Fernandez, Vicente Garcia
See also DLB 283; EWL 3; LAW

Huidobro Fernandez, Vicente Garcia
1893-1948 .... **TCLC 31**
See Huidobro, Vicente
See also CA 131; HW 1

Hulme, Keri 1947- .... **CLC 39, 130**
See also CA 125; CANR 69; CN 7; CP 7; CWP; EWL 3; FW; INT 125

Hulme, T(homas) E(rnest)
1883-1917 .... **TCLC 21**
See also BRWS 6; CA 117; 203; DLB 19

Hume, David 1711-1776 .... **LC 7, 56**
See also BRWS 3; DLB 104, 252; LMFS 1; TEA

Humphrey, William 1924-1997 .... **CLC 45**
See also AMWS 9; CA 77-80; 160; CANR 68; CN 7; CSW; DLB 6, 212, 234, 278; TCWW 2

Humphreys, Emyr Owen 1919- .... **CLC 47**
See also CA 5-8R; CANR 3, 24; CN 7; DLB 15

Humphreys, Josephine 1945- ..... **CLC 34, 57**
See also CA 121; 127; CANR 97; CSW; INT 127

Huneker, James Gibbons
1860-1921 .... **TCLC 65**
See also CA 193; DLB 71; RGAL 4

Hungerford, Hesba Fay
See Brinsmead, H(esba) F(ay)

Hungerford, Pixie
See Brinsmead, H(esba) F(ay)

Hunt, E(verette) Howard, (Jr.)
1918- .... **CLC 3**
See also AITN 1; CA 45-48; CANR 2, 47, 103; CMW 4

Hunt, Francesca
See Holland, Isabelle (Christian)

Hunt, Howard
See Hunt, E(verette) Howard, (Jr.)

Hunt, Kyle
See Creasey, John

Hunt, (James Henry) Leigh
1784-1859 .... **NCLC 1, 70**
See also DAM POET; DLB 96, 110, 144; RGEL 2; TEA

Hunt, Marsha 1946- .... **CLC 70**
See also BW 2, 3; CA 143; CANR 79

Hunt, Violet 1866(?)-1942 .... **TCLC 53**
See also CA 184; DLB 162, 197

Hunter, E. Waldo
See Sturgeon, Theodore (Hamilton)

Hunter, Evan 1926- .... **CLC 11, 31**
See McBain, Ed
See also AAYA 39; BPFB 2; CA 5-8R; CANR 5, 38, 62, 97; CMW 4; CN 7; CPW; DAM POP; DLBY 1982; INT CANR-5; MSW; MTCW 1; SATA 25; SFW 4

Hunter, Kristin 1931-
See Lattany, Kristin (Elaine Eggleston) Hunter

Hunter, Mary
See Austin, Mary (Hunter)

Hunter, Mollie 1922- .... **CLC 21**
See McIlwraith, Maureen Mollie Hunter
See also AAYA 13; BYA 6; CANR 37, 78; CLR 25; DLB 161; JRDA; MAICYA 1, 2; SAAS 7; SATA 54, 106, 139; WYA; YAW

Hunter, Robert (?)-1734 .... **LC 7**

Hurston, Zora Neale 1891-1960 .... **BLC 2; CLC 7, 30, 61; DC 12; HR 2; SSC 4; TCLC 121, 131; WLCS**
See also AAYA 15; AFAW 1, 2; AMWS 6; BW 1, 3; BYA 12; CA 85-88; CANR 61; CDALBS; DA; DA3; DAC; DAM MST, MULT, NOV; DFS 6; DLB 51, 86; EWL 3; EXPN; EXPS; FW; LAIT 3; LATS 1; LMFS 2; MAWW; MTCW 1, 2; NFS 3; RGAL 4; RGSF 2; SSFS 1, 6, 11; TUS; YAW

Husserl, E. G.
See Husserl, Edmund (Gustav Albrecht)

Husserl, Edmund (Gustav Albrecht)
1859-1938 .... **TCLC 100**
See also CA 116; 133

Huston, John (Marcellus)
1906-1987 .... **CLC 20**
See also CA 73-76; 123; CANR 34; DLB 26

Hustvedt, Siri 1955- .... **CLC 76**
See also CA 137

Hutten, Ulrich von 1488-1523 .... **LC 16**
See also DLB 179

Huxley, Aldous (Leonard)
1894-1963 .... **CLC 1, 3, 4, 5, 8, 11, 18, 35, 79; SSC 39; WLC**
See also AAYA 11; BPFB 2; BRW 7; CA 85-88; CANR 44, 99; CDBLB 1914-1945; DA; DA3; DAB; DAC; DAM MST, NOV; DLB 36, 100, 162, 195, 255; EWL 3; EXPN; LAIT 5; LMFS 2; MTCW 1, 2; NFS 6; RGEL 2; SATA 63; SCFW 2; SFW 4; TEA; YAW

Huxley, T(homas) H(enry)
1825-1895 .... **NCLC 67**
See also DLB 57; TEA

Huysmans, Joris-Karl 1848-1907 ... **TCLC 7, 69**
See also CA 104; 165; DLB 123; EW 7; GFL 1789 to the Present; LMFS 2; RGWL 2, 3

Hwang, David Henry 1957- .. **CLC 55; DC 4**
See also CA 127; 132; CAD; CANR 76; CD 5; DA3; DAM DRAM; DFS 11, 18; DLB 212, 228; INT CA-132; MTCW 2; RGAL 4

Hyde, Anthony 1946- .... **CLC 42**
See Chase, Nicholas
See also CA 136; CCA 1

Hyde, Margaret O(ldroyd) 1917- ..... **CLC 21**
See also CA 1-4R; CANR 1, 36; CLR 23; JRDA; MAICYA 1, 2; SAAS 8; SATA 1, 42, 76, 139

Hynes, James 1956(?)- .... **CLC 65**
See also CA 164; CANR 105

Hypatia c. 370-415 .... **CMLC 35**

Ian, Janis 1951- .... **CLC 21**
See also CA 105; 187

Ibanez, Vicente Blasco
See Blasco Ibanez, Vicente

Ibarbourou, Juana de 1895-1979 ..... **HLCS 2**
See also HW 1; LAW

Ibarguengoitia, Jorge 1928-1983 .... **CLC 37**
See also CA 124; 113; EWL 3; HW 1

Ibn Battuta, Abu Abdalla
1304-1368(?) .... **CMLC 57**
See also WLIT 2

Ibsen, Henrik (Johan) 1828-1906 .... **DC 2; TCLC 2, 8, 16, 37, 52; WLC**
See also AAYA 46; CA 104; 141; DA; DA3; DAB; DAC; DAM DRAM, MST; DFS 1, 6, 8, 10, 11, 15, 16; EW 7; LAIT 2; LATS 1; RGWL 2, 3

Ibuse, Masuji 1898-1993 .... **CLC 22**
See Ibuse Masuji
See also CA 127; 141; MJW; RGWL 3

Ibuse Masuji
See Ibuse, Masuji
See also DLB 180; EWL 3

Ichikawa, Kon 1915- .... **CLC 20**
See also CA 121

Ichiyo, Higuchi 1872-1896 .... **NCLC 49**
See also MJW

Idle, Eric 1943- .... **CLC 21**
See Monty Python
See also CA 116; CANR 35, 91

Ignatow, David 1914-1997 .... **CLC 4, 7, 14, 40; PC 34**
See also CA 9-12R; 162; CAAS 3; CANR 31, 57, 96; CP 7; DLB 5; EWL 3

Ignotus
See Strachey, (Giles) Lytton

Ihimaera, Witi 1944- .... **CLC 46**
See also CA 77-80; CN 7; RGSF 2

Ilf, Ilya .... **TCLC 21**
See Fainzilberg, Ilya Arnoldovich
See also EWL 3

Illyes, Gyula 1902-1983 .... **PC 16**
See also CA 114; 109; CDWLB 4; DLB 215; EWL 3; RGWL 2, 3

Immermann, Karl (Lebrecht)
1796-1840 .... **NCLC 4, 49**
See also DLB 133

Ince, Thomas H. 1882-1924 .... **TCLC 89**
See also IDFW 3, 4

Inchbald, Elizabeth 1753-1821 ...... **NCLC 62**
See also DLB 39, 89; RGEL 2

Inclan, Ramon (Maria) del Valle
See Valle-Inclan, Ramon (Maria) del

Infante, G(uillermo) Cabrera
See Cabrera Infante, G(uillermo)

Ingalls, Rachel (Holmes) 1940- .... **CLC 42**
See also CA 123; 127

Ingamells, Reginald Charles
See Ingamells, Rex

Ingamells, Rex 1913-1955 .... **TCLC 35**
See also CA 167; DLB 260

Inge, William (Motter) 1913-1973 ..... **CLC 1, 8, 19**
See also CA 9-12R; CDALB 1941-1968; DA3; DAM DRAM; DFS 1, 3, 5, 8; DLB 7, 249; EWL 3; MTCW 1, 2; RGAL 4; TUS

Ingelow, Jean 1820-1897 .... **NCLC 39, 107**
See also DLB 35, 163; FANT; SATA 33

Ingram, Willis J.
See Harris, Mark

Innaurato, Albert (F.) 1948(?)- ... **CLC 21, 60**
See also CA 115; 122; CAD; CANR 78; CD 5; INT CA-122

Innes, Michael
See Stewart, J(ohn) I(nnes) M(ackintosh)
See also DLB 276; MSW

Innis, Harold Adams 1894-1952 .... **TCLC 77**
See also CA 181; DLB 88

Insluis, Alanus de
See Alain de Lille

Iola
See Wells-Barnett, Ida B(ell)

Ionesco, Eugene 1912-1994 ... **CLC 1, 4, 6, 9, 11, 15, 41, 86; DC 12; WLC**
See also CA 9-12R; 144; CANR 55; CWW 2; DA; DA3; DAB; DAC; DAM DRAM, MST; DFS 4, 9; EW 13; EWL 3; GFL 1789 to the Present; LMFS 2; MTCW 1, 2; RGWL 2, 3; SATA 7; SATA-Obit 79; TWA

Iqbal, Muhammad 1877-1938 .... **TCLC 28**
See also CA 215; EWL 3

Ireland, Patrick
See O'Doherty, Brian

Irenaeus St. 130- .... **CMLC 42**

Irigaray, Luce 1930- .... **CLC 164**
See also CA 154; CANR 121; FW

Iron, Ralph
See Schreiner, Olive (Emilie Albertina)

Irving, John (Winslow) 1942- ... **CLC 13, 23, 38, 112, 175**
See also AAYA 8; AMWS 6; BEST 89:3; BPFB 2; CA 25-28R; CANR 28, 73, 112; CN 7; CPW; DA3; DAM NOV, POP; DLB 6, 278; DLBY 1982; EWL 3; MTCW 1, 2; NFS 12, 14; RGAL 4; TUS

Irving, Washington 1783-1859 . **NCLC 2, 19, 95; SSC 2, 37; WLC**
See also AMW; CDALB 1640-1865; DA; DA3; DAB; DAC; DAM MST; DLB 3, 11, 30, 59, 73, 74, 183, 186, 250, 254; EXPS; LAIT 1; RGAL 4; RGSF 2; SSFS 1, 8, 16; SUFW 1; TUS; WCH; YABC 2

Irwin, P. K.
See Page, P(atricia) K(athleen)

Isaacs, Jorge Ricardo 1837-1895 ... **NCLC 70**
See also LAW

Isaacs, Susan 1943- .... **CLC 32**
See also BEST 89:1; BPFB 2; CA 89-92; CANR 20, 41, 65, 112; CPW; DA3; DAM POP; INT CANR-20; MTCW 1, 2

Isherwood, Christopher (William Bradshaw) 1904-1986 .... **CLC 1, 9, 11, 14, 44; SSC 56**
See also BRW 7; CA 13-16R; 117; CANR 35, 97; DA3; DAM DRAM, NOV; DLB 15, 195; DLBY 1986; EWL 3; IDTP; MTCW 1, 2; RGAL 4; RGEL 2; TUS; WLIT 4

Ishiguro, Kazuo 1954- .. **CLC 27, 56, 59, 110**
See also BEST 90:2; BPFB 2; BRWS 4; CA 120; CANR 49, 95; CN 7; DA3; DAM NOV; DLB 194; EWL 3; MTCW 1, 2; NFS 13; WLIT 4

Ishikawa, Hakuhin
See Ishikawa, Takuboku

Ishikawa, Takuboku 1886(?)-1912 ..... **PC 10; TCLC 15**
See Ishikawa Takuboku
See also CA 113; 153; DAM POET

Iskander, Fazil (Abdulovich) 1929- .. **CLC 47**
See also CA 102; EWL 3

Isler, Alan (David) 1934- .... **CLC 91**
See also CA 156; CANR 105

Ivan IV 1530-1584 .... **LC 17**

Ivanov, Vyacheslav Ivanovich 1866-1949 .... **TCLC 33**
See also CA 122; EWL 3

Ivask, Ivar Vidrik 1927-1992 .... **CLC 14**
See also CA 37-40R; 139; CANR 24

Ives, Morgan
See Bradley, Marion Zimmer
See also GLL 1

Izumi Shikibu c. 973-c. 1034 .... **CMLC 33**

J. R. S.
See Gogarty, Oliver St. John

Jabran, Kahlil
See Gibran, Kahlil

Jabran, Khalil
See Gibran, Kahlil

Jackson, Daniel
See Wingrove, David (John)

Jackson, Helen Hunt 1830-1885 .... **NCLC 90**
See also DLB 42, 47, 186, 189; RGAL 4

Jackson, Jesse 1908-1983 .... **CLC 12**
See also BW 1; CA 25-28R; 109; CANR 27; CLR 28; CWRI 5; MAICYA 1, 2; SATA 2, 29; SATA-Obit 48

Jackson, Laura (Riding) 1901-1991 .... **PC 44**
See Riding, Laura
See also CA 65-68; 135; CANR 28, 89; DLB 48

Jackson, Sam
See Trumbo, Dalton

Jackson, Sara
See Wingrove, David (John)

Jackson, Shirley 1919-1965 . **CLC 11, 60, 87; SSC 9, 39; WLC**
See also AAYA 9; AMWS 9; BPFB 2; CA 1-4R; 25-28R; CANR 4, 52; CDALB 1941-1968; DA; DA3; DAC; DAM MST; DLB 6, 234; EXPS; HGG; LAIT 4; MTCW 2; RGAL 4; RGSF 2; SATA 2; SSFS 1; SUFW 1, 2

Jacob, (Cyprien-)Max 1876-1944 .... **TCLC 6**
See also CA 104; 193; DLB 258; EWL 3; GFL 1789 to the Present; GLL 2; RGWL 2, 3

Jacobs, Harriet A(nn) 1813(?)-1897 .... **NCLC 67**
See also AFAW 1, 2; DLB 239; FW; LAIT 2; RGAL 4

Jacobs, Jim 1942- .... **CLC 12**
See also CA 97-100; INT 97-100

Jacobs, W(illiam) W(ymark) 1863-1943 .... **TCLC 22**
See also CA 121; 167; DLB 135; EXPS; HGG; RGEL 2; RGSF 2; SSFS 2; SUFW 1

Jacobsen, Jens Peter 1847-1885 .... **NCLC 34**

Jacobsen, Josephine 1908- .... **CLC 48, 102**
See also CA 33-36R; CAAS 18; CANR 23, 48; CCA 1; CP 7; DLB 244

Jacobson, Dan 1929- .... **CLC 4, 14**
See also AFW; CA 1-4R; CANR 2, 25, 66; CN 7; DLB 14, 207, 225; EWL 3; MTCW 1; RGSF 2

Jacqueline
See Carpentier (y Valmont), Alejo

Jacques de Vitry c. 1160-1240 .... **CMLC 63**
See also DLB 208

Jagger, Mick 1944- .... **CLC 17**

Jahiz, al- c. 780-c. 869 .... **CMLC 25**

Jakes, John (William) 1932- .... **CLC 29**
See also AAYA 32; BEST 89:4; BPFB 2; CA 57-60; CAAE 214; CANR 10, 43, 66, 111; CPW; CSW; DA3; DAM NOV, POP; DLB 278; DLBY 1983; FANT; INT CANR-10; MTCW 1, 2; RHW; SATA 62; SFW 4; TCWW 2

James I 1394-1437 .... **LC 20**
See also RGEL 2

James, Andrew
See Kirkup, James

James, C(yril) L(ionel) R(obert) 1901-1989 .... **BLCS; CLC 33**
See also BW 2; CA 117; 125; 128; CANR 62; DLB 125; MTCW 1

James, Daniel (Lewis) 1911-1988
See Santiago, Danny
See also CA 174; 125

James, Dynely
See Mayne, William (James Carter)

James, Henry Sr. 1811-1882 .... **NCLC 53**

James, Henry 1843-1916 .... **SSC 8, 32, 47; TCLC 2, 11, 24, 40, 47, 64; WLC**
See also AMW; AMWC 1; AMWR 1; BPFB 2; BRW 6; CA 104; 132; CDALB 1865-1917; DA; DA3; DAB; DAC; DAM MST, NOV; DLB 12, 71, 74, 189; DLBD 13; EWL 3; EXPS; HGG; LAIT 2; MTCW 1, 2; NFS 12, 16; RGAL 4; RGEL 2; RGSF 2; SSFS 9; SUFW 1; TUS

James, M. R.
See James, Montague (Rhodes)
See also DLB 156, 201

James, Montague (Rhodes) 1862-1936 .... **SSC 16; TCLC 6**
See James, M. R.
See also CA 104; 203; HGG; RGEL 2; RGSF 2; SUFW 1

James, P. D. .... **CLC 18, 46, 122**
See White, Phyllis Dorothy James
See also BEST 90:2; BPFB 2; BRWS 4; CDBLB 1960 to Present; DLB 87, 276; DLBD 17; MSW

James, Philip
See Moorcock, Michael (John)

James, Samuel
See Stephens, James

James, Seumas
See Stephens, James

James, Stephen
See Stephens, James

James, William 1842-1910 .... **TCLC 15, 32**
See also AMW; CA 109; 193; DLB 270, 284; NCFS 5; RGAL 4

Jameson, Anna 1794-1860 .... **NCLC 43**
See also DLB 99, 166

Jameson, Fredric (R.) 1934- .... **CLC 142**
See also CA 196; DLB 67; LMFS 2

Jami, Nur al-Din 'Abd al-Rahman 1414-1492 .... **LC 9**

Jammes, Francis 1868-1938 .... **TCLC 75**
See also CA 198; EWL 3; GFL 1789 to the Present

Jandl, Ernst 1925-2000 .... **CLC 34**
See also CA 200; EWL 3

Janowitz, Tama 1957- .... **CLC 43, 145**
See also CA 106; CANR 52, 89; CN 7; CPW; DAM POP

Japrisot, Sebastien 1931- .... **CLC 90**
See Rossi, Jean-Baptiste
See also CMW 4; NFS 18

Jarrell, Randall 1914-1965 .... **CLC 1, 2, 6, 9, 13, 49; PC 41**
See also AMW; BYA 5; CA 5-8R; 25-28R; CABS 2; CANR 6, 34; CDALB 1941-1968; CLR 6; CWRI 5; DAM POET; DLB 48, 52; EWL 3; EXPP; MAICYA 1, 2; MTCW 1, 2; PAB; PFS 2; RGAL 4; SATA 7

Jarry, Alfred 1873-1907 .... **SSC 20; TCLC 2, 14**
See also CA 104; 153; DA3; DAM DRAM; DFS 8; DLB 192, 258; EW 9; EWL 3; GFL 1789 to the Present; RGWL 2, 3; TWA

Jarvis, E. K.
See Ellison, Harlan (Jay)

Jawien, Andrzej
See John Paul II, Pope

Jaynes, Roderick
See Coen, Ethan

Jeake, Samuel, Jr.
See Aiken, Conrad (Potter)

Jean Paul 1763-1825 .... **NCLC 7**

Jefferies, (John) Richard 1848-1887 .... **NCLC 47**
See also DLB 98, 141; RGEL 2; SATA 16; SFW 4

Jeffers, (John) Robinson 1887-1962 .. **CLC 2, 3, 11, 15, 54; PC 17; WLC**
See also AMWS 2; CA 85-88; CANR 35; CDALB 1917-1929; DA; DAC; DAM MST, POET; DLB 45, 212; EWL 3; MTCW 1, 2; PAB; PFS 3, 4; RGAL 4

Jefferson, Janet
See Mencken, H(enry) L(ouis)

Jefferson, Thomas 1743-1826 . **NCLC 11, 103**
See also ANW; CDALB 1640-1865; DA3; DLB 31, 183; LAIT 1; RGAL 4

Jeffrey, Francis 1773-1850 .... **NCLC 33**
See Francis, Lord Jeffrey

Jelakowitch, Ivan
See Heijermans, Herman

Jelinek, Elfriede 1946- .... **CLC 169**
See also CA 154; DLB 85; FW

Jellicoe, (Patricia) Ann 1927- .... **CLC 27**
See also CA 85-88; CBD; CD 5; CWD; CWRI 5; DLB 13, 233; FW

Jelloun, Tahar ben 1944- .... **CLC 180**
See Ben Jelloun, Tahar
See also CA 162; CANR 100

Jemyma
See Holley, Marietta

Jen, Gish .... **AAL; CLC 70**
See Jen, Lillian
See also AMWC 2

Jen, Lillian 1956(?)-
See Jen, Gish
See also CA 135; CANR 89

Jenkins, (John) Robin 1912- .... **CLC 52**
See also CA 1-4R; CANR 1; CN 7; DLB 14, 271

Jennings, Elizabeth (Joan)
1926-2001 .... **CLC 5, 14, 131**
See also BRWS 5; CA 61-64; 200; CAAS 5; CANR 8, 39, 66; CP 7; CWP; DLB 27; EWL 3; MTCW 1; SATA 66

Jennings, Waylon 1937- .... **CLC 21**

Jensen, Johannes V(ilhelm)
1873-1950 .... **TCLC 41**
See also CA 170; DLB 214; EWL 3; RGWL 3

Jensen, Laura (Linnea) 1948- .... **CLC 37**
See also CA 103

Jerome, Saint 345-420 .... **CMLC 30**
See also RGWL 3

Jerome, Jerome K(lapka)
1859-1927 .... **TCLC 23**
See also CA 119; 177; DLB 10, 34, 135; RGEL 2

Jerrold, Douglas William
1803-1857 .... **NCLC 2**
See also DLB 158, 159; RGEL 2

Jewett, (Theodora) Sarah Orne
1849-1909 .... **SSC 6, 44; TCLC 1, 22**
See also AMW; AMWC 2; AMWR 2; CA 108; 127; CANR 71; DLB 12, 74, 221; EXPS; FW; MAWW; NFS 15; RGAL 4; RGSF 2; SATA 15; SSFS 4

Jewsbury, Geraldine (Endsor)
1812-1880 .... **NCLC 22**
See also DLB 21

Jhabvala, Ruth Prawer 1927- . **CLC 4, 8, 29, 94, 138**
See also BRWS 5; CA 1-4R; CANR 2, 29, 51, 74, 91; CN 7; DAB; DAM NOV; DLB 139, 194; EWL 3; IDFW 3, 4; INT CANR-29; MTCW 1, 2; RGSF 2; RGWL 2; RHW; TEA

Jibran, Kahlil
See Gibran, Kahlil

Jibran, Khalil
See Gibran, Kahlil

Jiles, Paulette 1943- .... **CLC 13, 58**
See also CA 101; CANR 70; CWP

Jimenez (Mantecon), Juan Ramon
1881-1958 .... **HLC 1; PC 7; TCLC 4**
See also CA 104; 131; CANR 74; DAM MULT, POET; DLB 134; EW 9; EWL 3; HW 1; MTCW 1, 2; RGWL 2, 3

Jimenez, Ramon
See Jimenez (Mantecon), Juan Ramon

Jimenez Mantecon, Juan
See Jimenez (Mantecon), Juan Ramon

Jin, Ha .... **CLC 109**
See Jin, Xuefei
See also CA 152; DLB 244; SSFS 17

Jin, Xuefei 1956-
See Jin, Ha
See also CANR 91; SSFS 17

Joel, Billy .... **CLC 26**
See Joel, William Martin

Joel, William Martin 1949-
See Joel, Billy
See also CA 108

John, Saint 10(?)-100 .... **CMLC 27, 63**

John of Salisbury c. 1115-1180 ..... **CMLC 63**

John of the Cross, St. 1542-1591 .... **LC 18**
See also RGWL 2, 3

John Paul II, Pope 1920- .... **CLC 128**
See also CA 106; 133

Johnson, B(ryan) S(tanley William)
1933-1973 .... **CLC 6, 9**
See also CA 9-12R; 53-56; CANR 9; DLB 14, 40; EWL 3; RGEL 2

Johnson, Benjamin F., of Boone
See Riley, James Whitcomb

Johnson, Charles (Richard) 1948- .... **BLC 2; CLC 7, 51, 65, 163**
See also AFAW 2; AMWS 6; BW 2, 3; CA 116; CAAS 18; CANR 42, 66, 82; CN 7; DAM MULT; DLB 33, 278; MTCW 2; RGAL 4; SSFS 16

Johnson, Charles S(purgeon)
1893-1956 .... **HR 3**
See also BW 1, 3; CA 125; CANR 82; DLB 51, 91

Johnson, Denis 1949- . **CLC 52, 160; SSC 56**
See also CA 117; 121; CANR 71, 99; CN 7; DLB 120

Johnson, Diane 1934- .... **CLC 5, 13, 48**
See also BPFB 2; CA 41-44R; CANR 17, 40, 62, 95; CN 7; DLBY 1980; INT CANR-17; MTCW 1

Johnson, E. Pauline 1861-1913 .... **NNAL**
See also CA 150; DAC; DAM MULT; DLB 92, 175

Johnson, Eyvind (Olof Verner)
1900-1976 .... **CLC 14**
See also CA 73-76; 69-72; CANR 34, 101; DLB 259; EW 12; EWL 3

Johnson, Fenton 1888-1958 .... **BLC 2**
See also BW 1; CA 118; 124; DAM MULT; DLB 45, 50

Johnson, Georgia Douglas (Camp)
1880-1966 .... **HR 3**
See also BW 1; CA 125; DLB 51, 249; WP

Johnson, Helene 1907-1995 .... **HR 3**
See also CA 181; DLB 51; WP

Johnson, J. R.
See James, C(yril) L(ionel) R(obert)

Johnson, James Weldon 1871-1938 .. **BLC 2; HR 3; PC 24; TCLC 3, 19**
See also AFAW 1, 2; BW 1, 3; CA 104; 125; CANR 82; CDALB 1917-1929; CLR 32; DA3; DAM MULT, POET; DLB 51; EWL 3; EXPP; LMFS 2; MTCW 1, 2; PFS 1; RGAL 4; SATA 31; TUS

Johnson, Joyce 1935- .... **CLC 58**
See also BG 3; CA 125; 129; CANR 102

Johnson, Judith (Emlyn) 1936- .... **CLC 7, 15**
See Sherwin, Judith Johnson
See also CA 25-28R; 153; CANR 34

Johnson, Lionel (Pigot)
1867-1902 .... **TCLC 19**
See also CA 117; 209; DLB 19; RGEL 2

Johnson, Marguerite Annie
See Angelou, Maya

Johnson, Mel
See Malzberg, Barry N(athaniel)

Johnson, Pamela Hansford
1912-1981 .... **CLC 1, 7, 27**
See also CA 1-4R; 104; CANR 2, 28; DLB 15; MTCW 1, 2; RGEL 2

Johnson, Paul (Bede) 1928- .... **CLC 147**
See also BEST 89:4; CA 17-20R; CANR 34, 62, 100

Johnson, Robert .... **CLC 70**

Johnson, Robert 1911(?)-1938 .... **TCLC 69**
See also BW 3; CA 174

Johnson, Samuel 1709-1784 ...... **LC 15, 52; WLC**
See also BRW 3; BRWR 1; CDBLB 1660-1789; DA; DAB; DAC; DAM MST; DLB 39, 95, 104, 142, 213; LMFS 1; RGEL 2; TEA

Johnson, Uwe 1934-1984 .. **CLC 5, 10, 15, 40**
See also CA 1-4R; 112; CANR 1, 39; CD-WLB 2; DLB 75; EWL 3; MTCW 1; RGWL 2, 3

Johnston, Basil H. 1929- .... **NNAL**
See also CA 69-72; CANR 11, 28, 66; DAC; DAM MULT; DLB 60

Johnston, George (Benson) 1913- .... **CLC 51**
See also CA 1-4R; CANR 5, 20; CP 7; DLB 88

Johnston, Jennifer (Prudence)
1930- .... **CLC 7, 150**
See also CA 85-88; CANR 92; CN 7; DLB 14

Joinville, Jean de 1224(?)-1317 ..... **CMLC 38**

Jolley, (Monica) Elizabeth 1923- ...... **CLC 46; SSC 19**
See also CA 127; CAAS 13; CANR 59; CN 7; EWL 3; RGSF 2

Jones, Arthur Llewellyn 1863-1947
See Machen, Arthur
See also CA 104; 179; HGG

Jones, D(ouglas) G(ordon) 1929- ...... **CLC 10**
See also CA 29-32R; CANR 13, 90; CP 7; DLB 53

Jones, David (Michael) 1895-1974 .... **CLC 2, 4, 7, 13, 42**
See also BRW 6; BRWS 7; CA 9-12R; 53-56; CANR 28; CDBLB 1945-1960; DLB 20, 100; EWL 3; MTCW 1; PAB; RGEL 2

Jones, David Robert 1947-
See Bowie, David
See also CA 103; CANR 104

Jones, Diana Wynne 1934- .... **CLC 26**
See also AAYA 12; BYA 6, 7, 9, 11, 13, 16; CA 49-52; CANR 4, 26, 56, 120; CLR 23; DLB 161; FANT; JRDA; MAICYA 1, 2; SAAS 7; SATA 9, 70, 108; SFW 4; SUFW 2; YAW

Jones, Edward P. 1950- .... **CLC 76**
See also BW 2, 3; CA 142; CANR 79; CSW

Jones, Gayl 1949- ...... **BLC 2; CLC 6, 9, 131**
See also AFAW 1, 2; BW 2, 3; CA 77-80; CANR 27, 66, 122; CN 7; CSW; DA3; DAM MULT; DLB 33, 278; MTCW 1, 2; RGAL 4

Jones, James 1921-1977 .... **CLC 1, 3, 10, 39**
See also AITN 1, 2; AMWS 11; BPFB 2; CA 1-4R; 69-72; CANR 6; DLB 2, 143; DLBD 17; DLBY 1998; EWL 3; MTCW 1; RGAL 4

Jones, John J.
See Lovecraft, H(oward) P(hillips)

Jones, LeRoi .... **CLC 1, 2, 3, 5, 10, 14**
See Baraka, Amiri
See also MTCW 2

Jones, Louis B. 1953- .... **CLC 65**
See also CA 141; CANR 73

Jones, Madison (Percy, Jr.) 1925- .... **CLC 4**
See also CA 13-16R; CAAS 11; CANR 7, 54, 83; CN 7; CSW; DLB 152

Jones, Mervyn 1922- .... **CLC 10, 52**
See also CA 45-48; CAAS 5; CANR 1, 91; CN 7; MTCW 1

Jones, Mick 1956(?)- .... **CLC 30**

Jones, Nettie (Pearl) 1941- .... **CLC 34**
See also BW 2; CA 137; CAAS 20; CANR 88

Jones, Peter 1802-1856 .... **NNAL**

Jones, Preston 1936-1979 .... **CLC 10**
See also CA 73-76; 89-92; DLB 7

Jones, Robert F(rancis) 1934- .... **CLC 7**
See also CA 49-52; CANR 2, 61, 118

Jones, Rod 1953- .... **CLC 50**
See also CA 128

Jones, Terence Graham Parry
1942- .... **CLC 21**
See Jones, Terry; Monty Python
See also CA 112; 116; CANR 35, 93; INT 116; SATA 127

Jones, Terry
See Jones, Terence Graham Parry
See also SATA 67; SATA-Brief 51

Jones, Thom (Douglas) 1945(?)- ..... **CLC 81; SSC 56**
See also CA 157; CANR 88; DLB 244

Jong, Erica 1942- .... **CLC 4, 6, 8, 18, 83**
See also AITN 1; AMWS 5; BEST 90:2; BPFB 2; CA 73-76; CANR 26, 52, 75; CN 7; CP 7; CPW; DA3; DAM NOV, POP; DLB 2, 5, 28, 152; FW; INT CANR-26; MTCW 1, 2

Jonson, Ben(jamin) 1572(?)-1637 . **DC 4; LC 6, 33; PC 17; WLC**
See also BRW 1; BRWC 1; BRWR 1; CDBLB Before 1660; DA; DAB; DAC; DAM DRAM, MST, POET; DFS 4, 10; DLB 62, 121; LMFS 1; RGEL 2; TEA; WLIT 3

Jordan, June (Meyer) 1936-2002 .. **BLCS; CLC 5, 11, 23, 114; PC 38**
See also AAYA 2; AFAW 1, 2; BW 2, 3; CA 33-36R; 206; CANR 25, 70, 114; CLR 10; CP 7; CWP; DAM MULT, POET; DLB 38; GLL 2; LAIT 5; MAICYA 1, 2; MTCW 1; SATA 4, 136; YAW

Jordan, Neil (Patrick) 1950- .... **CLC 110**
See also CA 124; 130; CANR 54; CN 7; GLL 2; INT 130

Jordan, Pat(rick M.) 1941- .... **CLC 37**
See also CA 33-36R; CANR 121

Jorgensen, Ivar
See Ellison, Harlan (Jay)

Jorgenson, Ivar
See Silverberg, Robert

Joseph, George Ghevarughese .... **CLC 70**

Josephson, Mary
See O'Doherty, Brian

Josephus, Flavius c. 37-100 .... **CMLC 13**
See also AW 2; DLB 176

Josiah Allen's Wife
See Holley, Marietta

Josipovici, Gabriel (David) 1940- ...... **CLC 6, 43, 153**
See also CA 37-40R; CAAS 8; CANR 47, 84; CN 7; DLB 14

Joubert, Joseph 1754-1824 .... **NCLC 9**

Jouve, Pierre Jean 1887-1976 .... **CLC 47**
See also CA 65-68; DLB 258; EWL 3

Jovine, Francesco 1902-1950 .... **TCLC 79**
See also DLB 264; EWL 3

Joyce, James (Augustine Aloysius) 1882-1941 .... **DC 16; PC 22; SSC 3, 26, 44, 64; TCLC 3, 8, 16, 35, 52; WLC**
See also AAYA 42; BRW 7; BRWC 1; BRWR 1; BYA 11, 13; CA 104; 126; CDBLB 1914-1945; DA; DA3; DAB; DAC; DAM MST, NOV, POET; DLB 10, 19, 36, 162, 247; EWL 3; EXPN; EXPS; LAIT 1; LMFS 1, 2; MTCW 1, 2; NFS 7; RGSF 2; SSFS 1; TEA; WLIT 4

Jozsef, Attila 1905-1937 .... **TCLC 22**
See also CA 116; CDWLB 4; DLB 215; EWL 3

Juana Ines de la Cruz, Sor 1651(?)-1695 ...... **HLCS 1; LC 5; PC 24**
See also FW; LAW; RGWL 2, 3; WLIT 1

Juana Inez de La Cruz, Sor
See Juana Ines de la Cruz, Sor

Judd, Cyril
See Kornbluth, C(yril) M.; Pohl, Frederik

Juenger, Ernst 1895-1998 .... **CLC 125**
See Junger, Ernst
See also CA 101; 167; CANR 21, 47, 106; DLB 56

Julian of Norwich 1342(?)-1416(?) . **LC 6, 52**
See also DLB 146; LMFS 1

Julius Caesar 100B.C.-44B.C.
See Caesar, Julius
See also CDWLB 1; DLB 211

Junger, Ernst
See Juenger, Ernst
See also CDWLB 2; EWL 3; RGWL 2, 3

Junger, Sebastian 1962- .... **CLC 109**
See also AAYA 28; CA 165

Juniper, Alex
See Hospital, Janette Turner

Junius
See Luxemburg, Rosa

Just, Ward (Swift) 1935- .... **CLC 4, 27**
See also CA 25-28R; CANR 32, 87; CN 7; INT CANR-32

Justice, Donald (Rodney) 1925- .. **CLC 6, 19, 102**
See also AMWS 7; CA 5-8R; CANR 26, 54, 74, 121, 122; CP 7; CSW; DAM POET; DLBY 1983; EWL 3; INT CANR-26; MTCW 2; PFS 14

Juvenal c. 60-c. 130 .... **CMLC 8**
See also AW 2; CDWLB 1; DLB 211; RGWL 2, 3

Juvenis
See Bourne, Randolph S(illiman)

K., Alice
See Knapp, Caroline

Kabakov, Sasha .... **CLC 59**

Kacew, Romain 1914-1980
See Gary, Romain
See also CA 108; 102

Kadare, Ismail 1936- .... **CLC 52**
See also CA 161; EWL 3; RGWL 3

Kadohata, Cynthia .... **CLC 59, 122**
See also CA 140

Kafka, Franz 1883-1924 ... **SSC 5, 29, 35, 60; TCLC 2, 6, 13, 29, 47, 53, 112; WLC**
See also AAYA 31; BPFB 2; CA 105; 126; CDWLB 2; DA; DA3; DAB; DAC; DAM MST, NOV; DLB 81; EW 9; EWL 3; EXPS; LATS 1; LMFS 2; MTCW 1, 2; NFS 7; RGSF 2; RGWL 2, 3; SFW 4; SSFS 3, 7, 12; TWA

Kahanovitsch, Pinkhes
See Der Nister

Kahn, Roger 1927- .... **CLC 30**
See also CA 25-28R; CANR 44, 69; DLB 171; SATA 37

Kain, Saul
See Sassoon, Siegfried (Lorraine)

Kaiser, Georg 1878-1945 .... **TCLC 9**
See also CA 106; 190; CDWLB 2; DLB 124; EWL 3; LMFS 2; RGWL 2, 3

Kaledin, Sergei .... **CLC 59**

Kaletski, Alexander 1946- .... **CLC 39**
See also CA 118; 143

Kalidasa fl. c. 400-455 .... **CMLC 9; PC 22**
See also RGWL 2, 3

Kallman, Chester (Simon) 1921-1975 .... **CLC 2**
See also CA 45-48; 53-56; CANR 3

Kaminsky, Melvin 1926-
See Brooks, Mel
See also CA 65-68; CANR 16

Kaminsky, Stuart M(elvin) 1934- ..... **CLC 59**
See also CA 73-76; CANR 29, 53, 89; CMW 4

Kandinsky, Wassily 1866-1944 .... **TCLC 92**
See also CA 118; 155

Kane, Francis
See Robbins, Harold

Kane, Henry 1918-
See Queen, Ellery
See also CA 156; CMW 4

Kane, Paul
See Simon, Paul (Frederick)

Kanin, Garson 1912-1999 .... **CLC 22**
See also AITN 1; CA 5-8R; 177; CAD; CANR 7, 78; DLB 7; IDFW 3, 4

Kaniuk, Yoram 1930- .... **CLC 19**
See also CA 134

Kant, Immanuel 1724-1804 ..... **NCLC 27, 67**
See also DLB 94

Kantor, MacKinlay 1904-1977 .... **CLC 7**
See also CA 61-64; 73-76; CANR 60, 63; DLB 9, 102; MTCW 2; RHW; TCWW 2

Kanze Motokiyo
See Zeami

Kaplan, David Michael 1946- .... **CLC 50**
See also CA 187

Kaplan, James 1951- .... **CLC 59**
See also CA 135; CANR 121

Karadzic, Vuk Stefanovic 1787-1864 .... **NCLC 115**
See also CDWLB 4; DLB 147

Karageorge, Michael
See Anderson, Poul (William)

Karamzin, Nikolai Mikhailovich 1766-1826 .... **NCLC 3**
See also DLB 150; RGSF 2

Karapanou, Margarita 1946- .... **CLC 13**
See also CA 101

Karinthy, Frigyes 1887-1938 .... **TCLC 47**
See also CA 170; DLB 215; EWL 3

Karl, Frederick R(obert) 1927- .... **CLC 34**
See also CA 5-8R; CANR 3, 44

Kastel, Warren
See Silverberg, Robert

Kataev, Evgeny Petrovich 1903-1942
See Petrov, Evgeny
See also CA 120

Kataphusin
See Ruskin, John

Katz, Steve 1935- .... **CLC 47**
See also CA 25-28R; CAAS 14, 64; CANR 12; CN 7; DLBY 1983

Kauffman, Janet 1945- .... **CLC 42**
See also CA 117; CANR 43, 84; DLB 218; DLBY 1986

Kaufman, Bob (Garnell) 1925-1986 . **CLC 49**
See also BG 3; BW 1; CA 41-44R; 118; CANR 22; DLB 16, 41

Kaufman, George S. 1889-1961 ...... **CLC 38; DC 17**
See also CA 108; 93-96; DAM DRAM; DFS 1, 10; DLB 7; INT CA-108; MTCW 2; RGAL 4; TUS

Kaufman, Sue .... **CLC 3, 8**
See Barondess, Sue K(aufman)

Kavafis, Konstantinos Petrou 1863-1933
See Cavafy, C(onstantine) P(eter)
See also CA 104

Kavan, Anna 1901-1968 .... **CLC 5, 13, 82**
See also BRWS 7; CA 5-8R; CANR 6, 57; DLB 255; MTCW 1; RGEL 2; SFW 4

Kavanagh, Dan
See Barnes, Julian (Patrick)

Kavanagh, Julie 1952- .... **CLC 119**
See also CA 163

Kavanagh, Patrick (Joseph) 1904-1967 .... **CLC 22; PC 33**
See also BRWS 7; CA 123; 25-28R; DLB 15, 20; EWL 3; MTCW 1; RGEL 2

Kawabata, Yasunari 1899-1972 ..... **CLC 2, 5, 9, 18, 107; SSC 17**
See Kawabata Yasunari
See also CA 93-96; 33-36R; CANR 88; DAM MULT; MJW; MTCW 2; RGSF 2; RGWL 2, 3

Kawabata Yasunari
See Kawabata, Yasunari
See also DLB 180; EWL 3

Kaye, M(ary) M(argaret) 1909- .... **CLC 28**
See also CA 89-92; CANR 24, 60, 102; MTCW 1, 2; RHW; SATA 62

Kaye, Mollie
See Kaye, M(ary) M(argaret)

Kaye-Smith, Sheila 1887-1956 .... **TCLC 20**
See also CA 118; 203; DLB 36

Kaymor, Patrice Maguilene
See Senghor, Leopold Sedar

Kazakov, Yuri Pavlovich 1927-1982 . **SSC 43**
See Kazakov, Yury
See also CA 5-8R; CANR 36; MTCW 1; RGSF 2

Kazakov, Yury
See Kazakov, Yuri Pavlovich
See also EWL 3

Kazan, Elia 1909-2003 .... **CLC 6, 16, 63**
See also CA 21-24R; CANR 32, 78

Kazantzakis, Nikos 1883(?)-1957 .... **TCLC 2, 5, 33**
See also BPFB 2; CA 105; 132; DA3; EW 9; EWL 3; MTCW 1, 2; RGWL 2, 3

Kazin, Alfred 1915-1998 ..... **CLC 34, 38, 119**
See also AMWS 8; CA 1-4R; CAAS 7; CANR 1, 45, 79; DLB 67; EWL 3

Keane, Mary Nesta (Skrine) 1904-1996
See Keane, Molly
See also CA 108; 114; 151; CN 7; RHW

Keane, Molly .... **CLC 31**
See Keane, Mary Nesta (Skrine)
See also INT 114

Keates, Jonathan 1946(?)- .... **CLC 34**
See also CA 163

Keaton, Buster 1895-1966 .... **CLC 20**
See also CA 194

Keats, John 1795-1821 ...... **NCLC 8, 73, 121; PC 1; WLC**
See also BRW 4; BRWR 1; CDBLB 1789-1832; DA; DA3; DAB; DAC; DAM MST, POET; DLB 96, 110; EXPP; LMFS 1; PAB; PFS 1, 2, 3, 9, 17; RGEL 2; TEA; WLIT 3; WP

Keble, John 1792-1866 .... **NCLC 87**
See also DLB 32, 55; RGEL 2

Keene, Donald 1922- .... **CLC 34**
See also CA 1-4R; CANR 5, 119

Keillor, Garrison .... **CLC 40, 115**
See Keillor, Gary (Edward)
See also AAYA 2; BEST 89:3; BPFB 2; DLBY 1987; EWL 3; SATA 58; TUS

Keillor, Gary (Edward) 1942-
See Keillor, Garrison
See also CA 111; 117; CANR 36, 59; CPW; DA3; DAM POP; MTCW 1, 2

Keith, Carlos
See Lewton, Val

Keith, Michael
See Hubbard, L(afayette) Ron(ald)

Keller, Gottfried 1819-1890 .... **NCLC 2; SSC 26**
See also CDWLB 2; DLB 129; EW; RGSF 2; RGWL 2, 3

Keller, Nora Okja 1965- .... **CLC 109**
See also CA 187

Kellerman, Jonathan 1949- .... **CLC 44**
See also AAYA 35; BEST 90:1; CA 106; CANR 29, 51; CMW 4; CPW; DA3; DAM POP; INT CANR-29

Kelley, William Melvin 1937- .... **CLC 22**
See also BW 1; CA 77-80; CANR 27, 83; CN 7; DLB 33; EWL 3

Kellogg, Marjorie 1922- .... **CLC 2**
See also CA 81-84

Kellow, Kathleen
See Hibbert, Eleanor Alice Burford

Kelly, M(ilton) T(errence) 1947- .... **CLC 55**
See also CA 97-100; CAAS 22; CANR 19, 43, 84; CN 7

Kelly, Robert 1935- .... **SSC 50**
See also CA 17-20R; CAAS 19; CANR 47; CP 7; DLB 5, 130, 165

Kelman, James 1946- .... **CLC 58, 86**
See also BRWS 5; CA 148; CANR 85; CN 7; DLB 194; RGSF 2; WLIT 4

Kemal, Yashar 1923- .... **CLC 14, 29**
See also CA 89-92; CANR 44; CWW 2

Kemble, Fanny 1809-1893 .... **NCLC 18**
See also DLB 32

Kemelman, Harry 1908-1996 .... **CLC 2**
See also AITN 1; BPFB 2; CA 9-12R; 155; CANR 6, 71; CMW 4; DLB 28

Kempe, Margery 1373(?)-1440(?) ... **LC 6, 56**
See also DLB 146; RGEL 2

Kempis, Thomas a 1380-1471 .... **LC 11**

Kendall, Henry 1839-1882 .... **NCLC 12**
See also DLB 230

Keneally, Thomas (Michael) 1935- ... **CLC 5, 8, 10, 14, 19, 27, 43, 117**
See also BRWS 4; CA 85-88; CANR 10, 50, 74; CN 7; CPW; DA3; DAM NOV; DLB 289; EWL 3; MTCW 1, 2; NFS 17; RGEL 2; RHW

Kennedy, Adrienne (Lita) 1931- .... **BLC 2; CLC 66; DC 5**
See also AFAW 2; BW 2, 3; CA 103; CAAS 20; CABS 3; CANR 26, 53, 82; CD 5; DAM MULT; DFS 9; DLB 38; FW

Kennedy, John Pendleton 1795-1870 .... **NCLC 2**
See also DLB 3, 248, 254; RGAL 4

Kennedy, Joseph Charles 1929-
See Kennedy, X. J.
See also CA 1-4R; CAAE 201; CANR 4, 30, 40; CP 7; CWRI 5; MAICYA 2; MAICYAS 1; SATA 14, 86; SATA-Essay 130

Kennedy, William 1928- ... **CLC 6, 28, 34, 53**
See also AAYA 1; AMWS 7; BPFB 2; CA 85-88; CANR 14, 31, 76; CN 7; DA3; DAM NOV; DLB 143; DLBY 1985; EWL 3; INT CANR-31; MTCW 1, 2; SATA 57

Kennedy, X. J. .... **CLC 8, 42**
See Kennedy, Joseph Charles
See also CAAS 9; CLR 27; DLB 5; SAAS 22

Kenny, Maurice (Francis) 1929- ..... **CLC 87; NNAL**
See also CA 144; CAAS 22; DAM MULT; DLB 175

Kent, Kelvin
See Kuttner, Henry

Kenton, Maxwell
See Southern, Terry

Kenyon, Robert O.
See Kuttner, Henry

Kepler, Johannes 1571-1630 .... **LC 45**

Ker, Jill
See Conway, Jill K(er)

Kerkow, H. C.
See Lewton, Val

Kerouac, Jack 1922-1969 ...... **CLC 1, 2, 3, 5, 14, 29, 61; TCLC 117; WLC**
See Kerouac, Jean-Louis Lebris de
See also AAYA 25; AMWC 1; AMWS 3; BG 3; BPFB 2; CDALB 1941-1968; CPW; DLB 2, 16, 237; DLBD 3; DLBY 1995; EWL 3; GLL 1; LATS 1; LMFS 2; MTCW 2; NFS 8; RGAL 4; TUS; WP

Kerouac, Jean-Louis Lebris de 1922-1969
See Kerouac, Jack
See also AITN 1; CA 5-8R; 25-28R; CANR 26, 54, 95; DA; DA3; DAB; DAC; DAM MST, NOV, POET, POP; MTCW 1, 2

Kerr, (Bridget) Jean (Collins) 1923(?)-2003 .... **CLC 22**
See also CA 5-8R; 212; CANR 7; INT CANR-7

Kerr, M. E. .... **CLC 12, 35**
See Meaker, Marijane (Agnes)
See also AAYA 2, 23; BYA 1, 7, 8; CLR 29; SAAS 1; WYA

Kerr, Robert .... **CLC 55**

Kerrigan, (Thomas) Anthony 1918- .. **CLC 4, 6**
See also CA 49-52; CAAS 11; CANR 4

Kerry, Lois
See Duncan, Lois

Kesey, Ken (Elton) 1935-2001 ... **CLC 1, 3, 6, 11, 46, 64; WLC**
See also AAYA 25; BG 3; BPFB 2; CA 1-4R; 204; CANR 22, 38, 66; CDALB 1968-1988; CN 7; CPW; DA; DA3; DAB; DAC; DAM MST, NOV, POP; DLB 2, 16, 206; EWL 3; EXPN; LAIT 4; MTCW 1, 2; NFS 2; RGAL 4; SATA 66; SATA-Obit 131; TUS; YAW

Kesselring, Joseph (Otto) 1902-1967 .... **CLC 45**
See also CA 150; DAM DRAM, MST

Kessler, Jascha (Frederick) 1929- ...... **CLC 4**
See also CA 17-20R; CANR 8, 48, 111

Kettelkamp, Larry (Dale) 1933- .... **CLC 12**
See also CA 29-32R; CANR 16; SAAS 3; SATA 2

Key, Ellen (Karolina Sofia) 1849-1926 .... **TCLC 65**
See also DLB 259

Keyber, Conny
See Fielding, Henry

Keyes, Daniel 1927- .... **CLC 80**
See also AAYA 23; BYA 11; CA 17-20R, 181; CAAE 181; CANR 10, 26, 54, 74; DA; DA3; DAC; DAM MST, NOV; EXPN; LAIT 4; MTCW 2; NFS 2; SATA 37; SFW 4

Keynes, John Maynard 1883-1946 .... **TCLC 64**
See also CA 114; 162, 163; DLBD 10; MTCW 2

Khanshendel, Chiron
See Rose, Wendy

Khayyam, Omar 1048-1131 ... **CMLC 11; PC 8**
See Omar Khayyam
See also DA3; DAM POET

Kherdian, David 1931- .... **CLC 6, 9**
See also AAYA 42; CA 21-24R; CAAE 192; CAAS 2; CANR 39, 78; CLR 24; JRDA; LAIT 3; MAICYA 1, 2; SATA 16, 74; SATA-Essay 125

Khlebnikov, Velimir .... **TCLC 20**
See Khlebnikov, Viktor Vladimirovich
See also EW 10; EWL 3; RGWL 2, 3

Khlebnikov, Viktor Vladimirovich 1885-1922
See Khlebnikov, Velimir
See also CA 117

Khodasevich, Vladislav (Felitsianovich) 1886-1939 .... **TCLC 15**
See also CA 115; EWL 3

Kielland, Alexander Lange 1849-1906 .... **TCLC 5**
See also CA 104

Kiely, Benedict 1919- ... **CLC 23, 43; SSC 58**
See also CA 1-4R; CANR 2, 84; CN 7; DLB 15

Kienzle, William X(avier) 1928-2001 .... **CLC 25**
See also CA 93-96; 203; CAAS 1; CANR 9, 31, 59, 111; CMW 4; DA3; DAM POP; INT CANR-31; MSW; MTCW 1, 2

Kierkegaard, Soren 1813-1855 ..... **NCLC 34, 78, 125**
See also EW 6; LMFS 2; RGWL 3; TWA

Kieslowski, Krzysztof 1941-1996 .... **CLC 120**
See also CA 147; 151

Killens, John Oliver 1916-1987 .... **CLC 10**
See also BW 2; CA 77-80; 123; CAAS 2; CANR 26; DLB 33; EWL 3

Killigrew, Anne 1660-1685 .... **LC 4, 73**
See also DLB 131

Killigrew, Thomas 1612-1683 .... **LC 57**
See also DLB 58; RGEL 2

Kim
See Simenon, Georges (Jacques Christian)

Kincaid, Jamaica 1949- ...... **BLC 2; CLC 43, 68, 137**
See also AAYA 13; AFAW 2; AMWS 7; BRWS 7; BW 2, 3; CA 125; CANR 47, 59, 95; CDALBS; CDWLB 3; CLR 63; CN 7; DA3; DAM MULT, NOV; DLB 157, 227; DNFS 1; EWL 3; EXPS; FW; LATS 1; LMFS 2; MTCW 2; NCFS 3; SSFS 5, 7; TUS; YAW

King, Francis (Henry) 1923- .... **CLC 8, 53, 145**
See also CA 1-4R; CANR 1, 33, 86; CN 7; DAM NOV; DLB 15, 139; MTCW 1

King, Kennedy
See Brown, George Douglas

King, Martin Luther, Jr. 1929-1968 . **BLC 2; CLC 83; WLCS**
See also BW 2, 3; CA 25-28; CANR 27, 44; CAP 2; DA; DA3; DAB; DAC; DAM MST, MULT; LAIT 5; LATS 1; MTCW 1, 2; SATA 14

King, Stephen (Edwin) 1947- .... **CLC 12, 26, 37, 61, 113; SSC 17, 55**
See also AAYA 1, 17; AMWS 5; BEST 90:1; BPFB 2; CA 61-64; CANR 1, 30, 52, 76, 119; CPW; DA3; DAM NOV, POP; DLB 143; DLBY 1980; HGG; JRDA; LAIT 5; MTCW 1, 2; RGAL 4; SATA 9, 55; SUFW 1, 2; WYAS 1; YAW

King, Steve
See King, Stephen (Edwin)

King, Thomas 1943- .... **CLC 89, 171; NNAL**
See also CA 144; CANR 95; CCA 1; CN 7; DAC; DAM MULT; DLB 175; SATA 96

Kingman, Lee .... **CLC 17**
See Natti, (Mary) Lee
See also CWRI 5; SAAS 3; SATA 1, 67

Kingsley, Charles 1819-1875 .... **NCLC 35**
See also CLR 77; DLB 21, 32, 163, 178, 190; FANT; MAICYA 2; MAICYAS 1; RGEL 2; WCH; YABC 2

Kingsley, Henry 1830-1876 .... **NCLC 107**
See also DLB 21, 230; RGEL 2

Kingsley, Sidney 1906-1995 .... **CLC 44**
See also CA 85-88; 147; CAD; DFS 14; DLB 7; RGAL 4

Kingsolver, Barbara 1955- . **CLC 55, 81, 130**
See also AAYA 15; AMWS 7; CA 129; 134; CANR 60, 96; CDALBS; CPW; CSW; DA3; DAM POP; DLB 206; INT CA-134; LAIT 5; MTCW 2; NFS 5, 10, 12; RGAL 4

Kingston, Maxine (Ting Ting) Hong 1940- .... **AAL; CLC 12, 19, 58, 121; WLCS**
See also AAYA 8; AMWS 5; BPFB 2; CA 69-72; CANR 13, 38, 74, 87; CDALBS; CN 7; DA3; DAM MULT, NOV; DLB 173, 212; DLBY 1980; EWL 3; FW; INT CANR-13; LAIT 5; MAWW; MTCW 1, 2; NFS 6; RGAL 4; SATA 53; SSFS 3

Kinnell, Galway 1927- ..... **CLC 1, 2, 3, 5, 13, 29, 129; PC 26**
See also AMWS 3; CA 9-12R; CANR 10, 34, 66, 116; CP 7; DLB 5; DLBY 1987; EWL 3; INT CANR-34; MTCW 1, 2; PAB; PFS 9; RGAL 4; WP

Kinsella, Thomas 1928- .... **CLC 4, 19, 138**
See also BRWS 5; CA 17-20R; CANR 15, 122; CN 7; DLB 27; EWL 3; MTCW 1, 2; RGEL 2; TEA

Kinsella, W(illiam) P(atrick) 1935- . **CLC 27, 43, 166**
See also AAYA 7; BPFB 2; CA 97-100; CAAS 7; CANR 21, 35, 66, 75; CN 7; CPW; DAC; DAM NOV, POP; FANT; INT CANR-21; LAIT 5; MTCW 1, 2; NFS 15; RGSF 2

Kinsey, Alfred C(harles) 1894-1956 .... **TCLC 91**
See also CA 115; 170; MTCW 2

Kipling, (Joseph) Rudyard 1865-1936 . **PC 3; SSC 5, 54; TCLC 8, 17; WLC**
See also AAYA 32; BRW 6; BRWC 1, 2; BYA 4; CA 105; 120; CANR 33; CDBLB 1890-1914; CLR 39, 65; CWRI 5; DA; DA3; DAB; DAC; DAM MST, POET; DLB 19, 34, 141, 156; EWL 3; EXPS; FANT; LAIT 3; LMFS 1; MAICYA 1, 2; MTCW 1, 2; RGEL 2; RGSF 2; SATA 100; SFW 4; SSFS 8; SUFW 1; TEA; WCH; WLIT 4; YABC 2

Kirk, Russell (Amos) 1918-1994 .. **TCLC 119**
See also AITN 1; CA 1-4R; 145; CAAS 9; CANR 1, 20, 60; HGG; INT CANR-20; MTCW 1, 2

Kirkland, Caroline M. 1801-1864 . **NCLC 85**
See also DLB 3, 73, 74, 250, 254; DLBD 13

Kirkup, James 1918- .... **CLC 1**
See also CA 1-4R; CAAS 4; CANR 2; CP 7; DLB 27; SATA 12

Kirkwood, James 1930(?)-1989 .... **CLC 9**
See also AITN 2; CA 1-4R; 128; CANR 6, 40; GLL 2

Kirsch, Sarah 1935- .... **CLC 176**
See also CA 178; CWW 2; DLB 75; EWL 3

Kirshner, Sidney
See Kingsley, Sidney

Kis, Danilo 1935-1989 .... **CLC 57**
See also CA 109; 118; 129; CANR 61; CDWLB 4; DLB 181; EWL 3; MTCW 1; RGSF 2; RGWL 2, 3

Kissinger, Henry A(lfred) 1923- ...... **CLC 137**
See also CA 1-4R; CANR 2, 33, 66, 109; MTCW 1

Kivi, Aleksis 1834-1872 .... **NCLC 30**

Kizer, Carolyn (Ashley) 1925- ... **CLC 15, 39, 80**
See also CA 65-68; CAAS 5; CANR 24, 70; CP 7; CWP; DAM POET; DLB 5, 169; EWL 3; MTCW 2; PFS 18

Klabund 1890-1928 .... **TCLC 44**
See also CA 162; DLB 66

Klappert, Peter 1942- .... **CLC 57**
See also CA 33-36R; CSW; DLB 5

Klein, A(braham) M(oses) 1909-1972 .... **CLC 19**
See also CA 101; 37-40R; DAB; DAC; DAM MST; DLB 68; EWL 3; RGEL 2

Klein, Joe
See Klein, Joseph

Klein, Joseph 1946- .... **CLC 154**
See also CA 85-88; CANR 55

Klein, Norma 1938-1989 .... **CLC 30**
See also AAYA 2, 35; BPFB 2; BYA 6, 7, 8; CA 41-44R; 128; CANR 15, 37; CLR 2, 19; INT CANR-15; JRDA; MAICYA 1, 2; SAAS 1; SATA 7, 57; WYA; YAW

Klein, T(heodore) E(ibon) D(onald) 1947- .... **CLC 34**
See also CA 119; CANR 44, 75; HGG

Kleist, Heinrich von 1777-1811 .... **NCLC 2, 37; SSC 22**
See also CDWLB 2; DAM DRAM; DLB 90; EW 5; RGSF 2; RGWL 2, 3

Klima, Ivan 1931- .... **CLC 56, 172**
See also CA 25-28R; CANR 17, 50, 91; CDWLB 4; CWW 2; DAM NOV; DLB 232; EWL 3; RGWL 3

Klimentev, Andrei Platonovich
See Klimentov, Andrei Platonovich

Klimentov, Andrei Platonovich 1899-1951 .... **SSC 42; TCLC 14**
See Platonov, Andrei Platonovich; Platonov, Andrey Platonovich
See also CA 108

Klinger, Friedrich Maximilian von 1752-1831 .... **NCLC 1**
See also DLB 94

Klingsor the Magician
See Hartmann, Sadakichi

Klopstock, Friedrich Gottlieb 1724-1803 .... **NCLC 11**
See also DLB 97; EW 4; RGWL 2, 3

Kluge, Alexander 1932- .... **SSC 61**
See also CA 81-84; DLB 75

Knapp, Caroline 1959-2002 .... **CLC 99**
See also CA 154; 207

Knebel, Fletcher 1911-1993 .... **CLC 14**
See also AITN 1; CA 1-4R; 140; CAAS 3; CANR 1, 36; SATA 36; SATA-Obit 75

Knickerbocker, Diedrich
See Irving, Washington

Knight, Etheridge 1931-1991 ... **BLC 2; CLC 40; PC 14**
See also BW 1, 3; CA 21-24R; 133; CANR 23, 82; DAM POET; DLB 41; MTCW 2; RGAL 4

Knight, Sarah Kemble 1666-1727 .... **LC 7**
See also DLB 24, 200

Knister, Raymond 1899-1932 .... **TCLC 56**
See also CA 186; DLB 68; RGEL 2

Knowles, John 1926-2001 ... **CLC 1, 4, 10, 26**
See also AAYA 10; AMWS 12; BPFB 2; BYA 3; CA 17-20R; 203; CANR 40, 74, 76; CDALB 1968-1988; CN 7; DA; DAC; DAM MST, NOV; DLB 6; EXPN; MTCW 1, 2; NFS 2; RGAL 4; SATA 8, 89; SATA-Obit 134; YAW

Knox, Calvin M.
See Silverberg, Robert

Knox, John c. 1505-1572 .... **LC 37**
See also DLB 132

Knye, Cassandra
See Disch, Thomas M(ichael)

Koch, C(hristopher) J(ohn) 1932- .... **CLC 42**
See also CA 127; CANR 84; CN 7; DLB 289

Koch, Christopher
See Koch, C(hristopher) J(ohn)

Koch, Kenneth (Jay) 1925-2002 .... **CLC 5, 8, 44**
See also CA 1-4R; 207; CAD; CANR 6, 36, 57, 97; CD 5; CP 7; DAM POET; DLB 5; INT CANR-36; MTCW 2; SATA 65; WP

Kochanowski, Jan 1530-1584 .... **LC 10**
See also RGWL 2, 3

Kock, Charles Paul de 1794-1871 . **NCLC 16**

Koda Rohan
See Koda Shigeyuki

Koda Rohan
See Koda Shigeyuki
See also DLB 180

Koda Shigeyuki 1867-1947 .... **TCLC 22**
See Koda Rohan
See also CA 121; 183

Koestler, Arthur 1905-1983 ... **CLC 1, 3, 6, 8, 15, 33**
See also BRWS 1; CA 1-4R; 109; CANR 1, 33; CDBLB 1945-1960; DLBY 1983; EWL 3; MTCW 1, 2; RGEL 2

Kogawa, Joy Nozomi 1935- ...... **CLC 78, 129**
See also AAYA 47; CA 101; CANR 19, 62; CN 7; CWP; DAC; DAM MST, MULT; FW; MTCW 2; NFS 3; SATA 99

Kohout, Pavel 1928- .... **CLC 13**
See also CA 45-48; CANR 3

Koizumi, Yakumo
See Hearn, (Patricio) Lafcadio (Tessima Carlos)

Kolmar, Gertrud 1894-1943 .... **TCLC 40**
See also CA 167; EWL 3

Komunyakaa, Yusef 1947- .. **BLCS; CLC 86, 94; PC 51**
See also AFAW 2; AMWS 13; CA 147; CANR 83; CP 7; CSW; DLB 120; EWL 3; PFS 5; RGAL 4

Konrad, George
See Konrad, Gyorgy
See also CWW 2

Konrad, Gyorgy 1933- .... **CLC 4, 10, 73**
See Konrad, George
See also CA 85-88; CANR 97; CDWLB 4; CWW 2; DLB 232; EWL 3

Konwicki, Tadeusz 1926- .... **CLC 8, 28, 54, 117**
See also CA 101; CAAS 9; CANR 39, 59; CWW 2; DLB 232; EWL 3; IDFW 3; MTCW 1

Koontz, Dean R(ay) 1945- .... **CLC 78**
See also AAYA 9, 31; BEST 89:3, 90:2; CA 108; CANR 19, 36, 52, 95; CMW 4; CPW; DA3; DAM NOV, POP; HGG; MTCW 1; SATA 92; SFW 4; SUFW 2; YAW

Kopernik, Mikolaj
See Copernicus, Nicolaus

Kopit, Arthur (Lee) 1937- ...... **CLC 1, 18, 33**
See also AITN 1; CA 81-84; CABS 3; CD 5; DAM DRAM; DFS 7, 14; DLB 7; MTCW 1; RGAL 4

Kopitar, Jernej (Bartholomaus) 1780-1844 .... **NCLC 117**

Kops, Bernard 1926- .... **CLC 4**
See also CA 5-8R; CANR 84; CBD; CN 7; CP 7; DLB 13

Kornbluth, C(yril) M. 1923-1958 .... **TCLC 8**
See also CA 105; 160; DLB 8; SFW 4

Korolenko, V. G.
See Korolenko, Vladimir Galaktionovich

Korolenko, Vladimir
See Korolenko, Vladimir Galaktionovich

Korolenko, Vladimir G.
See Korolenko, Vladimir Galaktionovich

Korolenko, Vladimir Galaktionovich 1853-1921 .... **TCLC 22**
See also CA 121; DLB 277

Korzybski, Alfred (Habdank Skarbek) 1879-1950 .... **TCLC 61**
See also CA 123; 160

Kosinski, Jerzy (Nikodem) 1933-1991 .... **CLC 1, 2, 3, 6, 10, 15, 53, 70**
See also AMWS 7; BPFB 2; CA 17-20R; 134; CANR 9, 46; DA3; DAM NOV; DLB 2; DLBY 1982; EWL 3; HGG; MTCW 1, 2; NFS 12; RGAL 4; TUS

Kostelanetz, Richard (Cory) 1940- .. **CLC 28**
See also CA 13-16R; CAAS 8; CANR 38, 77; CN 7; CP 7

Kostrowitzki, Wilhelm Apollinaris de 1880-1918
See Apollinaire, Guillaume
See also CA 104

Kotlowitz, Robert 1924- .... **CLC 4**
See also CA 33-36R; CANR 36

Kotzebue, August (Friedrich Ferdinand) von 1761-1819 .... **NCLC 25**
See also DLB 94

Kotzwinkle, William 1938- ..... **CLC 5, 14, 35**
See also BPFB 2; CA 45-48; CANR 3, 44, 84; CLR 6; DLB 173; FANT; MAICYA 1, 2; SATA 24, 70; SFW 4; SUFW 2; YAW

Kowna, Stancy
See Szymborska, Wislawa

Kozol, Jonathan 1936- .... **CLC 17**
See also AAYA 46; CA 61-64; CANR 16, 45, 96

Kozoll, Michael 1940(?)- .... **CLC 35**

Kramer, Kathryn 19(?)- .... **CLC 34**

Kramer, Larry 1935- .... **CLC 42; DC 8**
See also CA 124; 126; CANR 60; DAM POP; DLB 249; GLL 1

Krasicki, Ignacy 1735-1801 .... **NCLC 8**

Krasinski, Zygmunt 1812-1859 .... **NCLC 4**
See also RGWL 2, 3

Kraus, Karl 1874-1936 .... **TCLC 5**
See also CA 104; 216; DLB 118; EWL 3

Kreve (Mickevicius), Vincas 1882-1954 .... **TCLC 27**
See also CA 170; DLB 220; EWL 3

Kristeva, Julia 1941- .... **CLC 77, 140**
See also CA 154; CANR 99; DLB 242; EWL 3; FW; LMFS 2

Kristofferson, Kris 1936- .... **CLC 26**
See also CA 104

Krizanc, John 1956- .... **CLC 57**
See also CA 187

Krleza, Miroslav 1893-1981 .... **CLC 8, 114**
See also CA 97-100; 105; CANR 50; CDWLB 4; DLB 147; EW 11; RGWL 2, 3

Kroetsch, Robert 1927- .. **CLC 5, 23, 57, 132**
See also CA 17-20R; CANR 8, 38; CCA 1; CN 7; CP 7; DAC; DAM POET; DLB 53; MTCW 1

Kroetz, Franz
See Kroetz, Franz Xaver

Kroetz, Franz Xaver 1946- .... **CLC 41**
See also CA 130; EWL 3

Kroker, Arthur (W.) 1945- .... **CLC 77**
See also CA 161

Kropotkin, Peter (Alekseevich) 1842-1921 .... **TCLC 36**
See Kropotkin, Petr Alekseevich
See also CA 119

Kropotkin, Petr Alekseevich
See Kropotkin, Peter (Alekseevich)
See also DLB 277

Krotkov, Yuri 1917-1981 .... **CLC 19**
See also CA 102

Krumb
See Crumb, R(obert)

Krumgold, Joseph (Quincy) 1908-1980 .... **CLC 12**
See also BYA 1, 2; CA 9-12R; 101; CANR 7; MAICYA 1, 2; SATA 1, 48; SATA-Obit 23; YAW

Krumwitz
See Crumb, R(obert)

Krutch, Joseph Wood 1893-1970 ..... **CLC 24**
See also ANW; CA 1-4R; 25-28R; CANR 4; DLB 63, 206, 275

Krutzch, Gus
See Eliot, T(homas) S(tearns)

Krylov, Ivan Andreevich 1768(?)-1844 .... **NCLC 1**
See also DLB 150

Kubin, Alfred (Leopold Isidor) 1877-1959 .... **TCLC 23**
See also CA 112; 149; CANR 104; DLB 81

Kubrick, Stanley 1928-1999 .... **CLC 16; TCLC 112**
See also AAYA 30; CA 81-84; 177; CANR 33; DLB 26

Kueng, Hans 1928-
See Kung, Hans
See also CA 53-56; CANR 66; MTCW 1, 2

Kumin, Maxine (Winokur) 1925- ..... **CLC 5, 13, 28, 164; PC 15**
See also AITN 2; AMWS 4; ANW; CA 1-4R; CAAS 8; CANR 1, 21, 69, 115; CP 7; CWP; DA3; DAM POET; DLB 5; EWL 3; EXPP; MTCW 1, 2; PAB; PFS 18; SATA 12

Kundera, Milan 1929- . **CLC 4, 9, 19, 32, 68, 115, 135; SSC 24**
See also AAYA 2; BPFB 2; CA 85-88; CANR 19, 52, 74; CDWLB 4; CWW 2; DA3; DAM NOV; DLB 232; EW 13; EWL 3; MTCW 1, 2; NFS 18; RGSF 2; RGWL 3; SSFS 10

Kunene, Mazisi (Raymond) 1930- ... **CLC 85**
See also BW 1, 3; CA 125; CANR 81; CP 7; DLB 117

Kung, Hans .... **CLC 130**
See Kueng, Hans

Kunikida Doppo 1869(?)-1908
See Doppo, Kunikida
See also DLB 180; EWL 3

Kunitz, Stanley (Jasspon) 1905- .. **CLC 6, 11, 14, 148; PC 19**
See also AMWS 3; CA 41-44R; CANR 26, 57, 98; CP 7; DA3; DLB 48; INT CANR-26; MTCW 1, 2; PFS 11; RGAL 4

Kunze, Reiner 1933- .... **CLC 10**
See also CA 93-96; CWW 2; DLB 75; EWL 3

Kuprin, Aleksander Ivanovich 1870-1938 .... **TCLC 5**
See Kuprin, Alexandr Ivanovich
See also CA 104; 182

Kuprin, Alexandr Ivanovich
See Kuprin, Aleksander Ivanovich
See also EWL 3

Kureishi, Hanif 1954(?)- .... **CLC 64, 135**
See also CA 139; CANR 113; CBD; CD 5; CN 7; DLB 194, 245; GLL 2; IDFW 4; WLIT 4

Kurosawa, Akira 1910-1998 ..... **CLC 16, 119**
See also AAYA 11; CA 101; 170; CANR 46; DAM MULT

Kushner, Tony 1957(?)- .... **CLC 81; DC 10**
See also AMWS 9; CA 144; CAD; CANR 74; CD 5; DA3; DAM DRAM; DFS 5; DLB 228; EWL 3; GLL 1; LAIT 5; MTCW 2; RGAL 4

Kuttner, Henry 1915-1958 .... **TCLC 10**
See also CA 107; 157; DLB 8; FANT; SCFW 2; SFW 4

Kutty, Madhavi
See Das, Kamala

Kuzma, Greg 1944- .... **CLC 7**
See also CA 33-36R; CANR 70

Kuzmin, Mikhail 1872(?)-1936 ...... **TCLC 40**
See also CA 170; EWL 3

Kyd, Thomas 1558-1594 .... **DC 3; LC 22**
See also BRW 1; DAM DRAM; DLB 62; IDTP; LMFS 1; RGEL 2; TEA; WLIT 3

Kyprianos, Iossif
See Samarakis, Antonis

L. S.
See Stephen, Sir Leslie

Labrunie, Gerard
See Nerval, Gerard de

La Bruyere, Jean de 1645-1696 .... **LC 17**
See also DLB 268; EW 3; GFL Beginnings to 1789

Lacan, Jacques (Marie Emile) 1901-1981 .... **CLC 75**
See also CA 121; 104; EWL 3; TWA

Laclos, Pierre Ambroise Francois 1741-1803 .... **NCLC 4, 87**
See also EW 4; GFL Beginnings to 1789; RGWL 2, 3

Lacolere, Francois
See Aragon, Louis

La Colere, Francois
See Aragon, Louis

La Deshabilleuse
See Simenon, Georges (Jacques Christian)

Lady Gregory
See Gregory, Lady Isabella Augusta (Persse)

Lady of Quality, A
See Bagnold, Enid

La Fayette, Marie-(Madelaine Pioche de la Vergne) 1634-1693 .... **LC 2**
See Lafayette, Marie-Madeleine
See also GFL Beginnings to 1789; RGWL 2, 3

Lafayette, Marie-Madeleine
See La Fayette, Marie-(Madelaine Pioche de la Vergne)
See also DLB 268

Lafayette, Rene
See Hubbard, L(afayette) Ron(ald)

La Flesche, Francis 1857(?)-1932 ...... **NNAL**
See also CA 144; CANR 83; DLB 175

La Fontaine, Jean de 1621-1695 .... **LC 50**
See also DLB 268; EW 3; GFL Beginnings to 1789; MAICYA 1, 2; RGWL 2, 3; SATA 18

Laforgue, Jules 1860-1887 . **NCLC 5, 53; PC 14; SSC 20**
See also DLB 217; EW 7; GFL 1789 to the Present; RGWL 2, 3

Layamon
See Layamon
See also DLB 146

Lagerkvist, Paer (Fabian)
1891-1974 .... **CLC 7, 10, 13, 54**
See Lagerkvist, Par
See also CA 85-88; 49-52; DA3; DAM DRAM, NOV; MTCW 1, 2; TWA

Lagerkvist, Par .... **SSC 12**
See Lagerkvist, Paer (Fabian)
See also DLB 259; EW 10; EWL 3; MTCW 2; RGSF 2; RGWL 2, 3

Lagerloef, Selma (Ottiliana Lovisa)
1858-1940 .... **TCLC 4, 36**
See Lagerlof, Selma (Ottiliana Lovisa)
See also CA 108; MTCW 2; SATA 15

Lagerlof, Selma (Ottiliana Lovisa)
See Lagerloef, Selma (Ottiliana Lovisa)
See also CLR 7; SATA 15

La Guma, (Justin) Alex(ander)
1925-1985 . **BLCS; CLC 19; TCLC 140**
See also AFW; BW 1, 3; CA 49-52; 118; CANR 25, 81; CDWLB 3; DAM NOV; DLB 117, 225; EWL 3; MTCW 1, 2; WLIT 2

Laidlaw, A. K.
See Grieve, C(hristopher) M(urray)

Lainez, Manuel Mujica
See Mujica Lainez, Manuel
See also HW 1

Laing, R(onald) D(avid) 1927-1989 . **CLC 95**
See also CA 107; 129; CANR 34; MTCW 1

Lamartine, Alphonse (Marie Louis Prat) de
1790-1869 .... **NCLC 11; PC 16**
See also DAM POET; DLB 217; GFL 1789 to the Present; RGWL 2, 3

Lamb, Charles 1775-1834 ..... **NCLC 10, 113; WLC**
See also BRW 4; CDBLB 1789-1832; DA; DAB; DAC; DAM MST; DLB 93, 107, 163; RGEL 2; SATA 17; TEA

Lamb, Lady Caroline 1785-1828 ... **NCLC 38**
See also DLB 116

Lamb, Mary Ann 1764-1847 .... **NCLC 125**
See also DLB 163; SATA 17

Lame Deer 1903(?)-1976 .... **NNAL**
See also CA 69-72

Lamming, George (William) 1927- ... **BLC 2; CLC 2, 4, 66, 144**
See also BW 2, 3; CA 85-88; CANR 26, 76; CDWLB 3; CN 7; DAM MULT; DLB 125; EWL 3; MTCW 1, 2; NFS 15; RGEL 2

L'Amour, Louis (Dearborn)
1908-1988 .... **CLC 25, 55**
See Burns, Tex; Mayo, Jim
See also AAYA 16; AITN 2; BEST 89:2; BPFB 2; CA 1-4R; 125; CANR 3, 25, 40; CPW; DA3; DAM NOV, POP; DLB 206; DLBY 1980; MTCW 1, 2; RGAL 4

Lampedusa, Giuseppe (Tomasi) di
.... **TCLC 13**
See Tomasi di Lampedusa, Giuseppe
See also CA 164; EW 11; MTCW 2; RGWL 2, 3

Lampman, Archibald 1861-1899 ... **NCLC 25**
See also DLB 92; RGEL 2; TWA

Lancaster, Bruce 1896-1963 .... **CLC 36**
See also CA 9-10; CANR 70; CAP 1; SATA 9

Lanchester, John 1962- .... **CLC 99**
See also CA 194; DLB 267

Landau, Mark Alexandrovich
See Aldanov, Mark (Alexandrovich)

Landau-Aldanov, Mark Alexandrovich
See Aldanov, Mark (Alexandrovich)

Landis, Jerry
See Simon, Paul (Frederick)

Landis, John 1950- .... **CLC 26**
See also CA 112; 122

Landolfi, Tommaso 1908-1979 .... **CLC 11, 49**
See also CA 127; 117; DLB 177; EWL 3

Landon, Letitia Elizabeth
1802-1838 .... **NCLC 15**
See also DLB 96

Landor, Walter Savage
1775-1864 .... **NCLC 14**
See also BRW 4; DLB 93, 107; RGEL 2

Landwirth, Heinz 1927-
See Lind, Jakov
See also CA 9-12R; CANR 7

Lane, Patrick 1939- .... **CLC 25**
See also CA 97-100; CANR 54; CP 7; DAM POET; DLB 53; INT 97-100

Lang, Andrew 1844-1912 .... **TCLC 16**
See also CA 114; 137; CANR 85; DLB 98, 141, 184; FANT; MAICYA 1, 2; RGEL 2; SATA 16; WCH

Lang, Fritz 1890-1976 .... **CLC 20, 103**
See also CA 77-80; 69-72; CANR 30

Lange, John
See Crichton, (John) Michael

Langer, Elinor 1939- .... **CLC 34**
See also CA 121

Langland, William 1332(?)-1400(?) ..... **LC 19**
See also BRW 1; DA; DAB; DAC; DAM MST, POET; DLB 146; RGEL 2; TEA; WLIT 3

Langstaff, Launcelot
See Irving, Washington

Lanier, Sidney 1842-1881 . **NCLC 6, 118; PC 50**
See also AMWS 1; DAM POET; DLB 64; DLBD 13; EXPP; MAICYA 1; PFS 14; RGAL 4; SATA 18

Lanyer, Aemilia 1569-1645 ...... **LC 10, 30, 83**
See also DLB 121

Lao-Tzu
See Lao Tzu

Lao Tzu c. 6th cent. B.C.-3rd cent. B.C. .... **CMLC 7**

Lapine, James (Elliot) 1949- .... **CLC 39**
See also CA 123; 130; CANR 54; INT 130

Larbaud, Valery (Nicolas)
1881-1957 .... **TCLC 9**
See also CA 106; 152; EWL 3; GFL 1789 to the Present

Lardner, Ring
See Lardner, Ring(gold) W(ilmer)
See also BPFB 2; CDALB 1917-1929; DLB 11, 25, 86, 171; DLBD 16; RGAL 4; RGSF 2

Lardner, Ring W., Jr.
See Lardner, Ring(gold) W(ilmer)

Lardner, Ring(gold) W(ilmer)
1885-1933 .... **SSC 32; TCLC 2, 14**
See Lardner, Ring
See also AMW; CA 104; 131; MTCW 1, 2; TUS

Laredo, Betty
See Codrescu, Andrei

Larkin, Maia
See Wojciechowska, Maia (Teresa)

Larkin, Philip (Arthur) 1922-1985 ... **CLC 3, 5, 8, 9, 13, 18, 33, 39, 64; PC 21**
See also BRWS 1; CA 5-8R; 117; CANR 24, 62; CDBLB 1960 to Present; DA3; DAB; DAM MST, POET; DLB 27; EWL 3; MTCW 1, 2; PFS 3, 4, 12; RGEL 2

La Roche, Sophie von
1730-1807 .... **NCLC 121**
See also DLB 94

Larra (y Sanchez de Castro), Mariano Jose de 1809-1837 .... **NCLC 17, 130**

Larsen, Eric 1941- .... **CLC 55**
See also CA 132

Larsen, Nella 1893(?)-1963 .... **BLC 2; CLC 37; HR 3**
See also AFAW 1, 2; BW 1; CA 125; CANR 83; DAM MULT; DLB 51; FW; LATS 1; LMFS 2

Larson, Charles R(aymond) 1938- ... **CLC 31**
See also CA 53-56; CANR 4, 121

Larson, Jonathan 1961-1996 .... **CLC 99**
See also AAYA 28; CA 156

Las Casas, Bartolome de
1474-1566 .... **HLCS; LC 31**
See Casas, Bartolome de las
See also LAW

Lasch, Christopher 1932-1994 .... **CLC 102**
See also CA 73-76; 144; CANR 25, 118; DLB 246; MTCW 1, 2

Lasker-Schueler, Else 1869-1945 ... **TCLC 57**
See Lasker-Schuler, Else
See also CA 183; DLB 66, 124

Lasker-Schuler, Else
See Lasker-Schueler, Else
See also EWL 3

Laski, Harold J(oseph) 1893-1950 . **TCLC 79**
See also CA 188

Latham, Jean Lee 1902-1995 .... **CLC 12**
See also AITN 1; BYA 1; CA 5-8R; CANR 7, 84; CLR 50; MAICYA 1, 2; SATA 2, 68; YAW

Latham, Mavis
See Clark, Mavis Thorpe

Lathen, Emma .... **CLC 2**
See Hennissart, Martha; Latsis, Mary J(ane)
See also BPFB 2; CMW 4

Lathrop, Francis
See Leiber, Fritz (Reuter, Jr.)

Latsis, Mary J(ane) 1927(?)-1997
See Lathen, Emma
See also CA 85-88; 162; CMW 4

Lattany, Kristin
See Lattany, Kristin (Elaine Eggleston) Hunter

Lattany, Kristin (Elaine Eggleston) Hunter
1931- .... **CLC 35**
See also AITN 1; BW 1; BYA 3; CA 13-16R; CANR 13, 108; CLR 3; CN 7; DLB 33; INT CANR-13; MAICYA 1, 2; SAAS 10; SATA 12, 132; YAW

Lattimore, Richmond (Alexander)
1906-1984 .... **CLC 3**
See also CA 1-4R; 112; CANR 1

Laughlin, James 1914-1997 .... **CLC 49**
See also CA 21-24R; 162; CAAS 22; CANR 9, 47; CP 7; DLB 48; DLBY 1996, 1997

Laurence, (Jean) Margaret (Wemyss)
1926-1987 . **CLC 3, 6, 13, 50, 62; SSC 7**
See also BYA 13; CA 5-8R; 121; CANR 33; DAC; DAM MST; DLB 53; EWL 3; FW; MTCW 1, 2; NFS 11; RGEL 2; RGSF 2; SATA-Obit 50; TCWW 2

Laurent, Antoine 1952- .... **CLC 50**

Lauscher, Hermann
See Hesse, Hermann

Lautreamont 1846-1870 .. **NCLC 12; SSC 14**
See Lautreamont, Isidore Lucien Ducasse
See also GFL 1789 to the Present; RGWL 2, 3

Lautreamont, Isidore Lucien Ducasse
See Lautreamont
See also DLB 217

Laverty, Donald
See Blish, James (Benjamin)

Lavin, Mary 1912-1996 . **CLC 4, 18, 99; SSC 4**
See also CA 9-12R; 151; CANR 33; CN 7; DLB 15; FW; MTCW 1; RGEL 2; RGSF 2

Lavond, Paul Dennis
See Kornbluth, C(yril) M.; Pohl, Frederik

Lawler, Ray
See Lawler, Raymond Evenor
See also DLB 289

Lawler, Raymond Evenor 1922- .... **CLC 58**
See Lawler, Ray
See also CA 103; CD 5; RGEL 2

Lawrence, D(avid) H(erbert Richards)
1885-1930 ... **SSC 4, 19; TCLC 2, 9, 16, 33, 48, 61, 93; WLC**
See Chambers, Jessie
See also BPFB 2; BRW 7; BRWR 2; CA 104; 121; CDBLB 1914-1945; DA; DA3; DAB; DAC; DAM MST, NOV, POET; DLB 10, 19, 36, 98, 162, 195; EWL 3; EXPP; EXPS; LAIT 2, 3; MTCW 1, 2; NFS 18; PFS 6; RGEL 2; RGSF 2; SSFS 2, 6; TEA; WLIT 4; WP

Lawrence, T(homas) E(dward)
1888-1935 .... **TCLC 18**
See Dale, Colin
See also BRWS 2; CA 115; 167; DLB 195

Lawrence of Arabia
See Lawrence, T(homas) E(dward)

Lawson, Henry (Archibald Hertzberg)
1867-1922 .... **SSC 18; TCLC 27**
See also CA 120; 181; DLB 230; RGEL 2; RGSF 2

Lawton, Dennis
See Faust, Frederick (Schiller)

Laxness, Halldor .... **CLC 25**
See Gudjonsson, Halldor Kiljan
See also EW 12; EWL 3; RGWL 2, 3

Layamon fl. c. 1200- .... **CMLC 10**
See Layamon
See also RGEL 2

Laye, Camara 1928-1980 ..... **BLC 2; CLC 4, 38**
See Camara Laye
See also AFW; BW 1; CA 85-88; 97-100; CANR 25; DAM MULT; MTCW 1, 2; WLIT 2

Layton, Irving (Peter) 1912- .... **CLC 2, 15, 164**
See also CA 1-4R; CANR 2, 33, 43, 66; CP 7; DAC; DAM MST, POET; DLB 88; EWL 3; MTCW 1, 2; PFS 12; RGEL 2

Lazarus, Emma 1849-1887 .... **NCLC 8, 109**

Lazarus, Felix
See Cable, George Washington

Lazarus, Henry
See Slavitt, David R(ytman)

Lea, Joan
See Neufeld, John (Arthur)

Leacock, Stephen (Butler)
1869-1944 .... **SSC 39; TCLC 2**
See also CA 104; 141; CANR 80; DAC; DAM MST; DLB 92; EWL 3; MTCW 2; RGEL 2; RGSF 2

Lead, Jane Ward 1623-1704 .... **LC 72**
See also DLB 131

Leapor, Mary 1722-1746 .... **LC 80**
See also DLB 109

Lear, Edward 1812-1888 .... **NCLC 3**
See also AAYA 48; BRW 5; CLR 1, 75; DLB 32, 163, 166; MAICYA 1, 2; RGEL 2; SATA 18, 100; WCH; WP

Lear, Norman (Milton) 1922- .... **CLC 12**
See also CA 73-76

Leautaud, Paul 1872-1956 .... **TCLC 83**
See also CA 203; DLB 65; GFL 1789 to the Present

Leavis, F(rank) R(aymond)
1895-1978 .... **CLC 24**
See also BRW 7; CA 21-24R; 77-80; CANR 44; DLB 242; EWL 3; MTCW 1, 2; RGEL 2

Leavitt, David 1961- .... **CLC 34**
See also CA 116; 122; CANR 50, 62, 101; CPW; DA3; DAM POP; DLB 130; GLL 1; INT 122; MTCW 2

Leblanc, Maurice (Marie Emile)
1864-1941 .... **TCLC 49**
See also CA 110; CMW 4

Lebowitz, Fran(ces Ann) 1951(?)- ... **CLC 11, 36**
See also CA 81-84; CANR 14, 60, 70; INT CANR-14; MTCW 1

Lebrecht, Peter
See Tieck, (Johann) Ludwig

le Carre, John .... **CLC 3, 5, 9, 15, 28**
See Cornwell, David (John Moore)
See also AAYA 42; BEST 89:4; BPFB 2; BRWS 2; CDBLB 1960 to Present; CMW 4; CN 7; CPW; DLB 87; EWL 3; MSW; MTCW 2; RGEL 2; TEA

Le Clezio, J(ean) M(arie) G(ustave)
1940- .... **CLC 31, 155**
See also CA 116; 128; DLB 83; EWL 3; GFL 1789 to the Present; RGSF 2

Leconte de Lisle, Charles-Marie-Rene
1818-1894 .... **NCLC 29**
See also DLB 217; EW 6; GFL 1789 to the Present

Le Coq, Monsieur
See Simenon, Georges (Jacques Christian)

Leduc, Violette 1907-1972 .... **CLC 22**
See also CA 13-14; 33-36R; CANR 69; CAP 1; EWL 3; GFL 1789 to the Present; GLL 1

Ledwidge, Francis 1887(?)-1917 .... **TCLC 23**
See also CA 123; 203; DLB 20

Lee, Andrea 1953- .... **BLC 2; CLC 36**
See also BW 1, 3; CA 125; CANR 82; DAM MULT

Lee, Andrew
See Auchincloss, Louis (Stanton)

Lee, Chang-rae 1965- .... **CLC 91**
See also CA 148; CANR 89; LATS 1

Lee, Don L. .... **CLC 2**
See Madhubuti, Haki R.

Lee, George W(ashington)
1894-1976 .... **BLC 2; CLC 52**
See also BW 1; CA 125; CANR 83; DAM MULT; DLB 51

Lee, (Nelle) Harper 1926- .... **CLC 12, 60; WLC**
See also AAYA 13; AMWS 8; BPFB 2; BYA 3; CA 13-16R; CANR 51; CDALB 1941-1968; CSW; DA; DA3; DAB; DAC; DAM MST, NOV; DLB 6; EXPN; LAIT 3; MTCW 1, 2; NFS 2; SATA 11; WYA; YAW

Lee, Helen Elaine 1959(?)- .... **CLC 86**
See also CA 148

Lee, John .... **CLC 70**

Lee, Julian
See Latham, Jean Lee

Lee, Larry
See Lee, Lawrence

Lee, Laurie 1914-1997 .... **CLC 90**
See also CA 77-80; 158; CANR 33, 73; CP 7; CPW; DAB; DAM POP; DLB 27; MTCW 1; RGEL 2

Lee, Lawrence 1941-1990 .... **CLC 34**
See also CA 131; CANR 43

Lee, Li-Young 1957- .... **CLC 164; PC 24**
See also CA 153; CANR 118; CP 7; DLB 165; LMFS 2; PFS 11, 15, 17

Lee, Manfred B(ennington)
1905-1971 .... **CLC 11**
See Queen, Ellery
See also CA 1-4R; 29-32R; CANR 2; CMW 4; DLB 137

Lee, Shelton Jackson 1957(?)- .. **BLCS; CLC 105**
See Lee, Spike
See also BW 2, 3; CA 125; CANR 42; DAM MULT

Lee, Spike
See Lee, Shelton Jackson
See also AAYA 4, 29

Lee, Stan 1922- .... **CLC 17**
See also AAYA 5, 49; CA 108; 111; INT 111

Lee, Tanith 1947- .... **CLC 46**
See also AAYA 15; CA 37-40R; CANR 53, 102; DLB 261; FANT; SATA 8, 88, 134; SFW 4; SUFW 1, 2; YAW

Lee, Vernon .... **SSC 33; TCLC 5**
See Paget, Violet
See also DLB 57, 153, 156, 174, 178; GLL 1; SUFW 1

Lee, William
See Burroughs, William S(eward)
See also GLL 1

Lee, Willy
See Burroughs, William S(eward)
See also GLL 1

Lee-Hamilton, Eugene (Jacob)
1845-1907 .... **TCLC 22**
See also CA 117

Leet, Judith 1935- .... **CLC 11**
See also CA 187

Le Fanu, Joseph Sheridan
1814-1873 .... **NCLC 9, 58; SSC 14**
See also CMW 4; DA3; DAM POP; DLB 21, 70, 159, 178; HGG; RGEL 2; RGSF 2; SUFW 1

Leffland, Ella 1931- .... **CLC 19**
See also CA 29-32R; CANR 35, 78, 82; DLBY 1984; INT CANR-35; SATA 65

Leger, Alexis
See Leger, (Marie-Rene Auguste) Alexis Saint-Leger

Leger, (Marie-Rene Auguste) Alexis Saint-Leger 1887-1975 .. **CLC 4, 11, 46; PC 23**
See Perse, Saint-John; Saint-John Perse
See also CA 13-16R; 61-64; CANR 43; DAM POET; MTCW 1

Leger, Saintleger
See Leger, (Marie-Rene Auguste) Alexis Saint-Leger

Le Guin, Ursula K(roeber) 1929- ..... **CLC 8, 13, 22, 45, 71, 136; SSC 12**
See also AAYA 9, 27; AITN 1; BPFB 2; BYA 5, 8, 11, 14; CA 21-24R; CANR 9, 32, 52, 74; CDALB 1968-1988; CLR 3, 28, 91; CN 7; CPW; DA3; DAB; DAC; DAM MST, POP; DLB 8, 52, 256, 275; EXPS; FANT; FW; INT CANR-32;

JRDA; LAIT 5; MAICYA 1, 2; MTCW 1, 2; NFS 6, 9; SATA 4, 52, 99; SCFW; SFW 4; SSFS 2; SUFW 1, 2; WYA; YAW

Lehmann, Rosamond (Nina)
1901-1990 .... **CLC 5**
See also CA 77-80; 131; CANR 8, 73; DLB 15; MTCW 2; RGEL 2; RHW

Leiber, Fritz (Reuter, Jr.)
1910-1992 .... **CLC 25**
See also BPFB 2; CA 45-48; 139; CANR 2, 40, 86; DLB 8; FANT; HGG; MTCW 1, 2; SATA 45; SATA-Obit 73; SCFW 2; SFW 4; SUFW 1, 2

Leibniz, Gottfried Wilhelm von
1646-1716 .... **LC 35**
See also DLB 168

Leimbach, Martha 1963-
See Leimbach, Marti
See also CA 130

Leimbach, Marti .... **CLC 65**
See Leimbach, Martha

Leino, Eino .... **TCLC 24**
See Lonnbohm, Armas Eino Leopold
See also EWL 3

Leiris, Michel (Julien) 1901-1990 ..... **CLC 61**
See also CA 119; 128; 132; EWL 3; GFL 1789 to the Present

Leithauser, Brad 1953- .... **CLC 27**
See also CA 107; CANR 27, 81; CP 7; DLB 120, 282

Lelchuk, Alan 1938- .... **CLC 5**
See also CA 45-48; CAAS 20; CANR 1, 70; CN 7

Lem, Stanislaw 1921- ...... **CLC 8, 15, 40, 149**
See also CA 105; CAAS 1; CANR 32; CWW 2; MTCW 1; SCFW 2; SFW 4

Lemann, Nancy (Elise) 1956- .... **CLC 39**
See also CA 118; 136; CANR 121

Lemonnier, (Antoine Louis) Camille
1844-1913 .... **TCLC 22**
See also CA 121

Lenau, Nikolaus 1802-1850 .... **NCLC 16**

L'Engle, Madeleine (Camp Franklin)
1918- .... **CLC 12**
See also AAYA 28; AITN 2; BPFB 2; BYA 2, 4, 5, 7; CA 1-4R; CANR 3, 21, 39, 66, 107; CLR 1, 14, 57; CPW; CWRI 5; DA3; DAM POP; DLB 52; JRDA; MAICYA 1, 2; MTCW 1, 2; SAAS 15; SATA 1, 27, 75, 128; SFW 4; WYA; YAW

Lengyel, Jozsef 1896-1975 .... **CLC 7**
See also CA 85-88; 57-60; CANR 71; RGSF 2

Lenin 1870-1924
See Lenin, V. I.
See also CA 121; 168

Lenin, V. I. .... **TCLC 67**
See Lenin

Lennon, John (Ono) 1940-1980 .. **CLC 12, 35**
See also CA 102; SATA 114

Lennox, Charlotte Ramsay
1729(?)-1804 .... **NCLC 23**
See also DLB 39; RGEL 2

Lentricchia, Frank, (Jr.) 1940- .... **CLC 34**
See also CA 25-28R; CANR 19, 106; DLB 246

Lenz, Gunter .... **CLC 65**

Lenz, Siegfried 1926- .... **CLC 27; SSC 33**
See also CA 89-92; CANR 80; CWW 2; DLB 75; EWL 3; RGSF 2; RGWL 2, 3

Leon, David
See Jacob, (Cyprien-)Max

Leonard, Elmore (John, Jr.) 1925- . **CLC 28, 34, 71, 120**
See also AAYA 22; AITN 1; BEST 89:1, 90:4; BPFB 2; CA 81-84; CANR 12, 28, 53, 76, 96; CMW 4; CN 7; CPW; DA3; DAM POP; DLB 173, 226; INT CANR-28; MSW; MTCW 1, 2; RGAL 4; TCWW 2

Leonard, Hugh .... **CLC 19**
See Byrne, John Keyes
See also CBD; CD 5; DFS 13; DLB 13

Leonov, Leonid (Maximovich)
1899-1994 .... **CLC 92**
See also CA 129; CANR 74, 76; DAM NOV; EWL 3; MTCW 1, 2

Leonov, Leonid Maksimovich
See Leonov, Leonid (Maximovich)
See also DLB 272

Leopardi, (Conte) Giacomo
1798-1837 .... **NCLC 22, 129; PC 37**
See also EW 5; RGWL 2, 3; WP

Le Reveler
See Artaud, Antonin (Marie Joseph)

Lerman, Eleanor 1952- .... **CLC 9**
See also CA 85-88; CANR 69

Lerman, Rhoda 1936- .... **CLC 56**
See also CA 49-52; CANR 70

Lermontov, Mikhail Iur'evich
See Lermontov, Mikhail Yuryevich
See also DLB 205

Lermontov, Mikhail Yuryevich
1814-1841 .... **NCLC 5, 47, 126; PC 18**
See Lermontov, Mikhail Iur'evich
See also EW 6; RGWL 2, 3; TWA

Leroux, Gaston 1868-1927 .... **TCLC 25**
See also CA 108; 136; CANR 69; CMW 4; SATA 65

Lesage, Alain-Rene 1668-1747 .... **LC 2, 28**
See also EW 3; GFL Beginnings to 1789; RGWL 2, 3

Leskov, N(ikolai) S(emenovich) 1831-1895
See Leskov, Nikolai (Semyonovich)

Leskov, Nikolai (Semyonovich)
1831-1895 .... **NCLC 25; SSC 34**
See Leskov, Nikolai Semenovich

Leskov, Nikolai Semenovich
See Leskov, Nikolai (Semyonovich)
See also DLB 238

Lesser, Milton
See Marlowe, Stephen

Lessing, Doris (May) 1919- ... **CLC 1, 2, 3, 6, 10, 15, 22, 40, 94, 170; SSC 6, 61; WLCS**
See also AFW; BRWS 1; CA 9-12R; CAAS 14; CANR 33, 54, 76, 122; CD 5; CDBLB 1960 to Present; CN 7; DA; DA3; DAB; DAC; DAM MST, NOV; DLB 15, 139; DLBY 1985; EWL 3; EXPS; FW; LAIT 4; MTCW 1, 2; NFS 12; RGEL 2; RGSF 2; SFW 4; SSFS 1, 12; TEA; WLIT 2, 4

Lessing, Gotthold Ephraim 1729-1781 . **LC 8**
See also CDWLB 2; DLB 97; EW 4; RGWL 2, 3

Lester, Richard 1932- .... **CLC 20**

Levenson, Jay .... **CLC 70**

Lever, Charles (James)
1806-1872 .... **NCLC 23**
See also DLB 21; RGEL 2

Leverson, Ada Esther
1862(?)-1933(?) .... **TCLC 18**
See Elaine
See also CA 117; 202; DLB 153; RGEL 2

Levertov, Denise 1923-1997 .. **CLC 1, 2, 3, 5, 8, 15, 28, 66; PC 11**
See also AMWS 3; CA 1-4R, 178; 163; CAAE 178; CAAS 19; CANR 3, 29, 50, 108; CDALBS; CP 7; CWP; DAM POET; DLB 5, 165; EWL 3; EXPP; FW; INT CANR-29; MTCW 1, 2; PAB; PFS 7, 17; RGAL 4; TUS; WP

Levi, Carlo 1902-1975 .... **TCLC 125**
See also CA 65-68; 53-56; CANR 10; EWL 3; RGWL 2, 3

Levi, Jonathan .... **CLC 76**
See also CA 197

Levi, Peter (Chad Tigar)
1931-2000 .... **CLC 41**
See also CA 5-8R; 187; CANR 34, 80; CP 7; DLB 40

Levi, Primo 1919-1987 .... **CLC 37, 50; SSC 12; TCLC 109**
See also CA 13-16R; 122; CANR 12, 33, 61, 70; DLB 177; EWL 3; MTCW 1, 2; RGWL 2, 3

Levin, Ira 1929- .... **CLC 3, 6**
See also CA 21-24R; CANR 17, 44, 74; CMW 4; CN 7; CPW; DA3; DAM POP; HGG; MTCW 1, 2; SATA 66; SFW 4

Levin, Meyer 1905-1981 .... **CLC 7**
See also AITN 1; CA 9-12R; 104; CANR 15; DAM POP; DLB 9, 28; DLBY 1981; SATA 21; SATA-Obit 27

Levine, Norman 1924- .... **CLC 54**
See also CA 73-76; CAAS 23; CANR 14, 70; DLB 88

Levine, Philip 1928- .. **CLC 2, 4, 5, 9, 14, 33, 118; PC 22**
See also AMWS 5; CA 9-12R; CANR 9, 37, 52, 116; CP 7; DAM POET; DLB 5; EWL 3; PFS 8

Levinson, Deirdre 1931- .... **CLC 49**
See also CA 73-76; CANR 70

Levi-Strauss, Claude 1908- .... **CLC 38**
See also CA 1-4R; CANR 6, 32, 57; DLB 242; EWL 3; GFL 1789 to the Present; MTCW 1, 2; TWA

Levitin, Sonia (Wolff) 1934- .... **CLC 17**
See also AAYA 13, 48; CA 29-32R; CANR 14, 32, 79; CLR 53; JRDA; MAICYA 1, 2; SAAS 1; SATA 4, 68, 119; SATA-Essay 131; YAW

Levon, O. U.
See Kesey, Ken (Elton)

Levy, Amy 1861-1889 .... **NCLC 59**
See also DLB 156, 240

Lewes, George Henry 1817-1878 ... **NCLC 25**
See also DLB 55, 144

Lewis, Alun 1915-1944 .... **SSC 40; TCLC 3**
See also BRW 7; CA 104; 188; DLB 20, 162; PAB; RGEL 2

Lewis, C. Day
See Day Lewis, C(ecil)

Lewis, C(live) S(taples) 1898-1963 .... **CLC 1, 3, 6, 14, 27, 124; WLC**
See also AAYA 3, 39; BPFB 2; BRWS 3; BYA 15, 16; CA 81-84; CANR 33, 71; CDBLB 1945-1960; CLR 3, 27; CWRI 5; DA; DA3; DAB; DAC; DAM MST, NOV, POP; DLB 15, 100, 160, 255; EWL 3; FANT; JRDA; LMFS 2; MAICYA 1, 2; MTCW 1, 2; RGEL 2; SATA 13, 100; SCFW; SFW 4; SUFW 1; TEA; WCH; WYA; YAW

Lewis, Cecil Day
See Day Lewis, C(ecil)

Lewis, Janet 1899-1998 .... **CLC 41**
See Winters, Janet Lewis
See also CA 9-12R; 172; CANR 29, 63; CAP 1; CN 7; DLBY 1987; RHW; TCWW 2

Lewis, Matthew Gregory
1775-1818 .... **NCLC 11, 62**
See also DLB 39, 158, 178; HGG; LMFS 1; RGEL 2; SUFW

Lewis, (Harry) Sinclair 1885-1951 . **TCLC 4, 13, 23, 39; WLC**
See also AMW; AMWC 1; BPFB 2; CA 104; 133; CDALB 1917-1929; DA; DA3; DAB; DAC; DAM MST, NOV; DLB 9, 102, 284; DLBD 1; EWL 3; LAIT 3; MTCW 1, 2; NFS 15; RGAL 4; TUS

Lewis, (Percy) Wyndham
1884(?)-1957 .. **SSC 34; TCLC 2, 9, 104**
See also BRW 7; CA 104; 157; DLB 15; EWL 3; FANT; MTCW 2; RGEL 2

Lewisohn, Ludwig 1883-1955 .... **TCLC 19**
See also CA 107; 203; DLB 4, 9, 28, 102

Lewton, Val 1904-1951 .... **TCLC 76**
See also CA 199; IDFW 3, 4

Leyner, Mark 1956- .... **CLC 92**
See also CA 110; CANR 28, 53; DA3; MTCW 2

Lezama Lima, Jose 1910-1976 .... **CLC 4, 10, 101; HLCS 2**
See also CA 77-80; CANR 71; DAM MULT; DLB 113, 283; EWL 3; HW 1, 2; LAW; RGWL 2, 3

L'Heureux, John (Clarke) 1934- ...... **CLC 52**
See also CA 13-16R; CANR 23, 45, 88; DLB 244

Liddell, C. H.
See Kuttner, Henry

Lie, Jonas (Lauritz Idemil) 1833-1908(?) .... **TCLC 5**
See also CA 115

Lieber, Joel 1937-1971 .... **CLC 6**
See also CA 73-76; 29-32R

Lieber, Stanley Martin
See Lee, Stan

Lieberman, Laurence (James) 1935- .... **CLC 4, 36**
See also CA 17-20R; CANR 8, 36, 89; CP 7

Lieh Tzu fl. 7th cent. B.C.-5th cent. B.C. .... **CMLC 27**

Lieksman, Anders
See Haavikko, Paavo Juhani

Li Fei-kan 1904-
See Pa Chin
See also CA 105; TWA

Lifton, Robert Jay 1926- .... **CLC 67**
See also CA 17-20R; CANR 27, 78; INT CANR-27; SATA 66

Lightfoot, Gordon 1938- .... **CLC 26**
See also CA 109

Lightman, Alan P(aige) 1948- .... **CLC 81**
See also CA 141; CANR 63, 105

Ligotti, Thomas (Robert) 1953- ...... **CLC 44; SSC 16**
See also CA 123; CANR 49; HGG; SUFW 2

Li Ho 791-817 .... **PC 13**

Liliencron, (Friedrich Adolf Axel) Detlev von 1844-1909 .... **TCLC 18**
See also CA 117

Lille, Alain de
See Alain de Lille

Lilly, William 1602-1681 .... **LC 27**

Lima, Jose Lezama
See Lezama Lima, Jose

Lima Barreto, Afonso Henrique de 1881-1922 .... **TCLC 23**
See also CA 117; 181; LAW

Lima Barreto, Afonso Henriques de
See Lima Barreto, Afonso Henrique de

Limonov, Edward 1944- .... **CLC 67**
See also CA 137

Lin, Frank
See Atherton, Gertrude (Franklin Horn)

Lincoln, Abraham 1809-1865 .... **NCLC 18**
See also LAIT 2

Lind, Jakov .... **CLC 1, 2, 4, 27, 82**
See Landwirth, Heinz
See also CAAS 4; EWL 3

Lindbergh, Anne (Spencer) Morrow 1906-2001 .... **CLC 82**
See also BPFB 2; CA 17-20R; 193; CANR 16, 73; DAM NOV; MTCW 1, 2; SATA 33; SATA-Obit 125; TUS

Lindsay, David 1878(?)-1945 .... **TCLC 15**
See also CA 113; 187; DLB 255; FANT; SFW 4; SUFW 1

Lindsay, (Nicholas) Vachel 1879-1931 .... **PC 23; TCLC 17; WLC**
See also AMWS 1; CA 114; 135; CANR 79; CDALB 1865-1917; DA; DA3; DAC; DAM MST, POET; DLB 54; EWL 3; EXPP; RGAL 4; SATA 40; WP

Linke-Poot
See Doeblin, Alfred

Linney, Romulus 1930- .... **CLC 51**
See also CA 1-4R; CAD; CANR 40, 44, 79; CD 5; CSW; RGAL 4

Linton, Eliza Lynn 1822-1898 .... **NCLC 41**
See also DLB 18

Li Po 701-763 .... **CMLC 2; PC 29**
See also WP

Lipsius, Justus 1547-1606 .... **LC 16**

Lipsyte, Robert (Michael) 1938- ...... **CLC 21**
See also AAYA 7, 45; CA 17-20R; CANR 8, 57; CLR 23, 76; DA; DAC; DAM MST, NOV; JRDA; LAIT 5; MAICYA 1, 2; SATA 5, 68, 113; WYA; YAW

Lish, Gordon (Jay) 1934- ... **CLC 45; SSC 18**
See also CA 113; 117; CANR 79; DLB 130; INT 117

Lispector, Clarice 1925(?)-1977 .... **CLC 43; HLCS 2; SSC 34**
See also CA 139; 116; CANR 71; CDWLB 3; DLB 113; DNFS 1; EWL 3; FW; HW 2; LAW; RGSF 2; RGWL 2, 3; WLIT 1

Littell, Robert 1935(?)- .... **CLC 42**
See also CA 109; 112; CANR 64, 115; CMW 4

Little, Malcolm 1925-1965
See Malcolm X
See also BW 1, 3; CA 125; 111; CANR 82; DA; DA3; DAB; DAC; DAM MST, MULT; MTCW 1, 2; NCFS 3

Littlewit, Humphrey Gent.
See Lovecraft, H(oward) P(hillips)

Litwos
See Sienkiewicz, Henryk (Adam Alexander Pius)

Liu, E. 1857-1909 .... **TCLC 15**
See also CA 115; 190

Lively, Penelope (Margaret) 1933- .. **CLC 32, 50**
See also BPFB 2; CA 41-44R; CANR 29, 67, 79; CLR 7; CN 7; CWRI 5; DAM NOV; DLB 14, 161, 207; FANT; JRDA; MAICYA 1, 2; MTCW 1, 2; SATA 7, 60, 101; TEA

Livesay, Dorothy (Kathleen) 1909-1996 .... **CLC 4, 15, 79**
See also AITN 2; CA 25-28R; CAAS 8; CANR 36, 67; DAC; DAM MST, POET; DLB 68; FW; MTCW 1; RGEL 2; TWA

Livy c. 59B.C.-c. 12 .... **CMLC 11**
See also AW 2; CDWLB 1; DLB 211; RGWL 2, 3

Lizardi, Jose Joaquin Fernandez de 1776-1827 .... **NCLC 30**
See also LAW

Llewellyn, Richard
See Llewellyn Lloyd, Richard Dafydd Vivian
See also DLB 15

Llewellyn Lloyd, Richard Dafydd Vivian 1906-1983 .... **CLC 7, 80**
See Llewellyn, Richard
See also CA 53-56; 111; CANR 7, 71; SATA 11; SATA-Obit 37

Llosa, (Jorge) Mario (Pedro) Vargas
See Vargas Llosa, (Jorge) Mario (Pedro)
See also RGWL 3

Llosa, Mario Vargas
See Vargas Llosa, (Jorge) Mario (Pedro)

Lloyd, Manda
See Mander, (Mary) Jane

Lloyd Webber, Andrew 1948-
See Webber, Andrew Lloyd
See also AAYA 1, 38; CA 116; 149; DAM DRAM; SATA 56

Llull, Ramon c. 1235-c. 1316 .... **CMLC 12**

Lobb, Ebenezer
See Upward, Allen

Locke, Alain (Le Roy) 1886-1954 .... **BLCS; HR 3; TCLC 43**
See also BW 1, 3; CA 106; 124; CANR 79; DLB 51; LMFS 2; RGAL 4

Locke, John 1632-1704 .... **LC 7, 35**
See also DLB 31, 101, 213, 252; RGEL 2; WLIT 3

Locke-Elliott, Sumner
See Elliott, Sumner Locke

Lockhart, John Gibson 1794-1854 .. **NCLC 6**
See also DLB 110, 116, 144

Lockridge, Ross (Franklin), Jr. 1914-1948 .... **TCLC 111**
See also CA 108; 145; CANR 79; DLB 143; DLBY 1980; RGAL 4; RHW

Lockwood, Robert
See Johnson, Robert

Lodge, David (John) 1935- .... **CLC 36, 141**
See also BEST 90:1; BRWS 4; CA 17-20R; CANR 19, 53, 92; CN 7; CPW; DAM POP; DLB 14, 194; EWL 3; INT CANR-19; MTCW 1, 2

Lodge, Thomas 1558-1625 .... **LC 41**
See also DLB 172; RGEL 2

Loewinsohn, Ron(ald William) 1937- .... **CLC 52**
See also CA 25-28R; CANR 71

Logan, Jake
See Smith, Martin Cruz

Logan, John (Burton) 1923-1987 .... **CLC 5**
See also CA 77-80; 124; CANR 45; DLB 5

Lo Kuan-chung 1330(?)-1400(?) .... **LC 12**

Lombard, Nap
See Johnson, Pamela Hansford

London, Jack 1876-1916 .. **SSC 4, 49; TCLC 9, 15, 39; WLC**
See London, John Griffith
See also AAYA 13; AITN 2; AMW; BPFB 2; BYA 4, 13; CDALB 1865-1917; DLB 8, 12, 78, 212; EWL 3; EXPS; LAIT 3; NFS 8; RGAL 4; RGSF 2; SATA 18; SFW 4; SSFS 7; TCWW 2; TUS; WYA; YAW

London, John Griffith 1876-1916
See London, Jack
See also CA 110; 119; CANR 73; DA; DA3; DAB; DAC; DAM MST, NOV; JRDA; MAICYA 1, 2; MTCW 1, 2

Long, Emmett
See Leonard, Elmore (John, Jr.)

Longbaugh, Harry
See Goldman, William (W.)

Longfellow, Henry Wadsworth 1807-1882 .... **NCLC 2, 45, 101, 103; PC 30; WLCS**
See also AMW; AMWR 2; CDALB 1640-1865; DA; DA3; DAB; DAC; DAM MST, POET; DLB 1, 59, 235; EXPP; PAB; PFS 2, 7, 17; RGAL 4; SATA 19; TUS; WP

Longinus c. 1st cent. - .... **CMLC 27**
See also AW 2; DLB 176

Longley, Michael 1939- .... **CLC 29**
See also BRWS 8; CA 102; CP 7; DLB 40

Longus fl. c. 2nd cent. - .... **CMLC 7**

Longway, A. Hugh
See Lang, Andrew

Lonnbohm, Armas Eino Leopold 1878-1926
See Leino, Eino
See also CA 123

Lonnrot, Elias 1802-1884 .... **NCLC 53**
See also EFS 1

Lonsdale, Roger ed. .... **CLC 65**
Lopate, Phillip 1943- .... **CLC 29**
    See also CA 97-100; CANR 88; DLBY 1980; INT 97-100
Lopez, Barry (Holstun) 1945- .... **CLC 70**
    See also AAYA 9; ANW; CA 65-68; CANR 7, 23, 47, 68, 92; DLB 256, 275; INT CANR-7, -23; MTCW 1; RGAL 4; SATA 67
Lopez Portillo (y Pacheco), Jose
    1920- .... **CLC 46**
    See also CA 129; HW 1
Lopez y Fuentes, Gregorio
    1897(?)-1966 .... **CLC 32**
    See also CA 131; EWL 3; HW 1
Lorca, Federico Garcia
    See Garcia Lorca, Federico
    See also DFS 4; EW 11; RGWL 2, 3; WP
Lord, Audre
    See Lorde, Audre (Geraldine)
    See also EWL 3
Lord, Bette Bao 1938- .... **AAL; CLC 23**
    See also BEST 90:3; BPFB 2; CA 107; CANR 41, 79; INT CA-107; SATA 58
Lord Auch
    See Bataille, Georges
Lord Brooke
    See Greville, Fulke
Lord Byron
    See Byron, George Gordon (Noel)
Lorde, Audre (Geraldine)
    1934-1992 .. **BLC 2; CLC 18, 71; PC 12**
    See Domini, Rey; Lord, Audre
    See also AFAW 1, 2; BW 1, 3; CA 25-28R; 142; CANR 16, 26, 46, 82; DA3; DAM MULT, POET; DLB 41; FW; MTCW 1, 2; PFS 16; RGAL 4
Lord Houghton
    See Milnes, Richard Monckton
Lord Jeffrey
    See Jeffrey, Francis
Loreaux, Nichol .... **CLC 65**
Lorenzini, Carlo 1826-1890
    See Collodi, Carlo
    See also MAICYA 1, 2; SATA 29, 100
Lorenzo, Heberto Padilla
    See Padilla (Lorenzo), Heberto
Loris
    See Hofmannsthal, Hugo von
Loti, Pierre .... **TCLC 11**
    See Viaud, (Louis Marie) Julien
    See also DLB 123; GFL 1789 to the Present
Lou, Henri
    See Andreas-Salome, Lou
Louie, David Wong 1954- .... **CLC 70**
    See also CA 139; CANR 120
Louis, Adrian C. .... **NNAL**
Louis, Father M.
    See Merton, Thomas (James)
Louise, Heidi
    See Erdrich, Louise
Lovecraft, H(oward) P(hillips)
    1890-1937 .... **SSC 3, 52; TCLC 4, 22**
    See also AAYA 14; BPFB 2; CA 104; 133; CANR 106; DA3; DAM POP; HGG; MTCW 1, 2; RGAL 4; SCFW; SFW 4; SUFW
Lovelace, Earl 1935- .... **CLC 51**
    See also BW 2; CA 77-80; CANR 41, 72, 114; CD 5; CDWLB 3; CN 7; DLB 125; EWL 3; MTCW 1
Lovelace, Richard 1618-1657 .... **LC 24**
    See also BRW 2; DLB 131; EXPP; PAB; RGEL 2
Lowe, Pardee 1904- .... **AAL**
Lowell, Amy 1874-1925 ... **PC 13; TCLC 1, 8**
    See also AMW; CA 104; 151; DAM POET; DLB 54, 140; EWL 3; EXPP; LMFS 2; MAWW; MTCW 2; RGAL 4; TUS

Lowell, James Russell 1819-1891 ... **NCLC 2, 90**
    See also AMWS 1; CDALB 1640-1865; DLB 1, 11, 64, 79, 189, 235; RGAL 4
Lowell, Robert (Traill Spence, Jr.)
    1917-1977 .... **CLC 1, 2, 3, 4, 5, 8, 9, 11, 15, 37, 124; PC 3; WLC**
    See also AMW; AMWC 2; AMWR 2; CA 9-12R; 73-76; CABS 2; CANR 26, 60; CDALBS; DA; DA3; DAB; DAC; DAM MST, NOV; DLB 5, 169; EWL 3; MTCW 1, 2; PAB; PFS 6, 7; RGAL 4; WP
Lowenthal, Michael (Francis)
    1969- .... **CLC 119**
    See also CA 150; CANR 115
Lowndes, Marie Adelaide (Belloc)
    1868-1947 .... **TCLC 12**
    See also CA 107; CMW 4; DLB 70; RHW
Lowry, (Clarence) Malcolm
    1909-1957 .... **SSC 31; TCLC 6, 40**
    See also BPFB 2; BRWS 3; CA 105; 131; CANR 62, 105; CDBLB 1945-1960; DLB 15; EWL 3; MTCW 1, 2; RGEL 2
Lowry, Mina Gertrude 1882-1966
    See Loy, Mina
    See also CA 113
Loxsmith, John
    See Brunner, John (Kilian Houston)
Loy, Mina .... **CLC 28; PC 16**
    See Lowry, Mina Gertrude
    See also DAM POET; DLB 4, 54
Loyson-Bridet
    See Schwob, Marcel (Mayer Andre)
Lucan 39-65 .... **CMLC 33**
    See also AW 2; DLB 211; EFS 2; RGWL 2, 3
Lucas, Craig 1951- .... **CLC 64**
    See also CA 137; CAD; CANR 71, 109; CD 5; GLL 2
Lucas, E(dward) V(errall)
    1868-1938 .... **TCLC 73**
    See also CA 176; DLB 98, 149, 153; SATA 20
Lucas, George 1944- .... **CLC 16**
    See also AAYA 1, 23; CA 77-80; CANR 30; SATA 56
Lucas, Hans
    See Godard, Jean-Luc
Lucas, Victoria
    See Plath, Sylvia
Lucian c. 125-c. 180 .... **CMLC 32**
    See also AW 2; DLB 176; RGWL 2, 3
Lucretius c. 94B.C.-c. 49B.C. .... **CMLC 48**
    See also AW 2; CDWLB 1; DLB 211; EFS 2; RGWL 2, 3
Ludlam, Charles 1943-1987 .... **CLC 46, 50**
    See also CA 85-88; 122; CAD; CANR 72, 86; DLB 266
Ludlum, Robert 1927-2001 .... **CLC 22, 43**
    See also AAYA 10; BEST 89:1, 90:3; BPFB 2; CA 33-36R; 195; CANR 25, 41, 68, 105; CMW 4; CPW; DA3; DAM NOV, POP; DLBY 1982; MSW; MTCW 1, 2
Ludwig, Ken .... **CLC 60**
    See also CA 195; CAD
Ludwig, Otto 1813-1865 .... **NCLC 4**
    See also DLB 129
Lugones, Leopoldo 1874-1938 .... **HLCS 2; TCLC 15**
    See also CA 116; 131; CANR 104; DLB 283; EWL 3; HW 1; LAW
Lu Hsun .... **SSC 20; TCLC 3**
    See Shu-Jen, Chou
    See also EWL 3
Lukacs, George .... **CLC 24**
    See Lukacs, Gyorgy (Szegeny von)

Lukacs, Gyorgy (Szegeny von) 1885-1971
    See Lukacs, George
    See also CA 101; 29-32R; CANR 62; CDWLB 4; DLB 215, 242; EW 10; EWL 3; MTCW 2
Luke, Peter (Ambrose Cyprian)
    1919-1995 .... **CLC 38**
    See also CA 81-84; 147; CANR 72; CBD; CD 5; DLB 13
Lunar, Dennis
    See Mungo, Raymond
Lurie, Alison 1926- ..... **CLC 4, 5, 18, 39, 175**
    See also BPFB 2; CA 1-4R; CANR 2, 17, 50, 88; CN 7; DLB 2; MTCW 1; SATA 46, 112
Lustig, Arnost 1926- .... **CLC 56**
    See also AAYA 3; CA 69-72; CANR 47, 102; CWW 2; DLB 232; EWL 3; SATA 56
Luther, Martin 1483-1546 .... **LC 9, 37**
    See also CDWLB 2; DLB 179; EW 2; RGWL 2, 3
Luxemburg, Rosa 1870(?)-1919 ..... **TCLC 63**
    See also CA 118
Luzi, Mario 1914- .... **CLC 13**
    See also CA 61-64; CANR 9, 70; CWW 2; DLB 128; EWL 3
L'vov, Arkady .... **CLC 59**
Lydgate, John c. 1370-1450(?) .... **LC 81**
    See also BRW 1; DLB 146; RGEL 2
Lyly, John 1554(?)-1606 .... **DC 7; LC 41**
    See also BRW 1; DAM DRAM; DLB 62, 167; RGEL 2
L'Ymagier
    See Gourmont, Remy(-Marie-Charles) de
Lynch, B. Suarez
    See Borges, Jorge Luis
Lynch, David (Keith) 1946- ...... **CLC 66, 162**
    See also CA 124; 129; CANR 111
Lynch, James
    See Andreyev, Leonid (Nikolaevich)
Lyndsay, Sir David 1485-1555 .... **LC 20**
    See also RGEL 2
Lynn, Kenneth S(chuyler)
    1923-2001 .... **CLC 50**
    See also CA 1-4R; 196; CANR 3, 27, 65
Lynx
    See West, Rebecca
Lyons, Marcus
    See Blish, James (Benjamin)
Lyotard, Jean-Francois
    1924-1998 .... **TCLC 103**
    See also DLB 242; EWL 3
Lyre, Pinchbeck
    See Sassoon, Siegfried (Lorraine)
Lytle, Andrew (Nelson) 1902-1995 ... **CLC 22**
    See also CA 9-12R; 150; CANR 70; CN 7; CSW; DLB 6; DLBY 1995; RGAL 4; RHW
Lyttelton, George 1709-1773 .... **LC 10**
    See also RGEL 2
Lytton of Knebworth, Baron
    See Bulwer-Lytton, Edward (George Earle Lytton)
Maas, Peter 1929-2001 .... **CLC 29**
    See also CA 93-96; 201; INT CA-93-96; MTCW 2
Macaulay, Catherine 1731-1791 .... **LC 64**
    See also DLB 104
Macaulay, (Emilie) Rose
    1881(?)-1958 .... **TCLC 7, 44**
    See also CA 104; DLB 36; EWL 3; RGEL 2; RHW
Macaulay, Thomas Babington
    1800-1859 .... **NCLC 42**
    See also BRW 4; CDBLB 1832-1890; DLB 32, 55; RGEL 2

MacBeth, George (Mann)
1932-1992 .... **CLC 2, 5, 9**
See also CA 25-28R; 136; CANR 61, 66; DLB 40; MTCW 1; PFS 8; SATA 4; SATA-Obit 70

MacCaig, Norman (Alexander)
1910-1996 .... **CLC 36**
See also BRWS 6; CA 9-12R; CANR 3, 34; CP 7; DAB; DAM POET; DLB 27; EWL 3; RGEL 2

MacCarthy, Sir (Charles Otto) Desmond
1877-1952 .... **TCLC 36**
See also CA 167

MacDiarmid, Hugh .... **CLC 2, 4, 11, 19, 63; PC 9**
See Grieve, C(hristopher) M(urray)
See also CDBLB 1945-1960; DLB 20; EWL 3; RGEL 2

MacDonald, Anson
See Heinlein, Robert A(nson)

Macdonald, Cynthia 1928- .... **CLC 13, 19**
See also CA 49-52; CANR 4, 44; DLB 105

MacDonald, George 1824-1905 .... **TCLC 9, 113**
See also BYA 5; CA 106; 137; CANR 80; CLR 67; DLB 18, 163, 178; FANT; MAICYA 1, 2; RGEL 2; SATA 33, 100; SFW 4; SUFW; WCH

Macdonald, John
See Millar, Kenneth

MacDonald, John D(ann)
1916-1986 .... **CLC 3, 27, 44**
See also BPFB 2; CA 1-4R; 121; CANR 1, 19, 60; CMW 4; CPW; DAM NOV, POP; DLB 8; DLBY 1986; MSW; MTCW 1, 2; SFW 4

Macdonald, John Ross
See Millar, Kenneth

Macdonald, Ross ...... **CLC 1, 2, 3, 14, 34, 41**
See Millar, Kenneth
See also AMWS 4; BPFB 2; DLBD 6; MSW; RGAL 4

MacDougal, John
See Blish, James (Benjamin)

MacDougal, John
See Blish, James (Benjamin)

MacDowell, John
See Parks, Tim(othy Harold)

MacEwen, Gwendolyn (Margaret)
1941-1987 .... **CLC 13, 55**
See also CA 9-12R; 124; CANR 7, 22; DLB 53, 251; SATA 50; SATA-Obit 55

Macha, Karel Hynek 1810-1846 .... **NCLC 46**

Machado (y Ruiz), Antonio
1875-1939 .... **TCLC 3**
See also CA 104; 174; DLB 108; EW 9; EWL 3; HW 2; RGWL 2, 3

Machado de Assis, Joaquim Maria
1839-1908 .... **BLC 2; HLCS 2; SSC 24; TCLC 10**
See also CA 107; 153; CANR 91; LAW; RGSF 2; RGWL 2, 3; TWA; WLIT 1

Machen, Arthur .... **SSC 20; TCLC 4**
See Jones, Arthur Llewellyn
See also CA 179; DLB 156, 178; RGEL 2; SUFW 1

Machiavelli, Niccolo 1469-1527 ... **DC 16; LC 8, 36; WLCS**
See also DA; DAB; DAC; DAM MST; EW 2; LAIT 1; LMFS 1; NFS 9; RGWL 2, 3; TWA

MacInnes, Colin 1914-1976 .... **CLC 4, 23**
See also CA 69-72; 65-68; CANR 21; DLB 14; MTCW 1, 2; RGEL 2; RHW

MacInnes, Helen (Clark)
1907-1985 .... **CLC 27, 39**
See also BPFB 2; CA 1-4R; 117; CANR 1, 28, 58; CMW 4; CPW; DAM POP; DLB 87; MSW; MTCW 1, 2; SATA 22; SATA-Obit 44

Mackay, Mary 1855-1924
See Corelli, Marie
See also CA 118; 177; FANT; RHW

Mackenzie, Compton (Edward Montague)
1883-1972 .... **CLC 18; TCLC 116**
See also CA 21-22; 37-40R; CAP 2; DLB 34, 100; RGEL 2

Mackenzie, Henry 1745-1831 .... **NCLC 41**
See also DLB 39; RGEL 2

Mackey, Nathaniel (Ernest) 1947- .... **PC 49**
See also CA 153; CANR 114; CP 7; DLB 169

Mackintosh, Elizabeth 1896(?)-1952
See Tey, Josephine
See also CA 110; CMW 4

MacLaren, James
See Grieve, C(hristopher) M(urray)

Mac Laverty, Bernard 1942- .... **CLC 31**
See also CA 116; 118; CANR 43, 88; CN 7; DLB 267; INT CA-118; RGSF 2

MacLean, Alistair (Stuart)
1922(?)-1987 .... **CLC 3, 13, 50, 63**
See also CA 57-60; 121; CANR 28, 61; CMW 4; CPW; DAM POP; DLB 276; MTCW 1; SATA 23; SATA-Obit 50; TCWW 2

Maclean, Norman (Fitzroy)
1902-1990 .... **CLC 78; SSC 13**
See also CA 102; 132; CANR 49; CPW; DAM POP; DLB 206; TCWW 2

MacLeish, Archibald 1892-1982 ... **CLC 3, 8, 14, 68; PC 47**
See also AMW; CA 9-12R; 106; CAD; CANR 33, 63; CDALBS; DAM POET; DFS 15; DLB 4, 7, 45; DLBY 1982; EWL 3; EXPP; MTCW 1, 2; PAB; PFS 5; RGAL 4; TUS

MacLennan, (John) Hugh
1907-1990 .... **CLC 2, 14, 92**
See also CA 5-8R; 142; CANR 33; DAC; DAM MST; DLB 68; EWL 3; MTCW 1, 2; RGEL 2; TWA

MacLeod, Alistair 1936- .... **CLC 56, 165**
See also CA 123; CCA 1; DAC; DAM MST; DLB 60; MTCW 2; RGSF 2

Macleod, Fiona
See Sharp, William
See also RGEL 2; SUFW

MacNeice, (Frederick) Louis
1907-1963 .... **CLC 1, 4, 10, 53**
See also BRW 7; CA 85-88; CANR 61; DAB; DAM POET; DLB 10, 20; EWL 3; MTCW 1, 2; RGEL 2

MacNeill, Dand
See Fraser, George MacDonald

Macpherson, James 1736-1796 .... **LC 29**
See Ossian
See also BRWS 8; DLB 109; RGEL 2

Macpherson, (Jean) Jay 1931- .... **CLC 14**
See also CA 5-8R; CANR 90; CP 7; CWP; DLB 53

Macrobius fl. 430- .... **CMLC 48**

MacShane, Frank 1927-1999 .... **CLC 39**
See also CA 9-12R; 186; CANR 3, 33; DLB 111

Macumber, Mari
See Sandoz, Mari(e Susette)

Madach, Imre 1823-1864 .... **NCLC 19**

Madden, (Jerry) David 1933- .... **CLC 5, 15**
See also CA 1-4R; CAAS 3; CANR 4, 45; CN 7; CSW; DLB 6; MTCW 1

Maddern, Al(an)
See Ellison, Harlan (Jay)

Madhubuti, Haki R. 1942- ... **BLC 2; CLC 6, 73; PC 5**
See Lee, Don L.
See also BW 2, 3; CA 73-76; CANR 24, 51, 73; CP 7; CSW; DAM MULT, POET; DLB 5, 41; DLBD 8; EWL 3; MTCW 2; RGAL 4

Madison, James 1751-1836 .... **NCLC 126**
See also DLB 37

Maepenn, Hugh
See Kuttner, Henry

Maepenn, K. H.
See Kuttner, Henry

Maeterlinck, Maurice 1862-1949 ..... **TCLC 3**
See also CA 104; 136; CANR 80; DAM DRAM; DLB 192; EW 8; EWL 3; GFL 1789 to the Present; LMFS 2; RGWL 2, 3; SATA 66; TWA

Maginn, William 1794-1842 .... **NCLC 8**
See also DLB 110, 159

Mahapatra, Jayanta 1928- .... **CLC 33**
See also CA 73-76; CAAS 9; CANR 15, 33, 66, 87; CP 7; DAM MULT

Mahfouz, Naguib (Abdel Aziz Al-Sabilgi)
1911(?)- .... **CLC 153**
See Mahfuz, Najib (Abdel Aziz al-Sabilgi)
See also AAYA 49; BEST 89:2; CA 128; CANR 55, 101; CWW 2; DA3; DAM NOV; MTCW 1, 2; RGWL 2, 3; SSFS 9

Mahfuz, Najib (Abdel Aziz al-Sabilgi)
.... **CLC 52, 55**
See Mahfouz, Naguib (Abdel Aziz Al-Sabilgi)
See also AFW; DLBY 1988; EWL 3; RGSF 2; WLIT 2

Mahon, Derek 1941- .... **CLC 27**
See also BRWS 6; CA 113; 128; CANR 88; CP 7; DLB 40; EWL 3

Maiakovskii, Vladimir
See Mayakovski, Vladimir (Vladimirovich)
See also IDTP; RGWL 2, 3

Mailer, Norman 1923- ... **CLC 1, 2, 3, 4, 5, 8, 11, 14, 28, 39, 74, 111**
See also AAYA 31; AITN 2; AMW; AMWC 2; AMWR 2; BPFB 2; CA 9-12R; CABS 1; CANR 28, 74, 77; CDALB 1968-1988; CN 7; CPW; DA; DA3; DAB; DAC; DAM MST, NOV, POP; DLB 2, 16, 28, 185, 278; DLBD 3; DLBY 1980, 1983; EWL 3; MTCW 1, 2; NFS 10; RGAL 4; TUS

Maillet, Antonine 1929- .... **CLC 54, 118**
See also CA 115; 120; CANR 46, 74, 77; CCA 1; CWW 2; DAC; DLB 60; INT 120; MTCW 2

Mais, Roger 1905-1955 .... **TCLC 8**
See also BW 1, 3; CA 105; 124; CANR 82; CDWLB 3; DLB 125; EWL 3; MTCW 1; RGEL 2

Maistre, Joseph 1753-1821 .... **NCLC 37**
See also GFL 1789 to the Present

Maitland, Frederic William
1850-1906 .... **TCLC 65**

Maitland, Sara (Louise) 1950- .... **CLC 49**
See also CA 69-72; CANR 13, 59; DLB 271; FW

Major, Clarence 1936- ... **BLC 2; CLC 3, 19, 48**
See also AFAW 2; BW 2, 3; CA 21-24R; CAAS 6; CANR 13, 25, 53, 82; CN 7; CP 7; CSW; DAM MULT; DLB 33; EWL 3; MSW

Major, Kevin (Gerald) 1949- .... **CLC 26**
See also AAYA 16; CA 97-100; CANR 21, 38, 112; CLR 11; DAC; DLB 60; INT CANR-21; JRDA; MAICYA 1, 2; MAICYAS 1; SATA 32, 82, 134; WYA; YAW

Maki, James
See Ozu, Yasujiro

Malabaila, Damiano
See Levi, Primo

Malamud, Bernard 1914-1986 .. **CLC 1, 2, 3, 5, 8, 9, 11, 18, 27, 44, 78, 85; SSC 15; TCLC 129; WLC**
See also AAYA 16; AMWS 1; BPFB 2; BYA 15; CA 5-8R; 118; CABS 1; CANR 28, 62, 114; CDALB 1941-1968; CPW;

DA; DA3; DAB; DAC; DAM MST, NOV,
POP; DLB 2, 28, 152; DLBY 1980, 1986;
EWL 3; EXPS; LAIT 4; LATS 1; MTCW
1, 2; NFS 4, 9; RGAL 4; RGSF 2; SSFS
8, 13, 16; TUS
Malan, Herman
See Bosman, Herman Charles; Bosman,
Herman Charles
Malaparte, Curzio 1898-1957 .... **TCLC 52**
See also DLB 264
Malcolm, Dan
See Silverberg, Robert
Malcolm X .... **BLC 2; CLC 82, 117; WLCS**
See Little, Malcolm
See also LAIT 5
Malherbe, Francois de 1555-1628 .... **LC 5**
See also GFL Beginnings to 1789
Mallarme, Stephane 1842-1898 ...... **NCLC 4, 41; PC 4**
See also DAM POET; DLB 217; EW 7;
GFL 1789 to the Present; LMFS 2; RGWL
2, 3; TWA
Mallet-Joris, Francoise 1930- .... **CLC 11**
See also CA 65-68; CANR 17; DLB 83;
EWL 3; GFL 1789 to the Present
Malley, Ern
See McAuley, James Phillip
Mallon, Thomas 1951- .... **CLC 172**
See also CA 110; CANR 29, 57, 92
Mallowan, Agatha Christie
See Christie, Agatha (Mary Clarissa)
Maloff, Saul 1922- .... **CLC 5**
See also CA 33-36R
Malone, Louis
See MacNeice, (Frederick) Louis
Malone, Michael (Christopher)
1942- .... **CLC 43**
See also CA 77-80; CANR 14, 32, 57, 114
Malory, Sir Thomas 1410(?)-1471(?) . **LC 11, 88; WLCS**
See also BRW 1; BRWR 2; CDBLB Before
1660; DA; DAB; DAC; DAM MST; DLB
146; EFS 2; RGEL 2; SATA 59; SATA-
Brief 33; TEA; WLIT 3
Malouf, (George Joseph) David
1934- .... **CLC 28, 86**
See also CA 124; CANR 50, 76; CN 7; CP
7; DLB 289; EWL 3; MTCW 2
Malraux, (Georges-)Andre
1901-1976 .... **CLC 1, 4, 9, 13, 15, 57**
See also BPFB 2; CA 21-22; 69-72; CANR
34, 58; CAP 2; DA3; DAM NOV; DLB
72; EW 12; EWL 3; GFL 1789 to the
Present; MTCW 1, 2; RGWL 2, 3; TWA
Malzberg, Barry N(athaniel) 1939- ... **CLC 7**
See also CA 61-64; CAAS 4; CANR 16;
CMW 4; DLB 8; SFW 4
Mamet, David (Alan) 1947- .. **CLC 9, 15, 34, 46, 91, 166; DC 4**
See also AAYA 3; CA 81-84; CABS 3;
CANR 15, 41, 67, 72; CD 5; DA3; DAM
DRAM; DFS 2, 3, 6, 12, 15; DLB 7; EWL
3; IDFW 4; MTCW 1, 2; RGAL 4
Mamoulian, Rouben (Zachary)
1897-1987 .... **CLC 16**
See also CA 25-28R; 124; CANR 85
Mandelshtam, Osip
See Mandelstam, Osip (Emilievich)
See also EW 10; EWL 3; RGWL 2, 3
Mandelstam, Osip (Emilievich)
1891(?)-1943(?) .... **PC 14; TCLC 2, 6**
See Mandelshtam, Osip
See also CA 104; 150; MTCW 2; TWA
Mander, (Mary) Jane 1877-1949 ... **TCLC 31**
See also CA 162; RGEL 2
Mandeville, Bernard 1670-1733 .... **LC 82**
See also DLB 101
Mandeville, Sir John fl. 1350- ...... **CMLC 19**
See also DLB 146

Mandiargues, Andre Pieyre de .... **CLC 41**
See Pieyre de Mandiargues, Andre
See also DLB 83
Mandrake, Ethel Belle
See Thurman, Wallace (Henry)
Mangan, James Clarence
1803-1849 .... **NCLC 27**
See also RGEL 2
Maniere, J.-E.
See Giraudoux, Jean(-Hippolyte)
Mankiewicz, Herman (Jacob)
1897-1953 .... **TCLC 85**
See also CA 120; 169; DLB 26; IDFW 3, 4
Manley, (Mary) Delariviere
1672(?)-1724 .... **LC 1, 42**
See also DLB 39, 80; RGEL 2
Mann, Abel
See Creasey, John
Mann, Emily 1952- .... **DC 7**
See also CA 130; CAD; CANR 55; CD 5;
CWD; DLB 266
Mann, (Luiz) Heinrich 1871-1950 ... **TCLC 9**
See also CA 106; 164, 181; DLB 66, 118;
EW 8; EWL 3; RGWL 2, 3
Mann, (Paul) Thomas 1875-1955 .... **SSC 5; TCLC 2, 8, 14, 21, 35, 44, 60; WLC**
See also BPFB 2; CA 104; 128; CDWLB 2;
DA; DA3; DAB; DAC; DAM MST, NOV;
DLB 66; EW 9; EWL 3; GLL 1; LATS 1;
LMFS 1; MTCW 1, 2; NFS 17; RGSF 2;
RGWL 2, 3; SSFS 4, 9; TWA
Mannheim, Karl 1893-1947 .... **TCLC 65**
See also CA 204
Manning, David
See Faust, Frederick (Schiller)
See also TCWW 2
Manning, Frederic 1882-1935 .... **TCLC 25**
See also CA 124; 216; DLB 260
Manning, Olivia 1915-1980 .... **CLC 5, 19**
See also CA 5-8R; 101; CANR 29; EWL 3;
FW; MTCW 1; RGEL 2
Mano, D. Keith 1942- .... **CLC 2, 10**
See also CA 25-28R; CAAS 6; CANR 26,
57; DLB 6
Mansfield, Katherine . **SSC 9, 23, 38; TCLC 2, 8, 39; WLC**
See Beauchamp, Kathleen Mansfield
See also BPFB 2; BRW 7; DAB; DLB 162;
EWL 3; EXPS; FW; GLL 1; RGEL 2;
RGSF 2; SSFS 2, 8, 10, 11
Manso, Peter 1940- .... **CLC 39**
See also CA 29-32R; CANR 44
Mantecon, Juan Jimenez
See Jimenez (Mantecon), Juan Ramon
Mantel, Hilary (Mary) 1952- .... **CLC 144**
See also CA 125; CANR 54, 101; CN 7;
DLB 271; RHW
Manton, Peter
See Creasey, John
Man Without a Spleen, A
See Chekhov, Anton (Pavlovich)
Manzoni, Alessandro 1785-1873 ... **NCLC 29, 98**
See also EW 5; RGWL 2, 3; TWA
Map, Walter 1140-1209 .... **CMLC 32**
Mapu, Abraham (ben Jekutiel)
1808-1867 .... **NCLC 18**
Mara, Sally
See Queneau, Raymond
Maracle, Lee 1950- .... **NNAL**
See also CA 149
Marat, Jean Paul 1743-1793 .... **LC 10**
Marcel, Gabriel Honore 1889-1973 . **CLC 15**
See also CA 102; 45-48; EWL 3; MTCW 1, 2
March, William 1893-1954 .... **TCLC 96**
See also CA 216

Marchbanks, Samuel
See Davies, (William) Robertson
See also CCA 1
Marchi, Giacomo
See Bassani, Giorgio
Marcus Aurelius
See Aurelius, Marcus
See also AW 2
Marguerite
See de Navarre, Marguerite
Marguerite d'Angouleme
See de Navarre, Marguerite
See also GFL Beginnings to 1789
Marguerite de Navarre
See de Navarre, Marguerite
See also RGWL 2, 3
Margulies, Donald 1954- .... **CLC 76**
See also CA 200; DFS 13; DLB 228
Marie de France c. 12th cent. - ...... **CMLC 8; PC 22**
See also DLB 208; FW; RGWL 2, 3
Marie de l'Incarnation 1599-1672 ...... **LC 10**
Marier, Captain Victor
See Griffith, D(avid Lewelyn) W(ark)
Mariner, Scott
See Pohl, Frederik
Marinetti, Filippo Tommaso
1876-1944 .... **TCLC 10**
See also CA 107; DLB 114, 264; EW 9;
EWL 3
Marivaux, Pierre Carlet de Chamblain de
1688-1763 .... **DC 7; LC 4**
See also GFL Beginnings to 1789; RGWL
2, 3; TWA
Markandaya, Kamala .... **CLC 8, 38**
See Taylor, Kamala (Purnaiya)
See also BYA 13; CN 7; EWL 3
Markfield, Wallace 1926-2002 .... **CLC 8**
See also CA 69-72; 208; CAAS 3; CN 7;
DLB 2, 28; DLBY 2002
Markham, Edwin 1852-1940 .... **TCLC 47**
See also CA 160; DLB 54, 186; RGAL 4
Markham, Robert
See Amis, Kingsley (William)
Markoosie .... **NNAL**
See Markoosie, Patsauq
See also CLR 23; DAM MULT
Marks, J
See Highwater, Jamake (Mamake)
Marks, J.
See Highwater, Jamake (Mamake)
Marks-Highwater, J
See Highwater, Jamake (Mamake)
Marks-Highwater, J.
See Highwater, Jamake (Mamake)
Markson, David M(errill) 1927- .... **CLC 67**
See also CA 49-52; CANR 1, 91; CN 7
Marlatt, Daphne (Buckle) 1942- .... **CLC 168**
See also CA 25-28R; CANR 17, 39; CN 7;
CP 7; CWP; DLB 60; FW
Marley, Bob .... **CLC 17**
See Marley, Robert Nesta
Marley, Robert Nesta 1945-1981
See Marley, Bob
See also CA 107; 103
Marlowe, Christopher 1564-1593 . **DC 1; LC 22, 47; WLC**
See also BRW 1; BRWR 1; CDBLB Before
1660; DA; DA3; DAB; DAC; DAM
DRAM, MST; DFS 1, 5, 13; DLB 62;
EXPP; LMFS 1; RGEL 2; TEA; WLIT 3
Marlowe, Stephen 1928- .... **CLC 70**
See Queen, Ellery
See also CA 13-16R; CANR 6, 55; CMW
4; SFW 4
Marmion, Shakerley 1603-1639 .... **LC 89**
See also DLB 58; RGEL 2

Marmontel, Jean-Francois 1723-1799 .. **LC 2**
Maron, Monika 1941- .... **CLC 165**
See also CA 201
Marquand, John P(hillips)
1893-1960 .... **CLC 2, 10**
See also AMW; BPFB 2; CA 85-88; CANR 73; CMW 4; DLB 9, 102; EWL 3; MTCW 2; RGAL 4
Marques, Rene 1919-1979 .. **CLC 96; HLC 2**
See also CA 97-100; 85-88; CANR 78; DAM MULT; DLB 113; EWL 3; HW 1, 2; LAW; RGSF 2
Marquez, Gabriel (Jose) Garcia
See Garcia Marquez, Gabriel (Jose)
Marquis, Don(ald Robert Perry)
1878-1937 .... **TCLC 7**
See also CA 104; 166; DLB 11, 25; RGAL 4
Marquis de Sade
See Sade, Donatien Alphonse Francois
Marric, J. J.
See Creasey, John
See also MSW
Marryat, Frederick 1792-1848 .... **NCLC 3**
See also DLB 21, 163; RGEL 2; WCH
Marsden, James
See Creasey, John
Marsh, Edward 1872-1953 .... **TCLC 99**
Marsh, (Edith) Ngaio 1899-1982 .. **CLC 7, 53**
See also CA 9-12R; CANR 6, 58; CMW 4; CPW; DAM POP; DLB 77; MSW; MTCW 1, 2; RGEL 2; TEA
Marshall, Garry 1934- .... **CLC 17**
See also AAYA 3; CA 111; SATA 60
Marshall, Paule 1929- .. **BLC 3; CLC 27, 72; SSC 3**
See also AFAW 1, 2; AMWS 11; BPFB 2; BW 2, 3; CA 77-80; CANR 25, 73; CN 7; DA3; DAM MULT; DLB 33, 157, 227; EWL 3; LATS 1; MTCW 1, 2; RGAL 4; SSFS 15
Marshallik
See Zangwill, Israel
Marsten, Richard
See Hunter, Evan
Marston, John 1576-1634 .... **LC 33**
See also BRW 2; DAM DRAM; DLB 58, 172; RGEL 2
Martha, Henry
See Harris, Mark
Marti (y Perez), Jose (Julian)
1853-1895 .... **HLC 2; NCLC 63**
See also DAM MULT; HW 2; LAW; RGWL 2, 3; WLIT 1
Martial c. 40-c. 104 .... **CMLC 35; PC 10**
See also AW 2; CDWLB 1; DLB 211; RGWL 2, 3
Martin, Ken
See Hubbard, L(afayette) Ron(ald)
Martin, Richard
See Creasey, John
Martin, Steve 1945- .... **CLC 30**
See also AAYA 53; CA 97-100; CANR 30, 100; MTCW 1
Martin, Valerie 1948- .... **CLC 89**
See also BEST 90:2; CA 85-88; CANR 49, 89
Martin, Violet Florence 1862-1915 .. **SSC 56; TCLC 51**
Martin, Webber
See Silverberg, Robert
Martindale, Patrick Victor
See White, Patrick (Victor Martindale)
Martin du Gard, Roger
1881-1958 .... **TCLC 24**
See also CA 118; CANR 94; DLB 65; EWL 3; GFL 1789 to the Present; RGWL 2, 3

Martineau, Harriet 1802-1876 .... **NCLC 26**
See also DLB 21, 55, 159, 163, 166, 190; FW; RGEL 2; YABC 2
Martines, Julia
See O'Faolain, Julia
Martinez, Enrique Gonzalez
See Gonzalez Martinez, Enrique
Martinez, Jacinto Benavente y
See Benavente (y Martinez), Jacinto
Martinez de la Rosa, Francisco de Paula
1787-1862 .... **NCLC 102**
See also TWA
Martinez Ruiz, Jose 1873-1967
See Azorin; Ruiz, Jose Martinez
See also CA 93-96; HW 1
Martinez Sierra, Gregorio
1881-1947 .... **TCLC 6**
See also CA 115; EWL 3
Martinez Sierra, Maria (de la O'LeJarraga)
1874-1974 .... **TCLC 6**
See also CA 115; EWL 3
Martinsen, Martin
See Follett, Ken(neth Martin)
Martinson, Harry (Edmund)
1904-1978 .... **CLC 14**
See also CA 77-80; CANR 34; DLB 259; EWL 3
Martyn, Edward 1859-1923 .... **TCLC 131**
See also CA 179; DLB 10; RGEL 2
Marut, Ret
See Traven, B.
Marut, Robert
See Traven, B.
Marvell, Andrew 1621-1678 .... **LC 4, 43; PC 10; WLC**
See also BRW 2; BRWR 2; CDBLB 1660-1789; DA; DAB; DAC; DAM MST, POET; DLB 131; EXPP; PFS 5; RGEL 2; TEA; WP
Marx, Karl (Heinrich)
1818-1883 .... **NCLC 17, 114**
See also DLB 129; LATS 1; TWA
Masaoka, Shiki -1902 .... **TCLC 18**
See Masaoka, Tsunenori
See also RGWL 3
Masaoka, Tsunenori 1867-1902
See Masaoka, Shiki
See also CA 117; 191; TWA
Masefield, John (Edward)
1878-1967 .... **CLC 11, 47**
See also CA 19-20; 25-28R; CANR 33; CAP 2; CDBLB 1890-1914; DAM POET; DLB 10, 19, 153, 160; EWL 3; EXPP; FANT; MTCW 1, 2; PFS 5; RGEL 2; SATA 19
Maso, Carole 19(?)- .... **CLC 44**
See also CA 170; GLL 2; RGAL 4
Mason, Bobbie Ann 1940- ... **CLC 28, 43, 82, 154; SSC 4**
See also AAYA 5, 42; AMWS 8; BPFB 2; CA 53-56; CANR 11, 31, 58, 83; CDALBS; CN 7; CSW; DA3; DLB 173; DLBY 1987; EWL 3; EXPS; INT CANR-31; MTCW 1, 2; NFS 4; RGAL 4; RGSF 2; SSFS 3,8; YAW
Mason, Ernst
See Pohl, Frederik
Mason, Hunni B.
See Sternheim, (William Adolf) Carl
Mason, Lee W.
See Malzberg, Barry N(athaniel)
Mason, Nick 1945- .... **CLC 35**
Mason, Tally
See Derleth, August (William)
Mass, Anna .... **CLC 59**
Mass, William
See Gibson, William
Massinger, Philip 1583-1640 .... **LC 70**
See also DLB 58; RGEL 2

Master Lao
See Lao Tzu
Masters, Edgar Lee 1868-1950 ...... **PC 1, 36; TCLC 2, 25; WLCS**
See also AMWS 1; CA 104; 133; CDALB 1865-1917; DA; DAC; DAM MST, POET; DLB 54; EWL 3; EXPP; MTCW 1, 2; RGAL 4; TUS; WP
Masters, Hilary 1928- .... **CLC 48**
See also CA 25-28R; CANR 13, 47, 97; CN 7; DLB 244
Mastrosimone, William 19(?)- .... **CLC 36**
See also CA 186; CAD; CD 5
Mathe, Albert
See Camus, Albert
Mather, Cotton 1663-1728 .... **LC 38**
See also AMWS 2; CDALB 1640-1865; DLB 24, 30, 140; RGAL 4; TUS
Mather, Increase 1639-1723 .... **LC 38**
See also DLB 24
Matheson, Richard (Burton) 1926- .. **CLC 37**
See also AAYA 31; CA 97-100; CANR 88, 99; DLB 8, 44; HGG; INT 97-100; SCFW 2; SFW 4; SUFW 2
Mathews, Harry 1930- .... **CLC 6, 52**
See also CA 21-24R; CAAS 6; CANR 18, 40, 98; CN 7
Mathews, John Joseph 1894-1979 .. **CLC 84; NNAL**
See also CA 19-20; 142; CANR 45; CAP 2; DAM MULT; DLB 175
Mathias, Roland (Glyn) 1915- .... **CLC 45**
See also CA 97-100; CANR 19, 41; CP 7; DLB 27
Matsuo Basho 1644-1694 .... **LC 62; PC 3**
See Basho, Matsuo
See also DAM POET; PFS 2, 7
Mattheson, Rodney
See Creasey, John
Matthews, (James) Brander
1852-1929 .... **TCLC 95**
See also DLB 71, 78; DLBD 13
Matthews, Greg 1949- .... **CLC 45**
See also CA 135
Matthews, William (Procter III)
1942-1997 .... **CLC 40**
See also AMWS 9; CA 29-32R; 162; CAAS 18; CANR 12, 57; CP 7; DLB 5
Matthias, John (Edward) 1941- .... **CLC 9**
See also CA 33-36R; CANR 56; CP 7
Matthiessen, F(rancis) O(tto)
1902-1950 .... **TCLC 100**
See also CA 185; DLB 63
Matthiessen, Peter 1927- ... **CLC 5, 7, 11, 32, 64**
See also AAYA 6, 40; AMWS 5; ANW; BEST 90:4; BPFB 2; CA 9-12R; CANR 21, 50, 73, 100; CN 7; DA3; DAM NOV; DLB 6, 173, 275; MTCW 1, 2; SATA 27
Maturin, Charles Robert
1780(?)-1824 .... **NCLC 6**
See also BRWS 8; DLB 178; HGG; LMFS 1; RGEL 2; SUFW
Matute (Ausejo), Ana Maria 1925- .. **CLC 11**
See also CA 89-92; EWL 3; MTCW 1; RGSF 2
Maugham, W. S.
See Maugham, W(illiam) Somerset
Maugham, W(illiam) Somerset
1874-1965 .. **CLC 1, 11, 15, 67, 93; SSC 8; WLC**
See also AAYA 53; BPFB 2; BRW 6; CA 5-8R; 25-28R; CANR 40; CDBLB 1914-1945; CMW 4; CN 4; DA; DA3; DAB; DAC; DAM DRAM, MST, NOV; DLB 10, 36, 77, 100, 162, 195; EWL 3; LAIT 3; MTCW 1, 2; RGEL 2; RGSF 2; SATA 54; SSFS 17

Maugham, William Somerset
See Maugham, W(illiam) Somerset

Maupassant, (Henri Rene Albert) Guy de
1850-1893 . NCLC **1, 42, 83**; SSC **1, 64**;
WLC
See also BYA 14; DA; DA3; DAB; DAC;
DAM MST; DLB 123; EW 7; EXPS; GFL
1789 to the Present; LAIT 2; LMFS 1;
RGSF 2; RGWL 2, 3; SSFS 4; SUFW;
TWA

Maupin, Armistead (Jones, Jr.)
1944- .... CLC **95**
See also CA 125; 130; CANR 58, 101;
CPW; DA3; DAM POP; DLB 278; GLL
1; INT 130; MTCW 2

Maurhut, Richard
See Traven, B.

Mauriac, Claude 1914-1996 .... CLC **9**
See also CA 89-92; 152; CWW 2; DLB 83;
EWL 3; GFL 1789 to the Present

Mauriac, Francois (Charles)
1885-1970 .... CLC **4, 9, 56**; SSC **24**
See also CA 25-28; CAP 2; DLB 65; EW
10; EWL 3; GFL 1789 to the Present;
MTCW 1, 2; RGWL 2, 3; TWA

Mavor, Osborne Henry 1888-1951
See Bridie, James
See also CA 104

Maxwell, William (Keepers, Jr.)
1908-2000 .... CLC **19**
See also AMWS 8; CA 93-96; 189; CANR
54, 95; CN 7; DLB 218, 278; DLBY
1980; INT CA-93-96; SATA-Obit 128

May, Elaine 1932- .... CLC **16**
See also CA 124; 142; CAD; CWD; DLB
44

Mayakovski, Vladimir (Vladimirovich)
1893-1930 .... TCLC **4, 18**
See Maiakovskii, Vladimir; Mayakovsky,
Vladimir
See also CA 104; 158; EWL 3; MTCW 2;
SFW 4; TWA

Mayakovsky, Vladimir
See Mayakovski, Vladimir (Vladimirovich)
See also EW 11; WP

Mayhew, Henry 1812-1887 .... NCLC **31**
See also DLB 18, 55, 190

Mayle, Peter 1939(?)- .... CLC **89**
See also CA 139; CANR 64, 109

Maynard, Joyce 1953- .... CLC **23**
See also CA 111; 129; CANR 64

Mayne, William (James Carter)
1928- .... CLC **12**
See also AAYA 20; CA 9-12R; CANR 37,
80, 100; CLR 25; FANT; JRDA; MAI-
CYA 1, 2; MAICYAS 1; SAAS 11; SATA
6, 68, 122; SUFW 2; YAW

Mayo, Jim
See L'Amour, Louis (Dearborn)
See also TCWW 2

Maysles, Albert 1926- .... CLC **16**
See also CA 29-32R

Maysles, David 1932-1987 .... CLC **16**
See also CA 191

Mazer, Norma Fox 1931- .... CLC **26**
See also AAYA 5, 36; BYA 1, 8; CA 69-72;
CANR 12, 32, 66; CLR 23; JRDA; MAI-
CYA 1, 2; SAAS 1; SATA 24, 67, 105;
WYA; YAW

Mazzini, Guiseppe 1805-1872 .... NCLC **34**

McAlmon, Robert (Menzies)
1895-1956 .... TCLC **97**
See also CA 107; 168; DLB 4, 45; DLBD
15; GLL 1

McAuley, James Phillip 1917-1976 .. CLC **45**
See also CA 97-100; DLB 260; RGEL 2

McBain, Ed
See Hunter, Evan
See also MSW

McBrien, William (Augustine)
1930- .... CLC **44**
See also CA 107; CANR 90

McCabe, Patrick 1955- .... CLC **133**
See also BRWS 9; CA 130; CANR 50, 90;
CN 7; DLB 194

McCaffrey, Anne (Inez) 1926- .... CLC **17**
See also AAYA 6, 34; AITN 2; BEST 89:2;
BPFB 2; BYA 5; CA 25-28R; CANR 15,
35, 55, 96; CLR 49; CPW; DA3; DAM
NOV, POP; DLB 8; JRDA; MAICYA 1,
2; MTCW 1, 2; SAAS 11; SATA 8, 70,
116; SFW 4; SUFW 2; WYA; YAW

McCall, Nathan 1955(?)- .... CLC **86**
See also BW 3; CA 146; CANR 88

McCann, Arthur
See Campbell, John W(ood, Jr.)

McCann, Edson
See Pohl, Frederik

McCarthy, Charles, Jr. 1933-
See McCarthy, Cormac
See also CANR 42, 69, 101; CN 7; CPW;
CSW; DA3; DAM POP; MTCW 2

McCarthy, Cormac .... CLC **4, 57, 59, 101**
See McCarthy, Charles, Jr.
See also AAYA 41; AMWS 8; BPFB 2; CA
13-16R; CANR 10; DLB 6, 143, 256;
EWL 3; LATS 1; TCWW 2

McCarthy, Mary (Therese)
1912-1989 .. CLC **1, 3, 5, 14, 24, 39, 59**;
SSC **24**
See also AMW; BPFB 2; CA 5-8R; 129;
CANR 16, 50, 64; DA3; DLB 2; DLBY
1981; EWL 3; FW; INT CANR-16;
MAWW; MTCW 1, 2; RGAL 4; TUS

McCartney, (James) Paul 1942- . CLC **12, 35**
See also CA 146; CANR 111

McCauley, Stephen (D.) 1955- .... CLC **50**
See also CA 141

McClaren, Peter .... CLC **70**

McClure, Michael (Thomas) 1932- ... CLC **6, 10**
See also BG 3; CA 21-24R; CAD; CANR
17, 46, 77; CD 5; CP 7; DLB 16; WP

McCorkle, Jill (Collins) 1958- .... CLC **51**
See also CA 121; CANR 113; CSW; DLB
234; DLBY 1987

McCourt, Frank 1930- .... CLC **109**
See also AMWS 12; CA 157; CANR 97;
NCFS 1

McCourt, James 1941- .... CLC **5**
See also CA 57-60; CANR 98

McCourt, Malachy 1931- .... CLC **119**
See also SATA 126

McCoy, Horace (Stanley)
1897-1955 .... TCLC **28**
See also AMWS 13; CA 108; 155; CMW 4;
DLB 9

McCrae, John 1872-1918 .... TCLC **12**
See also CA 109; DLB 92; PFS 5

McCreigh, James
See Pohl, Frederik

McCullers, (Lula) Carson (Smith)
1917-1967 .... CLC **1, 4, 10, 12, 48, 100**;
SSC **9, 24**; WLC
See also AAYA 21; AMW; AMWC 2; BPFB
2; CA 5-8R; 25-28R; CABS 1, 3; CANR
18; CDALB 1941-1968; DA; DA3; DAB;
DAC; DAM MST, NOV, POP; DFS 5, 18; DLB
2, 7, 173, 228; EWL 3; EXPS; FW; GLL
1; LAIT 3, 4; MAWW; MTCW 1, 2; NFS
6, 13; RGAL 4; RGSF 2; SATA 27; SSFS
5; TUS; YAW

McCulloch, John Tyler
See Burroughs, Edgar Rice

McCullough, Colleen 1938(?)- .. CLC **27, 107**
See also AAYA 36; BPFB 2; CA 81-84;
CANR 17, 46, 67, 98; CPW; DA3; DAM
NOV, POP; MTCW 1, 2; RHW

McCunn, Ruthanne Lum 1946- .... AAL
See also CA 119; CANR 43, 96; LAIT 2;
SATA 63

McDermott, Alice 1953- .... CLC **90**
See also CA 109; CANR 40, 90

McElroy, Joseph 1930- .... CLC **5, 47**
See also CA 17-20R; CN 7

McEwan, Ian (Russell) 1948- .... CLC **13, 66, 169**
See also BEST 90:4; BRWS 4; CA 61-64;
CANR 14, 41, 69, 87; CN 7; DAM NOV;
DLB 14, 194; HGG; MTCW 1, 2; RGSF
2; SUFW 2; TEA

McFadden, David 1940- .... CLC **48**
See also CA 104; CP 7; DLB 60; INT 104

McFarland, Dennis 1950- .... CLC **65**
See also CA 165; CANR 110

McGahern, John 1934- ... CLC **5, 9, 48, 156**;
SSC **17**
See also CA 17-20R; CANR 29, 68, 113;
CN 7; DLB 14, 231; MTCW 1

McGinley, Patrick (Anthony) 1937- . CLC **41**
See also CA 120; 127; CANR 56; INT 127

McGinley, Phyllis 1905-1978 .... CLC **14**
See also CA 9-12R; 77-80; CANR 19;
CWRI 5; DLB 11, 48; PFS 9, 13; SATA
2, 44; SATA-Obit 24

McGinniss, Joe 1942- .... CLC **32**
See also AITN 2; BEST 89:2; CA 25-28R;
CANR 26, 70; CPW; DLB 185; INT
CANR-26

McGivern, Maureen Daly
See Daly, Maureen

McGrath, Patrick 1950- .... CLC **55**
See also CA 136; CANR 65; CN 7; DLB
231; HGG; SUFW 2

McGrath, Thomas (Matthew)
1916-1990 .... CLC **28, 59**
See also AMWS 10; CA 9-12R; 132; CANR
6, 33, 95; DAM POET; MTCW 1; SATA
41; SATA-Obit 66

McGuane, Thomas (Francis III)
1939- .... CLC **3, 7, 18, 45, 127**
See also AITN 2; BPFB 2; CA 49-52;
CANR 5, 24, 49, 94; CN 7; DLB 2, 212;
DLBY 1980; EWL 3; INT CANR-24;
MTCW 1; TCWW 2

McGuckian, Medbh 1950- .... CLC **48, 174**;
PC **27**
See also BRWS 5; CA 143; CP 7; CWP;
DAM POET; DLB 40

McHale, Tom 1942(?)-1982 .... CLC **3, 5**
See also AITN 1; CA 77-80; 106

McIlvanney, William 1936- .... CLC **42**
See also CA 25-28R; CANR 61; CMW 4;
DLB 14, 207

McIlwraith, Maureen Mollie Hunter
See Hunter, Mollie
See also SATA 2

McInerney, Jay 1955- .... CLC **34, 112**
See also AAYA 18; BPFB 2; CA 116; 123;
CANR 45, 68, 116; CN 7; CPW; DA3;
DAM POP; INT 123; MTCW 2

McIntyre, Vonda N(eel) 1948- .... CLC **18**
See also CA 81-84; CANR 17, 34, 69;
MTCW 1; SFW 4; YAW

McKay, Claude .... BLC **3**; HR **3**; PC **2**;
TCLC **7, 41**; WLC
See McKay, Festus Claudius
See also AFAW 1, 2; AMWS 10; DAB;
DLB 4, 45, 51, 117; EWL 3; EXPP; GLL
2; LAIT 3; LMFS 2; PAB; PFS 4; RGAL
4; WP

McKay, Festus Claudius 1889-1948
See McKay, Claude
See also BW 1, 3; CA 104; 124; CANR 73;
DA; DAC; DAM MST, MULT, NOV,
POET; MTCW 1, 2; TUS

McKuen, Rod 1933- .... **CLC 1, 3**
See also AITN 1; CA 41-44R; CANR 40

McLoughlin, R. B.
See Mencken, H(enry) L(ouis)

McLuhan, (Herbert) Marshall
1911-1980 .... **CLC 37, 83**
See also CA 9-12R; 102; CANR 12, 34, 61; DLB 88; INT CANR-12; MTCW 1, 2

McManus, Declan Patrick Aloysius
See Costello, Elvis

McMillan, Terry (L.) 1951- . **BLCS; CLC 50, 61, 112**
See also AAYA 21; AMWS 13; BPFB 2; BW 2, 3; CA 140; CANR 60, 104; CPW; DA3; DAM MULT, NOV, POP; MTCW 2; RGAL 4; YAW

McMurtry, Larry (Jeff) 1936- .. **CLC 2, 3, 7, 11, 27, 44, 127**
See also AAYA 15; AITN 2; AMWS 5; BEST 89:2; BPFB 2; CA 5-8R; CANR 19, 43, 64, 103; CDALB 1968-1988; CN 7; CPW; CSW; DA3; DAM NOV, POP; DLB 2, 143, 256; DLBY 1980, 1987; EWL 3; MTCW 1, 2; RGAL 4; TCWW 2

McNally, T. M. 1961- .... **CLC 82**

McNally, Terrence 1939- .... **CLC 4, 7, 41, 91**
See also AMWS 13; CA 45-48; CAD; CANR 2, 56, 116; CD 5; DA3; DAM DRAM; DFS 16; DLB 7, 249; EWL 3; GLL 1; MTCW 2

McNamer, Deirdre 1950- .... **CLC 70**

McNeal, Tom .... **CLC 119**

McNeile, Herman Cyril 1888-1937
See Sapper
See also CA 184; CMW 4; DLB 77

McNickle, (William) D'Arcy
1904-1977 .... **CLC 89; NNAL**
See also CA 9-12R; 85-88; CANR 5, 45; DAM MULT; DLB 175, 212; RGAL 4; SATA-Obit 22

McPhee, John (Angus) 1931- .... **CLC 36**
See also AMWS 3; ANW; BEST 90:1; CA 65-68; CANR 20, 46, 64, 69, 121; CPW; DLB 185, 275; MTCW 1, 2; TUS

McPherson, James Alan 1943- . **BLCS; CLC 19, 77**
See also BW 1, 3; CA 25-28R; CAAS 17; CANR 24, 74; CN 7; CSW; DLB 38, 244; EWL 3; MTCW 1, 2; RGAL 4; RGSF 2

McPherson, William (Alexander)
1933- .... **CLC 34**
See also CA 69-72; CANR 28; INT CANR-28

McTaggart, J. McT. Ellis
See McTaggart, John McTaggart Ellis

McTaggart, John McTaggart Ellis
1866-1925 .... **TCLC 105**
See also CA 120; DLB 262

Mead, George Herbert 1863-1931 . **TCLC 89**
See also CA 212; DLB 270

Mead, Margaret 1901-1978 .... **CLC 37**
See also AITN 1; CA 1-4R; 81-84; CANR 4; DA3; FW; MTCW 1, 2; SATA-Obit 20

Meaker, Marijane (Agnes) 1927-
See Kerr, M. E.
See also CA 107; CANR 37, 63; INT 107; JRDA; MAICYA 1, 2; MAICYAS 1; MTCW 1; SATA 20, 61, 99; SATA-Essay 111; YAW

Medoff, Mark (Howard) 1940- .... **CLC 6, 23**
See also AITN 1; CA 53-56; CAD; CANR 5; CD 5; DAM DRAM; DFS 4; DLB 7; INT CANR-5

Medvedev, P. N.
See Bakhtin, Mikhail Mikhailovich

Meged, Aharon
See Megged, Aharon

Meged, Aron
See Megged, Aharon

Megged, Aharon 1920- .... **CLC 9**
See also CA 49-52; CAAS 13; CANR 1; EWL 3

Mehta, Gita 1943- .... **CLC 179**
See also DNFS 2

Mehta, Ved (Parkash) 1934- .... **CLC 37**
See also CA 1-4R; CAAE 212; CANR 2, 23, 69; MTCW 1

Melanchthon, Philipp 1497-1560 .... **LC 90**
See also DLB 179

Melanter
See Blackmore, R(ichard) D(oddridge)

Meleager c. 140B.C.-c. 70B.C. .... **CMLC 53**

Melies, Georges 1861-1938 .... **TCLC 81**

Melikow, Loris
See Hofmannsthal, Hugo von

Melmoth, Sebastian
See Wilde, Oscar (Fingal O'Flahertie Wills)

Melo Neto, Joao Cabral de
See Cabral de Melo Neto, Joao
See also EWL 3

Meltzer, Milton 1915- .... **CLC 26**
See also AAYA 8, 45; BYA 2, 6; CA 13-16R; CANR 38, 92, 107; CLR 13; DLB 61; JRDA; MAICYA 1, 2; SAAS 1, 50, 80, 128; SATA-Essay 124; WYA; YAW

Melville, Herman 1819-1891 ..... **NCLC 3, 12, 29, 45, 49, 91, 93, 123; SSC 1, 17, 46; WLC**
See also AAYA 25; AMW; AMWR 1; CDALB 1640-1865; DA; DA3; DAB; DAC; DAM MST, NOV; DLB 3, 74, 250, 254; EXPN; EXPS; LAIT 1, 2; NFS 7, 9; RGAL 4; RGSF 2; SATA 59; SSFS 3; TUS

Members, Mark
See Powell, Anthony (Dymoke)

Membreno, Alejandro .... **CLC 59**

Menander c. 342B.C.-c. 293B.C. .... **CMLC 9, 51; DC 3**
See also AW 1; CDWLB 1; DAM DRAM; DLB 176; LMFS 1; RGWL 2, 3

Menchu, Rigoberta 1959- .. **CLC 160; HLCS 2**
See also CA 175; DNFS 1; WLIT 1

Mencken, H(enry) L(ouis)
1880-1956 .... **TCLC 13**
See also AMW; CA 105; 125; CDALB 1917-1929; DLB 11, 29, 63, 137, 222; EWL 3; MTCW 1, 2; NCFS 4; RGAL 4; TUS

Mendelsohn, Jane 1965- .... **CLC 99**
See also CA 154; CANR 94

Menton, Francisco de
See Chin, Frank (Chew, Jr.)

Mercer, David 1928-1980 .... **CLC 5**
See also CA 9-12R; 102; CANR 23; CBD; DAM DRAM; DLB 13; MTCW 1; RGEL 2

Merchant, Paul
See Ellison, Harlan (Jay)

Meredith, George 1828-1909 ... **TCLC 17, 43**
See also CA 117; 153; CANR 80; CDBLB 1832-1890; DAM POET; DLB 18, 35, 57, 159; RGEL 2; TEA

Meredith, William (Morris) 1919- .... **CLC 4, 13, 22, 55; PC 28**
See also CA 9-12R; CAAS 14; CANR 6, 40; CP 7; DAM POET; DLB 5

Merezhkovsky, Dmitry Sergeevich
See Merezhkovsky, Dmitry Sergeyevich
See also EWL 3

Merezhkovsky, Dmitry Sergeyevich
1865-1941 .... **TCLC 29**
See Merezhkovsky, Dmitry Sergeyevich
See also CA 169

Merimee, Prosper 1803-1870 ... **NCLC 6, 65; SSC 7**
See also DLB 119, 192; EW 6; EXPS; GFL 1789 to the Present; RGSF 2; RGWL 2, 3; SSFS 8; SUFW

Merkin, Daphne 1954- .... **CLC 44**
See also CA 123

Merlin, Arthur
See Blish, James (Benjamin)

Mernissi, Fatima 1940- .... **CLC 171**
See also CA 152; FW

Merrill, James (Ingram) 1926-1995 .. **CLC 2, 3, 6, 8, 13, 18, 34, 91; PC 28**
See also AMWS 3; CA 13-16R; 147; CANR 10, 49, 63, 108; DA3; DAM POET; DLB 5, 165; DLBY 1985; EWL 3; INT CANR-10; MTCW 1, 2; PAB; RGAL 4

Merriman, Alex
See Silverberg, Robert

Merriman, Brian 1747-1805 .... **NCLC 70**

Merritt, E. B.
See Waddington, Miriam

Merton, Thomas (James)
1915-1968 . **CLC 1, 3, 11, 34, 83; PC 10**
See also AMWS 8; CA 5-8R; 25-28R; CANR 22, 53, 111; DA3; DLB 48; DLBY 1981; MTCW 1, 2

Merwin, W(illiam) S(tanley) 1927- ... **CLC 1, 2, 3, 5, 8, 13, 18, 45, 88; PC 45**
See also AMWS 3; CA 13-16R; CANR 15, 51, 112; CP 7; DA3; DAM POET; DLB 5, 169; EWL 3; INT CANR-15; MTCW 1, 2; PAB; PFS 5, 15; RGAL 4

Metcalf, John 1938- .... **CLC 37; SSC 43**
See also CA 113; CN 7; DLB 60; RGSF 2; TWA

Metcalf, Suzanne
See Baum, L(yman) Frank

Mew, Charlotte (Mary) 1870-1928 .. **TCLC 8**
See also CA 105; 189; DLB 19, 135; RGEL 2

Mewshaw, Michael 1943- .... **CLC 9**
See also CA 53-56; CANR 7, 47; DLBY 1980

Meyer, Conrad Ferdinand
1825-1898 .... **NCLC 81**
See also DLB 129; EW; RGWL 2, 3

Meyer, Gustav 1868-1932
See Meyrink, Gustav
See also CA 117; 190

Meyer, June
See Jordan, June (Meyer)

Meyer, Lynn
See Slavitt, David R(ytman)

Meyers, Jeffrey 1939- .... **CLC 39**
See also CA 73-76; CAAE 186; CANR 54, 102; DLB 111

Meynell, Alice (Christina Gertrude Thompson) 1847-1922 .... **TCLC 6**
See also CA 104; 177; DLB 19, 98; RGEL 2

Meyrink, Gustav .... **TCLC 21**
See Meyer, Gustav
See also DLB 81; EWL 3

Michaels, Leonard 1933-2003 ..... **CLC 6, 25; SSC 16**
See also CA 61-64; 216; CANR 21, 62, 119; CN 7; DLB 130; MTCW 1

Michaux, Henri 1899-1984 .... **CLC 8, 19**
See also CA 85-88; 114; DLB 258; EWL 3; GFL 1789 to the Present; RGWL 2, 3

Micheaux, Oscar (Devereaux)
1884-1951 .... **TCLC 76**
See also BW 3; CA 174; DLB 50; TCWW 2

Michelangelo 1475-1564 .... **LC 12**
See also AAYA 43

Michelet, Jules 1798-1874 .... **NCLC 31**
See also EW 5; GFL 1789 to the Present

Michels, Robert 1876-1936 .... **TCLC 88**
See also CA 212

Michener, James A(lbert)
1907(?)-1997 .. **CLC 1, 5, 11, 29, 60, 109**
See also AAYA 27; AITN 1; BEST 90:1; BPFB 2; CA 5-8R; 161; CANR 21, 45, 68; CN 7; CPW; DA3; DAM NOV, POP; DLB 6; MTCW 1, 2; RHW

Mickiewicz, Adam 1798-1855 . **NCLC 3, 101; PC 38**
See also EW 5; RGWL 2, 3

Middleton, (John) Christopher
1926- .... **CLC 13**
See also CA 13-16R; CANR 29, 54, 117; CP 7; DLB 40

Middleton, Richard (Barham)
1882-1911 .... **TCLC 56**
See also CA 187; DLB 156; HGG

Middleton, Stanley 1919- .... **CLC 7, 38**
See also CA 25-28R; CAAS 23; CANR 21, 46, 81; CN 7; DLB 14

Middleton, Thomas 1580-1627 ...... **DC 5; LC 33**
See also BRW 2; DAM DRAM, MST; DFS 18; DLB 58; RGEL 2

Migueis, Jose Rodrigues 1901-1980 . **CLC 10**
See also DLB 287

Mikszath, Kalman 1847-1910 .... **TCLC 31**
See also CA 170

Miles, Jack .... **CLC 100**
See also CA 200

Miles, John Russiano
See Miles, Jack

Miles, Josephine (Louise)
1911-1985 .... **CLC 1, 2, 14, 34, 39**
See also CA 1-4R; 116; CANR 2, 55; DAM POET; DLB 48

Militant
See Sandburg, Carl (August)

Mill, Harriet (Hardy) Taylor
1807-1858 .... **NCLC 102**
See also FW

Mill, John Stuart 1806-1873 .... **NCLC 11, 58**
See also CDBLB 1832-1890; DLB 55, 190, 262; FW 1; RGEL 2; TEA

Millar, Kenneth 1915-1983 .... **CLC 14**
See Macdonald, Ross
See also CA 9-12R; 110; CANR 16, 63, 107; CMW 4; CPW; DA3; DAM POP; DLB 2, 226; DLBD 6; DLBY 1983; MTCW 1, 2

Millay, E. Vincent
See Millay, Edna St. Vincent

Millay, Edna St. Vincent 1892-1950 .... **PC 6; TCLC 4, 49; WLCS**
See Boyd, Nancy
See also AMW; CA 104; 130; CDALB 1917-1929; DA; DA3; DAB; DAC; DAM MST, POET; DLB 45, 249; EWL 3; EXPP; MAWW; MTCW 1, 2; PAB; PFS 3, 17; RGAL 4; TUS; WP

Miller, Arthur 1915- ...... **CLC 1, 2, 6, 10, 15, 26, 47, 78, 179; DC 1; WLC**
See also AAYA 15; AITN 1; AMW; AMWC 1; CA 1-4R; CABS 3; CAD; CANR 2, 30, 54, 76; CD 5; CDALB 1941-1968; DA; DA3; DAB; DAC; DAM DRAM, MST; DFS 1, 3, 8; DLB 7, 266; EWL 3; LAIT 1, 4; LATS 1; MTCW 1, 2; RGAL 4; TUS; WYAS 1

Miller, Henry (Valentine)
1891-1980 .... **CLC 1, 2, 4, 9, 14, 43, 84; WLC**
See also AMW; BPFB 2; CA 9-12R; 97-100; CANR 33, 64; CDALB 1929-1941; DA; DA3; DAB; DAC; DAM MST, NOV, DLB 4, 9; DLBY 1980; EWL 3; MTCW 1, 2; RGAL 4; TUS

Miller, Jason 1939(?)-2001 .... **CLC 2**
See also AITN 1; CA 73-76; 197; CAD; DFS 12; DLB 7

Miller, Sue 1943- .... **CLC 44**
See also AMWS 12; BEST 90:3; CA 139; CANR 59, 91; DA3; DAM POP; DLB 143

Miller, Walter M(ichael, Jr.)
1923-1996 .... **CLC 4, 30**
See also BPFB 2; CA 85-88; CANR 108; DLB 8; SCFW; SFW 4

Millett, Kate 1934- .... **CLC 67**
See also AITN 1; CA 73-76; CANR 32, 53, 76, 110; DA3; DLB 246; FW; GLL 1; MTCW 1, 2

Millhauser, Steven (Lewis) 1943- .... **CLC 21, 54, 109; SSC 57**
See also CA 110; 111; CANR 63, 114; CN 7; DA3; DLB 2; FANT; INT CA-111; MTCW 2

Millin, Sarah Gertrude 1889-1968 ... **CLC 49**
See also CA 102; 93-96; DLB 225; EWL 3

Milne, A(lan) A(lexander)
1882-1956 .... **TCLC 6, 88**
See also BRWS 5; CA 104; 133; CLR 1, 26; CMW 4; CWRI 5; DA3; DAB; DAC; DAM MST; DLB 10, 77, 100, 160; FANT; MAICYA 1, 2; MTCW 1, 2; RGEL 2; SATA 100; WCH; YABC 1

Milner, Ron(ald) 1938- .... **BLC 3; CLC 56**
See also AITN 1; BW 1; CA 73-76; CAD; CANR 24, 81; CD 5; DAM MULT; DLB 38; MTCW 1

Milnes, Richard Monckton
1809-1885 .... **NCLC 61**
See also DLB 32, 184

Milosz, Czeslaw 1911- ...... **CLC 5, 11, 22, 31, 56, 82; PC 8; WLCS**
See also CA 81-84; CANR 23, 51, 91; CDWLB 4; CWW 2; DA3; DAM MST, POET; DLB 215; EW 13; EWL 3; MTCW 1, 2; PFS 16; RGWL 2, 3

Milton, John 1608-1674 ..... **LC 9, 43, 92; PC 19, 29; WLC**
See also BRW 2; BRWR 2; CDBLB 1660-1789; DA; DA3; DAB; DAC; DAM MST, POET; DLB 131, 151, 281; EFS 1; EXPP; LAIT 1; PAB; PFS 3, 17; RGEL 2; TEA; WLIT 3; WP

Min, Anchee 1957- .... **CLC 86**
See also CA 146; CANR 94

Minehaha, Cornelius
See Wedekind, (Benjamin) Frank(lin)

Miner, Valerie 1947- .... **CLC 40**
See also CA 97-100; CANR 59; FW; GLL 2

Minimo, Duca
See D'Annunzio, Gabriele

Minot, Susan 1956- .... **CLC 44, 159**
See also AMWS 6; CA 134; CANR 118; CN 7

Minus, Ed 1938- .... **CLC 39**
See also CA 185

Mirabai 1498(?)-1550(?) .... **PC 48**

Miranda, Javier
See Bioy Casares, Adolfo
See also CWW 2

Mirbeau, Octave 1848-1917 .... **TCLC 55**
See also CA 216; DLB 123, 192; GFL 1789 to the Present

Mirikitani, Janice 1942- .... **AAL**
See also CA 211; RGAL 4

Miro (Ferrer), Gabriel (Francisco Victor)
1879-1930 .... **TCLC 5**
See also CA 104; 185; EWL 3

Misharin, Alexandr .... **CLC 59**

Mishima, Yukio ... **CLC 2, 4, 6, 9, 27; DC 1; SSC 4**
See Hiraoka, Kimitake
See also AAYA 50; BPFB 2; GLL 1; MJW; MTCW 2; RGSF 2; RGWL 2, 3; SSFS 5, 12

Mistral, Frederic 1830-1914 .... **TCLC 51**
See also CA 122; 213; GFL 1789 to the Present

Mistral, Gabriela
See Godoy Alcayaga, Lucila
See also DLB 283; DNFS 1; EWL 3; LAW; RGWL 2, 3; WP

Mistry, Rohinton 1952- .... **CLC 71**
See also CA 141; CANR 86, 114; CCA 1; CN 7; DAC; SSFS 6

Mitchell, Clyde
See Ellison, Harlan (Jay)

Mitchell, Emerson Blackhorse Barney
1945- .... **NNAL**
See also CA 45-48

Mitchell, James Leslie 1901-1935
See Gibbon, Lewis Grassic
See also CA 104; 188; DLB 15

Mitchell, Joni 1943- .... **CLC 12**
See also CA 112; CCA 1

Mitchell, Joseph (Quincy)
1908-1996 .... **CLC 98**
See also CA 77-80; 152; CANR 69; CN 7; CSW; DLB 185; DLBY 1996

Mitchell, Margaret (Munnerlyn)
1900-1949 .... **TCLC 11**
See also AAYA 23; BPFB 2; BYA 1; CA 109; 125; CANR 55, 94; CDALBS; DA3; DAM NOV, POP; DLB 9; LAIT 2; MTCW 1, 2; NFS 9; RGAL 4; RHW; TUS; WYAS 1; YAW

Mitchell, Peggy
See Mitchell, Margaret (Munnerlyn)

Mitchell, S(ilas) Weir 1829-1914 .... **TCLC 36**
See also CA 165; DLB 202; RGAL 4

Mitchell, W(illiam) O(rmond)
1914-1998 .... **CLC 25**
See also CA 77-80; 165; CANR 15, 43; CN 7; DAC; DAM MST; DLB 88

Mitchell, William (Lendrum)
1879-1936 .... **TCLC 81**
See also CA 213

Mitford, Mary Russell 1787-1855 ... **NCLC 4**
See also DLB 110, 116; RGEL 2

Mitford, Nancy 1904-1973 .... **CLC 44**
See also CA 9-12R; DLB 191; RGEL 2

Miyamoto, (Chujo) Yuriko
1899-1951 .... **TCLC 37**
See Miyamoto Yuriko
See also CA 170, 174

Miyamoto Yuriko
See Miyamoto, (Chujo) Yuriko
See also DLB 180

Miyazawa, Kenji 1896-1933 .... **TCLC 76**
See Miyazawa Kenji
See also CA 157; RGWL 3

Miyazawa Kenji
See Miyazawa, Kenji
See also EWL 3

Mizoguchi, Kenji 1898-1956 .... **TCLC 72**
See also CA 167

Mo, Timothy (Peter) 1950(?)- ... **CLC 46, 134**
See also CA 117; CN 7; DLB 194; MTCW 1; WLIT 4

Modarressi, Taghi (M.) 1931-1997 ... **CLC 44**
See also CA 121; 134; INT 134

Modiano, Patrick (Jean) 1945- .... **CLC 18**
See also CA 85-88; CANR 17, 40, 115; CWW 2; DLB 83; EWL 3

Mofolo, Thomas (Mokopu)
1875(?)-1948 .... **BLC 3; TCLC 22**
See also AFW; CA 121; 153; CANR 83; DAM MULT; DLB 225; EWL 3; MTCW 2; WLIT 2

Mohr, Nicholasa 1938- .... **CLC 12; HLC 2**
See also AAYA 8, 46; CA 49-52; CANR 1, 32, 64; CLR 22; DAM MULT; DLB 145; HW 1, 2; JRDA; LAIT 5; MAICYA 2; MAICYAS 1; RGAL 4; SAAS 8; SATA 8, 97; SATA-Essay 113; WYA; YAW

Moi, Toril 1953- .... **CLC 172**
See also CA 154; CANR 102; FW

Mojtabai, A(nn) G(race) 1938- ..... **CLC 5, 9, 15, 29**
See also CA 85-88; CANR 88

Moliere 1622-1673 ..... **DC 13; LC 10, 28, 64; WLC**
See also DA; DA3; DAB; DAC; DAM DRAM, MST; DFS 13, 18; DLB 268; EW 3; GFL Beginnings to 1789; LATS 1; RGWL 2, 3; TWA

Molin, Charles
See Mayne, William (James Carter)

Molnar, Ferenc 1878-1952 .... **TCLC 20**
See also CA 109; 153; CANR 83; CDWLB 4; DAM DRAM; DLB 215; EWL 3; RGWL 2, 3

Momaday, N(avarre) Scott 1934- .... **CLC 2, 19, 85, 95, 160; NNAL; PC 25; WLCS**
See also AAYA 11; AMWS 4; ANW; BPFB 2; CA 25-28R; CANR 14, 34, 68; CDALBS; CN 7; CPW; DA; DA3; DAB; DAC; DAM MST, MULT, NOV, POP; DLB 143, 175, 256; EWL 3; EXPP; INT CANR-14; LAIT 4; LATS 1; MTCW 1, 2; NFS 10; PFS 2, 11; RGAL 4; SATA 48; SATA-Brief 30; WP; YAW

Monette, Paul 1945-1995 .... **CLC 82**
See also AMWS 10; CA 139; 147; CN 7; GLL 1

Monroe, Harriet 1860-1936 .... **TCLC 12**
See also CA 109; 204; DLB 54, 91

Monroe, Lyle
See Heinlein, Robert A(nson)

Montagu, Elizabeth 1720-1800 .... **NCLC 7, 117**
See also FW

Montagu, Mary (Pierrepont) Wortley
1689-1762 .... **LC 9, 57; PC 16**
See also DLB 95, 101; RGEL 2

Montagu, W. H.
See Coleridge, Samuel Taylor

Montague, John (Patrick) 1929- ...... **CLC 13, 46**
See also CA 9-12R; CANR 9, 69, 121; CP 7; DLB 40; EWL 3; MTCW 1; PFS 12; RGEL 2

Montaigne, Michel (Eyquem) de
1533-1592 .... **LC 8; WLC**
See also DA; DAB; DAC; DAM MST; EW 2; GFL Beginnings to 1789; LMFS 1; RGWL 2, 3; TWA

Montale, Eugenio 1896-1981 ... **CLC 7, 9, 18; PC 13**
See also CA 17-20R; 104; CANR 30; DLB 114; EW 11; EWL 3; MTCW 1; RGWL 2, 3; TWA

Montesquieu, Charles-Louis de Secondat
1689-1755 .... **LC 7, 69**
See also EW 3; GFL Beginnings to 1789; TWA

Montessori, Maria 1870-1952 .... **TCLC 103**
See also CA 115; 147

Montgomery, (Robert) Bruce 1921(?)-1978
See Crispin, Edmund
See also CA 179; 104; CMW 4

Montgomery, L(ucy) M(aud)
1874-1942 .... **TCLC 51, 140**
See also AAYA 12; BYA 1; CA 108; 137; CLR 8, 91; DA3; DAC; DAM MST; DLB 92; DLBD 14; JRDA; MAICYA 1, 2; MTCW 2; RGEL 2; SATA 100; TWA; WCH; WYA; YABC 1

Montgomery, Marion H., Jr. 1925- .... **CLC 7**
See also AITN 1; CA 1-4R; CANR 3, 48; CSW; DLB 6

Montgomery, Max
See Davenport, Guy (Mattison, Jr.)

Montherlant, Henry (Milon) de
1896-1972 .... **CLC 8, 19**
See also CA 85-88; 37-40R; DAM DRAM; DLB 72; EW 11; EWL 3; GFL 1789 to the Present; MTCW 1

Monty Python
See Chapman, Graham; Cleese, John (Marwood); Gilliam, Terry (Vance); Idle, Eric; Jones, Terence Graham Parry; Palin, Michael (Edward)
See also AAYA 7

Moodie, Susanna (Strickland)
1803-1885 .... **NCLC 14, 113**
See also DLB 99

Moody, Hiram (F. III) 1961-
See Moody, Rick
See also CA 138; CANR 64, 112

Moody, Minerva
See Alcott, Louisa May

Moody, Rick .... **CLC 147**
See Moody, Hiram (F. III)

Moody, William Vaughan
1869-1910 .... **TCLC 105**
See also CA 110; 178; DLB 7, 54; RGAL 4

Mooney, Edward 1951-
See Mooney, Ted
See also CA 130

Mooney, Ted .... **CLC 25**
See Mooney, Edward

Moorcock, Michael (John) 1939- ...... **CLC 5, 27, 58**
See Bradbury, Edward P.
See also AAYA 26; CA 45-48; CAAS 5; CANR 2, 17, 38, 64, 122; CN 7; DLB 14, 231, 261; FANT; MTCW 1, 2; SATA 93; SCFW 2; SFW 4; SUFW 1, 2

Moore, Brian 1921-1999 ... **CLC 1, 3, 5, 7, 8, 19, 32, 90**
See Bryan, Michael
See also BRWS 9; CA 1-4R; 174; CANR 1, 25, 42, 63; CCA 1; CN 7; DAB; DAC; DAM MST; DLB 251; EWL 3; FANT; MTCW 1, 2; RGEL 2

Moore, Edward
See Muir, Edwin
See also RGEL 2

Moore, G. E. 1873-1958 .... **TCLC 89**
See also DLB 262

Moore, George Augustus
1852-1933 .... **SSC 19; TCLC 7**
See also BRW 6; CA 104; 177; DLB 10, 18, 57, 135; EWL 3; RGEL 2; RGSF 2

Moore, Lorrie .... **CLC 39, 45, 68**
See Moore, Marie Lorena
See also AMWS 10; DLB 234

Moore, Marianne (Craig)
1887-1972 ..... **CLC 1, 2, 4, 8, 10, 13, 19, 47; PC 4, 49; WLCS**
See also AMW; CA 1-4R; 33-36R; CANR 3, 61; CDALB 1929-1941; DA; DA3; DAB; DAC; DAM MST, POET; DLB 45; DLBD 7; EWL 3; EXPP; MAWW; MTCW 1, 2; PAB; PFS 14, 17; RGAL 4; SATA 20; TUS; WP

Moore, Marie Lorena 1957- .... **CLC 165**
See Moore, Lorrie
See also CA 116; CANR 39, 83; CN 7; DLB 234

Moore, Thomas 1779-1852 .... **NCLC 6, 110**
See also DLB 96, 144; RGEL 2

Moorhouse, Frank 1938- .... **SSC 40**
See also CA 118; CANR 92; CN 7; DLB 289; RGSF 2

Mora, Pat(ricia) 1942- .... **HLC 2**
See also AMWS 13; CA 129; CANR 57, 81, 112; CLR 58; DAM MULT; DLB 209; HW 1, 2; MAICYA 2; SATA 92, 134

Moraga, Cherrie 1952- .... **CLC 126**
See also CA 131; CANR 66; DAM MULT; DLB 82, 249; FW; GLL 1; HW 1, 2

Morand, Paul 1888-1976 .... **CLC 41; SSC 22**
See also CA 184; 69-72; DLB 65; EWL 3

Morante, Elsa 1918-1985 .... **CLC 8, 47**
See also CA 85-88; 117; CANR 35; DLB 177; EWL 3; MTCW 1, 2; RGWL 2, 3

Moravia, Alberto .... **CLC 2, 7, 11, 27, 46; SSC 26**
See Pincherle, Alberto
See also DLB 177; EW 12; EWL 3; MTCW 2; RGSF 2; RGWL 2, 3

More, Hannah 1745-1833 .... **NCLC 27**
See also DLB 107, 109, 116, 158; RGEL 2

More, Henry 1614-1687 .... **LC 9**
See also DLB 126, 252

More, Sir Thomas 1478(?)-1535 .... **LC 10, 32**
See also BRWC 1; BRWS 7; DLB 136, 281; LMFS 1; RGEL 2; TEA

Moreas, Jean .... **TCLC 18**
See Papadiamantopoulos, Johannes
See also GFL 1789 to the Present

Moreton, Andrew Esq.
See Defoe, Daniel

Morgan, Berry 1919-2002 .... **CLC 6**
See also CA 49-52; 208; DLB 6

Morgan, Claire
See Highsmith, (Mary) Patricia
See also GLL 1

Morgan, Edwin (George) 1920- .... **CLC 31**
See also BRWS 9; CA 5-8R; CANR 3, 43, 90; CP 7; DLB 27

Morgan, (George) Frederick 1922- .. **CLC 23**
See also CA 17-20R; CANR 21; CP 7

Morgan, Harriet
See Mencken, H(enry) L(ouis)

Morgan, Jane
See Cooper, James Fenimore

Morgan, Janet 1945- .... **CLC 39**
See also CA 65-68

Morgan, Lady 1776(?)-1859 .... **NCLC 29**
See also DLB 116, 158; RGEL 2

Morgan, Robin (Evonne) 1941- .... **CLC 2**
See also CA 69-72; CANR 29, 68; FW; GLL 2; MTCW 1; SATA 80

Morgan, Scott
See Kuttner, Henry

Morgan, Seth 1949(?)-1990 .... **CLC 65**
See also CA 185; 132

Morgenstern, Christian (Otto Josef Wolfgang) 1871-1914 .... **TCLC 8**
See also CA 105; 191; EWL 3

Morgenstern, S.
See Goldman, William (W.)

Mori, Rintaro
See Mori Ogai
See also CA 110

Moricz, Zsigmond 1879-1942 .... **TCLC 33**
See also CA 165; DLB 215; EWL 3

Morike, Eduard (Friedrich)
1804-1875 .... **NCLC 10**
See also DLB 133; RGWL 2, 3

Mori Ogai 1862-1922 .... **TCLC 14**
See Ogai
See also CA 164; DLB 180; EWL 3; RGWL 3; TWA

Moritz, Karl Philipp 1756-1793 .... **LC 2**
See also DLB 94

Morland, Peter Henry
See Faust, Frederick (Schiller)

Morley, Christopher (Darlington)
1890-1957 .... **TCLC 87**
See also CA 112; DLB 9; RGAL 4

Morren, Theophil
See Hofmannsthal, Hugo von

Morris, Bill 1952- .... **CLC 76**

Morris, Julian
See West, Morris L(anglo)

Morris, Steveland Judkins 1950(?)-
See Wonder, Stevie
See also CA 111

Morris, William 1834-1896 .... **NCLC 4**
See also BRW 5; CDBLB 1832-1890; DLB 18, 35, 57, 156, 178, 184; FANT; RGEL 2; SFW 4; SUFW

Morris, Wright 1910-1998 .. **CLC 1, 3, 7, 18, 37; TCLC 107**
See also AMW; CA 9-12R; 167; CANR 21, 81; CN 7; DLB 2, 206, 218; DLBY 1981; EWL 3; MTCW 1, 2; RGAL 4; TCWW 2

Morrison, Arthur 1863-1945 .... **SSC 40; TCLC 72**
See also CA 120; 157; CMW 4; DLB 70, 135, 197; RGEL 2

Morrison, James Douglas 1943-1971
See Morrison, Jim
See also CA 73-76; CANR 40

Morrison, Jim .... **CLC 17**
See Morrison, James Douglas

Morrison, Toni 1931- ..... **BLC 3; CLC 4, 10, 22, 55, 81, 87, 173**
See also AAYA 1, 22; AFAW 1, 2; AMWC 1; AMWS 3; BPFB 2; BW 2, 3; CA 29-32R; CANR 27, 42, 67, 113; CDALB 1968-1988; CN 7; CPW; DA; DA3; DAB; DAC; DAM MST, MULT, NOV, POP; DLB 6, 33, 143; DLBY 1981; EWL 3; EXPN; FW; LAIT 2, 4; LATS 1; LMFS 2; MAWW; MTCW 1, 2; NFS 1, 6, 8, 14; RGAL 4; RHW; SATA 57, 144; SSFS 5; TUS; YAW

Morrison, Van 1945- .... **CLC 21**
See also CA 116; 168

Morrissy, Mary 1957- .... **CLC 99**
See also CA 205; DLB 267

Mortimer, John (Clifford) 1923- ..... **CLC 28, 43**
See also CA 13-16R; CANR 21, 69, 109; CD 5; CDBLB 1960 to Present; CMW 4; CN 7; CPW; DA3; DAM DRAM, POP; DLB 13, 245, 271; INT CANR-21; MSW; MTCW 1, 2; RGEL 2

Mortimer, Penelope (Ruth)
1918-1999 .... **CLC 5**
See also CA 57-60; 187; CANR 45, 88; CN 7

Mortimer, Sir John
See Mortimer, John (Clifford)

Morton, Anthony
See Creasey, John

Morton, Thomas 1579(?)-1647(?) .... **LC 72**
See also DLB 24; RGEL 2

Mosca, Gaetano 1858-1941 .... **TCLC 75**

Moses, Daniel David 1952- .... **NNAL**
See also CA 186

Mosher, Howard Frank 1943- .... **CLC 62**
See also CA 139; CANR 65, 115

Mosley, Nicholas 1923- .... **CLC 43, 70**
See also CA 69-72; CANR 41, 60, 108; CN 7; DLB 14, 207

Mosley, Walter 1952- .... **BLCS; CLC 97**
See also AAYA 17; AMWS 13; BPFB 2; BW 2; CA 142; CANR 57, 92; CMW 4; CPW; DA3; DAM MULT, POP; MSW; MTCW 2

Moss, Howard 1922-1987 . **CLC 7, 14, 45, 50**
See also CA 1-4R; 123; CANR 1, 44; DAM POET; DLB 5

Mossgiel, Rab
See Burns, Robert

Motion, Andrew (Peter) 1952- .... **CLC 47**
See also BRWS 7; CA 146; CANR 90; CP 7; DLB 40

Motley, Willard (Francis)
1909-1965 .... **CLC 18**
See also BW 1; CA 117; 106; CANR 88; DLB 76, 143

Motoori, Norinaga 1730-1801 .... **NCLC 45**

Mott, Michael (Charles Alston)
1930- .... **CLC 15, 34**
See also CA 5-8R; CAAS 7; CANR 7, 29

Mountain Wolf Woman 1884-1960 . **CLC 92; NNAL**
See also CA 144; CANR 90

Moure, Erin 1955- .... **CLC 88**
See also CA 113; CP 7; CWP; DLB 60

Mourning Dove 1885(?)-1936 .... **NNAL**
See also CA 144; CANR 90; DAM MULT; DLB 175, 221

Mowat, Farley (McGill) 1921- .... **CLC 26**
See also AAYA 1, 50; BYA 2; CA 1-4R; CANR 4, 24, 42, 68, 108; CLR 20; CPW; DAC; DAM MST; DLB 68; INT CANR-24; JRDA; MAICYA 1, 2; MTCW 1, 2; SATA 3, 55; YAW

Mowatt, Anna Cora 1819-1870 ..... **NCLC 74**
See also RGAL 4

Moyers, Bill 1934- .... **CLC 74**
See also AITN 2; CA 61-64; CANR 31, 52

Mphahlele, Es'kia
See Mphahlele, Ezekiel
See also AFW; CDWLB 3; DLB 125, 225; RGSF 2; SSFS 11

Mphahlele, Ezekiel 1919- ... **BLC 3; CLC 25, 133**
See Mphahlele, Es'kia
See also BW 2, 3; CA 81-84; CANR 26, 76; CN 7; DA3; DAM MULT; EWL 3; MTCW 2; SATA 119

Mqhayi, S(amuel) E(dward) K(rune Loliwe)
1875-1945 .... **BLC 3; TCLC 25**
See also CA 153; CANR 87; DAM MULT

Mrozek, Slawomir 1930- .... **CLC 3, 13**
See also CA 13-16R; CAAS 10; CANR 29; CDWLB 4; CWW 2; DLB 232; EWL 3; MTCW 1

Mrs. Belloc-Lowndes
See Lowndes, Marie Adelaide (Belloc)

Mrs. Fairstar
See Horne, Richard Henry Hengist

M'Taggart, John M'Taggart Ellis
See McTaggart, John McTaggart Ellis

Mtwa, Percy (?)- .... **CLC 47**

Mueller, Lisel 1924- .... **CLC 13, 51; PC 33**
See also CA 93-96; CP 7; DLB 105; PFS 9, 13

Muggeridge, Malcolm (Thomas)
1903-1990 .... **TCLC 120**
See also AITN 1; CA 101; CANR 33, 63; MTCW 1, 2

Muhammad 570-632 .... **WLCS**
See also DA; DAB; DAC; DAM MST

Muir, Edwin 1887-1959 . **PC 49; TCLC 2, 87**
See Moore, Edward
See also BRWS 6; CA 104; 193; DLB 20, 100, 191; EWL 3; RGEL 2

Muir, John 1838-1914 .... **TCLC 28**
See also AMWS 9; ANW; CA 165; DLB 186, 275

Mujica Lainez, Manuel 1910-1984 ... **CLC 31**
See Lainez, Manuel Mujica
See also CA 81-84; 112; CANR 32; EWL 3; HW 1

Mukherjee, Bharati 1940- ..... **AAL; CLC 53, 115; SSC 38**
See also AAYA 46; BEST 89:2; CA 107; CANR 45, 72; CN 7; DAM NOV; DLB 60, 218; DNFS 1, 2; EWL 3; FW; MTCW 1, 2; RGAL 4; RGSF 2; SSFS 7; TUS

Muldoon, Paul 1951- .... **CLC 32, 72, 166**
See also BRWS 4; CA 113; 129; CANR 52, 91; CP 7; DAM POET; DLB 40; INT 129; PFS 7

Mulisch, Harry 1927- .... **CLC 42**
See also CA 9-12R; CANR 6, 26, 56, 110; EWL 3

Mull, Martin 1943- .... **CLC 17**
See also CA 105

Muller, Wilhelm .... **NCLC 73**

Mulock, Dinah Maria
See Craik, Dinah Maria (Mulock)
See also RGEL 2

Munday, Anthony 1560-1633 .... **LC 87**
See also DLB 62, 172; RGEL 2

Munford, Robert 1737(?)-1783 .... **LC 5**
See also DLB 31

Mungo, Raymond 1946- .... **CLC 72**
See also CA 49-52; CANR 2

Munro, Alice 1931- .... **CLC 6, 10, 19, 50, 95; SSC 3; WLCS**
See also AITN 2; BPFB 2; CA 33-36R; CANR 33, 53, 75, 114; CCA 1; DA3; DAC; DAM MST, NOV; DLB 53; EWL 3; MTCW 1, 2; RGEL 2; RGSF 2; SATA 29; SSFS 5, 13

Munro, H(ector) H(ugh) 1870-1916 .... **WLC**
See Saki
See also AAYA 53; CA 104; 130; CANR 104; CDBLB 1890-1914; DA; DA3; DAB; DAC; DAM MST, NOV; DLB 34, 162; EXPS; MTCW 1, 2; RGEL 2; SSFS 15

Murakami, Haruki 1949- .... **CLC 150**
See Murakami Haruki
See also CA 165; CANR 102; MJW; RGWL 3; SFW 4

Murakami Haruki
See Murakami, Haruki
See also DLB 182; EWL 3

Murasaki, Lady
See Murasaki Shikibu

Murasaki Shikibu 978(?)-1026(?) ... **CMLC 1**
See also EFS 2; LATS 1; RGWL 2, 3

Murdoch, (Jean) Iris 1919-1999 ... **CLC 1, 2, 3, 4, 6, 8, 11, 15, 22, 31, 51**
See also BRWS 1; CA 13-16R; 179; CANR 8, 43, 68, 103; CDBLB 1960 to Present; CN 7; CWD; DA3; DAB; DAC; DAM MST, NOV; DLB 14, 194, 233; EWL 3; INT CANR-8; MTCW 1, 2; NFS 18; RGEL 2; TEA; WLIT 4

Murfree, Mary Noailles 1850-1922 .. **SSC 22; TCLC 135**
See also CA 122; 176; DLB 12, 74; RGAL 4

Murnau, Friedrich Wilhelm
See Plumpe, Friedrich Wilhelm

Murphy, Richard 1927- .... **CLC 41**
See also BRWS 5; CA 29-32R; CP 7; DLB 40; EWL 3

Murphy, Sylvia 1937- .... **CLC 34**
See also CA 121

Murphy, Thomas (Bernard) 1935- ... **CLC 51**
See also CA 101

Murray, Albert L. 1916- .... **CLC 73**
See also BW 2; CA 49-52; CANR 26, 52, 78; CSW; DLB 38

Murray, James Augustus Henry
1837-1915 .... **TCLC 117**

Murray, Judith Sargent
1751-1820 .... **NCLC 63**
See also DLB 37, 200

Murray, Les(lie Allan) 1938- .... **CLC 40**
See also BRWS 7; CA 21-24R; CANR 11, 27, 56, 103; CP 7; DAM POET; DLB 289; DLBY 2001; EWL 3; RGEL 2

Murry, J. Middleton
See Murry, John Middleton

Murry, John Middleton
1889-1957 .... **TCLC 16**
See also CA 118; DLB 149

Musgrave, Susan 1951- .... **CLC 13, 54**
See also CA 69-72; CANR 45, 84; CCA 1; CP 7; CWP

Musil, Robert (Edler von)
1880-1942 .... **SSC 18; TCLC 12, 68**
See also CA 109; CANR 55, 84; CDWLB 2; DLB 81, 124; EW 9; EWL 3; MTCW 2; RGSF 2; RGWL 2, 3

Muske, Carol .... **CLC 90**
See Muske-Dukes, Carol (Anne)

Muske-Dukes, Carol (Anne) 1945-
See Muske, Carol
See also CA 65-68; CAAE 203; CANR 32, 70; CWP

Musset, (Louis Charles) Alfred de
1810-1857 .... **NCLC 7**
See also DLB 192, 217; EW 6; GFL 1789 to the Present; RGWL 2, 3; TWA

Mussolini, Benito (Amilcare Andrea)
1883-1945 .... **TCLC 96**
See also CA 116

My Brother's Brother
See Chekhov, Anton (Pavlovich)

Myers, L(eopold) H(amilton)
1881-1944 .... **TCLC 59**
See also CA 157; DLB 15; EWL 3; RGEL 2

Myers, Walter Dean 1937- .. **BLC 3; CLC 35**
See also AAYA 4, 23; BW 2; BYA 6, 8, 11; CA 33-36R; CANR 20, 42, 67, 108; CLR 4, 16, 35; DAM MULT, NOV; DLB 33; INT CANR-20; JRDA; LAIT 5; MAICYA 1, 2; MAICYAS 1; MTCW 2; SAAS 2; SATA 41, 71, 109; SATA-Brief 27; WYA; YAW

Myers, Walter M.
See Myers, Walter Dean

Myles, Symon
See Follett, Ken(neth Martin)

Nabokov, Vladimir (Vladimirovich)
1899-1977 .... **CLC 1, 2, 3, 6, 8, 11, 15, 23, 44, 46, 64; SSC 11; TCLC 108; WLC**
See also AAYA 45; AMW; AMWC 1; AMWR 1; BPFB 2; CA 5-8R; 69-72; CANR 20, 102; CDALB 1941-1968; DA; DA3; DAB; DAC; DAM MST, NOV; DLB 2, 244, 278; DLBD 3; DLBY 1980, 1991; EWL 3; EXPS; LATS 1; MTCW 1, 2; NCFS 4; NFS 9; RGAL 4; RGSF 2; SSFS 6, 15; TUS

Naevius c. 265B.C.-201B.C. .... **CMLC 37**
See also DLB 211

Nagai, Kafu .... **TCLC 51**
See Nagai, Sokichi
See also DLB 180

Nagai, Sokichi 1879-1959
See Nagai, Kafu
See also CA 117

Nagy, Laszlo 1925-1978 .... **CLC 7**
See also CA 129; 112

Naidu, Sarojini 1879-1949 .... **TCLC 80**
See also EWL 3; RGEL 2

Naipaul, Shiva(dhar Srinivasa)
1945-1985 .... **CLC 32, 39**
See also CA 110; 112; 116; CANR 33; DA3; DAM NOV; DLB 157; DLBY 1985; EWL 3; MTCW 1, 2

Naipaul, V(idiadhar) S(urajprasad)
1932- .... **CLC 4, 7, 9, 13, 18, 37, 105; SSC 38**
See also BPFB 2; BRWS 1; CA 1-4R; CANR 1, 33, 51, 91; CDBLB 1960 to Present; CDWLB 3; CN 7; DA3; DAB; DAC; DAM MST, NOV; DLB 125, 204, 207; DLBY 1985, 2001; EWL 3; LATS 1; MTCW 1, 2; RGEL 2; RGSF 2; TWA; WLIT 4

Nakos, Lilika 1899(?)- .... **CLC 29**

Napoleon
See Yamamoto, Hisaye

Narayan, R(asipuram) K(rishnaswami)
1906-2001 . **CLC 7, 28, 47, 121; SSC 25**
See also BPFB 2; CA 81-84; 196; CANR 33, 61, 112; CN 7; DA3; DAM NOV; DNFS 1; EWL 3; MTCW 1, 2; RGEL 2; RGSF 2; SATA 62; SSFS 5

Nash, (Frediric) Ogden 1902-1971 . **CLC 23; PC 21; TCLC 109**
See also CA 13-14; 29-32R; CANR 34, 61; CAP 1; DAM POET; DLB 11; MAICYA 1, 2; MTCW 1, 2; RGAL 4; SATA 2, 46; WP

Nashe, Thomas 1567-1601(?) .... **LC 41, 89**
See also DLB 167; RGEL 2

Nathan, Daniel
See Dannay, Frederic

Nathan, George Jean 1882-1958 .... **TCLC 18**
See Hatteras, Owen
See also CA 114; 169; DLB 137

Natsume, Kinnosuke
See Natsume, Soseki

Natsume, Soseki 1867-1916 .... **TCLC 2, 10**
See Natsume Soseki; Soseki
See also CA 104; 195; RGWL 2, 3; TWA

Natsume Soseki
See Natsume, Soseki
See also DLB 180; EWL 3

Natti, (Mary) Lee 1919-
See Kingman, Lee
See also CA 5-8R; CANR 2

Navarre, Marguerite de
See de Navarre, Marguerite

Naylor, Gloria 1950- ..... **BLC 3; CLC 28, 52, 156; WLCS**
See also AAYA 6, 39; AFAW 1, 2; AMWS 8; BW 2, 3; CA 107; CANR 27, 51, 74; CN 7; CPW; DA; DA3; DAC; DAM MST, MULT, NOV, POP; DLB 173; EWL 3; FW; MTCW 1, 2; NFS 4, 7; RGAL 4; TUS

Neff, Debra .... **CLC 59**

Neihardt, John Gneisenau
1881-1973 .... **CLC 32**
See also CA 13-14; CANR 65; CAP 1; DLB 9, 54, 256; LAIT 2

Nekrasov, Nikolai Alekseevich
1821-1878 .... **NCLC 11**
See also DLB 277

Nelligan, Emile 1879-1941 .... **TCLC 14**
See also CA 114; 204; DLB 92; EWL 3

Nelson, Willie 1933- .... **CLC 17**
See also CA 107; CANR 114

Nemerov, Howard (Stanley)
1920-1991 .... **CLC 2, 6, 9, 36; PC 24; TCLC 124**
See also AMW; CA 1-4R; 134; CABS 2; CANR 1, 27, 53; DAM POET; DLB 5, 6; DLBY 1983; EWL 3; INT CANR-27; MTCW 1, 2; PFS 10, 14; RGAL 4

Neruda, Pablo 1904-1973 .. **CLC 1, 2, 5, 7, 9, 28, 62; HLC 2; PC 4; WLC**
See also CA 19-20; 45-48; CAP 2; DA; DA3; DAB; DAC; DAM MST, MULT, POET; DLB 283; DNFS 2; EWL 3; HW 1; LAW; MTCW 1, 2; PFS 11; RGWL 2, 3; TWA; WLIT 1; WP

Nerval, Gerard de 1808-1855 ... **NCLC 1, 67; PC 13; SSC 18**
See also DLB 217; EW 6; GFL 1789 to the Present; RGSF 2; RGWL 2, 3

Nervo, (Jose) Amado (Ruiz de)
1870-1919 .... **HLCS 2; TCLC 11**
See also CA 109; 131; EWL 3; HW 1; LAW

Nesbit, Malcolm
See Chester, Alfred

Nessi, Pio Baroja y
See Baroja (y Nessi), Pio

Nestroy, Johann 1801-1862 .... **NCLC 42**
See also DLB 133; RGWL 2, 3

Netterville, Luke
See O'Grady, Standish (James)

Neufeld, John (Arthur) 1938- .... **CLC 17**
See also AAYA 11; CA 25-28R; CANR 11, 37, 56; CLR 52; MAICYA 1, 2; SAAS 3; SATA 6, 81; SATA-Essay 131; YAW

Neumann, Alfred 1895-1952 .... **TCLC 100**
See also CA 183; DLB 56

Neumann, Ferenc
See Molnar, Ferenc

Neville, Emily Cheney 1919- .... **CLC 12**
See also BYA 2; CA 5-8R; CANR 3, 37, 85; JRDA; MAICYA 1, 2; SAAS 2; SATA 1; YAW

Newbound, Bernard Slade 1930-
See Slade, Bernard
See also CA 81-84; CANR 49; CD 5; DAM DRAM

Newby, P(ercy) H(oward)
1918-1997 .... **CLC 2, 13**
See also CA 5-8R; 161; CANR 32, 67; CN 7; DAM NOV; DLB 15; MTCW 1; RGEL 2

Newcastle
See Cavendish, Margaret Lucas

Newlove, Donald 1928- .... **CLC 6**
See also CA 29-32R; CANR 25

Newlove, John (Herbert) 1938- .... **CLC 14**
See also CA 21-24R; CANR 9, 25; CP 7

Newman, Charles 1938- .... **CLC 2, 8**
See also CA 21-24R; CANR 84; CN 7

Newman, Edwin (Harold) 1919- ...... **CLC 14**
See also AITN 1; CA 69-72; CANR 5

Newman, John Henry 1801-1890 . **NCLC 38, 99**
See also BRWS 7; DLB 18, 32, 55; RGEL 2

Newton, (Sir) Isaac 1642-1727 ...... **LC 35, 53**
See also DLB 252

Newton, Suzanne 1936- .... **CLC 35**
See also BYA 7; CA 41-44R; CANR 14; JRDA; SATA 5, 77

New York Dept. of Ed. .... **CLC 70**

Nexo, Martin Andersen
1869-1954 .... **TCLC 43**
See also CA 202; DLB 214; EWL 3

Nezval, Vitezslav 1900-1958 .... **TCLC 44**
See also CA 123; CDWLB 4; DLB 215; EWL 3

Ng, Fae Myenne 1957(?)- .... **CLC 81**
See also CA 146

Ngema, Mbongeni 1955- .... **CLC 57**
See also BW 2; CA 143; CANR 84; CD 5

Ngugi, James T(hiong'o) .... **CLC 3, 7, 13**
See Ngugi wa Thiong'o

Ngugi wa Thiong'o
See Ngugi wa Thiong'o
See also DLB 125; EWL 3

Ngugi wa Thiong'o 1938- .... **BLC 3; CLC 36**
See Ngugi, James T(hiong'o); Ngugi wa Thiong'o
See also AFW; BRWS 8; BW 2; CA 81-84; CANR 27, 58; CDWLB 3; DAM MULT, NOV; DNFS 2; MTCW 1, 2; RGEL 2

Niatum, Duane 1938- .... **NNAL**
  See also CA 41-44R; CANR 21, 45, 83; DLB 175
Nichol, B(arrie) P(hillip) 1944-1988 . **CLC 18**
  See also CA 53-56; DLB 53; SATA 66
Nicholas of Cusa 1401-1464 .... **LC 80**
  See also DLB 115
Nichols, John (Treadwell) 1940- .... **CLC 38**
  See also AMWS 13; CA 9-12R; CAAE 190; CAAS 2; CANR 6, 70, 121; DLBY 1982; LATS 1; TCWW 2
Nichols, Leigh
  See Koontz, Dean R(ay)
Nichols, Peter (Richard) 1927- .... **CLC 5, 36, 65**
  See also CA 104; CANR 33, 86; CBD; CD 5; DLB 13, 245; MTCW 1
Nicholson, Linda ed. .... **CLC 65**
Ni Chuilleanain, Eilean 1942- .... **PC 34**
  See also CA 126; CANR 53, 83; CP 7; CWP; DLB 40
Nicolas, F. R. E.
  See Freeling, Nicolas
Niedecker, Lorine 1903-1970 ..... **CLC 10, 42; PC 42**
  See also CA 25-28; CAP 2; DAM POET; DLB 48
Nietzsche, Friedrich (Wilhelm) 1844-1900 .... **TCLC 10, 18, 55**
  See also CA 107; 121; CDWLB 2; DLB 129; EW 7; RGWL 2, 3; TWA
Nievo, Ippolito 1831-1861 .... **NCLC 22**
Nightingale, Anne Redmon 1943-
  See Redmon, Anne
  See also CA 103
Nightingale, Florence 1820-1910 ... **TCLC 85**
  See also CA 188; DLB 166
Nijo Yoshimoto 1320-1388 .... **CMLC 49**
  See also DLB 203
Nik. T. O.
  See Annensky, Innokenty (Fyodorovich)
Nin, Anais 1903-1977 ..... **CLC 1, 4, 8, 11, 14, 60, 127; SSC 10**
  See also AITN 2; AMWS 10; BPFB 2; CA 13-16R; 69-72; CANR 22, 53; DAM NOV, POP; DLB 2, 4, 152; EWL 3; GLL 2; MAWW; MTCW 1, 2; RGAL 4; RGSF 2
Nisbet, Robert A(lexander) 1913-1996 .... **TCLC 117**
  See also CA 25-28R; 153; CANR 17; INT CANR-17
Nishida, Kitaro 1870-1945 .... **TCLC 83**
Nishiwaki, Junzaburo
  See Nishiwaki, Junzaburo
  See also CA 194
Nishiwaki, Junzaburo 1894-1982 .... **PC 15**
  See Nishiwaki, Junzaburo; Nishiwaki Junzaburo
  See also CA 194; 107; MJW; RGWL 3
Nishiwaki Junzaburo
  See Nishiwaki, Junzaburo
  See also EWL 3
Nissenson, Hugh 1933- .... **CLC 4, 9**
  See also CA 17-20R; CANR 27, 108; CN 7; DLB 28
Nister, Der
  See Der Nister
  See also EWL 3
Niven, Larry .... **CLC 8**
  See Niven, Laurence Van Cott
  See also AAYA 27; BPFB 2; BYA 10; CAAE 207; DLB 8; SCFW 2
Niven, Laurence Van Cott 1938-
  See Niven, Larry
  See also CA 21-24R; CAAE 207; CAAS 12; CANR 14, 44, 66, 113; CPW; DAM POP; MTCW 1, 2; SATA 95; SFW 4

Nixon, Agnes Eckhardt 1927- .... **CLC 21**
  See also CA 110
Nizan, Paul 1905-1940 .... **TCLC 40**
  See also CA 161; DLB 72; EWL 3; GFL 1789 to the Present
Nkosi, Lewis 1936- .... **BLC 3; CLC 45**
  See also BW 1, 3; CA 65-68; CANR 27, 81; CBD; CD 5; DAM MULT; DLB 157, 225
Nodier, (Jean) Charles (Emmanuel) 1780-1844 .... **NCLC 19**
  See also DLB 119; GFL 1789 to the Present
Noguchi, Yone 1875-1947 .... **TCLC 80**
Nolan, Christopher 1965- .... **CLC 58**
  See also CA 111; CANR 88
Noon, Jeff 1957- .... **CLC 91**
  See also CA 148; CANR 83; DLB 267; SFW 4
Norden, Charles
  See Durrell, Lawrence (George)
Nordhoff, Charles Bernard 1887-1947 .... **TCLC 23**
  See also CA 108; 211; DLB 9; LAIT 1; RHW 1; SATA 23
Norfolk, Lawrence 1963- .... **CLC 76**
  See also CA 144; CANR 85; CN 7; DLB 267
Norman, Marsha 1947- .... **CLC 28; DC 8**
  See also CA 105; CABS 3; CAD; CANR 41; CD 5; CSW; CWD; DAM DRAM; DFS 2; DLB 266; DLBY 1984; FW
Normyx
  See Douglas, (George) Norman
Norris, (Benjamin) Frank(lin, Jr.) 1870-1902 .... **SSC 28; TCLC 24**
  See also AMW; AMWC 2; BPFB 2; CA 110; 160; CDALB 1865-1917; DLB 12, 71, 186; LMFS 2; NFS 12; RGAL 4; TCWW 2; TUS
Norris, Leslie 1921- .... **CLC 14**
  See also CA 11-12; CANR 14, 117; CAP 1; CP 7; DLB 27, 256
North, Andrew
  See Norton, Andre
North, Anthony
  See Koontz, Dean R(ay)
North, Captain George
  See Stevenson, Robert Louis (Balfour)
North, Captain George
  See Stevenson, Robert Louis (Balfour)
North, Milou
  See Erdrich, Louise
Northrup, B. A.
  See Hubbard, L(afayette) Ron(ald)
North Staffs
  See Hulme, T(homas) E(rnest)
Northup, Solomon 1808-1863 .... **NCLC 105**
Norton, Alice Mary
  See Norton, Andre
  See also MAICYA 1; SATA 1, 43
Norton, Andre 1912- .... **CLC 12**
  See Norton, Alice Mary
  See also AAYA 14; BPFB 2; BYA 4, 10, 12; CA 1-4R; CANR 68; CLR 50; DLB 8, 52; JRDA; MAICYA 2; MTCW 1; SATA 91; SUFW 1, 2; YAW
Norton, Caroline 1808-1877 .... **NCLC 47**
  See also DLB 21, 159, 199
Norway, Nevil Shute 1899-1960
  See Shute, Nevil
  See also CA 102; 93-96; CANR 85; MTCW 2
Norwid, Cyprian Kamil 1821-1883 .... **NCLC 17**
  See also RGWL 3
Nosille, Nabrah
  See Ellison, Harlan (Jay)
Nossack, Hans Erich 1901-1978 .... **CLC 6**
  See also CA 93-96; 85-88; DLB 69; EWL 3

Nostradamus 1503-1566 .... **LC 27**
Nosu, Chuji
  See Ozu, Yasujiro
Notenburg, Eleanora (Genrikhovna) von
  See Guro, Elena
Nova, Craig 1945- .... **CLC 7, 31**
  See also CA 45-48; CANR 2, 53
Novak, Joseph
  See Kosinski, Jerzy (Nikodem)
Novalis 1772-1801 .... **NCLC 13**
  See also CDWLB 2; DLB 90; EW 5; RGWL 2, 3
Novick, Peter 1934- .... **CLC 164**
  See also CA 188
Novis, Emile
  See Weil, Simone (Adolphine)
Nowlan, Alden (Albert) 1933-1983 ... **CLC 15**
  See also CA 9-12R; CANR 5; DAC; DAM MST; DLB 53; PFS 12
Noyes, Alfred 1880-1958 .... **PC 27; TCLC 7**
  See also CA 104; 188; DLB 20; EXPP; FANT; PFS 4; RGEL 2
Nugent, Richard Bruce 1906(?)-1987 ... **HR 3**
  See also BW 1; CA 125; DLB 51; GLL 2
Nunn, Kem .... **CLC 34**
  See also CA 159
Nwapa, Flora (Nwanzuruaha) 1931-1993 .... **BLCS; CLC 133**
  See also BW 2; CA 143; CANR 83; CDWLB 3; CWRI 5; DLB 125; EWL 3; WLIT 2
Nye, Robert 1939- .... **CLC 13, 42**
  See also CA 33-36R; CANR 29, 67, 107; CN 7; CP 7; CWRI 5; DAM NOV; DLB 14, 271; FANT; HGG; MTCW 1; RHW; SATA 6
Nyro, Laura 1947-1997 .... **CLC 17**
  See also CA 194
Oates, Joyce Carol 1938- .. **CLC 1, 2, 3, 6, 9, 11, 15, 19, 33, 52, 108, 134; SSC 6; WLC**
  See also AAYA 15, 52; AITN 1; AMWS 2; BEST 89:2; BPFB 2; BYA 11; CA 5-8R; CANR 25, 45, 74, 113, 113; CDALB 1968-1988; CN 7; CP 7; CPW; CWP; DA; DA3; DAB; DAC; DAM MST, NOV, POP; DLB 2, 5, 130; DLBY 1981; EWL 3; EXPS; FW; HGG; INT CANR-25; LAIT 4; MAWW; MTCW 1, 2; NFS 8; RGAL 4; RGSF 2; SSFS 17; SUFW 2; TUS
O'Brian, E. G.
  See Clarke, Arthur C(harles)
O'Brian, Patrick 1914-2000 .... **CLC 152**
  See also CA 144; 187; CANR 74; CPW; MTCW 2; RHW
O'Brien, Darcy 1939-1998 .... **CLC 11**
  See also CA 21-24R; 167; CANR 8, 59
O'Brien, Edna 1936- ...... **CLC 3, 5, 8, 13, 36, 65, 116; SSC 10**
  See also BRWS 5; CA 1-4R; CANR 6, 41, 65, 102; CDBLB 1960 to Present; CN 7; DA3; DAM NOV; DLB 14, 231; EWL 3; FW; MTCW 1, 2; RGSF 2; WLIT 4
O'Brien, Fitz-James 1828-1862 ...... **NCLC 21**
  See also DLB 74; RGAL 4; SUFW
O'Brien, Flann .... **CLC 1, 4, 5, 7, 10, 47**
  See O Nuallain, Brian
  See also BRWS 2; DLB 231; EWL 3; RGEL 2
O'Brien, Richard 1942- .... **CLC 17**
  See also CA 124
O'Brien, (William) Tim(othy) 1946- . **CLC 7, 19, 40, 103**
  See also AAYA 16; AMWS 5; CA 85-88; CANR 40, 58; CDALBS; CN 7; CPW; DA3; DAM POP; DLB 152; DLBD 9; DLBY 1980; MTCW 2; RGAL 4; SSFS 5, 15

Obstfelder, Sigbjoern 1866-1900 .... **TCLC 23**
See also CA 123

O'Casey, Sean 1880-1964 .... **CLC 1, 5, 9, 11, 15, 88; DC 12; WLCS**
See also BRW 7; CA 89-92; CANR 62; CBD; CDBLB 1914-1945; DA3; DAB; DAC; DAM DRAM, MST; DLB 10; EWL 3; MTCW 1, 2; RGEL 2; TEA; WLIT 4

O'Cathasaigh, Sean
See O'Casey, Sean

Occom, Samson 1723-1792 .... **LC 60; NNAL**
See also DLB 175

Ochs, Phil(ip David) 1940-1976 .... **CLC 17**
See also CA 185; 65-68

O'Connor, Edwin (Greene) 1918-1968 .... **CLC 14**
See also CA 93-96; 25-28R

O'Connor, (Mary) Flannery 1925-1964 .... **CLC 1, 2, 3, 6, 10, 13, 15, 21, 66, 104; SSC 1, 23, 61; TCLC 132; WLC**
See also AAYA 7; AMW; AMWR 2; BPFB 3; BYA 16; CA 1-4R; CANR 3, 41; CDALB 1941-1968; DA; DA3; DAB; DAC; DAM MST, NOV; DLB 2, 152; DLBD 12; DLBY 1980; EWL 3; EXPS; LAIT 5; MAWW; MTCW 1, 2; NFS 3; RGAL 4; RGSF 2; SSFS 2, 7, 10; TUS

O'Connor, Frank .... **CLC 23; SSC 5**
See O'Donovan, Michael Francis
See also DLB 162; EWL 3; RGSF 2; SSFS 5

O'Dell, Scott 1898-1989 .... **CLC 30**
See also AAYA 3, 44; BPFB 3; BYA 1, 2, 3, 5; CA 61-64; 129; CANR 12, 30, 112; CLR 1, 16; DLB 52; JRDA; MAICYA 1, 2; SATA 12, 60, 134; WYA; YAW

Odets, Clifford 1906-1963 ..... **CLC 2, 28, 98; DC 6**
See also AMWS 2; CA 85-88; CAD; CANR 62; DAM DRAM; DFS 3, 17; DLB 7, 26; EWL 3; MTCW 1, 2; RGAL 4; TUS

O'Doherty, Brian 1928- .... **CLC 76**
See also CA 105; CANR 108

O'Donnell, K. M.
See Malzberg, Barry N(athaniel)

O'Donnell, Lawrence
See Kuttner, Henry

O'Donovan, Michael Francis 1903-1966 .... **CLC 14**
See O'Connor, Frank
See also CA 93-96; CANR 84

Oe, Kenzaburo 1935- .. **CLC 10, 36, 86; SSC 20**
See Oe Kenzaburo
See also CA 97-100; CANR 36, 50, 74; CWW 2; DA3; DAM NOV; DLB 182; DLBY 1994; EWL 3; LATS 1; MJW; MTCW 1, 2; RGSF 2; RGWL 2, 3

Oe Kenzaburo
See Oe, Kenzaburo
See also EWL 3

O'Faolain, Julia 1932- .... **CLC 6, 19, 47, 108**
See also CA 81-84; CAAS 2; CANR 12, 61; CN 7; DLB 14, 231; FW; MTCW 1; RHW

O'Faolain, Sean 1900-1991 .... **CLC 1, 7, 14, 32, 70; SSC 13**
See also CA 61-64; 134; CANR 12, 66; DLB 15, 162; MTCW 1, 2; RGEL 2; RGSF 2

O'Flaherty, Liam 1896-1984 .... **CLC 5, 34; SSC 6**
See also CA 101; 113; CANR 35; DLB 36, 162; DLBY 1984; MTCW 1, 2; RGEL 2; RGSF 2; SSFS 5

Ogai
See Mori Ogai
See also MJW

Ogilvy, Gavin
See Barrie, J(ames) M(atthew)

O'Grady, Standish (James) 1846-1928 .... **TCLC 5**
See also CA 104; 157

O'Grady, Timothy 1951- .... **CLC 59**
See also CA 138

O'Hara, Frank 1926-1966 .... **CLC 2, 5, 13, 78; PC 45**
See also CA 9-12R; 25-28R; CANR 33; DA3; DAM POET; DLB 5, 16, 193; EWL 3; MTCW 1, 2; PFS 8; 12; RGAL 4; WP

O'Hara, John (Henry) 1905-1970 . **CLC 1, 2, 3, 6, 11, 42; SSC 15**
See also AMW; BPFB 3; CA 5-8R; 25-28R; CANR 31, 60; CDALB 1929-1941; DAM NOV; DLB 9, 86; DLBD 2; EWL 3; MTCW 1, 2; NFS 11; RGAL 4; RGSF 2

O Hehir, Diana 1922- .... **CLC 41**
See also CA 93-96

Ohiyesa
See Eastman, Charles A(lexander)

Okada, John 1923-1971 .... **AAL**
See also BYA 14; CA 212

Okigbo, Christopher (Ifenayichukwu) 1932-1967 .... **BLC 3; CLC 25, 84; PC 7**
See also AFW; BW 1, 3; CA 77-80; CANR 74; CDWLB 3; DAM MULT, POET; DLB 125; EWL 3; MTCW 1, 2; RGEL 2

Okri, Ben 1959- .... **CLC 87**
See also AFW; BRWS 5; BW 2, 3; CA 130; 138; CANR 65; CN 7; DLB 157, 231; EWL 3; INT CA-138; MTCW 2; RGSF 2; WLIT 2

Olds, Sharon 1942- .. **CLC 32, 39, 85; PC 22**
See also AMWS 10; CA 101; CANR 18, 41, 66, 98; CP 7; CPW; DAM POET; DLB 120; MTCW 2; PFS 17

Oldstyle, Jonathan
See Irving, Washington

Olesha, Iurii
See Olesha, Yuri (Karlovich)
See also RGWL 2

Olesha, Iurii Karlovich
See Olesha, Yuri (Karlovich)
See also DLB 272

Olesha, Yuri (Karlovich) 1899-1960 . **CLC 8; TCLC 136**
See Olesha, Iurii; Olesha, Iurii Karlovich; Olesha, Yury Karlovich
See also CA 85-88; EW 11; RGWL 3

Olesha, Yury Karlovich
See Olesha, Yuri (Karlovich)
See also EWL 3

Oliphant, Mrs.
See Oliphant, Margaret (Oliphant Wilson)
See also SUFW

Oliphant, Laurence 1829(?)-1888 .. **NCLC 47**
See also DLB 18, 166

Oliphant, Margaret (Oliphant Wilson) 1828-1897 .... **NCLC 11, 61; SSC 25**
See Oliphant, Mrs.
See also DLB 18, 159, 190; HGG; RGEL 2; RGSF 2

Oliver, Mary 1935- .... **CLC 19, 34, 98**
See also AMWS 7; CA 21-24R; CANR 9, 43, 84, 92; CP 7; CWP; DLB 5, 193; EWL 3; PFS 15

Olivier, Laurence (Kerr) 1907-1989 . **CLC 20**
See also CA 111; 150; 129

Olsen, Tillie 1912- ... **CLC 4, 13, 114; SSC 11**
See also AAYA 51; AMWS 13; BYA 11; CA 1-4R; CANR 1, 43, 74; CDALBS; CN 7; DA; DA3; DAB; DAC; DAM MST; DLB 28, 206; DLBY 1980; EWL 3; EXPS; FW; MTCW 1, 2; RGAL 4; RGSF 2; SSFS 1; TUS

Olson, Charles (John) 1910-1970 .. **CLC 1, 2, 5, 6, 9, 11, 29; PC 19**
See also AMWS 2; CA 13-16; 25-28R; CABS 2; CANR 35, 61; CAP 1; DAM POET; DLB 5, 16, 193; EWL 3; MTCW 1, 2; RGAL 4; WP

Olson, Toby 1937- .... **CLC 28**
See also CA 65-68; CANR 9, 31, 84; CP 7

Olyesha, Yuri
See Olesha, Yuri (Karlovich)

Olympiodorus of Thebes c. 375-c. 430 .... **CMLC 59**

Omar Khayyam
See Khayyam, Omar
See also RGWL 2, 3

Ondaatje, (Philip) Michael 1943- .... **CLC 14, 29, 51, 76, 180; PC 28**
See also CA 77-80; CANR 42, 74, 109; CN 7; CP 7; DA3; DAB; DAC; DAM MST; DLB 60; EWL 3; LATS 1; LMFS 2; MTCW 2; PFS 8; TWA

Oneal, Elizabeth 1934-
See Oneal, Zibby
See also CA 106; CANR 28, 84; MAICYA 1, 2; SATA 30, 82; YAW

Oneal, Zibby .... **CLC 30**
See Oneal, Elizabeth
See also AAYA 5, 41; BYA 13; CLR 13; JRDA; WYA

O'Neill, Eugene (Gladstone) 1888-1953 ... **DC 20; TCLC 1, 6, 27, 49; WLC**
See also AITN 1; AMW; AMWC 1; CA 110; 132; CAD; CDALB 1929-1941; DA; DA3; DAB; DAC; DAM DRAM, MST; DFS 2, 4, 5, 6, 9, 11, 12, 16; DLB 7; EWL 3; LAIT 3; LMFS 2; MTCW 1, 2; RGAL 4; TUS

Onetti, Juan Carlos 1909-1994 ... **CLC 7, 10; HLCS 2; SSC 23; TCLC 131**
See also CA 85-88; 145; CANR 32, 63; CDWLB 3; DAM MULT, NOV; DLB 113; EWL 3; HW 1, 2; LAW; MTCW 1, 2; RGSF 2

O Nuallain, Brian 1911-1966
See O'Brien, Flann
See also CA 21-22; 25-28R; CAP 2; DLB 231; FANT; TEA

Ophuls, Max 1902-1957 .... **TCLC 79**
See also CA 113

Opie, Amelia 1769-1853 .... **NCLC 65**
See also DLB 116, 159; RGEL 2

Oppen, George 1908-1984 ..... **CLC 7, 13, 34; PC 35; TCLC 107**
See also CA 13-16R; 113; CANR 8, 82; DLB 5, 165

Oppenheim, E(dward) Phillips 1866-1946 .... **TCLC 45**
See also CA 111; 202; CMW 4; DLB 70

Opuls, Max
See Ophuls, Max

Origen c. 185-c. 254 .... **CMLC 19**

Orlovitz, Gil 1918-1973 .... **CLC 22**
See also CA 77-80; 45-48; DLB 2, 5

Orris
See Ingelow, Jean

Ortega y Gasset, Jose 1883-1955 .... **HLC 2; TCLC 9**
See also CA 106; 130; DAM MULT; EW 9; EWL 3; HW 1, 2; MTCW 1, 2

Ortese, Anna Maria 1914-1998 .... **CLC 89**
See also DLB 177; EWL 3

Ortiz, Simon J(oseph) 1941- .... **CLC 45; NNAL; PC 17**
See also AMWS 4; CA 134; CANR 69, 118; CP 7; DAM MULT, POET; DLB 120, 175, 256; EXPP; PFS 4, 16; RGAL 4

Orton, Joe .... **CLC 4, 13, 43; DC 3**
See Orton, John Kingsley
See also BRWS 5; CBD; CDBLB 1960 to Present; DFS 3, 6; DLB 13; GLL 1; MTCW 2; RGEL 2; TEA; WLIT 4

Orton, John Kingsley 1933-1967
See Orton, Joe
See also CA 85-88; CANR 35, 66; DAM DRAM; MTCW 1, 2

Orwell, George . **TCLC 2, 6, 15, 31, 51, 128, 129; WLC**
See Blair, Eric (Arthur)
See also BPFB 3; BRW 7; BYA 5; CDBLB 1945-1960; CLR 68; DAB; DLB 15, 98, 195, 255; EWL 3; EXPN; LAIT 4, 5; LATS 1; NFS 3, 7; RGEL 2; SCFW 2; SFW 4; SSFS 4; TEA; WLIT 4; YAW

Osborne, David
See Silverberg, Robert

Osborne, George
See Silverberg, Robert

Osborne, John (James) 1929-1994 .... **CLC 1, 2, 5, 11, 45; WLC**
See also BRWS 1; CA 13-16R; 147; CANR 21, 56; CDBLB 1945-1960; DA; DAB; DAC; DAM DRAM, MST; DFS 4; DLB 13; EWL 3; MTCW 1, 2; RGEL 2

Osborne, Lawrence 1958- .... **CLC 50**
See also CA 189

Osbourne, Lloyd 1868-1947 .... **TCLC 93**

Oshima, Nagisa 1932- .... **CLC 20**
See also CA 116; 121; CANR 78

Oskison, John Milton 1874-1947 .... **NNAL; TCLC 35**
See also CA 144; CANR 84; DAM MULT; DLB 175

Ossian c. 3rd cent. - .... **CMLC 28**
See Macpherson, James

Ossoli, Sarah Margaret (Fuller) 1810-1850 .... **NCLC 5, 50**
See Fuller, Margaret; Fuller, Sarah Margaret
See also CDALB 1640-1865; FW; LMFS 1; SATA 25

Ostriker, Alicia (Suskin) 1937- .... **CLC 132**
See also CA 25-28R; CAAS 24; CANR 10, 30, 62, 99; CWP; DLB 120; EXPP

Ostrovsky, Aleksandr Nikolaevich
See Ostrovsky, Alexander
See also DLB 277

Ostrovsky, Alexander 1823-1886 .. **NCLC 30, 57**
See Ostrovsky, Aleksandr Nikolaevich

Otero, Blas de 1916-1979 .... **CLC 11**
See also CA 89-92; DLB 134; EWL 3

O'Trigger, Sir Lucius
See Horne, Richard Henry Hengist

Otto, Rudolf 1869-1937 .... **TCLC 85**

Otto, Whitney 1955- .... **CLC 70**
See also CA 140; CANR 120

Ouida .... **TCLC 43**
See De la Ramee, Marie Louise (Ouida)
See also DLB 18, 156; RGEL 2

Ouologuem, Yambo 1940- .... **CLC 146**
See also CA 111; 176

Ousmane, Sembene 1923- ... **BLC 3; CLC 66**
See Sembene, Ousmane
See also BW 1, 3; CA 117; 125; CANR 81; CWW 2; MTCW 1

Ovid 43B.C.-17 .... **CMLC 7; PC 2**
See also AW 2; CDWLB 1; DA3; DAM POET; DLB 211; RGWL 2, 3; WP

Owen, Hugh
See Faust, Frederick (Schiller)

Owen, Wilfred (Edward Salter) 1893-1918 ... **PC 19; TCLC 5, 27; WLC**
See also BRW 6; CA 104; 141; CDBLB 1914-1945; DA; DAB; DAC; DAM MST, POET; DLB 20; EWL 3; EXPP; MTCW 2; PFS 10; RGEL 2; WLIT 4

Owens, Louis (Dean) 1948-2002 .... **NNAL**
See also CA 137, 179; 207; CAAE 179; CAAS 24; CANR 71

Owens, Rochelle 1936- .... **CLC 8**
See also CA 17-20R; CAAS 2; CAD; CANR 39; CD 5; CP 7; CWD; CWP

Oz, Amos 1939- .... **CLC 5, 8, 11, 27, 33, 54**
See also CA 53-56; CANR 27, 47, 65, 113; CWW 2; DAM NOV; EWL 3; MTCW 1, 2; RGSF 2; RGWL 3

Ozick, Cynthia 1928- .... **CLC 3, 7, 28, 62, 155; SSC 15, 60**
See also AMWS 5; BEST 90:1; CA 17-20R; CANR 23, 58, 116; CN 7; CPW; DA3; DAM NOV, POP; DLB 28, 152; DLBY 1982; EWL 3; EXPS; INT CANR-23; MTCW 1, 2; RGAL 4; RGSF 2; SSFS 3, 12

Ozu, Yasujiro 1903-1963 .... **CLC 16**
See also CA 112

Pabst, G. W. 1885-1967 .... **TCLC 127**

Pacheco, C.
See Pessoa, Fernando (Antonio Nogueira)

Pacheco, Jose Emilio 1939- .... **HLC 2**
See also CA 111; 131; CANR 65; DAM MULT; EWL 3; HW 1, 2; RGSF 2

Pa Chin .... **CLC 18**
See Li Fei-kan
See also EWL 3

Pack, Robert 1929- .... **CLC 13**
See also CA 1-4R; CANR 3, 44, 82; CP 7; DLB 5; SATA 118

Padgett, Lewis
See Kuttner, Henry

Padilla (Lorenzo), Heberto 1932-2000 .... **CLC 38**
See also AITN 1; CA 123; 131; 189; EWL 3; HW 1

Page, James Patrick 1944-
See Page, Jimmy
See also CA 204

Page, Jimmy 1944- .... **CLC 12**
See Page, James Patrick

Page, Louise 1955- .... **CLC 40**
See also CA 140; CANR 76; CBD; CD 5; CWD; DLB 233

Page, P(atricia) K(athleen) 1916- .... **CLC 7, 18; PC 12**
See Cape, Judith
See also CA 53-56; CANR 4, 22, 65; CP 7; DAC; DAM MST; DLB 68; MTCW 1; RGEL 2

Page, Stanton
See Fuller, Henry Blake

Page, Stanton
See Fuller, Henry Blake

Page, Thomas Nelson 1853-1922 .... **SSC 23**
See also CA 118; 177; DLB 12, 78; DLBD 13; RGAL 4

Pagels, Elaine Hiesey 1943- .... **CLC 104**
See also CA 45-48; CANR 2, 24, 51; FW; NCFS 4

Paget, Violet 1856-1935
See Lee, Vernon
See also CA 104; 166; GLL 1; HGG

Paget-Lowe, Henry
See Lovecraft, H(oward) P(hillips)

Paglia, Camille (Anna) 1947- .... **CLC 68**
See also CA 140; CANR 72; CPW; FW; GLL 2; MTCW 2

Paige, Richard
See Koontz, Dean R(ay)

Paine, Thomas 1737-1809 .... **NCLC 62**
See also AMWS 1; CDALB 1640-1865; DLB 31, 43, 73, 158; LAIT 1; RGAL 4; RGEL 2; TUS

Pakenham, Antonia
See Fraser, Antonia (Pakenham)

Palamas, Costis
See Palamas, Kostes

Palamas, Kostes 1859-1943 .... **TCLC 5**
See Palamas, Kostis
See also CA 105; 190; RGWL 2, 3

Palamas, Kostis
See Palamas, Kostes
See also EWL 3

Palazzeschi, Aldo 1885-1974 .... **CLC 11**
See also CA 89-92; 53-56; DLB 114, 264; EWL 3

Pales Matos, Luis 1898-1959 .... **HLCS 2**
See Pales Matos, Luis
See also HW 1; LAW

Paley, Grace 1922- .. **CLC 4, 6, 37, 140; SSC 8**
See also AMWS 6; CA 25-28R; CANR 13, 46, 74, 118; CN 7; CPW; DA3; DAM POP; DLB 28, 218; EWL 3; EXPS; FW; INT CANR-13; MAWW; MTCW 1, 2; RGAL 4; RGSF 2; SSFS 3

Palin, Michael (Edward) 1943- .... **CLC 21**
See Monty Python
See also CA 107; CANR 35, 109; SATA 67

Palliser, Charles 1947- .... **CLC 65**
See also CA 136; CANR 76; CN 7

Palma, Ricardo 1833-1919 .... **TCLC 29**
See also CA 168; LAW

Pancake, Breece Dexter 1952-1979
See Pancake, Breece D'J
See also CA 123; 109

Pancake, Breece D'J .... **CLC 29; SSC 61**
See Pancake, Breece Dexter
See also DLB 130

Panchenko, Nikolai .... **CLC 59**

Pankhurst, Emmeline (Goulden) 1858-1928 .... **TCLC 100**
See also CA 116; FW

Panko, Rudy
See Gogol, Nikolai (Vasilyevich)

Papadiamantis, Alexandros 1851-1911 .... **TCLC 29**
See also CA 168; EWL 3

Papadiamantopoulos, Johannes 1856-1910
See Moreas, Jean
See also CA 117

Papini, Giovanni 1881-1956 .... **TCLC 22**
See also CA 121; 180; DLB 264

Paracelsus 1493-1541 .... **LC 14**
See also DLB 179

Parasol, Peter
See Stevens, Wallace

Pardo Bazan, Emilia 1851-1921 .... **SSC 30**
See also EWL 3; FW; RGSF 2; RGWL 2, 3

Pareto, Vilfredo 1848-1923 .... **TCLC 69**
See also CA 175

Paretsky, Sara 1947- .... **CLC 135**
See also AAYA 30; BEST 90:3; CA 125; 129; CANR 59, 95; CMW 4; CPW; DA3; DAM POP; INT CA-129; MSW; RGAL 4

Parfenie, Maria
See Codrescu, Andrei

Parini, Jay (Lee) 1948- .... **CLC 54, 133**
See also CA 97-100; CAAS 16; CANR 32, 87

Park, Jordan
See Kornbluth, C(yril) M.; Pohl, Frederick

Park, Robert E(zra) 1864-1944 ..... **TCLC 73**
See also CA 122; 165

Parker, Bert
See Ellison, Harlan (Jay)

Parker, Dorothy (Rothschild) 1893-1967 .. **CLC 15, 68; PC 28; SSC 2**
See also AMWS 9; CA 19-20; 25-28R; CAP 2; DA3; DAM POET; DLB 11, 45, 86; EXPP; FW; MAWW; MTCW 1, 2; PFS 18; RGAL 4; RGSF 2; TUS

Parker, Robert B(rown) 1932- .... **CLC 27**
See also AAYA 28; BEST 89:4; BPFB 3; CA 49-52; CANR 1, 26, 52, 89; CMW 4; CPW; DAM NOV, POP; INT CANR-26; MSW; MTCW 1

Parkin, Frank 1940- .... **CLC 43**
See also CA 147

Parkman, Francis, Jr. 1823-1893 .. **NCLC 12**
See also AMWS 2; DLB 1, 30, 183, 186, 235; RGAL 4

Parks, Gordon (Alexander Buchanan) 1912- .... **BLC 3; CLC 1, 16**
See also AAYA 36; AITN 2; BW 2, 3; CA 41-44R; CANR 26, 66; DA3; DAM MULT; DLB 33; MTCW 2; SATA 8, 108

Parks, Tim(othy Harold) 1954- ...... **CLC 147**
See also CA 126; 131; CANR 77; DLB 231; INT CA-131

Parmenides c. 515B.C.-c. 450B.C. .... **CMLC 22**
See also DLB 176

Parnell, Thomas 1679-1718 .... **LC 3**
See also DLB 95; RGEL 2

Parr, Catherine c. 1513(?)-1548 .... **LC 86**
See also DLB 136

Parra, Nicanor 1914- ... **CLC 2, 102; HLC 2; PC 39**
See also CA 85-88; CANR 32; CWW 2; DAM MULT; DLB 283; EWL 3; HW 1; LAW; MTCW 1

Parra Sanojo, Ana Teresa de la 1890-1936 .... **HLCS 2**
See de la Parra, (Ana) Teresa (Sonojo)
See also LAW

Parrish, Mary Frances
See Fisher, M(ary) F(rances) K(ennedy)

Parshchikov, Aleksei 1954- .... **CLC 59**
See Parshchikov, Aleksei Maksimovich

Parshchikov, Aleksei Maksimovich
See Parshchikov, Aleksei
See also DLB 285

Parson, Professor
See Coleridge, Samuel Taylor

Parson Lot
See Kingsley, Charles

Parton, Sara Payson Willis 1811-1872 .... **NCLC 86**
See also DLB 43, 74, 239

Partridge, Anthony
See Oppenheim, E(dward) Phillips

Pascal, Blaise 1623-1662 .... **LC 35**
See also DLB 268; EW 3; GFL Beginnings to 1789; RGWL 2, 3; TWA

Pascoli, Giovanni 1855-1912 .... **TCLC 45**
See also CA 170; EW 7; EWL 3

Pasolini, Pier Paolo 1922-1975 .. **CLC 20, 37, 106; PC 17**
See also CA 93-96; 61-64; CANR 63; DLB 128, 177; EWL 3; MTCW 1; RGWL 2, 3

Pasquini
See Silone, Ignazio

Pastan, Linda (Olenik) 1932- .... **CLC 27**
See also CA 61-64; CANR 18, 40, 61, 113; CP 7; CSW; CWP; DAM POET; DLB 5; PFS 8

Pasternak, Boris (Leonidovich) 1890-1960 ...... **CLC 7, 10, 18, 63; PC 6; SSC 31; WLC**
See also BPFB 3; CA 127; 116; DA; DA3; DAB; DAC; DAM MST, NOV, POET; EW 10; MTCW 1, 2; RGSF 2; RGWL 2, 3; TWA; WP

Patchen, Kenneth 1911-1972 .... **CLC 1, 2, 18**
See also BG 3; CA 1-4R; 33-36R; CANR 3, 35; DAM POET; DLB 16, 48; EWL 3; MTCW 1; RGAL 4

Pater, Walter (Horatio) 1839-1894 . **NCLC 7, 90**
See also BRW 5; CDBLB 1832-1890; DLB 57, 156; RGEL 2; TEA

Paterson, A(ndrew) B(arton) 1864-1941 .... **TCLC 32**
See also CA 155; DLB 230; RGEL 2; SATA 97

Paterson, Banjo
See Paterson, A(ndrew) B(arton)

Paterson, Katherine (Womeldorf) 1932- .... **CLC 12, 30**
See also AAYA 1, 31; BYA 1, 2, 7; CA 21-24R; CANR 28, 59, 111; CLR 7, 50; CWRI 5; DLB 52; JRDA; LAIT 4; MAICYA 1, 2; MAICYAS 1; MTCW 1; SATA 13, 53, 92, 133; WYA; YAW

Patmore, Coventry Kersey Dighton 1823-1896 .... **NCLC 9**
See also DLB 35, 98; RGEL 2; TEA

Paton, Alan (Stewart) 1903-1988 ...... **CLC 4, 10, 25, 55, 106; WLC**
See also AAYA 26; AFW; BPFB 3; BRWS 2; BYA 1; CA 13-16; 125; CANR 22; CAP 1; DA; DA3; DAB; DAC; DAM MST, NOV; DLB 225; DLBD 17; EWL 3; EXPN; LAIT 4; MTCW 1, 2; NFS 3, 12; RGEL 2; SATA 11; SATA-Obit 56; TWA; WLIT 2

Paton Walsh, Gillian 1937- .... **CLC 35**
See Paton Walsh, Jill; Walsh, Jill Paton
See also AAYA 11; CANR 38, 83; CLR 2, 65; DLB 161; JRDA; MAICYA 1, 2; SAAS 3; SATA 4, 72, 109; YAW

Paton Walsh, Jill
See Paton Walsh, Gillian
See also AAYA 47; BYA 1, 8

Patterson, (Horace) Orlando (Lloyd) 1940- .... **BLCS**
See also BW 1; CA 65-68; CANR 27, 84; CN 7

Patton, George S(mith), Jr. 1885-1945 .... **TCLC 79**
See also CA 189

Paulding, James Kirke 1778-1860 ... **NCLC 2**
See also DLB 3, 59, 74, 250; RGAL 4

Paulin, Thomas Neilson 1949-
See Paulin, Tom
See also CA 123; 128; CANR 98; CP 7

Paulin, Tom .... **CLC 37, 177**
See Paulin, Thomas Neilson
See also DLB 40

Pausanias c. 1st cent. - .... **CMLC 36**

Paustovsky, Konstantin (Georgievich) 1892-1968 .... **CLC 40**
See also CA 93-96; 25-28R; DLB 272; EWL 3

Pavese, Cesare 1908-1950 .... **PC 13; SSC 19; TCLC 3**
See also CA 104; 169; DLB 128, 177; EW 12; EWL 3; RGSF 2; RGWL 2, 3; TWA

Pavic, Milorad 1929- .... **CLC 60**
See also CA 136; CDWLB 4; CWW 2; DLB 181; EWL 3; RGWL 3

Pavlov, Ivan Petrovich 1849-1936 . **TCLC 91**
See also CA 118; 180

Payne, Alan
See Jakes, John (William)

Paz, Gil
See Lugones, Leopoldo

Paz, Octavio 1914-1998 . **CLC 3, 4, 6, 10, 19, 51, 65, 119; HLC 2; PC 1, 48; WLC**
See also AAYA 50; CA 73-76; 165; CANR 32, 65, 104; CWW 2; DA; DA3; DAB; DAC; DAM MST, MULT, POET; DLBY 1990, 1998; DNFS 1; EWL 3; HW 1, 2; LAW; LAWS 1; MTCW 1, 2; PFS 18; RGWL 2, 3; SSFS 13; TWA; WLIT 1

p'Bitek, Okot 1931-1982 ..... **BLC 3; CLC 96**
See also AFW; BW 2, 3; CA 124; 107; CANR 82; DAM MULT; DLB 125; EWL 3; MTCW 1, 2; RGEL 2; WLIT 2

Peacock, Molly 1947- .... **CLC 60**
See also CA 103; CAAS 21; CANR 52, 84; CP 7; CWP; DLB 120, 282

Peacock, Thomas Love 1785-1866 .... **NCLC 22**
See also BRW 4; DLB 96, 116; RGEL 2; RGSF 2

Peake, Mervyn 1911-1968 .... **CLC 7, 54**
See also CA 5-8R; 25-28R; CANR 3; DLB 15, 160, 255; FANT; MTCW 1; RGEL 2; SATA 23; SFW 4

Pearce, Philippa
See Christie, Philippa
See also CA 5-8R; CANR 4, 109; CWRI 5; FANT; MAICYA 2

Pearl, Eric
See Elman, Richard (Martin)

Pearson, T(homas) R(eid) 1956- .... **CLC 39**
See also CA 120; 130; CANR 97; CSW; INT 130

Peck, Dale 1967- .... **CLC 81**
See also CA 146; CANR 72; GLL 2

Peck, John (Frederick) 1941- .... **CLC 3**
See also CA 49-52; CANR 3, 100; CP 7

Peck, Richard (Wayne) 1934- .... **CLC 21**
See also AAYA 1, 24; BYA 1, 6, 8, 11; CA 85-88; CANR 19, 38; CLR 15; INT CANR-19; JRDA; MAICYA 1, 2; SAAS 2; SATA 18, 55, 97; SATA-Essay 110; WYA; YAW

Peck, Robert Newton 1928- .... **CLC 17**
See also AAYA 3, 43; BYA 1, 6; CA 81-84, 182; CAAE 182; CANR 31, 63; CLR 45; DA; DAC; DAM MST; JRDA; LAIT 3; MAICYA 1, 2; SAAS 1; SATA 21, 62, 111; SATA-Essay 108; WYA; YAW

Peckinpah, (David) Sam(uel) 1925-1984 .... **CLC 20**
See also CA 109; 114; CANR 82

Pedersen, Knut 1859-1952
See Hamsun, Knut
See also CA 104; 119; CANR 63; MTCW 1, 2

Peeslake, Gaffer
See Durrell, Lawrence (George)

Peguy, Charles (Pierre) 1873-1914 .... **TCLC 10**
See also CA 107; 193; DLB 258; EWL 3; GFL 1789 to the Present

Peirce, Charles Sanders 1839-1914 .... **TCLC 81**
See also CA 194; DLB 270

Pellicer, Carlos 1900(?)-1977 .... **HLCS 2**
See also CA 153; 69-72; EWL 3; HW 1

Pena, Ramon del Valle y
See Valle-Inclan, Ramon (Maria) del

Pendennis, Arthur Esquir
See Thackeray, William Makepeace

Penn, William 1644-1718 .... **LC 25**
See also DLB 24

PEPECE
See Prado (Calvo), Pedro

Pepys, Samuel 1633-1703 ... **LC 11, 58; WLC**
See also BRW 2; CDBLB 1660-1789; DA; DA3; DAB; DAC; DAM MST; DLB 101, 213; NCFS 4; RGEL 2; TEA; WLIT 3

Percy, Thomas 1729-1811 .... **NCLC 95**
See also DLB 104

Percy, Walker 1916-1990 .... **CLC 2, 3, 6, 8, 14, 18, 47, 65**
See also AMWS 3; BPFB 3; CA 1-4R; 131; CANR 1, 23, 64; CPW; CSW; DA3; DAM NOV, POP; DLB 2; DLBY 1980, 1990, 1998; EWL 3; MTCW 1, 2; RGAL 4; TUS

Percy, William Alexander
1885-1942 .... **TCLC 84**
See also CA 163; MTCW 2
Perec, Georges 1936-1982 .... **CLC 56, 116**
See also CA 141; DLB 83; EWL 3; GFL 1789 to the Present; RGWL 3
Pereda (y Sanchez de Porrua), Jose Maria de 1833-1906 .... **TCLC 16**
See also CA 117
Pereda y Porrua, Jose Maria de
See Pereda (y Sanchez de Porrua), Jose Maria de
Peregoy, George Weems
See Mencken, H(enry) L(ouis)
Perelman, S(idney) J(oseph)
1904-1979 .. **CLC 3, 5, 9, 15, 23, 44, 49; SSC 32**
See also AITN 1, 2; BPFB 3; CA 73-76; 89-92; CANR 18; DAM DRAM; DLB 11, 44; MTCW 1, 2; RGAL 4
Peret, Benjamin 1899-1959 .... **PC 33; TCLC 20**
See also CA 117; 186; GFL 1789 to the Present
Peretz, Isaac Leib 1851(?)-1915
See Peretz, Isaac Loeb
See also CA 201
Peretz, Isaac Loeb 1851(?)-1915 ...... **SSC 26; TCLC 16**
See Peretz, Isaac Leib
See also CA 109
Peretz, Yitzkhok Leibush
See Peretz, Isaac Loeb
Perez Galdos, Benito 1843-1920 ..... **HLCS 2; TCLC 27**
See Galdos, Benito Perez
See also CA 125; 153; EWL 3; HW 1; RGWL 2, 3
Peri Rossi, Cristina 1941- .. **CLC 156; HLCS 2**
See also CA 131; CANR 59, 81; DLB 145; EWL 3; HW 1, 2
Perlata
See Peret, Benjamin
Perloff, Marjorie G(abrielle)
1931- .... **CLC 137**
See also CA 57-60; CANR 7, 22, 49, 104
Perrault, Charles 1628-1703 ... **DC 12; LC 2, 56**
See also BYA 4; CLR 79; DLB 268; GFL Beginnings to 1789; MAICYA 1, 2; RGWL 2, 3; SATA 25; WCH
Perry, Anne 1938- .... **CLC 126**
See also CA 101; CANR 22, 50, 84; CMW 4; CN 7; CPW; DLB 276
Perry, Brighton
See Sherwood, Robert E(mmet)
Perse, St.-John
See Leger, (Marie-Rene Auguste) Alexis Saint-Leger
Perse, Saint-John
See Leger, (Marie-Rene Auguste) Alexis Saint-Leger
See also DLB 258; RGWL 3
Perutz, Leo(pold) 1882-1957 .... **TCLC 60**
See also CA 147; DLB 81
Peseenz, Tulio F.
See Lopez y Fuentes, Gregorio
Pesetsky, Bette 1932- .... **CLC 28**
See also CA 133; DLB 130
Peshkov, Alexei Maximovich 1868-1936
See Gorky, Maxim
See also CA 105; 141; CANR 83; DA; DAC; DAM DRAM, MST, NOV; MTCW 2
Pessoa, Fernando (Antonio Nogueira)
1888-1935 ..... **HLC 2; PC 20; TCLC 27**
See also CA 125; 183; DAM MULT; DLB 287; EW 10; EWL 3; RGWL 2, 3; WP

Peterkin, Julia Mood 1880-1961 ...... **CLC 31**
See also CA 102; DLB 9
Peters, Joan K(aren) 1945- .... **CLC 39**
See also CA 158; CANR 109
Peters, Robert L(ouis) 1924- .... **CLC 7**
See also CA 13-16R; CAAS 8; CP 7; DLB 105
Petofi, Sandor 1823-1849 .... **NCLC 21**
See also RGWL 2, 3
Petrakis, Harry Mark 1923- .... **CLC 3**
See also CA 9-12R; CANR 4, 30, 85; CN 7
Petrarch 1304-1374 .... **CMLC 20; PC 8**
See also DA3; DAM POET; EW 2; LMFS 1; RGWL 2, 3
Petronius c. 20-66 .... **CMLC 34**
See also AW 2; CDWLB 1; DLB 211; RGWL 2, 3
Petrov, Evgeny .... **TCLC 21**
See Kataev, Evgeny Petrovich
Petry, Ann (Lane) 1908-1997 .. **CLC 1, 7, 18; TCLC 112**
See also AFAW 1, 2; BPFB 3; BW 1, 3; BYA 2; CA 5-8R; 157; CAAS 6; CANR 4, 46; CLR 12; CN 7; DLB 76; EWL 3; JRDA; LAIT 1; MAICYA 1, 2; MAICYAS 1; MTCW 1; RGAL 4; SATA 5; SATA-Obit 94; TUS
Petursson, Hallgrimur 1614-1674 .... **LC 8**
Peychinovich
See Vazov, Ivan (Minchov)
Phaedrus c. 15B.C.-c. 50 .... **CMLC 25**
See also DLB 211
Phelps (Ward), Elizabeth Stuart
See Phelps, Elizabeth Stuart
See also FW
Phelps, Elizabeth Stuart
1844-1911 .... **TCLC 113**
See Phelps (Ward), Elizabeth Stuart
See also DLB 74
Philips, Katherine 1632-1664 . **LC 30; PC 40**
See also DLB 131; RGEL 2
Philipson, Morris H. 1926- .... **CLC 53**
See also CA 1-4R; CANR 4
Phillips, Caryl 1958- .... **BLCS; CLC 96**
See also BRWS 5; BW 2; CA 141; CANR 63, 104; CBD; CD 5; CN 7; DA3; DAM MULT; DLB 157; EWL 3; MTCW 2; WLIT 4
Phillips, David Graham
1867-1911 .... **TCLC 44**
See also CA 108; 176; DLB 9, 12; RGAL 4
Phillips, Jack
See Sandburg, Carl (August)
Phillips, Jayne Anne 1952- .... **CLC 15, 33, 139; SSC 16**
See also BPFB 3; CA 101; CANR 24, 50, 96; CN 7; CSW; DLBY 1980; INT CANR-24; MTCW 1, 2; RGAL 4; RGSF 2; SSFS 4
Phillips, Richard
See Dick, Philip K(indred)
Phillips, Robert (Schaeffer) 1938- .... **CLC 28**
See also CA 17-20R; CAAS 13; CANR 8; DLB 105
Phillips, Ward
See Lovecraft, H(oward) P(hillips)
Philostratus, Flavius c. 179-c.
244 .... **CMLC 62**
Piccolo, Lucio 1901-1969 .... **CLC 13**
See also CA 97-100; DLB 114; EWL 3
Pickthall, Marjorie L(owry) C(hristie)
1883-1922 .... **TCLC 21**
See also CA 107; DLB 92
Pico della Mirandola, Giovanni
1463-1494 .... **LC 15**
See also LMFS 1

Piercy, Marge 1936- .... **CLC 3, 6, 14, 18, 27, 62, 128; PC 29**
See also BPFB 3; CA 21-24R; CAAE 187; CAAS 1; CANR 13, 43, 66, 111; CN 7; CP 7; CWP; DLB 120, 227; EXPP; FW; MTCW 1, 2; PFS 9; SFW 4
Piers, Robert
See Anthony, Piers
Pieyre de Mandiargues, Andre 1909-1991
See Mandiargues, Andre Pieyre de
See also CA 103; 136; CANR 22, 82; EWL 3; GFL 1789 to the Present
Pilnyak, Boris 1894-1938 . **SSC 48; TCLC 23**
See Vogau, Boris Andreyevich
See also EWL 3
Pinchback, Eugene
See Toomer, Jean
Pincherle, Alberto 1907-1990 ...... **CLC 11, 18**
See Moravia, Alberto
See also CA 25-28R; 132; CANR 33, 63; DAM NOV; MTCW 1
Pinckney, Darryl 1953- .... **CLC 76**
See also BW 2, 3; CA 143; CANR 79
Pindar 518(?)B.C.-438(?)B.C. .... **CMLC 12; PC 19**
See also AW 1; CDWLB 1; DLB 176; RGWL 2
Pineda, Cecile 1942- .... **CLC 39**
See also CA 118; DLB 209
Pinero, Arthur Wing 1855-1934 .... **TCLC 32**
See also CA 110; 153; DAM DRAM; DLB 10; RGEL 2
Pinero, Miguel (Antonio Gomez)
1946-1988 .... **CLC 4, 55**
See also CA 61-64; 125; CAD; CANR 29, 90; DLB 266; HW 1
Pinget, Robert 1919-1997 .... **CLC 7, 13, 37**
See also CA 85-88; 160; CWW 2; DLB 83; EWL 3; GFL 1789 to the Present
Pink Floyd
See Barrett, (Roger) Syd; Gilmour, David; Mason, Nick; Waters, Roger; Wright, Rick
Pinkney, Edward 1802-1828 .... **NCLC 31**
See also DLB 248
Pinkwater, Daniel
See Pinkwater, Daniel Manus
Pinkwater, Daniel Manus 1941- .... **CLC 35**
See also AAYA 1, 46; BYA 9; CA 29-32R; CANR 12, 38, 89; CLR 4; CSW; FANT; JRDA; MAICYA 1, 2; SAAS 3; SATA 8, 46, 76, 114; SFW 4; YAW
Pinkwater, Manus
See Pinkwater, Daniel Manus
Pinsky, Robert 1940- .... **CLC 9, 19, 38, 94, 121; PC 27**
See also AMWS 6; CA 29-32R; CAAS 4; CANR 58, 97; CP 7; DA3; DAM POET; DLBY 1982, 1998; MTCW 2; PFS 18; RGAL 4
Pinta, Harold
See Pinter, Harold
Pinter, Harold 1930- .. **CLC 1, 3, 6, 9, 11, 15, 27, 58, 73; DC 15; WLC**
See also BRWR 1; BRWS 1; CA 5-8R; CANR 33, 65, 112; CBD; CD 5; CDBLB 1960 to Present; DA; DA3; DAB; DAC; DAM DRAM, MST; DFS 3, 5, 7, 14; DLB 13; EWL 3; IDFW 3, 4; LMFS 2; MTCW 1, 2; RGEL 2; TEA
Piozzi, Hester Lynch (Thrale)
1741-1821 .... **NCLC 57**
See also DLB 104, 142
Pirandello, Luigi 1867-1936 .. **DC 5; SSC 22; TCLC 4, 29; WLC**
See also CA 104; 153; CANR 103; DA; DA3; DAB; DAC; DAM DRAM, MST; DFS 4, 9; DLB 264; EW 8; EWL 3; MTCW 2; RGSF 2; RGWL 2, 3

Pirsig, Robert M(aynard) 1928- ... **CLC 4, 6, 73**
See also CA 53-56; CANR 42, 74; CPW 1; DA3; DAM POP; MTCW 1, 2; SATA 39

Pisarev, Dmitrii Ivanovich
See Pisarev, Dmitry Ivanovich
See also DLB 277

Pisarev, Dmitry Ivanovich 1840-1868 .... **NCLC 25**
See Pisarev, Dmitrii Ivanovich

Pix, Mary (Griffith) 1666-1709 .... **LC 8**
See also DLB 80

Pixerecourt, (Rene Charles) Guilbert de 1773-1844 .... **NCLC 39**
See also DLB 192; GFL 1789 to the Present

Plaatje, Sol(omon) T(shekisho) 1878-1932 .... **BLCS; TCLC 73**
See also BW 2, 3; CA 141; CANR 79; DLB 125, 225

Plaidy, Jean
See Hibbert, Eleanor Alice Burford

Planche, James Robinson 1796-1880 .... **NCLC 42**
See also RGEL 2

Plant, Robert 1948- .... **CLC 12**

Plante, David (Robert) 1940- . **CLC 7, 23, 38**
See also CA 37-40R; CANR 12, 36, 58, 82; CN 7; DAM NOV; DLBY 1983; INT CANR-12; MTCW 1

Plath, Sylvia 1932-1963 ..... **CLC 1, 2, 3, 5, 9, 11, 14, 17, 50, 51, 62, 111; PC 1, 37; WLC**
See also AAYA 13; AMWR 2; AMWS 1; BPFB 3; CA 19-20; CANR 34, 101; CAP 2; CDALB 1941-1968; DA; DA3; DAB; DAC; DAM MST, POET; DLB 5, 6, 152; EWL 3; EXPN; EXPP; FW; LAIT 4; MAWW; MTCW 1, 2; NFS 1; PAB; PFS 1, 15; RGAL 4; SATA 96; TUS; WP; YAW

Plato c. 428B.C.-347B.C. ... **CMLC 8; WLCS**
See also AW 1; CDWLB 1; DA; DA3; DAB; DAC; DAM MST; DLB 176; LAIT 1; LATS 1; RGWL 2, 3

Platonov, Andrei
See Klimentov, Andrei Platonovich

Platonov, Andrei Platonovich
See Klimentov, Andrei Platonovich
See also DLB 272

Platonov, Andrey Platonovich
See Klimentov, Andrei Platonovich
See also EWL 3

Platt, Kin 1911- .... **CLC 26**
See also AAYA 11; CA 17-20R; CANR 11; JRDA; SAAS 17; SATA 21, 86; WYA

Plautus c. 254B.C.-c. 184B.C. ...... **CMLC 24; DC 6**
See also AW 1; CDWLB 1; DLB 211; RGWL 2, 3

Plick et Plock
See Simenon, Georges (Jacques Christian)

Plieksans, Janis
See Rainis, Janis

Plimpton, George (Ames) 1927-2003 .... **CLC 36**
See also AITN 1; CA 21-24R; CANR 32, 70, 103; DLB 185, 241; MTCW 1, 2; SATA 10

Pliny the Elder c. 23-79 .... **CMLC 23**
See also DLB 211

Pliny the Younger c. 61-c. 112 ...... **CMLC 62**
See also AW 2; DLB 211

Plomer, William Charles Franklin 1903-1973 .... **CLC 4, 8**
See also AFW; CA 21-22; CANR 34; CAP 2; DLB 20, 162, 191, 225; EWL 3; MTCW 1; RGEL 2; RGSF 2; SATA 24

Plotinus 204-270 .... **CMLC 46**
See also CDWLB 1; DLB 176

Plowman, Piers
See Kavanagh, Patrick (Joseph)

Plum, J.
See Wodehouse, P(elham) G(renville)

Plumly, Stanley (Ross) 1939- .... **CLC 33**
See also CA 108; 110; CANR 97; CP 7; DLB 5, 193; INT 110

Plumpe, Friedrich Wilhelm 1888-1931 .... **TCLC 53**
See also CA 112

Plutarch c. 46-c. 120 .... **CMLC 60**
See also AW 2; CDWLB 1; DLB 176; RGWL 2, 3; TWA

Po Chu-i 772-846 .... **CMLC 24**

Poe, Edgar Allan 1809-1849 ..... **NCLC 1, 16, 55, 78, 94, 97, 117; PC 1; SSC 1, 22, 34, 35, 54; WLC**
See also AAYA 14; AMW; AMWC 1; AMWR 2; BPFB 3; BYA 5, 11; CDALB 1640-1865; CMW 4; DA; DA3; DAB; DAC; DAM MST, POET; DLB 3, 59, 73, 74, 248, 254; EXPP; EXPS; HGG; LAIT 2; LATS 1; LMFS 1; MSW; PAB; PFS 1, 3, 9; RGAL 4; RGSF 2; SATA 23; SCFW 2; SFW 4; SSFS 2, 4, 7, 8, 16; SUFW; TUS; WP; WYA

Poet of Titchfield Street, The
See Pound, Ezra (Weston Loomis)

Pohl, Frederik 1919- .... **CLC 18; SSC 25**
See also AAYA 24; CA 61-64; CAAE 188; CAAS 1; CANR 11, 37, 81; CN 7; DLB 8; INT CANR-11; MTCW 1, 2; SATA 24; SCFW 2; SFW 4

Poirier, Louis 1910-
See Gracq, Julien
See also CA 122; 126; CWW 2

Poitier, Sidney 1927- .... **CLC 26**
See also BW 1; CA 117; CANR 94

Pokagon, Simon 1830-1899 .... **NNAL**
See also DAM MULT

Polanski, Roman 1933- .... **CLC 16, 178**
See also CA 77-80

Poliakoff, Stephen 1952- .... **CLC 38**
See also CA 106; CANR 116; CBD; CD 5; DLB 13

Police, The
See Copeland, Stewart (Armstrong); Summers, Andrew James; Sumner, Gordon Matthew

Polidori, John William 1795-1821 . **NCLC 51**
See also DLB 116; HGG

Pollitt, Katha 1949- .... **CLC 28, 122**
See also CA 120; 122; CANR 66, 108; MTCW 1, 2

Pollock, (Mary) Sharon 1936- .... **CLC 50**
See also CA 141; CD 5; CWD; DAC; DAM DRAM, MST; DFS 3; DLB 60; FW

Pollock, Sharon 1936- .... **DC 20**

Polo, Marco 1254-1324 .... **CMLC 15**

Polonsky, Abraham (Lincoln) 1910-1999 .... **CLC 92**
See also CA 104; 187; DLB 26; INT 104

Polybius c. 200B.C.-c. 118B.C. ...... **CMLC 17**
See also AW 1; DLB 176; RGWL 2, 3

Pomerance, Bernard 1940- .... **CLC 13**
See also CA 101; CAD; CANR 49; CD 5; DAM DRAM; DFS 9; LAIT 2

Ponge, Francis 1899-1988 .... **CLC 6, 18**
See also CA 85-88; 126; CANR 40, 86; DAM POET; DLBY 2002; EWL 3; GFL 1789 to the Present; RGWL 2, 3

Poniatowska, Elena 1933- . **CLC 140; HLC 2**
See also CA 101; CANR 32, 66, 107; CDWLB 3; DAM MULT; DLB 113; EWL 3; HW 1, 2; LAWS 1; WLIT 1

Pontoppidan, Henrik 1857-1943 .... **TCLC 29**
See also CA 170

Poole, Josephine .... **CLC 17**
See Helyar, Jane Penelope Josephine
See also SAAS 2; SATA 5

Popa, Vasko 1922-1991 .... **CLC 19**
See also CA 112; 148; CDWLB 4; DLB 181; EWL 3; RGWL 2, 3

Pope, Alexander 1688-1744 ...... **LC 3, 58, 60, 64; PC 26; WLC**
See also BRW 3; BRWC 1; BRWR 1; CDBLB 1660-1789; DA; DA3; DAB; DAC; DAM MST, POET; DLB 95, 101, 213; EXPP; PAB; PFS 12; RGEL 2; WLIT 3; WP

Popov, Evgenii Anatol'evich
See Popov, Yevgeny
See also DLB 285

Popov, Yevgeny .... **CLC 59**
See Popov, Evgenii Anatol'evich

Poquelin, Jean-Baptiste
See Moliere

Porter, Connie (Rose) 1959(?)- .... **CLC 70**
See also BW 2, 3; CA 142; CANR 90, 109; SATA 81, 129

Porter, Gene(va Grace) Stratton .. **TCLC 21**
See Stratton-Porter, Gene(va Grace)
See also BPFB 3; CA 112; CWRI 5; RHW

Porter, Katherine Anne 1890-1980 ... **CLC 1, 3, 7, 10, 13, 15, 27, 101; SSC 4, 31, 43**
See also AAYA 42; AITN 2; AMW; BPFB 3; CA 1-4R; 101; CANR 1, 65; CDALBS; DA; DA3; DAB; DAC; DAM MST, NOV; DLB 4, 9, 102; DLBD 12; DLBY 1980; EWL 3; EXPS; LAIT 3; MAWW; MTCW 1, 2; NFS 14; RGAL 4; RGSF 2; SATA 39; SATA-Obit 23; SSFS 1, 8, 11, 16; TUS

Porter, Peter (Neville Frederick) 1929- .... **CLC 5, 13, 33**
See also CA 85-88; CP 7; DLB 40, 289

Porter, William Sydney 1862-1910
See Henry, O.
See also CA 104; 131; CDALB 1865-1917; DA; DA3; DAB; DAC; DAM MST; DLB 12, 78, 79; MTCW 1, 2; TUS; YABC 2

Portillo (y Pacheco), Jose Lopez
See Lopez Portillo (y Pacheco), Jose

Portillo Trambley, Estela 1927-1998 .. **HLC 2**
See Trambley, Estela Portillo
See also CANR 32; DAM MULT; DLB 209; HW 1

Posey, Alexander (Lawrence) 1873-1908 .... **NNAL**
See also CA 144; CANR 80; DAM MULT; DLB 175

Posse, Abel .... **CLC 70**

Post, Melville Davisson 1869-1930 .... **TCLC 39**
See also CA 110; 202; CMW 4

Potok, Chaim 1929-2002 ... **CLC 2, 7, 14, 26, 112**
See also AAYA 15, 50; AITN 1, 2; BPFB 3; BYA 1; CA 17-20R; 208; CANR 19, 35, 64, 98; CLR 92; CN 7; DA3; DAM NOV; DLB 28, 152; EXPN; INT CANR-19; LAIT 4; MTCW 1, 2; NFS 4; SATA 33, 106; SATA-Obit 134; TUS; YAW

Potok, Herbert Harold -2002
See Potok, Chaim

Potok, Herman Harold
See Potok, Chaim

Potter, Dennis (Christopher George) 1935-1994 .... **CLC 58, 86, 123**
See also CA 107; 145; CANR 33, 61; CBD; DLB 233; MTCW 1

Pound, Ezra (Weston Loomis) 1885-1972 .. **CLC 1, 2, 3, 4, 5, 7, 10, 13, 18, 34, 48, 50, 112; PC 4; WLC**
See also AAYA 47; AMW; AMWR 1; CA 5-8R; 37-40R; CANR 40; CDALB 1917-1929; DA; DA3; DAB; DAC; DAM MST,

POET; DLB 4, 45, 63; DLBD 15; EFS 2; EWL 3; EXPP; LMFS 2; MTCW 1, 2; PAB; PFS 2, 8, 16; RGAL 4; TUS; WP

Povod, Reinaldo 1959-1994 .... **CLC 44**
See also CA 136; 146; CANR 83

Powell, Adam Clayton, Jr.
1908-1972 .... **BLC 3; CLC 89**
See also BW 1, 3; CA 102; 33-36R; CANR 86; DAM MULT

Powell, Anthony (Dymoke)
1905-2000 .... **CLC 1, 3, 7, 9, 10, 31**
See also BRW 7; CA 1-4R; 189; CANR 1, 32, 62, 107; CDBLB 1945-1960; CN 7; DLB 15; EWL 3; MTCW 1, 2; RGEL 2; TEA

Powell, Dawn 1896(?)-1965 .... **CLC 66**
See also CA 5-8R; CANR 121; DLBY 1997

Powell, Padgett 1952- .... **CLC 34**
See also CA 126; CANR 63, 101; CSW; DLB 234; DLBY 01

Powell, (Oval) Talmage 1920-2000
See Queen, Ellery
See also CA 5-8R; CANR 2, 80

Power, Susan 1961- .... **CLC 91**
See also BYA 14; CA 160; NFS 11

Powers, J(ames) F(arl) 1917-1999 ..... **CLC 1, 4, 8, 57; SSC 4**
See also CA 1-4R; 181; CANR 2, 61; CN 7; DLB 130; MTCW 1; RGAL 4; RGSF 2

Powers, John J(ames) 1945-
See Powers, John R.
See also CA 69-72

Powers, John R. .... **CLC 66**
See Powers, John J(ames)

Powers, Richard (S.) 1957- .... **CLC 93**
See also AMWS 9; BPFB 3; CA 148; CANR 80; CN 7

Pownall, David 1938- .... **CLC 10**
See also CA 89-92, 180; CAAS 18; CANR 49, 101; CBD; CD 5; CN 7; DLB 14

Powys, John Cowper 1872-1963 ... **CLC 7, 9, 15, 46, 125**
See also CA 85-88; CANR 106; DLB 15, 255; EWL 3; FANT; MTCW 1, 2; RGEL 2; SUFW

Powys, T(heodore) F(rancis)
1875-1953 .... **TCLC 9**
See also BRWS 8; CA 106; 189; DLB 36, 162; EWL 3; FANT; RGEL 2; SUFW

Prado (Calvo), Pedro 1886-1952 ... **TCLC 75**
See also CA 131; DLB 283; HW 1; LAW

Prager, Emily 1952- .... **CLC 56**
See also CA 204

Pratolini, Vasco 1913-1991 .... **TCLC 124**
See also CA 211; DLB 177; EWL 3; RGWL 2, 3

Pratt, E(dwin) J(ohn) 1883(?)-1964 . **CLC 19**
See also CA 141; 93-96; CANR 77; DAC; DAM POET; DLB 92; EWL 3; RGEL 2; TWA

Premchand .... **TCLC 21**
See Srivastava, Dhanpat Rai
See also EWL 3

Preseren, France 1800-1849 .... **NCLC 127**
See also CDWLB 4; DLB 147

Preussler, Otfried 1923- .... **CLC 17**
See also CA 77-80; SATA 24

Prevert, Jacques (Henri Marie)
1900-1977 .... **CLC 15**
See also CA 77-80; 69-72; CANR 29, 61; DLB 258; EWL 3; GFL 1789 to the Present; IDFW 3, 4; MTCW 1; RGWL 2, 3; SATA-Obit 30

Prevost, (Antoine Francois)
1697-1763 .... **LC 1**
See also EW 4; GFL Beginnings to 1789; RGWL 2, 3

Price, (Edward) Reynolds 1933- ... **CLC 3, 6, 13, 43, 50, 63; SSC 22**
See also AMWS 6; CA 1-4R; CANR 1, 37, 57, 87; CN 7; CSW; DAM NOV; DLB 2, 218, 278; EWL 3; INT CANR-37; NFS 18

Price, Richard 1949- .... **CLC 6, 12**
See also CA 49-52; CANR 3; DLBY 1981

Prichard, Katharine Susannah
1883-1969 .... **CLC 46**
See also CA 11-12; CANR 33; CAP 1; DLB 260; MTCW 1; RGEL 2; RGSF 2; SATA 66

Priestley, J(ohn) B(oynton)
1894-1984 .... **CLC 2, 5, 9, 34**
See also BRW 7; CA 9-12R; 113; CANR 33; CDBLB 1914-1945; DA3; DAM DRAM, NOV; DLB 10, 34, 77, 100, 139; DLBY 1984; EWL 3; MTCW 1, 2; RGEL 2; SFW 4

Prince 1958- .... **CLC 35**
See also CA 213

Prince, F(rank) T(empleton) 1912- .. **CLC 22**
See also CA 101; CANR 43, 79; CP 7; DLB 20

Prince Kropotkin
See Kropotkin, Peter (Alekseevich)

Prior, Matthew 1664-1721 .... **LC 4**
See also DLB 95; RGEL 2

Prishvin, Mikhail 1873-1954 .... **TCLC 75**
See Prishvin, Mikhail Mikhailovich

Prishvin, Mikhail Mikhailovich
See Prishvin, Mikhail
See also DLB 272; EWL 3

Pritchard, William H(arrison)
1932- .... **CLC 34**
See also CA 65-68; CANR 23, 95; DLB 111

Pritchett, V(ictor) S(awdon)
1900-1997 ... **CLC 5, 13, 15, 41; SSC 14**
See also BPFB 3; BRWS 3; CA 61-64; 157; CANR 31, 63; CN 7; DA3; DAM NOV; DLB 15, 139; EWL 3; MTCW 1, 2; RGEL 2; RGSF 2; TEA

Private 19022
See Manning, Frederic

Probst, Mark 1925- .... **CLC 59**
See also CA 130

Prokosch, Frederic 1908-1989 ...... **CLC 4, 48**
See also CA 73-76; 128; CANR 82; DLB 48; MTCW 2

Propertius, Sextus c. 50B.C.-c. 16B.C. .... **CMLC 32**
See also AW 2; CDWLB 1; DLB 211; RGWL 2, 3

Prophet, The
See Dreiser, Theodore (Herman Albert)

Prose, Francine 1947- .... **CLC 45**
See also CA 109; 112; CANR 46, 95; DLB 234; SATA 101

Proudhon
See Cunha, Euclides (Rodrigues Pimenta) da

Proulx, Annie
See Proulx, E(dna) Annie

Proulx, E(dna) Annie 1935- ...... **CLC 81, 158**
See also AMWS 7; BPFB 3; CA 145; CANR 65, 110; CN 7; CPW 1; DA3; DAM POP; MTCW 2; SSFS 18

Proust, (Valentin-Louis-George-Eugene) Marcel 1871-1922 .... **TCLC 7, 13, 33; WLC**
See also BPFB 3; CA 104; 120; CANR 110; DA; DA3; DAB; DAC; DAM MST, NOV; DLB 65; EW 8; EWL 3; GFL 1789 to the Present; MTCW 1, 2; RGWL 2, 3; TWA

Prowler, Harley
See Masters, Edgar Lee

Prus, Boleslaw 1845-1912 .... **TCLC 48**
See also RGWL 2, 3

Pryor, Richard (Franklin Lenox Thomas)
1940- .... **CLC 26**
See also CA 122; 152

Przybyszewski, Stanislaw
1868-1927 .... **TCLC 36**
See also CA 160; DLB 66; EWL 3

Pteleon
See Grieve, C(hristopher) M(urray)
See also DAM POET

Puckett, Lute
See Masters, Edgar Lee

Puig, Manuel 1932-1990 .... **CLC 3, 5, 10, 28, 65, 133; HLC 2**
See also BPFB 3; CA 45-48; CANR 2, 32, 63; CDWLB 3; DA3; DAM MULT; DLB 113; DNFS 1; EWL 3; GLL 1; HW 1, 2; LAW; MTCW 1, 2; RGWL 2, 3; TWA; WLIT 1

Pulitzer, Joseph 1847-1911 .... **TCLC 76**
See also CA 114; DLB 23

Purchas, Samuel 1577(?)-1626 .... **LC 70**
See also DLB 151

Purdy, A(lfred) W(ellington)
1918-2000 .... **CLC 3, 6, 14, 50**
See also CA 81-84; 189; CAAS 17; CANR 42, 66; CP 7; DAC; DAM MST, POET; DLB 88; PFS 5; RGEL 2

Purdy, James (Amos) 1923- .... **CLC 2, 4, 10, 28, 52**
See also AMWS 7; CA 33-36R; CAAS 1; CANR 19, 51; CN 7; DLB 2, 218; EWL 3; INT CANR-19; MTCW 1; RGAL 4

Pure, Simon
See Swinnerton, Frank Arthur

Pushkin, Aleksandr Sergeevich
See Pushkin, Alexander (Sergeyevich)
See also DLB 205

Pushkin, Alexander (Sergeyevich)
1799-1837 .... **NCLC 3, 27, 83; PC 10; SSC 27, 55; WLC**
See Pushkin, Aleksandr Sergeevich
See also DA; DA3; DAB; DAC; DAM DRAM, MST, POET; EW 5; EXPS; RGSF 2; RGWL 2, 3; SATA 61; SSFS 9; TWA

P'u Sung-ling 1640-1715 .... **LC 49; SSC 31**

Putnam, Arthur Lee
See Alger, Horatio, Jr.

Puzo, Mario 1920-1999 .... **CLC 1, 2, 6, 36, 107**
See also BPFB 3; CA 65-68; 185; CANR 4, 42, 65, 99; CN 7; CPW; DA3; DAM NOV, POP; DLB 6; MTCW 1, 2; NFS 16; RGAL 4

Pygge, Edward
See Barnes, Julian (Patrick)

Pyle, Ernest Taylor 1900-1945
See Pyle, Ernie
See also CA 115; 160

Pyle, Ernie .... **TCLC 75**
See Pyle, Ernest Taylor
See also DLB 29; MTCW 2

Pyle, Howard 1853-1911 .... **TCLC 81**
See also BYA 2, 4; CA 109; 137; CLR 22; DLB 42, 188; DLBD 13; LAIT 1; MAICYA 1, 2; SATA 16, 100; WCH; YAW

Pym, Barbara (Mary Crampton)
1913-1980 .... **CLC 13, 19, 37, 111**
See also BPFB 3; BRWS 2; CA 13-14; 97-100; CANR 13, 34; CAP 1; DLB 14, 207; DLBY 1987; EWL 3; MTCW 1, 2; RGEL 2; TEA

Pynchon, Thomas (Ruggles, Jr.)
1937- .... **CLC 2, 3, 6, 9, 11, 18, 33, 62, 72, 123; SSC 14; WLC**
See also AMWS 2; BEST 90:2; BPFB 3; CA 17-20R; CANR 22, 46, 73; CN 7; CPW 1; DA; DA3; DAB; DAC; DAM MST, NOV, POP; DLB 2, 173; EWL 3; MTCW 1, 2; RGAL 4; SFW 4; TUS

Pythagoras c. 582B.C.-c. 507B.C. . **CMLC 22**
See also DLB 176

Q
See Quiller-Couch, Sir Arthur (Thomas)

Qian, Chongzhu
See Ch'ien, Chung-shu

Qian Zhongshu
See Ch'ien, Chung-shu

Qroll
See Dagerman, Stig (Halvard)

Quarrington, Paul (Lewis) 1953- ..... **CLC 65**
See also CA 129; CANR 62, 95

Quasimodo, Salvatore 1901-1968 .... **CLC 10; PC 47**
See also CA 13-16; 25-28R; CAP 1; DLB 114; EW 12; EWL 3; MTCW 1; RGWL 2, 3

Quatermass, Martin
See Carpenter, John (Howard)

Quay, Stephen 1947- .... **CLC 95**
See also CA 189

Quay, Timothy 1947- .... **CLC 95**
See also CA 189

Queen, Ellery .... **CLC 3, 11**
See Dannay, Frederic; Davidson, Avram (James); Deming, Richard; Fairman, Paul W.; Flora, Fletcher; Hoch, Edward D(entinger); Kane, Henry; Lee, Manfred B(ennington); Marlowe, Stephen; Powell, (Oval) Talmage; Sheldon, Walter J(ames); Sturgeon, Theodore (Hamilton); Tracy, Don(ald Fiske); Vance, John Holbrook
See also BPFB 3; CMW 4; MSW; RGAL 4

Queen, Ellery, Jr.
See Dannay, Frederic; Lee, Manfred B(ennington)

Queneau, Raymond 1903-1976 ..... **CLC 2, 5, 10, 42**
See also CA 77-80; 69-72; CANR 32; DLB 72, 258; EW 12; EWL 3; GFL 1789 to the Present; MTCW 1, 2; RGWL 2, 3

Quevedo, Francisco de 1580-1645 .... **LC 23**

Quiller-Couch, Sir Arthur (Thomas)
1863-1944 .... **TCLC 53**
See also CA 118; 166; DLB 135, 153, 190; HGG; RGEL 2; SUFW 1

Quin, Ann (Marie) 1936-1973 .... **CLC 6**
See also CA 9-12R; 45-48; DLB 14, 231

Quincey, Thomas de
See De Quincey, Thomas

Quinn, Martin
See Smith, Martin Cruz

Quinn, Peter 1947- .... **CLC 91**
See also CA 197

Quinn, Simon
See Smith, Martin Cruz

Quintana, Leroy V. 1944- .... **HLC 2; PC 36**
See also CA 131; CANR 65; DAM MULT; DLB 82; HW 1, 2

Quiroga, Horacio (Sylvestre)
1878-1937 .... **HLC 2; TCLC 20**
See also CA 117; 131; DAM MULT; EWL 3; HW 1; LAW; MTCW 1; RGSF 2; WLIT 1

Quoirez, Francoise 1935- .... **CLC 9**
See Sagan, Francoise
See also CA 49-52; CANR 6, 39, 73; CWW 2; MTCW 1, 2; TWA

Raabe, Wilhelm (Karl) 1831-1910 . **TCLC 45**
See also CA 167; DLB 129

Rabe, David (William) 1940- .. **CLC 4, 8, 33; DC 16**
See also CA 85-88; CABS 3; CAD; CANR 59; CD 5; DAM DRAM; DFS 3, 8, 13; DLB 7, 228; EWL 3

Rabelais, Francois 1494-1553 .... **LC 5, 60; WLC**
See also DA; DAB; DAC; DAM MST; EW 2; GFL Beginnings to 1789; LMFS 1; RGWL 2, 3; TWA

Rabinovitch, Sholem 1859-1916
See Aleichem, Sholom
See also CA 104

Rabinyan, Dorit 1972- .... **CLC 119**
See also CA 170

Rachilde
See Vallette, Marguerite Eymery; Vallette, Marguerite Eymery
See also EWL 3

Racine, Jean 1639-1699 .... **LC 28**
See also DA3; DAB; DAM MST; DLB 268; EW 3; GFL Beginnings to 1789; LMFS 1; RGWL 2, 3; TWA

Radcliffe, Ann (Ward) 1764-1823 ... **NCLC 6, 55, 106**
See also DLB 39, 178; HGG; LMFS 1; RGEL 2; SUFW; WLIT 3

Radclyffe-Hall, Marguerite
See Hall, (Marguerite) Radclyffe

Radiguet, Raymond 1903-1923 ...... **TCLC 29**
See also CA 162; DLB 65; EWL 3; GFL 1789 to the Present; RGWL 2, 3

Radnoti, Miklos 1909-1944 .... **TCLC 16**
See also CA 118; 212; CDWLB 4; DLB 215; EWL 3; RGWL 2, 3

Rado, James 1939- .... **CLC 17**
See also CA 105

Radvanyi, Netty 1900-1983
See Seghers, Anna
See also CA 85-88; 110; CANR 82

Rae, Ben
See Griffiths, Trevor

Raeburn, John (Hay) 1941- .... **CLC 34**
See also CA 57-60

Ragni, Gerome 1942-1991 .... **CLC 17**
See also CA 105; 134

Rahv, Philip .... **CLC 24**
See Greenberg, Ivan
See also DLB 137

Raimund, Ferdinand Jakob
1790-1836 .... **NCLC 69**
See also DLB 90

Raine, Craig (Anthony) 1944- .. **CLC 32, 103**
See also CA 108; CANR 29, 51, 103; CP 7; DLB 40; PFS 7

Raine, Kathleen (Jessie) 1908- ...... **CLC 7, 45**
See also CA 85-88; CANR 46, 109; CP 7; DLB 20; EWL 3; MTCW 1; RGEL 2

Rainis, Janis 1865-1929 .... **TCLC 29**
See also CA 170; CDWLB 4; DLB 220; EWL 3

Rakosi, Carl .... **CLC 47**
See Rawley, Callman
See also CAAS 5; CP 7; DLB 193

Ralegh, Sir Walter
See Raleigh, Sir Walter
See also BRW 1; RGEL 2; WP

Raleigh, Richard
See Lovecraft, H(oward) P(hillips)

Raleigh, Sir Walter 1554(?)-1618 .... **LC 31, 39; PC 31**
See Ralegh, Sir Walter
See also CDBLB Before 1660; DLB 172; EXPP; PFS 14; TEA

Rallentando, H. P.
See Sayers, Dorothy L(eigh)

Ramal, Walter
See de la Mare, Walter (John)

Ramana Maharshi 1879-1950 .... **TCLC 84**

Ramoacn y Cajal, Santiago
1852-1934 .... **TCLC 93**

Ramon, Juan
See Jimenez (Mantecon), Juan Ramon

Ramos, Graciliano 1892-1953 .... **TCLC 32**
See also CA 167; EWL 3; HW 2; LAW; WLIT 1

Rampersad, Arnold 1941- .... **CLC 44**
See also BW 2, 3; CA 127; 133; CANR 81; DLB 111; INT 133

Rampling, Anne
See Rice, Anne
See also GLL 2

Ramsay, Allan 1686(?)-1758 .... **LC 29**
See also DLB 95; RGEL 2

Ramsay, Jay
See Campbell, (John) Ramsey

Ramuz, Charles-Ferdinand
1878-1947 .... **TCLC 33**
See also CA 165; EWL 3

Rand, Ayn 1905-1982 ...... **CLC 3, 30, 44, 79; WLC**
See also AAYA 10; AMWS 4; BPFB 3; BYA 12; CA 13-16R; 105; CANR 27, 73; CDALBS; CPW; DA; DA3; DAC; DAM MST, NOV, POP; DLB 227, 279; MTCW 1, 2; NFS 10, 16; RGAL 4; SFW 4; TUS; YAW

Randall, Dudley (Felker) 1914-2000 . **BLC 3; CLC 1, 135**
See also BW 1, 3; CA 25-28R; 189; CANR 23, 82; DAM MULT; DLB 41; PFS 5

Randall, Robert
See Silverberg, Robert

Ranger, Ken
See Creasey, John

Rank, Otto 1884-1939 .... **TCLC 115**

Ransom, John Crowe 1888-1974 .. **CLC 2, 4, 5, 11, 24**
See also AMW; CA 5-8R; 49-52; CANR 6, 34; CDALBS; DA3; DAM POET; DLB 45, 63; EWL 3; EXPP; MTCW 1, 2; RGAL 4; TUS

Rao, Raja 1909- .... **CLC 25, 56**
See also CA 73-76; CANR 51; CN 7; DAM NOV; EWL 3; MTCW 1, 2; RGEL 2; RGSF 2

Raphael, Frederic (Michael) 1931- ... **CLC 2, 14**
See also CA 1-4R; CANR 1, 86; CN 7; DLB 14

Ratcliffe, James P.
See Mencken, H(enry) L(ouis)

Rathbone, Julian 1935- .... **CLC 41**
See also CA 101; CANR 34, 73

Rattigan, Terence (Mervyn)
1911-1977 .... **CLC 7; DC 18**
See also BRWS 7; CA 85-88; 73-76; CBD; CDBLB 1945-1960; DAM DRAM; DFS 8; DLB 13; IDFW 3, 4; MTCW 1, 2; RGEL 2

Ratushinskaya, Irina 1954- .... **CLC 54**
See also CA 129; CANR 68; CWW 2

Raven, Simon (Arthur Noel)
1927-2001 .... **CLC 14**
See also CA 81-84; 197; CANR 86; CN 7; DLB 271

Ravenna, Michael
See Welty, Eudora (Alice)

Rawley, Callman 1903-
See Rakosi, Carl
See also CA 21-24R; CANR 12, 32, 91

Rawlings, Marjorie Kinnan
1896-1953 .... **TCLC 4**
See also AAYA 20; AMWS 10; ANW; BPFB 3; BYA 3; CA 104; 137; CANR 74; CLR 63; DLB 9, 22, 102; DLBD 17; JRDA; MAICYA 1, 2; MTCW 2; RGAL 4; SATA 100; WCH; YABC 1; YAW

Ray, Satyajit 1921-1992 .... **CLC 16, 76**
See also CA 114; 137; DAM MULT

Read, Herbert Edward 1893-1968 ..... **CLC 4**
See also BRW 6; CA 85-88; 25-28R; DLB 20, 149; EWL 3; PAB; RGEL 2

Read, Piers Paul 1941- .... **CLC 4, 10, 25**
See also CA 21-24R; CANR 38, 86; CN 7; DLB 14; SATA 21

Reade, Charles 1814-1884 .... **NCLC 2, 74**
See also DLB 21; RGEL 2

Reade, Hamish
See Gray, Simon (James Holliday)

Reading, Peter 1946- .... **CLC 47**
See also BRWS 8; CA 103; CANR 46, 96; CP 7; DLB 40

Reaney, James 1926- .... **CLC 13**
See also CA 41-44R; CAAS 15; CANR 42; CD 5; CP 7; DAC; DAM MST; DLB 68; RGEL 2; SATA 43

Rebreanu, Liviu 1885-1944 .... **TCLC 28**
See also CA 165; DLB 220; EWL 3

Rechy, John (Francisco) 1934- ...... **CLC 1, 7, 14, 18, 107; HLC 2**
See also CA 5-8R; CAAE 195; CAAS 4; CANR 6, 32, 64; CN 7; DAM MULT; DLB 122, 278; DLBY 1982; HW 1, 2; INT CANR-6; RGAL 4

Redcam, Tom 1870-1933 .... **TCLC 25**

Reddin, Keith .... **CLC 67**
See also CAD

Redgrove, Peter (William) 1932- . **CLC 6, 41**
See also BRWS 6; CA 1-4R; CANR 3, 39, 77; CP 7; DLB 40

Redmon, Anne .... **CLC 22**
See Nightingale, Anne Redmon
See also DLBY 1986

Reed, Eliot
See Ambler, Eric

Reed, Ishmael 1938- ..... **BLC 3; CLC 2, 3, 5, 6, 13, 32, 60, 174**
See also AFAW 1, 2; AMWS 10; BPFB 3; BW 2, 3; CA 21-24R; CANR 25, 48, 74; CN 7; CP 7; CSW; DA3; DAM MULT; DLB 2, 5, 33, 169, 227; DLBD 8; EWL 3; LMFS 2; MSW; MTCW 1, 2; PFS 6; RGAL 4; TCWW 2

Reed, John (Silas) 1887-1920 .... **TCLC 9**
See also CA 106; 195; TUS

Reed, Lou .... **CLC 21**
See Firbank, Louis

Reese, Lizette Woodworth 1856-1935 . **PC 29**
See also CA 180; DLB 54

Reeve, Clara 1729-1807 .... **NCLC 19**
See also DLB 39; RGEL 2

Reich, Wilhelm 1897-1957 .... **TCLC 57**
See also CA 199

Reid, Christopher (John) 1949- .... **CLC 33**
See also CA 140; CANR 89; CP 7; DLB 40; EWL 3

Reid, Desmond
See Moorcock, Michael (John)

Reid Banks, Lynne 1929-
See Banks, Lynne Reid
See also AAYA 49; CA 1-4R; CANR 6, 22, 38, 87; CLR 24; CN 7; JRDA; MAICYA 1, 2; SATA 22, 75, 111; YAW

Reilly, William K.
See Creasey, John

Reiner, Max
See Caldwell, (Janet Miriam) Taylor (Holland)

Reis, Ricardo
See Pessoa, Fernando (Antonio Nogueira)

Reizenstein, Elmer Leopold
See Rice, Elmer (Leopold)
See also EWL 3

Remarque, Erich Maria 1898-1970 . **CLC 21**
See also AAYA 27; BPFB 3; CA 77-80; 29-32R; CDWLB 2; DA; DA3; DAB; DAC; DAM MST, NOV; DLB 56; EWL 3; EXPN; LAIT 3; MTCW 1, 2; NFS 4; RGWL 2, 3

Remington, Frederic 1861-1909 ..... **TCLC 89**
See also CA 108; 169; DLB 12, 186, 188; SATA 41

Remizov, A.
See Remizov, Aleksei (Mikhailovich)

Remizov, A. M.
See Remizov, Aleksei (Mikhailovich)

Remizov, Aleksei (Mikhailovich) 1877-1957 .... **TCLC 27**
See Remizov, Alexey Mikhaylovich
See also CA 125; 133

Remizov, Alexey Mikhaylovich
See Remizov, Aleksei (Mikhailovich)
See also EWL 3

Renan, Joseph Ernest 1823-1892 .. **NCLC 26**
See also GFL 1789 to the Present

Renard, Jules(-Pierre) 1864-1910 .. **TCLC 17**
See also CA 117; 202; GFL 1789 to the Present

Renault, Mary .... **CLC 3, 11, 17**
See Challans, Mary
See also BPFB 3; BYA 2; DLBY 1983; EWL 3; GLL 1; LAIT 1; MTCW 2; RGEL 2; RHW

Rendell, Ruth (Barbara) 1930- .. **CLC 28, 48**
See Vine, Barbara
See also BPFB 3; BRWS 9; CA 109; CANR 32, 52, 74; CN 7; CPW; DAM POP; DLB 87, 276; INT CANR-32; MSW; MTCW 1, 2

Renoir, Jean 1894-1979 .... **CLC 20**
See also CA 129; 85-88

Resnais, Alain 1922- .... **CLC 16**

Revard, Carter (Curtis) 1931- .... **NNAL**
See also CA 144; CANR 81; PFS 5

Reverdy, Pierre 1889-1960 .... **CLC 53**
See also CA 97-100; 89-92; DLB 258; EWL 3; GFL 1789 to the Present

Rexroth, Kenneth 1905-1982 .... **CLC 1, 2, 6, 11, 22, 49, 112; PC 20**
See also BG 3; CA 5-8R; 107; CANR 14, 34, 63; CDALB 1941-1968; DAM POET; DLB 16, 48, 165, 212; DLBY 1982; EWL 3; INT CANR-14; MTCW 1, 2; RGAL 4

Reyes, Alfonso 1889-1959 .... **HLCS 2; TCLC 33**
See also CA 131; EWL 3; HW 1; LAW

Reyes y Basoalto, Ricardo Eliecer Neftali
See Neruda, Pablo

Reymont, Wladyslaw (Stanislaw) 1868(?)-1925 .... **TCLC 5**
See also CA 104; EWL 3

Reynolds, Jonathan 1942- .... **CLC 6, 38**
See also CA 65-68; CANR 28

Reynolds, Joshua 1723-1792 .... **LC 15**
See also DLB 104

Reynolds, Michael S(hane) 1937-2000 .... **CLC 44**
See also CA 65-68; 189; CANR 9, 89, 97

Reznikoff, Charles 1894-1976 .... **CLC 9**
See also CA 33-36; 61-64; CAP 2; DLB 28, 45; WP

Rezzori (d'Arezzo), Gregor von 1914-1998 .... **CLC 25**
See also CA 122; 136; 167

Rhine, Richard
See Silverstein, Alvin; Silverstein, Virginia B(arbara Opshelor)

Rhodes, Eugene Manlove 1869-1934 .... **TCLC 53**
See also CA 198; DLB 256

R'hoone, Lord
See Balzac, Honore de

Rhys, Jean 1894(?)-1979 ...... **CLC 2, 4, 6, 14, 19, 51, 124; SSC 21**
See also BRWS 2; CA 25-28R; 85-88; CANR 35, 62; CDBLB 1945-1960; CDWLB 3; DA3; DAM NOV; DLB 36, 117, 162; DNFS 2; EWL 3; LATS 1; MTCW 1, 2; RGEL 2; RGSF 2; RHW; TEA

Ribeiro, Darcy 1922-1997 .... **CLC 34**
See also CA 33-36R; 156; EWL 3

Ribeiro, Joao Ubaldo (Osorio Pimentel) 1941- .... **CLC 10, 67**
See also CA 81-84; EWL 3

Ribman, Ronald (Burt) 1932- .... **CLC 7**
See also CA 21-24R; CAD; CANR 46, 80; CD 5

Ricci, Nino 1959- .... **CLC 70**
See also CA 137; CCA 1

Rice, Anne 1941- .... **CLC 41, 128**
See Rampling, Anne
See also AAYA 9, 53; AMWS 7; BEST 89:2; BPFB 3; CA 65-68; CANR 12, 36, 53, 74, 100; CN 7; CPW; CSW; DA3; DAM POP; GLL 2; HGG; MTCW 2; SUFW 2; YAW

Rice, Elmer (Leopold) 1892-1967 .... **CLC 7, 49**
See Reizenstein, Elmer Leopold
See also CA 21-22; 25-28R; CAP 2; DAM DRAM; DFS 12; DLB 4, 7; MTCW 1, 2; RGAL 4

Rice, Tim(othy Miles Bindon) 1944- .... **CLC 21**
See also CA 103; CANR 46; DFS 7

Rich, Adrienne (Cecile) 1929- ... **CLC 3, 6, 7, 11, 18, 36, 73, 76, 125; PC 5**
See also AMWR 2; AMWS 1; CA 9-12R; CANR 20, 53, 74; CDALBS; CP 7; CSW; CWP; DA3; DAM POET; DLB 5, 67; EWL 3; EXPP; FW; MAWW; MTCW 1, 2; PAB; PFS 15; RGAL 4; WP

Rich, Barbara
See Graves, Robert (von Ranke)

Rich, Robert
See Trumbo, Dalton

Richard, Keith .... **CLC 17**
See Richards, Keith

Richards, David Adams 1950- .... **CLC 59**
See also CA 93-96; CANR 60, 110; DAC; DLB 53

Richards, I(vor) A(rmstrong) 1893-1979 .... **CLC 14, 24**
See also BRWS 2; CA 41-44R; 89-92; CANR 34, 74; DLB 27; EWL 3; MTCW 2; RGEL 2

Richards, Keith 1943-
See Richard, Keith
See also CA 107; CANR 77

Richardson, Anne
See Roiphe, Anne (Richardson)

Richardson, Dorothy Miller 1873-1957 .... **TCLC 3**
See also CA 104; 192; DLB 36; EWL 3; FW; RGEL 2

Richardson (Robertson), Ethel Florence Lindesay 1870-1946
See Richardson, Henry Handel
See also CA 105; 190; DLB 230; RHW

Richardson, Henry Handel .... **TCLC 4**
See Richardson (Robertson), Ethel Florence Lindesay
See also DLB 197; EWL 3; RGEL 2; RGSF 2

Richardson, John 1796-1852 .... **NCLC 55**
See also CCA 1; DAC; DLB 99

Richardson, Samuel 1689-1761 ...... **LC 1, 44; WLC**
See also BRW 3; CDBLB 1660-1789; DA; DAB; DAC; DAM MST, NOV; DLB 39; RGEL 2; TEA; WLIT 3

Richardson, Willis 1889-1977 .... **HR 3**
See also BW 1; CA 124; DLB 51; SATA 60
Richler, Mordecai 1931-2001 .... **CLC 3, 5, 9, 13, 18, 46, 70**
See also AITN 1; CA 65-68; 201; CANR 31, 62, 111; CCA 1; CLR 17; CWRI 5; DAC; DAM MST, NOV; DLB 53; EWL 3; MAICYA 1, 2; MTCW 1, 2; RGEL 2; SATA 44, 98; SATA-Brief 27; TWA
Richter, Conrad (Michael) 1890-1968 .... **CLC 30**
See also AAYA 21; BYA 2; CA 5-8R; 25-28R; CANR 23; DLB 9, 212; LAIT 1; MTCW 1, 2; RGAL 4; SATA 3; TCWW 2; TUS; YAW
Ricostranza, Tom
See Ellis, Trey
Riddell, Charlotte 1832-1906 .... **TCLC 40**
See Riddell, Mrs. J. H.
See also CA 165; DLB 156
Riddell, Mrs. J. H.
See Riddell, Charlotte
See also HGG; SUFW
Ridge, John Rollin 1827-1867 .... **NCLC 82; NNAL**
See also CA 144; DAM MULT; DLB 175
Ridgeway, Jason
See Marlowe, Stephen
Ridgway, Keith 1965- .... **CLC 119**
See also CA 172
Riding, Laura .... **CLC 3, 7**
See Jackson, Laura (Riding)
See also RGAL 4
Riefenstahl, Berta Helene Amalia 1902-2003
See Riefenstahl, Leni
See also CA 108
Riefenstahl, Leni .... **CLC 16**
See Riefenstahl, Berta Helene Amalia
Riffe, Ernest
See Bergman, (Ernst) Ingmar
Riggs, (Rolla) Lynn 1899-1954 .... **NNAL; TCLC 56**
See also CA 144; DAM MULT; DLB 175
Riis, Jacob A(ugust) 1849-1914 ..... **TCLC 80**
See also CA 113; 168; DLB 23
Riley, James Whitcomb 1849-1916 .... **PC 48; TCLC 51**
See also CA 118; 137; DAM POET; MAICYA 1, 2; RGAL 4; SATA 17
Riley, Tex
See Creasey, John
Rilke, Rainer Maria 1875-1926 .... **PC 2; TCLC 1, 6, 19**
See also CA 104; 132; CANR 62, 99; CDWLB 2; DA3; DAM POET; DLB 81; EW 9; EWL 3; MTCW 1, 2; RGWL 2, 3; TWA; WP
Rimbaud, (Jean Nicolas) Arthur 1854-1891 .... **NCLC 4, 35, 82; PC 3; WLC**
See also DA; DA3; DAB; DAC; DAM MST, POET; DLB 217; EW 7; GFL 1789 to the Present; LMFS 2; RGWL 2, 3; TWA; WP
Rinehart, Mary Roberts 1876-1958 .... **TCLC 52**
See also BPFB 3; CA 108; 166; RGAL 4; RHW
Ringmaster, The
See Mencken, H(enry) L(ouis)
Ringwood, Gwen(dolyn Margaret) Pharis 1910-1984 .... **CLC 48**
See also CA 148; 112; DLB 88
Rio, Michel 1945(?)- .... **CLC 43**
See also CA 201
Ritsos, Giannes
See Ritsos, Yannis

Ritsos, Yannis 1909-1990 .... **CLC 6, 13, 31**
See also CA 77-80; 133; CANR 39, 61; EW 12; EWL 3; MTCW 1; RGWL 2, 3
Ritter, Erika 1948(?)- .... **CLC 52**
See also CD 5; CWD
Rivera, Jose Eustasio 1889-1928 ... **TCLC 35**
See also CA 162; EWL 3; HW 1, 2; LAW
Rivera, Tomas 1935-1984 .... **HLCS 2**
See also CA 49-52; CANR 32; DLB 82; HW 1; RGAL 4; SSFS 15; TCWW 2; WLIT 1
Rivers, Conrad Kent 1933-1968 .... **CLC 1**
See also BW 1; CA 85-88; DLB 41
Rivers, Elfrida
See Bradley, Marion Zimmer
See also GLL 1
Riverside, John
See Heinlein, Robert A(nson)
Rizal, Jose 1861-1896 .... **NCLC 27**
Roa Bastos, Augusto (Antonio) 1917- .... **CLC 45; HLC 2**
See also CA 131; DAM MULT; DLB 113; EWL 3; HW 1; LAW; RGSF 2; WLIT 1
Robbe-Grillet, Alain 1922- .... **CLC 1, 2, 4, 6, 8, 10, 14, 43, 128**
See also BPFB 3; CA 9-12R; CANR 33, 65, 115; DLB 83; EW 13; EWL 3; GFL 1789 to the Present; IDFW 3, 4; MTCW 1, 2; RGWL 2, 3; SSFS 15
Robbins, Harold 1916-1997 .... **CLC 5**
See also BPFB 3; CA 73-76; 162; CANR 26, 54, 112; DA3; DAM NOV; MTCW 1, 2
Robbins, Thomas Eugene 1936-
See Robbins, Tom
See also CA 81-84; CANR 29, 59, 95; CN 7; CPW; CSW; DA3; DAM NOV, POP; MTCW 1, 2
Robbins, Tom .... **CLC 9, 32, 64**
See Robbins, Thomas Eugene
See also AAYA 32; AMWS 10; BEST 90:3; BPFB 3; DLBY 1980; MTCW 2
Robbins, Trina 1938- .... **CLC 21**
See also CA 128
Roberts, Charles G(eorge) D(ouglas) 1860-1943 .... **TCLC 8**
See also CA 105; 188; CLR 33; CWRI 5; DLB 92; RGEL 2; RGSF 2; SATA 88; SATA-Brief 29
Roberts, Elizabeth Madox 1886-1941 .... **TCLC 68**
See also CA 111; 166; CWRI 5; DLB 9, 54, 102; RGAL 4; RHW; SATA 33; SATA-Brief 27; WCH
Roberts, Kate 1891-1985 .... **CLC 15**
See also CA 107; 116
Roberts, Keith (John Kingston) 1935-2000 .... **CLC 14**
See also CA 25-28R; CANR 46; DLB 261; SFW 4
Roberts, Kenneth (Lewis) 1885-1957 .... **TCLC 23**
See also CA 109; 199; DLB 9; RGAL 4; RHW
Roberts, Michele (Brigitte) 1949- .... **CLC 48, 178**
See also CA 115; CANR 58, 120; CN 7; DLB 231; FW
Robertson, Ellis
See Ellison, Harlan (Jay); Silverberg, Robert
Robertson, Thomas William 1829-1871 .... **NCLC 35**
See Robertson, Tom
See also DAM DRAM
Robertson, Tom
See Robertson, Thomas William
See also RGEL 2

Robeson, Kenneth
See Dent, Lester
Robinson, Edwin Arlington 1869-1935 .... **PC 1, 35; TCLC 5, 101**
See also AMW; CA 104; 133; CDALB 1865-1917; DA; DAC; DAM MST, POET; DLB 54; EWL 3; EXPP; MTCW 1, 2; PAB; PFS 4; RGAL 4; WP
Robinson, Henry Crabb 1775-1867 .... **NCLC 15**
See also DLB 107
Robinson, Jill 1936- .... **CLC 10**
See also CA 102; CANR 120; INT 102
Robinson, Kim Stanley 1952- .... **CLC 34**
See also AAYA 26; CA 126; CANR 113; CN 7; SATA 109; SCFW 2; SFW 4
Robinson, Lloyd
See Silverberg, Robert
Robinson, Marilynne 1944- ...... **CLC 25, 180**
See also CA 116; CANR 80; CN 7; DLB 206
Robinson, Smokey .... **CLC 21**
See Robinson, William, Jr.
Robinson, William, Jr. 1940-
See Robinson, Smokey
See also CA 116
Robison, Mary 1949- .... **CLC 42, 98**
See also CA 113; 116; CANR 87; CN 7; DLB 130; INT 116; RGSF 2
Rochester
See Wilmot, John
See also RGEL 2
Rod, Edouard 1857-1910 .... **TCLC 52**
Roddenberry, Eugene Wesley 1921-1991
See Roddenberry, Gene
See also CA 110; 135; CANR 37; SATA 45; SATA-Obit 69
Roddenberry, Gene .... **CLC 17**
See Roddenberry, Eugene Wesley
See also AAYA 5; SATA-Obit 69
Rodgers, Mary 1931- .... **CLC 12**
See also BYA 5; CA 49-52; CANR 8, 55, 90; CLR 20; CWRI 5; INT CANR-8; JRDA; MAICYA 1, 2; SATA 8, 130
Rodgers, W(illiam) R(obert) 1909-1969 .... **CLC 7**
See also CA 85-88; DLB 20; RGEL 2
Rodman, Eric
See Silverberg, Robert
Rodman, Howard 1920(?)-1985 .... **CLC 65**
See also CA 118
Rodman, Maia
See Wojciechowska, Maia (Teresa)
Rodo, Jose Enrique 1871(?)-1917 .... **HLCS 2**
See also CA 178; EWL 3; HW 2; LAW
Rodolph, Utto
See Ouologuem, Yambo
Rodriguez, Claudio 1934-1999 .... **CLC 10**
See also CA 188; DLB 134
Rodriguez, Richard 1944- .... **CLC 155; HLC 2**
See also CA 110; CANR 66, 116; DAM MULT; DLB 82, 256; HW 1, 2; LAIT 5; NCFS 3; WLIT 1
Roelvaag, O(le) E(dvart) 1876-1931
See Rolvaag, O(le) E(dvart)
See also CA 117; 171
Roethke, Theodore (Huebner) 1908-1963 .... **CLC 1, 3, 8, 11, 19, 46, 101; PC 15**
See also AMW; CA 81-84; CABS 2; CDALB 1941-1968; DA3; DAM POET; DLB 5, 206; EWL 3; EXPP; MTCW 1, 2; PAB; PFS 3; RGAL 4; WP
Rogers, Carl R(ansom) 1902-1987 .... **TCLC 125**
See also CA 1-4R; 121; CANR 1, 18; MTCW 1

Rogers, Samuel 1763-1855 .... **NCLC 69**
See also DLB 93; RGEL 2
Rogers, Thomas Hunton 1927- .... **CLC 57**
See also CA 89-92; INT 89-92
Rogers, Will(iam Penn Adair)
1879-1935 .... **NNAL; TCLC 8, 71**
See also CA 105; 144; DA3; DAM MULT;
DLB 11; MTCW 2
Rogin, Gilbert 1929- .... **CLC 18**
See also CA 65-68; CANR 15
Rohan, Koda
See Koda Shigeyuki
Rohlfs, Anna Katharine Green
See Green, Anna Katharine
Rohmer, Eric .... **CLC 16**
See Scherer, Jean-Marie Maurice
Rohmer, Sax .... **TCLC 28**
See Ward, Arthur Henry Sarsfield
See also DLB 70; MSW; SUFW
Roiphe, Anne (Richardson) 1935- .. **CLC 3, 9**
See also CA 89-92; CANR 45, 73; DLBY
1980; INT 89-92
Rojas, Fernando de 1475-1541 ... **HLCS 1, 2;
LC 23**
See also DLB 286; RGWL 2, 3
Rojas, Gonzalo 1917- .... **HLCS 2**
See also CA 178; HW 2; LAWS 1
**Rolfe, Frederick (William Serafino Austin
Lewis Mary)** 1860-1913 .... **TCLC 12**
See Al Siddik
See also CA 107; 210; DLB 34, 156; RGEL
2
Rolland, Romain 1866-1944 .... **TCLC 23**
See also CA 118; 197; DLB 65, 284; EWL
3; GFL 1789 to the Present; RGWL 2, 3
Rolle, Richard c. 1300-c. 1349 ...... **CMLC 21**
See also DLB 146; LMFS 1; RGEL 2
Rolvaag, O(le) E(dvart) .... **TCLC 17**
See Roelvaag, O(le) E(dvart)
See also DLB 9, 212; NFS 5; RGAL 4
Romain Arnaud, Saint
See Aragon, Louis
Romains, Jules 1885-1972 .... **CLC 7**
See also CA 85-88; CANR 34; DLB 65;
EWL 3; GFL 1789 to the Present; MTCW
1
Romero, Jose Ruben 1890-1952 .... **TCLC 14**
See also CA 114; 131; EWL 3; HW 1; LAW
Ronsard, Pierre de 1524-1585 . **LC 6, 54; PC
11**
See also EW 2; GFL Beginnings to 1789;
RGWL 2, 3; TWA
Rooke, Leon 1934- .... **CLC 25, 34**
See also CA 25-28R; CANR 23, 53; CCA
1; CPW; DAM POP
Roosevelt, Franklin Delano
1882-1945 .... **TCLC 93**
See also CA 116; 173; LAIT 3
Roosevelt, Theodore 1858-1919 ..... **TCLC 69**
See also CA 115; 170; DLB 47, 186, 275
Roper, William 1498-1578 .... **LC 10**
Roquelaure, A. N.
See Rice, Anne
Rosa, Joao Guimaraes 1908-1967 ... **CLC 23;
HLCS 1**
See also CA 89-92; DLB 113; EWL 3;
WLIT 1
Rose, Wendy 1948- . **CLC 85; NNAL; PC 13**
See also CA 53-56; CANR 5, 51; CWP;
DAM MULT; DLB 175; PFS 13; RGAL
4; SATA 12
Rosen, R. D.
See Rosen, Richard (Dean)
Rosen, Richard (Dean) 1949- .... **CLC 39**
See also CA 77-80; CANR 62, 120; CMW
4; INT CANR-30
Rosenberg, Isaac 1890-1918 .... **TCLC 12**
See also BRW 6; CA 107; 188; DLB 20,
216; EWL 3; PAB; RGEL 2

Rosenblatt, Joe .... **CLC 15**
See Rosenblatt, Joseph
Rosenblatt, Joseph 1933-
See Rosenblatt, Joe
See also CA 89-92; CP 7; INT 89-92
Rosenfeld, Samuel
See Tzara, Tristan
Rosenstock, Sami
See Tzara, Tristan
Rosenstock, Samuel
See Tzara, Tristan
Rosenthal, M(acha) L(ouis)
1917-1996 .... **CLC 28**
See also CA 1-4R; 152; CAAS 6; CANR 4,
51; CP 7; DLB 5; SATA 59
Ross, Barnaby
See Dannay, Frederic
Ross, Bernard L.
See Follett, Ken(neth Martin)
Ross, J. H.
See Lawrence, T(homas) E(dward)
Ross, John Hume
See Lawrence, T(homas) E(dward)
Ross, Martin 1862-1915
See Martin, Violet Florence
See also DLB 135; GLL 2; RGEL 2; RGSF
2
Ross, (James) Sinclair 1908-1996 ... **CLC 13;
SSC 24**
See also CA 73-76; CANR 81; CN 7; DAC;
DAM MST; DLB 88; RGEL 2; RGSF 2;
TCWW 2
Rossetti, Christina (Georgina)
1830-1894 .... **NCLC 2, 50, 66; PC 7;
WLC**
See also AAYA 51; BRW 5; BYA 4; DA;
DA3; DAB; DAC; DAM MST, POET;
DLB 35, 163, 240; EXPP; LATS 1; MAI-
CYA 1, 2; PFS 10, 14; RGEL 2; SATA
20; TEA; WCH
Rossetti, Dante Gabriel 1828-1882 . **NCLC 4,
77; PC 44; WLC**
See also AAYA 51; BRW 5; CDBLB 1832-
1890; DA; DAB; DAC; DAM MST,
POET; DLB 35; EXPP; RGEL 2; TEA
Rossi, Cristina Peri
See Peri Rossi, Cristina
Rossi, Jean-Baptiste 1931-2003
See Japrisot, Sebastien
See also CA 201; 215
Rossner, Judith (Perelman) 1935- . **CLC 6, 9,
29**
See also AITN 2; BEST 90:3; BPFB 3; CA
17-20R; CANR 18, 51, 73; CN 7; DLB 6;
INT CANR-18; MTCW 1, 2
Rostand, Edmond (Eugene Alexis)
1868-1918 .... **DC 10; TCLC 6, 37**
See also CA 104; 126; DA; DA3; DAB;
DAC; DAM DRAM, MST; DFS 1; DLB
192; LAIT 1; MTCW 1; RGWL 2, 3;
TWA
Roth, Henry 1906-1995 ..... **CLC 2, 6, 11, 104**
See also AMWS 9; CA 11-12; 149; CANR
38, 63; CAP 1; CN 7; DA3; DLB 28;
EWL 3; MTCW 1, 2; RGAL 4
Roth, (Moses) Joseph 1894-1939 ..... **TCLC 33**
See also CA 160; DLB 85; EWL 3; RGWL
2, 3
Roth, Philip (Milton) 1933- ... **CLC 1, 2, 3, 4,
6, 9, 15, 22, 31, 47, 66, 86, 119; SSC
26; WLC**
See also AMWR 2; AMWS 3; BEST 90:3;
BPFB 3; CA 1-4R; CANR 1, 22, 36, 55,
89; CDALB 1968-1988; CN 7; CPW 1;
DA; DA3; DAB; DAC; DAM MST, NOV,
POP; DLB 2, 28, 173; DLBY 1982; EWL
3; MTCW 1, 2; RGAL 4; RGSF 2; SSFS
12, 18; TUS

Rothenberg, Jerome 1931- .... **CLC 6, 57**
See also CA 45-48; CANR 1, 106; CP 7;
DLB 5, 193
Rotter, Pat ed. .... **CLC 65**
Roumain, Jacques (Jean Baptiste)
1907-1944 .... **BLC 3; TCLC 19**
See also BW 1; CA 117; 125; DAM MULT;
EWL 3
Rourke, Constance Mayfield
1885-1941 .... **TCLC 12**
See also CA 107; 200; YABC 1
Rousseau, Jean-Baptiste 1671-1741 ...... **LC 9**
Rousseau, Jean-Jacques 1712-1778 .... **LC 14,
36; WLC**
See also DA; DA3; DAB; DAC; DAM
MST; EW 4; GFL Beginnings to 1789;
LMFS 2, 3; RGWL 2, 3; TWA
Roussel, Raymond 1877-1933 .... **TCLC 20**
See also CA 117; 201; EWL 3; GFL 1789
to the Present
Rovit, Earl (Herbert) 1927- .... **CLC 7**
See also CA 5-8R; CANR 12
Rowe, Elizabeth Singer 1674-1737 ..... **LC 44**
See also DLB 39, 95
Rowe, Nicholas 1674-1718 .... **LC 8**
See also DLB 84; RGEL 2
Rowlandson, Mary 1637(?)-1678 .... **LC 66**
See also DLB 24; RGAL 4
Rowley, Ames Dorrance
See Lovecraft, H(oward) P(hillips)
Rowling, J(oanne) K(athleen)
1965- .... **CLC 137**
See also AAYA 34; BYA 13, 14; CA 173;
CLR 66, 80; MAICYA 2; SATA 109;
SUFW 2
Rowson, Susanna Haswell
1762(?)-1824 .... **NCLC 5, 69**
See also DLB 37, 200; RGAL 4
Roy, Arundhati 1960(?)- .... **CLC 109**
See also CA 163; CANR 90; DLBY 1997;
EWL 3; LATS 1
Roy, Gabrielle 1909-1983 .... **CLC 10, 14**
See also CA 53-56; 110; CANR 5, 61; CCA
1; DAB; DAC; DAM MST; DLB 68;
EWL 3; MTCW 1; RGWL 2, 3; SATA 104
Royko, Mike 1932-1997 .... **CLC 109**
See also CA 89-92; 157; CANR 26, 111;
CPW
Rozanov, Vasily Vasilyevich
See Rozanov, Vassili
See also EWL 3
Rozanov, Vassili 1856-1919 .... **TCLC 104**
See Rozanov, Vasily Vasilyevich
Rozewicz, Tadeusz 1921- ...... **CLC 9, 23, 139**
See also CA 108; CANR 36, 66; CWW 2;
DA3; DAM POET; DLB 232; EWL 3;
MTCW 1, 2; RGWL 3
Ruark, Gibbons 1941- .... **CLC 3**
See also CA 33-36R; CAAS 23; CANR 14,
31, 57; DLB 120
Rubens, Bernice (Ruth) 1923- ...... **CLC 19, 31**
See also CA 25-28R; CANR 33, 65; CN 7;
DLB 14, 207; MTCW 1
Rubin, Harold
See Robbins, Harold
Rudkin, (James) David 1936- .... **CLC 14**
See also CA 89-92; CBD; CD 5; DLB 13
Rudnik, Raphael 1933- .... **CLC 7**
See also CA 29-32R
Ruffian, M.
See Hasek, Jaroslav (Matej Frantisek)
Ruiz, Jose Martinez .... **CLC 11**
See Martinez Ruiz, Jose
Rukeyser, Muriel 1913-1980 . **CLC 6, 10, 15,
27; PC 12**
See also AMWS 6; CA 5-8R; 93-96; CANR
26, 60; DA3; DAM POET; DLB 48; EWL
3; FW; GLL 2; MTCW 1, 2; PFS 10;
RGAL 4; SATA-Obit 22

Rule, Jane (Vance) 1931- .... **CLC 27**
See also CA 25-28R; CAAS 18; CANR 12, 87; CN 7; DLB 60; FW

Rulfo, Juan 1918-1986 .. **CLC 8, 80; HLC 2; SSC 25**
See also CA 85-88; 118; CANR 26; CD-WLB 3; DAM MULT; DLB 113; EWL 3; HW 1, 2; LAW; MTCW 1, 2; RGSF 2; RGWL 2, 3; WLIT 1

Rumi, Jalal al-Din 1207-1273 ...... **CMLC 20; PC 45**
See also RGWL 2, 3; WP

Runeberg, Johan 1804-1877 .... **NCLC 41**

Runyon, (Alfred) Damon 1884(?)-1946 .... **TCLC 10**
See also CA 107; 165; DLB 11, 86, 171; MTCW 2; RGAL 4

Rush, Norman 1933- .... **CLC 44**
See also CA 121; 126; INT CA-126

Rushdie, (Ahmed) Salman 1947- .... **CLC 23, 31, 55, 100; WLCS**
See also BEST 89:3; BPFB 3; BRWS 4; CA 108; 111; CANR 33, 56, 108; CN 7; CPW 1; DA3; DAB; DAC; DAM MST, NOV, POP; DLB 194; EWL 3; FANT; INT CA-111; LATS 1; LMFS 2; MTCW 1, 2; RGEL 2; RGSF 2; TEA; WLIT 4

Rushforth, Peter (Scott) 1945- .... **CLC 19**
See also CA 101

Ruskin, John 1819-1900 .... **TCLC 63**
See BRW 5; BYA 5; CA 114; 129; CDBLB 1832-1890; DLB 55, 163, 190; RGEL 2; SATA 24; TEA; WCH

Russ, Joanna 1937- .... **CLC 15**
See also BPFB 3; CA 5-28R; CANR 11, 31, 65; CN 7; DLB 8; FW; GLL 1; MTCW 1; SCFW 2; SFW 4

Russ, Richard Patrick
See O'Brian, Patrick

Russell, George William 1867-1935
See A.E.; Baker, Jean H.
See also BRWS 8; CA 104; 153; CDBLB 1890-1914; DAM POET; EWL 3; RGEL 2

Russell, Jeffrey Burton 1934- .... **CLC 70**
See also CA 25-28R; CANR 11, 28, 52

Russell, (Henry) Ken(neth Alfred) 1927- .... **CLC 16**
See also CA 105

Russell, William Martin 1947-
See Russell, Willy
See also CA 164; CANR 107

Russell, Willy .... **CLC 60**
See Russell, William Martin
See also CBD; CD 5; DLB 233

Rutherford, Mark .... **TCLC 25**
See White, William Hale
See also DLB 18; RGEL 2

Ruyslinck, Ward .... **CLC 14**
See Belser, Reimond Karel Maria de

Ryan, Cornelius (John) 1920-1974 ..... **CLC 7**
See also CA 69-72; 53-56; CANR 38

Ryan, Michael 1946- .... **CLC 65**
See also CA 49-52; CANR 109; DLBY 1982

Ryan, Tim
See Dent, Lester

Rybakov, Anatoli (Naumovich) 1911-1998 .... **CLC 23, 53**
See also CA 126; 135; 172; SATA 79; SATA-Obit 108

Ryder, Jonathan
See Ludlum, Robert

Ryga, George 1932-1987 .... **CLC 14**
See also CA 101; 124; CANR 43, 90; CCA 1; DAC; DAM MST; DLB 60

S. H.
See Hartmann, Sadakichi

S. S.
See Sassoon, Siegfried (Lorraine)

Saba, Umberto 1883-1957 .... **TCLC 33**
See also CA 144; CANR 79; DLB 114; EWL 3; RGWL 2, 3

Sabatini, Rafael 1875-1950 .... **TCLC 47**
See also BPFB 3; CA 162; RHW

Sabato, Ernesto (R.) 1911- .... **CLC 10, 23; HLC 2**
See also CA 97-100; CANR 32, 65; CD-WLB 3; DAM MULT; DLB 145; EWL 3; HW 1, 2; LAW; MTCW 1, 2

Sa-Carneiro, Mario de 1890-1916 . **TCLC 83**
See also DLB 287; EWL 3

Sacastru, Martin
See Bioy Casares, Adolfo
See also CWW 2

Sacher-Masoch, Leopold von 1836(?)-1895 .... **NCLC 31**

Sachs, Hans 1494-1576 .... **LC 95**
See also CDWLB 2; DLB 179; RGWL 2, 3

Sachs, Marilyn (Stickle) 1927- .... **CLC 35**
See also AAYA 2; BYA 6; CA 17-20R; CANR 13, 47; CLR 2; JRDA; MAICYA 1, 2; SAAS 2; SATA 3, 68; SATA-Essay 110; WYA; YAW

Sachs, Nelly 1891-1970 .... **CLC 14, 98**
See also CA 17-18; 25-28R; CANR 87; CAP 2; EWL 3; MTCW 2; RGWL 2, 3

Sackler, Howard (Oliver) 1929-1982 .... **CLC 14**
See also CA 61-64; 108; CAD; CANR 30; DFS 15; DLB 7

Sacks, Oliver (Wolf) 1933- .... **CLC 67**
See also CA 53-56; CANR 28, 50, 76; CPW; DA3; INT CANR-28; MTCW 1, 2

Sadakichi
See Hartmann, Sadakichi

Sade, Donatien Alphonse Francois 1740-1814 .... **NCLC 3, 47**
See also EW 4; GFL Beginnings to 1789; RGWL 2, 3

Sade, Marquis de
See Sade, Donatien Alphonse Francois

Sadoff, Ira 1945- .... **CLC 9**
See also CA 53-56; CANR 5, 21, 109; DLB 120

Saetone
See Camus, Albert

Safire, William 1929- .... **CLC 10**
See also CA 17-20R; CANR 31, 54, 91

Sagan, Carl (Edward) 1934-1996 .... **CLC 30, 112**
See also AAYA 2; CA 25-28R; 155; CANR 11, 36, 74; CPW; DA3; MTCW 1, 2; SATA 58; SATA-Obit 94

Sagan, Francoise .... **CLC 3, 6, 9, 17, 36**
See Quoirez, Francoise
See also CWW 2; DLB 83; EWL 3; GFL 1789 to the Present; MTCW 2

Sahgal, Nayantara (Pandit) 1927- .... **CLC 41**
See also CA 9-12R; CANR 11, 88; CN 7

Said, Edward W. 1935-2003 .... **CLC 123**
See also CA 21-24R; CANR 45, 74, 107; DLB 67; MTCW 2

Saint, H(arry) F. 1941- .... **CLC 50**
See also CA 127

St. Aubin de Teran, Lisa 1953-
See Teran, Lisa St. Aubin de
See also CA 118; 126; CN 7; INT CA-126

Saint Birgitta of Sweden c. 1303-1373 .... **CMLC 24**

Sainte-Beuve, Charles Augustin 1804-1869 .... **NCLC 5**
See also DLB 217; EW 6; GFL 1789 to the Present

Saint-Exupery, Antoine (Jean Baptiste Marie Roger) de 1900-1944 .... **TCLC 2, 56; WLC**
See also BPFB 3; BYA 3; CA 108; 132; CLR 10; DA3; DAM NOV; DLB 72; EW 12; EWL 3; GFL 1789 to the Present; LAIT 3; MAICYA 1, 2; MTCW 1, 2; RGWL 2, 3; SATA 20; TWA

St. John, David
See Hunt, E(verette) Howard, (Jr.)

St. John, J. Hector
See Crevecoeur, Michel Guillaume Jean de

Saint-John Perse
See Leger, (Marie-Rene Auguste) Alexis Saint-Leger
See also EW 10; EWL 3; GFL 1789 to the Present; RGWL 2

Saintsbury, George (Edward Bateman) 1845-1933 .... **TCLC 31**
See also CA 160; DLB 57, 149

Sait Faik .... **TCLC 23**
See Abasiyanik, Sait Faik

Saki .... **SSC 12; TCLC 3**
See Munro, H(ector) H(ugh)
See also BRWS 6; LAIT 2; MTCW 2; RGEL 2; SSFS 1; SUFW

Sala, George Augustus 1828-1895 . **NCLC 46**

Saladin 1138-1193 .... **CMLC 38**

Salama, Hannu 1936- .... **CLC 18**
See also EWL 3

Salamanca, J(ack) R(ichard) 1922- .. **CLC 4, 15**
See also CA 25-28R; CAAE 193

Salas, Floyd Francis 1931- .... **HLC 2**
See also CA 119; CAAS 27; CANR 44, 75, 93; DAM MULT; DLB 82; HW 1, 2; MTCW 2

Sale, J. Kirkpatrick
See Sale, Kirkpatrick

Sale, Kirkpatrick 1937- .... **CLC 68**
See also CA 13-16R; CANR 10

Salinas, Luis Omar 1937- ... **CLC 90; HLC 2**
See also AMWS 13; CA 131; CANR 81; DAM MULT; DLB 82; HW 1, 2

Salinas (y Serrano), Pedro 1891(?)-1951 .... **TCLC 17**
See also CA 117; DLB 134; EWL 3

Salinger, J(erome) D(avid) 1919- .. **CLC 1, 3, 8, 12, 55, 56, 138; SSC 2, 28, 65; WLC**
See also AAYA 2, 36; AMW; AMWC 1; BPFB 3; CA 5-8R; CANR 39; CDALB 1941-1968; CLR 18; CN 7; CPW 1; DA; DA3; DAB; DAC; DAM MST, NOV, POP; DLB 2, 102, 173; EWL 3; EXPN; LAIT 4; MAICYA 1, 2; MTCW 1, 2; NFS 1; RGAL 4; RGSF 2; SATA 67; SSFS 17; TUS; WYA; YAW

Salisbury, John
See Caute, (John) David

Salter, James 1925- .. **CLC 7, 52, 59; SSC 58**
See also AMWS 9; CA 73-76; CANR 107; DLB 130

Saltus, Edgar (Everton) 1855-1921 . **TCLC 8**
See also CA 105; DLB 202; RGAL 4

Saltykov, Mikhail Evgrafovich 1826-1889 .... **NCLC 16**
See also DLB 238;

Saltykov-Shchedrin, N.
See Saltykov, Mikhail Evgrafovich

Samarakis, Andonis
See Samarakis, Antonis
See also EWL 3

Samarakis, Antonis 1919- .... **CLC 5**
See Samarakis, Andonis
See also CA 25-28R; CAAS 16; CANR 36

Sanchez, Florencio 1875-1910 .... **TCLC 37**
See also CA 153; EWL 3; HW 1; LAW

Sanchez, Luis Rafael 1936- .... **CLC 23**
  See also CA 128; DLB 145; EWL 3; HW 1; WLIT 1
Sanchez, Sonia 1934- .... **BLC 3; CLC 5, 116; PC 9**
  See also BW 2, 3; CA 33-36R; CANR 24, 49, 74, 115; CLR 18; CP 7; CSW; CWP; DA3; DAM MULT; DLB 41; DLBD 8; EWL 3; MAICYA 1, 2; MTCW 1, 2; SATA 22, 136; WP
Sancho, Ignatius 1729-1780 .... **LC 84**
Sand, George 1804-1876 ..... **NCLC 2, 42, 57; WLC**
  See also DA; DA3; DAB; DAC; DAM MST, NOV; DLB 119, 192; EW 6; FW; GFL 1789 to the Present; RGWL 2, 3; TWA
Sandburg, Carl (August) 1878-1967 . **CLC 1, 4, 10, 15, 35; PC 2, 41; WLC**
  See also AAYA 24; AMW; BYA 1, 3; CA 5-8R; 25-28R; CANR 35; CDALB 1865-1917; CLR 67; DA; DA3; DAB; DAC; DAM MST, POET; DLB 17, 54, 284; EWL 3; EXPP; LAIT 2; MAICYA 1, 2; MTCW 1, 2; PAB; PFS 3, 6, 12; RGAL 4; SATA 8; TUS; WCH; WP; WYA
Sandburg, Charles
  See Sandburg, Carl (August)
Sandburg, Charles A.
  See Sandburg, Carl (August)
Sanders, (James) Ed(ward) 1939- .... **CLC 53**
  See Sanders, Edward
  See also BG 3; CA 13-16R; CAAS 21; CANR 13, 44, 78; CP 7; DAM POET; DLB 16, 244
Sanders, Edward
  See Sanders, (James) Ed(ward)
  See also DLB 244
Sanders, Lawrence 1920-1998 .... **CLC 41**
  See also BEST 89:4; BPFB 3; CA 81-84; 165; CANR 33, 62; CMW 4; CPW; DA3; DAM POP; MTCW 1
Sanders, Noah
  See Blount, Roy (Alton), Jr.
Sanders, Winston P.
  See Anderson, Poul (William)
Sandoz, Mari(e Susette) 1900-1966 .. **CLC 28**
  See also CA 1-4R; 25-28R; CANR 17, 64; DLB 9, 212; LAIT 2; MTCW 1, 2; SATA 5; TCWW 2
Sandys, George 1578-1644 .... **LC 80**
  See also DLB 24, 121
Saner, Reg(inald Anthony) 1931- .... **CLC 9**
  See also CA 65-68; CP 7
Sankara 788-820 .... **CMLC 32**
Sannazaro, Jacopo 1456(?)-1530 .... **LC 8**
  See also RGWL 2, 3
Sansom, William 1912-1976 . **CLC 2, 6; SSC 21**
  See also CA 5-8R; 65-68; CANR 42; DAM NOV; DLB 139; EWL 3; MTCW 1; RGEL 2; RGSF 2
Santayana, George 1863-1952 .... **TCLC 40**
  See also AMW; CA 115; 194; DLB 54, 71, 246, 270; DLBD 13; EWL 3; RGAL 4; TUS
Santiago, Danny .... **CLC 33**
  See James, Daniel (Lewis)
  See also DLB 122
Santmyer, Helen Hooven
  1895-1986 .... **CLC 33; TCLC 133**
  See also CA 1-4R; 118; CANR 15, 33; DLBY 1984; MTCW 1; RHW
Santoka, Taneda 1882-1940 .... **TCLC 72**
Santos, Bienvenido N(uqui)
  1911-1996 .... **AAL; CLC 22**
  See also CA 101; 151; CANR 19, 46; DAM MULT; EWL; RGAL 4

Sapir, Edward 1884-1939 .... **TCLC 108**
  See also CA 211; DLB 92
Sapper .... **TCLC 44**
  See McNeile, Herman Cyril
Sapphire
  See Sapphire, Brenda
Sapphire, Brenda 1950- .... **CLC 99**
Sappho fl. 6th cent. B.C.- ...... **CMLC 3; PC 5**
  See also CDWLB 1; DA3; DAM POET; DLB 176; RGWL 2, 3; WP
Saramago, Jose 1922- ..... **CLC 119; HLCS 1**
  See also CA 153; CANR 96; DLB 287; EWL 3; LATS 1
Sarduy, Severo 1937-1993 .... **CLC 6, 97; HLCS 2**
  See also CA 89-92; 142; CANR 58, 81; CWW 2; DLB 113; EWL 3; HW 1, 2; LAW
Sargeson, Frank 1903-1982 .... **CLC 31**
  See also CA 25-28R; 106; CANR 38, 79; EWL 3; GLL 2; RGEL 2; RGSF 2
Sarmiento, Domingo Faustino
  1811-1888 .... **HLCS 2**
  See also LAW; WLIT 1
Sarmiento, Felix Ruben Garcia
  See Dario, Ruben
Saro-Wiwa, Ken(ule Beeson)
  1941-1995 .... **CLC 114**
  See also BW 2; CA 142; 150; CANR 60; DLB 157
Saroyan, William 1908-1981 ... **CLC 1, 8, 10, 29, 34, 56; SSC 21; TCLC 137; WLC**
  See also CA 5-8R; 103; CAD; CANR 30; CDALBS; DA; DA3; DAB; DAC; DAM DRAM, MST, NOV; DFS 17; DLB 7, 9, 86; DLBY 1981; EWL 3; LAIT 4; MTCW 1, 2; RGAL 4; RGSF 2; SATA 23; SATA-Obit 24; SSFS 14; TUS
Sarraute, Nathalie 1900-1999 .... **CLC 1, 2, 4, 8, 10, 31, 80**
  See also BPFB 3; CA 9-12R; 187; CANR 23, 66; CWW 2; DLB 83; EW 12; EWL 3; GFL 1789 to the Present; MTCW 1, 2; RGWL 2, 3
Sarton, (Eleanor) May 1912-1995 ..... **CLC 4, 14, 49, 91; PC 39; TCLC 120**
  See also AMWS 8; CA 1-4R; 149; CANR 1, 34, 55, 116; CN 7; CP 7; DAM POET; DLB 48; DLBY 1981; EWL 3; FW; INT CANR-34; MTCW 1, 2; RGAL 4; SATA 36; SATA-Obit 86; TUS
Sartre, Jean-Paul 1905-1980 . **CLC 1, 4, 7, 9, 13, 18, 24, 44, 50, 52; DC 3; SSC 32; WLC**
  See also CA 9-12R; 97-100; CANR 21; DA; DA3; DAB; DAC; DAM DRAM, MST, NOV; DFS 5; DLB 72; EW 12; EWL 3; GFL 1789 to the Present; LMFS 2; MTCW 1, 2; RGSF 2; RGWL 2, 3; SSFS 9; TWA
Sassoon, Siegfried (Lorraine)
  1886-1967 .... **CLC 36, 130; PC 12**
  See also BRW 6; CA 104; 25-28R; CANR 36; DAB; DAM MST, NOV, POET; DLB 20, 191; DLBD 18; EWL 3; MTCW 1, 2; PAB; RGEL 2; TEA
Satterfield, Charles
  See Pohl, Frederik
Satyremont
  See Peret, Benjamin
Saul, John (W. III) 1942- .... **CLC 46**
  See also AAYA 10; BEST 90:4; CA 81-84; CANR 16, 40, 81; CPW; DAM NOV, POP; HGG; SATA 98
Saunders, Caleb
  See Heinlein, Robert A(nson)
Saura (Atares), Carlos 1932-1998 .... **CLC 20**
  See also CA 114; 131; CANR 79; HW 1

Sauser, Frederic Louis
  See Sauser-Hall, Frederic
Sauser-Hall, Frederic 1887-1961 ...... **CLC 18**
  See Cendrars, Blaise
  See also CA 102; 93-96; CANR 36, 62; MTCW 1
Saussure, Ferdinand de
  1857-1913 .... **TCLC 49**
  See also DLB 242
Savage, Catharine
  See Brosman, Catharine Savage
Savage, Thomas 1915- .... **CLC 40**
  See also CA 126; 132; CAAS 15; CN 7; INT CA-132; TCWW 2
Savan, Glenn (?)- .... **CLC 50**
Sax, Robert
  See Johnson, Robert
Saxo Grammaticus c. 1150-c.
  1222 .... **CMLC 58**
Saxton, Robert
  See Johnson, Robert
Sayers, Dorothy L(eigh)
  1893-1957 .... **TCLC 2, 15**
  See also BPFB 3; BRWS 3; CA 104; 119; CANR 60; CDBLB 1914-1945; CMW 4; DAM POP; DLB 10, 36, 77, 100; MSW; MTCW 1, 2; RGEL 2; SSFS 12; TEA
Sayers, Valerie 1952- .... **CLC 50, 122**
  See also CA 134; CANR 61; CSW
Sayles, John (Thomas) 1950- . **CLC 7, 10, 14**
  See also CA 57-60; CANR 41, 84; DLB 44
Scammell, Michael 1935- .... **CLC 34**
  See also CA 156
Scannell, Vernon 1922- .... **CLC 49**
  See also CA 5-8R; CANR 8, 24, 57; CP 7; CWRI 5; DLB 27; SATA 59
Scarlett, Susan
  See Streatfeild, (Mary) Noel
Scarron 1847-1910
  See Mikszath, Kalman
Schaeffer, Susan Fromberg 1941- ..... **CLC 6, 11, 22**
  See also CA 49-52; CANR 18, 65; CN 7; DLB 28; MTCW 1, 2; SATA 22
Schama, Simon (Michael) 1945- ..... **CLC 150**
  See also BEST 89:4; CA 105; CANR 39, 91
Schary, Jill
  See Robinson, Jill
Schell, Jonathan 1943- .... **CLC 35**
  See also CA 73-76; CANR 12, 117
Schelling, Friedrich Wilhelm Joseph von
  1775-1854 .... **NCLC 30**
  See also DLB 90
Scherer, Jean-Marie Maurice 1920-
  See Rohmer, Eric
  See also CA 110
Schevill, James (Erwin) 1920- .... **CLC 7**
  See also CA 5-8R; CAAS 12; CAD; CD 5
Schiller, Friedrich von 1759-1805 ...... **DC 12; NCLC 39, 69**
  See also CDWLB 2; DAM DRAM; DLB 94; EW 5; RGWL 2, 3; TWA
Schisgal, Murray (Joseph) 1926- .... **CLC 6**
  See also CA 21-24R; CAD; CANR 48, 86; CD 5
Schlee, Ann 1934- .... **CLC 35**
  See also CA 101; CANR 29, 88; SATA 44; SATA-Brief 36
Schlegel, August Wilhelm von
  1767-1845 .... **NCLC 15**
  See also DLB 94; RGWL 2, 3
Schlegel, Friedrich 1772-1829 .... **NCLC 45**
  See also DLB 90; EW 5; RGWL 2, 3; TWA

Schlegel, Johann Elias (von)
1719(?)-1749 .... **LC 5**

Schleiermacher, Friedrich
1768-1834 .... **NCLC 107**
See also DLB 90

Schlesinger, Arthur M(eier), Jr.
1917- .... **CLC 84**
See also AITN 1; CA 1-4R; CANR 1, 28, 58, 105; DLB 17; INT CANR-28; MTCW 1, 2; SATA 61

Schlink, Bernhard 1944- .... **CLC 174**
See also CA 163; CANR 116

Schmidt, Arno (Otto) 1914-1979 ...... **CLC 56**
See also CA 128; 109; DLB 69; EWL 3

Schmitz, Aron Hector 1861-1928
See Svevo, Italo
See also CA 104; 122; MTCW 1

Schnackenberg, Gjertrud (Cecelia)
1953- .... **CLC 40; PC 45**
See also CA 116; CANR 100; CP 7; CWP; DLB 120, 282; PFS 13

Schneider, Leonard Alfred 1925-1966
See Bruce, Lenny
See also CA 89-92

Schnitzler, Arthur 1862-1931 ..... **DC 17; SSC 15, 61; TCLC 4**
See also CA 104; CDWLB 2; DLB 81, 118; EW 8; EWL 3; RGSF 2; RGWL 2, 3

Schoenberg, Arnold Franz Walter
1874-1951 .... **TCLC 75**
See also CA 109; 188

Schonberg, Arnold
See Schoenberg, Arnold Franz Walter

Schopenhauer, Arthur 1788-1860 .. **NCLC 51**
See also DLB 90; EW 5

Schor, Sandra (M.) 1932(?)-1990 ..... **CLC 65**
See also CA 132

Schorer, Mark 1908-1977 .... **CLC 9**
See also CA 5-8R; 73-76; CANR 7; DLB 103

Schrader, Paul (Joseph) 1946- .... **CLC 26**
See also CA 37-40R; CANR 41; DLB 44

Schreber, Daniel 1842-1911 .... **TCLC 123**

Schreiner, Olive (Emilie Albertina)
1855-1920 .... **TCLC 9**
See also AFW; BRWS 2; CA 105; 154; DLB 18, 156, 190, 225; EWL 3; FW; RGEL 2; TWA; WLIT 2

Schulberg, Budd (Wilson) 1914- .. **CLC 7, 48**
See also BPFB 3; CA 25-28R; CANR 19, 87; CN 7; DLB 6, 26, 28; DLBY 1981, 2001

Schulman, Arnold
See Trumbo, Dalton

Schulz, Bruno 1892-1942 .. **SSC 13; TCLC 5, 51**
See also CA 115; 123; CANR 86; CDWLB 4; DLB 215; EWL 3; MTCW 2; RGSF 2; RGWL 2, 3

Schulz, Charles M(onroe)
1922-2000 .... **CLC 12**
See also AAYA 39; CA 9-12R; 187; CANR 6; INT CANR-6; SATA 10; SATA-Obit 118

Schumacher, E(rnst) F(riedrich)
1911-1977 .... **CLC 80**
See also CA 81-84; 73-76; CANR 34, 85

Schuyler, George Samuel 1895-1977 .... **HR 3**
See also BW 2; CA 81-84; 73-76; CANR 42; DLB 29, 51

Schuyler, James Marcus 1923-1991 .. **CLC 5, 23**
See also CA 101; 134; DAM POET; DLB 5, 169; EWL 3; INT CA-101; WP

Schwartz, Delmore (David)
1913-1966 ... **CLC 2, 4, 10, 45, 87; PC 8**
See also AMWS 2; CA 17-18; 25-28R; CANR 35; CAP 2; DLB 28, 48; EWL 3; MTCW 1, 2; PAB; RGAL 4; TUS

Schwartz, Ernst
See Ozu, Yasujiro

Schwartz, John Burnham 1965- .... **CLC 59**
See also CA 132; CANR 116

Schwartz, Lynne Sharon 1939- .... **CLC 31**
See also CA 103; CANR 44, 89; DLB 218; MTCW 2

Schwartz, Muriel A.
See Eliot, T(homas) S(tearns)

Schwarz-Bart, Andre 1928- .... **CLC 2, 4**
See also CA 89-92; CANR 109

Schwarz-Bart, Simone 1938- . **BLCS; CLC 7**
See also BW 2; CA 97-100; CANR 117; EWL 3

Schwerner, Armand 1927-1999 .... **PC 42**
See also CA 9-12R; 179; CANR 50, 85; CP 7; DLB 165

Schwitters, Kurt (Hermann Edward Karl Julius) 1887-1948 .... **TCLC 95**
See also CA 158

Schwob, Marcel (Mayer Andre)
1867-1905 .... **TCLC 20**
See also CA 117; 168; DLB 123; GFL 1789 to the Present

Sciascia, Leonardo 1921-1989 .. **CLC 8, 9, 41**
See also CA 85-88; 130; CANR 35; DLB 177; EWL 3; MTCW 1; RGWL 2, 3

Scoppettone, Sandra 1936- .... **CLC 26**
See Early, Jack
See also AAYA 11; BYA 8; CA 5-8R; CANR 41, 73; GLL 1; MAICYA 2; MAICYAS 1; SATA 9, 92; WYA; YAW

Scorsese, Martin 1942- .... **CLC 20, 89**
See also AAYA 38; CA 110; 114; CANR 46, 85

Scotland, Jay
See Jakes, John (William)

Scott, Duncan Campbell
1862-1947 .... **TCLC 6**
See also CA 104; 153; DAC; DLB 92; RGEL 2

Scott, Evelyn 1893-1963 .... **CLC 43**
See also CA 104; 112; CANR 64; DLB 9, 48; RHW

Scott, F(rancis) R(eginald)
1899-1985 .... **CLC 22**
See also CA 101; 114; CANR 87; DLB 88; INT CA-101; RGEL 2

Scott, Frank
See Scott, F(rancis) R(eginald)

Scott, Joan .... **CLC 65**

Scott, Joanna 1960- .... **CLC 50**
See also CA 126; CANR 53, 92

Scott, Paul (Mark) 1920-1978 ...... **CLC 9, 60**
See also BRWS 1; CA 81-84; 77-80; CANR 33; DLB 14, 207; EWL 3; MTCW 1; RGEL 2; RHW

Scott, Sarah 1723-1795 .... **LC 44**
See also DLB 39

Scott, Sir Walter 1771-1832 .... **NCLC 15, 69, 110; PC 13; SSC 32; WLC**
See also AAYA 22; BRW 4; BYA 2; CDBLB 1789-1832; DA; DAB; DAC; DAM MST, NOV, POET; DLB 93, 107, 116, 144, 159; HGG; LAIT 1; RGEL 2; RGSF 2; SSFS 10; SUFW 1; TEA; WLIT 3; YABC 2

Scribe, (Augustin) Eugene 1791-1861 . **DC 5; NCLC 16**
See also DAM DRAM; DLB 192; GFL 1789 to the Present; RGWL 2, 3

Scrum, R.
See Crumb, R(obert)

Scudery, Georges de 1601-1667 .... **LC 75**
See also GFL Beginnings to 1789

Scudery, Madeleine de 1607-1701 .. **LC 2, 58**
See also DLB 268; GFL Beginnings to 1789

Scum
See Crumb, R(obert)

Scumbag, Little Bobby
See Crumb, R(obert)

Seabrook, John
See Hubbard, L(afayette) Ron(ald)

Sealy, I(rwin) Allan 1951- .... **CLC 55**
See also CA 136; CN 7

Search, Alexander
See Pessoa, Fernando (Antonio Nogueira)

Sebastian, Lee
See Silverberg, Robert

Sebastian Owl
See Thompson, Hunter S(tockton)

Sebestyen, Igen
See Sebestyen, Ouida

Sebestyen, Ouida 1924- .... **CLC 30**
See also AAYA 8; BYA 7; CA 107; CANR 40, 114; CLR 17; JRDA; MAICYA 1, 2; SAAS 10; SATA 39, 140; WYA; YAW

Secundus, H. Scriblerus
See Fielding, Henry

Sedges, John
See Buck, Pearl S(ydenstricker)

Sedgwick, Catharine Maria
1789-1867 .... **NCLC 19, 98**
See also DLB 1, 74, 183, 239, 243, 254; RGAL 4

Seelye, John (Douglas) 1931- .... **CLC 7**
See also CA 97-100; CANR 70; INT CA-97-100; TCWW 2

Seferiades, Giorgos Stylianou 1900-1971
See Seferis, George
See also CA 5-8R; 33-36R; CANR 5, 36; MTCW 1

Seferis, George .... **CLC 5, 11**
See Seferiades, Giorgos Stylianou
See also EW 12; EWL 3; RGWL 2, 3

Segal, Erich (Wolf) 1937- .... **CLC 3, 10**
See also BEST 89:1; BPFB 3; CA 25-28R; CANR 20, 36, 65, 113; CPW; DAM POP; DLBY 1986; INT CANR-20; MTCW 1

Seger, Bob 1945- .... **CLC 35**

Seghers, Anna .... **CLC 7**
See Radvanyi, Netty
See also CDWLB 2; DLB 69; EWL 3

Seidel, Frederick (Lewis) 1936- .... **CLC 18**
See also CA 13-16R; CANR 8, 99; CP 7; DLBY 1984

Seifert, Jaroslav 1901-1986 . **CLC 34, 44, 93; PC 47**
See also CA 127; CDWLB 4; DLB 215; EWL 3; MTCW 1, 2

Sei Shonagon c. 966-1017(?) .... **CMLC 6**

Sejour, Victor 1817-1874 .... **DC 10**
See also DLB 50

Sejour Marcou et Ferrand, Juan Victor
See Sejour, Victor

Selby, Hubert, Jr. 1928- .... **CLC 1, 2, 4, 8; SSC 20**
See also CA 13-16R; CANR 33, 85; CN 7; DLB 2, 227

Selzer, Richard 1928- .... **CLC 74**
See also CA 65-68; CANR 14, 106

Sembene, Ousmane
See Ousmane, Sembene
See also AFW; CWW 2; EWL 3; WLIT 2

Senancour, Etienne Pivert de
1770-1846 .... **NCLC 16**
See also DLB 119; GFL 1789 to the Present

Sender, Ramon (Jose) 1902-1982 ...... **CLC 8; HLC 2; TCLC 136**
See also CA 5-8R; 105; CANR 8; DAM MULT; EWL 3; HW 1; MTCW 1; RGWL 2, 3

Seneca, Lucius Annaeus c. 4B.C.-c. 65 .... **CMLC 6; DC 5**
See also AW 2; CDWLB 1; DAM DRAM; DLB 211; RGWL 2, 3; TWA

Senghor, Leopold Sedar 1906-2001 ... **BLC 3; CLC 54, 130; PC 25**
See also AFW; BW 2; CA 116; 125; 203; CANR 47, 74; DAM MULT, POET; DNFS 2; EWL 3; GFL 1789 to the Present; MTCW 1, 2; TWA

Senna, Danzy 1970- .... **CLC 119**
See also CA 169

Serling, (Edward) Rod(man) 1924-1975 .... **CLC 30**
See also AAYA 14; AITN 1; CA 162; 57-60; DLB 26; SFW 4

Serna, Ramon Gomez de la
See Gomez de la Serna, Ramon

Serpieres
See Guillevic, (Eugene)

Service, Robert
See Service, Robert W(illiam)
See also BYA 4; DAB; DLB 92

Service, Robert W(illiam) 1874(?)-1958 .... **TCLC 15; WLC**
See Service, Robert
See also CA 115; 140; CANR 84; DA; DAC; DAM MST, POET; PFS 10; RGEL 2; SATA 20

Seth, Vikram 1952- .... **CLC 43, 90**
See also CA 121; 127; CANR 50, 74; CN 7; CP 7; DA3; DAM MULT; DLB 120, 271, 282; EWL 3; INT CA-127; MTCW 2

Seton, Cynthia Propper 1926-1982 .. **CLC 27**
See also CA 5-8R; 108; CANR 7

Seton, Ernest (Evan) Thompson 1860-1946 .... **TCLC 31**
See also ANW; BYA 3; CA 109; 204; CLR 59; DLB 92; DLBD 13; JRDA; SATA 18

Seton-Thompson, Ernest
See Seton, Ernest (Evan) Thompson

Settle, Mary Lee 1918- .... **CLC 19, 61**
See also BPFB 3; CA 89-92; CAAS 1; CANR 44, 87; CN 7; CSW; DLB 6; INT CA-89-92

Seuphor, Michel
See Arp, Jean

Sevigne, Marie (de Rabutin-Chantal) 1626-1696 .... **LC 11**
See Sevigne, Marie de Rabutin Chantal
See also GFL Beginnings to 1789; TWA

Sevigne, Marie de Rabutin Chantal
See Sevigne, Marie (de Rabutin-Chantal)
See also DLB 268

Sewall, Samuel 1652-1730 .... **LC 38**
See also DLB 24; RGAL 4

Sexton, Anne (Harvey) 1928-1974 ..... **CLC 2, 4, 6, 8, 10, 15, 53, 123; PC 2; WLC**
See also AMWS 2; CA 1-4R; 53-56; CABS 2; CANR 3, 36; CDALB 1941-1968; DA; DA3; DAB; DAC; DAM MST, POET; DLB 5, 169; EWL 3; EXPP; FW; MAWW; MTCW 1, 2; PAB; PFS 4, 14; RGAL 4; SATA 10; TUS

Shaara, Jeff 1952- .... **CLC 119**
See also CA 163; CANR 109

Shaara, Michael (Joseph, Jr.) 1929-1988 .... **CLC 15**
See also AITN 1; BPFB 3; CA 102; 125; CANR 52, 85; DAM POP; DLBY 1983

Shackleton, C. C.
See Aldiss, Brian W(ilson)

Shacochis, Bob .... **CLC 39**
See Shacochis, Robert G.

Shacochis, Robert G. 1951-
See Shacochis, Bob
See also CA 119; 124; CANR 100; INT CA-124

Shaffer, Anthony (Joshua) 1926-2001 .... **CLC 19**
See also CA 110; 116; 200; CBD; CD 5; DAM DRAM; DFS 13; DLB 13

Shaffer, Peter (Levin) 1926- .. **CLC 5, 14, 18, 37, 60; DC 7**
See also BRWS 1; CA 25-28R; CANR 25, 47, 74, 118; CBD; CD 5; CDBLB 1960 to Present; DA3; DAB; DAM DRAM, MST; DFS 5, 13; DLB 13, 233; EWL 3; MTCW 1, 2; RGEL 2; TEA

Shakespeare, William 1564-1616 .... **WLC**
See also AAYA 35; BRW 1; CDBLB Before 1660; DA; DA3; DAB; DAC; DAM DRAM, MST, POET; DLB 62, 172, 263; EXPP; LAIT 1; LATS 1; LMFS 1; PAB; PFS 1, 2, 3, 4, 5, 8, 9; RGEL 2; TEA; WLIT 3; WP; WS; WYA

Shakey, Bernard
See Young, Neil

Shalamov, Varlam (Tikhonovich) 1907(?)-1982 .... **CLC 18**
See also CA 129; 105; RGSF 2

Shamloo, Ahmad
See Shamlu, Ahmad

Shamlou, Ahmad
See Shamlu, Ahmad

Shamlu, Ahmad 1925-2000 .... **CLC 10**
See also CA 216; CWW 2

Shammas, Anton 1951- .... **CLC 55**
See also CA 199

Shandling, Arline
See Berriault, Gina

Shange, Ntozake 1948- ... **BLC 3; CLC 8, 25, 38, 74, 126; DC 3**
See also AAYA 9; AFAW 1, 2; BW 2; CA 85-88; CABS 3; CAD; CANR 27, 48, 74; CD 5; CP 7; CWD; CWP; DA3; DAM DRAM, MULT; DFS 2, 11; DLB 38, 249; FW; LAIT 5; MTCW 1, 2; NFS 11; RGAL 4; YAW

Shanley, John Patrick 1950- .... **CLC 75**
See also CA 128; 133; CAD; CANR 83; CD 5

Shapcott, Thomas W(illiam) 1935- .. **CLC 38**
See also CA 69-72; CANR 49, 83, 103; CP 7; DLB 289

Shapiro, Jane 1942- .... **CLC 76**
See also CA 196

Shapiro, Karl (Jay) 1913-2000 ...... **CLC 4, 8, 15, 53; PC 25**
See also AMWS 2; CA 1-4R; 188; CAAS 6; CANR 1, 36, 66; CP 7; DLB 48; EWL 3; EXPP; MTCW 1, 2; PFS 3; RGAL 4

Sharp, William 1855-1905 .... **TCLC 39**
See Macleod, Fiona
See also CA 160; DLB 156; RGEL 2

Sharpe, Thomas Ridley 1928-
See Sharpe, Tom
See also CA 114; 122; CANR 85; INT CA-122

Sharpe, Tom .... **CLC 36**
See Sharpe, Thomas Ridley
See also CN 7; DLB 14, 231

Shatrov, Mikhail .... **CLC 59**

Shaw, Bernard
See Shaw, George Bernard
See also DLB 190

Shaw, G. Bernard
See Shaw, George Bernard

Shaw, George Bernard 1856-1950 .. **TCLC 3, 9, 21, 45; WLC**
See Shaw, Bernard
See also BRW 6; BRWC 1; BRWR 2; CA 104; 128; CDBLB 1914-1945; DA; DA3; DAB; DAC; DAM DRAM, MST; DFS 1, 3, 6, 11; DLB 10, 57; EWL 3; LAIT 3; LATS 1; MTCW 1, 2; RGEL 2; TEA; WLIT 4

Shaw, Henry Wheeler 1818-1885 .. **NCLC 15**
See also DLB 11; RGAL 4

Shaw, Irwin 1913-1984 .... **CLC 7, 23, 34**
See also AITN 1; BPFB 3; CA 13-16R; 112; CANR 21; CDALB 1941-1968; CPW; DAM DRAM, POP; DLB 6, 102; DLBY 1984; MTCW 1, 21

Shaw, Robert 1927-1978 .... **CLC 5**
See also AITN 1; CA 1-4R; 81-84; CANR 4; DLB 13, 14

Shaw, T. E.
See Lawrence, T(homas) E(dward)

Shawn, Wallace 1943- .... **CLC 41**
See also CA 112; CAD; CD 5; DLB 266

Shchedrin, N.
See Saltykov, Mikhail Evgrafovich

Shea, Lisa 1953- .... **CLC 86**
See also CA 147

Sheed, Wilfrid (John Joseph) 1930- . **CLC 2, 4, 10, 53**
See also CA 65-68; CANR 30, 66; CN 7; DLB 6; MTCW 1, 2

Sheehy, Gail 1937- .... **CLC 171**
See also CA 49-52; CANR 1, 33, 55, 92; CPW; MTCW 1

Sheldon, Alice Hastings Bradley 1915(?)-1987
See Tiptree, James, Jr.
See also CA 108; 122; CANR 34; INT CA-108; MTCW 1

Sheldon, John
See Bloch, Robert (Albert)

Sheldon, Walter J(ames) 1917-1996
See Queen, Ellery
See also AITN 1; CA 25-28R; CANR 10

Shelley, Mary Wollstonecraft (Godwin) 1797-1851 ...... **NCLC 14, 59, 103; WLC**
See also AAYA 20; BPFB 3; BRW 3; BRWC 2; BRWS 3; BYA 5; CDBLB 1789-1832; DA; DA3; DAB; DAC; DAM MST, NOV; DLB 110, 116, 159, 178; EXPN; HGG; LAIT 1; LMFS 1, 2; NFS 1; RGEL 2; SATA 29; SCFW; SFW 4; TEA; WLIT 3

Shelley, Percy Bysshe 1792-1822 .. **NCLC 18, 93; PC 14; WLC**
See also BRW 4; BRWR 1; CDBLB 1789-1832; DA; DA3; DAB; DAC; DAM MST, POET; DLB 96, 110, 158; EXPP; LMFS 1; PAB; PFS 2; RGEL 2; TEA; WLIT 3; WP

Shepard, Jim 1956- .... **CLC 36**
See also CA 137; CANR 59, 104; SATA 90

Shepard, Lucius 1947- .... **CLC 34**
See also CA 128; 141; CANR 81; HGG; SCFW 2; SFW 4; SUFW 2

Shepard, Sam 1943- .... **CLC 4, 6, 17, 34, 41, 44, 169; DC 5**
See also AAYA 1; AMWS 3; CA 69-72; CABS 3; CAD; CANR 22, 120; CD 5; DA3; DAM DRAM; DFS 3, 6, 7, 14; DLB 7, 212; EWL 3; IDFW 3, 4; MTCW 1, 2; RGAL 4

Shepherd, Michael
See Ludlum, Robert

Sherburne, Zoa (Lillian Morin) 1912-1995 .... **CLC 30**
See also AAYA 13; CA 1-4R; 176; CANR 3, 37; MAICYA 1, 2; SAAS 18; SATA 3; YAW

Sheridan, Frances 1724-1766 .... **LC 7**
See also DLB 39, 84

Sheridan, Richard Brinsley 1751-1816 .... **DC 1; NCLC 5, 91; WLC**
See also BRW 3; CDBLB 1660-1789; DA; DAB; DAC; DAM DRAM, MST; DFS 15; DLB 89; WLIT 3

Sherman, Jonathan Marc .... **CLC 55**

Sherman, Martin 1941(?)- .... **CLC 19**
See also CA 116; 123; CAD; CANR 86; CD 5; DLB 228; GLL 1; IDTP

Sherwin, Judith Johnson
See Johnson, Judith (Emlyn)
See also CANR 85; CP 7; CWP

Sherwood, Frances 1940- .... **CLC 81**
See also CA 146

Sherwood, Robert E(mmet)
1896-1955 .... **TCLC 3**
See also CA 104; 153; CANR 86; DAM DRAM; DFS 11, 15, 17; DLB 7, 26, 249; IDFW 3, 4; RGAL 4

Shestov, Lev 1866-1938 .... **TCLC 56**

Shevchenko, Taras 1814-1861 .... **NCLC 54**

Shiel, M(atthew) P(hipps)
1865-1947 .... **TCLC 8**
See Holmes, Gordon
See also CA 106; 160; DLB 153; HGG; MTCW 2; SFW 4; SUFW

Shields, Carol 1935-2003 .... **CLC 91, 113**
See also AMWS 7; CA 81-84; CANR 51, 74, 98; CCA 1; CN 7; CPW; DA3; DAC; MTCW 2

Shields, David 1956- .... **CLC 97**
See also CA 124; CANR 48, 99, 112

Shiga, Naoya 1883-1971 ..... **CLC 33; SSC 23**
See Shiga Naoya
See also CA 101; 33-36R; MJW; RGWL 3

Shiga Naoya
See Shiga, Naoya
See also DLB 180; EWL 3; RGWL 3

Shilts, Randy 1951-1994 .... **CLC 85**
See also AAYA 19; CA 115; 127; 144; CANR 45; DA3; GLL 1; INT CA-127; MTCW 2

Shimazaki, Haruki 1872-1943
See Shimazaki Toson
See also CA 105; 134; CANR 84; RGWL 3

Shimazaki Toson .... **TCLC 5**
See Shimazaki, Haruki
See also DLB 180; EWL 3

Sholokhov, Mikhail (Aleksandrovich)
1905-1984 .... **CLC 7, 15**
See also CA 101; 112; DLB 272; EWL 3; MTCW 1, 2; RGWL 2, 3; SATA-Obit 36

Shone, Patric
See Hanley, James

Showalter, Elaine 1941- .... **CLC 169**
See also CA 57-60; CANR 58, 106; DLB 67; FW; GLL 2

Shreve, Susan Richards 1939- .... **CLC 23**
See also CA 49-52; CAAS 5; CANR 5, 38, 69, 100; MAICYA 1, 2; SATA 46, 95; SATA-Brief 41

Shue, Larry 1946-1985 .... **CLC 52**
See also CA 145; 117; DAM DRAM; DFS 7

Shu-Jen, Chou 1881-1936
See Lu Hsun
See also CA 104

Shulman, Alix Kates 1932- .... **CLC 2, 10**
See also CA 29-32R; CANR 43; FW; SATA 7

Shusaku, Endo
See Endo, Shusaku

Shuster, Joe 1914-1992 .... **CLC 21**
See also AAYA 50

Shute, Nevil .... **CLC 30**
See Norway, Nevil Shute
See also BPFB 3; DLB 255; NFS 9; RHW; SFW 4

Shuttle, Penelope (Diane) 1947- .... **CLC 7**
See also CA 93-96; CANR 39, 84, 92, 108; CP 7; CWP; DLB 14, 40

Shvarts, Elena 1948- .... **PC 50**
See also CA 147

Sidhwa, Bapsy (N.) 1938- .... **CLC 168**
See also CA 108; CANR 25, 57; CN 7; FW

Sidney, Mary 1561-1621 .... **LC 19, 39**
See Sidney Herbert, Mary

Sidney, Sir Philip 1554-1586 . **LC 19, 39; PC 32**
See also BRW 1; BRWR 2; CDBLB Before 1660; DA; DA3; DAB; DAC; DAM MST, POET; DLB 167; EXPP; PAB; RGEL 2; TEA; WP

Sidney Herbert, Mary
See Sidney, Mary
See also DLB 167

Siegel, Jerome 1914-1996 .... **CLC 21**
See Siegel, Jerry
See also CA 116; 169; 151

Siegel, Jerry
See Siegel, Jerome
See also AAYA 50

Sienkiewicz, Henryk (Adam Alexander Pius)
1846-1916 .... **TCLC 3**
See also CA 104; 134; CANR 84; EWL 3; RGSF 2; RGWL 2, 3

Sierra, Gregorio Martinez
See Martinez Sierra, Gregorio

Sierra, Maria (de la O'LeJarraga) Martinez
See Martinez Sierra, Maria (de la O'LeJarraga)

Sigal, Clancy 1926- .... **CLC 7**
See also CA 1-4R; CANR 85; CN 7

Sigourney, Lydia H.
See Sigourney, Lydia Howard (Huntley)
See also DLB 73, 183

Sigourney, Lydia Howard (Huntley)
1791-1865 .... **NCLC 21, 87**
See Sigourney, Lydia H.; Sigourney, Lydia Huntley
See also DLB 1

Sigourney, Lydia Huntley
See Sigourney, Lydia Howard (Huntley)
See also DLB 42, 239, 243

Siguenza y Gongora, Carlos de
1645-1700 .... **HLCS 2; LC 8**
See also LAW

Sigurjonsson, Johann 1880-1919 ... **TCLC 27**
See also CA 170; EWL 3

Sikelianos, Angelos 1884-1951 .... **PC 29; TCLC 39**
See also EWL 3; RGWL 2, 3

Silkin, Jon 1930-1997 .... **CLC 2, 6, 43**
See also CA 5-8R; CAAS 5; CANR 89; CP 7; DLB 27

Silko, Leslie (Marmon) 1948- .... **CLC 23, 74, 114; NNAL; SSC 37; WLCS**
See also AAYA 14; AMWS 4; ANW; BYA 12; CA 115; 122; CANR 45, 65, 118; CN 7; CP 7; CPW 1; CWP; DA; DA3; DAC; DAM MST, MULT, POP; DLB 143, 175, 256, 275; EWL 3; EXPP; EXPS; LAIT 4; MTCW 2; NFS 4; PFS 9, 16; RGAL 4; RGSF 2; SSFS 4, 8, 10, 11

Sillanpaa, Frans Eemil 1888-1964 ... **CLC 19**
See also CA 129; 93-96; EWL 3; MTCW 1

Sillitoe, Alan 1928- .. **CLC 1, 3, 6, 10, 19, 57, 148**
See also AITN 1; BRWS 5; CA 9-12R; CAAE 191; CAAS 2; CANR 8, 26, 55; CDBLB 1960 to Present; CN 7; DLB 14, 139; EWL 3; MTCW 1, 2; RGEL 2; RGSF 2; SATA 61

Silone, Ignazio 1900-1978 .... **CLC 4**
See also CA 25-28; 81-84; CANR 34; CAP 2; DLB 264; EW 12; EWL 3; MTCW 1; RGSF 2; RGWL 2, 3

Silone, Ignazione
See Silone, Ignazio

Silver, Joan Micklin 1935- .... **CLC 20**
See also CA 114; 121; INT CA-121

Silver, Nicholas
See Faust, Frederick (Schiller)
See also TCWW 2

Silverberg, Robert 1935- .... **CLC 7, 140**
See also AAYA 24; BPFB 3; BYA 7, 9; CA 1-4R, 186; CAAE 186; CAAS 3; CANR 1, 20, 36, 85; CLR 59; CN 7; CPW; DAM POP; DLB 8; INT CANR-20; MAICYA 1, 2; MTCW 1, 2; SATA 13, 91; SATA-Essay 104; SCFW 2; SFW 4; SUFW 2

Silverstein, Alvin 1933- .... **CLC 17**
See also CA 49-52; CANR 2; CLR 25; JRDA; MAICYA 1, 2; SATA 8, 69, 124

Silverstein, Shel(don Allan)
1932-1999 .... **PC 49**
See also AAYA 40; BW 3; CA 107; 179; CANR 47, 74, 81; CLR 5; CWRI 5; JRDA; MAICYA 1, 2; MTCW 2; SATA 33, 92; SATA-Brief 27; SATA-Obit 116

Silverstein, Virginia B(arbara Opshelor)
1937- .... **CLC 17**
See also CA 49-52; CANR 2; CLR 25; JRDA; MAICYA 1, 2; SATA 8, 69, 124

Sim, Georges
See Simenon, Georges (Jacques Christian)

Simak, Clifford D(onald) 1904-1988 . **CLC 1, 55**
See also CA 1-4R; 125; CANR 1, 35; DLB 8; MTCW 1; SATA-Obit 56; SFW 4

Simenon, Georges (Jacques Christian)
1903-1989 .... **CLC 1, 2, 3, 8, 18, 47**
See also BPFB 3; CA 85-88; 129; CANR 35; CMW 4; DA3; DAM POP; DLB 72; DLBY 1989; EW 12; EWL 3; GFL 1789 to the Present; MSW; MTCW 1, 2; RGWL 2, 3

Simic, Charles 1938- .... **CLC 6, 9, 22, 49, 68, 130**
See also AMWS 8; CA 29-32R; CAAS 4; CANR 12, 33, 52, 61, 96; CP 7; DA3; DAM POET; DLB 105; MTCW 2; PFS 7; RGAL 4; WP

Simmel, Georg 1858-1918 .... **TCLC 64**
See also CA 157

Simmons, Charles (Paul) 1924- .... **CLC 57**
See also CA 89-92; INT CA-89-92

Simmons, Dan 1948- .... **CLC 44**
See also AAYA 16; CA 138; CANR 53, 81; CPW; DAM POP; HGG; SUFW 2

Simmons, James (Stewart Alexander)
1933- .... **CLC 43**
See also CA 105; CAAS 21; CP 7; DLB 40

Simms, William Gilmore
1806-1870 .... **NCLC 3**
See also DLB 3, 30, 59, 73, 248, 254; RGAL 4

Simon, Carly 1945- .... **CLC 26**
See also CA 105

Simon, Claude (Henri Eugene)
1913-1984 .... **CLC 4, 9, 15, 39**
See also CA 89-92; CANR 33, 117; DAM NOV; DLB 83; EW 13; EWL 3; GFL 1789 to the Present; MTCW 1

Simon, Myles
See Follett, Ken(neth Martin)

Simon, (Marvin) Neil 1927- ... **CLC 6, 11, 31, 39, 70; DC 14**
See also AAYA 32; AITN 1; AMWS 4; CA 21-24R; CANR 26, 54, 87; CD 5; DA3; DAM DRAM; DFS 2, 6, 12, 18; DLB 7, 266; LAIT 4; MTCW 1, 2; RGAL 4; TUS

Simon, Paul (Frederick) 1941(?)- ...... **CLC 17**
See also CA 116; 153

Simonon, Paul 1956(?)- .... **CLC 30**

Simonson, Rick ed. .... **CLC 70**

Simpson, Harriette
See Arnow, Harriette (Louisa) Simpson

Simpson, Louis (Aston Marantz)
1923- .... **CLC 4, 7, 9, 32, 149**
See also AMWS 9; CA 1-4R; CAAS 4; CANR 1, 61; CP 7; DAM POET; DLB 5; MTCW 1, 2; PFS 7, 11, 14; RGAL 4

Simpson, Mona (Elizabeth) 1957- ... **CLC 44, 146**
See also CA 122; 135; CANR 68, 103; CN 7; EWL 3

Simpson, N(orman) F(rederick) 1919- .... **CLC 29**
See also CA 13-16R; CBD; DLB 13; RGEL 2

Sinclair, Andrew (Annandale) 1935- . **CLC 2, 14**
See also CA 9-12R; CAAS 5; CANR 14, 38, 91; CN 7; DLB 14; FANT; MTCW 1

Sinclair, Emil
See Hesse, Hermann

Sinclair, Iain 1943- .... **CLC 76**
See also CA 132; CANR 81; CP 7; HGG

Sinclair, Iain MacGregor
See Sinclair, Iain

Sinclair, Irene
See Griffith, D(avid Lewelyn) W(ark)

Sinclair, Mary Amelia St. Clair 1865(?)-1946
See Sinclair, May
See also CA 104; HGG; RHW

Sinclair, May .... **TCLC 3, 11**
See Sinclair, Mary Amelia St. Clair
See also CA 166; DLB 36, 135; EWL 3; RGEL 2; SUFW

Sinclair, Roy
See Griffith, D(avid Lewelyn) W(ark)

Sinclair, Upton (Beall) 1878-1968 ..... **CLC 1, 11, 15, 63; WLC**
See also AMWS 5; BPFB 3; BYA 2; CA 5-8R; 25-28R; CANR 7; CDALB 1929-1941; DA; DA3; DAB; DAC; DAM MST, NOV; DLB 9; EWL 3; INT CANR-7; LAIT 3; MTCW 1, 2; NFS 6; RGAL 4; SATA 9; TUS; YAW

Singe, (Edmund) J(ohn) M(illington) 1871-1909 .... **WLC**

Singer, Isaac
See Singer, Isaac Bashevis

Singer, Isaac Bashevis 1904-1991 .. **CLC 1, 3, 6, 9, 11, 15, 23, 38, 69, 111; SSC 3, 53; WLC**
See also AAYA 32; AITN 1, 2; AMW; AMWR 2; BPFB 3; BYA 1, 4; CA 1-4R; 134; CANR 1, 39, 106; CDALB 1941-1968; CLR 1; CWRI 5; DA; DA3; DAB; DAC; DAM MST, NOV; DLB 6, 28, 52, 278; DLBY 1991; EWL 3; EXPS; HGG; JRDA; LAIT 3; MAICYA 1, 2; MTCW 1, 2; RGAL 4; RGSF 2; SATA 3, 27; SATA-Obit 68; SSFS 2, 12, 16; TUS; TWA

Singer, Israel Joshua 1893-1944 .... **TCLC 33**
See also CA 169; EWL 3

Singh, Khushwant 1915- .... **CLC 11**
See also CA 9-12R; CAAS 9; CANR 6, 84; CN 7; EWL 3; RGEL 2

Singleton, Ann
See Benedict, Ruth (Fulton)

Singleton, John 1968(?)- .... **CLC 156**
See also AAYA 50; BW 2, 3; CA 138; CANR 67, 82; DAM MULT

Sinjohn, John
See Galsworthy, John

Sinyavsky, Andrei (Donatevich) 1925-1997 .... **CLC 8**
See Sinyavsky, Andrey Donatovich; Tertz, Abram
See also CA 85-88; 159

Sinyavsky, Andrey Donatovich
See Sinyavsky, Andrei (Donatevich)
See also EWL 3

Sirin, V.
See Nabokov, Vladimir (Vladimirovich)

Sissman, L(ouis) E(dward) 1928-1976 .... **CLC 9, 18**
See also CA 21-24R; 65-68; CANR 13; DLB 5

Sisson, C(harles) H(ubert) 1914-2003 .... **CLC 8**
See also CA 1-4R; CAAS 3; CANR 3, 48, 84; CP 7; DLB 27

Sitting Bull 1831(?)-1890 .... **NNAL**
See also DA3; DAM MULT

Sitwell, Dame Edith 1887-1964 ..... **CLC 2, 9, 67; PC 3**
See also BRW 7; CA 9-12R; CANR 35; CDBLB 1945-1960; DAM POET; DLB 20; EWL 3; MTCW 1, 2; RGEL 2; TEA

Siwaarmill, H. P.
See Sharp, William

Sjoewall, Maj 1935- .... **CLC 7**
See Sjowall, Maj
See also CA 65-68; CANR 73

Sjowall, Maj
See Sjoewall, Maj
See also BPFB 3; CMW 4; MSW

Skelton, John 1460(?)-1529 ..... **LC 71; PC 25**
See also BRW 1; DLB 136; RGEL 2

Skelton, Robin 1925-1997 .... **CLC 13**
See Zuk, Georges
See also AITN 2; CA 5-8R; 160; CAAS 5; CANR 28, 89; CCA 1; CP 7; DLB 27, 53

Skolimowski, Jerzy 1938- .... **CLC 20**
See also CA 128

Skram, Amalie (Bertha) 1847-1905 .... **TCLC 25**
See also CA 165

Skvorecky, Josef (Vaclav) 1924- ...... **CLC 15, 39, 69, 152**
See also CA 61-64; CAAS 1; CANR 10, 34, 63, 108; CDWLB 4; DA3; DAC; DAM NOV; DLB 232; EWL 3; MTCW 1, 2

Slade, Bernard .... **CLC 11, 46**
See Newbound, Bernard Slade
See also CAAS 9; CCA 1; CN 7; DLB 53

Slaughter, Carolyn 1946- .... **CLC 56**
See also CA 85-88; CANR 85; CN 7

Slaughter, Frank G(ill) 1908-2001 ... **CLC 29**
See also AITN 2; CA 5-8R; 197; CANR 5, 85; INT CANR-5; RHW

Slavitt, David R(ytman) 1935- ...... **CLC 5, 14**
See also CA 21-24R; CAAS 3; CANR 41, 83; CP 7; DLB 5, 6

Slesinger, Tess 1905-1945 .... **TCLC 10**
See also CA 107; 199; DLB 102

Slessor, Kenneth 1901-1971 .... **CLC 14**
See also CA 102; 89-92; DLB 260; RGEL 2

Slowacki, Juliusz 1809-1849 .... **NCLC 15**
See also RGWL 3

Smart, Christopher 1722-1771 . **LC 3; PC 13**
See also DAM POET; DLB 109; RGEL 2

Smart, Elizabeth 1913-1986 .... **CLC 54**
See also CA 81-84; 118; DLB 88

Smiley, Jane (Graves) 1949- ...... **CLC 53, 76, 144**
See also AMWS 6; BPFB 3; CA 104; CANR 30, 50, 74, 96; CN 7; CPW 1; DA3; DAM POP; DLB 227, 234; EWL 3; INT CANR-30

Smith, A(rthur) J(ames) M(arshall) 1902-1980 .... **CLC 15**
See also CA 1-4R; 102; CANR 4; DAC; DLB 88; RGEL 2

Smith, Adam 1723(?)-1790 .... **LC 36**
See also DLB 104, 252; RGEL 2

Smith, Alexander 1829-1867 .... **NCLC 59**
See also DLB 32, 55

Smith, Anna Deavere 1950- .... **CLC 86**
See also CA 133; CANR 103; CD 5; DFS 2

Smith, Betty (Wehner) 1904-1972 .... **CLC 19**
See also BPFB 3; BYA 3; CA 5-8R; 33-36R; DLBY 1982; LAIT 3; RGAL 4; SATA 6

Smith, Charlotte (Turner) 1749-1806 .... **NCLC 23, 115**
See also DLB 39, 109; RGEL 2; TEA

Smith, Clark Ashton 1893-1961 .... **CLC 43**
See also CA 143; CANR 81; FANT; HGG; MTCW 2; SCFW 2; SFW 4; SUFW

Smith, Dave .... **CLC 22, 42**
See Smith, David (Jeddie)
See also CAAS 7; DLB 5

Smith, David (Jeddie) 1942-
See Smith, Dave
See also CA 49-52; CANR 1, 59, 120; CP 7; CSW; DAM POET

Smith, Florence Margaret 1902-1971
See Smith, Stevie
See also CA 17-18; 29-32R; CANR 35; CAP 2; DAM POET; MTCW 1, 2; TEA

Smith, Iain Crichton 1928-1998 .... **CLC 64**
See also BRWS 9; CA 21-24R; 171; CN 7; CP 7; DLB 40, 139; RGSF 2

Smith, John 1580(?)-1631 .... **LC 9**
See also DLB 24, 30; TUS

Smith, Johnston
See Crane, Stephen (Townley)

Smith, Joseph, Jr. 1805-1844 .... **NCLC 53**

Smith, Lee 1944- .... **CLC 25, 73**
See also CA 114; 119; CANR 46, 118; CSW; DLB 143; DLBY 1983; EWL 3; INT CA-119; RGAL 4

Smith, Martin
See Smith, Martin Cruz

Smith, Martin Cruz 1942- .. **CLC 25; NNAL**
See also BEST 89:4; BPFB 3; CA 85-88; CANR 6, 23, 43, 65, 119; CMW 4; CPW; DAM MULT, POP; HGG; INT CANR-23; MTCW 2; RGAL 4

Smith, Patti 1946- .... **CLC 12**
See also CA 93-96; CANR 63

Smith, Pauline (Urmson) 1882-1959 .... **TCLC 25**
See also DLB 225; EWL 3

Smith, Rosamond
See Oates, Joyce Carol

Smith, Sheila Kaye
See Kaye-Smith, Sheila

Smith, Stevie .... **CLC 3, 8, 25, 44; PC 12**
See Smith, Florence Margaret
See also BRWS 2; DLB 20; EWL 3; MTCW 2; PAB; PFS 3; RGEL 2

Smith, Wilbur (Addison) 1933- .... **CLC 33**
See also CA 13-16R; CANR 7, 46, 66; CPW; MTCW 1, 2

Smith, William Jay 1918- .... **CLC 6**
See also AMWS 13; CA 5-8R; CANR 44, 106; CP 7; CSW; CWRI 5; DLB 5; MAICYA 1, 2; SAAS 22; SATA 2, 68

Smith, Woodrow Wilson
See Kuttner, Henry

Smith, Zadie 1976- .... **CLC 158**
See also AAYA 50; CA 193

Smolenskin, Peretz 1842-1885 .... **NCLC 30**

Smollett, Tobias (George) 1721-1771 ... **LC 2, 46**
See also BRW 3; CDBLB 1660-1789; DLB 39, 104; RGEL 2; TEA

Snodgrass, W(illiam) D(e Witt) 1926- .... **CLC 2, 6, 10, 18, 68**
See also AMWS 6; CA 1-4R; CANR 6, 36, 65, 85; CP 7; DAM POET; DLB 5; MTCW 1, 2; RGAL 4

Snorri Sturluson 1179-1241 .... **CMLC 56**
See also RGWL 2, 3

Snow, C(harles) P(ercy) 1905-1980 ... **CLC 1, 4, 6, 9, 13, 19**
See also BRW 7; CA 5-8R; 101; CANR 28; CDBLB 1945-1960; DAM NOV; DLB 15, 77; DLBD 17; EWL 3; MTCW 1, 2; RGEL 2; TEA

Snow, Frances Compton
See Adams, Henry (Brooks)
Snyder, Gary (Sherman) 1930- . **CLC 1, 2, 5, 9, 32, 120; PC 21**
See also AMWS 8; ANW; BG 3; CA 17-20R; CANR 30, 60; CP 7; DA3; DAM POET; DLB 5, 16, 165, 212, 237, 275; EWL 3; MTCW 2; PFS 9; RGAL 4; WP
Snyder, Zilpha Keatley 1927- .... **CLC 17**
See also AAYA 15; BYA 1; CA 9-12R; CANR 38; CLR 31; JRDA; MAICYA 1, 2; SAAS 2; SATA 1, 28, 75, 110; SATA-Essay 112; YAW
Soares, Bernardo
See Pessoa, Fernando (Antonio Nogueira)
Sobh, A.
See Shamlu, Ahmad
Sobh, Alef
See Shamlu, Ahmad
Sobol, Joshua 1939- .... **CLC 60**
See Sobol, Yehoshua
See also CA 200; CWW 2
Sobol, Yehoshua 1939-
See Sobol, Joshua
See also CWW 2
Socrates 470B.C.-399B.C. .... **CMLC 27**
Soderberg, Hjalmar 1869-1941 ...... **TCLC 39**
See also DLB 259; EWL 3; RGSF 2
Soderbergh, Steven 1963- .... **CLC 154**
See also AAYA 43
Sodergran, Edith (Irene) 1892-1923
See Soedergran, Edith (Irene)
See also CA 202; DLB 259; EW 11; EWL 3; RGWL 2, 3
Soedergran, Edith (Irene) 1892-1923 .... **TCLC 31**
See Sodergran, Edith (Irene)
Softly, Edgar
See Lovecraft, H(oward) P(hillips)
Softly, Edward
See Lovecraft, H(oward) P(hillips)
Sokolov, Alexander V(sevolodovich) 1943-
See Sokolov, Sasha
See also CA 73-76
Sokolov, Raymond 1941- .... **CLC 7**
See also CA 85-88
Sokolov, Sasha .... **CLC 59**
See Sokolov, Alexander V(sevolodovich)
See also CWW 2; DLB 285; EWL 3; RGWL 2, 3
Sokolov, Sasha .... **CLC 59**
Solo, Jay
See Ellison, Harlan (Jay)
Sologub, Fyodor .... **TCLC 9**
See Teternikov, Fyodor Kuzmich
See also EWL 3
Solomons, Ikey Esquir
See Thackeray, William Makepeace
Solomos, Dionysios 1798-1857 .... **NCLC 15**
Solwoska, Mara
See French, Marilyn
Solzhenitsyn, Aleksandr I(sayevich) 1918- .. **CLC 1, 2, 4, 7, 9, 10, 18, 26, 34, 78, 134; SSC 32; WLC**
See Solzhenitsyn, Aleksandr Isaevich
See also AAYA 49; AITN 1; BPFB 3; CA 69-72; CANR 40, 65, 116; DA; DA3; DAB; DAC; DAM MST, NOV; EW 13; EXPS; LAIT 4; MTCW 1, 2; NFS 6; RGSF 2; RGWL 2, 3; SSFS 9; TWA
Solzhenitsyn, Aleksandr Isaevich
See Solzhenitsyn, Aleksandr I(sayevich)
See also EWL 3
Somers, Jane
See Lessing, Doris (May)
Somerville, Edith Oenone 1858-1949 .... **SSC 56; TCLC 51**
See also CA 196; DLB 135; RGEL 2; RGSF 2

Somerville & Ross
See Martin, Violet Florence; Somerville, Edith Oenone
Sommer, Scott 1951- .... **CLC 25**
See also CA 106
Sondheim, Stephen (Joshua) 1930- . **CLC 30, 39, 147**
See also AAYA 11; CA 103; CANR 47, 67; DAM DRAM; LAIT 4
Sone, Monica 1919- .... **AAL**
Song, Cathy 1955- .... **AAL; PC 21**
See also CA 154; CANR 118; CWP; DLB 169; EXPP; FW; PFS 5
Sontag, Susan 1933- .... **CLC 1, 2, 10, 13, 31, 105**
See also AMWS 3; CA 17-20R; CANR 25, 51, 74, 97; CN 7; CPW; DA3; DAM POP; DLB 2, 67; EWL 3; MAWW; MTCW 1, 2; RGAL 4; RHW; SSFS 10
Sophocles 496(?)B.C.-406(?)B.C. .... **CMLC 2, 47, 51; DC 1; WLCS**
See also AW 1; CDWLB 1; DA; DA3; DAB; DAC; DAM DRAM, MST; DFS 1, 4, 8; DLB 176; LAIT 1; LATS 1; LMFS 1; RGWL 2, 3; TWA
Sordello 1189-1269 .... **CMLC 15**
Sorel, Georges 1847-1922 .... **TCLC 91**
See also CA 118; 188
Sorel, Julia
See Drexler, Rosalyn
Sorokin, Vladimir .... **CLC 59**
See Sorokin, Vladimir Georgievich
Sorokin, Vladimir Georgievich
See Sorokin, Vladimir
See also DLB 285
Sorrentino, Gilbert 1929- .. **CLC 3, 7, 14, 22, 40**
See also CA 77-80; CANR 14, 33, 115; CN 7; CP 7; DLB 5, 173; DLBY 1980; INT CANR-14
Soseki
See Natsume, Soseki
See also MJW
Soto, Gary 1952- ... **CLC 32, 80; HLC 2; PC 28**
See also AAYA 10, 37; BYA 11; CA 119; 125; CANR 50, 74, 107; CLR 38; CP 7; DAM MULT; DLB 82; EWL 3; EXPP; HW 1, 2; INT CA-125; JRDA; MAICYA 2; MAICYAS 1; MTCW 2; PFS 7; RGAL 4; SATA 80, 120; WYA; YAW
Soupault, Philippe 1897-1990 .... **CLC 68**
See also CA 116; 147; 131; EWL 3; GFL 1789 to the Present; LMFS 2
Souster, (Holmes) Raymond 1921- .... **CLC 5, 14**
See also CA 13-16R; CAAS 14; CANR 13, 29, 53; CP 7; DA3; DAC; DAM POET; DLB 88; RGEL 2; SATA 63
Southern, Terry 1924(?)-1995 .... **CLC 7**
See also AMWS 11; BPFB 3; CA 1-4R; 150; CANR 1, 55, 107; CN 7; DLB 2; IDFW 3, 4
Southey, Robert 1774-1843 .... **NCLC 8, 97**
See also BRW 4; DLB 93, 107, 142; RGEL 2; SATA 54
Southworth, Emma Dorothy Eliza Nevitte 1819-1899 .... **NCLC 26**
See also DLB 239
Souza, Ernest
See Scott, Evelyn
Soyinka, Wole 1934- .. **BLC 3; CLC 3, 5, 14, 36, 44, 179; DC 2; WLC**
See also AFW; BW 2, 3; CA 13-16R; CANR 27, 39, 82; CD 5; CDWLB 3; CN 7; CP 7; DA; DA3; DAB; DAC; DAM DRAM, MST, MULT; DFS 10; DLB 125; EWL 3; MTCW 1, 2; RGEL 2; TWA; WLIT 2

Spackman, W(illiam) M(ode) 1905-1990 .... **CLC 46**
See also CA 81-84; 132
Spacks, Barry (Bernard) 1931- .... **CLC 14**
See also CA 154; CANR 33, 109; CP 7; DLB 105
Spanidou, Irini 1946- .... **CLC 44**
See also CA 185
Spark, Muriel (Sarah) 1918- ..... **CLC 2, 3, 5, 8, 13, 18, 40, 94; SSC 10**
See also BRWS 1; CA 5-8R; CANR 12, 36, 76, 89; CDBLB 1945-1960; CN 7; CP 7; DA3; DAB; DAC; DAM MST, NOV; DLB 15, 139; EWL 3; FW; INT CANR-12; LAIT 4; MTCW 1, 2; RGEL 2; TEA; WLIT 4; YAW
Spaulding, Douglas
See Bradbury, Ray (Douglas)
Spaulding, Leonard
See Bradbury, Ray (Douglas)
Spelman, Elizabeth .... **CLC 65**
Spence, J. A. D.
See Eliot, T(homas) S(tearns)
Spencer, Anne 1882-1975 .... **HR 3**
See also BW 2; CA 161; DLB 51, 54
Spencer, Elizabeth 1921- .... **CLC 22; SSC 57**
See also CA 13-16R; CANR 32, 65, 87; CN 7; CSW; DLB 6, 218; EWL 3; MTCW 1; RGAL 4; SATA 14
Spencer, Leonard G.
See Silverberg, Robert
Spencer, Scott 1945- .... **CLC 30**
See also CA 113; CANR 51; DLBY 1986
Spender, Stephen (Harold) 1909-1995 .... **CLC 1, 2, 5, 10, 41, 91**
See also BRWS 2; CA 9-12R; 149; CANR 31, 54; CDBLB 1945-1960; CP 7; DA3; DAM POET; DLB 20; EWL 3; MTCW 1, 2; PAB; RGEL 2; TEA
Spengler, Oswald (Arnold Gottfried) 1880-1936 .... **TCLC 25**
See also CA 118; 189
Spenser, Edmund 1552(?)-1599 ...... **LC 5, 39; PC 8, 42; WLC**
See also BRW 1; CDBLB Before 1660; DA; DA3; DAB; DAC; DAM MST, POET; DLB 167; EFS 2; EXPP; PAB; RGEL 2; TEA; WLIT 3; WP
Spicer, Jack 1925-1965 .... **CLC 8, 18, 72**
See also BG 3; CA 85-88; DAM POET; DLB 5, 16, 193; GLL 1; WP
Spiegelman, Art 1948- .... **CLC 76, 178**
See also AAYA 10, 46; CA 125; CANR 41, 55, 74; MTCW 2; SATA 109; YAW
Spielberg, Peter 1929- .... **CLC 6**
See also CA 5-8R; CANR 4, 48; DLBY 1981
Spielberg, Steven 1947- .... **CLC 20**
See also AAYA 8, 24; CA 77-80; CANR 32; SATA 32
Spillane, Frank Morrison 1918-
See Spillane, Mickey
See also CA 25-28R; CANR 28, 63; DA3; MTCW 1, 2; SATA 66
Spillane, Mickey .... **CLC 3, 13**
See Spillane, Frank Morrison
See also BPFB 3; CMW 4; DLB 226; MSW; MTCW 2
Spinoza, Benedictus de 1632-1677 .. **LC 9, 58**
Spinrad, Norman (Richard) 1940- ... **CLC 46**
See also BPFB 3; CA 37-40R; CAAS 19; CANR 20, 91; DLB 8; INT CANR-20; SFW 4
Spitteler, Carl (Friedrich Georg) 1845-1924 .... **TCLC 12**
See also CA 109; DLB 129; EWL 3
Spivack, Kathleen (Romola Drucker) 1938- .... **CLC 6**
See also CA 49-52

Spoto, Donald 1941- .... **CLC 39**
See also CA 65-68; CANR 11, 57, 93
Springsteen, Bruce (F.) 1949- .... **CLC 17**
See also CA 111
Spurling, Hilary 1940- .... **CLC 34**
See also CA 104; CANR 25, 52, 94
Spyker, John Howland
See Elman, Richard (Martin)
Squared, A.
See Abbott, Edwin A.
Squires, (James) Radcliffe
1917-1993 .... **CLC 51**
See also CA 1-4R; 140; CANR 6, 21
Srivastava, Dhanpat Rai 1880(?)-1936
See Premchand
See also CA 118; 197
Stacy, Donald
See Pohl, Frederik
Stael
See Stael-Holstein, Anne Louise Germaine Necker
See also EW 5; RGWL 2, 3
Stael, Germaine de
See Stael-Holstein, Anne Louise Germaine Necker
See also DLB 119, 192; FW; GFL 1789 to the Present; TWA
Stael-Holstein, Anne Louise Germaine Necker 1766-1817 .... **NCLC 3, 91**
See also Stael; Stael, Germaine de
Stafford, Jean 1915-1979 .. **CLC 4, 7, 19, 68; SSC 26**
See also CA 1-4R; 85-88; CANR 3, 65; DLB 2, 173; MTCW 1, 2; RGAL 4; RGSF 2; SATA-Obit 22; TCWW 2; TUS
Stafford, William (Edgar)
1914-1993 .... **CLC 4, 7, 29**
See also AMWS 11; CA 5-8R; 142; CAAS 3; CANR 5, 22; DAM POET; DLB 5, 206; EXPP; INT CANR-22; PFS 2, 8, 16; RGAL 4; WP
Stagnelius, Eric Johan 1793-1823 . **NCLC 61**
Staines, Trevor
See Brunner, John (Kilian Houston)
Stairs, Gordon
See Austin, Mary (Hunter)
See also TCWW 2
Stalin, Joseph 1879-1953 .... **TCLC 92**
Stampa, Gaspara c. 1524-1554 .... **PC 43**
See also RGWL 2, 3
Stampflinger, K. A.
See Benjamin, Walter
Stancykowna
See Szymborska, Wislawa
Standing Bear, Luther
1868(?)-1939(?) .... **NNAL**
See also CA 113; 144; DAM MULT
Stannard, Martin 1947- .... **CLC 44**
See also CA 142; DLB 155
Stanton, Elizabeth Cady
1815-1902 .... **TCLC 73**
See also CA 171; DLB 79; FW
Stanton, Maura 1946- .... **CLC 9**
See also CA 89-92; CANR 15, 123; DLB 120
Stanton, Schuyler
See Baum, L(yman) Frank
Stapledon, (William) Olaf
1886-1950 .... **TCLC 22**
See also CA 111; 162; DLB 15, 255; SFW 4
Starbuck, George (Edwin)
1931-1996 .... **CLC 53**
See also CA 21-24R; 153; CANR 23; DAM POET
Stark, Richard
See Westlake, Donald E(dwin)
Staunton, Schuyler
See Baum, L(yman) Frank

Stead, Christina (Ellen) 1902-1983 ... **CLC 2, 5, 8, 32, 80**
See also BRWS 4; CA 13-16R; 109; CANR 33, 40; DLB 260; EWL 3; FW; MTCW 1, 2; RGEL 2; RGSF 2
Stead, William Thomas
1849-1912 .... **TCLC 48**
See also CA 167
Stebnitsky, M.
See Leskov, Nikolai (Semyonovich)
Steele, Sir Richard 1672-1729 .... **LC 18**
See also BRW 3; CDBLB 1660-1789; DLB 84, 101; RGEL 2; WLIT 3
Steele, Timothy (Reid) 1948- .... **CLC 45**
See also CA 93-96; CANR 16, 50, 92; CP 7; DLB 120, 282
Steffens, (Joseph) Lincoln
1866-1936 .... **TCLC 20**
See also CA 117; 198
Stegner, Wallace (Earle) 1909-1993 .. **CLC 9, 49, 81; SSC 27**
See also AITN 1; AMWS 4; ANW; BEST 90:3; BPFB 3; CA 1-4R; 141; CAAS 9; CANR 1, 21, 46; DAM NOV; DLB 9, 206, 275; DLBY 1993; EWL 3; MTCW 1, 2; RGAL 4; TCWW 2; TUS
Stein, Gertrude 1874-1946 ..... **DC 19; PC 18; SSC 42; TCLC 1, 6, 28, 48; WLC**
See also AMW; AMWC 2; CA 104; 132; CANR 108; CDALB 1917-1929; DA; DA3; DAB; DAC; DAM MST, NOV, POET; DLB 4, 54, 86, 228; DLBD 15; EWL 3; EXPS; GLL 1; MAWW; MTCW 1, 2; NCFS 4; RGAL 4; RGSF 2; SSFS 5; TUS; WP
Steinbeck, John (Ernst) 1902-1968 ... **CLC 1, 5, 9, 13, 21, 34, 45, 75, 124; SSC 11, 37; TCLC 135; WLC**
See also AAYA 12; AMW; BPFB 3; BYA 2, 3, 13; CA 1-4R; 25-28R; CANR 1, 35; CDALB 1929-1941; DA; DA3; DAB; DAC; DAM DRAM, MST, NOV; DLB 7, 9, 212, 275; DLBD 2; EWL 3; EXPS; LAIT 3; MTCW 1, 2; NFS 1, 5, 7, 17; RGAL 4; RGSF 2; RHW; SATA 9; SSFS 3, 6; TCWW 2; TUS; WYA; YAW
Steinem, Gloria 1934- .... **CLC 63**
See also CA 53-56; CANR 28, 51; DLB 246; FW; MTCW 1, 2
Steiner, George 1929- .... **CLC 24**
See also CA 73-76; CANR 31, 67, 108; DAM NOV; DLB 67; EWL 3; MTCW 1, 2; SATA 62
Steiner, K. Leslie
See Delany, Samuel R(ay), Jr.
Steiner, Rudolf 1861-1925 .... **TCLC 13**
See also CA 107
Stendhal 1783-1842 .. **NCLC 23, 46; SSC 27; WLC**
See also DA; DA3; DAB; DAC; DAM MST, NOV; DLB 119; EW 5; GFL 1789 to the Present; RGWL 2, 3; TWA
Stephen, Adeline Virginia
See Woolf, (Adeline) Virginia
Stephen, Sir Leslie 1832-1904 .... **TCLC 23**
See also BRW 5; CA 123; DLB 57, 144, 190
Stephen, Sir Leslie
See Stephen, Sir Leslie
Stephen, Virginia
See Woolf, (Adeline) Virginia
Stephens, James 1882(?)-1950 .... **SSC 50; TCLC 4**
See also CA 104; 192; DLB 19, 153, 162; EWL 3; FANT; RGEL 2; SUFW
Stephens, Reed
See Donaldson, Stephen R(eeder)
Steptoe, Lydia
See Barnes, Djuna
See also GLL 1

Sterchi, Beat 1949- .... **CLC 65**
See also CA 203
Sterling, Brett
See Bradbury, Ray (Douglas); Hamilton, Edmond
Sterling, Bruce 1954- .... **CLC 72**
See also CA 119; CANR 44; SCFW 2; SFW 4
Sterling, George 1869-1926 .... **TCLC 20**
See also CA 117; 165; DLB 54
Stern, Gerald 1925- .... **CLC 40, 100**
See also AMWS 9; CA 81-84; CANR 28, 94; CP 7; DLB 105; RGAL 4
Stern, Richard (Gustave) 1928- ... **CLC 4, 39**
See also CA 1-4R; CANR 1, 25, 52, 120; CN 7; DLB 218; DLBY 1987; INT CANR-25
Sternberg, Josef von 1894-1969 .... **CLC 20**
See also CA 81-84
Sterne, Laurence 1713-1768 .... **LC 2, 48; WLC**
See also BRW 3; BRWC 1; CDBLB 1660-1789; DA; DAB; DAC; DAM MST, NOV; DLB 39; RGEL 2; TEA
Sternheim, (William Adolf) Carl
1878-1942 .... **TCLC 8**
See also CA 105; 193; DLB 56, 118; EWL 3; RGWL 2, 3
Stevens, Mark 1951- .... **CLC 34**
See also CA 122
Stevens, Wallace 1879-1955 . **PC 6; TCLC 3, 12, 45; WLC**
See also AMW; AMWR 1; CA 104; 124; CDALB 1929-1941; DA; DA3; DAB; DAC; DAM MST, POET; DLB 54; EWL 3; EXPP; MTCW 1, 2; PAB; PFS 13, 16; RGAL 4; TUS; WP
Stevenson, Anne (Katharine) 1933- .. **CLC 7, 33**
See also BRWS 6; CA 17-20R; CAAS 9; CANR 9, 33, 123; CP 7; CWP; DLB 40; MTCW 1; RHW
Stevenson, Robert Louis (Balfour)
1850-1894 ...... **NCLC 5, 14, 63; SSC 11, 51; WLC**
See also AAYA 24; BPFB 3; BRW 5; BRWC 1; BRWR 1; BYA 1, 2, 4, 13; CDBLB 1890-1914; CLR 10, 11; DA; DA3; DAB; DAC; DAM MST, NOV; DLB 18, 57, 141, 156, 174; DLBD 13; HGG; JRDA; LAIT 1, 3; MAICYA 1, 2; NFS 11; RGEL 2; RGSF 2; SATA 100; SUFW; TEA; WCH; WLIT 4; WYA; YABC 2; YAW
Stewart, J(ohn) I(nnes) M(ackintosh)
1906-1994 .... **CLC 7, 14, 32**
See Innes, Michael
See also CA 85-88; 147; CAAS 3; CANR 47; CMW 4; MTCW 1, 2
Stewart, Mary (Florence Elinor)
1916- .... **CLC 7, 35, 117**
See also AAYA 29; BPFB 3; CA 1-4R; CANR 1, 59; CMW 4; CPW; DAB; FANT; RHW; SATA 12; YAW
Stewart, Mary Rainbow
See Stewart, Mary (Florence Elinor)
Stifle, June
See Campbell, Maria
Stifter, Adalbert 1805-1868 .. **NCLC 41; SSC 28**
See also CDWLB 2; DLB 133; RGSF 2; RGWL 2, 3
Still, James 1906-2001 .... **CLC 49**
See also CA 65-68; 195; CAAS 17; CANR 10, 26; CSW; DLB 9; DLBY 01; SATA 29; SATA-Obit 127
Sting 1951-
See Sumner, Gordon Matthew
See also CA 167

Stirling, Arthur
See Sinclair, Upton (Beall)
Stitt, Milan 1941- .... **CLC 29**
See also CA 69-72
Stockton, Francis Richard 1834-1902
See Stockton, Frank R.
See also CA 108; 137; MAICYA 1, 2; SATA 44; SFW 4
Stockton, Frank R. .... **TCLC 47**
See Stockton, Francis Richard
See also BYA 4, 13; DLB 42, 74; DLBD 13; EXPS; SATA-Brief 32; SSFS 3; SUFW; WCH
Stoddard, Charles
See Kuttner, Henry
Stoker, Abraham 1847-1912
See Stoker, Bram
See also CA 105; 150; DA; DA3; DAC; DAM MST, NOV; HGG; SATA 29
Stoker, Bram .... **SSC 62; TCLC 8; WLC**
See Stoker, Abraham
See also AAYA 23; BPFB 3; BRWS 3; BYA 5; CDBLB 1890-1914; DAB; DLB 36, 70, 178; LATS 1; NFS 18; RGEL 2; SUFW; TEA; WLIT 4
Stolz, Mary (Slattery) 1920- .... **CLC 12**
See also AAYA 8; AITN 1; CA 5-8R; CANR 13, 41, 112; JRDA; MAICYA 1, 2; SAAS 3; SATA 10, 71, 133; YAW
Stone, Irving 1903-1989 .... **CLC 7**
See also AITN 1; BPFB 3; CA 1-4R; 129; CAAS 3; CANR 1, 23; CPW; DA3; DAM POP; INT CANR-23; MTCW 1, 2; RHW; SATA 3; SATA-Obit 64
Stone, Oliver (William) 1946- .... **CLC 73**
See also AAYA 15; CA 110; CANR 55
Stone, Robert (Anthony) 1937- ... **CLC 5, 23, 42, 175**
See also AMWS 5; BPFB 3; CA 85-88; CANR 23, 66, 95; CN 7; DLB 152; EWL 3; INT CANR-23; MTCW 1
Stone, Zachary
See Follett, Ken(neth Martin)
Stoppard, Tom 1937- ... **CLC 1, 3, 4, 5, 8, 15, 29, 34, 63, 91; DC 6; WLC**
See also BRWC 1; BRWR 2; BRWS 1; CA 81-84; CANR 39, 67; CBD; CD 5; CDBLB 1960 to Present; DA; DA3; DAB; DAC; DAM DRAM, MST; DFS 2, 5, 8, 11, 13, 16; DLB 13, 233; DLBY 1985; EWL 3; LATS 1; MTCW 1, 2; RGEL 2; TEA; WLIT 4
Storey, David (Malcolm) 1933- . **CLC 2, 4, 5, 8**
See also BRWS 1; CA 81-84; CANR 36; CBD; CD 5; CN 7; DAM DRAM; DLB 13, 14, 207, 245; EWL 3; MTCW 1; RGEL 2
Storm, Hyemeyohsts 1935- ... **CLC 3; NNAL**
See also CA 81-84; CANR 45; DAM MULT
Storm, (Hans) Theodor (Woldsen) 1817-1888 .... **NCLC 1; SSC 27**
See also CDWLB 2; DLB 129; EW; RGSF 2; RGWL 2, 3
Storni, Alfonsina 1892-1938 . **HLC 2; PC 33; TCLC 5**
See also CA 104; 131; DAM MULT; DLB 283; HW 1; LAW
Stoughton, William 1631-1701 .... **LC 38**
See also DLB 24
Stout, Rex (Todhunter) 1886-1975 ..... **CLC 3**
See also AITN 2; BPFB 3; CA 61-64; CANR 71; CMW 4; MSW; RGAL 4
Stow, (Julian) Randolph 1935- ... **CLC 23, 48**
See also CA 13-16R; CANR 33; CN 7; DLB 260; MTCW 1; RGEL 2

Stowe, Harriet (Elizabeth) Beecher 1811-1896 .... **NCLC 3, 50; WLC**
See also AAYA 53; AMWS 1; CDALB 1865-1917; DA; DA3; DAB; DAC; DAM MST, NOV; DLB 1, 12, 42, 74, 189, 239, 243; EXPN; JRDA; LAIT 2; MAICYA 1, 2; NFS 6; RGAL 4; TUS; YABC 1
Strabo c. 64B.C.-c. 25 .... **CMLC 37**
See also DLB 176
Strachey, (Giles) Lytton 1880-1932 .... **TCLC 12**
See also BRWS 2; CA 110; 178; DLB 149; DLBD 10; EWL 3; MTCW 2; NCFS 4
Stramm, August 1874-1915 .... **PC 50**
See also CA 195; EWL 3
Strand, Mark 1934- .... **CLC 6, 18, 41, 71**
See also AMWS 4; CA 21-24R; CANR 40, 65, 100; CP 7; DAM POET; DLB 5; EWL 3; PAB; PFS 9, 18; RGAL 4; SATA 41
Stratton-Porter, Gene(va Grace) 1863-1924
See Porter, Gene(va Grace) Stratton
See also ANW; CA 137; CLR 87; DLB 221; DLBD 14; MAICYA 1, 2; SATA 15
Straub, Peter (Francis) 1943- ... **CLC 28, 107**
See also BEST 89:1; BPFB 3; CA 85-88; CANR 28, 65, 109; CPW; DAM POP; DLBY 1984; HGG; MTCW 1, 2; SUFW 2
Strauss, Botho 1944- .... **CLC 22**
See also CA 157; CWW 2; DLB 124
Strauss, Leo 1899-1973 .... **TCLC 141**
See also CA 101; 45-48; CANR 122
Streatfeild, (Mary) Noel 1897(?)-1986 .... **CLC 21**
See also CA 81-84; 120; CANR 31; CLR 17, 83; CWRI 5; DLB 160; MAICYA 1, 2; SATA 20; SATA-Obit 48
Stribling, T(homas) S(igismund) 1881-1965 .... **CLC 23**
See also CA 189; 107; CMW 4; DLB 9; RGAL 4
Strindberg, (Johan) August 1849-1912 ... **DC 18; TCLC 1, 8, 21, 47; WLC**
See also CA 104; 135; DA; DA3; DAB; DAC; DAM DRAM, MST; DFS 4, 9; DLB 259; EW 7; EWL 3; IDTP; LMFS 2; MTCW 2; RGWL 2, 3; TWA
Stringer, Arthur 1874-1950 .... **TCLC 37**
See also CA 161; DLB 92
Stringer, David
See Roberts, Keith (John Kingston)
Stroheim, Erich von 1885-1957 ..... **TCLC 71**
Strugatskii, Arkadii (Natanovich) 1925-1991 .... **CLC 27**
See also CA 106; 135; SFW 4
Strugatskii, Boris (Natanovich) 1933- .... **CLC 27**
See also CA 106; SFW 4
Strummer, Joe 1953(?)- .... **CLC 30**
Strunk, William, Jr. 1869-1946 ...... **TCLC 92**
See also CA 118; 164; NCFS 5
Stryk, Lucien 1924- .... **PC 27**
See also CA 13-16R; CANR 10, 28, 55, 110; CP 7
Stuart, Don A.
See Campbell, John W(ood, Jr.)
Stuart, Ian
See MacLean, Alistair (Stuart)
Stuart, Jesse (Hilton) 1906-1984 ... **CLC 1, 8, 11, 14, 34; SSC 31**
See also CA 5-8R; 112; CANR 31; DLB 9, 48, 102; DLBY 1984; SATA 2; SATA-Obit 36
Stubblefield, Sally
See Trumbo, Dalton

Sturgeon, Theodore (Hamilton) 1918-1985 .... **CLC 22, 39**
See Queen, Ellery
See also AAYA 51; BPFB 3; BYA 9, 10; CA 81-84; 116; CANR 32, 103; DLB 8; DLBY 1985; HGG; MTCW 1, 2; SCFW; SFW 4; SUFW
Sturges, Preston 1898-1959 .... **TCLC 48**
See also CA 114; 149; DLB 26
Styron, William 1925- .... **CLC 1, 3, 5, 11, 15, 60; SSC 25**
See also AMW; AMWC 2; BEST 90:4; BPFB 3; CA 5-8R; CANR 6, 33, 74; CDALB 1968-1988; CN 7; CPW; CSW; DA3; DAM NOV, POP; DLB 2, 143; DLBY 1980; EWL 3; INT CANR-6; LAIT 2; MTCW 1, 2; NCFS 1; RGAL 4; RHW; TUS
Su, Chien 1884-1918
See Su Man-shu
See also CA 123
Suarez Lynch, B.
See Bioy Casares, Adolfo; Borges, Jorge Luis
Suassuna, Ariano Vilar 1927- .... **HLCS 1**
See also CA 178; HW 2; LAW
Suckert, Kurt Erich
See Malaparte, Curzio
Suckling, Sir John 1609-1642 . **LC 75; PC 30**
See also BRW 2; DAM POET; DLB 58, 126; EXPP; PAB; RGEL 2
Suckow, Ruth 1892-1960 .... **SSC 18**
See also CA 193; 113; DLB 9, 102; RGAL 4; TCWW 2
Sudermann, Hermann 1857-1928 .. **TCLC 15**
See also CA 107; 201; DLB 118
Sue, Eugene 1804-1857 .... **NCLC 1**
See also DLB 119
Sueskind, Patrick 1949- .... **CLC 44**
See Suskind, Patrick
Suetonius c. 70-c. 130 .... **CMLC 60**
See also AW 2; DLB 211; RGWL 2, 3
Sukenick, Ronald 1932- .... **CLC 3, 4, 6, 48**
See also CA 25-28R; CAAE 209; CAAS 8; CANR 32, 89; CN 7; DLB 173; DLBY 1981
Suknaski, Andrew 1942- .... **CLC 19**
See also CA 101; CP 7; DLB 53
Sullivan, Vernon
See Vian, Boris
Sully Prudhomme, Rene-Francois-Armand 1839-1907 .... **TCLC 31**
See also GFL 1789 to the Present
Su Man-shu .... **TCLC 24**
See Su, Chien
See also EWL 3
Summerforest, Ivy B.
See Kirkup, James
Summers, Andrew James 1942- .... **CLC 26**
Summers, Andy
See Summers, Andrew James
Summers, Hollis (Spurgeon, Jr.) 1916- .... **CLC 10**
See also CA 5-8R; CANR 3; DLB 6
Summers, (Alphonsus Joseph-Mary Augustus) Montague 1880-1948 .... **TCLC 16**
See also CA 118; 163
Sumner, Gordon Matthew .... **CLC 26**
See Police, The; Sting
Sun Tzu c. 400B.C.-c. 320B.C. .... **CMLC 56**
Surtees, Robert Smith 1805-1864 .. **NCLC 14**
See also DLB 21; RGEL 2
Susann, Jacqueline 1921-1974 .... **CLC 3**
See also AITN 1; BPFB 3; CA 65-68; 53-56; MTCW 1, 2
Su Shi
See Su Shih
See also RGWL 2, 3

Su Shih 1036-1101 .... **CMLC 15**
  See Su Shi
Suskind, Patrick
  See Sueskind, Patrick
  See also BPFB 3; CA 145; CWW 2
Sutcliff, Rosemary 1920-1992 .... **CLC 26**
  See also AAYA 10; BYA 1, 4; CA 5-8R; 139; CANR 37; CLR 1, 37; CPW; DAB; DAC; DAM MST, POP; JRDA; LATS 1; MAICYA 1, 2; MAICYAS 1; RHW; SATA 6, 44, 78; SATA-Obit 73; WYA; YAW
Sutro, Alfred 1863-1933 .... **TCLC 6**
  See also CA 105; 185; DLB 10; RGEL 2
Sutton, Henry
  See Slavitt, David R(ytman)
Suzuki, D. T.
  See Suzuki, Daisetz Teitaro
Suzuki, Daisetz T.
  See Suzuki, Daisetz Teitaro
Suzuki, Daisetz Teitaro
  1870-1966 .... **TCLC 109**
  See also CA 121; 111; MTCW 1, 2
Suzuki, Teitaro
  See Suzuki, Daisetz Teitaro
Svevo, Italo .... **SSC 25; TCLC 2, 35**
  See Schmitz, Aron Hector
  See also DLB 264; EW 8; EWL 3; RGWL 2, 3
Swados, Elizabeth (A.) 1951- .... **CLC 12**
  See also CA 97-100; CANR 49; INT CA-97-100
Swados, Harvey 1920-1972 .... **CLC 5**
  See also CA 5-8R; 37-40R; CANR 6; DLB 2
Swan, Gladys 1934- .... **CLC 69**
  See also CA 101; CANR 17, 39
Swanson, Logan
  See Matheson, Richard (Burton)
Swarthout, Glendon (Fred)
  1918-1992 .... **CLC 35**
  See also CA 1-4R; 139; CANR 1, 47; LAIT 5; SATA 26; TCWW 2; YAW
Sweet, Sarah C.
  See Jewett, (Theodora) Sarah Orne
Swenson, May 1919-1989 ...... **CLC 4, 14, 61, 106; PC 14**
  See also AMWS 4; CA 5-8R; 130; CANR 36, 61; DA; DAB; DAC; DAM MST, POET; DLB 5; EXPP; GLL 2; MTCW 1, 2; PFS 16; SATA 15; WP
Swift, Augustus
  See Lovecraft, H(oward) P(hillips)
Swift, Graham (Colin) 1949- ...... **CLC 41, 88**
  See also BRWC 2; BRWS 5; CA 117; 122; CANR 46, 71; CN 7; DLB 194; MTCW 2; NFS 18; RGSF 2
Swift, Jonathan 1667-1745 .. **LC 1, 42; PC 9; WLC**
  See also AAYA 41; BRW 3; BRWC 1; BRWR 1; BYA 5, 14; CDBLB 1660-1789; CLR 53; DA; DA3; DAB; DAC; DAM MST, NOV, POET; DLB 39, 95, 101; EXPN; LAIT 1; NFS 6; RGEL 2; SATA 19; TEA; WCH; WLIT 3
Swinburne, Algernon Charles
  1837-1909 ... **PC 24; TCLC 8, 36; WLC**
  See also BRW 5; CA 105; 140; CDBLB 1832-1890; DA; DA3; DAB; DAC; DAM MST, POET; DLB 35, 57; PAB; RGEL 2; TEA
Swinfen, Ann .... **CLC 34**
  See also CA 202
Swinnerton, Frank Arthur
  1884-1982 .... **CLC 31**
  See also CA 108; DLB 34
Swithen, John
  See King, Stephen (Edwin)
Sylvia
  See Ashton-Warner, Sylvia (Constance)

Symmes, Robert Edward
  See Duncan, Robert (Edward)
Symonds, John Addington
  1840-1893 .... **NCLC 34**
  See also DLB 57, 144
Symons, Arthur 1865-1945 .... **TCLC 11**
  See also CA 107; 189; DLB 19, 57, 149; RGEL 2
Symons, Julian (Gustave)
  1912-1994 .... **CLC 2, 14, 32**
  See also CA 49-52; 147; CAAS 3; CANR 3, 33, 59; CMW 4; DLB 87, 155; DLBY 1992; MSW; MTCW 1
Synge, (Edmund) J(ohn) M(illington)
  1871-1909 .... **DC 2; TCLC 6, 37**
  See also BRW 6; BRWR 1; CA 104; 141; CDBLB 1890-1914; DAM DRAM; DFS 18; DLB 10, 19; EWL 3; RGEL 2; TEA; WLIT 4
Syruc, J.
  See Milosz, Czeslaw
Szirtes, George 1948- .... **CLC 46; PC 51**
  See also CA 109; CANR 27, 61, 117; CP 7
Szymborska, Wislawa 1923- ..... **CLC 99; PC 44**
  See also CA 154; CANR 91; CDWLB 4; CWP; CWW 2; DA3; DLB 232; DLBY 1996; EWL 3; MTCW 2; PFS 15; RGWL 3
T. O., Nik
  See Annensky, Innokenty (Fyodorovich)
Tabori, George 1914- .... **CLC 19**
  See also CA 49-52; CANR 4, 69; CBD; CD 5; DLB 245
Tacitus c. 55-c. 117 .... **CMLC 56**
  See also AW 2; CDWLB 1; DLB 211; RGWL 2, 3
Tagore, Rabindranath 1861-1941 .... **PC 8; SSC 48; TCLC 3, 53**
  See also CA 104; 120; DA3; DAM DRAM, POET; EWL 3; MTCW 1, 2; PFS 18; RGEL 2; RGSF 2; RGWL 2, 3; TWA
Taine, Hippolyte Adolphe
  1828-1893 .... **NCLC 15**
  See also EW 7; GFL 1789 to the Present
Talayesva, Don C. 1890-(?) .... **NNAL**
Talese, Gay 1932- .... **CLC 37**
  See also AITN 1; CA 1-4R; CANR 9, 58; DLB 185; INT CANR-9; MTCW 1, 2
Tallent, Elizabeth (Ann) 1954- .... **CLC 45**
  See also CA 117; CANR 72; DLB 130
Tallmountain, Mary 1918-1997 .... **NNAL**
  See also CA 146; 161; DLB 193
Tally, Ted 1952- .... **CLC 42**
  See also CA 120; 124; CAD; CD 5; INT CA-124
Talvik, Heiti 1904-1947 .... **TCLC 87**
  See also EWL 3
Tamayo y Baus, Manuel
  1829-1898 .... **NCLC 1**
Tammsaare, A(nton) H(ansen)
  1878-1940 .... **TCLC 27**
  See also CA 164; CDWLB 4; DLB 220; EWL 3
Tam'si, Tchicaya U
  See Tchicaya, Gerald Felix
Tan, Amy (Ruth) 1952- . **AAL; CLC 59, 120, 151**
  See also AAYA 9, 48; AMWS 10; BEST 89:3; BPFB 3; CA 136; CANR 54, 105; CDALBS; CN 7; CPW 1; DA3; DAM MULT, NOV, POP; DLB 173; EXPN; FW; LAIT 3, 5; MTCW 2; NFS 1, 13, 16; RGAL 4; SATA 75; SSFS 9; YAW
Tandem, Felix
  See Spitteler, Carl (Friedrich Georg)

Tanizaki, Jun'ichiro 1886-1965 ... **CLC 8, 14, 28; SSC 21**
  See Tanizaki Jun'ichiro
  See also CA 93-96; 25-28R; MJW; MTCW 2; RGSF 2; RGWL 2
Tanizaki Jun'ichiro
  See Tanizaki, Jun'ichiro
  See also DLB 180; EWL 3
Tanner, William
  See Amis, Kingsley (William)
Tao Lao
  See Storni, Alfonsina
Tapahonso, Luci 1953- .... **NNAL**
  See also CA 145; CANR 72; DLB 175
Tarantino, Quentin (Jerome)
  1963- .... **CLC 125**
  See also CA 171
Tarassoff, Lev
  See Troyat, Henri
Tarbell, Ida M(inerva) 1857-1944 . **TCLC 40**
  See also CA 122; 181; DLB 47
Tarkington, (Newton) Booth
  1869-1946 .... **TCLC 9**
  See also BPFB 3; BYA 3; CA 110; 143; CWRI 5; DLB 9, 102; MTCW 2; RGAL 4; SATA 17
Tarkovskii, Andrei Arsen'evich
  See Tarkovsky, Andrei (Arsenyevich)
Tarkovsky, Andrei (Arsenyevich)
  1932-1986 .... **CLC 75**
  See also CA 127
Tartt, Donna 1964(?)- .... **CLC 76**
  See also CA 142
Tasso, Torquato 1544-1595 .... **LC 5, 94**
  See also EFS 2; EW 2; RGWL 2, 3
Tate, (John Orley) Allen 1899-1979 .. **CLC 2, 4, 6, 9, 11, 14, 24; PC 50**
  See also AMW; CA 5-8R; 85-88; CANR 32, 108; DLB 4, 45, 63; DLBD 17; EWL 3; MTCW 1, 2; RGAL 4; RHW
Tate, Ellalice
  See Hibbert, Eleanor Alice Burford
Tate, James (Vincent) 1943- ...... **CLC 2, 6, 25**
  See also CA 21-24R; CANR 29, 57, 114; CP 7; DLB 5, 169; EWL 3; PFS 10, 15; RGAL 4; WP
Tauler, Johannes c. 1300-1361 ...... **CMLC 37**
  See also DLB 179; LMFS 1
Tavel, Ronald 1940- .... **CLC 6**
  See also CA 21-24R; CAD; CANR 33; CD 5
Taviani, Paolo 1931- .... **CLC 70**
  See also CA 153
Taylor, Bayard 1825-1878 .... **NCLC 89**
  See also DLB 3, 189, 250, 254; RGAL 4
Taylor, C(ecil) P(hilip) 1929-1981 .... **CLC 27**
  See also CA 25-28R; 105; CANR 47; CBD
Taylor, Edward 1642(?)-1729 .... **LC 11**
  See also AMW; DA; DAB; DAC; DAM MST, POET; DLB 24; EXPP; RGAL 4; TUS
Taylor, Eleanor Ross 1920- .... **CLC 5**
  See also CA 81-84; CANR 70
Taylor, Elizabeth 1932-1975 ..... **CLC 2, 4, 29**
  See also CA 13-16R; CANR 9, 70; DLB 139; MTCW 1; RGEL 2; SATA 13
Taylor, Frederick Winslow
  1856-1915 .... **TCLC 76**
  See also CA 188
Taylor, Henry (Splawn) 1942- .... **CLC 44**
  See also CA 33-36R; CAAS 7; CANR 31; CP 7; DLB 5; PFS 10
Taylor, Kamala (Purnaiya) 1924-
  See Markandaya, Kamala
  See also CA 77-80; NFS 13

Taylor, Mildred D(elois) 1943- .... **CLC 21**
See also AAYA 10, 47; BW 1; BYA 3, 8; CA 85-88; CANR 25, 115; CLR 9, 59, 90; CSW; DLB 52; JRDA; LAIT 3; MAICYA 1, 2; SAAS 5; SATA 135; WYA; YAW

Taylor, Peter (Hillsman) 1917-1994 .. **CLC 1, 4, 18, 37, 44, 50, 71; SSC 10**
See also AMWS 5; BPFB 3; CA 13-16R; 147; CANR 9, 50; CSW; DLB 218, 278; DLBY 1981, 1994; EWL 3; EXPS; INT CANR-9; MTCW 1, 2; RGSF 2; SSFS 9; TUS

Taylor, Robert Lewis 1912-1998 .... **CLC 14**
See also CA 1-4R; 170; CANR 3, 64; SATA 10

Tchekhov, Anton
See Chekhov, Anton (Pavlovich)

Tchicaya, Gerald Felix 1931-1988 .. **CLC 101**
See Tchicaya U Tam'si
See also CA 129; 125; CANR 81

Tchicaya U Tam'si
See Tchicaya, Gerald Felix
See also EWL 3

Teasdale, Sara 1884-1933 .... **PC 31; TCLC 4**
See also CA 104; 163; DLB 45; GLL 1; PFS 14; RGAL 4; SATA 32; TUS

Tecumseh 1768-1813 .... **NNAL**
See also DAM MULT

Tegner, Esaias 1782-1846 .... **NCLC 2**

Teilhard de Chardin, (Marie Joseph) Pierre 1881-1955 .... **TCLC 9**
See also CA 105; 210; GFL 1789 to the Present

Temple, Ann
See Mortimer, Penelope (Ruth)

Tennant, Emma (Christina) 1937- .. **CLC 13, 52**
See also BRWS 9; CA 65-68; CAAS 9; CANR 10, 38, 59, 88; CN 7; DLB 14; EWL 3; SFW 4

Tenneshaw, S. M.
See Silverberg, Robert

Tenney, Tabitha Gilman 1762-1837 .... **NCLC 122**
See also DLB 37, 200

Tennyson, Alfred 1809-1892 ... **NCLC 30, 65, 115; PC 6; WLC**
See also AAYA 50; BRW 4; CDBLB 1832-1890; DA; DA3; DAB; DAC; DAM MST, POET; DLB 32; EXPP; PAB; PFS 1, 2, 4, 11, 15; RGEL 2; TEA; WLIT 4; WP

Teran, Lisa St. Aubin de .... **CLC 36**
See St. Aubin de Teran, Lisa

Terence c. 184B.C.-c. 159B.C. ...... **CMLC 14; DC 7**
See also AW 1; CDWLB 1; DLB 211; RGWL 2, 3; TWA

Teresa de Jesus, St. 1515-1582 .... **LC 18**

Terkel, Louis 1912-
See Terkel, Studs
See also CA 57-60; CANR 18, 45, 67; DA3; MTCW 1, 2

Terkel, Studs .... **CLC 38**
See Terkel, Louis
See also AAYA 32; AITN 1; MTCW 2; TUS

Terry, C. V.
See Slaughter, Frank G(ill)

Terry, Megan 1932- .... **CLC 19; DC 13**
See also CA 77-80; CABS 3; CAD; CANR 43; CD 5; CWD; DFS 18; DLB 7, 249; GLL 2

Tertullian c. 155-c. 245 .... **CMLC 29**

Tertz, Abram
See Sinyavsky, Andrei (Donatevich)
See also CWW 2; RGSF 2

Tesich, Steve 1943(?)-1996 .... **CLC 40, 69**
See also CA 105; 152; CAD; DLBY 1983

Tesla, Nikola 1856-1943 .... **TCLC 88**

Teternikov, Fyodor Kuzmich 1863-1927
See Sologub, Fyodor
See also CA 104

Tevis, Walter 1928-1984 .... **CLC 42**
See also CA 113; SFW 4

Tey, Josephine .... **TCLC 14**
See Mackintosh, Elizabeth
See also DLB 77; MSW

Thackeray, William Makepeace 1811-1863 .... **NCLC 5, 14, 22, 43; WLC**
See also BRW 5; BRWC 2; CDBLB 1832-1890; DA; DA3; DAB; DAC; DAM MST, NOV; DLB 21, 55, 159, 163; NFS 13; RGEL 2; SATA 23; TEA; WLIT 3

Thakura, Ravindranatha
See Tagore, Rabindranath

Thames, C. H.
See Marlowe, Stephen

Tharoor, Shashi 1956- .... **CLC 70**
See also CA 141; CANR 91; CN 7

Thelwell, Michael Miles 1939- .... **CLC 22**
See also BW 2; CA 101

Theobald, Lewis, Jr.
See Lovecraft, H(oward) P(hillips)

Theocritus c. 310B.C.- .... **CMLC 45**
See also AW 1; DLB 176; RGWL 2, 3

Theodorescu, Ion N. 1880-1967
See Arghezi, Tudor
See also CA 116

Theriault, Yves 1915-1983 .... **CLC 79**
See also CA 102; CCA 1; DAC; DAM MST; DLB 88; EWL 3

Theroux, Alexander (Louis) 1939- .... **CLC 2, 25**
See also CA 85-88; CANR 20, 63; CN 7

Theroux, Paul (Edward) 1941- ..... **CLC 5, 8, 11, 15, 28, 46**
See also AAYA 28; AMWS 8; BEST 89:4; BPFB 3; CA 33-36R; CANR 20, 45, 74; CDALBS; CN 7; CPW 1; DA3; DAM POP; DLB 2, 218; EWL 3; HGG; MTCW 1, 2; RGAL 4; SATA 44, 109; TUS

Thesen, Sharon 1946- .... **CLC 56**
See also CA 163; CP 7; CWP

Thespis fl. 6th cent. B.C.- .... **CMLC 51**
See also LMFS 1

Thevenin, Denis
See Duhamel, Georges

Thibault, Jacques Anatole Francois 1844-1924
See France, Anatole
See also CA 106; 127; DA3; DAM NOV; MTCW 1, 2; TWA

Thiele, Colin (Milton) 1920- .... **CLC 17**
See also CA 29-32R; CANR 12, 28, 53, 105; CLR 27; DLB 289; MAICYA 1, 2; SAAS 2; SATA 14, 72, 125; YAW

Thistlethwaite, Bel
See Wetherald, Agnes Ethelwyn

Thomas, Audrey (Callahan) 1935- .... **CLC 7, 13, 37, 107; SSC 20**
See also AITN 2; CA 21-24R; CAAS 19; CANR 36, 58; CN 7; DLB 60; MTCW 1; RGSF 2

Thomas, Augustus 1857-1934 .... **TCLC 97**

Thomas, D(onald) M(ichael) 1935- . **CLC 13, 22, 31, 132**
See also BPFB 3; BRWS 4; CA 61-64; CAAS 11; CANR 17, 45, 75; CDBLB 1960 to Present; CN 7; CP 7; DA3; DLB 40, 207; HGG; INT CANR-17; MTCW 1, 2; SFW 4

Thomas, Dylan (Marlais) 1914-1953 .... **PC 2, 52; SSC 3, 44; TCLC 1, 8, 45, 105; WLC**
See also AAYA 45; BRWS 1; CA 104; 120; CANR 65; CDBLB 1945-1960; DA; DA3; DAB; DAC; DAM DRAM, MST, POET; DLB 13, 20, 139; EWL 3; EXPP; LAIT 3; MTCW 1, 2; PAB; PFS 1, 3, 8; RGEL 2; RGSF 2; SATA 60; TEA; WLIT 4; WP

Thomas, (Philip) Edward 1878-1917 .... **TCLC 10**
See also BRW 6; BRWS 3; CA 106; 153; DAM POET; DLB 19, 98, 156, 216; EWL 3; PAB; RGEL 2

Thomas, Joyce Carol 1938- .... **CLC 35**
See also AAYA 12; BW 2, 3; CA 113; 116; CANR 48, 114; CLR 19; DLB 33; INT CA-116; JRDA; MAICYA 1, 2; MTCW 1, 2; SAAS 7; SATA 40, 78, 123, 137; WYA; YAW

Thomas, Lewis 1913-1993 .... **CLC 35**
See also ANW; CA 85-88; 143; CANR 38, 60; DLB 275; MTCW 1, 2

Thomas, M. Carey 1857-1935 .... **TCLC 89**
See also FW

Thomas, Paul
See Mann, (Paul) Thomas

Thomas, Piri 1928- .... **CLC 17; HLCS 2**
See also CA 73-76; HW 1

Thomas, R(onald) S(tuart) 1913-2000 .... **CLC 6, 13, 48**
See also CA 89-92; 189; CAAS 4; CANR 30; CDBLB 1960 to Present; CP 7; DAB; DAM POET; DLB 27; EWL 3; MTCW 1; RGEL 2

Thomas, Ross (Elmore) 1926-1995 .. **CLC 39**
See also CA 33-36R; 150; CANR 22, 63; CMW 4

Thompson, Francis (Joseph) 1859-1907 .... **TCLC 4**
See also BRW 5; CA 104; 189; CDBLB 1890-1914; DLB 19; RGEL 2; TEA

Thompson, Francis Clegg
See Mencken, H(enry) L(ouis)

Thompson, Hunter S(tockton) 1937(?)- .... **CLC 9, 17, 40, 104**
See also AAYA 45; BEST 89:1; BPFB 3; CA 17-20R; CANR 23, 46, 74, 77, 111; CPW; CSW; DA3; DAM POP; DLB 185; MTCW 1, 2; TUS

Thompson, James Myers
See Thompson, Jim (Myers)

Thompson, Jim (Myers) 1906-1977(?) .... **CLC 69**
See also BPFB 3; CA 140; CMW 4; CPW; DLB 226; MSW

Thompson, Judith .... **CLC 39**
See also CWD

Thomson, James 1700-1748 .... **LC 16, 29, 40**
See also BRWS 3; DAM POET; DLB 95; RGEL 2

Thomson, James 1834-1882 .... **NCLC 18**
See also DAM POET; DLB 35; RGEL 2

Thoreau, Henry David 1817-1862 .. **NCLC 7, 21, 61; PC 30; WLC**
See also AAYA 42; AMW; ANW; BYA 3; CDALB 1640-1865; DA; DA3; DAB; DAC; DAM MST; DLB 1, 183, 223, 270; LAIT 2; LMFS 1; NCFS 3; RGAL 4; TUS

Thorndike, E. L.
See Thorndike, Edward L(ee)

Thorndike, Edward L(ee) 1874-1949 .... **TCLC 107**
See also CA 121

Thornton, Hall
See Silverberg, Robert

Thorpe, Adam 1956- .... **CLC 176**
See also CA 129; CANR 92; DLB 231

Thubron, Colin (Gerald Dryden) 1939- .... **CLC 163**
See also CA 25-28R; CANR 12, 29, 59, 95; CN 7; DLB 204, 231

Thucydides c. 455B.C.-c. 395B.C. . **CMLC 17**
See also AW 1; DLB 176; RGWL 2, 3

Thumboo, Edwin Nadason 1933- .... **PC 30**
See also CA 194

Thurber, James (Grover)
1894-1961 .. **CLC 5, 11, 25, 125; SSC 1, 47**
See also AMWS 1; BPFB 3; BYA 5; CA 73-76; CANR 17, 39; CDALB 1929-1941; CWRI 5; DA; DA3; DAB; DAC; DAM DRAM, MST, NOV; DLB 4, 11, 22, 102; EWL 3; EXPS; FANT; LAIT 3; MAICYA 1, 2; MTCW 1, 2; RGAL 4; RGSF 2; SATA 13; SSFS 1, 10; SUFW; TUS

Thurman, Wallace (Henry)
1902-1934 .... **BLC 3; HR 3; TCLC 6**
See also BW 1, 3; CA 104; 124; CANR 81; DAM MULT; DLB 51

Tibullus c. 54B.C.-c. 18B.C. .... **CMLC 36**
See also AW 2; DLB 211; RGWL 2, 3

Ticheburn, Cheviot
See Ainsworth, William Harrison

Tieck, (Johann) Ludwig
1773-1853 .... **NCLC 5, 46; SSC 31**
See also CDWLB 2; DLB 90; EW 5; IDTP; RGSF 2; RGWL 2, 3; SUFW

Tiger, Derry
See Ellison, Harlan (Jay)

Tilghman, Christopher 1948(?)- .... **CLC 65**
See also CA 159; CSW; DLB 244

Tillich, Paul (Johannes)
1886-1965 .... **CLC 131**
See also CA 5-8R; 25-28R; CANR 33; MTCW 1, 2

Tillinghast, Richard (Williford)
1940- .... **CLC 29**
See also CA 29-32R; CAAS 23; CANR 26, 51, 96; CP 7; CSW

Timrod, Henry 1828-1867 .... **NCLC 25**
See also DLB 3, 248; RGAL 4

Tindall, Gillian (Elizabeth) 1938- ...... **CLC 7**
See also CA 21-24R; CANR 11, 65, 107; CN 7

Tiptree, James, Jr. .... **CLC 48, 50**
See Sheldon, Alice Hastings Bradley
See also DLB 8; SCFW 2; SFW 4

Tirone Smith, Mary-Ann 1944- .... **CLC 39**
See also CA 118; 136; CANR 113; SATA 143

Tirso de Molina 1580(?)-1648 .... **DC 13; HLCS 2; LC 73**
See also RGWL 2, 3

Titmarsh, Michael Angelo
See Thackeray, William Makepeace

Tocqueville, Alexis (Charles Henri Maurice Clerel Comte) de 1805-1859 .. **NCLC 7, 63**
See also EW 6; GFL 1789 to the Present; TWA

Toffler, Alvin 1928- .... **CLC 168**
See also CA 13-16R; CANR 15, 46, 67; CPW; DAM POP; MTCW 1, 2

Toibin, Colm
See Toibin, Colm
See also DLB 271

Toibin, Colm 1955- .... **CLC 162**
See Toibin, Colm
See also CA 142; CANR 81

Tolkien, J(ohn) R(onald) R(euel)
1892-1973 .... **CLC 1, 2, 3, 8, 12, 38; TCLC 137; WLC**
See also AAYA 10; AITN 1; BPFB 3; BRWC 2; BRWS 2; CA 17-18; 45-48; CANR 36; CAP 2; CDBLB 1914-1945; CLR 56; CPW 1; CWRI 5; DA; DA3; DAB; DAC; DAM MST, NOV, POP; DLB 15, 160, 255; EFS 2; EWL 3; FANT; JRDA; LAIT 1; LATS 1; LMFS 2; MAICYA 1, 2; MTCW 1, 2; NFS 8; RGEL 2; SATA 2, 32, 100; SATA-Obit 24; SFW 4; SUFW; TEA; WCH; WYA; YAW

Toller, Ernst 1893-1939 .... **TCLC 10**
See also CA 107; 186; DLB 124; EWL 3; RGWL 2, 3

Tolson, M. B.
See Tolson, Melvin B(eaunorus)

Tolson, Melvin B(eaunorus)
1898(?)-1966 .... **BLC 3; CLC 36, 105**
See also AFAW 1, 2; BW 1, 3; CA 124; 89-92; CANR 80; DAM MULT, POET; DLB 48, 76; RGAL 4

Tolstoi, Aleksei Nikolaevich
See Tolstoy, Alexey Nikolaevich

Tolstoi, Lev
See Tolstoy, Leo (Nikolaevich)
See also RGSF 2; RGWL 2, 3

Tolstoy, Aleksei Nikolaevich
See Tolstoy, Alexey Nikolaevich
See also DLB 272

Tolstoy, Alexey Nikolaevich
1882-1945 .... **TCLC 18**
See Tolstoi, Aleksei Nikolaevich
See also CA 107; 158; EWL 3; SFW 4

Tolstoy, Leo (Nikolaevich)
1828-1910 . **SSC 9, 30, 45, 54; TCLC 4, 11, 17, 28, 44, 79; WLC**
See Tolstoi, Lev
See also CA 104; 123; DA; DA3; DAB; DAC; DAM MST, NOV; DLB 238; EFS 2; EW 7; EXPS; IDTP; LAIT 2; LATS 1; LMFS 1; NFS 10; SATA 26; SSFS 5; TWA

Tolstoy, Count Leo
See Tolstoy, Leo (Nikolaevich)

Tomalin, Claire 1933- .... **CLC 166**
See also CA 89-92; CANR 52, 88; DLB 155

Tomasi di Lampedusa, Giuseppe 1896-1957
See Lampedusa, Giuseppe (Tomasi) di
See also CA 111; DLB 177; EWL 3

Tomlin, Lily .... **CLC 17**
See Tomlin, Mary Jean

Tomlin, Mary Jean 1939(?)-
See Tomlin, Lily
See also CA 117

Tomline, F. Latour
See Gilbert, W(illiam) S(chwenck)

Tomlinson, (Alfred) Charles 1927- .... **CLC 2, 4, 6, 13, 45; PC 17**
See also CA 5-8R; CANR 33; CP 7; DAM POET; DLB 40

Tomlinson, H(enry) M(ajor)
1873-1958 .... **TCLC 71**
See also CA 118; 161; DLB 36, 100, 195

Tonson, Jacob fl. 1655(?)-1736 .... **LC 86**
See also DLB 170

Toole, John Kennedy 1937-1969 ..... **CLC 19, 64**
See also BPFB 3; CA 104; DLBY 1981; MTCW 2

Toomer, Eugene
See Toomer, Jean

Toomer, Eugene Pinchback
See Toomer, Jean

Toomer, Jean 1894-1967 .. **BLC 3; CLC 1, 4, 13, 22; HR 3; PC 7; SSC 1, 45; WLCS**
See also AFAW 1, 2; AMWS 3, 9; BW 1; CA 85-88; CDALB 1917-1929; DA3; DAM MULT; DLB 45, 51; EWL 3; EXPP; EXPS; LMFS 2; MTCW 1, 2; NFS 11; RGAL 4; RGSF 2; SSFS 5

Toomer, Nathan Jean
See Toomer, Jean

Toomer, Nathan Pinchback
See Toomer, Jean

Torley, Luke
See Blish, James (Benjamin)

Tornimparte, Alessandra
See Ginzburg, Natalia

Torre, Raoul della
See Mencken, H(enry) L(ouis)

Torrence, Ridgely 1874-1950 .... **TCLC 97**
See also DLB 54, 249

Torrey, E(dwin) Fuller 1937- .... **CLC 34**
See also CA 119; CANR 71

Torsvan, Ben Traven
See Traven, B.

Torsvan, Benno Traven
See Traven, B.

Torsvan, Berick Traven
See Traven, B.

Torsvan, Berwick Traven
See Traven, B.

Torsvan, Bruno Traven
See Traven, B.

Torsvan, Traven
See Traven, B.

Tourneur, Cyril 1575(?)-1626 .... **LC 66**
See also BRW 2; DAM DRAM; DLB 58; RGEL 2

Tournier, Michel (Edouard) 1924- .... **CLC 6, 23, 36, 95**
See also CA 49-52; CANR 3, 36, 74; DLB 83; EWL 3; GFL 1789 to the Present; MTCW 1, 2; SATA 23

Tournimparte, Alessandra
See Ginzburg, Natalia

Towers, Ivar
See Kornbluth, C(yril) M.

Towne, Robert (Burton) 1936(?)- ...... **CLC 87**
See also CA 108; DLB 44; IDFW 3, 4

Townsend, Sue .... **CLC 61**
See Townsend, Susan Lilian
See also AAYA 28; CA 119; 127; CANR 65, 107; CBD; CD 5; CPW; CWD; DAB; DAC; DAM MST; DLB 271; INT CA-127; SATA 55, 93; SATA-Brief 48; YAW

Townsend, Susan Lilian 1946-
See Townsend, Sue

Townshend, Pete
See Townshend, Peter (Dennis Blandford)

Townshend, Peter (Dennis Blandford)
1945- .... **CLC 17, 42**
See also CA 107

Tozzi, Federigo 1883-1920 .... **TCLC 31**
See also CA 160; CANR 110; DLB 264; EWL 3

Tracy, Don(ald Fiske) 1905-1970(?)
See Queen, Ellery
See also CA 1-4R; 176; CANR 2

Trafford, F. G.
See Riddell, Charlotte

Traill, Catharine Parr 1802-1899 .. **NCLC 31**
See also DLB 99

Trakl, Georg 1887-1914 .... **PC 20; TCLC 5**
See also CA 104; 165; EW 10; EWL 3; LMFS 2; MTCW 2; RGWL 2, 3

Tranquilli, Secondino
See Silone, Ignazio

Transtroemer, Tomas Gosta
See Transtromer, Tomas (Goesta)

Transtromer, Tomas
See Transtromer, Tomas (Goesta)

Transtromer, Tomas (Goesta)
1931- .... **CLC 52, 65**
See also CA 117; 129; CAAS 17; CANR 115; DAM POET; DLB 257; EWL 3

Transtromer, Tomas Gosta
See Transtromer, Tomas (Goesta)

Traven, B. 1882(?)-1969 .... **CLC 8, 11**
See also CA 19-20; 25-28R; CAP 2; DLB 9, 56; EWL 3; MTCW 1; RGAL 4

Trediakovsky, Vasilii Kirillovich
1703-1769 .... **LC 68**
See also DLB 150

Treitel, Jonathan 1959- .... **CLC 70**
See also CA 210; DLB 267

Trelawny, Edward John
1792-1881 .... **NCLC 85**
See also DLB 110, 116, 144

Tremain, Rose 1943- .... **CLC 42**
See also CA 97-100; CANR 44, 95; CN 7;
DLB 14, 271; RGSF 2; RHW

Tremblay, Michel 1942- .... **CLC 29, 102**
See also CA 116; 128; CCA 1; CWW 2;
DAC; DAM MST; DLB 60; EWL 3; GLL
1; MTCW 1, 2

Trevanian .... **CLC 29**
See Whitaker, Rod(ney)

Trevor, Glen
See Hilton, James

Trevor, William .. **CLC 7, 9, 14, 25, 71, 116;
SSC 21, 58**
See Cox, William Trevor
See also BRWS 4; CBD; CD 5; CN 7; DLB
14, 139; EWL 3; LATS 1; MTCW 2;
RGEL 2; RGSF 2; SSFS 10

Trifonov, Iurii (Valentinovich)
See Trifonov, Yuri (Valentinovich)
See also RGWL 2, 3

Trifonov, Yuri (Valentinovich)
1925-1981 .... **CLC 45**
See Trifonov, Iurii (Valentinovich); Trifonov, Yury Valentinovich
See also CA 126; 103; MTCW 1

Trifonov, Yury Valentinovich
See Trifonov, Yuri (Valentinovich)
See also EWL 3

Trilling, Diana (Rubin) 1905-1996 . **CLC 129**
See also CA 5-8R; 154; CANR 10, 46; INT
CANR-10; MTCW 1, 2

Trilling, Lionel 1905-1975 .... **CLC 9, 11, 24**
See also AMWS 3; CA 9-12R; 61-64;
CANR 10, 105; DLB 28, 63; EWL 3; INT
CANR-10; MTCW 1, 2; RGAL 4; TUS

Trimball, W. H.
See Mencken, H(enry) L(ouis)

Tristan
See Gomez de la Serna, Ramon

Tristram
See Housman, A(lfred) E(dward)

Trogdon, William (Lewis) 1939-
See Heat-Moon, William Least
See also CA 115; 119; CANR 47, 89; CPW;
INT CA-119

Trollope, Anthony 1815-1882 .... **NCLC 6, 33,
101; SSC 28; WLC**
See also BRW 5; CDBLB 1832-1890; DA;
DA3; DAB; DAC; DAM MST, NOV;
DLB 21, 57, 159; RGEL 2; RGSF 2;
SATA 22

Trollope, Frances 1779-1863 .... **NCLC 30**
See also DLB 21, 166

Trotsky, Leon 1879-1940 .... **TCLC 22**
See also CA 118; 167

Trotter (Cockburn), Catharine
1679-1749 .... **LC 8**
See also DLB 84, 252

Trotter, Wilfred 1872-1939 .... **TCLC 97**

Trout, Kilgore
See Farmer, Philip Jose

Trow, George W. S. 1943- .... **CLC 52**
See also CA 126; CANR 91

Troyat, Henri 1911- .... **CLC 23**
See also CA 45-48; CANR 2, 33, 67, 117;
GFL 1789 to the Present; MTCW 1

Trudeau, G(arretson) B(eekman) 1948-
See Trudeau, Garry B.
See also CA 81-84; CANR 31; SATA 35

Trudeau, Garry B. .... **CLC 12**
See Trudeau, G(arretson) B(eekman)
See also AAYA 10; AITN 2

Truffaut, Francois 1932-1984 ... **CLC 20, 101**
See also CA 81-84; 113; CANR 34

Trumbo, Dalton 1905-1976 .... **CLC 19**
See also CA 21-24R; 69-72; CANR 10;
DLB 26; IDFW 3, 4; YAW

Trumbull, John 1750-1831 .... **NCLC 30**
See also DLB 31; RGAL 4

Trundlett, Helen B.
See Eliot, T(homas) S(tearns)

Truth, Sojourner 1797(?)-1883 ...... **NCLC 94**
See also DLB 239; FW; LAIT 2

Tryon, Thomas 1926-1991 .... **CLC 3, 11**
See also AITN 1; BPFB 3; CA 29-32R; 135;
CANR 32, 77; CPW; DA3; DAM POP;
HGG; MTCW 1

Tryon, Tom
See Tryon, Thomas

Ts'ao Hsueh-ch'in 1715(?)-1763 .... **LC 1**

Tsushima, Shuji 1909-1948
See Dazai Osamu
See also CA 107

Tsvetaeva (Efron), Marina (Ivanovna)
1892-1941 .... **PC 14; TCLC 7, 35**
See also CA 104; 128; CANR 73; EW 11;
MTCW 1, 2; RGWL 2, 3

Tuck, Lily 1938- .... **CLC 70**
See also CA 139; CANR 90

Tu Fu 712-770 .... **PC 9**
See Du Fu
See also DAM MULT; TWA; WP

Tunis, John R(oberts) 1889-1975 ..... **CLC 12**
See also BYA 1; CA 61-64; CANR 62; DLB
22, 171; JRDA; MAICYA 1, 2; SATA 37;
SATA-Brief 30; YAW

Tuohy, Frank .... **CLC 37**
See Tuohy, John Francis
See also DLB 14, 139

Tuohy, John Francis 1925-
See Tuohy, Frank
See also CA 5-8R; 178; CANR 3, 47; CN 7

Turco, Lewis (Putnam) 1934- ..... **CLC 11, 63**
See also CA 13-16R; CAAS 22; CANR 24,
51; CP 7; DLBY 1984

Turgenev, Ivan (Sergeevich)
1818-1883 ..... **DC 7; NCLC 21, 37, 122;
SSC 7, 57; WLC**
See also DA; DAB; DAC; DAM MST,
NOV; DFS 6; DLB 238, 284; EW 6;
LATS 1; NFS 16; RGSF 2; RGWL 2, 3;
TWA

Turgot, Anne-Robert-Jacques
1727-1781 .... **LC 26**

Turner, Frederick 1943- .... **CLC 48**
See also CA 73-76; CAAS 10; CANR 12,
30, 56; DLB 40, 282

Turton, James
See Crace, Jim

Tutu, Desmond M(pilo) 1931- .. **BLC 3; CLC 80**
See also BW 1, 3; CA 125; CANR 67, 81;
DAM MULT

Tutuola, Amos 1920-1997 ..... **BLC 3; CLC 5,
14, 29**
See also AFW; BW 2, 3; CA 9-12R; 159;
CANR 27, 66; CDWLB 3; CN 7; DA3;
DAM MULT; DLB 125; DNFS 2; EWL
3; MTCW 1, 2; RGEL 2; WLIT 2

Twain, Mark .. **SSC 34; TCLC 6, 12, 19, 36,
48, 59; WLC**
See Clemens, Samuel Langhorne
See also AAYA 20; AMW; AMWC 1; BPFB
3; BYA 2, 3, 11, 14; CLR 58, 60, 66; DLB
11; EXPN; EXPS; FANT; LAIT 2; NFS
1, 6; RGAL 4; RGSF 2; SFW 4; SSFS 1,
7; SUFW; TUS; WCH; WYA; YAW

Tyler, Anne 1941- . **CLC 7, 11, 18, 28, 44, 59,
103**
See also AAYA 18; AMWS 4; BEST 89:1;
BPFB 3; BYA 12; CA 9-12R; CANR 11,
33, 53, 109; CDALBS; CN 7; CPW;
CSW; DAM NOV, POP; DLB 6, 143;
DLBY 1982; EWL 3; EXPN; LATS 1;
MAWW; MTCW 1, 2; NFS 2, 7, 10;
RGAL 4; SATA 7, 90; SSFS 17; TUS;
YAW

Tyler, Royall 1757-1826 .... **NCLC 3**
See also DLB 37; RGAL 4

Tynan, Katharine 1861-1931 .... **TCLC 3**
See also CA 104; 167; DLB 153, 240; FW

Tyutchev, Fyodor 1803-1873 .... **NCLC 34**

Tzara, Tristan 1896-1963 ..... **CLC 47; PC 27**
See also CA 153; 89-92; DAM POET; EWL
3; MTCW 2

Uchida, Yoshiko 1921-1992 .... **AAL**
See also AAYA 16; BYA 2, 3; CA 13-16R;
139; CANR 6, 22, 47, 61; CDALBS; CLR
6, 56; CWRI 5; JRDA; MAICYA 1, 2;
MTCW 1, 2; SAAS 1; SATA 1, 53; SATA-
Obit 72

Udall, Nicholas 1504-1556 .... **LC 84**
See also DLB 62; RGEL 2

Ueda Akinari 1734-1809 .... **NCLC 131**

Uhry, Alfred 1936- .... **CLC 55**
See also CA 127; 133; CAD; CANR 112;
CD 5; CSW; DA3; DAM DRAM, POP;
DFS 11, 15; INT CA-133

Ulf, Haerved
See Strindberg, (Johan) August

Ulf, Harved
See Strindberg, (Johan) August

Ulibarri, Sabine R(eyes)
1919-2003 .... **CLC 83; HLCS 2**
See also CA 131; 214; CANR 81; DAM
MULT; DLB 82; HW 1, 2; RGSF 2

Unamuno (y Jugo), Miguel de
1864-1936 ..... **HLC 2; SSC 11; TCLC 2, 9**
See also CA 104; 131; CANR 81; DAM
MULT, NOV; DLB 108; EW 8; EWL 3;
HW 1, 2; MTCW 1, 2; RGSF 2; RGWL
2, 3; TWA

Uncle Shelby
See Silverstein, Shel(don Allan)

Undercliffe, Errol
See Campbell, (John) Ramsey

Underwood, Miles
See Glassco, John

Undset, Sigrid 1882-1949 ..... **TCLC 3; WLC**
See also CA 104; 129; DA; DA3; DAB;
DAC; DAM MST, NOV; EW 9; EWL 3;
FW; MTCW 1, 2; RGWL 2, 3

Ungaretti, Giuseppe 1888-1970 ... **CLC 7, 11, 15**
See also CA 19-20; 25-28R; CAP 2; DLB
114; EW 10; EWL 3; RGWL 2, 3

Unger, Douglas 1952- .... **CLC 34**
See also CA 130; CANR 94

Unsworth, Barry (Forster) 1930- .... **CLC 76, 127**
See also BRWS 7; CA 25-28R; CANR 30,
54; CN 7; DLB 194

Updike, John (Hoyer) 1932- . **CLC 1, 2, 3, 5,
7, 9, 13, 15, 23, 34, 43, 70, 139; SSC 13,
27; WLC**
See also AAYA 36; AMW; AMWC 1;
AMWR 1; BPFB 3; BYA 12; CA 1-4R;
CABS 1; CANR 4, 33, 51, 94; CDALB
1968-1988; CN 7; CP 7; CPW 1; DA;
DA3; DAB; DAC; DAM MST, NOV,
POET, POP; DLB 2, 5, 143, 218, 227;
DLBD 3; DLBY 1980, 1982, 1997; EWL
3; EXPP; HGG; MTCW 1, 2; NFS 12;
RGAL 4; RGSF 2; SSFS 3; TUS

Upshaw, Margaret Mitchell
See Mitchell, Margaret (Munnerlyn)

Upton, Mark
See Sanders, Lawrence

Upward, Allen 1863-1926 .... **TCLC 85**
See also CA 117; 187; DLB 36

Urdang, Constance (Henriette)
1922-1996 .... **CLC 47**
See also CA 21-24R; CANR 9, 24; CP 7; CWP

Uriel, Henry
See Faust, Frederick (Schiller)

Uris, Leon (Marcus) 1924-2003 ... **CLC 7, 32**
See also AITN 1, 2; BEST 89:2; BPFB 3; CA 1-4R; CANR 1, 40, 65, 123; CN 7; CPW 1; DA3; DAM NOV, POP; MTCW 1, 2; SATA 49

Urista, Alberto H. 1947- ...... **HLCS 1; PC 34**
See Alurista
See also CA 45-48, 182; CANR 2, 32; HW 1

Urmuz
See Codrescu, Andrei

Urquhart, Guy
See McAlmon, Robert (Menzies)

Urquhart, Jane 1949- .... **CLC 90**
See also CA 113; CANR 32, 68, 116; CCA 1; DAC

Usigli, Rodolfo 1905-1979 .... **HLCS 1**
See also CA 131; EWL 3; HW 1; LAW

Ustinov, Peter (Alexander) 1921- .... **CLC 1**
See also AITN 1; CA 13-16R; CANR 25, 51; CBD; CD 5; DLB 13; MTCW 2

U Tam'si, Gerald Felix Tchicaya
See Tchicaya, Gerald Felix

U Tam'si, Tchicaya
See Tchicaya, Gerald Felix

Vachss, Andrew (Henry) 1942- .... **CLC 106**
See also CA 118; CAAE 214; CANR 44, 95; CMW 4

Vachss, Andrew H.
See Vachss, Andrew (Henry)

Vaculik, Ludvik 1926- .... **CLC 7**
See also CA 53-56; CANR 72; CWW 2; DLB 232; EWL 3

Vaihinger, Hans 1852-1933 .... **TCLC 71**
See also CA 116; 166

Valdez, Luis (Miguel) 1940- ..... **CLC 84; DC 10; HLC 2**
See also CA 101; CAD; CANR 32, 81; CD 5; DAM MULT; DFS 5; DLB 122; EWL 3; HW 1; LAIT 4

Valenzuela, Luisa 1938- .... **CLC 31, 104; HLCS 1; SSC 14**
See also CA 101; CANR 32, 65, 123; CDWLB 3; CWW 2; DAM MULT; DLB 113; EWL 3; FW; HW 1, 2; LAW; RGSF 2; RGWL 3

Valera y Alcala-Galiano, Juan
1824-1905 .... **TCLC 10**
See also CA 106

Valery, (Ambroise) Paul (Toussaint Jules)
1871-1945 .... **PC 9; TCLC 4, 15**
See also CA 104; 122; DA3; DAM POET; DLB 258; EW 8; EWL 3; GFL 1789 to the Present; MTCW 1, 2; RGWL 2, 3; TWA

Valle-Inclan, Ramon (Maria) del
1866-1936 .... **HLC 2; TCLC 5**
See also CA 106; 153; CANR 80; DAM MULT; DLB 134; EW 8; EWL 3; HW 2; RGSF 2; RGWL 2, 3

Vallejo, Antonio Buero
See Buero Vallejo, Antonio

Vallejo, Cesar (Abraham)
1892-1938 .... **HLC 2; TCLC 3, 56**
See also CA 105; 153; DAM MULT; EWL 3; HW 1; LAW; RGWL 2, 3

Valles, Jules 1832-1885 .... **NCLC 71**
See also DLB 123; GFL 1789 to the Present

Vallette, Marguerite Eymery
1860-1953 .... **TCLC 67**
See Rachilde
See also CA 182; DLB 123, 192

Valle Y Pena, Ramon del
See Valle-Inclan, Ramon (Maria) del

Van Ash, Cay 1918- .... **CLC 34**

Vanbrugh, Sir John 1664-1726 .... **LC 21**
See also BRW 2; DAM DRAM; DLB 80; IDTP; RGEL 2

Van Campen, Karl
See Campbell, John W(ood, Jr.)

Vance, Gerald
See Silverberg, Robert

Vance, Jack .... **CLC 35**
See Vance, John Holbrook
See also DLB 8; FANT; SCFW 2; SFW 4; SUFW 1, 2

Vance, John Holbrook 1916-
See Queen, Ellery; Vance, Jack
See also CA 29-32R; CANR 17, 65; CMW 4; MTCW 1

Van Den Bogarde, Derek Jules Gaspard Ulric Niven 1921-1999 .... **CLC 14**
See Bogarde, Dirk
See also CA 77-80; 179

Vandenburgh, Jane .... **CLC 59**
See also CA 168

Vanderhaeghe, Guy 1951- .... **CLC 41**
See also BPFB 3; CA 113; CANR 72

van der Post, Laurens (Jan)
1906-1996 .... **CLC 5**
See also AFW; CA 5-8R; 155; CANR 35; CN 7; DLB 204; RGEL 2

van de Wetering, Janwillem 1931- ... **CLC 47**
See also CA 49-52; CANR 4, 62, 90; CMW 4

Van Dine, S. S. .... **TCLC 23**
See Wright, Willard Huntington
See also MSW

Van Doren, Carl (Clinton)
1885-1950 .... **TCLC 18**
See also CA 111; 168

Van Doren, Mark 1894-1972 .... **CLC 6, 10**
See also CA 1-4R; 37-40R; CANR 3; DLB 45, 284; MTCW 1, 2; RGAL 4

Van Druten, John (William)
1901-1957 .... **TCLC 2**
See also CA 104; 161; DLB 10; RGAL 4

Van Duyn, Mona (Jane) 1921- ...... **CLC 3, 7, 63, 116**
See also CA 9-12R; CANR 7, 38, 60, 116; CP 7; CWP; DAM POET; DLB 5

Van Dyne, Edith
See Baum, L(yman) Frank

van Itallie, Jean-Claude 1936- .... **CLC 3**
See also CA 45-48; CAAS 2; CAD; CANR 1, 48; CD 5; DLB 7

Van Loot, Cornelius Obenchain
See Roberts, Kenneth (Lewis)

van Ostaijen, Paul 1896-1928 .... **TCLC 33**
See also CA 163

Van Peebles, Melvin 1932- .... **CLC 2, 20**
See also BW 2, 3; CA 85-88; CANR 27, 67, 82; DAM MULT

van Schendel, Arthur(-Francois-Emile)
1874-1946 .... **TCLC 56**
See also EWL 3

Vansittart, Peter 1920- .... **CLC 42**
See also CA 1-4R; CANR 3, 49, 90; CN 7; RHW

Van Vechten, Carl 1880-1964 ... **CLC 33; HR 3**
See also AMWS 2; CA 183; 89-92; DLB 4, 9, 51; RGAL 4

van Vogt, A(lfred) E(lton) 1912-2000 . **CLC 1**
See also BPFB 3; BYA 13, 14; CA 21-24R; 190; CANR 28; DLB 8, 251; SATA 14; SATA-Obit 124; SCFW; SFW 4

Vara, Madeleine
See Jackson, Laura (Riding)

Varda, Agnes 1928- .... **CLC 16**
See also CA 116; 122

Vargas Llosa, (Jorge) Mario (Pedro)
1939- .... **CLC 3, 6, 9, 10, 15, 31, 42, 85; HLC 2**
See Llosa, (Jorge) Mario (Pedro) Vargas
See also BPFB 3; CA 73-76; CANR 18, 32, 42, 67, 116; CDWLB 3; DA; DA3; DAB; DAC; DAM MST, MULT, NOV; DLB 145; DNFS 2; EWL 3; HW 1, 2; LAIT 5; LATS 1; LAWS 1; MTCW 1, 2; RGWL 2; SSFS 14; TWA; WLIT 1

Varnhagen von Ense, Rahel
1771-1833 .... **NCLC 130**
See also DLB 90

Vasiliu, George
See Bacovia, George

Vasiliu, Gheorghe
See Bacovia, George
See also CA 123; 189

Vassa, Gustavus
See Equiano, Olaudah

Vassilikos, Vassilis 1933- .... **CLC 4, 8**
See also CA 81-84; CANR 75; EWL 3

Vaughan, Henry 1621-1695 .... **LC 27**
See also BRW 2; DLB 131; PAB; RGEL 2

Vaughn, Stephanie .... **CLC 62**

Vazov, Ivan (Minchov) 1850-1921 . **TCLC 25**
See also CA 121; 167; CDWLB 4; DLB 147

Veblen, Thorstein B(unde)
1857-1929 .... **TCLC 31**
See also AMWS 1; CA 115; 165; DLB 246

Vega, Lope de 1562-1635 .... **HLCS 2; LC 23**
See also EW 2; RGWL 2, 3

Vendler, Helen (Hennessy) 1933- ... **CLC 138**
See also CA 41-44R; CANR 25, 72; MTCW 1, 2

Venison, Alfred
See Pound, Ezra (Weston Loomis)

Verdi, Marie de
See Mencken, H(enry) L(ouis)

Verdu, Matilde
See Cela, Camilo Jose

Verga, Giovanni (Carmelo)
1840-1922 .... **SSC 21; TCLC 3**
See also CA 104; 123; CANR 101; EW 7; EWL 3; RGSF 2; RGWL 2, 3

Vergil 70B.C.-19B.C. ... **CMLC 9, 40; PC 12; WLCS**
See Virgil
See also AW 2; DA; DA3; DAB; DAC; DAM MST, POET; EFS 1; LMFS 1

Verhaeren, Emile (Adolphe Gustave)
1855-1916 .... **TCLC 12**
See also CA 109; EWL 3; GFL 1789 to the Present

Verlaine, Paul (Marie) 1844-1896 .. **NCLC 2, 51; PC 2, 32**
See also DAM POET; DLB 217; EW 7; GFL 1789 to the Present; LMFS 2; RGWL 2, 3; TWA

Verne, Jules (Gabriel) 1828-1905 ... **TCLC 6, 52**
See also AAYA 16; BYA 4; CA 110; 131; CLR 88; DA3; DLB 123; GFL 1789 to the Present; JRDA; LAIT 2; LMFS 2; MAICYA 1, 2; RGWL 2, 3; SATA 21; SCFW; SFW 4; TWA; WCH

Verus, Marcus Annius
See Aurelius, Marcus

Very, Jones 1813-1880 .... **NCLC 9**
See also DLB 1, 243; RGAL 4

Vesaas, Tarjei 1897-1970 .... **CLC 48**
See also CA 190; 29-32R; EW 11; EWL 3; RGWL 3

Vialis, Gaston
See Simenon, Georges (Jacques Christian)

Vian, Boris 1920-1959(?) .... **TCLC 9**
See also CA 106; 164; CANR 111; DLB 72; EWL 3; GFL 1789 to the Present; MTCW 2; RGWL 2, 3

Viaud, (Louis Marie) Julien 1850-1923
See Loti, Pierre
See also CA 107

Vicar, Henry
See Felsen, Henry Gregor

Vicker, Angus
See Felsen, Henry Gregor

Vidal, Gore 1925- ...... **CLC 2, 4, 6, 8, 10, 22, 33, 72, 142**
See Box, Edgar
See also AITN 1; AMWS 4; BEST 90:2; BPFB 3; CA 5-8R; CAD; CANR 13, 45, 65, 100; CD 5; CDALBS; CN 7; CPW; DA3; DAM NOV, POP; DFS 2; DLB 6, 152; EWL 3; INT CANR-13; MTCW 1, 2; RGAL 4; RHW; TUS

Viereck, Peter (Robert Edwin) 1916- .... **CLC 4; PC 27**
See also CA 1-4R; CANR 1, 47; CP 7; DLB 5; PFS 9, 14

Vigny, Alfred (Victor) de 1797-1863 .... **NCLC 7, 102; PC 26**
See also DAM POET; DLB 119, 192, 217; EW 5; GFL 1789 to the Present; RGWL 2, 3

Vilakazi, Benedict Wallet 1906-1947 .... **TCLC 37**
See also CA 168

Villa, Jose Garcia 1914-1997
See Villa, Jose Garcia

Villa, Jose Garcia 1914-1997 .... **AAL; PC 22**
See also CA 25-28R; CANR 12, 118; EWL 3; EXPP

Villarreal, Jose Antonio 1924- .... **HLC 2**
See also CA 133; CANR 93; DAM MULT; DLB 82; HW 1; LAIT 4; RGAL 4

Villaurrutia, Xavier 1903-1950 ...... **TCLC 80**
See also CA 192; EWL 3; HW 1; LAW

Villaverde, Cirilo 1812-1894 .... **NCLC 121**
See also LAW

Villehardouin, Geoffroi de 1150(?)-1218(?) .... **CMLC 38**

Villiers de l'Isle Adam, Jean Marie Mathias Philippe Auguste 1838-1889 ... **NCLC 3; SSC 14**
See also DLB 123, 192; GFL 1789 to the Present; RGSF 2

Villon, Francois 1431-1463(?) . **LC 62; PC 13**
See also DLB 208; EW 2; RGWL 2, 3; TWA

Vine, Barbara .... **CLC 50**
See Rendell, Ruth (Barbara)
See also BEST 90:4

Vinge, Joan (Carol) D(ennison) 1948- .... **CLC 30; SSC 24**
See also AAYA 32; BPFB 3; CA 93-96; CANR 72; SATA 36, 113; SFW 4; YAW

Viola, Herman J(oseph) 1938- .... **CLC 70**
See also CA 61-64; CANR 8, 23, 48, 91; SATA 126

Violis, G.
See Simenon, Georges (Jacques Christian)

Viramontes, Helena Maria 1954- .... **HLCS 2**
See also CA 159; DLB 122; HW 2

Virgil
See Vergil
See also CDWLB 1; DLB 211; LAIT 1; RGWL 2, 3; WP

Visconti, Luchino 1906-1976 .... **CLC 16**
See also CA 81-84; 65-68; CANR 39

Vitry, Jacques de
See Jacques de Vitry

Vittorini, Elio 1908-1966 .... **CLC 6, 9, 14**
See also CA 133; 25-28R; DLB 264; EW 12; EWL 3; RGWL 2, 3

Vivekananda, Swami 1863-1902 .... **TCLC 88**

Vizenor, Gerald Robert 1934- .... **CLC 103; NNAL**
See also CA 13-16R; CAAE 205; CAAS 22; CANR 5, 21, 44, 67; DAM MULT; DLB 175, 227; MTCW 2; TCWW 2

Vizinczey, Stephen 1933- .... **CLC 40**
See also CA 128; CCA 1; INT CA-128

Vliet, R(ussell) G(ordon) 1929-1984 .... **CLC 22**
See also CA 37-40R; 112; CANR 18

Vogau, Boris Andreyevich 1894-1937(?)
See Pilnyak, Boris
See also CA 123

Vogel, Paula A(nne) 1951- ... **CLC 76; DC 19**
See also CA 108; CAD; CANR 119; CD 5; CWD; DFS 14; RGAL 4

Voigt, Cynthia 1942- .... **CLC 30**
See also AAYA 3, 30; BYA 1, 3, 6, 7, 8; CA 106; CANR 18, 37, 40, 94; CLR 13, 48; INT CANR-18; JRDA; LAIT 5; MAICYA 1, 2; MAICYAS 1; SATA 48, 79, 116; SATA-Brief 33; WYA; YAW

Voigt, Ellen Bryant 1943- .... **CLC 54**
See also CA 69-72; CANR 11, 29, 55, 115; CP 7; CSW; CWP; DLB 120

Voinovich, Vladimir (Nikolaevich) 1932- .... **CLC 10, 49, 147**
See also CA 81-84; CAAS 12; CANR 33, 67; MTCW 1

Vollmann, William T. 1959- .... **CLC 89**
See also CA 134; CANR 67, 116; CPW; DA3; DAM NOV, POP; MTCW 2

Voloshinov, V. N.
See Bakhtin, Mikhail Mikhailovich

Voltaire 1694-1778 .... **LC 14, 79; SSC 12; WLC**
See also BYA 13; DA; DA3; DAB; DAC; DAM DRAM, MST; EW 4; GFL Beginnings to 1789; LATS 1; LMFS 1; NFS 7; RGWL 2, 3; TWA

von Aschendrof, Baron Ignatz
See Ford, Ford Madox

von Chamisso, Adelbert
See Chamisso, Adelbert von

von Daeniken, Erich 1935- .... **CLC 30**
See also AITN 1; CA 37-40R; CANR 17, 44

von Daniken, Erich
See von Daeniken, Erich

von Hartmann, Eduard 1842-1906 .... **TCLC 96**

von Hayek, Friedrich August
See Hayek, F(riedrich) A(ugust von)

von Heidenstam, (Carl Gustaf) Verner
See Heidenstam, (Carl Gustaf) Verner von

von Heyse, Paul (Johann Ludwig)
See Heyse, Paul (Johann Ludwig von)

von Hofmannsthal, Hugo
See Hofmannsthal, Hugo von

von Horvath, Odon
See von Horvath, Odon

von Horvath, Odon
See von Horvath, Odon

von Horvath, Odon 1901-1938 .... **TCLC 45**
See von Horvath, Oedoen
See also CA 118; 194; DLB 85, 124; RGWL 2, 3

von Horvath, Oedoen
See von Horvath, Odon
See also CA 184

von Kleist, Heinrich
See Kleist, Heinrich von

von Liliencron, (Friedrich Adolf Axel) Detlev
See Liliencron, (Friedrich Adolf Axel) Detlev von

Vonnegut, Kurt, Jr. 1922- . **CLC 1, 2, 3, 4, 5, 8, 12, 22, 40, 60, 111; SSC 8; WLC**
See also AAYA 6, 44; AITN 1; AMWS 2; BEST 90:4; BPFB 3; BYA 3, 14; CA 1-4R; CANR 1, 25, 49, 75, 92; CDALB 1968-1988; CN 7; CPW 1; DA; DA3; DAB; DAC; DAM MST, NOV, POP; DLB 2, 8, 152; DLBD 3; DLBY 1980; EWL 3; EXPN; EXPS; LAIT 4; LMFS 2; MTCW 1, 2; NFS 3; RGAL 4; SCFW 4; SFW 4; SSFS 5; TUS; YAW

Von Rachen, Kurt
See Hubbard, L(afayette) Ron(ald)

von Rezzori (d'Arezzo), Gregor
See Rezzori (d'Arezzo), Gregor von

von Sternberg, Josef
See Sternberg, Josef von

Vorster, Gordon 1924- .... **CLC 34**
See also CA 133

Vosce, Trudie
See Ozick, Cynthia

Voznesensky, Andrei (Andreievich) 1933- .... **CLC 1, 15, 57**
See Voznesensky, Andrey
See also CA 89-92; CANR 37; CWW 2; DAM POET; MTCW 1

Voznesensky, Andrey
See Voznesensky, Andrei (Andreievich)
See also EWL 3

Wace, Robert c. 1100-c. 1175 .... **CMLC 55**
See also DLB 146

Waddington, Miriam 1917- .... **CLC 28**
See also CA 21-24R; CANR 12, 30; CCA 1; CP 7; DLB 68

Wagman, Fredrica 1937- .... **CLC 7**
See also CA 97-100; INT CA-97-100

Wagner, Linda W.
See Wagner-Martin, Linda (C.)

Wagner, Linda Welshimer
See Wagner-Martin, Linda (C.)

Wagner, Richard 1813-1883 ...... **NCLC 9, 119**
See also DLB 129; EW 6

Wagner-Martin, Linda (C.) 1936- .... **CLC 50**
See also CA 159

Wagoner, David (Russell) 1926- .... **CLC 3, 5, 15; PC 33**
See also AMWS 9; CA 1-4R; CAAS 3; CANR 2, 71; CN 7; CP 7; DLB 5, 256; SATA 14; TCWW 2

Wah, Fred(erick James) 1939- .... **CLC 44**
See also CA 107; 141; CP 7; DLB 60

Wahloo, Per 1926-1975 .... **CLC 7**
See also BPFB 3; CA 61-64; CANR 73; CMW 4; MSW

Wahloo, Peter
See Wahloo, Per

Wain, John (Barrington) 1925-1994 . **CLC 2, 11, 15, 46**
See also CA 5-8R; 145; CAAS 4; CANR 23, 54; CDBLB 1960 to Present; DLB 15, 27, 139, 155; EWL 3; MTCW 1, 2

Wajda, Andrzej 1926- .... **CLC 16**
See also CA 102

Wakefield, Dan 1932- .... **CLC 7**
See also CA 21-24R; CAAE 211; CAAS 7; CN 7

Wakefield, Herbert Russell 1888-1965 .... **TCLC 120**
See also CA 5-8R; CANR 77; HGG; SUFW

Wakoski, Diane 1937- ...... **CLC 2, 4, 7, 9, 11, 40; PC 15**
See also CA 13-16R; CAAE 216; CAAS 1; CANR 9, 60, 106; CP 7; CWP; DAM POET; DLB 5; INT CANR-9; MTCW 2

Wakoski-Sherbell, Diane
See Wakoski, Diane

Walcott, Derek (Alton) 1930- ... **BLC 3; CLC 2, 4, 9, 14, 25, 42, 67, 76, 160; DC 7; PC 46**
See also BW 2; CA 89-92; CANR 26, 47, 75, 80; CBD; CD 5; CDWLB 3; CP 7; DA3; DAB; DAC; DAM MST, MULT, POET; DLB 117; DLBY 1981; DNFS 1; EFS 1; EWL 3; LMFS 2; MTCW 1, 2; PFS 6; RGEL 2; TWA

Waldman, Anne (Lesley) 1945- .... **CLC 7**
See also BG 3; CA 37-40R; CAAS 17; CANR 34, 69, 116; CP 7; CWP; DLB 16

Waldo, E. Hunter
See Sturgeon, Theodore (Hamilton)

Waldo, Edward Hamilton
See Sturgeon, Theodore (Hamilton)

Walker, Alice (Malsenior) 1944- .... **BLC 3; CLC 5, 6, 9, 19, 27, 46, 58, 103, 167; PC 30; SSC 5; WLCS**
See also AAYA 3, 33; AFAW 1, 2; AMWS 3; BEST 89:4; BPFB 3; BW 2, 3; CA 37-40R; CANR 9, 27, 49, 66, 82; CDALB 1968-1988; CN 7; CPW; CSW; DA; DA3; DAB; DAC; DAM MST, MULT, NOV, POET, POP; DLB 6, 33, 143; EWL 3; EXPN; EXPS; FW; INT CANR-27; LAIT 3; MAWW; MTCW 1, 2; NFS 5; RGAL 4; RGSF 2; SATA 31; SSFS 2, 11; TUS; YAW

Walker, David Harry 1911-1992 .... **CLC 14**
See also CA 1-4R; 137; CANR 1; CWRI 5; SATA 8; SATA-Obit 71

Walker, Edward Joseph 1934-
See Walker, Ted
See also CA 21-24R; CANR 12, 28, 53; CP 7

Walker, George F. 1947- .... **CLC 44, 61**
See also CA 103; CANR 21, 43, 59; CD 5; DAB; DAC; DAM MST; DLB 60

Walker, Joseph A. 1935- .... **CLC 19**
See also BW 1, 3; CA 89-92; CAD; CANR 26; CD 5; DAM DRAM, MST; DFS 12; DLB 38

Walker, Margaret (Abigail) 1915-1998 .... **BLC; CLC 1, 6; PC 20; TCLC 129**
See also AFAW 1, 2; BW 2, 3; CA 73-76; 172; CANR 26, 54, 76; CN 7; CP 7; CSW; DAM MULT; DLB 76, 152; EXPP; FW; MTCW 1, 2; RGAL 4; RHW

Walker, Ted .... **CLC 13**
See Walker, Edward Joseph
See also DLB 40

Wallace, David Foster 1962- ..... **CLC 50, 114**
See also AAYA 50; AMWS 10; CA 132; CANR 59; DA3; MTCW 2

Wallace, Dexter
See Masters, Edgar Lee

Wallace, (Richard Horatio) Edgar 1875-1932 .... **TCLC 57**
See also CA 115; CMW 4; DLB 70; MSW; RGEL 2

Wallace, Irving 1916-1990 .... **CLC 7, 13**
See also AITN 1; BPFB 3; CA 1-4R; 132; CAAS 1; CANR 1, 27; CPW; DAM NOV, POP; INT CANR-27; MTCW 1, 2

Wallant, Edward Lewis 1926-1962 ... **CLC 5, 10**
See also CA 1-4R; CANR 22; DLB 2, 28, 143; EWL 3; MTCW 1, 2; RGAL 4

Wallas, Graham 1858-1932 .... **TCLC 91**

Waller, Edmund 1606-1687 .... **LC 86**
See also BRW 2; DAM POET; DLB 126; PAB; RGEL 2

Walley, Byron
See Card, Orson Scott

Walpole, Horace 1717-1797 .... **LC 2, 49**
See also BRW 3; DLB 39, 104, 213; HGG; LMFS 1; RGEL 2; SUFW 1; TEA

Walpole, Hugh (Seymour) 1884-1941 .... **TCLC 5**
See also CA 104; 165; DLB 34; HGG; MTCW 2; RGEL 2; RHW

Walrond, Eric (Derwent) 1898-1966 .... **HR 3**
See also BW 1; CA 125; DLB 51

Walser, Martin 1927- .... **CLC 27**
See also CA 57-60; CANR 8, 46; CWW 2; DLB 75, 124; EWL 3

Walser, Robert 1878-1956 ..... **SSC 20; TCLC 18**
See also CA 118; 165; CANR 100; DLB 66; EWL 3

Walsh, Gillian Paton
See Paton Walsh, Gillian

Walsh, Jill Paton .... **CLC 35**
See Paton Walsh, Gillian
See also CLR 2, 65; WYA

Walter, Villiam Christian
See Andersen, Hans Christian

Walters, Anna L(ee) 1946- .... **NNAL**
See also CA 73-76

Walther von der Vogelweide c. 1170-1228 .... **CMLC 56**

Walton, Izaak 1593-1683 .... **LC 72**
See also BRW 2; CDBLB Before 1660; DLB 151, 213; RGEL 2

Wambaugh, Joseph (Aloysius), Jr. 1937- .... **CLC 3, 18**
See also AITN 1; BEST 89:3; BPFB 3; CA 33-36R; CANR 42, 65, 115; CMW 4; CPW 1; DA3; DAM NOV, POP; DLB 6; DLBY 1983; MSW; MTCW 1, 2

Wang Wei 699(?)-761(?) .... **PC 18**
See also TWA

Ward, Arthur Henry Sarsfield 1883-1959
See Rohmer, Sax
See also CA 108; 173; CMW 4; HGG

Ward, Douglas Turner 1930- .... **CLC 19**
See also BW 1; CA 81-84; CAD; CANR 27; CD 5; DLB 7, 38

Ward, E. D.
See Lucas, E(dward) V(errall)

Ward, Mrs. Humphry 1851-1920
See Ward, Mary Augusta
See also RGEL 2

Ward, Mary Augusta 1851-1920 ... **TCLC 55**
See Ward, Mrs. Humphry
See also DLB 18

Ward, Peter
See Faust, Frederick (Schiller)

Warhol, Andy 1928(?)-1987 .... **CLC 20**
See also AAYA 12; BEST 89:4; CA 89-92; 121; CANR 34

Warner, Francis (Robert le Plastrier) 1937- .... **CLC 14**
See also CA 53-56; CANR 11

Warner, Marina 1946- .... **CLC 59**
See also CA 65-68; CANR 21, 55, 118; CN 7; DLB 194

Warner, Rex (Ernest) 1905-1986 ...... **CLC 45**
See also CA 89-92; 119; DLB 15; RGEL 2; RHW

Warner, Susan (Bogert) 1819-1885 .... **NCLC 31**
See also DLB 3, 42, 239, 250, 254

Warner, Sylvia (Constance) Ashton
See Ashton-Warner, Sylvia (Constance)

Warner, Sylvia Townsend 1893-1978 .. **CLC 7, 19; SSC 23; TCLC 131**
See also BRWS 7; CA 61-64; 77-80; CANR 16, 60, 104; DLB 34, 139; EWL 3; FANT; FW; MTCW 1, 2; RGEL 2; RGSF 2; RHW

Warren, Mercy Otis 1728-1814 ..... **NCLC 13**
See also DLB 31, 200; RGAL 4; TUS

Warren, Robert Penn 1905-1989 .. **CLC 1, 4, 6, 8, 10, 13, 18, 39, 53, 59; PC 37; SSC 4, 58; WLC**
See also AITN 1; AMW; AMWC 2; BPFB 3; BYA 1; CA 13-16R; 129; CANR 10, 47; CDALB 1968-1988; DA; DA3; DAB; DAC; DAM MST, NOV, POET; DLB 2, 48, 152; DLBY 1980, 1989; EWL 3; INT CANR-10; MTCW 1, 2; NFS 13; RGAL 4; RGSF 2; RHW; SATA 46; SATA-Obit 63; SSFS 8; TUS

Warrigal, Jack
See Furphy, Joseph

Warshofsky, Isaac
See Singer, Isaac Bashevis

Warton, Joseph 1722-1800 .... **NCLC 118**
See also DLB 104, 109; RGEL 2

Warton, Thomas 1728-1790 .... **LC 15, 82**
See also DAM POET; DLB 104, 109; RGEL 2

Waruk, Kona
See Harris, (Theodore) Wilson

Warung, Price .... **TCLC 45**
See Astley, William
See also DLB 230; RGEL 2

Warwick, Jarvis
See Garner, Hugh
See also CCA 1

Washington, Alex
See Harris, Mark

Washington, Booker T(aliaferro) 1856-1915 .... **BLC 3; TCLC 10**
See also BW 1; CA 114; 125; DA3; DAM MULT; LAIT 2; RGAL 4; SATA 28

Washington, George 1732-1799 .... **LC 25**
See also DLB 31

Wassermann, (Karl) Jakob 1873-1934 .... **TCLC 6**
See also CA 104; 163; DLB 66; EWL 3

Wasserstein, Wendy 1950- .. **CLC 32, 59, 90; DC 4**
See also CA 121; 129; CABS 3; CAD; CANR 53, 75; CD 5; CWD; DA3; DAM DRAM; DFS 5, 17; DLB 228; EWL 3; FW; INT CA-129; MTCW 2; SATA 94

Waterhouse, Keith (Spencer) 1929- . **CLC 47**
See also CA 5-8R; CANR 38, 67, 109; CBD; CN 7; DLB 13, 15; MTCW 1, 2

Waters, Frank (Joseph) 1902-1995 ... **CLC 88**
See also CA 5-8R; 149; CAAS 13; CANR 3, 18, 63, 121; DLB 212; DLBY 1986; RGAL 4; TCWW 2

Waters, Mary C. .... **CLC 70**

Waters, Roger 1944- .... **CLC 35**

Watkins, Frances Ellen
See Harper, Frances Ellen Watkins

Watkins, Gerrold
See Malzberg, Barry N(athaniel)

Watkins, Gloria Jean 1952(?)- .... **CLC 94**
See also BW 2; CA 143; CANR 87; DLB 246; MTCW 2; SATA 115

Watkins, Paul 1964- .... **CLC 55**
See also CA 132; CANR 62, 98

Watkins, Vernon Phillips 1906-1967 .... **CLC 43**
See also CA 9-10; 25-28R; CAP 1; DLB 20; EWL 3; RGEL 2

Watson, Irving S.
See Mencken, H(enry) L(ouis)

Watson, John H.
See Farmer, Philip Jose

Watson, Richard F.
See Silverberg, Robert

Watts, Ephraim
See Horne, Richard Henry Hengist

Waugh, Auberon (Alexander) 1939-2001 .... **CLC 7**
See also CA 45-48; 192; CANR 6, 22, 92; DLB 14, 194

Waugh, Evelyn (Arthur St. John)
1903-1966 .. **CLC 1, 3, 8, 13, 19, 27, 44, 107; SSC 41; WLC**
See also BPFB 3; BRW 7; CA 85-88; 25-28R; CANR 22; CDBLB 1914-1945; DA; DA3; DAB; DAC; DAM MST, NOV, POP; DLB 15, 162, 195; EWL 3; MTCW 1, 2; NFS 13, 17; RGEL 2; RGSF 2; TEA; WLIT 4

Waugh, Harriet 1944- .... **CLC 6**
See also CA 85-88; CANR 22

Ways, C. R.
See Blount, Roy (Alton), Jr.

Waystaff, Simon
See Swift, Jonathan

Webb, Beatrice (Martha Potter)
1858-1943 .... **TCLC 22**
See also CA 117; 162; DLB 190; FW

Webb, Charles (Richard) 1939- .... **CLC 7**
See also CA 25-28R; CANR 114

Webb, James H(enry), Jr. 1946- ...... **CLC 22**
See also CA 81-84

Webb, Mary Gladys (Meredith)
1881-1927 .... **TCLC 24**
See also CA 182; 123; DLB 34; FW

Webb, Mrs. Sidney
See Webb, Beatrice (Martha Potter)

Webb, Phyllis 1927- .... **CLC 18**
See also CA 104; CANR 23; CCA 1; CP 7; CWP; DLB 53

Webb, Sidney (James) 1859-1947 .. **TCLC 22**
See also CA 117; 163; DLB 190

Webber, Andrew Lloyd .... **CLC 21**
See Lloyd Webber, Andrew
See also DFS 7

Weber, Lenora Mattingly
1895-1971 .... **CLC 12**
See also CA 19-20; 29-32R; CAP 1; SATA 2; SATA-Obit 26

Weber, Max 1864-1920 .... **TCLC 69**
See also CA 109; 189

Webster, John 1580(?)-1634(?) ...... **DC 2; LC 33, 84; WLC**
See also BRW 2; CDBLB Before 1660; DA; DAB; DAC; DAM DRAM, MST; DFS 17; DLB 58; IDTP; RGEL 2; WLIT 3

Webster, Noah 1758-1843 .... **NCLC 30**
See also DLB 1, 37, 42, 43, 73, 243

Wedekind, (Benjamin) Frank(lin)
1864-1918 .... **TCLC 7**
See also CA 104; 153; CANR 121, 122; CDWLB 2; DAM DRAM; DLB 118; EW 8; EWL 3; LMFS 2; RGWL 2, 3

Wehr, Demaris .... **CLC 65**

Weidman, Jerome 1913-1998 .... **CLC 7**
See also AITN 2; CA 1-4R; 171; CAD; CANR 1; DLB 28

Weil, Simone (Adolphine)
1909-1943 .... **TCLC 23**
See also CA 117; 159; EW 12; EWL 3; FW; GFL 1789 to the Present; MTCW 2

Weininger, Otto 1880-1903 .... **TCLC 84**

Weinstein, Nathan
See West, Nathanael

Weinstein, Nathan von Wallenstein
See West, Nathanael

Weir, Peter (Lindsay) 1944- .... **CLC 20**
See also CA 113; 123

Weiss, Peter (Ulrich) 1916-1982 .. **CLC 3, 15, 51**
See also CA 45-48; 106; CANR 3; DAM DRAM; DFS 3; DLB 69, 124; EWL 3; RGWL 2, 3

Weiss, Theodore (Russell)
1916-2003 .... **CLC 3, 8, 14**
See also CA 9-12R; 216; CAAE 189; CAAS 2; CANR 46, 94; CP 7; DLB 5

Welch, (Maurice) Denton
1915-1948 .... **TCLC 22**
See also BRWS 8, 9; CA 121; 148; RGEL 2

Welch, James 1940- ... **CLC 6, 14, 52; NNAL**
See also CA 85-88; CANR 42, 66, 107; CN 7; CP 7; CPW; DAM MULT, POP; DLB 175, 256; LATS 1; RGAL 4; TCWW 2

Weldon, Fay 1931- . **CLC 6, 9, 11, 19, 36, 59, 122**
See also BRWS 4; CA 21-24R; CANR 16, 46, 63, 97; CDBLB 1960 to Present; CN 7; CPW; DAM POP; DLB 14, 194; EWL 3; FW; HGG; INT CANR-16; MTCW 1, 2; RGEL 2; RGSF 2

Wellek, Rene 1903-1995 .... **CLC 28**
See also CA 5-8R; 150; CAAS 7; CANR 8; DLB 63; EWL 3; INT CANR-8

Weller, Michael 1942- .... **CLC 10, 53**
See also CA 85-88; CAD; CD 5

Weller, Paul 1958- .... **CLC 26**

Wellershoff, Dieter 1925- .... **CLC 46**
See also CA 89-92; CANR 16, 37

Welles, (George) Orson 1915-1985 .. **CLC 20, 80**
See also AAYA 40; CA 93-96; 117

Wellman, John McDowell 1945-
See Wellman, Mac
See also CA 166; CD 5

Wellman, Mac .... **CLC 65**
See Wellman, John McDowell; Wellman, John McDowell
See also CAD; RGAL 4

Wellman, Manly Wade 1903-1986 ... **CLC 49**
See also CA 1-4R; 118; CANR 6, 16, 44; FANT; SATA 6; SATA-Obit 47; SFW 4; SUFW

Wells, Carolyn 1869(?)-1942 .... **TCLC 35**
See also CA 113; 185; CMW 4; DLB 11

Wells, H(erbert) G(eorge)
1866-1946 .... **SSC 6; TCLC 6, 12, 19, 133; WLC**
See also AAYA 18; BPFB 3; BRW 6; CA 110; 121; CDBLB 1914-1945; CLR 64; DA; DA3; DAB; DAC; DAM MST, NOV; DLB 34, 70, 156, 178; EWL 3; EXPS; HGG; LAIT 3; LMFS 2; MTCW 1, 2; NFS 17; RGEL 2; RGSF 2; SATA 20; SCFW; SFW 4; SSFS 3; SUFW; TEA; WCH; WLIT 4; YAW

Wells, Rosemary 1943- .... **CLC 12**
See also AAYA 13; BYA 7, 8; CA 85-88; CANR 48, 120; CLR 16, 69; CWRI 5; MAICYA 1, 2; SAAS 1; SATA 18, 69, 114; YAW

Wells-Barnett, Ida B(ell)
1862-1931 .... **TCLC 125**
See also CA 182; DLB 23, 221

Welsh, Irvine 1958- .... **CLC 144**
See also CA 173; DLB 271

Welty, Eudora (Alice) 1909-2001 .. **CLC 1, 2, 5, 14, 22, 33, 105; SSC 1, 27, 51; WLC**
See also AAYA 48; AMW; AMWR 1; BPFB 3; CA 9-12R; 199; CABS 1; CANR 32, 65; CDALB 1941-1968; CN 7; CSW; DA; DA3; DAB; DAC; DAM MST, NOV; DLB 2, 102, 143; DLBD 12; DLBY 1987, 2001; EWL 3; EXPS; HGG; LAIT 3; MAWW; MTCW 1, 2; NFS 13, 15; RGAL 4; RGSF 2; RHW; SSFS 2, 10; TUS

Wen I-to 1899-1946 .... **TCLC 28**
See also EWL 3

Wentworth, Robert
See Hamilton, Edmond

Werfel, Franz (Viktor) 1890-1945 ... **TCLC 8**
See also CA 104; 161; DLB 81, 124; EWL 3; RGWL 2, 3

Wergeland, Henrik Arnold
1808-1845 .... **NCLC 5**

Wersba, Barbara 1932- .... **CLC 30**
See also AAYA 2, 30; BYA 6, 12, 13; CA 29-32R, 182; CAAE 182; CANR 16, 38; CLR 3, 78; DLB 52; JRDA; MAICYA 1, 2; SAAS 2; SATA 1, 58; SATA-Essay 103; WYA; YAW

Wertmueller, Lina 1928- .... **CLC 16**
See also CA 97-100; CANR 39, 78

Wescott, Glenway 1901-1987 .. **CLC 13; SSC 35**
See also CA 13-16R; 121; CANR 23, 70; DLB 4, 9, 102; RGAL 4

Wesker, Arnold 1932- .... **CLC 3, 5, 42**
See also CA 1-4R; CAAS 7; CANR 1, 33; CBD; CD 5; CDBLB 1960 to Present; DAB; DAM DRAM; DLB 13; EWL 3; MTCW 1; RGEL 2; TEA

Wesley, John 1703-1791 .... **LC 88**
See also DLB 104

Wesley, Richard (Errol) 1945- .... **CLC 7**
See also BW 1; CA 57-60; CAD; CANR 27; CD 5; DLB 38

Wessel, Johan Herman 1742-1785 .... **LC 7**

West, Anthony (Panther)
1914-1987 .... **CLC 50**
See also CA 45-48; 124; CANR 3, 19; DLB 15

West, C. P.
See Wodehouse, P(elham) G(renville)

West, Cornel (Ronald) 1953- .... **BLCS; CLC 134**
See also CA 144; CANR 91; DLB 246

West, Delno C(loyde), Jr. 1936- .... **CLC 70**
See also CA 57-60

West, Dorothy 1907-1998 .. **HR 3; TCLC 108**
See also BW 2; CA 143; 169; DLB 76

West, (Mary) Jessamyn 1902-1984 ... **CLC 7, 17**
See also CA 9-12R; 112; CANR 27; DLB 6; DLBY 1984; MTCW 1, 2; RGAL 4; RHW; SATA-Obit 37; TCWW 2; TUS; YAW

West, Morris
See West, Morris L(anglo)
See also DLB 289

West, Morris L(anglo) 1916-1999 ..... **CLC 6, 33**
See West, Morris
See also BPFB 3; CA 5-8R; 187; CANR 24, 49, 64; CN 7; CPW; MTCW 1, 2

West, Nathanael 1903-1940 .. **SSC 16; TCLC 1, 14, 44**
See also AMW; AMWR 2; BPFB 3; CA 104; 125; CDALB 1929-1941; DA3; DLB 4, 9, 28; EWL 3; MTCW 1, 2; NFS 16; RGAL 4; TUS

West, Owen
See Koontz, Dean R(ay)

West, Paul 1930- .... **CLC 7, 14, 96**
See also CA 13-16R; CAAS 7; CANR 22, 53, 76, 89; CN 7; DLB 14; INT CANR-22; MTCW 2

West, Rebecca 1892-1983 ... **CLC 7, 9, 31, 50**
See also BPFB 3; BRWS 3; CA 5-8R; 109; CANR 19; DLB 36; DLBY 1983; EWL 3; FW; MTCW 1, 2; NCFS 4; RGEL 2; TEA

Westall, Robert (Atkinson)
1929-1993 .... **CLC 17**
See also AAYA 12; BYA 2, 6, 7, 8, 9, 15; CA 69-72; 141; CANR 18, 68; CLR 13; FANT; JRDA; MAICYA 1, 2; MAICYAS 1; SAAS 2; SATA 23, 69; SATA-Obit 75; WYA; YAW

Westermarck, Edward 1862-1939 . **TCLC 87**
Westlake, Donald E(dwin) 1933- . **CLC 7, 33**
See also BPFB 3; CA 17-20R; CAAS 13; CANR 16, 44, 65, 94; CMW 4; CPW; DAM POP; INT CANR-16; MSW; MTCW 2
Westmacott, Mary
See Christie, Agatha (Mary Clarissa)
Weston, Allen
See Norton, Andre
Wetcheek, J. L.
See Feuchtwanger, Lion
Wetering, Janwillem van de
See van de Wetering, Janwillem
Wetherald, Agnes Ethelwyn 1857-1940 .... **TCLC 81**
See also CA 202; DLB 99
Wetherell, Elizabeth
See Warner, Susan (Bogert)
Whale, James 1889-1957 .... **TCLC 63**
Whalen, Philip (Glenn) 1923-2002 .... **CLC 6, 29**
See also BG 3; CA 9-12R; 209; CANR 5, 39; CP 7; DLB 16; WP
Wharton, Edith (Newbold Jones) 1862-1937 ... **SSC 6; TCLC 3, 9, 27, 53, 129; WLC**
See also AAYA 25; AMW; AMWC 2; AMWR 1; BPFB 3; CA 104; 132; CDALB 1865-1917; DA; DA3; DAB; DAC; DAM MST, NOV; DLB 4, 9, 12, 78, 189; DLBD 13; EWL 3; EXPS; HGG; LAIT 2, 3; LATS 1; MAWW; MTCW 1, 2; NFS 5, 11, 15; RGAL 4; RGSF 2; RHW; SSFS 6, 7; SUFW; TUS
Wharton, James
See Mencken, H(enry) L(ouis)
Wharton, William (a pseudonym) . **CLC 18, 37**
See also CA 93-96; DLBY 1980; INT CA-93-96
Wheatley (Peters), Phillis 1753(?)-1784 ... **BLC 3; LC 3, 50; PC 3; WLC**
See also AFAW 1, 2; CDALB 1640-1865; DA; DA3; DAC; DAM MST, MULT, POET; DLB 31, 50; EXPP; PFS 13; RGAL 4
Wheelock, John Hall 1886-1978 .... **CLC 14**
See also CA 13-16R; 77-80; CANR 14; DLB 45
Whim-Wham
See Curnow, (Thomas) Allen (Monro)
White, Babington
See Braddon, Mary Elizabeth
White, E(lwyn) B(rooks) 1899-1985 .... **CLC 10, 34, 39**
See also AITN 2; AMWS 1; CA 13-16R; 116; CANR 16, 37; CDALBS; CLR 1, 21; CPW; DA3; DAM POP; DLB 11, 22; EWL 3; FANT; MAICYA 1, 2; MTCW 1, 2; NCFS 5; RGAL 4; SATA 2, 29, 100; SATA-Obit 44; TUS
White, Edmund (Valentine III) 1940- .... **CLC 27, 110**
See also AAYA 7; CA 45-48; CANR 3, 19, 36, 62, 107; CN 7; DA3; DAM POP; DLB 227; MTCW 1, 2
White, Hayden V. 1928- .... **CLC 148**
See also CA 128; DLB 246
White, Patrick (Victor Martindale) 1912-1990 ...... **CLC 3, 4, 5, 7, 9, 18, 65, 69; SSC 39**
See also BRWS 1; CA 81-84; 132; CANR 43; DLB 260; EWL 3; MTCW 1; RGEL 2; RGSF 2; RHW; TWA

White, Phyllis Dorothy James 1920-
See James, P. D.
See also CA 21-24R; CANR 17, 43, 65, 112; CMW 4; CN 7; CPW; DA3; DAM POP; MTCW 1, 2; TEA
White, T(erence) H(anbury) 1906-1964 .... **CLC 30**
See also AAYA 22; BPFB 3; BYA 4, 5; CA 73-76; CANR 37; DLB 160; FANT; JRDA; LAIT 1; MAICYA 1, 2; RGEL 2; SATA 12; SUFW 1; YAW
White, Terence de Vere 1912-1994 ... **CLC 49**
See also CA 49-52; 145; CANR 3
White, Walter
See White, Walter F(rancis)
White, Walter F(rancis) 1893-1955 ... **BLC 3; HR 3; TCLC 15**
See also BW 1; CA 115; 124; DAM MULT; DLB 51
White, William Hale 1831-1913
See Rutherford, Mark
See also CA 121; 189
Whitehead, Alfred North 1861-1947 .... **TCLC 97**
See also CA 117; 165; DLB 100, 262
Whitehead, E(dward) A(nthony) 1933- .... **CLC 5**
See also CA 65-68; CANR 58, 118; CBD; CD 5
Whitehead, Ted
See Whitehead, E(dward) A(nthony)
Whiteman, Roberta J. Hill 1947- ...... **NNAL**
See also CA 146
Whitemore, Hugh (John) 1936- .... **CLC 37**
See also CA 132; CANR 77; CBD; CD 5; INT CA-132
Whitman, Sarah Helen (Power) 1803-1878 .... **NCLC 19**
See also DLB 1, 243
Whitman, Walt(er) 1819-1892 .. **NCLC 4, 31, 81; PC 3; WLC**
See also AAYA 42; AMW; AMWR 1; CDALB 1640-1865; DA; DA3; DAB; DAC; DAM MST, POET; DLB 3, 64, 224, 250; EXPP; LAIT 2; LMFS 1; PAB; PFS 2, 3, 13; RGAL 4; SATA 20; TUS; WP; WYAS 1
Whitney, Phyllis A(yame) 1903- .... **CLC 42**
See also AAYA 36; AITN 2; BEST 90:3; CA 1-4R; CANR 3, 25, 38, 60; CLR 59; CMW 4; CPW; DA3; DAM POP; JRDA; MAICYA 1, 2; MTCW 2; RHW; SATA 1, 30; YAW
Whittemore, (Edward) Reed, Jr. 1919- .... **CLC 4**
See also CA 9-12R; CAAS 8; CANR 4, 119; CP 7; DLB 5
Whittier, John Greenleaf 1807-1892 .... **NCLC 8, 59**
See also AMWS 1; DLB 1, 243; RGAL 4
Whittlebot, Hernia
See Coward, Noel (Peirce)
Wicker, Thomas Grey 1926-
See Wicker, Tom
See also CA 65-68; CANR 21, 46
Wicker, Tom .... **CLC 7**
See Wicker, Thomas Grey
Wideman, John Edgar 1941- ... **BLC 3; CLC 5, 34, 36, 67, 122; SSC 62**
See also AFAW 1, 2; AMWS 10; BPFB 4; BW 2, 3; CA 85-88; CANR 14, 42, 67, 109; CN 7; DAM MULT; DLB 33, 143; MTCW 2; RGAL 4; RGSF 2; SSFS 6, 12
Wiebe, Rudy (Henry) 1934- .. **CLC 6, 11, 14, 138**
See also CA 37-40R; CANR 42, 67, 123; CN 7; DAC; DAM MST; DLB 60; RHW

Wieland, Christoph Martin 1733-1813 .... **NCLC 17**
See also DLB 97; EW 4; LMFS 1; RGWL 2, 3
Wiene, Robert 1881-1938 .... **TCLC 56**
Wieners, John 1934- .... **CLC 7**
See also BG 3; CA 13-16R; CP 7; DLB 16; WP
Wiesel, Elie(zer) 1928- .... **CLC 3, 5, 11, 37, 165; WLCS**
See also AAYA 7; AITN 1; CA 5-8R; CAAS 4; CANR 8, 40, 65; CDALBS; DA; DA3; DAB; DAC; DAM MST, NOV; DLB 83; DLBY 1987; EWL 3; INT CANR-8; LAIT 4; MTCW 1, 2; NCFS 4; NFS 4; RGWL 3; SATA 56; YAW
Wiggins, Marianne 1947- .... **CLC 57**
See also BEST 89:3; CA 130; CANR 60
Wiggs, Susan .... **CLC 70**
See also CA 201
Wight, James Alfred 1916-1995
See Herriot, James
See also CA 77-80; SATA 55; SATA-Brief 44
Wilbur, Richard (Purdy) 1921- ..... **CLC 3, 6, 9, 14, 53, 110; PC 51**
See also AMWS 3; CA 1-4R; CABS 2; CANR 2, 29, 76, 93; CDALBS; CP 7; DA; DAB; DAC; DAM MST, POET; DLB 5, 169; EWL 3; EXPP; INT CANR-29; MTCW 1, 2; PAB; PFS 11, 12, 16; RGAL 4; SATA 9, 108; WP
Wild, Peter 1940- .... **CLC 14**
See also CA 37-40R; CP 7; DLB 5
Wilde, Oscar (Fingal O'Flahertie Wills) 1854(?)-1900 ...... **DC 17; SSC 11; TCLC 1, 8, 23, 41; WLC**
See also AAYA 49; BRW 5; BRWC 1, 2; BRWR 1; BYA 15; CA 104; 119; CANR 112; CDBLB 1890-1914; DA; DA3; DAB; DAC; DAM DRAM, MST, NOV; DFS 4, 8, 9; DLB 10, 19, 34, 57, 141, 156, 190; EXPS; FANT; LATS 1; RGEL 2; RGSF 2; SATA 24; SSFS 7; SUFW; TEA; WCH; WLIT 4
Wilder, Billy .... **CLC 20**
See Wilder, Samuel
See also DLB 26
Wilder, Samuel 1906-2002
See Wilder, Billy
See also CA 89-92; 205
Wilder, Stephen
See Marlowe, Stephen
Wilder, Thornton (Niven) 1897-1975 .. **CLC 1, 5, 6, 10, 15, 35, 82; DC 1; WLC**
See also AAYA 29; AITN 2; AMW; CA 13-16R; 61-64; CAD; CANR 40; CDALBS; DA; DA3; DAB; DAC; DAM DRAM, MST, NOV; DFS 1, 4, 16; DLB 4, 7, 9, 228; DLBY 1997; EWL 3; LAIT 3; MTCW 1, 2; RGAL 4; RHW; WYAS 1
Wilding, Michael 1942- ...... **CLC 73; SSC 50**
See also CA 104; CANR 24, 49, 106; CN 7; RGSF 2
Wiley, Richard 1944- .... **CLC 44**
See also CA 121; 129; CANR 71
Wilhelm, Kate .... **CLC 7**
See Wilhelm, Katie (Gertrude)
See also AAYA 20; BYA 16; CAAS 5; DLB 8; INT CANR-17; SCFW 2
Wilhelm, Katie (Gertrude) 1928-
See Wilhelm, Kate
See also CA 37-40R; CANR 17, 36, 60, 94; MTCW 1; SFW 4
Wilkins, Mary
See Freeman, Mary E(leanor) Wilkins

Willard, Nancy 1936- .... **CLC 7, 37**
   See also BYA 5; CA 89-92; CANR 10, 39, 68, 107; CLR 5; CWP; CWRI 5; DLB 5, 52; FANT; MAICYA 1, 2; MTCW 1; SATA 37, 71, 127; SATA-Brief 30; SUFW 2

William of Malmesbury c. 1090B.C.-c. 1140B.C. .... **CMLC 57**

William of Ockham 1290-1349 ..... **CMLC 32**

Williams, Ben Ames 1889-1953 ..... **TCLC 89**
   See also CA 183; DLB 102

Williams, C(harles) K(enneth) 1936- .... **CLC 33, 56, 148**
   See also CA 37-40R; CAAS 26; CANR 57, 106; CP 7; DAM POET; DLB 5

Williams, Charles
   See Collier, James Lincoln

Williams, Charles (Walter Stansby) 1886-1945 .... **TCLC 1, 11**
   See also BRWS 9; CA 104; 163; DLB 100, 153, 255; FANT; RGEL 2; SUFW 1

Williams, Ella Gwendolen Rees
   See Rhys, Jean

Williams, (George) Emlyn 1905-1987 .... **CLC 15**
   See also CA 104; 123; CANR 36; DAM DRAM; DLB 10, 77; IDTP; MTCW 1

Williams, Hank 1923-1953 .... **TCLC 81**
   See Williams, Hiram King

Williams, Hiram Hank
   See Williams, Hank

Williams, Hiram King
   See Williams, Hank
   See also CA 188

Williams, Hugo (Mordaunt) 1942- ... **CLC 42**
   See also CA 17-20R; CANR 45, 119; CP 7; DLB 40

Williams, J. Walker
   See Wodehouse, P(elham) G(renville)

Williams, John A(lfred) 1925- . **BLC 3; CLC 5, 13**
   See also AFAW 2; BW 2, 3; CA 53-56; CAAE 195; CAAS 3; CANR 6, 26, 51, 118; CN 7; CSW; DAM MULT; DLB 2, 33; EWL 3; INT CANR-6; RGAL 4; SFW 4

Williams, Jonathan (Chamberlain) 1929- .... **CLC 13**
   See also CA 9-12R; CAAS 12; CANR 8, 108; CP 7; DLB 5

Williams, Joy 1944- .... **CLC 31**
   See also CA 41-44R; CANR 22, 48, 97

Williams, Norman 1952- .... **CLC 39**
   See also CA 118

Williams, Sherley Anne 1944-1999 ... **BLC 3; CLC 89**
   See also AFAW 2; BW 2, 3; CA 73-76; 185; CANR 25, 82; DAM MULT, POET; DLB 41; INT CANR-25; SATA 78; SATA-Obit 116

Williams, Shirley
   See Williams, Sherley Anne

Williams, Tennessee 1911-1983 . **CLC 1, 2, 5, 7, 8, 11, 15, 19, 30, 39, 45, 71, 111; DC 4; WLC**
   See also AAYA 31; AITN 1, 2; AMW; AMWC 1; CA 5-8R; 108; CABS 3; CAD; CANR 31; CDALB 1941-1968; DA; DA3; DAB; DAC; DAM DRAM, MST; DFS 17; DLB 7; DLBD 4; DLBY 1983; EWL 3; GLL 1; LAIT 4; LATS 1; MTCW 1, 2; RGAL 4; TUS

Williams, Thomas (Alonzo) 1926-1990 .... **CLC 14**
   See also CA 1-4R; 132; CANR 2

Williams, William C.
   See Williams, William Carlos

Williams, William Carlos 1883-1963 .... **CLC 1, 2, 5, 9, 13, 22, 42, 67; PC 7; SSC 31**
   See also AAYA 46; AMW; AMWR 1; CA 89-92; CANR 34; CDALB 1917-1929; DA; DA3; DAB; DAC; DAM MST, POET; DLB 4, 16, 54, 86; EWL 3; EXPP; MTCW 1, 2; NCFS 4; PAB; PFS 1, 6, 11; RGAL 4; RGSF 2; TUS; WP

Williamson, David (Keith) 1942- ..... **CLC 56**
   See also CA 103; CANR 41; CD 5; DLB 289

Williamson, Ellen Douglas 1905-1984
   See Douglas, Ellen
   See also CA 17-20R; 114; CANR 39

Williamson, Jack .... **CLC 29**
   See Williamson, John Stewart
   See also CAAS 8; DLB 8; SCFW 2

Williamson, John Stewart 1908-
   See Williamson, Jack
   See also CA 17-20R; CANR 23, 70; SFW 4

Willie, Frederick
   See Lovecraft, H(oward) P(hillips)

Willingham, Calder (Baynard, Jr.) 1922-1995 .... **CLC 5, 51**
   See also CA 5-8R; 147; CANR 3; CSW; DLB 2, 44; IDFW 3, 4; MTCW 1

Willis, Charles
   See Clarke, Arthur C(harles)

Willy
   See Colette, (Sidonie-Gabrielle)

Willy, Colette
   See Colette, (Sidonie-Gabrielle)
   See also GLL 1

Wilmot, John 1647-1680 .... **LC 75**
   See Rochester
   See also BRW 2; DLB 131; PAB

Wilson, A(ndrew) N(orman) 1950- .. **CLC 33**
   See also BRWS 6; CA 112; 122; CN 7; DLB 14, 155, 194; MTCW 2

Wilson, Angus (Frank Johnstone) 1913-1991 . **CLC 2, 3, 5, 25, 34; SSC 21**
   See also BRWS 1; CA 5-8R; 134; CANR 21; DLB 15, 139, 155; EWL 3; MTCW 1, 2; RGEL 2; RGSF 2

Wilson, August 1945- ... **BLC 3; CLC 39, 50, 63, 118; DC 2; WLCS**
   See also AAYA 16; AFAW 2; AMWS 8; BW 2, 3; CA 115; 122; CAD; CANR 42, 54, 76; CD 5; DA; DA3; DAB; DAC; DAM DRAM, MST, MULT; DFS 3, 7, 15, 17; DLB 228; EWL 3; LAIT 4; LATS 1; MTCW 1, 2; RGAL 4

Wilson, Brian 1942- .... **CLC 12**

Wilson, Colin 1931- .... **CLC 3, 14**
   See also CA 1-4R; CAAS 5; CANR 1, 22, 33, 77; CMW 4; CN 7; DLB 14, 194; HGG; MTCW 1; SFW 4

Wilson, Dirk
   See Pohl, Frederik

Wilson, Edmund 1895-1972 .. **CLC 1, 2, 3, 8, 24**
   See also AMW; CA 1-4R; 37-40R; CANR 1, 46, 110; DLB 63; EWL 3; MTCW 1, 2; RGAL 4; TUS

Wilson, Ethel Davis (Bryant) 1888(?)-1980 .... **CLC 13**
   See also CA 102; DAC; DAM POET; DLB 68; MTCW 1; RGEL 2

Wilson, Harriet
   See Wilson, Harriet E. Adams
   See also DLB 239

Wilson, Harriet E.
   See Wilson, Harriet E. Adams
   See also DLB 243

Wilson, Harriet E. Adams 1827(?)-1863(?) .... **BLC 3; NCLC 78**
   See Wilson, Harriet; Wilson, Harriet E.
   See also DAM MULT; DLB 50

Wilson, John 1785-1854 .... **NCLC 5**

Wilson, John (Anthony) Burgess 1917-1993
   See Burgess, Anthony
   See also CA 1-4R; 143; CANR 2, 46; DA3; DAC; DAM NOV; MTCW 1, 2; NFS 15; TEA

Wilson, Lanford 1937- ... **CLC 7, 14, 36; DC 19**
   See also CA 17-20R; CABS 3; CAD; CANR 45, 96; CD 5; DAM DRAM; DFS 4, 9, 12, 16; DLB 7; EWL 3; TUS

Wilson, Robert M. 1941- .... **CLC 7, 9**
   See also CA 49-52; CAD; CANR 2, 41; CD 5; MTCW 1

Wilson, Robert McLiam 1964- .... **CLC 59**
   See also CA 132; DLB 267

Wilson, Sloan 1920-2003 .... **CLC 32**
   See also CA 1-4R; 216; CANR 1, 44; CN 7

Wilson, Snoo 1948- .... **CLC 33**
   See also CA 69-72; CBD; CD 5

Wilson, William S(mith) 1932- .... **CLC 49**
   See also CA 81-84

Wilson, (Thomas) Woodrow 1856-1924 .... **TCLC 79**
   See also CA 166; DLB 47

Wilson and Warnke eds. .... **CLC 65**

Winchilsea, Anne (Kingsmill) Finch 1661-1720
   See Finch, Anne
   See also RGEL 2

Windham, Basil
   See Wodehouse, P(elham) G(renville)

Wingrove, David (John) 1954- .... **CLC 68**
   See also CA 133; SFW 4

Winnemucca, Sarah 1844-1891 .... **NCLC 79; NNAL**
   See also DAM MULT; DLB 175; RGAL 4

Winstanley, Gerrard 1609-1676 .... **LC 52**

Wintergreen, Jane
   See Duncan, Sara Jeannette

Winters, Janet Lewis .... **CLC 41**
   See Lewis, Janet
   See also DLBY 1987

Winters, (Arthur) Yvor 1900-1968 .... **CLC 4, 8, 32**
   See also AMWS 2; CA 11-12; 25-28R; CAP 1; DLB 48; EWL 3; MTCW 1; RGAL 4

Winterson, Jeanette 1959- .... **CLC 64, 158**
   See also BRWS 4; CA 136; CANR 58, 116; CN 7; CPW; DA3; DAM POP; DLB 207, 261; FANT; FW; GLL 1; MTCW 2; RHW

Winthrop, John 1588-1649 .... **LC 31**
   See also DLB 24, 30

Wirth, Louis 1897-1952 .... **TCLC 92**
   See also CA 210

Wiseman, Frederick 1930- .... **CLC 20**
   See also CA 159

Wister, Owen 1860-1938 .... **TCLC 21**
   See also BPFB 3; CA 108; 162; DLB 9, 78, 186; RGAL 4; SATA 62; TCWW 2

Witkacy
   See Witkiewicz, Stanislaw Ignacy

Witkiewicz, Stanislaw Ignacy 1885-1939 .... **TCLC 8**
   See also CA 105; 162; CDWLB 4; DLB 215; EW 10; EWL 3; RGWL 2, 3; SFW 4

Wittgenstein, Ludwig (Josef Johann) 1889-1951 .... **TCLC 59**
   See also CA 113; 164; DLB 262; MTCW 2

Wittig, Monique 1935(?)-2003 .... **CLC 22**
   See also CA 116; 135; 212; CWW 2; DLB 83; EWL 3; FW; GLL 1

Wittlin, Jozef 1896-1976 .... **CLC 25**
   See also CA 49-52; 65-68; CANR 3; EWL 3

Wodehouse, P(elham) G(renville)
1881-1975 . **CLC 1, 2, 5, 10, 22; SSC 2; TCLC 108**
See also AITN 2; BRWS 3; CA 45-48; 57-60; CANR 3, 33; CDBLB 1914-1945; CPW 1; DA3; DAB; DAC; DAM NOV; DLB 34, 162; EWL 3; MTCW 1, 2; RGEL 2; RGSF 2; SATA 22; SSFS 10

Woiwode, L.
See Woiwode, Larry (Alfred)

Woiwode, Larry (Alfred) 1941- ... **CLC 6, 10**
See also CA 73-76; CANR 16, 94; CN 7; DLB 6; INT CANR-16

Wojciechowska, Maia (Teresa)
1927-2002 .... **CLC 26**
See also AAYA 8, 46; BYA 3; CA 9-12R, 183; 209; CAAE 183; CANR 4, 41; CLR 1; JRDA; MAICYA 1, 2; SAAS 1; SATA 1, 28, 83; SATA-Essay 104; SATA-Obit 134; YAW

Wojtyla, Karol
See John Paul II, Pope

Wolf, Christa 1929- .... **CLC 14, 29, 58, 150**
See also CA 85-88; CANR 45, 123; CDWLB 2; CWW 2; DLB 75; EWL 3; FW; MTCW 1; RGWL 2, 3; SSFS 14

Wolf, Naomi 1962- .... **CLC 157**
See also CA 141; CANR 110; FW

Wolfe, Gene (Rodman) 1931- .... **CLC 25**
See also AAYA 35; CA 57-60; CAAS 9; CANR 6, 32, 60; CPW; DAM POP; DLB 8; FANT; MTCW 2; SATA 118; SCFW 2; SFW 4; SUFW 2

Wolfe, George C. 1954- .... **BLCS; CLC 49**
See also CA 149; CAD; CD 5

Wolfe, Thomas (Clayton)
1900-1938 ...... **SSC 33; TCLC 4, 13, 29, 61; WLC**
See also AMW; BPFB 3; CA 104; 132; CANR 102; CDALB 1929-1941; DA; DA3; DAB; DAC; DAM MST, NOV; DLB 9, 102, 229; DLBD 2, 16; DLBY 1985, 1997; EWL 3; MTCW 1, 2; NFS 18; RGAL 4; TUS

Wolfe, Thomas Kennerly, Jr.
1930- .... **CLC 147**
See Wolfe, Tom
See also CA 13-16R; CANR 9, 33, 70, 104; DA3; DAM POP; DLB 185; EWL 3; INT CANR-9; MTCW 1, 2; SSFS 18; TUS

Wolfe, Tom .... **CLC 1, 2, 9, 15, 35, 51**
See Wolfe, Thomas Kennerly, Jr.
See also AAYA 8; AITN 2; AMWS 3; BEST 89:1; BPFB 3; CN 7; CPW; CSW; DLB 152; LAIT 5; RGAL 4

Wolff, Geoffrey (Ansell) 1937- .... **CLC 41**
See also CA 29-32R; CANR 29, 43, 78

Wolff, Sonia
See Levitin, Sonia (Wolff)

Wolff, Tobias (Jonathan Ansell)
1945- .... **CLC 39, 64, 172; SSC 63**
See also AAYA 16; AMWS 7; BEST 90:2; BYA 12; CA 114; 117; CAAS 22; CANR 54, 76, 96; CN 7; CSW; DA3; DLB 130; EWL 3; INT CA-117; MTCW 2; RGAL 4; RGSF 2; SSFS 4, 11

Wolfram von Eschenbach c. 1170-c. 1220 .... **CMLC 5**
See Eschenbach, Wolfram von
See also CDWLB 2; DLB 138; EW 1; RGWL 2

Wolitzer, Hilma 1930- .... **CLC 17**
See also CA 65-68; CANR 18, 40; INT CANR-18; SATA 31; YAW

Wollstonecraft, Mary 1759-1797 .... **LC 5, 50, 90**
See also BRWS 3; CDBLB 1789-1832; DLB 39, 104, 158, 252; FW; LAIT 1; RGEL 2; TEA; WLIT 3

Wonder, Stevie .... **CLC 12**
See Morris, Steveland Judkins

Wong, Jade Snow 1922- .... **CLC 17**
See also CA 109; CANR 91; SATA 112

Woodberry, George Edward
1855-1930 .... **TCLC 73**
See also CA 165; DLB 71, 103

Woodcott, Keith
See Brunner, John (Kilian Houston)

Woodruff, Robert W.
See Mencken, H(enry) L(ouis)

Woolf, (Adeline) Virginia 1882-1941 . **SSC 7; TCLC 1, 5, 20, 43, 56, 101, 123, 128; WLC**
See also AAYA 44; BPFB 3; BRW 7; BRWC 2; BRWR 1; CA 104; 130; CANR 64; CDBLB 1914-1945; DA; DA3; DAB; DAC; DAM MST, NOV; DLB 36, 100, 162; DLBD 10; EWL 3; EXPS; FW; LAIT 3; LATS 1; LMFS 2; MTCW 1, 2; NCFS 2; NFS 8, 12; RGEL 2; RGSF 2; SSFS 4, 12; TEA; WLIT 4

Woollcott, Alexander (Humphreys)
1887-1943 .... **TCLC 5**
See also CA 105; 161; DLB 29

Woolrich, Cornell .... **CLC 77**
See Hopley-Woolrich, Cornell George
See also MSW

Woolson, Constance Fenimore
1840-1894 .... **NCLC 82**
See also DLB 12, 74, 189, 221; RGAL 4

Wordsworth, Dorothy 1771-1855 .. **NCLC 25**
See also DLB 107

Wordsworth, William 1770-1850 .. **NCLC 12, 38, 111; PC 4; WLC**
See also BRW 4; BRWC 1; CDBLB 1789-1832; DA; DA3; DAB; DAC; DAM MST, POET; DLB 93, 107; EXPP; LATS 1; LMFS 1; PAB; PFS 2; RGEL 2; TEA; WLIT 3; WP

Wotton, Sir Henry 1568-1639 .... **LC 68**
See also DLB 121; RGEL 2

Wouk, Herman 1915- .... **CLC 1, 9, 38**
See also BPFB 2, 3; CA 5-8R; CANR 6, 33, 67; CDALBS; CN 7; CPW; DA3; DAM NOV, POP; DLBY 1982; INT CANR-6; LAIT 4; MTCW 1, 2; NFS 7; TUS

Wright, Charles (Penzel, Jr.) 1935- .. **CLC 6, 13, 28, 119, 146**
See also AMWS 5; CA 29-32R; CAAS 7; CANR 23, 36, 62, 88; CP 7; DLB 165; DLBY 1982; EWL 3; MTCW 1, 2; PFS 10

Wright, Charles Stevenson 1932- ..... **BLC 3; CLC 49**
See also BW 1; CA 9-12R; CANR 26; CN 7; DAM MULT, POET; DLB 33

Wright, Frances 1795-1852 .... **NCLC 74**
See also DLB 73

Wright, Frank Lloyd 1867-1959 .... **TCLC 95**
See also AAYA 33; CA 174

Wright, Jack R.
See Harris, Mark

Wright, James (Arlington)
1927-1980 .... **CLC 3, 5, 10, 28; PC 36**
See also AITN 2; AMWS 3; CA 49-52; 97-100; CANR 4, 34, 64; CDALBS; DAM POET; DLB 5, 169; EWL 3; EXPP; MTCW 1, 2; PFS 7, 8; RGAL 4; TUS; WP

Wright, Judith (Arundell)
1915-2000 .... **CLC 11, 53; PC 14**
See also CA 13-16R; 188; CANR 31, 76, 93; CP 7; CWP; DLB 260; EWL 3; MTCW 1, 2; PFS 8; RGEL 2; SATA 14; SATA-Obit 121

Wright, L(aurali) R. 1939- .... **CLC 44**
See also CA 138; CMW 4

Wright, Richard (Nathaniel)
1908-1960 ... **BLC 3; CLC 1, 3, 4, 9, 14, 21, 48, 74; SSC 2; TCLC 136; WLC**
See also AAYA 5, 42; AFAW 1, 2; AMW; BPFB 3; BW 1; BYA 2; CA 108; CANR 64; CDALB 1929-1941; DA; DA3; DAB; DAC; DAM MST, MULT, NOV; DLB 76, 102; DLBD 2; EWL 3; EXPN; LAIT 3, 4; MTCW 1, 2; NCFS 1; NFS 1, 7; RGAL 4; RGSF 2; SSFS 3, 9, 15; TUS; YAW

Wright, Richard B(ruce) 1937- .... **CLC 6**
See also CA 85-88; CANR 120; DLB 53

Wright, Rick 1945- .... **CLC 35**

Wright, Rowland
See Wells, Carolyn

Wright, Stephen 1946- .... **CLC 33**

Wright, Willard Huntington 1888-1939
See Van Dine, S. S.
See also CA 115; 189; CMW 4; DLBD 16

Wright, William 1930- .... **CLC 44**
See also CA 53-56; CANR 7, 23

Wroth, Lady Mary 1587-1653(?) .... **LC 30; PC 38**
See also DLB 121

Wu Ch'eng-en 1500(?)-1582(?) .... **LC 7**

Wu Ching-tzu 1701-1754 .... **LC 2**

Wulfstan c. 10th cent. -1023 .... **CMLC 59**

Wurlitzer, Rudolph 1938(?)- .... **CLC 2, 4, 15**
See also CA 85-88; CN 7; DLB 173

Wyatt, Sir Thomas c. 1503-1542 . **LC 70; PC 27**
See also BRW 1; DLB 132; EXPP; RGEL 2; TEA

Wycherley, William 1640-1716 .... **LC 8, 21**
See also BRW 2; CDBLB 1660-1789; DAM DRAM; DLB 80; RGEL 2

Wylie, Elinor (Morton Hoyt)
1885-1928 .... **PC 23; TCLC 8**
See also AMWS 1; CA 105; 162; DLB 9, 45; EXPP; RGAL 4

Wylie, Philip (Gordon) 1902-1971 ... **CLC 43**
See also CA 21-22; 33-36R; CAP 2; DLB 9; SFW 4

Wyndham, John .... **CLC 19**
See Harris, John (Wyndham Parkes Lucas Beynon)
See also DLB 255; SCFW 2

Wyss, Johann David Von
1743-1818 .... **NCLC 10**
See also CLR 92; JRDA; MAICYA 1, 2; SATA 29; SATA-Brief 27

Xenophon c. 430B.C.-c. 354B.C. ... **CMLC 17**
See also AW 1; DLB 176; RGWL 2, 3

Xingjian, Gao 1940-
See Gao Xingjian
See also CA 193; RGWL 3

Yakamochi 718-785 .... **CMLC 45; PC 48**

Yakumo Koizumi
See Hearn, (Patricio) Lafcadio (Tessima Carlos)

Yamada, Mitsuye (May) 1923- .... **PC 44**
See also CA 77-80

Yamamoto, Hisaye 1921- .... **AAL; SSC 34**
See also CA 214; DAM MULT; LAIT 4; SSFS 14

Yamauchi, Wakako 1924- .... **AAL**
See also CA 214

Yanez, Jose Donoso
See Donoso (Yanez), Jose

Yanovsky, Basile S.
See Yanovsky, V(assily) S(emenovich)

Yanovsky, V(assily) S(emenovich)
1906-1989 .... **CLC 2, 18**
See also CA 97-100; 129

Yates, Richard 1926-1992 .... **CLC 7, 8, 23**
See also AMWS 11; CA 5-8R; 139; CANR 10, 43; DLB 2, 234; DLBY 1981, 1992; INT CANR-10

Yeats, W. B.
See Yeats, William Butler

Yeats, William Butler 1865-1939 . **PC 20, 51; TCLC 1, 11, 18, 31, 93, 116; WLC**
See also AAYA 48; BRW 6; BRWR 1; CA 104; 127; CANR 45; CDBLB 1890-1914; DA; DA3; DAB; DAC; DAM DRAM, MST, POET; DLB 10, 19, 98, 156; EWL 3; EXPP; MTCW 1, 2; NCFS 3; PAB; PFS 1, 2, 5, 7, 13, 15; RGEL 2; TEA; WLIT 4; WP

Yehoshua, A(braham) B. 1936- .. **CLC 13, 31**
See also CA 33-36R; CANR 43, 90; EWL 3; RGSF 2; RGWL 3

Yellow Bird
See Ridge, John Rollin

Yep, Laurence Michael 1948- .... **CLC 35**
See also AAYA 5, 31; BYA 7; CA 49-52; CANR 1, 46, 92; CLR 3, 17, 54; DLB 52; FANT; JRDA; MAICYA 1, 2; MAICYAS 1; SATA 7, 69, 123; WYA; YAW

Yerby, Frank G(arvin) 1916-1991 ..... **BLC 3; CLC 1, 7, 22**
See also BPFB 3; BW 1, 3; CA 9-12R; 136; CANR 16, 52; DAM MULT; DLB 76; INT CANR-16; MTCW 1; RGAL 4; RHW

Yesenin, Sergei Alexandrovich
See Esenin, Sergei (Alexandrovich)

Yesenin, Sergey
See Esenin, Sergei (Alexandrovich)
See also EWL 3

Yevtushenko, Yevgeny (Alexandrovich) 1933- ...... **CLC 1, 3, 13, 26, 51, 126; PC 40**
See Evtushenko, Evgenii Aleksandrovich
See also CA 81-84; CANR 33, 54; CWW 2; DAM POET; EWL 3; MTCW 1

Yezierska, Anzia 1885(?)-1970 .... **CLC 46**
See also CA 126; 89-92; DLB 28, 221; FW; MTCW 1; RGAL 4; SSFS 15

Yglesias, Helen 1915- .... **CLC 7, 22**
See also CA 37-40R; CAAS 20; CANR 15, 65, 95; CN 7; INT CANR-15; MTCW 1

Yokomitsu, Riichi 1898-1947 .... **TCLC 47**
See also CA 170; EWL 3

Yonge, Charlotte (Mary) 1823-1901 .... **TCLC 48**
See also CA 109; 163; DLB 18, 163; RGEL 2; SATA 17; WCH

York, Jeremy
See Creasey, John

York, Simon
See Heinlein, Robert A(nson)

Yorke, Henry Vincent 1905-1974 ..... **CLC 13**
See Green, Henry
See also CA 85-88; 49-52

Yosano Akiko 1878-1942 .... **PC 11; TCLC 59**
See also CA 161; EWL 3; RGWL 3

Yoshimoto, Banana .... **CLC 84**
See Yoshimoto, Mahoko
See also AAYA 50; NFS 7

Yoshimoto, Mahoko 1964-
See Yoshimoto, Banana
See also CA 144; CANR 98; SSFS 16

Young, Al(bert James) 1939- ... **BLC 3; CLC 19**
See also BW 2, 3; CA 29-32R; CANR 26, 65, 109; CN 7; CP 7; DAM MULT; DLB 33

Young, Andrew (John) 1885-1971 ...... **CLC 5**
See also CA 5-8R; CANR 7, 29; RGEL 2

Young, Collier
See Bloch, Robert (Albert)

Young, Edward 1683-1765 .... **LC 3, 40**
See also DLB 95; RGEL 2

Young, Marguerite (Vivian) 1909-1995 .... **CLC 82**
See also CA 13-16; 150; CAP 1; CN 7

Young, Neil 1945- .... **CLC 17**
See also CA 110; CCA 1

Young Bear, Ray A. 1950- ... **CLC 94; NNAL**
See also CA 146; DAM MULT; DLB 175

Yourcenar, Marguerite 1903-1987 ... **CLC 19, 38, 50, 87**
See also BPFB 3; CA 69-72; CANR 23, 60, 93; DAM NOV; DLB 72; DLBY 1988; EW 12; EWL 3; GFL 1789 to the Present; GLL 1; MTCW 1, 2; RGWL 2, 3

Yuan, Chu 340(?)B.C.-278(?)B.C. . **CMLC 36**

Yurick, Sol 1925- .... **CLC 6**
See also CA 13-16R; CANR 25; CN 7

Zabolotsky, Nikolai Alekseevich 1903-1958 .... **TCLC 52**
See Zabolotsky, Nikolay Alekseevich
See also CA 116; 164

Zabolotsky, Nikolay Alekseevich
See Zabolotsky, Nikolai Alekseevich
See also EWL 3

Zagajewski, Adam 1945- .... **PC 27**
See also CA 186; DLB 232; EWL 3

Zalygin, Sergei -2000 .... **CLC 59**

Zamiatin, Evgenii
See Zamyatin, Evgeny Ivanovich
See also RGSF 2; RGWL 2, 3

Zamiatin, Evgenii Ivanovich
See Zamyatin, Evgeny Ivanovich
See also DLB 272

Zamiatin, Yevgenii
See Zamyatin, Evgeny Ivanovich

Zamora, Bernice (B. Ortiz) 1938- .. **CLC 89; HLC 2**
See also CA 151; CANR 80; DAM MULT; DLB 82; HW 1, 2

Zamyatin, Evgeny Ivanovich 1884-1937 .... **TCLC 8, 37**
See Zamiatin, Evgenii; Zamiatin, Evgenii Ivanovich; Zamyatin, Yevgeny Ivanovich
See also CA 105; 166; EW 10; SFW 4

Zamyatin, Yevgeny Ivanovich
See Zamyatin, Evgeny Ivanovich
See also EWL 3

Zangwill, Israel 1864-1926 ... **SSC 44; TCLC 16**
See also CA 109; 167; CMW 4; DLB 10, 135, 197; RGEL 2

Zappa, Francis Vincent, Jr. 1940-1993
See Zappa, Frank
See also CA 108; 143; CANR 57

Zappa, Frank .... **CLC 17**
See Zappa, Francis Vincent, Jr.

Zaturenska, Marya 1902-1982 .... **CLC 6, 11**
See also CA 13-16R; 105; CANR 22

Zeami 1363-1443 .... **DC 7; LC 86**
See also DLB 203; RGWL 2, 3

Zelazny, Roger (Joseph) 1937-1995 . **CLC 21**
See also AAYA 7; BPFB 3; CA 21-24R; 148; CANR 26, 60; CN 7; DLB 8; FANT; MTCW 1, 2; SATA 57; SATA-Brief 39; SCFW; SFW 4; SUFW 1, 2

Zhdanov, Andrei Alexandrovich 1896-1948 .... **TCLC 18**
See also CA 117; 167

Zhukovsky, Vasilii Andreevich
See Zhukovsky, Vasily (Andreevich)
See also DLB 205

Zhukovsky, Vasily (Andreevich) 1783-1852 .... **NCLC 35**
See Zhukovsky, Vasilii Andreevich

Ziegenhagen, Eric .... **CLC 55**

Zimmer, Jill Schary
See Robinson, Jill

Zimmerman, Robert
See Dylan, Bob

Zindel, Paul 1936-2003 .... **CLC 6, 26; DC 5**
See also AAYA 2, 37; BYA 2, 3, 8, 11, 14; CA 73-76; 213; CAD; CANR 31, 65, 108; CD 5; CDALBS; CLR 3, 45, 85; DA; DA3; DAB; DAC; DAM DRAM, MST, NOV; DFS 12; DLB 7, 52; JRDA; LAIT 5; MAICYA 1, 2; MTCW 1, 2; NFS 14; SATA 16, 58, 102; SATA-Obit 142; WYA; YAW

Zinov'Ev, A. A.
See Zinoviev, Alexander (Aleksandrovich)

Zinoviev, Alexander (Aleksandrovich) 1922- .... **CLC 19**
See also CA 116; 133; CAAS 10

Zoilus
See Lovecraft, H(oward) P(hillips)

Zola, Emile (Edouard Charles Antoine) 1840-1902 .... **TCLC 1, 6, 21, 41; WLC**
See also CA 104; 138; DA; DA3; DAB; DAC; DAM MST, NOV; DLB 123; EW 7; GFL 1789 to the Present; IDTP; LMFS 1, 2; RGWL 2, 3; TWA

Zoline, Pamela 1941- .... **CLC 62**
See also CA 161; SFW 4

Zoroaster 628(?)B.C.-551(?)B.C. ... **CMLC 40**

Zorrilla y Moral, Jose 1817-1893 .... **NCLC 6**

Zoshchenko, Mikhail (Mikhailovich) 1895-1958 .... **SSC 15; TCLC 15**
See also CA 115; 160; EWL 3; RGSF 2; RGWL 3

Zuckmayer, Carl 1896-1977 .... **CLC 18**
See also CA 69-72; DLB 56, 124; EWL 3; RGWL 2, 3

Zuk, Georges
See Skelton, Robin
See also CCA 1

Zukofsky, Louis 1904-1978 ... **CLC 1, 2, 4, 7, 11, 18; PC 11**
See also AMWS 3; CA 9-12R; 77-80; CANR 39; DAM POET; DLB 5, 165; EWL 3; MTCW 1; RGAL 4

Zweig, Paul 1935-1984 .... **CLC 34, 42**
See also CA 85-88; 113

Zweig, Stefan 1881-1942 .... **TCLC 17**
See also CA 112; 170; DLB 81, 118; EWL 3

Zwingli, Huldreich 1484-1531 .... **LC 37**
See also DLB 179

Literary Criticism Series
Cumulative Topic Index

This index lists all topic entries in Gale's *Classical and Medieval Literature Criticism* (CMLC), *Contemporary Literary Criticism* (CLC), *Drama Criticism* (DC), *Literature Criticism from 1400 to 1800* (LC), *Nineteenth-Century Literature Criticism* (NCLC), *Short Story Criticism* (SSC), and *Twentieth-Century Literary Criticism* (TCLC). The index also lists topic entries in the Gale Critical Companion Collection, which includes the following publications: *The Beat Generation* (BG), and *Harlem Renaissance* (HR).

Aborigine in Nineteenth-Century Australian Literature, The NCLC 120: 1-88
 overviews, 2-27
 representations of the Aborigine in Australian literature, 27-58
 Aboriginal myth, literature, and oral tradition, 58-88

Aesopic Fable, The LC 51: 1-100
 the British Aesopic Fable, 1-54
 the Aesopic tradition in non-English-speaking cultures, 55-66
 political uses of the Aesopic fable, 67-88
 the evolution of the Aesopic fable, 89-99

African-American Folklore and Literature TCLC 126: 1-67
 African-American folk tradition, 1-16
 representative writers, 16-34
 hallmark works, 35-48
 the study of African-American literature and folklore, 48-64

Age of Johnson LC 15: 1-87
 Johnson's London, 3-15
 aesthetics of neoclassicism, 15-36
 "age of prose and reason," 36-45
 clubmen and bluestockings, 45-56
 printing technology, 56-62
 periodicals: "a map of busy life," 62-74
 transition, 74-86

Age of Spenser LC 39: 1-70
 overviews and general studies, 2-21
 literary style, 22-34
 poets and the crown, 34-70

AIDS in Literature CLC 81: 365-416

Alcohol and Literature TCLC 70: 1-58
 overview, 2-8
 fiction, 8-48
 poetry and drama, 48-58

American Abolitionism NCLC 44: 1-73
 overviews and general studies, 2-26
 abolitionist ideals, 26-46
 the literature of abolitionism, 46-72

American Autobiography TCLC 86: 1-115
 overviews and general studies, 3-36
 American authors and autobiography, 36-82
 African-American autobiography, 82-114

American Black Humor Fiction TCLC 54: 1-85
 characteristics of black humor, 2-13
 origins and development, 13-38
 black humor distinguished from related literary trends, 38-60
 black humor and society, 60-75
 black humor reconsidered, 75-83

American Civil War in Literature NCLC 32: 1-109
 overviews and general studies, 2-20
 regional perspectives, 20-54
 fiction popular during the war, 54-79
 the historical novel, 79-108

American Frontier in Literature NCLC 28: 1-103
 definitions, 2-12
 development, 12-17
 nonfiction writing about the frontier, 17-30
 frontier fiction, 30-45
 frontier protagonists, 45-66
 portrayals of Native Americans, 66-86
 feminist readings, 86-98
 twentieth-century reaction against frontier literature, 98-100

American Humor Writing NCLC 52: 1-59
 overviews and general studies, 2-12
 the Old Southwest, 12-42
 broader impacts, 42-5
 women humorists, 45-58

American Novel of Manners TCLC 130: 1-42
 history of the Novel of Manners in America, 4-10
 representative writers, 10-18
 relevancy of the Novel of Manners, 18-24
 hallmark works in the Novel of Manners, 24-36
 Novel of Manners and other media, 36-40

American Mercury, The TCLC 74: 1-80

American Popular Song, Golden Age of TCLC 42: 1-49
 background and major figures, 2-34
 the lyrics of popular songs, 34-47

American Proletarian Literature TCLC 54: 86-175
 overviews and general studies, 87-95
 American proletarian literature and the American Communist Party, 95-111
 ideology and literary merit, 111-17
 novels, 117-36

Gastonia, 136-48
 drama, 148-54
 journalism, 154-9
 proletarian literature in the United States, 159-74

American Realism NCLC 120: 89-246
 overviews, 91-112
 background and sources, 112-72
 social issues, 172-223
 women and realism, 223-45

American Renaissance SSC 64: 46-193
 overviews and general studies, 47-103
 major authors of short fiction, 103-92

American Romanticism NCLC 44: 74-138
 overviews and general studies, 74-84
 sociopolitical influences, 84-104
 Romanticism and the American frontier, 104-15
 thematic concerns, 115-37

American Western Literature TCLC 46: 1-100
 definition and development of American Western literature, 2-7
 characteristics of the Western novel, 8-23
 Westerns as history and fiction, 23-34
 critical reception of American Western literature, 34-41
 the Western hero, 41-73
 women in Western fiction, 73-91
 later Western fiction, 91-9

American Writers in Paris TCLC 98: 1-156
 overviews and general studies, 2-155

Anarchism NCLC 84: 1-97
 overviews and general studies, 2-23
 the French anarchist tradition, 23-56
 Anglo-American anarchism, 56-68
 anarchism: incidents and issues, 68-97

Animals in Literature TCLC 106: 1-120
 overviews and general studies, 2-8
 animals in American literature, 8-45
 animals in Canadian literature, 45-57
 animals in European literature, 57-100
 animals in Latin American literature, 100-06
 animals in women's literature, 106-20

Antebellum South, Literature of the NCLC 112:1-188

overviews, 4-55
culture of the Old South, 55-68
antebellum fiction: pastoral and heroic romance, 68-120
role of women: a subdued rebellion, 120-59
slavery and the slave narrative, 159-85

The Apocalyptic Movement TCLC 106: 121-69

Aristotle CMLC 31:1-397
philosophy, 3-100
poetics, 101-219
rhetoric, 220-301
science, 302-397

Art and Literature TCLC 54: 176-248
overviews and general studies, 176-93
definitions, 193-219
influence of visual arts on literature, 219-31
spatial form in literature, 231-47

Arthurian Literature CMLC 10: 1-127
historical context and literary beginnings, 2-27
development of the legend through Malory, 27-64
development of the legend from Malory to the Victorian Age, 65-81
themes and motifs, 81-95
principal characters, 95-125

Arthurian Revival NCLC 36: 1-77
overviews and general studies, 2-12
Tennyson and his influence, 12-43
other leading figures, 43-73
the Arthurian legend in the visual arts, 73-6

Australian Cultural Identity in Nineteenth-Century Literature NCLC 124: 1-164
overviews and general studies, 4-22
poetry, 22-67
fiction, 67-135
role of women writers, 135-64

Australian Literature TCLC 50: 1-94
origins and development, 2-21
characteristics of Australian literature, 21-33
historical and critical perspectives, 33-41
poetry, 41-58
fiction, 58-76
drama, 76-82
Aboriginal literature, 82-91

Beat Generation, The BG 1:1-562
the Beat Generation: an overview, 1-137
primary sources, 3-32
overviews and general studies, 32-47
Beat Generation as a social phenomenon, 47-65
drugs, inspiration, and the Beat Generation, 65-92
religion and the Beat Generation, 92-124
women of the Beat Generation, 124-36
Beat "scene": East and West, 139-259
primary sources, 141-77
Beat scene in the East, 177-218
Beat scene in the West, 218-59
Beat Generation publishing: periodicals, small presses, and censorship, 261-349
primary sources, 263-74
overview, 274-88
Beat periodicals: "little magazines," 288-311
Beat publishing: small presses, 311-24
Beat battles with censorship, 324-49
performing arts and the Beat Generation, 351-417
primary sources, 353-58
Beats and film, 358-81
Beats and music, 381-415
visual arts and the Beat Generation, 419-91
primary sources, 421-24
critical commentary, 424-90

Beat Generation, Literature of the TCLC 42: 50-102
overviews and general studies, 51-9
the Beat generation as a social phenomenon, 59-62
development, 62-5
Beat literature, 66-96
influence, 97-100

The Bell Curve Controversy CLC 91: 281-330

***Bildungsroman* in Nineteenth-Century Literature** NCLC 20: 92-168
surveys, 93-113
in Germany, 113-40
in England, 140-56
female *Bildungsroman*, 156-67

Bloomsbury Group TCLC 34: 1-73
history and major figures, 2-13
definitions, 13-7
influences, 17-27
thought, 27-40
prose, 40-52
and literary criticism, 52-4
political ideals, 54-61
response to, 61-71

The Bloomsbury Group TCLC 138: 1-59
representative members of the Bloomsbury Group, 9-24
literary relevance of the Bloomsbury Group, 24-36
Bloomsbury's hallmark works, 36-48
other modernists studied with the Bloomsbury Group, 48-54

The Blues in Literature TCLC 82: 1-71

Bly, Robert, *Iron John: A Book about Men and Men's Work* CLC 70: 414-62

The Book of J CLC 65: 289-311

Brazilian Literature TCLC 134: 1-126
overviews and general studies, 3-33
Brazilian poetry, 33-48
contemporary Brazilian writing, 48-76
culture, politics, and race in Brazilian writing, 76-100
modernism and postmodernism in Brazil, 100-25

British Ephemeral Literature LC 59: 1-70
overviews and general studies, 1-9
broadside ballads, 10-40
chapbooks, jestbooks, pamphlets, and newspapers, 40-69

Buddhism and Literature TCLC 70: 59-164
eastern literature, 60-113
western literature, 113-63

The *Bulletin* and the Rise of Australian Literary Nationalism NCLC 116: 1-121
overviews, 3-32
legend of the nineties, 32-55
Bulletin style, 55-71
Australian literary nationalism, 71-98
myth of the bush, 98-120

Businessman in American Literature TCLC 26: 1-48
portrayal of the businessman, 1-32
themes and techniques in business fiction, 32-47

The Calendar LC 55: 1-92
overviews and general studies, 2-19
measuring time, 19-28
calendars and culture, 28-60
calendar reform, 60-92

Captivity Narratives LC 82: 71-172
overviews, 72-107
captivity narratives and Puritanism, 108-34
captivity narratives and Native Americans, 134-49
influence on American literature, 149-72

Caribbean Literature TCLC 138: 60-135
overviews and general studies, 61-9
ethnic and national identity, 69-107
expatriate Caribbean literature, 107-23
literary histoiography, 123-35

Catholicism in Nineteenth-Century American Literature NCLC 64: 1-58
overviews, 3-14
polemical literature, 14-46
Catholicism in literature, 47-57

Celtic Mythology CMLC 26: 1-111
overviews and general studies, 2-22
Celtic myth as literature and history, 22-48
Celtic religion: Druids and divinities, 48-80
Fionn MacCuhaill and the Fenian cycle, 80-111

Celtic Twilight See Irish Literary Renaissance

Chartist Movement and Literature, The NCLC 60: 1-84
overview: nineteenth-century working-class fiction, 2-19
Chartist fiction and poetry, 19-73
the Chartist press, 73-84

Child Labor in Nineteenth-Century Literature NCLC 108: 1-133
overviews, 3-10
climbing boys and chimney sweeps, 10-16
the international traffic in children, 16-45
critics and reformers, 45-82
fictional representations of child laborers, 83-132

Children's Literature, Nineteenth-Century NCLC 52: 60-135
overviews and general studies, 61-72
moral tales, 72-89
fairy tales and fantasy, 90-119
making men/making women, 119-34

Christianity in Twentieth-Century Literature TCLC 110: 1-79
overviews and general studies, 2-31
Christianity in twentieth-century fiction, 31-78

Chronicle Plays LC 89: 1-106
development of the genre, 2-33
historiography and literature, 33-56
genre and performance, 56-88
politics and ideology, 88-106

The City and Literature TCLC 90: 1-124
overviews and general studies, 2-9
the city in American literature, 9-86
the city in European literature, 86-124

Civic Critics, Russian NCLC 20: 402-46
principal figures and background, 402-9
and Russian Nihilism, 410-6
aesthetic and critical views, 416-45

The Cockney School NCLC 68: 1-64
overview, 2-7
Blackwood's Magazine and the contemporary critical response, 7-24
the political and social import of the Cockneys and their critics, 24-63

Colonial America: The Intellectual Background LC 25: 1-98
overviews and general studies, 2-17
philosophy and politics, 17-31
early religious influences in Colonial America, 31-60
consequences of the Revolution, 60-78
religious influences in post-revolutionary America, 78-87
colonial literary genres, 87-97

Colonialism in Victorian English Literature NCLC 56: 1-77
overviews and general studies, 2-34

colonialism and gender, 34-51
monsters and the occult, 51-76

Columbus, Christopher, Books on the Quincentennial of His Arrival in the New World CLC 70: 329-60

Comic Books TCLC 66: 1-139
historical and critical perspectives, 2-48
superheroes, 48-67
underground comix, 67-88
comic books and society, 88-122
adult comics and graphic novels, 122-36

Comedy of Manners LC 92: 1-75
overviews, 2-21
comedy of manners and society, 21-47
comedy of manners and women, 47-74

Commedia dell'Arte LC 83: 1-147
overviews, 2-7
origins and development, 7-23
characters and actors, 23-45
performance, 45-62
texts and authors, 62-100
influence in Europe, 100-46

Connecticut Wits NCLC 48: 1-95
overviews and general studies, 2-40
major works, 40-76
intellectual context, 76-95

Contemporary Feminist Criticism CLC 180: 1-103
overviews and general studies, 2–59
modern French feminist theory, 59-102

Contemporary Gay and Lesbian Literature CLC 171: 1-130
overviews and general studies, 2-43
contemporary gay literature, 44-95
lesbianism in contemporary literature, 95-129

Contemporary Southern Literature CLC 167: 1-132
criticism, 2-131

Crime in Literature TCLC 54: 249-307
evolution of the criminal figure in literature, 250-61
crime and society, 261-77
literary perspectives on crime and punishment, 277-88
writings by criminals, 288-306

Crime-Mystery-Detective Stories SSC 59:89-226
overviews and general studies, 90-140
origins and early masters of the crime-mystery-detective story, 140-73
hard-boiled crime-mystery-detective fiction, 173-209
diversity in the crime-mystery-detective story, 210-25

The Crusades CMLC 38: 1-144
history of the Crusades, 3-60
literature of the Crusades, 60-116
the Crusades and the people: attitudes and influences, 116-44

Cyberpunk TCLC 106: 170-366
overviews and general studies, 171-88
feminism and cyberpunk, 188-230
history and cyberpunk, 230-70
sexuality and cyberpunk, 270-98
social issues and cyberpunk, 299-366

Cyberpunk Short Fiction SSC 60: 44-108
overviews and general studies, 46-78
major writers of cyberpunk fiction, 78-81
sexuality and cyberpunk fiction, 81-97
additional pieces, 97-108

Czechoslovakian Literature of the Twentieth Century TCLC 42:103-96
through World War II, 104-35
de-Stalinization, the Prague Spring, and contemporary literature, 135-72

Slovak literature, 172-85
Czech science fiction, 185-93

Dadaism TCLC 46: 101-71
background and major figures, 102-16
definitions, 116-26
manifestos and commentary by Dadaists, 126-40
theater and film, 140-58
nature and characteristics of Dadaist writing, 158-70

Danish Literature See **Twentieth-Century Danish Literature**

Darwinism and Literature NCLC 32: 110-206
background, 110-31
direct responses to Darwin, 131-71
collateral effects of Darwinism, 171-205

Death in American Literature NCLC 92: 1-170
overviews and general studies, 2-32
death in the works of Emily Dickinson, 32-72
death in the works of Herman Melville, 72-101
death in the works of Edgar Allan Poe, 101-43
death in the works of Walt Whitman, 143-70

Death in Nineteenth-Century British Literature NCLC 68: 65-142
overviews and general studies, 66-92
responses to death, 92-102
feminist perspectives, 103-17
striving for immortality, 117-41

Death in Literature TCLC 78:1-183
fiction, 2-115
poetry, 115-46
drama, 146-81

Deconstruction TCLC 138: 136-256
overviews and general studies, 137-83
deconstruction and literature, 183-221
deconstruction in philosophy and history, 221-56

de Man, Paul, Wartime Journalism of CLC 55: 382-424

Detective Fiction, Nineteenth-Century NCLC 36: 78-148
origins of the genre, 79-100
history of nineteenth-century detective fiction, 101-33
significance of nineteenth-century detective fiction, 133-46

Detective Fiction, Twentieth-Century TCLC 38: 1-96
genesis and history of the detective story, 3-22
defining detective fiction, 22-32
evolution and varieties, 32-77
the appeal of detective fiction, 77-90

Detective Story See **Crime-Mystery-Detective Stories**

Dime Novels NCLC 84: 98-168
overviews and general studies, 99-123
popular characters, 123-39
major figures and influences, 139-52
socio-political concerns, 152-167

Disease and Literature TCLC 66: 140-283
overviews and general studies, 141-65
disease in nineteenth-century literature, 165-81
tuberculosis and literature, 181-94
women and disease in literature, 194-221
plague literature, 221-53
AIDS in literature, 253-82

El Dorado, The Legend of See **Legend of El Dorado, The**

The Double in Nineteenth-Century Literature NCLC 40: 1-95
genesis and development of the theme, 2-15
the double and Romanticism, 16-27
sociological views, 27-52
psychological interpretations, 52-87
philosophical considerations, 87-95

Dramatic Realism NCLC 44: 139-202
overviews and general studies, 140-50
origins and definitions, 150-66
impact and influence, 166-93
realist drama and tragedy, 193-201

Drugs and Literature TCLC 78: 184-282
overviews and general studies, 185-201
pre-twentieth-century literature, 201-42
twentieth-century literature, 242-82

Dystopias in Contemporary Literature CLC 168: 1-91
overviews and general studies, 2-52
dystopian views in Margaret Atwood's *The Handmaid's Tale* (1985), 52-71
feminist readings of dystopias, 71-90

Eastern Mythology CMLC 26: 112-92
heroes and kings, 113-51
cross-cultural perspective, 151-69
relations to history and society, 169-92

Eighteenth-Century British Periodicals LC 63: 1-123
rise of periodicals, 2-31
impact and influence of periodicals, 31-64
periodicals and society, 64-122

Eighteenth-Century Travel Narratives LC 77: 252-355
overviews and general studies, 254-79
eighteenth-century European travel narratives, 279-334
non-European eighteenth-century travel narratives, 334-55

Electronic "Books": Hypertext and Hyperfiction CLC 86: 367-404
books vs. CD-ROMS, 367-76
hypertext and hyperfiction, 376-95
implications for publishing, libraries, and the public, 395-403

Eliot, T. S., Centenary of Birth CLC 55: 345-75

Elizabethan Drama LC 22: 140-240
origins and influences, 142-67
characteristics and conventions, 167-83
theatrical production, 184-200
histories, 200-12
comedy, 213-20
tragedy, 220-30

Elizabethan Prose Fiction LC 41: 1-70
overviews and general studies, 1-15
origins and influences, 15-43
style and structure, 43-69

Enclosure of the English Common NCLC 88: 1-57
overviews and general studies, 1-12
early reaction to enclosure, 12-23
nineteenth-century reaction to enclosure, 23-56

The Encyclopedists LC 26: 172-253
overviews and general studies, 173-210
intellectual background, 210-32
views on esthetics, 232-41
views on women, 241-52

English Caroline Literature LC 13: 221-307
background, 222-41
evolution and varieties, 241-62
the Cavalier mode, 262-75
court and society, 275-91
politics and religion, 291-306

English Decadent Literature of the 1890s
NCLC 28: 104-200
  fin de siècle: the Decadent period, 105-19
  definitions, 120-37
  major figures: "the tragic generation," 137-50
  French literature and English literary Decadence, 150-7
  themes, 157-61
  poetry, 161-82
  periodicals, 182-96

English Essay, Rise of the LC 18: 238-308
  definitions and origins, 236-54
  influence on the essay, 254-69
  historical background, 269-78
  the essay in the seventeenth century, 279-93
  the essay in the eighteenth century, 293-307

English Mystery Cycle Dramas LC 34: 1-88
  overviews and general studies, 1-27
  the nature of dramatic performances, 27-42
  the medieval worldview and the mystery cycles, 43-67
  the doctrine of repentance and the mystery cycles, 67-76
  the fall from grace in the mystery cycles, 76-88

The English Realist Novel, 1740-1771 LC 51: 102-98
  overviews and general studies, 103-22
  from Romanticism to Realism, 123-58
  women and the novel, 159-175
  the novel and other literary forms, 176-197

English Revolution, Literature of the LC 43: 1-58
  overviews and general studies, 2-24
  pamphlets of the English Revolution, 24-38
  political sermons of the English Revolution, 38-48
  poetry of the English Revolution, 48-57

English Romantic Hellenism NCLC 68: 143-250
  overviews and general studies, 144-69
  historical development of English Romantic Hellenism, 169-91
  influence of Greek mythology on the Romantics, 191-229
  influence of Greek literature, art, and culture on the Romantics, 229-50

English Romantic Poetry NCLC 28: 201-327
  overviews and reputation, 202-37
  major subjects and themes, 237-67
  forms of Romantic poetry, 267-78
  politics, society, and Romantic poetry, 278-99
  philosophy, religion, and Romantic poetry, 299-324

The Epistolary Novel LC 59: 71-170
  overviews and general studies, 72-96
  women and the Epistolary novel, 96-138
  principal figures: Britain, 138-53
  principal figures: France, 153-69

Espionage Literature TCLC 50: 95-159
  overviews and general studies, 96-113
  espionage fiction/formula fiction, 113-26
  spies in fact and fiction, 126-38
  the female spy, 138-44
  social and psychological perspectives, 144-58

European Debates on the Conquest of the Americas LC 67: 1-129
  overviews and general studies, 3-56
  major Spanish figures, 56-98
  English perceptions of Native Americans, 98-129

European Romanticism NCLC 36: 149-284
  definitions, 149-77
  origins of the movement, 177-82
  Romantic theory, 182-200
  themes and techniques, 200-23
  Romanticism in Germany, 223-39
  Romanticism in France, 240-61
  Romanticism in Italy, 261-4
  Romanticism in Spain, 264-8
  impact and legacy, 268-82

Exile in Literature TCLC 122: 1-129
  overviews and general studies, 2-33
  exile in fiction, 33-92
  German literature in exile, 92-129

Existentialism and Literature TCLC 42: 197-268
  overviews and definitions, 198-209
  history and influences, 209-19
  Existentialism critiqued and defended, 220-35
  philosophical and religious perspectives, 235-41
  Existentialist fiction and drama, 241-67

Familiar Essay NCLC 48: 96-211
  definitions and origins, 97-130
  overview of the genre, 130-43
  elements of form and style, 143-59
  elements of content, 159-73
  the Cockneys: Hazlitt, Lamb, and Hunt, 173-91
  status of the genre, 191-210

Fashion in Nineteenth-Century Literature NCLC 128: 104-93
  overviews and general studies, 105-38
  fashion and American literature, 138-46
  fashion and English literature, 146-74
  fashion and French literature, 174-92

The Faust Legend LC 47: 1-117

Fear in Literature TCLC 74: 81-258
  overviews and general studies, 81
  pre-twentieth-century literature, 123
  twentieth-century literature, 182

Feminism in the 1990s: Commentary on Works by Naomi Wolf, Susan Faludi, and Camille Paglia CLC 76: 377-415

Feminist Criticism See Contemporary Feminist Criticism

Feminist Criticism in 1990 CLC 65: 312-60

Fifteenth-Century English Literature LC 17: 248-334
  background, 249-72
  poetry, 272-315
  drama, 315-23
  prose, 323-33

Film and Literature TCLC 38: 97-226
  overviews and general studies, 97-119
  film and theater, 119-34
  film and the novel, 134-45
  the art of the screenplay, 145-66
  genre literature/genre film, 167-79
  the writer and the film industry, 179-90
  authors on film adaptations of their works, 190-200
  fiction into film: comparative essays, 200-23

Finance and Money as Represented in Nineteenth-Century Literature NCLC 76: 1-69
  historical perspectives, 2-20
  the image of money, 20-37
  the dangers of money, 37-50
  women and money, 50-69

Folklore and Literature TCLC 86: 116-293
  overviews and general studies, 118-144
  Native American literature, 144-67
  African-American literature, 167-238
  folklore and the American West, 238-57
  modern and postmodern literature, 257-91

Food in Literature TCLC 114: 1-133
  food and children's literature, 2-14
  food as a literary device, 14-32
  rituals invloving food, 33-45
  food and social and ethnic identity, 45-90
  women's relationship with food, 91-132

Food in Nineteenth-Century Literature NCLC 108: 134-288
  overviews, 136-74
  food and social class, 174-85
  food and gender, 185-219
  food and love, 219-31
  food and sex, 231-48
  eating disorders, 248-70
  vegetarians, carnivores, and cannibals, 270-87

French Drama in the Age of Louis XIV LC 28: 94-185
  overview, 95-127
  tragedy, 127-46
  comedy, 146-66
  tragicomedy, 166-84

French Enlightenment LC 14: 81-145
  the question of definition, 82-9
  le siècle des lumières, 89-94
  women and the salons, 94-105
  censorship, 105-15
  the philosophy of reason, 115-31
  influence and legacy, 131-44

French New Novel TCLC 98: 158-234
  overviews and general studies, 158-92
  influences, 192-213
  themes, 213-33

French Realism NCLC 52: 136-216
  origins and definitions, 137-70
  issues and influence, 170-98
  realism and representation, 198-215

French Revolution and English Literature NCLC 40: 96-195
  history and theory, 96-123
  romantic poetry, 123-50
  the novel, 150-81
  drama, 181-92
  children's literature, 192-5

Futurism, Italian TCLC 42: 269-354
  principles and formative influences, 271-9
  manifestos, 279-88
  literature, 288-303
  theater, 303-19
  art, 320-30
  music, 330-6
  architecture, 336-9
  and politics, 339-46
  reputation and significance, 346-51

Gaelic Revival See Irish Literary Renaissance

Gates, Henry Louis, Jr., and African-American Literary Criticism CLC 65: 361-405

Gay and Lesbian Literature CLC 76: 416-39

Gay and Lesbian Literature See also Contemporary Gay and Lesbian Literature

German Exile Literature TCLC 30: 1-58
  the writer and the Nazi state, 1-10
  definition of, 10-4
  life in exile, 14-32
  surveys, 32-50
  Austrian literature in exile, 50-2
  German publishing in the United States, 52-7

German Expressionism TCLC 34: 74-160
  history and major figures, 76-85
  aesthetic theories, 85-109
  drama, 109-26
  poetry, 126-38
  film, 138-42

painting, 142-7
music, 147-53
and politics, 153-8

The Ghost Story SSC 58: 1-142
overviews and general studies, 1-21
the ghost story in American literature, 21-49
the ghost story in Asian literature, 49-53
the ghost story in European and English literature, 54-89
major figures, 89-141

The Gilded Age NCLC 84: 169-271
popular themes, 170-90
Realism, 190-208
Aestheticism, 208-26
socio-political concerns, 226-70

Glasnost **and Contemporary Soviet Literature** CLC 59: 355-97

Gothic Novel NCLC 28: 328-402
development and major works, 328-34
definitions, 334-50
themes and techniques, 350-78
in America, 378-85
in Scotland, 385-91
influence and legacy, 391-400

The Governess in Nineteenth-Century Literature NCLC 104: 1-131
overviews and general studies, 3-28
social roles and economic conditions, 28-86
fictional governesses, 86-131

The Grail Theme in Twentieth-Century Literature TCLC 142: 1-89
overviews and general studies, 2-20
major works, 20-89

Graphic Narratives CLC 86: 405-32
history and overviews, 406-21
the "Classics Illustrated" series, 421-2
reviews of recent works, 422-32

Graphic Novels CLC 177: 163-299
overviews and general studies, 165-198
critical readings of major works, 198-286
reviews of recent graphic novels, 286-299

Graveyard Poets LC 67: 131-212
origins and development, 131-52
major figures, 152-75
major works, 175-212

Greek Historiography CMLC 17: 1-49

Greek Mythology CMLC 26: 193-320
overviews and general studies, 194-209
origins and development of Greek mythology, 209-29
cosmogonies and divinities in Greek mythology, 229-54
heroes and heroines in Greek mythology, 254-80
women in Greek mythology, 280-320

Greek Theater CMLC 51: 1-58
criticism, 2-58

Hard-Boiled Fiction TCLC 118: 1-109
overviews and general studies, 2-39
major authors, 39-76
women and hard-boiled fiction, 76-109

The Harlem Renaissance HR 1: 1-563
overviews and general studies of the Harlem Renaissance, 1-137
primary sources, 3-12
overviews, 12-38
background and sources of the Harlem Renaissance, 38-56
the New Negro aesthetic, 56-91
patrons, promoters, and the New York Public Library, 91-121
women of the Harlem Renaissance, 121-37
social, economic, and political factors that influenced the Harlem Renaissance, 139-240
primary sources, 141-53
overviews, 153-87
social and economic factors, 187-213
Black intellectual and political thought, 213-40
publishing and periodicals during the Harlem Renaissance, 243-339
primary sources, 246-52
overviews, 252-68
African American writers and mainstream publishers, 268-91
anthologies: *The New Negro* and others, 291-309
African American periodicals and the Harlem Renaissance, 309-39
performing arts during the Harlem Renaissance, 341-465
primary sources, 343-48
overviews, 348-64
drama of the Harlem Renaissance, 364-92
influence of music on Harlem Renaissance writing, 437-65
visual arts during the Harlem Renaissance, 467-563
primary sources, 470-71
overviews, 471-517
painters, 517-36
sculptors, 536-58
photographers, 558-63

Harlem Renaissance TCLC 26: 49-125
principal issues and figures, 50-67
the literature and its audience, 67-74
theme and technique in poetry, fiction, and drama, 74-115
and American society, 115-21
achievement and influence, 121-2

Havel, Václav, Playwright and President CLC 65: 406-63

Heroic Drama LC 91: 249-373
definitions and overviews, 251-78
politics and heroic drama, 278-303
early plays: Dryden and Orrery, 303-51
later plays: Lee and Otway, 351-73

Historical Fiction, Nineteenth-Century NCLC 48: 212-307
definitions and characteristics, 213-36
Victorian historical fiction, 236-65
American historical fiction, 265-88
realism in historical fiction, 288-306

Hollywood and Literature TCLC 118: 110-251
overviews and general studies, 111-20
adaptations, 120-65
socio-historical and cultural impact, 165-206
theater and hollywood, 206-51

Holocaust and the Atomic Bomb: Fifty Years Later CLC 91: 331-82
the Holocaust remembered, 333-52
Anne Frank revisited, 352-62
the atomic bomb and American memory, 362-81

Holocaust Denial Literature TCLC 58: 1-110
overviews and general studies, 1-30
Robert Faurisson and Noam Chomsky, 30-52
Holocaust denial literature in America, 52-71
library access to Holocaust denial literature, 72-5
the authenticity of Anne Frank's diary, 76-90
David Irving and the "normalization" of Hitler, 90-109

Holocaust, Literature of the TCLC 42: 355-450
historical overview, 357-61
critical overview, 361-70
diaries and memoirs, 370-95
novels and short stories, 395-425
poetry, 425-41
drama, 441-8

Homosexuality in Nineteenth-Century Literature NCLC 56: 78-182
defining homosexuality, 80-111
Greek love, 111-44
trial and danger, 144-81

Humors Comedy LC 85: 194-324
overviews, 195-251
major figures: Ben Jonson, 251-93
major figures: William Shakespeare, 293-324

Hungarian Literature of the Twentieth Century TCLC 26: 126-88
surveys of, 126-47
Nyugat and early twentieth-century literature, 147-56
mid-century literature, 156-68
and politics, 168-78
since the 1956 revolt, 178-87

Hysteria in Nineteenth-Century Literature NCLC 64: 59-184
the history of hysteria, 60-75
the gender of hysteria, 75-103
hysteria and women's narratives, 103-57
hysteria in nineteenth-century poetry, 157-83

Image of the Noble Savage in Literature LC 79: 136-252
overviews and development, 136-76
the Noble Savage in the New World, 176-221
Rousseau and the French Enlightenment's view of the noble savage, 221-51

Imagism TCLC 74: 259-454
history and development, 260
major figures, 288
sources and influences, 352
Imagism and other movements, 397
influence and legacy, 431

Immigrants in Nineteenth-Century Literature, Representation of NCLC 112: 188-298
overview, 189-99
immigrants in America, 199-223
immigrants and labor, 223-60
immigrants in England, 260-97

Incest in Nineteenth-Century American Literature NCLC 76: 70-141
overview, 71-88
the concern for social order, 88-117
authority and authorship, 117-40

Incest in Victorian Literature NCLC 92: 172-318
overviews and general studies, 173-85
novels, 185-276
plays, 276-84
poetry, 284-318

Indian Literature in English TCLC 54: 308-406
overview, 309-13
origins and major figures, 313-25
the Indo-English novel, 325-55
Indo-English poetry, 355-67
Indo-English drama, 367-72
critical perspectives on Indo-English literature, 372-80
modern Indo-English literature, 380-9
Indo-English authors on their work, 389-404

The Industrial Revolution in Literature NCLC 56: 183-273

historical and cultural perspectives, 184-201
contemporary reactions to the machine, 201-21
themes and symbols in literature, 221-73

The Irish Famine as Represented in Nineteenth-Century Literature NCLC 64: 185-261
overviews and general studies, 187-98
historical background, 198-212
famine novels, 212-34
famine poetry, 234-44
famine letters and eye-witness accounts, 245-61

Irish Literary Renaissance TCLC 46: 172-287
overview, 173-83
development and major figures, 184-202
influence of Irish folklore and mythology, 202-22
Irish poetry, 222-34
Irish drama and the Abbey Theatre, 234-56
Irish fiction, 256-86

Irish Nationalism and Literature NCLC 44: 203-73
the Celtic element in literature, 203-19
anti-Irish sentiment and the Celtic response, 219-34
literary ideals in Ireland, 234-45
literary expressions, 245-73

Irish Novel, The NCLC 80: 1-130
overviews and general studies, 3-9
principal figures, 9-22
peasant and middle class Irish novelists, 22-76
aristocratic Irish and Anglo-Irish novelists, 76-129

Israeli Literature TCLC 94: 1-137
overviews and general studies, 2-18
Israeli fiction, 18-33
Israeli poetry, 33-62
Israeli drama, 62-91
women and Israeli literature, 91-112
Arab characters in Israeli literature, 112-36

Italian Futurism See **Futurism, Italian**

Italian Humanism LC 12: 205-77
origins and early development, 206-18
revival of classical letters, 218-23
humanism and other philosophies, 224-39
humanism and humanists, 239-46
the plastic arts, 246-57
achievement and significance, 258-76

Italian Romanticism NCLC 60: 85-145
origins and overviews, 86-101
Italian Romantic theory, 101-25
the language of Romanticism, 125-45

Jacobean Drama LC 33: 1-37
the Jacobean worldview: an era of transition, 2-14
the moral vision of Jacobean drama, 14-22
Jacobean tragedy, 22-3
the Jacobean masque, 23-36

Jazz and Literature TCLC 102: 3-124

Jewish-American Fiction TCLC 62: 1-181
overviews and general studies, 2-24
major figures, 24-48
Jewish writers and American life, 48-78
Jewish characters in American fiction, 78-108
themes in Jewish-American fiction, 108-43
Jewish-American women writers, 143-59
the Holocaust and Jewish-American fiction, 159-81

Jews in Literature TCLC 118: 252-417
overviews and general studies, 253-97
representing the Jew in literature, 297-351
the Holocaust in literature, 351-416

Journals of Lewis and Clark, The NCLC 100: 1-88
overviews and general studies, 4-30
journal-keeping methods, 30-46
Fort Mandan, 46-51
the Clark journal, 51-65
the journals as literary texts, 65-87

Kabuki LC 73: 118-232
overviews and general studies, 120-40
the development of Kabuki, 140-65
major works, 165-95
Kabuki and society, 195-231

Kit-Kat Club, The LC 71: 66-112
overviews and general studies, 67-88
major figures, 88-107
attacks on the Kit-Kat Club, 107-12

Knickerbocker Group, The NCLC 56: 274-341
overviews and general studies, 276-314
Knickerbocker periodicals, 314-26
writers and artists, 326-40

Lake Poets, The NCLC 52: 217-304
characteristics of the Lake Poets and their works, 218-27
literary influences and collaborations, 227-66
defining and developing Romantic ideals, 266-84
embracing Conservatism, 284-303

Language Poets TCLC 126: 66-172
overviews and general studies, 67-122
selected major figures in language poetry, 122-72

Larkin, Philip, Controversy CLC 81: 417-64

Latin American Literature, Twentieth-Century TCLC 58: 111-98
historical and critical perspectives, 112-36
the novel, 136-45
the short story, 145-9
drama, 149-60
poetry, 160-7
the writer and society, 167-86
Native Americans in Latin American literature, 186-97

Law and Literature TCLC 126: 173-347
overviews and general studies, 174-253
fiction critiquing the law, 253-88
literary responses to the law, 289-346

Legend of El Dorado, The LC 74: 248-350
overviews, 249-308
major explorations for El Dorado, 308-50

The Levellers LC 51: 200-312
overviews and general studies, 201-29
principal figures, 230-86
religion, political philosophy, and pamphleteering, 287-311

Literary Criticism in the Nineteenth Century, American NCLC 128: 1-103
overviews and general studies, 2-44
the trancendentalists, 44-65
"young America," 65-71
James Russell Lowell, 71-9
Edgar Allan Poe, 79-97
Walt Whitman, 97-102

Literary Expressionism TCLC 142: 90-185
overviews and general studies, 91-138
themes in literary expressionism, 138-61
expressionism in Germany, 161-84

Literary Marketplace, The Nineteenth-Century NCLC 128: 194-368
overviews and general studies, 197-228
British literary marketplace, 228-66
French literary marketplace, 266-82
American literary marketplace, 282-323
Women in the literary marketplace, 323-67

Literary Prizes TCLC 122: 130-203
overviews and general studies, 131-34
the Nobel Prize in Literature, 135-83
the Pulitzer Prize, 183-203

Literature and Millenial Lists CLC 119: 431-67
The Modern Library list, 433
The Waterstone list, 438-439

Literature in Response to the September 11 Attacks CLC 174: 1-46
Major works about September 11, 2001, 2-22
Critical, artistic, and journalistic responses, 22-45

Literature of the American Cowboy NCLC 96: 1-60
overview, 3-20
cowboy fiction, 20-36
cowboy poetry and songs, 36-59

Literature of the California Gold Rush NCLC 92: 320-85
overviews and general studies, 322-24
early California Gold Rush fiction, 324-44
Gold Rush folklore and legend, 344-51
the rise of Western local color, 351-60
social relations and social change, 360-385

Living Theatre, The DC 16: 154-214

Madness in Nineteenth-Century Literature NCLC 76: 142-284
overview, 143-54
autobiography, 154-68
poetry, 168-215
fiction, 215-83

Madness in Twentieth-Century Literature TCLC 50: 160-225
overviews and general studies, 161-71
madness and the creative process, 171-86
suicide, 186-91
madness in American literature, 191-207
madness in German literature, 207-13
madness and feminist artists, 213-24

Magic Realism TCLC 110: 80-327
overviews and general studies, 81-94
magic realism in African literature, 95-110
magic realism in American literature, 110-32
magic realism in Canadian literature, 132-46
magic realism in European literature, 146-66
magic realism in Asian literature, 166-79
magic realism in Latin-American literature, 179-223
magic realism in Israeli literature and the novels of Salman Rushdie, 223-38
magic realism in literature written by women, 239-326

Marxist Criticism TCLC 134: 127-57
overviews and general studies, 128-67
Marxist interpretations, 167-209
cultural and literary Marxist theory, 209-49
Marxism and feminist critical theory, 250-56

The Masque LC 63: 124-265
development of the masque, 125-62
sources and structure, 162-220
race and gender in the masque, 221-64

Medical Writing LC 55: 93-195
colonial America, 94-110
enlightenment, 110-24
medieval writing, 124-40
sexuality, 140-83
vernacular, 185-95

Memoirs of Trauma CLC 109: 419-466
overview, 420
criticism, 429

Metafiction TCLC 130: 43-228
  overviews and general studies, 44-85
  Spanish metafiction, 85-117
  studies of metafictional authors and works, 118-228

Metaphysical Poets LC 24: 356-439
  early definitions, 358-67
  surveys and overviews, 367-92
  cultural and social influences, 392-406
  stylistic and thematic variations, 407-38

Missionaries in the Nineteenth-Century, Literature of NCLC 112: 299-392
  history and development, 300-16
  uses of ethnography, 316-31
  sociopolitical concerns, 331-82
  David Livingstone, 382-91

Modern Essay, The TCLC 58: 199-273
  overview, 200-7
  the essay in the early twentieth century, 207-19
  characteristics of the modern essay, 219-32
  modern essayists, 232-45
  the essay as a literary genre, 245-73

Modern French Literature TCLC 122: 205-359
  overviews and general studies, 207-43
  French theater, 243-77
  gender issues and French women writers, 277-315
  ideology and politics, 315-24
  modern French poetry, 324-41
  resistance literature, 341-58

Modern Irish Literature TCLC 102: 125-321
  overview, 129-44
  dramas, 144-70
  fiction, 170-247
  poetry, 247-321

Modern Japanese Literature TCLC 66: 284-389
  poetry, 285-305
  drama, 305-29
  fiction, 329-61
  western influences, 361-87

Modernism TCLC 70: 165-275
  definitions, 166-184
  Modernism and earlier influences, 184-200
  stylistic and thematic traits, 200-229
  poetry and drama, 229-242
  redefining Modernism, 242-275

Muckraking Movement in American Journalism TCLC 34: 161-242
  development, principles, and major figures, 162-70
  publications, 170-9
  social and political ideas, 179-86
  targets, 186-208
  fiction, 208-19
  decline, 219-29
  impact and accomplishments, 229-40

Multiculturalism in Literature and Education CLC 70: 361-413

Music and Modern Literature TCLC 62: 182-329
  overviews and general studies, 182-211
  musical form/literary form, 211-32
  music in literature, 232-50
  the influence of music on literature, 250-73
  literature and popular music, 273-303
  jazz and poetry, 303-28

Mystery Story See Crime-Mystery-Detective Stories

Native American Literature CLC 76: 440-76

Natural School, Russian NCLC 24: 205-40
  history and characteristics, 205-25
  contemporary criticism, 225-40

Naturalism NCLC 36: 285-382
  definitions and theories, 286-305
  critical debates on Naturalism, 305-16
  Naturalism in theater, 316-32
  European Naturalism, 332-61
  American Naturalism, 361-72
  the legacy of Naturalism, 372-81

Negritude TCLC 50: 226-361
  origins and evolution, 227-56
  definitions, 256-91
  Negritude in literature, 291-343
  Negritude reconsidered, 343-58

New Criticism TCLC 34: 243-318
  development and ideas, 244-70
  debate and defense, 270-99
  influence and legacy, 299-315

New South, Literature of the NCLC 116: 122-240
  overviews, 124-66
  the novel in the New South, 166-209
  myth of the Old South in the New, 209-39

The New World in Renaissance Literature LC 31: 1-51
  overview, 1-18
  utopia vs. terror, 18-31
  explorers and Native Americans, 31-51

New York Intellectuals and *Partisan Review* TCLC 30: 117-98
  development and major figures, 118-28
  influence of Judaism, 128-39
  Partisan Review, 139-57
  literary philosophy and practice, 157-75
  political philosophy, 175-87
  achievement and significance, 187-97

The New Yorker TCLC 58: 274-357
  overviews and general studies, 274-95
  major figures, 295-304
  New Yorker style, 304-33
  fiction, journalism, and humor at *The New Yorker,* 333-48
  the new *New Yorker,* 348-56

Newgate Novel NCLC 24: 166-204
  development of Newgate literature, 166-73
  Newgate Calendar, 173-7
  Newgate fiction, 177-95
  Newgate drama, 195-204

New Zealand Literature TCLC 134: 258-368
  overviews and general studies, 260-300
  Maori literature, 300-22
  New Zealand drama, 322-32
  New Zealand fiction, 332-51
  New Zealand poetry, 351-67

Nigerian Literature of the Twentieth Century TCLC 30: 199-265
  surveys of, 199-227
  English language and African life, 227-45
  politics and the Nigerian writer, 245-54
  Nigerian writers and society, 255-62

Nihilism and Literature TCLC 110: 328-93
  overviews and general studies, 328-44
  European and Russian nihilism, 344-73
  nihilism in the works of Albert Camus, Franz Kafka, and John Barth, 373-92

Nineteenth-Century Captivity Narratives NCLC 80:131-218
  overview, 132-37
  the political significance of captivity narratives, 137-67
  images of gender, 167-96
  moral instruction, 197-217

Nineteenth-Century Euro-American Literary Representations of Native Americans NCLC 104: 132-264
  overviews and general studies, 134-53
  Native American history, 153-72
  the Indians of the Northeast, 172-93
  the Indians of the Southeast, 193-212
  the Indians of the West, 212-27
  Indian-hater fiction, 227-43
  the Indian as exhibit, 243-63

Nineteenth-Century Native American Autobiography NCLC 64: 262-389
  overview, 263-8
  problems of authorship, 268-81
  the evolution of Native American autobiography, 281-304
  political issues, 304-15
  gender and autobiography, 316-62
  autobiographical works during the turn of the century, 362-88

Norse Mythology CMLC 26: 321-85
  history and mythological tradition, 322-44
  Eddic poetry, 344-74
  Norse mythology and other traditions, 374-85

Northern Humanism LC 16: 281-356
  background, 282-305
  precursor of the Reformation, 305-14
  the Brethren of the Common Life, the Devotio Moderna, and education, 314-40
  the impact of printing, 340-56

Novel of Manners, The NCLC 56: 342-96
  social and political order, 343-53
  domestic order, 353-72
  depictions of gender, 373-83
  the American novel of manners, 383-95

Novels of the Ming and Early Ch'ing Dynasties LC 76: 213-356
  overviews and historical development, 214-45
  major works—overview, 245-85
  genre studies, 285-325
  cultural and social themes, 325-55

Nuclear Literature: Writings and Criticism in the Nuclear Age TCLC 46: 288-390
  overviews and general studies, 290-301
  fiction, 301-35
  poetry, 335-8
  nuclear war in Russo-Japanese literature, 338-55
  nuclear war and women writers, 355-67
  the nuclear referent and literary criticism, 367-88

Occultism in Modern Literature TCLC 50: 362-406
  influence of occultism on literature, 363-72
  occultism, literature, and society, 372-87
  fiction, 387-96
  drama, 396-405

Opium and the Nineteenth-Century Literary Imagination NCLC 20:250-301
  original sources, 250-62
  historical background, 262-71
  and literary society, 271-9
  and literary creativity, 279-300

Orientalism NCLC 96: 149-364
  overviews and general studies, 150-98
  Orientalism and imperialism, 198-229
  Orientalism and gender, 229-59
  Orientalism and the nineteenth-century novel, 259-321
  Orientalism in nineteenth-century poetry, 321-63

The Oxford Movement NCLC 72: 1-197
  overviews and general studies, 2-24
  background, 24-59
  and education, 59-69
  religious responses, 69-128
  literary aspects, 128-178
  political implications, 178-196

The Parnassian Movement NCLC 72: 198-241
  overviews and general studies, 199-231

and epic form, 231-38
and positivism, 238-41

Pastoral Literature of the English Renaissance LC 59: 171-282
overviews and general studies, 172-214
principal figures of the Elizabethan period, 214-33
principal figures of the later Renaissance, 233-50
pastoral drama, 250-81

Periodicals, Nineteenth-Century British NCLC 24: 100-65
overviews and general studies, 100-30
in the Romantic Age, 130-41
in the Victorian era, 142-54
and the reviewer, 154-64

Picaresque Literature of the Sixteenth and Seventeenth Centuries LC 78: 223-355
context and development, 224-71
genre, 271-98
the picaro, 299-326
the picara, 326-53

Plath, Sylvia, and the Nature of Biography CLC 86: 433-62
the nature of biography, 433-52
reviews of *The Silent Woman*, 452-61

Political Theory from the 15th to the 18th Century LC 36: 1-55
overview, 1-26
natural law, 26-42
empiricism, 42-55

Polish Romanticism NCLC 52: 305-71
overviews and general studies, 306-26
major figures, 326-40
Polish Romantic drama, 340-62
influences, 362-71

Politics and Literature TCLC 94: 138-61
overviews and general studies, 139-96
Europe, 196-226
Latin America, 226-48
Africa and the Caribbean, 248-60

Popular Literature TCLC 70: 279-382
overviews and general studies, 280-324
"formula" fiction, 324-336
readers of popular literature, 336-351
evolution of popular literature, 351-382

The Portrayal of Jews in Nineteenth-Century English Literature NCLC 72: 242-368
overviews and general studies, 244-77
Anglo-Jewish novels, 277-303
depictions by non-Jewish writers, 303-44
Hebraism versus Hellenism, 344-67

The Portrayal of Mormonism NCLC 96: 61-148
overview, 63-72
early Mormon literature, 72-100
Mormon periodicals and journals, 100-10
women writers, 110-22
Mormonism and nineteenth-century literature, 122-42
Mormon poetry, 142-47

Postcolonialism TCLC 114: 134-239
overviews and general studies, 135-153
African postcolonial writing, 153-72
Asian/Pacific literature, 172-78
postcolonial literary theory, 178-213
postcolonial women's writing, 213-38

Postmodernism TCLC 90:125-307
overview, 126-166
criticism, 166-224
fiction, 224-282
poetry, 282-300
drama, 300-307

Pre-Raphaelite Movement NCLC 20: 302-401
overview, 302-4
genesis, 304-12

Germ and *Oxford and Cambridge Magazine*, 312-20
Robert Buchanan and the "Fleshly School of Poetry," 320-31
satires and parodies, 331-4
surveys, 334-51
aesthetics, 351-75
sister arts of poetry and painting, 375-94
influence, 394-9

Pre-romanticism LC 40: 1-56
overviews and general studies, 2-14
defining the period, 14-23
new directions in poetry and prose, 23-45
the focus on the self, 45-56

Pre-Socratic Philosophy CMLC 22: 1-56
overviews and general studies, 3-24
the Ionians and the Pythagoreans, 25-35
Heraclitus, the Eleatics, and the Atomists, 36-47
the Sophists, 47-55

Prison in Nineteenth-Century Literature, The NCLC 116: 241-357
overview, 242-60
romantic prison, 260-78
domestic prison, 278-316
America as prison, 316-24
physical prisons and prison authors, 324-56

Protestant Hagiography and Martyrology LC 84: 106-217
overview, 106-37
John Foxe's *Book of Martyrs*, 137-97
martyrology and the feminine perspective, 198-216

Protestant Reformation, Literature of the LC 37: 1-83
overviews and general studies, 1-49
humanism and scholasticism, 49-69
the reformation and literature, 69-82

Psychoanalysis and Literature TCLC 38: 227-338
overviews and general studies, 227-46
Freud on literature, 246-51
psychoanalytic views of the literary process, 251-61
psychoanalytic theories of response to literature, 261-88
psychoanalysis and literary criticism, 288-312
psychoanalysis as literature/literature as psychoanalysis, 313-34

The Quarrel between the Ancients and the Moderns LC 63: 266-381
overviews and general studies, 267-301
Renaissance origins, 301-32
Quarrel between the Ancients and the Moderns in France, 332-58
Battle of the Books in England, 358-80

Racism in Literature TCLC 138: 257-373
overviews and general studies, 257-326
racism and literature by and about African Americans, 292-326
theme of racism in literature, 326-773

Rap Music CLC 76: 477-50

Realism in Short Fiction SSC 63: 128-57
overviews and general studies, 129-37
realist short fiction in France, 137-62
realist short fiction in Russia, 162-215
realist short fiction in England, 215-31
realist short fiction in the United States, 231-56

Regionalism and Local Color in Short Fiction SSC 65: 160-289
overviews and general studies, 163-205
regionalism/local color fiction of the west, 205-42
regionalism/local color fiction of the midwest, 242-57

regionalism/local color fiction of the south, 257-88

Renaissance Natural Philosophy LC 27: 201-87
cosmology, 201-28
astrology, 228-54
magic, 254-86

Representations of the Devil in Nineteenth-Century Literature NCLC 100: 89-223
overviews and general studies, 90-115
the Devil in American fiction, 116-43
English Romanticism: the satanic school, 143-89
Luciferian discourse in European literature, 189-222

Restoration Drama LC 21: 184-275
general overviews and general studies, 185-230
Jeremy Collier stage controversy, 230-9
other critical interpretations, 240-75

Revenge Tragedy LC 71: 113-242
overviews and general studies, 113-51
Elizabethan attitudes toward revenge, 151-88
the morality of revenge, 188-216
reminders and remembrance, 217-41

Revising the Literary Canon CLC 81: 465-509

Revising the Literary Canon TCLC 114: 240-84
overviews and general studies, 241-85
canon change in American literature, 285-339
gender and the literary canon, 339-59
minority and third-world literature and the canon, 359-84

Revolutionary Astronomers LC 51: 314-65
overviews and general studies, 316-25
principal figures, 325-51
Revolutionary astronomical models, 352-64

Robin Hood, Legend of LC 19: 205-58
origins and development of the Robin Hood legend, 206-20
representations of Robin Hood, 220-44
Robin Hood as hero, 244-56

Rushdie, Salman, *Satanic Verses* Controversy CLC 55: 214-63; 59:404-56

Russian Nihilism NCLC 28: 403-47
definitions and overviews, 404-17
women and Nihilism, 417-27
literature as reform: the Civic Critics, 427-33
Nihilism and the Russian novel: Turgenev and Dostoevsky, 433-47

Russian Thaw TCLC 26: 189-247
literary history of the period, 190-206
theoretical debate of socialist realism, 206-11
Novy Mir, 211-7
Literary Moscow, 217-24
Pasternak, *Zhivago*, and the Nobel prize, 224-7
poetry of liberation, 228-31
Brodsky trial and the end of the Thaw, 231-6
achievement and influence, 236-46

Salem Witch Trials LC 38: 1-145
overviews and general studies, 2-30
historical background, 30-65
judicial background, 65-78
the search for causes, 78-115
the role of women in the trials, 115-44

Salinger, J. D., Controversy Surrounding *In Search of J. D. Salinger* CLC 55: 325-44

Sanitation Reform, Nineteenth-Century NCLC 124: 165-257

overviews and general studies, 166
primary texts, 186-89
social context, 189-221
public health in literature, 221-56

Science and Modern Literature TCLC 90: 308-419
overviews and general studies, 295-333
fiction, 333-95
poetry, 395-405
drama, 405-19

Science in Nineteenth-Century Literature NCLC 100: 224-366
overviews and general studies, 225-65
major figures, 265-336
sociopolitical concerns, 336-65

Science Fiction, Nineteenth-Century NCLC 24: 241-306
background, 242-50
definitions of the genre, 251-56
representative works and writers, 256-75
themes and conventions, 276-305

Scottish Chaucerians LC 20: 363-412

Scottish Poetry, Eighteenth-Century LC 29: 95-167
overviews and general studies, 96-114
the Scottish Augustans, 114-28
the Scots Vernacular Revival, 132-63
Scottish poetry after Burns, 163-66

Sea in Literature, The TCLC 82: 72-191
drama, 73-9
poetry, 79-119
fiction, 119-91

Sea in Nineteenth-Century English and American Literature, The NCLC 104: 265-362
overviews and general studies, 267-306
major figures in American sea fiction—Cooper and Melville, 306-29
American sea poetry and short stories, 329-45
English sea literature, 345-61

Sensation Novel, The NCLC 80: 219-330
overviews and general studies, 221-46
principal figures, 246-62
nineteenth-century reaction, 262-91
feminist criticism, 291-329

Sentimental Novel, The NCLC 60: 146-245
overviews and general studies, 147-58
the politics of domestic fiction, 158-79
a literature of resistance and repression, 179-212
the reception of sentimental fiction, 213-44

September 11 Attacks, Literature in Response to See Literature in Response to the September 11 Attacks

Sex and Literature TCLC 82: 192-434
overviews and general studies, 193-216
drama, 216-63
poetry, 263-87
fiction, 287-431

Sherlock Holmes Centenary TCLC 26: 248-310
Doyle's life and the composition of the Holmes stories, 248-59
life and character of Holmes, 259-78
method, 278-79
Holmes and the Victorian world, 279-92
Sherlockian scholarship, 292-301
Doyle and the development of the detective story, 301-07
Holmes's continuing popularity, 307-09

Short-Short Fiction SSC 61: 311-36
overviews and general studies, 312-19
major short-short fiction writers, 319-35

The Silver Fork Novel NCLC 88: 58-140
criticism, 59-139

Slave Narratives, American NCLC 20: 1-91
background, 2-9
overviews and general studies, 9-24
contemporary responses, 24-7
language, theme, and technique, 27-70
historical authenticity, 70-5
antecedents, 75-83
role in development of Black American literature, 83-8

The Slave Trade in British and American Literature LC 59: 283-369
overviews and general studies, 284-91
depictions by white writers, 291-331
depictions by former slaves, 331-67

Social Conduct Literature LC 55: 196-298
overviews and general studies, 196-223
prescriptive ideology in other literary forms, 223-38
role of the press, 238-63
impact of conduct literature, 263-87
conduct literature and the perception of women, 287-96
women writing for women, 296-98

Social Protest Literature Outside England, Nineteenth-Century NCLC 124: 258-350
overviews and general studies, 259-72
oppression revealed, 272-306
literature to incite or prevent reform, 306-50

Socialism NCLC 88: 141-237
origins, 142-54
French socialism, 154-83
Anglo-American socialism, 183-205
Socialist-Feminism, 205-36

Southern Gothic Literature TCLC 142: 186-270
overviews and general studies, 187-97
major authors in southern gothic literature, 197-230
structure and technique in southern gothic literature, 230-50
themes in southern gothic literature, 250-70

Southern Literature See Contemporary Southern Literature

Southern Literature of the Reconstruction NCLC 108: 289-369
overview, 290-91
reconstruction literature: the consequences of war, 291-321
old south to new: continuities in southern culture, 321-68

Spanish Civil War Literature TCLC 26: 311-85
topics in, 312-33
British and American literature, 333-59
French literature, 359-62
Spanish literature, 362-73
German literature, 373-75
political idealism and war literature, 375-83

Spanish Golden Age Literature LC 23: 262-332
overviews and general studies, 263-81
verse drama, 281-304
prose fiction, 304-19
lyric poetry, 319-31

Spasmodic School of Poetry NCLC 24: 307-52
history and major figures, 307-21
the Spasmodics on poetry, 321-7
Firmilian and critical disfavor, 327-39
theme and technique, 339-47
influence, 347-51

Sports in Literature TCLC 86: 294-445
overviews and general studies, 295-324
major writers and works, 324-402
sports, literature, and social issues, 402-45

Steinbeck, John, Fiftieth Anniversary of *The Grapes of Wrath* CLC 59: 311-54

Sturm und Drang NCLC 40: 196-276
definitions, 197-238
poetry and poetics, 238-58
drama, 258-75

Supernatural Fiction in the Nineteenth Century NCLC 32: 207-87
major figures and influences, 208-35
the Victorian ghost story, 236-54
the influence of science and occultism, 254-66
supernatural fiction and society, 266-86

Supernatural Fiction, Modern TCLC 30: 59-116
evolution and varieties, 60-74
"decline" of the ghost story, 74-86
as a literary genre, 86-92
technique, 92-101
nature and appeal, 101-15

Surrealism TCLC 30: 334-406
history and formative influences, 335-43
manifestos, 343-54
philosophic, aesthetic, and political principles, 354-75
poetry, 375-81
novel, 381-6
drama, 386-92
film, 392-8
painting and sculpture, 398-403
achievement, 403-5

Symbolism, Russian TCLC 30: 266-333
doctrines and major figures, 267-92
theories, 293-8
and French Symbolism, 298-310
themes in poetry, 310-4
theater, 314-20
and the fine arts, 320-32

Symbolist Movement, French NCLC 20: 169-249
background and characteristics, 170-86
principles, 186-91
attacked and defended, 191-7
influences and predecessors, 197-211
and Decadence, 211-6
theater, 216-26
prose, 226-33
decline and influence, 233-47

Television and Literature TCLC 78: 283-426
television and literacy, 283-98
reading vs. watching, 298-341
adaptations, 341-62
literary genres and television, 362-90
television genres and literature, 390-410
children's literature/children's television, 410-25

Theater of the Absurd TCLC 38: 339-415
"The Theater of the Absurd," 340-7
major plays and playwrights, 347-58
and the concept of the absurd, 358-86
theatrical techniques, 386-94
predecessors of, 394-402
influence of, 402-13

Tin Pan Alley See American Popular Song, Golden Age of

Tobacco Culture LC 55: 299-366
social and economic attitudes toward tobacco, 299-344
tobacco trade between the old world and the new world, 344-55
tobacco smuggling in Great Britain, 355-66

Transcendentalism, American NCLC 24: 1-99
overviews and general studies, 3-23
contemporary documents, 23-41
theological aspects of, 42-52
and social issues, 52-74
literature of, 74-96

Travel Writing in the Nineteenth Century NCLC 44: 274-392

the European grand tour, 275-303
the Orient, 303-47
North America, 347-91

Travel Writing in the Twentieth Century TCLC 30: 407-56
conventions and traditions, 407-27
and fiction writing, 427-43
comparative essays on travel writers, 443-54

Tristan and Isolde Legend CMLC 42: 311-404

True-Crime Literature CLC 99: 333-433
history and analysis, 334-407
reviews of true-crime publications, 407-23
writing instruction, 424-29
author profiles, 429-33

Twentieth-Century Danish Literature TCLC 142: 271-344
major works, 272-84
major authors, 284-344

Ulysses **and the Process of Textual Reconstruction** TCLC 26:386-416
evaluations of the new *Ulysses,* 386-94
editorial principles and procedures, 394-401
theoretical issues, 401-16

Utilitarianism NCLC 84: 272-340
J. S. Mill's Utilitarianism: liberty, equality, justice, 273-313
Jeremy Bentham's Utilitarianism: the science of happiness, 313-39

Utopianism NCLC 88: 238-346
overviews: Utopian literature, 239-59
Utopianism in American literature, 259-99
Utopianism in British literature, 299-311
Utopianism and Feminism, 311-45

Utopian Literature, Nineteenth-Century NCLC 24: 353-473
definitions, 354-74
overviews and general studies, 374-88
theory, 388-408
communities, 409-26
fiction, 426-53
women and fiction, 454-71

Utopian Literature, Renaissance LC 32: 1-63
overviews and general studies, 2-25
classical background, 25-33
utopia and the social contract, 33-9
origins in mythology, 39-48
utopia and the Renaissance country house, 48-52
influence of millenarianism, 52-62

Vampire in Literature TCLC 46: 391-454
origins and evolution, 392-412
social and psychological perspectives, 413-44
vampire fiction and science fiction, 445-53

Vernacular Bibles LC 67: 214-388
overviews and general studies, 215-59
the English Bible, 259-355
the German Bible, 355-88

Victorian Autobiography NCLC 40: 277-363
development and major characteristics, 278-88
themes and techniques, 289-313
the autobiographical tendency in Victorian prose and poetry, 313-47
Victorian women's autobiographies, 347-62

Victorian Fantasy Literature NCLC 60: 246-384
overviews and general studies, 247-91
major figures, 292-366
women in Victorian fantasy literature, 366-83

Victorian Hellenism NCLC 68: 251-376
overviews and general studies, 252-78
the meanings of Hellenism, 278-335
the literary influence, 335-75

Victorian Illustrated Fiction NCLC 120: 247-356
overviews and development, 128-76
technical and material aspects of book illustration, 276-84
Charles Dickens and his illustrators, 284-320
William Makepeace Thackeray, 320-31
George Eliot and Frederic Leighton, 331-51
Lewis Carroll and John Tenniel, 351-56

Victorian Novel NCLC 32: 288-454
development and major characteristics, 290-310
themes and techniques, 310-58
social criticism in the Victorian novel, 359-97
urban and rural life in the Victorian novel, 397-406
women in the Victorian novel, 406-25
Mudie's Circulating Library, 425-34
the late-Victorian novel, 434-51

Vietnamese Literature TCLC 102: 322-386

Vietnam War in Literature and Film CLC 91: 383-437
overview, 384-8
prose, 388-412
film and drama, 412-24
poetry, 424-35

Violence in Literature TCLC 98: 235-358
overviews and general studies, 236-74
violence in the works of modern authors, 274-358

Vorticism TCLC 62: 330-426
Wyndham Lewis and Vorticism, 330-8
characteristics and principles of Vorticism, 338-65
Lewis and Pound, 365-82

Vorticist writing, 382-416
Vorticist painting, 416-26

Well-Made Play, The NCLC 80: 331-370
overviews and general studies, 332-45
Scribe's style, 345-56
the influence of the well-made play, 356-69

Women's Autobiography, Nineteenth Century NCLC 76: 285-368
overviews and general studies, 287-300
autobiographies concerned with religious and political issues, 300-15
autobiographies by women of color, 315-38
autobiographies by women pioneers, 338-51
autobiographies by women of letters, 351-68

Women's Diaries, Nineteenth-Century NCLC 48: 308-54
overview, 308-13
diary as history, 314-25
sociology of diaries, 325-34
diaries as psychological scholarship, 334-43
diary as autobiography, 343-8
diary as literature, 348-53

Women in Modern Literature TCLC 94: 262-425
overviews and general studies, 263-86
American literature, 286-304
other national literatures, 304-33
fiction, 333-94
poetry, 394-407
drama, 407-24

Women Writers, Seventeenth-Century LC 30: 2-58
overview, 2-15
women and education, 15-9
women and autobiography, 19-31
women's diaries, 31-9
early feminists, 39-58

World War I Literature TCLC 34: 392-486
overview, 393-403
English, 403-27
German, 427-50
American, 450-66
French, 466-74
and modern history, 474-82

Yellow Journalism NCLC 36: 383-456
overviews and general studies, 384-96
major figures, 396-413

Yiddish Literature TCLC 130: 229-364
overviews and general studies, 230-54
major authors, 254-305
Yiddish literature in America, 305-34
Yiddish and Judaism, 334-64

Young Playwrights Festival
1988 CLC 55: 376-81
1989 CLC 59: 398-403
1990 CLC 65: 444-8

TCLC Cumulative Nationality Index

AMERICAN

Adams, Andy **56**
Adams, Brooks **80**
Adams, Henry (Brooks) **4, 52**
Addams, Jane **76**
Agee, James (Rufus) **1, 19**
Aldrich, Bess (Genevra) Streeter **125**
Allen, Fred **87**
Anderson, Maxwell **2**
Anderson, Sherwood **1, 10, 24, 123**
Anthony, Susan B(rownell) **84**
Atherton, Gertrude (Franklin Horn) **2**
Austin, Mary (Hunter) **25**
Baker, Ray Stannard **47**
Baker, Carlos (Heard) **119**
Bambara, Toni Cade **116**
Barry, Philip **11**
Baum, L(yman) Frank **7, 132**
Beard, Charles A(ustin) **15**
Becker, Carl (Lotus) **63**
Belasco, David **3**
Bell, James Madison **43**
Benchley, Robert (Charles) **1, 55**
Benedict, Ruth (Fulton) **60**
Benét, Stephen Vincent **7**
Benét, William Rose **28**
Bierce, Ambrose (Gwinett) **1, 7, 44**
Biggers, Earl Derr **65**
Bishop, Elizabeth **121**
Bishop, John Peale **103**
Black Elk **33**
Boas, Franz **56**
Bodenheim, Maxwell **44**
Bok, Edward W. **101**
Bourne, Randolph S(illiman) **16**
Boyd, James **115**
Boyd, Thomas (Alexander) **111**
Bradford, Gamaliel **36**
Brautigan, Richard **133**
Brennan, Christopher John **17**
Brennan, Maeve **124**
Brodkey, Harold (Roy) **123**
Bromfield, Louis (Brucker) **11**
Broun, Heywood **104**
Bryan, William Jennings **99**
Burroughs, Edgar Rice **2, 32**
Burroughs, William S(eward) **121**
Cabell, James Branch **6**
Cable, George Washington **4**
Cahan, Abraham **71**
Caldwell, Erskine (Preston) **117**
Campbell, Joseph **140**
Cardozo, Benjamin N(athan) **65**
Carnegie, Dale **53**
Cather, Willa (Sibert) **1, 11, 31, 99, 132**
Chambers, Robert W(illiam) **41**
Chambers, (David) Whittaker **129**
Chandler, Raymond (Thornton) **1, 7**
Chapman, John Jay **7**
Chase, Mary Ellen **124**
Chesnutt, Charles W(addell) **5, 39**
Childress, Alice **116**

Chopin, Katherine **5, 14, 127**
Cobb, Irvin S(hrewsbury) **77**
Coffin, Robert P(eter) Tristram **95**
Cohan, George M(ichael) **60**
Comstock, Anthony **13**
Cotter, Joseph Seamon Sr. **28**
Cram, Ralph Adams **45**
Crane, (Harold) Hart **2, 5, 80**
Crane, Stephen (Townley) **11, 17, 32**
Crawford, F(rancis) Marion **10**
Crothers, Rachel **19**
Cullen, Countée **4, 37**
Cummings, E. E. **137**
Darrow, Clarence (Seward) **81**
Davis, Rebecca (Blaine) Harding **6**
Davis, Richard Harding **24**
Day, Clarence (Shepard Jr.) **25**
Dent, Lester **72**
De Voto, Bernard (Augustine) **29**
Dewey, John **95**
Dreiser, Theodore (Herman Albert) **10, 18, 35, 83**
Dulles, John Foster **72**
Dunbar, Paul Laurence **2, 12**
Duncan, Isadora **68**
Dunne, Finley Peter **28**
Eastman, Charles A(lexander) **55**
Eddy, Mary (Ann Morse) Baker **71**
Einstein, Albert **65**
Erskine, John **84**
Faulkner, William **141**
Faust, Frederick (Schiller) **49**
Fenollosa, Ernest (Francisco) **91**
Fields, W. C. **80**
Fisher, Dorothy (Frances) Canfield **87**
Fisher, Rudolph **11**
Fisher, Vardis **140**
Fitzgerald, F(rancis) Scott (Key) **1, 6, 14, 28, 55**
Fitzgerald, Zelda (Sayre) **52**
Fletcher, John Gould **35**
Foote, Mary Hallock **108**
Ford, Henry **73**
Forten, Charlotte L. **16**
Freeman, Douglas Southall **11**
Freeman, Mary E(leanor) Wilkins **9**
Fuller, Henry Blake **103**
Futrelle, Jacques **19**
Gale, Zona **7**
Garland, (Hannibal) Hamlin **3**
Gilman, Charlotte (Anna) Perkins (Stetson) **9, 37, 117**
Ginsberg, Allen **120**
Glasgow, Ellen (Anderson Gholson) **2, 7**
Glaspell, Susan **55**
Goldman, Emma **13**
Green, Anna Katharine **63**
Grey, Zane **6**
Griffith, D(avid Lewelyn) W(ark) **68**
Griggs, Sutton (Elbert) **77**
Guest, Edgar A(lbert) **95**
Guiney, Louise Imogen **41**
Hall, James Norman **23**

Handy, W(illiam) C(hristopher) **97**
Harper, Frances Ellen Watkins **14**
Harris, Joel Chandler **2**
Harte, (Francis) Bret(t) **1, 25**
Hartmann, Sadakichi **73**
Hatteras, Owen **18**
Hawthorne, Julian **25**
Hearn, (Patricio) Lafcadio (Tessima Carlos) **9**
Hecht, Ben **101**
Heller, Joseph **131**
Hellman, Lillian (Florence) **119**
Hemingway, Ernest (Miller) **115**
Henry, O. **1, 19**
Hergesheimer, Joseph **11**
Heyward, (Edwin) DuBose **59**
Higginson, Thomas Wentworth **36**
Himes, Chester **139**
Holley, Marietta **99**
Holly, Buddy **65**
Holmes, Oliver Wendell Jr. **77**
Hopkins, Pauline Elizabeth **28**
Horney, Karen (Clementine Theodore Danielsen) **71**
Howard, Robert E(rvin) **8**
Howe, Julia Ward **21**
Howells, William Dean **7, 17, 41**
Huneker, James Gibbons **65**
Hurston, Zora Neale **121, 131**
Ince, Thomas H. **89**
James, Henry **2, 11, 24, 40, 47, 64**
James, William **15, 32**
Jewett, (Theodora) Sarah Orne **1, 22**
Johnson, James Weldon **3, 19**
Johnson, Robert **69**
Kerouac, Jack **117**
Kinsey, Alfred C(harles) **91**
Kirk, Russell (Amos) **119**
Kornbluth, C(yril) M. **8**
Korzybski, Alfred (Habdank Skarbek) **61**
Kubrick, Stanley **112**
Kuttner, Henry **10**
Lardner, Ring(gold) W(ilmer) **2, 14**
Lewis, (Harry) Sinclair **4, 13, 23, 39**
Lewisohn, Ludwig **19**
Lewton, Val **76**
Lindsay, (Nicholas) Vachel **17**
Locke, Alain (Le Roy) **43**
Lockridge, Ross (Franklin) Jr. **111**
London, Jack **9, 15, 39**
Lovecraft, H(oward) P(hillips) **4, 22**
Lowell, Amy **1, 8**
Malamud, Bernard **129**
Mankiewicz, Herman (Jacob) **85**
March, William **96**
Markham, Edwin **47**
Marquis, Don(ald Robert Perry) **7**
Masters, Edgar Lee **2, 25**
Matthews, (James) Brander **95**
Matthiessen, F(rancis) O(tto) **100**
McAlmon, Robert (Menzies) **97**
McCoy, Horace (Stanley) **28**
Mead, George Herbert **89**
Mencken, H(enry) L(ouis) **13**

Micheaux, Oscar (Devereaux) **76**
Millay, Edna St. Vincent **4, 49**
Mitchell, Margaret (Munnerlyn) **11**
Mitchell, S(ilas) Weir **36**
Mitchell, William **81**
Monroe, Harriet **12**
Moody, William Vaughan **105**
Morley, Christopher (Darlington) **87**
Morris, Wright **107**
Muir, John **28**
Murfree, Mary Noailles **135**
Nash, (Frediric) Ogden **109**
Nathan, George Jean **18**
Nemerov, Howard (Stanley) **124F**
Neumann, Alfred **100**
Nisbet, Robert A(lexander) **117**
Nordhoff, Charles (Bernard) **23**
Norris, (Benjamin) Frank(lin Jr.) **24**
O'Connor, Flannery **132**
O'Neill, Eugene (Gladstone) **1, 6, 27, 49**
Oppen, George **107**
Osbourne, Lloyd **93**
Oskison, John Milton **35**
Park, Robert E(zra) **73**
Patton, George S(mith) Jr. **79**
Peirce, Charles Sanders **81**
Percy, William Alexander **84**
Petry, Ann (Lane) **112**
Phelps, Elizabeth Stuart **113**
Phillips, David Graham **44**
Post, Melville Davisson **39**
Pulitzer, Joseph **76**
Pyle, Ernie **75**
Pyle, Howard **81**
Rawlings, Marjorie Kinnan **4**
Reed, John (Silas) **9**
Reich, Wilhelm **57**
Remington, Frederic **89**
Rhodes, Eugene Manlove **53**
Riggs, (Rolla) Lynn **56**
Riis, Jacob A(ugust) **80**
Riley, James Whitcomb **51**
Rinehart, Mary Roberts **52**
Roberts, Elizabeth Madox **68**
Roberts, Kenneth (Lewis) **23**
Robinson, Edwin Arlington **5, 101**
Rogers, Carl **125**
Rogers, Will(iam Penn Adair) **8, 71**
Roosevelt, Franklin Delano **93**
Roosevelt, Theodore **69**
Rourke, Constance (Mayfield) **12**
Runyon, (Alfred) Damon **10**
Saltus, Edgar (Everton) **8**
Santayana, George **40**
Santmyer, Helen Hooven **133**
Sapir, Edward **108**
Saroyan, William **137**
Schoenberg, Arnold Franz Walter **75**
Sherwood, Robert E(mmet) **3**
Slesinger, Tess **10**
Stanton, Elizabeth Cady **73**
Steffens, (Joseph) Lincoln **20**
Stein, Gertrude **1, 6, 28, 48**
Steinbeck, John **135**
Sterling, George **20**
Stevens, Wallace **3, 12, 45**
Stockton, Frank R. **47**
Stroheim, Erich von **71**
Strunk, William Jr. **92**
Sturges, Preston **48**
Tarbell, Ida M(inerva) **40**
Tarkington, (Newton) Booth **9**
Taylor, Frederick Winslow **76**
Teasdale, Sara **4**
Tesla, Nikola **88**
Thomas, Augustus **97**
Thomas, M. Carey **89**
Thorndike, Edward L(ee) **107**
Thurman, Wallace (Henry) **6**
Torrence, Ridgely **97**
Twain, Mark **6, 12, 19, 36, 48, 59**
Van Doren, Carl (Clinton) **18**

Veblen, Thorstein B(unde) **31**
Walker, Margaret **129**
Washington, Booker T(aliaferro) **10**
Wells, Carolyn **35**
Wells-Barnett, Ida B(ell) **125**
West, Dorothy **108**
West, Nathanael **1, 14, 44**
Whale, James **63**
Wharton, Edith (Newbold Jones) **3, 9, 27, 53, 129**
White, Walter F(rancis) **15**
Williams, Ben Ames **89**
Williams, Hank **81**
Wilson, (Thomas) Woodrow **79**
Wirth, Louis **92**
Wister, Owen **21**
Wolfe, Thomas (Clayton) **4, 13, 29, 61**
Woodberry, George Edward **73**
Woollcott, Alexander (Humphreys) **5**
Wright, Frank Lloyd **95**
Wright, Richard **136**
Wylie, Elinor (Morton Hoyt) **8**

ARGENTINIAN

Arlt, Roberto (Godofredo Christophersen) **29**
Borges, Jorge Luis **109**
Güiraldes, Ricardo (Guillermo) **39**
Hudson, W(illiam) H(enry) **29**
Lugones, Leopoldo **15**
Storni, Alfonsina **5**

AUSTRALIAN

Baynton, Barbara **57**
Franklin, (Stella Maria Sarah) Miles (Lampe) **7**
Furphy, Joseph **25**
Ingamells, Rex **35**
Lawson, Henry (Archibald Hertzberg) **27**
Paterson, A(ndrew) B(arton) **32**
Warung, Price **45**

AUSTRIAN

Beer-Hofmann, Richard **60**
Broch, Hermann **20**
Brod, Max **115**
Freud, Sigmund **52**
Hayek, F(riedrich) A(ugust von) **109**
Hofmannsthal, Hugo von **11**
Kafka, Franz **2, 6, 13, 29, 47, 53, 112**
Kraus, Karl **5**
Kubin, Alfred (Leopold Isidor) **23**
Meyrink, Gustav **21**
Musil, Robert (Edler von) **12, 68**
Pabst, G. W. **127**
Perutz, Leo(pold) **60**
Rank, Otto **115**
Roth, (Moses) Joseph **33**
Schnitzler, Arthur **4**
Steiner, Rudolf **13**
Stroheim, Erich von **71**
Trakl, Georg **5**
Weininger, Otto **84**
Werfel, Franz (Viktor) **8**
Zweig, Stefan **17**

BELGIAN

Bosschere, Jean de **19**
Lemonnier, (Antoine Louis) Camille **22**
Maeterlinck, Maurice **3**
Sarton, May (Eleanor) **120**
van Ostaijen, Paul **33**
Verhaeren, Émile (Adolphe Gustave) **12**

BRAZILIAN

Cunha, Euclides (Rodrigues Pimenta) da **24**
Drummond de Andrade, Carlos **139**
Lima Barreto, Afonso Henrique de **23**
Machado de Assis, Joaquim Maria **10**
Ramos, Graciliano **32**

BULGARIAN

Vazov, Ivan (Minchov) **25**

CANADIAN

Campbell, Wilfred **9**
Carman, (William) Bliss **7**
Carr, Emily **32**
Connor, Ralph **31**
Drummond, William Henry **25**
Duncan, Sara Jeannette **60**
Engel, Marian **137**
Garneau, (Hector de) Saint-Denys **13**
Innis, Harold Adams **77**
Knister, Raymond **56**
Leacock, Stephen (Butler) **2**
Lewis, (Percy) Wyndham **2, 9, 104**
McCrae, John **12**
Montgomery, L(ucy) M(aud) **51, 140**
Nelligan, Emile **14**
Pickthall, Marjorie L(owry) C(hristie) **21**
Roberts, Charles G(eorge) D(ouglas) **8**
Scott, Duncan Campbell **6**
Service, Robert W(illiam) **15**
Seton, Ernest (Evan) Thompson **31**
Stringer, Arthur **37**
Wetherald, Agnes Ethelwyn **81**

CHILEAN

Donoso, José **133**
Godoy Alcayaga, Lucila **2**
Huidobro Fernandez, Vicente Garcia **31**
Prado (Calvo), Pedro **75**

CHINESE

Liu, E. **15**
Lu Hsun **3**
Su Man-shu **24**
Wen I-to **28**

COLOMBIAN

Rivera, José Eustasio **35**

CZECH

Brod, Max **115**
Chapek, Karel **6, 37**
Freud, Sigmund **52**
Hasek, Jaroslav (Matej Frantisek) **4**
Kafka, Franz **2, 6, 13, 29, 47, 53, 112**
Nezval, Vitezslav **44**

DANISH

Brandes, Georg (Morris Cohen) **10**
Hansen, Martin A(lfred) **32**
Jensen, Johannes V. **41**
Nexo, Martin Andersen **43**
Pontoppidan, Henrik **29**

DUTCH

Bok, Edward W. **101**
Couperus, Louis (Marie Anne) **15**
Heijermans, Herman **24**
Hillesum, Etty **49**
van Schendel, Arthur(-Francois-Émile) **56**

ENGLISH

Abercrombie, Lascelles **141**
Abbott, Edwin **139**
Alexander, Samuel **77**
Barbellion, W. N. P. **24**
Baring, Maurice **8**
Baring-Gould, Sabine **88**
Beerbohm, (Henry) Max(imilian) **1, 24**
Bell, Gertrude (Margaret Lowthian) **67**
Belloc, (Joseph) Hilaire (Pierre Sebastien Rene Swanton) **7, 18**
Bennett, (Enoch) Arnold **5, 20**
Benson, A.C. **123**
Benson, E(dward) F(rederic) **27**
Benson, Stella **17**

Bentley, E(dmund) C(lerihew) 12
Beresford, J(ohn) D(avys) 81
Besant, Annie (Wood) 9
Blackmore, R(ichard) D(oddridge) 27
Blackwood, Algernon (Henry) 5
Bottomley, Gordon 107
Braddon, Mary Elizabeth 111
Bramah, Ernest 72
Bridges, Robert (Seymour) 1
Brooke, Rupert (Chawner) 2, 7
Buchanan, Robert 107
Burke, Thomas 63
Butler, Samuel 1, 33
Butts, Mary 77
Byron, Robert 67
Caine, Hall 97
Carpenter, Edward 88
Carter, Angela 139
Chesterton, G(ilbert) K(eith) 1, 6, 64
Childers, (Robert) Erskine 65
Churchill, Winston (Leonard Spencer) 113
Coleridge, Mary E(lizabeth) 73
Collier, John 127
Collingwood, R(obin) G(eorge) 67
Conrad, Joseph 1, 6, 13, 25, 43, 57
Coppard, A(lfred) E(dgar) 5
Corelli, Marie 51
Crofts, Freeman Wills 55
Crowley, Aleister 7
Dale, Colin 18
Davies, William Henry 5
Delafield, E. M. 61
de la Mare, Walter (John) 4, 53
Dobson, Austin 79
Doughty, Charles M(ontagu) 27
Douglas, Keith (Castellain) 40
Dowson, Ernest (Christopher) 4
Doyle, Arthur Conan 7
Drinkwater, John 57
Dunsany 2, 59
Eddison, E(ric) R(ucker) 15
Elaine 18
Elizabeth 41
Ellis, (Henry) Havelock 14
Firbank, (Arthur Annesley) Ronald 1
Flecker, (Herman) James Elroy 43
Ford, Ford Madox 1, 15, 39, 57
Forster, E(dward) M(organ) 125
Freeman, R(ichard) Austin 21
Galsworthy, John 1, 45
Gilbert, W(illiam) S(chwenck) 3
Gill, Eric 85
Gissing, George (Robert) 3, 24, 47
Glyn, Elinor 72
Gosse, Edmund (William) 28
Grahame, Kenneth 64, 136
Granville-Barker, Harley 2
Gray, John (Henry) 19
Gurney, Ivor (Bertie) 33
Haggard, H(enry) Rider 11
Hall, (Marguerite) Radclyffe 12
Hardy, Thomas 4, 10, 18, 32, 48, 53, 72
Henley, William Ernest 8
Hilton, James 21
Hodgson, William Hope 13
Hope, Anthony 83
Housman, A(lfred) E(dward) 1, 10
Housman, Laurence 7
Hudson, W(illiam) H(enry) 29
Hulme, T(homas) E(rnest) 21
Hunt, Violet 53
Jacobs, W(illiam) W(ymark) 22
James, Montague (Rhodes) 6
Jerome, Jerome K(lapka) 23
Johnson, Lionel (Pigot) 19
Kaye-Smith, Sheila 20
Keynes, John Maynard 64
Kipling, (Joseph) Rudyard 8, 17
Laski, Harold J(oseph) 79
Lawrence, D(avid) H(erbert Richards) 2, 9, 16, 33, 48, 61, 93
Lawrence, T(homas) E(dward) 18

Lee, Vernon 5
Lee-Hamilton, Eugene (Jacob) 22
Leverson, Ada 18
Lindsay, David 15
Lowndes, Marie Adelaide (Belloc) 12
Lowry, (Clarence) Malcolm 6, 40
Lucas, E(dward) V(errall) 73
Macaulay, (Emilie) Rose 7, 44
MacCarthy, (Charles Otto) Desmond 36
Mackenzie, Compton (Edward Montague) 116
Maitland, Frederic William 65
Manning, Frederic 25
Marsh, Edward 99
McTaggart, John McTaggart Ellis 105
Meredith, George 17, 43
Mew, Charlotte (Mary) 8
Meynell, Alice (Christina Gertrude Thompson) 6
Middleton, Richard (Barham) 56
Milne, A(lan) A(lexander) 6, 88
Moore, G. E. 89
Morrison, Arthur 72
Muggeridge, Thomas (Malcom) 120
Murry, John Middleton 16
Myers, L(eopold) H(amilton) 59
Nightingale, Florence 85
Noyes, Alfred 7
Oppenheim, E(dward) Phillips 45
Orwell, George 2, 6, 15, 31, 51, 128, 129
Owen, Wilfred (Edward Salter) 5, 27
Pankhurst, Emmeline (Goulden) 100
Pinero, Arthur Wing 32
Powys, T(heodore) F(rancis) 9
Quiller-Couch, Arthur (Thomas) 53
Richardson, Dorothy Miller 3
Rolfe, Frederick (William Serafino Austin Lewis Mary) 12
Rosenberg, Isaac 12
Ruskin, John 20
Sabatini, Rafael 47
Saintsbury, George (Edward Bateman) 31
Sapper 44
Sayers, Dorothy L(eigh) 2, 15
Shiel, M(atthew) P(hipps) 8
Sinclair, May 3, 11
Stapledon, (William) Olaf 22
Stead, William Thomas 48
Stephen, Leslie 23
Strachey, (Giles) Lytton 12
Summers, (Alphonsus Joseph-Mary Augustus) Montague 16
Sutro, Alfred 6
Swinburne, Algernon Charles 8, 36
Symons, Arthur 11
Thomas, (Philip) Edward 10
Thompson, Francis (Joseph) 4
Tolkien, J. R. R. 137
Tomlinson, H(enry) M(ajor) 71
Trotter, Wilfred 97
Upward, Allen 85
Van Druten, John (William) 2
Wakefield, Herbert (Russell) 120
Wallace, (Richard Horatio) Edgar 57
Wallas, Graham 91
Walpole, Hugh (Seymour) 5
Ward, Mary Augusta 55
Warner, Sylvia Townsend 131
Warung, Price 45
Webb, Mary Gladys (Meredith) 24
Webb, Sidney (James) 22
Welch, (Maurice) Denton 22
Wells, H(erbert) G(eorge) 6, 12, 19, 133
Whitehead, Alfred North 97
Williams, Charles (Walter Stansby) 1, 11
Wodehouse, P(elham) G(renville) 108
Woolf, (Adeline) Virginia 1, 5, 20, 43, 56, 101, 128
Yonge, Charlotte (Mary) 48
Zangwill, Israel 16

ESTONIAN

Talvik, Heiti 87
Tammsaare, A(nton) H(ansen) 27

FINNISH

Leino, Eino 24
Soedergran, Edith (Irene) 31
Westermarck, Edward 87

FRENCH

Alain 41
Apollinaire, Guillaume 3, 8, 51
Arp, Jean 115
Artaud, Antonin (Marie Joseph) 3, 36
Bachelard, Gaston 128
Barbusse, Henri 5
Barrès, (Auguste-)Maurice 47
Barthes, Roland 135
Benda, Julien 60
Bergson, Henri(-Louis) 32
Bernanos, (Paul Louis) Georges 3
Bernhardt, Sarah (Henriette Rosine) 75
Bloy, Léon 22
Bourget, Paul (Charles Joseph) 12
Claudel, Paul (Louis Charles Marie) 2, 10
Cocteau, Jean (Maurice Eugene Clement) 119
Colette, (Sidonie-Gabrielle) 1, 5, 16
Coppee, Francois 25
Crevel, Rene 112
Daumal, Rene 14
Deleuze, Gilles 116
Desnos, Robert 22
Drieu la Rochelle, Pierre(-Eugène) 21
Dujardin, Edouard (Emile Louis) 13
Durkheim, Emile 55
Epstein, Jean 92
Fargue, Leon-Paul 11
Feydeau, Georges (Léon Jules Marie) 22
Genet, Jean 128
Gide, André (Paul Guillaume) 5, 12, 36
Giono, Jean 124
Giraudoux, Jean(-Hippolyte) 2, 7
Gourmont, Remy (-Marie-Charles) de 17
Halévy, Elie 104
Huysmans, Joris-Karl 7, 69
Jacob, (Cyprien-)Max 6
Jammes, Francis 75
Jarry, Alfred 2, 14
Larbaud, Valery (Nicolas) 9
Léautaud, Paul 83
Leblanc, Maurice (Marie Emile) 49
Leroux, Gaston 25
Lyotard, Jean-François 103
Martin du Gard, Roger 24
Melies, Georges 81
Mirbeau, Octave 55
Mistral, Frédéric 51
Nizan, Paul 40
Péguy, Charles (Pierre) 10
Péret, Benjamin 20
Proust, (Valentin-Louis-George-Eugène-)Marcel 7, 13, 33
Radiguet, Raymond 29
Renard, Jules 17
Rolland, Romain 23
Rostand, Edmond (Eugene Alexis) 6, 37
Roussel, Raymond 20
Saint-Exupéry, Antoine (Jean Baptiste Marie Roger) de 2, 56
Schwob, Marcel (Mayer André) 20
Sorel, Georges 91
Sully Prudhomme, René-François-Armand 31
Teilhard de Chardin, (Marie Joseph) Pierre 9
Valéry, (Ambroise) Paul (Toussaint Jules) 4, 15
Vallette, Marguerite Eymery 67
Verne, Jules (Gabriel) 6, 52
Vian, Boris 9
Weil, Simone (Adolphine) 23

Zola, Émile (Édouard Charles Antoine) **1, 6, 21, 41**

GERMAN

Adorno, Theodor W(iesengrund) **111**
Andreas-Salome, Lou **56**
Arp, Jean **115**
Auerbach, Erich **43**
Ball, Hugo **104**
Barlach, Ernst (Heinrich) **84**
Benjamin, Walter **39**
Benn, Gottfried **3**
Borchert, Wolfgang **5**
Brecht, (Eugen) Bertolt (Friedrich) **1, 6, 13, 35**
Carossa, Hans **48**
Cassirer, Ernst **61**
Doeblin, Alfred **13**
Einstein, Albert **65**
Ewers, Hanns Heinz **12**
Feuchtwanger, Lion **3**
Frank, Bruno **81**
George, Stefan (Anton) **2, 14**
Goebbels, (Paul) Joseph **68**
Haeckel, Ernst Heinrich (Philipp August) **83**
Hauptmann, Gerhart (Johann Robert) **4**
Heym, Georg (Theodor Franz Arthur) **9**
Heyse, Paul (Johann Ludwig von) **8**
Hitler, Adolf **53**
Horkheimer, Max **132**
Horney, Karen (Clementine Theodore Danielsen) **71**
Huch, Ricarda (Octavia) **13**
Husserl, Edmund (Gustav Albrecht) **100**
Kaiser, Georg **9**
Klabund **44**
Kolmar, Gertrud **40**
Lasker-Schueler, Else **57**
Liliencron, (Friedrich Adolf Axel) Detlev von **18**
Luxemburg, Rosa **63**
Mann, (Luiz) Heinrich **9**
Mann, (Paul) Thomas **2, 8, 14, 21, 35, 44, 60**
Mannheim, Karl **65**
Michels, Robert **88**
Morgenstern, Christian (Otto Josef Wolfgang) **8**
Neumann, Alfred **100**
Nietzsche, Friedrich (Wilhelm) **10, 18, 55**
Ophuls, Max **79**
Otto, Rudolf **85**
Plumpe, Friedrich Wilhelm **53**
Raabe, Wilhelm (Karl) **45**
Rilke, Rainer Maria **1, 6, 19**
Schreber, Daniel Paul **123**
Schwitters, Kurt (Hermann Edward Karl Julius) **95**
Simmel, Georg **64**
Spengler, Oswald (Arnold Gottfried) **25**
Sternheim, (William Adolf) Carl **8**
Strauss, Leo **141**
Sudermann, Hermann **15**
Toller, Ernst **10**
Vaihinger, Hans **71**
von Hartmann, Eduard **96**
Wassermann, (Karl) Jakob **6**
Weber, Max **69**
Wedekind, (Benjamin) Frank(lin) **7**
Wiene, Robert **56**

GHANIAN

Casely-Hayford, J(oseph) E(phraim) **24**

GREEK

Cavafy, C(onstantine) P(eter) **2, 7**
Kazantzakis, Nikos **2, 5, 33**
Palamas, Kostes **5**
Papadiamantis, Alexandros **29**
Sikelianos, Angelos **39**

HAITIAN

Roumain, Jacques (Jean Baptiste) **19**

HUNGARIAN

Ady, Endre **11**
Babits, Mihaly **14**
Csath, Geza **13**
Herzl, Theodor **36**
Horváth, Ödön von **45**
Jozsef, Attila **22**
Karinthy, Frigyes **47**
Mikszath, Kalman **31**
Molnár, Ferenc **20**
Moricz, Zsigmond **33**
Radnóti, Miklós **16**

ICELANDIC

Sigurjonsson, Johann **27**

INDIAN

Chatterji, Saratchandra **13**
Dasgupta, Surendranath **81**
Gandhi, Mohandas Karamchand **59**
Ghose, Aurabinda **63**
Iqbal, Muhammad **28**
Naidu, Sarojini **80**
Premchand **21**
Ramana Maharshi **84**
Tagore, Rabindranath **3, 53**
Vivekananda, Swami **88**

INDONESIAN

Anwar, Chairil **22**

IRANIAN

Hedabayat, Sādeq **21**

IRISH

A.E. **3, 10**
Baker, Jean H. **3, 10**
Cary, (Arthur) Joyce (Lunel) **1, 29**
Gogarty, Oliver St. John **15**
Gregory, Isabella Augusta (Persse) **1**
Harris, Frank **24**
Joyce, James (Augustine Aloysius) **3, 8, 16, 35, 52**
Ledwidge, Francis **23**
Martin, Violet Florence **51**
Martyn, Edward **131**
Moore, George Augustus **7**
O'Grady, Standish (James) **5**
Shaw, George Bernard **3, 9, 21, 45**
Somerville, Edith Oenone **51**
Stephens, James **4**
Synge, (Edmund) J(ohn) M(illington) **6, 37**
Tynan, Katharine **3**
Wilde, Oscar (Fingal O'Flahertie Wills) **1, 8, 23, 41**
Yeats, William Butler **1, 11, 18, 31, 93, 116**

ITALIAN

Alvaro, Corrado **60**
Betti, Ugo **5**
Brancati, Vitaliano **12**
Campana, Dino **20**
Carducci, Giosuè (Alessandro Giuseppe) **32**
Croce, Benedetto **37**
D'Annunzio, Gabriele **6, 40**
de Filippo, Eduardo **127**
Deledda, Grazia (Cosima) **23**
Gentile, Giovanni **96**
Giacosa, Giuseppe **7**
Jovine, Francesco **79**
Levi, Carlo **125**
Levi, Primo **109**
Malaparte, Curzio **52**
Marinetti, Filippo Tommaso **10**
Montessori, Maria **103**
Mosca, Gaetano **75**
Mussolini, Benito (Amilcare Andrea) **96**
Papini, Giovanni **22**
Pareto, Vilfredo **69**
Pascoli, Giovanni **45**
Pavese, Cesare **3**
Pirandello, Luigi **4, 29**
Protolini, Vasco **124**
Saba, Umberto **33**
Tozzi, Federigo **31**
Verga, Giovanni (Carmelo) **3**

JAMAICAN

De Lisser, H(erbert) G(eorge) **12**
Garvey, Marcus (Moziah Jr.) **41**
Mais, Roger **8**
Redcam, Tom **25**

JAPANESE

Abé, Kōbō **131**
Akutagawa Ryunosuke **16**
Dazai Osamu **11**
Futabatei, Shimei **44**
Hagiwara, Sakutaro **60**
Hayashi, Fumiko **27**
Ishikawa, Takuboku **15**
Kunikida, Doppo **99**
Masaoka, Shiki **18**
Miyamoto, (Chujo) Yuriko **37**
Miyazawa, Kenji **76**
Mizoguchi, Kenji **72**
Mori Ogai **14**
Nagai, Kafu **51**
Nishida, Kitaro **83**
Noguchi, Yone **80**
Santoka, Taneda **72**
Shimazaki Toson **5**
Suzuki, Daisetz Teitaro **109**
Yokomitsu, Riichi **47**
Yosano Akiko **59**

LATVIAN

Berlin, Isaiah **105**
Rainis, Jānis **29**

LEBANESE

Gibran, Kahlil **1, 9**

LESOTHAN

Mofolo, Thomas (Mokopu) **22**

LITHUANIAN

Kreve (Mickevicius), Vincas **27**

MEXICAN

Azuela, Mariano **3**
Gamboa, Federico **36**
Gonzalez Martinez, Enrique **72**
Nervo, (Jose) Amado (Ruiz de) **11**
Reyes, Alfonso **33**
Romero, José Rubén **14**
Villaurrutia, Xavier **80**

NEPALI

Devkota, Laxmiprasad **23**

NEW ZEALANDER

Mander, (Mary) Jane **31**

NICARAGUAN

Darío, Rubén **4**

NORWEGIAN

Bjoernson, Bjoernstjerne (Martinius) **7, 37**
Bojer, Johan **64**
Grieg, (Johan) Nordahl (Brun) **10**
Ibsen, Henrik (Johan) **2, 8, 16, 37, 52**
Kielland, Alexander Lange **5**
Lie, Jonas (Lauritz Idemil) **5**

Obstfelder, Sigbjoern **23**
Skram, Amalie (Bertha) **25**
Undset, Sigrid **3**

PAKISTANI

Iqbal, Muhammad **28**

PERUVIAN

Palma, Ricardo **29**
Vallejo, César (Abraham) **3, 56**

POLISH

Asch, Sholem **3**
Borowski, Tadeusz **9**
Conrad, Joseph **1, 6, 13, 25, 43, 57**
Peretz, Isaac Loeb **16**
Prus, Boleslaw **48**
Przybyszewski, Stanislaw **36**
Reymont, Wladyslaw (Stanislaw) **5**
Schulz, Bruno **5, 51**
Sienkiewicz, Henryk (Adam Alexander Pius) **3**
Singer, Israel Joshua **33**
Witkiewicz, Stanislaw Ignacy **8**

PORTUGUESE

Pessoa, Fernando (António Nogueira) **27**
Sa-Carniero, Mario de **83**

PUERTO RICAN

Hostos (y Bonilla), Eugenio Maria de **24**

ROMANIAN

Bacovia, George **24**
Caragiale, Ion Luca **76**
Rebreanu, Liviu **28**

RUSSIAN

Aldanov, Mark (Alexandrovich) **23**
Andreyev, Leonid (Nikolaevich) **3**
Annensky, Innokenty (Fyodorovich) **14**
Artsybashev, Mikhail (Petrovich) **31**
Babel, Isaak (Emmanuilovich) **2, 13**
Bagritsky, Eduard **60**
Balmont, Konstantin (Dmitriyevich) **11**
Bely, Andrey **7**
Berdyaev, Nikolai (Aleksandrovich) **67**
Bergelson, David **81**
Blok, Alexander (Alexandrovich) **5**
Bryusov, Valery Yakovlevich **10**
Bulgakov, Mikhail (Afanas'evich) **2, 16**
Bulgya, Alexander Alexandrovich **53**
Bunin, Ivan Alexeyevich **6**
Chekhov, Anton (Pavlovich) **3, 10, 31, 55, 96**
Der Nister **56**
Eisenstein, Sergei (Mikhailovich) **57**
Esenin, Sergei (Alexandrovich) **4**
Fadeyev, Alexander **53**
Gladkov, Fyodor (Vasilyevich) **27**
Gumilev, Nikolai (Stepanovich) **60**
Gurdjieff, G(eorgei) I(vanovich) **71**
Guro, Elena **56**
Hippius, Zinaida **9**
Ilf, Ilya **21**
Ivanov, Vyacheslav Ivanovich **33**
Kandinsky, Wassily **92**
Khlebnikov, Velimir **20**
Khodasevich, Vladislav (Felitsianovich) **15**
Klimentov, Andrei Platonovich **14**
Korolenko, Vladimir Galaktionovich **22**
Kropotkin, Peter (Aleksieevich) **36**
Kuprin, Aleksander Ivanovich **5**
Kuzmin, Mikhail **40**
Lenin, V. I. **67**
Mandelstam, Osip (Emilievich) **2, 6**
Mayakovski, Vladimir (Vladimirovich) **4, 18**
Merezhkovsky, Dmitry Sergeyevich **29**
Nabokov, Vladimir (Vladimirovich) **108**
Olesha, Yuri **136**
Pavlov, Ivan Petrovich **91**
Petrov, Evgeny **21**
Pilnyak, Boris **23**
Prishvin, Mikhail **75**
Remizov, Aleksei (Mikhailovich) **27**
Rozanov, Vassili **104**
Shestov, Lev **56**
Sologub, Fyodor **9**
Stalin, Joseph **92**
Tolstoy, Alexey Nikolaevich **18**
Tolstoy, Leo (Nikolaevich) **4, 11, 17, 28, 44, 79**
Trotsky, Leon **22**
Tsvetaeva (Efron), Marina (Ivanovna) **7, 35**
Zabolotsky, Nikolai Alekseevich **52**
Zamyatin, Evgeny Ivanovich **8, 37**
Zhdanov, Andrei Alexandrovich **18**
Zoshchenko, Mikhail (Mikhailovich) **15**

SCOTTISH

Barrie, J(ames) M(atthew) **2**
Brown, George Douglas **28**
Buchan, John **41**
Cunninghame Graham, Robert (Gallnigad) Bontine **19**
Davidson, John **24**
Doyle, Arthur Conan **7**
Frazer, J(ames) G(eorge) **32**
Lang, Andrew **16**
MacDonald, George **9, 113**
Muir, Edwin **2, 87**
Murray, James Augustus Henry **117**
Sharp, William **39**
Tey, Josephine **14**

SLOVENIAN

Cankar, Ivan **105**

SOUTH AFRICAN

Bosman, Herman Charles **49**
Campbell, (Ignatius) Roy (Dunnachie) **5**
La Guma, Alex **140**
Mqhayi, S(amuel) E(dward) K(rune Loliwe) **25**
Plaatje, Sol(omon) T(shekisho) **73**
Schreiner, Olive (Emilie Albertina) **9**
Smith, Pauline (Urmson) **25**
Vilakazi, Benedict Wallet **37**

SPANISH

Alas (y Urena), Leopoldo (Enrique Garcia) **29**
Aleixandre, Vicente **113**
Barea, Arturo **14**
Baroja (y Nessi), Pio **8**
Benavente (y Martinez), Jacinto **3**
Blasco Ibáñez, Vicente **12**
Echegaray (y Eizaguirre), Jose (Maria Waldo) **4**
García Lorca, Federico **1, 7, 49**
Jiménez (Mantecón), Juan Ramón **4**
Machado (y Ruiz), Antonio **3**
Martinez Sierra, Gregorio **6**
Martinez Sierra, Maria (de la O'LeJarraga) **6**
Miro (Ferrer), Gabriel (Francisco Victor) **5**
Onetti, Juan Carlos **131**
Ortega y Gasset, José **9**
Pereda (y Sanchez de Porrua), Jose Maria de **16**
Pérez Galdós, Benito **27**
Ramoacn y Cajal, Santiago **93**
Salinas (y Serrano), Pedro **17**
Sender, Ramón **136**
Unamuno (y Jugo), Miguel de **2, 9**
Valera y Alcala-Galiano, Juan **10**
Valle-Inclán, Ramón (Maria) del **5**

SWEDISH

Bengtsson, Frans (Gunnar) **48**
Dagerman, Stig (Halvard) **17**
Ekelund, Vilhelm **75**
Heidenstam, (Carl Gustaf) Verner von **5**
Key, Ellen (Karolina Sofia) **65**
Lagerloef, Selma (Ottiliana Lovisa) **4, 36**
Söderberg, Hjalmar **39**
Strindberg, (Johan) August **1, 8, 21, 47**

SWISS

Frisch, Max (Rudolf) **121**
Ramuz, Charles-Ferdinand **33**
Rod, Edouard **52**
Saussure, Ferdinand de **49**
Spitteler, Carl (Friedrich Georg) **12**
Walser, Robert **18**

SYRIAN

Gibran, Kahlil **1, 9**

TURKISH

Sait Faik **23**

UKRAINIAN

Aleichem, Sholom **1, 35**
Bialik, Chaim Nachman **25**

URUGUAYAN

Quiroga, Horacio (Sylvestre) **20**
Sánchez, Florencio **37**

WELSH

Davies, William Henry **5**
Evans, Caradoc **85**
Lewis, Alun **3**
Thomas, Dylan (Marlais) **1, 8, 45, 105**

YUGOSLAVIAN

Andrić, Ivo **135**

ISBN 0-7876-7041-3